Scotland

written and researched by

Rob Humphreys and Donald Reid

www.roughguides.com

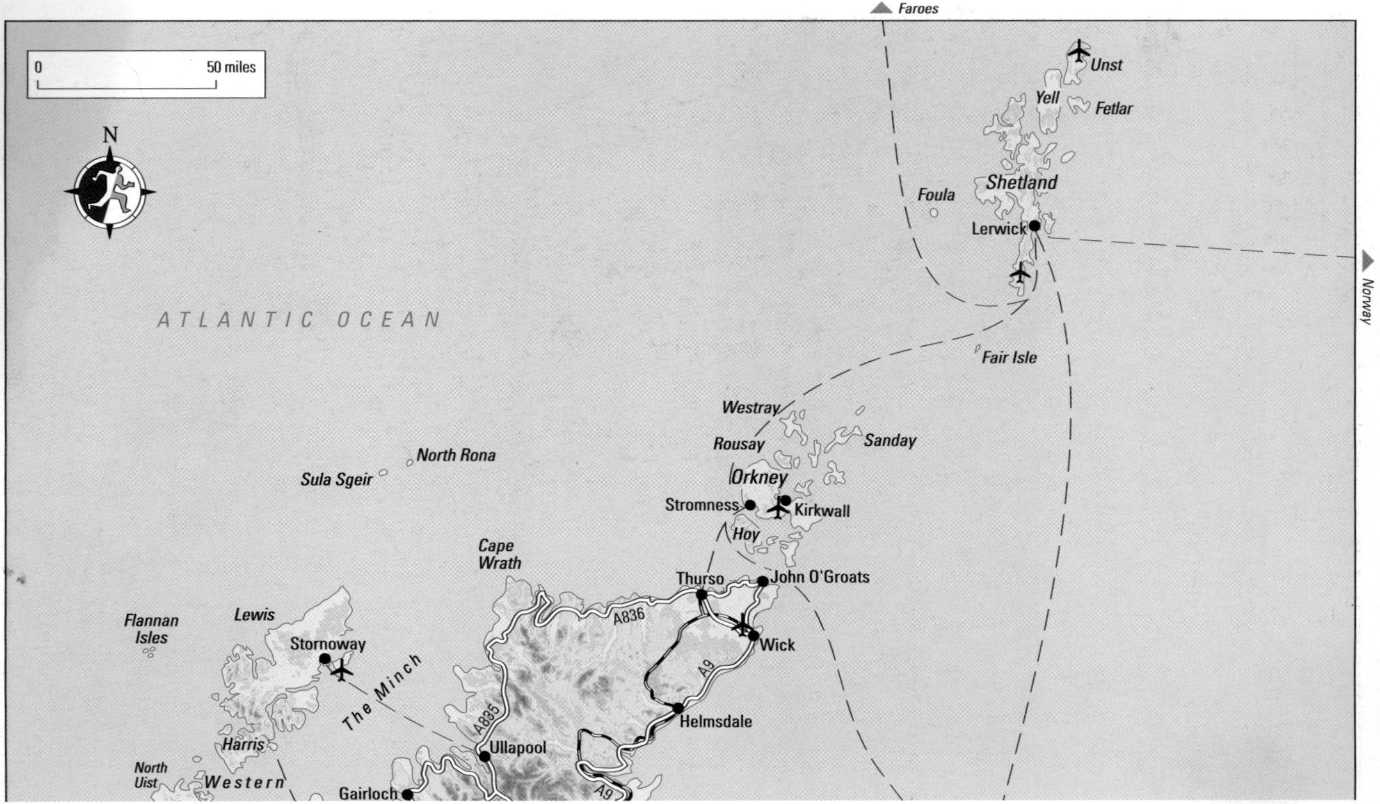

Faroes
Norway
0
50 miles
N
ATLANTIC OCEAN
Unst
Yell
Fetlar
Shetland
Foula
Lerwick
Fair Isle
Westray
Rousay
Sanday
Orkney
Stromness
Kirkwall
Hoy
North Rona
Sula Sgeir
Cape Wrath
Thurso
John O'Groats
A836
Wick
A9
Helmsdale
Flannan Isles
Lewis
Stornoway
The Minch
A835
Ullapool
Harris
North Uist
Western
Gairloch

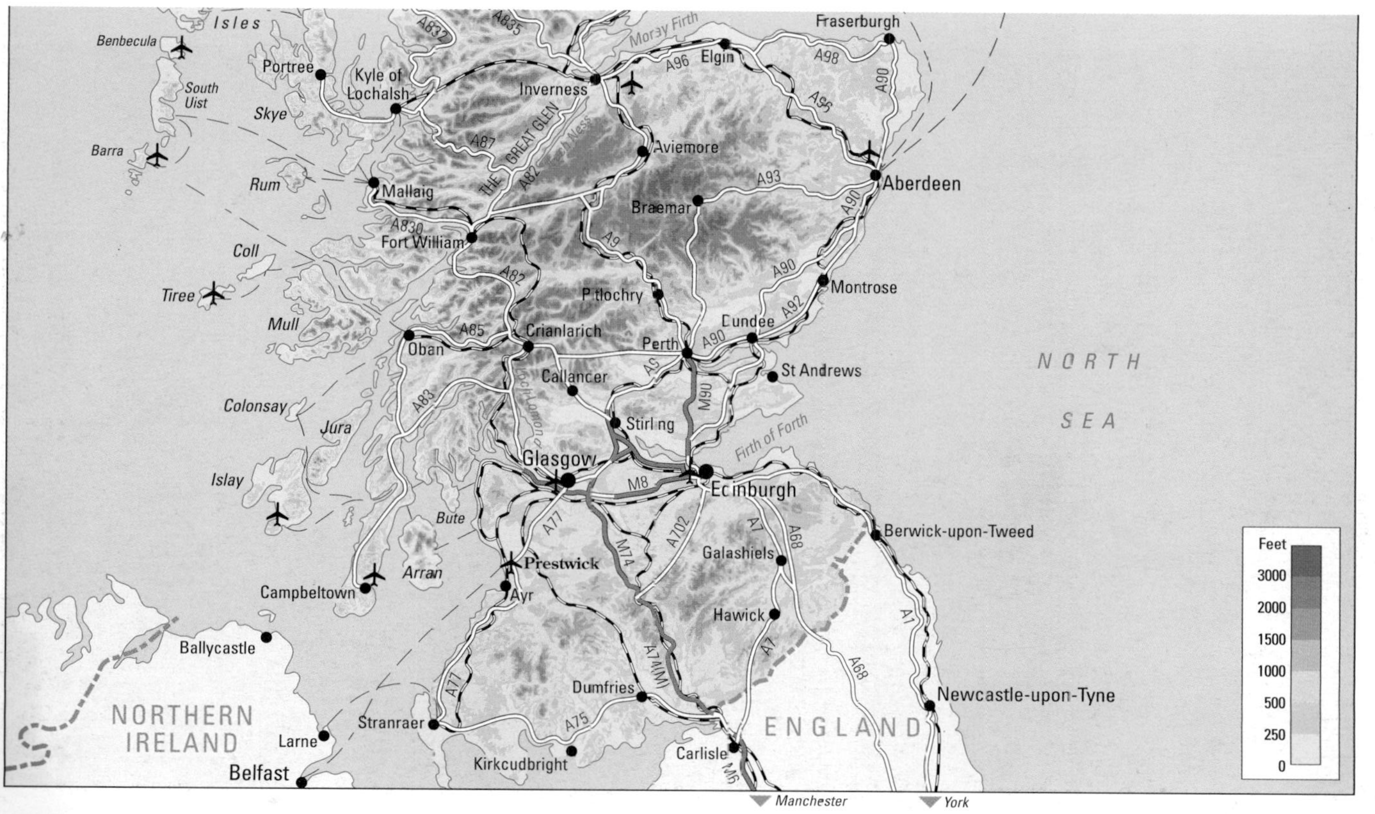
NORTH SEA
NORTHERN IRELAND
ENGLAND
Isles
Benbecula
South Uist
Barra
Skye
Rum
Coll
Tiree
Mull
Colonsay
Jura
Islay
Bute
Arran
Portree
Kyle of Lochalsh
Mallaig
Fort William
Inverness
THE GREAT GLEN
Loch Ness
Moray Firth
Elgin
Fraserburgh
Aviemore
Aberdeen
Braemar
Montrose
Pitlochry
Dundee
Perth
Crianlarich
Oban
Callander
Loch Lomond
St Andrews
Stirling
Firth of Forth
Glasgow
Edinburgh
Prestwick
Ayr
Campbeltown
Ballycastle
Larne
Belfast
Stranraer
Kirkcudbright
Dumfries
Galashiels
Hawick
Berwick-upon-Tweed
Newcastle-upon-Tyne
Carlisle
Manchester
York
A832
A835
A87
A82
A830
A85
A83
A9
A96
A98
A90
A93
A92
A5
M90
M8
M74
A77
A702
A7
A68
A1
A74(M)
A75
M6
Feet
3000
2000
1500
1000
500
250
0

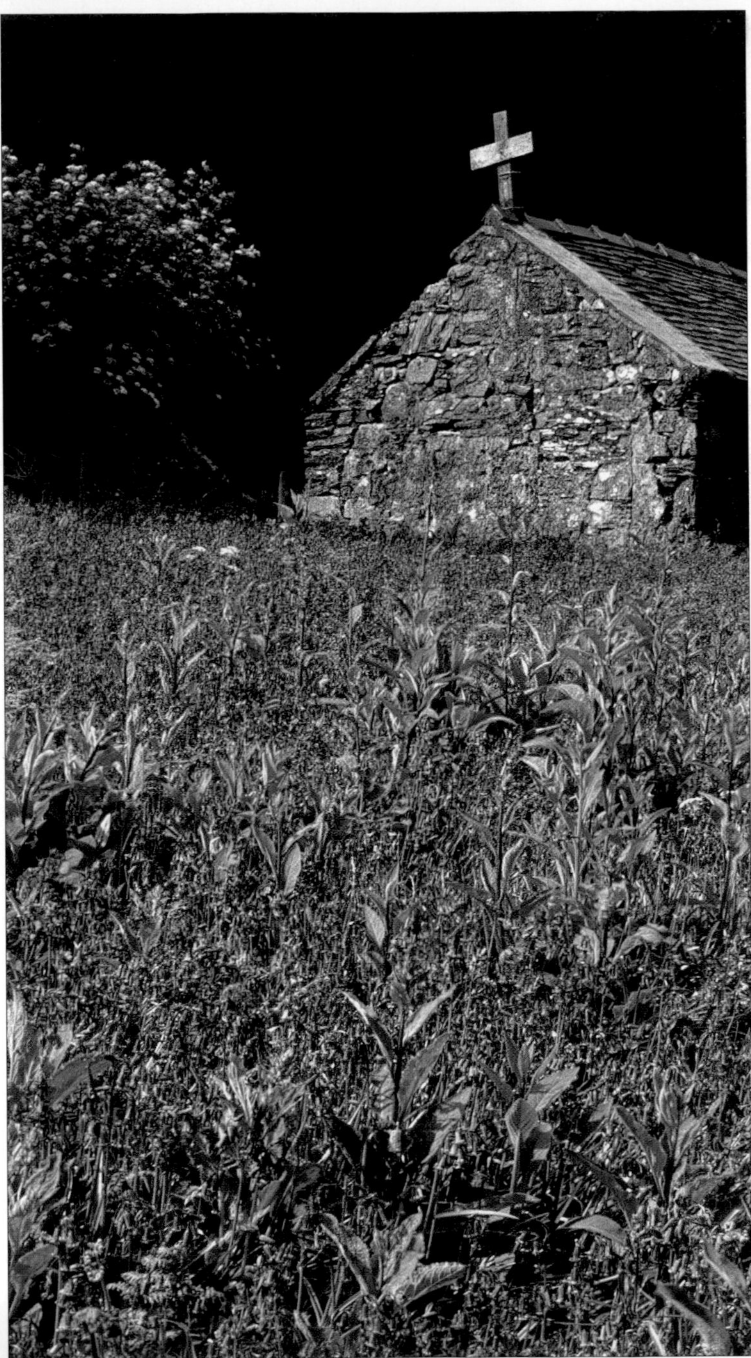

Introduction to

Scotland

Scotland not only defies description, it gets positively irritated by it. Clichéd images of the place abound – postcards of hairy Highland cows, tartan tins of shortbread, ranks of diamond-patterned golf jerseys... and they drive many Scots to apoplexy. And yet Scotland has a habit of delivering on its classic images: ruined castles really do perch on just about every hilltop, in summer the glens inevitably turn purple with heather and, if you're lucky, you just might bump into a formation of bagpipers marching down the village street on gala day.

Scotland is a difficult country, where Celtic hedonism intertwines, somehow, with stern Calvinism, where the losers of battles (and football games) are more romanticized than the winners. It's often defined by its scenery – known to make poets weep, but half the time hidden under a pall of drizzly mist. The country's major contribution to medieval warfare was the chaotic, blood-curdling charge of the half-naked Highlander, yet it's civilized enough to have given the world steam power, the television and penicillin. Chefs from Paris to Prague rhapsodize over Scottish wild salmon and Aberdeen Angus steaks, even while the locals are tucking happily into another deep-fried supper of haggis and chips.

Naturally, the tourist industry tends to play up the heritage and play down the contemporary, but beyond the tartan lies a modern, dynamic nation. Oil and microprocessors now matter more to the Scottish economy than

Munro-bagging

Just as the Inuit have hundreds of words for snow, so in Scotland a hill is rarely just a hill. Depending on where you are in the country, what it's shaped like and how high it is, a hill might be a ben, a mount, a law, a pen, a brae or even a pap. Even more confusing if you're keen on doing a bit of hill-walking are "Munros". These are the hills in Scotland over 3000 feet in height, defined by a list first drawn up by one Sir Hugh Munro in 1891. You "bag" a Munro by walking to the top of it, and once you've bagged all 284 you can call yourself a Munroist and let your chiropodist retire in peace. Of course, there's no need to do them all: at heart, Munro-bagging is simply about appreciating the great Scottish outdoors. It's advisable, however, not to get too obsessed by Sir Hugh's challenge: after the Munros you might hear the call of the "Corbetts" (hills between 2500 and 2999 feet) or even the "Donalds" (lowland hills above 2000 feet).

Harris tweed. Edinburgh still has its genteel Royal Mile, but just as many folk are drawn by its clubs and cappuccino culture, while out in the Hebrides, the locals are more likely to be teleworking via the internet than shearing sheep. The Highland huntin' shootin' fishin' set are these days outnumbered by mountain bikers and wide-eyed whale-watchers. Much as folk bands are knocking out old tunes on electronic fiddles, reinvention of tradition has become a Scottish artform.

Stuck in the far northwest corner of Europe, Scotland is remote, but it's not isolated. The inspiring emptiness of the wild northwest coast lies barely a couple of hours from Edinburgh and Glasgow, two of Britain's most dense and intriguing urban centres. Ancient ties to Ireland, Scandinavia, France and the Netherlands mean that – compared with the English at least – Scots are pretty enthusiastic about the European Union. EU money has been poured into the infrastructure, particularly in the Highlands and Islands, funding numerous arts projects and sustaining the national identity. By contrast, Scotland's relationship with the "auld enemy", England, remains as problematic as ever. Despite the new Scottish parliament established in Edinburgh in 1999, with its new-found power to shape Scottish life, many Scots still tend to view matters south of the border with a mixture of exaggerated disdain and well-hidden envy. Ask for a "full English breakfast" and you'll quickly find yourself put right. Old prejudices die hard.

Where to go

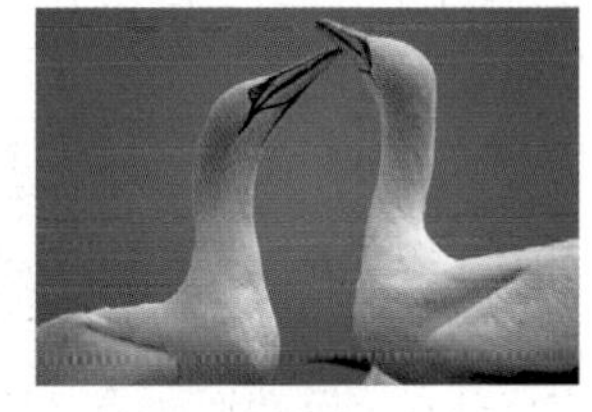

Even if you're planning a short visit, it's still perfectly possible, and quite common, to combine a stay in either Edinburgh or Glasgow with a brief foray into the Highlands. With more time at your disposal, the opportunity to experience the variety of landscapes in Scotland increases, but there's no escaping the fact that travel in the more remote regions of Scotland takes time, and – in the case of the outer islands – money. If you're planning to spend most of your time in the countryside, it's most rewarding to concentrate on just one or two small areas.

The initial focus for many visitors to Scotland is the capital, **Edinburgh**, a dramatically handsome and engaging city famous for its magnificent castle and historic Old Town. Come here in August and you'll find the city transformed by the Edinburgh Festival, the largest arts festival in the world.

Fact file

- Scotland covers an **area** of just over 30,000 square miles, has a 2300-mile-long coastline and contains over 31,460 **lochs**. Of its 790 **islands**, 130 are inhabited. The highest point is the summit of Ben Nevis (4406 feet), while the bottom of Loch Morar is 1017 feet below sea level.
- The **capital** is Edinburgh (population nearly 450,000), and the largest city is Glasgow (over 600,000). While the number of people worldwide who claim Scottish descent is estimated at over 25 million, the **population** of the country is just 5 million – 1.3 percent of whom (roughly 66,000 people) speak **Gaelic**.
- Scotland is a constituent territory of the **United Kingdom** of Great Britain and Northern Ireland. The head of state is Queen Elizabeth II. It is a **parliamentary democracy** whose sovereign parliament sits at Westminster in London, with elements of government business devolved to the separately elected Scottish Parliament which sits in Edinburgh.
- **Whisky** accounts for 13 percent of Scotland's exports and is worth £2.6 billion annually, but Scotland also manufactures 28 percent of Europe's personal computers and 12 percent of Europe's mobile phones.

An hour's travel to the west is the country's largest city, **Glasgow**, a place quite different in character from Edinburgh. Once a sprawling industrial metropolis, Glasgow has done much to improve its image by promoting its impressive architectural heritage and lively social and cultural life. Other urban centres are inevitably overshadowed by the big two, although the transformation from industrial grey to cultural colour is injecting life into **Dundee**, while there's a defiant separateness to **Aberdeen** with its silvery granite architecture and oil prosperity. **Stirling** is well worth visiting for its wonderful castle and historic importance, while **Perth**, **Dumfries** and **Inverness** are pleasant county towns serving a wide rural hinterland.

You don't have to travel far north of the Glasgow–Edinburgh axis to find the first hints of **Highland** landscape, a divide marked by the Highland Boundary Fault which cuts across central Scotland. The lochs, hills and wooded glens of the **Trossachs** and **Loch Lomond** are most easily reached, and as a consequence busier than other parts. Further north,

Perthshire and the Grampian hills of **Angus** and **Deeside** show the Scottish countryside at its richest, with colourful woodlands and long glens rising up to distinctive mountain peaks. South of Inverness the mighty **Cairngorm** massif offers hints of the raw wilderness Scotland can still provide, an aspect of the country which is at its finest in the lonely north and western Highlands. To get to the far north you'll have to cross the **Great Glen**, an ancient geological fissure which cuts right across the country from Ben Nevis to **Loch Ness**, a moody stretch of water rather choked with tourists hoping for a glimpse of its monster. Scotland's most memorable scenery is to be found on the jagged west coast, stretching from

Whisky

The Scots like a drink. Somehow, a Scot who doesn't like (or, worse, can't handle) a dram of "Scotch" – although whisky is rarely described as such in Scotland – isn't wholly credible. No Highland village or cobbled Edinburgh street would be complete without its cosy, convivial pub – and no pub complete without its array of amber-tinged bottles, the spirit within nurtured by a beguiling and well-marketed mix of soft Scottish rain, glistening Highland streams, rich peaty soil and tender Scots craftsmanship.

But not only is whisky the national drink, it's often regarded as the national pastime too, lubricating any social gathering from a Highland ceilidh to a Saturday night session. And the tradition that whisky be drunk neat says far more about Scottish society's machismo than its epicurean instincts: the truth is that a splash of water releases the whisky's flavours. It's no surprise, then, that the canny Scots also turn a healthy profit bottling the country's abundant spring water and selling it around the world.

Argyll all the way north to **Wester Ross** and the looming hills of Assynt. Not all of central and northern Scotland is rugged Highlands, however, with the east coast in particular mixing fertile farm land with pretty stone-built fishing villages and golf courses, most notably at the prosperous university town of **St Andrews**, the spiritual home of the game. Elsewhere the whisky trail of **Speyside** and the castles and Pictish stones of the **north-east** provide plenty of scope for exploration off the beaten track, while in the southern part of the country, the rolling hills and ruined abbeys of the **Borders** offer a refreshingly unaffected vision of rural Scotland.

The grand splendour of the Highlands would be bare without the **islands** off the west and north coasts. Assorted in size, flavour and accessibility, the long chain of rocky Hebrides which necklace Scotland's Atlantic shoreline include **Mull** and its nearby pilgrimage centre of **Iona**; **Islay** and **Jura**, famous for their wildlife and whisky; **Skye**, the most-visited of the Hebrides, where the snow-tipped Cuillin peaks rise up from deep sea lochs; and the **Western Isles**, an elongated archipelago that is the last bastion of Gaelic language and culture. Off the north coast, **Orkney** and **Shetland**, both with a rich Norse heritage, differ not only from each other, but also quite distinctly from mainland Scotland in dialect and culture – far-flung islands buffeted by wind and sea that offer some of the country's wildest scenery, finest bird-watching and best archeological sites.

When to go

The **summer** months of June, July and August are regarded as high season, with local school holidays making July and early August the busiest period. While the locals celebrate a single day of bright sunshine as "glorious", the weather at this time is, at best, unpredictable; however, days are generally mild or warm and, most importantly, long, with daylight lingering until 9pm or later. August in Edinburgh is Festival-time, which dominates everything in the city and means accommodation is hard to come by. Elsewhere, events such as Highland Games, folk festivals or sporting events – most of which take place in the summer months – can tie up accommodation, though normally only in a fairly concentrated local area. If you're out and about in the Highlands throughout the summer, you won't be able to avoid the clouds of small biting insects called **midges**, which can be a real annoyance on still days, particularly around dusk.

The weather

"There's no such thing as bad weather, only inadequate clothing," the poet laureate Ted Hughes is alleged to have said when asked why he liked holidaying on Scotland's west coast, given that it always rains there. For those who don't share Hughes' cavalier attitude to the elements, the weather is probably the single biggest factor to put you off visiting Scotland. It's not so much that the weather's always bad, it's just that it is unpredictable: you could enjoy the most fabulous week of sunshine in early April and suffer a week of low-lying fog and drizzle in August. Out in the islands, they say you can get all four seasons in a day. The saving grace is that even if the weather's not necessarily good, it's generally interesting, exhilarating, dramatic, and certainly photogenic. Then, the sun finally coming out is truly worth the wait. A week spent in a landscape swathed in thick mist can be transformed when the clouds lift to reveal a majestic mountain range or a hidden group of islands far offshore.

The Kirkcudbright Conundrum

At some point or other, most visitors will fall foul of the peculiarities of Scottish pronunciation. Hikers wishing to embark on the

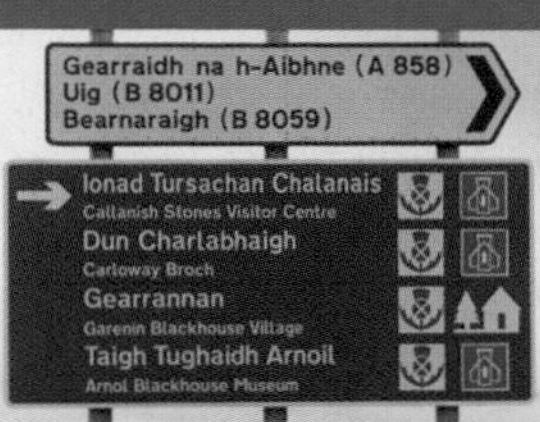

West Highland Way, for example, first have to negotiate the linguistic hurdle of the footpath's starting-point at Milngavie – pronounced "mill-guy". Seemingly innocuous place names, the unwary will discover, can be pronounced idiosyncratically: Avoch like "och"; Crovie as "crivie"; Culzean like "cullane"; Glamis most definitely as "glahms". Other common names to come a cropper on are Kirkcaldy ("kircoddy") and Kirkcudbright ("kircoobree"). Even the labels on some whiskies can be hard to swallow, particularly on Islay ("eye-la") in Argyll ("argyle"), where drinkers have to get their mouths around Bunnahabhainn ("bunna-have-an") and Caol Ila ("culleela"). Stress is important, too: the island of Benbecula must be pronounced with the stress on the second syllable; ditto the town and whisky of Bowmore. And when you think you've finally cracked Scots pronunciation, it's time to get really stuck into the nettlebed of Gaelic, in which the seemingly unpronounceable town of Gearraidh na h-Aibhne is anglicized to become Garynahine.

Commonly, **May** and **September** throw up weather every bit as good as, if not better than, the months of high summer. You're less likely to encounter crowds or struggle to find somewhere to stay, and the mild temperatures combined with the changing colours of nature mean both are great for outdoor activities, particularly hiking. Note, however, that September is stalking season for deer, which can disrupt access over parts of the Highlands.

The **spring** and **autumn** months of April and October bracket the season for many parts of rural Scotland. A large number of attractions, tourist offices and guesthouses often open for business on Easter weekend and shut up shop after the school half-term in mid-October. If places do stay open through the winter it's normally with reduced opening hours; this is the best time to pick up special offers at hotels and guesthouses. Note too that in more remote spots public transport will often operate on a reduced winter timetable.

Winter days, from November through to March, occasionally crisp and bright, are more often cold, gloomy and all too brief, although Hogmanay and New Year has traditionally been a time to visit Scotland for partying and warm hospitality – something which improves as the weather worsens. While even tourist hotspots such as Edinburgh are notably quieter during winter, a fall of snow in the Highlands will prompt plenty of activity around the ski resorts.

Scotland's climate

The table shows average daily maximum temperatures and monthly rainfall.

	Jan	Feb	Mar	Apr	May	June	July	Aug	Sept	Oct	Nov	Dec
Dumfries												
°C	6	6	8	11	14	17	18	18	16	13	9	7
mm	103	72	66	55	71	63	77	93	104	106	109	104
°F	42	43	47	52	58	63	65	65	61	55	47	44
inches	4	2.8	2.6	2.1	2.8	2.5	3	3.6	4	4.1	4.3	4.1
Edinburgh												
°C	6	6	9	11	14	17	18	18	16	13	9	7
mm	47	39	39	38	49	45	69	73	57	56	58	56
°F	43	44	47	52	58	63	65	65	61	56	48	45
inches	1.8	1.5	1.5	1.5	1.9	1.8	2.7	2.8	2.2	2.2	2.2	2.2
Fort William												
°C	6	7	9	11	15	17	17	17	15	13	9	7
mm	200	132	152	111	103	124	137	150	199	215	220	238
°F	43	44	47	52	58	62	63	63	60	55	48	45
inches	7.8	5.1	5.9	4.3	4	4.8	5.3	5.9	7.8	8.4	8.6	9.3
Lerwick												
°C	5	5	6	8	10	13	14	14	13	10	7	6
mm	127	93	93	72	64	64	67	78	113	119	140	147
°F	41	41	43	46	50	55	57	57	55	51	45	43
inches	5	3.6	3.6	2.8	2.5	2.5	2.6	3	4.4	4.6	5.5	5.7
Perth												
°C	6	6	8	12	15	18	19	19	16	13	9	7
mm	70	52	47	43	57	51	67	72	63	65	69	82
°F	42	43	47	53	59	64	66	65	61	55	47	44
inches	2.7	2	1.8	1.7	2.2	2	2.6	2.8	2.5	2.5	2.7	3.2
Tiree												
°C	7	7	8	10	13	15	16	16	15	13	10	8
mm	120	71	77	60	56	66	79	83	123	125	123	123
°F	45	45	47	51	55	59	60	61	58	55	49	47
inches	4.7	2.8	3	2.3	2.2	2.6	3.1	3.2	4.8	4.9	4.8	4.8
Wick												
°C	6	6	7	9	11	14	15	15	14	12	8	7
mm	81	58	55	45	47	49	61	74	68	73	90	82
°F	42	42	45	49	52	58	60	60	57	53	47	44
inches	3.2	2.3	2.1	1.8	1.8	1.9	2.4	2.9	2.7	2.8	3.5	3.2

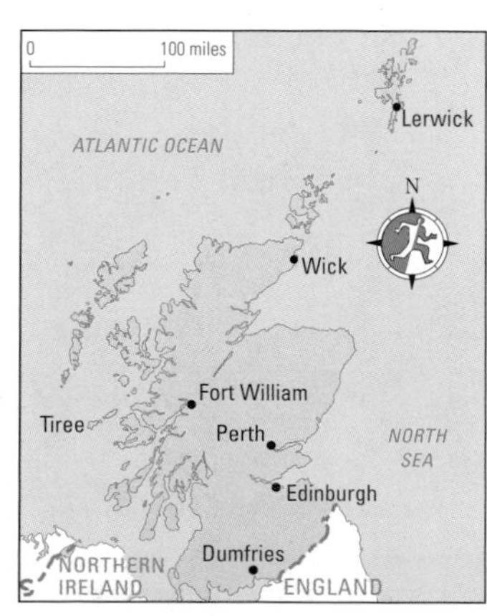

40 things not to miss

It's not possible to see everything that Scotland has to offer in one trip – and we don't suggest you try. What follows is a selective taste of the country's highlights: great places to visit, outstanding buildings, spectacular scenery and unforgettable journeys. They're arranged in five colour-coded categories, which you can browse through to find the very best things to see and experience. All entries have a page reference to take you straight into the guide, where you can find out more.

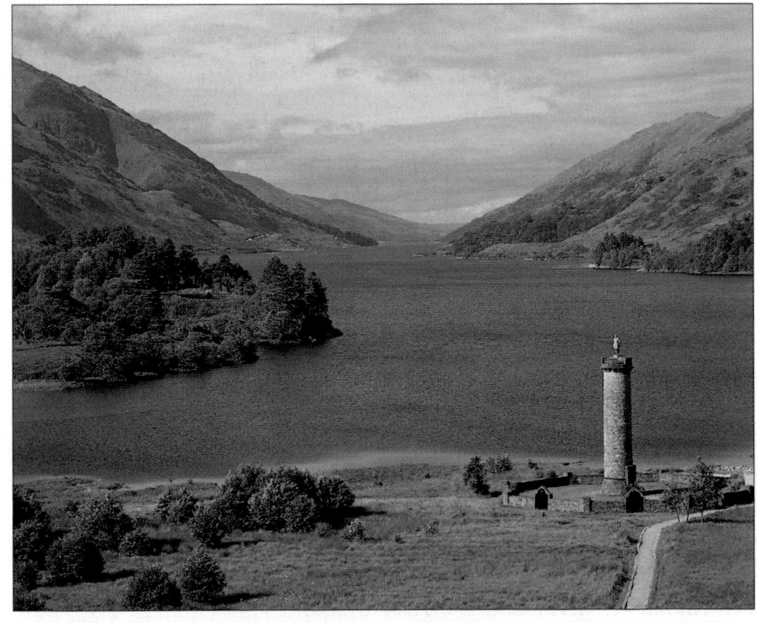

01 Loch Shiel Page **621** • Among Scotland's myriad lochs, Shiel stands out for its serene beauty and compelling history.

02 Museum of Scotland, Edinburgh Page **94** • The ivory Lewis chessmen are part of this superb collection of artefacts.

03 Glasgow School of Art Page **255** • Finest example of the unique style of Glasgow architect and designer Charles Rennie Mackintosh.

04 Edinburgh Old Town Page **74** • Lose yourself in the capital's medieval cobbled streets and closes.

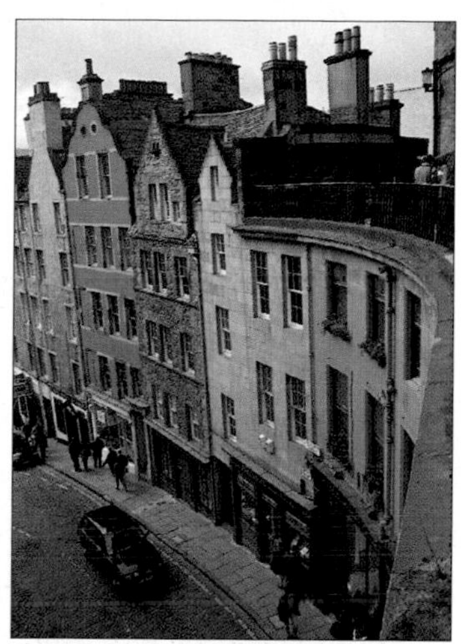

05 Calanais, Lewis Page **482** • Prehistoric standing stones that occupy a serene lochside setting in the Western Isles.

06 Glen Coe Page **612** • Moody, poignant and spectacular glen within easy reach of Fort William.

07 Hogmanay Page **125** • New Year celebrations, with whisky, dancing and fireworks staving off the midwinter chill.

08 Staffa and the Treshnish Isles Page **398** • View the basalt columns of Staffa's Fingal's Cave from the sea, and then picnic amidst the puffins on the Isle of Lunga.

09 Tobermory Page **394** • Scotland's most picturesque fishing port, bar none.

10 Highland Games Page **42** • An entertaining blend of summer sports day and traditional clan gathering, held in locations across the Highlands.

11 **West Highland railway** Page **578** • One of the great railway journeys of the world.

12 **Kinloch Castle, Rùm** Page **466** • Stay in the servants' quarters of this Edwardian hideaway or in one of its few remaining four-poster beds.

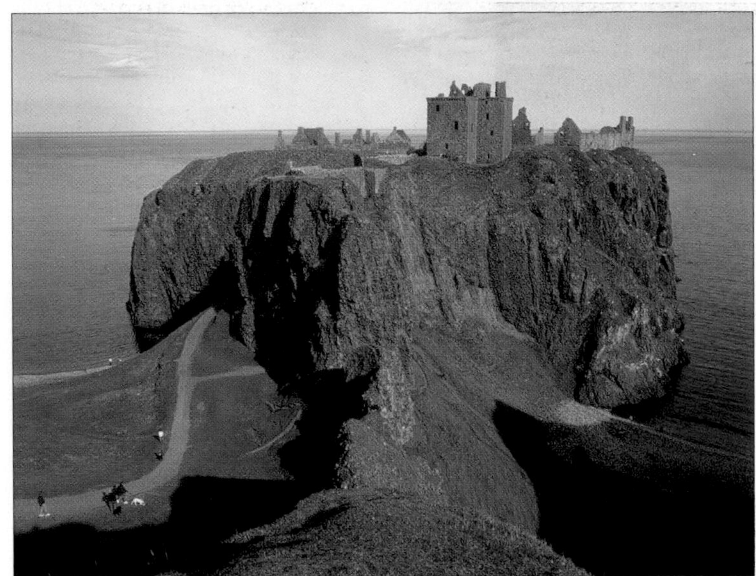

13 **Dunnottar Castle** Page **546** • Memorably dramatic ruined fortress, surrounded by giddy sea cliffs.

14 **St Magnus Cathedral, Kirkwall** Page **695** • A medieval cathedral in miniature, built by the Vikings using the local red and yellow sandstone.

15 **Hillwalking** Page **45** • The array of challenging but accessible hills makes walking one of the best ways to enjoy Scotland.

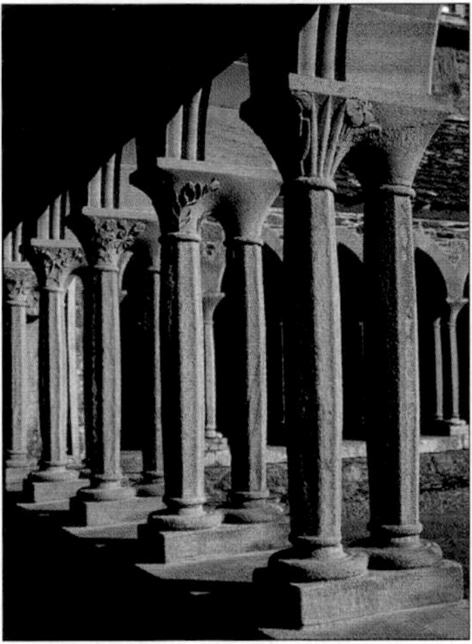

16 Iona Page **401** • The home of Celtic Christian spirituality, an island of pilgrimage today as in antiquity.

17 Caledonian forest Page **604** • The few gnarled survivors of the great ancient Highland forests are majestic characters.

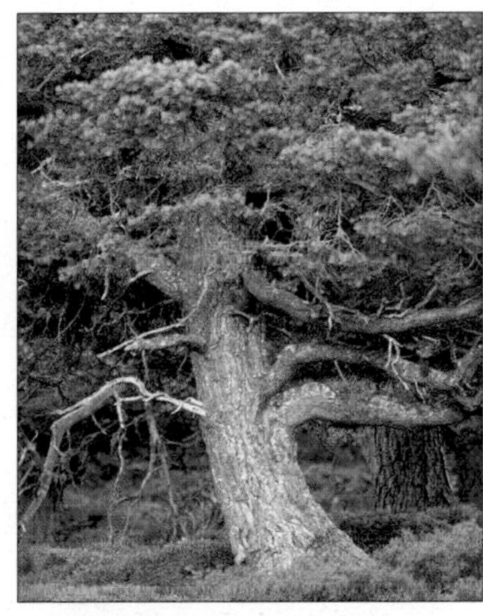

18 Flying above Orkney Page **683** • Take an exhilarating aerial tour of the archipelago in an eight-seater plane.

19 Eigg Page **468** • Perfect example of a tiny, friendly Hebridean island with a golden beach to lie on, a hill to climb and stunning views across the sea to its neighbour, Rùm.

20 Himalayas putting green, St Andrews Page **342** • Play for next-to-nothing right beside the most famous fairway in world golf.

22 Melrose Abbey Page **171** • Ruined Cistercian abbey situated in the most beguiling of Border towns.

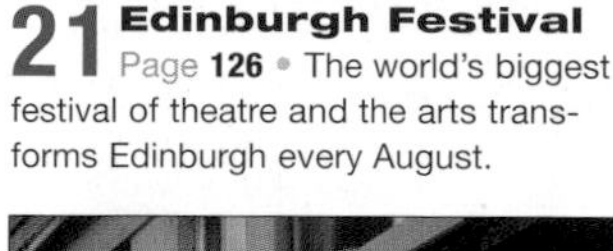

21 Edinburgh Festival Page **126** • The world's biggest festival of theatre and the arts transforms Edinburgh every August.

23 Islay Page **430** • Hebridean island with no fewer than seven whisky distilleries, and wonderfully varied birdlife that includes thousands of wintering geese.

24 Burrell Collection, Glasgow Page **267** • An unconventional but impressive museum at the heart of Glasgow's cultural renaissance.

25 Loch Fyne Oyster Bar Page **374** • Pick up a picnic or enjoy fine dining at Scotland's top smokehouse and seafood outlet, located just outside Inveraray.

26 Shetland folk festival Page **728** • Shetland is the place to experience traditional folk music, and the annual folk festival is the best time to do it.

27 Gearrannan, Lewis Page **481** • Stay in the thatched blackhouse hostel in this beautifully restored former crofting village.

28 The Cairngorm mountains Page **594** • Beguiling natural splendour mixed with terrific outdoor activities.

29 Ailsa Craig Page **223** • Distinctive muffin-shaped island off the Ayrshire coast that's home to thousands of cliff-nesting gannets.

30 Maes Howe, Orkney Page **687** • Europe's best-preserved Neolithic chambered cairn also contains fine examples of Viking runic inscriptions and drawings.

31 DCA, Dundee Page **513** • The Dundee Contemporary Arts centre, an inspiring focus for the town's up-and-coming cultural scene.

32 Stirling Castle Page **302** • The grandest castle in Scotland, with a commanding outlook over Highlands and Lowlands.

33 Jarlshof, Shetland Page **733** • An exceptional archeological site taking in Iron Age, Bronze Age, Pictish, Viking and medieval remains.

34 South Harris beaches Page **487** • Take your pick of deserted golden beaches in South Harris, or further south in the Uists.

35 Skye Cuillin Page **454** • The most spectacular mountain range on the west coast, for viewing or climbing.

36 Pubs Page **34** • Forget the great outdoors and install yourself in one of Scotland's cosy and convivial hostelries.

37 Mousa, Shetland Page **731** • The mother of all Iron Age brochs, on an island off the coast of Shetland.

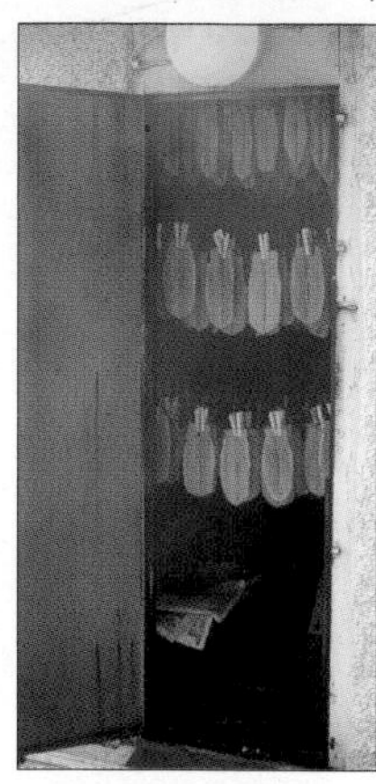

38 Arbroath "smokies" Page **517** • An unsung delicacy – haddock smoked over traditional wood fires, best savoured in this unpretentious east-coast port town.

39 Whale-watching, Gairloch Page **633** • Close encounters with a very different type of Highland wildlife.

40 Pictish stones Page **523** • Intriguing stone carvings by the ancient Picts are found up and down the east coast.

contents

Using the Rough Guide

We've tried to make this Rough Guide a good read and easy to use. The book is divided into five main sections, and you should be able to find whatever you want in one of them.

colour section

The front colour section offers a quick tour of Scotland. The **introduction** aims to give you a feel for the place, with suggestions on where to go. We also tell you what the weather is like and include a basic country fact file. Next, our authors round up their favourite aspects of Scotland in the **things not to miss** section – whether it's great food, amazing sights or a special journey. Right after this comes the Rough Guide's full **contents** list.

basics

You've decided to go and the Basics section covers all the **pre-departure** nitty-gritty to help you plan your trip. This is where to find out which airlines fly to your destination, what paperwork you'll need, what to do about money and insurance, about internet access, food, security, public transport, car rental – in fact just about every piece of **general practical information** you might need.

guide

This is the heart of the Rough Guide, divided into user-friendly chapters, each of which covers a specific region. Every chapter starts with a list of **highlights** and an **introduction** that helps you to decide where to go, depending on your time and budget. Likewise, introductions to the various towns and smaller regions within each chapter should help you plan your itinerary. We start most town accounts with information on arrival and accommodation, followed by a tour of the sights, and finally reviews of places to eat and drink, and details of nightlife. Longer accounts also have a directory of practical listings. Each chapter concludes with **public transport** details for that region.

contexts

Read Contexts to get a deeper understanding of what makes Scotland tick. We include a brief history, articles about **architecture** and **music**, a detailed further reading section that reviews dozens of **books** relating to the country, and a **language** section which gives useful guidance for speaking **Gaelic**, and a glossary of words and terms that are peculiar to the country.

index + small print

Apart from a **full index**, which includes maps as well as places, this section covers publishing information, credits and acknowledgements, and also has our contact details in case you want to send in updates and corrections to the book – or suggestions as to how we might improve it.

chapter map of **Scotland**

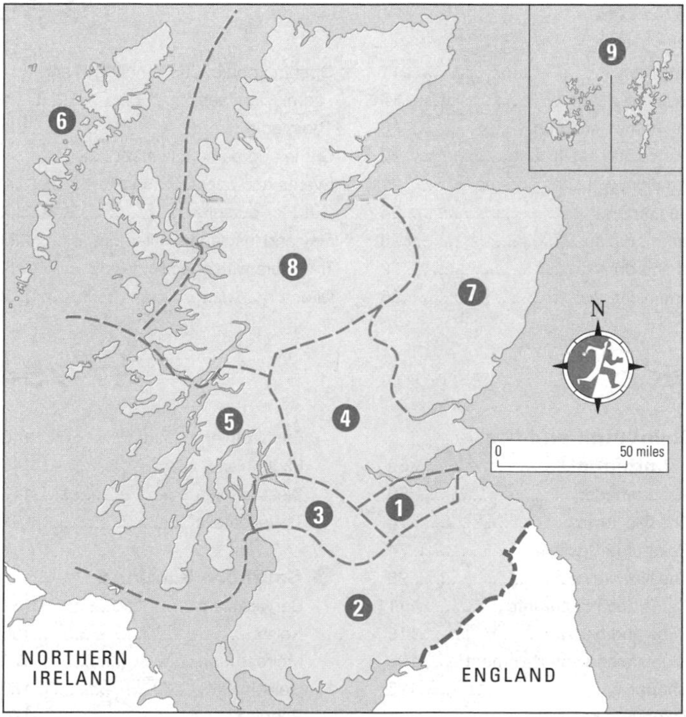

contents

colour section i–xxiv

basics 9–56

guide 57–754

contexts 755–832

language 833–842

index + small print 843–862

map symbols

maps are listed in the full index using coloured text

- Railway
- Motorway
- Road
- Tunnel
- Pedestrianized street
- Steps
- Footpath
- Wall
- Ferry route
- Coastline/river
- Chapter division boundary
- Regional boundary
- International boundary
- Highland boundary fault
- Point of interest
- Peak
- Viewpoint
- Rocks
- Lighthouse
- Airport
- Waterfall
- Cave
- Ruins/archeological site
- Castle
- Abbey
- Stately home
- Museum
- Gardens
- Battlefield
- Campsite
- Accommodation
- Hostel
- Underground station
- Bus stop
- Parking
- Hospital
- Tourist office
- Post office
- Whisky distillery
- Skiing
- Stadium
- Building
- Church
- Cemetery
- Park
- Forest
- Beach

basics

basics

Getting there

There are some nonstop flights to Scotland from North America, but not from Australia or New Zealand; in any case, you'll get a much wider choice – and usually lower fares – if you fly via London. From continental Europe and parts of Britain, the cheapest and quickest way to reach Scotland is by plane. However, road and rail connections from around Britain are pretty straightforward, and there are direct ferries to Scotland from Ireland, Belgium and Scandinavia.

Scotland has three main **international airports:** Glasgow International, Edinburgh and Aberdeen. Only Glasgow handles nonstop scheduled flights from North America; both it and Edinburgh have a reasonable spread of European flights; and Aberdeen has international arrivals only from Scandinavia. Glasgow Prestwick also has a few scheduled flights to and from Europe, and transatlantic flights via Dublin, but the majority of its custom comes from charter airlines. Note that although Glasgow International, Edinburgh and Aberdeen are well linked into the **domestic** network, there are no flights from Glasgow Prestwick to anywhere else in Scotland.

Airfares depend primarily on availability, but they also depend on the **season**, with the highest fares charged from mid-June to mid-September and around Christmas and New Year. Fares will ordinarily be cheaper during the rest of the year, which is considered low season, though some airlines also have a "shoulder" season – typically April to mid-June and mid-September to October.

You can often cut costs by going through a **specialist flight agent** – either a consolidator, who buys up blocks of tickets from the airlines and sells them at a discount, or a **discount agent**, who in addition to dealing with discounted flights may also offer special student and youth fares and a range of other travel-related services such as travel insurance, rail passes, car rentals, tours and the like. Some agents specialize in **charter flights**, which may be cheaper than anything available on a scheduled flight, but again departure dates are fixed and withdrawal penalties are high. You may even find it cheaper to pick up a bargain **package deal** from a tour operator and then find your own accommodation when you get there.

A further possibility is to see if you can arrange a **courier flight**, although you'll need a flexible schedule, and preferably be travelling alone with very little luggage. In return for shepherding a parcel through customs, you can expect to get a deeply discounted ticket. You'll probably also be restricted in the duration of your stay.

If Scotland is part of a planned longer journey, it might be worth considering buying a **Round-the-World** (RTW) ticket. Some travel agents can sell you an "off-the-shelf" RTW ticket that will have you touching down in about half-a-dozen major hub cities. London is a popular stop on RTW tickets, and it's easy to add on a side-trip to Scotland. Alternatively, agents can assemble a RTW routing for you which includes Glasgow.

Booking flights online

Many airlines and discount travel websites offer you the opportunity to book your tickets online, cutting out the costs of agents and middlemen. Good deals can often be found through discount or auction sites, as well as through the airlines' own websites.

Ⓦwww.etn.nl/discount.htm A hub of consolidator and discount agent web links, maintained by the nonprofit European Travel Network.

Ⓦwww.flyaow.com Online air travel info and reservations site.

Ⓦwww.cheaptickets.com Discount flight specialists.

Ⓦwww.cheapflights.com Flight deals, travel agents, plus links to other travel sites.

Ⓦwww.priceline.com Name-your-own-price website that has deals at around forty percent off standard fares. You cannot specify flight times (although you do specify dates). UK site at Ⓦwww.priceline.co.uk.

Ⓦwww.lastminute.com Offers good last-minute holiday package and flight-only deals.

Ⓦwww.deckchair.com Online tickets, drawing on a wide range of airlines.
Ⓦwww.expedia.com Discount airfares, all-airline search engine and daily deals.
Ⓦwww.travelocity.com Destination guides and hot fares. Provides access to the travel agent system SABRE, the most comprehensive central reservations system in the US.
Ⓦwww.hotwire.com Bookings from the US only. Last-minute savings of up to forty percent on regular published fares.
Ⓦwww.skyauction.com Bookings from the US only. Auctions tickets and travel packages using a "second bid" scheme. The best strategy is to bid the maximum you're willing to pay, since if you win you'll pay just enough to beat the runner-up regardless of your maximum bid.
Ⓦwww.travelshop.com.au Australian website offering discounted flights, packages, insurance, online bookings.
Ⓦwww.uniquetravel.com.au Australian site with a good range of packages and good value flights.

From North America

If you want to fly nonstop into Scotland from North America, you have to fly into Glasgow, and even then there's only a limited choice: American Airlines from Chicago, Continental from New York, or Air Canada from Toronto. Most other airlines, and all flights to other Scottish airports, route through London, Manchester or Dublin.

Figure on six to seven hours' **flight time** nonstop from the east coast to Glasgow, or seven hours to London plus an extra hour and a quarter from London to Glasgow or Edinburgh (not including stopover time). Add three or four hours more for travel from the west coast. Most eastbound flights cross the Atlantic overnight, reaching Britain the next morning; flying back, departure times tend to be morning or afternoon, arriving in the afternoon or evening.

Return **fares** (including taxes) to Glasgow from New York or Chicago are $700–800 low season, $800–1000 high season; from Toronto around C$1000 low season, C$1150 high season; from Vancouver (via either Toronto or London) C$1200 low season, C$1400 high season. Flying **into London** works out cheaper, with return fares from New York $400–600 low season, $600–800 high season; from LA add $200 across the board; from Toronto fares are around C$800 low or C$1000 high.

Airlines in North America

Aer Lingus Ⓣ1-800/223-6537, Ⓦwww.aerlingus.ie.
Air Canada Ⓣ1-888/247-2262, Ⓦwww.aircanada.ca.
American Airlines Ⓣ1-800/433-7300, Ⓦwww.aa.com.
British Airways Ⓣ1-800/247-9297, Ⓦwww.britishairways.com.
British Midland Ⓣ1-800/788-0555, Ⓦwww.flybmi.com.
Continental Ⓣ1-800/231-0856, Ⓦwww.continental.com.
Delta Ⓣ1-800/241-4141, Ⓦwww.delta.com.
TWA Ⓣ1-800/892-4141, Ⓦwww.twa.com.
United Airlines Ⓣ1-800/538-2929, Ⓦwww.ual.com.
US Airways Ⓣ1-800/622-1015, Ⓦwww.usairways.com.
Virgin Atlantic Airways Ⓣ1-800/862-8621, Ⓦwww.virgin-atlantic.com.

Flight agents in North America

Air Brokers International Ⓣ1-800/883-3273, Ⓦwww.airbrokers.com. Consolidator and specialist in RTW tickets.
Airhitch Ⓣ1-800/326-2009, Ⓦwww.airhitch.org. Standby-seat broker: for a set price, they guarantee to get you on a flight as close to your preferred destination as possible, within a week.
Airtech Ⓣ212/219-7000, Ⓦwww.airtech.com. Standby seat broker; also deals in consolidator fares and courier flights.
Council Travel Ⓣ1-800/226-8624, Ⓦwww.counciltravel.com. Nationwide organization that mostly, but by no means exclusively, specializes in student/budget travel.
Educational Travel Center Ⓣ1-800/747-5551, Ⓦwww.edtrav.com. Student/youth discount agent.
High Adventure Travel Ⓣ1-800/350-0612, Ⓦwww.airtreks.com. Round-the-world tickets. The website features an interactive database that lets you build and price your own RTW itinerary.
New Frontiers/Nouvelles Frontières Ⓣ1-800/677-0720, Ⓦwww.newfrontiers.com. Discount travel firm.
Skylink US Ⓣ1-800/AIR-ONLY, Canada Ⓣ1-800/SKY-LINK. Consolidator.
STA Travel Ⓣ1-800/777-0112 or Ⓣ1-800/781-4040, Ⓦwww.sta-travel.com. Worldwide specialists in independent travel; also student IDs, travel insurance, car rental, rail passes, and so on.
Student Flights Ⓣ1-800/255-8000, Ⓦwww.isecard.com. Student/youth fares, student IDs.

TFI Tours International ⓣ1-800/745-8000. Consolidator.
Travac ⓣ1-800/872-8800, ⓦwww.thetravelsite.com. Consolidator and charter broker.
Travel Avenue ⓣ1-800/333-3335, ⓦwww.travelavenue.com. Full-service travel agent that offers discounts in the form of rebates.
Travel Cuts US ⓣ416/979-2406, Canada ⓣ1-800/667-2887. Canadian student travel organization.
Travelers Advantage ⓣ1-877/259-2691, ⓦwww.travelersadvantage.com. Discount travel club; annual membership fee required.
Worldtek Travel ⓣ1/800-243-1723, ⓦwww.worldtek.com. Discount travel agency.
Worldwide Discount Travel Club ⓣ305/534-2642. Discount travel club.

Courier flights from North America

Air Courier Association ⓣ1-800/282-1202, ⓦwww.aircourier.org.
International Association of Air Travel Couriers ⓣ561/582-8320, ⓦwww.courier.org.

Tour operators in North America

Abercrombie & Kent ⓣ1-800/323-7308 or ⓣ630/954-2944, ⓦwww.abercrombiekent.com. Cruises, road and rail tours around Scotland.
Adventures Abroad ⓣ1-800/665-3998 or ⓣ604/303-1099, ⓦwww.adventures-abroad.com. Coach tours of Scotland.
BCT Scenic Walking ⓣ1-800/473-1210, ⓦwww.bctwalk.com. Guided walking packages in the Scottish Borders and the Highlands and Islands.
CIE Tours ⓣ1-800/243-8687 or ⓣ973/292-3899, ⓦwww.cietours.com. Escorted coach tours and self-drive packages.
Golf International Inc ⓣ1-800/833-1389, ⓦwww.golfinternational.com. Scottish golf vacation specialist.
Himalayan Travel ⓣ1-800/225-2380 or ⓣ203/743-2349, ⓦwww.gorp.com/himtravel.htm. Guided or self-guided walking and cycling tours in Scotland.
Home at First ⓣ1-800/523-5842, ⓦwww.homeatfirst.com. Flights, cottages, car rental and golf packages.
Jerry Quinlan's Celtic Golf ⓣ1-800/535-6148 or ⓣ609/884-8090, ⓦwww.jqcelticgolf.com. Customized golf tours of Scotland.
Lord Addison Travel ⓣ1-800/326-0170, ⓦwww.lordaddison.com. Escorted coach tours.
Mountain Travel-Sobek ⓣ1-888/687-6235, ⓦwww.mtsobek.com. Hiking holidays.
Prestige Tours ⓣ1-800/890-7375, ⓦwww.prestige-tours.com. Fly-drive, all-inclusive coach tours and city breaks.
Sterling Tours ⓣ1-800/727-4359, ⓦwww.sterlingtours.com. Scottish specialist offering a variety of independent itineraries, plus some packages.

From Australia and New Zealand

Flight time from **Australia and New Zealand** to Scotland is at least 24 hours, and can be more depending on routes and transfer times. There's a wide variety of routes, with those touching down in Southeast Asia the quickest and cheapest on average. To reach Scotland, you'll have to change planes either in London – the most popular choice – or in another European gateway such as Paris or Amsterdam. Given the length of the journey involved, you might be better off including a night's stopover in your itinerary, and indeed some airlines include one in the price of the flight.

The cheapest direct scheduled flights to London are usually to be found on one of the Asian airlines. Average return fares (including taxes) from eastern gateways to London are A$1500–2000 in low season, A$2000–2500 in high season. Fares from **Perth** or **Darwin** cost A$100–200 less. (You need to add A$100–200 onto all these for the flight from London to Glasgow or Edinburgh.) Return fares from **Auckland** to London range between NZ$2000 and NZ$2500 depending on the season, route and carrier.

Airlines in Australia and New Zealand

Air New Zealand Australia ⓣ13 2476, New Zealand ⓣ0800/737000, ⓦwww.airnz.com.
British Airways Australia ⓣ02/8904 8800, New Zealand ⓣ09/356 8690, ⓦwww.britishairways.com.
Cathay Pacific Australia ⓣ13 1747, New Zealand ⓣ09/379 0861, ⓦwww.cathaypacific.com.
Gulf Air Australia ⓣ02/9244 2199, New Zealand ⓣ09/308 3366, ⓦwww.gulfairco.com.
Japanese Airlines (JAL) Australia ⓣ02/9272 1111, New Zealand ⓣ09/379 9906, ⓦwww.jal.com.
KLM Australia ⓣ1300/303747, New Zealand ⓣ09/309 1782, ⓦwww.klm.com.
Korean Air Australia ⓣ02/9262 6000, New Zealand ⓣ09/307 3687, ⓦwww.koreanair.com.

Malaysia Airlines Australia ⓣ13 2627, New Zealand ⓣ09/373 2741, ⓦwww.malaysiaairlines.com.
Qantas Australia ⓣ13 1313, New Zealand ⓣ0800/808 767, ⓦwww.qantas.com.au.
Royal Brunei Airlines Australia ⓣ07/3221 7757, ⓦwww.bruneiair.com.
Singapore Airlines Australia ⓣ13 1011, New Zealand ⓣ0800/808909, ⓦwww.singaporeair.com.
SriLankan Airlines Australia ⓣ02/9244 2234, New Zealand ⓣ09/308 3353, ⓦwww.airlanka.com.
South African Airways Australia ⓣ1800/221 699, New Zealand ⓣ09/379 3708, ⓦwww.flysaa.com.
Thai Airways Australia ⓣ1300/651960, New Zealand ⓣ09/377 3886, ⓦwww.thaiair.com.
United Airlines Australia ⓣ13 1777, New Zealand ⓣ09/379 3800, ⓦwww.united.com.

Flight agents in Australia and New Zealand

Anywhere Travel Australia ⓣ02/9663 0411.
Budget Travel New Zealand ⓣ0800/808040.
Destinations Unlimited New Zealand ⓣ09/373 4033.
Flight Centres Australia ⓣ02/9235 3522 or for nearest branch ⓣ13 1600, New Zealand ⓣ09/358 4310, ⓦwww.flightcentre.com.au.
STA Travel Australia ⓣ1300/360 960, New Zealand ⓣ0800/874773, ⓦwww.statravel.com.au.
Student Uni Travel Australia ⓣ02/9232 8444.
Thomas Cook Australia ⓣ13 1771, New Zealand ⓣ09/379 3920, ⓦwww.thomascook.com.au.
Trailfinders Australia ⓣ02/9247 7666.
Usit Beyond New Zealand ⓣ0800/788336, ⓦwww.usitbeyond.co.nz.

Tour operators in Australia and New Zealand

Best of Britain Australia ⓣ02/9909 1055. Can arrange flights, accommodation, car rental, tours, canal boats and B&Bs throughout Scotland.
Explore Holidays Australia ⓣ02/9857 6200 or ⓣ1300/731000, ⓦwww.exploreholidays.com.au. Accommodation packages and coach tours.

From England and Wales

Crossing the border from England into Scotland is straightforward, with train and bus services forming part of the British national network. **Flying** is quicker than travelling by **train** or **coach** if you're heading out to the Highlands and Islands, though if you add on the time spent getting to and from the airport and checking in, the whole experience doesn't save you as much time as you might think, especially on journeys through the big London airports. Airfares are only competitive on popular routes such as London to Edinburgh and Glasgow and, again, if you add on the cost of travel to and from the airport (and remember to include airport tax), the savings on the same journey overland are often minimal.

By plane

The most competitive **airfares** from England are with the no-frills budget airlines: easyJet flies from **Luton** to Glasgow, Edinburgh, Aberdeen and Inverness; Ryanair from **Stansted** to Prestwick; and Go from Stansted and from **Bristol** to Glasgow and Edinburgh. As a broad guide to what you're likely to pay, reckon on around £30 for a rock-bottom one-way ticket and £50 for a return (including tax). However, the cheaper tickets need to be booked in advance, often apply only to early morning or late evening flights and are either non-refundable or only partially refundable, and non-exchangeable. For more reasonable flight times and/or a more flexible, refundable fare from these same budget airlines, you're looking at more like £100 return, a price that British Airways – with a range of flights out of many English airports – can often compete with. From **Wales**, BA flies from Cardiff to Glasgow or Edinburgh for around £100 return, or to Aberdeen for £140 return.

Airlines

British Airways ⓣ0845/773 3377, ⓦwww.britishairways.com.
British Midland ⓣ0870/607 0555, ⓦwww.flybmi.com.
easyJet ⓣ0870/600 0000, ⓦwww.easyjet.com.
Go ⓣ0870/607 6543, ⓦwww.go-fly.com.
KLM ⓣ0870/507 4074, ⓦwww.klmuk.com.
Ryanair ⓣ0870/156 9569, ⓦwww.ryanair.com.

Flight agents

North South Travel ⓣ01245/608291, ⓦwww.northsouthtravel.co.uk. Friendly, competitive travel agency, whose profits are used to support projects in the developing world.

STA Travel ⓣ0870/160 6070, ⓦwww.statravel.co.uk. Specialists in low-cost flights and tours for students and under-26s, though other customers welcome.
Usit Campus ⓣ0870/240 1010, ⓦwww.usitcampus.co.uk. Student/youth travel specialists, with branches also in YHA shops and on university campuses all over Britain.

By train

Glasgow and Edinburgh are both served by frequent direct **train** services from London, and are easily reached from other main English towns and cities, though you may have to change trains en route. GNER trains depart from **London King's Cross** and run up the east coast via Peterborough, York and Newcastle to Edinburgh, with some going on to Glasgow, Aberdeen or Inverness, while Virgin trains run up the west coast from **London Euston** via Crewe, Preston and Carlisle to Glasgow. The main long-distance direct service to Scotland that doesn't originate in London is on Virgin from **Penzance** to Edinburgh via Birmingham and Newcastle. **Journey times** from London can be as little as 4hr 30min to Edinburgh and 5hr to Glasgow; from Manchester or York, knock off about 2hr; from Bristol add about 2hr. Beyond Edinburgh or Glasgow, allow another 2hr 30min to reach Aberdeen, or 3hr 30min to Inverness.

Fare structures are fiendishly complex, but if you book far enough in advance you can get a London–Glasgow return for £30–50, though if you simply turn up at the station, the cheapest off-peak fare available will be more like £80 return. Virgin offer return fares from Manchester to Glasgow for as little as £10–15 if you book in advance, but £50 on the day; from Bristol to Edinburgh, advance returns cost £50–70, but over £100 on the day. Various discount **passes** are also available in Britain to nationals and foreign visitors alike, for those under 26, over 60, or travelling with children. For more details, and links to sites where you can book online, visit ⓦwww.nationalrail.co.uk.

If you're travelling up from London it's definitely worth considering taking one of the **Caledonian Sleepers**, run by ScotRail from London Euston (daily except Sat) to Glasgow, Edinburgh, Aberdeen, Inverness and Fort William. A sample return fare to Edinburgh or Glasgow is £89 if booked in advance. Sleeper cabins contain two beds, so you may have to share (with someone of the same sex) unless you pay a supplement; first-class customers automatically enjoy the luxury of a single-berth cabin. Otherwise, there's the budget option of a relatively comfortable reclining seat, starting at £25 single; while hardly the lap of luxury, this is still a more attractive option than the rather grim overnight bus journey (which is only a few pounds less expensive). You can usually board the train an hour before departure.

Train information

GNER ⓣ0845/722 5225, ⓦwww.gner.co.uk.
National Rail enquiries ⓣ0845/748 4950, ⓦwww.nationalrail.co.uk.
ScotRail ⓣ0845/755 0033, ⓦwww.scotrail.co.uk.
Virgin ⓣ0845/722 2333, ⓦwww.virgintrains.co.uk.

By coach

Inter-town bus services (known as **coaches** throughout Britain) duplicate many train routes, often at half the price or less. The frequency of service is usually comparable to the train, and in some instances the difference in journey time isn't that great; buses are also reasonably comfortable, and on longer routes often have drinks and sandwiches available on board.

The main operators are **National Express** (ⓣ0870/580 8080, ⓦwww.gobycoach.com) and its sister company **Scottish Citylink** (ⓣ0870/550 5050, ⓦwww.citylink.co.uk). Buses run direct from most British cities to Edinburgh, Glasgow, Aberdeen and Inverness. Typical **fares** from London to Glasgow or Edinburgh (daytime or overnight journeys take around 8hr) are £30 return if bought in advance, £36 on the day; from Cardiff £52 or £58; from Manchester £26 or £29. There are also various discount **passes** available, detailed on the websites.

By car

The two main **driving** routes to Scotland from the south are via the east of England on the A1, or via the west using the M6, A74(M) and M74. The A1, which passes by Peterborough, Doncaster, Newcastle and Berwick-upon-Tweed, gives you the option of branching off onto the A68, which takes the hilly but scenic route over the border at

than half the double-room rate). If you're visiting Edinburgh, which can be pricey, allow at least an extra £10 or so a day.

Tipping

There are no fixed rules for **tipping** in Scotland. If you think you've received good service, particularly in restaurants or cafés, you may want to leave a tip of ten to fifteen percent, but check first that service has not already been included. It is not normal to leave tips in pubs, although bar staff are sometimes offered drinks, which they may accept in the form of money (the assumption being that they'll spend the tip on a drink for themselves after closing time). Taxi drivers, on the other hand, will expect tips on long journeys: ten percent is the norm. The other occasion when you'll be expected to tip is in upmarket hotels where porters, bellboys and table waiters rely on being tipped to bump up their often dismal wages.

Youth and student discounts

Various official and quasi-official **youth/student ID cards** soon pay for themselves in savings; check out Ⓦwww.isic.org for full details. Full-time students are eligible for the International Student ID Card (**ISIC**), which entitles the bearer to special air, rail and bus fares and discounts at museums, theatres and other attractions. For Americans there's also a health benefit with ISIC, providing up to $3000 in emergency medical coverage and $100 a day for sixty days in the hospital, plus a 24-hour hotline to call in the event of a medical, legal or financial emergency. Anybody aged 26 or less qualifies for the **International Youth Travel Card**, which carries the same benefits. Teachers qualify for the **International Teacher Card**, offering similar discounts. Check the website for details of outlets selling the cards, all of which cost in the order of US$22, C$16, A$16.50, NZ$21 or £6.

Insurance and health

Even though EU health care privileges apply in Scotland, you'd do well to take out an insurance policy before travelling to cover against theft, loss and illness or injury. Before paying for a new policy, however, it's worth checking whether you are already covered: some all-risks home insurance policies may cover your possessions when overseas, and many private medical schemes include cover when abroad. In Canada, provincial health plans usually provide partial cover for medical mishaps overseas, while holders of official student/teacher/youth cards in Canada and the US are entitled to meagre accident coverage and hospital in-patient benefits. Students will often find that their student health coverage extends during the vacations and for one term beyond the date of last enrollment.

After exhausting the possibilities above, you'll probably want to contact a specialist travel insurance company, or consider the travel insurance deal we offer (see box). A typical travel insurance policy usually provides cover for the loss of baggage, tickets and – up to a certain limit – cash or cheques, as well as cancellation or curtailment of your journey. Most of them exclude so-called dangerous sports unless an extra premium is paid: in Scotland this can mean scuba diving, windsurfing and skiing. Many policies can be chopped and changed to exclude coverage you don't need: for example, sickness and accident benefits can often be excluded or included at will. If you do take medical coverage, ascertain whether benefits will be paid as treatment proceeds or only after return home, and whether there is a 24-hour medical emergency number. When securing baggage cover, make sure that the per-article limit – typically under £500 – will cover your most valuable possession. If you need to make a

Rough Guides travel insurance

Rough Guides offers its own travel insurance, customized for our readers by a leading UK broker and backed by a Lloyd's underwriter. It's available for anyone, of any nationality and any age, travelling anywhere in the world.

There are two main Rough Guide insurance plans: **Essential**, for basic, no-frills cover; and **Premier** – with more generous and extensive benefits. Alternatively, you can take out **annual multi-trip insurance**, which covers you for any number of trips throughout the year (with a maximum of sixty days for any one trip). Unlike many policies, the Rough Guides schemes are calculated by the day, so if you're travelling for 27 days rather than a month, that's all you pay for. If you intend to be away for the whole year, the **Adventurer** policy will cover you for 365 days. Each plan can be supplemented with a "Hazardous Activities Premium" if you plan to indulge in sports considered dangerous, such as skiing, scuba diving or trekking.

To get a quote and buy a policy, go to Ⓦwww.roughguides.com/insurance, or call the Rough Guides Insurance Line on US toll-free Ⓣ1-866/220 5588, UK freefone Ⓣ0800/015 0906, or, if you're calling from elsewhere, Ⓣ+44-1243/621046.

claim, you should keep receipts for medicines and medical treatment, and in the event you have anything stolen, you must obtain an official statement from the police.

Health

No vaccinations are required for entry to the UK. EU citizens are entitled to free medical treatment at National Health Service hospitals on production of an **E111** form. Australia, New Zealand and several non-EU European countries have reciprocal health-care arrangements with the UK. Citizens of other countries will be charged for all medical services except those administered by Accident and Emergency (A&E) units at National Health Service hospitals. In other words, if you've just been hit by a car, you would not be charged if the injuries simply required stitching and setting in the emergency unit, but would were admission to a hospital ward be necessary. Health insurance is therefore extremely advisable for all non-EU nationals.

Pharmacists can dispense only a limited range of drugs without a doctor's prescription. Most are open standard shop hours, though in large towns some may close as late as 10pm; local newspapers carry lists of late-opening pharmacies, or you can contact the local police for current details. **Doctors' surgeries** tend to be open from about 9am to noon and then for a couple of hours in the evening; outside surgery hours, you can turn up at the casualty department of the local hospital for complaints that require immediate attention – unless it's an emergency, in which case call for an ambulance on Ⓣ999.

Information, websites and maps

If you want to do a bit of research before arriving in Scotland, you should contact the British Tourist Authority (BTA) in your country or the main office of the Scottish Tourist Board (STB). Either will send you a wealth of free literature, much of it rose-tinted advertising copy, though some of it might prove useful – in particular the maps, city guides, event calendars and accommodation brochures. If you want more hard facts on a specific area, phone the regional tourist board or visit its website.

Tourist offices (often called Tourist Information Centres or "TICs") exist in virtually every Scottish town; you'll find their phone numbers and opening hours in the relevant sections throughout this book. **Opening hours** are frequently confusing and vary from place to place and month to month, with offices in many areas closing completely in the winter season. Often stacked full of souvenirs and other gifts, most TICs have a decent selection of leaflets, displays, maps and books relating to the local area. The staff are usually helpful and will do their best to help with enquiries about accommodation, local public transport, attractions and restaurants, although it is worth being aware that they are reluctant to divulge information about local attractions or accommodation which are not paid-up members of the Tourist Board – and a number of perfectly decent guesthouses and the like choose not to pay the fees. Some offices may make a small charge for a town guide with an accompanying street plan, or an accommodation list, and most will charge a fee of between £1 and £3 if they book accommodation for you (see p.28).

British Tourist Authority

Ⓦ **www.visitbritain.com**
Australia Level UK, Gateway, 1 MacQuarie Place, Circular Quay, Sydney, NSW 2000 Ⓣ02/9377 4400.
Canada 11 Avenue Rd #450, Toronto, ON M5R 3J8 Ⓣ1-888/VISIT-UK or Ⓣ905/405-1840.
Ireland 18–19 College Green, Dublin 2 Ⓣ01/670 8100.
New Zealand 17th floor, Fay Richwhite Building, 151 Queen St, Auckland 1 Ⓣ09/303 1446.
USA 551 Fifth Ave #701, New York, NY 10176 Ⓣ1-800/GO-2-BRITAIN or Ⓣ212/986-2200.

Scottish Tourist Board

Ⓦ **www.visitscotland.com**
Scotland 23 Ravelston Terrace, Edinburgh EH4 3EU Ⓣ0131/332 2433.
England 19 Cockspur St, London SW1Y 5BL Ⓣ020/7321 5000.

Regional tourist boards

Aberdeen and Grampian Ⓣ01224/288828, Ⓦwww.castlesandwhisky.com.
Angus and City of Dundee Ⓣ01382/527527, Ⓦwww.angusanddundee.co.uk.
Argyll, the Isles, Loch Lomond, Stirling and Trossachs Ⓣ01786/470945, Ⓦwww.scottish.heartlands.org.
Ayrshire and Arran Ⓣ01292/288688, Ⓦwww.ayrshire-arran.com.
Dumfries and Galloway Ⓣ01387/253862, Ⓦwww.dumfriesandgalloway.co.uk.
Edinburgh and the Lothians Ⓣ0131/473 3800, Ⓦwww.edinburgh.org.
Greater Glasgow and Clyde Valley Ⓣ0141/204 4480, Ⓦwww.seeglasgow.com.
Highlands of Scotland Ⓣ01997/421160, Ⓦwww.host.co.uk.
Kingdom of Fife Ⓣ01592/750066, Ⓦwww.standrews.com/fife.
Orkney Ⓣ01856/872856, Ⓦwww.visitorkney.com.
Perthshire Ⓣ01738/627958, Ⓦwww.perthshire.co.uk.
Scottish Borders Ⓣ01750/20555, Ⓦwww.scot-borders.co.uk.
Shetland Ⓣ01595/693434, Ⓦwww.visitshetland.com.
Western Isles Ⓣ01851/703088, Ⓦwww.witb.co.uk.

Useful websites

Ⓦ**www.aboutscotland.com** Useful for accommodation, easy to use and linked to holiday activities.
Ⓦ**ceolas.org/ceolas.html** A very informative Celtic music site, both historical and contemporary, with lots of music to listen to.
Ⓦ**www.geo.ed.ac.uk/home/scotland/scotland.html** Produced by the Geography Department of Edinburgh University – an introduction to all things Scottish, history, geography and politics. Excellent background information with a myriad of links.
Ⓦ**www.hebrides.com** Absorbing site on the islands off the west coast of Scotland, with masses of pages and links.
Ⓦ**www.highlanderweb.co.uk** Styled as a magazine aimed primarily at businesses, but with a mixture of radio, music, products and more.
Ⓦ**www.knowhere.co.uk** A self-styled user's guide to Britain. Up-to-date info, with readers' comments, including best-of and worst-of sections.
Ⓦ**www.rampantscotland.com** Index of links to everything Scottish; well worth going to if you're searching for something specific.
Ⓦ**www.scotland-info.co.uk** A big site covering the whole of the country, with a commercial bent – lots of links to shops, hotels and so on – but good on information for individual areas.

Ⓦ **www.scotlandthegreen.co.uk** Aimed at veggie, vegan and eco-friendly folk. As yet it's not very comprehensive, but it's getting there, with detail on travel, holidays, accommodation and shops.
Ⓦ **www.stonepages.com/scotland** An offbeat though perfectly sane and informative website for those hooked on cairns and stone circles.
Ⓦ **www.travelscotland.co.uk** Run in association with the STB, this is a lively magazine-format site, full of news, features and reviews, but perhaps less useful for arranging a holiday.
Ⓦ **www.wannabethere.com** Scottish adventure holidays for 16- to 35-year-olds, everything from pony trekking to all-night partying; well worth a look if you need inspiration.

Maps

The most comprehensive maps of Scotland are produced by the **Ordnance Survey** or OS (Ⓦwww.ordsvy.gov.uk), renowned for their accuracy and clarity. The 204 maps in their 1:50,000 (pink) Landranger series cover the whole of Britain and show enough detail to be useful for most walkers and cyclists. There's more detail still in the 1:25,000 (green) Pathfinder series, which also covers the whole of Britain, though it is currently being replaced by the new full-colour 1:25,000 (orange) Explorer series. The full Ordnance Survey range is only available at a few big-city stores, although in any walking district of Scotland you'll find the relevant maps in local shops or tourist offices. If you're planning a walk of more than a couple of hours in duration, or intend to walk in the Scottish hills at all, it is strongly recommended that you carry the relevant OS map and familiarize yourself with how to navigate using it.

Virtually every service station in Scotland stocks at least one large-format **road atlas**, covering all of Britain at around three miles to one inch, and generally including larger-scale plans of major towns. You could also invest in the excellent **fold-out maps** published by Michelin and Bartholomew; the latter includes clear town plans of the major cities. Another option is the official tourist map series published by Estate Publications, perfect if you're driving or cycling round one particular region since it marks all the major tourist sights as well as youth hostels and campsites. These are available from just about every tourist office in Scotland.

Map outlets

UK and Ireland

Blackwell's Map and Travel Shop 53 Broad St, Oxford OX1 3BQ Ⓣ01865/792792, Ⓦwww.bookshop.blackwell.co.uk.
Heffers Map and Travel 20 Trinity St, Cambridge CB2 1TJ Ⓣ01223/568568, Ⓦwww.heffers.co.uk.
Hodges Figgis Bookshop 56–58 Dawson St, Dublin 2 Ⓣ01/677 4754, Ⓦwww.hodgesfiggis.com.
James Thin Melven's 29 Union St, Inverness IV1 1QA Ⓣ01463/233500, Ⓦwww.jthin.co.uk.
John Smith 26 Colquhoun Ave, Glasgow G52 4PJ Ⓣ0141/552 3377, Ⓦwww.johnsmith.co.uk.
Stanfords 12–14 Long Acre, London WC2E 9LP Ⓣ020/7836 1321, Ⓦwww.stanfords.co.uk.

North America

Adventurous Traveler PO Box 64769, Burlington, VT 05406 Ⓣ1-800/282-3963, Ⓦwww.adventuroustraveler.com.
Forsyth Travel Library 226 Westchester Ave, White Plains, NY 10604 Ⓣ1-800/367-7984, Ⓦwww.forsyth.com.
Globe Corner 28 Church St, Cambridge, MA 02138 Ⓣ1-800/358-6013, Ⓦwww.globecorner.com.
Map Link 30 S La Patera Lane #5, Santa Barbara, CA 93117 Ⓣ805/692-6777, Ⓦwww.maplink.com.
Rand McNally 444 N Michigan Ave, Chicago, IL 60611 Ⓣ312/321-1751 and nationwide, Ⓦwww.randmcnally.com.
World of Maps 118 Holland Ave, Ottawa, ON K1Y 0X6 Ⓣ613/724-6776, Ⓦwww.itmb.com.
World Wide Books and Maps 1247 Granville St, Vancouver, BC V6Z 1G3 Ⓣ604/687-3320, Ⓦwww.worldofmaps.com.

Australia and New Zealand

Mapland 372 Little Bourke St, Melbourne Ⓣ03/9670 4383, Ⓦwww.mapland.com.au.
Map Shop 6 Peel St, Adelaide Ⓣ08/8231 2033, Ⓦwww.mapshop.net.au.
Mapworld 173 Gloucester St, Christchurch Ⓣ03/374 5399, Ⓦwww.mapworld.co.nz.
Perth Map Centre 1/884 Hay St, Perth Ⓣ08/9322 5733, Ⓦwww.perthmap.com.au.
Specialty Maps 46 Albert St, Auckland Ⓣ09/307 2217, Ⓦwww.ubd-online.co.nz/maps.

Getting around

The majority of Scots live in the central belt, which spreads from Glasgow in the west to Edinburgh, virtually on the east coast. Public transport here is efficient and most places are easily accessible by train and bus. To the south and north it can be a different story: off the main routes, public transport services are few and far between, particularly in more remote parts of the Highlands and Islands. With careful planning, however, practically everywhere is accessible and you'll have no trouble getting to the main tourist destinations. In most parts of Scotland, especially if you take the scenic back roads, the low level of traffic makes driving wonderfully unstressful.

By train

Scotland has a modest **rail** network, at its densest in the central belt, at its most skeletal in the Highlands, and all-but-nonexistent in the Islands. **ScotRail** runs the majority of train services, reaching all the major towns, sometimes on lines rated as among the great scenic routes of the world.

You can buy **tickets** for ScotRail trains at stations, from major travel agents, or over the phone and online with a credit card. If the ticket office at the station is closed, you can usually buy a ticket on board from the inspector using cash or a credit card. However, the inspector cannot always issue discounted or special-offer tickets. The cheapest tickets on ScotRail trains are APEX fares, which must be purchased at least 48 hours in advance of departure.

To find out about the numerous discounted national rail passes, contact National Rail enquiries. In addition, ScotRail offers a couple of **travel passes** worth considering. The most flexible is the **Freedom of Scotland Travelpass**, which gives unlimited train travel within Scotland. It's also valid on all CalMac ferries and on various buses in the remoter regions, and gives discounts on P&O ferries to Orkney and Shetland. Various versions of the pass are available, starting at £79 for four days' travel in an eight-day period, with discounts for national rail card holders. The **Highland Rover** is more limited in scope, allowing unlimited travel on trains within the Highland region, plus the West Highland Line, travel between Aberdeen and Aviemore and a few connecting bus routes; it starts at £49 for four out of eight consecutive days.

Much less tempting are the various national rail passes which allow unlimited travel in Scotland, England and Wales. The only one that can be bought in the UK is the **All-Line Rover**, which starts at a whopping £315 for seven consecutive days' travel (with discounts for national rail card holders). **BritRail passes** are only available for purchase before you leave your home country, through local travel agents or the specialist companies listed below. There are basically two versions of the pass: the standard BritRail Pass, which allows unlimited standard-class travel and starts at US$265/A$383/NZ$459 for eight consecutive days; and the BritRail Flexipass, which allows four days of travel within a two-month period, starting at US$235/A$336/NZ$403. There are various discounts available for those under 26 or over 60, and for those with children.

If you've been resident in a European country other than the UK for at least six months, an **InterRail** pass, allowing unlimited train travel within Britain might be a cost-effective way to travel, if Scotland is part of a longer European trip. For more details, visit Ⓦwww.inter-rail.co.uk.

On most ScotRail routes **bicycles** are carried free, but since there are only between two and six bike spaces available, it's essential that you reserve ahead.

Train information

UK

National Rail enquiries ⓣ0845/748 4950, Ⓦwww.nationalrail.co.uk. Gives details of timetables, fares and other information on rail travel throughout the UK.

ScotRail ⓣ0845/755 0033, ⓦwww.scotrail.co.uk. For booking tickets and seats on all trains within Scotland, and sleeper trains from London to Scotland.

North America

BritRail ⓣ1-877/677-1066, ⓦwww.britrail.net. Official BritRail site, with links to agents.

DER Travel ⓣ1-888/337-7350, ⓦwww.dertravel.com/rail. Eurail, Europass and individual country passes.

Europrail International ⓣ1-888/667-9734, ⓦwww.europrail.net. Eurail, Europass and individual country passes.

Online Travel ⓣ1-800/660-5300, ⓦwww.eurorail.com. Eurail, Europass and passes for Britain.

Rail Europe US ⓣ1-877/456-RAIL, Canada ⓣ1-800/361-RAIL, ⓦwww.raileurope.com. Official North American Eurail agent; also sells BritRail and other passes.

Australia and New Zealand

Rail Plus Australia ⓣ1300/555 003, New Zealand ⓣ09/303 2484, ⓦwww.railplus.com.au. Sells Eurail, Europass and Britrail passes.

By coach and bus

All Scotland's major towns and cities are served by long-distance bus services, known across Britain as **coaches**, the majority of which are run by the national operator, **Scottish Citylink** (ⓣ0870/550 5050, ⓦwww.citylink.co.uk). On the whole, coaches are cheaper than the equivalent train journey and, as a result, are very popular, so for busy routes and travel at weekends and holidays it's a good idea to buy a "reserved-journey ticket", which guarantees you a seat.

There are various **discount cards** on offer for those with children, those under 26 or over 50 and full-time students: contact Scottish Citylink for more on these. If you plan to do a lot of travelling by coach, it may be worth buying an **Explorer Pass**, which offers unlimited travel on Scottish Citylink: prices start at £33 for three consecutive days with reductions for discount card holders. If you're travelling a lot in England and Wales, too, you might be better off with a National Express **Tourist Trail Pass**, which gives you unlimited travel throughout Britain on National Express and Scottish Citylink coaches. You can buy these passes in North America from Britbus (ⓣ540/298-1395, ⓦwww.britbus.com).

Local bus services are run by a bewildering array of companies, many of which change routes and timetables frequently. As a general rule, the further away from urban areas you get, the less frequent and more expensive bus services become. On the

Minibus tours

If you're backpacking or don't have your own transport, a cheap, flexible and fun way of getting a flavour of Scotland is to join one of the popular **minibus tours** that operate out of Edinburgh and head off into the Highlands. The current leading operator, **Haggis** (ⓣ0131/557 9393, ⓦwww.haggisadventures.com), has bright yellow minibuses setting off daily on whistlestop tours of various parts of Scotland lasting between one and six days. In the company of a live-wire guide, the tours aim to show backpackers a mix of classic highlights with a few well-chosen spots off the tourist trail, with an emphasis on keeping the on-board atmosphere lively. A three-day round-trip from Edinburgh starts from £69 (food and accommodation not included). A popular variant on this is a **jump-on/jump-off** ticket (also from £69) which allows you to stop off where you want for as long as you want, but still take advantage of the guided tour and guaranteed transport connections as you go.

Several other companies offer similar packages, including **Macbackpackers** (ⓣ0131/558 9900, ⓦwww.macbackpackers.com), who run tours linking up their own hostels round the country, and **Wild in Scotland** (ⓣ0131/478 6500, ⓦwww.wild-in-scotland.com), who unlike the others take in the Outer Hebrides during their six-day tour. The popular **Rabbie's Trail Burners** tours (ⓣ0131/226 3133, ⓦwww.rabbies.com) don't aim squarely at the backpacker market and have a rather more mellow approach.

Other tours offering different slants on the Scottish experience are **Heart of Scotland** (ⓣ0131/558 8855, ⓦwww.heartofscotlandtours.co.uk), which organizes an informal traditional music session during its overnight stop, and **Walkabout Scotland** (ⓣ0131/661 7168, ⓦwww.walkaboutscotland.com), a company specializing in hill-walking day-trips from Edinburgh.

chores before leaving), many retain an institutionalized air about them. Bunk-bed accommodation in single-sex dormitories, 11.30pm curfews and no smoking/no alcohol policies are the norm outside the big cities. Breakfast is not normally included in the price, though most hostels have self-catering facilities.

In order to stay in an SYHA hostel, you must be a member of one of the hostelling organizations affiliated to **Hostelling International** (**HI**). If you aren't a member in your home country, you can join at any SYHA hostel for a £9 fee (£6 for people resident in Scotland). You can also choose to pay the fee in £1.50 instalments over your first six nights, meaning that you can avoid the full whack if you end up staying only a couple of nights in hostels.

Particularly in the popular city hostels, **advance booking** is recommended, and just about essential at Easter, Christmas and from May to August. You can book by post, phone and sometimes fax, and your bed will be held until 6pm on the day of arrival. If you have a credit card, you can use either the SYHA website or HI's **International Booking Network** (IBN) to book beds as far as six months in advance. The SYHA Handbook (£1) gives full details for every hostel.

The **Gatliff Hebridean Hostels Trust (GHHT)** is a charitable organization allied to the SYHA that rents out very simple croft accommodation in the Western Isles. Accommodation is very basic, almost primitive, and many of these hostels have no phone, but the settings are invariably spectacular. Elsewhere in the Highlands and Islands, these places tend to be known as "**bothies**" or "**bunkhouses**", and usually independently-run. In Shetland, camping böds, operated by the **Shetland Amenity Trust**, offer similarly plain accommodation: you need all your usual camping equipment to stay at one (except, of course, a tent). For more details about Gatliff hostels and camping böds, see the relevant chapters in the guide.

Many **independent hostels** now compete with the SYHA hostels. These are usually laid-back places with no membership, fewer rules and no curfew, housed in buildings ranging from croft houses to converted churches. These are detailed in the *Independent Hostels Guide to Britain & Europe* by Sam Dalley, which is updated annually and distributed by Cordee (Ⓦwww.cordee.co.uk). Many of them are affiliated to the **Independent Backpackers Hostels of Scotland** (Ⓦwww.hostel-scotland.co.uk), and some also feature in **Highland Hostels** (Ⓦwww.highland-hostels.co.uk), a more discerning association that concentrates on the best-run and more independent-minded places.

Hostelling organizations

Australia Ⓣ02/9261 1111, Ⓦwww.yha.com.au.
Canada Ⓣ1-800/663-5777, Ⓦwww.hostellingintl.ca.
England and Wales Ⓣ0870/870 8808, Ⓦwww.yha.org.uk.
Ireland Ⓣ01/830 4555, Ⓦwww.anoige.ie.
Northern Ireland Ⓣ028/9032 4733, Ⓦwww.hini.org.uk.
New Zealand Ⓣ03/379 9970, Ⓦwww.yha.co.nz.
Scotland Ⓣ0870/155 3255, Ⓦwww.syha.org.uk.
USA Ⓣ202/783-6161, Ⓦwww.hiayh.org.

Camping and self-catering

One option for campers is to head for one of the hundreds of official **caravan and camping parks** around Scotland, most of which are open from April to October. The most expensive sites, which charge about £10 to pitch a tent, are usually well equipped, with shops, a restaurant, a bar and, occasionally, sports facilities. The AA motoring organization lists and grades campsites in its publication *Camping and Caravanning in Britain and Ireland*, and regional tourist boards can all supply lists of their recommended sites. Most of these, however, are principally aimed at caravans, trailers and motorhomes, and generally don't offer the tranquil atmosphere and independence those travelling with a tent are seeking.

That said, informal sites of the kind tent campers relish do exist, and are described throughout this guide, though they are few and far between. Some hostels allow camping, and farmers sometimes let folk camp on their land for free or for a nominal sum. Scotland's relaxed trespass law allows you the freedom to **camp wild** in open country, though most outdoor enthusiasts who make use of this emphasize the importance of being discreet and responsible, ensuring that you camp well away from private residences, livestock and cultivated land, and that you remove all signs of your presence when you leave.

The great majority of **caravans** are permanently moored nose-to-tail in the vicinity of some of Scotland's finest scenery; others are positioned singly in back gardens or amidst farmland. Some can be booked for self-catering, and with prices hovering around £100 a week, this can work out as one of the cheapest options if you're travelling with kids in tow.

If you're planning to do a lot of camping at official camping and caravanning sites, it might be worthwhile joining the Camping and Caravanning Club (Ⓣ024/7669 4995, Ⓦwww.campingandcaravanningclub.co.uk). Membership costs around £30 and entitles you to pay only a per-person fee, not a pitch fee, at CCC sites. Those coming from abroad can get the same benefits by buying an international camping carnet, available from home motoring organizations or a CCC equivalent.

Self-catering

A **self-catering** cottage or apartment is a good way to cut down on costs. In most cases, however, and particularly during summer, the minimum period of let is a week, and therefore isn't a valid option if you're aiming to tour round the country. The least you can expect to pay is around £150 per week for a place sleeping four, but something special – such as a well-sited coastal cottage – might cost two or three times that amount. Such is the number and variety of self-catering places on offer that we've mentioned only a few in the guide; the prices given are weekly summer rates, which tend to fall dramatically out of season. A good source of information is the STB's self-catering guide, updated annually, and listing over 1200 properties.

CKD Finlayson Hughes Ⓣ01463/224343, Ⓦwww.ckdfh.co.uk. Fifty or so properties mainly in the Highlands and Islands, Perth and Aberfeldy; everything from castles to bothies.

Country Cottages in Scotland Ⓣ0870/444 1133, Ⓦwww.countrycottagesinscotland.co.uk. Superior cottages with lots of character scattered across the Scottish mainland, plus Skye and Mull.

Ecosse Unique Ⓣ01835/870779, Ⓦwww.uniquescotland.com. Carefully selected cottages across mainland Scotland, plus Skye and Mull.

Forest Holidays Ⓣ0131/334 0303, Ⓦwww.forestholidays.co.uk. Only two sites, at Loch Awe, and Strathyre near Callander: purpose-built cabins in beautiful woodland areas, sleeping five or six people.

Highland Hideaways Ⓣ01631/563901, Ⓦwww.highlandhideaways.co.uk. A range of self-catering properties, mainly on the Highlands and Islands, which range from a former bank in Oban to a converted boathouse on Loch Awe.

Landmark Trust Ⓣ01628/825925, Ⓦwww.landmarktrust.co.uk. Fifteen upmarket historical properties in Scotland.

National Trust for Scotland Ⓣ0131/243 9331, Ⓦwww.nts.org.uk. The NTS lets around forty of its converted historic cottages and houses.

Welcome Cottage Holidays Ⓣ01756/700599, Ⓦwww.welcome.cottages.co.uk. A wide range of unpretentious cottages all over Scotland (excluding the Outer and Northern Isles).

Campus accommodation

A different, equally cheap, self-catering option, especially if you're staying a week or more in one of the cities, is **campus accommodation**. The universities of Glasgow, Strathclyde, Edinburgh, Stirling, St Andrews and Dundee all open their halls of residence to overseas visitors during the summer break, and some also offer rooms during the Easter and Christmas vacations. Accommodation varies from tiny single rooms in long, lonely corridors to relatively comfortable places in small shared apartments. Prices per night for bed and breakfast tend to be no cheaper than local B&Bs, but they can work out decent value per week for self-catering. We've listed each place in the relevant city listings, or you can contact Venuemasters (Ⓣ0114/249 3090, Ⓦwww.venuemasters.co.uk) for a brochure.

Food and drink

Scottish cuisine may not be famous round the world but the quality of local produce – particularly meat, fish, shellfish and game – is outstanding, and eating out in Scotland has improved immensely in the last few years as these assets have been brought to the fore. In the larger towns and cities you'll normally find a clutch of reasonable restaurants, an awakening café/bistro culture and a couple of Indian, Italian or Chinese restaurants.

What to eat

In many hotels and B&Bs you'll be offered a **Scottish breakfast**, similar to its English counterpart of sausage, bacon and egg, but typically with the addition of local favourites such as black pudding (blood sausage) and potato scones. Porridge is another likely option, properly made with oatmeal and water and cooked with salt; it's traditional to add a little milk, though some folk like to sprinkle on some sugar as well. You may also be offered strongly flavoured kippers (hot smoked herring) or more delicate "Arbroath smokies" (smoked haddock). Oatcakes (plain, slightly salty oatmeal biscuits) and a "buttery" – a butter-enriched bread related to the French croissant and popular in the north of Scotland – might feature. Scotland's staple drink, like England's, is **tea**, made from dubious teabags and drunk strong and with milk, though **coffee** is just as readily available everywhere. However, while designer coffee shops are now a familiar feature in the cities, and decent coffee is available in more and more places across the country, execrable versions of espressos and cappuccinos, as well as dire instant coffee, are still all too familiar.

The quintessential Scots dish is **haggis**, a type of rich sausage meat made from spiced liver, offal, oatmeal and onion and cooked inside a bag made from a sheep's stomach. Though more frequently found on tourist-oriented menus than the dining tables of Scots at home, it's traditionally eaten with "bashed neeps" (mashed turnips) and "chappit tatties" (mashed potatoes). The humble haggis has become rather trendy in recent years, appearing in swanky restaurants wrapped in filo pastry or drizzled with berry sauce, and a vegetarian version is widely available. Other traditional dishes which you may well encounter include **stovies**, a tasty mash of onion and fried potato heated up with minced beef, or various forms of meat pie: a **Scotch pie** has mince inside a circular hard pastry case, while a **bridie**, famously associated with the town of Forfar, has mince and onions inside a flaky pastry crescent. In this cold climate, home-made soup is often welcome; try **Scots broth**, made with combinations of lentil, split pea, mutton stock or vegetables and barley. A more refined delicacy is **Cullen skink**, a rich soup made from smoked haddock, potatoes and cream.

Scots **beef** is delicious, especially the Aberdeen Angus breed; menus will specify if your steak falls into that fine category. Scots farmers, aware of the standards their produce has reached, have preciously guarded their stock from the recent troubles associated with BSE and foot and mouth disease. **Venison**, the meat of the red deer, also features large – low in cholesterol and very tasty, it's served roasted or in casseroles, often cooked with juniper and red wine. If you like **game** and can afford it, splash out on grouse, the most highly prized of all game birds, which when cooked properly is strong, dark and succulent. Pheasant is also worth a try and is less rich than other game, more like a tasty chicken; you can eat it stuffed with oatmeal or with a mealie pudding, a kind of vegetarian black pudding made from onion, oatmeal and spices.

Scottish **fish and shellfish** is the envy of Europe, with a vast array of different types of fish, prawns, lobster, mussels, oysters, crab and scallops found round the extensive Scottish coastline. Fresh fish is normally available in most coastal towns, as well as the big cities, where restaurants have well-organized supply lines. Elaborate dishes are sometimes concocted, though frankly the best seafood dishes are frequently the simplest. The prevalence of fish farming, now a significant industry in the Highlands and Islands, means that the once-treasured **salmon** is widespread and relatively inexpensive – its pale pink flesh is still delicious, though those concerned about the environment make sure to search out organic salmon, and connoisseurs keep an eye out for the more delicately flavoured (and more expensive) wild salmon. Both salmon and **trout**, another commonly farmed fish, are frequently smoked and served cold with bread and butter. **Herring**, once the staple fish in Scotland, is still popular in some parts fried in oatmeal or "soused" (pickled).

Another local product to enjoy an upsurge in popularity recently is **cheese**, which you'll find in a number of specialist shops and delis, while many classier restaurants making a point of serving only Scottish cheeses after dinner. The types on offer cover a wide spectrum: look out in particular for Isle of Mull, a tangy farmhouse cheddar; Dunsyre Blue, a Scottish Dolcelatte; and Howgate, a Camembert made near St Andrews.

Scotland is notorious for its sweet tooth, and **cakes and puddings** are taken very seriously. Bakers with extensive displays of of iced buns, cakes and cream-filled pastries are a typical feature of any Scottish high street, while home-made shortbread, scones or tablet (a hard, crystalline form of fudge) are considered great treats. Among traditional desserts, "clootie dumpling" is a sweet, stodgy fruit pudding soaked in a cloth for hours, while the rather over-elaborate Cranachan, made with toasted oatmeal steeped in whisky and folded into whipped cream flavoured with fresh raspberries, or the similar Atholl Brose, are considered more refined. In the summer months, Scottish berries, in particular raspberries and strawberries, are particularly tasty.

One Scottish institution that refuses to die out is **high tea**, consisting of a cooked main course and a plethora of cakes, washed down with lots of tea and eaten between about 5 and 6.30pm.

As for **fast food**, fish and chips is as popular as in England and chip shops, or "**chippies**", abound, the best often found in coastal towns within sight of the fishing boats tied up in harbour. Deep-fried battered fish is the standard choice – when served with chips it's known as a "fish supper", even if eaten at lunchtime – though everything from hamburgers to haggis suppers is normally on offer, all deep-fried, of course. Scotland is even credited with inventing the **deep-fried Mars bar** (a caramel-chocolate bar coated in batter and fried in fat) as the definitive badge of a nation with the worst heart-disease statistics in Europe. For alternative fast food, the major towns feature all the usual **pizza**, **burger** and **baked potato** outlets, as well as Chinese, Mexican and Indian take-aways.

Where to eat

For budget eating, you'll find **cafés** ranging from the most basic "greasy spoon" diners to French-style **brasseries**, where, if you're lucky, you'll find a wide-ranging menu and decent, interesting meals. For snacks and light lunches, **tearooms** are a common feature of tourist attractions and villages; it's generally not advisable to go into one with high expectations, though you may often find decent home baking.

Some of the cheapest places to eat out are the **pubs** or **hotel bars** – indeed, in the smallest villages these might be your only option. Bar menus generally have a standard line-up of unambitious options such as scampi and chips or steak pie and chips, with vegetarians in particular suffering from a paucity of choice. Having said that, some bar food is outstanding, with freshly prepared, filling food that equals the à la carte dishes served in the adjacent hotel restaurant.

As for **restaurants**, standards vary enormously, but Scotland has an ever-increasing number of top-class chefs producing superb dishes with a Scottish slant that certainly rival their English and European counterparts. Outside Edinburgh and Glasgow, the vast majority of these are hotel restaurants, which are nevertheless happy to serve non-residents. In some hotel restaurants, however, the food can be very ordinary despite the descriptions on the à la carte menu. Either way, you could easily end up paying £20–40 a head.

In central Scotland, particularly in Edinburgh and Glasgow, you can find restaurants offering a range of **international** styles including Japanese, Thai, Caribbean and Turkish, as well as the more common and familiar Indian, Chinese and Italian establishments. Glasgow, in particular, considers itself one of Britain's **curry** capitals, while Edinburgh's restaurant scene is expanding rapidly, with a particular strength in its **seafood** and **vegetarian** restaurants.

If you're primarily on a culinary pilgrimage, you might consider getting hold of a copy of *A Taste of Scotland* (ⓦwww.taste-of-scotland.com). While establishments do pay to be included, they have to be invited to join, and it remains the best annual foodie guide available.

Our restaurant listings include a mix of high-quality and budget establishments. To help give an idea of costs, each place we've reviewed is placed in one of three **price categories**: inexpensive (under £10 per person for a standard two courses, excluding alcohol), moderate (£10–20) or expensive (£20–30).

When to eat

Unfortunately, in many parts of Scotland outside the cities, inflexible and unenlightened **meal times** mean that you have to keep a close eye on your watch if you don't want to miss out on eating. B&Bs and hotels will frequently serve breakfast only until 9am at the latest, lunch is usually over by 2pm, and, despite the long summer evenings, pub and hotel kitchens often stop serving dinner as early as 8pm.

Drinking

As in the rest of Britain, Scottish **pubs**, which originated as travellers' hostelries and coaching inns, are the main social institution. The "pub crawl", a drunken stagger through as many pubs as possible in one night, is a national pastime in large towns and cities. The focal points of any community, Scottish pubs vary hugely, from old-fashioned inns with open fires and heaps of atmosphere, to raucous theme pubs with jukeboxes and satellite TV. Outside the big cities, many pubs are real no-nonsense, spit-and-sawdust public bars with an almost exclusively male clientele, making some visitors, especially women, feel highly uncomfortable. Out in the Islands, pubs are few and far between, with most drinking taking place in the local hotel bar. In Edinburgh and Glasgow, by contrast, you'll find traditional pubs supplemented by upbeat, trendy café-bars.

The national drink is **whisky** (for more on which, see below), though you might not guess it from the prodigious amount of "alcopops" (bottles of sweet fruit drinks laced with vodka or gin) and ready-made mixers consumed on a Friday and Saturday night. Similarly, Scotland produces some exceptionally good cask-conditioned real ales, yet lager is much more popular. In our listings, we've tended to steer folk towards those pubs that take their beer and whisky seriously, rather than those hell-bent on getting their punters drunk as quickly as possible.

Scotland has very relaxed licensing laws compared with England and Wales. Pub **opening hours** are generally 11am to 11pm, but in the cities and towns, or anywhere where there is demand, places stay open much later. Whatever time the pub closes, "last orders" will be called by the bar staff about fifteen minutes before closing time to allow a bit of "drinking-up time". In general, you have to be sixteen to enter a pub unaccompanied, though some places are easy about having folk with children in, or have special family rooms and beer gardens where the kids can run free. The legal drinking age is eighteen.

Whisky

Whisky – *uisge beatha*, or the "water of life" in Gaelic – has been produced in Scotland since the fifteenth century, but only really took off in popularity after the 1780 tax on claret made wine too expensive for most people. The taxman soon caught up with whisky distilling, however, and drove the stills underground. Today, many distilleries operate on the site of simple cottages that once distilled the stuff illegally. In 1823, Parliament revised its Excise Laws, in the process legalizing whisky production, and today the drink is Scotland's chief export. As with all spirits in Scotland, a standard single measure is 25ml, though some places serve 35ml.

There are two types of whisky: single malt, made from malted barley, and grain whisky, which is made from maize and a little malted barley in a continuous still – relatively cheap to produce, it was only introduced into Scotland in the 1830s. **Blended whisky**, which accounts for more than ninety percent of all sales, is a mixture of the two types. Grain whisky forms about seventy percent of the average bottle of blended whisky, but each brand's distinctive flavour comes from the malt whisky which is added to the grain in different quantities: the more expensive the blend, the higher the proportion of skilfully chosen and aged malts that have gone into it. Johnnie Walker, Bells, Teachers and The Famous Grouse are some of the best-known blended whiskies. All have a similar flavour, and are drunk neat or with water, sometimes with mixers such as soda or lemonade.

Despite the dominance of the blended whiskies, **single malt whisky** is infinitely superior, and, as a result, a great deal more expensive. Despite the snobbishness which surrounds the subject, malt whisky is best drunk neat or with a splash of water to release its distinctive flavours. Single malts vary enormously depending on the amount of peat used for drying the barley, the water used for mashing, and the type of oak cask used in the maturing process (for more on which, see the box). Traditionally they are divided into four distinct groups: Highland, Lowland, Campbeltown and Islay. However, with Campbeltown down to just two distilleries, and new distilleries springing up all over the country, there is a strong case for dispensing with the old labels.

The two most important whisky regions are **Speyside** (see p.557), which produces famous varieties such as Glenlivet, Glenfiddich and Macallan, and **Islay** (see p.433), which produces distinctively peaty whiskies such as Laphroaig, Lagavulin and Ardbeg. Many distilleries have a highly developed nose for PR and offer guided tours that range from slick and streamlined to small and friendly; details of some of the best are given in the main text of the guide. All of them offer visitors a "wee dram" as a finale, and those distilleries that charge an entrance fee often give you your money back if you buy a bottle at the end – though prices are no lower at source than in the shops, between £20 and £30 for the average 70cl bottle.

Beer

Traditional Scottish beer is a thick, dark ale known as **heavy**, served at room temperature in pints or half-pints, with a full head. Quite different in taste from English "bitter", heavy is a more robust, sweeter beer with less of an edge, and is served from a distinctive tall font. Scottish beers are graded by the shilling in a system used since the 1870s to indicate the level of potency: the higher the shilling mark (/-), the stronger or "heavier" the beer. A pint costs anything from £1.50 to £2.50, depending on the brew and the locale of the pub.

Both of Scotland's biggest-name breweries, McEwan's and Tennents, produce standard own-name lagers as well as a selection of heavies: McEwan's Special and Tennent's Velvet are varieties of a 70/- ale, while the stronger, tastier 80/- varieties are slightly less widespread but do qualify as "real ales".

Making malt whisky

Malt whisky is made by soaking barley in **steeps** (water cisterns) for two or three days until it swells, after which it is left to germinate for around seven days, during which the starch in the barley seed is converted into soluble sugars – this process is known as **malting**. The malted barley or "green malt" is then dried in a **kiln** over a furnace, which can be oil-fired, peat-fired or, more often than not, a combination of the two. Only a few distilleries still do their own malting and kilning in the traditional pagoda-style kilns; the rest simply have their malted barley delivered from an industrial maltings. The first process in most distilleries is therefore **milling**, which grinds the malted barley into "grist". Next comes the **mashing**, during which the grist is infused in hot water in mashtuns, producing a sugary concoction called "wort". After cooling, the wort passes into the washbacks, traditionally made of wood, where it is fermented with yeast for two to three days. During **fermentation**, the sugar is converted into alcohol, producing a brown foaming liquid known as "wash". **Distillation** now takes place, not once but twice: the wash is steam-heated, and the vapours siphoned off and condensed as a spirit. This is the point at which the whisky is poured into oak casks – usually ones which have already been used to store bourbon or sherry – and left to age for a minimum of three years. The average **maturation** period for a single malt whisky, however, is ten years; and the longer it matures, the more expensive it is, because two percent evaporates each year. Unlike wine, as soon as the whisky is bottled, maturation ceases.

However, if you really want to discover how good Scottish beer – once renowned throughout the world for its strength – can be, look out for the products of the small **local breweries**. Edinburgh's Caledonian Brewery makes nine good cask beers, and operates from Victorian premises using much of their original equipment, including the only direct-fired coppers left in Britain. Others names to look out for are Belhaven, brewed in Dunbar; Greenmantle, brewed by Broughton Ales in the Borders; and Fraoch, only available in bottles, a very refreshing, light ale made from heather according to an ancient recipe. Small local micro-breweries are beginning to spring up all over the country; depending where you are, the produce of the breweries at Aviemore, the Black Isle, Arran, Skye, Orkney or Shetland might be available. Your best chance of uncovering these beers is to head for pubs promising "real" or "cask-conditioned" ales – these are often pointed out in the guide, though for a more comprehensive list covering the whole of the UK get hold of a copy of the *Good Beer Guide*, published annually by the Campaign for Real Ale (Ⓦwww.camra.org.uk).

Water and soft drinks

Scotland produces a prodigious amount of **mineral water**, which is mainly exported, as the tap water tends to be chill and clean. In addition, Scotland has the distinction of being the only country in the world where neither Coke nor Pepsi is the most popular fizzy drink. That accolade belongs to **Irn-Bru**, a fizzy orange, sickly-sweet concoction sold in just about every shop in the country.

Communications

Communications are pretty modern and reliable in Scotland, although out in the more remote parts of the country, and particularly in the Highlands and Islands, you'll encounter difficulties: mobile phone coverage may well be patchy, though you'll usually find a payphone within easy walking distance. Internet cafés exist in most major towns and cities, but are surprisingly thin on the ground in rural areas.

Post

Most **post offices** In towns and cities are open Monday to Friday 9am to 5.30pm and Saturday 9am to 12.30 or 1pm. However, in small communities you'll find sub-post offices operating out of a shop, shed, or even a private house. In remote regions, the post office will often keep extremely restricted hours, even if the shop in which the post office counter is located keeps longer hours.

Stamps can be bought at post-office counters, from vending machines outside, or from many newsagents and shops. Domestic UK postage costs 27p first-class, 19p second-class. Airmail letters are 36p to Europe, 45p worldwide, or you can buy a pre-stamped air letter for 40p (from post offices only). Postcard stamps cost 37p to Europe, 40p worldwide. Royal Mail can answer all enquiries (Ⓣ0845/774 0740, Ⓦwww.royalmail.com).

Phones

Most public **payphones** in Scotland are operated by British Telecom, known as BT (Ⓦwww.bt.com) and, in towns, at least, are widespread. Many BT payphones take all coins from 10p upwards, with a minimum charge of 20p. Some payphones accept only credit cards and/or **phonecards**, which are available from post offices and some newsagents from £3; for international calls, it's best to buy a **global card** for £10 and upwards. Domestic calls are cheapest between 6pm and 8am Monday to Friday and all day on Saturday and Sunday.

Throughout this guide, every phone number is prefixed by the area code, separated

Useful numbers

UK operator ⓣ100
UK directory assistance ⓣ192
International operator ⓣ155
International directory assistance ⓣ153

from the number by an oblique slash. You don't have to dial the code if you're calling from within the same area, unless you're using a mobile phone. Any number with the prefix ⓣ0800 is toll-free; ⓣ0845 numbers are charged at local rate; ⓣ0870 at long-distance rate; and all ⓣ09 numbers at expensive premium rates. Any number beginning ⓣ07 is a mobile phone.

Phoning home

To the US or Canada ⓣ001 + area code + number.
To Ireland ⓣ00353 + area code without the zero + number.
To Australia ⓣ0061 + area code without the zero + number.
To New Zealand ⓣ0064 + area code without the zero + number.

Telephone charge cards

One of the most convenient ways of phoning home from abroad is with a **telephone charge card**. Using a toll-free UK access code and a PIN number, you can make calls from most hotel, public and private phones that will be charged to your own account. While rates are always cheaper from a residential phone at off-peak rates, that's normally not an option when you're travelling. You may be able to use the card to minimize hotel phone surcharges, but don't depend on it. However, the benefit of calling cards is mainly one of convenience, as rates aren't necessarily cheaper than calling from a public phone while abroad and can't compete with discounted off-peak times many local phone companies offer. But since most major charge cards are free to obtain, it's certainly worth getting one at least for emergencies.

AT&T, MCI, Sprint, Canada Direct and other **North American** long-distance companies all enable their customers to make credit-card calls while overseas. Call your company's customer service line to find out what the toll-free access code is in the UK. Calls made from Scotland will automatically be billed to your home number, although you can also choose to make a collect call via the operator. Elsewhere, charge cards such as Telstra Telecard or Optus Calling Card in **Australia**, and Telecom NZ's Calling Card in **New Zealand**, can be used to make calls abroad, which are charged back to a domestic account or credit card.

Calling Scotland from abroad

First dial your **international access code** (00 from Ireland and New Zealand; 011 from the US and Canada; 0011 from Australia), followed by **44** for the UK, then the Scottish area code minus its initial zero, then the number.

Mobile phones

If you want to use your **mobile phone** in Scotland, you'll need to check with your phone provider whether it is will work abroad, and what the call charges are. Technology in the UK is GSM (ⓦwww.gsmworld.com). Unless you have a tri-band phone, it is unlikely that a mobile bought for use in North America will work elsewhere; for details, contact your mobile service provider. Most mobiles in Australia and New Zealand use GSM, but it pays to check before you leave home. To save yourself money and hassle, it might be worth simply picking up a "pay-as-you-go" mobile once you've arrived in Britain; Vodaphone has the most reliable signal in Scotland, though you'll still find plenty of valleys and islands where there's no signal at all.

Email

An easy way to keep in touch while travelling is to sign up for a free internet **email** address that can be accessed from anywhere, for example YahooMail (ⓦwww.yahoo.com) or Hotmail (ⓦwww.hotmail.com). Once you've set up an account, you can use these sites to pick up and send mail from any café, library or hotel with internet access. Internet cafés are confined to the big cities and towns, with remarkably few in the Highlands and Islands. That said, the tourist office should be able to tell you of somewhere you can get online for a nominal fee; £4–5 an hour is the usual rate. ⓦwww.kropla.com gives useful details of how to plug your laptop in when abroad, phone country codes around the world, and information about electrical systems in different countries.

Opening hours, public holidays and admission fees

Traditional shop hours in Scotland are Monday to Saturday 9am to 5.30 or 6pm. In the bigger towns and cities, many places now stay open on Sundays and late at night (often on Thursdays or Fridays). Large supermarkets and out-of-town shopping centres also tend to stay open until 8 or 9pm Monday to Saturday, and for six hours on a Sunday. However, in the Highlands and Islands, you'll find precious little open on a Sunday, with many small towns also retaining an "early closing day" – often Wednesday – when shops close at 1pm.

Unlike in England, Scotland's **bank holidays** mean just that: they are literally days when the banks are closed, rather than general public holidays, and they vary from year to year. They include January 2; the Friday before Easter; the first and last Monday in May; the last Monday in August; Christmas Day (Dec 25); and Boxing Day (Dec 26).

New Year's Day (Jan 1) is the only fixed **public holiday**, but all Scottish towns and cities have one-day holidays in both spring and autumn – dates vary from place to place but normally fall on a Monday. You can get a booklet detailing the exact dates from the Glasgow Chamber of Commerce (ⓣ0141/204 2121, ⓦwww.glasgowchamber.org).

Admission to museums and monuments

Apart from the big city sights, and a number of attractions high on the tourist trail, Scotland's **tourist season** runs from Easter to October, and outside this period many indoor attractions are shut, though ruins, parks and gardens are normally accessible year-round. We've given full details of opening hours and adult admission charges in the guide. Note that last entrance can be an hour (or more) before published closing time.

Many of Scotland's most treasured sights – from castles and country houses to islands, gardens and tracts of protected landscape – come under the control of the privately run **National Trust for Scotland** (ⓣ0131/243 9331, ⓦwww.nts.org.uk) or the state-run **Historic Scotland** (ⓣ0131/668 8600, ⓦwww.historic-scotland.gov.uk); we've quoted **"NTS"** or **"HS"** respectively for each site reviewed in this guide. Both organizations charge an admission fee for most places, and these can be quite high, especially for the more grandiose NTS estates. If you think you'll be visiting more than half-a-dozen NTS properties, or more than a dozen HS ones, it's worth taking **annual membership**, which costs £28 for either organization, and allows free admission to their properties. In addition, both the NTS and HS offer short-term passes: the **National Trust Touring Pass** costs £18 for seven days' free admission, or £26 for fourteen days. The HS equivalent is a **Scottish Explorer**, at £17 for seven days, £22 for fourteen days.

A lot of Scottish **stately homes** remain in the hands of the landed gentry, who tend to charge around £5 for admission to edited highlights of their domain. Many other old buildings, albeit rarely the most momentous structures, are owned by local authorities; admission is often cheap and sometimes free. Municipal art galleries and museums are usually free, as are most of the **state-owned museums**, although "voluntary" donations may be solicited.

The majority of fee-charging attractions in Scotland give 25–50 percent **reductions** for senior citizens, the unemployed, full-time students and children under 16, with under-5s being admitted free almost everywhere. Proof of age will be required in most cases.

A further option, open to non-UK citizens only, is the **Great British Heritage Pass** (ⓦwww.visitbritain.com), which gives free admission to some 600 sites throughout Britain, including NTS or HS sites and many which are not run by either organization. Costing from £35/US$54 for seven days, it can be purchased through most travel agents at home, on arrival at any large UK airport, or from major tourist offices across Britain.

The media

In general, the Scots dismiss the UK's so-called "national media" as London-based and London-biased, and prefer to listen to Scottish radio programmes, read Scottish newspapers, and – albeit to a much lesser extent – watch Scottish TV. Local papers are also avidly consumed, with the weekly papers in places like Orkney and Shetland read by virtually the entire adult population.

The press

Many of Britain's national daily tabloid **newspapers** – from the reactionary *Sun* to the vaguely left-leaning *Daily Mirror* – appear in specific Scottish editions, although the "quality" press, ranging between the right-wing *Daily Telegraph* and the left-of-centre *Guardian*, are justifiably seen in Scotland as being London papers.

The **Scottish press** centres on two serious **dailies** – *The Scotsman*, based in Edinburgh, and *The Herald*, published in Glasgow, both of them broadsheets offering good coverage of the current issues affecting Scotland, along with British and foreign news, sport, arts and lifestyle pages. Scotland's biggest-selling daily is the downmarket *Daily Record*, a tabloid from the same stable as the *Daily Mirror*. The provincial daily press is more widely read than its English counterpart, with the two biggest-selling regional titles being Aberdeen's famously parochial *Press and Journal*, widely read in the northeast, Orkney and Shetland, and the right-wing *Dundee Courier*, mostly sold in Perth, Angus, Tayside and Fife. The **weekly** *Oban Times* gives an insight into life in the Highlands and Islands, but is staid compared with the radical, campaigning weekly *West Highland Free Press*, printed on Skye; both carry articles in Gaelic as well as English. Further north, the lively *Shetland Times* and sedate *Orcadian* are essential weekly reads.

Many national **Sunday newspapers** have a Scottish edition, although again Scotland has its own offerings – *Scotland on Sunday*, from the *Scotsman* stable, and the *Sunday Herald*, complementing its eponymous daily. Far more fun and widely read is the anachronistic *Sunday Post*, published by Dundee's mighty D.C. Thomson publishing group. It's a wholesome paper, uniquely Scottish, and has changed little since the 1950s, since which time its two long-running cartoon strips, *Oor Wullie* and *The Broons*, have acquired something of a cult status.

Scottish **monthlies** include the *Scottish Field*, a lowbrow version of England's *Tatler*, covering the interests and pursuits of the landed gentry; *Caledonia*, a glamorous glossy unashamedly aiming at the metropolitan elite; and the widely read *Scots Magazine*, an old-fashioned middle-of-the-road publication which promotes family values and lots of good fresh air. For visitors to Glasgow and Edinburgh, the fortnightly **listings magazine** *The List* is a must, covering all events in both cities and featuring lively interviews and articles. Another useful publication is the lively *Big Issue*, a weekly magazine with a Scottish edition, which contains listings, features and a focus on homelessness, the "issue" of the title; it's only available from official street vendors, who are themselves homeless, and to whom a large proportion of the cover price goes.

USA Today and the *International Herald Tribune* are the most widely available **North American papers**, though only the larger newsagents will stock them; you can also find *Time* and *Newsweek* in quality bookstores and newsagents.

TV and radio

In Scotland there are five main **TV channels**: the state-owned BBC1 and BBC2, and the independent commercial channels, ITV, Channel 4 and Channel 5. The **BBC** continues to maintain its worldwide reputation for in-house quality productions, ranging from expensive costume dramas to intelligent documentaries, split between the avowedly mainstream BBC1 and the more rarefied fare of BBC2. **BBC Scotland** produces news programmes and a regular crop of local-interest lifestyle, current affairs, drama and comedy shows which slot into the schedules of both BBC channels. The commercial channel, **ITV**, is divided between three regional companies: the populist STV, received in most of southern Scotland and parts of the West Highlands; Grampian, based in Aberdeen; and Border, which transmits from Carlisle. These are complemented by the more eclectic and less mainstream **Channel 4**, and thoroughly downmarket **Channel 5**, which (thankfully) still can't be received in some parts of Scotland. A plethora of **satellite** and, in the cities, **cable** channels are also available; the dominant force is Rupert Murdoch's **Sky**, which offers, among other channels, blanket sports coverage that plays wall-to-wall in pubs the length of the country.

The **BBC radio** network broadcasts six main channels in Scotland, five of which are national stations originating largely from London: Radio 1 (pop and dance music), Radio 2 (light music), Radio 3 (classical music), Radio 4 (current affairs, arts and drama) and Radio 5 Live (sports, news and live discussions and phone-ins). Only the award-winning BBC Radio Scotland offers a Scottish perspective on news, politics, arts, music, travel and sport, as well as providing a Gaelic network in the Highlands with local programmes in Shetland, Orkney and the Borders.

A web of local **commercial radio** stations covers the country, mostly mixing rock and pop music with news bulletins, but a few tiny community-based stations such as Lochbroom FM in Ullapool – famed for its daily midge count – transmit documentaries and discussions on local issues. The most populated areas of Scotland also receive UK-wide commercial radio, which competes with the BBC: Classic FM lures listeners from Radio 3, Virgin Radio competes head to head with Radio 1, and Talk Sport takes on Radio 5 Live.

Some Scottish radio stations

BBC Radio Scotland 92–95FM, 810MW Ⓦwww.bbc.co.uk/scotland/radioscotland. Nationwide news, sport, music, current affairs and arts.

Clyde 1 102.5FM Ⓦwww.radioclyde.co.uk. Glasgow's main contemporary rock and pop station. The slightly mellower Clyde 2 is at 1152MW.

Lochbroom FM 102.2FM Ⓦwww.btinternet.com/~lochbroomfm. Britain's smallest radio station, broadcasting to the northwest coast from Ullapool.

Moray Firth 99.4FM, 1107MW Ⓦwww.morayfirth.co.uk. Award-winning independent station for the Inverness area.

Nevis Radio 96.6FM Ⓦwww.nevisradio.co.uk. From the slopes of Ben Nevis, all that's happening in Fort William and surrounds.

North Sound 96.9FM, 1035MW Ⓦwww.northsound.co.uk. Pumps out the latest tunes to Aberdeen.

Radio Forth 97.3FM Ⓦwww.radioforth.co.uk. Rock and pop for Edinburgh and around. Max AM at 1548MW is their easier-listening stablemate.

Radio Tay 96.4 & 102.8FM, 1161 & 1584MW Ⓦwww.radiotay.co.uk. Dundee's local radio.

Scot FM 100.3 & 101.1FM Ⓦwww.scot-fm.com. Mainstream pop and shock-jocks for the central belt.

SIBC 96.2FM Ⓦwww.sibc.co.uk. Shetland's own independent station.

Crime and personal safety

For the most part the Scottish police are approachable and helpful to visitors. If you're lost in a major town, asking a police officer is generally the quickest way to get help; alternatively, you could ask a traffic warden, a much-maligned species of law enforcer responsible for parking restrictions and other vehicle-related matters.

As with any country, Scotland's major towns and cities have their danger spots, but these tend to be inner-city housing estates where no tourist has any reason to roam. The chief urban risk is **pickpocketing**, so carry only as much money as you need, and keep all bags and pockets fastened. Out in the Highlands and Islands, crime levels are very low. Should you have anything stolen or be involved in some incident that requires reporting, go to the local police station (addresses in the major cities are listed in this guide); the ⓣ999 number should only be used in dire emergencies.

Emergencies

To call out the **police**, **fire service**, **ambulance** and/or, in certain areas, mountain rescue or the coastguard, dial ⓣ**999**.

Events and spectator sports

Scotland offers a huge range of organized annual events, reflecting both vibrant contemporary culture and well-marketed heritage. Many tourists will want to home straight in on Highland Games and other tartan-draped theatricals, but it's worth bearing in mind that there's more to Scotland than this: numerous regional celebrations perpetuate ancient customs, and the fabulous Edinburgh Festival is an arts celebration unrivalled in size and variety in the world. A few of the smaller, more obscure events, particularly those with a pagan bent, are in no way created for tourists, and indeed do not always welcome the casual visitor; local tourist offices always have full information.

The STB publishes a weighty list of all Scottish events twice a year: it's free and you can get it from area tourist offices or direct from their headquarters. Full details are at ⓦwww.visitscotland.com.

Events calendar

Dec 31 and Jan 1 Hogmanay and Ne'er Day. Traditionally more important to the Scots than Christmas, known for the custom of "first-footing", when groups of revellers troop into neighbours' houses at midnight bearing gifts. More popular these days are huge and highly organized street parties, most notably in Edinburgh (ⓦwww.edinburghshogmanay.org), but also in Aberdeen, Glasgow and other centres.

Jan 1 Stonehaven fireball ceremony. Locals swing fireballs on long sticks to welcome New Year and ward off evil spirits. Also Kirkwall Boys' and Men's Ba' Games, Orkney: mass, drunken football game through the streets of the town, with the castle and the harbour the respective goals. As a grand finale the players jump into the harbour.

Jan 11 Burning of the Clavie, Burghead, Moray (ⓦwww.tartans.com/articles/clavie). A burning tar barrel is carried through the town and then rolled down Doorie Hill. Charred fragments of the Clavie offer protection against the evil eye.

Mid- to late Jan Celtic Connections, Glasgow. A major celebration of Celtic and folk music held in venues across the city.

Last Tues in Jan Up-Helly-Aa, Lerwick, Shetland (ⓦwww.shetlandpiper.com/Up-Helly-Aa). Norse fire festival culminating in the burning of a specially built Viking longship. Visitors will need an invite from one of the locals, or you can buy a ticket for the Town Hall celebrations.

Jan 25 Burns Night. Scots worldwide get stuck into haggis, whisky and vowel-grinding poetry to commemorate Scotland's greatest poet, Robert Burns.

Feb Scottish Curling Championship (ⓦwww.rccc.org.uk), held in a different (indoor) venue each year.

Feb–March Six Nations Rugby tournament. Between Scotland, England, Wales, Ireland, France and Italy (ⓦwww.6nations.co.uk). Scotland's home games are played at Murrayfield stadium in Edinburgh.

March 1 Whuppity Scourie, Lanark. Local children race round the church beating each other with home-made paper weapons in a representation (it's thought) of the chasing away of winter or the warding off of evil spirits.

April Scottish Grand National, Ayr (ⓦwww.ayr-racecourse.co.uk). Not quite as testing as the English equivalent steeplechase, but an important event on the Scottish racing calendar. Also Rugby

Sevens (seven-a-side tournament; Ⓦwww.melrose.bordernet.co.uk) in the Borders, plus the acclaimed **Shetland Folk Festival** (Ⓦwww.sffs.shetland.co.uk).
April 6 Tartan Day. Over-hyped celebration of ancestry by North Americans of Scottish descent on the anniversary of the Declaration of Arbroath in 1320. Ignored by most Scots in Scotland, other than journalists.
May 1 Beltane Fire Festival. Calton Hill in Edinburgh (Ⓦwww.beltane.org).
Early May Spirit of Speyside Scotch Whisky Festival (Ⓦwww.spiritofspeyside.com), and **Isle of Bute Jazz Festival.**
May Scottish FA Cup Final. In Glasgow: Scotland's premier football event.
Late May Atholl Highlanders Parade at Blair Castle, Perthshire (Ⓦwww.blairatholl.org.uk/bata/events). The annual parade and inspection of Britain's last private army by their colonel-in-chief, the Duke of Atholl. Also the **Highlands Festival**, a large celebration of arts, music, language, food and culture.
Early June Caledonian Brewery Beer Festival, Edinburgh (Ⓦwww.caledonian-events.co.uk). Also week-long festivities in Lanark culminating in the crowning of the Lanimer Queen, a ceremony dating back to the fifteenth century.
June–Aug Riding of the Marches. In the border towns of Hawick, Selkirk, Annan, Dumfries, Duns, Peebles, Jedburgh, Langholm and Lauder (Ⓦwww.scot-borders.co.uk). The Rides originated to check the boundaries of common land owned by the town and also to commemorate warfare between the Scots and the English. Nowadays individual Ridings have their own special ceremonies, though they all start with a parade of pipes and brass bands.
June Shinty Camanachd Cup Final (Ⓦwww.shinty.com). The climax of the season for Scotland's own stick-and-ball game, normally held in one of the main Highland towns. Also marks the beginning of the Highland Games season across the Highlands, northeast and Argyll. **St Magnus Festival, Orkney** (Ⓦwww.visitorkney.com), is a classical and folk music, drama, dance and literature celebrating the islands.
Late June Royal Highland Agricultural Show. At Ingliston near Edinburgh (Ⓦwww.rhass.org.uk).
Early July Glasgow International Jazz Festival (Ⓦwww.jazzfest.co.uk), and **T in the Park** (Ⓦwww.tinthepark.com). The latter is Scotland's biggest outdoor music event, held in Glasgow's Strathclyde Park with a star-studded line-up of contemporary bands.
July Scottish Open Golf Championship. Held at a different venue each year. Also **Highland Games** at Caithness, Elgin, Glengarry, North Uist, Inverness, Inveraray, Mull, Lewis, Durness, Lochaber, Dufftown, Halkirk.
Early Aug The two-day **Lammas Fair** at St Andrews (Ⓦwww.saint-andrews.co.uk). The oldest medieval market in the country.
Aug Edinburgh Festival (Ⓦwww.edinburghfestivals.com). One of the world's great arts jamborees, described in full on p.126. **The Edinburgh Military Tattoo** (Ⓦwww.edtattoo.co.uk) features floodlit massed pipe bands and drums on the castle esplanade. There's also the **World Pipe Band Championship** at Glasgow, and **Highland Games** at Dunoon (Cowal), Mallaig, Skye, Dornoch, Aboyne, Strathpeffer, Assynt, Bute, Glenfinnan, Argyllshire, Glenurquhart and Invergordon (Ⓦwww.albagames.co.uk).
Early Sept Ben Nevis Race (for amateurs). Held on the first weekend in the month, running to the top of Scotland's highest mountain and back again. Also **Highland Games** at Braemar.
Late Sept Doors Open Day (Ⓦwww.doorsopendays.co.uk). The one weekend a year when many public and private buildings are open to the public; actual dates vary. Also another **Spirit of Speyside Whisky Festival** (Ⓦwww.spiritofspeyside.com), and the **Scottish Book Town Festival** in Wigtown (Ⓦwww.wigtown-booktown.co.uk).
Oct The National Mod Competitive festival. All aspects of Gaelic performing arts, held in various venues (Ⓦwww.the-mod.co.uk).
Late Oct Glenfiddich Piping Championships. Held at Blair Atholl for the world's top ten solo pipers (Ⓦwww.thepipingcentre.co.uk).
Nov 30 St Andrew's Day. Celebrating Scotland's patron saint.

Highland Games

Despite their name, **Highland Games** are held all over Scotland between May and mid-September, varying in size and the range of events they offer; although the most famous are at Oban, Cowal and especially Braemar, the smaller events are often more fun. The Games probably originated in the fourteenth century as a means of recruiting the best fighting men for the clan chiefs, and were popularized by Queen Victoria to encourage the traditional dress, music, games and dance of the Highlands; various royals still attend the Games at Braemar. The most distinctive events are known as the **"heavies"** – tossing the caber, putting the stone, and tossing the weight over the bar – all of which require prodigious strength and skill. Tossing the caber is the most spectacular, when the athlete must run carrying an entire tree trunk and attempt to heave it end over end in a perfect, elegant throw. Just as important as the sporting events are the **piping** competitions – for individuals and bands – and **dancing** competitions, where you'll see girls as young as three tripping the quick, intricate steps of dances such as the Highland Fling.

Football

Football (soccer) is far and away Scotland's most popular spectator sport, and one of the areas of Scottish life that has remained truly independent from the English. A potent source of pride for Scots everywhere, the national team (always accompanied by its distinctive and vocal supporters, known as the "Tartan Army") has consistently managed to hold its own in international competitions, qualifying frequently for World Cup finals but at the same time cornering the market in gallant failure by failing to progress far on every occasion.

Scotland was one of the first countries in the world to establish a national domestic league, in 1874, but today most of the teams which play in it are little known beyond the boundaries of Scotland. The exceptions are the two massive Glasgow teams which dominate the Scottish scene, **Rangers** and **Celtic** (known collectively as the "Old Firm"; see p.266). The sectarian, and occasionally violent, rivalry between these two is one of the least attractive aspects of Scottish life, and their stranglehold over the **Scottish Premier League** or SPL (Ⓦwww.scotprem.com) has arguably been just as damaging. Although the 1980s saw Dundee United and Aberdeen break the deadlock, the old pattern reasserted itself during the 1990s, with Rangers winning nine titles in a row and Celtic taking over in 2000–01. During the past few seasons, calls have been mounting for the Old Firm to join either the English Premiership or a pan-European league, which would give them tougher opposition on a more regular basis. However, it's fairly claimed that the loss of the two flagship clubs would leave the Scottish league without a credible European contender, and serve an undeserved deathblow to the nation's rich footballing tradition.

With a couple of exceptions (notably Jock Stein's legendary Celtic sides of the late 1960s and early 1970s), Scottish soccer has traditionally been renowned less for its great teams than for its outstanding individuals – **players** such as Denis Law of Manchester United, Kenny Dalglish of Celtic and Liverpool, Billy Bremner at Leeds and Graeme Souness in the famous Liverpool side of the early 1980s, as well as **managers** of near-mythical status like Jock Stein, Matt Busby, Bill Shankly and, of course, Alex Ferguson of Manchester United. These days, as in England, foreign players have flooded the league, to the extent that home-grown players are the exception rather than the rule in the Rangers and Celtic teams. However, talented local players still have a stage on which to perform, and the new blend of continental sophistication mixed with Scottish passion and ruggedness makes for a distinctive spectacle which will appeal to soccer enthusiasts, who should definitely take in a game or two while they're here.

The **season** begins in early August and ends in mid-May, with matches on Saturday afternoons at 3pm, and also often on Sunday afternoons and Wednesday evenings. **Tickets** range from £10 to £20 for big games; the major clubs operate telephone credit-card booking services (see the relevant city's listings section for details). For a quick overview, Ⓦwww.soccernet.com features details of every Scottish club, with news and match-report archives.

Rugby

Rugby gets its name from Rugby public school in England, where the game mutated from football in the nineteenth century. A rugby match may at times look like a bunch of weightlifters grappling each other in the mud – as the old joke goes, rugby is a hooligan's game played by gentlemen, while football is a gentleman's game played by hooligans – but it is in reality highly tactical and athletic.

Although rugby has always lived under the shadow of football in Scotland, it ranks as one of the country's major sports, and the national team performs at a creditable level on the international stage. Weekends when the national team is playing a home international at **Murrayfield** stadium in Edinburgh are colourful occasions, with kilted masses filling the capital's pubs and lining the streets leading to the ground. Internationals take place in the spring, when Scotland take on the other "home nations", along with France and Italy, in the annual Six Nations tournament, although there are always fixtures in the autumn against international touring teams such as New Zealand, Australia and South Africa. Tickets for big games are hard to come by; contact the Scottish Rugby Union (Ⓣ0131/346 5000, Ⓦwww.sru.org.uk) for an indication of where and when tickets are available for any particular fixture.

The **club rugby** scene in Scotland is in a certain amount of disarray, with many of the country's top players finding better offers to play in England or France. The one area where the tradition runs deepest, however, is in the Borders, where towns such as Hawick, Kelso and Galashiels can be gripped by the fortunes of their local team on a Saturday afternoon. The Borders are also the home of **seven-a-side rugby**, an abridged version of the game which was invented in Melrose in the 1890s and is now played around the world, most notably at the glamorous annual event in Hong Kong. The Melrose Sevens (Ⓦwww.melrose.bordernet.co.uk) is still the biggest tournament of the year in Scotland, although you'll find events at one or other of the Border towns through the spring, most going on right through an afternoon and invoking a festival atmosphere in the large crowd.

Shinty

Played throughout Scotland but with particular strongholds in the West Highlands and Speyside, the game of **shinty** (the Gaelic *sinteag* means "leap") arrived from Ireland around 1500 years ago. Until the latter part of the nineteenth century, it was played on an informal basis and teams from neighbouring villages had to come to an agreement about rules before matches could begin. However, in 1893, the **Camanachd Association** – the Gaelic word for shinty is *camanachd* – was set up to formalize the rules, and the first Camanachd Cup Final was held in Inverness in 1896. Today, shinty is still fairly close to its Irish roots in the game of hurling, with each team having twelve players including a goalkeeper, and each goal counting for a point. The game, which bears similarities to an undisciplined version of hockey, isn't for the faint-hearted; it's played at a furious pace, with sticks – called camans or cammocks – flying alarmingly in all directions. Support is enthusiastic and vocal, and if you're in the Highlands during the season (roughly August to mid-May) it's well worth trying to catch a match: check with tourist offices or the local paper to see if there are any local fixtures, or go to Ⓦwww.shinty.com.

Curling

The one winter sport which enjoys a strong Scottish identity is **curling** (Ⓦwww.rccc.org.uk), occasionally still played on a frozen outdoor rink, or "pond", though most commonly these days seen in indoor ice rinks. The game, which involves gently sliding smooth-bottomed 18kg discs of granite called "stones" across the ice towards a target circle, is said to have been invented in Scotland, although its earliest representation is in a sixteenth-century Flemish painting. Played by two teams of four, it's a highly tactical and skilful sport, enlivened by team-members using brushes to furiously sweep the ice in front of a moving stone to help it travel further and straighter. If you're interested in seeing curling being played, go along to the ice rink in places such as Perth, Hamilton or Aviemore on a winter evening.

Outdoor pursuits

A large number of visitors to Scotland come specifically to enjoy a landscape that, weather conditions apart, is perfect for outdoor pursuits at all levels of fitness and ambition. Within striking distance of Glasgow and Edinburgh are vast stretches of glens and moorland and spectacular mountains, which in winter can provide great skiing. Throughout the country, numerous marked trails range from hour-long ambles to coast-to-coast treks. The shoreline, lochs and rivers give opportunities for fishing as well as sailing and watersports, including surfing, and there are plenty of fine beaches. Scotland, of course, is also the "home of golf": it's relatively cheap to play here, and there are proportionally more courses than anywhere else in the world.

Walking and climbing

The whole of Scotland offers superb opportunities for **hill walking**, from the smooth, grassy hills and moors of the Southern Uplands to the wild and rugged country of the northwest.

There are several **Long-Distance Footpaths** (LDPs) which take days to walk, though you can, of course, just do a section of them. Well signposted and increasingly well supported, with a range of services from bunkhouses to baggage-carrying services, these are a great way to respond to the challenge of walking in Scotland without taking on the dizzy heights. The **Southern Upland**

Midges and ticks

Despite being only just over a millimetre long, and enjoying a life span on the wing of just a few weeks, the **midge** (*culicoides*) – a tiny biting fly prevalent in the Highlands (mainly the west coast) and Islands – is considered to be second only to the weather as the major deterrent to tourism in Scotland. There are more than thirty varieties of midge, though only half of these bite humans. Ninety percent of all midge bites are down to the female *culicoides impunctatus* or Highland midge (the male does not bite), which has two sets of jaws sporting twenty teeth each; she needs a good meal of blood in order to produce eggs.

These persistent creatures can be a nuisance, but some people also have a violent allergic reaction to midge bites. The easiest way to avoid midges is to visit in the winter, since they only appear between April and October. Midges also favour still, damp, overcast or shady conditions and are at their meanest around sunrise and sunset, when clouds of them can descend on an otherwise idyllic spot. Direct sunlight, heavy rain, noise and smoke discourage them to some degree, though the most effective deterrent is, undoubtedly, wind. You'll soon notice if they're near; cover up arms and legs and try to avoid wearing dark colours, which attract the creatures. Various **repellents** are worth a try. Recommendations include Autan and Jungle Formula (widely available from pharmacists), the herbal remedy citronella, and Skin So Soft by Avon, which is said to be very effective, despite not being designed to fend off the critters. An alternative to repellents for protecting your face, especially if you're walking or camping, is a midge net, which you secure by tucking it under your hat; although they appear ridiculous at first, midge nets are commonplace and extremely useful.

If you're anywhere near woodland, there's a possibility you may receive attention from **ticks**, tiny parasites no bigger than a pin head, which bury themselves into your skin. Removing ticks by dabbing them with alcohol, butter or oil is now discouraged; the medically favoured way of extracting them is to pull them out carefully with small tweezers. There is a very slight risk of catching some very nasty diseases, such as encephalitis, from ticks. If flu-like symptoms persist after a tick bite, you should see a doctor immediately.

Staying safe in the hills

Beguiling though the hills of Scotland can seem, you have to be properly prepared before venturing out onto them. Due to rapid weather changes, the mountains are potentially extremely dangerous and should be treated with respect. Every year, in every season, climbers and walkers lose their lives in Scotland.

- Wear sturdy, ankle-supporting footwear and wear or carry with you warm, brightly coloured and waterproof layered clothing, even for what appears to be an easy expedition in apparently settled weather.
- Always carry adequate maps, a compass (which you should know how to use), food, water and a whistle. If it's sunny, make sure you use sun protection.
- Check out a weather forecast before you go. If the weather looks as if it's closing in, get down from the mountain fast.
- Always leave word with someone of your route and what time you expect to return, and remember to contact the person again to let them know that you are back.
- In an emergency, call mountain rescue on ⓣ999.

Way, which crosses the country from coast to coast in the south, is, at 212 miles, the longest. The best known, however, is the **West Highland Way**, a 95-mile hike from Glasgow to Fort William via Loch Lomond and Glen Coe. The gentler **Speyside Way**, in the northeast, leads for 84 miles from the Cairngorms to the Moray Firth past a number of whisky distilleries. The green signposts of the Scottish Rights of Way Society point to these and many other cross-country routes, which include "drove roads", long-established paths through the hills along which clansmen once led their cattle to or from markets held in the larger settlements.

Scotland's main climbing areas are in the **Highlands**, which boast many challenging peaks as well as great hill walks. There are 284 mountains over 3000ft (914m) in Scotland, known as **Munros** after the man who first classified them: many walkers "collect" or "bag" them, and it's possible to chalk up several in a day. Serious climbers will probably head for **Glen Coe** or **Torridon**, which offer difficult routes in spectacular surroundings. These and some of the other finest Highland areas (Lawers, Kintail, West Affric) are in the ownership of the National Trust for Scotland, while Blaven on Skye and Ladhar Bheinn (Knoydart) are John Muir Trust properties; both allow year-round access. Elsewhere, the accepted freedom to roam in wilder parts of the countryside allows extensive walking and climbing, although there may be restricted access during lambing (dogs are particularly unwelcome in April and May) and deerstalking seasons (mid-August to the third week in October). The booklet "Heading for the Scottish Hills", published by the Scottish Mountaineering Club or SMC, provides such information on all areas.

Numerous short walks (from accessible towns and villages) and several major walks are touched on in this guide. However, you should only use our notes as general outlines, and always in conjunction with a good map. Where possible, we have given details of the best maps to use – in most cases one of the excellent and reliable Ordnance Survey (OS) series (see p.23), usually available from local tourist offices, which can also supply other local maps, safety advice and guidebooks/leaflets. Among the many **guidebooks** available for serious walking and climbing, the SMC's series of District Guides offer blow-by-blow accounts of climbs written by professional mountaineers; for other good walking guides see the "Books" section of Contexts (p.819). These, as well as a wide range of maps, are available from most of the good **outdoor stores** scattered around the country (most notably Tiso and Nevisport), which are normally staffed by experienced climbers and walkers, and are a good source of candid advice about the equipment you'll need and favourite hiking areas.

For relatively gentle walking in the company of knowledgeable locals, look out for **guided walks** offered by rangers at many National Trust for Scotland, Forest Enterprise and Scottish Natural Heritage sites. These often focus on local wildlife, and the best can lead to some special sightings, such as a badger's sett or a golden eagle's eyrie.

Useful contacts for walkers

General information

Ⓦ **www.walkscotland.com** Comprehensive site with lists of specific walks, mountain routes, news, gear and even a few shaggy dog stories.
Ⓦ **www.walkingwild.com** Smart official site from the tourist board, with good lists of operators and information on long distance footpaths.

Clubs and associations

Mountain Bothies Association
Ⓦ www.mountainbothies.org.uk. Charity dedicated to maintaining huts and shelters in the Scottish highlands.
Mountaineering Council of Scotland
Ⓣ 01738/638227, Ⓦ www.mountaineering-scotland.org.uk. The representative body for all mountain activities, which publishes details of estate boundaries and contact phone numbers.
Ramblers Association Scotland
Ⓣ 01592/611177, Ⓦ www.ramblers.org.uk. Campaigning organization with network of local groups and news on events and issues.
Scottish Mountaineering Club
Ⓦ www.smc.org.uk. The largest mountaineering club in the country. A well-respected organization which publishes a popular series of mountain guidebooks.

Tour operators

Assynt Guided Holidays Ⓣ 01854/666215, Ⓔ tomraystrang@btinternet.com. Sutherland mountain walks, glen and lochside ambles, and fishing trips, with one of Scotland's most knowledgeable guides.
C-N-Do Scotland Ⓣ 01786/445703, Ⓦ www.btinternet.com/cndoscotland. Munro-bagging for novices and experts, in small groups and with qualified leaders, as well as day-long winter skills and navigation courses.
Glen Coe Mountain Sport Ⓣ 01855/811472, Ⓦ www.glencoe-mountain-sport.co.uk. Year-round programme of gentle walks and scrambles on Skye, and around Glen Coe and Ben Nevis.
Mountain Innovations Ⓣ 01479/831331, Ⓦ www.scotmountain.co.uk. Cairngorm-based outfit offering imaginative tailor-made tours for mountaineers and fly-drive packages.
North-West Frontiers Ⓣ 01854/612628, Ⓦ www.nwfrontiers.com. Guided mountain trips with small groups in the northwest Highlands, starting in Inverness; May to October only.
Ossian Guides Ⓣ 01540/673402, Ⓦ www.ossianguides.co.uk. Walking, scrambling and climbing with qualified leaders throughout the Highlands.
Rua Reidh Lighthouse Holidays
Ⓣ 01445/771263, Ⓦ www.ruareidh.co.uk. Accompanied and self-guided wilderness walks on the west coast, from three-night to one-week itineraries. Family multiactivity holidays also available.
Walkabout Scotland Ⓣ 0131/661 7168, Ⓦ www.walkaboutscotland.com. A great way to get a taste of hiking in the Highlands, with guided hillwalking day-trips from Edinburgh for £40 per person, with all transport included.

Winter sports

Skiing and **snowboarding** take place at five different locations in Scotland – Glen Coe, the Nevis Range beside Fort William, Glenshee, the Lecht and the Cairngorms near Aviemore – but as none of these can offer anything even vaguely approaching an alpine experience it is as well not to come with high expectations. They can go for months on end through the winter with insufficient snow, then see the approach roads suddenly made impassable by a glut of the stuff.

All the resorts have a combination of chairlifts and tows – Nevis Range boasts a gondola while Cairngorm has a new funicular railway – and equipment can always be rented nearby. Expect to pay up to £20 for a standard day pass at one of the resorts, or £55 for a three-day pass; rental of skis or snowboard comes in at around £15 per day, with reductions for multiday rents. At weekends, in good weather with decent snow, expect the slopes to be packed with trippers from the Central Belt, although mid-week usually sees queues dissolving and the experience improving immeasurably. We've given details in the guide for each of the resorts, including phone numbers to check on ski conditions. For more general information, check the comprehensive Ⓦ www.ski.scotland.net.

Nordic, or cross-country, skiing, can be done in a few places around Scotland, notably around Braemar near Glenshee and the Cairngorms. This can be a great way to free yourself from the crowds of the resorts and explore the Highland wilderness made pristine by the snow, although the demands on fitness and navigational abilities are higher. The best way to get started or to find out about good routes is to contact an outdoor pursuits company that offers Nordic rental and instruction; try Cairnwell Ski School in

Glenshee (☎01250/885255) or Huntly Nordic Ski Centre in Huntly, Aberdeenshire (☎01466/794428, Ⓦwww.huntly.net/hnoc).

Pony trekking and horse riding

Pony trekking as an organized leisure activity originated in Scotland; the late Lieutenant-Commander Jock Kerr Hunter set up the first **riding school** here fifty or so years ago, to encourage people to explore the country via its old drove roads. Since then, equestrian centres have mushroomed, and miles of the most beautiful loch-sides, heather-clad moorland and long sandy beaches are now accessible on horseback, to novices as well as experienced riders.

The Scottish Tourist Board produces a glossy "Trekking and Riding" brochure which lists around sixty **riding centres** across the country (Ⓦwww.visitscotland.com/outdoor), all of them approved by either the Trekking and Riding Society of Scotland (TRSS ☎01821/650210) or the British Horse Society (BHS). As a rule, any centre will offer the option of pony trekking (leisurely ambles on sure-footed Highland ponies), **hacking** (for experienced riders who want to go for a short ride at a fastish pace) and **trail riding** (over longer distances, for riders who feel secure at a canter). In addition, a network of special **horse-and-rider B&Bs** means you can ride independently on your own horse.

A four-day route – the **Buccleuch Country Ride** – was recently inaugurated in the Borders region, using private tracks, open country and quiet bridleways. For more information about this, and the B&B network for riders, contact the Scottish Borders Tourist Board (see p.22), or the TRSS.

Cycling and mountain biking

Despite the recent boom in the sale of mountain bikes, **cyclists** are still treated with notorious neglect by many motorists and by the people who plan the country's traffic systems. Very few of Scotland's towns have proper cycle routes, but if you're hellbent on tackling the congestion, pollution and aggression of city traffic, get a **helmet** and a secure **lock**: cycle theft in Scotland is an organized and highly effective racket. The rural back roads are infinitely more enjoyable, particularly in the gentle landscape of the south and east of the country, where generally amiable gradients and a decent density of pubs and B&Bs make it a perfect area for cycle touring. Your main problem out in the countryside will be finding spare parts: anything more complex than inner tubes or tyres can be very hard to come by.

Mountain biking is popular in the Highland walking areas, but riders should always keep to tracks where a right to cycle exists, and pass walkers at considerate speeds. Footpaths, unless otherwise marked, are for pedestrian use only. The Forestry Commission has recently established 1150 miles of excellent off-road routes all over the country, which are detailed in numerous "Cycling in the Forest" leaflets (available from Forest Enterprise offices listed below, and from most tourist offices). Waymarked and graded, these are best attempted on mountain bikes with multi-gears, although many of the gentler routes may be tackled on hybrid and standard road cycles.

A number of **long-distance routes** have been established in Scotland over the last few years using a combination of specially built cycle paths and quieter back roads. Up-to-date information on these, along with a list of publications detailing specific routes, are available from the cyclists campaigning group Sustrans (☎0131/623 7600, Ⓦwww.sustrans.co.uk), as well as some of the organizations listed in the box below.

Transporting your bike by train is a good way of getting to the interesting parts of Scotland without a lot of hard pedalling. Bikes are allowed on mainline GNER and Virgin Intercity trains (subject to availability of space) for a £3 charge: you should book the space as far in advance as possible. Bikes are carried free on ScotRail trains, but again, subject to availability. Bus and coach companies, including National Express and Scottish Citylink, rarely accept cycles unless they are dismantled and boxed; one notable exception is the Bike Bus Company (☎0131/229 6274, Ⓦwww.bikebus.co.uk), which operates a minibus and trailer service for cyclists out of Edinburgh.

Bike rental is available at shops in most large towns and many tourist centres, although only a few more enlightened establishments offer much more than pretty heavy and basic standard models – OK for a brief spin, but not for any serious touring. Expect to pay £10–20 per day; most rental outlets also give good discounts for multiday rents.

Another option is to shell out on a **cycling holiday package**. These take many forms, but generally include transport of your luggage to each stop, pre-booked accommodation, detailed route instructions, a packed lunch and backup support. Most holiday companies offer some budget packages, with hostel instead of hotel or B&B accommodation, and the cost-cutting option of using your own bike. A week-long tour starts at around £250 per person for hostel accommodation, including bike rental. Britain's biggest cycling organization, the **Cycle Touring Club** or CTC, provides lists of tour operators and rental outlets in Scotland, and supplies members with touring and technical advice, as well as insurance. As a general introduction, the Scottish Tourist Board's "Cycling in Scotland" brochure is worth getting hold of, with practical advice and suggestions for itineraries around the country. The STB's recently introduced "Cyclists Welcome" scheme gives guesthouses and B&Bs around the country a chance to advertise that they're cyclist-friendly, and able to provide such things as an overnight laundry service, a late meal or a packed lunch.

Useful contacts for cyclists

Bespoke Highland Tours ⓣ01687/450272, ⓦwww.scotland-inverness.co.uk/bht-main.htm. Organizes cycle touring in the Highlands and Islands, using a reliable and long-standing network of B&Bs and hostels, and arranges transport links and baggage transfer.

Cyclists' Touring Club ⓣ01483/417217, ⓦwww.ctc.org.uk. Britain's largest cycling organization, and a good source of general advice; their handbook has lists of cyclist-friendly B&Bs and cafés in Scotland. Annual membership £25.

Forest Enterprise ⓣ01463/243846, ⓦwww.forestry.gov.uk. The best source of information on Scotland's extensive network of forest trails – ideal for mountain biking at all levels of ability.

North Sea Cycle Route ⓦwww.northsea-cycle.co.uk. Signposted 6000-km route round seven countries fringing the North Sea, including 1242km in Scotland along the east coast and in Orkney and Shetland.

Scottish Border Trails ⓣ01721/720336, ⓔarthur@trails.scotborders.co.uk. Good contact for routes in Scotland's prime mountain-biking territory.

Scottish Cycle Safaris ⓣ0131/556 5560, ⓦwww.cyclescotland.co.uk. Fully organized cycle tours at all levels, from camping to country house hotels, with a good range of bikes available for rent, from tandems to chidrens' bikes.

Scottish Cyclists' Union ⓣ0131/652 0187, ⓦwww.scuweb.com. Produces an annual handbook and calendar of cycling events (£5) – mainly road, mountain-bike and track races.

Spokes ⓣ0131/313 2114, ⓦwww.spokes.org.uk. Active Edinburgh cycle campaign group with plenty of good links and news on events and cycle-friendly developments.

ⓦ**www.visitscotland.com/outdoor** has lots of practical information and advice, including lists of bike-rental centres. They can also sell you a Cycle Scotland map with information.

Golf

There are over 400 **golf courses** in Scotland, where the game is less elitist and more accessible than anywhere else in the world. Golf in its present form took shape in the fifteenth century on the dunes of Scotland's east coast, and today you'll find some of the oldest courses in the world on these early coastal sites, known as "links". It's often possible just to turn up and play, though it's sensible to phone ahead; booking is essential for the championship courses.

Public courses are owned by the local council, while **private** courses belong to a club. You can play on both – occasionally the private courses require that you are a member of another club, and the odd one asks for introductions from a member, but these rules are often waived for overseas visitors and all you need to do is pay a one-off fee. The cost of a round will set you back around £10 on a small nine-hole course, and more than £40 for many good quality eighteen-hole courses. In remote areas the courses are sometimes unstaffed; just put the admission fee into the honesty box. Most courses have **resident professionals** who give lessons, and some rent equipment at reasonable rates. Renting a caddie car will add a few pounds to the cost.

Scotland's **championship** courses, which often host the British Open, are renowned for their immaculately kept greens and challenging holes and, though they're favoured by serious players, anybody with a valid handicap certificate can enjoy them. **St Andrews** is the top destination for golfers: it's the home of the Royal and Ancient Golf Club, the worldwide controlling body that regulates the rules of the game. Of its six courses, the Old Course is probably the most famous in the world; unlike many exclusive courses it is possible for anyone with a valid handicap certificate (under 24 for men, or 36 for women) to play a round, either by booking a tee-time well in advance or striking lucky in the daily lottery, which allocates half of each day's tee-times. All the St Andrews courses are operated by the St Andrews Links Trust (Ⓣ01334/466666, Ⓦwww.standrews.org.uk). One of the easiest championship courses to get into is the notoriously tough **Carnoustie** in Angus (Ⓣ01241/853249; £75), though you should still try to book as far ahead as possible. Other championship courses include **Gleneagles** in Perthshire (Ⓣ01764/662231; £100), **Royal Dornoch** in Sutherland (Ⓣ01862/810219; £60), and **Turnberry** in Ayrshire (Ⓣ01655/331000; £120). Professional players consider **Muirfield** in Gullane, near Edinburgh (Ⓣ01620/842123; £85; Tues & Thurs only) to be one of the most testing courses in the world and it's also one of the most elitist – women can play only if accompanied by a man, and they aren't allowed into the clubhouse. Ⓦwww.scotlands-golf-courses.com has information, contacts, photographs and even maps of "signature" holes.

If you're coming to Scotland primarily to play golf, it's worth shelling out for a ticket which gives you access to a number of courses in any one region. There's more information at Ⓦwww.scottishgolf.com and Ⓦwww.visitscotland.com/golf.

Fishing

Scotland's serrated coastline – with the deep sea lochs of the west, the firths of the east and the myriad offshore islands – encompasses the full gamut of marine habitats, and ranks among the cleanest coasts in Europe. Combine this with an abundance of **salmon**, **sea trout**, **brown trout** and **pike**, acres of open space and easy access, and you have an angler's paradise. Whether you're into game-, coarse- or sea-fishing, you'll be spoilt for choice. The only element in short supply is company; Scotland may offer wonderful fishing, but its unpolluted, open waters don't attract anywhere near the numbers of anglers you'd expect.

Nor will you get bogged down in fishing bureaucracy. No licence is needed to fish in Scotland, although nearly all land is privately owned and its fishing therefore controlled by a landlord/lady or his/her agent. Permission, however, is usually easy to obtain: **permits** can be bought without hassle at local tackle shops, or through fishing clubs in the area – if in doubt, ask at the nearest tourist office. The other thing to bear in mind is that salmon and sea trout have strict **seasons**, which vary between districts but usually stretch from late August to late February. Once again, individual tourist offices will know the precise dates, or you can check in the Scottish Tourist Board's excellent "Fish Scotland" brochure (Ⓦwww.visitscotland.com/outdoor). It provides a rough introduction to game-, coarse- and sea-angling, with tips on how to find the famous sea marks and salmon beats, and a rundown of less-well-known fishing spots. More useful information and contacts are at Ⓦwww.where-to-fish.com and Ⓦwww.fishing-uk-scotland.com.

Sailing

Like many of the outdoor sports on offer in Scotland, the opportunities for **sailing** are outstanding, tainted only by the unreliability of the weather. While you'll find keen sailors all over Scotland, the protected Firth of Clyde sees the most concentrated activity through the year, though in the summer months the scenery, lack of crowds and sheer explorability of the entire west coast are in their element. Yacht racing is popular in the Clyde, while **cruising** is the main focus on the west coast, where a number of marinas in the area between Crinan and Oban are the common starting point of voyages which commonly take in a mix of islands and sheltered sea lochs. Even in summer, however, the full force of North Atlantic weather can be felt, and changeable conditions combined with tricky tides and rocky shores demand good sailing and navigational skills.

Yacht charters are available from various ports, either bareboat or in yachts run by a skipper and crew; contact Sail Scotland (see below) or the Associated Scottish Yacht Charters (Ⓦwww.asyc.co.uk).

An alternative way to enjoy Scotland under sail is to spend a week at one of the **sailing schools** around the country. These normally offer either dinghy-based tuition from a single onshore centre, or a cruise on a larger boat mixing instruction with exploration. Many sailing schools, as well as small boat rental operations dotted along the coast, will **rent** sailing dinghies by the hour or day, giving you the chance to get out on the water and, in the right circumstances, set off for a nearby island or headland for a picnic. These companies will also often rent **windsurfers**, though the chilly water means you'll always need a wetsuit. Scotland's top spot for windsurfing is the island of Tiree, an unusually flat island which has the advantage of stopping the waves but not the wind, which frequently whips in straight off the Atlantic.

For more information, get hold of the tourist board's comprehensive "Sail Scotland" brochure (ⓣ01309/676757, ⓦwww.sailscotland.co.uk).

Beaches and surfing

Scotland is ringed by fine **beaches** and bays, most of them clean and many of them deserted even in high summer – perhaps hardly surprising, given the bracing winds and chilly water which often accompany them. Few people come to Scotland for a beach holiday, but it's worth sampling a beach or two, even if you keep your sweater on. A rash of slightly melancholy seaside towns lie within easy reach of Glasgow, while on the east coast the relatively low cliffs and miles of sandy beaches are ideal for walking. Bizarrely enough, given the low temperature of the water, the beaches in the northeast are beginning to figure on surfers' itineraries, attracting enthusiasts from all over Europe (see below). Perhaps the most beautiful beaches of all are to be found on Scotland's islands: endless, isolated stretches that on a sunny day can be paradisal.

The Marine Conservation Society monitors bathing-water quality, and in 2001 recommended twenty beaches in Scotland, from North Berwick to Dornoch. Notable sandy beaches which failed to meet the strict EU standards include Ayr, Largs and Troon South (all in Ayrshire), and Rockcliffe and Sandyhills (in Dumfries and Galloway).

Surfing

Unlikely though it may seem, Scotland is fast gaining a reputation as a **surfing** destination, with a good selection of excellent quality breaks. It may not have the sunshine of Hawaii, and the water is generally steely-grey rather than turquoise-blue, but there are world-class waves to be found. **Thurso** is the number-one spot on the **north coast**, and boasts one of the finest reef breaks in Europe. In addition, the rest of this coastline – Sango Bay, Torrisdale, Farr Bay and Armadale, in particular – offers waves comparable to those in Hawaii, Australia and Indonesia. However, Scotland's northern coastline lies on the same latitude as Alaska and Iceland, so the water temperature is very low: even in midsummer it rarely exceeds 15°C, and in winter can drop to as low as to 7°C. The one vital accessory, therefore, is a good wet suit (ideally a 5/3mm steamer), wet-suit boots and, outside summer, gloves and a hood, too.

In addition to Thurso, there are several other excellent breaks, many of which lie within easy reach of large cities, such as **Pease Bay** near Edinburgh, and **Fraserburgh** near Aberdeen. The beaches of the **Moray Firth** also offer a good North Sea swell. Of the islands, the west coasts of **Coll**, **Tiree** and **Islay** get great swell from the Atlantic and have good beaches, while the spectacular west coast offers numerous possibilities, in particular one of Britain's most isolated beaches, **Sandwood Bay**. In the Outer Hebrides, the best breaks are along the northern coastline of **Lewis**, near Carloway and Bragar.

Many of these beaches are surrounded by stunning scenery, and you'd be unlucky to encounter another surfer for miles. However, this isolation – combined with the cold water and big, powerful waves – means that, in general, much of Scottish surf is best left to **experienced surfers**. If you're a beginner, get local advice before you go in, and be aware of your limitations; remember, if you get caught in a current off the west coast the next stop might be Iceland.

The popularity of surfing in Scotland has led to a spate of **surf shops** opening up, all of which rent or sell equipment, and provide good information about the local breaks and events on the surfing scene (Granite Reef and Momentum also offer surfing lessons).

Two further sources of information are *Surf UK* by Wayne "Alf" Alderson (Fernhurst Books; £13.95), with details on over 400 breaks around Britain, and the bimonthly *Surf* magazine (£3).

Surf shops

Boardwise, 1146 Argyle St, Glasgow ⓣ0141/334 5559; 4 Lady Lawson St, Edinburgh ⓣ0131/229 5887.
Clan 45 Hyndland St, Partick, Glasgow ⓣ0141/339 6523.
ESP, 5–7 Moss St, Elgin ⓣ01343/550129.
Granite Reef, 45 The Green, Aberdeen ⓣ01224/252752.
Momentum, 22 Bruntsfield Place, Edinburgh ⓣ0131/229 6665.
Outback Surfing, 92d High St, Elgin ⓣ01343/540750.

The top ten Scottish breaks

*__Brimm's Ness__, five miles west of Thurso; p.652. A selection of reef breaks that pick up the smallest of swells.
Fraserburgh, 39 miles north of Aberdeen; p.564. A number of beach and reef breaks – beginners should stick to the beach.
Machrihanish Bay, Mull of Kintyre; p.419. Four miles of beach breaks on one of Scotland's loneliest peninsulas.
Pease Bay, near Dunbar, 26 miles east of Edinburgh; p.143. A popular break suited to all abilities; can get very crowded.
Sandside Bay, on the north coast, ten miles west of Thurso; p.652. Reef and beach breaks, but dubious water quality due to the proximity of the Dounreay nuclear power station.
Sandwood Bay, a day's hike south of Cape Wrath in Sutherland; p.647. Beach breaks on one of the most scenic and remote shorelines in Britain, only accessible on foot.
*__Skirza Harbour__, three miles south of John O'Groats; p.654. An excellent left-hand reef break on the far northeast tip of Scotland.
*__Thurso East__, just below the castle; p.652. One of the best right-hand reef breaks in Europe.
*__Torrisdale Bay__, Bettyhill, on the north coast of the Highlands; p.651. An excellent right-hand river-mouth break.
*__Valtos__, on the Uig peninsula, Lewis; p.483. A break on one of the Outer Hebrides' most exquisite shell-sand beaches.
**Experienced surfers only*

Gay and lesbian travellers

Both Glasgow and Edinburgh have reasonably prominent gay and lesbian communities, with a well-established network of bars, cafés, nightclubs, support groups and events.

In Edinburgh, the area around Broughton Street is the heart of the city's "pink triangle", while in Glasgow the scene is mostly found in the Merchant City area; our entertainment listings for both cities include a number of gay bars and clubs. Elsewhere in Scotland, there are one or two gay bars in both Aberdeen and Dundee, with support and advice groups dotted around the country. Details for these, and many other aspects of the gay scene in Scotland, are on the websites for the campaigning Equality Network (ⓦwww.diversity.org.uk) and the monthly *Scotsgay* newspaper (ⓦwww.scotsgay.co.uk). The links page on the Glasgow Lesbian, Gay, Bisexual & Transgender Centre website (ⓣ0141/221 7203, ⓦwww.gglc.org.uk) is particularly useful. Glasgow and Edinburgh's fortnightly *List* magazine has useful news and what's-on listings.

Contacts for gay and lesbian travellers

UK

ⓦwww.gaytravel.co.uk Online gay and lesbian travel agent, offering good deals on all types of holiday. Also lists gay- and lesbian-friendly hotels.

North America

Ferrari Publications ⓣ 1-800/962-2912, ⓦ www.ferrariguides.com. Publishes *Ferrari Gay Travel A to Z*, a worldwide gay and lesbian guide; *Inn Places*, a worldwide accommodation guide; the guides *Men's Travel in Your Pocket* and *Women's Travel in Your Pocket*, and the quarterly *Ferrari Travel Report*.
International Gay/Lesbian Travel Association ⓣ 1-800/448-8550, ⓦ www.iglta.org. Trade group that can provide a list of gay and lesbian owned or friendly travel agents, accommodation and other travel businesses.

Australia and New Zealand

Gay and Lesbian Travel ⓦ www.galta.com.au. Directory and links for worldwide gay and lesbian travel.
Gay Travel ⓦ www.gaytravel.com. Trip planning, bookings and general information about international travel.
Parkside Travel ⓣ 1800/888501, ⓔ hwtravel@senet.com.au. Gay travel agent associated with local branch of Hervey World Travel; all aspects of gay and lesbian travel worldwide.
Pinkstay ⓦ www.pinkstay.com. Everything from visa information to finding accommodation and work around the world.
Silke's Travel ⓣ 1800/807860, ⓔ silba@magna.com.au. Long-established gay and lesbian specialist, with the emphasis on women's travel.
Tearaway Travel ⓣ 03/9510 6344, ⓔ tearaway@bigpond.com. Gay-specific business dealing with international and domestic travel.

Travellers with specific needs

Travellers with disabilities

Scottish attitudes towards **travellers with disabilities** are far behind advances towards independence made in North America and Australia. Access to theatres, cinemas and other public places has improved recently, but public transport companies rarely make any effort to help, though some ScotRail InterCity services now accommodate wheelchair users in comfort. Wheelchair users and blind or partially sighted people are automatically given 30–50 percent reductions on train fares, and people with other disabilities are eligible for the **Disabled Persons Railcard** (£20 per year), which gives a third off most tickets. There are no bus discounts for the disabled, and of the major **car-rental** firms only Hertz offers models with hand controls at the same rate as conventional vehicles, and even these are only available in the more expensive categories. It's the same story for **accommodation**, with modified suites for people with disabilities available only at higher-priced establishments and perhaps the odd B&B.

Contacts for travellers with disabilities

UK and Ireland

ⓦ **www.everybody.co.uk** Provides information on accommodation suitable for disabled travellers throughout the UK.
Capability Scotland ⓣ 0131/337 9876, ⓦ www.capability-scotland.org.uk. Primarily a charity concerned with spina bifida, this is a well-run, well-connected organization for all disability issues and information.
Irish Wheelchair Association ⓣ 01/833 8241, ⓔ iwa@iol.ie. Useful information provided about travelling abroad with a wheelchair.
RADAR (Royal Association for Disability and Rehabilitation) ⓣ 020/7250 3222, Minicom 7250 4119, ⓦ www.radar.org.uk. A good source of advice on holidays and travel in the UK. They produce an annual holiday guide *Holidays in Britain and Ireland* for £8.
Tripscope ⓣ 0845/758 5641, ⓦ www.justmobility.co.uk/tripscope. Provides a national phone information service offering free advice on UK transport for those with a mobility problem.

North America

Access-Able Ⓦwww.access-able.com. Online resource for travellers with disabilities.

Directions Unlimited Ⓣ1-800/533-5343. Tour operator specializing in custom tours for people with disabilities.

Mobility International USA Ⓣ541/343-1284, Ⓦwww.miusa.org. Information and referral services, access guides, tours and exchange programmes. Annual membership $35 (includes quarterly newsletter).

Society for the Advancement of Travel for the Handicapped (SATH) Ⓣ212/447-7284, Ⓦwww.sath.org. Non-profit educational organization that has actively represented travellers with disabilities since 1976.

Travel Information Service Ⓣ215/456-9600. Telephone-only information and referral service.

Twin Peaks Press Ⓣ360/694-2462, Ⓦhome.pacifier.com/~twinpeak. Publisher of the *Directory of Travel Agencies for the Disabled* ($19.95), listing more than 370 agencies worldwide; *Travel for the Disabled* ($19.95); the *Directory of Accessible Van Rentals* ($12.95) and *Wheelchair Vagabond* ($19.95), loaded with personal tips.

Wheels Up! Ⓣ1-888/389-4335, Ⓦwww.wheelsup.com. Provides discounted airfare, tour and cruise prices for disabled travellers; also publishes a free monthly newsletter and has a comprehensive website.

Australia and New Zealand

ACROD (Australian Council for Rehabilitation of the Disabled) Ⓣ02/6282 4333, Ⓦwww.acrod.org.au. Provides lists of travel agencies and tour operators for people with disabilities.

Disabled Persons Assembly Ⓣ04/801 9100, Ⓦwww.dpa.org.nz. New Zealand resource centre with lists of travel agencies and tour operators for people with disabilities.

Senior travellers

Senior citizens, whether resident in the UK or not, are usually eligible for some kind of discount at sights all over Scotland, so it's always worth asking. Those aged sixty or over might also consider buying a **Senior Railcard**, which costs £18 and gives a third off standard rail fares. On the coaches, you only need to be fifty or over to buy a **Smart Card** (£6), valid for one year and giving you a thirty percent discount. The best-known package company specializing in worldwide group travel for seniors is, of course, Saga Holidays (UK Ⓣ01303/771111, US Ⓣ1-877/265-6862, Ⓦwww.sagaholidays.com).

Travelling with children

Scottish attitudes to those **travelling with children** can be discouraging, particularly if you've experienced the more indulgent approach of the French or Italians. Restaurateurs would basically prefer it if parents and carers left the kids at home. Obviously, out in rural areas, particularly in the Islands, attitudes are much more relaxed, and the sight of kids in the hotel lounge bar not so unusual. However, most families with young children opt for self-catering cottages (see p.30) precisely to avoid the hassle of trying to eat out with kids. It's always worth asking about discounted "family tickets" when visiting any attractions or sight. If you're travelling on public transport, it's definitely worthwhile buying a **Family Railcard** (£20), which gives you sixty percent off kids' fares and thirty percent off adult fares.

Directory

Electricity The current is 240v AC. North American appliances need a transformer and adapter; Australasian appliances need only an adapter.

Gaelic In some areas of Scotland, particularly in the Highlands and Hebrides, road signs are bilingual English–Gaelic. Throughout the guide, where appropriate, we've given the Gaelic translation (in italics and parentheses) the first time any village or island is mentioned, after which the English name is used. The main exception to this rule is in the Western Isles, where signposting is exclusively in Gaelic; we've reflected this by giving the Gaelic first and putting the English in parentheses, and thereafter using the Gaelic (except for the islands and ferry ports, which are more familiar in the English form they're given on ferry timetables).

Laundry Coin-operated laundries are found in nearly all Scottish cities and towns, and are open about twelve hours a day from Monday to Friday, less on weekends. A wash followed by a spin or tumble dry costs about £3; a "service wash" (having your laundry done for you in a few hours) costs about £2 extra. In the remoter regions of Scotland, you'll have to rely on hostel and campsite laundry facilities.

Smoking The last decade or so has seen a dramatic change in attitudes towards smoking, and a significant reduction in the consumption of cigarettes. Smoking is now outlawed from just about all public buildings and on public transport, and many restaurants and hotels have become totally non-smoking. Smokers are advised, when booking a table or a room, to check their vice is tolerated there.

Time From late October to late March, Scotland is on Greenwich Mean Time (GMT), which is five hours ahead of US Eastern Standard Time and ten hours behind Australian Eastern Standard Time. Over the summer, clocks go forward an hour for British Summer Time (BST).

Toilets Public loos are found at all train and bus stations and signposted on town high streets; a fee of 10p or 20p is sometimes charged.

guide

guide

Edinburgh and the Lothians

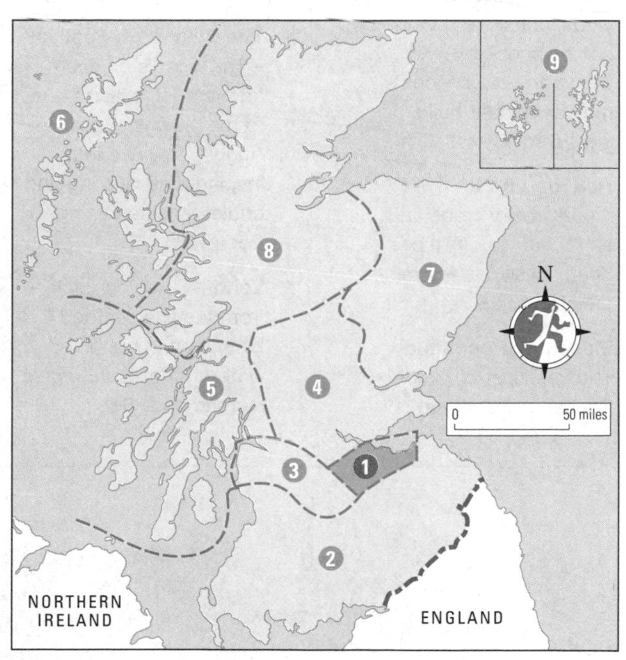

CHAPTER 1

Highlights

* **Edinburgh Castle** – Perched on an imposing volcanic crag, the castle still dominates Scotland's capital, its ancient battlements protecting the Crown Jewels. See p.74
* **The Old Town** – The evocative heart of the historic city, with its tenements, closes, courtyards, ghosts and catacombs cheek-by-jowl with many of Scotland's most important buildings. See p.74
* **Holyrood Park** – Wild moors, rocky crags and an 800-ft peak (Arthur's Seat), all slap in the middle of the city. See p.92
* **Museum of Scotland** – The treasures of Scotland's past in a dynamic and superbly conceived new building. See p.94
* **Café Royal Circle Bar** – In a city filled with fine drinking spots, there are few finer pubs in which to sample a pint of local 80 shilling beer; order six oysters (once the city's staple food) to complete the experience. See p.120
* **The Edinburgh Festival** – The world's biggest arts festival, which transforms the city every August. Bewildering, inspiring, exhausting and endlessly entertaining. See p.126
* **Leith** – Take your pick from the fine seafood bistros on the cobbled waterfront of Edinburgh's historic port. See p.135

1

Edinburgh and the Lothians

Venerable, dramatic **EDINBURGH**, the showcase capital of Scotland, is a historic, cosmopolitan and cultured city. The setting is wonderfully striking; the city is perched on a series of extinct volcanoes and rocky crags which rise from the generally flat landscape of the Lothians, with the sheltered shoreline of the Firth of Forth to the north. "My own Romantic town", Sir Walter Scott called it, although it was another native author, Robert Louis Stevenson, who perhaps best captured the feel of his "precipitous city", declaring that "No situation could be more commanding for the head of a kingdom; none better chosen for noble prospects."

The centre has two distinct parts, divided by **Princes Street Gardens**, which run roughly east–west under the shadow of **Castle Rock**. To the north, the dignified, Grecian-style **New Town** was immaculately laid out during the Age of Reason, after the announcement of a plan to improve conditions in the city. The **Old Town**, on the other hand, with its tortuous alleys and tightly packed closes, is unrelentingly medieval, associated in popular imagination with the underworld lore of schizophrenic Deacon Brodie, inspiration for Stevenson's *Dr Jekyll and Mr Hyde*, and the body snatchers Burke and Hare. Edinburgh earned its nickname "Auld Reekie" for the smog and smell generated by the Old Town, which for centuries swam in sewage tipped out of the windows of cramped tenements.

Accommodation price codes

Throughout this book, accommodation **prices** have been graded with the codes below, corresponding to the cost of the least expensive double room in high season. Price codes are not given for **campsites**, most of which charge less than £10 per person. Almost all **hostels** and **bunkhouses** charge between £8 and £12 per person per night; the few exceptions to this rule have the prices quoted in the text. For a full account of these codes, see p.28.

❶ under £40	❹ £60–70	❼ £110–150
❷ £40–50	❺ £70–90	❽ £150–200
❸ £50–60	❻ £90–110	❾ £200 and over

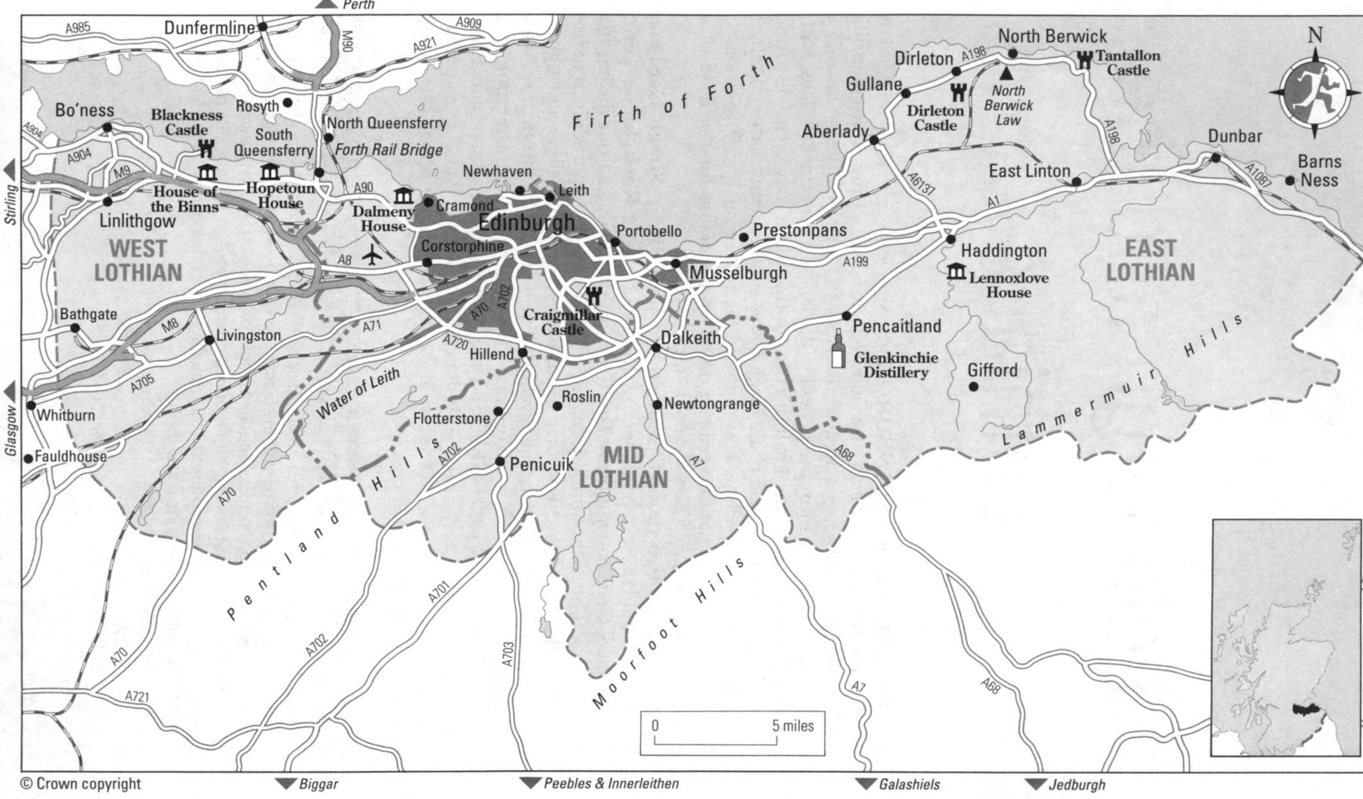
Perth
Stirling
Glasgow
Biggar
Peebles & Innerleithen
Galashiels
Jedburgh
Berwick-upon-Tweed
N
Firth of Forth
Dunfermline
Rosyth
North Queensferry
Forth Rail Bridge
South Queensferry
Bo'ness
Blackness Castle
House of the Binns
Hopetoun House
Linlithgow
WEST LOTHIAN
Dalmeny House
Cramond
Newhaven
Leith
Edinburgh
Portobello
Corstorphine
Musselburgh
Prestonpans
Craigmillar Castle
Dalkeith
Hillend
Roslin
Newtongrange
Flotterstone
Penicuik
MID LOTHIAN
Bathgate
Livingston
Whitburn
Fauldhouse
Water of Leith
Pentland Hills
Moorfoot Hills
Lammermuir Hills
Aberlady
Gullane
Dirleton
Dirleton Castle
North Berwick
North Berwick Law
Tantallon Castle
East Linton
Dunbar
Barns Ness
Haddington
Lennoxlove House
EAST LOTHIAN
Pencaitland
Glenkinchie Distillery
Gifford
A985
A904
M9
M90
A909
A921
A90
A8
M8
A71
A705
A70
A720
A702
A701
A703
A7
A68
A721
A199
A1
A6137
A198
A1087
0
5 miles

Set on the crag which sweeps down from the towering fairy-tale **Castle** to the royal **Palace of Holyroodhouse**, the Old Town preserves all the key reminders of its role as a capital, plus a brand new **parliament building** rising up opposite the palace. A few hundred yards away a tantalizing glimpse of the wild beauty of Scotland's scenery can be had immediately beyond the palace in **Holyrood Park**, an extensive area of open countryside dominated by **Arthur's Seat**, the largest and most impressive of the volcanoes.

In August and early September, around a million visitors flock to the city for the **Edinburgh Festival**, in fact a series of separate festivals that make up the largest arts extravaganza in the world. Among the many museums, the exciting new **National Museum of Scotland** houses 10,000 of Scotland's most precious artefacts, while the **National Gallery of Scotland** and its offshoot, the **Scottish National Gallery of Modern Art**, have two of Britain's finest collections of paintings.

On a less elevated theme, the city's distinctive howffs (pubs), allied to its brewing and distilling traditions, make it a great **drinking** city. The presence of three **universities**, plus several colleges, means that there is a youthful presence for most of the year – a welcome corrective to the stuffiness which is often regarded as Edinburgh's Achilles heel.

Beyond the city centre, the most lively area is **Leith**, the city's medieval port, whose seedy edge is softened by a series of great bars and upmarket seafood restaurants, along with the presence of the former royal yacht **Britannia**, now open to visitors. The wider rural hinterland of Edinburgh, known as the **Lothians**, mixes rolling countryside and attractive country towns with some dramatic historic ruins. In East Lothian, blustery cliff-top paths lead to the romantic battlements of **Tantallon Castle**, while nearby North Berwick, home of the **Scottish Seabird Centre**, looks out to the gannet-covered Bass Rock. The most famous sight in Midlothian is the mysterious fifteenth-century **Rosslyn Chapel**, while West Lothian boasts the towering, roofless **Linlithgow Palace**, thirty minutes from Edinburgh by train. To the northwest of the city, the dramatic curves of the **Forth Rail Bridge** are best seen by walking across the parallel road bridge, starting at **South Queensferry**.

Some history

It was during the **Dark Ages** that the name of Edinburgh – at least in its early forms of Dunedin or Din Eidyn ("fort of Eidyn") – first appeared. Castle Rock, a strategic fort atop one of the volcanoes, served as the nation's **southernmost border post** until 1018, when King Malcolm I established the River Tweed as the permanent frontier. In the reign of Malcolm Canmore, the Castle became one of the main seats of the court, and the town, which was given privileged status as a **royal burgh**, began to grow. In 1128 King David established Holyrood Abbey at the foot of the slope, later allowing its monks to found a separate burgh, known as **Canongate**.

Robert the Bruce granted Edinburgh a **new charter** in 1329, giving it jurisdiction over the nearby port of **Leith**, and during the following century the prosperity brought by foreign trade enabled the newly fortified city to establish itself as the permanent **capital of Scotland**. Under King James IV, the city enjoyed a short but brilliant **Renaissance era**, which saw not only the construction of a new palace alongside Holyrood Abbey, but also the granting of a royal charter to the College of Surgeons, the earliest in the city's long line of academic and professional bodies.

This period came to an abrupt end in 1513 with the calamitous defeat by the English at the Battle of Flodden, which led to several decades of political instability. In the 1540s, King Henry VIII's attempt to force a royal union with Scotland led to the sack of Edinburgh, prompting the Scots to turn to France: French troops arrived to defend the city, while the young queen Mary was dispatched to Paris as the promised bride of the Dauphin. While the French occupiers succeeded in removing the English threat, they themselves antagonized the locals, who had become increasingly sympathetic to the ideals of the **Reformation**. When the radical preacher John Knox returned from exile in 1555, he quickly won over the city to his Calvinist message.

James VI's rule saw the foundation of the University of Edinburgh in 1582, but following the **Union of the Crowns** in 1603 the city was totally upstaged by London: although James promised to visit every three years, it was not until 1617 that he made his only return trip. In 1633 Charles I visited Edinburgh for his coronation, but soon afterwards precipitated a crisis by introducing episcopacy to the Church of Scotland, in the process making Edinburgh a bishopric for the first time. Fifty years of religious turmoil followed, culminating in the triumph of **Presbyterianism**. Despite these vicissitudes, Edinburgh expanded throughout the seventeenth century and, constrained by its walls, was forced to build both upwards and inwards.

The **Union of the Parliaments** of 1707 dealt a further blow to Edinburgh's political prestige, though the guaranteed preservation of the national church and the legal and educational systems ensured that it was never relegated to a purely provincial role. On the contrary, it was in the second half of the eighteenth century that Edinburgh achieved the height of its intellectual influence, led by an outstanding group, including David Hume and Adam Smith. Around the same time, the city began to expand beyond its medieval boundaries, laying out a **New Town**, a masterpiece of the Neoclassical style.

Industrialization affected Edinburgh less than any other major city in the nation, and it never lost its white-collar character. Nevertheless, the city underwent an enormous **urban expansion** in the course of the century, annexing, among many other small burghs, the large port of Leith.

In 1947 Edinburgh was chosen to host the great **International Festival** which served as a symbol of the new peaceful European order; despite some hiccups, it has flourished ever since, in the process helping to make tourism a mainstay of the local economy. In 1975 the city carried out another territorial expansion, moving its boundaries westwards as far as the old burgh of South Queensferry and the Forth Bridges. Four years later, an inconclusive referendum on Scottish devolution delayed Edinburgh's revival of its role as a governmental capital, and Glasgow, previously the poor relation but always a tenacious rival, began to challenge the city's status as a cultural centre.

However, while the 1990s saw Glasgow establish a clear lead in driving Scotland's contemporary arts scene, they also marked the return of power and influence to Edinburgh. Following a referendum in 1997, in which Scotland voted resoundingly in favour of re-establishing its own **parliament**, elections were held in May 1999. On July 1, 1999, the Queen formally opened the parliament, temporarily housed in the twin-towered Church of Scotland Assembly Halls on the Mound. Inevitably, the early years of the parliament have seen petty squabbling mixed with rather dizzying constitutional manoeuvring, but with debates, decisions and demonstrations about crucial aspects of the government of Scotland now taking place in Edinburgh, there has been a notable upturn in the sense of importance of the city. Added to this, recent acquisitions and mergers involving Scotland's two major banks, the Royal Bank of Scotland and the Bank of Scotland, have affirmed Edinburgh's significant place as a financial centre not just in Britain, but also Europe. Meanwhile, construction teams are at work on the Parliament building, which will take its place opposite the ancient Palace of Holyroodhouse at the foot of the Royal Mile.

Arrival, information and transport

Although Edinburgh occupies a large area relative to its population – less than half a million people – most places worth visiting lie within the compact city centre, which is easily explored on foot. This is divided clearly and unequivocally between the maze-like **Old Town**, which lies on and around the crag linking the Castle and the Palace, and the **New Town**, laid out in a symmetrical pattern on the undulating ground to the north.

Edinburgh International Airport (Ⓣ0131/333 1000) is at Turnhouse, seven miles west of the city centre, close to the start of the M8 motorway to Glasgow. Regular Airlink shuttle buses (£3.30) connect to Waverley Bridge in the town centre; taxis charge around £15 for the same journey. Conveniently situated at the eastern end of Princes Street in the New Town, **Waverley Station** (timetable and fare enquiries Ⓣ0845/748 4950) is the terminus for all mainline trains. The main central exits take you out onto Waverley Bridge, where the Castle appears dramatically ahead of you and the Old Town skyline is to the south, with Princes Street to the north. The northern exit from Waverley leads up a stairway to Princes Street itself, while the southern exit leads to Market Street, the outer fringe of the Old Town.

There's a second mainline train stop, **Haymarket Station**, just under two miles west on the lines from Waverley to Glasgow, Fife and the Highlands, although this is only really of use if you're staying nearby. The **bus** terminal for local and intercity services is on St Andrew Square, two minutes' walk from Waverley Station, on the opposite side of Princes Street.

Information

Edinburgh's main **tourist office** is found on top of Princes Mall near the northern entrance to the station (April & Oct Mon–Sat 9am–6pm, Sun 10am–6pm; May, June & Sept 9am–7pm, Sun 10am–7pm; July & Aug Mon–Sat 9am–8pm, Sun 10am–8pm; Nov–March Mon–Sat 9am–5pm, Sun 10am–4pm; Ⓣ0131/473 3800, Ⓦwww.edinburgh.org). Although inevitably flustered at the height of the season, it's efficiently run, with scores of free leaflets and a bank of computers available if you want to search for information on the web. The much smaller **airport branch** is in the main concourse, directly opposite Gate 5 (daily: April–Oct 6.30am–10.30pm; Nov–March 7.30am–9.30pm). For backpacker-related information head to the **Haggis Office** at 60 High St (daily 9am–6pm; Ⓣ0131/557 9393, Ⓦwww.haggisadventures.com). Although their main function is to run minibus tours of Scotland, they're a good source of general information about the backpacker scene around Scotland and you can book hostels and intercity coaches from here, as well as change money. For up-to-date maps of the city head for one of the major book stores: Waterstone's, 13–14 Princes St, is the nearest to Waverley Station.

Open-top bus tours are big business in Edinburgh, with three rival companies taking largely similar routes around the main sights. All depart from Waverley Bridge and all allow you to get on and off at leisure. The most entertaining of the three are MacTours, who use a fleet of characterful vintage buses.

New Town

Balmoral Hotel 1 Princes St (ⓣ0131/556 2414, ⓦwww.rfhotels.com. Originally known as the *North British*, this elegant Edinburgh landmark is the finest grand hotel in the city. The *Balmoral* boasts nearly two hundred rooms, full business facilities, a swimming pool and gym, and two highly rated restaurants. ❽

Bonham Hotel 35 Drumsheugh Gardens ⓣ0131/226 6050, ⓦwww.thebonham.com. One of Edinburgh's most stylish modern hotels, cheekily hiding behind a grand West End Victorian facade. An interesting mix of period and modern furniture. ❽

Caledonian Hotel corner of Princes St & Lothian Rd ⓣ0131/459 9988. Built by the railway for the well-to-do travelling between London and their Highland estates, this red-sandstone building lords it over the west end of Princes Street. Recently taken over by the Hilton Group, it still attracts the stars despite falling behind the standards of its competitors. ❾

Christopher North Hotel 6 Gloucester Place ⓣ0131/225 2720, ⓦwww.christophernorth.co.uk. Elegant and comfortable town-house hotel in a typical New Town terrace. Decor is modern and dramatic, if a little overwhelming. ❻

Frederick House Hotel 42 Frederick St ⓣ0131/226 1999, ⓦwww.townhousehotels.co.uk. A reasonable if slightly plain hotel in a superb location just off George Street in the New Town. ❹

Howard Hotel 34 Great King St ⓣ0131/557 3500, ⓦwww.thehoward.com. Top-of-the-range elegant town-house hotel, with fifteen exclusive rooms lavishly decorated in grand and rather refined style. ❾

Melvin House Hotel 3 Rothesay Terrace ⓣ0131/225 5084, ⓦwww.melvinhouse.co.uk. One of Edinburgh's grandest Victorian terrace houses, with exquisite internal wood panelling, a galleried library and decent rooms, some with outstanding views over Dean village and the city skyline. ❼

Old Waverley Hotel 43 Princes St ⓣ0131/556 4648. Rather old-fashioned but ideally placed grand hotel, right across from Waverley Station and with sweeping city views. ❽

Parliament House Hotel 15 Calton Hill ⓣ0131/478 4000, ⓦwww.scotland-hotels.co.uk. The parliament has now moved, but this smart hotel in a discreet but central location halfway up Calton Hill remains pleasant and well run. Includes three rooms for disabled visitors. ❽

Leith

Malmaison 1 Tower Place ⓣ0131/468 5000, ⓦwww.malmaison.com. Chic modern hotel in a converted harbourside building with bright, bold original designs in each room, as well as CD players and cable TV. Also has gym, room service, Parisian brasserie and café-bar serving lighter meals. ❼

South of the centre

Allison House Hotel 15–17 Mayfield Gardens, Mayfield ⓣ0131/667 8049, ⓦwww.allisonhousehotel.com. Well run and recently expanded suburban hotel with 23 rooms located on one of the main bus routes into town. ❹

Braid Hills Hotel 134 Braid Rd, Braid Hills ⓣ0131/447 8888, ⓔbookings@braidhillshotel.co.uk. Old-fashioned baronial-style hotel in a residential area up in the hilly southern outskirts, with fine views (a ten-minute drive from the city). ❼

Bruntsfield Hotel 69–74 Bruntsfield Place, Bruntsfield ⓣ0131/229 1393, ⓦwww.thebruntsfield.co.uk. Large, comfortable and peaceful hotel overlooking Bruntsfield Links, a mile south of Princes Street. ❻

Prestonfield House Hotel Priestfield Road, Bruntsfield ⓣ0131/668 3346, ⓦwww.prestonfieldhouse.com. A unique Edinburgh hotel: a seventeenth-century mansion set in its own park below Arthur's Seat with upmarket rooms in the main house and a tasteful annex. Peacocks strut around on the lawns and Highland cattle low in the adjacent fields. ❼

Simpson's Hotel 79 Lauriston Place ⓣ0131/622 7979, ⓦwww.simpsons-hotel.com. Well priced and smart medium-sized hotel located in the former maternity hospital near Tollcross and the Meadows. Named after Sir James Young Simpson, pioneer of modern anaesthetics. ❺

West of the centre

Jarvis Ellersly Country House Hotel 4 Ellersly Rd, Corstorphine ⓣ0131/337 6888. Edwardian country mansion set in a walled garden in quiet suburban Corstorphine, between the city centre and the airport. Predominantly business clientele. ❼

The Original Raj Hotel 6 West Coates ⓣ0131/346 1333. Imaginatively conceived and lavishly executed, a town-house hotel with seventeen rooms themed on India and the splendour of the Raj. ❻

Guesthouses

Generally offering much better value for money and a far more homely experience than the larger city hotels are Edinburgh's vast range of **guesthouses**, **small hotels** and **bed & breakfast** establishments. A few of these, commanding a premium rate, can be found in the very centre of the city, but areas such as the edges of the New Town and the inner suburbs of Bruntsfield and the Grange offer a perfect balance of accessibility and good value. Elsewhere, almost all suburbs are well served by regular buses.

Old Town

Bank Hotel 1 South Bridge ⓣ0131/556 9043, ⓦwww.festival-inns.co.uk. Notable location in a 1920s bank at the crossroads of the Royal Mile and South Bridge, with Logie Baird's bar downstairs and nine unusual but comfortable rooms upstairs on the theme of famous Scots. ❺

The Witchery Apartments Castlehill, Royal Mile ⓣ0131/225 5613, ⓦwww.thewitchery.com. Two riotously indulgent apartments above the famously spooky Royal Mile restaurant. Top of the range, unique and memorable. ❽

New Town

Ardenlee Guest House 9 Eyre Place ⓣ0131/556 2838. Welcoming, non-smoking guesthouse near the Royal Botanic Garden, with exceptionally comfortable and spacious rooms. Breakfast includes some vegetarian options, and large family rooms are available. ❸

Brodies Guest House 22 E Claremont St ⓣ0131/556 4032, ⓔrose.olbert@saqnet.co.uk. Standard but friendly B&B in a Victorian town house near the Broughton area on the eastern edge of the New Town. ❸

Davenport House 58 Great King St ⓣ0131/558 8495, ⓔdavenporthouse@btinternet.com. A grand, regally decorated guesthouse in an attractive New Town town house; a well-priced and intimate alternative to some of the nearby hotels. ❹

Galloway Guest House 22 Dean Park Crescent ⓣ0131/332 3672. Friendly, family-run option in elegant Stockbridge, within walking distance of the centre. ❷

Gerald's Place 21b Abercromby Place ⓣ0131/558 7017, ⓦwww.scotland2000.com/geraldsplace. A real taste of New Town life at an upmarket but wonderfully hospitable and comfy basement B&B. ❺

Greenside Hotel 9 Royal Terrace ⓣ0131/557 0022, ⓦwww.townhousehotels.co.uk. One of a number of small hotels on Calton Hill with great views from the top floors – in this case across to Leith and beyond to the Firth of Forth. Value for money considering the location. ❹

Rick's Restaurant with rooms 55a Frederick St ⓣ0131/622 7800, ⓦwww.ricksedinburgh.co.uk. Four much sought-after rooms at the back of the popular New Town bar and restaurant. Beautifully styled and fitted with walnut headboards and top quality fabrics, they look out onto a cobbled lane behind. ❻

Six Mary's Place Raeburn Place ⓣ0131/332 8965, ⓔsixmarysplace@btinternet.com. Collectively run "alternative" guesthouse; has a no-smoking policy and offers excellent home-cooked vegetarian meals. ❹

Stuart House 12 E Claremont St ⓣ0131/557 9030, ⓔstuartho@globalnet.co.uk. Homely, bright Georgian house in the Broughton area. No smoking. ❹

South of the centre

Ashdene House 23 Fountainhall Rd, Grange ⓣ0131/667 6026, ⓔAshdene_House_Edinburgh@compuserve.com. Well-run, non-smoking and environmentally friendly guesthouse in the quiet southern suburbs. ❸

Cluaran House 47 Leamington Terrace, Viewforth ⓣ0131/221 0047, ⓦwww.scotland2000.com/cluaran. Pleasant B&B in a nicely decorated, non-smoking house near Brunstfield serving wholefood breakfasts. ❸

The Greenhouse 14 Hartington Gardens, Viewforth ⓣ0131/622 7634, ⓔgreenhouse_edin@hotmail.com. A fully vegetarian/vegan guesthouse, right down to the soaps and duvets, though a relaxed rather than right-on atmosphere prevails. The rooms are neat and tastefully furnished, with fresh fruit and flowers in each. ❸

Hopetoun Guest House 15 Mayfield Rd, Mayfield ⓣ0131/667 7691, ⓔhopetoun@aol.com. Bright, friendly non-smoking guesthouse with just three rooms. Great views of Arthur's Seat and Blackford Hill. ❷

International Guest House 37 Mayfield Gardens, Mayfield ⓣ0131/667 2511, ⓔintergh@easynet.co.uk. One of the best of the Mayfield guesthouses, with comfortable well equipped rooms. ❷

The Stuarts B&B 17 Glengyle Terrace, Bruntsfield ⓣ0131/229 9559, ⓔreservations@the-stuarts.com. A five-star bed and breakfast in central Edinburgh, with three comfortable and well-equipped rooms in a basement beside Bruntsfield Links. ❺

Teviotdale House Hotel 53 Grange Loan, Grange ⓣ0131/667 4376, ⓔteviotdale.house@btinternet.com. Peaceful non-smoking hotel, offering luxurious standards at reasonable prices. Particularly good (and huge) home-cooked Scottish breakfasts. ❸

Leith and Inverleith

A-Haven Town House 180 Ferry Rd, Leith ⓣ0131/554 6559, ⓔreservations@a-haven.co.uk. A terrifically friendly place – among the best of a number of guesthouses on one of Edinburgh's main east–west arteries. ❺

Ashlyn Guest House 42 Inverleith Row, Inverleith ⓣ0131/552 2954. Right by the Botanic Garden, a half-hour walk to the centre or an easy bus trip. Non-smoking. ❸

Bar Java 48–50 Constitution St, Leith ⓣ0131/467 7527, ⓦwww.java-bedandbreakfast.com. Simple but brightly designed rooms above one of Leith's funkiest bars. Great breakfasts served, and food and drink available till late in the bar itself. ❷

East of the centre

Joppa Turrets Guest House 1 Lower Joppa, Joppa ⓣ0131/669 5806, ⓦwww.joppaturrets.demon.co.uk. The place to come if you want an Edinburgh holiday by the sea: a quiet establishment right by the beach in Joppa, five miles east of the city centre. ❷

Portobello House 2 Pittville St, Portobello ⓣ0131/669 6067. Pleasant rooms and good (organic) breakfasts at this family-run guesthouse, only two minutes from the shore. ❷

Stra'ven Guest House 3 Brunstane Rd North, Joppa ⓣ0131/669 5580. Splendid lounge and friendly service in an elegant well-kept guesthouse. No smoking. ❷

Self-catering apartments and campus accommodation

Custom-built **self-catering apartments** are popular with business travellers, but with no minimum let are a viable alternatives to guesthouses. They're also well worth considering for longer stays, for example during the Festival. **Campus accommodation** is available in the city during the summer months, though it's neither as useful or cheap as might be expected.

Canon Court Apartments 20 Canonmills ⓣ0131/474 7000, ⓦwww.canoncourt.co.uk. All mod cons available in these smart, comfortable self-catering apartments on the northern edge of the New Town, near the Water of Leith. Prices start at £87 a night for a studio apartment.

Napier University 219 Colinton Rd, Merchiston ⓣ0131/455 4331, ⓔvacation.lets@napier.ac.uk. Three- to five-person self-catering flats in the Tollcross/Bruntsfield area of the city. Minimum stay one week; from £315 per week.

National Trust for Scotland 5 Charlotte Square ⓣ0131/243 9331, ⓔholidays@nts.org.uk. Has a two-room apartment in Gladstone's Land (the finest house on the Royal Mile) available for rent. Minimum period one week in summer and three nights in winter. Sleeps two and costs from £240 per week.

Royal Garden Apartments York Buildings, Queen St ⓣ0131/625 1234. Superbly equipped, comfortable modern one- and two-bedroom apartments very centrally located opposite the National Portrait Gallery. Prices start at £85 per night.

University of Edinburgh Pollock Halls of Residence 18 Holyrood Park Rd, Newington ⓣ0131/651 2007 or 0800/028 7118, ⓦwww.edinburghfirst.com. Unquestionably the best setting of any of the campuses, right beside the Royal Commonwealth Pool and Holyrood Park, but relatively expensive (rates are for bed and breakfast). Easter & late June to mid-Sept. ❺

West End Apartments c/o Brian Matheson, 2 Learmonth Terrace, Comely Bank ⓣ0131/332 0717 or 226 6512, ⓔbrian@sias.co.uk. Five apartments in a West End town house; minimum let two nights. Sleeps up to five and costs £200–800 per week.

Hostels

Edinburgh now has a wealth of **hostels**, including two grand SYHA-run establishments and a cluster of independent outfits on or near the Royal Mile. Competition is fierce, so be prepared for a bit of enthusiastic marketing when you make an enquiry. All hostels are open all year round, unless stated.

Argyle Backpackers Hotel 14 Argyle Place, Marchmont ⓣ0131/667 9991, ⓦwww.sol.co.uk/a/argyle. Quieter, less intense version of the typical backpackers' hostel, with small dorms with single beds and a dozen double/twin rooms, though prices are a pound or two higher. Pleasantly located near the Meadows in studenty Marchmont.
Belford Hostel 6–8 Douglas Gardens, West End ⓣ0131/225 6209; booking hotline 0800/096 6868, ⓦwww.hoppo.com. Housed in a converted Arts and Crafts church, just west of the centre close to St Mary's Cathedral and the Gallery of Modern Art. The dorms are in box rooms with the vaulted church ceiling above.
Brodies Backpackers Hostel 12 High St, Old Town ⓣ0131/556 6770, ⓦwww.brodieshostels.co.uk. Tucked down a typical Old Town close, with four fairly straightforward dorms and limited communal areas. Smaller than many others, and a little bit more homely.
Bruntsfield Hostel 7 Bruntsfield Crescent, Bruntsfield ⓣ0131/447 2994, ⓦwww.syha.org.uk. Large SYHA youth hostel overlooking Bruntsfield Links a mile south of Princes Street; take bus #10, #11 or #16. Note that as well as the similarly sized Eglinton hostel (see below), SYHA also take over two central student residences with single rooms during July and August – one on The Pleasance and one on Cowgate; both have over 100 single bedrooms for around £16 per night (ⓣ0131/556 5566 or book on the central reservations line).
Castle Rock Hostel 15 Johnston Terrace, Old Town ⓣ0131/225 9666, ⓦwww.scotlands-top-hostels.com. Busy 200-bed hostel tucked below the Castle ramparts. Dorms are large and bright, and the communal areas include a games room with pool and ping-pong tables.
Cowgate Tourist Hostel 94–116 Cowgate, Old Town ⓣ0131/226 2153, ⓦwww.cowgatetourist hostel.co.uk. Basic but usefully central accommodation in small three-, four- and five-bedroom apartments with kitchens, in the heart of the Old Town.
Edinburgh Backpackers Hostel 65 Cockburn St, Old Town ⓣ0131/539 8695; booking hotline 0800/096 6868, ⓦwww.hoppo.com. Big hostel with a great central location in a side street off the Royal Mile. Accommodation is mostly in large but bright dorms, although a few doubles are available.
Eglinton Hostel 18 Eglinton Crescent, Haymarket ⓣ0131/337 1120, ⓦwww.syha.org.uk. Slightly more expensive but the more central of the two main SYHA hostels, in a characterful town house west of the centre, near Haymarket Station.
High Street Hostel 8 Blackfriars St, Old Town ⓣ0131/557 3984, ⓦwww.scotlands-top-hostels.com. Large but lively and well-known hostel in a sixteenth-century building just off the Royal Mile. Linked to *Castle Rock Hostel* and *Royal Mile Backpackers*.
Royal Mile Backpackers 105 High St, Old Town ⓣ0131/557 6120, ⓦwww.scotlands-top-hostels.com. Small, friendly hostel popular with longer term residents, with limited communal areas but shared facilities with the nearby *High Street Hostel*.
St Christopher's Inns 9–13 Market St, Old Town ⓣ0131/226 1446, ⓦwww.st-christophers.co.uk. Edinburgh's first sighting of the mega hostels now common in London; 110 beds (all bunks) with smaller rooms as well as dorms. There's a small communal area and a noisy bar for beer and food on ground level. A little corporate but clean and with good service; slightly more expensive than most other hostels.

Campsites

Davidson's Mains Caravan Site Marine Drive, Silverknowes ⓣ0131/312 6874. Edinburgh Caravan Club site in a pleasant location close to the shore in the north-western suburbs, a thirty-minute ride from the centre by bus #14. Open year-round.
Drummohr Caravan Park Levenhall, Musselburgh ⓣ0131/665 6867. A large, pleasant site in this coastal satellite town to the east of Edinburgh, with excellent transport connections to the city, including buses #15, #15A, #26, #44, #66 (SMT) and #85. Open March–Oct.
Mortonhall Caravan Park 38 Mortonhall Gate, Frogston Rd E ⓣ0131/664 1533. A good site, five miles south of the centre, near the Braid Hills; take bus #11 from Princes Street. Open March–Oct.

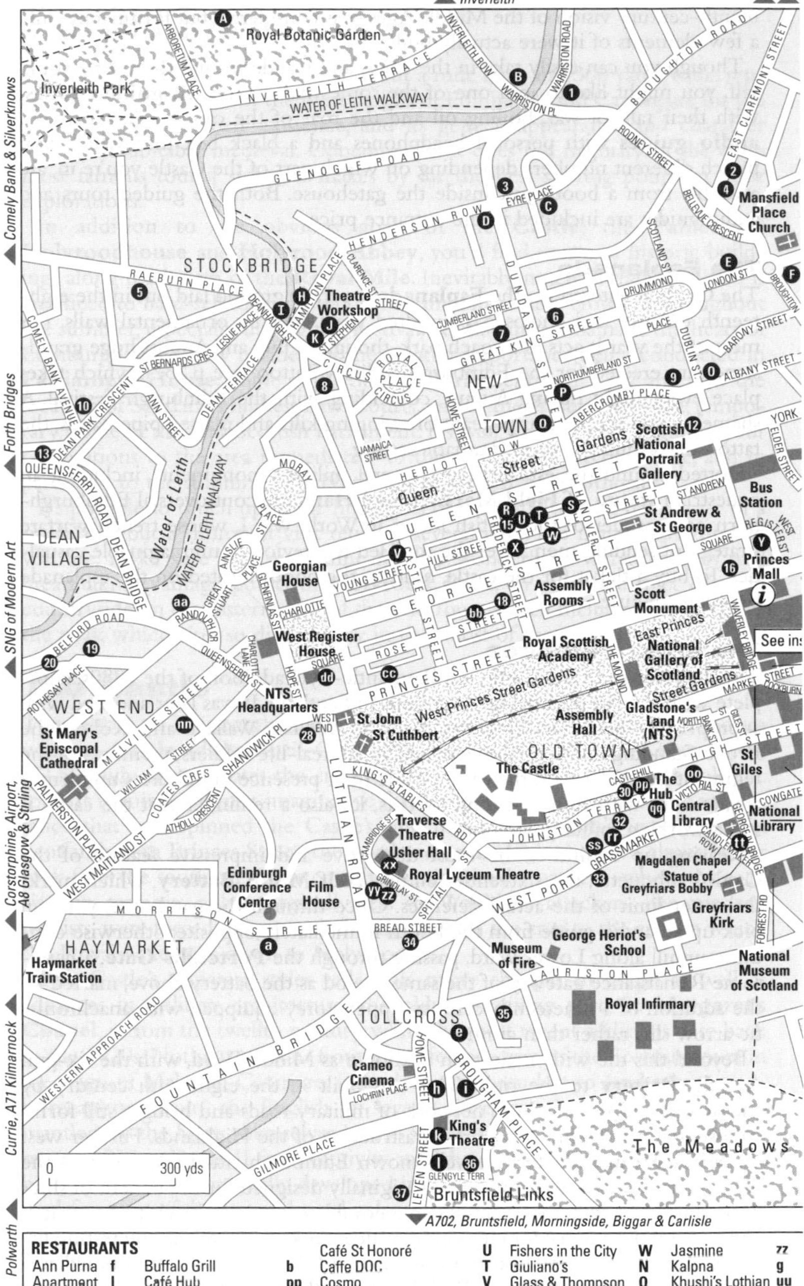

RESTAURANTS

Ann Purna	f	Buffalo Grill	b	Café St Honoré	U	Fishers in the City	W	Jasmine	zz
Apartment	l	Café Hub	pp	Caffe DOC	T	Giuliano's	N	Kalpna	g
Bann UK	jj	Café Marlayne	X	Cosmo	V	Glass & Thompson	Q	Khushi's Lothian	uu
Bell's Diner	K	Café Mediterraneo	L	Creelers	jj	Grain Store	oo	King's Balti	j
Black Bo's	ll	Café Odile	ee	Duck's at Le Marché Noir	C	Henderson's	S	Kweilin	P
Blue Parrot	J	Café Royal Oyster Bar	Y	Elephant House	tt	Howies at Waterloo	Z	L'Alba d'Oro	D
				Favorit	k	Igg's	hh	La Bagatelle	i

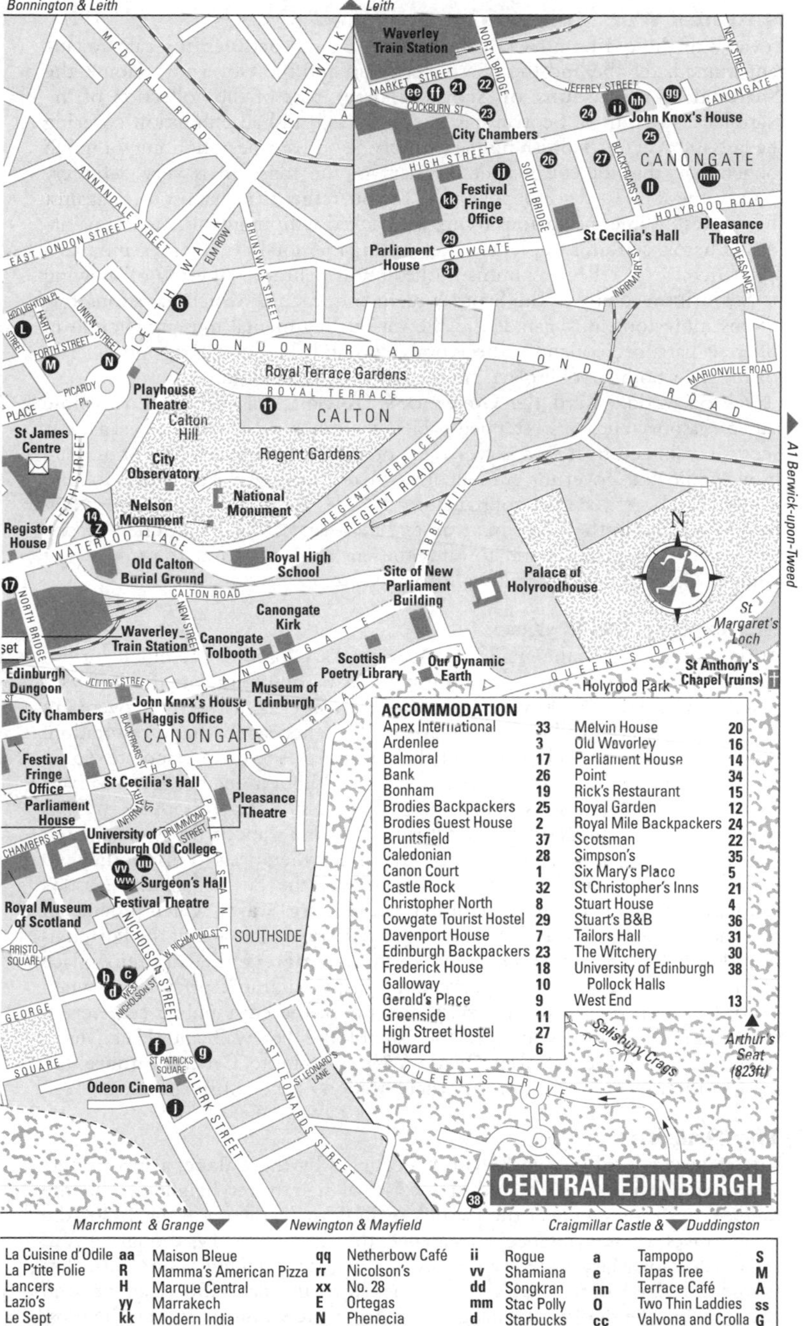

La Cuisine d'Odile	aa	Maison Bleue	qq	Netherbow Café	ii	Rogue	a	Tampopo	S
La P'tite Folie	R	Mamma's American Pizza	rr	Nicolson's	vv	Shamiana	e	Tapas Tree	M
Lancers	H	Marque Central	xx	No. 28	dd	Songkran	nn	Terrace Café	A
Lazio's	yy	Marrakech	E	Ortegas	mm	Stac Polly	O	Two Thin Laddies	ss
Le Sept	kk	Modern India	N	Phenecia	d	Starbucks	cc	Valvona and Crolla	G
Loon Fung	B	Mussel Inn	bb	Pizza Express	I	Suruchi	ww	Viva Mexico	ff
Lost Sock	F	Ndebele	h	Plaisir du Chocolat	gg	Susie's Diner	c		

National War Museum of Scotland

Located in the old hospital buildings, down a ramp between the café/restaurant immediately behind the one o'clock gun and the Governor's House, the **National War Museum of Scotland** (free), part of the collection of the National Museums of Scotland, is a recently refurbished exhibition covering the last 400 years of Scottish military history. Scots have been fighting for much longer than that, of course, but the slant of the museum is very definitely towards the soldiers who fought *for* the Union, rather than against it (or against themselves). While the various rooms are packed with uniforms, medals, paintings of heroic actions and plenty of interesting memorabilia, the museum manages to convey a reflective, human tone. Just as delicate is the job of showing no favouritism to any of the Scottish regiments, each of which has strong traditions more forcefully paraded in the various regimental museums found in different parts of Scotland – the Royal Scots and the Scots Dragoon Guards, for instance, both have displays in other parts of Edinburgh Castle.

Back on Middle Ward, the **Governor's House** is a 1740s mansion whose harled masonry and crow-stepped gables are archetypal features of vernacular Scottish architecture. It now serves as the officers' mess for members of the garrison, while the governor himself lives in the northern side wing. Behind stands the largest single construction in the Castle complex, the **New Barracks**, built in the 1790s in an austere Neoclassical style. From here a cobbled road then snakes round towards the enclosed citadel at the uppermost point of Castle Rock, entered via **Foog's Gate**.

St Margaret's Chapel

At the eastern end of the citadel, **St Margaret's Chapel** is the oldest surviving building in the Castle, and probably also in Edinburgh itself. Used as a powder magazine for 300 years, this tiny Norman church was rediscovered in 1845 and was eventually rededicated in 1934, after sympathetic restoration. Externally, it is plain and severe, but the interior preserves an elaborate zigzag archway dividing the nave from the sanctuary. Although once believed to have been built by the saint herself, and mooted as the site of her death in 1093, its architectural style suggests that it actually dates from about thirty years later, and was thus probably built by King David I as a memorial to his mother.

The battlements in front of the chapel offer the best of all the Castle's panoramic views. They are interrupted by the **Lang Stairs**, which provide an alternative means of access from the Argyle Battery via the side of the Portcullis Gate. Just below the battlements there's a small **cemetery**, the last resting place of the **soldiers' pets**: it is kept in immaculate condition, particularly when contrasted with the dilapidated state of some of the city's public cemeteries. Continuing eastwards, you skirt the top of the Forewall and Half Moon Batteries, passing the 110-foot **Castle Well** en route to **Crown Square**, the highest, most secure and most important section of the entire complex.

The Palace

The eastern side of Crown Square is occupied by the **Palace**, a surprisingly unassuming edifice built round an octagonal stair turret heightened in the nineteenth century to bear the Castle's main flagpole. Begun in the 1430s, the Palace owes its Renaissance appearance to King James IV, though it was remodelled for Mary, Queen of Scots and her consort Henry, Lord Darnley, whose entwined initials (MAH), together with the date 1566, can be seen above one of the doorways. This gives access to a few historic rooms, the most interesting of which is the tiny panelled bedchamber at the extreme south

The Stone of Destiny

Legend has it that the **Stone of Destiny** (also called the Stone of Scone) was "Jacob's Pillow", on which he dreamed of the ladder of angels from earth to heaven. Its real history is obscure, but it is known that it was moved from Ireland to Dunadd by missionaries, and thence to Dunstaffnage, from where Kenneth MacAlpine, king of the Dalriada Scots, brought it to the abbey at Scone in 838. There it remained for almost five hundred years, used as a coronation throne on which all kings of Scotland were crowned.

In 1296, an over-eager Edward I stole what he believed to be the Stone and installed it at Westminster Abbey, where, apart from a brief interlude in 1950 when it was removed by Scottish nationalists and hidden in Arbroath for several months, it remained for seven hundred years. All this changed in December 1996 when, after an elaborate ceremony-laden journey from London, the Stone returned to Scotland, in one of the doomed attempts by the Conservative government to convince the Scottish people that the Union was a good thing. Much to the annoyance of the people of Perth and the curators of Scone Palace (see p.352), and to the general indifference of the people of Scotland, the Stone was placed in Edinburgh Castle.

However, speculation surrounds the authenticity of the Stone, for the original is said to have been intricately carved, while the one seen today is a plain block of sandstone. Many believe that the canny monks at Scone palmed this off onto the English king (some say that it's nothing more sacred than the cover for a medieval septic tank), and that the real Stone of Destiny lies hidden in an underground chamber, its whereabouts a mystery to all but the chosen few.

eastern corner, where Mary gave birth to James VI. Along with the rest of the Palace, the room was revamped for James's triumphant homecoming in 1617, though this was to be the last time it served as a royal residence.

Another section of the Palace has recently been refurbished with a detailed audiovisual presentation on the **Honours of Scotland**, the originals of which are housed in the Crown Room at the very end of the display. Though you might be put off by the slow-moving, claustrophobic queues that shuffle past the displays, the interest in them is justified: these magnificent crown jewels – the only pre-Restoration set in the United Kingdom – serve as one of the most potent images of Scotland's nationhood. They were last used for the Scottish-only coronation of Charles II in 1651, an event which provoked the wrath of Oliver Cromwell, who made exhaustive attempts to have the jewels melted down. Having narrowly escaped his clutches by being smuggled out of the Castle and hidden in a rural church, the jewels later served as symbols of the absent monarch at sittings of the Scottish Parliament before being locked away in a chest following the Union of 1707. For over a century they were out of sight and eventually presumed lost, before being rediscovered in 1818 as a result of a search initiated by Sir Walter Scott.

Of the three pieces comprising the Honours, the oldest is the **sceptre**, which bears statuettes of the Virgin and Child, St James and St Andrew, rounded off by a polished globe of rock crystal: it was given to James IV in 1494 by Pope Alexander VI, and refashioned by Scottish craftsmen for James V. Even finer is the **sword**, a swaggering Italian High Renaissance masterpiece by the silversmith Domenico da Sutri, presented to James IV by the great artistic patron Pope Julius II. Both the hilt and the scabbard are engraved with Julius's personal emblem, showing the oak tree and its acorns, the symbols of the Risen Christ, together with dolphins, symbols of the Church. The jewel-encrusted **crown**, made for James V by the Scottish goldsmith James Mosman, incorpo-

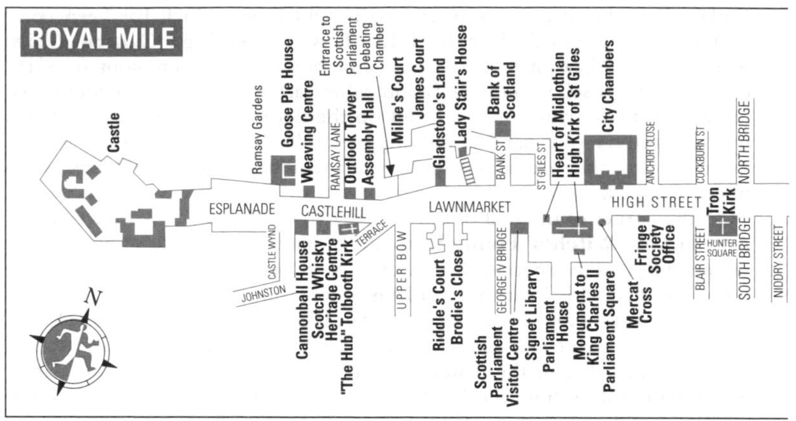

Parliament by going to the public entrance in Milne's Court, one of the closes off the Royal Mile just past the Assembly Hall (Mon–Fri 10am–noon & 2–4pm; free). When Parliament is in session, you can sit and watch the **debates** from the large public gallery – tickets are available on an ad hoc basis either from the desk at the public entrance or from the Scottish Parliament **visitor centre** on the corner of George IV Bridge and High Street, although they can also be booked (Ⓣ0131/348 5000, Ⓦwww.scottish.parliament.uk) up to a week before the date you wish to attend. The best time to see a debate is First Minister's Questions on Thursday afternoon, but the visitor centre will be able tell you when Parliament is in session, and which debates are taking place on particular days. If Parliament is not in session, it is still possible to view the empty debating chamber from the public gallery, where stewards are on hand to answer questions. For more about the background to the Parliament, see p.772 of Contexts.

The imposing black church building opposite the Assembly Hall at the foot of Castlehill is **The Hub** (daily 8am–late; Ⓣ0131/473 2010, Ⓦwww.eif.co.uk/thehub), also known as "Edinburgh's Festival Centre", the first permanent home of the Edinburgh International Festival since its inception in 1947. Although the Festival only takes place for three weeks every August and early September, The Hub is open year-round, providing performance, rehearsal and exhibition space, a ticket centre and a café. The building itself was constructed in 1845 to designs by James Gillespie Graham and Augustus Pugin, one of the co-architects of the Houses of Parliament in London – a connection obvious from the superb neo-Gothic detailing and the sheer presence of the building, whose spire is the highest in Edinburgh. It was built as an Assembly Hall for the Church of Scotland, and became a parish church when the assembly moved to the United Free Church hall across the road. On the ground floor level is the *Hub Café* (daily 8am–11pm), which serves drinks, coffees and a small selection of tasty snacks and meals in a vivid yellow interior space as well as on the large terrace area outside. Also worth checking out is the main hall upstairs, where the original neo-Gothic woodwork and high-vaulted ceiling is enlivened with a fabulous fabric design in Rastafarian colours. Permanent works of art have been incorporated into the centre, including over 200 delightful foot-high sculptures by Scottish sculptor Jill Watson, depicting Festival performers and audiences.

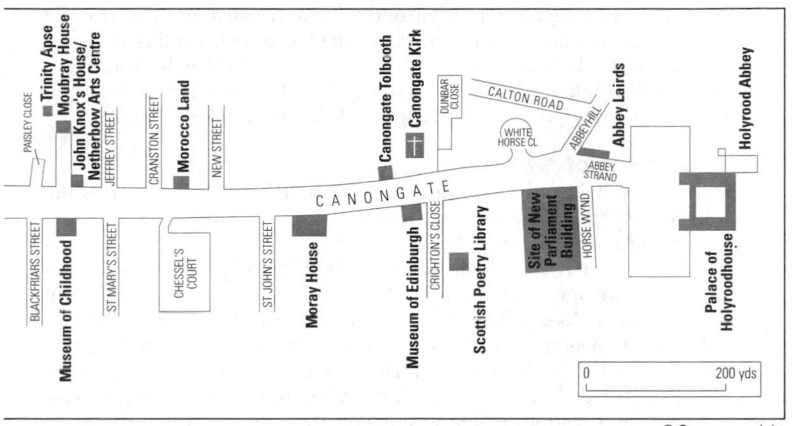

Lawnmarket

Below the Tolbooth Kirk, the Royal Mile opens out into the broader expanse of **Lawnmarket**, which, as its name suggests, was once a marketplace. At its northern end is the entry to **Milne's Court**, whose excellently restored tenements now serve as student residences, and immediately beyond, **James Court**, one of Edinburgh's most fashionable addresses prior to the advent of the New Town, with David Hume and James Boswell among those who lived there.

Back on Lawnmarket itself, **Gladstone's Land** (April–Oct Mon–Sat 10am–5pm, Sun 2–5pm; £3.50) takes its name from the merchant Thomas Gledstane (sic), who in 1617 acquired a modest dwelling on the site, transforming it into a magnificent six-storey mansion. The Gledstane family are thought to have occupied the third floor, renting out the rest to merchants, in the style of tenement occupation still widespread in the city today. The arcaded ground floor, the only authentic example left of what was once a common feature of Royal Mile houses, has been restored to illustrate its early function as a shopping booth. Several other rooms have been kitted out in authentic period style to give an impression of the lifestyle of a well-to-do household of the late seventeenth century; the Painted Chamber, with its decorated wooden ceiling and wall friezes, is particularly impressive. You can also stay here (see p.72).

A few paces further on, steps lead down to Lady Stair's Close, in which stands the **Writers' Museum** (Mon–Sat 10am–5pm; also Sun 2–5pm during the Festival; free), housed in Lady Stair's House, another fine seventeenth-century residence. Dedicated to the three lions of Scottish literature – Robert Burns, Sir Walter Scott and Robert Louis Stevenson the museum shows off various manuscripts, first editions and portraits, plus personal mementoes (among them locks of hair and walking sticks). Continuing the literary theme, the courtyard outside, called the **Makars' Court** after the Scots word for the "maker" of poetry or prose, has quotations by Scotland's most famous writers and poets inscribed on paving stones.

On the south side of Lawnmarket is **Brodie's Close**, named after the father of one of Edinburgh's most morbid characters, Deacon William Brodie, burglar by night and apparent pillar of society by day. Following his eventual capture, he managed to escape to Holland, but was betrayed, brought back to Edinburgh and hanged in 1788 on gallows of his own design. His ruse of trying to cheat death by secretly wearing an iron collar under his shirt failed. You can visit the popular *Deacon Brodie's Tavern* on the corner of the Lawnmarket and Bank Street and ruminate over a beer on the connections between Brodie, Robert Louis Stevenson's similarly themed tale *Dr Jekyll and Mr Hyde*, and the various split personalities of Edinburgh itself, not least its Old Town and New Town.

The High Kirk of St Giles

Across George IV Bridge is the third section of the Royal Mile, known as the **High Street**, which occupies two blocks either side of the intersection between North Bridge and South Bridge. The dominant building of the southern side of the street is the **High Kirk of St Giles** (April–Sept Mon–Fri 9am–7pm, Sat 9am–5pm, Sun 1–5pm; Oct–March Mon–Sat 9am–5pm, Sun 1–5pm; free) which closes off Parliament Square from High Street. The sole parish church of medieval Edinburgh, where John Knox (see box below) launched and directed the Scottish Reformation, the Kirk is almost invariably referred to as a cathedral, although it has only been the seat of a bishop on two brief and unhappy occasions in the seventeenth century. According to one of the city's best-known legends, the attempt in 1637 to introduce the English prayer book, and thus Episcopal government, so incensed a humble stallholder named Jenny Geddes that she hurled her stool at the preacher, prompting the rest of the congregation to chase the offending clergy out of the building. A tablet in the north aisle marks the spot from where she let rip.

John Knox

The Protestant reformer **John Knox** has been alternately credited with, or blamed for, the distinctive national culture that emerged from the Calvinist Reformation, which has cast its shadow over Scottish history and the Scottish character right up to the present.

Little is known about Knox's early years: he was born between 1505 and 1514 in East Lothian, and trained for the priesthood at St Andrews University under John Major, author of a *History of Great Britain* that advocated the union of Scotland and England. Ordained in 1540, Knox then served as a private tutor, in league with Scotland's first significant Protestant leader, **George Wishart**. After Wishart was burnt at the stake for heresy in 1546, Knox became involved with the group who had carried out the revenge murder of the Scottish primate, Cardinal David Beaton, subsequently taking over his castle in St Andrews. The following year this was captured by the French, and Knox was carted off to work as a galley slave.

He was freed in 1548, as a result of the intervention of the English, who invited him to play an evangelizing role in the spread of their own Reformation. Following successful ministries in Berwick-upon-Tweed and Newcastle-upon-Tyne, Knox turned down the bishopric of Rochester, less from an intrinsic opposition to episcopacy than from a wish to avoid becoming embroiled in the turmoil he guessed would ensue if the Catholic Mary Tudor acceded to the English throne. When this duly happened in 1553, Knox fled to the Continent, ending up as minister to the English-speaking community in Geneva, which was then in the grip of the theocratic government of the Frenchman **Jean Calvin**. Knox was quickly won over to his radical version of Protestantism, declaring Geneva to be "the most perfect school of Christ since the days of the Apostles".

In exile, Knox was much preoccupied with the question of the influence wielded by political rulers, believing that the future of the Reformation in Europe was at risk because of the opposition of a few powerful sovereigns. This prompted him to write his infamous treatise, *The First Blast of the Trumpet Against the Monstrous Regiment*

In the early nineteenth century, St Giles received a much-needed but over-drastic restoration, covering most of the Gothic exterior with a smooth stone coating that gives it a certain Georgian dignity while sacrificing its medieval character almost completely. The only part to survive this treatment is the late fifteenth-century tower, whose resplendent crown spire is formed by eight flying buttresses. The **interior** has survived in much better shape. Especially notable are the four massive piers supporting the tower, which date back, at least in part, to the church's Norman predecessor. In the nineteenth century, St Giles was adorned with a whole series of funerary monuments in order to give it the character of a national pantheon on the model of Westminster Abbey. It was also equipped with several Pre-Raphaelite stained-glass windows. The best of these, designed by Edward Burne-Jones and William Morris, showing Old Testament prophets and the Israelites crossing the River Jordan, can be seen on the facade wall of the **north aisle**. Alongside is the great **west window**, whose dedication to Robbie Burns in 1985 caused enormous controversy – as a hardened drinker and womanizer, the national bard was far from being an upholder of accepted Presbyterian values. Look out, also, for an elegant bronze relief of Robert Louis Stevenson on the south side of the church.

At the southeastern corner of St Giles, the **Thistle Chapel** was built by Sir Robert Lorimer in 1911 as the private chapel of the sixteen knights of the Most Noble Order of the Thistle, the highest chivalric order in Scotland. Self-consciously derivative of St George's Chapel in Windsor, it's an exquisite piece

of Women, a specific attack on the three Catholic women then ruling Scotland, England and France, which has made his name synonymous with misogyny ever since.

When Knox was allowed to return to Scotland in 1555, he took over as spiritual leader of the Reformation, becoming minister of St Giles in Edinburgh, where he established a reputation as a charismatic preacher. However, the establishment of Protestantism as the official religion of Scotland in 1560 was dependent on the forging of an alliance with Elizabeth I, which Knox himself rigorously championed: the swift deployment of English troops against the French garrison in Edinburgh dealt a fatal blow to Franco-Spanish hopes of re-establishing Catholicism in both Scotland and England. Although the return of Mary, Queen of Scots the following year placed a Catholic monarch on the Scottish throne, reputedly Knox was always able to retain the upper hand in his famous disputes with her.

Before his death in 1572, Knox began mapping out the organization of the Scots Kirk, sweeping away all vestiges of Episcopal control and giving lay people a role of unprecedented importance. He also proposed a nationwide education system, to be compulsory for the very young and free for the poor, though lack of funds meant this could not be implemented in full. His final legacy was the posthumously published *History of the Reformation of Religion in the Realm of Scotland*, a justification of his life's work.

For all his considerable influence, Knox was not responsible for many of the features which have created the popular image of Scottish Presbyterianism – and of Knox himself – as austere and joyless. A man of refined cultural tastes, he did not encourage the iconoclasm that destroyed so many of Scotland's churches and works of art: indeed, much of this was carried out by English hands. Nor did he promote unbending Sabbatarianism, an obsessive work ethic or even the inflexible view of the doctrine of predestination favoured by his far more fanatical successors. Ironically, though, by fostering an irrevocable rift in the "Auld Alliance" with France, he did more than anyone else to ensure that Scotland's future was to be linked with that of England.

and sundial adorned with a statue of Moses, it gives a good impression of how the Royal Mile must have once looked. Whether or not it was ever really the home of Knox is debatable: he may have moved here for safety at the height of the religious troubles. The house did, however, once belong to goldsmith James Mosman, son of the designer of the Scottish crown, who was executed for his dogged loyalty to Knox's *bête noire*, Mary, Queen of Scots. The rather bare interiors, which give a good idea of the labyrinthine layout of Old Town houses, display explanatory material on Knox's life and career. The house is linked to the neighbouring **Netherbow Arts Centre**, a busy venue during the Festival which displays paintings and photography throughout the year and has a popular lunch-time café selling wholesome soups and light meals.

Canongate

For over seven hundred years, the district through which Canongate runs was a burgh in its own right, officially separate from the capital, which was entered through the Netherbow Port. A notorious slum area even into the 1960s, it has been the subject of some of the most ambitious **restoration** programmes in the Old Town, though the lack of harmony between the buildings renovated in different decades can be seen fairly clearly. For such a central district, it's interesting to note that most of the buildings here are residential, and by no means are they all bijou apartments. The development of the Canongate is ongoing, particularly at its lower end around the site of the new Parliament building. This section of the Royal Mile look features an eclectic range of shops, from a gallery of historic maps and sea charts to genuine bagpipe makers.

Near the top of Canongate, a good example of the restoration work can be seen at **Chessel's Court**, a mid-eighteenth-century development with fanciful Rococo chimneys. It was formerly the site of the Excise Office, scene of the robbery that led to the arrest and execution of Deacon Brodie. Over the road the **Morocco Land** is a reasonably faithful reproduction of an old tenement, incorporating the original bust of a Moor from which its name derives.

Dominated by a turreted steeple and an odd external box clock, the late sixteenth-century **Canongate Tolbooth**, a little further down the north side of the street, has served both as the headquarters of the burgh administration and as a prison, and now houses **The People's Story** (Mon–Sat 10am–5pm, during the Festival also Sun 2–5pm; free), a lively museum devoted to the everyday life and work of Edinburgh people down the centuries, with sounds and tableaux on various aspects of city living – including a typical Edinburgh pub. Next door, **Canongate Kirk** was built in the 1680s to house the congregation expelled from Holyrood Abbey when the latter was commandeered by James VII (James II in England) to serve as the chapel for the Order of the Thistle. It's a curiously archaic design, still Renaissance in outline, and built to a cruciform plan wholly at odds with the ideals and requirements of Protestant worship. Its churchyard, one of the city's most exclusive cemeteries, commands a superb view across to Calton Hill. Among those buried here are Adam Smith, Mrs Agnes McLehose (better known as Robert Burns' "Clarinda") and Robert Fergusson, regarded by some as Edinburgh's greatest poet, despite his death at the age of 24; his headstone was donated by Burns, a fervent admirer, who also wrote the inscription.

Opposite the church, the **Museum of Edinburgh** in Huntly House (Mon–Sat 10am–5pm; Festival period Mon–Sat 10am–5pm Sun 2–5pm; free) includes a quirky array of old shop signs, some dating back to the eighteenth century, as well as displays on indigenous industries such as glass, silver, pottery and clockmaking, and on the dubious military career of Earl Haig. Also on view is the original version of the National Covenant of 1638; modern science has failed to resolve whether or not some of the signatories signed with their own blood, as tradition has it.

Among the intriguing series of closes and entries on this stretch of Canongate, **Dunbar's Close**, on the north side of the street, has a beautiful seventeenth-century walled garden tucked in behind the tenements. Opposite this is the entry to Crichton's Close, through which you'll find the **Scottish Poetry Library** (Mon–Fri noon–6pm, Sat noon–4pm; free), a small island of modern architectural eloquence amid a sea of construction work and large-scale developments. Visitors are free to read the books, periodicals and leaflets, or listen to recordings of poetry in English, Scots and Gaelic. Readings and events are organized through the year.

At the very foot of the street, the entrance to the residential **Whitehorse Close** was once the site of the inn from where stagecoaches began the journey to London. Stridently quaint, it drips with the characteristic features of Scottish vernacular architecture: crow-stepped gables, dormer windows, overhanging upper storeys and curving outside stairways.

Holyrood

At the foot of Canongate lies **Holyrood**, Edinburgh's royal quarter, the **legend** of whose foundation in 1128 is described in a fifteenth-century manuscript which is still kept there. The story goes that King David I, son of Malcolm Canmore and St Margaret, went out hunting one day and was suddenly confronted by a stag who threw him from his horse and seemed ready to gore him. In desperation, the king tried to protect himself by grasping its antlers, but instead found himself holding a crucifix, whereupon the animal ran off. In a dream that night, he heard a voice commanding him to "make a house for Canons devoted to the Cross"; he duly obeyed, naming the abbey Holyrood (rood being an alternative name for a cross). A more prosaic explanation is that David, the most pious of all Scotland's monarchs, simply acquired a relic of the True Cross and decided to build a suitable home for it.

Holyrood soon became a favoured **royal residence**, its situation in a secluded valley making it far more agreeable than the draughty Castle. At first, monarchs lodged in the monastic guesthouse, to which a wing for the exclusive use of the court was added during the reign of James II. This was transformed into a full-blown palace for James IV, which in turn was replaced by a much larger building for Charles II, although he never actually lived there. Indeed, it was something of a white elephant until Queen Victoria started making regular trips to her northern kingdom, a custom that has been maintained by her successors.

Admissions to Holyrood

Guided tours of Holyrood take place only from November to March; at other times of the year, visitors are free to move at their own pace. It is worth remembering that Holyrood is still a working palace, so the buildings are closed to the public for long periods during state functions; you won't be able to visit for a fortnight in the middle of May, and during the annual royal visit which usually takes place in the last two weeks of June and the first in July.

The precincts

On the north side of **Abbey Strand**, which forms a sort of processional way linking Canongate with Holyrood, Abbey Lairds is a four-storey sixteenth-century mansion which once served as a home for aristocratic debtors and is now occupied by royal flunkies during the summer seat of the court. Historic Scotland have an information centre and bookshop in the building (April–Oct 9.30am–6pm; Nov–March 9.30am–5pm).

Legend has it that Mary, Queen of Scots used to bathe in sweet white wine in the curious little turreted structure nearby known as **Queen Mary's Bath House**; it is more likely, however, that it was either a summer pavilion or a dovecote. Its architecture is mirrored in the **Croft an Righ**, a picturesque L-shaped house in a quiet, generally overlooked corner beside the eastern wall of the complex.

The Palace of Holyroodhouse

In its present form, the **Palace of Holyroodhouse** (April–Oct daily 9.30am–6pm; Nov–March daily 9.30am–4.30pm; £6.50) is largely a seventeenth-century creation, planned for Charles II. However, the tower house of the old palace was skilfully incorporated to form the northwestern block, with a virtual mirror image of it erected as a counterbalance at the other end. The three-storey **courtyard** is an early exercise in Palladian style, exhibiting a punctiliously accurate knowledge of the main Classical orders to create a sense of absolute harmony and unity.

Inside, the **State Apartments**, as Charles II's palace is known, are decked out with oak panelling, tapestries, portraits and decorative paintings, all overshadowed by the magnificent white stucco **ceilings**, especially in the Morning Drawing Room. The most eye-catching chamber, however, is the **Great Gallery**, which takes up the entire first floor of the northern wing. During the 1745 sojourn of the Young Pretender this was the setting for a banquet, described in detail in Scott's novel *Waverley*, and it is still used for big ceremonial occasions. Along the walls are 89 portraits commissioned from the seventeenth-century Dutch artist Jacob de Wit to illustrate the royal lineage of Scotland from its mythical origins in the fourth century BC; the result is unintentionally hilarious, as it is clear that the artist's imagination was taxed to bursting point by the need to paint so many different facial types without having an inkling as to what the subjects actually looked like. In the adjacent **King's Closet**, de Wet's *The Finding of Moses* provides a biblical link to the portraits, the Scottish royal family claiming descent from Scota, the Egyptian pharaoh's daughter, who discovered Moses in the bulrushes.

The oldest parts of the palace, the **Historical Apartments**, are mainly of note for their associations with Mary, Queen of Scots and in particular for the brutal murder, organized by her husband, Lord Darnley, of her private secretary, David Rizzio, who was stabbed 56 times and dragged from the small closet, through the Queen's Bedchamber, and into the Outer Chamber. Until a few years ago, visitors were shown apparently indelible bloodstains on the floor of the latter, but these are now admitted to be fakes, and have been covered up. A display cabinet in the same room shows some pieces of **needlework** woven by the deposed queen while in English captivity; another case has an outstanding **miniature portrait** of her by the French court painter, François Clouet.

Holyrood Abbey

In the grounds of the Palace are the wonderfully evocative ruins of **Holyrood Abbey**. Of King David's original Norman church, the only surviving fragment is a doorway in the far southeastern corner. Most of the remainder dates from a late twelfth- and early thirteenth-century rebuilding in the Early Gothic style.

The surviving parts of the **west front**, including one of the twin towers and the elaborately carved entrance portal, show how resplendent the abbey must once have been. Unfortunately, its sacking by the English in 1547, followed by the demolition of the transept and chancel during the Reformation, all but destroyed the building. Charles I attempted to restore some semblance of unity by ordering the erection of the great east window and a new stone roof, but the latter collapsed in 1768, causing grievous damage to the rest of the structure. By this time, the Canongate congregation had another place of worship, and schemes to rebuild the abbey were abandoned.

The Scottish Parliament site

Immediately opposite Abbey Strand, the massive construction site between the Royal Mile and Holyrood Road is where the new **Scottish Parliament** is being built. For decades, campaigners for home rule for Scotland envisaged the Old Royal High School building on Calton Hill (see p.106) as the place where the long-awaited Scottish parliament would sit. In the run-up to the devolution referendum, however, the Scottish Office unexpectedly announced that the Old Royal High School was too small to accommodate the proposed parliament and its offices, and various alternative sites were suggested, including the empty docklands at Leith.

Eventually a disused brewery at the foot of the Royal Mile was identified as the ideal location, and a competition to design the building was won by Catalan architect **Enric Miralles**, in association with Edinburgh-based architects RMJM. Their concept centres on a series of petal-shaped buildings which have been compared (both favourably and unfavourably) to upturned boats. Miralles died in 2000, causing a few ripples of uncertainty as to whether the famously whimsical designer had in fact set down his final vision. The structure will cost something in the region of £100 million, and is due to be ready by late 2002, until which time the parliament is sitting in the Church of Scotland Assembly Hall on the Mound (see p.81).

While the building is being completed, a temporary **visitor centre** (daily 10am–4pm; free) has been established on Holyrood Road, next door to Dynamic Earth, where you can view plans, models and computer images of the proposed structure.

Our Dynamic Earth

The New Parliament Building is by no means the only newcomer to this historic area. On the Holyrood Road, beneath a pincushion of white metal struts which make it look like a miniature version of London's Millennium Dome, **Our Dynamic Earth** (April–Oct daily 10am–6pm; Nov–March Wed–Sat 10am–5pm; £7.95/families from £21), is a hi-tech attraction about the natural world aimed mainly at families. Although James Hutton, the Edinburgh-born "Father of Geology", lived nearby in the eighteenth century, there are few specific links to Edinburgh or Scotland, as you're taken in a "time machine" elevator to a room where the creation of the universe, 15 billion years ago, is described using wide-screen video graphics, eerie music and a deep-throated commentary. Subsequent galleries describe the formation of the earth and continents with crashing sound effects and a shaking floor, the calmer grandeur of glaciers and oceans being explored through magnificent large-screen landscape footage. The "Casualties and Survivors" gallery describes the history of life on earth, from primordial swamps to life-size models of some of the odd creatures who once inhabited the earth, while, further on, the polar regions – complete with a real iceberg – and tropical jungles are imaginatively recreated, with interactive computer screens and special effects at every turn. Outside, the dramatic **amphitheatre** which incorporates the steps leading up to the entrance to Our Dynamic Earth makes for a great venue for outdoor theatre and music performances – notably during the Festival.

Holyrood Park

Holyrood Park – or Queen's Park – a natural wilderness in the very heart of the modern city, is unquestionably one of Edinburgh's main assets, as locals (though relatively few tourists) readily appreciate. Packed into an area no more than five miles in diameter is an amazing variety of landscapes – hills, crags, moorland, marshes, glens, lochs and fields – representing something of a microcosm of Scotland's scenery. The park is a great place for outdoor activities, with toddlers, cyclists and rock climbers all being catered for. A single tarred road, the **Queen's Drive**, circles the park, enabling many of its features to be seen by car, though you really need to stroll around to appreciate it fully. In a small stone-built gate lodge at the entrance to the park from Holyrood Road, the **Holyrood Park Ranger Service** has a small information point (Mon–Thurs 10am–4pm, Fri 10am–3.30pm) where you can pick up a map of suggested walks or find out about ranger-led walks which depart from the lodge at 2pm on Wednesdays. Note that sometime in 2002 the ranger service will move to a brand-new Park HQ in the area behind the Palace of Holyroodhouse.

Two of the most rewarding walks begin opposite the southern gates of the Palace: one, a pathway nicknamed the Radical Road, traverses the ridge immediately below the **Salisbury Crags**, one of the main features of the Edinburgh skyline, while you can also walk along the top of the basalt crags, from where there are excellent views of the Palace of Holyroodhouse and Holyrood Abbey.

From the Palace gates, the best way to follow Queen's Drive is in a clockwise direction. Soon you arrive at **St Margaret's Loch**, a nineteenth-century man-made pond, above which stand the scanty ruins of **St Anthony's Chapel**, another fine vantage point. From here, the road's loop is one-way only for vehicular traffic, ascending to **Dunsapie Loch**, again an artificial stretch of water, which makes an excellent foil to the crag behind.

This is the usual starting point for the ascent of **Arthur's Seat**, a majestic extinct volcano rising 823ft above sea level. The Seat is Edinburgh's single most prominent landmark, resembling a huge crouched lion when seen from the west. The climb from Dunsapie, up a grassy slope, followed by a rocky path near the summit, is considerably less arduous than it looks, a fairly straightforward twenty-minute stomp, though there are several other, somewhat longer and more taxing ways up from other points in the park. The views from the top are all you'd expect, covering the entire city and much of the Firth of Forth; on a clear day, you can even see the southernmost mountains of the Highlands. The composer, Felix Mendelssohn climbed Arthur's Seat in July 1829, noting: "It is beautiful here! In the evening a cool breeze is wafted from the sea, and then all objects appear clearly and sharply defined against the grey sky; the lights from the windows glitter brilliantly." As there is little reason to associate it with the British king of the Holy Grail legends, there's no satisfactory story to explain the name.

From Dunsapie Loch, Queen's Drive continues round beneath the summit to meet itself again at a roundabout near the southern point of the Salisbury Crags. At a second roundabout the second exit leads out of the park; the first exit takes you beneath **Samson's Ribs**, a group of basalt pillars strikingly reminiscent of the Hebridean island of Staffa (see p.398), and onto **Duddingston Loch**, the only natural stretch of water in the park, now a bird sanctuary. Perched above it, just outside the park boundary, **Duddingston Kirk** dates back in part to the twelfth century and is the focus of one of the most unspoilt old villages within modern Edinburgh. In the village, the *Sheep Heid Inn* (see p.122) is a great spot to pull in for a drink or a bar meal, and you can also try your hand at the traditional skittle alley.

Cowgate and the Grassmarket

At the bottom of the valley immediately south of the Royal Mile, and following a roughly parallel course from the Lawnmarket to St Mary's Street, is the **Cowgate**. One of Edinburgh's oldest surviving streets, it was also formerly one of the city's most prestigious addresses. However, the construction of the great **viaducts** of George IV Bridge and South Bridge entombed it below street level, condemning it to decay and neglect and leading the nineteenth-century writer, Alexander Smith, to declare that "the condition of the inhabitants is as little known to respectable Edinburgh as are the habits of moles, earthworms, and the mining population". In the last decade or so the Cowgate has experienced something of a revival, with various nightclubs and Festival venues establishing themselves, though few tourists venture here and the contrast with the neighbouring Royal Mile remains stark.

At the corner with Niddry Street, which runs down from the High Street near its junction with North Bridge and South Bridge, unprepossessing **St Cecilia's Hall** (Wed & Sat 2–5pm, also Mon–Sat 10.30am–12.30pm during the Edinburgh Festival; £1) was built in the 1760s for the Musical Society of Edinburgh. Inside, Scotland's oldest and most beautiful concert room, oval in shape and set under a shallow dome, makes a perfect venue for concerts of Baroque and early music, held during the Festival and occasionally at other times of the year. The building is primarily worth visiting for the **Russell Collection** of antique keyboard instruments.

Towards the western end of Cowgate stands the **Magdalen Chapel** (Mon–Fri 9.30am–4pm; free), a sixteenth-century almshouse under the jurisdiction of the Incorporation of Hammermen, a guild to which most Edinburgh workers, other than goldsmiths, belonged. A few years later, as one of the focal points of the Reformation, it was probably the setting for the first ever General Assembly of the Church of Scotland. The Hammermen added a handsome tower and steeple in the 1620s, and later transformed the chapel into their guildhall, which was suitably adorned with fine ironwork. However, the main feature of the interior is the only significant pre-Reformation stained glass in Scotland still in its original location. That it escaped the iconoclasts is probably due to the fact that it is purely heraldic.

The Grassmarket

At its western end, Cowgate opens out into the **Grassmarket**, which has played an important role in the murkier aspects of Edinburgh's turbulent history. The public gallows were located here, and it was the scene of numerous riots and other disturbances down the centuries. It was here, in 1736, that Captain Porteous was lynched after he had ordered shots to be fired at the crowd watching a public execution. The notorious duo William Burke and William Hare had their lair in a now-vanished close just off the western end of the Grassmarket, luring to it victims whom they murdered with the intention of selling their bodies to the eminent physician Robert Knox. Eventually,

Hare betrayed his partner, who was duly executed in 1829, and Knox's career was finished off as a result. Today, the Grassmarket can still be seamy, though the cluster of busy bars and restaurants along its northern side are evidence of a serious attempt to clean up its image.

At the northeastern corner of the Grassmarket are five old tenements of the old **West Bow**, which formerly zigzagged up to the Royal Mile. The rest of this was replaced in the 1840s by curving **Victoria Street**, an unusual two-tier thoroughfare, with arcaded shops below, and a pedestrian terrace above. This sweeps up to **George IV Bridge** and the **National Library of Scotland** which holds a rich collection of illuminated manuscripts, early printed books, historical documents, and the letters and papers of prominent Scottish literary figures, displayed in regularly changing thematic exhibitions (usually Mon–Sat 10am–5pm, Sun 2–5pm; free).

Greyfriars and around

The **statue of Greyfriars Bobby** at the southwestern corner of **George IV Bridge** must rank as Edinburgh's most sentimental tourist attraction. Bobby was a Skye terrier acquired as a working dog by a police constable named John Gray. When John Gray died in 1858, Bobby began a vigil on his grave which he maintained until he died fourteen years later. In the process, he became an Edinburgh celebrity, fed and cared for by locals who gave him a special collar (now in the Huntly House museum; see p.88) to prevent him being impounded as a stray. His statue, originally a fountain, was modelled from life, and erected soon after his death; his story has gained international renown, thanks to a spate of cloying books and tear-jerking movies.

The grave Bobby mourned over is in the **Greyfriars Kirkyard**, which among its clutter of grandiose seventeenth- and eighteenth-century funerary monuments boasts the striking mausoleum of the Adam family of architects. Greyfriars is particularly associated with the long struggle to establish Presbyterianism in Scotland: in 1638, it was the setting for the signing of the National Covenant, while in 1679 some 1200 Covenanters were imprisoned in the enclosure at the southwestern end of the yard. Set against the northern wall is the Martyrs' Monument, a defiantly worded memorial commemorating all those who died in pursuit of the eventual victory.

The graveyard rather overshadows **Greyfriars Kirk** itself, completed in 1620 as the first new church in Edinburgh since the Reformation. It's a real oddball in both layout and design, having a nave and aisles but no chancel, and adopting the anachronistic architectural language of the friary that preceded it, complete with medieval-looking windows, arches and buttresses.

At the western end of Greyfriars Kirkyard is one of the most significant surviving portions of the **Flodden Wall**, the city fortifications erected in the wake of Scotland's disastrous military defeat of 1513. When open, the gateway beyond offers a short-cut to **George Heriot's Hospital**, otherwise approached from Lauriston Place to the south. Founded as a home for poor boys by "Jinglin Geordie" Heriot, James VI's goldsmith, it is now one of Edinburgh's most prestigious fee-paying schools; although you can't go inside, you can wander round the quadrangle, whose array of towers, turrets, chimneys, carved doorways and traceried windows is one of the finest achievements of the Scottish Renaissance.

The National Museum of Scotland

Immediately opposite Greyfriars Bobby, on the south side of Chambers Street, stands the striking honey-coloured sandstone **National Museum of**

Scotland (Mon–Sat 10am–5pm, Tues 10am–8pm, Sun noon–5pm; free). Opened in 1998 to deserved acclaim, both for its elegant design and for its respectful but imaginative treatment of the nation's treasures, this is undoubtedly Scotland's premier museum. The fresh, open atmosphere of the building is combined with terrific features: specially commissioned art works; the **Discovery Centre**, specifically aimed at 5–14 year olds; the **exhibIT** computer bank with databases of the museum's collections; and the **Tower** restaurant, a sleek, stylish place with fabulous views which is also open in the evenings (for a review, see p.112).

The lack of a figurehead national museum had been keenly felt for decades, but it wasn't until the late 1980s that funding was made available, with construction beginning in 1996. Designed by the architects Benson & Forsyth, and built principally from sandstone quarried near Elgin in northeast Scotland, the most obvious feature of the exterior is the cylindrical entrance tower, which breaks up the angular, modern lines of the building and deliberately echoes the shape of the Half Moon Battery of Edinburgh Castle. Tall windows reveal glimpses of the interior, an effect continued inside, where unexpected views of the floors above and below, as well as out on to the street, emphasise the interconnectedness of the layers of Scotland's history.

The main entrance to the museum is at the base of the tower (although it is also possible to enter through the neighbouring Royal Museum of Scotland; see p.97). Make your way to the information desk in **Hawthornden Court**, the central atrium of the museum and a useful orientation point; on this level you'll also find the museum shop and access to the Royal Museum café. The glossy **brochure** on sale (£4.99) is more a photographic souvenir than a guidebook, but free guided tours on different themes take place through the day, and audio headsets (free) give detailed information on artefacts and displays.

Beginnings and Early People

To get to the first section, "**Beginnings**", take the lift or stairs from Hawthornden Court down to Level 0. Here, Scotland's story before the arrival of man is presented with audiovisual displays, artistic recreations and a selection of rocks and fossils, including some Lewisian gneiss, the oldest rock in Europe, and "Lizzie" (*Westlothiana lizziae*), the oldest known fossil reptile in world.

The second section, "**Early People**", also on Level 0, covers the period from the arrival of the first people to the end of the first millennium AD. This, in many ways, is the most engrossing section of the entire museum, an eloquent testament to the remarkable craftsmanship, artistry and practicality of Scotland's early people. The best way to approach this section is from the doors of the main lift, where you are confronted by eight giant bronze figures in the distinctive post-industrial style of Edinburgh-born sculptor **Sir Eduardo Paolozzi**. His trademark incorporation of geometric shapes into the human form allows the figures to "wear" different artefacts such as prehistoric bracelets and necklaces in small display compartments. The innovative use of contemporary art is continued with installations by the environmental artist **Andy Goldsworthy**, who shapes natural materials into sinuously beautiful geometrical patterns. Look out for *Hearth*, created from pieces of wood found on the construction site of the new museum, and *Enclosure*, four curved walls of slate roof tiles and four panels of cracked clay. Among the artefacts on display, highlights are the **Trappain treasure** hoard, 20kg of silver plates, cutlery and goblets found buried in East Lothian; the **Cramond Lioness**, a sculpture from a

Roman tombstone found recently in the Firth of Forth (see p.137); and the beautifully detailed gold, silver and amber **Hunterston brooch**, dating from around 700AD.

The Kingdom of the Scots

The "**Kingdom of the Scots**" on Level 1 covers the period between Scotland's development as a single independent nation and the union with England in 1707. At the entrance to the section in Hawthornden Court is the **Dupplin Cross**, a symbol of the different peoples who united under king Kenneth MacAlpine, to form a single kingdom in 843. Many famous Scots are represented here, including Robert the Bruce, Mary, Queen of Scots and her son James VI, under whom the crowns of Scotland and England became united in 1603. Star exhibits include the **Monymusk reliquary**, an intricately decorated box said to have carried the remains of St Columba; the **Lewis chessmen**, exquisitely idiosyncratic twelfth-century pieces carved from walrus ivory; and the "**Maiden**", an early form of the guillotine. The section on the church is of interest not only for the craftsmanship of some of the objects, most notably the silver gilt **St Fillan's crozier**, but also because just outside the window you can glimpse Greyfriars Kirkyard, where the National Covenant – the document which demanded a Presbyterian rather than Episcopalian form of worship in Scotland and provoked numerous battles in the sixteenth and seventeenth centuries – was signed in 1638.

Scotland Transformed

Level 3 shows exhibits under the theme "**Scotland Transformed**", covering the century or so following the Union of Parliaments in 1707. This was the period which saw the last of the Highland uprisings under Bonnie Prince Charlie (whose silver travelling canteen is on display), yet also witnessed the expansion of trade links with the Americas and developments in industries such as weaving and iron and steel production. Dominating the floor is a reconstructed steam-driven **Newcomen engine**, which was still being used to pump water from a coal mine in Ayrshire in 1901. Alongside it, in contrast, is part of a thatched, cruck-frame house of the 1720s of a type in which many Scots still lived during this time.

Industry and empire

Following the early innovations of steam and mechanical engineering, Scotland went on to pioneer many aspects of heavy engineering, with ship and locomotive production to the fore. Largest of the exhibits in "**Industry and Empire**" on Level 4 is the steam locomotive *Ellesmere*. As well as industrial progress, other fields are covered too, including domestic life, leisure activities and the influence of Scots around the world, both as a result of emigration, and through such luminaries as James Watt, Charles Rennie Mackintosh and Robert Louis Stevenson.

The Twentieth Century Gallery

For the **Twentieth Century Gallery** on Level 6, a range of Scots, from schoolchildren to celebrities, were asked to pick a single object to represent the twentieth century. Choices are intriguing, controversial and unexpected, from computers to football strips, cans of Irn Bru to a black Saab convertible. Tony Blair, who went to Fettes school in Edinburgh, chose a guitar, and former Edinburgh "milkie" Sean Connery a milk bottle. The obvious challenge is implicitly made: what would you choose, and why? Other features worth taking in here include a small **cinema** showing black-and-white documentary films about life in Scotland in the 1930s, and the **roof garden**, accessed by a lift. Up here, sweeping views open out to the Firth of Forth, the Pentland hills, and across to the Castle and Royal Mile skyline.

The Royal Museum of Scotland

Interlinked with the National Museum, though also with its own entrance, is the Royal Museum of Scotland (same hours), a dignified Venetian-style palace with a cast-iron interior modelled on that of the Crystal Palace in London. Intended as Scotland's answer to the museum complex in London's South Kensington, the Royal Museum has been an Edinburgh institution for over 100 years. It contains an extraordinarily eclectic range of exhibits, from exotic stuffed animals to colonial loot – the neat slogan used to describe the different roles of the sister museums is that the National Museum shows Scotland to the world, and the Royal Museum shows the world to Scotland.

The **sculpture** in the lofty entrance hall begins with a superb Assyrian relief from the royal palace at Nimrud, and ranges via Classical Greece, Rome and Nubia to Buddhas from Japan and Burma and a totem pole from British Columbia. Also on the ground floor are collections of stuffed animals and birds, and the **Power Collections**, with a double-action beam engine designed by James Watt in 1786 alongside a section of the Inchkeith lighthouse and the control desk from Hunterston A nuclear reactor. Upstairs there's a fine array of Egyptian mummies, ceramics from ancient Greece to the present day, costumes, jewellery, natural-history displays and a splendid selection of European decorative art, ranging from early medieval liturgical objects via Limoges enamels and sixteenth-century German woodcarving to stunning **French silverware** made during the reign of Louis XIV. Finally, on the top floor, you'll come to a distinguished collection of historic scientific instruments, a small selection of arms and armour, plus sections on geology, fossils, ethnology, and the arts of Islam, Japan and China.

The University of Edinburgh

Immediately alongside the Royal Museum is the earliest surviving part of the **University of Edinburgh**, variously referred to as Old College or Old Quad, although nowadays it houses only a few University departments; the main campus colonizes the streets and squares to the south. Founded in 1582 by James VI (later James I of England), the university is now the largest in Scotland, with over 13,000 students.

The Old College was designed by Robert Adam, but was built after his death in a considerably modified form by William Playfair (1789–1857), one of Edinburgh's greatest architects. Playfair built just one of Adam's two quadrangles (the dome, topped by a golden "Youth", was not added until 1879) and his magnificent Upper Library is now mostly used for ceremonial occasions. The small **Talbot Rice Art Gallery** (Tues–Sat 10am–5pm; free), housed in the southwest corner of the Old College, displays in rather lacklustre fashion some of the University's large art and bronze collection, including a number of twentieth-century works by Scots Joan Eardley and William McTaggart. The best part of the gallery, worth navigating the complex entrance route to find, are the rooms given to touring and temporary avant garde exhibitions which are mounted here on a regular basis – the show held during the Festival is normally of a high standard.

A little further up Nicolson Street, the southern extension of South Bridge, is the glass-fronted **Festival Theatre** (see p.124), a refurbished music hall which opened in 1994, giving the city a long-awaited venue for presenting opera and dance on a large scale. Opposite this is the stately facade of **Surgeons' Hall**, a handsome Ionic temple built by Playfair as the headquarters of the Royal College of Surgeons. Most of it is accessible to the public only one day a year, an exception being the **museum**, entered from 9 Hill Square (Mon–Fri 2–4pm; free), which has intriguing, if somewhat specialist exhibits on the history of medicine, including a book bound with the skin of body snatcher William Hare.

Lothian Road and around

The area immediately **west** and **southwest** of the Old Town was formerly known as **Portsburgh**, a theoretically separate burgh outside the city walls that was nonetheless a virtual fiefdom of Edinburgh. Since the 1880s and the construction of the **Royal Lyceum Theatre** on Grindlay Street, the area has gradually developed into something of a theatre district, with the Usher Hall, Traverse Theatre and Filmhouse cinema, along with a collection of good restaurants and bars, all within a few hundred yards of each other. Running north–south through the area is the wide Lothian Road, which together with perpendicular Morrison Street has seen a good deal of construction in recent years, most prominently various large financial headquarters and the Edinburgh Conference Centre. The **Museum of Fire** (by appointment only; ⓣ0131/228 2401; free) situated on Lauriston Place next to the Art School, records the history of the oldest municipal fire brigade in Britain, formed in 1824. It contains a small collection of well-preserved manual-, horse-drawn and motorized fire appliances.

Lothian Road meets Lauriston Place at **Tollcross** – marked by a clock in the middle of a busy crossroads; this area is lively at night, and features the intimate art-house cinema *The Cameo*. Beyond Tollcross, the open parkland areas of the Meadows and Bruntsfield Links mark the transition to Edinburgh's genteel Victorian villa suburbs. The streets closest to the meadows in the suburbs of Newington, Marchmont and Bruntsfield are dominated by students' flats; further south again is **Morningside**, whose prim and proper outlook was immortalized in Muriel Spark's *The Prime of Miss Jean Brodie*, and remains a favourite target for ridicule.

The New Town

The **NEW TOWN**, itself well over two hundred years old, stands in total contrast to the Old Town: the layout is symmetrical, the streets are broad and straight, and most of the buildings are Neoclassical. Originally intended to be residential, the entire area, right down to the names of its streets, is something of a celebration of the Union, which was then generally regarded as a proud development in Scotland's history. Today the New Town is the bustling hub of the city's professional, commercial and business life, dominated by shops, banks and offices.

The existence of the New Town is chiefly due to the vision of **George Drummond**, who made schemes for the expansion of the city soon after becoming Lord Provost in 1725. Work began on the draining of the Nor' Loch below the Castle in 1759, a job that was to last some sixty years. The North Bridge, linking the Old Town with the port of Leith, was built between 1763 and 1772 and, in 1766, following a public competition, a plan for the New

Town by 22-year-old architect **James Craig** was chosen. Its gridiron pattern was perfectly matched to the site: central George Street, flanked by showpiece squares, was laid out along the main ridge, with parallel Princes Street and Queen Street on either side below, and two smaller streets, Thistle Street and Rose Street in between the three major thoroughfares providing coach houses, artisans' dwellings and shops. Princes and Queen streets were built up on one side only, so as not to block the spectacular views of the Old Town and Fife. Architects were accordingly afforded a wonderful opportunity to play with vistas and spatial relationships, particularly well exploited by Robert Adam, who contributed extensively to the later phases of the work. The First New Town, as the area covered by Craig's plan came to be known, received a whole series of extensions in the first few decades of the nineteenth century, all carefully in harmony with the Neoclassical idiom.

In many ways, the layout of the New Town is its own most remarkable sight, an extraordinary grouping of squares, circuses, terraces, crescents and parks with a few set pieces such as **Register House**, the north frontage of **Charlotte Square** and the assemblage of curiosities on and around **Calton Hill**. However, it also contains assorted of Victorian additions, notably the **Scott Monument**, as well as two of the city's most important public collections – the **National Gallery of Scotland** and, further afield, the **Scottish National Gallery of Modern Art**.

Princes Street

Although only allocated a subsidiary role in the original plan of the New Town, **Princes Street** had developed into Edinburgh's principal thoroughfare by the middle of the nineteenth century, a role it has retained ever since. Its unobstructed views across to the Castle and the Old Town are undeniably magnificent. Indeed, without the views, Princes Street would lose much of its appeal; its northern side, dominated by ugly department stores, is almost always crowded with shoppers, and few of the original eighteenth-century buildings remain.

It was the coming of the railway, which follows a parallel course to the south, that ensured Princes Street's rise to prominence. The tracks are well concealed at the far end of the sunken **gardens** that replaced the Nor' Loch, which provide ample space to relax or picnic during the summer. Thomas de Quincey (1785–1859), author of the classic account of drug addiction, *Confessions of an English Opium Eater* (published in 1821), spent the last thirty years of his life in Edinburgh and is buried in the graveyard of St Cuthbert's Church, beneath the Castle at the western end of the gardens.

The East End

Register House (Mon–Fri 9am–4.45pm; free), Princes Street's most distinguished building, is at its extreme northeastern corner, framing the perspective down North Bridge, and providing a good visual link between the Old and New Towns. Unfortunately, the majesty of the setting is marred by the **St James Centre** to the rear, a covered shopping arcade now regarded as the city's worst ever planning blunder. Register House was designed in the 1770s by Robert Adam to hold Scotland's historic records, a function it has maintained ever since. Its exterior is a model of restrained Neoclassicism; the interior, centred on a glorious Roman rotunda, has a dome lavishly decorated with plasterwork and antique-style medallions.

Opposite is one of the few buildings on the south side of Princes Street, the **Balmoral Hotel**, formerly known as the *North British*. Among the most luxurious hotels in the city, it has always been associated with the railway, and the timepiece on its bulky clock tower is always kept two minutes fast in order to encourage passengers to hurry to catch their trains. Alongside the hotel, **Princes Mall** is a fairly sensitive modern commercial development. The open-air piazza on its street-level roof is home to Edinburgh's tourist office (see p.65), and a favourite haunt of street theatre groups and other performing artists during the Festival.

Located on Market Street, on the other side of Waverley Station from Princes Mall, the **Edinburgh Dungeon** (daily 10am–6pm; £6.95), which describes itself as "an orgy of grisly entertainment", is a self-consciously OTT horror theme park with actors and gruesome special effects. A populist attraction, the dungeon inevitably revels in Edinburgh's real-life tales of blood and gore, from sixteenth-century witchhunts to the body-snatchers Burke and Hare.

The Scott Monument and the Royal Scottish Academy

Facing the Victorian shopping emporium Jenners, and set within East Princes Street Gardens, the 200ft-high **Scott Monument** (March–May daily 9am–6pm; June–Sept Mon–Sat 9am–8pm, Sun 10am–6pm; Oct daily 9am–6pm; Nov–Feb daily 9am–4pm; £2.50) was erected in memory of the writer by public subscription within a few years of his death. The largest monument in the world to a man of letters, the elaborate Gothic spire was created by George Meikle Kemp, a carpenter and joiner whose only building this is; while it was still under construction, he stumbled into a canal one foggy evening and drowned. The architecture is closely modelled on Scott's beloved Melrose Abbey (see p.171), while the rich sculptural decoration shows 16 Scottish writers and 64 characters from Scott's famous *Waverley* novels. Underneath the archway is a **statue** of Scott with his deerhound Maida, carved from a thirty-ton block of Carrara marble.

The monument's rather mottled appearance is a result of a recent project which saw parts of the eroded, blackened stonework replaced with new honey-coloured sandstone. The restoration work is impressive and visitors are able to use a tightly winding internal spiral staircase to climb up to a series of platforms which offer some inspiring – if heady – vistas of the city below and hills and firths beyond.

The Princes Street Gardens are bisected by the **Mound**, which provides one of only two direct road links between the Old and New Towns (the other is the Northbridge). Its name is an accurate description: it was formed in the 1780s by dumping piles of earth and other waste brought from the New Town's building plots. At the foot of the Mound on the Princes Street level are two grand sandstone buildings; nearest to Princes Street, Playfair's **Royal Scottish Academy** (Mon–Sat 10am–5pm, Sun 2–5pm; price varies depending on exhibition) is the more elaborate of the two, a Grecian-style Doric temple topped with a statue of Queen Victoria and four sphinxes. It is used somewhat infrequently for temporary exhibitions during the year, notably for the RSA annual exhibition held from April to July, although the £26-million Playfair Project, due for completion in 2005, will eventually see it used as an extension of its more important neighbour, the National Gallery.

The National Gallery of Scotland

To the rear of the Royal Scottish Academy, the less elaborate **National Gallery of Scotland** (Mon–Sat 10am–5pm, Sun noon–5pm; free, entrance charge for some temporary exhibitions) is another of Playfair's Athenian constructions, built in the 1840s and now housing Scotland's premier collection of pre-twentieth-century European art. Though by no means as vast as national collections found elsewhere in Europe, the National Gallery of Scotland benefits not just from a clutch of exquisite Old Masters and Impressionist works, but also from the fact that it is a manageable gallery enlivened by imaginative displays and a pleasantly unrushed atmosphere. Elsewhere in the city, the Scottish National Portrait Gallery (see p.105), the Scottish National Gallery of Modern Art (p.109) and its neighbour the Dean Gallery (p.110), display other parts of the National Galleries' collection. A free bus service (Mon–Sat 11am–5pm, Sun 12–5pm; ⓣ0131/624 6200) connects all four buildings.

The innovative and often controversial influence of the National Galleries' flamboyant director, Timothy Clifford, is immediately apparent on the ground floor, where the rooms have been restored to their 1840s appearance, with the pictures hung closely together on claret-coloured walls, often on two levels, and intermingled with sculptures and *objets d'art* to produce a deliberately cluttered effect. As a result some lesser works, which would otherwise languish in the vaults, are displayed a good 15ft up. Two small, late nineteenth-century works in Room 12 – one anonymous, the other by A.E. Moffat – show the gallery as it was in the nineteenth century, with paintings stacked up even higher than at present.

Though individual works are frequently rearranged, the layout is broadly chronological, starting in the upper rooms above the entrance, and continuing clockwise around the ground floor. The upper part of the rear extension is devoted to smaller panels of the eighteenth and nineteenth centuries, while the basement contains the majority of the Scottish collection. The gallery has a programme of temporary exhibitions, which may mean that some of the paintings described below will not be on display. There are no guided tours; instead, audio guides available in five languages (£2) provide commentaries on the gallery's more important works.

Early Netherlandish and German works

Among the gallery's most valuable treasures are the *Trinity Panels*, the remaining parts of the only surviving pre-Reformation altarpiece made for a Scottish church. Painted by **Hugo van der Goes** in the mid-fifteenth century, they were commissioned for the Holy Trinity Collegiate Church (which was demolished to make way for Edinburgh's Waverley Station) by its provost Edward Bonkil, who appears in the company of organ-playing angels in the finest and best preserved of the four panels. On the reverse sides are portraits of James III, his son (the future James IV) and Queen Margaret of Denmark. Their feebly characterized heads, which stand in jarring contrast to the superlative figures of the patron saints accompanying them, were modelled from life by an unknown local painter after the altar had been shipped to Edinburgh. The panels are turned every half-hour.

Of the later Netherlandish works, **Gerard David** is represented by the touchingly anecdotal *Three Legends of St Nicholas*, while the *Portrait of a Man* by **Quentin Massys** is an excellent early example of northern European assimilation of the forms and techniques of the Italian Renaissance. Many of his German contemporaries developed their own variations on this style, among them **Lucas Cranach**, whose splendidly erotic *Venus and Cupid* is sometimes on view.

Italian Renaissance works

The Italian section includes a wonderful array of **Renaissance** masterpieces, the latest addition to which is a superb painting by Botticelli, *The Virgin*

Adoring the Sleeping Christ Child, which was carefully restored and now positively glows with colour and light. Equally graceful are three works by **Raphael**, particularly *The Bridgewater Madonna* and the tondo *The Holy Family with a Palm Tree*, the latter another example of the striking luminosity restoration can reveal.

Of the four mythological scenes by **Titian**, the sensuous *Three Ages of Man*, an allegory of childhood, adulthood and old age, is one of the most accomplished compositions of his early period. The companion pair *Diana and Acteon* and *Diana and Calisto*, painted for Philip II of Spain, show the almost impressionistic freedom of his late style. **Bassano**'s truly regal *Adoration of the Kings*, a dramatic altarpiece *The Deposition of Christ* by **Tintoretto**, and several other works by **Veronese**, complete a fine Venetian collection.

Seventeenth-century southern European works

Among the seventeenth-century works, **El Greco**'s *A Fable*, painted during his early years in Italy, takes a mysterious subject whose exact meaning is unclear. Indigenous Spanish art is represented by **Velázquez**'s *An Old Woman Cooking Eggs*, an astonishingly assured work for a lad of nineteen, and by **Zurbaran**'s *The Immaculate Conception*, part of his ambitious decorative scheme of the Carthusian monastery in Jerez. There are two small copper panels by the short-lived but enormously influential Rome-based German painter **Adam Elsheimer**; of these, *The Stoning of St Stephen* is a *tour de force* of technical precision.

The series of *The Seven Sacraments* by **Poussin** are displayed in their own room, whose floor and central octagonal seat repeat some of the motifs in the paintings. Based on the artist's extensive research into biblical times, the series marks the first attempt to portray scenes from the life of Jesus and the early Christians in an authentic manner, rather than one overlaid by artistic conventions. The result is profoundly touching, with a myriad of imaginative and subtle details. Poussin's younger contemporary **Claude**, who also left France to live in Rome, is represented by his largest canvas, *Landscape with Apollo and the Muse*, which radiates his characteristically idealized vision of Classical antiquity.

Seventeenth-century Flemish and Dutch works

Rubens' *The Feast of Herod* is an archetypal example of his grand manner, in which the gory subject matter is overshadowed by the lively depiction of the delights of the table; the painting's rich colours have been revived by recent restoration. Like all his large works, it was executed with extensive studio assistance, whereas the three small *modellos*, including the highly finished *Adoration of the Shepherds*, are all from his own hand. The trio of large upright canvases by **Van Dyck** date from his early Genoese period; of these, *The Lomellini Family* shows his mastery in creating a definitive dynastic image. Among the four canvases by **Rembrandt** is a poignant *Self-Portrait Aged 51*, and the ripely suggestive *Woman in Bed*, which probably represents the biblical figure of Sarah on her wedding night, waiting for her husband Tobias to put the devil to flight. *Christ in the House of Martha and Mary* is the largest and probably the earliest of the thirty or so surviving paintings by **Vermeer**; as the only one with a religious subject, it inspired a notorious series of forgeries by Han van Meegeren. There are two portraits by **Hals**, while his *Verdonck* stands in animated contrast to Rembrandt's self-portrait. There's also an excellent cross section of the specialist Dutch painters of the age, including the strangely haunting *Interior of the Church of St Bavo in Haarlem* by **Pieter Saenredam**.

European works of the eighteenth and nineteenth centuries

Of the large-scale eighteenth-century works, **Tiepolo**'s *The Finding of Moses*, a gloriously bravura fantasy (the Pharaoh's daughter and her attendants appear in sixteenth-century garb) stands out; despite its enormous size, it has lost a sizeable portion from the right-hand side. By way of contrast, the gems of the French section are the smaller panels, in particular **Watteau**'s *Fêtes Vénitiennes*, an effervescent Rococo idyll, and **Chardin**'s *Vase of Flowers*, a copybook example of still-life painting. One of the gallery's most recent major purchases is **Canova**'s 1817 statue *The Three Graces* – saved at the last minute from the hands of the J. Paul Getty Museum in California. However, as part of the purchase agreement it is on loan to the Victoria and Albert Museum in London until 2006.

There's also a superb group of early Impressionist works such Jean Bastien Lepage's beautifully innocent *Pas Meche* and Camille Pissarro's *Kitchen Garden L'Hermitage*. Impressionist masters are also well represented; there's a collection of sketches, painting and bronzes by **Degas**, including the influential *Portrait of Diego Marteli*, as well as Monet's *Haystacks (Snow)* and Renoir's *Woman Nursing Child*. Representing the post-Impressionists are three outstanding examples of **Gauguin**'s work, including *Vision After the Sermon*, set in Brittany; Van Gogh's *Olive Trees*; and **Cézanne**'s *The Big Trees* – a clear forerunner of modern abstraction.

English and American works

The gallery has relatively few English paintings, but those here are impressive. **Hogarth**'s *Sarah Malcolm*, painted in Newgate Prison the day the murderess was executed, once belonged to Horace Walpole, who also commissioned **Reynolds**' *The Ladies Waldegrave*, a group portrait of his three great-nieces. **Gainsborough**'s *The Honourable Mrs Graham* is one of his most memorable society portraits, while **Constable** himself described *Dedham Vale* as being "perhaps my best". The gallery owns a wonderful array of watercolours by **Turner**, faithfully displayed each January when damaging sunlight is at its weakest, though visitors at other times of year can enjoy two of his fine Roman views displayed in one of the darker galleries.

More unexpected than the scarcity of English works is the presence of some exceptional American canvases, among them **Benjamin West**'s Romantic fantasy *King Alexander III Rescued from a Stag* and **John Singer Sargent**'s virtuoso *Lady Agnew of Lochnaw*.

Scottish works

On the face of it, the gallery's Scottish collection, which shows the entire gamut of Scottish painting from seventeenth-century portraiture to the Arts and Crafts movement, is something of an anticlimax. There are, however, some important works displayed within a broad European context; **Gavin Hamilton**'s *Achilles Mourning the Death of Patroclus*, for example, painted in Rome, is an unquestionably arresting image. **Allan Ramsay**, who became court painter to George III, is represented by his *Portrait of a Lady*, once thought to be of Flora MacDonald, Bonnie Prince Charlie's much romanticized rescuer.

Of **Sir Henry Raeburn**'s large portraits, the swaggering masculinity of *Sir John Sinclair* in Highland dress is a fine example of Raeburn's technical mastery. He was equally sure when working on a small scale, as shown in one of the gallery's most popular pictures, *The Rev Robert Walker Skating on Duddingston Loch*.

Other Scottish painters represented include the versatile **Sir David Wilkie**, whose huge historical painting, *Sir David Baird Discovering the Body of Sultan Tippo Saib*, is in marked contrast to the genre scenes displayed in the basement, and **Alexander Nasmyth**, whose tendency to gild the lily can be seen in his *View of Tantallon Castle and the Bass Rock*, where the dramatic scenery is further spiced up by the inclusion of a shipwreck.

George Street

The street parallel to Princes Street to the north is **George Street**, rapidly changing its role from a thoroughfare of august financial institutions to a high-brow version of Princes Street, where the big deals are these days done in designer-label shops. George Street was designed to be the centrepiece of the First New Town, joining two grand squares. At its eastern end lies **St Andrew Square**, in the middle of which is the Melville Monument, a statue of Lord Melville, Pitt the Younger's Navy Treasurer. Rather going against its dignified role, St Andrew Square is home to Edinburgh's bus station; originally this was housed in an ugly concrete construction in the northeastern corner of the square, but this has been demolished and it now shares space with the city's newest shopping mall, home of Harvey Nichols and other designer outlets. Beside this on the eastern side stands a handsome eighteenth-century town mansion, designed by Sir William Chambers. Headquarters of the Royal Bank of Scotland since 1825, the palatial mid-nineteenth-century banking hall is a symbol of the success of the New Town.

Heading west along George Street, on the south side of the street, the oval-shaped church of **St Andrew** (now known as St Andrew and St George) is chiefly famous as the scene of the 1843 Disruption led by Thomas Chalmers, which split the Church of Scotland in two. Famous visitors to George Street have included Percy Bysshe Shelley, who stayed at no. 60 with the 16-year-old Harriet Westbrook during the summer of 1811, and Charles Dickens, who gave a number of readings of his works in the Assembly Rooms in the 1840s and 1850s.

Charlotte Square

At the western end of George Street, **Charlotte Square** was designed by Robert Adam in 1791, a year before his death. For the most part, his plans were faithfully implemented, an exception being the domed and porticoed church of St George, which was simplified on grounds of expense. Its interior was gutted in the 1960s and refurbished as **West Register House**; like its counterpart at the opposite end of Princes Street, it features changing documentary exhibitions (Mon–Fri 9am–4.45pm; free).

Once the most exclusive quarter of the city, when the New Town began to change to commercial use, the square maintained its prestige by attracting the offices of the city's most august law firms. By the 1980s, however, it was becoming more and more difficult for the expanding companies to fit into the space available, and for a period in the 1990s the square was eerily empty. However, the wheel has turned again and the **north side** of the square is once more the city's premier address, with the official residence of the First Minister of the Scottish Parliament at number 6, also the place where the Scottish cabinet meets.

Restored by the NTS, the lower floors of neighbouring number 7 are open to the public under the name of the **Georgian House** (March–Oct Mon–Sat 10am–5pm, Sun 2–5pm; £5), whose contents give a good idea of what the house must have looked like during the period of the first owner, the head of the clan Lamont. The rooms are decked out in period furniture, including a working barrel organ which plays a selection of Scottish airs, and hung with fine paintings, including portraits by Ramsay and Raeburn, seventeenth-century Dutch cabinet pictures, and a beautiful *Marriage of the Virgin* by El Greco's teacher, the Italian miniaturist Giulio Clovio. In the basement are the original wine cellar, lined with roughly made bins, and a kitchen, complete with an open fire for roasting, and a separate oven for baking; video reconstructions of life below and above stairs are shown in a nearby room.

Meanwhile the love affair of the NTS with the square is continued on the south side, most of which they occupy as their main **headquarters** in Scotland; the buildings have been superbly restored over the past few years to something approaching their Georgian grandeur. It's well worth paying a visit through the entrance of number 28 to peer at the sumptuous interior. One floor up, a small **gallery** (Mon–Sat 10am–5pm, Sun noon–5pm; free) shows a collection of twentieth-century Scottish art, including a number of attractive examples of the work of the Scottish Colourists, while two adjoining rooms offer an introduction to the Trust in general, with a video showing highlights of their properties around Scotland. Downstairs there's a **shop** selling National Trust books and souvenirs, as well as a very pleasant **café**. Authentically decked out with severe Georgian family portraits, the same room is used in the evenings as a dining room where rather grand "Taste of Scotland" style meals are served (see p.113).

Queen Street

Queen Street, the last of the three main streets of the First New Town, is bordered to the north by gardens, and commands sweeping views across to Fife. Occupied mostly by offices, it's the best preserved of the area's three main streets, although it's principally notable for the striking late nineteenth-century home of the National Portrait Gallery.

The Scottish National Portrait Gallery

At the eastern end of Queen Street is the **Scottish National Portrait Gallery** (Mon–Sat 10am–5pm, Sun noon–5pm; free). The remarkable building is itself a fascinating period piece, its red sandstone exterior, modelled on the Doge's Palace in Venice, encrusted with statues of famous Scots – a theme taken up in the stunning entrance hall, which has a mosaic-like frieze procession by William Hole of great figures from Scotland's past, with heroic murals by the same artist adorning the balcony above.

Temporary exhibitions are displayed in the galleries on the ground floor; elsewhere on this floor are the gallery shop and **café** (which closes 30min before the gallery), a favourite spot with locals. The **permanent collection** is located on the two upper floors. In contrast to the more global outlook of its sister National Galleries, the Portrait Gallery devotes itself to images of famous Scots – a definition stretched to include anyone with the slightest Scottish connection – and is dominated by Scottish artists. Taken as a whole, the gallery offers an engaging procession through Scottish history, with familiar images of famous Scots such as Bonnie Prince Charlie, Mary, Queen of Scots and Robert Burns. The gallery in fact owns two portraits of Prince Charlie (not always shown at the same time), one by Antonio David showing him as an aristocratic, rosy-cheeked 12 year old; the other, by Maurice-Quentin de la Tour, depicting him as an older, dashing warrior in armour, was originally purchased by the prince himself. From the seventeenth century there's an excellent portrait of Charles Seton, second Earl of Dunfermline, attributed to Van Dyck, and one of the tartan-clad Lord Mungo Murray, who died in the disastrous attempt to establish a Scottish colony in Panama.

Eighteenth-century highlights include portraits of the philosopher–historian David Hume by Allan Ramsay, and the bard Robert Burns by his friend Alexander Nasmyth, plus a varied group by Raeburn: subjects include Sir Walter Scott, the fiddler Niel Gow and the artist himself. Thomas Gainsborough's portrait *John, 4th Duke of Argyll* (1768) depicts the man who "pacified" the Highlands after the Jacobite rebellion – though an enemy to many he was feted by the establishment. The star portrait from the nineteenth century is that of physician Sir Alexander Morison by his patient, the mad painter Richard Dadd. Twentieth-century portraits occupy the first floor and include clever photomontages of sporting stars Stephen Hendry and Alex Ferguson, a larger-than-life bright red bust of socialist Jimmy Reid by Kenny Hunter, and many other royals, inventors, politicians, tycoons and celebrities. Visitors to the café can enjoy the company of Sean Connery, captured by acclaimed Scottish artist John Bellany.

Calton

Of the various extensions to the New Town, the most intriguing is **Calton**, which branches out from the eastern end of Princes Street and encircles a volcanic hill. For years the centre of a thriving **gay** scene (see p.122), it is an area of extraordinary showpiece architecture, dating from the time of the Napoleonic Wars or just after, and intended as an ostentatious celebration of the British victory. While the predominantly Grecian architecture led to Calton being regarded as a Georgian Acropolis, it is, in fact, more of a shrine to local heroes.

Waterloo Place forms a ceremonial way from Princes Street to Calton Hill. On its southern side is the sombre and overgrown **Old Calton Burial Ground**, in which you can see Robert Adam's plain, cylindrical memorial to David Hume and a monument, complete with a statue of Abraham Lincoln, to the Scots who died in the American Civil War. Hard up against the cemetery's eastern wall, perched above a sheer rockface, is a picturesque castellated building which many visitors arriving at Waverley Station below imagine to be Edinburgh Castle itself. In fact, it's the only surviving part of the **Calton Gaol**, once Edinburgh's main prison. Next door is the massive **St Andrew's House**, built in the 1930s to house civil servants.

Further on, set majestically in a confined site below Calton Hill, sits one of Edinburgh's greatest buildings, the Grecian **Old Royal High School**, which for many years was assumed to be where Scotland's new parliament would sit. Less than a year before the first elections, however, it was announced that the building was too small for the parliament envisaged, and that a brand new building would be commissioned (see p.91), while the Church of Scotland Assembly Hall (see p.81) would act as a temporary home. Previously in the Old Town, the new site for Edinburgh's oldest school – alma mater to, among others, Robert Adam, Walter Scott and Alexander Graham Bell – was built by Thomas Hamilton, himself an old boy. Across the road, Hamilton also built the **Burns Monument**, a circular Corinthian temple modelled on the Monument to Lysicrates in Athens, as a memorial to the national bard.

Robert Louis Stevenson reckoned that **Calton Hill** was the best place to view Edinburgh, "since you can see the Castle, which you lose from the Castle, and Arthur's Seat, which you cannot see from Arthur's Seat". Though the panoramas from ground level are spectacular enough, those from the top of the **Nelson Monument** (April–Sept Mon 1–6pm, Tues–Sat 10am–6pm; Oct–March Mon–Sat 10am–3pm; £2, or £4 joint ticket with Scott Monument), perched near the summit of Calton Hill, are even better. Begun just two years after Nelson's death at Trafalgar, this is one of Edinburgh's oddest buildings, resembling a gigantic spyglass. Each day at 1pm a white ball drops down a mast at the top of the monument; together with the one o'clock gun fired from the castle battlements these were a daily check for the mariners of Leith who needed accurate chronometers to ensure reliable navigation at sea.

Alongside, the **National Monument** was begun in 1822 by Playfair to plans by the English architect Charles Cockerell. Had it been completed, it would have been a reasonably accurate replica of the Parthenon, but funds ran out with only twelve columns built. Various later schemes to finish it similarly foundered, earning it the nickname "Edinburgh's Disgrace". At the opposite side of the hill, the grandeur of Playfair's Classical **Monument to Dugald Stewart** seems totally disproportionate to the stature of the man it commemorates – a now-forgotten professor of philosophy at the University.

Playfair also built the **City Observatory** for his uncle, the mathematician and astronomer John Playfair, whom he honoured in the cenotaph outside. Because of pollution and the advent of street lighting, which impaired views of the stars, the observatory proper had to be relocated to Blackford Hill before the end of the century, though the equipment here continues to be used by students. At the opposite end of the complex is the **Old Observatory**, one of the few surviving buildings by James Craig, designer of the New Town. New schemes for the development of Calton Hill, either grandiose or foolish (or both), are regularly proposed: with the possibility of cash from the Lottery Fund, one of these may some day be carried out.

The Northern New Town

The **Northern New Town** was the earliest extension to the First New Town, begun in 1801, and today roughly covers the area north of Queen Street between India Street to the west and Broughton Street to the east, and as far as Fettes Row to the north. This has survived in far better shape than its predecessor: with the exception of one street, almost all of it is intact, and it has managed to preserve a predominantly residential character.

One of the area's most intriguing buildings is the neo-Norman **Mansfield Place Church**, on the corner of Broughton and East London streets, designed in the late nineteenth century for the strange, now defunct Catholic Apostolic sect. Having lain redundant and neglected for three decades, it has suddenly acquired cult status, its preservation the current obsession of local conservation groups. The chief reason for this is its cycle of **murals** by the Dublin-born **Phoebe Anna Traquair**, a leading light in the Scottish Arts and Crafts movement. She laboured for eight years on this decorative scheme, which has all the freshness and luminosity of a medieval manuscript, yet it was almost lost due to leaks and rot in the fabric of the building in recent decades. It was only when the building was acquired by a trust in 1998 that its future was secured and the precious murals saved. The building is currently undergoing major refurbishment, with the basement being turned into offices for Scottish voluntary groups and the upper level beside the murals being used as a large performance and exhibition space.

The Royal Botanic Garden

Just beyond the northern boundaries of the New Town, with entrances on Inverleith Row and Arboretum Place, is the seventy-acre site of the **Royal Botanic Garden** (daily: March & Sept 9.30am–6pm; April–Aug 9.30am–7pm; Oct & Feb 9.30am–5pm; Nov–Jan 9.30am–4pm; free), particularly renowned for the rhododendrons, which blaze out in a glorious patchwork of colours in April and May. In the heart of the grounds a group of hothouses designated the **Glasshouse Experience** (daily: March–Oct 10am–5pm; Nov–Feb 10am–3.30pm; free, but donation requested) displays orchids, giant Amazonian water lilies, and a 200-year-old West Indian palm tree, the latter being in the elegant 1850s glass-topped Palm House. Many of the most exotic plants were brought to Edinburgh by the aptly named George Forrest, who made seven expeditions to southwestern China between 1904 and 1932. There is also a major new Chinese-style garden, featuring a pavilion, waterfall and the world's biggest collection of Chinese wild plants outside China. **Guided tours** of the garden (£2) leave from the West Gate on Arboretum Place at 11am and 2pm from April to September.

Dean Village and Stockbridge

Work began on the western end of the New Town in 1822, in a small area of land north of Charlotte Square and west of George Street. Instead of the straight lines of the earlier sections, there were now the gracious curves of Randolph Crescent, Ainslie Place and the magnificent twelve-sided Moray Place, designed by the vainglorious James Gillespie Graham who described himself, with no authority to do so, as "architect in Scotland to the Prince Regent". Round the corner from Randolph Crescent, the four-arched **Dean Bridge**, a bravura feat of 1830s engineering by Thomas Telford, carries the main road high above Edinburgh's placid little river, the **Water of Leith**. Down to the left lies **Dean Village**, an old milling community that is one of central Edinburgh's most picturesque yet oddest corners, its atmosphere of decay arrested by the conversion of some of the mills into designer flats. There's now a riverside path which runs almost the entire length of the river; though a little gloomy in parts, some stretches are charming and colourful. The section leading to Stockbridge passes **St Bernard's Well**, a pump room covered by a mock Roman temple. Commissioned in 1788 by Lord Gardenstone to draw mineral waters from the Water of Leith, it has recently been restored, and is occasionally open to the public (contact Water of Leith Conservation Trust; ⓣ0131/445 7367).

Stockbridge, which straddles both sides of the Water of Leith on the other side of Dean Bridge, is another old village which has retained its distinctive identity, in spite of its absorption into the Georgian face of the New Town, and is particularly renowned for its antique shops and collection of bars and restaurants. The residential upper streets on the far side of the river were developed by Sir Henry Raeburn, who named the finest of them **Ann Street**, which after Charlotte Square is the most prestigious address in Edinburgh (writers Thomas de Quincey and J.M. Ballantyne were residents); alone among New Town streets, its houses each have a front garden.

The West End and around

The western extension to the New Town was the last part to be built, deviating from the area's overriding Neoclassicism with a number of Victorian additions, including the city's principal Episcopal church, **St Mary's Cathedral**. With its proximity to the city centre the West End is now mostly used for offices, with a decent clutch of bars and restaurants, though there is some elegant terraced housing towards its outer edges. Here, enjoying some green space and a dignified setting are two compelling collections of contemporary art, the well-established **Scottish National Gallery of Modern Art** and its newer neighbour, the **Dean Gallery**, both of which regularly host worthwhile seasonal and touring exhibitions. Further out, Edinburgh's **Zoo**, a popular family attraction, is located on one of the city's prominent rises, Corstorphine Hill.

St Mary's Cathedral

In amongst the West End's blend of Georgian and Victorian styles, the huge **St Mary's Episcopal Cathedral**, an addition of the 1870s, is less intrusive than it would otherwise be, its three spires forming an eminently satisfying landmark for the far end of the city centre. Located between Manor Place and Palmerston Place, it was the last major work of Sir George Gilbert Scott. The cathedral is built in imitation of the Early English Gothic style and was, at the time of its construction, the most ambitious church built in Britain since the Reformation.

The Scottish National Gallery of Modern Art

Set in spacious wooded grounds at the far northwestern fringe of the New Town, about ten minutes' walk from either the cathedral or Dean Village, the **Scottish National Gallery of Modern Art** on Belford Road (Mon–Sat 10am–5pm, Sun noon–5pm; free), was established as the first collection in Britain devoted solely to twentieth-century painting and sculpture. The grounds serve as a sculpture park, featuring works by Jacob Epstein, Henry Moore and Barbara Hepworth, while inside the display space is divided between temporary loan exhibitions and selections from the gallery's own holdings; the latter are arranged thematically, but are almost constantly moved around. What you get to see at any particular time is therefore a matter of chance, though the most important works are nearly always on view. The establishment of the complementary Dean Gallery across the road (see p.110) has widened the scope of the displays, and linked exhibitions are a common feature. Both galleries have excellent **cafés**; if it's a sunny day head for the one at the Gallery of Modern Art, which has a pleasant outdoor terrace.

French painters are particularly well represented, beginning with early twentieth-century work such as **Bonnard**'s *Lane at Vernonnet* and **Vuillard**'s jewel-like *Two Seamstresses*. There are a few examples of the Fauves, notably **Matisse**'s *The Painting Session* and **Derain**'s dazzlingly brilliant *Still Life*, as well as a fine group of late canvases by **Leger**, notably *The Constructors*. Among some striking examples of German Expressionism are **Kirchner**'s *Japanese Theatre*, **Feininger**'s *Gelmeroda III*, and a wonderfully soulful wooden sculpture of a woman by **Barlach** entitled *The Terrible Year, 1937*. Cubism is represented by **Picasso**'s *Soles* and **Braque**'s *Candlestick*.

Of works by Americans, **Roy Lichtenstein**'s *In the Car* is a fine example of his Pop Art style, while **Duane Hanson**'s fibreglass *Tourists* is typically unflinching. English artists on show include Sickert, Nicholson, Spencer, Freud, Hockney and Hirst but, as you'd expect, slightly more space is allocated to Scottish artists. Of particular note are the Colourists – **S.J. Peploe**, **J.D. Fergusson**, **Francis Cadell** and **George Leslie Hunter** – whose works are attracting fancy prices on the art market, as well as ever-growing posthumous critical acclaim. Although they did not form a recognizable school, they all

Approaches to the Modern Art and Dean galleries

The best way of getting to the neighbouring Modern Art and Dean galleries is along the **Water of Leith walkway**, which can be joined at Stockbridge or the Dean Village. Alternatively, a **free bus** runs on the hour (Mon–Sat 11am–5pm, Sun noon–5pm) from outside the National Gallery on the Mound, stopping at the National Portrait Gallery on the way. The only regular **public transport** running along Belford Road is bus #13, which leaves from the western end of George Street.

worked in France and displayed considerable French influence in their warm, bright palettes. Also worth exploring is the vivid realism of the more recent Edinburgh School, whose members include **Anne Redpath**, **Sir Robin Philipson** and **William Gillies**, and the distinctive styles of contemporary Scots such as **John Bellany**, a portraitist of striking originality, and the poet–artist–gardener **Ian Hamilton Finlay**. There are also works by **Steven Campbell**, **Ken Currie** and **Peter Howson**, a group of artists based in Glasgow whose work came to international attention in the 1980s and 90s.

The Dean Gallery

Opposite the Modern Art Gallery on the other side of Belford Road is the latest addition to the National Galleries of Scotland, the **Dean Gallery** (same hours; free), housed in an equally impressive Neoclassical building completed in 1833. The interior of the gallery, built as an orphanage and later an education centre, has been dramatically refurbished specifically to make room for the work of Edinburgh-born sculptor **Sir Eduardo Paolozzi**, partly assembled from a bequest by Gabrielle Keiller (of the marmalade family), and partly from a gift of the artist himself, which included some 3000 sculptures, 2000 prints and drawings, and 3000 books.

Visitors are given an awesome introduction to Paolozzi's work by the huge *Vulcan*, a half-man, half-machine which squeezes into the Great Hall immediately opposite the main entrance. No less persuasive of Paolozzi's dynamic creative talents are the rooms to the right of the main entrance, where his London studio has been expertly re-created, right down to the clutter of half-finished casts, toys and empty pots of glue. Hidden amongst this chaos is a large part of his bequest, with incomplete models piled four or five deep on the floor and designs stacked randomly on shelves. In the adjoining room a selection of his sculptures and drawings are exhibited in a more traditional manner.

Also on the ground floor is the **Roland Penrose Gallery**, which houses an impressive collection of Dada and Surrealist art; Penrose was a close friend and patron of many of the movements' leading figures. **Marcel Duchamp**, **Max Ernst** and **Man Ray** are all represented in the gallery, and look out also for **Dali**'s *The Signal of Anguish* and **Magritte**'s *Magic Mirror* along with work by **Miró** and **Giacometti** – all hung on crowded walls with an assortment of artefacts and ethnic souvenirs gathered by Penrose and his artist companions while travelling. The adjoining **Gabrielle Keiller Library** contains a unique collection of surrealist literature, manuscripts and correspondence, and there's a wonderful pen and ink caricature of Picasso by **De Chirico**, as well as a series of Picasso's own cartoons satirizing General Franco. The rooms upstairs are normally given over to special touring exhibitions, which usually carry an entrance charge.

The Zoo

A couple of miles west of the galleries, **Edinburgh Zoo** (daily: April–Sept 9am–6pm; Oct & March 9am–5pm; Nov–Feb 9am–4.30pm; £7, family from £20) is set on an eighty-acre site on the slopes of Corstorphine Hill (buses from town: #2, #26, #31, #36, #69, #85, #86). Here you can see over 1000 animals, including a number of endangered species such as white rhinos, red pandas, pygmy hippos and poison-arrow frogs. Making the most of the space offered by Corstorphine Hill, the **African Plains Experience** has a walkway leading you out over the animals to viewing platforms, while other popular new additions include the Magic Forest, showcasing smaller primates, and a water-filled Evolution Maze. However, the zoo's chief claim to fame is its crowd of penguins (the largest number in captivity anywhere in the world), a legacy of Leith's whaling trade in the South Atlantic. The **penguin parade**, which takes place daily at 2.15pm from April to September, and on sunny March and October days, has gained something of a cult status.

Cafés and restaurants

The last decade has seen an upsurge in style, sophistication and good taste in Edinburgh's cafés and restaurants. **Café culture** has hit the centre of the city, with tables spilling onto the pavements in the summer, and this has been matched by the rise of a clutch of original, upmarket and stylish restaurants, many identifying their cuisine as **contemporary** or **modern Scottish** and championing top-quality meat, game and fish. As with most large cities in Britain, the culinary map of Edinburgh is colourful and **global**, with long-established Chinese, Indian and Mexican places competing with Thai, Japanese, North African and Spanish cuisine.

Generally, small **diners** and **bistros** predominate, many adopting a casual French style and offering good-value set menus. Traditional **Scottish cooking** can still be found at some of the more formal restaurants, and inevitably some tourist-oriented places offer haggis and other classic clichés. Edinburgh excels in **vegetarian** restaurants, including a couple of classic Indian vegetarian places, and **seafood** – it's long been a speciality of the **Leith** waterfront, and you'll now also find a number of great seafood bistros in the centre of town.

Most of Edinburgh's restaurants serve from noon to 2.30pm and 6pm to 10pm, and many are closed at least one day a week – it's worth checking before heading out on a Sunday or Monday. During the **Festival** the majority of restaurants keep longer hours, but they are also much busier. Many **pubs** (see p.118) also serve food, either in the bar itself or an attached restaurant.

Cafés and restaurant are shown on the maps on pp.66–67 & pp.76–77.

Royal Mile and around

Generally, the cafés and restaurants of the **Royal Mile** are less obviously tourist traps than the shops of the ancient thoroughfare, and you can find plenty of places brimming with character and imagination. Many are tucked away down the lanes and closes of the Old Town, or located in unusual and interesting buildings. In summer, this is the busiest part of town, so it's advisable to book a table for an evening meal.

Bistros, cafés and diners

Café Hub Lawnmarket ☎0131/473 2067. Colourful, well-run café in the Edinburgh Festival centre, with light modern meals served right through the day and evening. Teas, coffees, snacks and drinks also served. The large terrace is usefully central on sunny days. Inexpensive.

Café Odile Stills Gallery, 23 Cockburn St ☎0131/225 1333. Not the easiest place to find, but worth seeking out. French home cooking at its best, with tasty, original savoury tarts, flans, salads and sandwiches, as well as delicious cakes and coffee. Inexpensive.

Elephant House 21 George IV Bridge ☎0131/220 5355. A popular café with a large selection of coffees, teas, sandwiches, light meals and big cakes. The cavernous back room is great for reading newspapers and having philosophical discussions. Open every day 8am–11pm. Inexpensive.

Lower Aisle In the High Kirk of St Giles, High Street ☎0131/225 5147. Popular with bewigged advocates from the High Court, this café in the crypt serves good-value light lunches, with excellent home baking. Closed evenings and all day Sat. Inexpensive.

Netherbow Café Netherbow Arts Centre, 43 High St ☎0131/556 9579. Decent wholefood and vegetarian soups and light meals, with a courtyard for sunny days and kid's corner. Lunchtimes only. Closed Sun. Inexpensive.

Plaisir du Chocolat 251–253 Canongate ☎0131/556 9524. Unexpectedly classy Parisian tearoom serving delicious, if expensive, lunches, luxurious patisserie treats, an array of gourmet teas and real hot chocolates (though no coffee). Open every day 10am–6pm. Moderate.

Two Thin Laddies 6 Grassmarket ☎0131/476 2721. An antidote to chain coffee shops and plastic sandwich bars, this tiny Old Town café thrives on an irreverent attitude and a tasty range of sandwiches, snacks and daily specials. Open daytime only. Inexpensive.

French

Le Sept Old Fishmarket Close ☎0131/225 5428. Long-established French brasserie tucked down a cobbled close off the Royal Mile specializing in fish dishes and filling savoury crepes. Moderate.

Maison Bleue 36 Victoria St ☎0131/226 1900. A contemporary French bistro with an eclectic menu of tapas-style plates of food including sushi or haggis balls in beer batter. Good value at lunch and early evening menus. Moderate.

Indian

Khushi's Lothian Restaurant 16 Drummond St ☎0131/556 8996. One of the first Indian places to open in the capital, *Khushi's* is still essentially a basic cafeteria with few frills, but it's a characterful and friendly place and the food is reliable and cheap. Bring your own drink. Closed Sun. Inexpensive.

Suruchi 14a Nicolson St ☎0131/556 6583. Popular establishment serving genuine South Indian dishes – the menu is written in bizarre but entertaining broad Scots. Look out for cross-cultural specials such as tandoori trout. Moderate.

Italian-American

Mamma's American Pizza Company 30 Grassmarket ☎0131/225 6464. The best pizzas in this part of town, popular with students and larger groups, with outside tables in the summer and reasonably priced wine. Open till midnight Sun–Thurs, 1am Fri & Sat. Inexpensive–moderate.

Mexican

Viva Mexico 10 Anchor Close, off Cockburn Street ☎0131/226 5145. One of Edinburgh's best Mexicans for many years, doing the staples well in a friendly, easy going atmosphere. Moderate.

Scottish and seafood

Creelers 3 Hunter Square ☎0131/220 4447. The only specialist seafood restaurant in the Old Town, with fresh produce brought in from a sister restaurant/fish shop on Arran. Go for the more relaxed bistro section at the front rather than the lifeless, more expensive restaurant at the back. Moderate–expensive.

The Grain Store 30 Victoria St ☎0131/225 7635. Often missed by passers by, this unpretentious restaurant on eclectic Victoria Street is worth knowing about as a relaxing haven above the tourist bustle of the Old Town. Serves fairly uncomplicated but good-quality modern Scottish food, with reasonable lunchtime and set-price options. Expensive.

Nicolson's 6a Nicolson St ☎0131/557 4567. Now an Art Deco restaurant serving modern Scottish food, but most famous these days as the location of the tearoom where J.K. Rowling penned the first Harry Potter book between cappuccinos. Closed Sun. Moderate.

Ortegas 38 St Mary's St ☎0131/557 5754. Comfortable local bistro with some refreshingly original dishes, including good vegetarian options. Although the name sounds Spanish, the food isn't easily pigeonholed. Moderate.

The Tower Museum of Scotland, Chambers Street ☎0131/225 3003. Unique setting on Level 5 of the new Museum of Scotland; at night you are escorted along the empty corridors to the restaurant, where spectacular views to the floodlit Castle are revealed. Excellent modern Scottish food in a self-consciously chic setting. Expensive.

The Witchery by the Castle 352 Castlehill, Royal Mile ☎0131/225 5613. The restaurant that only Edinburgh could create, with Gothic panelling, tapestries and heavy stonework only a broomstick-hop from the Castle. The superb fish and game dishes are pricey, but you can steal a sense of it all with a pre- or post-theatre set menu (£10). Expensive.

Spanish

Igg's 15 Jeffrey St ☎0131/557 8184. A Spanish-owned hybrid, offering tapas snacks and Mediterranean dishes alongside traditional Scottish food. Smart but not intimidating. Closed Sun. Expensive.

Vegetarian

Bann UK 5 Hunter Square ☎0131/226 1112. Thoroughly modern vegetarian restaurant, with interesting, non-conventional dishes, stylish design and DJs playing ambient music late on. Mon–Thurs & Sun 10am–1am, Fri & Sat 10am–3am. Moderate.

Black Bo's 57 Blackfriars St ☎0131/557 6136. Inventive non-meat diner with an earthy atmosphere and friendly service. Open evenings daily and lunch Fri & Sat. Moderate.

New Town & West End

For eating places, as well as clubs and bars, this is the happening part of town. Many nationwide chains have restaurants on George Street; it's worth exploring some of the side streets and back lanes to find more authentic, home-grown places. Recently Thistle Street Lane has attracted interesting and varied restaurants.

Bistros, cafés and diners

Glass & Thompson 2 Dundas St ☎0131/557 0909. An unusually airy deli with huge bowls of olives and an extensive cheese counter; scattered tables and chairs mean you can linger over a made-to-order sandwich, an irresistible cake and coffee. Closed evenings. Inexpensive.

Hadrian's 2 North Bridge ☎0131/557 5000. Although it's strictly part of the upmarket *Balmoral Hotel*, this brasserie isn't too overpriced, and the elegance of the design and atmosphere, along with good quality modern British cooking, make it worth seeking out. Moderate.

Howies at Waterloo 29 Waterloo Place ☎0131/556 5766. Flagship of the small local Howies chain, with a pleasant dining area on the fringe of Calton Hill and reliably well-priced, comforting modern Scottish food. Moderate.

L'Alba d'Oro 5 Henderson Row, Canonmills ☎0131/557 2580. Italian voices fill the air in this classic takeaway, with fish and chips served on one side and pizzas, filled Italian rolls and ready-made pasta dishes on the other. Open till midnight. Inexpensive.

No. 28 28 Charlotte Square ☎0131/243 9339. Refined and very pleasant café within the Georgian National Trust for Scotland headquarters, serving classy light lunches and upmarket Scottish options. Next door is *No. 27* (same number), for evening dining. Inexpensive–moderate.

Starbucks Coffee Waterstone's, 128 Princes St ☎0131/226 3610. One chain coffee shop worth mentioning, surrounded by books and with fantastic views across Princes Street Gardens to the Castle. Inexpensive.

Chinese

Kweilin 19–21 Dundas St ☎0131/557 1875. One of the most reliable Chinese restaurants in town, serving Cantonese and Szechuan dishes in a pleasant atmosphere. Slightly more expensive than some. Moderate.

Loon Fung 2 Warriston Place, Canonmills ☎0131/556 1781. Something of a trailblazer for Cantonese cuisine in Scotland, near the eastern entrance to the Botanic Garden. Moderate.

French

Café Marlayne 76 Thistle St ☎0131/226 2230. An intimate venue for French farmhouse cooking, with plenty of hearty dishes. Moderate.

Café St Honoré 34 Thistle St Lane ☎0131/226 2211. A little piece of Paris tucked away in a New Town back lane. Fairly traditional French fare, but top quality. Closed Sun. Expensive.

La Cuisine d'Odile 13 Randolph Crescent, West End ☎0131/225 5685. Genuine French home cooking in a West End basement under the French Institute. Lunch only (noon–2pm). Closed Sun, Mon & July. Inexpensive.

La P'tite Folie 61 Frederick St ☎0131/225 7983. Another by-product of the Pierre Victoire school of reliable French cuisine in an uncomplicated, lively setting. Set lunches (around £6) and an à la carte evening menu. Moderate.

Italian

Caffe DOC 49a Thistle St ⓣ0131/220 6846. Modern Italian style and a genuine dedication to good food are evident here, with a dining room rather hidden behind the sleek street-front coffee bar. Moderate–expensive.

Cosmo 58a N Castle St ⓣ0131/226 6743. Straightforward but genuine and delicious Italian cuisine in a long-established, fairly exclusive restaurant. Closed Sun. Expensive.

Japanese

Tampopo 25a Thistle St ⓣ0131/220 5254. Tiny budget noodle bar offering filling meals from around £5, but engaging owner Katsuo Honjigawa will guide you through more interesting meals including sushi and bento boxes. Tues–Sat noon–2.30pm & 6–9pm. Inexpensive–moderate.

Scottish

Duck's at Le Marché Noir 2–4 Eyre Place, Canonmills ⓣ0131/558 1608. An upmarket Scottish–French restaurant with an endearingly unconventional attitude, serving reliably imaginative, high–quality food. Closed lunchtime Sat & Sun. Expensive.

Stac Polly 29–33 Dublin St ⓣ0131/556 2231. Teetering on the edge of overbearing Scottishness, *Stac Polly* avoids the kitsch with some classy touches, atmospheric surroundings and a hearty menu of game, fish and meat dishes. Closed lunchtimes Sat & Sun. Expensive.

Seafood

Café Royal Oyster Bar 17a W Register St ⓣ0131/556 4124. An Edinburgh classic, with its splendidly ornate Victorian interior (featured in *Chariots of Fire*), stained-glass windows, marble floor and Doulton tiling. Classic seafood dishes, including freshly caught oysters, served in a civilized, chatty atmosphere. Very expensive.

Fishers in the City 58 Thistle Lane ⓣ0131/225 5109. New Town incarnation of Leith's best-loved seafood bistro. This one has a sleek modern interior, great service and some stunning seafood. Expensive.

Mussel Inn 61–65 Rose St ⓣ0131/225 5979. After feasting on a kilo of mussels and a basket of chips for under £10 you'll realize why there's a demand to get in here. Owned by two west-coast shellfish farmers, which ensures that the time from sea to stomach is minimal. Closed Sun. Moderate.

Thai

Songkran 24a Stafford St, West End ⓣ0131/225 7889. A simple basement restaurant with some nice authentic decor and good value tasty Thai food, including "banquet" options. Moderate.

Vegetarian

Henderson's Salad Table 94 Hanover St ⓣ0131/225 2131. A much-loved Edinburgh institution with a self-service basement restaurant offering freshly prepared hot dishes, plus a great choice of salads, soups, sweets and cheeses. The slightly antiquated cafeteria feel can put people off, but the food is rarely short of outstanding. Light jazz every evening. Open Mon–Sat 8am–10.30pm. Inexpensive–moderate. *Henderson's Bistro*, next door at 25 Thistle St (ⓣ0131/225 2605) offers moderately priced bistro-style vegetarian meals, and is open during the day and Thurs–Sat evenings. Closed Mon.

Broughton & Leith Walk

On the eastern edge of the New Town, the area around Broughton Street is young, trendy and less upmarket than the very centre of the city. The city's gay community is an obvious influence here, and you'll find a strong Italian presence, including Valvona & Crolla, Edinburgh's outstanding deli. The restaurants at the top of Leith Walk may not be the most sophisticated in town, but many are open into the small hours.

Bistros, cafés and diners

Lost Sock Diner 11 East London St, Broughton ⓣ0131/557 6097. Fill up on burgers, wraps and blackboard specials, all at surprising low prices, while your dirty clothes take a spin in the adjacent laundrette. Try the parsnip chips. Open till 9pm Tues–Wed, 10pm Thurs–Sat. Inexpensive.

Valvona and Crolla 19 Elm Row, Leith Walk ⓣ0131/556 6066. The café at the back of this exquisite Italian deli serves authentic and delicious breakfasts, lunches and snacks. The best advert for the café is the walk through the shop – which has food stacked from floor to ceiling, with display cabinets full of sublime olives, meats and cheeses. Open Mon–Sat 8am–5pm. Moderate.

Indian

Modern India 20 Union Place ⓣ0131/556 4547. Edinburgh's best example of the contemporary curry-house, with bright new decor and a menu daring to stray from the conventional. A little bit of Bollywood right across from the Playhouse theatre. Moderate.

Italian

Café Mediterraneo 73 Broughton St ⓣ0131/557 6900. A great little place with a deli counter and a small dining space serving Italian food in unpretentious style. Not a red-checked table cloth to be seen. Moderate.

Giuliano's 18–19 Union Place, Broughton ⓣ0131/556 6590. Raucous trattoria across from the Playhouse, much favoured for family and office nights out. Does its best to conjure up the full Italian atmosphere. Open till 2am every night. Moderate.

North African

Marrakech 30 London St, Broughton ⓣ0131/556 4444. Scotland's only Moroccan restaurant and very reasonably priced, dishing up superb, authentic couscous and *tajine*, plus a range of soups, fresh bread and pastries. Unlicensed, but you can take your own bottle and there's no corkage charge. Moderate.

Spanish

The Tapas Tree 1 Forth St, Broughton ⓣ0131/556 7118. Authentic, lively and extremely friendly tapas bar, featuring Spanish guitar music on Wednesday evenings and flamenco on Thursday evenings. Moderate.

Stockbridge and around

The northern fringe of the New Town, **Stockbridge** is the home for many of the city's young professionals, and the eating scene here is straightforward and pleasant.

Bistros, cafés and diners

Bell's Diner 7 St Stephen St, Stockbridge ⓣ0131/225 8116. This unpretentious little diner is a long-standing Stockbridge favourite. Good, inexpensive burgers, plus a wide choice of steaks and pancakes. Open daily until 11pm. Moderate.

The Gallery Café Scottish National Gallery of Modern Art, Belford Road, Dean ⓣ0131/332 8600. Far more than a standard refreshment stop for gallery visitors, the cultured setting and strong menu attracts reassuring numbers of locals. Serves salads, filled croissants, light meals, coffee and cakes. Open Mon–Sat 10am–4.30pm, Sun noon–4.30pm. Moderate.

Terrace Café Royal Botanic Garden, Inverleith ⓣ0131/552 0616. Superior spot with outside tables offering stunning views of the city skyline, though the food is not that exciting. Their changing menu includes hot dishes, sandwiches and cakes. Inexpensive.

Indian

Lancers 5 Hamilton Place, Stockbridge ⓣ0131/332 3444. Mostly rich, filling Bengali and Punjabi curries in a slightly dated setting. Non-curry options include steak au poivre and the like. Moderate.

Italian

Pizza Express 1 Deanhaugh St, Stockbridge ⓣ0131/332 7229. The chain with the winning formula for smart interiors and decent pizzas. This one boasts a terrific location in a clocktower building overlooking the Water of Leith. Open till midnight. Inexpensive–moderate.

Mexican

Blue Parrot Cantina 49 St Stephen's St, Stockbridge ⓣ0131/225 2941. Cosy Stockbridge basement restaurant, with a small, frequently changing menu which deviates from the Mexican clichés. Moderate.

Lothian Road and Tollcross

This is Edinburgh's theatre district, featuring sophisticated, lively places to eat and drink, and good-value pre- and post-theatre deals. **Lothian Road** is another of the city's popular late-night stops, while **Tollcross**, a bit closer to the student areas of the Southside, is an up-and-coming area with a growing number of attractive cafés and restaurants.

Bistros, cafés and diners

blue 10 Cambridge St ⓣ0131/221 1222. Long-standing super-stylish café/bistro in the same building as the avant-garde Traverse Theatre. Modern minimalist decor, with tasty modern dishes for under £10 per main course. Open till 11pm. Closed Sun. Moderate.

Ndebele 57 Home St ⓣ0131/221 1141. Colourful African café offering sandwiches with lots of alternative fillings, imaginative salads and biltong for homesick South Africans. Open daily till 10pm. Inexpensive.

Chinese

Jasmine 32 Grindlay St ⓣ0131/229 5757. Modern looking, good-value Cantonese restaurant, with a strong line in fresh fish. Across the street from the Lyceum and the Usher Hall. Moderate.

French

La Bagatelle 22a Brougham Place, Tollcross ⓣ0131/229 0869. Fine French food in an authentic if slightly intense atmosphere, with a good-value three-course lunch for £10.50. Closed Sun. Expensive.

Indian

Shamiana 14 Brougham Place, Tollcross ⓣ0131/228 2265. Established, first-class North Indian and Kashmiri restaurant located midway between the King's and Lyceum theatres. One of the more expensive places in this category, and an oddly stark interior, but well worth it. Mon–Sat 6–10pm, Sun 6–9pm. Moderate.

Italian

Lazio's 95 Lothian Rd ⓣ0131/229 7788. Pick of the family-run trattorias on this block, handy for a late-night meal after a show in the nearby theatre district. Closes 1.30am during the week and 3am at weekends. Moderate.

Scottish and seafood

The Atrium 10 Cambridge St ⓣ0131/228 8882. Proving resilient in its position among the most impressive restaurants in the city. Quirky arty design with railway-sleeper tables and innovative nouvelle focusing on high-quality Scottish produce. Closed Sunday. Very expensive.

Marque Central 30b Grindlay St ⓣ0131/229 9859. Sister restaurant to the original Southside venture, moving into the theatreland patch with its great value pre- and post-theatre deals. At any time a place for imaginative modern Scottish food. Closed Sun. Moderate–expensive.

Point Hotel 34 Bread St ⓣ0131/221 5555. A classy feel with modern decor, white linen tablecloths and smartly dressed waiters, and well-presented food based on fresh local fish and meat. One of the best-value deals in town: a three-course set menu is just £12.90. Moderate.

The Rogue Restaurant Scottish Widows Building, 69 Morrison St ⓣ0131/228 2700. A typically unconventional venture by Edinburgh's most adventurous restaurateur, David Ramsden. Inexpensive toasted panini plus lobster and top-grade fillet steaks in a large avant-garde dining area with white linen and smooth service. Moderate.

Southside

As the student quarter of the city, the **Southside** boasts plenty of good-value eating, but you'll also find an appealing number of ambitious, attractive restaurants staked out here on the fringe of the more expensive city-centre area.

Bistros, cafés and diners

The Apartment 7–13 Barclay Place, Bruntsfield ⓣ0131/228 6456. Hugely popular, highly fashionable modern diner, with IKEA furniture, sisal flooring and abstract modern art on the walls. Their "Chunky, Healthy Lines" feature filling kebabs of meat, fish or vegetables. Moderate.

Buffalo Grill 14 Chapel St, Newington ⓣ0131/667 7427. Popular local steakhouse serving (they claim) "BSE – the best steaks in Edinburgh". Moderate.

Favorit 30–32 Leven St, Bruntsfield ⓣ0131/221 1800. Thoroughly modern café-diner dishing up coffees, fruit shakes, cakes and big sandwiches, as well as drinks, right through to 3am.

Kaffe Politik 146–148 Marchmont Rd, Marchmont ⓣ0131/446 9873. Café culture hits the student fiefdom of deepest Marchmont, in a relaxed and stylish venue serving coffees and substantial snacks. Open till 10pm. Inexpensive.

Peckhams Underground 155–169 Bruntsfield Place, Bruntsfield ⓣ0131/228 2888. Stylish booths in a hidden cellar underneath one of the area's top delis. Good place for brunches, snacks or filling evening meals. Moderate.

Parrots 3 Viewforth, Bruntsfield ⓣ0131/229 3252. Rather heavy velvety decor and a bizarre parrot theme, but it's a great place for friendly service and a satisfying, old-fashioned feed based on stews, curries and stodgy puddings. No smoking. Closed Sun & Mon. Inexpensive–moderate.

Chinese

Chinese Home Cooking 34 West Preston St, Newington ⓣ0131/668 4946. Cheap and cheerful BYOB café, popular with lively student nights out. Inexpensive.

Szechuan House 12 Leamington Terrace, Viewforth ⓣ0131/229 4655. Unassuming setting in a shabby-looking hotel, but a real find for lovers of genuine spicy Chinese food. BYOB. Closed Mon. Moderate.

French

La Bon Vie 49 Causewayside, Newington ☎0131/667 1110. Popular, well-run French restaurant serving reasonable set-price Scottish-French fare. Moderate.

Indian

Ann Purna 45 St Patrick Square, Newington ☎0131/662 1807. Excellent-value and authentic Gujarati and southern Indian cuisine (so mainly vegetarian) – try the three-course lunch for £4.95. Moderate.

Kalpna 2 St Patrick Square, Newington ☎0131/667 9890. Outstanding vegetarian restaurant serving authentic Gujarati dishes. Four set meals, including a vegan option, stand alongside the main menu. Closed Sun. Moderate.

King's Balti 79 Buccleuch St, Newington ☎0131/662 9212. Edinburgh's best balti establishment is very popular with students and features an evening banquet for £25.95. You can bring your own bottle, but 50p corkage per person is charged. Moderate.

North African

Phenecia 55–57 W Nicolson St, Newington ☎0131/662 4493. A basic, easy-going joint beside the main University campus, serving mostly Tunisian food but drawing on a variety of Mediterranean cuisines; the three-course lunch for under £5 is very good value. Moderate.

Scottish and seafood

The New Bell 233 Causewayside ☎0131/668 2868. Located above a pub, but its tasty meat and fish dishes are streets ahead of standard pub fare. Closed Mon. Moderate.

The Marque 19–21 Causewayside, Newington ☎0131/466 6660. One of the best exponents of classy-but-casual dining in Edinburgh, with modern Scottish recipes and some top-value pre- and post-theatre deals. Closed Mon. Moderate–expensive.

Sweet Melinda's 11 Roseneath St, Marchmont ☎0131/229 7953. A smart seafood restaurant in a single, timber-panelled room with a friendly neighbourhood feel. Closed Sun & lunchtimes Mon. Moderate.

Vegetarian

Susie's Diner 51 W Nicolson St, Newington ☎0131/667 8729. Popular café serving inventive soups, savouries and puddings, and a range of vegan food, to crowds of students. Inexpensive.

Leith and Newhaven

The area around the cobbled Shore of **Leith**, along the edge of the Water of Leith just as it reaches the sea, is the best-known dining location in Edinburgh, and lives up to its billing with good-quality, laid-back seafood bistros. It's worth coming down here at least once during your stay, especially on a summer evening.

Bistros, cafés and diners

Daniel's, 88 Commercial St ☎0131/553 5933. Top-grade bistro in an attractive setting on the ground floor of a converted warehouse in Leith. Food is from the Alsace region of France; the *tarte flambée*, one of the specialist dishes, is a sort of pizza with a French name and German ingredients. Moderate.

Malmaison Café Bar 1 Tower Place ☎0131/468 5001. Successful attempt to create the feel of a French café, serving excellent steak and chips as well as indulgent breakfasts and brunches. Moderate.

Chinese

Joanna's Cuisine 42 Dalmeny St ☎0131/554 5833. Homely little place, on a side street leading east off the middle of Leith Walk. The menu includes wonderful Pekinese specialities, notably delicious duck. Moderate.

French

Restaurant Martin Wishart 52 The Shore ☎0131/553 3557. Edinburgh's only Michelin-star holder wows the gourmets with French-influenced Scottish food right by the Water of Leith. The food's incredible but the ambience is rather stark. Closed Sun & Mon. Expensive.

The Vintner's Rooms 87 Giles St ☎0131/554 6767. Splendid restaurant in a seventeenth-century warehouse; the ornate Rococo dining room is a marvel and the food – ranging from seafood to game – isn't bad either. Very expensive.

Indian

Britannia Spice 150 Commercial St ☎0131/555 2255. The decor's nautical, the food is prepared by specialist chefs from the sub-continent and the awards for this relatively new but ambitious Indian restaurant have been piling up. Moderate.

Raj 89–91a Henderson St ☎0131/553 3980. A decent ethnic alternative to the waterfront brasseries, serving Bangladeshi and North Indian dishes, but few vegetarian choices. Moderate.

Italian

Tinelli 139 Easter Rd ☎0131/652 1932. Long-standing, very popular restaurant in an unlikely part of town, reputed to be Edinburgh's best traditional Italian. Specializes in northern Italian food – try the spinach and pumpkin-stuffed pasta. Closed Sun & Mon. Moderate.

Umberto's 2 Bonnington Road Lane, Bonnington ☎0131/554 1314. The best place in Edinburgh for anyone with children. Play areas, sympathetic staff and the food's good as well. Moderate.

Seafood

Ship on the Shore 24–26 The Shore ☎0131/555 0409. The homeliest and least expensive of the waterfront brasseries, serving good fresh fish and with a changing range of cask ales. Moderate.

The Shore 3 The Shore ☎0131/553 5080. A bar/restaurant with huge mirrors, wood panelling and aproned waiters who serve up good fish dishes and decent wines. Live jazz, folk and hubbub floats through from the adjoining bar. Moderate.

Skippers Bistro 1a Dock Place ☎0131/554 1018. More relaxed than it looks from the outside, with a vaguely nautical atmosphere and a superb fish-oriented menu that changes according to what's fresh. Worth booking ahead. Expensive.

Waterfront Wine Bar 1c Dock Place ☎0131/554 7427. Housed in the former lock-keeper's cottage, you can eat in the wonderfully characterful wine bar (smoking) or non-smoking conservatory attached. Fish dishes dominate. Moderate.

Pubs and bars

Many of Edinburgh's **pubs**, especially in the Old Town, have histories that stretch back centuries, while others, particularly in the New Town, are unaltered Victorian or Edwardian period pieces. Add a plentiful supply of trendy modern **bars**, and there's a variety of styles and atmospheres to cater for all tastes. The standard licensing hours are 11am–11pm (12.30–11pm on Sundays), but many honest howffs stay open later and, during the Festival especially, it's no problem to find bars open till at least 1am.

Edinburgh has a long history of brewing beer, though only two principal **breweries** remain: the giant Scottish and Newcastle (who produce McEwan's and Younger's) and the small independent Caledonian Brewery, which uses old techniques and equipment to produce some of the best beers in Britain. The Caledonian Brewery, Slateford Road (☎0131/623 8066) runs one-hour tours at 11am, 12.30pm and 2.30pm (Mon–Fri), though it's best to phone ahead before you visit. For more on Scottish beer, see p.35.

Once upon a time Edinburgh's main drinking strip was the near-legendary **Rose Street**, a pedestrianized lane tucked between Princes and George streets in the New Town, and the ultimate Edinburgh pub crawl was to drink a half-pint in each of its dozen or so establishments. Things are a bit more sophisticated these days, with **George Street** itself taking a lead: various former financial institutions have been converted into bars, with a predictable invasion of suits by day and style by night. On the outer fringes of the New Town, **Stockbridge** features pleasant drinking establishments, while the **Broughton** area is one of the city's liveliest, as well as the established meeting point for the gay community. While many of the **Royal Mile**'s pubs aren't ashamed to make the most of local historical connections to draw in the tourists, you don't have to travel far to find some lively places, notably the student-filled pubs in and around the **Grassmarket**, with a further batch on the studenty **Southside**. **Leith** has a range of bars, from rough spit-and-sawdust places to polished pseudo-Victoriana, while we've also listed a number of characterful places further away from the centre.

A fun way to explore Edinburgh's pubs is to take the **Edinburgh Literary Pub Tour**, a pub crawl with culture around Old and New Town watering

△ Canongate Tolbooth, Edinburgh

holes. Led by professional actors, the tour introduces you to the scenes, characters and words of the major figures of Scottish literature, including Burns, Scott and MacDiarmid. The tour starts from the *Beehive Inn*, 18–20 Grassmarket (March–May & Oct Thurs–Sun 7.30pm; June & Sept daily 6pm & 8.30pm; July & Aug daily 2pm, 6pm & 8.30pm; Nov–Feb Fri 7.30pm; £7).

The Royal Mile and around

Bannermans 212 Cowgate. Once the best pub in the street, now the late-night music can be a bit intrusive. Still atmospheric, however – a former vintner's cellar, it has a labyrinthine interior deep under the Old Town and good beer on tap. Open daily till 1am.

Black Bo's 55 Blackfriars St. No music, and no decent ales, but a good example of how to stay trendy without going minimalist. Next to, but separate from, the vegetarian restaurant of the same name.

Bow Bar 80 West Bow. Wonderful old wood-panelled bar that won an award as the best drinkers' pub in Britain a few years back. Choose from among nearly 150 whiskies or a changing selection of first-rate Scottish and English cask beers. Closed Sun afternoons.

City Café 19 Blair St. Longstanding but determinedly trendy bar on the street linking the Royal Mile to the clubbers' hub along the Cowgate. The blue pool tables are always popular and you can buy candies behind the American-style bar.

Doric Tavern 15 Market St. Long-established upstairs wine bar (open till 1am) is a favoured watering hole of journalists and artists. The downstairs *McGuffie's Tavern* is a traditional Edinburgh howff, while the brasserie beside the wine bar serves reliable good quality Scottish food.

EH1 197 High St. Wrought iron and cool aqua colours dominate in this contemporary Royal Mile bar, popular with a pre-club set. Serves up food throughout the day, plus pitchers of vividly coloured cocktails. Open till 1am.

Greyfriars Bobby 34 Candlemaker Row. Slightly nondescript but long-established favourite with both students and tourists, named after the statue outside. Open till 1am.

Hebrides Bar 17 Market St. Home from home for Edinburgh's Highland community; there's a ceilidh atmosphere with lots of jigs, strathspeys and reels, but no tartan kitsch.

Jolly Judge 7a James Court. Atmospheric, low-ceilinged bar in a close just down from the Castle. Cosy in winter and pleasant outside in summer.

Last Drop 74–78 Grassmarket. The "Drop" refers to the Edinburgh gallows, which were located in front, and whose former presence is symbolized in the red paintwork of the exterior. Cheapish pub food and, like its competitors in the same block, patronized mainly by students. Open till 1am.

New Town and West End

Abbotsford 3 Rose St. A large-scale pub whose original Victorian decor, complete with wood panelling and island bar, is among the finest in the city. Good range of ales, including a house ale brewed by Broughton. The restaurant upstairs serves hearty Scottish food.

Café Royal Circle Bar 17 W Register St. As notable as the *Oyster Bar* restaurant next door, the *Café Royal* is worth a visit just for its Victorian decor, notably the huge elliptical "island" counter and the tiled portraits of renowned inventors. Thurs open until midnight, Fri & Sat till 1am. Upstairs, the *Café Royal Bistro Bar* is an unlovely rugby-themed affair.

Cumberland Bar 1 Cumberland St. Mellow and highly regarded New Town bar with no jukebox, no TV and a wide variety of ales. There's a garden in the summer and good, reasonably priced food is served from noon to 2pm.

The Dome 14 George St. Opulent conversion of a massive New Town bank, thronging with well-dressed locals. Probably the most impressive bar interior in Edinburgh, though the ultra-chic atmosphere can be a bit intense. Sun–Thurs open till 11.30pm, Fri & Sat till 1am.

Indigo Yard 7 Charlotte Lane, West End. For many years one of Edinburgh's "it" bars, although the moment has probably passed. Still busy and lively, with decent food as well as designer lager. Daily till 1am.

Kay's Bar 39 Jamaica St. Small, dark, civilized one-time wine shop, warmed by a roaring log fire in winter, and serving fine cask ales. Mon–Thurs open till midnight, Fri & Sat till 1am.

Milne's Bar 35 Hanover St. Cellar bar once beloved of Edinburgh's literati, earning the nickname "The Poets' Pub" courtesy of Hugh MacDiarmid et al. Recent redevelopment hasn't done it many favours. Serves a good range of cask beers.

Oxford Bar 8 Young St. Traditional city bar, unpretentious and somewhat of a shrine for rugby fans, off-duty policemen and readers of the books of Ian Rankin. Open until 1am.

Pivo Caffé 2–6 Calton Rd. The theme is essentially Czech, but the result is a laid-back and popular bar with good DJs. Eastern European food and beer is prominent. Open daily till 1am.

Broughton and Leith Walk

The Barony Bar 81–85 Broughton St. A fine old-fashioned bar, which manages to be big and lively without being spoilt. Real ale and some good food, though it can be a wait to get served. Open till midnight.

The Basement 10a Broughton St. Packed out, especially at the weekends, with a pre-club crowd, this trendy bar is run by young and enthusiastic staff and serves cheap Mexican food till 10pm every day. Open till 1am.

The Outhouse 12a Broughton Street Lane. Busy pre-club bar tucked away down a cobbled lane off Broughton Street, with a lively beer garden and funky music. Open till 1am.

Stockbridge

Baillie Bar 2 St Stephen St. Traditional basement bar at the corner of Edinburgh's most self-consciously Bohemian street. English and Scottish ales are available, as well as better-than-average pub grub. Open Mon–Thurs till midnight, Fri & Sat till 1am, Sun till 11pm.

Bert's Bar 2–4 Raeburn Place, Stockbridge, and 29 William St, West End. Popular locals' pubs, despite their relatively recent arrival. Both have excellent beer, tasty pies and strive to be authentic, non-theme-oriented venues, though the telly rarely misses any sporting action.

Hector's 47–49 Deanhaugh St. A magnet for trendy Stockbridgers, full of tall stools, chocolate-coloured leather couches and rough-hewn walls. Good place for weekend brunches; food is served all day in a dining area to the rear.

Lothian Road and Tollcross

Bennets Bar 8 Leven St, Tollcross. Edwardian pub with mahogany-framed mirrors and Art Nouveau stained glass; gets packed in the evening, particularly when there's a show at the King's Theatre next door. Mon–Sat serves lunch and opens till midnight.

Blue Blazer 2 Spittal St. Traditional Edinburgh howff with oak-clad bar and church pews; serves a good selection of ales. Open till midnight Wed & Thurs, 1am Fri & Sat.

Cloisters Brougham Place. Fine real-ale pub located in an old manse – the attitude to beer is appropriately reverential.

Monboddo 36 Bread St. Stylish modern bar on the street level of the chic *Point Hotel*. Serves fine food at lunchtimes and beer in tall glasses by evening.

Traverse Bar Café Traverse Theatre, 10 Cambridge St. Much more than just a theatre bar, attracting a lively, sophisticated crowd which dispels any notion of a quiet interval drink. Good food available in the bar and also at *blue* upstairs. One of *the* places to be during the Festival.

The Southside

Human Be-In 2–8 West Crosscauseway, Newington. Despite the silly name, this is one of the trendiest student bars around, with huge plate glass windows to admire the beautiful people and tables outside for summer posing. Good food too. Open till 1am.

Drouthy Neebors Causewayside, Newington. What a Scottish theme bar will look like when it's exported around the world to countries bored of Irish theme bars. Popular with students, and often lively. Open till 1am.

Peartree House 36 W Nicolson St, Newington. Fine bar in an eighteenth-century house with old sofas and a large courtyard, one of central Edinburgh's very few beer gardens; serves budget bar lunches. Open Mon–Wed & Sun until midnight, Thurs–Sat until 1am.

Leith

Bar Java 48–50 Constitution St. Friendly bar in an area you'd expect all the pubs to have sawdust on the floor. Serves decent food, has a small courtyard beer garden and even B&B rooms upstairs. Open Sun–Wed till midnight; Thurs–Sat till 1am.

Carriers' Quarters 42 Bernard St. Intimate pub that dates back to 1785, with many original features, including a tiny "snug" and blazing log fire. Open till 1am Fri & Sat.

Kings Wark 36 The Shore. Real ale in an atmospheric restored eighteenth-century pub right in the heart of Leith, with bar meals chalked up on the rafters. Open till midnight Fri & Sat.

Starbank Inn 64 Laverockbank Rd, Newhaven. Fine old stone-built pub overlooking the Forth with a high reputation for cask ales and bar food. Open till midnight Thurs–Sat.

Elsewhere in the city

Athletic Arms (The Diggers) 1 Angle Park Terrace, Polwarth. Out in the western suburbs, not far from Hearts football ground and Murrayfield rugby stadium; the pub's nickname comes from the cemetery nearby. For decades it has had the reputation of being Edinburgh's best pub for serious ale drinkers. Open Mon–Sat till midnight; Sun till 6pm.

plus some antiquarian booksellers. Along and around the **Royal Mile** there are several distinctly offbeat places among the tacky-souvenir sellers. For antique shops the two best areas are **St Stephen Street** in Stockbridge and **Causewayside** in Southside.

Bagpipes Bagpipes Galore, 118 Canongate ⓣ0131/556 4073; Clan Bagpipes, 13a James Court, Lawnmarket ⓣ0131/225 2415.
Books Longstanding Edinburgh bookseller James Thin has large shops at 53–59 South Bridge (ⓣ0131/556 6743) and 57 George St (ⓣ0131/225 4495): the first is a labyrinthine, rambling general and academic shop, the second smaller and more genteel, with a good café. Waterstone's is, at present, the only major chain in Edinburgh, with branches at 128 Princes St (ⓣ0131/226 2666), 13–14 Princes St (ⓣ0131/556 3034) and 83 George St ⓣ0131/225 3436. There's a good selection of antiquarian bookshops in the city: Peter Bell, 68 West Port ⓣ0131/229 0562; Castle Books, 20 Rankeillor St ⓣ0131/667 5174; West Port Books, 147 West Port ⓣ0131/229 4431; and McNaughtan's Bookshop 3a–4a Haddington Place, Leith Walk ⓣ0131/556 5897. Most of these sell a wide range of secondhand books: for shelves of cheap secondhand paperbacks also try Broughton Books, 2a Broughton Place (ⓣ0131/557 8010), and Second Edition, 9 Howard St (ⓣ0131/556 9403).
Clothes (secondhand) Wm Armstrong, 81–83 Grassmarket ⓣ0131/220 5557; 64 Clerk St ⓣ0131/667 3056; Echo, 66 West Port ⓣ0131/229 6344; Herman Brown, 151 West Port ⓣ0131/228 2589; Paddy Barras, 15 Grassmarket ⓣ0131/226 3087; and Flip, 60–62 South Bridge ⓣ0131/556 4966.
Haggis Charles MacSween & Son, Dryden Rd, Bilston Glen, Loanhead (ⓣ0131/440 2555), has an international reputation, and also makes a tasty vegetarian version; buy it from the factory or various outlets around Edinburgh, such as the Food Hall in Jenners at 48 Princes St, or Peckhams, 155–159 Bruntsfield Place.
Maps Carson Clark, 181–183 Canongate (ⓣ0131/556 4710), sells antique maps, charts and globes.
Music Check out Avalanche, 17 West Nicolson St (ⓣ0131/668 2374), 28 Lady Lawson St (ⓣ0131/228 1939) and 63 Cockburn St (ⓣ0131/225 3939) for indie music; Coda, 12 Bank St (ⓣ0131/622 7246) for contemporary Scottish folk and roots music; Fopp, 55 Cockburn St (ⓣ0131/220 0133) for a wide range of CDs; Underground Solu'shun, 9 Cockburn St (ⓣ0131/226 2242) for house, garage, techno and drum'n'bass vinyl; and Vinyl Villains, 5 Elm Row (ⓣ0131/558 1170), for secondhand records, tapes and ephemera.
Tartan Kinloch Anderson, on the corner of Commercial and Dock streets, Leith (ⓣ0131/555 1390), has a large showroom; James Pringle Woollen Mill, 70 Bangor Rd, Leith (ⓣ0131/553 5161) has an archive computer which tells you if you're entitled to wear a clan tartan, and gives full historic information; Geoffrey Tailor, 57–59 High St (ⓣ0131/557 0256) is one of the largest and most respected retailers on the Royal Mile – they also have a shop in the Edinburgh Old Town Weaving Co by the Castle Esplanade, where "live" weaving takes place.
Tweed Romanes and Paterson, 62 Princes St ⓣ0131/225 4966.
Whisky Royal Mile Whiskies, 379–381 High St ⓣ0131/225 3383; William Cadenhead, 172 Canongate ⓣ0131/556 5864.
Woollen goods Bill Baber Knitwear, 66 Grassmarket (ⓣ0131/225 3249), has garments designed and made on the premises; Ragamuffin, 2a St Mary's St (ⓣ0131/557 6007), features Skye knitwear; and Shetland Connection, 491 Lawnmarket (ⓣ0131/225 3525) sells Shetland knitting wool, lace and cobweb.

The Edinburgh Festival

The world's largest celebration of the arts, the **Edinburgh Festival** is a massive explosion of cultural and artistic expression, with every available performance space in **August** – from the grandest concert halls to pub courtyards – helping play host to a packed programme of drama, comedy, performance, music and film. All over the city the streets fill with buskers, craft stalls, tourists, celebrities, performers, media types and festival-goers; posters plaster every vertical space and the centre of town takes on a slightly surreal, vital atmosphere.

The Edinburgh Festival is actually an umbrella term which encompasses different festivals taking place at around the same time in the city. The principal events are the **Edinburgh International Festival** and the much larger **Edinburgh Festival Fringe**, but there are also **film**, **book**, **jazz and blues** and **television** festivals, the **Military Tattoo** on the Castle Esplanade, and the **Edinburgh Mela**, an Asian festival held during the first weekend in September.

The Edinburgh Festival began in 1947, when, driven by a desire for postwar reconciliation and escape from austerity, the Viennese-born former manager of the Glyndebourne Opera, Rudolf Bing, brought together a host of distinguished musicians from the war-ravaged countries of central Europe. At the same time, eight theatre groups turned up in Edinburgh, uninvited, performing in an unlikely variety of local venues; the next year a critic dubbed their enterprise "the fringe of the official festival drama", and the name and the spirit of the Fringe was born.

Doing the Festival

For the visitor, the sheer volume of the Festival's output can be bewildering: virtually every branch of arts and entertainment is represented somewhere, and world-famous stars mix with pub singers in the daily line-up. It can be a struggle to find **accommodation**, get hold of the tickets, book a table in a restaurant or simply get from one side of town to another; you can end up seeing something truly dire, or something mind-blowing and you'll inevitably try to do too much.

The unpredictable nature of the Edinburgh Festival is one of it's greatest charms, so while the following information will help you get to grips with it, be prepared for – and enjoy – the unexpected. If you want up-to-the-minute information at any time of year, Ⓦ **www.edinburghfestivals.co.uk** has links to the home pages of most of Edinburgh's main festivals.

What's on

In addition to each festival's own programme, various publications give information about what's on day by day during the Festival. Every day the Fringe Office publishes **The Guide**, giving a chronological listing of virtually every Fringe show scheduled for that day. It's available free from the Office and hundreds of other spots around Edinburgh. Of the local newspapers, the best coverage is in **The Scotsman**, which issues an excellent daily Festival supplement. Their reviews and star-rating system carry a lot of weight. **The Herald**, published in Glasgow, also has good if slightly detached coverage. Most London-based newspapers print daily festival news and reviews, notably **The Guardian**, which publishes a daily Festival supplement, available only in Edinburgh. For a local view, the **Edinburgh Evening News** provides a no-nonsense round-up of news and festival issues. **The List**, a locally produced arts and entertainment guide, comes out weekly during the Festival and manages to combine comprehensive coverage with a reliably on-the-pulse sense of what's hot and what's not.

There's also coverage of the Festival on radio and TV. **BBC Radio Scotland** (94.3FM and 810MW) and **BBC2 TV** cover the shiny end of the Festival spectrum with informed specialized arts shows. **Radio Forth** (97.3FM), Edinburgh's independent local radio station, is much less highbrow and likes to broadcast the latest Festival news and gossip.

The Edinburgh International Festival

The legacy of Rudolf Bing's Glyndebourne connections ensured that, for many years, the **Edinburgh International Festival** (sometimes called the "Official Festival") was dominated by opera. Although in the 1980s an international theatre, ballet, dance and classical music was introduced, it's still very much a highbrow event, and forays into populist territory remain rare.

The International Festival attracts truly international stars, along with some of the world's finest orchestras and opera, theatre and ballet companies. Performances take place at the city's larger venues such as the Usher Hall and the Festival Theatre and, while ticket prices at the top end run to over £35, it is possible to see shows for £10 or less. The most popular events sell out quickly, although for every show fifty tickets are kept back and sold at The Hub on the morning of the performance, when queues can begin forming at dawn.

The most popular single event in the Festival is the dramatic **Fireworks Concert**, held late at night on the final Saturday of the International Festival: the Scottish Chamber Orchestra belts out pop classics from the Ross Bandstand in Princes Street Gardens, accompanied by a spectacular fireworks display high up above the ramparts of the Castle. Unless you want a seat right by the orchestra you don't need a ticket for this event: hundreds of thousands of people view the display from various vantage points throughout the city, the prime spots being Princes Street, Northbridge, Calton Hill or Inverleith Park and the Botanic Gardens by Stockbridge.

Since 1999, the International Festival's headquarters have been located at **The Hub** (see p.82); you can contact them for further **information**, including the annual programme, which is released in April.

The Edinburgh Festival Fringe

Even standing alone from its sister festivals, the **Edinburgh Festival Fringe** is easily the world's largest arts gathering. Each year sees over 15,000 performances from over 600 companies, with more than 10,000 participants from all over the world. There are something in the region of 1500 shows every day, round the clock, in 200 venues around the city. While the headlining names at the International Festival reinforce the Festival's cultural credibility, it is the Fringe which dominates Edinburgh every August, giving the city its unique buzz.

For the first three decades of its existence, the Fringe was a fairly intimate affair, dominated by drama, and peopled largely by graduating Oxbridge students and talent-spotting producers (often Oxbridge graduates themselves). The burgeoning of the Fringe began in earnest in the late 1970s as other forms of entertainment established themselves, notably new comedy, which over the next quarter of a century became almost synonymous with the Edinburgh Fringe. Nowadays, the Fringe is *the* place where artists of every conceivable description come to get discovered.

The first **Fringe Programme** appeared in 1951, the bright idea of a local printer. A single sheet of paper then, it's now a fat magazine crammed with information on most, though not all, participating shows. In 1959, the **Fringe Society** was founded by participants to provide basic marketing and co-ordination between events. Crucially, no artistic control was imposed on those who wanted to produce a show, a defining element of the Fringe which continues to this day – anyone who can afford the registration fee can take part. This means that the shows range from the inspired to the diabolical, and ensures a highly competitive atmosphere, in which one bad review in a prominent

Making it big at the Festival

There's hardly a serious **entertainer** worth their salt who hasn't played the Edinburgh Festival at some time. Best known are the satirists of *Beyond the Fringe*, the 1960 Edinburgh revue which launched the careers of Peter Cook, Jonathan Miller, Alan Bennett and Dudley Moore. Miller and Cook had come fresh from the Cambridge Footlights; other Footlighters have included the entire casts of *Monty Python* and *The Goodies*, David Frost, Germaine Greer, Richard Harris, Douglas Adams, Clive James, Griff Rhys-Jones, Stephen Fry and Emma Thompson. From Oxford came Rowan Atkinson and Mel Smith, while Manchester University graduates Ben Elton, Rik Mayall and Adrian Edmondson were first seen in Edinburgh in a revue called *Twentieth Century Coyote.* They teamed up with a duo called The Outer Limits (Nigel Planer and Peter Richardson) to form *The Young Ones.*

Comedian Arthur Smith first attracted attention in the student revue *Hamalongayorick*, while his bogus historical tours shepherding unsuspecting tourists down the Royal Mile became the stuff of legend. Actor Robbie Coltrane was seen in the Traverse's original *Slab Boys Trilogy* long before fame struck, while Billy Connolly's serious play *The Red Runner*, part of the International Festival, was panned by the critics, but was a hit with the crowds. Other celebs who got their break at the Fringe include Paul Merton, Jo Brand, Steve Coogan, Frank Skinner and drag queen Lily Savage, while various soap stars have arrived in Edinburgh to reinvent themselves, including Nigel Pivaro (*Coronation Street*), Tom Watt (*Eastenders*), Dannii Minogue (*Home and Away*) and Mark Little (*Neighbours*).

publication means box-office disaster. Many unknowns rely on self-publicity, taking to the streets to perform highlights from their show, or pressing leaflets into the hands of every passer-by. Performances go on round the clock: if so inclined, you could sit through twenty shows in a day.

The full Fringe **programme** is usually available in June from the Festival Fringe Office (ⓣ0131/226 5257, ⓦwww.edfringe.com). Postal and telephone **bookings** (ⓣ0131/226 5138) for shows can be made immediately afterwards, while during the Festival, tickets are sold at the Fringe office (daily 10am–7pm), the venue itself, or at various locations around the city (in recent years, James Thin Booksellers at 53–59 Southbridge; Waterstones bookshop at 83 George St; and HMV, 93 Princes St).

Ticket prices for most Fringe shows start at £5, and average from £8 to £12 at the main venues, with the better-known acts going for even more. Although some theatre and music acts can be longer, most performances are scheduled to run for an hour, which means that you can easily spend £40–50 on admission alone in the course of a hard day's festivalling.

The International Festival and the Fringe don't quite coincide: the former tends to run over the last two weeks of **August** and the first week of **September**, whereas the latter starts a week earlier, culminating on the last weekend in August, traditionally an English (but, confusingly, not a Scottish) Bank Holiday weekend.

Theatre

Comedy grabs more headlines, but **theatre** still makes up the bulk of the Fringe. Right from the start, innovative, controversial, wonderful and sometimes downright ghastly productions have characterized the Fringe's drama content. Content ranges from Molière to Berkoff, from Shakespeare to Beckett (someone, somewhere, always puts on *Krapp's Last Tape*). There are numerous student productions, as well as the appearance of Scottish favourites, such as

Kennedy are good for an appearance most years, while visitors from further afield have included Doris Lessing, Louis de Bernières, Ben Okri, John Updike and Vikram Seth. In addition, there are cook-ups by celebrity chefs promoting their latest tomes and a dedicated programme of children's activities and book-related events. An on-site café and, of course, a bookshop, ensure that all the participants' needs are met.

For further **information**, contact the Scottish Book Centre, 137 Dundee St, EH11 1BG ⓣ0131/228 5444, ⓦwww.edbookfest.co.uk.

Edinburgh International Jazz and Blues Festival

The **Edinburgh International Jazz and Blues Festival**, which used to run concurrently with the other festivals, now runs immediately prior to the Fringe in the first week in August, easing the city into the festival spirit with a full programme of gigs in many different locations. Like all the other festivals, this one has grown over the years from a concentrated international summer camp to a bigger, more modern affair, reflecting the panoply of generations and styles which appear under the banner of jazz and blues. Scotland's own varied and vibrant jazz scene is always fully represented, and late-night clubs with atmosphere complement major concerts given by international stars. Past visitors have included B.B. King, Bill Wyman, Dizzy Gillespie, Dave Brubeck, Van Morrison, Carol Kidd and the Blues Band. Highlights include **Jazz On A Summer's Day**, a musical extravaganza in Princes Street Gardens, and a colourful New Orleans-style **street parade**.

The **programme** is available at the end of May from the office at 29 St Stephen's St, EH3 5AN ⓣ0131/225 2202, ⓦwww.jazzmusic.co.uk.

The Military Tattoo

Staged in the spectacular stadium of the Edinburgh Castle Esplanade, the **Military Tattoo** is an unashamed display of pomp and military pride. The programme of choreographed drills, massed pipe bands, historical tableaux, energetic battle re-enactments, national dancing and pyrotechnics has been a feature of the Festival for fifty years, the emotional climax provided by a lone piper on the Castle battlements. Followed by a quick firework display (longer and more splendid on Saturdays), it's a successful formula barely tampered with over the years.

Tickets need to be booked well in advance, and it's advisable to take a cushion and rainwear. Tickets and information are available from the Tattoo Office, 32 Market St, EH1 1QB ⓣ0131/225 1188, ⓦwww.edintattoo.co.uk.

The Edinburgh Mela

A festival within a festival, the **Edinburgh Mela** is held at Meadowbank Stadium, off London Road, just to the north of Holyrood Park, over the first weekend in September, coinciding with the finale of the International Festival. Truly a people's event, it was introduced to Edinburgh in the mid-1990s by the capital's Asian community. The word "Mela" is a Sanskrit term meaning "gathering", and is used to describe many different community events and festivals on the Asian subcontinent. In Edinburgh, the Mela is about cultural diversity, and the family-oriented programme is designed to celebrate the many different cultures in the city. Music, dance, foods, carnivals, fashion shows, sports, children's events, crafts and a two-day careers fair for school-leavers see the festival season out with a bang rather than a whimper. Further **details** from The Edinburgh Mela, 14 Forth St ⓣ0131/557 1400, ⓦwww.edinburgh-mela.co.uk.

Listings

Airlines British Airways ⓣ0845/773 3377; British European ⓣ0870/567 6676; British Midland ⓣ0870/607 0555; EasyJet ⓣ0870/600 0000; Go ⓣ0870/607 6543.

American Express 139 Princes St (Mon–Fri 9am–5.30pm, Sat 9am–4pm; ⓣ0131/718 2501).

Banks Bank of Scotland, The Mound (head office), 38 St Andrew Square; Barclays, 1 St Andrew Square; Clydesdale, 20 Hanover St; HSBC, 76 Hanover St; Lloyds TSB, 120 George St; NatWest, 80 George St; Royal Bank of Scotland, 42 St Andrew Square.

Bike rental Biketrax, 11 Lochrin Place ⓣ0131/228 6633; Edinburgh Cycle Hire, 29 Blackfriars St ⓣ0131/556 5560.

Car rental Arnold Clark, Lochrin Place ⓣ0131/229 8911; Avis, 100 Dalry Rd ⓣ0131/337 6363; Budget, 394 Ferry Rd ⓣ0800/181181; Easy Rent-a-Car ⓣ0906/586 0586; Europcar, 24 E London St ⓣ0131/557 3456; Hertz, Waverley Station ⓣ0131/557 5272; Mitchells, 32 Torphichen St ⓣ0131/229 5384; Thrifty Car Rental, 42 Haymarket Terrace ⓣ0131/337 1319.

Consulates Australia, 69 George St ⓣ0131/624 3333; Canada, 30 Lothian Rd ⓣ0131/220 4333; Denmark, 215 Balgreen Rd ⓣ0131/337 6352; France, 11 Randolph Crescent ⓣ0131/225 7954; Germany, 16 Eglington Crescent ⓣ0131/337 2323; Italy, 32 Melville St ⓣ0131/226 3631; Netherlands, 53 George St ⓣ0131/220 3226; Norway, 86 George St ⓣ0131/226 5701; Poland, 2 Kinnear Rd ⓣ0131/552 0301; Spain, 63 N Castle St ⓣ0131/220 1843; Sweden, 22 Hanover St ⓣ0131/220 6050; Switzerland, 66 Hanover Place ⓣ0131/226 5660; USA, 3 Regent Terrace ⓣ0131/556 8315.

Dentist The National Health Service Line ⓣ0800/224488 will tell you where your nearest surgery is. For emergencies go to Edinburgh Dental Institute, Lauriston Place (ⓣ0131/536 4920) or the Western General Hospital, Crewe Rd South (ⓣ0131/537 1338).

Exchange Post Offices will exchange currency commission-free; Thomas Cook, 28 Frederick St (Mon–Sat 9am–5.30pm; ⓣ0131/465 7700); currency exchange bureaus in the main tourist office (Mon–Wed 9am–5pm, Thurs–Sat 9am–6pm & Sun 10am–5pm) and beside platform 1 at Waverley Station (Sept–June Mon–Sat 7.30am–9pm, Sun 8.30am–9pm; July–Aug Mon–Sat 7am–10pm, Sun 8am–10pm). To change money after hours, try one of the upmarket hotels – but expect to pay a hefty commission charge.

Football Edinburgh has two Scottish Premier Division teams, who are normally at home on alternate weekends. Heart of Midlothian (known as Hearts) play at Tynecastle Stadium, Gorgie Road (ⓣ0131/200 7201), a couple of miles west of the centre; Hibernian (or Hibs) play at Easter Road Stadium (ⓣ0131/661 1895), a similar distance northeast of the centre. Between them, the two clubs dominated Scottish football in the 1950s, but neither has won more than the odd trophy since, though one or the other periodically threatens to make a major breakthrough. Tickets from £12.

Gay and lesbian contacts Gay & Lesbian Switchboard (ⓣ0131/556 4049), Edinburgh LGB Centre, 60 Broughton St (ⓣ0131/478 7069).

Genealogical research Scottish Genealogy Society, 15 Victoria Terrace ⓣ0131/220 3677; Scottish Roots, 16 Forth St ⓣ0131/477 8214.

Golf Edinburgh is awash with fine golf courses, but most of them are private. The best public courses are the two on the Braid Hills (ⓣ0131/447 6666); others are Carrick Knowe (ⓣ0131/337 1096), Craigentinny (ⓣ0131/554 7501) and Silverknowes (ⓣ0131/336 3843).

Hospital Royal Infirmary, 1 Lauriston Place (ⓣ0131/536 1000), has a 24hr casualty department. The Royal Infirmary is moving in stages to a new location to the southeast of the centre, but the casualty department will be the last to move, some time in 2003. There are also casualty departments at the Western Infirmary, Crewe Road North, and for children at the Sick Kid's hospital, Sciennes Road.

Internet The Cottage, 136 Nicolson St (daily 24hr; ⓣ0131/531 1881, ⓦwww.cottagecopies.com); easyEverything, 58 Rose St (daily 24hr; ⓣ0131/220 3580); Web 13, 13 Bread St (Mon–Fri 9am–5.30pm, Thurs until 7pm, Sat 9am–6pm, Sun 11am–5pm; ⓣ0131/229 8883, ⓦwww.web13.co.uk).

Laundry Capital Launderette, 208 Dalkeith Rd, Newington (ⓣ0131/667 0825); Sundial Launderette at 7–9 East London St, Broughton (ⓣ0131/556 2743); Tarvit Launderette, 7–9 Tarvit St, Tollcross (ⓣ0131/229 6382).

Left luggage Lockers at Waverley Station and St Andrew Square bus station.
Libraries Central Library, George IV Bridge (Mon–Thurs 10am–8pm, Fri 10am–5pm, Sat 9am–1pm; ☎0131/225 5584). In addition to the usual departments, there's a separate Scottish section, plus an Edinburgh Room which is a mine of information on the city. The National Library of Scotland, George IV Bridge (Mon–Fri 9.30am–8.30pm, Sat 9.30am–1pm; ☎0131/226 4531), a magnificent copyright library, is for research purposes only, although accreditation is necessary to use the facilities. There is freer access to an annex which contains the Map Room, 33 Salisbury Place (Mon–Fri 9.30am–5pm, Sat 9.30am–1pm).
Lost property Edinburgh Airport ☎0131/333 1000; Edinburgh Police HQ ☎0131/311 3141; Lothian Regional Transport ☎0131/554 4494; Scotrail ☎0141/335 3276.
Motoring organizations AA, 18–22 Melville St ☎0870/550 0600; RAC, 35 Kinnaird Park ☎0800/550550.
Pharmacy Boots, 48 Shandwick Place (Mon–Fri 8am–9pm, Sat 8am–7pm, Sun 10am–5pm; ☎0131/225 6757) has the longest opening hours.
Police In an emergency call 999. Otherwise contact Lothian and Borders Police HQ, Fettes Ave ☎0131/311 3131; or the local police stations at Gayfield Square, Broughton ☎0131/556 9270; Queen Charlotte St, Leith ☎0131/554 9350; St Leonard's St, Southside ☎0131/662 5000; or Torphichen Place, West End ☎0131/229 2323.
Post office 8–10 St James Centre (Mon 9am–5.30pm, Tues–Fri 8.30am–5.30pm, Sat 8.30am–6pm; ☎0845/722 3344).
Rape crisis centre ☎0131/556 9437.
Rugby Scotland's international fixtures are played at Murrayfield Stadium, a couple of miles west of the city centre. Phone the stadium on ☎0131/346 5000 for advice on ticket sales, but be warned that tickets can be very hard to come by for the big games.
Sports stadium Meadowbank Sports Centre and Stadium, 139 London Rd (☎0131/661 5351), is Edinburgh's main venue for most spectator and participatory sports. Facilities include an athletics track, a velodrome and indoor halls.
Swimming pools The city has one Olympic-standard modern pool, the Royal Commonwealth Pool, 21 Dalkeith Rd (☎0131/667 7211); and a number of considerably older pools at Caledonian Crescent (☎0131/313 3964); Glenogle Road (☎0131/343 6376); 15 Bellfield St, Portobello (☎0131/669 6888) and 6 Thirlestane Rd (☎0131/447 0052).
Taxis Airport Taxis ☎0131/344 3344; Central Radio Taxis ☎0131/229 2468; and City Cabs ☎0131/228 1211.
Travel agents Usit Campus Travel (student and youth specialist), 53 Forrest Rd (☎0131/225 6111) and 92 South Clerk St (☎0131/668 3303); Edinburgh Travel Centre (student and youth specialist) 3 Bristo Square (☎0131/668 2221); STA, 27 Forest Rd (☎0131/226 7747). For three- and six-day coach trips to the Highlands, try Haggis Backpackers, 11 Blackfriars St (☎0131/557 9393) or MacBackpackers, 105 High St (☎0131/558 9900).

Out from the centre

There's a great deal to be discovered by exploring beyond the compact centre of Edinburgh, in particular along the Firth of Forth coastline to the north and the rise of the Pentland Hills to the south. Just over a mile northeast of the city centre is **Leith**, the historic port of Edinburgh, a fascinating mix of cobbled streets and new developments, run-down housing and some of the city's top restaurants. Nearby you can find a flavour of the city's maritime and fishing heritage at the atmospheric harbour of **Newhaven**, while the long beach at **Portobello** is still a popular spot on a sunny day. To the northwest of the city are the more placid charms of the old Roman village of **Cramond** and the country mansions **Lauriston Castle** and **Dalmeny House**.

In the southern suburbs of the city, the imposing fifteenth-century **Craigmillar Castle** is incongruously set amid a rather grim housing estate, but there is also a rural aspect to the area, with various hills, parks and, on the southern edge of the city, the range of the **Pentland Hills** which offer some wild walking country and terrific views.

Leith and around

For several hundred years, **LEITH** was separate from Edinburgh. As Scotland's major east coast port, it played a key role in the nation's history, even serving as the seat of government for a time, and in 1833 finally became a burgh in its own right. In 1920, however, it was incorporated into the capital and, in the decades that followed, went into seemingly terminal decline: the population dropped dramatically, and much of its centre was ripped out, to be replaced by grim housing schemes.

The 1980s, however, saw an unexpected turnaround. Against all the odds, a couple of waterfront bistros proved enormously successful; competitors followed apace, and today the port boasts arguably the best concentration of good restaurants (particularly seafood) in Edinburgh (see p.117 & 121 for reviews). The surviving historic buildings were spruced up and large blocks of yuppie flats appeared among the crumbling tenements and council housing. Meanwhile the dock areas are being transformed by Europe's largest current waterfront development, most notably the vast building housing civil servants from the Scottish Executive and the new Ocean Terminal, a shopping and entertainment complex beside which the former royal yacht **Britannia** is settling into retirement.

To reach Leith from the city centre, take one of the many buses going down Leith Walk, near the top end of which is a statue of Sherlock Holmes, whose creator, Sir Arthur Conan Doyle, was born nearby.

Around the port

While you're most likely to come to Leith for the bars and restaurants, the area itself warrants exploration; though the shipbuilding yards have gone, it remains an active port with a rough-edged character. Most of the showpiece Neoclassical buildings lie on or near **The Shore**, the tenement-lined road along the final stretch of the Water of Leith, just before it disgorges into the Firth of Forth. Note the former **Town Hall**, on the parallel Constitution Street, now the headquarters of the local constabulary, immortalized in the tongue twister, "The Leith police dismisseth us"; the Classical Trinity House on Kirkgate, built in 1816; and the massive Customs House on Commercial Street. To the west, set back from The Shore, is **Lamb's House**, a seventeenth-century mansion comparable to Gladstone's Land in the Old Town. Built as the home of the prosperous merchant Andro Lamb, it currently functions as an old people's day centre.

Leith Links is an area of predominantly flat parkland, just east of the police station. Documentary evidence suggests that The Links was a golf course in the fifteenth century, giving rise to Leith's claim to be regarded as the birthplace of the sport: in 1744 its first written rules were drawn up here, ten years before they were formalized in St Andrews.

Britannia

A little to the west of The Shore, moored alongside **Ocean Terminal**, a huge shopping and entertainment centre designed by Terence Conran, is one of the world's most famous ships, **Britannia** (daily: April–May 9.30am–4pm; July–Sept 9.30am–4.30pm; Oct–March 10am–3.30pm; bookings advised ⓣ0131/555 5566; £7.75). Launched in 1953 at John Brown's shipyard on Clydeside, *Britannia* was used by the royal family for 44 years for state visits, diplomatic functions and royal holidays. Leith acquired her following decommission in 1997, against the wishes of many of the royal family, who felt that scuttling would have been a more dignified end.

Visits to *Britannia* begin in the **visitor centre**, within Ocean Terminal, which uses the royal barge and a reconstructed sergeant's mess to display royal holiday snaps and video clips of *Britannia*'s most famous moments, which included the evacuation of Aden and the British handover of Hong Kong in 1997. An audio handset is then handed out and you are allowed to roam around the yacht: the **bridge**, the **admiral's quarters**, the **officers' mess** and a large part of the **state apartments**, including the state dining and drawing rooms and the (separate) cabins used by the Queen and the Duke of Edinburgh, viewed through a glass partition. The ship has been largely kept as she was when she was in service, with a well-preserved 1950s dowdiness which the audio guide loyally attributes to the Queen's good taste and astute frugality in the lean postwar years. Certainly the atmosphere is a far cry from the opulent splendour which many expect.

The audio guide also reveals quirkier aspects of *Britannia*'s history: a full Marine Band was always part of the 300-strong crew; hand signals were used by the sailors to communicate orders as shouting was forbidden; and a special solid mahogany rail was built onto the royal bridge to allow the Queen to stand on deck as *Britannia* came into port, without fear of a gust of wind lifting the royal skirt.

To get to Ocean Terminal, jump on one of the tour buses which leave from Waverley Bridge; otherwise, buses #10 and #16 from Princes Street and #22 from St Andrews Square run down Leith Walk to the junction of Commercial Street and North Junction Street, from where it's a five-minute walk down to the visitor centre.

Newhaven

To the west of Leith lies the village of **NEWHAVEN**, built by James IV at the start of the sixteenth century as an alternative shipbuilding centre to Leith: his massive warship, the *Great Michael*, capable of carrying 120 gunners, 300 mariners and 1000 troops, and said to have used up all the trees in Fife, was built here. It has also been a ferry station and an important fishing centre, landing some six million oysters a year at the height of its success (in the 1860s). Today, the harbour still has a pleasantly salty feel. Among various modern developments, the old fish market remains, housing *Harry Ramsden's* fish and chip café, a couple of fish merchants and the small **Newhaven Heritage Museum** (daily noon–5pm; free), a fascinating collection of costumes and other memorabilia staffed by enthusiastic members of local fishing families. From the harbour itself, the high-speed inflatable boats of **Seafari Adventures** (☎0131/331 5000) whizz out to the Forth Islands and South Queensferry (see p.150) on trips to view bird and sea life.

Portobello

Among Edinburgh's least expected assets is its **beach**, most of which falls within **PORTOBELLO**, the suburb to the southeast of Leith. Once a lively **seaside resort** it's now a forlorn kind of place, its funfairs and amusement arcades decidedly down-at-heel. Nonetheless, it retains a certain faded charm, and – on hot summer weekends at least – the beach can be a mass of swimmers, sunbathers, surfers and pleasure boats. A walk along the promenade is a pleasure at any time of the year. Portobello is about three miles east of the centre of town, and can be reached on buses #15, #26, #46 or #86.

Lauriston Castle and Cramond

Lauriston Castle (40min obligatory guided tours April–Oct daily except Friday 11.20am–4.20pm; Nov–March Sat & Sun 2.20pm & 3.20pm; £4.50) is a country mansion set in its own parkland overlooking the Firth of Forth, about five miles west of the centre. The original sixteenth-century tower house forms the centrepiece of what is otherwise a neo-Jacobean structure, which in 1902 became the retirement home of a prosperous local cabinet-maker. He decked out the interior with his private collection of furniture and antiques, which includes Flemish tapestries and ornaments made of Blue John from Derbyshire. The castle can be reached from the city centre by bus #40.

One mile further west, **CRAMOND** is one of the city's most atmospheric – and poshest – old villages. The enduring image of Cramond is of step-gabled whitewashed houses rising uphill from the waterfront, though it also boasts the foundations of a Roman fort, a medieval bridge and tower house, and a church, inn and mansion, all from the seventeenth century. In December 1996, a wonderful Roman sculpture of a lioness devouring a man was discovered in the River Almond: it is thought that it was simply thrown into the river after the departure of the Romans. It is now on display in the National Museum of Scotland on Chambers Street (see p.94). There are a number of interesting **short walks** in the area: across the causeway at low tide to the uninhabited (except for seabirds) **Cramond Island**; eastwards along the seafront towards the gasometers of **Granton** with sweeping views out to sea; upstream along the River Almond past former mills and their adjoining cottages towards the sixteenth-century **Old Cramond Brig**; and, after a short ferry crossing, through the Dalmeny estate to **Dalmeny House** (see below). Apart from the last one, which is just a little longer, these walks should take around an hour each.

Dalmeny

In 1975, Edinburgh's boundaries were extended to include a number of towns and villages which were formerly part of West Lothian. Among them is **DALMENY**, two miles west of Cramond and accessible directly from the city centre by bus (#43 SMT) or train. Another option is to take the short ferry and coastal path from Cramond, which passes through the estate of **Dalmeny House** (July & Aug Mon, Tues & Sun noon–5.30pm; £4), the seat of the Earls of Rosebery. Built in 1815 by the English architect William Wilkins, it was the first stately home in Scotland in the neo-Gothic style, vividly evoking Tudor architecture in its picturesque turreted roofline, and in its fan vaults and hammerbeam ceilings. The family portraits include one of the fourth Earl (who commissioned the house) by Raeburn, and of the fifth Earl (a former British prime minister) by Millais; there are also likenesses of other famous society figures by Reynolds, Gainsborough and Lawrence. Among the furnishings are a set of tapestries made from cartoons by Goya, and the Rothschild Collection of eighteenth-century French furniture and *objets d'art*. There's also a fascinating collection of memorabilia of Napoleon Bonaparte – notably some items he used during his exile in St Helena – amassed by the fifth Earl, who wrote a biography of the French emperor.

Dalmeny **village** is a quiet community built around a spacious green. Its focal point is the mid-twelfth-century **St Cuthbert's Kirk**, a wonderful Norman church that has remained more or less intact. Although very weather-beaten, the south doorway is particularly notable for its depictions of strange beasts. More vivaciously grotesque carvings can be seen inside on the chancel corbels and arch.

Craigmillar Castle

Craigmillar Castle (April–Sept daily 9.30am–6.30pm; Oct–March Mon–Wed & Sat 9.30am–4.30pm, Thurs 9.30am–noon, Fri & Sun 2–4.30pm; HS; £2), where the murder of Lord Darnley, second husband of Mary, Queen of Scots was plotted, lies in a green belt five miles southeast of the centre. It's one of the best-preserved medieval fortresses in Scotland, and before Queen Victoria set her heart on Balmoral, it was being considered as her royal castle north of the border, a possibility which seems odd now given its proximity to the ugly council housing scheme of Craigmillar, one of Edinburgh's most deprived districts.

The oldest part of the complex is the L-shaped **tower house**, which dates back to the early 1400s: it remains substantially intact, and the great hall, with its resplendent late Gothic chimneypiece, is in good enough shape to be rented out for functions. A few decades after Craigmillar's completion, the tower house was surrounded by a quadrangular wall with cylindrical corner towers pierced by some of the earliest surviving gunholes in Britain. The west range was remodelled as an aristocratic mansion in the mid-seventeenth century, but its owners abandoned the place a hundred years later, leaving it to picturesque decay. Take bus #30, #33 or #82, or any bus heading for Hawick or Jedburgh, from the city centre to the district called Little France, from where the castle is a ten-minute walk along Craigmillar Castle Road.

The southern hills

The **hills** of Edinburgh's southern suburbs offer good, not overly demanding, walking opportunities, with plenty of sweeping panoramic views. The **Royal Observatory** (Mon–Sat 10am–5pm, Sun noon–5pm; £3.50) stands at the top of Blackford Hill, just a short walk south of Morningside, or accessible by buses #24 and #41 direct from the centre. The visitor centre here seeks to explain the mysteries of the solar system by means of various hands-on exhibits and CD-Roms, and you also get to see the observatory's two main telescopes.

At the foot of the hill, the bird sanctuary of Blackford Pond is the starting point for one of the many trails running through the **Hermitage of Braid** local nature reserve, a lovely shady area along the course of the Braid Burn. The castellated eighteenth-century mansion along the burn, after which the reserve is named, now serves as a visitor centre (Mon–Fri 1–4pm, Sun noon–5pm). Immediately to the south are the **Braid Hills**, most of whose area is occupied by two golf courses, which are closed on alternate Sundays in order to allow access for walkers.

Further south are the **Pentland Hills**, a chain some eighteen miles long and five wide. Numerous walks, from gentle strolls along well-marked paths to a ten-mile traverse of the hills and moors, are outlined on a pamphlet available from the Regional Park Information Centre at **FLOTTERSTONE**, ten miles south of the city centre on the A702, an old staging post on the route south. There's been an inn here since the seventeenth century; the present *Flotterstone Inn* is a good spot for a drink or a pub meal after your exertions. The best entry point from within Edinburgh is **SWANSTON**, an unspoiled, highly exclusive hamlet of whitewashed thatched roof dwellings separated from the rest of the city by almost a mile of farmland. **Robert Louis Stevenson** (see box opposite) spent his boyhood summers in Swanston Cottage, the largest of the houses, immortalizing it in the novel *St Ives*. To get a taste of the scenery of the Pentlands, the simplest way is to set off from the car park by the ski centre at **Hillend** at the north-east end of the range; take the path up the right-hand side of the dry ski

Robert Louis Stevenson

Though **Robert Louis Stevenson** (1850–94) is sometimes dismissed for his straight-up writing style, he was undoubtedly one of the best-loved writers of his generation, and one whose travelogues, novels, short stories and essays remain enormously popular a century after his death.

Born in Edinburgh into a distinguished family of engineers, Stevenson was a sickly child, with a solitary childhood dominated by his governess, Alison "Cummie" Cunningham, who regaled him with tales drawn from Calvinist folklore. Sent to the University to study engineering, Stevenson rebelled against his upbringing by spending much of his time in the lowlife howffs and brothels of the city, and eventually switching to law. Although called to the bar in 1875, by then he had decided to channel his energies into literature: while still a student, he had already made his mark as an **essayist** – he eventually had over a hundred essays published, ranging from light-hearted whimsy to trenchant political analysis. A set of topographical pieces about his native city was later collected together as *Edinburgh: Picturesque Notes*, which conjure up nicely its atmosphere, character and appearance – warts and all.

Stevenson's other early successes were two **travelogues**, *An Inland Voyage* and *Travels with a Donkey in the Cevennes*, kaleidoscopic jottings based on his journeys in France, where he went to escape Scotland's weather, which was damaging his health. It was there that he met Fanny Osbourne, an American ten years his senior, who was estranged from her husband and had two children in tow. His voyage to join her in San Francisco formed the basis for his most important factual work, *The Amateur Emigrant*, a vivid first-hand account of the great nineteenth-century European migration to the United States.

Having married the now-divorced Fanny, Stevenson began an elusive search for an agreeable climate that led to Switzerland, the French Riviera and the Scottish Highlands. He belatedly turned to the novel, achieving immediate acclaim in 1881 for **Treasure Island**, a highly moralistic adventure yarn that began as an entertainment for his stepson and future collaborator, Lloyd Osbourne. In 1886, his most famous short story, **Dr Jekyll and Mr Hyde**, despite its nominal London setting, offered a vivid evocation of Edinburgh's Old Town: an allegory of its dual personality of prosperity and squalor, and an analysis of its Calvinistic preoccupations with guilt and damnation. The same year saw the publication of the historical romance **Kidnapped**, an adventure novel which exemplified Stevenson's view that literature should seek above all to entertain.

In 1887 Stevenson left Britain for good, travelling first to the United States where he began one of his most ambitious novels, *The Master of Ballantrae*. A year later, he set sail for the South Seas, and eventually settled in **Samoa**; his last works include a number of stories with a local setting, such as the grimly realistic *The Ebb Tide* and *The Beach of Falesà*. However, Scotland continued to be his main inspiration: he wrote *Catriona* as a sequel to *Kidnapped*, and was at work on two more novels with Scottish settings, *St Ives* and *Weir of Hermiston*, a dark story of father and son confrontation, at the time of his sudden death from a brain haemorrhage in 1894. He was buried on the top of Mount Vaea overlooking the Pacific Ocean.

slopes, turning left shortly after crossing a style to reach a point with outstanding views over Edinburgh and Fife. If you're feeling energetic, the views get even better higher up, and you'll get more of an idea of the unexpected green emptiness of the Pentland range running away to the south. By the **chair lift** for the dry ski slopes (Mon–Fri 1–9pm, Sun 10am–7pm; £1.20) there's a downhill mountain bike course, though with no bike rental facilities at Hillend you'll have to bring a bike here from town. Hillend is connected with the city centre by buses #4 and #15, while the hourly Lowland Omnibus #315 carries on to Flotterstone.

East Lothian

East Lothian consists of the coastal strip and hinterland immediately east of Edinburgh, bounded by the Firth of Forth to the north and the Lammermuir Hills to the south. All of it is within easy day-trip range from the capital though there are places you can stay overnight if you're keen to explore it properly. Often mocked as the "home counties" of Edinburgh, there's no denying its well-ordered feel, with prosperous farms and large estate houses dominating the scenery. The most immediately attractive part of the area is the coastline, extending from **Musselburgh**, all but joined onto Edinburgh, round to **Dunbar**. There's something for most tastes here, including the wide sandy beaches by **Aberlady**, the famous golf course of **Gullane**, the enjoyable Seabird Centre at **North Berwick** which looks out to the volcanic plug of the Bass Rock, and the dramatic – and romantic – clifftop ruins at **Tantallon**. The inland region is often ignored in favour of the coast, or by traffic speeding along the main A1 road from Edinburgh which cuts through the region before turning south for Berwick. At the foot of the Lammermuirs is the county town of **Haddington**, a pleasant enough place, though the attractions nearby of Gifford, a neat village deeper into the hills, or Edinburgh's "local" whisky distillery by Pencaitland, are always likely to be a stronger draw.

Musselburgh to Dirleton

Though strictly the largest town in East Lothian, with a long history connected to the development of mussel beds at the mouth of the River Esk, you're unlikely to linger long at **MUSSELBURGH**, if only for the feeling that you've hardly shaken off the dust of Edinburgh. There is, however, a **race course** here, one of the busiest in Scotland, with a regular programme of decent quality National Hunt and Flat meetings. For details of what's on, contact the course on ⓣ0131/665 2859.

Bypassing the chimneys of the Cockenzie power station, the East Lothian coastline takes a turn for the better by **ABERLADY**, an elongated conservation village of Gothic-style cottages and mansions just sixteen miles east of Edinburgh. The village served as Haddington's port until its river silted up in the sixteenth century, the costly stained-glass windows of the honey-coloured medieval church acting as a reminder of more affluent times. The salt marshes and sand dunes of the adjacent **Aberlady Bay Nature Reserve**, a birdwatchers' haven, mark the site of the old harbour.

From the nature reserve, it's a couple of miles to **GULLANE** (pronounced "Gillin"), the location of the famous shoreline links of **Muirfield Golf Course**, home course of the grandly named Honourable Company of Edinburgh Golfers and venue for the Open Championship in 2002. If golf isn't your thing (there are three other courses around Gullane, not to mention dozens more around East Lothian), you might prefer the fine sandy **beaches** of Gullane Bay or one of the museums which lie inland. A half-mile detour off the Aberlady to Gullane Road takes you to the **Myreton Motor Museum** (Easter–Oct daily 10am–6pm; Nov–Easter daily 10am–5pm; £3), a small stash of vintage cars, motorbikes, military vehicles and motoring memorabilia. A few miles east of this, by East Fortune, the **Museum of Flight** (daily 10.30am–5pm; £3), has over fifty vintage aircraft including a Vulcan bomber, a Comet airliner, a Spitfire and a Tigermoth packed into old World War II hangars. Nearby, in the hamlet of Athelstaneford, an old church houses the **National Flag Heritage Centre** (April–Sept daily 10am–5pm; free) tracing the history of Scotland's national flag, the white St Andrew's Cross on a blue background.

Two miles east of Gullane lies the genteel hamlet of **DIRLETON**, where a pair of triangular greens are bordered by tastefully refurbished cottages with thriving gardens. **Dirleton Castle** (daily: April–Sept 9.30am–6.30pm; Oct–March 9.30am–4.30pm; HS; £2.80) is a romantic thirteenth-century ruin with gardens, leading to a volcanic knoll crowned by Cromwell-shattered ruins. Scrambling round the castle is fun, and if the weather's good you can take the mile-long path from the village church to the sandy, rock-framed beach at **Yellowcraigs**, which overlooks **Fidra Island**, a large lump of basalt that's home to thousands of (noisy) seabirds. Also near the beach, the *Yellowcraig Caravan Club Site* (Ⓣ01620/850217; April–Oct), with pleasant woodland walks to the shore, is the only budget place to **stay**; the splendid *Open Arms Hotel* opposite the castle (Ⓣ01620/850241, Ⓔopenarms@clara.co.uk; ❼), on the other hand, has every luxury, including a fantastic restaurant serving moderate to expensive food from a varied and imaginative menu. Across the green, the *Castle Inn* (Ⓣ01620/850221; ❸), an old coaching inn, serves decent afternoon teas from 3pm to 5pm on Sundays.

North Berwick

NORTH BERWICK has a great deal of charm and a somewhat faded, old-fashioned air, its guesthouses and hotels extending along the shore in all their Victorian and Edwardian sobriety. The town's small harbour is set on a headland which cleaves two crescents of sand, providing the town with an attractive coastal setting, though its the two nearby volcanic heaps, the **Bass Rock** and **North Berwick Law**, which are the town's defining physical features. The Bass Rock, home to some 100,000 nesting gannets in summer, is closely watched from North Berwick's principal attraction, the Scottish Seabird Centre, located by the harbour. The small **museum** on School Road (April–Oct daily 11am–5pm; free), housed in the old school house, displays local curios including the old town stocks.

Little now remains of the original medieval town, but the fragmentary ruins of the **Auld Kirk**, next to the harbour, bear witness to one of the most extraordinary events of sixteenth-century Scotland. In 1590, while **King James VI** spent the summer in Denmark wooing his prospective wife, the **Earl of Bothwell**, Francis Stuart, was plotting against him. On hearing of the king's imminent return, Bothwell, a keen practitioner of the "black arts", summoned the witches of Lothian to meet the Devil in the Auld Kirk. Bothwell turned up disguised as the Devil and instructed his 200 acolytes to raise a storm that would shipwreck the king. To cast the spell, they opened a few graves and engaged in a little flagellation before kissing the bare buttocks of the "Devil" – reportedly "as cold as ice and as hard as iron" as it hung over the pulpit. Despite these shenanigans, the king returned safely – when rumours reached him of Bothwell's treachery he refused to believe them, and the earl went unpunished, possibly because James was reassured by his failure. After all, if the Devil himself was unable to harm him, he must surely be blessed by God, a belief the monarch was later to elaborate as the "Divine Right of Kings".

Scottish Seabird Centre and the Bass Rock

Located in an attractively designed new building by the harbour, the **Scottish Seabird Centre** (daily: April–Oct 10am–6pm; Nov–March 10am–4pm; £4.50, family tickets from £12.50) opened in 2000, and offers an introduction to all types of seabird found around the Scottish coast, particularly the 100,000-plus gannets and puffins which nest on the Bass Rock every summer. Such is the connection between the rock and its annual visitors that the gannet, once known as the solan goose, takes its Latin name, *Morus bassana*, from the Bass Rock. Thanks to a live link from the centre to cameras mounted on the volcanic island, you're able to view close-up pictures of the birds in their nesting grounds. At each of three different screens there are controls which allow you to zoom in, or pan over the rock and out to sea, where you can normally see the gannets diving spectacularly in pursuit of fish. At different times of year the cameras are mounted in different locations, depending on the movement of birds – in winter, for example, the gannets aren't around so it's more interesting to watch the shore birds or some peregrine falcons which have nested on Fidra Island. Elsewhere in the centre, hands-on games and exhibits explain more about different seabirds, and a mock-up of a cliff face has various stuffed birds nesting on it – all the birds, the centre insists, have been ethically gathered.

Resembling a giant molar, the **Bass Rock** rises 350ft above the sea some three miles east of North Berwick. This massive chunk of basalt has had an interesting history, having held out as a Jacobite stronghold for six years longer than anywhere else in the country, then served as a prison, a fortress and a monastic retreat. The last lighthouse keepers left in 1988, leaving it, quite literally, to the birds – its Scotland's second-largest gannet colony after St Kilda but also hosts razorbills, terns, puffins, guillemots and fulmars. If you're not content with viewing the birds on the video link-up in the Seabird Centre, there are, weather permitting, **boat trips** round the island from North Berwick harbour (Easter to Sept daily; £5) – contact Fred Marr on *Sula* (ⓣ01620/892838).

North Berwick Law

The other volcanic monolith, 613ft-high **North Berwick Law**, which dominates the Lothian landscape for miles around, is about an hour's walk from the beach (take Law Road off High Street and follow the signs). On a clear day, the views out across the Firth of Forth, Fife and the Lammermuirs make the effort worthwhile, and at the top you can see the remains of a Napoleonic watchtower and an arch made from the jawbone of a whale.

Practicalities

North Berwick is served by a regular half-hour **train** from Edinburgh Waverley, with special travel and entry deals available for those heading for the Seabird Centre (ask at Waverley ticket office). From the station it's a ten-minute walk east to the town centre along Abbey Road, Westgate and High Street. **Buses** from Edinburgh (every 30min) run along the coast via Aberlady, Gullane and Dirleton and stop on High Street, while the hourly service from Haddington and Dunbar terminates outside the **tourist office**, on Quality Street (April & May Mon–Sat 9am–6pm; June & Sept Mon–Sat 9am–6pm, Sun 11am–4pm; July Mon–Sat 9am–7pm, Sun 11am–6pm; Aug Mon–Sat 9am–8pm, Sun 11am–6pm; Oct–March Mon–Sat 9am–5pm; ⓣ01620/892197).

As befits a well-to-do holiday resort, there are several excellent **B&Bs**, including *Windrow*, at 20 Marmion Rd (ⓣ01620/892066; ❷; April–Sept), a Victorian house within easy walking distance of the sea, and *Tantallon House* at 2 West Bay Rd (ⓣ01620/892873; ❸; April–Oct), next to the golf course while *Glebe House*, Law Road (ⓣ01620/892608; ❹), is a beautiful eighteenth-century manse in secluded grounds overlooking the sea. Of the **guesthouses**, the seafront *Craigview*, 5 Beach Rd (ⓣ01620/892257; ④), has four-poster beds and serves good vegetarian breakfasts. The nearest **campsite**, *Tantallon Caravan Park* (ⓣ01620/893348, ⓔTantallonP@aol.com; March–Oct), occupies a prime clifftop location a couple of miles east of the centre – take the Dunbar bus (Mon–Sat 6 daily, Sun 2 daily).

One of the best **cafés** in town is at the Seabird Centre, which has panoramic views over the beach. As well as lunches, coffees and cakes, it's also open as a **bistro** in the evenings (May–Sept Wed–Sat; for bookings and winter opening hours call ⓣ01620/893342). In town, the *Grange* at 35 High St (ⓣ01620/893344; closed Mon) is a pleasant restaurant serving good quality, moderately priced meals, while both the *Tantallon Inn* on Marine Parade and the *Marine Hotel* on Cromwell Road do decent bar food.

Tantallon Castle

The melodramatic ruins of **Tantallon Castle** (April–Sept daily 9.30am–6.30pm; Oct–March Mon–Wed & Sat 9.30am–4.30pm, Thurs 9.30am–noon, Fri & Sun 2–4.30pm; HS; £2.80), three miles east of North Berwick on the A198, stand on the precipitous cliffs facing the Bass Rock. With a sheer drop down to the sea on three sides and a sequence of moats and ditches on the fourth, the castle's desolate invincibility is daunting, especially when the wind howls over the remaining battlements and the surf crashes on the rocks far below. Built at the end of the fourteenth century, the castle was a stronghold of the Douglases, the Earls of Angus, one of the most powerful noble families in Scotland. A Douglas had been regent early in the reign of James II and guardian to James IV, while another had married James IV's widow, Margaret Tudor – their grandson was Lord Darnley, second husband of Mary, Queen of Scots and father of James VI (James I of England).

Besieged several times, the castle was finally destroyed by Cromwell in 1651 after a twelve-day bombardment. The ruins, including a seventeenth-century dovecote left untouched by Cromwell's men, enjoy a wonderfully photogenic setting, with the Bass Rock and the Firth of Forth in the background. You can reach Tantallon Castle from North Berwick by the Dunbar **bus** (Mon–Sat 6 daily, Sun 2 daily), which takes fifteen minutes, or you can walk there from town along the cliffs in around an hour.

Dunbar

Twelve miles further along the coast lies **DUNBAR**, which bears some resemblance to North Berwick with its wide, recently spruced-up High Street graced by several grand old stone buildings. One of the oldest is the **Town House** (April–Oct daily 12.30–4.30pm; free), formerly a prison and now home to a small archeology room and local-history centre. Of greater significance is the three-storey **John Muir House**, 128 High St (call ⓣ01368/860187 for opening hours; free), birthplace of the explorer and naturalist who created the United States national park system. Recently refurbished, the house now acts as an interpretative and education centre inspired by the pioneer's life and legacy. A more appropriate tribute, in some respects, is the **country park** in Muir's honour, where an easy three-mile walk west of the harbour takes you along a rugged stretch of coast to the sands of Belhaven Bay.

The delightfully intricate double **harbour** merits a stroll, with its narrow channels, cobbled quays and roughened rocks, set beside the shattered remains of the castle. The town's one other claim to fame is as the home of **Belhaven**

beers, which are still made on the original site of the monks' brewery, signposted off the Edinburgh road (guided tours can be arranged for groups; phone ⓣ01368/864488 for details).

The **tourist office**, 143 High St (May Mon–Sat 9am–6pm, Sun 11am–4pm; June, July & Sept Mon–Sat 9am–7pm, Sun 11am–4pm; Aug Mon–Sat 9am–8pm, Sun 11am–6pm; Oct–April Mon–Sat 9am–5pm; ⓣ01368/863353) will help with **accommodation**; try the pleasant bay-windowed *Overcliffe Guest House*, 11 Bayswell Park (ⓣ01368/864004; ❸), a short walk west from the castle, or the non-smoking *Woodside* B&B, 13 North St (ⓣ01368/862384; ❶; April–Oct). The nearest **campsite** is *Belhaven Bay Caravan and Camping Park*, in the John Muir Park, just off the A1087 (ⓣ01368/865956; March–Oct), while the Camping and Caravanning Club maintain a site at *Barns Ness*, off the A1 (ⓣ01368/863536; March–Oct).

For a light **lunch**, the *Food Hamper* and *William Smith's* on the High Street do good sandwiches, while the best evening meal options are the *Creel* (ⓣ01368/863279) by the old harbour, where you can eat steaks and seafood, including a speciality Jamaican seafood dish served with bananas, or *Cuckoo Wrasse* (ⓣ01368/865384), also by the harbour at 1 Shore Street, which serves rather pricey seafood dishes in a bistro-style setting.

Haddington

The East Lothian gentry keep a careful eye on **HADDINGTON**, their favourite country town. Its compact centre preserves an intriguing ensemble of seventeenth- to nineteenth-century architectural styles where everything of any interest has been labelled and plaqued. Yet the town's staid appearance belies a long history of innovation. During the early 1700s, Haddington became a byword for modernization as its merchants supplied the district's progressive landowners with all sorts of new-fangled equipment, stock and seed, and in only a few decades utterly transformed Lothian agriculture.

The Town

Haddington's centre is best approached from the west, where tree-trimmed **Court Street** ends suddenly with the soaring spire, stately stonework and dignified Venetian windows of the **Town House**, designed by William Adam in 1748. Close by, to the right and next door to a fine Italianate facade, the **Jane Welsh Carlyle House** (April–Sept Wed–Sat 2–5pm; £1.50) was the childhood home of the wife of essayist and historian Thomas Carlyle (see p.187). The dining room – the only part of the house open to the public – has been restored to its early nineteenth-century appearance and sports pictures of the influential personalities of the day, while the lovely garden is pretty much as Jane would have known it.

Heading east from the town centre along High Street, it's a brief walk down Church Street – past the hooped arches of **Nungate Bridge** – to the hulking mass of **St Mary's Church** (April–Sept Mon–Sat 11am–4pm, Sun 1–4.30pm; free), Scotland's largest parish church. Built close to the reedy River Tyne, the church dates from the fourteenth century but it's a real hotch-potch of styles, the squat grey tower uneasy above clumsy buttressing and pinkish-ochre stone walls. Inside, on the **Lauderdale Aisle**, a munificent tomb features the best of Elizabethan alabaster carving, moustached knights and their ruffed ladies lying beneath a finely ornamented canopy. In stark contrast, a plain slab in the choir is inscribed with Thomas Carlyle's beautiful tribute to his wife, "Suddenly snatched away from him, and the light of his life as if gone out." The church also offers brass rubbing, has a good tearoom and in the summer hosts internationally acclaimed concerts organized by the Lamp of Lothian Collegiate Trust (call ☎01620/823738 or 824609 for details). At nearby Haddington House, on Sidegate, the seventeenth-century medicinal gardens of **St Mary's Pleasance** (open during daylight hours; free) merit a brief stroll.

Practicalities

Fast and frequent **buses** connect Haddington with Edinburgh, fifteen miles to the west, and with North Berwick on the east coast, with all services stopping on High Street. There's no **tourist office**, but orientation is easy and *A Walk Around Haddington* (£1), detailing every building of any conceivable consequence, is available from local newsagents.

The *Plough Tavern*, 11 Court St (☎01620/823326; ❷), is a welcoming traditional **inn** right in the town centre. Alternatively, try the more luxurious *Brown's Hotel*, 1 West Rd (☎01620/822254; ❻), occupying a fine Regency town house. *Monks' Muir Caravan Park* (☎01620/860340), which takes its environmental credentials very seriously, is on the eastern edge of town by the A1, and also takes tents.

For **daytime snacks** and lovely deli lunch platters, the place to seek out is *Jaques & Lawrence* at 37 Court St, opposite the post office. The best place for an **evening meal** is the *Waterside Bistro* (☎01620/825674), on the far side of Nungate Bridge, justifiably popular for its delicious seafood and varied vegetarian dishes. Alternatively, try *Poldrate's Restaurant* (☎01620/826882) at Poldrate Mill on Gifford Road, where the menu changes daily, or the restaurant at *Brown's Hotel*, though you'll need to book in advance. Decent bar meals are available at the *Victoria Inn* in Court Street, while real-ale fans should head to *The Pheasant* in Poldrate, rumoured to serve the best pint in East Lothian.

Around Haddington

A thorough exploration of Haddington will only take two or three hours, but there are several other attractions in its vicinity. A mile south of Haddington, **Lennoxlove House** (June–Oct Wed, Thurs, Sat & Sun 2–4.30pm; £4), a sprawling pile incorporating a medieval tower house, displays a splendid fine- and applied-art collection belonging to the Duke of Hamilton. An hour-long tour takes in portraits of the family, French furniture, porcelain and damask wall hangings, with the highlight being the death mask of Mary, Queen of Scots, and a silver casket in which she kept the letters that allegedly proved her involvement in Darnley's murder.

A further three miles south along the B6369 on the edge of the Lammermuir Hills, the pretty hamlet of **Gifford**, whose eighteenth-century estate cottages edge a trim whitewashed church, was the birthplace (in 1723) of the Reverend John Witherspoon, a signatory of the American Declaration of Independence. The hamlet makes a good base for walkers, with several footpaths setting out across the surrounding red-soiled farmland for the Lammermuir Hills, while longer trails connect with the Southern Upland Way. If you want **to stay**, try the traditional *Tweeddale Arms* (☎01620/810240; ❹), which has a fine **restaurant**, or *Eaglescairne Mains* (☎01620/810491; ❹), a substantial farmhouse with open fires and a tennis court. You can also eat at the *Goblin Ha Hotel*, Main Street (☎01620/810244), which has a wonderful beer garden and serves excellent healthy country fare. Alternatively you may prefer to make up a picnic from the deli-style *Little Bread Shop* opposite the green.

Glenkinchie Distillery

Six miles west of Gifford, and about the same distance from Haddington along the A6093, the village of Pencaitland is the closest place to Edinburgh where malt whisky is made. Set in a peaceful dip in the rolling countryside about two miles outside Pencaitland, the **Glenkinchie Distillery** (June–Oct Mon–Sat 9.30am–5pm, Sun noon–5pm; Nov–Feb Mon–Fri 11am–4pm; March–May Mon–Fri 10am–5pm; £3.50) is one of only a handful found in the Lowlands of Scotland. Here, of course, they emphasise the qualities which set Glenkinchie, a lighter, drier malt, apart from the peaty, smoky whiskies of the north. Also in the tour there's an impressive scale model of a distillery, allowing you to place all the different processes in context, and a room where the art of blending is explained.

Midlothian

Immediately south of Edinburgh lies the old county of **MIDLOTHIAN**, once called Edinburghshire. It's one of the hilliest parts of the Central Lowlands, with the Pentland chain running down its western side, and the Moorfoots defining its boundary with the Borders to the south. Though predominantly rural, it contains a belt of former mining communities, which are struggling to come to terms with the recent decline of the industry. Such charms as it has are mostly low-key, with the exception of the riotously ornate chapel at **Roslin**.

Dalkeith and around

Despite its Victorian demeanour, **DALKEITH**, eight miles southeast of central Edinburgh – to which it is linked by very regular buses (#3, #30, #82) – grew up in the Middle Ages as a baronial burgh under the successive control of the Douglases and Buccleuchs. Today it's a bustling shopping centre, with an unusually broad High Street at its heart.

At the far end of the street is the entrance to **Dalkeith Country Park** (April–Oct daily 10am–6pm; £2), the estate of the Dukes of Buccleuch, whose seat, the early eighteenth-century **Dalkeith Palace**, can only be seen from the outside. You can, however, visit its one-time chapel, now the Episcopalian parish church of **St Mary**, adorned inside with extremely rich furnishings. Further north, Robert Adam's **Montagu Bridge** straddles the River North Esk in a graceful arch; beyond are some derelict but once wonderfully grandiose garden follies. There is also a large woodland playground, suitable for all but the youngest children.

A mile or so south of Dalkeith is **NEWTONGRANGE**, whose Lady Victoria Colliery is now open to the public as the **Scottish Mining Museum** (daily: Feb–Oct 10am–5pm, Nov–Jan 11am–4pm; £4, family tickets from £10), with a 1625-foot shaft, and a winding tower powered by Scotland's largest steam engine. A great place for kids, the visitor centre brings the mine and the local community to life with "magic helmets", which enable you to go on shift and experience a virtual-reality tour of life below ground.

Roslin

The tranquil village of **ROSLIN** lies seven miles south of the centre of Edinburgh, from where it can be reached by bus #87A or by regular Eastern

Scottish services from St Andrew Square. An otherwise nondescript place, the village has two unusual claims to fame: it was near here, at the Roslin Institute, that the world's first cloned sheep, Dolly, was created in 1997; and it also boasts the mysterious, richly decorated late-Gothic **Rosslyn Chapel** (Mon–Sat 10am–5pm, Sun noon–4.45pm; £4). Only the choir, Lady Chapel and part of the transepts were built of what was intended to be a huge collegiate church dedicated to St Matthew: construction halted soon after the founder's death in 1484, and the vestry built onto the facade nearly four hundred years later is the sole subsequent addition. After a long period of neglect, a massive restoration project has recently been undertaken: a canopy has been placed over the chapel which will remain in place for several years in order to dry out the saturated ceiling and walls, and other essential repairs are due to be carried out within the chapel.

The outside of the chapel bristles with pinnacles, gargoyles, flying buttresses and canopies, while inside the foliage carving is particularly outstanding, with botanically accurate depictions of over a dozen different leaves and plants. Among them are cacti and Indian corn, providing fairly convincing evidence that the founder's grandfather, the daring sea adventurer Prince Henry of Orkney, did indeed, as legend has it, set foot in the New World a century before Columbus. The rich and subtle figurative sculptures have given Rosslyn the nickname of "a Bible in stone", though they're more allegorical than literal, with portrayals of the Dance of Death, the Seven Acts of Mercy and the Seven Deadly Sins.

The greatest and most original carving of all is the extraordinary knotted **Prentice Pillar** at the southeastern corner of the Lady Chapel. According to local legend, the pillar was made by an apprentice during the absence of the master mason, who killed him in a fit of jealousy on seeing the finished work. A tiny head of a man with a slashed forehead, set at the apex of the ceiling at the far northwestern corner of the building, is popularly supposed to represent the apprentice, his murderer the corresponding head at the opposite side. The entwined dragons at the foot are symbols of Satan, and were probably inspired by Norse mythology.

A number of books have been published in recent years about Rosslyn Chapel, drawing on everything from Freemasons and the Turin Shroud to the True Gospels and the regular sightings of UFOs over Midlothian. Conspiracy theories notwithstanding, the chapel is very definitely worth a visit.

West Lothian

To many, West Lothian is a poor relative to the rolling, rich farmland of East and Midlothian, with a landscape dominated by motorways, industrial estates and giant hillocks of ochre-coloured mine waste called "bings". However, anywhere this close to the centres of power through Scottish history would find it hard not to have something to show for itself, and in the ruined royal palace at **Linlithgow** the area boasts one of Scotland's more magnificent ruins. There's some interesting industrial heritage, too, including the prettiest stretch of the recently upgraded **Union Canal**, and the restored railway at **Bo'ness**, a popular family attraction. Although strictly no longer part of West Lothian, the village of **South Queensferry** is only a few miles east of Bo'ness. An interesting enough place in its own right, it lies under the considerable shadow of the **Forth rail and road bridges**. A mile or two beyond South Queensferry is **Hopetoun House**, an impressive stately home.

Linlithgow

Roughly equidistant (fifteen miles) from Falkirk and Edinburgh is the ancient royal burgh of **LINLITHGOW**. The town itself has largely kept its medieval layout, but development since the 1960s has sadly stripped it of some fine buildings, notably close to the **Town Hall** and **Cross** – the former marketplace – on the long High Street.

Though hidden from the main street, **Linlithgow Palace** (April–Sept daily 9.30am–6.30pm; Oct–March Mon–Sat 9.30am–4.30pm, Sun 2–4.30pm; HS; £2.80), is a splendid fifteenth-century ruin romantically set on the edge of Linlithgow Loch and associated with some of Scotland's best-known historical figures – including Mary, Queen of Scots, who was born here in on 8 December 1542 and became queen six days later. A royal manor house is believed to have existed on this site since the time of David I. Fire razed the manor in 1424, after which James I began construction of the present palace, a process that continued through two centuries and the reign of no fewer than eight monarchs. From the top of the northwest tower, Queen Margaret looked out in vain for the return of James IV from the field of Flodden in 1513 – indeed, the views from her bower, six giddy storeys up from the ground, are exceptional. The ornate octagonal **fountain** in the inner courtyard, with its wonderfully intricate figures and medallion heads, flowed with wine for the wedding of James V and Mary of Guise. Bonnie Prince Charlie visited during the 1745 rebellion, and a year later the palace was burnt, probably accidentally, whilst occupied by General Hawley's troops.

This is a great place to take children: the rooflessness of the castle creates unexpected vistas and the elegant, the bare rooms echo with footsteps and the fluttering of birds flying out through the empty windows, and there's a labyrinthine feel to the place with spiral staircases and endless nooks and crannies. The galleried **Great Hall** is magnificent, as is the adjoining kitchen, which has a truly cavernous fireplace. Don't miss the dank downstairs **brewery**, which produced vast quantities of ale; 24 gallons was apparently a good nightly consumption in the sixteenth century.

St Michael's Church, adjacent to the palace, is one of Scotland's largest pre-Reformation churches, consecrated in the thirteenth century. The present building was completed three hundred years later, with the exception of the hugely incongruous aluminium spire, tacked on in 1946. Inside, decorative woodcarving around the pulpit depicts queens Margaret, Mary and Victoria.

A foil to the romantic historicism of the palace, the **Linlithgow Story**, 143 High St (April–Oct Mon–Sat 10am–5pm, Sun 1–4pm; £1), tries to recreate the town's transition from royal burgh via industrial centre to suburban backwater with videos and life-sized models. The second floor looks at local industries from paper mills to tanneries, where, it is said, the use of materials derived from animals was so efficient that "only the moo was left".

Running through Linlithgow is part of the **Union Canal**, the 31-mile artery opened in 1822, which together with the Forth & Clyde Canal linked Edinburgh with Glasgow. At Falkirk, ten miles west of here, the incredible Falkirk Wheel (see p.310) transfers boats from one canal to the other. On summer weekend afternoons the Linlithgow Union Canal Society runs short trips on the *Victoria* (£2.50), a diesel-powered replica of a Victorian steam packet boat, and longer trips to the splendid Avon Aqueduct on the *St Magdalene*, an electric canal boat (Ⓣ01506/843194; £6). The boats depart from the Manse Road canal basin, uphill from the train station at the southern end of town, where the small Linlithgow Canal Centre (Easter–Oct Sat & Sun 2–5pm) is also located. An eighteen-mile walk along the canal towpath leads eventually to the centre of Edinburgh.

Practicalities

Frequent **buses** between Stirling and Edinburgh stop at the Cross, and the town is on the main train routes from Edinburgh to both Glasgow Queen Street and Stirling; the **train station** lies at the southern end of town. The **tourist office** is in the Town Hall building at the Cross (April–Sept daily 10am–5pm; ⓣ01506/844600), between the Palace and the High Street.

For **accommodation** try *The Star and Garter*, 1 High St (ⓣ01506/846362; ❸), at the east end of town, a comfortable old coaching inn that serves inexpensive bar meals. Victorian *Pardovan House* is an excellent **B&B** (ⓣ01506/834219; ❷; April–Sept) at Philipstoun, a couple of miles west of Linlithgow, or you could try friendly *Belsyde Farm*, Lanark Road (ⓣ01506/842098; ❶), a late-eighteenth-century house on a sheep and cattle farm beside the Union Canal.

There are a few decent places to **eat** in Linlithgow: for good pub food try *The Four Marys*, opposite the Cross on High Street, which also has real ales or, for more expensive Scottish cuisine, *Livingston's* (ⓣ01506/846565), through an arch at 52 High Street, serves upmarket, expensive meals in a small garden observatory, while *Marynka* (ⓣ01506/840123), also on the High Street at number 57, is a brighter, more modern bistro-style place. Best of the lot is a place just outside Linlithgow on the way to Blackness called the *Champany Inn* (ⓣ01506/834532), which serves delicious steaks, chops and seafood.

The only official **campsite** in the area is at *Beecraigs Caravan Park* (ⓣ01506/844516), about four miles south of town and part of the larger Beecraigs Country Park. There are only 39 pitches, however, so get there early or phone first.

Around Linlithgow

The small hillside town of **BO'NESS**, roughly four miles north of Linlithgow – which has traditionally looked down its nose at its pint-sized neighbour – sprawls in a less than genteel fashion down to the Forth, where a riverside path is separated from the road by a strip of scrub. On a clear day there are good views across the Forth to Culross (see p.327). The **Bo'ness and Kinneil Railway**, whose headquarters are in the old station at the eastern end of the waterfront road, is Scotland's largest vintage train centre with half a dozen sheds full of locomotives, carriages, wagons and so on. In summer (July & Aug Tues–Sun; April–Oct Sat & Sun; ⓣ01506/822298) it runs lovingly kept steam trains to Birkhill, just over three miles away (£4.50 return). Here you can wander along the wooded Avon Gorge, or take a guided tour through the **Birkhill Fireclay Mine** (four tours a day coincide with train times; £3), where 300 million-year-old fossils line the walls.

Further down the coast from Bo'ness and four miles northeast of Linlithgow, boldly positioned on a rocky promontory in the Forth, lies the village of **BLACKNESS**, once Linlithgow's seaport and location of the dramatic fourteenth-century **Blackness Castle** (April–Sept daily 9.30am–6.30pm; Oct–March Mon–Wed & Sat 9.30am–4.30pm, Thurs 9.30am–noon, Fri & Sun 2–4.30pm; HS; £2), which, after the Treaty of Union in 1707, was one of only four castles in Scotland to be garrisoned. Built in the shape of a galleon, the castle, which was used as one of the location shots for Mel Gibson's film version of *Hamlet*, offers grand views of the Forth bridges from the narrow gun slits in its northern tower.

General Tam Dalyell, the seventeenth-century Scottish royalist, spent part of his youth at the **House of the Binns** (May–Sept daily except Fri 1.30–5pm; grounds open year-round 10am–dusk; NTS; £4), occupying a hilltop site about a mile inshore from Blackness and three miles east of Linlithgow. Today it's the home of the veteran Labour MP Tam Dalyell, a regular thorn in the flesh of governments of all hues and the man who first articulated the West Lothian Question (see p.774), which has troubled politicians in Edinburgh and London ever since. Inside you can see ornate plaster ceilings, paintings, period furniture and family relics not much changed since (the original) Tam's day.

South Queensferry and around

Less than a mile of countryside separates Dalmeny from **SOUTH QUEENSFERRY**, a compact little town used by St Margaret as a crossing point for her frequent trips between her palaces in Edinburgh and Dunfermline. The **High Street**, squeezed into the narrow gap between the seashore and the hillside above, is lined by a picturesque array of old buildings, among them an unusual two-tiered row of shops, the roofs of the lower level serving as the walkway for the upper storey. The small **museum**, 53 High St (Mon & Thurs–Sat 10am–1pm & 2.15–5pm, Sun noon–5pm; free), contains relics of the town's history and information on the building of the two bridges which loom over the village. A dedicated museum to the bridge can be found in North Queensferry (see p.331), while the best way to get a good view of the magnificent Rail Bridge is to walk (or cycle) across the Road Bridge.

Inchcolm

From South Queensferry's Hawes Pier, just west of the rail bridge, pleasure boats (Easter, May & June Sat & Sun; July to mid-Sept daily; confirm sailing in advance on ⓣ0131/331 4857; £10) head out onto the Forth in the direction of the island of **Inchcolm**, whose beautiful ruined **Abbey** was founded in 1123 by King Alexander I in gratitude for the hospitality he received from a hermit (whose cell survives at the northwestern corner of the island) when his ship was forced ashore in a storm. The best-preserved medieval monastic complex in Scotland, the abbey's surviving buildings date from the thirteenth to the fifteenth centuries, and include a splendid octagonal chapterhouse. Although the church is almost totally dilapidated, its tower can be ascended for a great aerial view of the island, which is populated by a variety of nesting birds and a colony of grey seals. The pier here is a pick up point for *Sea.fari* (ⓣ0131/331 5000) which also operates out of Newhaven harbour (see p.136), taking high-speed wildlife-spotting trips out past Inchcolm and round various other islands in the estuary.

Hopetoun House

Immediately beyond the western edge of South Queensferry, just over the West Lothian border, **Hopetoun House** (April–Sept daily 10am–5.30pm; £5.30 house and grounds, £2.90 grounds only) is one of Scotland's grandest stately homes. The original house was built at the turn of the eighteenth century for the first Earl of Hopetoun by Sir William Bruce, the architect of Holyroodhouse. A couple of decades later, William Adam carried out an enormous extension, engulfing the house in a curvaceous main facade and two projecting wings – superb examples of Roman Baroque pomp and swagger. The scale and lavishness of the Adam interiors, most of whose decoration was carried out by his sons after the architect's death, make for a stark contrast with the intimacy of those designed by Bruce. Particularly impressive are the Red and Yellow Drawing Rooms, with their splendid ceilings by the young Robert Adam. Among the house's furnishings are seventeenth-century tapestries, Meissen porcelain, and a distinguished collection of paintings, including portraits by Gainsborough, Ramsay and Raeburn. The grounds of Hopetoun House are also open, with magnificent walks along the banks of the Forth and great opportunities for picnics.

Travel details

Trains

Edinburgh to: Aberdeen (hourly; 2hr 40min); Birmingham (6 daily; 5hr 30min); Dunbar (hourly; 30min); Dundee (hourly; 1hr 45min); Falkirk (every 30min; 25min); Fort William (change at Glasgow, 3 daily; 4hr 55min); Glasgow (2–4 hourly; 50min); Inverness (4 daily; 3hr 50min); London (20 daily; 4hr 30min); Manchester (direct, 4 daily; 4hr; change at Preston, 7 daily; 4hr); Newcastle-upon-Tyne (27 daily; 1hr 30min); North Berwick (hourly; 30 min); Oban (3 daily, change at Glasgow; 4hr 10min); Perth (6 daily; 1hr 15min); Stirling (every 30min; 45min); York (24 daily; 2hr 30min).

Buses

Edinburgh (St Andrew Square) to: Aberdeen (22 daily; express 3hr, standard 3hr 50min); Birmingham (2 daily; 6hr 50min); Dundee (22 daily; express 1hr 25min–2hr); Fort William (4 daily direct; 4hr); Glasgow (every 30min; 1hr 10min); Inverness (13 daily; 3–4hr); London (6 daily; 7hr 50min); Newcastle-upon-Tyne (3 daily; 3hr 15min); Oban (3 daily; 5hr); Perth (21 daily; 1hr 20min); York (1 daily; 5hr).

Flights

Edinburgh to: Dublin (Mon–Fri 5 daily, Sat & Sun 4 daily; 1hr); Kirkwall (Mon–Sat 1 daily; 1hr 20min); Lerwick (1 daily; 1hr 30min); London City (Mon–Fri 16 daily, Sat 1, Sun 6 daily; 1hr 15min); London Gatwick (Mon–Fri 6 daily, Sat & Sun 4 daily; 1hr 15min); London Heathrow (Mon–Fri 20 daily, Sat & Sun 15 daily; 1hr); London Luton (Mon–Fri 6, Sat & Sun 4 daily; 1hr 20min); London Stansted (Mon–Fri 8 daily, Sat & Sun 4–6 daily; 1hr 10min); Stornoway (Mon–Fri 1 daily; 1hr 10 min).

Southern Scotland

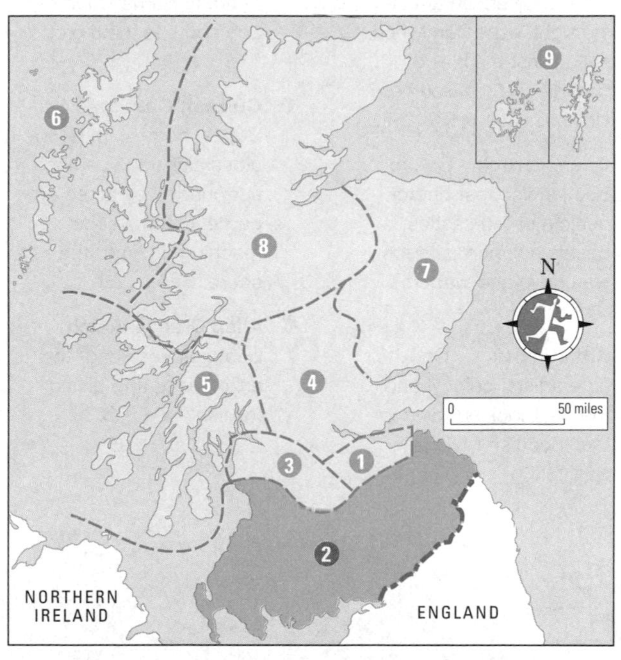

CHAPTER 2 Highlights

* **Melrose Abbey** – The Border Abbey with the best-preserved sculptural detail, set within most charming of the Border towns. See p.171

* **Samye Ling Monastery** – The golden domes of Eskdalemuir's Tibetan monastery are an arresting sight, especially when set against the bleak backdrop of the Southern Uplands. See p.189

* **Caerlaverock** – One of Scotland's most photogenic moated castles, beside a superb site for waterfowl and waders. See p.195

* **Kirkcudbright** – One-time artists' colony, and the best-looking town in the "Scottish Riviera". See p.203

* **Galloway Forest Park** – Go mountain biking along remote forest tracks, or hiking on the Southern Upland Way. See p.208

* **Alloway** – The village where poet Robert Burns was born, and the best of many Burns' pilgrimage spots in the region. See p.219

* **Culzean Castle** – Stately home with a fabulous cliff-edge setting, surrounded by acres of gardens and woods reaching down to the shore. See p.221

* **Ailsa Craig** – Watch baby gannets learn the art of flying and diving for fish. See p.223

2

Southern Scotland

Southern Scotland divides neatly into three distinct regions: the Borders, Dumfries and Galloway, and Ayrshire. Although none of the regions has the highest of tourist profiles, those visitors who whizz past on their way to Edinburgh, Glasgow or the Highlands are missing out on a huge swathe of Scotland that is in many ways the very heart of the country. Its inhabitants, particularly in the Borders, bore the brunt of long wars with the English, its farms have fed Scotland's cities since industrialization, and two of the country's literary icons, Sir Walter Scott and Robbie Burns, lived and died here.

Geographically, the region is dominated by the **Southern Uplands**, a chain of bulging round-topped hills and weather-beaten moorland, punctuated by narrow glens, fast-flowing rivers and blue-black lochs. This region is at its most dramatic in the **Galloway Forest Park** to the southwest, with peaks reaching to over 2000ft, crisscrossed by numerous popular walking trails. Back in the valleys, and down by the coast, the landscape is fairly lush – farming country for the most part, with tourism an important, but secondary, industry. On the coast, you'll find enormous variety: the east coast is fairly bleak, with dramatic cliffs interspersed with tiny fishing villages; the **Solway coast**, in the southwest, is much gentler, indented by sandy coves and estuaries; while the Ayrshire coast, by contrast, is much more heavily populated, and in parts an almost continuous stretch of seaside resorts and industrial centres.

Lying north of the inhospitable Cheviot Hills, which separate Scotland from England, the **Borders** region is dominated by the meanderings of the **River Tweed**. None of the towns along the Tweed is of any great size, yet they have provided inspiration for countless folkloric ballads telling of bloody battles with the English and clashes between the notorious warring families, the Border Reivers (see box on p.167). The small but delightful town of **Melrose**,

Accommodation price codes

Throughout this book, accommodation **prices** have been graded with the codes below, corresponding to the cost of the least expensive double room in high season. Price codes are not given for **campsites**, most of which charge less than £10 per person. Almost all **hostels** and **bunkhouses** charge between £8 and £12 per person per night; the few exceptions to this rule have the prices quoted in the text. For a full account of these codes, see p.28.

❶ under £40	❹ £60–70	❼ £110–150
❷ £40–50	❺ £70–90	❽ £150–200
❸ £50–60	❻ £90–110	❾ £200 and over

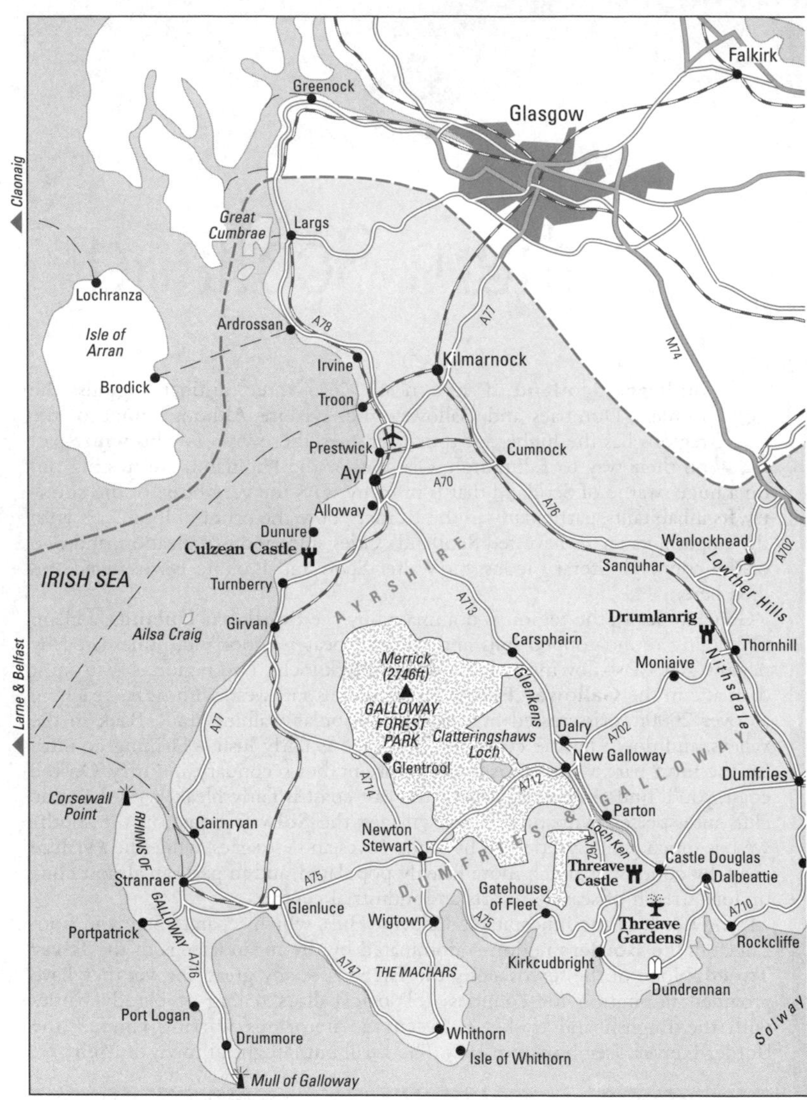

in the heart of the Borders, is the most obvious base for exploring the region, and has the most impressive of the four **Border abbeys** founded by the medieval Canmore kings, all of which are now reduced to romantic ruins.

Dumfries and Galloway, occupying the southwestern corner of Scotland, gets even more overlooked than the Borders, though the region remains popular with Lowland Scots and folk from the north of England. If you do make the effort to get off the main north–south highway to Glasgow, you'll find several more ruined abbeys, medieval castles, forested hills and dramatic tidal flats and seacliffs ideal for bird-watching. The key resort is the charming town of

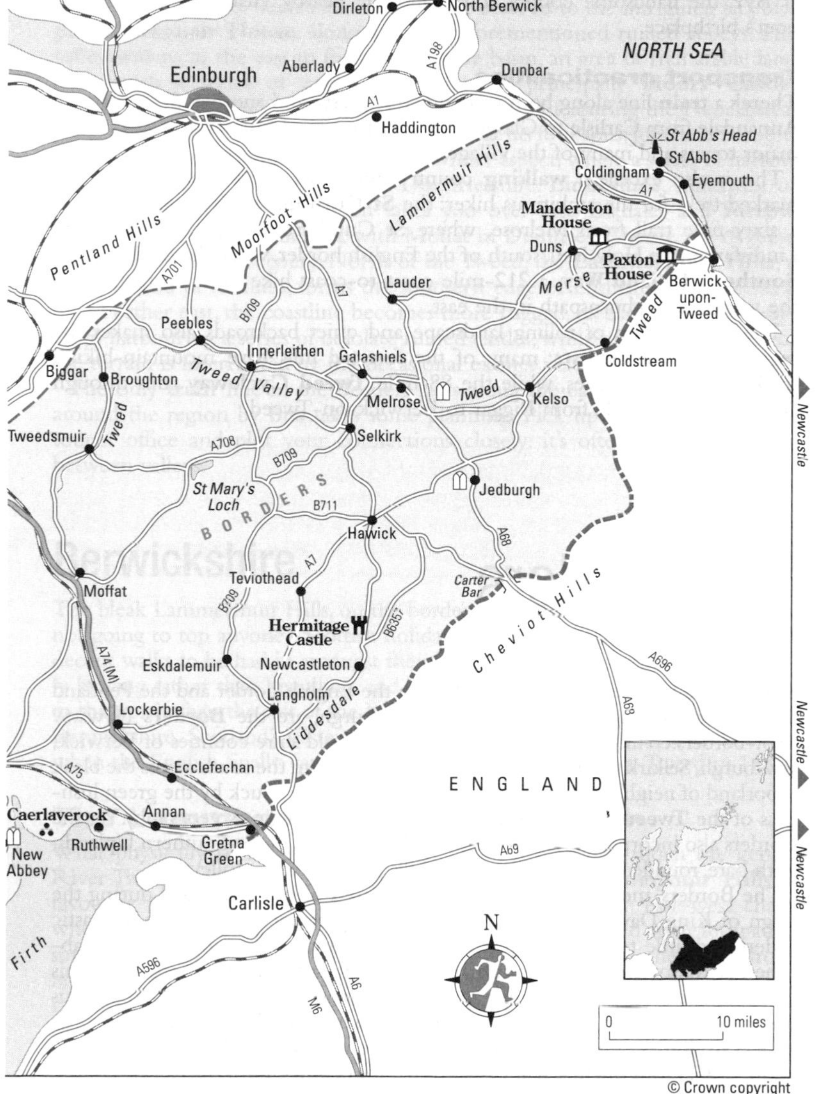

© Crown copyright

Kirkcudbright halfway along the marshy Solway coast, well placed for exploring the rest of the county.

Ayrshire is rich farming country, and not an obvious destination for first-time visitors to Scotland. It has fewer sights than its neighbours, with almost everything of interest confined to the coast. However, the **golf courses** along its gentle coastline are among the finest links courses in the country, and golfers can buy three- and five-day passes from tourist offices allowing free or reduced-fee access to many of the region's golf courses. Fans of Robert Burns could happily spend several days exploring the author's old haunts, especially

terwork. Also on display is a stunning collection of Chippendale and Regency rosewood furniture. Finally, the expansive **Picture Gallery**, completed in the 1810s, blends aspects of earlier Neoclassicism into a more austere design, with most of the plasterwork moulded to look like masonry. The National Gallery of Scotland uses this room as an outstation, displaying some of its lesser works here and changing the exhibits frequently.

The **grounds**, eighty acres of mixed parkland and woodland abutting the Tweed, laid out by an assistant of Capability Brown, boast gentle footpaths, a croquet lawn, an army-built adventure playground, a tearoom, Highland cattle, Shetland ponies, a Victorian boathouse housing a salmon-netting museum, and a hide, from where you can spy on red squirrels.

Duns and around

Heading inland from Eyemouth, the B6355 and then the A6105 cross the fertile farmland of the Merse to **DUNS**, the tiny, former county town of Berwickshire (Berwick itself lying over the border in England). Duns gets few visitors nowadays, though it has a nice little market square. A few folk come to pay their respects at the **Jim Clark Room**, 44 Newtown St (April–Sept Mon–Sat 10.30am–1pm & 2–4.30pm, Sun 2–4pm; Oct Mon–Sat 1–4pm; £1), dedicated to a local farmer-turned-motor-racing ace, twice world champion, whose brilliant career ended in death on the track at Hockenheim in Germany in 1968. Duns is also the (disputed) birthplace of **John Duns Scotus** (c.1265–1308), a medieval scholar, vehemently opposed to modern theology, whose followers were known as "Scotists" or "Dunses", hence the word "dunce" for someone who is slow to learn.

There are several easy walks in the near vicinity. It's only a twenty-minute walk to the 714ft summit of **Duns Law** (take North Castle Street and follow the signs) – most people make the trek up for the view, some to see the **Covenanters' Stone**, marking the spot where Alexander Leslie's army camped in 1639. Leslie assembled his troops on the Law to watch for Charles I's mercenaries, who had been sent north to crush the Covenanters. In the event, the royalist army faded away without even forcing a battle, and the king, by refusing to accept defeat, took one more step towards the Civil War. Other local **walks** are detailed in the leaflet "Walks Around Duns", available from *The Cherry Tree*, a tearoom on the market square.

Duns is well connected by **bus** to all the major settlements of the east Borders, and has a couple of excellent **B&Bs**: the central *St Albans* (Ⓣ01361/883285; ❹), a former eighteenth-century manse, situated on an unlikely sounding street called Clouds, off Preston Road; and *Wellfield House* (Ⓣ01361/883189, Ⓦwww.wellfieldhouse.com; ❸), a rather grand Georgian house on Preston Road, with a library/billiard room and real fires. The wooden bar of the venerable *Whip and Saddle* on the market square is the best place for a **drink** and traditional bar **food**.

Two places near Duns raise the tone significantly. **SWINTON**, an ordinary-looking village six miles southeast, boasts the award-winning *Wheatsheaf* (Ⓣ01890/860257; ❺), a **restaurant** (closed Mon) whose rather twee dining room, overlooking the rectangular village green, nevertheless offers traditional Scottish dishes sourced locally and served with finesse; the two-course set lunch for under £10 is a bargain, and there are six nicely furnished rooms up above. Set in its own grounds to the east of **CHIRNSIDE** village, seven miles northeast of Duns, is *Chirnside Hall* (Ⓣ01890/818219, Ⓦwww.chirnsidehall-hotel.co.uk; ❻), more of a full-blown **country house hotel**, with a splendid restaurant attached.

Manderston House

Manderston House (mid-May to Sept Thurs & Sun 2–5.30pm; ⓦ www.manderston.co.uk; £6, gardens only £3), two miles east of Duns on the A6105, is the very embodiment of Edwardian Britain. Between 1871 and 1905, the Miller family spent most of their herring and hemp fortune on turning their Georgian home into a prestigious country house, with no expense spared as architect John Kinross added entire suites of rooms in the Neoclassical style of Robert Adam. It's certainly a staggering sight, from the intricate plasterwork ceilings to the inlaid marble floor in the hall and the extravagant silver staircase, the whole lot sumptuously furnished with trappings worthy of a new member of the aristocracy: James Miller married Eveline Curzon, the daughter of Lord Scarsdale, in 1893. The house is currently the home of Lord and Lady Palmer, of Huntley & Palmers biscuits fame – there's even a Biscuit Tin Museum in the house just to prove it. When you've finished inside the house, stroll round the fifty or so acres of **gardens**, noted for their courtyard stables, cloistered marble dairy, mock tower house and rhododendrons and azaleas.

The Tweed Valley

Rising in the hills far to the west, the **River Tweed** snakes its way across the Borders until it reaches the North Sea at Berwick-upon-Tweed, most of its final stretch forming the boundary between Scotland and England. This is the area known as the **Merse**, a gentle, rural landscape of rich farmland and wooded river banks where the occasional military ruin, usually on the south side of the border, serves as a reminder of more violent days. The **Border Abbeys** – perhaps the best reason for visiting the region – also lie in ruins, not because of the Reformation, but because they were burnt to the ground by the English, for whom the lower Tweed was the obvious point at which to cross the border into Scotland: time and again they launched themselves north, destroying everything in their way. Indeed, the English turned Berwick-upon-Tweed into one of the most heavily guarded frontier towns in northern Europe, and its massive Elizabethan fortifications survive today.

On the Scottish side, the lower Tweed has just one town of note, **Kelso**, a busy agricultural centre distinguished by the Georgian elegance of its main square and its proximity to **Floors Castle** and **Mellerstain House**. Kelso is also visited for its abbey, though the ruins of the colossal twelfth-century foundation, whose abbots claimed precedence over St Andrews, are easily upstaged by those at **Melrose** and **Dryburgh**, further upstream. Melrose makes a great base for exploring the middle reaches of the Tweed Valley. The rich, forested scenery inspired Sir Walter Scott, whose own purpose-built creation, **Abbotsford House**, stands a few miles outside Melrose. Perhaps fortunately, Scott died before the textile boom industrialized parts of the Tweed Valley, turning his beloved **Selkirk** and **Galashiels** into mill towns. The Tweed is at its most beguiling in the stretch between Melrose and pleasant country town of **Peebles**, when it winds through the hills past numerous stately homes, most notably **Traquair House**. Public transport is no problem, with frequent buses travelling along the valley. Just west of Peebles, the Tweed curves south towards Tweedsmuir, from where it's just a few miles further to Moffat in Dumfriesshire (see p.189).

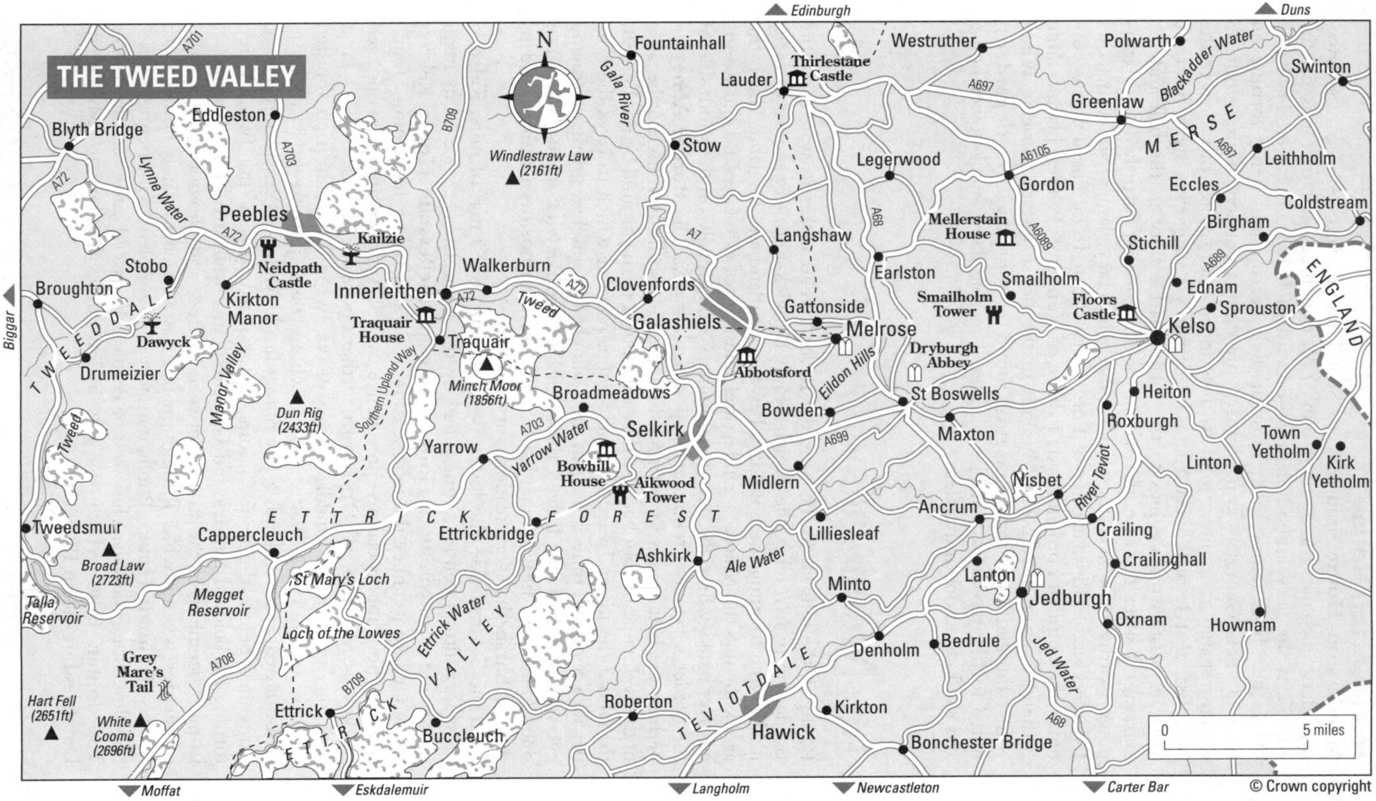
THE TWEED VALLEY
Edinburgh
Duns
Biggar
Moffat
Eskdalemuir
Langholm
Newcastleton
Carter Bar
N
Fountainhall
Thirlestane Castle
Lauder
Westruther
Polwarth
Blackadder Water
Swinton
Greenlaw
MERSE
A697
A701
Eddleston
Blyth Bridge
A703
B709
Windlestraw Law (2161ft)
Gala River
Stow
Legerwood
A6105
Gordon
Leitholm
Eccles
Coldstream
Lynne Water
A72
Peebles
Kailzie
Neidpath Castle
A7
Langshaw
A68
Mellerstain House
A6089
Stichill
Birgham
Stobo
Kirkton Manor
Walkerburn
Innerleithen
Clovenfords
Earlston
Smailholm
A689
Ednam
Sprouston
ENGLAND
Broughton
TWEEDDALE
Dawyck
Drumeizier
Manor Valley
Traquair House
Traquair
Tweed
Gattonside
Galashiels
Melrose
Smailholm Tower
Floors Castle
Kelso
Abbotsford
Eildon Hills
Dryburgh Abbey
Minch Moor (1856ft)
Southern Upland Way
Dun Rig (2433ft)
Broadmeadows
St Boswells
Heiton
Bowden
Roxburgh
A703
Yarrow Water
Selkirk
Maxton
Town Yetholm
Kirk Yetholm
A699
Yarrow
Bowhill House
Aikwood Tower
Midlern
Linton
Nisbet
River Teviot
Tweedsmuir
ETTRICK FOREST
Ettrickbridge
Cappercleuch
Ancrum
Lilliesleaf
Crailing
Ashkirk
Ale Water
Crailinghall
Broad Law (2723ft)
Megget Reservoir
St Mary's Loch
Minto
Lanton
Jedburgh
Talla Reservoir
Ettrick Water
VALLEY
Oxnam
Hownam
Loch of the Lowes
Denholm
Bedrule
Jed Water
Grey Mare's Tail
A708
B709
TEVIOTDALE
Hart Fell (2651ft)
White Coomb (2696ft)
Ettrick
ETTRICK
Roberton
Kirkton
A68
Buccleuch
Hawick
Bonchester Bridge
0
5 miles

Coldstream

The tiny border town of **COLDSTREAM**, which sits tight against the Tweed, is famous for its association with the Second Regiment of the Foot Guards, popularly known as the **Coldstream Guards**. Formed in 1650 from Cromwell's New Model Army by General George Monck in order to fight the Scottish Presbyterians, they switched sides along with their general in 1660 and marched on London for Charles II. Monck's regiment was thereafter recognized as the "Coldstream Guards" and the general became the first Duke of Albemarle – a handsome payoff for his timely change of heart. Oddly enough, in the sort of detail beloved of military historians, the Coldstreamers still sport the crownless tunic buttons they first wore as part of Cromwell's Model Army. The regiment's deeds are recorded in the **Coldstream Museum** (April–Sept Mon–Sat 10am–4pm; Oct Mon–Sat 1–4pm; free), on the rather desolate little Market Square, hidden away off the High Street.

Coldstream has long been an important border crossing, but the town's ford was replaced only in 1766 by the handsome five-arched **Smeaton's Bridge** you now see across the Tweed. Like Gretna Green (see p.186), Coldstream issued "irregular marriages" to runaway English couples, in this case from the Toll House at the far end of the bridge (where three English Lord Chancellors were married). You might suspect the huge fluted **column** near the bridge to be dedicated to the local regiment, but in fact it celebrates the victory of the

The Battle of Flodden

We'll here nae mair lilting at our ewe milking
Women and barins are heartless and wae
Sighing and moaning on a ilka green loaning
The flowers of the forest are a wede away.

A Lament for Flodden by Jane Elliot (1727–1805)

The Borders region witnessed one of the most devastating of sixteenth-century battles when the possibly the largest Scots army ever to invade England was decimated by the English at **Flodden Field** in 1513. For once, it wasn't English aggression which brought the two sides to battle, but the "Auld Alliance" between Scotland and France. James IV's brother-in-law, the English king Henry VIII, had invaded France, and the Scots opted to stand by their French allies. The Scots army, under James's command, took the English strongholds of Norham, Etal, Ford and Wark before being confronted to the south of the village of Branxton, three miles southeast of Coldstream, by an English force of roughly equal size under the Earl of Surrey. However, the English artillery was lighter and more manoeuvrable, and forced the Scots to come down off their advantageous position on Branxton Hill. Subsequently, the heavily armoured Scottish noblemen got stuck in the mud, and their over-long pikes and lances proved no match for the shorter and sturdier English halberds. English losses were heavy, but the Scots lost as many as ten thousand men, including the king himself, fighting at the head of his troops, along with his son (an archbishop), nine earls, fourteen lords and even the chiefs of many of the great Highland clans. After the battle was over, James's body was taken to his brother-in-law, but Henry denied it burial and no one knows what became of it.

If Bannockburn was Scotland's greatest victory over the English, and Bonnie Prince Charlie's last stand at Culloden their most noble defeat, Flodden was simply an unmitigated disaster. It became the subject of numerous songs and ballads (like the one quoted above), and remains a painful memory for Scots even today. The English, meanwhile, have forgotten all about it.

local MP following the Reform Act in 1832. Coldstream's long High Street forms part of the trunk road linking Newcastle and Edinburgh, now the A697, and as such is busy with traffic most days. If you want to stretch your legs, you're best off walking along the **Nun's Walk** which gives fine views over the Tweed into England and as far the Cheviots. To reach the path, head for the pocket-size **Henderson Park**, opposite the tourist office, which also boasts an aromatic garden for the blind with signs in braille.

Slightly further afield, on the western side of Coldstream, you can visit the 3000-acre **Hirsel Country Park** (parking: Easter–Sept £2; Oct–Easter £1). Hirsel House, home to the Douglas-Home family (of Tory prime minister fame), is not open to the public, but you can walk around the attractive grounds, complete with lake, picnic area and rhododendron woods, which are particularly resplendent in early summer. The **Homestead Museum** (Mon–Fri 10am–5pm, Sat & Sun noon–5pm; free), housed in the old out-houses, shows the workings of the estate, past and present.

Practicalities

Coldstream's **tourist office**, roughly halfway down the High Street (July & Aug Mon–Sat 10am–6pm, Sun 10am–2pm; April–June & Sept Mon–Sat 10am–5pm, Sun 10am–1pm; Oct Mon–Sat 10am–12.30pm & 1.30–4.30pm; ⓣ01890/882607), has a comprehensive supply of brochures and booklets on the Borders. There's a handful of **B&Bs** in the town, but you're probably better off pushing on to Kelso or Melrose; if you're looking for a bit of luxury, head for the *Wheatsheaf Hotel* in nearby Swinton (see p.162). Your best bet for a **drink** and a bite to **eat** is the cosy *Besom Inn*, next to the tourist office, its tiny series of bars decked out with a sprinkling of militaria. For a decent **tea-room**, head into the Hirsel estate (see above).

Kelso and around

KELSO, eight miles upstream from Coldstream, at the confluence of the Tweed and Teviot, grew up in the shadow of its now-ruined Benedictine **Abbey** (April–Sept Mon–Sat 9.30am–6pm, Sun 2–6pm; Oct–March Mon–Sat 9.30am–4pm, Sun 2–4pm; free), once the richest and most powerful of the Border abbeys. Unfortunately, the English savaged Kelso three times in the first half of the sixteenth century: the last (and by far the worst) assault was part of the "Rough Wooing" led by the Earl of Hertford when the Scots refused to ratify a marriage treaty between Henry VIII's son and the infant Mary, Queen of Scots. Such was the extent of the devastation – compounded by the Reformation – that less survives of Kelso than any of the Border abbeys. Nevertheless, at first sight, it looks pretty impressive, with the heavy Norman west end of the abbey church almost entirely intact. Beyond, little remains, though it is possible to make out the two transepts and towers which gave the abbey the shape of a double cross, unique in Scotland. Just across the leafy cemetery from the abbey stands the **Old Parish Church**, constructed in 1773 by a local man to an octagonal design that excited universal execration. "It is," wrote one contemporary, "a misshapen pile, the ugliest Parish Church in Scotland, but it is an excellent model for a circus." While you're in the vicinity, pop into the **Kelso Pottery** (Mon–Sat 10am–1pm & 2–5pm), close by at The Knowes, to see ceramics fired in a large outdoor pit kiln.

Kelso town managed to rebuild itself and is now centred on the **Square**, an unusually large cobbled expanse presided over by the honey-hued Ionic columns, pediment and oversized clock belltower of the elegant **Town Hall**.

The Border Reivers

From the thirteenth to the early seventeenth centuries, the wild, inhospitable border country stretching from the Solway Firth in the west to the Tweed Valley in the east, well away from the power bases of both the Scottish and English monarchs, was overrun by outlaws known as the **Border Reivers**, *reive* being a Scots word for plunder. As George MacDonald Fraser put it in his book *The Steel Bonnets*, "The great border tribes of both Scotland and England feuded continuously among themselves. Robbery and blackmail were everyday professions; raiding, arson, kidnapping, murder and extortion were an accepted part of the social system." This, then, was no cross-border dispute, but an open struggle for power among the tribes of the region. Those who "shook loose the Border" included people from all walks of life – agricultural labourers, gentleman farmers, smallholders, even peers of the realm – for whom theft, raiding, tracking and ambush became second nature.

The source of this behaviour was the destruction and devastation wrought upon the region by virtually continual warfare between England and Scotland, and the "slash and burn" policy of the era. With many residents no longer able to find sustenance from the land, crime became the only way to survive. Cattle-rustling, blackmail and kidnapping led to an anarchical mindset, where feuding families would wreak havoc and devastation on each other almost as a way of life.

The legacy of the Border Reivers can still be seen today in the fortified farms and churches of the region's architecture; in the **Common Riding** traditions of many border towns; in the language – the words "blackmail" and "bereaved" have their roots in the destructive behaviour that was so characteristic of this period; and in the great family names such as Armstrong, Graham, Kerr and Nixon, which once filled the hearts of Borderers with dread.

To one side stands the imposing *Cross Keys Hotel*, with its distinctive rooftop balustrade, with a supporting chorus of three-storey eighteenth- and nineteenth-century pastel buildings on every side. Leaving the Square along Roxburgh Street, take the alley down to the **Cobby Riverside Walk**, where a brief stroll leads to Floors Castle (see below). En route, but hidden from view by the islet in the middle of the river, is the spot where the Teviot meets the Tweed. This bit of river, known as The Junction, has long been famous for its **salmon fishing**, with permits – costing thousands – booked years in advance. Permits for fishing other, less expensive reaches of the Tweed and Teviot are available from Tweedside Tackle, 36 Bridge St (Ⓣ01573/225306). Details of last-minute fishing lets are available from the Tweedline on Ⓣ0906/866 6412; for fishing catches and prospects, phone Ⓣ0906/866 6410.

Practicalities

With good connections to Melrose and Jedburgh to the west and a less regular service to Coldstream and Duns, Kelso **bus station** on Roxburgh Street is a brief walk from The Square, where you'll find the **tourist office** in the Town Hall (July & Aug Mon–Sat 9am–6pm, Sun 10am–5pm; April–June & Sept Mon–Sat 10am–5pm, Sun 10am–1pm; Oct Mon–Sat 10am–4.30pm, Sun 10am–1pm; Ⓣ01573/223464).

Other than during Kelso's main **festivals** – the Border Union Dog Show in late June, the Border Union Agricultural Show in late July, the Kelso Rugby Sevens in early September and the Ram Sales a week or so later – **accommodation** is not a problem. One of the best B&Bs in town is *Abbey Bank*, near Kelso Pottery on The Knowes (Ⓣ01573/226550, Ⓔdiah@abbeybank.freeserve.co.uk; ❷), a Georgian house with large double beds and a lovely south-facing garden. Another good choice is the *Ednam House Hotel* (Ⓣ01573/224168, Ⓦwww.ednamhouse.com; ❺), a splendid Georgian mansion set back off Bridge Street, with antique furnishings and fittings and gardens that abut the Tweed; make sure, though, that you're not put in the modern extension. Lastly, there's the *Roxburghe Hotel* (Ⓣ01573/450331, Ⓦwww.roxburghe.net; ❼), a luxury hotel two miles south of Kelso on the A698 at Heiton, owned by the Duke and Duchess of Roxburghe, which also boasts an eighteen-hole championship golf course.

Most **eating** places are just off The Square: the *Cobbles Inn* restaurant is housed in a former pub just up Bowmont Street – check the specials menu for the best dishes – and *The Queen's Head*, on Bridge Street, has an extremely adventurous bar meal menu. The moderately expensive *Ednam House Hotel* (see above) restaurant is more upmarket and often features some unusual dishes, while the restaurant at the *Roxburghe Hotel* is even more formal, its top-quality food and service matched by correspondingly high prices.

Floors Castle

If you stand on Kelso's handsome bridge over the Tweed, you can easily make out the pepperpot turrets and castellations of **Floors Castle** (Easter–Oct daily 10am–4.30pm; Ⓦwww.floorscastle.com; £5.50), a vast, pompous mansion a mile or so northwest of the town. The bulk of the building was designed by William Adam in the 1720s and, picking through the Victorian modifications, the interior still demonstrates his uncluttered style. However, you won't see much of it, as just ten rooms and a basement are open to the public. Highlights include Hendrick Danckert's splendid panorama of Horse Guards Parade in London in the entrance hall; the Brussels tapestries in the ante and drawing rooms; paintings by Augustus John and Henri Matisse in the Needle Room; and all sorts of snuff boxes and cigarette cases in the gallery. Floors remains privately owned, the property of the tenth Duke of Roxburghe, whose imperious features can be seen in a variety of portraits. The duke is a close friend of royalty: it was here, apparently, that Prince Andrew proposed to Sarah Ferguson in 1986.

Kirk Yetholm and Town Yetholm

Yetholm, perched on the edge of the Cheviot Hills six miles southeast of Kelso along the B6352, is two separate places, **KIRK YETHOLM** and **TOWN YETHOLM**, lying a quarter of a mile apart. The villages, accessible by bus from Kelso, lie at the northern end of the **Pennine Way**, a long-distance footpath which travels the length of northern England finishing at the Kirk Yetholm SYHA **hostel** (Ⓣ01573/420631, Ⓦwww.syha.org.uk; April–Sept). The hostel also marks the end of the second leg of **St Cuthbert's Way** (see p.170). Walkers who have completed the Pennine Way clutching a copy of Wainwright's guidebook to the long-distance footpath are entitled to a celebratory free half-pint at the *Border Hotel* (Ⓣ01573/420637, Ⓦwww.theborderhotel.co.uk; ❸) in Kirk Yetholm, which serves good food, too.

Mellerstain House

Six miles northwest of Kelso off the A6089, **Mellerstain House** (Easter & May–Sept daily except Sat 12.30–5pm; Ⓦwww.scot-borders.co.uk/mellerstain; £5) represents the very best of the Adams' brothers' work: William designed the wings in 1725, and his son Robert the castellated centre fifty years later. Robert's love of columns, roundels and friezes culminates in a stunning sequence of plaster-moulded, pastel-shaded ceilings, from the looping symmetry of the library ceiling, adorned by medallion oil paintings *Learning* and

Reading on either side of *Minerva*, to the whimsical griffin and vase pattern in the drawing room. The art collection, which includes works by Constable, Van Dyck, Gainsborough, Ramsay and Veronese, is also noteworthy. It takes an hour to tour the house, which is still the home of the thirteenth Earl and Countess of Haddington, descendants of the Baillie family who acquired the estate in 1642; afterwards you can wander the formal Edwardian **gardens**, which slope down to the lake.

Smailholm Tower

In marked contrast to Mellerstain is the craggy **Smailholm Tower** (April–Sept daily 9.30am–6.30pm; HS; £2), perched on a rocky outcrop a few miles to the south. A remote and evocative fastness recalling Reivers' raids and border skirmishes, the fifteenth-century tower was designed to withstand sudden attack. The rough rubble walls average six feet in thickness and both the entrance – once guarded by a heavy door plus an iron yett (gate) – and the windows are disproportionately small. These were necessary precautions: on both sides of the border, clans were engaged in endless feuds, a violent history that stirred the imagination of a "wee, sick laddie" who was brought here to live in 1773. The boy was Walter Scott and his epic poem *Marmion* resounds to the clamour of Smailholm's ancient quarrels:

> [The forayers], home returning, fill'd the hall
> With revel, wassel-rout, and brawl.
> Methought that still with trump and clang,
> The gateway's broken arches rang;
> Methought grim features, seam'd with scars,
> Glared through the window's rusty bars.

Inside, ignore the inept costumed models and press on up to the roof, where two narrow **wall-walks**, jammed against the barrel-vaulted roof and the crow-stepped gables, provide panoramic views. On the north side the watchman's seat has also survived, stuck against the chimney stack for warmth and with a recess for a lantern.

Dryburgh Abbey

Hidden away in a U-bend in the Tweed, ten miles upstream from Kelso, the remains of **Dryburgh Abbey** (April–Sept daily 9.30am–6.30pm; Oct–March Mon–Sat 9.30am–4.30pm, Sun 2–4.30pm; HS; £2.80) occupy an idyllic position against a hilly backdrop, with ancient cedars, redwoods, beech and lime trees and wide lawns flattering the pinkish-red hues of the stonework. The Premonstratensians, or White Canons, founded the abbey in the twelfth century, but they were never as successful – or apparently as devout – as their Cistercian neighbours in Melrose. Their chronicles detail interminable disputes about land and money: in one incident, a fourteenth-century canon called Marcus flattened the abbot with his fist. Later, the abbey attained its own folklore: Scott's *Minstrelsy* records the tale of a woman who lived in the vaults with a sprite called Fatlips. She only came out after dark to beg from her neighbours and was variously thought mad or demonic.

The romantic setting is second to none, but the ruins of the **Abbey Church** are much less substantial than, say, at Melrose or Jedburgh. Virtually nothing survives of the nave, but the transepts have fared better, their chapels now serving as private burial grounds for, among others, Sir Walter Scott and Field Marshal Haig, the World War I commander whose ineptitude cost thousands of soldiers' lives. The night stairs, down which the monks stumbled in the early hours of the morning, survive in the south transept, and lead even today to the monks' dormitory. Leaving the church via the east processional door in the south aisle, with its dog-tooth decoration, you enter the cloisters, the highlight of which is the barrel-vaulted **Chapter House**, complete with low stone benches and blind interlaced arcading.

Next door to the abbey is the *Dryburgh Abbey Hotel* (Ⓣ01835/822261, Ⓦwww.dryburgh.co.uk; ❼), a sprawling red-sandstone **hotel** that's a hunting, shooting, fishing kind of place. You can enjoy the indoor pool, or simply have a cup of tea or a drink in the bar. Dryburgh is not easy to get to by **public transport**, though it's only a mile's walk north from St Boswell's on the A68, and a pleasant three or four miles from Melrose. Drivers and cyclists should approach the abbey via the much-visited **Scott's View**, to the north on the B6356, overlooking the Tweed Valley, where the writer and his friends often picnicked and where Scott's horse stopped out of habit during the writer's own funeral procession. The scene inspired Joseph Turner's *Melrose 1831*, now on display in the National Gallery of Scotland (see p.100).

Melrose

Tucked in between the Tweed and the gorse-backed Eildon Hills, minuscule **MELROSE** is the most beguiling of towns, its narrow streets trimmed by a harmonious ensemble of styles, from pretty little cottages and tweedy shops to high-standing Georgian and Victorian facades. Its chief draw is its ruined abbey, by far the best of the Border abbeys, but it's also perfectly positioned for exploring the Tweed valley. Most of the year it's a sleepy little place, but as the

Walking in the Eildons and St Cuthbert's Way

Ordnance Survey Landranger map No. 44

From the centre of Melrose, it's a vigorous three-mile walk to the top of the **Eildon Hills**, whose triple volcanic peaks are the Central Borders' most distinctive landmark. The tourist office sells a leaflet detailing the hike, which begins about ninety yards south of – and up the hill from – Market Square, along the B6359 to Lilliesleaf. The path is signposted to the left and leads to the saddle between the North and Mid Hills. To the right of the saddle are **Mid Hill**, the highest summit at 1385ft, and further south, **West Hill**; to the left, **North Hill** is topped by the scant remains of an Iron Age fort and a Roman signal station. There are several routes back to town; one heading down from the northeast picks up a path to Newstead and you can return to Melrose by the river.

The hills have been associated with all sorts of legends, beginning with tales of their creation by the wizard-cum-alchemist Michael Scott (1175–1230) who, in the words of Sir Walter Scott, "cleft the Eildon Hills in three". It was here that the mystic **Thomas the Rhymer** received the gift of prophecy from the Faerie Queen, and Arthur and his knights are reckoned to lie asleep deep within the hills, victims of a powerful spell. The ancient Celts, who revered the number three, also considered the site a holy place and maintained their settlements on the slopes long after the Romans' departure.

Melrose is also the starting point for the popular **St Cuthbert's Way**, a sixty-mile walk which finishes at Lindisfarne (Holy Island of Northumberland) on the east coast. The tourist office can give details of the walk, though the trail is well marked by yellow arrows from the abbey up over the Eildons to the pretty village of **Bowden**, where you can make a detour to see a twelfth-century kirk, half a mile down the hill from the square.

birthplace in 1883 of the **Rugby Sevens** (seven-a-side games), it swarms during Sevens Week (second week in April), and again in early September when it hosts the **Melrose Music Festival**, a popular weekend of traditional music attracting folkies from afar.

The town and abbey

To the north of the town square, the pink- and red-tinted stone ruins of **Melrose Abbey** (April–Sept daily 9.30am–6.30pm; Oct–March Mon–Sat 9.30am–4.30pm, Sun 2–4.30pm; HS; £3.50) soar above their riverside surroundings. Founded in 1136 by King David I, Melrose was the first Cistercian settlement in Scotland and grew rich selling wool and hides to Flanders, but its prosperity was fragile: the English repeatedly razed Melrose, most viciously under Richard II in 1385 and the Earl of Hertford in 1545. Most of the present remains date from the intervening period, when extensive rebuilding abandoned the original Cistercian austerity for an elaborate, Gothic style inspired by the abbeys of northern England, though it seems likely that the abbey was never fully finished before the Reformation. The sculptural detailing at Melrose is of the highest quality, but it's easy to miss if you don't know where to look, so taking advantage of the free audioguide, or buying yourself a guidebook, is a good idea.

The site is dominated by the **Abbey Church**, which has lost its west front, and whose nave is reduced to the elegant window arches and chapels of the south aisle. Amazingly, however, the stone **pulpitum** (screen), separating the choir monks from their lay brothers, is preserved. Beyond, the **presbytery** has its magnificent perpendicular window, lierne vaulting and ceiling bosses intact, with the capitals of the surrounding columns sporting the most intricate of curly kale carving. In the **south transept**, another fine fifteenth-century window sprouts yet more delicate, foliate tracery and the adjacent cornice is enlivened by angels playing musical instruments, though these figures are badly weathered. This kind of finely carved detail is repeated everywhere you look in Melrose. Outside, the exterior sculpturing on the south transept is even more impressive, lower niche-corbels are decorated with crouching figures holding scrolls bearing inscriptions such as "He suffered because he willed it". Elsewhere, look for the statue of the Virgin and Child, high on the south side of the westernmost surviving buttress, the Coronation of the Virgin on the east end gable, and the numerous mischievous **gargoyles**, from peculiar crouching beasts to the pig playing the bagpipes on the roof on the south side of the nave.

Legend has it that the heart of **Robert the Bruce** is buried here (his body having been buried at Dunfermline Abbey), and in 1997, when a heart cask was publicly exhumed, this theory received an unexpected boost. However, the burial location was not in accordance with Bruce's own wishes. In 1329, the dying king told his friend, Sir James Douglas, to carry his heart on a Crusade to the Holy Land in fulfilment of an old vow: "Seeing therefore, that my body cannot go to achieve what my heart desires, I will send my heart instead of my body, to accomplish my vow." Douglas tried his best, but was killed fighting the Moors in Spain – and Bruce's heart ended up in Melrose. A new commemorative stone marks its current resting place in the chapter house, to the north of the sacristy.

The paltry ruins of the old monastic buildings edge the church to the north and lead over the road to the **Commendator's House** (same hours as the abbey), a lovely red sandstone building converted into a private house in 1590 by the abbey's last Commendator, and now housing a modest collection of ecclesiastical bric-a-brac. Beyond the house is the mill-lade, where water used to flow in order to power the abbey's mills, and was also diverted to flush the monks' latrines. Back towards the town, to the south of the abbey, you should pop into the delightful **Priorwood Garden** (April–Sept Mon–Sat 10am–5.30pm, Sun 1.30–5.30pm; Oct–Dec Mon–Sat 10am–4pm, Sun 1.30–4pm; NTS; free), whose compact walled precincts, are given over to an orchard and flowers that are suitable for drying; there's a dried flower shop, too.

Melrose's other museum, the **Trimontium Exhibition**, just off Market Square (April–Oct Mon–Fri 10.30am–4.30pm, Sat & Sun 10.30am–1pm & 2–4.30pm; Ⓦwww.trimontium.freeserve.co.uk; £1.50), is a quirky little centre that merits a browse. Its displays include Celtic bronze axe-heads excavated from the Eildon hills, dioramas, models and the odd archeological find outlining the three Roman occupations of the region. For further Roman adventures, the four-mile circular **Trimontium Walk** (April–Oct Thurs 1.30–5pm; book on Ⓣ01896/822651; £2.50) visits various Roman sites in the area, including the Leaderfoot viaduct, and the most northerly amphitheatre in the Roman Empire. The walk begins at the exhibition, includes a guide and tea in Newstead, the site of the Trimontium fort (Three Hills), whose remains are on display in the National Museum of Scotland in Edinburgh (see p.94).

Practicalities

Buses to Melrose stop in Market Square, from where it's a brief walk north to the abbey ruins and the **tourist office** opposite (July & Aug Mon–Sat 9.30am–6.30pm, Sun 10am–6pm; June & Sept Mon–Sat 10am–6pm, Sun 10am–2pm; March–May & Oct Mon–Sat 10am–5pm, Sun 10am–1pm; Ⓣ01896/822555).

Melrose has a clutch of **hotels**, though prices are generally higher than you might expect. The best of the bunch is *Burt's*, a smartly converted old inn on Market Square (Ⓣ01896/822285, Ⓦwww.burtshotel.co.uk; ❻); rooms are small, but very comfortable. Across the street is the ten-bedroom *Millars* (Ⓣ01896/822645; ❺), recently smartened up and with fewer pretensions than *Burt's*. It's among Melrose's simple **B&Bs**, however, that you'll get the real flavour of the place, most notably at the easygoing and comfortable *Braidwood*, on Buccleuch Street (Ⓣ01896/822488; ❷), a stone's throw from the abbey, and the equally agreeable *Dunfermline House* (Ⓣ01896/822148, Ⓦwww.dunmel. freeserve.co.uk; ❷) opposite – advance booking is recommended at both during the summer. The town also has an SYHA **hostel** (Ⓣ01896/822521, Ⓦwww.syha.org.uk; Feb–Oct & New Year) in a sprawling Georgian villa overlooking the abbey from beside the access road into the bypass. The *Gibson Caravan Park* **campsite** (Ⓣ01896/822969) is in the town centre, just off the High Street, opposite the Greenyards rugby grounds.

Melrose offers a reasonable choice of **eating** options. *Marmion's Brasserie* (Ⓣ01896/822245), housed in a spacious Victorian house on Buccleuch Street, serves well-prepared meals from an imaginative, moderately expensive menu. *Burt's* does excellent bar meals, and if you're feeling energetic, walk past the abbey and across the old suspension bridge to Gattonside, where the *Hoebridge Inn* (Ⓣ01896/823082; closed Mon), once a bobbin mill and now one of the Borders' best restaurants, serves home-made Scottish food in relaxed, low-key surroundings. If you want a light lunch or snack, head to *Russell's* (closed Thurs out of season), a popular, very traditional tearoom on Market Square; or *Haldane's Fish & Chip Shop* (closed Wed), next door. For **pubs**, try the friendly *King's Arms* on the High Street, or the *Ship Inn*, on East Port at the top of the square, the liveliest in town, especially during the Folk Festival and on Saturday afternoons when the Melrose rugby team have played at home. Be sure to check out what's on at *The Wynd* (Ⓣ01896/823854, Ⓦwww.the-wynd-theatre.co.uk), Melrose's very own pint-sized **theatre**, tucked away down the alleyway, north off the main square, which shows films and puts on gigs as well as live drama.

Abbotsford

Abbotsford (June–Sept daily 9.30am–5pm; mid-March to May & Oct Mon–Sat 9.30am–5pm, Sun 2–5pm; £4), a stately home three miles up the Tweed from Melrose, was designed to satisfy the Romantic inclinations of **Sir Walter Scott**, who lived here from 1812 until his death twenty years later. Built on the site of a farmhouse Scott bought and subsequently demolished, Abbotsford (as Scott chose to call it) took twelve years to evolve, with the fanciful turrets and castellations of the Scots Baronial exterior incorporating copies of medieval originals: the entrance porch imitates that of Linlithgow Palace and the screen wall in the garden echoes Melrose Abbey's cloister. Scott was proud of his *folie de grandeur*, writing to a friend, "It is a kind of conundrum castle to be sure [which] pleases a fantastic person in style and manner." That said, it was undoubtedly one of the chief causes of Scott's subsequent bankruptcy.

Despite all the exterior pomp, the interior is surprisingly small and poky, with just six rooms open for viewing on the upper floor. Visitors start in the wood-panelled **study**, with its small writing desk made of salvage from the Spanish Armada, at which Scott banged out the Waverley novels at a furious rate. The heavy wood-panelled **library** boasts Scott's collection of more than nine thousand rare books and an extraordinary assortment of memorabilia, the centrepiece of which is Napoleon's pen case and blotting book, but which also includes Rob Roy's purse and *skene dhu* (knife), a lock of Nelson's hair, and of Bonnie Prince Charlie's and the latter's *quaich* (drinking cup), Flora Macdonald's pocketbook, the inlaid pearl crucifix that accompanied Mary, Queen of Scots to the scaffold, and even a piece of oatcake found in the pocket of a dead Highlander at Culloden. You can also see Henry Raeburn's famous portrait of Scott hanging in the **drawing room**, and all sorts of weapons – notably Rob Roy's sword, dagger and gun – in the **armoury**. In the barbaric-looking **entrance hall**, hung with elk and wild cattle skulls, and spoils gathered from the battlefield of Waterloo by Scott himself, is a model of the skull of Robert the Bruce and some of Scott's dandyish clothes.

The fast and frequent Melrose–Galashiels **bus** provides easy access to Abbotsford: ask for the Tweedbank island on the A6091, from where the house is a ten-minute walk up the road.

Galashiels

It's hard to avoid **GALASHIELS**, or "Gala" as it's known locally, a hard-working textile town four miles west of Melrose whose workers' terraces of grey-green spread along the valley of the Gala Water near its junction with the Tweed. It occupies a pivotal position in the Borders, and has the region's principal **bus station**, situated close to (and north of the river from) the town centre. The main street runs parallel with the river, its eastern end cheered by a melodramatic equestrian statue of a Border Reiver above the town's war memorial. You could while away half an hour at the sixteenth-century **Old Gala House** (April–Oct Tues–Sat 10am–4pm, Sun 2–4pm; free), the town's oldest house and now the local museum, up St John's Street and then left down Scott Crescent. The long-demolished New Gala House, a mansion

Sir Walter Scott

Walter Scott (1771–1832) was born in Edinburgh to a solidly bourgeois family whose roots were in Selkirkshire. As a child he was left lame by polio and his anxious parents sent him to recuperate at his grandfather's farm in Smailholm, where the boy's imagination was fired by his relatives' tales of derring-do, the violent history of the Borders retold amidst the rugged landscape that he spent long summer days exploring. Scott returned to Edinburgh to resume his education and take up a career in law, but his real interests remained elsewhere. Throughout the 1790s he transcribed hundreds of old Border ballads, publishing a three-volume collection entitled *Minstrelsy of the Scottish Borders* in 1802. An instant success, *Minstrelsy* was followed by Scott's own *Lay of the Last Minstrel*, a narrative poem whose strong story and rose-tinted regionalism proved very popular.

More poetry was to come, most successfully *Marmion* (1808) and *The Lady of the Lake* (1810), not to mention an eighteen-volume edition of the works of John Dryden and nineteen volumes of Jonathan Swift. However, despite having two paid jobs, one as the Sheriff-Depute of Selkirkshire, the other as clerk to the Court of Session in Edinburgh, his finances remained shaky. He had become a partner in a printing firm, which put him deeply into debt, not helped by the enormous sums he spent on his mansion, Abbotsford. From 1813, Scott was writing to pay the bills and thumped out a veritable flood of historical novels using his extensive knowledge of Scottish history and folklore. He produced his best work within the space of ten years: *Waverley* (1814), *The Antiquary* (1816), *Rob Roy* and *The Heart of Midlothian* (both 1818), as well as two notable novels set in England, *Ivanhoe* (1819) and *Kenilworth* (1821). In 1824 he returned to Scottish tales with *Redgauntlet*, the last of his quality work.

A year later Scott's money problems reached crisis proportions after an economic crash bankrupted his printing business. Attempting to pay his creditors in full, he found the quality of his writing deteriorating with its increased speed and the effort broke his health. His last years were plagued by illness, and in 1832 he died at Abbotsford and was buried within the ruins of Dryburgh Abbey.

Although Scott's interests were diverse, his historical novels mostly focused on the Jacobites, whose loyalty to the Stuarts had riven Scotland since the "Glorious Revolution" of 1688. That the nation was prepared to be entertained by such tales was essentially a matter of timing: by the 1760s it was clear the Jacobite cause was lost for good and Scotland, emerging from its isolated medievalism, had been firmly welded into the United Kingdom. Thus its turbulent history and independent spirit was safely in the past, and ripe for romancing – as shown by the arrival of King George IV in Edinburgh during 1822 decked out in Highland dress. Yet, for Sir Walter the romance was tinged with a genuine sense of loss. Loyal to the Hanoverians, he still grieved for Bonnie Prince Charlie; he welcomed a commercial Scotland but lamented the passing of feudal ties, and so his heroes are transitional, fighting men of action superseded by bourgeois figures searching for a clear identity.

With the 1997 televised serial of *Ivanhoe*, British interest in Scott has been revived, and although many of his works are currently out of print, Edinburgh University Press has recently begun a long-term project to issue proper critical editions of the Waverley novels for the first time, correcting hitherto heavily corrupted texts and restoring passages and endings that had been altered – often drastically – by the original publishers. See "Books" on p.821 for details of works by Scott that are currently in print.

which stood at the top of the town, was taken over during World War II by an Edinburgh girls' school, **St Trinnean's**; the artist Ronald Searle met two of the pupils in 1941, inspiration for the unruly schoolgirls in his St Trinian's novels. Galashiels **tourist office** is at 3 St John's St (July & Aug Mon–Sat 10am–6pm, Sun 1–5pm; April–June & Sept Mon–Sat 10am–5pm, Sun 2–4pm; Oct Mon–Sat 10am–12.30pm & 1.30–4.30pm; ⓣ01896/755551), and can help point you in the right direction to find the **Lochcarron Visitor Centre** (Mon–Sat 9am–5pm; June–Sept also Sun noon–5pm; Ⓦwww.lochcarron.com; £2.50), a woollen mill on Huddersfield Street, that offers guided tours of its factory, which specializes in cashmere.

Innerleithen and around

If you're driving west and want to avoid Galashiels, then simply follow the Tweed instead of the main road. Whichever way you go, you'll eventually pass through **INNERLEITHEN**, a rural village which gained prominence in eighteenth century as a mill town and spa centre. Aside from its main attraction, the wonderful Traquair House (see below), the town boasts **Robert Smail's Printing Works** (Easter & May–Sept Mon–Sat 10am–1pm & 2–5pm, Sun 2–5pm; Oct Sat 10am–1pm & 2–5pm, Sun 2–5pm; NTS; £2.50), a working museum on the main street, with original nineteenth-century machinery where you can try your hand at typesetting. Ten to fifteen minutes' walk north of the main street are the quaint **St Ronan's Wells** (Easter–Oct daily 2–5pm; free), where Walter Scott used to imbibe the sulphur waters, and where you can still taste them from a tap under the porch (and buy the stuff bottled from Pearce & Sons on Miller Street). The current building is a Victorian reconstruction of the original 1826 pump room, with its striking peacock-blue and white weatherboarding and its pepperpot towers sporting thistle finials. This was built to accommodate the tourists drawn here by the success of Scott's novel *St Ronan's Well*.

Most visitors make Peebles their base, but you could **stay** in Innerleithen at the central *Traquair Arms Hotel*, on Traquair Road (Ⓣ01896/830229, Ⓦwww.trad-inns.co.uk/traquair; ④), a cosy old inn that's also a great place for a pint, a cup of tea, and some filling bar food. Alternatively, there's the *Caddon View Guest House* (Ⓣ01896/830208, Ⓔcaddonview@aol.com; ③), a nice spacious double-fronted Victorian villa at 14 Pirn Rd. For either place, you'll need to book early during the Traquair Fair in August. Campers should head for the *Tweedside Caravan Park* **campsite** (Ⓣ01896/831271; April–Oct), by the river down Montgomery Street; it has a laundry facilities and a games rooms. **Bike rental** is available from Bikesport on Peebles Road (Ⓣ01896/830880), should you feel like checking out the many graded cycle routes through Glentress, Cardrona, or the Elibank and Traquair forests.

Traquair House

Peeping out from the trees a mile or so south of Innerleithen on the B709, **Traquair House** (daily: June–Aug 10.30am–5.30pm; April, May, Sept & Oct 12.30–5.30pm; Ⓦwww.traquair.co.uk; £5.30, grounds only £2) is the oldest continuously inhabited house in Scotland, with the present owners – the Maxwell Stuarts – having lived here since 1491. The first Laird of Traquair (pronounced "tra-queer"), inherited an elementary fortified tower, which his powerful descendants gradually converted into a mansion, visited, it is said, by 27 monarchs including Mary, Queen of Scots. Persistently Catholic, the family paid for its principles: the fifth earl got two years in the Tower of London for his support of Bonnie Prince Charlie, Protestant mill workers repeatedly attacked their property, and by 1800 little remained of the family's once enormous estates – certainly not enough to fund any major rebuilding.

Consequently, Traquair's main appeal is in its ancient shape and structure. The whitewashed facade is strikingly handsome, with narrow windows and trim turrets surrounding the tiniest of front doors – an organic, homogeneous edifice that's a welcome change from other grandiose stately homes. Inside, the house has kept many of its oldest features. You can see original vaulted cellars, where locals once hid their cattle from raiders; the twisting main staircase as well as the earlier medieval version, later a secret escape route for persecuted Catholics; a carefully camouflaged priest's hole; and even a **priest's room** where a string of resident chaplains lived in hiding until the Catholic Emancipation Act freed things up in 1829. Of the furniture and fittings, the carved oak door at the foot of the stairs is outstanding, as are the Dutch trompe l'oeil carvings in the **still room** and the bright-yellow four-poster of the **king's room**, with a bedspread allegedly embroidered by Mary, Queen of Scots. That said, it's not any particular piece that impresses, but rather the accumulation of family possessions that give a real insight into the Maxwell Stuarts' revolving-door fortunes and eccentricities. In the **museum room** there are several fine examples of Jacobite or **Amen glass**, inscribed with pictures of the Bonnie Prince or verses in his honour; a handful of personal items thought to have been owned by Mary, Queen of Scots; and the cloak worn by the fourth earl during his dramatic escape from the Tower of London. (Under sentence of death for his part in the Jacobite Rising of 1715, the earl was saved by his wife, Lady Winifred Herbert, who got his jailers drunk and smuggled him out disguised as a maid.)

It's worth sparing time for the surrounding **gardens** where you'll find a **hedge maze**, several craft workshops and the **Traquair House Brewery** dating back to 1566, which was revived in 1965, and claims to be the only British brewery that still ferments totally in oak. You can learn about the brewery and taste the ales in the Brewery Shop, as well as buy them from the laid-back tearoom and gift shop. There's also a redundant avenue which leads to the locked **Bear Gates**; Bonnie Prince Charlie departed the house through the gates, and the then owner promised to keep them locked till a Stuart should ascend the throne.

If you're really taken by the place, you can stay in one of its two double guest **rooms** (Ⓣ01896/830323; ❸), decked out with antiques and four-posters, on a bed-and-breakfast basis only.

Peebles

Fast, wide, tree-lined and fringed with grassy banks, the Tweed looks at its best at **PEEBLES**, a handsome royal burgh that sits on the north bank, seven miles upstream from Innerleithen. The town itself has a genteel, relaxed air, its wide, handsome High Street bordered by houses in a medley of architectural styles, mostly dating from Victorian times. The soaring crown spire of the **Old Parish Church** (daily 10am–4pm) rises up at the western end of the High Street and, inside, the church has some unusual features in its elegant oak, bronze and engraved-glass entrance screen and 22 modern oil paintings illustrating the scriptures. Suspended from the ceiling are tattered Napoleonic flags, emblems of 1816, the year the Peebleshire Militia disbanded.

Further down the High Street is the **Tweedale Museum & Gallery** (Mon–Fri 10am–noon & 2–5pm, Sat 10am–1pm, Sun 2–4pm; Nov–March closed Sat & Sun; free), housed in the Chambers Institute, which is heralded by two wonderfully ornate wrought-iron street lamps painted up in magenta and silver. William Chambers, a local worthy, presented the building to the town in 1859, complete with an art gallery dedicated to the enlightenment of his neighbours. He stuffed the place with casts of the world's most famous sculptures and, although most were lost long ago, today's "Secret Room", once the Museum Room, boasts two handsome friezes: one a copy of the Elgin marbles taken from the Parthenon; the other of the Triumph of Alexander, originally cast in 1812 to honour Napoleon.

Walks and bike-rides around Peebles

A series of **footpaths** snake through the hills surrounding Peebles with their rough-edged burns, bare peaks and deep woods. The five-mile **Sware Trail** is one of the easiest and most scenic, weaving west along the north bank of the river and looping back to the south. On the way, it passes **Neidpath Castle** (Easter, Whitsun, July & Aug daily 11am–6pm; £3), a gaunt medieval tower house perched high above the river on a rocky buff. It's a superb setting, and the interior possesses a pit prison and a great hall bedecked with stunning batik wall hangings depicting the life of Mary, Queen of Scots. The walk also goes by the splendid skew rail bridge, part of the Glasgow line which was finished in 1850. Other, longer footpaths follow the old **drove roads**, like the thirteen-mile haul to St Mary's Loch or the fourteen-mile route to Selkirk via Traquair House (see p.175). For either of these, you'll need an Ordnance Survey map, a compass and proper hiking gear (see p.46). A more gentle stroll is the 2.5-mile amble to the privately owned **Kailzie Gardens** (daily 11am–5.30pm; £2), whose fifteen acres include a walled garden, trout pond (fly-fishing tackle is available for rent), a lovely wood-panelled tearoom, a souvenir shop and small gallery.

From Peebles, you can link up to the clearly signposted ninety-mile **Tweed Cycleway**: mountain bikes can be rented from The Bicycle Works, 3 High St (ⓣ01721/723423), or Scottish Border Trails (ⓣ01721/722934), at the entrance to Glentress Forest two miles east of town on the A72.

Practicalities

Buses to Peebles from Selkirk, Galashiels and Edinburgh stop outside the post office, a few doors down from the well-stocked **tourist office** on the High Street (July & Aug Mon–Sat 9am–7pm, Sun 10am–6pm; June Mon–Sat 10am–5.30pm, Sun 10am–4pm; Sept Mon–Sat 9.30am–5.30pm, Sun 10am–4pm; April & May Mon–Sat 10am–5pm, Sun 10am–2pm; Oct Mon–Sat 9.30am–5.30pm, Sun 10am–2pm; Nov–March Mon–Sat 9.30am–4.30pm; ⓣ01721/720138).

Peebles boasts a vast number of **B&Bs**; try *Rowanbrae*, a trim, pint-sized Victorian place on a quiet cul-de-sac on Northgate, off the east end of High Street (ⓣ01721/721630, ⓔjohn@rowanbrae.freeserve.co.uk; ❶); or *Viewfield*, 1 Rosetta Rd (ⓣ01721/721232, ⓔmmitchell38@yahoo.com; ❶), an attractive detached Victorian house a ten-minute walk west of the bridge, with rooms overlooking a lovely garden – take the Old Town road (the A72) and follow it round, turning right up Young Street. For upmarket **hotels** you have to head out of town: *Castle Venlaw Hotel* (ⓣ01721/720384, ⓦwww.venlaw.co.uk; ❻) is a Scots Baronial house set in its own grounds on the edge of town up the Edinburgh Road; the *Cringletie House Hotel* (ⓣ01721/730233, ⓦwww.cringletie.com; ❽) is a still more splendid Baronial pile a couple of miles further up the Edinburgh Road; and finally, there's the *Peebles Hotel Hydro* (ⓣ01721/720602, ⓦwww.peebleshotelhydro.co.uk; ❽), a massive Edwardian purpose-built hotel, which prides itself on welcomng families with kids and/or grandparents in tow. Of the two **campsites** on the edge of town, the *Rosetta Caravan Park* (ⓣ01721/720770; April–Oct) is the quieter, set in field surrounded by mature woods, a fifteen-minute walk north of the High Street (directions as for *Viewfield* B&B).

The best place to **eat** is the *Sunflower* (ⓣ017221/722420), a tiny, brightly coloured restaurant at 4 Bridgegate, just off Northgate, which does inexpensive hot sandwiches and a few main dishes for lunch, and more adventurous (and slightly pricier) evening meals, for which it's advisable to book. *Tatlers*, on the High Street, is a normal café, though it does serve good coffee. As for **pubs**, the *Crown Hotel* on the High Street, is a cosy place to hunker down; the *Tontine Hotel*, opposite, is a grander place with the views south over the Tweed. For really good pub food, try one of the bar meals at the *Castle Venlaw Hotel*.

Tweeddale

Upstream from Peebles, the Tweed valley is more commonly known as **Tweeddale**. The valley sides gradually narrow as the road follows the river upstream and south to the source of the Tweed, at the border with Dumfries and Galloway. Eight miles southwest of Peebles, near Strobo, the Tweed passes **Dawyck Botanic Garden** (March–Oct daily 9.30am–6pm; £3), an arboretum outstation of the Royal Botanic Garden in Edinburgh, which specializes in rare trees and shrubs, but also has an impressive display of rhododendrons and azaleas.

Two miles west of Dawyck stands the village of **BROUGHTON**, home of the excellent Broughton Ales. Inside the old Free Church, the **John Buchan Centre** (Easter & May to mid-Oct daily 2–5pm; £1.50) commemorates John Buchan, first Baron Tweedsmuir (1875–1940), author and diplomat, who spent his childhood holidays in the district. Three miles down a dead-end road in pretty, secluded **Holmswater Glen**, the *Glenholm Centre* (Ⓣ01899/830408, Ⓦwww.glenholm.co.uk; closed Jan; ❸) is a working farm with a cosy four-room guesthouse, the perfect base for exploring the surrounding hills.

Ten miles or so further south on the A701, the Tweed eventually reaches tiny **TWEEDSMUIR**, en route passing *The Crook Inn* (Ⓣ01899/880272; ❹), one-time watering hole of Robbie Burns and a good base for climbing **Broad Law** (2723ft), the Southern Uplands' second highest hill. Behind the hotel, there's a small workshop and craft centre, where you can watch glass-blowing displays. At Tweedsmuir, you can either head over the pass to the Devil's Beef Tub and Moffat (see p.189), or east over the **Tweedsmuir Hills** to St Mary's Loch (see below). The eleven-mile single-track road to St Mary's Loch, inaccessible in winter, climbs at a twenty percent gradient past **Talla Reservoir**, where many men lost their lives constructing a water supply for Edinburgh in 1905. Fishing permits for Talla and the neighbouring Megget Reservoir are available from *Tibbie Shiels Inn* at St Mary's Loch (see p.178).

Selkirk and around

Just south of the River Tweed, some five miles southwest of Melrose, lies the royal burgh of **SELKIRK**. The old town sits high up above Ettrick Water; down in the valley by the riverside, the town's imposing greystone woollen mills are mostly boarded up now, an eerie reminder of a once prosperous era. There's precious little reason to linger in Selkirk itself, though the town sits on the edge of some lovely countryside, and serves as the gateway to the picturesque, sparsely populated valleys of Yarrow Water and Ettrick Water, to the west.

At the centre of Selkirk, at one end of the High Street, you'll find the tiny **Market Square**, where you should pop into *Graeve's Snack Attack* and purchase the local "Selkirk Bannock", a sort of fruit cake. While munching it, you can admire Selkirk's statues, the most prominent being that of Sir Walter Scott, which stands outside the former Town House, now dubbed **Sir Walter Scott's Courtroom** (April–Sept Mon–Sat 10am–4pm; July & Aug also Sun 2–4pm; Oct–March Mon–Sat 1–4pm; free), where he served as sheriff for 33 years. At the other end of the High Street is a rather more unusual statue of **Mungo Park**, the renowned explorer and anti-slavery advocate, born in the county in

1771. The base displays two finely cast bas-reliefs depicting his exploits along the River Niger, which came to an end with his accidental drowning in 1805; his son, who died searching for his father's body in 1827, is also commemorated. The bronze life-size African mourners, *Peace*, *War*, *Slavery* and *Home Life in the Niger,* were added in 1913, after several petitions and newspaper editorials demanded that Park be further commemorated.

Just off Market Square to the south is **Halliwell's House Museum** (April–Oct Mon–Sat 10am–5pm, Sun 2–4pm; July & Aug Sun until 6pm; free), an old-style hardware shop and an informative exhibit on the industrialization of the Tweed Valley, while the adjacent Robson Gallery hosts a series of temporary exhibitions of paintings and ceramics. Down by the river at the junction of the A7 with the B7014, **Selkirk Glass** (Mon–Sat 9am–5pm, Sun 11am–5pm; free) is a thriving craft industry that stands in stark contrast to the neighbouring mills. Visitors arrive by the coachload to sit in the café and watch glass-blowers making intricate paperweights and the like.

The **tourist office** (same hours as Halliwell's House; ⓣ01750/720054) is in Halliwell's House off Market Square, and can help with **accommodation**. First choice for those with an unlimited budget is the upmarket *Philipburn House Hotel* (ⓣ01750/720747, ⓦwww.philipburnhousehotel.co.uk; ❻), an unusual eighteenth-century house set in its own grounds a mile west of the town centre; the hotel offers expensive, but excellent Scottish cuisine. More modest in price, but still full of character is the *Heatherlie House Hotel* (ⓣ01750/721200, ⓦwww.heatherlie.freeserve.co.uk; ❹), a Victorian mansion a sharp left turn up from the road to Ettrick at Heatherlie Park. **Camping** is possible beside the river, next to the swimming pool at *Victoria Park* (ⓣ01750/720897; April–Oct), though the campsites in the Ettrick Valley are far more scenic (see p.181).

Bowhill House

Three miles west of Selkirk off the A708, **Bowhill House** (July daily 1–4.30pm; £4.50) is the property of the Duke of Buccleuch and Queensberry, a seriously wealthy man. Beyond the grandiose mid-nineteenth-century mansion's facade of dark whinstone is an outstanding collection of French antiques and European **paintings**: in the dining room, for example, there are portraits by Reynolds and Gainsborough and a Canaletto cityscape, while the drawing room boasts Boulle furniture, Meissen tableware, paintings by Ruysdael, Leandro Bassano and Claude Lorraine, as well as two more family portraits by Reynolds. Look out also for the Scott Room, which features another splendid portrait of Sir Walter by Henry Raeburn, and the Monmouth Room, commemorating James, Duke of Monmouth, the illegitimate son of Charles II, who married Anne of the Buccleuchs. After several years in exile, Monmouth returned to England when his father died in 1685, hoping to wrest the crown from James II. He was defeated at the Battle of Sedgemoor in Somerset and subsequently sent to the scaffold; among other items, his execution shirt is on display.

The wooded hills of **Bowhill Country Park** adjoining the house (July daily noon–5pm; Easter–June & Aug daily except Fri noon–5pm; £2) are criss-crossed by scenic footpaths and cycle trails: you can rent **mountain bikes** from the visitor centre.

Getting to Bowhill by **public transport** is difficult. The Peebles bus, leaving Selkirk daily at 2pm, will drop you at General's Bridge (takes 10min), from where it's a mile or so's walk through the grounds to the house.

Yarrow Water

The A708, which passes by Bowhill, follows **Yarrow Water** upstream towards Dumfriesshire. A couple of miles west of Bowhill there's the Broadmeadows SYHA **hostel** at Yarrowford (Ⓣ01750/76262, Ⓦwww.syha.org.uk; April–Sept), which serves as a convenient starting-point for some good hill walks. From here, you can reach the hilltop cairns of **The Three Brethren**, whose 1530-ft summit offers excellent views over the Borders. You can also link up with stretches of the Southern Upland Way by heading east down through Yair Forest, or by following an old drove road west to the Cheese Well at Minchmoor (so called because of offerings left by travellers for the faerie folk), and ending up at Traquair House near Innerleithen.

Eight miles further west, the A708 is crossed by the B709 going north through the hills to Innerleithen and southeast to Hawick. The junction is marked by the **Gordon Arms Hotel** (Ⓣ01750/82232; ❷), reputedly the last meeting place of Walter Scott and James Hogg, the "Shepherd poet of Ettrick" (see below), where framed fragments of letters from Scott are on display in an otherwise basic bar serving meals and real ale. From the hotel, which offers a transport service and a cheap **bunkhouse** for walkers, you can follow the course of the lovely Yarrow Water further east for about seventeen miles to Selkirk (see p.178). Buses along the Yarrow Valley take you only as far as the *Gordon Arms Hotel* and then turn north to Traquair and Peebles.

A couple of miles further up the A708 at the top of Yarrow Water lies a pair of icy lakes: **St Mary's Loch**, and its diminutive neighbour, **Loch of the Lowes**, separated by a slender isthmus and magnificently set beneath the surrounding hills. This spot was popular with the nineteenth-century Scottish literati, especially Scott and Hogg, who wrote:

> Oft had he viewed, as morning rose
> the bosom of the lonely Lowes.
> Oft thrilled his heart at close of even
> to see the dappled vales of heaven
> with many a mountain, moor and tree
> asleep upon Saint Mary.

The pair gathered to chew the fat at **Tibbie Shiels Inn** on the isthmus, which takes its name from Isabella Shiel, a formidable and, by all accounts, amusing woman who ruled the place till her death in 1878 at the age of 96. Today, the inn is a famous watering hole on the Southern Upland Way and serves a limited range of bar meals. For a short and enjoyable walk, follow the footpath from the inn along the east side of St Mary's Loch into **Bowerhope Forest**. Alternatively, the Southern Upland Way heads across the moors north to Traquair House and south to the valley of the Ettrick Water, both strenuous hikes that require an Ordnance Survey map, a compass and proper clothing (see p.46).

Aikwood Tower and Ettrick Water

Aikwood Tower (April–Sept Tues, Thurs & Sun 2–5pm; £1.50), four miles west of Selkirk on the B7009, is a sixteenth-century fortified tower house, whose stern rubble walls stand surrounded by forests of the Ettrick Water Valley. Inside, an exhibition explores the life and work of **James Hogg**, a friend of Sir Walter Scott's known as the "Ettrick Shepherd". Hogg was born locally, in sheep-farming Ettrick valley, in 1770 and became a self-taught poet of some contemporary renown who spent several years living among the

Edinburgh literary elite. Today he's largely forgotten, which – considering his style – is not entirely surprising. The old byres adjoining the tower are given over to temporary displays of local artists' work and during the summer months sculpture is exhibited in the gardens. Aikwood is also the home of the Speaker of the Scottish Parliament, Sir David Steel.

Running alongside **Ettrick Water** towards Langholm (see p.188), the B7009 passes through some of the Borders' loveliest scenery, from gentle, open hills dotted with the occasional sheep farm to the progressively bleak moors of Eskdalemuir (see p.188). A couple of miles beyond Aikwood Tower lies the hamlet of **ETTRICKBRIDGE**, which, like every border town, boasts a *Cross Keys Inn* (Ⓣ01750/52224; ❸), in this case a seventeenth-century coaching inn with a cosy, oak-beamed bar. Ten miles further on, just north of Ettrick, you'll find the *Honey Cottage Caravan Park* (Ⓣ01750/62246), a picturesque, family-run campsite on Ettrick Water.

Teviotdale

To the south of the Tweed, **Teviotdale** is an altogether gentler valley, stretched between Teviothead, in the western hills, and Kelso, where the river joins the Tweed. The chief draw here is the best-preserved of all the Border abbeys, at **Jedburgh**, which lies on a tributary of the Teviot called Jed Water. The main town on the Teviot itself is **Hawick**, famous for its knitwear factories, but hardly a must on most people's itinerary. From Hawick the busy A7 tracks up the most dramatic section of **Teviotdale** towards Langholm in Dumfriesshire. The alternative is to take the B6399 – or, if you're coming straight from Jedburgh, the B6357 – both slower but even more picturesque, remote roads flanked by dense forests, barren moors and secluded heaths. If you do come this way, stop off at solitary **Hermitage Castle**, a well-preserved fourteenth-century fortress.

The Galashiels-to-Carlisle **bus** travels along much of Teviotdale via Hawick, where buses connect with Jedburgh.

Jedburgh

Just ten miles north of the border with England, **JEDBURGH** nestles in the lush valley of the Jed Water near its confluence with the Teviot out on the edge of the wild Cheviot Hills. During the interminable Anglo-Scottish Wars, Jedburgh was the quintessential frontier town, a heavily garrisoned royal burgh incorporating a mighty castle and abbey. Though the castle was destroyed by the Scots in 1409 to keep it out of the hands of the English, its memory has been kept alive by stories: in 1285, for example, King Alexander III was celebrating his wedding feast in the great hall when a ghostly apparition predicted his untimely death and a bloody civil war; sure enough, he died in a hunting accident shortly afterwards and chaos ensued. Today, Jedburgh is the first place of any size that you come to on the A68, having crossed over Carter Bar from England, and as such gets quite a bit of passing tourist trade, The ruined **abbey** is the main event, though a stroll round Jedburgh's old town centre is a pleasant way to while away an hour or so.

The abbey and town

Despite its ruinous state, **Jedburgh Abbey** (April–Sept daily 9.30am–6.30pm; Oct–March Mon–Sat 9.30am–4.30pm, Sun 2–4.30pm; HS; £3.30) still

Aug Mon–Sat 10am–6pm, Sun noon–5pm; June & Sept Mon–Sat 10am–5.30pm, Sun noon–5pm; Easter–May & Oct Mon–Sat 10am–5pm, Sun noon–5pm; Nov–Easter Mon–Sat 11am–3.45pm; £2), not a tower at all, but a former inn and hotel. However, it started out in life as a medieval fortified keep, and now houses a rather good town **museum**, spread out over three floors; you can even climb out onto the roof, from which you get a good view of the near-by medieval motte. Hawick's other formal attraction is the **Hawick Museum & Scott Art Gallery** (April–Sept Mon–Fri 10am–noon & 1–5pm, Sat & Sun 2–4.45pm; Oct–March Mon–Fri 1–4pm, Sun 2–4pm; £1.25), a mile or so west of the town centre in Wilton Lodge Park. The museum has displays reflecting the manufacturing life of the area and a special section on Jimmie Guthrie, a local motorcycle ace who died during the German Grand Prix in 1937. There's also a gallery housing nineteenth- and twentieth-century Scottish art; more exciting, though, are the regular travelling exhibitions which Hawick manages to attract.

The **tourist office** is on the ground floor of Drumlanrig Tower (same hours as Hawick Museum; ⓣ01450/372547, ⓦwww.hawick.org). A good choice for **accommodation** is the *Kirklands Hotel* (ⓣ01450/372263; ❹), a genuinely friendly, unpretentious place, which serves reasonably priced bar and restaurant meals. Hawick's most celebrated annual event is its **Common Riding**, which is held in early June, and commemorates a skirmish in 1514 when the local Hawick callants defeated a small English force and captured their banner. Another date for the diary is the Borders **festival of jazz and blues**, which takes place in Hawick in early September (ⓦwww.hawick.org/jazz.htm).

Liddesdale

Either forming the border with England, or sticking close to it, **Liddesdale** is the only valley in the Borders whose river flows westwards. It's best approached via the hamlet of Bonchester Bridge, which sits on the A6088 from Hawick to Carter Bar. From here, the B6357 cuts south through Wauchope Forest before reaching Liddesdale.

The valley's wild beauty is at its most striking between Saughtree and Newcastleton, where there's a turning to **Hermitage Castle** (April–Sept daily 9.30am–6.30pm; HS; £1.80), a bleak and forbidding fastness bedevilled by all sorts of horrifying legends: one owner, William Douglas, starved his prisoners to death, whilst Lord de Soulis, another occupant, engaged the help of demons to fortify the castle in defiance of the king, Robert the Bruce. Not entirely trusting his demonic assistants, Soulis also drilled holes into the shoulders of his vassals, the better to yoke them to sledges of building materials. Bruce became so tired of the complaints that he exclaimed, "Boil him if you please, but let me hear no more of him." Bruce's henchmen took him at his word and ambushed the rebellious baron. Convinced, however, that Soulis had a pact with his demonic familiar, Redcap, that made him difficult to kill ("ropes could not bind him, nor steel weapons touch"), they bound him with ropes of sifted sand, wrapped him in lead and boiled him slowly. From the outside, the castle remains an imposing structure, its heavy walls topped by stepped gables and a tidy corbelled parapet. However, the apparent homogeneity is deceptive: certain features were invented during a Victorian restoration, a confusing supplement to the ad hoc alterations that had already transformed the fourteenth-century original. The ruinous interior is a bit of a letdown, but look out for the tight Gothic doorways and gruesome dungeon.

It's a short journey on to **NEWCASTLETON**, a classic estate village built for the hand-loom weavers of the third Duke of Buccleuch in 1793. The grid-iron streets fall either side of a long main road that connects three geometrically arranged squares, with the largest, Douglas Square, as the centrepiece. You can have a **drink**, sample some local trout or pheasant, or even **stay** the night at the *Liddesdale Hotel* (ⓣ01387/375255; ❷), a family-run inn on Douglas Square itself. Book ahead if you plan to stay during the hugely popular **Newcastleton Folk Festival** in July. There are no buses along the length of Liddesdale.

Dumfries and Galloway

The southwest corner of Scotland, now known as **Dumfries and Galloway** (ⓦwww.dumfriesandgalloway.co.uk), is a region set apart. A lot of people heading north from England might pause to explore the Borders region, but few bother to exit the main Carlisle–Glasgow motorway. Yet Dumfries and Galloway have stately homes, deserted hills and ruined abbeys to compete with the best of the Borders. They also have something the Borders don't have, and that's the Solway coast, a long, indented coastline of sheltered sandy coves that's been dubbed the "Scottish Riviera" – an exaggeration perhaps, but it's certainly Scotland's warmest, southernmost stretch of coastline. Also, being off the beaten track, and not crossed by any motorways Galloway, in particular, suffers little of the tourist crush familiar further north.

The region has a fascinatingly diverse heritage: originally inhabited by southern Picts, it has at various times been overrun by Romans, Anglo-Saxons from Northumberland and Celts from Ireland: the name Galloway means the "land of the stranger Gaels". It was an unruly land, where independent chieftains maintained close contacts with the Vikings rather than the Scots, right up until medieval times. Gradually, this autonomy was whittled away, as the area became swallowed up by the Scottish crown, though Galloway, in particular, has continued to be a fiercely independent region, typified by local hero, Robert the Bruce. Later, Galloway became a stronghold of the Covenanters, and suffered terribly during the "Killing Times" following the Restoration, when the government forces came to impose episcopalianism. From around the seventeenth century, the ports of the Solway coast prospered with the expansion of local shipping routes over to Ireland. The region subsequently experienced economic decline as trade routes changed, turning busy ports into sleepy backwaters, and these days southwest Scotland is one of the most agreeably laid-back areas of the country.

Dumfries is the obvious gateway to the region, a pleasant enough town that's only really a must for those on the trail of **Robert Burns**, who spent the last part of his life here. More compelling is the nearby coast, overlooking the Solway Firth, the shallow estuary wedged between Scotland and England, famed for its wildlife and for the nearby red sandstone ruins of **Caerlaverock Castle** and **Sweetheart Abbey**. Edged by tidal marsh and mud bank, much of the Solway shoreline is flat and eerily remote, but there are also some fine rocky bays sheltering beneath wooded hills, most notably along the **Colvend coast.** Further along the coast is **Kirkcudbright**, once a bustling port thronged with sailing ships, later an artists' retreat, and now a tranquil, well-preserved little eighteenth- and early nineteenth-century town. Like Kirkcudbright, **Threave Garden and Castle**, just outside Castle Douglas, are popular with – but not crowded by – tourists.

Contrasting with the essentially gentle landscape of the Solway coast, is the brooding presence of the **Galloway Hills** to the north, their beautiful moors, mountains, lakes and rivers centred on the 150,000-acre **Galloway Forest Park**, a seriously underused hill-walking and mountain-biking paradise. Continuing west into what used to be Wigtownshire, the landscape becomes flatter and more relentlessly agricultural. The three main points of interest here are **Whithorn**, where St Ninian introduced Christianity to Scotland, the attractive seaport of **Portpatrick** on the hammer-headed Rhinns of Galloway, and the **Mull of Galloway**, Scotland's southernmost point, and a nesting site for thousands of seabirds.

Travelling the region by **bus** presents few problems and there's a good **train** service from Dumfries along Nithsdale to Sanquhar and eventually to Kilmarnock. It's also easy to travel on from southwest Scotland by **ferry** to Northern Ireland, from Stranraer to Belfast and from Cairnryan to Larne.

Annandale

Cutting through **Annandale**, the A74(M) and the main railway line connect Carlisle with Glasgow. This is the fastest route for crossing southern Scotland but it's a fairly bleak landscape and an unpleasantly busy motorway, jam-packed with trucks and lorries. If you simply need to break your journey, then the market town of **Moffat**, thirty miles or so north of the border (and bypassed by the motorway), is the best choice – it's also a feasible base for exploring the surrounding Southern Uplands. Alternatively, if you're heading east into the Borders, you could leave the motorway earlier, either at **Lockerbie**, and head up via **Eskdalemuir**, or even before that, and head towards Teviotdale, via **Langholm**.

Gretna Green

GRETNA GREEN (Ⓦ www.gretnagreen.com) is synonymous with elopements and quick **weddings**, thanks to an anomaly between the English and Scottish legal systems. Up until 1753 English couples could buy a quick and secret wedding at London's Fleet Prison, bribing imprisoned clerics with small amounts of money. The Hardwicke Marriage Act brought an end to this seedy wheeze, enforcing the requirement of a licence and a church ceremony. However, in Scotland, a marriage declaration made before two witnesses remained legal. The consequences of this difference in the law verged on farce: hundreds of runaway couples dashed north to Scotland, their weddings witnessed by just about anyone who came to hand – ferrymen, farmers, tollgate keepers and even self-styled "priests" who set up their own "marriage houses".

Gretna Green, due to its position beside the border on the main turnpike road to Edinburgh, became the most popular destination for the fugitives. In their rush, many people tied the knot at the first place to hand after dismounting from the stagecoach, which happened to be a **blacksmith's shop** situated at the crossroads, though the better-off maintained class distinctions, heading for the staging post at Gretna Hall. The association with blacksmiths was strengthened by one of the first "priests", the redoubtable Joseph Paisley, a

25-stone Goliath who – in business from 1754 to 1812 – gave a certain style to the ceremony by straightening a horseshoe, a show of strength rather than a symbolic act. His melodramatic act led to stories of Gretna Green weddings being performed over the blacksmith's **anvil**, and later "priests" were more than happy to act out the rumour. Gretna Green boomed until the marriage laws were further amended in 1856, but some business continued right down to 1940, when marriage by declaration was made illegal.

Gretna still makes its money from the marriage charade, which is fair enough given that there's not much else going for the place. The only marriages that take place in Gretna Green nowadays, however, are for couples taken in by the "romance" of the name, and English couples under eighteen, who want to get married without the permission of their parents. Most of the money comes from the car and coachloads of tourists who roll up at the **World Famous Old Blacksmith's Shop Centre**, a vast complex of tartan and whisky shops, arts gallery, café, restaurant, toilets and museum, all to the backdrop hum of the nearby A74(M). Not to be outdone, the *Gretna Hall Hotel*, on the other side of the motorway, have built themselves a rival blacksmith's and also run their own museum. There's no conceivable reason to stop at either place, and even less in the neighbouring settlement of Gretna, which was built between the wars to house those working at the nearby munitions factory. There is, however, a useful **tourist office** (daily: July & Aug 10am–6pm; May, June & Sept 10am–5pm; April & Oct 10am–4.30pm; ⓣ01461/337834), opposite the blacksmith's.

Ecclefechan

It's about nine miles from the border to the tidy hamlet of **ECCLEFECHAN**, birthplace of the historian and essayist **Thomas Carlyle** (1795–1881). Born into a strongly Calvinist family, Carlyle's highly successful account of the French Revolution (1837) set out his theory of history as "Divine Scripture":

Lockerbie

The quiet country town of **Lockerbie**, halfway between the border and Moffat, was catapulted into the headlines on Wednesday, December 21, 1988, when a 747 jumbo jet, on Pan-Am flight 103 from Frankfurt to New York via London Heathrow, was blown up at 31,000 feet by a terrorist bomb concealed in a transistor radio. All 259 crew and passengers died, plus 11 residents of Sherwood Crescent in Lockerbie where the plane's fuselage landed. The impact of this event caused terrible trauma in Lockerbie, both physically and psychologically, and continues to do so even now, more than a decade on. A memorial was set up, and links were forged with the families of the US victims, but there was also a strong suspicion among the victims' groups of a cover-up by the powers that be. Jim Swire, a doctor from the English Midlands, who lost his 23-year-old daughter in the crash, was instrumental in pressing for those responsible to be brought to trial, and for the truth to be told about the whole incident. He even went as far as visiting Libya, meeting with relatives of those who were killed in the revenge air attacks launched by the US, and personally asking Colonel Gaddafi (who lost his own two-year-old daughter in one of the raids) to allow the two Libyans charged with the crime to stand trial. Eventually, more than ten years after the event, a trial was held under Scottish law in a specially created court in the Netherlands, and resulted in the conviction of one of the two suspects. At the time of going to press, the convicted Libyan was appealing against the verdict, while Jim Swire was continuing to press for a public inquiry into the many unanswered questions, not least why various intelligence warnings prior to the bombing were ignored.

the French aristocracy had reaped the rewards of their corruption and indulgence. However, with no clearly defined political ideology his radicalism soon began to wane, reinforced by the failure of contemporary activist movements to live up to his idealistic expectations. Disillusioned, Carlyle was eventually to become the strongest voice for the moral concerns of the Victorian bourgeoisie, and as such a litmus paper for his age. His long marriage was turbulent, but when his wife died in 1866 he never recovered and was a semi-recluse for many years before his death. His old home, the whitewashed **Arched House** (May–Sept Mon & Fri–Sun 1.30–5.30pm; NTS; £2.50), a typical two-storey house with a central pend (passage), was built by his father and uncle, and is now a tiny museum, featuring among the personal memorabilia a bronze cast of his hands, old smoking caps and his cradle. The family moved from the Arched House while Thomas was in his infancy; in 1828, he moved to Craigenputtock, thirteen miles northwest of Dumfries, and from 1834 until his death, he lived in London. He's buried in the local churchyard.

The double bay-fronted Victorian *Cressfield Country House Hotel*, on Townfoot (Ⓣ01576/300281; ❸), designed by Carlyle's father, is a good choice of **accommodation**; to get there follow the signs to the nearby *Cressfield Caravan Park* **campsite** (Ⓣ01576/300702), a pristinely kept site set within a country park.

Langholm and around

While not strictly in Annandale, **LANGHOLM** is on the road from Carlisle and Gretna Green to the Borders. A quiet, stone-built mill town at the confluence of the Esk, Ewes and Wauchope waters, Langholm flourished during the eighteenth-century textile boom, and is still dominated by the industry. This was the birthplace of the poet **Hugh MacDiarmid** (1892–1978), a key player in the Scottish nationalist literary renaissance between the two world wars, a cofounder of the Scottish National Party, and later a Communist Party member; he was expelled from each in turn. MacDiarmid, born Christopher Murray Grieve, looked to the hard Scots language of the Border ballads and medieval poets such as Dunbar and Henryson, but had little time for the naïve sentimentality of Burns, and the Tory politics of Scott, heaping scorn on the local anglicized gentry. This didn't go down well with some of the burghers of Langholm, who, when MacDiarmid died at the age of 86, tried to prevent him being buried in the local churchyard.

A generation on, and how times have changed: the local tourist board now hands out a leaflet on the "MacDiarmid Trail", tracing the roots of "Scotland's greatest twentieth-century poet". First stop is the old library where MacDiarmid's mother was caretaker; not far away is his birthplace at 17 Arkinholm Terrace; you'll find his grave in the Langholm Cemetery on the A7 heading south out of town. Even if you've no interest in MacDiarmid, it's worth heading out to the striking **MacDiarmid Memorial**, a giant metal book on a hill two miles up the road to Newcastleton, off the A7. The path past the sculpture continues up the hill to an earlier monument, the **Malcolm Memorial**, commemorating another local boy, albeit a rather more conventional one, Sir John "Boy" Malcolm (1769–1833), an ambitious, reactionary colonialist who became Governor of Bombay; the views from his monument are terrific.

Eskdalemuir

Three roads lead out of Langholm into the Borders, the most stunning being the narrow country lane that snakes its way east over the empty hills to Newcastleton in Liddesdale (see p.184), followed by the far slower trip northwest up Eskdale for Selkirk and the Tweed Valley (see p.178). Thirteen miles up Eskdale, the fluttering prayer flags, scarlet-robed Buddhists and golden temple domes of the **Tibetan Monastery** (T 01387/373232, W www.samyeling.org) make a surreal sight against the bleak expanse of the tiny village of **ESKDALEMUIR**. Visitors are welcome to look round the impressive Samye Ling temple, and to attend courses on Buddhist meditation and Eastern philosophy. **Accommodation** and a basic vegetarian canteen are available for people staying on retreats or attending courses, and there's a small shop and café for passing visitors.

Moffat and around

Encircled by hills and dales, **MOFFAT** is an old market town whose heyday was during the eighteenth century, when it was briefly a modish spa, its sulphur springs attracting the rich and famous. One disappointed customer suggested they smelt of bilge water, but they were good enough for Robbie Burns and James Boswell, who came to "wash off the scurvy spots". Moffat is no longer so fashionable; its shops now sell tartan and tat, and its hotels and inns have all seen better days. Nevertheless, the wide **High Street** has a pleasingly eclectic mixture of buildings, from the *Victorian Star Hotel*, "famous" as Britain's narrowest free-standing hotel, to the Neoclassical town hall, on the opposite side of the street. The most obvious reminder of Moffat's halcyon period is the John Adam-designed **Moffat House Hotel**, a three-storey greystone house, with characteristic red sandstone trim around the windows, flanked by matching outbuildings. Inside, only the central oval staircase hints at former days, the rest of the place resembling every other hotel run by the multinational Best Western chain. Back on the High Street, don't miss the nearby **Colvin Fountain**, whose sturdy bronze ram was accidentally cast without any ears.

For details of the town's history as a spa, among other topics, and a retreat from bad weather, pop into the **Moffat Museum** (Easter & Whitsun–Sept Mon, Tues & Thurs–Sat 10.30am–1pm & 2.30–5pm, Sun 2.30–5pm; £1), in an old bakehouse at Church Gate, at the bottom of the High Street. A little way further south along the road to Dumfries is the giant **Moffat Woollen Mill** (daily March–Oct 9am–5.30pm; Nov–Feb 9.30am–5pm; free), where you can watch weaving demonstrations, and visit the inevitable clan tartan centre and whisky shop. In sunny weather, those with small children might like to take their kids to **Moffatasia** (May–Aug Mon–Sat 10am–8pm, Sun 1–7pm; free), an outdoor water-feature playground where the little ones can soak themselves under various mushroom jets, fountains and water cannon.

Moffat is also a good base for **walking** in the surrounding countryside. The tourist office has a helpful compendium of local walks, one of the best being the short but brisk hike up to the top of Gallow Hill, from where there are great views out over Annandale (allow a couple of hours). For a more gentle stroll round the outskirts of the town by the River Annan, follow the "waterside walk" sign opposite Station Park. More strenuous walking is within reach in the Lowther Hills (see p.199), and nearby Beattock marks the midway point of the Southern Upland Way.

Practicalities

Buses drop passengers off on the High Street, in the town centre. The **tourist office** (daily: June–Aug 9.30am–6.30pm; April, May, Sept & Oct 10am–5pm; T 01683/220620) is hidden away in a corner of the large car park of the Moffat Woollen Mill to the south of the town centre. There is no shortage of **accommodation**, though you're much better off avoiding the hotels that line the High Street, all of which have seen better days. Instead, head off into the quiet backstreets to the east of the High Street and try an attractive Victorian villa like *Burnside* (Ⓣ01683/221900, Ⓔkate.burnside@btinternet.com; ❷; March– Nov), or *Kirkland House* (Ⓣ01683/221133; ❷), the town's former manse, both on Well Road. Moving up the price range, there's the large, double-fronted *Wellview Hotel* (Ⓣ01683/220184, Ⓦwww.wellview.co.uk; ❺), on Ballplay Road on the eastern edge of Moffat, which also has an excellent restaurant. The fourteen-acre *Hammerland's Farm* **caravan** and **camping** site (Ⓣ01683/220436; March–Oct) is a short walk from the centre of town, near the tourist office.

Apart from the *Wellview Hotel*, the best **restaurant** is *The Lime Tree* (Ⓣ01683/221654), which serves imaginative food in a small place at the top of the High Street opposite the *Moffat House Hotel*. Otherwise, head for *Claudio's*, a popular, cosy Italian restaurant housed in the attractive Victorian former police station on Burnside. For snacks and decent coffee, go to *Arietes* **café** on the High Street; for a drink, penetrate the dark shadows of the *Black Bull*, at the bottom of the High Street on Churchgate, a **pub** which once quartered John Graham of Claverhouse as he planned his persecution of the Covenanters on behalf of Charles II.

Around Moffat

From Moffat, there are two beautiful routes you can take through the most dramatic parts of the Southern Uplands and into the Borders region. Of the two, the finest is the A708, which heads northeast up Moffat Water over to Selkirk in the Borders (see p.178). On the way, the 200ft **Grey Mare's Tail Waterfall** (NTS), which tumbles down a rocky crevasse, provides one of Dumfriesshire's best-known beauty spots. The base of the falls is approached by a precipitous footpath along the left side of the stream, a ten-minute clamber each way from the road. There's a longer hike, too, up the steep right-hand bank, past the head of the falls and on to the remote **Loch Skeen**, where you can fish without permits. Further northeast in the Borders, St Mary's Loch gives easy access to an especially stimulating section of the Southern Upland Way (see p.158).

The second route, to the west, uses the A701, which ascends the west side of Annandale to skirt the impressive box canyon at its head, and cuts down Tweeddale towards Peebles (see p.176). Best viewed from the road about six miles from town, the gorge – the **Devil's Beef Tub** – takes its name from the days when rustling Reivers hid their herds here. Walter Scott described the place aptly: "It looks as if four hills were laying their heads together to shut out daylight from the dark hollow place between them." The gorge was also a suitably secret hideaway for persecuted Covenanters during Charles II's "Killing Times".

Travelling these routes by **bus** remains difficult. The only service along the A708 is the Scenic Bus Service #130, which runs from Moffat to Selkirk twice on a Saturday.

Dumfries and around

Situated on the wide banks of the River Nith a short distance inland from the Solway Firth, **DUMFRIES** is by far the largest town in southwest Scotland, with a population of more than thirty thousand. Long known as the "Queen of the South" (as is its football club), the town flourished as a medieval seaport

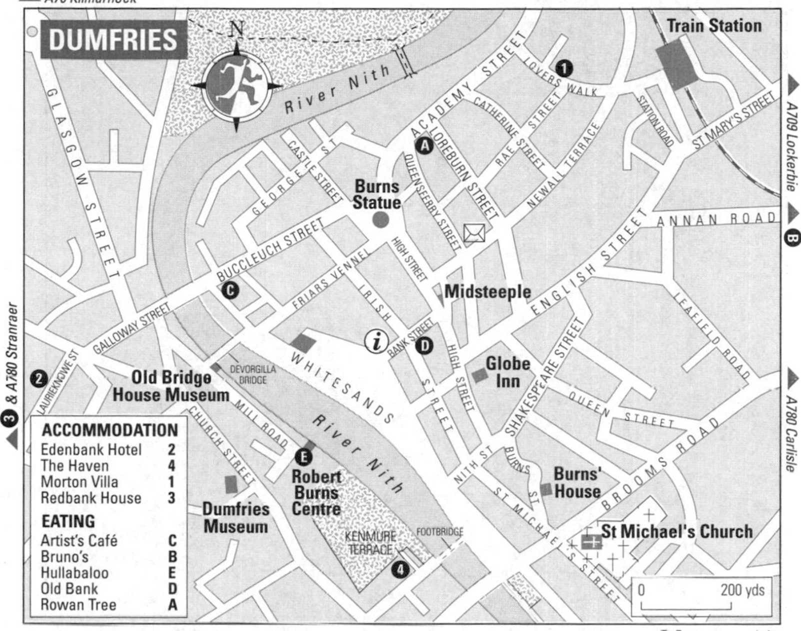

© Crown copyright

and trading centre, its success attracting the attention of many English armies. The invaders managed to polish off most of the early settlement in 1448, 1536 and again in 1570, but Dumfries survived to prosper with its light industries and port supplying the agricultural hinterland. The town planners of the 1960s badly damaged the town, but enough remains of the warm red sandstone buildings that distinguish Dumfries from other towns in the southwest to make it worth at least a brief stop. It's also acts a convenient base for exploring the Solway coast, to the east and west, and is second only to Ayr for its associations with Robbie Burns, who spent the last five years of his life here employed as an exciseman.

The Town

Orientation around Dumfries is easy, with the railway to the east, and the river to the north and west. The pedestrianized **High Street** runs roughly parallel to the Nith; at its northern end, presiding over a floral roundabout, is the **Burns Statue**, a sentimental piece of Victorian frippery in white Carrara marble, featuring the great man holding a posy in one hand while the other clutches at his heart. His faithful hound, Luath, lies curled around his feet – though it doesn't look much like a Scots collie (as Luath was). Further down the High Street, Burns' body lay in state at the town's most singular building, the **Midsteeple**, an appealingly wonky hotchpotch of a building, built in 1707 to fulfil the multiple functions of town prison, clocktower, courthouse and arsenal.

If you're on Burns' trail, make sure you duck down the alleyway to the **Globe Inn**, just past the ornate red and gold Victorian fountain, a little further down the High Street. This whitewashed inn, with its own suntrap courtyard, is

△ Dumfries

Burns' most famous "howff" (pub), headquarters of the local Burns' society, and one of the town's few surviving seventeenth-century buildings. Burns had a fling with Annie Park, a barmaid at the Globe Inn, and the resultant child was taken into the Burns household by the long suffering Jean Armour, who apparently opined that "our Robbie should have had twa wives".

Southeast of the High Street, in what was once Mill Vennel and is now, inevitably, Burns Street, stands **Burns' House** (April–Sept Mon–Sat 10am–5pm, Sun 2–5pm; Oct–March Tues–Sat 10am–1pm & 2–5pm; free), a simple sandstone building where the poet died of rheumatic heart disease in 1796, a few days before the birth of his last son, Maxwell. Burns lived here just three years before he died, though his wife, Jean Armour, stayed on until her own death, some 38 years later. Inside, there's the usual collection of Burns memorabilia – manuscripts, letters, his nutmeg grater and the like – while one of the bedroom windows bears his signature, scratched with his diamond ring. As a member of the Dumfries Volunteers, Burns was given a military funeral, before being buried nearby in a simple grave by **St Michael's Church** (Mon–Fri 10am–4pm; free), a large red sandstone church, built in 1745, with a slightly ill-fitting Gothic tower. In 1815, Burns was dug up and moved across the graveyard to a purpose-built **Mausoleum**, a bright white Neoclassical eyesore, which houses a slightly ludicrous statue of Burns being accosted by the Poetic Muse. The rest of the graveyard is packed full of large red sandstone tombstones, including many of the poet's friends, all architecturally plain, but inscribed with the most wonderfully verbose epitaphs.

From the church, head down to the Nith, which is shallow and fast-running, especially as it rushes down the weir. This side of the river, known as **Whitesands**, was once busy with timberyards, tanneries, breweries, boats and the local cattle market; nowadays, it serves as the town's main car park, and is architecturally a bit of a mess. More impressive is the pedestrian-only **Devorgilla Bridge**, a little further upstream, built in 1431 and one of the oldest bridges in Scotland. Attached to its southwestern end is the town's oldest house, built in 1660, now housing the tiny **Old Bridge House Museum** (April–Sept Mon–Sat 10am–5pm, Sun 2–5pm; free), stuffed full of Victorian domestic bric-a-brac, including a teeth-chattering range of Victorian dental gear.

Downstream from the Old Bridge House, an old water mill has been converted into the **Robert Burns Centre**, or RBC (April–Sept Mon–Sat 10am–8pm, Sun 2–5pm; Oct–March Tues–Sat 10am–1pm & 2–5pm; free), with an optional twenty-minute slide show (£1.50) and a simple exhibition on the poet's years in Dumfries upstairs. On the hill above the RBC stands the **Dumfries Museum** (April–Sept Mon–Sat 10am–5pm, Sun 2–5pm; Oct–March Tues–Sat 10am–1pm & 2–5pm; free), from which there are great views over the town. The museum is housed partly in an eighteenth-century windmill, which was converted into the town's observatory in the 1830s, and features a **camera obscura** on its top floor (April–Sept; £1.50), well worth a visit on a clear day. Outside the museum, don't miss the statuary that shelters within a Neoclassical mausoleum, featuring Robert Paterson, the model for Scott's "Old Mortality", lounging around by his pony.

One last sight worth mentioning, though slightly out of the way, is the ruin of the red sandstone **Lincluden Collegiate Church**, which lies within a housing estate to the north of the centre (signposted off the A76). Built in the early fifteenth century on the site of a Benedictine nunnery, the south transept and choir are well preserved, with the latter harbouring an ornately carved tomb and effigy of the widow of the founder, Archibald, third Earl of Douglas, thought to be the work of a master mason from Melrose Abbey.

Practicalities

Dumfries **train** station is five minutes' walk east of the town centre, while **buses** drop you off at Whitesands beside the River Nith. The **tourist office** (Mon–Sat 10am–5pm; June–Sept also Sun noon–5pm; ⓣ01387/253862) is also on Whitesands, and stocks a "Burns trail" leaflet for the afflicted.

Dumfries abounds in handsome sandstone villas, several of which have been turned into **guesthouses** and **B&Bs**. For value and convenience, you can't beat *Morton Villa*, 28 Lovers Walk (ⓣ01387/255825; ❷), a large Victorian house with a pleasant garden near the station. For a more distinctive setting, try *The Haven*, 1 Kenmure Terrace (ⓣ01387/251281; ❶), on a short block of attractive old houses overlooking the Nith from beside the suspension footbridge below the RBC. If you're looking for a **hotel**, head for Laurieknowe Street, a five- to ten-minute walk west of Devorgilla Bridge, where you'll find the welcoming, family-run *Edenbank* (ⓣ01387/252759; ❸). *Redbank House* (ⓣ01387/247034, ⓦwww.redbankhouse.co.uk; ❷) is a pristine red-brick mansion set within its own wooded garden at the edge of town on the A710, boasting a sauna, snooker room and gym.

By far the best option for **food** is *Hullabaloo* (ⓣ01387/259679), a stylish restaurant on the top floor of the RBC, with a summer terrace overlooking the river. Lunchtimes are for wraps, bagels and ciabatta sandwiches; in the evening, when it's advisable to book, there are moderately expensive Mediterranean-influenced dishes on offer. Another daytime option is the *Artists' Café*, 6 Buccleuch St, which has an eclectic, inexpensive menu featuring wraps, tortillas, toasties and soup. The *Old Bank*, a café on Irish Street, offers more predictable fare. For the evening, there's also the *Rowan Tree Bistro*, 20 Academy St (closed Mon & Tues), which offers a small, but simple selection of inexpensive local fish meat dishes. *Bruno's* is a family-friendly Italian restaurant on Balmoral Road that's become a Dumfries institution, with the equally popular *Balmoral* chippie round the side which justifiably claims to sell the best chips in the southwest.

Two of Burns' favourite drinking places are still in operation: the *Hole in the Wa'* **pub**, down an alley opposite Woolworth's on High Street, serves the usual bar food, but for somewhere with a bit more atmosphere, make for the smoky, oak-panelled *Globe Inn* on the High Street, which is crammed with memorabilia connected with the poet but is otherwise little changed since his time. The *Robert the Bruce* pub, with its Neoclassical portico at the top of Buccleuch Street, is a typical and very popular church conversion by the J.D. Wetherspoons chain. **Films** are regularly shown at the RBC (ⓣ01387/264808; Tues–Sat). Grierson and Graham, 10 Academy St (ⓣ01387/259483), offer **bike rental**, useful for reaching the nearby Solway coast.

Around Dumfries

Dumfries itself might be short on top-drawer sights, but the countryside immediately around it, within easy reach, more than makes up for the lack. To the north, **Ellisland Farm**, where Burns made his final stab at running his own farm, is much more atmospheric than any of the Burns' sights in Dumfries. To the southeast, the medieval ruins of **Caerlaverock Castle** are simply magnificent, as is the adjacent nature reserve and the early Christian cross at nearby **Ruthwell**. On the west bank of the Nith estuary, the star attraction is **Sweetheart Abbey**, the best preserved of the trio of Cistercian abbeys in Dumfries and Galloway. Regular **buses** run to all these sights, with timetables available from the Dumfries tourist office.

Ellisland Farm

North of Dumfries, the A76 passes **Ellisland Farm** (April–Sept Mon–Sat 10am–1pm & 2–5pm, Sun 2–5pm; Oct–March Tues–Sat 10am–5pm; Ⓦ www.ellislandfarm.co.uk; £2.50), built by Robert Burns in 1788 as a family home and working farmhouse. His three years at Ellisland were very productive: Burns wrote over 130 poems and songs, including *Tam o' Shanter* and *Auld Lang Syne*. The farm, though, didn't prosper – "a ruinous affair", Burns called it – due to the boggy soil, and eventually Burns got a salaried post as an exciseman. Ellisland remains a working farm, though it also houses a museum, where you can see Burns' personal effects – his fishing rod and flute – the original range installed by the poet for his wife, and many of the agricultural implements Burns used, not to mention his pistol and sword, essential possessions when carrying out the unpopular job of levying taxes.

Caerlaverock Castle and around

Caerlaverock Castle, eight miles southeast of Dumfries (April–Sept daily 9.30am–6.30pm; Oct–March Mon–Sat 9.30am–4.30pm, Sun 2–4.30pm; HS; £2.80), is a picture-perfect ruined castle. Not only is it moated, it's built from the rich local red sandstone, is triangular in shape and has preserved its mighty double-towered gatehouse. Built in the late thirteenth century, it clearly impressed medieval chroniclers. During the siege of 1300 by Edward I, a contemporary bard commented: "In shape it was like a shield, for it had but three sides round it, with a tower at each corner… and good ditches filled right up to the brim with water. And I think you will never see a more finely situated castle." Caerlaverock sustained further damage in 1312, this time from the Scots, and again in 1356–57 from the English, forcing numerous rebuilding programmes. Close inspection of the main gatehouse reveals several phases of construction: the fifteenth-century machicolations of the gatehouse top earlier towers that are themselves studded with wide-mouthed gunports from around 1590. The most surprising addition, however, lies inside, where you're confronted by the ornate Renaissance facade of the **Nithsdale Lodging**, erected in the 1630s by the first Earl of Nithsdale. The decorated tympana above the windows feature lively mythological and heraldic scenes in what was clearly the latest style. Sadly, Nithsdale didn't get much value for money: just six years later he and his royal garrison were forced to surrender after a thirteen-week siege and bombardment by the Covenanters, who proceeded to wreck the place. It was never inhabited again.

Caerlaverock Castle makes for a popular family day out; it has a siege-engine playground, a tearoom and an exhibition and video on the siege of 1300, where kids can do their own heraldry – a useful wet weather retreat. There are also various walks marked out along the edge of the neighbouring national nature reserve, including one leading to the earthworks of the old castle which preceded Caerlaverock; en route, you should look out for the rare natterjack toad. Three miles further east, at Eastpark, is the **Caerlaverock Wildfowl and Wetlands Trust (WWT) Centre** (daily 10am–5pm; Ⓦ www.wwtck.free-online.co.uk; £4, with concessions for those arriving by public transport, bicycle or on foot), 1350 acres of protected salt marsh and mud flat edging the Solway Firth. The centre is equipped with screened approaches that link the main observatory to a score of well-situated birdwatchers' hides. It's famous for the 25,000 or so barnacle geese which winter here between September and April. The rest of the year, when the geese are away nesting in Svalbard, there's plenty of other flora and fauna to look out for, as well as the aforementioned natterjack toad. Throughout the year the wild whooper swans have a daily

Threave Garden

Threave Garden (daily 9.30am to sunset; NTS; £4.50), the premier horticultural sight in Dumfries and Galloway, is a pleasant mile or so's walk or cycle south of Castle Douglas, along the shores of Loch Carlingwark. The garden features a magnificent spread of flowers and woodland, sixty acres subdivided into more than a dozen areas, from the bright, old-fashioned blooms of the Rose Garden to the brilliant banks of rhododendrons in the Woodland Garden and the ranks of primula, astilbe and gentian in the Peat Garden. In springtime, thousands of visitors turn up for the flowering of more than two hundred types of daffodil and, from late May onwards, the herbaceous beds are the main attraction, with most of them arranged like islets in a sea of lawn (so that they can be viewed from all sides). The exception is the more formal beds of the Walled Garden which adjoin the greenhouses and the nursery.

Threave is also used by the National Trust for Scotland as a teaching garden, and its postgraduate students occupy Threave House, the hulking Victorian mansion that was the residence of the last laird. The **visitor centre** (April–Oct daily 9.30am–5.30pm; March, Nov & Dec Wed–Sun 10am–4pm) has maps of and an exhibition about the garden and the surrounding estate (also NTS property), though the restaurant's fruit pies, and outdoor terrace, are more immediately appealing.

Threave Castle

The nicest way of reaching **Threave Castle** (April–Sept daily 9.30am–6.30pm; HS; £2), a mile or so north of the gardens, is to walk through the estate. However you decide to get there, you should follow the signs to the Open Farm (which has the *Bothy* tearoom serving soup and sandwiches), from where it's a lovely fifteen-minute walk down to the River Dee, where you ring a brass bell for the boat to take you over to the flat and grassy island on which the stern-looking tower house stands. Built for one of the Black Douglases, Archibald the Grim, first Lord of Galloway and third Earl of Douglas, in around 1370, the fortress was among the first of its kind, a sturdy, rectangular structure completed shortly after the War of Independence when clan feuding spurred a frenzy of castle building. During the reign of James II, there was a sustained campaign to crush the Black Douglases: the nine-year-old king was present at the Black Dinner in Edinburgh Castle when the sixth Earl of Douglas was executed. Some years later, after another dinner in Stirling the king personally murdered the eighth earl.

The rickety curtain wall to the south and east is all that remains of the **artillery fortifications**, hurriedly constructed in the 1450s by the ninth earl in a desperate – and unsuccessful – attempt to defend the castle against James II's new-fangled cannon. The castle fell to the English in 1545 and 1588, but a royalist garrison withstood a thirteen-week siege by the Covenanters in 1640, only surrendering after orders from the king. As at Caerlaverock, the castle was then partially dismantled, but enough remains of the interior to make out its general plan, beginning with the storage areas and spitefully gloomy **prison** in the basement. Up above, the entrance level was once reached from the outside by removable timber stairs, while inside a spiral staircase ascended to the upper floors; you can still make out its course. The **roof** was flat to accommodate stone-throwing machinery, and had a projecting wooden gallery to enable the defenders to drop nasty objects onto the heads of the attackers: from the outside you can clearly see the holes where the timber supports were lodged.

Kirkcudbright and around

KIRKCUDBRIGHT (pronounced "kir-coo-bree"), hugging the muddy banks of the River Dee ten miles southwest of Castle Douglas, is the only major town along the Solway coast to have retained a working harbour. In addition, it has a ruined castle and the most attractive of town centres, a charming medley of simple two-storey cottages with medieval pends, Georgian villas and Victorian town houses, all built in a mixture of sandstone, granite and brick, and attractively painted up, with their windows and quoins picked out. It comes as little surprise, then, to find that Kirkcudbright became something of a magnet for Scottish artists from the late nineteenth century onwards. It may no longer live up to the tourist board's "artists' town" label, but it does have a rich artistic heritage that's easy and enjoyable to explore.

The Town

The most surprising sight in Kirkcudbright is **MacLellan's Castle** (April–Sept daily 9.30am–12.30pm & 1.30–6pm; HS; £1.80), a pink-flecked sixteenth-century tower house that sits at one end of the High Street by the harbourside. Part fortified keep and part spacious mansion, the castle was built in 1570s for the then-Provost of Kirkcudbright, Sir Thomas MacLellan of Bombie, when a degree of law and order permitted the aristocracy to relax its former defensive preoccupations and satisfy its increasing desire for comfort and domestic convenience. As a consequence, chimneys have replaced battlements at the wall-heads and windows begin at the ground floor. Nevertheless, the walls remain impressively thick, and there are a handful of wide-mouthed gun loops, though these are haphazard affairs designed to deter intruders rather than beat off an invading army. The interior is well preserved from the kitchen (complete with bread oven), and vaulted storerooms in the basement, to the rabbit warren of well-appointed domestic apartments above. Keep an eye out for the spyhole known as the "**laird's lug**", behind the fireplace of the Great Hall. MacLellan's son, Robert, rose to even greater social heights than his father, but amassed so many debts that on his death in 1639, the house had to be sold off along with most of the family's estate, and from then on the place was more or less abandoned. Sir Thomas MacLellan is buried in the neighbouring **Greyfriars Kirk** (daily 10am–noon & 2–4pm; key from 7 Castle St), where his tomb is an eccentrically crude attempt at Neoclassicism; it even incorporates parts of someone else's gravestone.

Near the castle, on the L-shaped High Street, is **Broughton House** (daily: Easter, July & Aug 11am–5.30pm; April–June, Sept & Oct 1–5.30pm; Nov garden only Mon–Fri 11am–4pm; NTS; £3.50), a smart Georgian town house set back from, and elevated above, the surrounding terraces. This is the former home of the artist, **Edward Hornel** (1863–1933), an important member of the late nineteenth-century Scottish art scene, who spent his childhood a few doors down the street, and returned in 1900 to establish an artists' colony in Kirkcudbright with some of the "Glasgow Boys" (see p.260). Hornel bought Broughton House in 1901 and added a studio and a vast, glass-roofed, mahogany-panelled gallery at the back of the house. The gallery, now filled with the mannered, vibrantly coloured paintings of girls at play, which he churned out in the latter part of the his career, also features a scaled-down plaster cast of the Elgin Marbles decorating the cornice (which determined the size of the room). Note, too the model of the extraordinary war memorial which stands outside MacLellan's Castle, and which Hornel helped to choose.

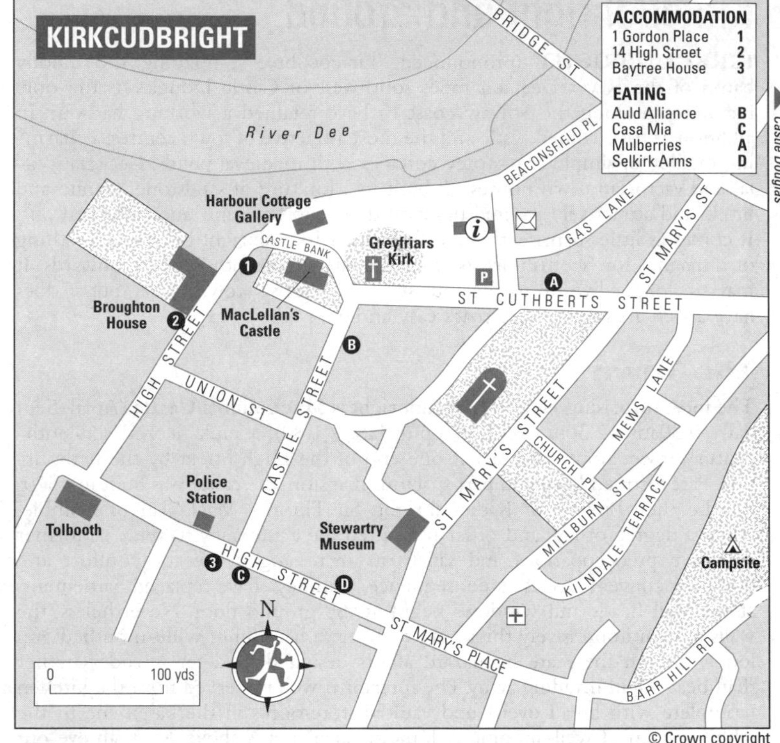

Hornel's trip to Japan in 1893 imbued him with a life-long affection for the country, and his surprisingly large, densely packed, wonderful, rambling **gardens** have a strong Japanese influence.

Before visiting Broughton House, you should really pay a visit to Kirkcudbirght's imposing, church-like **Tollbooth**, with its stone-built clock-tower and spire. Built in the 1620s, it used to serve as town council, court-house, debtors' prison, water supply and town hall: outside on the forestair, you also see the mercat cross and a pair of cast-iron "jougs", in which felons were publicly displayed. Unfortunately, the interior has much less character, but it does house the **Tolbooth Art Centre** (Mon–Sat 11am–4pm; June–Sept also Sun 2–5pm; £1.50), which has, on the upper floor, a small permanent display of works by some of Kirkcudbrught's erstwhile resident artists, including Hornel's striking *Japanese Girl*, and S.J. Peploe's Colourist view of the Tolbooth. The ten-minute video gives you a good, succinct overview of Kirkcudbright's artistic heritage. The town's artistic connections are furthered by its several art galleries, including the picturesque **Harbour Cottage Gallery**, which hosts a variety of temporary exhibitions (March–Dec Mon–Sat 10.30am–12.30pm & 2–5pm, Sun 2–5pm; 75p).

Don't miss the **Stewartry Museum** on St Mary Street (Mon–Sat 11am–4pm; June–Sept also Sun 2–5pm; £1.50), where, packed into a purpose-built Victorian building, hundreds of local exhibits illuminate the life and times of the Solway coast. It's an extraordinary collection, cabinets crammed with anything from glass bottles, weaving equipment, pipes, pictures and postcards to stuffed birds, pickled fish and the tricornered hats once worn by town officials. There are also examples of book jackets designed by Jessie King and E.A. Taylor, two of Hornel's coterie. Incidentally, the "Stewartry" is the old name for the former county of Kirkcudbrightshire, as for centuries it was ruled by a royal steward appointed by the Balliol family.

Tongland Power Station and the Wildlife Park

There are a couple of minor sights just outside Kirkcudbright where you could while away bad weather and/or entertain the kids. The most interesting is the **Tongland Power Station** (late May to mid-Sept Mon–Fri 9.30am–5pm; July & Aug also Sat 9.30am–5pm; £2.50), whose hydroelectric turbines and generators are housed in a fine Art Deco building a couple of miles up the River Dee. More appealing to children is the local **Wildlife Park** (daily: April–Aug 10am–6pm; March & Sept–Nov 10am–5.30pm; £4.50), a mile or so up the B727 east of Kirkcudbright. Lesser pandas, collared peccaries and Scottish wildcats are just some of the animals you can expect to see, and you can feed the goats, deer and llama – and have an encounter with a snake.

Practicalities

Buses to Kirkcudbright stop by the harbour car park, next to the **tourist office** (July & Aug Mon–Sat 9.30am–6pm, Sun 10am–5pm; April–June, Sept & Oct Mon–Sat 10am–5pm, Sun noon–4pm; ⓣ01557/330494), where you can get help finding a place to stay, a service you will probably need in high season.

The town has some excellent **accommodation** choices, worth booking in advance: one of the best is *14 High St* (ⓣ01557/330766, ⓔ14highstreet@kirkcudbright.co.uk; ❸), next door to Broughton House, with a garden overlooking the river, or *Baytree House*, at no. 110 (ⓣ01557/330824; ❹), another Georgian house with comfortable rooms, good cooking, and a beautiful garden with sundeck. Cheaper B&B can be had from 1 Gordon Place (ⓣ01557/330472; ❷), at the castle end of the High Street. The *Silvercraigs* caravan and **campsite** (ⓣ01557/330123; Easter to late Oct) is five or ten minutes' walk from the centre down St Mary's Street and Place, on a bluff overlooking town. Alternatively, you could head to the *Seaward* caravan and campsite at Brighouse Bay (ⓣ01557/331079, ⓦwww.gillespie-leisure.co.uk; March–Oct), six miles southwest of town, offering the full range of facilities in a new leisure complex.

Kirkcudbright is strangely limited when it comes to **restaurants**. Top choice is the *Auld Alliance*, 5 Castle St (ⓣ01557/330569), a superior, if pricey, restaurant offering an imaginative mixture of French and Scottish cuisine. More reasonable is the *Casa Mia*, an Italo–Scottish restaurant within the *Gordon House Hotel*, 116 High St. Otherwise, there's the usual bar food at the Best–Western-run *Selkirk Arms Hotel* on the High Street, which boasts a large garden out the back. A stylish daytime **café**, *Mulberries*, is on St Cuthbert's Street. For a **drink**, the busy *Masonic Arms*, on Castle Street, pulls a reasonable pint. Kirkcudbright has a small **jazz festival** in mid-June and a host of **summer festivities** in the middle of August.

Gatehouse of Fleet

Like Castle Douglas, **GATEHOUSE OF FLEET**, ten miles west of Kirkcudbright, has a distinctive long, dead straight main street. However, the quiet streets of Gatehouse have none of the life and bustle of Castle Douglas. By contrast, in the late eighteenth and early nineteenth century, the town was a thriving industrial centre with cotton mills, shipbuilding and a brewery. The man who made all this happen (and made himself immeasurably rich in the process) was the local laird James Murray (1727–99). Yorkshire mill owners provided the industrial expertise, imported engineers designed aqueducts to improve the water supply, and dispossessed crofters – and their children – contributed the labour. Between 1760 and 1790, Murray achieved much success, but his custom-built town failed to match its better-placed rivals. By 1850 the boom was over, the town was bypassed by the railway, the mills slipped into disrepair, and nowadays tiny Gatehouse is sustained by tourism and forestry.

It's the country setting that sets Gatehouse apart, rather than any particular sight. As at Castle Douglas, the sloping whitewashed High Street has a landmark clocktower, in this case an incongruous free-standing one, built in grey granite and topped by strange mitre-shaped crenellations. More picturesque is Ann Street, beside the tower, at the end of which you can gain access to the wooded grounds of **Cally House** (now the *Cally Palace Hotel*), and its gardens (Easter–Sept Tues–Fri 2–5pm, Sat & Sun 10am–5.30pm; £1.50). A palatial Neoclassical country mansion, Cally House was built in the 1760s, and is proof positive of the fortune already owned by the Murray family, even before James Murray began his cotton enterprise. Back in town, the **Mill on the Fleet** (March–Oct daily 10.30am–4.30pm; £1.50), opposite the car park by the river at the bottom of the High Street, traces the economic and social history of Gatehouse and Galloway from inside a restored grey granite bobbin mill; its café has an attractive terrace overlooking the river.

Perched on a hill a mile southwest of Gatehouse stands **Cardoness Castle** (April–Sept daily 9.30am–6.30pm; Oct–March Sat 9.30am–4.30pm, Sun 2–4.30pm; HS; £2), a classic late fifteenth-century fortified tower house. It once edged the Water of Fleet river, but this was canalized long ago and today Cardoness overlooks the minor road linking Gatehouse with the busy, nearby A75. Ancient seat of the McCullochs, it was mortgaged and bought by the Gordon family in 1622, a state of affairs that was unacceptable to some of the McCullochs, who subjected the Gordons to extreme acts of violence on more than one occasion. Inside, it has some fashionably decorated fireplaces and plenty of en-suite latrines. The views out to Fleet Bay in the distance are excellent, though, of course, they're even better from the monument at the top of the hill behind the castle.

Also worth a visit are the ruins of **Anwoth Church**, a couple of miles west of Gatehouse. The centre of the old nave is occupied by the ornate seventeenth-century sarcophagus of the Gordon family, decorated with some wonderful wordy, stirring epitaphs, as is the table-top grave of some Covenanter martyrs, to the west of the church, in the atmospheric graveyard.

Practicalities

The **tourist office** (July & Aug Mon–Sat 10am–5.30pm, Sun 10.30am–4.30pm; May, June & Sept Mon–Sat 10am–5pm, Sun 11am–4pm; March, April & Oct Mon–Sat 10am–4.30pm, Sun noon–4pm; ⓣ01557/814212) is situated by the car park by the river. The place to stay is the sumptuous *Cally Palace* **hotel** (ⓣ01557/814341, ⓦwww.callypalace.co.uk; ❼; closed Jan), though make sure you're placed in the old house rather than the ugly modern extension. The Cally has its own leisure centre, tennis courts and 18-hole golf course. The best **B&B** in Gatehouse itself is the *Bay Horse*, 9 Ann St (ⓣ01557/814073; March–Oct; ❷). The *Murray Arms Hotel*, the old coaching inn next to the clocktower, is where Robbie Burns wrote *Scots wha hae*, but the *Masonic Arms*, just up Ann Street, is more welcoming and serves good **pub food** in the bar or in its conservatory. For the ultimate array of whiskies, head for the *Anwoth Hotel*, at the bottom of the High Street. The *Gatehouse* **tearoom**, inside the original "Gatehouse", the oldest (and once the only) house in town, serves snacks washed down with Sulwath ales from Castle Douglas.

Galloway Forest Park and around

The strange thing about Galloway is that while the area around the coast is all rolling farmland, stately homes, sandy coves and estuarine mudflats, you only have to head north ten or twenty miles and you're transported to the entirely different landscape of the Galloway Hills, an environment of glassy lochs, wooded hills and bare, rounded peaks. Much of this landscape is now incorporated into the **Galloway Forest Park**, Britain's largest forest park, which stretches all the way from the southern part of Ayrshire right down to Gatehouse of Fleet, laid out on land owned by the Forestry Commission. Few people actually live here, but the park is a major draw for hikers and mountain bikers, who are both well catered for with lots of trails clearly marked out. Accommodation is thin on the ground in the park itself, except for the Forestry Commission campsite in Glen Trool, though **Newton Stewart** and **New Galloway** are both feasible to use as bases for exploring the park.

Newton Stewart

NEWTON STEWART, famous for its salmon and trout fishing, is an unassuming market town on the west bank of the River Cree, which used to form the county boundary between Kirkcudbrightshire and Wigtownshire. As the largest town within easy reach of the Galloway Forest Park, with some excellent accommodation choices and good bus connections, it's a popular choice as a base for hikers and cyclists. Originally known as Fordhouse of Cree, it was renamed in the seventeenth century by the local laird, William Stewart. A hundred years late, the estate was bought by William Douglas (of Castle Douglas fame), who preferred Newton Douglas, though neither the name, nor the cotton and carpet industry he established lasted long.

Newton Stewart's most intriguing sight is on the eastern riverbank in what used to be the separate village of Minnigaff, where the **Minnigaff parish church** (mid-June to mid-Sept Mon & Fri 1.30–4pm; free) houses three eleventh-century carved grave-slabs. Otherwise, the town's attractions are pretty much confined to the local **museum** (July & Aug Mon–Fri 10am-12.30pm & 2–5pm, Sat & Sun 2–5pm; Easter–June Mon–Sat 2–5pm; Sept daily 2–5pm; £1), housed in the deconsecrated Church of St Andrew, to the west of the main street. There's also a remarkable collection of over fifty dolls' houses on display at **Sophie's Puppenstube and Dolls' House Museum** (April–Dec Mon–Sat 10am–5pm; Jan–March Tues–Sat 10am–4pm; £2.75), located at 29 Queen St, on the road heading west from the main square.

Practicalities

On the main square itself, by the bus station, you'll find the local **tourist office** (July & Aug 10am–6pm; May, June & Sept 10am–5pm; April & Oct 10am–4.30pm; ⓣ01671/402431), which has plenty of helpful literature. The finest **hotel** is the warm and friendly *Creebridge House Hotel* (ⓣ01671/402121,

Ⓦwww.creebridge.co.uk; ❺), in an appealing eighteenth-century granite hunting lodge near the main bridge. It's a haunt of serious anglers, and can arrange fishing permits, personal gillies (guides), and even tackle (March to mid-Oct). A cheaper option is to go for one of the substantial red sandstone Victorian villa **B&Bs**, such as *Rowallan House* (Ⓣ01671/402520), on Corsbie Road, west of the main street up Church Lane. There's also an SYHA **hostel** (Ⓣ01671/402211, Ⓦwww.syha.org.uk; April–Sept) in an old schoolhouse in Minnigaff, up Millcroft Road from the bridge.

The best place **to eat** is the *Creebridge*, which has a wonderful but pricey restaurant as well as serving great pub food with its real ales. Another, more formal option is to eat at the restaurant at the *Kirroughtree Hotel* (Ⓣ01671/402141, Ⓦwww.kirroughtreehouse.co.uk; ❽; mid-Feb to Dec), a whitewashed mansion surrounded by beautiful gardens of azaleas and rhododendrons on the south-eastern outskirts of town near the A75/A712 junction.

Galloway Forest Park

The only tarmacked road to cross the **Galloway Forest Park** is the desolate twenty-mile stretch of the A712 from Newton Stewart east to New Galloway, known as the **Queen's Way**, which cuts through the southern half of the park. Travelling this road, you'll pass all sorts of hiking trails, some the gentlest of strolls, others long-distance treks. For a short walk, stop at the **Grey Mare's Tail Bridge**, about seven miles east of Newton Stewart, where the Forestry Commission has laid out various trails, all delving into the pine forests beside the road, crossing gorges, waterfalls and burns. A few miles further on is **Clatteringshaws Loch**, a reservoir surrounded by pine forest, with a visitor centre and tearoom (daily: March–Sept 10am–5pm; Oct 10.30am–4.30pm) and a fourteen-mile footpath running right round the loch. This runs past the **Bruce's Stone**, a huge boulder where Robert the Bruce is supposed to have rested after victory over the English. The trail also connects with the Southern Upland Way as it meanders north towards the **Rhinns of Kells**, the bumpy hill range marking the park's eastern boundary. Heading southeast from Clatteringshaws is the **Raiders Road**, a ten-mile-long former drovers' road, now a forest drive popular with cyclists, but sadly also open to cars in the summer.

Many hikers aim for **Glen Trool** at the western edge of the park, about ten miles north of Newton Stewart, where a narrow lane twists the five miles over to **Loch Trool**. Buses only go as far as the village of Glentrool, at the foot of the glen, where the *House O'Hill Hotel* (Ⓣ01671/840243; ❷) provides basic **accommodation**, beer, food and, occasionally, great music. The Forestry Commission *Caldons* **campsite** (Ⓣ01671/840218, Ⓦwww.forestholidays.co.uk; Easter–Sept) sits in the woods close to the western edge of the loch. Halfway up the loch stands another **Bruce Stone**, this one marking the spot where Robert the Bruce ambushed an English force in 1307 after routing the main body of the army at Solway Moss. From here, there's a choice of magnificent hiking trails, including access to **Merrick** (2746ft), the highest hill in the southwest, as well as lesser tracks laid out by the Forestry Commission. Several longer routes curve round the grassy peaks and icy lochs of the Awful Hand and Dungeon ranges, whilst another includes part of the Southern Upland Way, which threads through the Minnigaff hills to Clatteringshaws Loch (see above). The Forestry Commission produces leaflets on its various walks, organizes guided tours of the Red Deer Range and other activities in the park: for further details, call Ⓣ01671/402420.

The Glenkens

At the eastern edge of the forest park is the river valley of the **Glenkens**, which extends south as far as Castle Douglas along Loch Ken, and north along the Water of Ken as far as Carsphairn, a desolate hamlet surrounded by wild moors near the border with Ayrshire. The wooded banks of **Loch Ken** are particularly stunning in autumn, and the area is a haven for the watersports fans, with waterskiing, powerboating, rowing, sailing, windsurfing, angling, bird-watching and more on offer. Contact the Loch Ken Marina and Water Sports Club (Ⓣ0705/009 2792) for the action sports or Galloway Sailing Centre (Ⓣ01644/420626) for the non-powered variety; angling permits and boats are available from all the marinas and caravan parks. The village of **PARTON**, halfway up the loch, is home to the **Scottish Alternative Games**, which takes place on a Sunday in early August and features lots of frivolous and obscure games such as the world "gird'n'cleek" championships, "spinnin' the peerie", "hurlin' the curlin' stane" and snail racing.

New Galloway and around

NEW GALLOWAY, nineteen miles east of Newton Stewart, is a smart, little one-street town of stone-built whitewashed cottages at the northern tip of Loch Ken. The *Smithy* **tearoom** (March–Oct), at the bottom of the high street, is a good source of local information, and serves toasties, baked potatoes and other snacks. New Galloway's accommodation is undistinguished, and you're better of heading north a few miles to the neighbouring village of St John's Town of Dalry, more commonly known simply as **DALRY**. Its main street has a more spacious feel than New Galloway's, with the Southern Upland Way actually passing through it. The *Lochinvar Hotel* (Ⓣ01644/430210; ❷) is an attractive, creeper-clad inn on the road in from New Galloway, while the nearest SYHA **hostel** is at **KENDOON** (Ⓣ01644/460680, Ⓦwww.syha.org.uk; April–Sept), five miles north of Dalry along the B7000. The hostel is about twenty minutes' very pleasant walk through the woods from the A713 to the west; if you're travelling there on the Castle Douglas–Ayr bus, ask the driver to tell you when to get off.

The Machars

The Machars is the name given to the triangular peninsula of rolling farmland and open landscapes south of Newton Stewart. Its title comes from the Gaelic *machair*, which is the name for the low-lying sandy grasslands by the coast. It's a neglected part of the coastline, a bit out on a limb, and with a somewhat disconsolate air. However, you could easily while away an hour or two in **Wigtown**'s various bookshops and, as the birthplace of Scottish Christianity, **Whithorn** is well worth a visit.

Wigtown

Seven miles south of Newton Stewart, **WIGTOWN** is a tiny place, considering it was once the county town of Wigtownshire. Despite its modest size, it has a remarkable main square, a vast, triangular-shaped affair, its layout unchanged since medieval times. Overlooking and dominating the square and its central bowling green are the gargantuan and rather exotic-looking County Buildings, built in French Gothic style. Wigtown has recently reinvented itself as "Scotland's national Booktown" (Ⓦwww.wigtown-booktown.co.uk), with ten to fifteen **bookshops** occupying some of the modest houses which line the square; for a map of their locations, head for the information centre (Mon–Fri 10am–4pm, Sat 9am–noon), on the main square. Most are closed on Sundays, the one notable exception being *Readinglasses*, which also has a small **café** inside. It's a five-minute walk from the square down Harbour Street to the tidal flats below, where a simple stone post commemorates two **Covenanter martyrs**, Margaret McLachlan (aged 63) and Margaret Wilson (aged 18), who in 1685 were tied to stakes on the flats and drowned by the rising tide; their tombstones lie in the local churchyard, smothered in stirring epitaphs.

If you're looking for somewhere to eat or sleep, the best thing to do is to head to **BLADNOCH**, a little village by the river a mile or so southwest. Here, by the bridge you'll find a pretty little cottage **B&B**, *The Old Coach House* (Ⓣ01988/402316; ❷), next door to the equally lovely *Bladnoch Inn* pub. Across the road stands the greystone **Bladnoch distillery** (Easter–Oct Mon–Fri 9am–5pm; July & Aug also Sun noon–5pm; Nov–Easter by appointment; Ⓣ01988/402605, Ⓦwww.bladnoch.co.uk; £1), Scotland's southernmost whisky distillery, and the only one in the southwest. Resurrected in 2000, having been closed for seven years, Bladnoch offers frequent **guided tours** daily from 10am, at the end of which you'll get the traditional generous dram.

Whithorn and around

Fifteen miles south of Wigtown is **WHITHORN** (Ⓦwww.whithorn.com), a one-street town which nevertheless occupies an important place in Scottish history, for it is thought that here in 397 **St Ninian** founded the first Christian church north of Hadrian's Wall. According to the Venerable Bede, Ninian built a church in "a manner to which the Britons were not accustomed", and it became known as *Candida Casa*, "a bright and shining place", translated by the southern Picts he had come to convert as "Hwiterne" (White House) – hence Whithorn. No one can be sure where the *Candida Casa* actually stood, and very little is known about Ninian's life, but his tomb at Whithorn soon became a popular place of pilgrimage and, in the twelfth century, a Premonstratensian priory was established to service the shrine. For generations the rich and the royal made the trek here, the last being Mary, Queen of Scots in 1563, but then came the Reformation and the prohibition of pilgrimages in 1581.

These days, it takes a serious leap of the imagination to envisage Whithorn as a medieval pilgrimage centre. For this reason, it's a good idea to start by watching the audiovisual show at the **Whithorn Dig** (April–Oct daily 10.30am–5pm; £2.70; HS members £1.90), to the right of the pend (arched house) on the main street, which leads to the remains of the priory. In the adjacent exhibition, there's a handful of archeological finds from the 1990s dig, including a Viking cat-skinning trough; the upstairs Discovery Centre, meanwhile, is a hands-on affair, aimed primarily at kids and school groups. Heading outside, the dig site is pretty uninspiring, as are the nearby ruins of the nave of **Whithorn Priory**, though the latter does have a couple of finely carved thirteenth-century south-facing doorways. The most compelling early Christian relics found in the vicinity – a series of standing crosses and headstones – are housed in the onsite **Whithorn Museum**. The oldest is the Latinus stone from the mid-fifth century, the earliest Christian stone in Scotland; the Petrus stone, with its *chi-rho* symbol and Latin inscription "the place of Peter the Apostle", dates from the mid-seventh century; while the best-preserved is the tenth-century Monteith Cross, decorated with interlaced patterns. Should you be picnic-less, grab a snack at the Whithorn Dig's *Pilgrims' Tearoom*.

The pilgrims who crossed the Solway to visit St Ninian's shrine landed at the **ISLE OF WHITHORN**, four miles south of Whithorn, no longer an island, but an antique and picturesque little seaport. If you continue to the end of the harbour, you'll pick up signs to the minuscule remains of the thirteenth-century **St Ninian's Chapel**, which some believe was the site of the original *Candida Casa*. You can still follow in the pilgrims' footsteps by walking, cycling or riding the marked **Pilgrim Way** in a hundred-mile round-trip, starting from Glenluce and winding along paths and quiet roads to the Isle of Whithorn. For the less energetic, there's a pleasant twelve-mile round-walk between Whithorn and the Isle of Whithorn, which takes in **St Ninian's Cave**, three miles to the west, where the saint allegedly first put foot on Scottish soil. If you want to **stay**, try the unassuming *Steam Packet Inn* (Ⓣ01988/500334; ❸), right on the quay in Isle of Whithorn; it does pub food that's above average in quality and price, and has a moderately expensive **restaurant**.

The Rhinns of Galloway

West of the Machars, the hilly, hammer-shaped peninsula at the end of the Solway coast, known as the **Rhinns of Galloway**, encompasses two contrasting towns: the grimy port of **Stranraer**, from where there are regular ferries over to Northern Ireland, and the beguiling seaside resort of **Portpatrick**. At either end of the peninsula are two lighthouses: one stands above Corsewall Point, and is now home to a luxury hotel, the other stands on the **Mull of Galloway**, a windswept headland at the southwest tip of Scotland, which is home to a vast array of nesting seabirds.

Stranraer and around

No one could say that **STRANRAER** was beautiful, and if you're heading to (or coming from) Northern Ireland, there's really no reason to linger longer than you have to. If you find yourself with time to kill, head for the town's one specific attraction, the **Castle of St John** (Easter to mid-Sept Mon–Sat 10am–1pm & 2–5pm; £1.20), a ruined four-storey tower house built around 1500, which stands on the main street, one block inland from the harbour front. Inside, an exhibition traces the history of the castle, which was notorious in the 1680s as the headquarters of Graham of Claverhouse, sheriff of Wigtown and known as "bloody Clavers" for his brutal campaigns against the local Covenanters. Later, the tower was used as a police station and prison, and still retains the old exercise yard on the roof. If you've yet more time on your hands, pop into the **Stranraer Museum** in the Old Town Hall a short distance west along George Street (Mon–Fri 10am–5pm, Sat 10am–1pm & 2–5pm; free) for a brief foray into local history.

Practicalities

The **train station** is right by the Stena Line **ferry** terminal (Ⓣ0870/570 7070, Ⓦwww.stenaline.co.uk) on the East Pier, from where boats depart for Belfast. A couple of minutes' walk away, on Port Rodie, is the **bus station**. Stena Line's fast HSS **catamarans** depart for Belfast from the West Pier on the other side of the harbour. P&O Irish Sea ferries (Ⓣ0870/242 4777, Ⓦwww.poirishsea.com) to and from Larne, arrive not in Stranraer, but at the port of **CAIRNRYAN**, some five miles north; note, though, that bus services to Cairnryan are infrequent and aren't integrated with the ferry times.

Stranraer's **tourist office** is at 28 Harbour St (April–Oct 9.30am–5.30pm, Sun 10am–4.30pm; Nov–March Mon–Sat 10am–4pm; ⓣ01776/702595) between the two piers. Should you need **accommodation**, head for the *Harbour Guest House* (ⓣ01776/704626, ⓦwww.harbourguesthouse.com; ❷), a decent **B&B** on the seafront on Market Street, just a short stroll from either pier. You'll have few problems **eating out** if you're after fish and chips, pizzas or pub grub, but for something more edifying, aim for the moderately expensive restaurant of the *North West Castle* (ⓣ01776/704413, ⓦwww.mcmillanhotels.com; ❺), the vast, whitewashed crenellated pile next to the police station on Port Rodie. Built in 1820 as a double bay-fronted house for the Arctic explorer Sir John Ross, who tried in vain to discover the Northwest Passage, and later went in search of Sir John Franklin, the whole place has been vastly extended since then to provide a slightly dowdy, but grandiose place in which to hide away from the rest of Stranraer. For **campers**, *Aird Donald Caravan Park* (ⓣ01776/702025, ⓦcome-to/airddonald.co.uk) is ten minutes' walk east of the town centre along London Road, though there are much nicer sites elsewhere on the Rhinns.

A better bet, if you want to splash out on a posh hotel, is to head out to **Corsewall Point**, eleven miles north of Stranraer, at the northern tip of the Rhinns of Galloway, where the (still functioning) lighthouse has been incorporated into the luxury *Corsewall Lighthouse Hotel* (ⓣ01776/853220, ⓔcorsewall-lighthouse@msn.com; ❻), set in twenty acres of garden. If you don't have your own transport, the owners will collect you from the town, as long as you book in advance.

Castle Kennedy Gardens

The approach to **Castle Kennedy Gardens** (April–Sept daily 10am–5pm; £3), three miles east of Stranraer, is splendid, passing along a tree-lined avenue which frames the ruined medieval fortress of Castle Kennedy beyond, and then across a palm-fringed canal. The castle forms the centrepiece of the gardens, on a hill squeezed between two lochs, though its ruins can no longer be visited. The 75-acre landscaped gardens, which include a lovely walled garden, stretch west as far as nearby Lochinch Castle, seat of the Earl of Stair (and also inaccessible), via a giant lily pond and a stupendous avenue of one hundred-year old monkey puzzle trees.

Glenluce Abbey

Seven miles east of Castle Kennedy, along the A75, you'll pick up signs for **Glenluce Abbey** (April–Sept daily 9.30am–6.30pm; Oct–March Sat 9.30am–4.30pm, Sun 2–4.30pm; HS; £1.80), whose ruins lie in a gentle valley by the railway, a couple of miles north of the main road. Founded in 1192 as a daughter-house of Dundrennan, Glenluce is the most ruinous of the trio of Cistercian monasteries in the southwest. However, it does have one surviving gem: the fifteenth-century **Chapter House**, which has survived pretty much intact, its ribbed-vault ceiling generating the clearest of acoustics; opera singers practise here and so should you. Notice, too, the green man motif carved into the corbels and ceiling bosses. Popularized in the twelfth century, these grotesques have human or cat-like faces, with large, glaring eyes, frowning foreheads and prominent teeth or fangs. All have greenery sprouting from their faces, a feature that originated with pagan leaf masks and the Celtic concept of fertility. The one other remarkable relic at Glenluce is the monks' water-supply system, whose clay pipes (and even a lidded junction box), can be seen in and around the cloisters. Glenluce is also known for the wizard and alchemist **Michael Scott** who lived here in the thirteenth century, supposedly luring the plague into a secret vault where he promptly imprisoned it. Scott, one-time magician to the court of the Emperor Frederick in Sicily, appears in Dante's *Inferno*. Note that there are no direct **buses** to the abbey, but the Glenluce–Newton Stewart bus will drop you off along the main road and you can walk the mile or so from there.

Portpatrick and around

Situated roughly halfway along the west shore of the Rhinns, **PORTPATRICK** has an attractive pastel-painted seafront that wraps itself round a small rocky bay, sheltered by equally rocky cliffs. Until the mid-nineteenth century, when sailing ships were replaced by steamboats, Portpatrick was a thriving seaport, serving as the main embarkation point for Northern Ireland, with coal, cotton and British troops heading in one direction, Ulster cattle and linen in the other. Nowadays, it's a quiet, comely resort enjoyed for its rugged scenery, sea-angling and coastal hikes, including the twenty-minute stroll along the sea cliffs to the shattered ruins of **Dunskey Castle**, an L-shaped tower house dating from the early sixteenth century (take the steep steps near the garages beyond the lighthouse then follow the public footpath). Walkers can also tackle the first stretch of the 212-mile coast-to-coast **Southern Upland Way**, which starts at the quayside.

Practicalities

Portpatrick has several good **hotels** and **guesthouses**, the best of which is the lilac-painted *Waterfront Hotel* (ⓣ01776/810800, ⓦwww.waterfronthotel; ❹), which has gone for the contemporary look inside. Cheaper choices include the neighbouring *Knowe Guest House* (ⓣ01776/810441; ❶), a bright, white B&B which runs a tearoom in its conservatory, and the equally comfortable Victorian *Carlton Guest House*, also on the harbour at 21 South Crescent (ⓣ01776/810253; ❶). It's impossible to miss the *Portpatrick Hotel* (ⓣ01942/824824, ⓦwww.shearingsholidays.com; Feb–Nov; ❺), a grand turreted Edwardian mansion on the hill above the harbour; inside, it's a bit tatty round the edges, but it goes down well with the tour groups, for whom there's live music more or less every night. Another option, if you're on an unlimited budget, is *Knockinaam Lodge* (ⓣ01776/810471; ❾), a rather self-consciously exclusive small country house hotel hidden away in its own private cove a couple of miles south of Portpatrick.

There are several caravan and **campsites** in a row on the hill overlooking Portpatrick and Dunskey Castle, quite a distance from town (and the sea), but accessed by a pleasant walk along the disused railway and clifftop trail; *Sunnymeade* (ⓣ01776/810293) has the better facilities, but *Castle Bay* (ⓣ01776/810462) has the more informal atmosphere.

The best place for a **meal** and a **drink** is the *Crown* pub on the seafront. For something more formal and slightly pricier, head to the *Waterfront Bistro* next door. Portpatrick has an annual **folk festival** in the first weekend of September (call ⓣ01776/810717 for more details).

Port Logan

The remoter reaches of the Rhinns of Galloway, extending about twenty miles south from Portpatrick, consist of gorse-covered hills and pastureland crossed by narrow country lanes and dotted with farming hamlets. Of the two shorelines, the west has a sharper, rockier aspect and it's here, near the village of **PORT LOGAN**, you'll find the uncrowded **Logan Botanic Garden**

(March–Oct daily 9.30am–6pm; £3), an outpost of Edinburgh's Royal Botanic Garden. There are three main areas: a peat garden, a woodland and a walled garden noted for its tree ferns and cabbage palms. The Gulf Stream keeps the Rhinns almost completely free of frost, allowing subtropical species to grow, including plants from South and Central America, southern Africa, Australasia and the Mediterranean. Closer to the village, there's also the **Logan Fish Pond** (daily: mid-March to Sept noon–5pm; Oct noon–4pm; £3) a fully restored Victorian fish larder set within a natural tidal pool created by a blow hole formed during the Ice Age.

The Mull of Galloway

It's a further twelve miles south from Port Logan to the **Mull of Galloway** (Ⓦwww.mull-of-galloway.co.uk), a bleak and precipitous headland, where wheeling guillemots, razorbills and kittiwakes and whistling winds circle a bright whitewashed lighthouse. This is the southernmost point in Scotland and on clear days you can see over to Cumbria, Ireland and the Isle of Man. The headland is also an RSPB reserve and there's a new **visitor centre** (Easter to mid-Oct daily 10am–5pm) in a building near the lighthouse.

Ayrshire

The rolling hills and rich soil of **Ayrshire** (Ⓦwww.ayrshire-arran.com) make for prime farming country and, as such, are not really top of most visitors' Scottish itinerary. **Ayr**, the county town and birthplace of Robert Burns, is handsome enough, but won't keep you long, and **Kilmarnock**, the largest place in the region, sees virtually no tourists whatsoever. However, with Ireland only a short ferry ride away, and Glasgow a short train ride away, Ayrshire still gets plenty of visitors. Most wisely stick to the coastline, attracted by the wide, flat sandy **beaches** and the region's vast number of **golf** courses. South of Ayr, the most obvious points of interest are **Culzean Castle**, with its Robert Adam interior and extensive wooded grounds, and the off-shore islands of **Ailsa Craig**, home to the world's second largest gannetry. North of Ayr, where the towns benefited from the industrialization of Glasgow, there are even fewer places to detain you, with the exception of **Irvine**, home to the ever-expanding Scottish Maritime Museum.

Ayrshire disappeared from official maps in 1975, but has recently returned, due to redrawing of administrative boundaries, but divided into three: South Ayrshire (which includes Ayr), East Ayrshire (which includes Kilmarnock) and North Ayrshire (from Irvine northwards, including the Isle of Arran). Happily, the tourist board covers the whole of Ayrshire and the Isle of Arran (for coverage of Arran, see p.423).

There's a useful **train** line from Ayr down the coast to Stranraer, and north to Largs. From Troon, north of Ayr, fast **ferries** depart to Belfast, and from the port of Ardrossan, further north still, you can cross to the Isle of Arran, from where you can hopscotch on to the Hebrides in summer.

Glasgow Prestwick airport

Ayr is the nearest large town to **Glasgow Prestwick airport** (Ⓦwww.gpia.co.uk), which lies three miles north and has regular transport to Ayr and Glasgow. **Buses** depart from directly outside the terminal: there's an express bus to Glasgow (hourly; £3.50; 50min), or Airbus #4 (Mon–Sat every 30min, Sun hourly), which costs just 50p if you have an air ticket but takes an hour and a half to reach Glasgow. The **train** station is a short walk from the terminal (alight at the airport not Prestwick Town), with trains taking 45 minutes to reach Glasgow (Mon–Sat every 30min, Sun hourly; £4.90). To reach **Ayr**, you've a choice of Airbus #4 (50p; 15min), the train (£2.30; 20min), or a taxi (around £6).

Ayr and around

With a population of around fifty thousand, **AYR** is by far the largest town on the Firth of Clyde coast. It was an important seaport and trading centre for many centuries, and rivalled Glasgow in size and significance right up until the late seventeenth century. In recognition, Cromwell made it a centre of his administration and built an enormous fortress here, long since destroyed. With the relative decline of its seaborne trade, Ayr reinvented itself in the nineteenth century as an administrative centre and a popular resort for middle-class Victorians. Nowadays, the town won't detain you long, though its prestigious racecourse, venue for the Scottish Grand National, pulls in huge crowds, and the local tourist industry continues to do steady business out of the fact that Robbie Burns was born in the neighbouring village of **Alloway** (see p.219).

Arrival and accommodation

The **train** station is ten minutes' walk southeast of the town centre. The **bus** station is in the centre at the foot of Sandgate; nearby is the **tourist office**, at 22 Sandgate (July & Aug Mon–Sat 9am–6pm, Sun 10am–5pm; Oct–June Mon–Sat 9am–5pm; Ⓣ01292/290300), which can help with accommodation, a particularly useful service during big race meetings.

Ayr is one of many towns on this stretch of coast, and along the Firth of Clyde, visited each summer by the *Waverley*, the last seagoing **paddle steamer** in the world; call Ⓣ0141/243 2224 or visit Ⓦwww.waverleyexcursions.co.uk for exact details.

Accommodation

The majority of Ayr's **accommodation** is clustered in the area between the town centre and the Esplanade. Of the numerous choices on Queen's Terrace, head for *Craggallan* (Ⓣ01292/264998, Ⓦwww.craggallan.com; ❷), a friendly little guesthouse with a dining table that converts into a billiards table. You might prefer to opt for the *Horizon Hotel* (Ⓣ01292/264384, Ⓦwww.horizonhotel.com; ❹), a purpose-built modern hotel, and the only one actually on the seafront. The best-value luxury option is the *Savoy Park Hotel*, 16 Racecourse Rd (Ⓣ01292/266112, Ⓦwww.savoypark.com; ❺), a splendid red sandstone Scots Baronial building, with a lovely garden complete with gazebo and swings; the public rooms are suitably grand and the bedrooms have all mod cons. Ayr's SYHA **hostel** (Ⓣ01292/262322, Ⓦwww.syha.org.uk; March–Oct) also occupies a Scots Baronial mansion, at 5 Craigweil Rd off Racecourse Road; inside, the single-sex dorms are pretty basic and utilitarian, though the sea views are excellent. Those wishing to camp should head for the *Heads of Ayr* caravan and

campsite (Ⓣ01292/442269; March–Nov), three miles south of town along the coastal A719, beside the popular Heads of Ayr Farm Park (Easter–Oct daily 10am–5pm).

The Town

NEW BRIG
Will your poor narrow foot-path of a street,
Where twa wheel-barrows tremble when they meet,
Your ruin'd formless bulk o' stane and lime,
Compare wi' bonnie brigs o' modern time?...

AULD BRIG
Conceited gowk! puff'd up wi' windy pride!
This mony a year I've stood the flood an' tide;
And tho' wi' crazy eild I'm sair forfairn,
I'll be brig, when ye're a shapeless cairn!

The Brigs of Ayr by Robbie Burns

Burns' words proved prophetic, since Ayr's New Bridge, designed by none other than Robert Adam himself, and erected in 1787, was pulled down and replaced by the current structure in 1877. By contrast, the cobbled, four-arched **Auld Brig** survived the threat of demolition in the early twentieth century, thanks largely to Burns' poem, and is now one of the oldest stone bridges in Scotland, having been built during the reign of James IV (1488–1513). A short stroll upstream from the bridge stands the much restored **Auld Kirk**, the church funded by Cromwell as recompense for the one he incorporated into his stronghold. At the lych gate, notice the coffin-shaped mort-safe (heavy grating) on the walls; placed over newly dug graves, these mort-safes were an early nineteenth-century security system, meant to deter bodysnatchers at a time when dead bodies were swiftly bought up by medical schools with no questions asked. The church's dark and gloomy interior retains the original pulpit (call Ⓣ01292/262580 for access).

The rest of Ayr's busy town centre, wedged between Sandgate and the south bank of the treacly River Ayr, was rebuilt by the Victorians, and is now busy most days with shoppers from all over the county. The most conspicuous landmark is the big, grey, rather ugly castellated **Wallace Tower**, erected in 1828 at the southern end of the High Street. It stands on what is thought to have been the site of the Edward I's barracks, which was set alight by Wallace in 1297. At the junction of the High Street and Sandgate stands the rather more impressive Neoclassical **Town Buildings**, completed in 1832, whose spectacular 226ft spire is guarded by griffins, eagles and a Triton.

All you can see of Cromwell's zigzag **Citadel**, built to the west of the town centre in 1650s, is a small section of the old walls – the area was built over, for the most part, in Victorian times, but is still known locally as "the Fort". The best-preserved section of the fortifications lies on South Harbour Street, though the one surviving corbelled corner turret is, in fact, a Victorian addition known as **Miller's Folly** after its eccentric former owner. Another survivor from the distant past is the **St John's Tower**, which stands on its own in a walled garden at the heart of the old citadel, and is all that remains of the medieval church, where the Scottish parliament met after the Battle of Bannockburn in 1315 to decide the royal succession, and which Cromwell later used as an armoury.

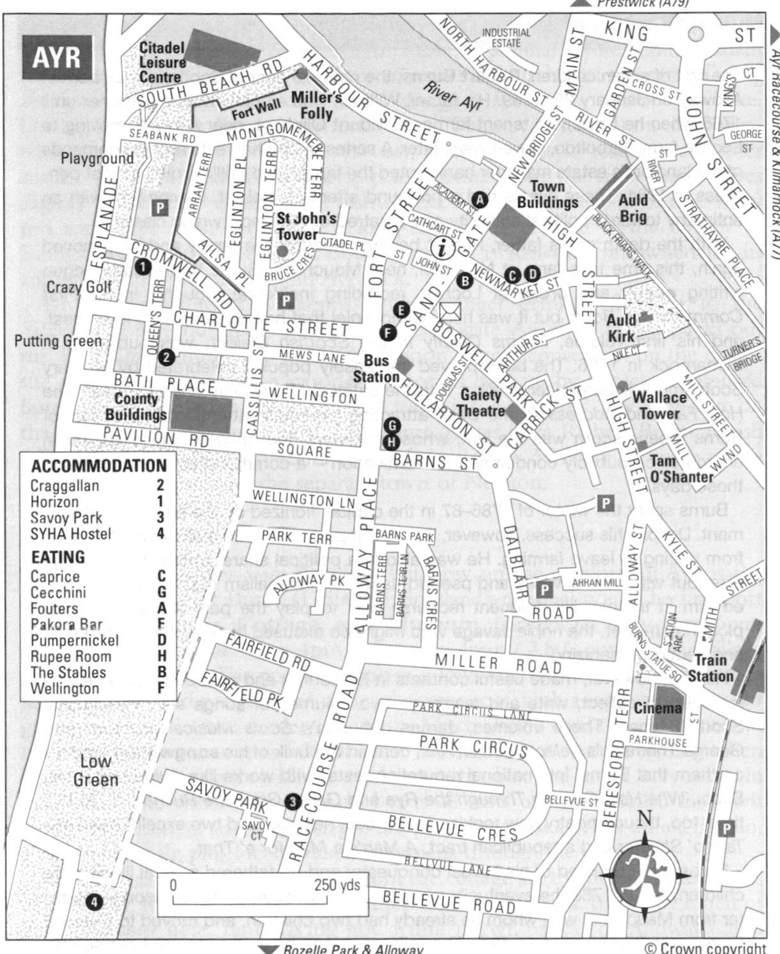

To the south of the citadel are the wide, gridiron streets of Ayr's main Georgian and Regency residential development. **Wellington Square**, whose first occupants were "Gentlemen of Rich Fortune and Retired Army Officers", is the area's showpiece, its trim gardens and terraces overlooked by the **County Buildings**, a vast, imposing Palladian pile from 1820. The opening of the Glasgow-to-Ayr train line in 1840 brought the first major influx of holiday-makers to the town, but today, only a few hardy visitors and local dog-walkers take a stroll along Ayr's bleak, long **Esplanade** and beach, which look out to the Isle of Arran.

Eating, drinking and nightlife

Ayr is blessed when it comes to **eating** options. Arguably the town's best restaurant is *Fouters*, 2a Academy St, a cellar bistro off Sandgate (ⓣ01292/261391, ⓦwww.fouters.co.uk; closed Sun & Mon); its small but

On the Burns trail

The number of memorials, museums, pubs and places across the region associated with **Robert Burns** is quite staggering, given how brief his short life was. If you've only a passing interest in the poet, then you're best off visiting either his birthplace in **Alloway**, near Ayr (see p.219), or the town where he died and is buried, **Dumfries** (see p.193). However, the dedicated Burns' fan can also visit a couple more minor Burns sights in Ayrshire.

The **Bachelors' Club** (April–Sept 1.30–5.30pm; Oct Sat & Sun 1.30–5.30pm; NTS; £2.50) is a wee thatched house in the tiny village of Tarbolton, some six miles northeast of Ayr. It was here in the upstairs room – the largest in the village at the time – that the twenty-year-old Burns attended dancing classes, set up a debating society, and became a freemason.

In Kirkoswald, fourteen miles southwest of Ayr, is **Souter Johnnie's Cottage** (April–Sept daily 11.30am–5pm; Oct Sat & Sun 11.30am–5pm; NTS; £2.50), the simple thatched house that was once the home of John Davidson, the boon companion of Robert Burns and original Souter (cobbler) Johnnie of the poet's *Tam o' Shanter*. To the rear of the house, the restored alehouse has life-size stone figures of Johnnie, Tam himself (called after his boat, Shanter being his farm) and other Burnsian characters, all of whom are buried in the nearby graveyard.

President Eisenhower and his rather bizarre association with Culzean: the castle's top floor was gifted to him out of the blue in 1945 by the Kennedy family, for his lifetime, and the president duly visited four times before his death in 1969. Last of all, there's an **exhibition** on the Kennedy family, though they weren't a very nice bunch over the centuries.

Many folk come here purely to stroll and picnic in the woods, mess about by the beach, or simply have tea and cakes, rather than admire the interior of the castle, and it's certainly worth leaving enough time for an exploration of the **country park**. A web of wooded trails lead you through the park, taking in several lakes, cliff walks, a beach, a lovely Camellia House and a walled garden, where the blooms are at their best in July and August. There are also one or two reminders of earlier days. The twelfth earl, for example, took his role as defender of the realm seriously, and the battery and earthworks he constructed to the south of the house, to thwart a Napoleonic invasion, are still visible. Down by the shore, the old **Gas House**, has an exhibition on the coal gas system introduced to Culzean in the 1840s, and on the Ayrshire-born William Murdoch (1754–1839), the "father of British Gas". Talks, children's events, band recitals and a nature walks are laid on throughout the year; get details from the visitor centre, nearby tourist offices or the castle website.

Crossraguel Abbey and around

The substantial remains of **Crossraguel Abbey** (April–Sept Mon–Sat 9.30am–6.30pm, Sun 2–6.30pm; HS; £2), three miles inland from Culzean, right by the A77, are mostly overlooked – something of a surprise considering their singularity. Founded in 1250 as a Cluniac monastery in the thirteenth century – one of only two in Scotland – Crossraguel benefited from royal patronage, with its abbots holding land "for ever in free regality". The Cluniac order was famous for its elaborate ritual, which kept the choir monks busy all day long, but the abbots took the temporal side of their work just as seriously and became powerful local lords. By the early sixteenth century, they had constructed an extensive and well-fortified private compound complete with a massive gatehouse and sturdy tower house, both of which still stand.

The best place to start is in the choir of the **abbey church**, where only the ornate carving over the piscina and sedilia, in the polygonal apse, gives any indication of the quality of architecture that once must have existed throughout the building. Better still is the fifteenth-century vaulted **sacristy**, which has kept its vaulted ceiling and its decorative capitals, corbels and bosses, embellished with various images: squirrels, lions and other creatures, plus a triple-faced head, and a green man. Next door, off the cloisters, the vaulted **chapter house** is also intact, with stone benches on every side and a fancy canopied seat for the abbot; it also boasts the most wonderful acoustics. The **tower house**, tacked onto the eastern end of the complex, was built around 1480 to provide the kind of luxury accommodation more in keeping with the abbot's high status in the outside world, and clearly illustrates the corruption of the monastic ideal that spurred the Reformation. On the opposite side of the abbey, the **gatehouse** is equally grand and has been restored, so that you can climb to right up to the cap house and walk out onto the battlements. Clearly visible nearby is the abbey's well-preserved dovecote, a beehive-shaped affair that was a crucial part of the abbey's economy; the monks not only ate the doves but also relied on them for eggs.

Turnberry

Beyond Crossraguel, the A77 eventually reaches the coast at the village of **TURNBERRY**, a vast purpose-built Edwardian golfing resort, which has recently been massively expanded to make room for the Colin Montgomerie Links Golf Academy. Turnberry's links courses are occasional home to the Open championship, and rooms at the luxurious *Turnberry Hotel* (ⓣ01655/331000, ⓦwww.turnberry.co.uk; ❾) will set you back a cool £230 and upwards – and that's before you've paid for your round of golf. Visible out on the rocks on the point to the north of the village is a lighthouse and the ruined **castle** where Robert the Bruce was born in 1274, and which was in all likelihood left to fall into rack and ruin in 1307, after Bruce himself attacked and routed the English troops garrisoned within.

Girvan and around

Set beneath a ridge of grassy hills, **GIRVAN**, five miles south of Turnberry, is at its prettiest round the busy harbour, a narrow slit beside the mouth of the Girvan Water. Here, overlooked by old stone houses, the fishing fleet sets about its business, and, for a moment, it's possible to ignore the rundown nature of the rest of the town. The long beaches around Girvan's otherwise rugged coastline are great for seaside strolls, though clambering down the cliff to the caves where the legendary Sawney Bean and his cannibal family lived is not recommended.

Girvan has a seasonal **tourist office**, on Bridge Street, just up from the harbour (July & Aug Mon–Sat 10am–5pm, Sun 11am–4pm; April–June, Sept & Oct call for hours; ⓣ01465/712183) which can help with **accommodation**. One of the nicest places to stay is *Southfield House* (ⓣ01465/714222, ⓦwww.southfieldhotel.fsnet.co.uk; ❸), a handsome whitewashed hotel on The Avenue, which also does bar meals and has more formal and moderately expensive restaurant.

Ailsa Craig

The best reason for visiting Girvan is to take the boat excursion to the island of **Ailsa Craig**, which lies ten miles off the coast in the middle of the Firth of Clyde. The island's name means "Fairy Rock" in Gaelic, though the island looks more like an enormous muffin than a place of enchantment. It would certainly have been less than enchanting for the persecuted Catholics who escaped to the island during the Reformation. With its jagged cliffs and 1114ft summit, Ailsa Craig is now a privately owned **bird sanctuary** that's home to thousands of gannets. The best time to make the trip is at the end of May and in June when the fledglings are trying to fly. Several companies **cruise** round the island, but only Mark McCrindle, who also organizes sea-angling trips, is licensed to land (May to late Sept 1–2 daily; exact timings and prices depend on the length of trip and the tides; ⓣ01465/713219). It takes about an hour to reach the island, so you've enough time to walk up to the summit of the rock and watch the birds, weather permitting.

North of Ayr

The Ayrshire coast extends some thirty miles or so north of Ayr. A train line and the busy coastal road, the A78, cut across this disparate shoreline, where rolling farmland is interrupted by the pockmarks of industrialization, interspersed with moribund seaside resorts, and internationally famous links golf courses. One place that is worth a visit is **Irvine**, home not only to the excellent Scottish Maritime Museum, but also the Big Idea, an innovative science museum aimed primarily at kids. The northernmost town on the Ayrshire coast, and also easily the area's most agreeable seaside resort, is **Largs**, from where you can catch a ferry across to the nearby island of **Great Cumbrae**, a low-key but popular holiday spot.

Public transport is pretty good, with frequent **buses** and a **train** line reaching as far as Largs. In addition, fast ferries depart from **Troon** to Belfast, and **Ardrossan** is the departure point for CalMac ferries to the Isle of Arran (see p.229).

Prestwick and Troon

Leaving Ayr, the A78 trims the outskirts of **PRESTWICK**, whose golf club initiated the Open Championship in 1860, and whose old links course was the competition's exclusive venue for the first decade. Unless you're a golf fan, however, Prestwick can be happily bypassed, as can **TROON**, another uninspiring seaside resort and port three miles further north, which boasts no fewer than six golf courses surrounding the town on every side and a fast ferry Seacat link with Belfast (ⓦwww.seacat.co.uk).

More intriguing than either town is **Dundonald Castle** (April–Sept daily 10am–5pm; HS; £2), three miles inland from Troon on the A759. Built in the 1370s by Robert Stewart, the first of the family to hold the Scottish crown (as Robert II), the castle has some impressively large medieval barrel vaulting, a grand but roofless great hall, a very nasty dungeon, and commanding views over neighbouring Kilmarnock.

Kilmarnock

Twelve miles northeast from Ayr, **KILMARNOCK** is, by and large, a shabby and depressed manufacturing town, known principally for being the home of Johnnie Walker whisky. The town planners of the 1960s and 1970s didn't do the place any favours, saddling it with some terrible shopping centres, and a grim one-way road system. Yet it isn't a bad-looking town in parts, thanks to the local red sandstone, and it has one or two sights.

One of the town's most handsome buildings is the **Dick Institute** (Mon, Tues, Thurs & Fri 9am–8pm, Wed 10am–5pm, Sat 9am–5pm; free), a splendid edifice with a Corinthian portico flanked by monkey-puzzle trees, just off the B7073 London Road. Opened in 1901, and completely rebuilt ten years later after a disastrous fire, the institute was paid for with money donated by local boy James Dick, who made his fortune in gutta-percha (a type of rubber used in shoemaking). On the ground floor is the town library, and a space for temporary exhibitions; upstairs is the local museum, an endearingly old-fashioned place piled high with fossils, stuffed fauna, model boats and a lace loom. Also on display is a selection of the institute's artworks, which include a couple of top-notch Pre-Raphaelite paintings by Alma-Tadema and Millais, and several works by Edward Hornel.

To the north of the Dick Institute, beyond Kilmarnock College and the railway, is Kay Park, site of the largest **Burns Monument** in Scotland, a Scots Baronial monstrosity erected in 1879. It currently stands rather forlorn at the highest point in the town, closed up and surrounded by security fencing. More uplifting is **Dean Castle** (April–Oct daily noon–5pm; Nov–March Sat & Sun noon–4pm; free), set in beautiful wooded grounds a mile or so to the north up Kilmarnock Water. The keep dates back to around 1360, while the adjacent palace was built a hundred years later, though both were accidentally burnt to the ground in 1735. The whole complex was restored and lived in by the eighth Lord Howard de Walden in the early part of the twentieth century, before being gifted to the local council in 1975. The grounds are open all year round during daylight hours, but to visit the castle you must go on a 45-minute guided tour, which set off hourly. Highlights include several fifteenth- and sixteenth-century Brussels tapestries, plus a collection of musical instruments and a large armoury from the same period.

Practicalities

Kilmarnock's **train station** lies at the north end of John Finnie Street, which is lined with impressive red sandstone Victorian buildings, and runs parallel with the main shopping drag, King Street, to the east. There is currently no tourist office, but if you need a place to **stay**, look no further than the *Burnside Hotel* (Ⓣ01563/522952, Ⓦwww.burnsidehotel.co.uk; ❷), which occupies a large, relaxed Victorian mansion at 18 London Rd. You can get a bite to eat at *Marmita's*, a half-decent **coffee shop** at 37 Bank St, off the southern end of John Finnie Street, while J.D. Wetherspoon have kindly provided the eminently civilized, though entirely modern, *Wheatsheaf* **pub**, just up from The Cross, at the northern end of King Street.

Irvine

IRVINE, twelve miles north of Ayr, was once the principal port for trade between Glasgow and Ireland, and later for coal from Kilmarnock, its halcyon days recalled by the enjoyable **Scottish Maritime Museum** (April–Oct daily 10am–5pm; £2.50), which is spread across several locations down at the town's beautifully restored old harbour. The best place to start is in the **Linthouse Engine Shop**, on Harbour Road, a late nineteenth-century hanger-like building held up with massive iron girders, moved here brick by brick from Govan in 1990. Inside, the ad hoc displays include everything from old sailing dinghies and canoes to a giant ship's turbines, and a kids' corner for learning Morse code and semaphore. Free guided tours set off roughly four times a day round the nearby **Shipbuilder's Flat**, which has been restored to something

CHAPTER 3

Highlights

* **Gallery of Modern Art** – Idiosyncratic but populist collection of contemporary artworks, bang in the heart of the city. See p.246
* **Necropolis** – Elegantly crumbling graveyard on a city centre hill, behind the ancient cathedral. See p.254
* **Glasgow School of Art** – Take a student-led tour of Charles Rennie Mackintosh's architectural masterpiece. See p.255
* **Clydeside** – The river that made Glasgow: walk or cycle along it, take a boat on it, cross a bridge over it, or get a view of it from the top of the Glasgow Tower. See p.263
* **Burrell Collection** – An inspired and eclectic art collection displayed in a purpose-built museum in Pollok Park. See p.267
* **"Glaesga nightlife"** – Sample the glitz and the grit with cocktails at the *Rogano* followed by a pint of heavy at the *Horseshoe Bar*. See p.274
* **New Lanark** – Stay for next-to-nothing at this fascinating nineteenth-century planned village. See p.289

Glasgow and the Clyde

Rejuvenated, upbeat **Glasgow**, Scotland's largest city, has not traditionally enjoyed the best of reputations. Once an industrial giant set on the banks of the mighty River Clyde, it can still initially seem a grey and depressing place, with the M8 motorway screeching through the centre and dilapidated housing estates on its outskirts. However, the effects of Glasgow's remarkable overhaul, set in motion in the 1980s by the "Glasgow's Miles Better" campaign and crowned by the awarding of the title of European City of Culture in 1990, are still much in evidence, even if the momentum has slowed. Glasgow's image of itself has changed irrevocably and few visitors will be left in any doubt that the city is, in its own idiosyncratic way, a cultured and dynamic place well worth getting to know.

The city has much to offer: here are some of the best-financed and most imaginative museums and galleries in Britain – among them the showcase **Burrell Collection** of art and antiquities – and nearly all of them are free. Glasgow's **architecture** is some of the most striking in the UK, from the restored eighteenth-century warehouses of the **Merchant City** to the hulking Victorian prosperity of George Square. Most distinctive of all is the work of local luminary Charles Rennie Mackintosh, whose elegantly streamlined Art Nouveau designs appear all over the city, reaching their apotheosis in the stunning **School of Art**. Recent development of the old shipyards of the Clyde, notably in the space-age shapes of the new **Glasgow Science Centre**, hint at yet another string to the city's bow: combining design with innovation. The city boasts thriving live-music venues, distinctive places to eat and drink, busy

Accommodation price codes

Throughout this book, accommodation **prices** have been graded with the codes below, corresponding to the cost of the least expensive double room in high season. Price codes are not given for **campsites**, most of which charge less than £10 per person. Almost all **hostels** and **bunkhouses** charge between £8 and £12 per person per night; the few exceptions to this rule have the prices quoted in the text. For a full account of these codes, see p.28.

1 under £40	4 £60–70	7 £110–150
2 £40–50	5 £70–90	8 £150–200
3 £50–60	6 £90–110	9 £200 and over

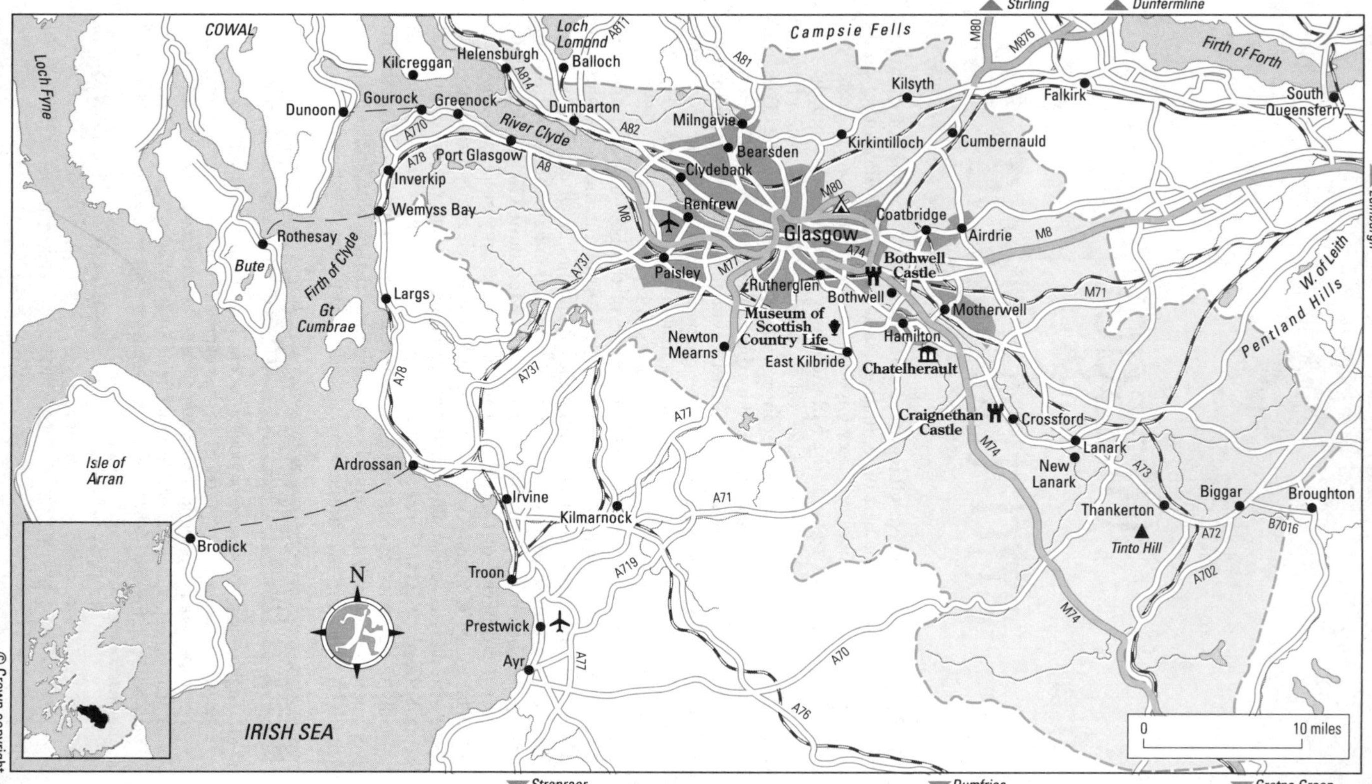

Stirling
Dunfermline
Edinburgh
Stranraer
Dumfries
Gretna Green
COWAL
Loch Fyne
Loch Lomond
Campsie Fells
Firth of Forth
Kilcreggan
Helensburgh
Balloch
Kilsyth
Falkirk
South Queensferry
Dunoon
Gourock
Greenock
Dumbarton
Milngavie
Kirkintilloch
Cumbernauld
River Clyde
Port Glasgow
Bearsden
Clydebank
Inverkip
Wemyss Bay
Renfrew
Glasgow
Coatbridge
Airdrie
Rothesay
Bute
Firth of Clyde
Paisley
Rutherglen
Bothwell Castle
Bothwell
Motherwell
W. of Leith
Pentland Hills
Largs
Gt Cumbrae
Museum of Scottish Country Life
Newton Mearns
East Kilbride
Hamilton
Chatelherault
Craignethan Castle
Crossford
Lanark
New Lanark
Isle of Arran
Ardrossan
Irvine
Kilmarnock
Thankerton
Biggar
Broughton
Tinto Hill
Brodick
Troon
Prestwick
Ayr
N
IRISH SEA
0
10 miles
A811
A81
M80
M876
A814
A82
A770
A78
A8
M8
M80
A74
M77
M71
A737
A77
A71
A719
M74
A73
A72
B7016
A702
A70
A76

theatres, concert halls and an opera house. Above all, the feature that best defines the individualism and peculiar attraction of the city is its **people**, whether rough-edged comedians on the football terraces or bright young things dressed to the nines in the trendiest of style bars.

Despite all the upbeat hype, Glasgow's gentrification has passed by deprived inner-city areas such as the **East End**, home of the **Barras market** and some staunchly change-resistant pubs. This area, along with isolated housing schemes such as Castlemilk and Easterhouse, needs more than a facelift to resolve its complex social and economic problems, and has historically been the breeding ground for the city's much-lauded **socialism**, celebrated in the wonderful **People's Palace** social history museum. Indeed, even in the more stylish quarters of Glasgow there's a gritty edge that's never far away, reinforcing a peculiar mix of grime and glitz which the city seems to have patented.

Quite apart from its own attractions, Glasgow makes an excellent base from which to explore the **Clyde Valley and coast**, made easily accessible by a reliable train service. Chief among the draws is the remarkable eighteenth-century **New Lanark** mills and workers' village, a World Heritage Site, while other day-trips might take you to the new **National Museum of Scottish Country Life** near East Kilbride or on a boat heading "doon the watter" past the old shipbuilding centres on the Clyde estuary.

Glasgow

GLASGOW's earliest history, like so much else in this surprisingly romantic city, is obscured in a swirl of myth. The city's name is said to derive from the Celtic *Glas-cu*, which loosely translates as "the dear, green place" – a tag that the tourist board is keen to exploit as an antidote to the sooty images of popular imagination. It is generally agreed that the first settlers arrived in the sixth century to join Christian missionary **Kentigern** – later to become St Mungo – in his newly founded monastery on the banks of the tiny Molendinar Burn.

William the Lionheart gave the town an official charter in 1175, after which it continued to grow in importance, peaking in the mid-fifteenth century when the **university** was founded on Kentigern's site – the second in Scotland after St Andrews. This led to the establishment of an archbishopric, and hence city status, in 1492, and, due to its situation on a large, navigable river, Glasgow soon expanded into a major industrial **port**. The first cargo of tobacco from Virginia offloaded in Glasgow in 1674, and the 1707 Act of Union between Scotland and England – despite demonstrations against it in Glasgow – led to a boom in trade with the colonies until American independence. Following the **Industrial Revolution** and James Watt's innovations in steam power, coal from the abundant seams of Lanarkshire fuelled the ironworks all around the Clyde, worked by the cheap hands of the Highlanders and, later, those fleeing the Irish potato famine of the 1840s.

The **Victorian** age transformed Glasgow beyond recognition. The population boomed from 77,000 in 1801 to nearly 800,000 at the end of the century, and new tenement blocks swept into the suburbs in an attempt to cope with the choking influxes of people. Two vast and stately **International Exhibitions** were held in 1888 and 1901 to showcase the city and its industries to the outside world, necessitating the construction of huge civic monoliths such as the Kelvingrove Art Gallery and the Council Chambers in George Square. At this time Glasgow became known as the "Second City of the Empire" – a curious epithet for a place that today rarely acknowledges second place in anything.

By the turn of the twentieth century, Glasgow's industries had been honed into one massive **shipbuilding** culture. Everything from tugboats to transatlantic liners were fashioned out of sheet metal in the yards that straddled the Clyde from Gourock to Rutherglen. In the harsh economic climate of the 1930s, however, unemployment spiralled, and Glasgow could do little to counter its popular image as a city dominated by inebriate violence and, having absorbed vast numbers of Irish emigrants, sectarian tensions. The **Gorbals** area in particular became notorious as one of the worst slums in Europe. The city's image has never been helped by the depth of animosity between its two great rival football teams, Catholic **Celtic** and Protestant **Rangers**.

Shipbuilding, and many associated industries, died away almost completely in the 1960s and 1970s, leaving the city depressed, jobless and directionless. Then, in the 1980s, the self-promotion campaign began, snowballing towards the 1988 Garden Festival and year-long party as European City of Culture in 1990. More recently, Glasgow beat off competition from Edinburgh and Liverpool to become **UK City of Architecture and Design** in 1999, an event which strove valiantly to showcase the city's rich architectural heritage and highlight the role of design in modern everyday living. These various titles have helped to reinforce the impression that Glasgow, despite its many problems, has successfully broken the industrial shackles of the past and evolved into a city of stature and confidence.

Arrival, orientation and information

Glasgow International airport (Ⓣ0141/887 1111, Ⓦwww.glasgow-airport.com) is at Abbotsinch, eight miles southwest of the city – not to be confused with Glasgow Prestwick airport, which is thirty miles south near Ayr. From the international airport, the Glasgow Airport Link bus (£3.30; information Ⓣ0870/608 2608) runs from bus stops 1 or 2 into the central Buchanan Street bus station every fifteen minutes during the day. White airport taxis charge around £15.

From **Glasgow Prestwick** airport (Ⓣ01292/511000, Ⓦwww.gpia.co.uk), buses to Glasgow depart from directly outside the terminal: there's an express bus (hourly; £3.50; 50min), or Airbus #4 (Mon–Sat every 30min, Sun hourly), which costs just 50p if you have an air ticket but takes an hour and a half. The **train** station is a short walk from the terminal (alight at the airport not Prestwick Town), with trains taking 45 minutes to reach Glasgow (Mon–Sat every 30min, Sun hourly; £4.90).

Nearly all **trains** from England come into **Central station**, which sits over Argyle Street, one of the city's main shopping thoroughfares. Bus #398 from the front entrance on Gordon Street shuttles every ten minutes to **Queen Street station**, at the corner of George Square, terminus for trains serving Edinburgh and the north. The walk between the two takes about ten minutes. Bus #398 also stops at **Buchanan Street bus station**, arrival point for regional and inter-city **coaches**.

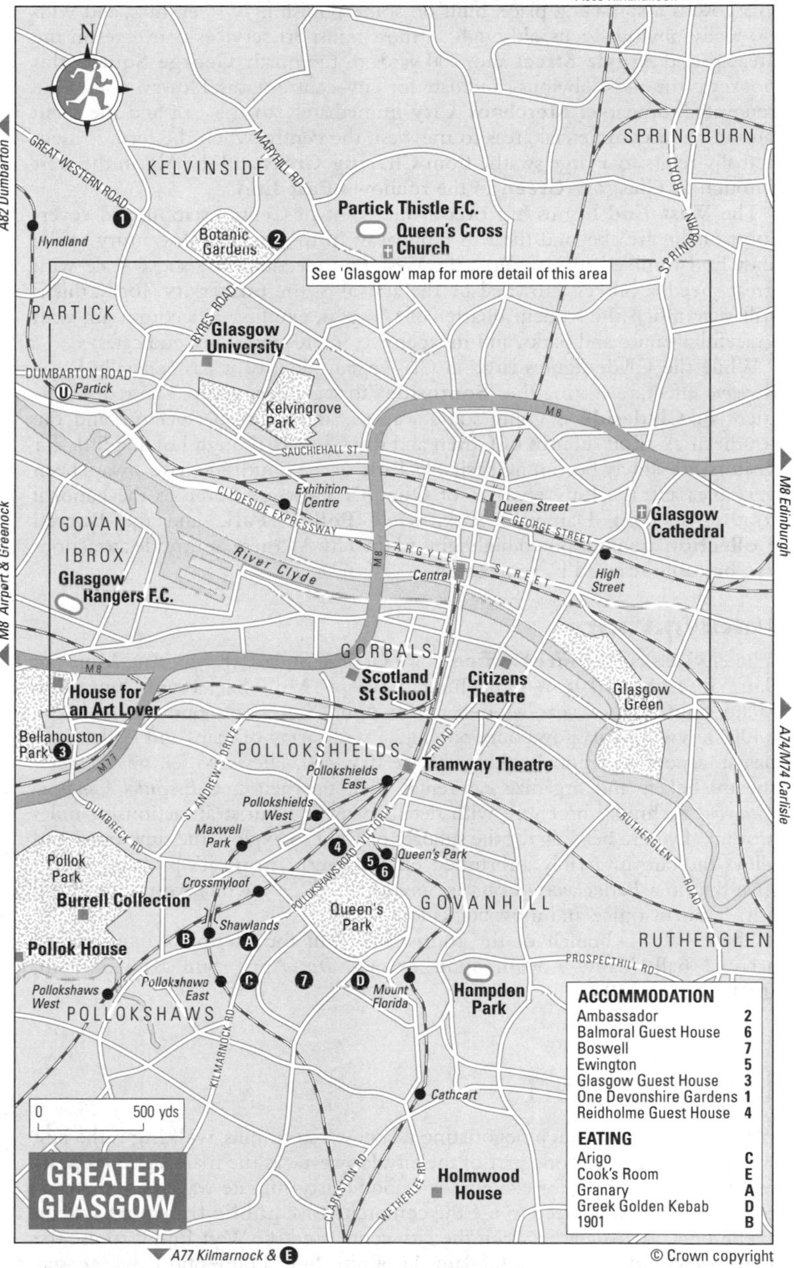
GREATER GLASGOW
A803 Kirkintilloch
A82 Dumbarton
M8 Airport & Greenock
M8 Edinburgh
A74/M74 Carlisle
A77 Kilmarnock & E
KELVINSIDE
SPRINGBURN
PARTICK
GOVAN
IBROX
GORBALS
POLLOKSHIELDS
GOVANHILL
RUTHERGLEN
POLLOKSHAWS
Partick Thistle F.C.
Queen's Cross Church
Botanic Gardens
Hyndland
See 'Glasgow' map for more detail of this area
Glasgow University
Kelvingrove Park
Exhibition Centre
Queen Street
Glasgow Cathedral
Central
High Street
Glasgow Rangers F.C.
Scotland St School
Citizens Theatre
Glasgow Green
House for an Art Lover
Bellahouston Park
Tramway Theatre
Pollokshields East
Pollokshields West
Maxwell Park
Queen's Park
Pollok Park
Burrell Collection
Crossmyloof
Shawlands
Pollok House
Pollokshaws West
Pollokshaws East
Mount Florida
Hampden Park
Cathcart
Holmwood House
0 500 yds
River Clyde
ACCOMMODATION
Ambassador 2
Balmoral Guest House 6
Boswell 7
Ewington 5
Glasgow Guest House 3
One Devonshire Gardens 1
Reidholme Guest House 4
EATING
Arigo C
Cook's Room E
Granary A
Greek Golden Kebab D
1901 B

Orientation

Glasgow is a sprawling place, built on some punishingly steep hills, and with no really obvious focus, although, as most transport services converge on the area around **Argyle Street** and, 200 yards to the north, **George Square**, this pocket is the most obvious candidate for city-centre status. However, with the renovated, upmarket **Merchant City** immediately to the east and the main business and commercial areas to the west, the centre, when the term is used, actually refers to a large swathe from **Charing Cross** and the M8 in the west through to **Glasgow Green** in the rundown **East End**.

The **West End** begins just over a mile west of Central station, and covers most of the area beyond the M8 motorway. In the nineteenth century, as the East End tumbled into poverty, the West End ascended the social scale with great speed, a process crowned by the arrival of the **university**. Today, this is still very much the student quarter of Glasgow, exuding a decorous air, with graceful avenues and parks, and inexpensive, interesting shops and cafés.

While the Clyde figures large in Glaswegian identity, it has generally had a divisive effect, relegating the "**Southside**" to secondary status. The redevelopment of **Clydeside** is going some way to adjust that perspective, and the southern ex-slum suburbs of Govan and the Gorbals, though holding little for visitors, are slowly becoming desirable. Parts of the Southside have always been very pleasant: the leafy enclaves of **Queen's Park** are home to the national football stadium, Hampden Park, while **Pollok Park** and the **Burrell Collection** are undisputed highlights of the city. All these Southside attractions can be easily reached by train or bus.

Information

The city's efficient **tourist office**, at 11 George Square (July & Aug Mon–Sat 9am–8pm, Sun 10am–6pm; June & Sept Mon–Sat 10am–7pm, Sun 10am–6pm; rest of year Mon–Sat 9am–6pm, Sun 10am–6pm; Ⓣ0141/204 4400, Ⓦwww.seeglasgow.com), provides a wide array of maps and leaflets, and has an accommodation-booking service (fee £2). They also sell travel passes, theatre tickets and organize car rental. Pick up their free *Essential Guide to Glasgow*, a chunky brochure with details of every tourist attraction for miles around. If you're heading for the suburbs or want to explore the tiny streets and alleys that are invariably airbrushed off the tourist maps, it's probably worth investing in a *Bartholomew Glasgow Streetfinder* (£2.99), which you can pick up at the tourist office and most bookshops.

There's also a branch of the tourist office in the **airport's** international arrivals hall (daily 7.30am–5pm, except Oct–April Sun 8am–3.30pm; Ⓣ0141/848 4440).

City transport

Although it can be tough negotiating Glasgow's steep hills, **walking** is the best way of exploring any one part of the city. However, as the main sights are scattered – the West End, for example, is a good thirty-minute walk from the centre – you'll probably need to use the comprehensive **public transport** system.

The best way to get between the city centre and the West End is to use the **Underground** (Mon–Sat 6.30am–11.30pm, Sun 11am–6pm), whose stations are marked with a large orange U. Affectionately known as the "Clockwork Orange" (there's only one, circular route and the trains are a garish bright orange), the service is extremely easy to use. There's a flat fare of 90p, or you can buy a **day ticket** for £1.60 (Mon–Fri after 9.30am and all day weekends). The main stations are **Buchanan Street**, near George Square and connected to Queen Street train station by a moving walkway, and **St Enoch**, at the junction of Buchanan Street pedestrian precinct and Argyle Street. **Hillhead** station is bang in the heart of the West End, near the university.

If you're travelling beyond the city centre or the West End, or to the main sights on the Southside, you may need to use the bus and train networks. The array of different **bus** companies and the various routes they take is perplexing even to locals, and there's no easy guide to using them other than picking up individual timetables at the Travel Centre on St Enoch's Square (see below). The main operator is First Glasgow (☎0141/423 6600), which runs the "Overground" buses; Arriva (☎0141/885 4040) also operates many services. Information on relevant services is given at some bus stops.

The suburban **train** network is swift and convenient. Suburbs south of the Clyde are connected to Central station, either at the mainline station or the subterranean low-level station, while trains from Queen Street (which also has mainline and low-level stations) head into the northeast suburbs. There are two grim but functional **cross-city lines**: the one running through Central station connects to southeastern districts as far out as Lanark, while the Queen Street line links to the East End and points east. Trains on both lines go through **Partick** station, near the West End, which is also an underground stop; beyond Partick, the trains are an excellent way to link to points west and northwest of Glasgow, including Milngavie (for the start of the West Highland Way), Dumbarton and Helensburgh.

You can hail a black **taxi** from anywhere in the city centre, day or night. There are also taxi ranks at Central and Queen Street train stations and Buchanan Street bus station. Fares are very reasonable; from the city centre to the West End costs £4–5, or the three-mile journey from Central station to Pollok Park and the Burrell Collection costs £7–8.

As for **driving**, the M8 motorway runs right through the heart of Glasgow, making the centre very accessible; once you're there, however, the grid of one-way streets and pedestrian precincts can be frustrating to navigate. You'll find plenty of parking meters and there are expensive 24-hour multistorey **car parks** at Waterloo Street, Mitchell Street, Oswald Street and Cambridge Street.

Transport passes and information

Various **public transport passes** are available if you plan to do lots of travelling on one day or are in the city for more than a few days. For train and underground travel the **Roundabout Glasgow** ticket (£3.50; available Mon–Fri after 9am, and all day Sat & Sun) gives unlimited travel for a day. The simplest of a complicated system of **Zonecards** costs £11.20 and gives travel for a week in central Glasgow, including Partick in the west and the Burrell Collection in the south. Neither of these are valid on the buses, which have their own systems of daily and weekly tickets.

To help demystify the system, and get detailed information on local public transport, make for the neo-Gothic hut of the **Travel Centre** (Mon–Sat 9.30am–5.30pm), located a couple of hundred yards southwest of the tourist office above St Enoch underground station, where you can pick up sheaves of maps, leaflets and bus timetables. There are smaller Travel Centres at Buchanan Street bus station and Hillhead underground station. For information on all transport within the city and further afield, call ☎0870/608 2608.

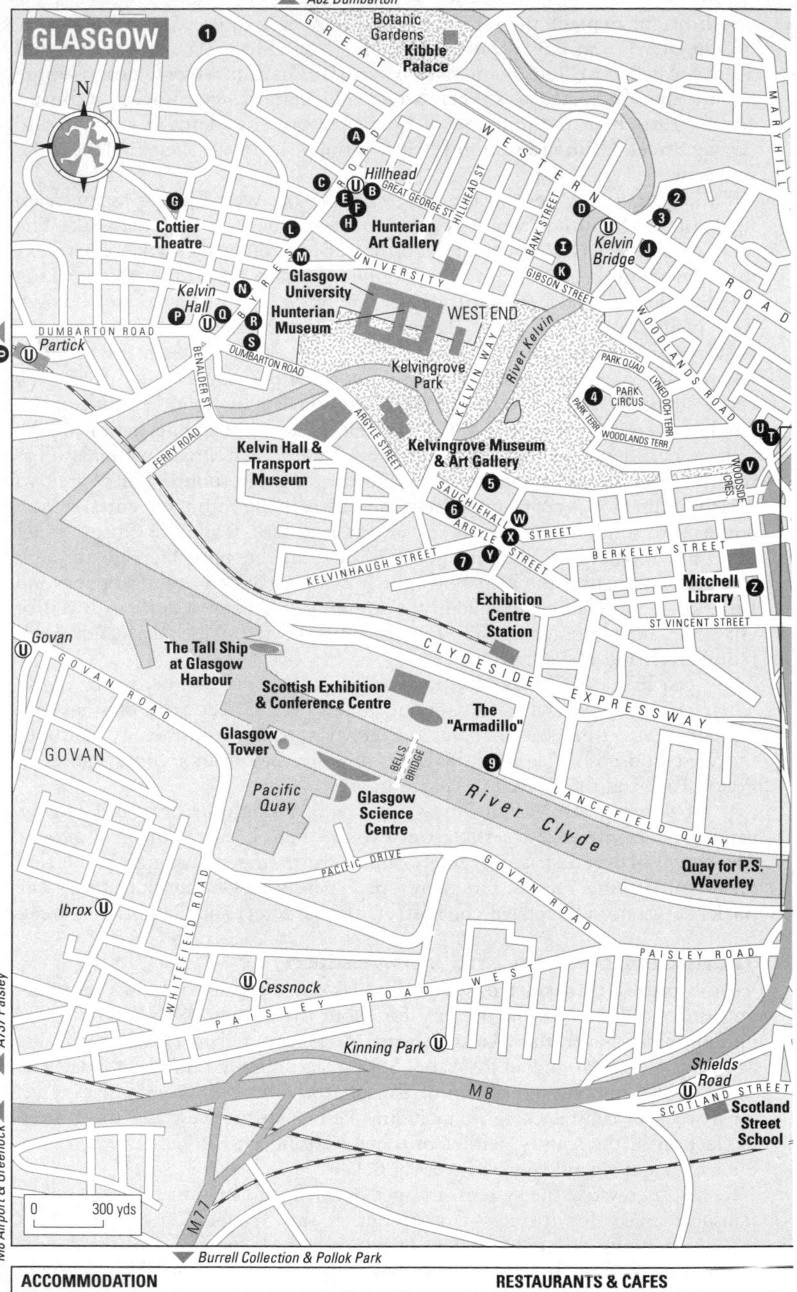

ACCOMMODATION

Alamo Guest House	5	Embassy Appartments	2	Number 36	7
Argyll	6	Inn on the Green	10	Scott Guest House	3
Cathedral House	8	Kirklee Hotel	1	SYHA hostel	4
City Inn	9				

RESTAURANTS & CAFES

Air Organic	W	Brel	H
Ashoka Ashton Lane	B	Cabin	O
Bay Tree Café	J	Café Antipasti	A
Big Blue	D	Café Serghei	AA

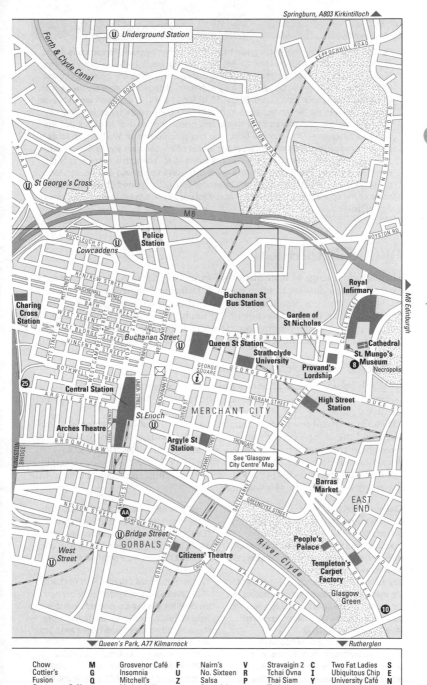

Springburn, A803 Kirkintilloch

Underground Station
Forth & Clyde Canal
KEPPOCHHILL ROAD
GARSCUBE ROAD
POSSIL ROAD
PINKSTON ROAD
SPRINGBURN ROAD
St George's Cross
M8
ROYSTON RD
BUCCLEUCH ST
Cowcaddens
Police Station
RENFREW STREET
SAUCHIEHALL STREET
BATH STREET
WEST REGENT STREET
WEST GEORGE STREET
VINCENT STREET
BOTHWELL STREET
ARGYLE STREET
PITT STREET
WEST CAMPBELL STREET
HOPE STREET
RENFIELD STREET
WEST NILE STREET
Charing Cross Station
Buchanan Street
Buchanan St Bus Station
Royal Infirmary
M8 Edinburgh
Garden of St Nicholas
CATHEDRAL STREET
CASTLE STREET
Queen St Station
Cathedral
St. Mungo's Museum
Necropolis
Strathclyde University
Provand's Lordship
GEORGE SQUARE
GEORGE STREET
Central Station
UNION STREET
BUCHANAN ST
QUEEN ST
INGRAM STREET
HIGH STREET
High Street Station
DUKE ST
MERCHANT CITY
St Enoch
Arches Theatre
OSWALD STREET
BROOMIELAW
KINGSTON BRIDGE
Argyle St Station
STOCKWELL STREET
TRONGATE
See 'Glasgow City Centre' Map
GALLOWGATE
Barras Market
EAST END
SALTMARKET
GREENDYKE STREET
BRIDGE ST
NELSON STREET
NORFOLK STREET
Bridge Street
COOK STREET
GORBALS
GORBALS STREET
CROWN STREET
Citizens' Theatre
River Clyde
People's Palace
LONDON ROAD
THE GREEN
Templeton's Carpet Factory
West Street
CROW
BALLATER STREET
Glasgow Green

Queen's Park, A77 Kilmarnock
Rutherglen

Chow	M	Grosvenor Café	F	Nairn's	V	Stravaigin 2	C	Two Fat Ladies	S
Cottier's	G	Insomnia	U	No. Sixteen	R	Tchai Ovna	I	Ubiquitous Chip	E
Fusion	Q	Mitchell's	Z	Salsa	P	Thai Siam	Y	University Café	N
Grassroots Café	T	Mother India	X	Stravaigin	K	Tinderbox	L		

City tours

Guide Friday and City Sightseeing run tours of the sights by **open-topped bus** (both April–Oct Mon–Sat 9.30am–4pm; £7.50), which leave every half-hour from George Square on a continuous circuit of all the major attractions in the city centre and West End, allowing you to get on and off as you please. Altogether more bizarre is the **Glasgow Ducks** tour (book on ⓣ0870/013 6140; £11.50), in which an amphibious vehicle which looks like an escapee from a Disney theme park takes in a few city highlights before plunging into the Clyde and heading downriver to check out the sights of Clydeside. Back on dry land, you can pick up one of **Walkabout Tours**' personal cassette players and maps at the tourist office, allowing you to walk at your own pace round the main city centre sights listening to a historical commentary (£5 per day). **Mercat Tours** also offers a guided historic tour (June–Sept daily 2pm; ⓣ0141/772 0022; £5), as well as a "Gruesome Glasgow" guided ghost tour round some of the spookier parts of the city (April–Oct daily 7pm & 9pm; March & Nov daily 7pm; Dec–Feb Fri 7pm; £5).

Accommodation

There's a good range of **accommodation** in Glasgow, from a couple of large, well-run hostels through to some highly fashionable designer hotels in the centre. The city centre is dominated by hotels, while cosier guesthouses and B&Bs can be found in the West End or in the southern suburb of Queen's Park. In general, prices are significantly lower than in Edinburgh, and given that many hotels are business-oriented, you can often negotiate good deals at weekends.

Hotels and guesthouses

It's worth booking ahead at **hotels and guesthouses** to ensure a good room, especially in summer – either directly or through the tourist office (which charges a £2 fee).

If you're prepared to sacrifice character, ambience and home comforts, you'll often find the cheapest rooms in the city at the **budget chain hotels** found throughout the city centre. Big players include Novotel/Ibis ⓣ020/8283 4530, ⓦwww.accorhotels.com; Travelodge ⓣ0870/085 0950, ⓦwww.travelodge.co.uk; Travel Inn ⓣ0870/242 8000, ⓦwww.travelinn.co.uk; and Holiday Inn Express ⓣ0800/897121, ⓦwww.hiexpress.com.

City centre

Adelaide's 209 Bath St ⓣ0141/248 4970, ⓦwww.adelaides.co.uk. Eight simple, well-appointed rooms in a beautifully restored church building, with pleasant staff and an attractive café. Breakfast excluded. ❷

Baird Hall 460 Sauchiehall St ⓣ0141/553 4148. The most distinctive student halls of residence in the country, in a lavish Art Deco building near the School of Art and the upper end of Sauchiehall Street (June to mid-Sept). ❶

Bewley's 110 Bath St ⓣ0141/353 0800, ⓦwww.bewleyshotel.com. Oddly shaped new central hotel, part of the famous Irish chain, with large windows and double, triple and family rooms at a year-round flat rate. ❸

Brunswick 106 Brunswick St ⓣ0141/552 0001, ⓦwww.brunswickhotel.co.uk. Under the banner "Eat Drink Sleep" in the heart of the Merchant City, a fashionable but good-value designer hotel with minimalist furniture and a smart bar and restaurant. ❹

Cathedral House 28 Cathedral Sq ⓣ0141/552 3519. Located in the oldest part of the city near the cathedral, this free-standing red sandstone Victorian building with turrets and high chimney stacks has comfortable modern rooms and a popular downstairs bar. ❹

Groucho St Judes 190 Bath St ⓣ0141/352 8800, ⓦwww.grouchosaintjudes.com. Elegant contemporary boutique hotel with six rooms and some exquisite designer touches. ❻

Inn on the Green 25 Greenhead St ⓣ0141/554 0165, ⓦwww.theinnonthegreen.co.uk. Neat and tasteful small hotel off the beaten track on the edge of Glasgow Green, with live jazz most evenings in the restaurant downstairs. Breakfast excluded. ❺

Langs 2 Port Dundas Place ⓣ0141/333 1500, ⓦwww.langshotels.co.uk. Big, sassy, classy modern hotel with a spa, trendy restaurants and lots of mod cons. Breakfast excluded. ❹

Malmaison 278 West George St ⓣ0141/572 1000, ⓦwww.malmaison.com. Glasgow's version of the sleek, chic mini-chain, an austere Grecian-temple frontage masking a superbly comfortable designer hotel. Breakfast excluded. ❼

Pipers' Tryst 30–34 McPhater St ⓣ0141/353 0220, ⓦwww.thepipingcentre.co.uk. Eight fortunately soundproofed, hotel-grade rooms attached to the bagpiping centre; a café on the ground floor (Mon–Sat) serves breakfasts and evening meals. ❹

Rennie Mackintosh 218–220 Renfrew St ⓣ0141/333 9992, ⓦwww.renniemackintoshhotels. com. An obvious theme, but the "Mockintosh" furniture and designs are elegant rather than tacky, and the hotel is small, smart and intimate. ❸

The Old School House 194 Renfrew St ⓣ0141/332 7600, ⓦwww.hotelsglasgow.com. Attractive stand-alone villa with 17 well-equipped rooms right next to the School of Art. ❸

West End and Clydeside

Alamo Guest House 46 Gray St ⓣ0141/339 2395. Good-value, family-run boarding house next to Kelvingrove Park. Small but comfortable rooms. ❷

Ambassador 7 Kelvin Drive ⓣ0141/946 1018, ⓦwww.glasgowhotelsandapartments.co.uk. Smallish and comfortable, a standard mid-sized guesthouse in lovely surroundings next to the River Kelvin and Botanic Gardens. ❸

Argyll 973 Sauchiehall St ⓣ0141/337 3313, ⓦwww.argyllhotelglasgow.co.uk. Lots of tartan trimmings, but this well-run hotel near Kelvingrove Museum and Art Gallery has neat rooms and friendly staff. ❸

City Inn Finnieston Quay ⓣ0141/240 1002, ⓦwww.cityinn.com. Chain hotel with stylish rooms and decent rates made interesting by its riverside location right under the Finnieston crane. Breakfast excluded. ❸

Kirklee 11 Kensington Gate ⓣ0141/334 5555, ⓦwww.scotland2000.com/kirklee. Characterful West End B&B in an Edwardian town house, with antique furniture and walls crammed with paintings and etchings. ❹

Number 36 36 St Vincent Crescent ⓣ0141/248 2086, ⓦwww.no36.co.uk. Neat, comfortable guesthouse in a lovely crescent well located for Kelvingrove, the SECC and transport links to the city centre. ❷

One Devonshire Gardens 1 Devonshire Gardens, Great Western Road ⓣ0141/339 2001, ⓦwww.one-devonshire-gardens.co.uk. Glasgow's most exclusive and exquisite small hotel, a ten-minute walk up the Great Western Road from the Botanic Gardens. Well-known for its gourmet restaurant run by celebrity chef Gordon Ramsay. ❽

Scott Guest House 417 Woodside Rd ⓣ0141/339 3750. Friendly B&B, well situated close to Kelvinbridge underground station. ❶

Southside

Balmoral Guest House 124 Queens Drive ⓣ0141/401 8866, ⓦwww.balmoral.kirion.net. Smart five-room guesthouse in a honey-coloured sandstone terrace right beside Queen's Park. ❸

Boswell 27 Mansionhouse Rd ⓣ0141/632 9812. Informal, relaxing hotel in an old Queen's Park villa with a superb real-ale bar. ❹

Ewington 132 Queen's Drive ⓣ0141/423 1152, ⓦwww.scotland-hotels.co.uk. A few doors down from the *Balmoral Guest House* with a similar outlook onto Queen's Park, but this is a much grander, upmarket hotel with a subterranean restaurant. Prices can drop dramatically at weekends. Breakfast excluded. ❻

Glasgow Guest House 56 Dumbreck Rd ⓣ0141/427 0129. Pleasant four-room guesthouse with old furniture, good disabled facilities and handy transport links into the city centre. ❷

Reidholme Guest House 36 Regent Park Square ⓣ0141/423 1855. Small, friendly guesthouse in a quiet side street, designed by Alexander "Greek" Thomson (see p.248). ❷

Hostels, campsites and self-catering

Glasgow doesn't have nearly as many **hostels** as Edinburgh, though it isn't short of bed space, thanks to the arrival of the bright-pink liveried, seven-storey *Euro Hostel* smack in the centre of the city at 318 Clyde St (ⓣ0141/222 2828, ⓦwww.euro-hostels.com), which tries to bridge the gap between backpacker hostel and budget hotel. Its 360 beds are all bunks but they're in smart en-suite rooms sleeping two, four, six or more – some of which have great views. Bed and continental breakfast is from £13.75.

The popular SYHA hostel, 7–8 Park Terrace (ⓣ0141/332 3004, ⓦwww.syha.org.uk), is located in a large town house in one of the West End's grandest terraces. It's a ten-minute walk south of Kelvinbridge underground station; bus #11 or #44 from the city centre leaves you with a short stroll west up Woodlands Road. Beds, mainly in en-suite four-bed dorms, are £11.50 per person in July and August and £11 the rest of the year; book in advance.

Campsite

The only **campsite** within a decent distance of Glasgow is *Craigendmuir Park*, Campsie View, Stepps (ⓣ0141/779 4159, ⓦwww.craigendmuir.co.uk), four miles northeast of the centre, about fifteen minutes' walk from Stepps train station. It has adequate facilities with showers, a laundry and a shop, but there are only ten pitches.

Self-catering

Low-priced **self-catering** rooms and flats are available at the University of Glasgow (ⓣ0141/330 5385, ⓦwww.glas.ac.uk) from June to mid-September, mostly located in the West End, with prices starting at £13.50 per night. The University of Strathclyde (ⓣ0141/553 4148, ⓦwww.strath.ac.uk) has various sites available during the same period, most of which are gathered around the cathedral: B&B in single rooms is available near the main campus in Cathedral Street starting at £18.50 per person per night, though you can pick up rooms for as little as £10 if you have your own bedding and spurn breakfast.

Embassy Apartments, at 8 Kelvin Drive (ⓣ0141/946 6698, ⓦwww.glasgowhotelsandapartments.co.uk; ❸), have useful self-catering apartments located near Kelvinbridge underground, available on a nightly basis.

The City Centre

Glasgow's large **City Centre** is ranged across the north bank of the River Clyde. At its geographical heart is **George Square**, a nineteenth-century municipal showpiece crowned by the enormous **City Chambers** at its eastern end. Behind this lies one of the greatest marketing successes of the 1980s', the **Merchant City**, an area which blends magnificent Victorian architecture with yuppie conversions. The grand buildings and trendy cafés cling to the borders of the run-down **East End**, a strongly working-class district that chooses to ignore its rather showy neighbour. The oldest part of Glasgow, around the **Cathedral**, lies immediately north of the East End.

Called by poet John Betjeman "the greatest Victorian city in the world", Glasgow's commercial core spreads west of George Square, and is mostly built on a large grid system – possibly inspired by Edinburgh's New Town – with ruler-straight roads soon rising up severe hills to grand, sandblasted buildings. The same style was copied by many North American cities, and indeed parts of Glasgow have been pressed into service as nineteenth-century New York in films such as *House of Mirth*. The main shopping areas here are **Argyle Street**, running parallel to the river, and **Buchanan Street**, which links Argyle Street to the pedestrianized shopping thoroughfare, **Sauchiehall Street**. Just to the northwest of here is Charles Rennie Mackintosh's famous **Glasgow School of Art**. Lying between the commercial bustle of Argyle and

© Crown copyright

ACCOMMODATION

Adelaide's	7
Baird Hall	4
Bewley's	8
Brunswick	10
Euro Hostel	11
Groucho St Judes	6
Langs	5
Malmaison	9
Old School House	3
Rennie Mackintosh	2
Pipers' Tryst	1

CAFÉS AND RESTAURANTS

Amber Regent	J	Gamba	K	Oko	N
Arta	V	Granary	Z	Pancho Villas	W
Café Gandolfi	P	Ho Wong	T	Pattaya	B
Canton Express	C	Ichiban	S	Primo Piatto	E
City Merchant	O	Kama Sutra	D	Rogano	M
El Sabor	Q	Le Bouchon	X	The 13th Note	AA
Esca	Y	Le Chardon d'Or	I	Wee Curry Shop	A
Farfelu	R	Mao	U	Where the Monkey Sleeps	G
Fratelli Sarti	H	Mussel Inn	L	Willow Tea Rooms	F

Sauchiehall streets, and to the immediate west of Buchanan Street, are the contours of an Ice Age drumlin (one of three main drumlins in the area), now known as **Blythswood Hill**. In comparison with the bustling shopping parades surrounding it on three sides, this area is remarkably quiet and reserved, with streets of Georgian buildings crowned by neat Blythswood Square.

George Square and around

Now hemmed in by the city's grinding traffic, the imposing architecture of **George Square** reflects the confidence of Glasgow's Victorian age. The wide-open plaza almost has a continental airiness about it, although there isn't much subtlety about the eighty-foot column rising up at its centre. It's topped by a statue of Sir Walter Scott, even though his links with Glasgow are, at best, sketchy. Haphazardly dotted around the great writer's plinth are a number of dignified statues of assorted luminaries, ranging from Queen Victoria to Scots heroes such as James Watt and wee Robbie Burns. The florid splendour of the **City Chambers**, opened by Queen Victoria in 1888, occupies the entire eastern end of the square. Built from wealth gained by colonial trade and heavy industry, it epitomizes the aspirations and optimism of late-Victorian city elders. Its intricately detailed facade includes high-minded friezes typical of the era: the four nations which then comprised the United Kingdom (England, Scotland, Wales and Ireland) at the feet of the throned queen, the British colonies and allegorical figures representing Religion, Virtue and Knowledge. It's worth taking a free **guided tour** of the labyrinthine interior (Mon–Fri 10.30am & 2.30pm; booking recommended on ⓣ0141/287 4018) to get a look at the acres of intricate gold leaf and Italian marble.

Equally opulent is the **Merchant's House** opposite Queen Street station (appointment only; ⓣ0141/221 8272; free), where the grand Banqueting Hall and silk-lined Directors' Room are highlights. Even if you don't get inside, look out for the golden square-rigged ship on a globe perched on the top of the building.

The Gallery of Modern Art

Queen Street leads south from George Square to **Royal Exchange Square**, where the focal point is the graceful mansion built in 1780 for tobacco lord William Cunninghame. This was the most ostentatious of the Glasgow merchants' homes and, having served as the city's Royal Exchange and central library, now houses the **Gallery of Modern Art** (Mon–Thurs & Sat 10am–5pm, Fri & Sun 11am–5pm; free). Surrounded by controversy from the day it opened in 1996, the gallery has tended to please the punters more than the critics, who have damned the place for emphasizing presentation over content. The presentation is certainly unusual: the main part of the gallery is divided into four levels, named Fire, Earth, Water and Air, though these themes bear only a tenuous link to the work displayed.

The mirrored reception area leads you straight into the **Earth Gallery**, a spacious zone that effortlessly absorbs large-scale socially committed works by the "New Glasgow Boys" – Peter Howson, Adrian Wiszniewski, Ken Currie and Steven Campbell. Felipe Linares' beautifully painted papier-mâché skeletons, exploring the Seven Deadly Sins, shine defiantly from the end of the gallery, along with the evocative monochrome photographs of Sebastião Salgado, whose work records the plight of the world's economic underclasses. Right in the middle of the gallery the kinetic sculpture *Titanic* by Eduard Bersudsky, made of scrap metal and old junk, whirrs into life every hour on the half-hour.

Downstairs is the **Fire Gallery**, containing an imaginative new art library, while upstairs you'll find the **Water Gallery**, a brightly lit room dealing with the flow of life and death through art, ranging from Andy Goldsworthy's cracked and sun-baked red clay floor to intricate aboriginal paintings on canvas and bark. Here you'll also find a significant collection of the work of Scottish east-coast artist John Bellany, including his nightmarish triptych *Journey to End of the Night*, depicting a black lobster embracing a ghostly white woman.

The blinding-white upper-floor **Air Gallery** generally features work with vivid visual impact, though in the summer it is filled by major temporary exhibitions. A small set of stairs at the far end of the gallery leads down to an area filled with pop art such as the wavy lines of Bridget Riley's *Arrest III* and Alan Davie's jazz-inspired *Cornucopia*, along with the gruesome row of guillotined heads in baskets by Scottish conceptual artist Ian Hamilton Finlay.

Don't miss the top-floor **café** (see p.270), where a huge mural by Adrian Wiszniewski competes with the view over the rooftops.

Along Buchanan Street

Buchanan Street runs north–south one block west of George Square, defining Glasgow's main shopping district. At the southern end of the street is **Princes Square**, one of the most stylish and imaginative shopping centres in the country, hollowed out of the innards of a soft sandstone building. The interior, all recherché Art Deco and ornate ironwork, has lots of pricey, highly fashionable shops, the whole place set to a soothing background of classical music. A short walk south is the **St Enoch Shopping Centre**, sandwiched between Argyle and Howard streets – a lofty glass pyramid built around a redundant train station.

Glaswegians' voracious appetite for shopping is fed further at the northern end of Buchanan Street, just beyond the underground station, where the **Buchanan Galleries** is a bewilderingly vast shopping mall of some 600,000 square feet which includes the largest Habitat store in Europe. Next door, almost anonymous beside its massive neighbouring auditorium of consumerism, is the £30-million **Royal Concert Hall**, with only three huge flagpoles protruding to proclaim that this is, in fact, a building of note. The showpiece hall does, however, have an excellent auditorium which plays host to world-class musical events from touring orchestras to rock acts, while the lobbies are used for temporary art exhibitions. These can be seen for free, or you can take a **guided tour** of the huge hall and its backstage areas (phone for schedule ⓣ0141/353 8000; £1.50).

The Lighthouse

At 11 Mitchell Lane, an otherwise nondescript alleyway between Buchanan Street and Union Street, is **The Lighthouse** (Mon, Wed, Fri & Sat 10.30am–5.30pm, Tues 11am–5.30pm, Thurs 10.30am–7pm, Sun noon–5pm; free; ⓦwww.thelighthouse.co.uk), a spectacularly converted Charles Rennie Mackintosh building which has found new life as Scotland's Centre for Architecture, Design and the City. The 1895 building was Mackintosh's first public commission, and housed the offices of the *Glasgow Herald* newspaper; despite glass and sandstone additions by architects Page & Park, it retains many original features, including the distinctive tower from which the building takes its name. The venue played a central role in Glasgow's reign as City of Architecture and Design in 1999, and acts as a permanent legacy of that year, mounting temporary exhibitions on design and architecture alongside the permanent **Mackintosh Interpretation Centre** (£2.50), a great place to learn more about the man and his work. It features plans, models, photographs, original objects and computer and video displays which explore many of Mackintosh's unique buildings and interiors, while the Lighthouse Tower itself gives fantastic views out over the city skyline to a number of his important buildings, including the School of Art and Scotland Street School.

The Merchant City

The grid of streets that lies immediately east of the City Chambers is known as the **Merchant City** (ⓦwww.glasgowmerchantcity.net), an area of eighteenth-century warehouses and homes once bustling with cotton, tobacco and sugar traders, which in the last two decades has been sandblasted and swabbed clean with greater enthusiasm and municipal money than any other part of Glasgow

Glasgow's architecture

Glasgow, founded on religion, built on trade and now well established as a cultural centre, has become recognized for its architectural riches, from the medieval cathedral to the modern glass-lined galleries of the Burrell Collection. Most dominant is the legacy of the **Victorian age**, when booming trade and industry allowed merchants to commission the finest architects of the day. The celebrated work of **Charles Rennie Mackintosh** (see box on p.256) took Glasgow architecture to the forefront of early twentieth-century design, a final flowering of homespun genius before economic conditions effectively stopped the architectural trade in its tracks, its revival only really taking hold in the 1980s and 1990s.

The city's expansion: 1750–1850

Glasgow's great expansion was initiated in the eighteenth century by wealthy tobacco merchants who built the grand edifices of public and municipal importance that still make up much of the **Merchant City**. One of the finest Merchant City views is down Garth Street, which frames the Venetian windows and Ionic columns of **Trades House**, designed by Robert Adam in 1791, while nearby **Hutcheson Hall** boasts an elegant tower that moves from a square through octagonals to a drum – an early nineteenth-century architectural nod to the Renaissance by the architect David Hamilton.

Further west, **Royal Exchange Square** is one of the best examples of a typical Glasgow square: treeless, bare and centred around a building of importance, the 1829 **Royal Exchange**, now housing the Gallery of Modern Art. As workers piled into the centre of Glasgow in the early nineteenth century, filling up the already crowded tenements, wealthy residents began moving west to the gridded streets that line **Blythswood Hill** (mostly developed after 1820) with two- or three-storey terraces, their porches and heavy cornices providing textural relief to the endless sandstone monotony. The dignified proportions and design of **Blythswood Square** are a highlight of this area; at no. 5 the later Art Nouveau doorway designed by Charles Rennie Mackintosh sits incongruously amongst the Georgian solidity. Above all, the long streets provide a beautiful selection of open-ended views, one moment leading into the heart of the city, the next filled with distant hills and sky.

Desiring to surround themselves with trees and fields, the well-to-do continued their migration west; in the early 1830s, the Woodlands Hill development was completed beyond Charing Cross – a leafy parkland area in contrast to the treeless town squares of the city centre. Here **Woodside Crescent**, leading into Woodside Terrace, is a severe line of buildings with splendid Doric porches and neatly organized gardens. **Park Circus**, on the other hand, is a parade of uninterrupted Georgian magnificence, with delicate detail – such as narrow window slots on either side of the doors – enhancing the dignified crescent. It's an excellent example of grand planning which, having changed from residential to commercial use, is rapidly being transformed again into upmarket designer apartments.

Greek Thomson and the Victorians

Long since overshadowed by Charles Rennie Mackintosh, the design of **Alexander "Greek" Thomson**, in the latter half of the nineteenth century, though well respected in its time, has been sadly neglected. As his nickname suggests, his work took the principles of Greek architecture, but reprocessed them in a highly unique manner. Energetic and talented, he designed buildings from lowly tene-

in an attempt to bring residents back into the city centre. The expected flood of yuppies, however, was more like a trickle, and the latest efforts to woo them centre on New York-style loft conversions. Yet the expensive designer shops, style bars and bijou cafés continue to flock here, giving the area a pervasive air of sophistication and chic.

ments to grand suburban villas. The 1857 **St Vincent Street Church**, his best work, has a massive simplicity and serenity lightened by the use of exotic Egyptian and Hindu motifs, particularly in the tower with its decorated egg-shaped dome. This fusion of the Classical and the Eastern stands out for its originality at a time when Gothic Revival or Renaissance work was all the rage. Thomson's buildings are now coming to the prominence they deserve, though some were tragically torn down in the municipal clearances of the 1970s. Most recently, the National Trust has opened his finest domestic dwelling, **Holmwood House**, on the Southside, to the public (see p.269).

West from Park Circus lies **Glasgow University** (1866–86), its Gothic Revivalism – the work of Sir George Gilbert Scott – representing everything that Greek Thomson despised; he called it "sixteenth-century Scottish architecture clothed in fourteenth-century French details". Scottish features abound, such as crow-stepped gables, round turrets with conical caps and the top-heavy central tower. Inside, cloisters and quadrants sum up a suitably scholastic severity.

Originally conceived as a convenient way to house the influx of workers in the late 1800s, the Glasgow **tenement** design became more refined as the wealthy middle-classes began to realize its potential. Mainly constructed between 1860 and 1910, tenements have three to five storeys with two or three apartments per floor. Important rooms are picked out with bay windows, middle storeys are emphasized by architraves or decorated panels below sill or above lintel, and street junctions are given importance by swelling bay windows, turrets and domes. A fascinating example of the style of these buildings, as well as the typical style of life inside them, can be seen at the **Tenement House** (see p.257), while west of the university, the streets off **Byres Road** are lined with similarly grand tenement buildings, in particular the Baronial red sandstone of Great George Street.

From World War I to the present

World War I put an end to the glorious century of Glasgow building, and the Depression years did little to enhance the city. However, since World War II bombing was targeted on the shipbuilding district of Clydebank, west of the centre, most of the city's legacy of fine sandstone buildings survived intact.

Glassy office buildings have sprung up in recent years, their mirrored walls basking in the reflected glory of the surrounding buildings to disguise their banality of design. Modern domestic architecture has proved relentlessly utilitarian, with the exception of the experimental **Homes for the Future** complex on the north side of Glasgow Green, conceived as part of Glasgow's Year of Architecture and Deisgn in 1999 to introduce practical protypes of urban living in the twenty-first century. However, the 1980s onwards have seen the return of the grand public building as inheritor of architectural innovation. Beginning with the imaginative **Burrell Collection**, the theme has been taken up by the titanium-clad behemoths of Clydeside: the unmistakeable Clyde Auditorium, better known as the **"Armadillo"**, and the futuristic glass-walled **Science Centre**, flanked by a bubble-like IMAX theatre and the 100-metre-high Glasgow Tower. This is not to ignore the poverty of artistry which went into great works such as the Kingston Bridge and Royal Concert Hall, but few could argue that Glasgow has failed to open itself to innovation and ideas. Above all, the city can be credited with involving its citizens in an awareness that everyone is influenced, as well as represented, by the buildings around them.

At the junction of Ingram and John streets, look out for the **Italian Centre**, a revitalized eighteenth-century warehouse now housing lively cafés, outdoor sculpture and some of the city's most fashionable boutiques – Versace established his first shop in Britain here. Immediately opposite, across John Street, is the delicate white spire of the National Trust for Scotland's regional headquarters,

Hutcheson Hall, at 158 Ingram St (Mon–Sat 10am–5pm; free). The ground floor houses an exhibition of "Glasgow Style", with some attractive work by contemporary designers and craftsmen on sale, while there's a particularly fine ornately decorated hall upstairs. Here you can pick up a Merchant City Trail leaflet, which guides you around a dozen of the most interesting buildings in the area.

Almost opposite in the other direction, a little way down Glassford Street, the Robert Adam-designed **Trades House** (Mon–Sat 9am–6pm, depending on functions; free) is easily distinguished by its neat, green copper dome. Purpose-built in 1794, it still functions as the headquarters of the Glasgow trade guilds. Its history can be traced back to 1605 when fourteen societies of well-to-do city merchants, who were the forerunners of the trade unions, first incorporated. These included a Bakers' Guild, and societies for Hammermen, Gardeners, Bonnet-Makers, Wrights and Weavers, although today they have limited connections to their respective trades and act as charitably minded associations from all sections of Glasgow's business community (mostly male). The former civic pride and status of the guilds is still evident, however, from the rich assortment of carvings and stained-glass windows, with a lively pictorial representation of the different trades in the silk frieze around the walls of the first-floor banqueting hall.

Glasgow Cross

Before 1846, **Glasgow Cross** – the junction of Trongate, Gallowgate and the High Street, at the southeastern corner of the Merchant City – was the city's principal intersection, until the construction of the new train station near George Square shifted the city's emphasis west. The turreted seventeenth-century **Tolbooth Steeple** still stands here, although the rest of the building has long since disappeared, and today the stern tower is little more than a traffic hazard at a busy junction.

The East End

East of Glasgow Cross, down Gallowgate beyond the train lines, lies the **East End**, the district that perhaps most closely corresponds to the old perception of Glasgow. Hemmed in by Glasgow Green to the south and the old university to the west, this densely packed industrial area essentially created the city's wealth. The Depression caused the closure of many factories, leaving communities stranded in an industrial wasteland. Today isolated pubs, tatty shops and cafés sit amidst this dereliction, in sharp contrast to the gloss of the Merchant City only a few blocks to the west. Walking around here you definitely get the sense that you're off the tourist trail, but unless you're here after dark it's not as threatening as it may feel, and there's no doubt that the area advertises a rich flavour of working-class Glasgow.

Three hundred yards down either London Road or Gallowgate is **The Barras**, Glasgow's largest and most popular weekend market (Sat & Sun 9am–5pm). Red iron gates announce its official entrance, but boundaries are breached as the stalls – selling household goods, bric-a-brac, secondhand clothes and records, none of it of particularly high quality – spill out into the surrounding cobbled streets. The fast-talking traders, lively atmosphere and entertaining vignettes of Glasgow life make it an off-beat diversion from shopping-mall banality.

Between London Road and the River Clyde are the wide and tree-lined spaces of **Glasgow Green**. Reputedly the oldest public park in Britain, the

Green has been common land since at least 1178, when it was first mentioned in records. Glaswegians hold it very dear, considering it to be an immortal link between themselves and their ancestors, for whom a stroll on the Green was a favourite Sunday afternoon jaunt. It has also been the site of many of the city's major political demonstrations – the Chartists in the 1830s and Scottish republican campaigners in the 1920s – and was the traditional culmination of the May Day marches until the 1950s, when the celebrations were moved to Queen's Park. Various memorials (some in bad states of disrepair) are dotted around the lawns: the 146-foot **Nelson Monument**; the ornate but derelict terracotta **Doulton Fountain**, rising like a wedding cake to a pinnacle where a forlorn Queen Victoria oversees her crumbling Empire; and the stern monument extolling the evils of drink and the glory of God that was erected by the nineteenth-century **Temperance movement** – now quite a meeting place for local drunks. On the northeast side of the Green, just beyond the People's Palace, it's worth taking a look at the extraordinary **Templeton's Carpet Factory**, a massive brick edifice of turrets, arched windows, mosaic-style patterns and castellated grandeur designed in the style of the Doge's Palace in Venice and built in 1892. Subsequent to its days as a carpet factory it has been a small business centre and health centre, but is now disused.

The People's Palace

Opposite the Templeton's carpet factory on Glasgow Green you can still see some poles erected to hang out washing, recalling the days when the Green was very much a public space in daily use. Beside these, the **People's Palace** (Mon–Thurs & Sat 10am–5pm, Fri & Sun 11am–5pm; free) houses a wonderfully haphazard evocation of the city's history. This squat, red-sandstone Victorian building, with a vast semicircular glasshouse tacked on the back, was purpose-built as a museum back in 1898 – almost a century before the rest of the country caught on to the fashion for social history collections. While many of the displays are designed to instil a warm glow in the memories of older locals, the museum is refreshingly unpretentious, and visitors are almost always outnumbered by Glaswegian families.

On the **top floor**, glowing murals by local artist Ken Currie powerfully evoke the spirit of radical Glasgow, from the Carlton Weavers strike in 1787 to the Red Clydesiders of the 1920s (a radical Independent Labour Party formed during the post-World War I economic slump), and look down upon a potted history of Glasgow's social and economic development. Decorated by Suffragette flags and trade union banners, the room contains a host of memorabilia, including the desk of John MacLean, who became consul to the Russian Bolshevik government in 1918. The **west wing** looks at famous Glasgow products through history, with displays of everything from cast-iron railings and biscuit wrappers to a giant portrait of Billy Connolly. In the **East Gallery**, an entertaining sound-and-light show reconstructs a "single-end" or one-roomed house, a typical setting for the daily life of hundreds of thousands of Glasgow people through the years. Downstairs, various themes with a particular resonance in Glasgow are explored, including alcohol, the traditional holiday excursion "doon the watter" by steamer to various Clyde coastal resorts, and some guidance to understanding "the Patter", Glaswegians' idiosyncratic version of the Queen's English.

The glasshouse at the back of the palace contains the **Winter Gardens**, with a café, water garden, twittering birds and assorted tropical plants and shrubs.

The Cathedral area

Rising north up the hill from the Tolbooth Steeple at Glasgow Cross is Glasgow's **High Street**. In British cities, the name is commonly associated with the busiest central thoroughfare, and it's a surprise to see how forlorn and dilapidated Glasgow's version is, long superseded by the grander thoroughfares further west. The High Street leads up to the **Cathedral**, on the site of Glasgow's original settlement.

Glasgow Cathedral

Built in 1136, destroyed in 1192 and rebuilt soon after, stumpy-spired **Glasgow Cathedral** (April–Sept Mon–Sat 9.30am–6pm, Sun 2–5pm; Oct–March Mon–Sat 9.30am–4pm, Sun 2–4pm; free) was not completed until the late fifteenth century, with the final reconstruction of the chapterhouse and the aisle designed by Robert Blacader, the city's first archbishop. Thanks to the intervention of the city guilds, it is the only Scottish mainland cathedral to have escaped the hands of religious reformers in the sixteenth century. The cathedral is dedicated to the city's patron saint and reputed founder, St Mungo, about whom four popular stories are frequently told – they even make an appearance on the city's coat of arms. These involve a bird that he brought back to life, the bell with which he summoned the faithful to prayer, a tree that he managed to make spontaneously combust and a fish that he caught with a repentant adulterous queen's ring on its tongue.

Because of the sloping ground on which it is built, at its east end the cathedral is effectively on two levels, the crypt being part of the lower church. On entering, you arrive in the impressively lofty nave of the **upper church**, with the lower church entirely hidden from view. Most of this upper church was completed under the direction of Bishop William de Bondington (1233–58), although later design elements came from Blacader. Either side of the nave, the narrow **aisles** are illuminated by vivid stained-glass windows, most of which date from the last century. Threadbare Union flags and military pennants hang listlessly beneath them, serving as a reminder that the cathedral is very much a part of the Unionist Protestant tradition. Beyond the nave, the **choir** is hidden from view by the curtained stone pulpit, making the interior feel a great deal smaller than might be expected from the outside. In the choir's northeastern corner, a small door leads into the gloomy **sacristy**, in which Glasgow University was first founded over five hundred years ago. Wooden boards mounted on the walls detail the alternating Roman Catholic and Protestant clergy of the cathedral, testimony to the turbulence and fluctuations of the Church in Scotland.

Two sets of steps from the nave lead down into the **lower church**, where you'll see the dark and musty **chapel** surrounding the tomb of St Mungo. The saint's relics were removed in the late Middle Ages, although the tomb still forms the centrepiece. The chapel itself is one of the most glorious examples of medieval architecture in Scotland, best seen in the delicate fan vaulting rising up from the thicket of cool stone columns. Scots designer Robert Stewart was commissioned in 1979 to produce a tapestry detailing the four myths of St Mungo, which can be illuminated using the button at the bottom of the north-side stairs to reveal its swirl of browns and oranges. Also in the lower church, the spaciously light **Blacader Aisle** was originally built as a two-storey extension; today only this lower section survives, where the bright, and frequently gory, medieval ceiling bosses stand out superbly against the simple whitewashed vaulting.

△ Statue of Mercury, Merchant City, Glasgow

The Necropolis

Rising up behind the Cathedral, the atmospheric **Necropolis** is a grassy mound covered in a fantastic assortment of crumbling and tumbling gravestones, ornate urns, gloomy catacombs and Neoclassical temples. Inspired by the Père Lachaise cemetery in Paris, developer John Strong created a garden of death in 1833, and it quickly became a fitting spot for the great and the good of wealthy nineteenth-century Glasgow to indulge their vanity. Various paths lead through the rows of eroding, neglected graves, and from the summit, next to the column topped with an indignant John Knox, there are superb **views** which capture the city and its trademark mix of grit and grace – the steaming chimneys of the Tennants brewery, the traffic on the M8 motorway, the crowded city-centre offices, the serene cathedral itself, and a wide cityscape of spires and high-rise blocks to the south and east.

Cathedral Square

Back in Cathedral Square, the **St Mungo Museum of Religious Life and Art** (Mon–Thurs & Sat 10am–5pm, Fri & Sun 11am–5pm; free) focuses on objects, beliefs and art from Christianity, Buddhism, Judaism, Islam, Hinduism and Sikhism. Portrayals of Hindu gods are juxtaposed with the stunning Salvador Dali painting *St John of the Cross* – the focus of huge controversy when it was purchased by the city in 1952 for what was regarded as the vast sum of £9200 – that draws the viewer into its morose depths. In addition to the main exhibition there is a small collection of photographs, papers and archive material looking at religion in Glasgow, the power and zealotry of the nineteenth-century Temperance movement and Christian missionaries (local boy David Livingstone in particular). Outside is Britain's only permanent "dry stone" Zen Buddhist garden, with slabs of rock, white gravel and moss arranged to suggest the forms of land and sea.

Across the square, the oldest house in the city, the **Provand's Lordship** (same times; free) dates from 1471, and has been used, among other things, as an ecclesiastical residence and an inn. Inside, the re-creations of life in the fifteenth century aren't particularly arresting unless you've an interest in period furniture. As a reminder of the manse's earthier history, the upper floor contains pictures of assorted lowlife characters, such as the notorious drunkards and prostitutes of eighteenth- and nineteenth-century Glasgow.

Behind the Provand's Lordship lies the small **Garden of St Nicholas**, a herb garden contrasting medieval and Renaissance aesthetics and approaches to medicine, with muddled clusters of herbs amid stone carvings of the heart and other organs, and a controlled arrangement of plants around a small ornate fountain. The garden, bordered by sandstone walkways where you can sit, is an aromatic and peaceful haven away from the High Street.

Sauchiehall Street and around

Glasgow's most famous street, **Sauchiehall Street**, runs in a straight line west from the northern end of Buchanan Street, past some unexciting shopping malls to a few of the city's most interesting sights. Charles Rennie Mackintosh fans should head for the **Willow Tea Rooms**, not all that easy to spot at first, above a jewellery shop at 217 Sauchiehall St. This is a faithful reconstruction on the site of the 1904 original, which was created for Kate Cranston, one of Rennie Mackintosh's few contemporary supporters in the city, opened in 1980 after more than fifty years of closure. Everything from the fixtures and fittings right down to the teaspoons and menu cards were designed by Mackintosh.

Taking inspiration from the word *Sauchiehall*, which means "avenue of willow", he chose the willow leaf as a theme to unify the whole structure from the tables to the mirrors and the ironwork. The motif is most apparent in the stylized linear panels of the bow window which continues into the intimate dining room as if to surround the sitter, like a willow grove, and is echoed in the distinctively high-backed silver-and-purple chairs. These elongated forms were used to enhance the small space and demonstrate Mackintosh's superb ability to fuse function with decoration. Tea is served here daily from 9.30am until 5pm (for a review, see p.270).

One block west are the **McLellan Galleries**, 270 Sauchiehall St (daily 10am–6pm, Thurs until 8pm; free, apart from admission to some exhibitions), which, despite its inauspicious frontage is as soothing an example of Neoclassical architecture as anywhere in the city. A grand staircase sweeps you up into the main exhibition space, lit naturally by beautiful pedimented windows.

Another artistic space a few blocks further west at no. 350, albeit of a different tone entirely, is the recently remodelled **CCA** (Centre for Contemporary Arts; ⓣ0141/332 7521, ⓦwww.cca-glasgow.com), where eclectically internationalist exhibitions and performances consistently make the centre one of the city's cultural hotspots.

The Glasgow School of Art

Rising above Sauchiehall Street to the north is one of the city centre's steepest hills, where Dalhousie and Scott streets veer up to Renfrew Street, where you'll find Charles Rennie Mackintosh's **Glasgow School of Art**, 167 Renfrew St (guided tours Mon–Fri 11am & 2pm, Sat 10.30 & 11.30am; July & August also Sat 1pm, Sun 10.30 & 11.30am; booking advised; ⓣ0141/353 4526, ⓦwww.gsa.ac.uk; £5). This is one of the most prestigious art schools in the country, with such notable alumni as artists Robert Colquhoun and Robert Macbryde and, more recently, Steven Campbell, Ken Currie and actor Robbie Coltrane. Widely considered to be the pinnacle of Mackintosh's work, the school is a characteristically angular building of warm sandstone which, due to financial constraints, had to be constructed in two sections (1897–99 and 1907–09). There's a clear change in the architect's style from the earlier severity of the mock-Baronial east wing to the softer lines of the western half.

The only way to see the school is to take one of the student-led **guided tours**, the extent of which are dependent on curricular activities. You can, however, be sure of seeing at least some of the differences between the two halves and a handful of the most impressive rooms. All over the school, from the roof to the stairwells, Mackintosh's unique touches recur – light Oriental reliefs, tall-backed chairs and stylized Celtic illuminations. Even before entering the building up the gently curving stairway, you cannot fail to be struck by the soaring height of the north-facing windows, which light the art studios and were designed, in the architect's inimitable style, to combine aesthetics with practicality.

In the main entrance hall, the school shop sells tour tickets and a good selection of Mackintosh books, posters and cards. Hanging in the hall stairwell is the artist's highly personal wrought-iron version of the legend of St Mungo represented on the city's coat of arms. You'll see excellent examples of his early furniture in the tranquil **Mackintosh Room**, flooded with soft, natural light, while the **Furniture Gallery**, tucked up in the eaves, shelters an Aladdin's cave of designs that weren't able to be housed elsewhere in the school – numerous tall-backed chairs, a semicircular settle designed for the Willow Tea

Charles Rennie Mackintosh

The work of the architect **Charles Rennie Mackintosh** (1868–1928), has come to be synonymous with the image of Glasgow. Historians may disagree over whether his work was a forerunner of the Modernist movement or merely a sunset of Victorianism, but he nonetheless undoubtedly created buildings of great beauty, idiosyncratically fusing Scots Baronial with Gothic, Art Nouveau and modern design. Though the bulk of his work was conceived at the turn of the twentieth century, since the postwar years Mackintosh's ideas have become particularly fashionable, giving rise to a certain amount of ersatz "**Mockintosh**" in his home city, with his distinctive lettering and small design features used time and again by shops, pubs and businesses. Fortunately, there are also plenty of examples of the genuine article, making the city something of a pilgrimage centre for art and design students from all over the world.

Although his family did little to encourage his artistic ambitions, as a young child Mackintosh began to cultivate his interest in drawing from nature during walks in the countryside, taken to improve his health. This talent was to flourish when he joined the Glasgow School of Art in 1884, where the vibrant new director, Francis Newberry, encouraged his pupils to create original and individual work. Here he met Herbert MacNair and the sisters Margaret and Frances MacDonald, whose work seemed to be sympathetic with his, fusing the organic forms of nature with a linear, symbolic Art Nouveau style. Nicknamed "**The Spook School**", the four created a new artistic language, using extended vertical design, stylized abstract organic forms and muted colours, reflecting their interest in Japanese design and the work of Whistler and Beardsley. However, it was architecture that truly challenged Mackintosh, allowing him to use his creative artistic impulse in a three-dimensional and cohesive manner.

His big break came in 1896, when he won the competition to design a new home for the **Glasgow School of Art** (see p.255). This is his most famous work, but a number of smaller buildings created during his tenure with the architects Honeyman and Keppie, which began in 1889, document the development of his style. One of his earliest commissions was for a new building to house the *Glasgow Herald* on Mitchell Lane, off Argyle Street. A massive tower rises up from the corner, giving the building its popular name of **The Lighthouse**; it now houses the Mackintosh Interpretation Centre (see p.247).

In the 1890s Glasgow went wild for tearooms, where the middle classes could play billiards and chess, read in the library or merely chat over some fine dining. The imposing Miss Cranston, who dominated the Glasgow teashop scene, running the most elegant establishments, gave Mackintosh great freedom of design, and in

Rooms, domino tables, a chest of drawers with highlighted silver panels and two bedroom suites. Around the room are mounted building designs including the House for an Art Lover, which now stands in the Bellahouston Park (see p.265).

You can peer down from the Furniture Gallery into the school's most spectacular room, the glorious two-storey **Library**. Here, sombre oak panelling is set against angular lights adorned with primary colours, dangling down in seemingly random clusters. The dark bookcases sit precisely in their fitted alcoves, while of the furniture, the most unusual feature is the central periodical desk, whose oval central strut displays perfect and quite beautiful symmetry.

The school also puts on various **exhibitions** through the year, which you can view without going on a tour. For details, contact the school or check up-to-date listings.

1896 he started to plan the interiors for her growing business. Over the next twenty years he designed articles from teaspoons to furniture and, finally, as in the case of the **Willow Tea Rooms** (see p.254), the structure itself.

Mackintosh designed few **religious buildings**: the Queens Cross Church of 1896, still at the junction of Garscube and Maryhill roads in the northwest of the city, is the only completed example standing. Hallmarks include the sturdy box-shaped tower and asymmetrical exterior with complex heart-shaped floral motifs in the large chancel window. To give height to the small and peaceful interior, he used an open-arched timber ceiling, enhanced by carved detail and an oak pulpit decorated with tulip-form relief. It isn't the most unified of structures, but shows the flexibility of his distinctive style. It is now home to the **Charles Rennie Mackintosh Society** (Mon–Fri 10am–5pm, Sat 10am–2pm, Sun 2–5pm; ⓣ0141/946 6600, ⓦwww.crmsociety.com).

The spectre of limited budgets was to haunt Mackintosh throughout his career, and he never had the chance to design and construct with complete freedom. However, these constraints didn't manage to dull his creativity, as demonstrated by the **Scotland Street School** of 1904, just south of the river (see p.265). Here, the two main stairways that frame the entrance are lit by glass-filled bays that protrude from the building. It is his most symmetrical work, with a whimsical nod to history in the Scots Baronial conical tower roofs and sandstone building material. Mackintosh's forceful personality and originality did not endear him to construction workers: he would frequently change his mind or add details at the last minute, often over-stretching a budget. This lost him the support of local builders and architects, despite his being admired on the continent, and prompted him to move to Suffolk in 1914 to escape the "philistines" of Glasgow and to re-evaluate his achievements. Indeed, the building which arguably displays Mackintosh at his most flamboyant was one he never saw built, the **House for an Art Lover** (see p.265), constructed in Bellahouston Park in 1996, 95 years after plans for it were submitted to a German architectural competition.

Having moved away from Glasgow, Mackintosh made use of his natural ability to draw flora and fauna, often in botanical detail and coloured with delicate watercolour washes. While living in 1923–27 in Port Vendres, on the Mediterranean coast of southwestern France, he produced a series of still-lifes and landscape works which express something of his architectural style: houses and rocks are painted in precise detail with a massive solidity and geometric form, and bold colours unite the patterned texture of the landscape, within an eerie stillness unbroken by human activity. These are a final flowering of his creative talent, a delicate contrast to the massive legacy of stonework left behind in the city that he loved.

The Tenement House

Just a few hundred yards north of the School of Art – on the other side of a sheer hill – is the **Tenement House**, 145 Buccleuch Street (March–Oct daily 2–5pm; Nov–Feb by appointment only; NTS; £3.20). This is a typical tenement block still lived in on most floors, except for the ground and first floor, where you can see the perfectly preserved home of Agnes Toward, who moved here with her mother in 1911, changing nothing and throwing very little out until she was hospitalized in 1965. On the ground floor, the National Trust for Scotland has constructed a fascinating display on the development of the humble tenement block as the bedrock of urban Scottish housing, with a display of relics – ration books, letters, bills, holiday snaps and so forth – from Miss Toward's life. Upstairs, you have to ring the doorbell to enter the flat, which gives every impression of still being inhabited, with a cluttered hearth and range, kitchen utensils, recess beds, framed religious tracts and sewing machine all untouched. The only major change since Miss Toward left has been the re-installation of the flickering gas lamps she would have used in the early days. Tenement flats were home for the vast majority of Glaswegians for much of the twentieth century, and as such developed a culture and vocabulary all of its own: the "hurley", for example, was the bed on castors which was kept below the box bed in an alcove off the kitchen.

The Piping Centre

Behind the hulking Royal Scottish Academy for Music and Drama, a short way east of the Tenement House, the immaculate **Piping Centre**, at 30–34 McPhater Street, prides itself on being a national centre for the promotion of the bagpipe. Equipped with rehearsal rooms, performance halls, conference centre, accommodation (see p.243), museum and an attractive café, it is a meeting place for fans and performers from all over the world. For the casual visitor, the single-room **museum** (daily 10am–4.30pm; £3; Ⓦwww.thepipingcentre.co.uk) is of most interest, with a collection of instruments and related artefacts from the fourteenth century to the present day. Headsets provide a taped commentary with musical examples at relevant stages and the museum shop contains a stack of related material, from tapes and videos to manuscripts and piping accessories.

The West End

The urbane veneer of the **West End** seems a world away from Glasgow's industrial image and the hustle and bustle of the city centre. In the 1800s, the city's wealthy merchants established huge estates away from the soot and grime of city life, and in 1870 the ancient university was moved from its cramped home near the cathedral to a spacious new site overlooking the River Kelvin. Elegant housing swiftly followed, the Kelvingrove Art Gallery was built to house the 1888 International Exhibition and, in 1896, the Glasgow District Subway – today's Underground – started its circuitous shuffle from here to the city centre.

The hub of life in this part of Glasgow is **Byres Road**, running between Great Western Road and Dumbarton Road past Hillhead underground station. Shops, restaurants, cafés, some enticing pubs and hordes of roving young people, including thousands of students, give the area a sense of style and vitality. Glowing red sandstone tenements and graceful terraces provide a suitably upmarket backdrop to this cosmopolitan district.

The main sights straddle the banks of the cleaned-up River Kelvin, where the slopes, trees and statues of **Kelvingrove Park** are framed by a backdrop of the Gothic towers and turrets of **Glasgow University** and the **Kelvingrove Museum and Art Gallery**, off Argyle Street.

Kelvingrove Museum and Art Gallery

Founded on donations from the city's chief industrialists, the huge, red-brick fantasy castle of **Kelvingrove Museum and Art Gallery** (Mon–Thurs & Sat 10am–5pm, Fri & Sun 11am–5pm; free) is a brash statement of Glasgow's nineteenth-century self-confidence. On the ground floor, the central hall is an impressive, airy introduction to the style of the place. On summer Sundays, the organ, which dates from the 1901 exhibition, comes to life with recitals by Scotland's top organists. In the east wing off the main atrium a dusty hall con-

At the time of going to press, the Kelvingrove Museum and Art Gallery was on the point of securing a grant for a complete **refurbishment** of the building. This would mean that the museum would be closed to the public from early 2003 for about one year. For the latest information, contact the tourist office or the Kelvingrove project office on ⓣ0141/287 2757.

tains the **Scottish Natural History** display, where local and global events are marked in the rings of a slice of ancient Douglas fir. On the opposite side of the main hall sits an unremarkable exhibition of European and Scottish weapons.

However, it's the art collections, the majority of which are upstairs, that are of most interest. **Room 22** contains some superb Italian paintings, notably Botticelli's delicate *Annunciation*, Giorgione's rich and vibrant *The Adulteress Brought Before Christ*, and some fervent landscapes by Salvator Rosa. Further down the gallery, Rembrandt's symbolic portrayal of a carcass of an ox stands out darkly, along with his quiet portrait, *The Man in Armour*. Continuing from the seventeenth century and leading up to the early nineteenth century, **room 23** contains predominantly British work. The space is dominated by two paintings by Jacob More, a Scottish artist who worked in the elegiacally classical style of Claude; the spread of classicism in eighteenth-century Europe is also attested by pieces such as *Vestals Attending the Sacred Fire*, by David Allan, whose figures languish amongst ancient temples.

Room 24 is filled with quality work from Scottish and European artists from the eighteenth century to the early twentieth century, among them Corot, Degas and Millet. As for the Scots, the angelic face of *Mrs William Urquhart* is testimony to Sir Henry Raeburn's skill as an informal portraitist, while the meticulous detail of *South and North Western View from Ben Lomond* – a dramatic pair of paintings by John Knox – makes a striking contrast with Turner's radiant *Modern Italy – The Pifferari*, a picture that glows amongst the dark glens and sombre portraits. **Room 25** is dominated by French Impressionists and Postimpressionists, including work by Monet and Van Gogh, while **room 26** sets such continental luminaries as Picasso and Derain alongside excellent work by the increasingly popular Scottish Colourists. *The Pink Parasol* by J.D. Fergusson, for example, reveals what he learned from Matisse and Cézanne, while Cadell's *Orange Blind*, with its unexpectedly strident blocks of colour contrasting with the precise, flat brushwork, is one of the gallery's best-loved works. Nearby, the grittier *Two Children* by Joan Eardley makes use of collage and thick paint to convey the energy of Gorbals children in the 1960s.

Crossing over to the **east wing**, take time to look at some of the superb sculptures and busts arrayed around the balcony overlooking the main hall. These include a bust by Archie Forest of Donald Dewar, a champion of Scottish devolution who died suddenly in 2000. In the east wing, **The Scottish Gallery** is entirely devoted to native artists. Here Raeburn's magnificent *Mr and Mrs Robert N. Campbell of Kailzie* almost overwhelms the room, the golden, life-size figures emerging from the loosely brushed background. A statue of Sir Walter Scott gazes upon a row of paintings depicting the romantic, Victorian view of Scotland, as exemplified by Horatio McCullochs' depiction of Loch Maree. On the far wall hangs the famous portrait of Robert Burns by Alexander Naysmyth, now found on biscuit tins the world over.

The **Glasgow Style** room is dedicated to the era when Charles Rennie Mackintosh was in his prime: this marvellous collection of furniture is crowned

The Glasgow Boys

The traditional rivalry between Glasgow and Edinburgh was alive and kicking in the late nineteenth century when the Royal Scottish Academy resolutely refused to accept the work of any west-coast artist. That was soon to change, however, when in the 1870s a group of painters formed a loose association, centred in Glasgow, that was to invest Scottish painting with a fresh approach inspired by contemporary European trends (in particular the *plein air* painting of the Impressionists). Derisively nicknamed **"The Glasgow Boys"**, only in later years did their work come to be seen as quintessentially Glaswegian and reclaimed with considerable pride. The group was dominated by five men – Guthrie, Lavery, Henry, Hornel and Crawhall – who, despite coming from very different backgrounds, all violently rejected the eighteenth-century conservatism which spawned little other than sentimental, anecdotal renditions of Scottish history peopled by "poor but happy" families, in a detailed, exacting manner. They dubbed these paintings "**gluepots**" for their use of megilp, an oily substance that gave the work the brown patina of age, and instead began to experiment with colour, liberally splashing paint across the canvas. The content and concerns of the paintings, often showing peasant life and work, were as offensive to the effete art establishment as their style: until then most of Glasgow's public art collections had been accrued by wealthy tobacco lords and merchants.

The five Glasgow Boys came from dissimilar backgrounds. **Sir James Guthrie** spent his summers in the countryside, surrounded by like-minded artists, painting in the outdoors and observing everyday life. Instead of happy peasants, his work shows individuals staring out of the canvas, detached and unrepentant, painted with rich tones but without undue attention to detail or the play of light. Typical of his finest work during the 1880s, *A Highland Funeral* (on display in St Mungo's Museum; see p.254) was hugely influential for the rest of the group, who found inspiration in its restrained emotional content, colour and unaffected realism. Seeing it persuaded **Sir John Lavery**, then studying in France, to return to Glasgow. Lavery was eventually to become an internationally popular society portraitist, his subtle use of paint revealing his debt to Whistler, but his earlier work, depicting the middle class at play, is filled with fresh colour and figures in motion. In 1888 Lavery documented the Glasgow International Exhibition and went on to paint a number of large-scale works, one of which – a massive depiction of Queen Victoria's visit to Glasgow – hangs in the Royal Concert Hall.

Rather than a realistic aesthetic, an interest in colour and decoration united the work of friends **George Henry** and **E.A. Hornel**. The predominance of colour, pattern and design in Henry's *Galloway Landscape*, for example, is remarkable, while their joint work *The Druids* (both on display in the Glasgow Style room at Kelvingrove; see p.258), in thickly applied impasto, is full of Celtic symbolism. In 1893 both artists set off for Japan, funded by Alexander Reid and later William Burrell, where their work used vibrant tone and texture for expressive effect and took Scottish painting to the forefront of European trends.

Newcastle-born **Joseph Crawhall** was, by all accounts, a reserved and quiet individual. He combined superb draughtsmanship and simplicity of line with a photographic memory to create watercolours of an outstanding naturalism and freshness. Unlike the forceful Guthrie and Lavery, who craved wealth and success, Crawhall was a shy man who enjoyed hunting and riding in the countryside and was quite happy to paint delicate animal studies throughout his career. William Burrell was an important patron, and a good collection of Crawhall's works resides at the Burrell Collection (see p.267).

The Glasgow Boys school reached its height by 1900, and once its members had achieved the artistic respect – and for some the commercial success – they craved, it began to disintegrate and did not outlast World War I. However, the influence of their work cannot be underestimated, shaking the foundations of the artistic elite and inspiring the next generation of Edinburgh painters, now known as the "Colourists".

by a pair of domino tables and chairs designed by Mackintosh for the tearooms of Miss Cranston (see p.254). The **Glasgow Boys** are well represented, with the decoratively patterned *In a Japanese Garden* by George Henry alongside his colaborative work with Hornel, *The Druids Bringing in the Mistletoe*. Works by Guthrie, Crawhall and Lavery are also on display.

The Transport Museum

Twin-towered **Kelvin Hall** opposite the Kelvingrove Museum is home to the excellent **Transport Museum**, an enormous collection of trains, cars, trams, circus caravans and prams, along with an array of old Glaswegian ephemera (Mon–Thurs & Sat 10am–5pm, Fri & Sun 11am–5pm; free). Just inside the Bunhouse Road entrance, "Kelvin Street" is a re-created 1938 cobbled street featuring an old Italian coffee shop, a butcher (complete with plastic meat joints dangling in the window), a bakery (where labels claim that the buns were provided by the university's taxidermy department) and an old-time underground station. A cinema shows fascinating films – mostly on themes based loosely around transport – of old Glasgow life, with crackly footage of Sauchiehall Street packed solid with trams and shoppers and hordes of pasty-faced Glaswegians setting off for their annual jaunts down the coast. The Clyde Room displays intricate models of ships forged in Glasgow's yards, everything from tiny schooners to ostentatious ocean liners such as the QE2.

Glasgow University and the Hunterian bequests

Dominating the West End skyline, the gloomy turreted tower of **Glasgow University**, designed by Sir Gilbert Scott in the mid-nineteenth century, overlooks the glades of the River Kelvin. Access to the main buildings and museums is from University Avenue, running east from Byres Road. In the dark neo-Gothic pile under the tower you'll find the **University Visitor Centre** (Mon–Sat 9.30am–5pm; May–Sept also Sun 2–5pm), which, as well as giving information for potential students, distributes leaflets about the various university buildings and the statues around the campus. From May to September **historical tours** of the campus are run from here (check schedules on ⓣ0141/330 5511; £2). It's possible to join a tour up the sky-piercing university **tower** (May–Sept Fri 2pm; free), climbing 228 narrow spiral-staircase steps to some heady views; places, though, are limited to twenty people, with tickets available only in person that morning from the Visitor Centre.

Beside the Visitor Centre is the **Hunterian Museum** (Mon–Sat 9.30am–5pm; free), Scotland's oldest public museum, dating back to 1807. The collection was donated to the university by ex-student William Hunter, a pathologist and anatomist whose eclectic tastes form the basis of a fairly diverting zoological and archeological jaunt. Exhibitions include Scotland's only dinosaur, a look at the Romans in Scotland – the furthest outpost of their massive empire – and a vast numismatic collection.

The Hunterian Art Gallery

Opposite the university, across University Avenue, is Hunter's more frequently visited bequest, the **Hunterian Art Gallery** (Mon–Sat 9.30am–5pm; free), best known for its wonderful works by James Abbott McNeill Whistler: only Washington DC has a larger collection. Whistler's breathy landscapes are less compelling than his portraits of women, which give his subjects a resolute strength in addition to their fey and occasionally winsome qualities: look out especially for the trio of full-length portraits, *Harmony of Flesh Colour* and *Black, Pink and Gold – the Tulip* and *Red and Black – the Fan*.

The gallery's other major collection is of nineteenth- and twentieth-century Scottish art, including the quasi-Impressionist Scottish landscapes of William McTaggart, a forerunner of the Glasgow Boys movement, itself represented here by Guthrie and Hornel. Taking the aims of this group one step further, the monumental dancing figures of J.D. Fergusson's *Les Eus* preside over a small collection of work by the Scottish Colourists, such as Peploe, Hunter and Cadell, who left a vibrant legacy of thickly textured, colourful landscapes and portraits. A small selection of French Impressionism includes works by Boudin and Pissarro, with Corot's soothing *Distant View of Corbeil* being a highlight from the Barbizon school.

A side gallery leads to the **Mackintosh House** (closed 12.30–1.30pm; free), a re-creation of the interior of the now-demolished Glasgow home of Margaret and Charles Rennie Mackintosh. An introductory display contains photographs of the original house sliding irrevocably into terminal decay, from where you are led into an exquisitely cool interior that contains over sixty pieces of Mackintosh furniture on three floors. Among the highlights are the Studio Drawing Room, whose cream and white furnishings are bathed in expansive pools of natural light, and the Japanese-influenced guest bedroom in dazzling, monochrome geometrics. In addition, a permanent Mackintosh exhibition gallery shows an interesting selection of his work, from watercolours to architectural drawings.

The Botanic Gardens

At the northern, top end of Byres Road, where it meets the Great Western Road, is the main entrance to the **Botanic Gardens** (daily 7am–dusk; free). The best-known glasshouse here, the hulking, domed **Kibble Palace** (daily 10am–4.45pm; winter closes 4.15pm; closed for restoration after autumn 2002), was built in 1863 for wealthy landowner John Kibble's estate on the shores of Loch Long, where it stood for ten years before he decided to transport it into Glasgow, drawing it up the Clyde on a vast raft pulled by a steamer. For over two decades it was used not as a greenhouse but as a Victorian pleasure palace, before the gardens' owners put a stop to the drunken revels that wreaked havoc with the lawns and plant beds. Today the palace is far more sedate, housing a damp, musty collection of swaying palms from around the world, along with an unremarkable but well-placed café. Nearby, the **Main Range Glasshouse** (same times) is home to lurid, blooming flowers and plants luxuriating in the humidity, including stunning orchids, cacti, ferns and tropical fruit. Between the two in the old curator's house is a small **visitor centre** (daily 11am–4pm; free) with art exhibitions an interactive computer aimed at younger visitors.

In addition to the area around the main glasshouses, there are some beautifully remote paths in the gardens that weave and dive along the closely wooded banks of the deep-set River Kelvin, linking up with the walkway which runs alongside the river all the way down to Dumbarton Road, near its confluence with the Clyde.

Clydeside

"The **Clyde** made Glasgow and Glasgow made the Clyde" runs an old saw, full of sentimentality for the days when the river was the world's premier shipbuilding centre, and when its industry lent an innovation and confidence which made Glasgow the second city of the British Empire. Despite the hardships heavy industry brought, every Glaswegian would follow the progress of the skeleton ships under construction in the riverside yards, cheering them on their way down the Clyde as they were launched. The last of the great liners to be built on **Clydeside** was the *QE2* in 1967, yet such events are hard to visualize today, with the banks of the river all but devoid of any industry: shipbuilding is now restricted to a couple of barely viable yards, as derelict warehouses, crumbling docks and overgrown wastelands crowd the river's flanks.

Glasgow is often accused of failing to capitalize on its river, and it's only in the last few years, with a number of large, striking Clydeside buildings going up, such as the Scottish Exhibition and Conference Centre, or **SECC**, the **Armadillo** and the **Science Centre**, that the river is once again becoming a focus of attention. If the talk of further development is to believed, the Clyde may well return to its position as the heart and soul of Glasgow. But in the meantime, mileage is being made of the shipbuilding heritage, with attractions such as the **Tall Ship at Glasgow Harbour** and **Clydebuilt** striving to recreate the river's heyday.

The easiest way to reach the cluster of Clydeside attractions is to **walk** the mile or so west along the riverside footpath from the city centre. Otherwise, **trains** from Glasgow Central low-level station and half-hourly **bus** #30 from the centre of town run to the Exhibition Centre. Bell's Bridge runs across the river to the Science Centre on the south bank, also served by bus #24 from Renfield Street.

The north bank

On Clydeside immediately south of the West End, just over a mile west of the city centre, is the harshly re-landscaped Scottish Exhibition and Conference Centre, or **SECC**. It was built on a reclaimed dock in 1985 to kick-start the revival of the riverbank: two vast adjoining red and grey sheds that make a dutifully utilitarian venue for travelling fairs, mega-concerts and anonymous bars and cafés. Although the huge **Finnieston Crane**, retained as an icon of shipbuilding days, stands alongside the SECC, the site was rescued from bland obscurity by the arrival in 1997 of a supplementary concert hall officially entitled the Clyde Auditorium but universally nicknamed "**the Armadillo**" for its rounded exterior of armour-plating. It resembles a poor man's version of the Sydney Opera House but has quickly established itself as one of the city's architectural landmarks.

The Waverley

One of Glasgow's best-loved treasures is the **Waverley**, the last sea-going paddlesteamer in the world, which spends the summer cruising "doon the watter" to various ports on the Firth of Clyde and the Ayrshire coast from its base at Anderson Quay between Finnieston and the Kingston Bridge. Built on Clydeside as recently as 1947, she's an elegant vessel to look at, not least when she's thrashing away at full steam with the hills of Argyll or Arran in the background. Call the booking office on ⓣ0141/243 2224 or check ⓦwww.waverleyexcursions.co.uk for her sailing times and itinerary.

A few hundred yards downstream on the north bank of the river, the masts and rigging of the huge square-rigger *Glenlee* draw you to an attraction known as the **Tall Ship at Glasgow Harbour** (daily: April–Sept 10am–5pm; Oct–March 11am–4pm; £4.50). A 245-foot-long, three-masted barque, the *Glenlee* was launched on the river in 1896 and is now one of only five large sailing vessels built on Clydeside still afloat. Although the lovingly careful restoration project of the Clyde Maritime Trust is ongoing, you're able to snoop around most of the ship, including three main decks and the ship's hold. The sheer scale of the *Glenlee* is her most impressive feature, though various parts of the ship are imaginatively set up to offer an insight into life aboard when she was a hard-working merchant vessel carrying cargo round Cape Horn. In the Pumphouse Visitor Centre, on the quay alongside, changing exhibitions highlight different aspects of the ship's links to Glasgow and the city's maritime history.

The Glasgow Science Centre

On the south bank of the river, linked to the SECC by Bell's Bridge, are the three space-age, titanium-clad constructions which make up the **Glasgow Science Centre**, a massive, hands-on collection opened in 2001 (Tower £5.50, Science Mall £6.50, IMAX £5.50; any two £9.50; all three £14; Ⓦwww.gsc.org.uk). Of the three buildings, the most obvious from afar is the 127-metre **Glasgow Tower** (daily 10am–6pm, Thurs–Sat until 9pm), an aerofoil-like construction which can rotate to face into the prevailing wind and which is the tallest free-standing structure in Scotland. Glass lifts ascend to the viewing cabin at the top, offering suitably panoramic views.

Alongside the tower is the centrepiece of the development, the curvaceous, wedge-shaped **Science Mall** (daily 10am–6pm). Behind the vast glass wall which faces the river are four floors of interactive exhibits ranging from lift-you-own-weight pulleys to high-tech thermograms. Described as "hands-on info-tainment for the genome generation", it's like all your most enjoyable school science experiments packed into one building, with in-house boffins demonstrating chemical reactions, and pensioners and toddlers equally captivated by cockroach colonies or jigsaw puzzles of human organs. The centre covers almost every aspect of science from simple optical illusions to cutting-edge computer technology, including a section on moral and environmental issues – lots of good fun, although weekends and school holidays are busy and noisy.

The smallest of the three buildings on the site is the bubble-like **IMAX theatre**, which shows a range of mostly science- and nature-based documentaries on its giant screen, with programmes changing regularly.

Clydebuilt at Braehead

Three miles downriver (west) from the Science Centre, a further tribute to the Clyde shipbuilding legacy can be found at **Clydebuilt** (Mon–Sat 10am–6pm, Sun 11am–5pm; £3.50), a small outpost of Irvine's Scottish Maritime Museum (see p.225). The attraction, a single building with a couple of retired working boats moored alongside, is completely overwhelmed by the massive **Braehead** shopping centre which surrounds it, though the fact that a **water-taxi** runs here from beside King George V bridge in Glasgow city centre – one of the few opportunities that exists to travel on the river – makes a visit here more appealing. The museum takes a look at Glasgow's rise as a trading port and shipbuilding centre, with a series of displays, reconstructions and films, with the old Clyde puffer tied up to the pontoon beside it offering the most tangible sense of bygone days.

The Southside

On the Clyde's **Southside**, immediately facing the city centre, are the notoriously deprived districts of the Gorbals and Govan – sprinkled with new developments but still obviously derelict and tatty in many parts. There's little reason to venture here unless you're making your way to the Science Centre (see opposite), the famously innovative Citizen's Theatre (see p.278), or one of the revived architectural gems of Charles Rennie Mackintosh, the **Scotland Street School** and the **House for an Art Lover**.

Moving further south, inner-city decay fades into altogether gentler and more salubrious suburbs, including Queen's Park, home to Scotland's national football stadium, **Hampden Park**; Pollokshaws and the rural landscape of Pollok Park, which contains two of Glasgow's major museums, the **Burrell Collection** and **Pollok House**; and Cathcart, location of Alexander "Greek" Thomson's **Holmwood House**.

Southside attractions are fairly widely spread. The **underground** will get you to Scotland Street School and the House for an Art Lover, while a **train** from Central station is best for Hampden Park (Mount Florida station) and Holmwood House (Cathcart station). For Pollok Park either take the train to Pollokshaws West station (not to be confused with Pollokshields West), or **bus** #45, #47, #48 or #57 to Pollokshaws Road, or a **taxi** (£12–14 from the centre). From the park gates a **free minibus** runs every half-hour between 10am and 4.30pm to both the Burrell Collection and Pollok House.

Scotland Street School Museum of Education

Opposite Shields Road underground station is the **Scotland Street School Museum of Education** (Mon–Thurs & Sat 10am–5pm, Fri & Sun 11am–5pm; free), another of the city's Charles Rennie Mackintosh treasures. Opened as a school in 1906 to Mackintosh's distinctively angular design, it closed in 1979, since when it has been entertainingly refurbished to house a fascinating collection of memorabilia related to classroom life. There are reconstructed classrooms from the Victorian and Edwardian eras, World War II and the 1960s, as well as changing rooms, a primitive domestic science room and re-creations of the school matron's sanatorium and a janitor's lair. If you visit on a weekday during term time, you may stumble on a period lesson going on, local schoolkids struggling with their ink blotters, gas masks and archly unsympathetic teachers. You may find the faint smell of antiseptic conjuring up memories of scuffed knees and playground tantrums.

House for an Art Lover

West of Scotland Street School, tucked just inside Bellahouston Park, is Charles Rennie Mackintosh's **House for an Art Lover** (April–Sept daily except Fri 10am–4pm; Oct–March Sat & Sun 10am–4pm but closed occasionally for functions; ⓣ0141/353 4449; £3.50). Designed in 1901 for a German competition, it was not until 1996, after years of detailed research and painstaking work, that the building was actually constructed and opened as a centre for Glasgow School of Art postgraduate students, with a limited number of rooms open to the public.

It's all quintessential Mackintosh, almost unimaginable as a living space but exquisitely stylish and original at the same time. On the upper floor, you can watch a video giving a detailed account of the building's history, then pass into the delicate **Oval Room**, intended for women to retire to after dinner. From here, a small corridor leads into the main **hallway**, where massive windows cast a cool light upon an area designed for large parties. In direct contrast, the dazzling, white **Music Room** has bow windows opening out to a large balcony, though the garden view is marred by an artificial ski slope. The **Dining Room** is decorated with darkened stained wood and enhanced by some beautiful gesso tiles.

On the ground floor, the **café** (Ⓣ0141/353 4779) is particularly popular with locals on Sunday mornings; there's an attractive menu, and it's open through the day and sometimes also in the evenings.

Hampden Park and the Scottish Football Museum

Two and a half miles due south of the city centre, just to the west of the tree-filled Queen's Park, the floodlights and giant stands of Scotland's national football stadium, **Hampden Park**, loom over the surrounding suburban tenements and terraces. Home of Queen's Park Football Club, these days not one of Scotland's more esteemed outfits despite the grandeur of their home turf, the fact that it's the venue for Scotland's international fixtures and major cup finals

Football in Glasgow

Football, or *fitba'* as it's pronounced locally, is one of Glasgow's great passions – and one of its great blights. While the city can claim to be one of Europe's premier footballing centres, it's known above all for one of the most bitter rivalries in any sport, that between **Celtic** and **Rangers**. Two of the largest clubs in Britain, with weekly crowds regularly topping 60,000, the Old Firm, as they're collectively known, have dominated Scottish football for a century, most notably in the last fifteen years as they have lavished vast sums of money on foreign talent in an often frantic effort to out-do the other while at the same time stay in touch with the standards of the top English and European teams.

The roots of Celtic, who play at Celtic Park in the eastern district of Parkhead (Ⓣ0141/551 8653), lie in the city's immigrant Irish and **Catholic** population, while Rangers, based at Ibrox Park in Govan on the Southside (Ⓣ0870/600 1993), have traditionally drawn support from local **Protestants**. As a result, sporting rivalries have been enmeshed in a sectarian divide which many argue would not have remained so long, nor so deep, had it been divorced from the footballing scene: although Catholics do play for Rangers, and Protestants for Celtic, sections of supporters of both clubs seem intent on perpetuating the feud. While large-scale violence on the terraces and streets has not been seen for some time – thanks in large measure to canny policing – Old Firm matches often seethe with bitter passions, and sectarian-related assaults do still occur in parts of the city.

However, there is a less intense side to the game, found not just in the fun-loving "Tartan Army" which follows the (often rollercoaster) fortunes of the Scottish national team, but also in Glasgow's smaller clubs, who actively distance themselves from the distasteful aspects of the Old Firm and plod along with homegrown talent in the lower reaches of the Scottish league. **Queen's Park**, residents of Hampden (Ⓣ0141/632 1275), **St Mirren**, the Paisley team (Ⓣ0141/889 2558), and the much-maligned **Partick Thistle**, who play at Firhill Stadium in the West End (Ⓣ0141/579 1971), offer the best chances of experiencing the more down-to-earth side of Glaswegian football – mixed with all-important reminders that it is, in the end, only a game.

makes it a place of pilgrimage for the country's football fans. Regular **guided tours** (daily 10.30am–3.30pm; £2.50; Ⓦwww.hampdenpark.co.uk) offer the chance to see the changing rooms, warm-up areas and inside the stadium itself, complete with anecdotes of players past and the story of the ground and its recent renovation (which almost bankrupted the Scottish Football Association). Also here is the engaging **Scottish Football Museum** (Mon–Sat 10am–5pm, Sun 11am–5pm; £5), with extensive collections of memorabilia, video clips and displays covering almost every aspect of the game. On view is the Scottish Cup, the world's oldest footballing trophy, and a re-creation of the old changing room at Hampden, though there's also a light-hearted side to the museum, with one of the more bizarre exhibits a life-size reconstruction of various Dutch defenders floundering in the wake of Archie Gemmill as he slots home the most famous goal in Scottish footballing history during the otherwise embarrassing 1978 World Cup campaign in Argentina.

The Burrell Collection

Located in Pollok Park some six miles southwest of the city centre, the outstanding **Burrell Collection** (Mon–Thurs & Sat 10am–5pm, Fri & Sun 11am–5pm; free), the lifetime collection of shipping magnate Sir William Burrell (1861–1958), is, for some, the principal reason for visiting Glasgow. Unlike many other art collectors, Sir William's only real criterion for buying a piece was whether he liked it or not, enabling him to buy many "unfashionable" works, which cost comparatively little but subsequently proved their worth. He wanted to leave his collection of art, sculpture and antiquities for public display, but stipulated in 1943 that they should be housed "in a rural setting far removed from the atmospheric pollution of urban conurbations, not less than sixteen miles from the Royal Exchange". For decades, these conditions proved too difficult to meet, with few open spaces available and a pall of industrial smoke ruling out any city site. However, by the late 1960s, after the nationwide Clean Air Act had reduced pollution, and the vast land of **Pollok Park**, previously privately owned, had been donated to the city, plans began for a new, purpose-built gallery, which finally opened in 1983. Today the simplicity and clean lines of the Burrell building are its greatest assets, with large picture windows giving sweeping views over woodland and serving as a tranquil backdrop to the objects inside. The sculpture and antiques are on the **ground floor**, arranged in six sections that overlap and occasionally backtrack, while a **mezzanine** above displays most of the paintings.

The courtyard

On entering the building, head past the information desk and shop to an airy covered **courtyard** where the most striking piece, by virtue of sheer size, is the **Warwick Vase**, a huge bowl containing fragments of a second-century AD vase from Emperor Hadrian's villa in Tivoli. Next to it is a series of sinewy and naturalistic bronze casts of **Rodin sculptures**, among them *The Age of Bronze*, *A Call to Arms* and the famous *Thinker*. On three sides of the courtyard, a trio of dark and sombre panelled rooms have been re-erected in faithful detail from the Burrells' Hutton Castle home, their heavy tapestries, antique furniture and fireplaces displaying the same eclectic taste as the rest of the museum.

The ground floor

From the courtyard, go through the massive sandstone portal and door from Hornby Castle which was incorporated into the design of the building, to the start of the **Ancient Civilizations** collection – a catch-all title for Greek, Roman and earlier artefacts – which includes an exquisite mosaic Roman cockerel from the first century BC and a 4000-year-old Mesopotamian lion's head. The bulk of it is Egyptian, however, with rows of inscrutable gods and kings. Nearby, also illuminated by enormous windows, the **Oriental Art** collection forms nearly one-quarter of the whole display, ranging from Neolithic jades through bronze vessels and Tang funerary horses to cloisonné. The earliest piece, from around the second century BC, is a loveable earthenware watchdog from the Han Dynasty, but most dominant is the serene fifteenth-century *Lohan* (disciple of Buddha), who sits cross-legged and contemplative up against the window and the trees of Pollok Park. Near Eastern art is also represented, in a dazzling array of turquoise- and cobalt-decorated jugs, and a swathe of intricate carpets.

Burrell considered his **Medieval and Post-Medieval European Art**, which encompasses silverware, glass, textiles and sculpture, to be the most valuable part of his collection. Ranged across a maze of small galleries, the most impressive sections are the sympathetically lit stained glass – note the homely image of a man warming his toes by the fire – and the numerous tapestries, among them the riotous fifteenth-century *Peasants Hunting Rabbits with Ferrets*. Among the church art and reliquary are simple thirteenth-century Spanish wooden images and cool fifteenth-century English alabaster, while a trio of period interiors span the period from the Gothic era to the eighteenth century. This is interrupted by a selection from Burrell's vast art collection, the highlight of which is one of Rembrandt's evocative early self-portraits.

The mezzanine

Upstairs, the cramped and comparatively gloomy **mezzanine** is probably the least satisfactory section of the gallery, not the best setting for its sparkling array of paintings. The selection incongruously leaps from a small gathering of fifteenth-century religious works to Géricault's darkly dynamic *Prancing Grey Horse* and Degas's thoughtful and perceptive *Portrait of Émile Duranty*. Pissarro, Manet and Boudin are also represented, along with some exquisite watercolours by Glasgow Boy Joseph Crawhall, revealing his accurate and tender observations of the animal world.

Pollok House

Within Pollok Park, a quarter of a mile down rutted tracks west of the Burrell Collection, lies the lovely eighteenth-century **Pollok House** (daily 10am–5pm; NTS; April–Oct £4, rest of year free; café and gardens free year-round), the manor of the Pollok Park estate and once home of the Maxwell family, local lords and owners of most of southern Glasgow until well into the last century. Designed by William Adam in the mid-1700s, the house is typical of its age: graciously light and sturdily built, looking out onto the pristine raked and parterre gardens, whose stylized daintiness contrasts with the heavy Spanish paintings inside, among them two El Greco portraits and works by Murillo and Goya.

The house recently came under the management of the National Trust for Scotland – a happy reunion, as it was in the upstairs smoking room in 1931 that the then-owner, Sir John Stirling Maxwell, held the first meetings with the 8th Duke of Atholl and Lord Colquhoun of Luss that led to the formation of the NTS. The Trust has made a deliberate effort to return the house to the layout and style it would have enjoyed when the Stirling Maxwells were living here in the 1920s and 1930s. As a result, the **paintings** range from the Spanish masterpieces in the morning room and some splendid Dutch hunting scenes in the dining room to Sir John's own worthy but noticeably amateur efforts which line the upstairs corridors. Generally the rooms have the flavour of a well-to-do but unstuffy country house, with the odd piece of attractive furniture and some pleasant rooms, but little that can be described as outstanding. The servants' quarters downstairs do manage to capture the imagination – a virtually untouched labyrinth of tiled Victorian parlours and corridors that includes a good tearoom in the old kitchen. Free tours of the house are available from the front desk, or you can wander around at your own pace.

Holmwood House

Four miles south of the city centre in the suburb of Cathcart, the finest domestic design by rediscovered Glasgow architect Alexander "Greek" Thomson, **Holmwood House** (April–Oct daily 1.30–5.30pm; NTS; £3.50), has recently been restored and opened to the public. A commission by James Couper, co-owner of a paper mill on the nearby River Carth, the house shows off Thomson's bold Classical concepts, with exterior pillars on two levels and a raised main door, as well as his detailed and highly imaginative interiors. The restoration is ongoing, as you'll see from the patches of exquisite stencilling revealed beneath the wallpaper, and the fact that the rooms are unfurnished. A free audioguide provides some background information and explanation in each of the rooms. One room upstairs is given over to a series of displays about Thomson and the history of the house. Also on the upper floor is the **drawing room** – look for the white marble fireplace and the night-time star decorations on the ceiling, which contrast with a black marble fireplace and sunburst decorations in the room immediately underneath on the downstairs level, the **parlour**, which also boasts a delightful round bay window. Across the corridor, the **dining room** has a frieze of scenes from the *Iliad*, along with a skylight at the back of the room designed to allow the Greek gods to peer down on the feasts being consumed inside. One unusual feature not designed by Thomson is the small hatch cut in the interconnecting door between the dining room and the butler's pantry; the house was last occupied by a sisterhood of nuns, who used the dining room as a chapel and created the small hatch for use as a confessional.

Eating

The huge growth in restaurants, bars and cafés in Glasgow over recent years shows little sign of abating. **Eating** options are fairly diverse, fuelled by an ethnically mixed population, a stream of international tourists, enough slick business types and a lively social scene: the city's restaurants offer everything from tapas to sushi, dim sum to every variety of dansak at the city's renowned Indian restaurants. Contemporary Scottish cuisine – fresh local produce prepared under French and other international influences – has seen a boom in recent years. Also on the increase are fish and seafood offerings, and while the number of exclusively **vegetarian** restaurants is somewhat limited, practically every restaurant in the city serves non-meat options.

Most of Glasgow's more formal restaurants are open for lunch between around noon and 2.30pm, and then again for dinner from around 6pm to

10.30pm. More casual café-bars and bistros are frequently open from 9am (often later on Sundays) right through the day and evening. We have indicated below where restaurants are closed on any particular day or where the hours they keep diverge from the norm.

Worth knowing about if you're watching the pennies is the restaurant-booking website Ⓦwww.5pm.co.uk, which every day receives a significant number of good-quality restaurants around Glasgow posting special good-value dining deals (sometimes with restrictions, for example that a table should be clear for a certain time).

Cafés, diners and café-bars

For budget food, **cafés** and **café-bars** – in addition, of course, to local **diners**, fast-food outlets and that perennial fall-back, the fish and chip shop – are the best bets, serving filling snacks all day and often into the evening. The best of these are mainly concentrated in the places where younger folk keeping irregular hours are found, namely the Merchant City and the West End, particularly around the university.

City centre

Café Gandolfi 64 Albion St ⓣ0141/552 6813. This bona fide landmark (now also with a branch in Buchanan Street's Habitat shop) was one of the first to test the waters in the Merchant City. Designed with distinctive wooden furniture that creator Tim Stead once called "sculpture in disguise", it serves up healthy and hearty portions of soup, salad, fish dishes, and more. Only drawback is the queue. Moderate.

Gallery of Modern Art rooftop café Queen St. Serving light meals during lunch hours (with cakes and coffee at other times), this café is worth a visit for Adrian Wiszniewski's massive mural and, of course, the views. Open Mon–Sat 10am–4.30pm, Sun 11am–4.30pm. Inexpensive.

Granary 82 Howard St. Cosy daytime café near the St Enoch shopping centre, serving a raft of home-cooked vegetarian favourites, complemented by a salad bar and some notable patisserie. Inexpensive.

Grassroots Café 93 St Georges Rd. Although the competition is not particularly stiff, this is the best vegetarian outlet in the city. Fresh, creative cooking and a relaxed atmosphere. Inexpensive.

The 13th Note 50–60 King St. One of Glasgow's hipper drinking and music haunts on the southern edge of the Merchant City (see p.247), also offering vegetarian and vegan fare with Greek and other Mediterranean influences. Inexpensive.

Tron Theatre Chisholm St off the Trongate. Another arty hangout (see p.278), this time for writers and theatrical types in either the modern designed street-side pub/café or a more traditional Victorian bar. One all-day menu serves both spaces with pre-theatre specials most evenings. Mon–Sat noon–10pm, Sun 10.30am–4pm. Moderate.

Where the Monkey Sleeps 182 West Regent St. Staffed by cordial art graduates who acquired their barista skills while still in school, and carrying an unstudied hipness. While food is limited to soups and sandwiches, the espresso is supreme and the space doubles as a gallery. Mon–Sat 8am–11pm, Sun 10am–11pm. Inexpensive.

Willow Tea Rooms 217 Sauchiehall St. Refined elevenses, lunches and afternoon tea amid the splendour of the Mackintosh-designed building and interiors. A similarly themed branch at 97 Buchanan Street is less authentic but less frenetic. Moderate.

West End

Air Organic 36 Kelvingrove St ⓣ0141/564 5200. This hip bistro (and pre-club bar downstairs) has earned design awards, while the menu is dominated by veg and meaty organic offerings cooked with an Asian touch. Excellent for Sunday brunch, and open late on Fri & Sat until 2am. Moderate.

Bay Tree Café 403 Great Western Rd. Middle Eastern flavours and dishes dominate this tiny vegetarian café, which also does veggie burgers and Indian pakora. Counter service. Inexpensive.

Brel 39–43 Ashton Lane. Popular with students and post-grads, offering a smattering of Belgian food *(moules et frites)* and beers. The rear conservatory which opens on to a grassy knoll is an attractive spot on fine days. Moderate.

Grosvenor Café 31 Ashton Lane. This small, traditional café recently became fully licensed, but maintains a cosy atmosphere and serves good-value no-nonsense food (pizzas, fried food, burgers) during the day, while the evening menu is a bit more fussy. Inexpensive.

Insomnia 38–42 Woodlands Rd. A classic 24/7 café conveniently located about halfway between the city centre and the middle of the West End. Very crowded once the clubs close, it is renowned for its convenience rather than its cuisine. Daily 24hr. Inexpensive.

Stravaigin 2 8 Ruthven Lane ☎0141/334 7165. A deservedly popular diner (formerly known as the *Back Alley*) that serves excellent burgers alongside a menu in line with the award-wining modern Scottish *Stravaigin* restaurant (see p.273). Moderate.

Tchai Ovna 42 Otago Lane. With live acoustic gigs and pre-club nights, this largely alcohol-free zone with lovely cakes and an array of sixty teas is a bohemian favourite. Inexpensive.

Tinderbox 189 Byres Rd. A style café which aspires – with an array of espresso-based drinks and its designer looks – to lure people who might ordinarily fancy a pint at the pub. Even in trendy Glasgow, it is amazingly successful. Inexpensive.

University Café 87 Byres Rd. A 70-year-old institution dearly loved by generations of students and West End residents. Formica tables in snug booths, glass counters and other original features, where the favourites are fish'n'chips or mince'n'-tatties rounded off with an ice-cream cone. Inexpensive.

Southside

The Granary 10–16 Kilmarnock Rd ☎0141/632 8487. At Shawlands Cross, in the commercial heart of the Southside, this bar with a bistro-style dining room to the rear serves an international selection of food and rich satisfying desserts. Moderate.

1901 1534 Pollokshaws Rd. Formerly the *Stoat & Ferret*, this bistro/pub near Pollok Country Park is a lesser-known gem serving a basic French-Mediterranean menu. There's often live jazz on a Sunday afternoon. Moderate.

Restaurants

The liveliest quarter of the **city centre** for eating out is the Merchant City (southeast of George Square), with its high concentration of trendy bars, clubs and restaurants amid loft conversions and a smattering of hip, chic shops. However, Bath Street has also established itself more recently as a hotbed of dining and drinking, and, reassuringly, Glasgow still boasts a fairly high quotient of independent establishments to off-set the rash of chain restaurants and café-bars. For all the predictable fast-food names, seek out the pedestrianized stretches of Argyle, Buchanan and Sauchiehall streets, with the last of these also offering a concentration of late-night eateries in the Charing Cross district.

The **West End** boasts an attractive range of stylish bars, cafés and restaurants, thanks to the local university population and the area's perennially young, affluent and creative vibe. The hub of the area is around the Hillhead underground station on Byres Road, with nearby cobbled Ashton Lane and its chock-a-block restaurants and pubs always the liveliest area. The **Southside** is quieter and less intense, featuring some family-run restaurants with a welcoming ambience.

City centre restaurants

Chinese and East Asian

Amber Regent 50 West Regent St ☎0141/331 1655. Quality service, a restrained ambience and excellent Chinese food. The extensive Cantonese menu offers half-price main courses early evening on weekdays (5.30–7pm). Closed Sun. Moderate.

Canton Express 407 Sauchiehall St. Late-night cheap eating near *The Garage* and other night-clubs. During the day, however, it is popular with local Chinese residents – testimony to its authentic cooking. Daily noon–4am. Inexpensive.

Ho Wong 82 York St, south of Argyle Street, west of Central station ☎0141/221 3550. Off-beat location for a posh restaurant with first-class Cantonese and Sichuan food. Expensive.

Ichiban Japanese Noodle Café 50 Queen St. Japanese-style setting, with long benches you share with fellow diners. Bowls of noodles and sushi selections are the staples here; service is friendly and efficient. Completely non-smoking. Inexpensive.

Mao 84 Brunswick St. Bright, fully glazed corner café-bar in the Merchant City offering a range of Asian cuisine, with spicy Korean and Indonesian specialities of particular note, and a pre-club feel at the weekend. Moderate.

Oko 68 Ingram St ⓣ0141/572 1500. Locally owned restaurant bringing freshly prepared sushi on colour-coded plates and the conveyor belt thing to the stylish Merchant City. Closed Sun. Moderate.

Pattaya 437 Sauchiehall St. In order to cater to post-clubbing crowds, this basic and satisfying Thai restaurant has decided to stop serving lunches and instead stay open into the wee small hours. Daily 5pm–5am. Moderate.

European

Arta Old Cheese Market, 13–19 Walls St ⓣ0141/552 2101. The huge ground floor bar is decked out like a Spanish town house, while the restaurant upstairs is modern minimalism. Good, freshly prepared tapas. Closed Mon & Tues. Moderate.

El Sabor Merchant Sq, Bell St ⓣ0141/552 3400. Casual split-level Spanish cantina with a frequently changing tapas menu as well as mains such as chicken rellenos. Moderate.

Esca 27 Chisholm St ⓣ0141/553 0880. Italian place across from the Tron Theatre, a relative newcomer that is casual and brightly designed, with a light touch in the kitchen. Moderate.

Fratelli Sarti 133 Wellington St or 121 Bath St. This Italian café/deli/restaurant all under one roof is both authentic and popular. The more formal dining space is off Bath Street, but the same selection of pizzas, pastas and daily specials is also available in the atmospheric café. Open from 8am Mon–Sat, and noon on Sun. Moderate.

Le Bouchon 17 King St ⓣ0141/552 7411. Fairly traditional French cooking in a basic brasserie setting, with excellent pre-theatre offers. Closed Sun. Moderate.

Le Chardon d'Or 176 West Regent St ⓣ0141/248 3801. Backed by the Roux brothers and featuring the Scottish-born head chef from their *Le Gavroche* restaurant in London, this recently opened French restaurant has Michelin star potential. Closed Sun. Expensive.

Primo Piatto 244a Bath St ⓣ0141/564 1236. Lesser-known basement Italian restaurant near the King's Theatre offering fresh ingredients, interesting dishes and a great home-made tiramisu. Closed Sun. Moderate.

Indian

Kama Sutra 331 Sauchiehall St ⓣ0141/332 0055. Deep velvet curtains and wrought-iron decoration highlight the unusual design, while a wide-ranging menu which includes dishes from the Northeast frontier make this a favourite central curry house. Daytime buffet is a popular bargain. Open Sun–Thurs until midnight, Fri & Sat until 1am. Moderate.

Wee Curry Shop 7 Buccleuch St. Tiny Indian café near the Glasgow Film Theatre, serving home-made, inexpensive meals to compete with the best in town. BYOB and marvel. Closed Sun. Inexpensive.

Mexican

Pancho Villas 26 Bell St ⓣ0141/552 7737. Glasgow's Mexican selection is limited and this one repeatedly gets the best notices. In addition to staples, it also offers some authentic but less seen dishes such as ceviche. Moderate.

Scottish and seafood

City Merchant 97 Candleriggs ⓣ0141/553 1577. Popular Merchant City brasserie serving excellent food using fresh Scottish produce from Ayrshire lamb to its speciality of west coast seafood. Expensive.

Farfelu 89 Candleriggs ⓣ0141/552 5345. On the floor above and adjacent to the *City Merchant*, a cool and casual spot with views over the early nineteenth-century city halls. Modern fine dining with combos like seared scallops with horseradish potatoes. Closed Sun. Moderate–Expensive.

Gamba 225a West George St ⓣ0141/572 0899. A stylish modern basement restaurant that acknowledges the Mediterranean both in decor and seafood menu, and has been known to impress hard-to-please visitors from London. Closed Sun. Expensive.

Groucho St Judes 190 Bath St ⓣ0141/352 8800. Part of booming Bath St, the ground floor restaurant is a hip, comfortable place for filling meals of a mostly Scottish nature, whether Aberdeen Angus steaks or mussels. Meanwhile the basement bar is a real scene spot. Moderate or Expensive.

Mitchell's 157 North St ⓣ0141/204 4312. Next to the domed Mitchell's Library, this is a comfortable brasserie without airs. The menu is fairly meaty and moderately priced. Good beer and an excellent refuge. Mon–Thurs noon–2.30pm & 5–10pm, Fri noon–2.30pm & 5–11pm, Sat 5–11pm.

Mussel Inn 157 Hope St ⓣ0141/572 1405. Like its Edinburgh flagship, this branch concentrates on simply prepared pots of fresh mussels and grilled scallops in casual environs. Mon–Sat noon–10pm, Sun 1.30–6pm. Moderate.

Rogano 11 Exchange Place ⓣ0141/248 4055. A shockingly expensive fish restaurant decked out as an Art Deco replica of the *Queen Mary* that has long been a Glasgow institution. *Café Rogano*, in the basement, is cheaper. Restaurant: daily noon–2.30pm & 6.30–10.30pm. Café: daily noon–11pm, Fri & Sat until midnight. Expensive.

West End restaurants

Chinese and East Asian

Chow 98 Byres Rd. Proof that Chinese restaurants can be modern and not crammed with Oriental kitsch. This bijou diner with extra tables upstairs offers excellent value-for-money meals. No smoking. Moderate.

Fusion Sushi Bar 41 Byres Rd ⓣ0141/339 3666. Funky sushi bar with rolls and sashimi at various prices as well as yakitori, teriyaki, katsu and the like. No smoking. Moderate.

Thai Siam 1191 Argyle St ⓣ0141/229 1191. A bit off the beaten track but worth the effort to find, boasting a friendly neighbourhood ambience with notable Thai specialities such as green curry with coconut. Closed Sun. Moderate.

European

Amaryllis At "Number 1 Devonshire Gardens", corner of Great Western and Hyndland roads ⓣ0141/337 3434. Gordon Ramsay, the Glaswegian celebrity chef who made it big in London, opened this long-awaited and critically acclaimed French restaurant in spring 2001. It's less pricey than you'd expect, though the main man still spends most of his time down south. Closed Sun evening. Expensive.

The Big Blue 445 Great Western Rd ⓣ0141/357 1038. Owned by the same family which runs the nearby and pricey *La Parmigiana*, this is a popular Italian restaurant and bar with casual attitude and outdoor tables overlooking the River Kelvin. Good for pizza and seafood dishes. Inexpensive.

Café Antipasti 337 Byres Rd ⓣ0141/337 2737. A busy Italian bistro near the Botanic Gardens serving tasty and well-priced pastas and salads. No bookings are taken, so expect a queue on busy nights. Second branch in town on Sauchiehall Street. Inexpensive.

Indian

Ashoka Ashton Lane 19 Ashton Lane ⓣ0141/337 1115. Lively curry house in the Harlequin chain, which dominates the Indian restaurant community throughout the west of Scotland; all have consistent quality and this branch is particularly popular with students. There are other Ashoka restaurants at 1284 Argyle St, and on the Southside at 268 Clarkston Rd. Mon–Sat noon–midnight, Sun 5pm–midnight. Moderate.

Mother India 28 Westminster Terrace, off Sauchiehall St ⓣ0141/221 1663. By near-unanimous consent, this is the best Indian restaurant in Glasgow. Excellent authentic home cooking with some original Goanese specials as well as the old favourites at affordable prices in refreshingly laid-back surroundings. BYOB; small corkage fee. Moderate.

Mexican

Cottier's 93–95 Hyndland St ⓣ0141/357 5825. Welcoming, classic West End vibe on the top floor of a church annexe adjacent to Cottier's Theatre. Wide-ranging menu including daily specials, all with a Latin American spin. Moderate.

Salsa 184 Dumbarton Rd ⓣ0141/337 1416. A smaller version of sister restaurant *Cantina Del Rey* in the Merchant City, this West End branch serves similar, basic Mexican-style favourites, whether burritos or fajitas, in a colourful and laid-back atmosphere. Moderate.

Scottish and seafood

The Cabin 996 Dumbarton Rd ⓣ0141/569 1036. Unique in Glasgow, perhaps the world. With one seating per night serving a three-course *table d'hôte* menu of upmarket Scottish food with a hint of Irish influence, unforgetable post-meal entertainment is provided by host/chanteuse Wilma, who belts out a series of classic songs and arias and has everyone singing along by the evening's end. Best for parties of four or more. Book in advance; deposit sometimes requested. Tues–Sat from 7.30pm. Expensive.

Nairn's 13 Woodside Crescent ⓣ0141/353 0707. Showcase restaurant for Scotland's celebrity chef Nick Nairn, on the garden level of a lovely Georgian town house. Fresh, specially sourced ingredients go into artfully presented dishes. Closed Sun & Mon. Expensive.

No. Sixteen 16 Byres Rd ⓣ0141/339 2544. Undoubtedly the best under-£15 meal in Glasgow, in a tiny, family-run neighbourhood bistro that is a rising star. Booking essential. Closed Sun. Moderate.

Stravaigin 28–30 Gibson St ⓣ0141/334 2665. Local meats and fish are given an international make-over using a host of unexpected ingredients. Adventurous fine-dining selections and an exceptional-value bar menu, too. Basement restaurant open until 10.30pm, bar until 11pm Sun–Thurs, midnight Fri & Sat. Moderate upstairs, expensive downstairs.

Two Fat Ladies 88 Dumbarton Rd ⓣ0141/339 1944. The second-best fish restaurant in Glasgow, after *Gamba* (see opposite). Tiny, intimate space with the kitchen right up front, serving fixed-price, three-course meals. Closed Sun & Mon. Expensive.

The Ubiquitous Chip 12 Ashton Lane ⓣ0141/334 5007. Opened in 1971, *The Chip*, as it's affectionately known, led the way in Glasgow in headlining Scotland's quality fresh produce at the heart of its contemporary, upmarket dining experience. Some say it's living on its well-deserved reputation, but it's still up there. Less expensive options upstairs. Expensive.

Southside restaurants

European

Arigo 67 Kilmarnock Rd ☎0141/636 6616. Some claim this is the best Italian restaurant in the city. Lamb and veal dishes are noteworthy, with everything made fresh to order. Moderate.

Café Serghei 67 Bridge St ☎0141/429 1547. A converted bank near the Clyde (within easy walking distance of the city centre), this restaurant looks formal but is quite relaxed, serving hearty Greek favourites. Excellent pre-theatre offer. Moderate.

Greek Golden Kebab 34 Sinclair Drive ☎0141/649 7581. The longest-running Greek restaurant in Glasgow hasn't changed its rustic cooking in probably thirty years. Worth seeking out. Thurs–Sun 5pm–1am. Moderate.

Scottish

Art Lovers' Café In House for an Art Lover, Bellahouston Park, 10 Dumbreck Rd ☎0141/353 4779. This showcase Rennie Mackintosh house (see p.265) offers sublime lunches with views of the garden. Moderate.

The Cook's Room 205 Fenwick Rd, Giffnock ☎0141/621 1903. Chef/owner Tom Battersby has earned an admirable reputation, and his restaurant with its rustic furniture and friendly service merits a special trip for dinner or a weekend brunch. Moderate.

Buying your own food

There are plenty of specialist outlets where you can **buy your own food**. Of the more interesting options, Peckhams, with late-opening branches at 65 Glassford St, 100 Byres Rd, 42 Clarence Drive and in Central Station, is a reliable up-market **deli** with an impressive range including lots of tasty takeaway options. Fratelli Sarti, 133 Wellington St, is a traditional Italian deli, piled high with directly imported delicacies, and has a wonderful stock of Italian wines plus a café/restaurant attached (see p.272). Grassroots, 93 Woodlands Rd, is the best **vegetarian** deli in the city, with a tasty range of food as well as a next-door café (see p.270) and an extensive range of health and alternative health products. Heart Buchanan, 380 Byres Rd, has excellent, upmarket prepared meals and dry goods, while Iain Mellis, 492 Great Western Rd, is a wonderful, old-fashioned **cheesemonger** specializing in farmhouse cheeses from the British Isles; they also keep a selection of the best from overseas, and stock olives, bacon, teas and other treats.

Drinking

Glasgow's tough image was once inextricably associated with its **pubs**, widely – if mistakenly – thought of as no-go areas for visitors. Today, many of the dark, slightly threatening, nicotine-stained working men's pubs have been converted into airy bars, though in truth any drinking spot is a great place to get a handle on real Glaswegian bonhomie.

If you tire of the trendier pre-club bars in the **city centre** and its buzzing Merchant City, set out for the **East End** or the **Saltmarket** district near the Clyde, where the local spit-and-sawdust establishments offer a welcome change. The liveliest area is the **West End**, with students mixing with fun-seeking locals around Byres Road, and the nearby Woodlands and Kelvingrove neighborhoods offering alternatives. Decent pubs are more widely scattered in the **Southside**, but you'll find a handful of pleasant spots, ranging from stylish hangouts to historic locals.

As for **opening hours**, Glasgow's pubs and bars often keep serving until midnight; some do close at 11pm during the week, but then again in certain areas you'll find pubs open at the weekend until 1am. After closing-time, your only option is to head to a nightclub (see below), some of which don't close until 5am.

City centre pubs and bars

The Arches 253 Argyle St. This contemporary arts centre under Central station made its new bar one of the focal points in a recent interior redesign. Good happy-hour bargains; arty clientele.

Babbity Bowster 16–18 Blackfriars St, off the High Street. Lively place with a natural Scottish feel – and thankfully without any kitsch. Good place to hear spontaneous folk sessions. Excellent beer and good basic food all day and night, with pricier restaurant upstairs.

Bar 10 10 Mitchell St. Across from the Lighthouse architecture centre, and considered the grand-daddy of Glasgow style bars, designed by Ben Kelly of Manchester's *Hacienda* club fame. Still popular and suitably chic, though a healthy dose of Glaswegian humour softens any posey edge.

Bar 91 91 Candleriggs. Merchant City style bar that tends to be friendlier and less pretentious than some others.

Bargo 80 Albion St. Design-award winner with a spacious wood and stainless-steel interior that opens onto the pavement. Popular with students who appreciate the scene and the cheap eats.

Budda 142 St Vincent St. Despite its name, the look here is more Arab bazaar than Far Eastern minimalism. Comfy sofas and a club upstairs, too.

Corinthian 191 Ingram St. A remarkable renovation of an old bank, with some over-the-top Italianate architecture dating to early Victoriana. Three distinct bars, one restaurant and a private club: dress smartly.

The Griffin 226 Bath St. Three-bars-in-one pub with classic Glasgow-style Art Nouveau design. Across from the Kings Theatre, and originally named the Kings Arms.

Horseshoe Bar 17 Drury St. A must for visiting real-pub aficionados. Traditional 'Gin Palace pub', with the longest continuous bar in the UK, this is reputedly Glasgow's busiest drinking hole, with a mixed clientele, including recent rock darlings Travis; karaoke upstairs for aspiring Fran Healys.

Mitre Bar 12–16 Brunswick St. Tucked away up a lane between Wilson Street and the Trongate, this tiny unpretentious traditional retreat festooned with football banners sells decent beer to a mixed bunch of locals.

Monkey Bar 100 Bath St. City-centre style bar, with office staff making it loud at lunchtimes and the pre-club crowd thronging in at weekends. Pool table, too.

Moskito 200 Bath St. Newer arrival, less full of posing youth than some but nonetheless hip and stylish, with inexpensive food and ambient tunes.

Nice'n'Sleazy 421 Sauchiehall St. Better known for its indie rock performance space (see p.278), the ground-floor bar has the feel of New York's East Village, with slightly tatty booths and the best jukebox in the city.

Republic Bier Halle 9 Gordon St. Intense modern industrial design using shuttered concrete and caissons of stone with chunky seating. Serves 130 different beers and hearty Eastern European grub from sausages to goulash.

Variety Bar 401 Sauchiehall St. Crowded with faded faux Art Nouveau details and frequented by nearby Glasgow Art School students, here for the eclectic array of different DJs every night.

East End and Saltmarket pubs and bars

Baird's Bar 224 Gallowgate. In general, it's a wise idea to avoid discussing local football in Glasgow bars. If you're a diehard Celtic supporter, however, come here and you'll be as close to "Paradise" as possible – short of going to Celtic Park itself.

Clutha Vaults 167 Stockwell St. Slightly more scrubbed and less atmospheric than the *Scotia* (see below) but host to a similar line-up of free live music.

McChuill's 40 High St. Just skirting the Merchant City, this converted railway shed with vaulted brick ceilings manages to be neither style bar nor traditional pub. Popular for music, ranging from hip-hop DJ to salsa and jazz.

Saracen Head 209 Gallowgate, opposite the Barras market and near the Barrowland ballroom. The *Sarry Heid* is notorious for its rough-edged atmosphere and its historic relics displayed in glass cabinets. The mildly mental atmosphere is pure Glasgow. Look out for the tax demand from Robbie Burns up on the wall, dating from the days when he was the local tax collector. Often open weekends only.

Scotia Bar 112 Stockwell St. Management says this is the oldest pub in the city – not convincingly proven, but it looks the part, with low, exposed timber ceilings. Still the place for live blues, folk and skiffle sessions; Billy Connolly began his career here, telling jokes in between singing folk songs.
Victoria Bar 157–159 Bridgegate. Time-honoured, basic pub serving a wide selection of real ales and hosting a range of live music, with monthly bluegrass and even Morris dancers.

West End pubs and bars

Attic 44–46 Ashton Lane. Proof that New York doesn't have a monopoly on creative loft conversions, this bar above the *Cul-de-Sac* restaurant is the smart place to drink on busy Ashton Lane.
Bar Bola 144 Park Rd. Style bar with less pretensions than usual, featuring wrought iron and swirls of wood. Located near the Kelvin River and away from the well-trodden pub-crawl routes.
Bonham's Wine Bar 194 Byres Rd. Two-level bar with splendid stained-glass windows and good wine list. Popular, unpretentious, and with reasonable daytime food.
54 Below 3 Kelvingrove St, at Argyle St. One of the more recent bars converted from gloom to glam – but not too much of the latter. Hints at an Eastern European theme.
Firebird 1321 Argyle St. Fully glazed, airy drinking spot near the Kelvingrove Art Gallery, with a wood-stoked pizza oven producing some tasty snacks plus DJs to keep the pre-clubbing crowd entertained.
The Halt 106 Woodlands Rd. A good beer and whisky selection in this relaxed pub, where live rockin' music is played almost every night in the adjoining lounge.
Lismore Lounge 206 Dumbarton Rd. One-time working man's pub, tastefully redecorated with specially commissioned stained-glass panels depicting the Highland Clearances, this friendly bar is a meeting point for the local Gaels, who come here to chat, relax and listen to the impromptu music sessions.
Living Room 5–9 Byres Rd. Hotbed for the young and hip, at the southern end of Byres Road. Wrought iron and candles enhance the pre-club atmosphere.
Tennent's 191 Byres Rd. No-nonsense, beery pub that offers a refreshing antidote to designer-driven bars nearby. Large and popular, with real ale and a no-music policy.
Uisge Beatha 232 Woodlands Rd. Unexceptional white frontage belies the eclectic interior, with lots of sofas and ironic Scots kitsch. Barmen wear kilts and keep the atmosphere lively. The name is Gaelic for "the water of life" – that is, whisky.
Whistler's Mother 116–122 Byres Rd. Combines a relaxed restaurant with a more basic student-oriented bar, popular with legions of young folk.

Southside pubs and bars

Brazen Head 1–3 Cathcart Rd. Local Irish–Italian bar close to the Citizens' Theatre and decorated with football strips.
Clockwork Beer Company 1153 Cathcart Rd, near Mt Florida train station. Spacious pub that brews its own ales and has an excellent selection of malt whiskies, plus a daytime family area with toys.
Cul de Sac Southside 1179 Pollokshaws Rd. Relaxing if fashionable spot; the only calculated style bar on the Southside, with the *Attic* upstairs serving food.
Heraghty's Free House 708 Pollokshaws Rd. Authentic Irish pub on the corner of Pollokshaws and Nithsdale roads which prides itself on pouring the perfect pint of Guinness. Still living down its history of not having a women's loo: one's been installed for several years now.
The Taverna 778 Pollokshaws Rd. A favourite for many who stay in this neck of the Southside; fully glazed corner location with potted palms and selection of real ales.

Nightlife and entertainment

Nightlife is well served, with many bars now open until 1am at the weekends, and some offering even later hours. Glasgow's **clubbing scene** is highly rated, with the city attracting top DJs from around the world and also breeding a good deal of local talent. Establishments are pretty mixed and an underground scene thrives, although some outdated mega-discos still have dress codes. Opening hours hover between 11pm to 3am, though some stay open until 5am. Cover charges are variable: expect to pay around £4 during the week and up to £15 at the weekend. Drinks are usually about thirty percent more expensive than in the pubs.

Glasgow is home to Scottish Opera, Scottish Ballet and the Royal Scottish National Orchestra, and the city's cultural programme offers a breadth of **music** (from hip contemporary to heavyweight classical), plus **dance**, **theatre**, **film** and performance art. The larger theatres, cinema multiplexes and concert halls are in the city centre, while the West End is home to venues such as the quirky Grosvenor repertory cinema and friendly Cottier Theatre. The Southside has two theatres noted for cutting-edge drama, the Citizens' and the Tramway.

For detailed **listings**, pick up the comprehensive fortnightly magazine *The List* (£1.95), which also covers Edinburgh, or consult Glasgow's *Herald* or *Evening Times* newspapers. To book **tickets** for theatre productions or big concerts, call at the Ticket Centre, City Hall, Candleriggs (Mon–Sat 10.30am–6.30pm, Sun noon–5pm), or call Ticket Link on ⓣ0141/287 5511.

Clubs

Alaska 142 Bath Lane ⓣ0141/248 1777. Rated for weekly Friday and monthly Saturday techno and house clubs in tastefully designed environs.
Archaos 25 Queen St ⓣ0141/204 3189. Massive, multi-level place with designer décor and a mainstream music policy.
The Arches 30 Midland St, off Jamaica St ⓣ0141/221 4001. In converted railway arches under Central station, the club portion of this arts venue offers an eclectic array of music: hard house, trance, techno and funk.
Fury Murray's 96 Maxwell St, behind the St Enoch Centre ⓣ0141/221 6511. Student-oriented and lively, with music spanning the 1960s to recent indie and chart favourites.
The Garage 490 Sauchiehall St ⓣ0141/332 1120. Medium-sized club that also hosts gigs across the rock'n'roll spectrum.
Glasgow School of Art 167 Renfrew St ⓣ0141/332 0691. Blissfully unadorned space for hipsters with music that ranges from *Hi Karate*'s funk, hip hop and jungle mix every Thursday to Northern soul and techno.
Trash 197 Pitt St ⓣ0141/572 3372. Three-room venue geared towards students and recent graduates looking to get dressed up.
The Tunnel 84 Mitchell St ⓣ0141/204 1000. Pre-eminent contemporary and progressive house music club with arty décor (dig the gents' cascading waterfall walls) and fairly strict dress codes.
The Velvet Rooms 520 Sauchiehall St ⓣ0141/332 0755. Consists of a small bar with postage-stamp dance area for mainstream dance, garage and soul.

Gay clubs and bars

Bennett's 90 Glassford St, Merchant City ⓣ0141/552 5761. Glasgow's longest running gay club, predominantly male, fairly traditional, and with commercially oriented music.
Candle Bar 20 Candleriggs ⓣ0141/564 1285. Relaxed and unpretentious fairly recent addition to the scene, with karaoke nights.
Delmonica's 68 Virginia St ⓣ0141/552 4803. One of Glasgow's liveliest gay bars, in a popular area, with a mixed, hedonistic crowd and some kind of entertainment or event nightly.
Gay and Lesbian Centre 11 Dixon St ⓣ0141/221 7203. Licensed café in addition to more institutional support such as information and reading rooms.
Polo Lounge 84 Wilson St, off Glassford Street ⓣ0141/553 1221. The original decor – marble tiles and open fires – and gentleman's club atmosphere upstairs combine with the dark, pounding nightclubs underneath which attract a gay and gay-friendly crowd.
Revolver 6a John St ⓣ0141/553 2456. Recently opened gay bar geared more towards the art of conversation than dance, with a popular Sunday chill-out.
Sadie Frosts 8–10 West George St, Queen Street station ⓣ0141/332 8005. In the train station facing George Square, Sadie's house DJs alternate with karaoke through the week.

Live music venues

Barrowland 244 Gallowgate ⓣ0141/552 4601. Legendary East End ballroom that hosts some of the liveliest, sweatiest and best gigs you may ever encounter. With room for a couple of thousand, it mostly books bands securely on the rise but still hosts some big-time acts who return to it as their favourite venue in Scotland.
The Garage 490 Sauchiehall St ⓣ0141/332

1120. Club which converts to a medium-size venue for bands that are just about to make it big.

King Tut's Wah Wah Hut 272a St Vincent St ☎0141/221 5279. Famous as the place where Oasis were discovered, and still presenting one of the city's best live music programmes. Also has a good downstairs bar, with an excellent jukebox should you want to sit out the gig.

Nice'n'Sleazy 421 Sauchiehall St ☎0141/333 9637. Alternative and indie-orientated acts play most nights in the appropriately dingy performance space below this city-centre bar (see p.275).

Queen Margaret Union 22 University Gardens ☎0141/339 9784. Once an indie showcase but now more likely to feature dance-oriented acts.

Scotia Bar 112 Stockwell St ☎0141/552 8681. The folkies' favourite, a mellow musical pub with regular live gigs and jam sessions. Free.

The 13th Note 50–60 King St ☎0141/553 1638. The basement of this relaxed bar and vegetarian restaurant (see p.270) is the place to sample local and cutting-edge musical talent, including jazz and R&B; the club of the same name at 260 Clyde St is a bit louder and livelier.

Theatres and comedy venues

Arches Theatre 253 Argyle St ☎0901/022 0300. Andy Arnold runs the *Arches* theatre company, reviving old classics and introducing new talent in this recently refurbished, hip venue.

Citizens' Theatre 119 Gorbals St ☎0141/429 0022. The "Citz" has evolved from its 1960s working-class roots into one of the most respected contemporary theatres in Britain. Three stages, concession rates for students and free preview nights.

Cottier Theatre 935 Hyndland St ☎0141/357 3868. This performance space in the old Dowanhill church hosts touring shows, dance and music gigs. An adjoining bar with beer garden is a favourite on dry summer evenings.

Mitchell Theatre 6 Granville St, Charing Cross ☎0141/287 5511. Small but popular venue located at rear of Glasgow's huge reference library for touring groups and occasional music acts.

Ramshorn Theatre 98 Ingram St ☎0141/552 3489. Another church conversion, this Merchant City venue features student and post-student productions at bargain prices.

The Stand 333 Woodlands Rd ☎0870/600 6055. Recent addition and sister to the first-rate comedy club in Edinburgh, booking national and international acts.

State Bar 148 Holland St ☎0141/357 5387. Saturday's Madcap Comedy Club rules the roost downstairs here, with local and national stars.

Tramway Theatre 25 Albert Drive, off Pollokshaws Road ☎0141/287 3900. Premier avant-garde venue for experimental theatre, dance and music, as well as art exhibitions.

Tron Theatre 63 Trongate ☎0141/552 4267. Varied repertoire of mainstream and more challenging productions from itinerant companies, such as Glasgow's *Vanishing Point.*

Concert halls

Glasgow Royal Concert Hall 2 Sauchiehall St ☎0141/287 5511. Chunky modern monstrosity that is the venue for big-name touring orchestras and the home to the Royal Scottish National Orchestra, as well as booking some big-name rock and soul stars and middle-of-the-road music hall acts.

Scottish Exhibition and Conference Centre, and Clyde Auditorium Finnieston Quay ☎0870/040 4000. The SECC is a gigantic airplane hangar-like space with dreadful acoustics that, unfortunately, is the only indoor venue in Scotland for world-touring megastars from Tom Jones to Eminem. The adjacent Clyde Auditorium – better known as the Armadillo – is smaller but more melodic.

Theatre Royal 282 Hope St ☎0141/332 9000. This late-nineteenth-century theatre was revived in the mid-1970s as the opulent home of Scottish Opera, and plays regular host to visiting orchestras, opera and theatre groups, including the Royal Shakespeare Company.

Cinemas

Glasgow Film Theatre 12 Rose St ☎0141/332 8128. Dedicated art, independent and repertory cinema house. Its in-house *Café Cosmo* is an excellent place for pre-show drinks.

Grosvenor Ashton Lane ☎0141/339 4298. Eclectic mix of mainstream and art-house movies on two screens in this eighty-year-old cinema, which has plans to open a restaurant and bar. Occasional theme nights and frequent late shows for local students.

Odeon City Centre 56 Renfield St ☎0141/332 3413. Multiscreen cinema with the latest releases.

Odeon at the Quay Paisley Road ☎0141/418 0111. Another multiplex, just over the river on the Southside.

Listings

American Express 115 Hope St ⓣ0141/222 1401. Mon–Fri 8.30am–5.30pm (except Wed 9.30am–5.30pm), Sat 9am–2pm (winter Sat closes noon).

Banks and exchange Bank of Scotland, 110 Queen St, 55 Bath St and 2 Trongate; Clydesdale Bank, 14 Bothwell St, 150 Buchanan St, 30 St Vincent Place; Royal Bank of Scotland, 22 St Enoch Square, 393 Sauchiehall St. English banks in Glasgow include Barclays, 90 St Vincent St and Lloyds/TSB, 52–60 St Vincent St. Thomas Cook (Mon–Sat 8.30am–6.30pm, Sun 10am–4pm; Nov–May closed Sun) is at Central station ⓣ0141/207 3407.

Bike rental Only a few bike shops rent out bikes. Dales, 150 Dobbies Loan ⓣ0141/332 2705, a block north of the Buchanan Street bus station, has a few bikes available. There's a better selection at West End Cycles, 16 Chancellor St ⓣ0141/357 1344, conveniently placed close to the start of the Glasgow to Loch Lomond route, one of a number of special cycle routes which radiate out from the city. For further details, check ⓦwww.sustrans.co.uk.

Books Borders, 98 Buchanan St; Waterstone's, 153 Sauchiehall St. For secondhand: Caledonian Bookshop, 483 Great Western Rd, or Voltaire & Rousseau, 12–14 Otago Lane.

Bus and coach information Buchanan Street bus station ⓣ0141/333 3708; City Link coaches ⓣ0870/550 5050; First Glasgow (local service) ⓣ0141/423 6600, ⓦwww.firstglasgow.co.uk. The comprehensive Traveline ⓣ0870/608 2608 has full information.

Camping and outdoors gear Tiso, 129 Buchanan St ⓣ0141/248 4877 and Couper St (off Kyle St), Townhead ⓣ0141/559 5450, which features an ice-climbing wall, a waterfall (to test cagoules) and 100m track for trying out walking boots and mountain bikes.

Car rental Arnold Clark, Castlebank St ⓣ0141/339 9886; Avis, 161 North St ⓣ0141/221 2827; Budget, 101 Waterloo St ⓣ0141/221 9241; Europcar, 38 Anderston Quay ⓣ0141/248 8788. Car-rental firms at the airport include Budget ⓣ0141/889 1479, Europcar ⓣ0141/887 0414 and Hertz ⓣ0141/887 2451.

Dentist National Health Service line ⓣ0800/224488 lists local and emergency dentists. Glasgow Dental Hospital, 378 Sauchiehall St (ⓣ0141/211 9600).

Flight information Glasgow International airport ⓣ0141/887 1111, ⓦwww.glasgow-airport.com. Glasgow Prestwick airport ⓣ01292/511000, ⓦwww.gpia.co.uk.

Gay and lesbian contacts Strathclyde Lesbian and Gay Switchboard ⓣ0141/332 8372; Glasgow Women's Library, Lesbian Archive & Information Centre, 109 Trongate ⓣ0141/552 8345; Glasgow Lesbian, Gay, Bisexual and Transgender Centre, 11 Dixon St ⓣ0141/221 7203, ⓦwww.gglc.org.uk.

Hospital 24hr casualty department at the Royal Infirmary, 84 Castle St ⓣ0141/211 4000.

Internet EasyEverything is open 24hr at 57–61 St Vincent St. Internet Exchange is at 136 Sauchiehall St.

Laundry Harvey's, 161 Great Western Rd; Laundromat, 39 Bank St; Majestic Laundrette, 1110 Argyle St.

Left luggage Staffed office at Buchanan Street bus station (daily 6.30am–10.30pm) and 24hr lockers at both Central and Queen Street train stations.

Music Fopp, 358 Byres Rd & 19 Union St; Tower Records, 217–221 Argyle St; Missing Records, 9–11 Wellington St.

Pharmacies Boots, Buchanan Galleries (Mon–Sat 9am–6pm, Thurs until 8pm, Sun 11am–5pm; ⓣ0141/333 9306); Munro, 693 Great Western Rd (daily 9am–9pm; ⓣ0141/339 0012).

Police Strathclyde Police HQ, Pitt Street ⓣ0141/532 2000; Stewart Street station, Cowcaddens ⓣ0141/532 3000.

Post office General information ⓣ0845/722 3344. Main office at 47 St Vincent St (Mon–Fri 8.30am–5.45pm, Sat 9am–5.30pm); other city centre offices at 87–91 Bothwell St and 228 Hope St.

Taxis TOA ⓣ0141/429 7070.

Train information National Rail enquiries ⓣ0845/748 4950, ⓦwww.nationalrail.co.uk.

Travel agents Campus Travel, The Hub, Hillhead St ⓣ0141/357 0608 and 122 George St ⓣ0141/553 1818.

The Clyde

The **River Clyde** is the dominant physical feature of Glasgow and its environs, the largest urban concentration in Scotland, with almost two million people living in the city and satellite towns. Little of this immediate hinterland can be described as beautiful, with crisscrossing motorways and relentlessly grim housing estates dominating much of the landscape. However, there are pockets of interest, many related to the river itself or the industries which grew up from it. Beyond the urban sprawl, rolling green hills, open expanses of water and attractive countryside eventually begin to dominate, not always captivating initially, but holding promises of wilder country beyond.

West of the city, regular trains and the M8 motorway dip down from the southern bank of the Clyde to **Paisley**, where the distinctive cloth pattern gained its name, before heading back up to the edge of the river again as it broadens into the **Firth of Clyde**. Here the former ship-building towns of **Port Glasgow**, **Greenock** and **Gourock** look out over the water to the lochs and hills of Argyll, a prospect which also serves as a backdrop to two towns on the north bank of the firth – the ancient Strathclyde capital of **Dumbarton**, and **Helensburgh**, birthplace of architect Charles Rennie Mackintosh and television pioneer John Logie Baird.

North of Glasgow lies some wonderful upland countryside. Trains terminate at tiny Milngavie (pronounced "mill-guy"), which makes great play of its status as the start of the long-distance walk, the **West Highland Way** (for details of which, see p.317). Nearby, the rolling beauty of the Campsie Fells (see p.309) provides excellent walking and stunning views down onto Glasgow and the glinting river that runs through it.

Heading southeast out of Glasgow, the industrial landscape of the **Clyde Valley** eventually gives way to a far more attractive scenery of gorges and towering castles. Here lie the stoic town of **Lanark**, where eighteenth-century philanthropists built their model workers' community around the mills of **New Lanark**, and the spectacular **Falls of Clyde**, a mile upstream. Even further beyond, deep into the rolling countryside of South Lanarkshire where the Clyde is little more than a widening stream, the market town of **Biggar** with its unusual clutch of museums serves as a useful orientation point to the hill farming country of the Scottish Borders beyond.

The Firth of Clyde – south bank

The swift journey from Glasgow along the M8, coupled with the proximity of the international airport, can belie the fact that **Paisley** is not a suburb of Glasgow but a town in its own right, with a long and distinctive history, particularly in the textile trade. Further west, the motorway and train line rejoin the Clyde by the **Erskine Bridge**, a huge concrete parabola which carries cars between the two banks of the river. As the estuary widens, the former ship-building centres of Port Glasgow and **Greenock** crowd the river bank, followed by the old-fashioned seaside resort of **Gourock**, and eventually **Wemyss Bay**, jumping-off point for the ferry to Rothesay on Bute. Of the four, Greenock is by far the most interesting, with an excellent town museum that examines the life and achievements of local boy James Watt.

Paisley

Founded in the twelfth century as a monastic settlement around an abbey, **PAISLEY** expanded rapidly after the eighteenth century as a linen manufacturing town, specializing in the production of highly fashionable imitation Kashmiri shawls. Paisley quickly eclipsed other British centres producing the cloth, eventually lending its name to the swirling pine-cone design.

South of the train station, down Gilmour or Smithills streets, lies the bridge over the White Cart Water and the borough's ponderous **Town Hall**, seemingly built back to front as its municipal clock and mismatched double towers loom incongruously over the river instead of facing onto the town. Opposite the town hall, the **Abbey** (Mon–Sat 10am–3.30pm; free) was built on the site of the town's original settlement and was massively overhauled in the Victorian age. The unattractive, fat grey facade of the church does little justice to the renovated interior, which is tall, spacious and elaborately decorated; the elongated choir, rebuilt extensively throughout the last two centuries, is illuminated by jewel-coloured stained glass from a variety of ages and styles. The abbey's oldest monument is the tenth-century Celtic cross of St Barochan, which lurks like a gnarled old bone at the eastern end of the north aisle.

Paisley's bland pedestrianised **High Street** leads westwards from the town hall towards two churches that make far more of an impression on the town's skyline than the modest abbey. The steep cobbles of Church Hill rise away from the High Street up to the grand steps and five-stage spire of the **High Church**, while beyond the civic museum at the bottom of the High Street stands the **Thomas Coats Memorial Church** (May–Sept Mon, Wed & Fri 2–4pm; free), a Victorian masterpiece of hugely overstated grandeur. Sitting squat like a giant red predator waiting to pounce, the church is one of the most opulent Baptist centres in Britain, with huge tower-top buttresses and an interior of seemingly endless marble and alabaster.

Between the two churches, Paisley's civic **Museum and Art Gallery** (Tues–Sat 10am–5pm, Sun 2–5pm; free) shelters behind pompous Ionic columns that face the grim buildings of Paisley University. Inside, it's a reasonably attractive civic building, with grand domes and self-important staircases. The main reason for coming here is to see the Shawl Gallery, which deals with the growth and development of the Paisley pattern and shawls, showing the familiar pine-cone (or teardrop) pattern from its simplistic beginnings to elaborate later incarnations. Paisley's identity as a centre for craftsmanship is also celebrated in displays of the work of contemporary local artisans, found on the balcony overlooking the entrance hall, and alongside these a number of working looms are looked after by a weaver-in-residence. Leading on from this is the largest gallery, mixing local social history with blown-up photos of locals (or "buddies", as inhabitants of Paisley like to be known) selecting their favourite exhibits in the museum. The Upper Gallery houses a small art collection including works by Glasgow Boys Hornel, Guthrie and Lavery (see box on p.260), as well as one or two paintings by local boy John Byrne, artist and playwright best known for his plays *The Slab Boys* and *Tutti Frutti*.

On Oakshaw Street, which runs along the crest of the hill above the Art Gallery, the **Coats Observatory** (Tues–Sat 10am–5pm, Sun 2–5pm; free) has recorded astronomical and meteorological information since 1884. Today it houses a ten-inch telescope under its dome, and a couple of small exhibition areas display seismic recorders that documented the cataclysmic San Francisco earthquake of 1906. The telescopes are used for public viewing on Thursday evenings from the last Thursday in October until the last Thursday in March (7.30–9.30pm, weather permitting).

spectacular backdrop of the Argyll mountains, which can be seen in their full glory from Tower Hill, reached from John Street past the health centre; it's a steep climb but the view makes the effort worthwhile.

Wemyss Bay

There's not much south of Gourock apart from a gruesome power-station chimney and large yacht marina at **Inverkip**, until you reach **WEMYSS BAY**, the terminus of the southern branch of the train line from Port Glasgow, which clips the edge of Greenock before curling around the mountains and moors, playing a flirtatious game of peek-a-boo with the Clyde estuary. The most memorable part of the journey is the arrival at the breathtaking Wemyss Bay station, a startling wrought-iron and glass palace which serves as a reminder of the great glory days when thousands of Glaswegians would alight for their steamer trip "doon the watter". Today the only steamer connection is the rather prosaic CalMac **ferry** over to Rothesay, capital of the Isle of Bute (see p.377).

The Firth of Clyde – north bank

Heading west out of Glasgow, the A82 road and the train tracks both follow the north bank of the river, passing through Clydebank, another ex-shipbuilding centre, and Bowling, the western entry point of the newly reopened Forth & Clyde canal (see p.310). At **Dumbarton**, an ancient regional capital, the main road swings north towards Loch Lomond (see p.315), while the railway and A814 carry on along the shores of the Firth of Clyde to wealthy **Helensburgh**, before themselves turning north along the shores of Gare Loch and Loch Long to Arrochar, which marks the beginning of Argyll (see p.373).

Dumbarton

Founded in the fifth century, today the town of **DUMBARTON** is a brutal concrete sprawl, fulfilling every last cliché about postwar planning and architecture. Avoid the town itself – though Talking Heads fans might be interested to know that David Byrne was born here – and head one mile southeast to **Dumbarton Castle** (April–Sept Mon–Sat 9.30am–6.30pm, Sun 2–6.30pm; Oct–March Mon–Wed & Sat 9.30–4.30pm, Thurs 9.30am–1pm, Sun 2–4.30pm; £2), which sits atop a twin outcrop of volcanic rock overlooking the Clyde. It's best reached from Dumbarton East train station, from where you turn right and take the second left, Victoria Street, continuing straight for just over half a mile. As a natural site, Dumbarton Rock could not be bettered – surrounded by water on three sides and with commanding views. First founded as a Roman fort, the structure was expanded in the fifth century by the Damnonii tribe, and remained Strathclyde's capital until its absorption into the greater kingdom of Scotland in 1034. The castle then became a royal seat, from which Mary, Queen of Scots sailed for France to marry Henri II's son in 1548, and to which she was attempting to escape when she and her troops were defeated twenty years later at the Battle of Langside. Since the 1600s, the castle has been used as a garrison and artillery fortress to guard the approaches to Glasgow; most of the current buildings date from this period.

The solid eighteenth-century **Governor's House** lies at the base of the rock, from where you enter the castle complex proper by climbing the steep steps up into the narrow cleft between the two rocks, crowned by the oldest remaining structure in the complex, a fourteenth-century **portcullis arch**. Vertiginous steps ascend to each peak: to see both you must climb more than five hundred steps. The **eastern rock** is the higher, with a windy summit that affords excellent views over to the lakes, rivers and mountains beyond Dumbarton town.

Dumbarton is also home to a quirky but fascinating piece of industrial heritage relating to the glory days of Clyde shipbuilding, housed on Castle Street, three streets west of Victoria Street. The **Denny Tank** (Mon–Sat 10am–4pm; £1.50), an outpost of the Scottish Maritime museum, houses the world's oldest working ship-model experiment tank, at around 110 yards long. It's still used to test scale models of ships prior to the expensive business of construction, and explanatory panels cover the whole process from wax modelling up to the experiments themselves.

Practicalities

Regular **trains** run from Glasgow's Queen Street station to Dumbarton East and Dumbarton Central stations; the former gives best access to the castle and accommodation. The **tourist office** (daily: July & Aug 10am–7pm; June & Sept 10am–6pm; May & Oct 10am–5pm; Nov–April 10am–4pm; ⓣ01389/742306, ⓦwww.visitscottishheartlands.org) is situated a couple of miles east of town on the A82 and mainly caters for the vast number of car-bound tourists on their way to the Highlands. Most **accommodation** is also clustered around this traffic artery and the busy Glasgow road that leads into Dumbarton proper. The *Dumbuck House Hotel*, Glasgow Road (ⓣ01389/734336, ⓔdumbuckhot@aol.com; ❺), offers spacious and comfortable rooms, while *Kilmalid House*, 17 Glenpath, is a quiet **B&B** off Barnhill Road (ⓣ01389/732030; ❶). To reach this area from Dumbarton East train station, exit left and continue until you reach Greenhead Road, which will take you straight up to the A82. Closer to Dumbarton Central, Mrs Valentine, at 87 Glasgow Rd (ⓣ01389/732819; ❶), also offers inexpensive B&B. There is the usual selection of takeaways focused on the High Street in the centre of town or, for decent **pub food** during the day, try the High Street's *Burgh Bar*.

Helensburgh

HELENSBURGH, twenty miles or so northwest of Glasgow, is a smart, Georgian grid-plan settlement laid out in an imitation of Edinburgh's New Town and overlooking the Clyde estuary. In the eighteenth century it was a well-to-do commuter town for Glasgow and also a seaside resort, whose bathing-master, **Henry Bell**, invented one of the first steamboats, the *Comet*, to transport Glaswegians "doon the watter". Today, Helensburgh is a stop on the route of the paddlesteamer **Waverley** (see p.263), and in addition, there's a passenger-only **ferry** service across the Clyde to Gourock (see p.283); pick up timetables for both services from the **tourist office**, on the ground floor of the old Italianate church tower by the Clyde (daily: July & Aug 10am–6pm; June & Sept 10am–5.30pm; April & May 10am–5pm; early Oct 10am–4.30pm; ⓣ01436/672642).

The inventor of TV, John Logie Baird, was born here, as was Charles Rennie Mackintosh, who in 1902 was commissioned by the Glaswegian publisher Walter Blackie to design **Hill House** on Upper Colquhoun Street (April–Oct daily 1.30–5.30pm; NTS; £6). You may have to join a queue to get in: the house is so popular it can barely cope with the current tide of visitors, and the number of people who can be in the house at any one time is restricted. Without doubt the best surviving example of Mackintosh's domestic architecture, the house is stamped with his very personal interpretation of Art Nouveau, right down to the light fittings, characterized by his sparing use of colour and stylized floral patterns. The effect is occasionally overwhelming – it's difficult to imagine actually living in such an environment – yet it is precisely Mackintosh's attention to detail that makes the place so special. A new exhibition gallery in the east wing of the house displays contemporary domestic design from around Britain. After exploring the house, head for the kitchen quarters, which have been sensitively transformed into a **tearoom**.

Practicalities

Hill House is a good twenty-minute walk up Sinclair Street from Helensburgh Central **train** station, or just five minutes from Helensburgh Upper train station (where trains from Oban and Fort William stop). There's not a lot of choice when it comes to **hotels**: the purpose-built *Commodore*, 112–117 West Clyde St (ⓣ01436/676924; ❹), overlooking the Clyde, is probably the first choice. The town's **B&Bs** are a better bet: *Lethamhill*, 20 West Dhuhill Drive (ⓣ01436/676016, ⓔlethamhill@talk21.com; ❸), is set in the attractive, leafy villa district near Helensburgh Upper, as is the Art Deco *Greenpark* on Charlotte Street near Hill House (ⓣ01436/671545; ❷; April–Oct). Helensburgh isn't short of tearooms and coffee shops; for evening **meals** the choice isn't inspired but you can try the *Commodore Hotel* or the *Upper Crust* Scottish restaurant (ⓣ01436/678035), 88a West Clyde St.

The Clyde valley

The journey southeast of Glasgow into Lanarkshire, while mostly following the course of the Clyde upstream, is dominated by endless suburbs, industrial parks and wide strips of concrete highway. The principal road here is the M74, though you'll have to get off the motorway to find the main points of interest, which tend to lie on or near the banks of the river. Less than ten miles from central Glasgow, **Bothwell Castle** lies about a mile northeast of the **Blantyre** millworkers' tenement in which the explorer David Livingstone was born. Five miles west of Blantyre, on the outskirts of the new town of East Kilbride, the **National Museum of Scottish Country Life**, set on a historic farm, offers a in-depth look at the history of agriculture in Scotland. Back by the Clyde, the valley's largest settlements, **Motherwell** and **Hamilton**, straddle either side of the river and motorway; Motherwell is a depressed town, hard-hit by the closure of its steel works in 1992 and, although Hamilton fancies itself as more upscale, there is little to visit in either place. Sandwiched between the two, the enormous **Strathclyde Country Park** features a huge, glassy, artificial loch, the focus of watersports and various other outdoor pursuits.

From here, the Clyde winds through lush market gardens and orchards that bloom far below the austere lines of **Craignethan Castle**, before passing beneath the sturdy little town of **Lanark**, probably the best base from which to explore the valley. **New Lanark**, on the riverbank, is a remarkable eighteenth-century planned village. Ten miles further upstream, the country town of **Biggar** is a pleasant spot with a surprising number of rather quirky museums, and marks the transition from the industrial central belt to rolling Border country.

Blantyre and around

BLANTYRE, now a colourless suburb of Hamilton, was a remote hamlet based around a mill on the banks of the Clyde when explorer and missionary David Livingstone was born there in 1813. First Bus's **bus** #263 or #267 from

Glasgow (Buchanan St) to Hamilton runs via Blantyre, or there are frequent **trains** from Glasgow Central's lower level. From Blantyre station, a right turn brings you through suburban housing to a quiet country park. The separate tenement block near the river, now painted a brilliant white, has been taken over by the **David Livingstone Centre** (April-Oct Mon–Sat 10am–5.30pm, Sun 12.30–5.30pm; Nov–March Mon–Sat 10am–4.30pm, Sun 12.30–4.30pm; NTS; £3), exploring his life, from his boyhood up until his death in 1873 when he was searching for the source of the Nile. In 1813, the block consisted of 24 one-room tenements, each occupied by an entire family of mill workers. Today, the Livingstone family room shows the claustrophobic conditions under which he was brought up; all the others feature slightly defensive exhibitions on the missionary movement, with tableaux of scenes from his life in Africa, including his "discovery" of the Victoria Falls and the famous meeting of November 10, 1871, with Henry Stanley (who wrote, after having spent ten months searching for the "lost" explorer, that he greeted him with the words, "Dr Livingstone, I presume?"). Also of interest are the displays which indicate the extent to which Livingstone was a much-feted hero of nineteenth-century Britain, and the fact that his belief that "commerce and Christianity" would offer an alternative to slavery and poverty in Africa were behind his intrepid, if somewhat self-concerned, adventures into the Dark Continent.

A mile or so north of Blantyre, **Bothwell Castle** (April–Sept daily 9.30am–6.30pm; Oct–March Sat–Wed 9.30am–4.30pm, Thurs 9.30am–12.30pm, Sun 2–4.30pm; HS; £2) is one of Scotland's most dramatic citadels, its great red sandstone bulk looming high above a loop in the river. The oldest section is the solid donjon, or circular tower, at the western end, built by the Moray family in the late thirteenth century to protect themselves against the English king Edward I during the Scottish wars of independence. Such was the might of the castle that Edward finally succeeded in capturing it only in September 1301, after ordering the construction and deployment of a massive siege engine, wheeled in from Glasgow in order to lob huge stones at the castle walls. Over the next two centuries, the castle changed hands numerous times and was added to by each successive owner, with the last section, the Great Hall, overlooking the grassy inner courtyard. Despite its jigsaw construction, today the overwhelming impression is of the near-impenetrable strength of the castle, its solid red towers – whose walls stand almost sixteen feet thick in places – holding firm centuries after their construction. First Bus operates **bus** #255 from Glasgow (Buchanan St) to Hamilton, which will drop you off on the Bothwell Road near the castle entrance. By car, it is best approached from the B7071 Bothwell–Uddingston road.

National Museum of Scottish Country Life

On the edge of **EAST KILBRIDE** new town, five miles west of Blantyre and seven miles southeast of Glasgow centre, the **National Museum of Scottish Country Life** (daily 10am–5pm; NTS; £3), one of six national museums, is a slightly unexpected union of historic farm and modern museum. The site of the museum, **Kittochside**, is a 170-acre farm which had formerly been in the hands of the same family for ten generations, spanning four centuries of changing land use and agricultural development. Crucially, the land here was never subject to the intensive farming which came to dominate farming in Britain after World War II, and part of the function of the museum is to keep Kittochside as a working farm where traditional methods of farming can be observed.

The custom-built, £6-million museum building on the edge of the farm was opened in 2001, and while it has all the charm of a small factory from the outside, the interior uses space and light creatively. The exhibition has three principal sections: the **Land Gallery** is concerned with how Scots have used the land over centuries, and how the landscape has changed as a result; the **People Gallery** looks at the way of life for farmers and their families; and the **Tools Gallery**, occupying the large central hall, displays all kinds of farm equipment from early ploughs to a combine harvester. More of these are parked up in a downstairs store, and there's also a room full of tractors of various vintages.

What really makes the museum, however, is its contextual setting. A tractor and trailer shuttles visitors the half-mile up to the eighteenth-century **farmhouse** and its steading, still in daily use for hand-milking cows and, in season, threshing grain. You can wander round the farmhouse, furnished much as it would have been in the 1950s, the crucial decade that the farm as a whole is meant to capture, just before traditional methods using horses and hand-tools were replaced by tractors and mechanization. There are **paths** leading from the farmhouse around the surrounding fields, and you're encouraged to wander along these, not just to get a sense of the wider farm, but also to see and experience the farm in use. At different times of year different activities, from ploughing to harvesting, will be taking place: a board in the exhibition building should advertise what's going on that day.

Transport isn't straightforward. If you don't have your own vehicle, aim for East Kilbride by **bus** #31 from Glasgow's St Enoch Centre or #205 from Blantyre shopping centre, or **train** from Glasgow Central, and then take a taxi for the final three miles to the museum.

Hamilton and around

Although the town of **HAMILTON**, a mile upstream from Blantyre, has little to offer, it lies under the watchful gaze of an old hunting lodge built in 1732 for the aristocratic Hamilton family. Designed by Scots architect William Adam, this building is the centrepiece of **Chatelherault Park** (Mon–Sat 10am–5pm, Sun noon–5pm; park open until 9pm; free), a pleasant area with walks that follow the Avon water and wind through the surrounding countryside, past the ruins of Cadzow Castle and some 600-year-old oaks. Frequent **trains** leave Glasgow Central's lower level for Hamilton via Blantyre, and there's also express **bus** #X1 to Hamilton from Glasgow Buchanan St. Bus #253 or #254 from Hamilton Central station stops at the park entrance.

Once known as the "Steelopolis" of Scotland, the small town of **MOTHERWELL**, separated from Hamilton by the river and motorway, is a fairly uninspiring place, with the exception of the informative **Motherwell Heritage Centre** (Wed–Sat 10am–5pm, Thurs until 7pm, Sun noon–5pm; free), looming above the station on the High Road. The foyer holds changing exhibitions on local themes, while the multimedia exhibition takes you through the history of the town: reconstructed streets, cinemas and exhibits document the lives of the local community, and the future of Motherwell is explored with optimism despite widespread unemployment. On the upper floor is a local history lab, and from the top of the glass tower stretch spectacular views across Lanarkshire.

Craignethan Castle

The section of the Clyde Valley southeast from Hamilton to Lanark has become appropriately known as "Greenhouse Glen", where the winding road, lined with small stone villages and inordinate numbers of garden centres, gives occasional glimpses of the river through the trees. Buses #17 and #217 from

Hamilton and Lanark stop off at **CROSSFORD**, five miles northwest of Lanark, where the River Nethan joins the Clyde. From here, to reach the gaunt clifftop ruins of **Craignethan Castle** (April–Sept daily 9.30am–6.30pm; Oct & Nov Mon–Wed & Sat 9.30am–4.30pm, Thurs 9.30am–12.30pm, Sun 2–4.30pm; HS; £2), you can either climb a difficult mile up through the wooded Nethan valley or, if driving, take the tortuous three-mile signposted route. Craignethan was the last major castle to be built in Scotland, constructed in 1530 by Sir James Hamilton of Finnart, Master of Works to James V. Hamilton, inspired by new styles of artillery fortification in Italy, built a unique *caponier*, a dank vault wedged into the dry moat between the two sections of the castle. From here, defenders could spray the ditch with small-arms fire from behind the safety of walls five feet thick. It was from Craignethan that Mary, Queen of Scots left on May 13, 1568, ultimately for defeat at Langside, followed by exile and imprisonment in England. The castle, like so many others in Scotland, is said to be inhabited by her ghost, as her stay at Craignethan was probably the last time she was ever amongst true friends. Craignethan certainly has a spooky quality about it, its stillness interrupted only by the shriek of circling crows. The most intact parts of the castle are the gloomy *caponier* and the musty cellars underneath the vast main tower, from which gun holders still protrude.

Lanark and New Lanark

The neat little market town of **LANARK** is an old and distinguished burgh, sitting in the purple hills high above the River Clyde, its rooftops and spires visible for miles around. Beyond the **world's oldest bell**, cast in 1130 and visible in the Georgian Church of St Nicholas, there's little to see in town unless you around during the lively **Lanimer** celebrations in early June, one of Scotland's oldest ceremonies of riding the marches or boundaries, which goes back to 1140. Most people head straight on to the village of **NEW LANARK** (Ⓦ www.newlanark.org), a mile below the main town on Braxfield Road, whose importance as a centre of social and industrial innovation has recently been recognized by UNESCO, who included it on their list of World Heritage Sites.

Although New Lanark is served by an hourly **bus** from Lanark train station, it's well worth the steep downhill walk to get there. The first sight of the village, hidden away down in the gorge, is unforgettable: large broken curving walls of honeyed warehouses and tenements, built in Palladian style, are lined up along the turbulent river's edge. The community was founded by David Dale and Richard Arkwright in 1785 to harness the power of the Clyde waterfalls in their cotton-spinning industry, but it was Dale's son-in-law, Robert Owen, who revolutionized the social side of the experiment in 1798, creating a "village of unity". Believing the welfare of the workers to be crucial to industrial success, Owen built adult educational facilities, the world's first day nursery and playground, and schools in which dancing and music were obligatory and there was no punishment or reward.

While you're free to wander around the village, which rather unexpectedly for such a historical site is still partially residential, to get into any of the **exhibitions** (all daily 11am–5pm) you need to buy a passport ticket (£4.75; various discount tickets are available, including an all-in ticket covering admission and the return train and bus trip from Glasgow). The Neoclassical building at the heart of the village was opened by Owen in 1816 under the utopian title of **The Institute for the Formation of Character**. With a library, chapel and dance hall, the Institute became the main focus of the community, and

(every 30min; 40min); Hamilton (every 30min; 25min); Kilmarnock (hourly; 40min); Lanark (Mon–Sat hourly; 50min); Largs (hourly; 1hr); London (10 daily; 5hr 45min); Manchester (1 daily; 3hr 50min); Motherwell (every 20min; 30min); Newcastle-upon-Tyne (8 daily; 2hr 30min); Paisley (every 15min; 10min); Port Glasgow (every 15min; 30min); Queen's Park (every 15min; 6min); Rutherglen (every 20min; 10min); Stranraer (6 daily; 2hr 10min); Wemyss Bay (hourly; 55min); York (7 daily; 3hr 30min).

Glasgow Queen St to: Aberdeen (hourly; 2hr 35min); Aviemore (3 daily; 2hr 40min); Balloch (Mon–Sat every 30min; 45min); Dumbarton (every 20min; 25min); Dundee (hourly; 1hr 20min); Edinburgh (every 15min; 50min); Fort William (3 daily; 3hr 40min); Helensburgh (every 30min; 45min); Inverness (3 daily; 3hr 25min); Mallaig (3 daily; 5hr 15min); Milngavie (every 30min; 22min); Oban (3 daily; 3hr); Perth (hourly; 1hr); Springburn (every 30min; 13min); Stirling (hourly; 30min).

Buses

Glasgow Buchanan St to: Aberdeen (20 daily; 4hr 15min); Aviemore (hourly; 3hr 30min); Campbeltown (4 daily; 4hr 20min); Dundee (hourly; 2hr 15min); Edinburgh (every 15min; 1hr 10min); Fort William (4 daily; 3hr); Glen Coe (4 daily; 2hr 30min); Inverness (hourly; 4–5hr); Kyle of Lochalsh (3 daily; 5hr); Lochgilphead (3 daily; 2hr 40min); Loch Lomond (hourly; 45min); London (5 daily; 7hr 30min); Newcastle-upon-Tyne (2 daily; 4hr); Oban (4 daily; 3hr); Perth (hourly; 1hr 35min); Pitlochry (hourly; 2hr 20min); Portree (3 daily; 6hr); Stirling (hourly; 45min); York (1 daily; 6hr 30min).

Flights

Glasgow International to: Barra (Mon–Fri 2 daily; 1hr 5min); Dublin (4 daily; 1hr); Islay (Mon–Fri 2 daily; 40min); Kirkwall (Mon–Sat 1 daily; 2hr); Lerwick (Mon–Fri 2 daily, Sat & Sun 1 daily; 2hr 20min); London City (Mon–Fri 6 daily, Sun 1 daily; 1hr 30min); London Gatwick (Mon–Fri 6 daily, Sat & Sun 4 daily; 1hr 30min); London Heathrow (Mon–Fri 20 daily, Sat & Sun 12 daily; 1hr 30min); London Luton (Mon–Fri 7 daily, Sat 3 daily, Sun 4 daily; 1hr 15min); London Stansted (Mon–Fri 4 daily, Sat 3 daily, Sun 4 daily; 1hr 30min); Stornoway (Mon–Sat 2 daily; 1hr).

Glasgow Prestwick to: Dublin (Mon–Fri 3 daily, Sat & Sun 2 daily; 45min); London Stansted (Mon–Fri 8 daily, Sat & Sun 6 daily; 1hr 10min).

Central Scotland

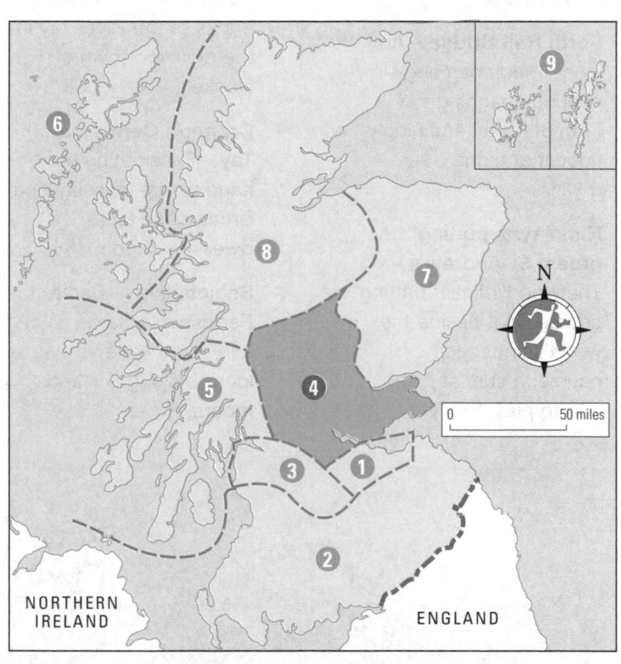

CHAPTER 4

Highlights

* **Stirling Castle** – Impregnable, explorable and resonant with history. If you see only one castle in Scotland, make it this one. See p.302
* **The Trossachs** – Pocket Highlands with shining lochs, wooded glens and noble peaks. See p.319
* **Forth Rail Bridge** – An icon of Victorian engineering spanning the Firth of Forth, stunningly floodlit at night. See p.331
* **Himalayas putting green, St Andrew's** – The world's finest putting course right beside the world's finest golf course; a snip at just 80p to play. See p.342
* **The East Neuk** – Buy freshly cooked lobster at Crail's historic stone harbour or dine in style at the *Cellar* restaurant in the fishing town of Anstruther. See p.345
* **Folk music** – Join in a session at *Maclean's Real Music Bar* by the banks of the River Tay in the dignified town of Dunkeld. See p.358
* **Crannog Centre, Loch Tay** – Fascinating heritage centre investigating Bronze Age lake dwellings. See p.360
* **Schiehallion** – Scale Perthshire's "fairy mountain" for the views over lochs, hills, glens and moors. See p.363

Central Scotland

Central Scotland, the strip of mainland north of the densely populated Glasgow–Edinburgh axis and south of the main swathe of Highlands, is an accessible, popular and richly varied region. The Highland Boundary Fault, the dramatic physical divide running southwest-to-northeast across the region, has rendered central Scotland the main stage from medieval to modern times for some of the most important events in Scottish history. Today the landscape is not only littered with remnants of the past – well-preserved medieval towns and castles, royal residences and battle sites – but also coloured by the many romantic myths and legends that have grown up around it.

Stirling, its imposing castle perched high above the town, was historically the most important bridging point across the River Forth, and from the castle battlements you can see the site of two of Scotland's most famous battlefield victories during the Wars of Independence (1296–1328). Stirling's strategic location can be seen in the settlements which surround it: to the south on the road to Edinburgh lies **Falkirk**, its industrial heritage now enlivened by the extraordinary Falkirk Wheel which transfers boats between two recently restored canals; while to the west and north lie attractive country villages and fertile farmland. Beyond are the fabled mountains, glens, lochs and forests of the **Trossachs**, stretching west from **Callander** to Loch Lomond. The geography and history of the Trossachs caught the imagination of **Sir Walter Scott**, whose poetic idolization of the region inspired a flood of trippers which has hardly been stemmed since. Often conveniently described as the Highlands-in-miniature, the area does indeed offer a taste of archetypal Scottish scenery.

Popular for walking and, in particular, cycling, much of the Trossachs, together with the attractive islands and "bonnie banks" of **Loch Lomond**, form part of Scotland's first National Park, established in 2001.

Accommodation price codes

Throughout this book, accommodation **prices** have been graded with the codes below, corresponding to the cost of the least expensive double room in high season. Price codes are not given for **campsites**, most of which charge less than £10 per person. Almost all **hostels** and **bunkhouses** charge between £8 and £12 per person per night; the few exceptions to this rule have the prices quoted in the text. For a full account of these codes, see p.28.

❶ under £40	❹ £60–70	❼ £110–150
❷ £40–50	❺ £70–90	❽ £150–200
❸ £50–60	❻ £90–110	❾ £200 and over

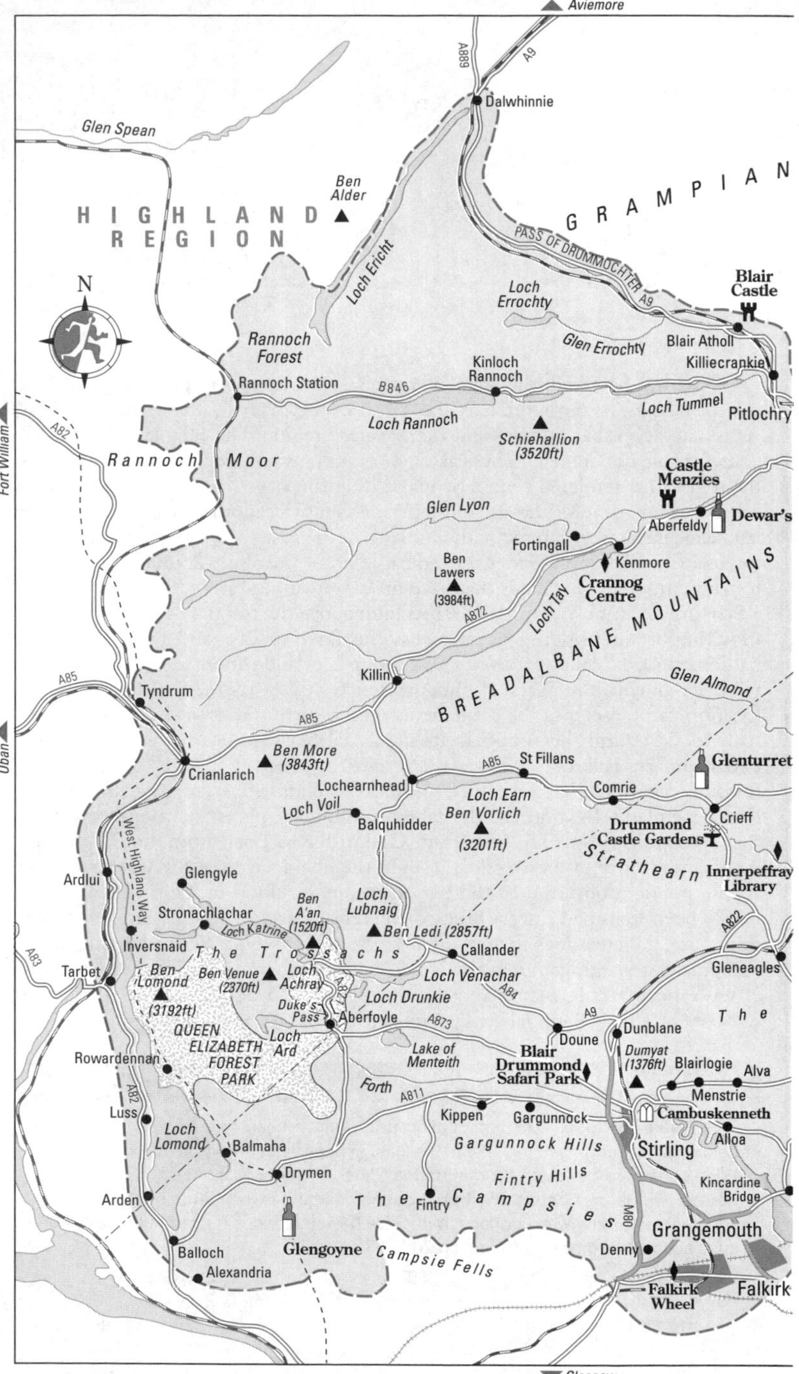
Aviemore
A889
A9
Dalwhinnie
Glen Spean
GRAMPIAN
Ben Alder
HIGHLAND REGION
PASS OF DRUMMOCHTER
Loch Ericht
Loch Errochty
Blair Castle
A9
Glen Errochty
Blair Atholl
Rannoch Forest
Kinloch Rannoch
Killiecrankie
Rannoch Station
B846
Loch Tummel
Pitlochry
Fort William
A82
Loch Rannoch
Schiehallion (3520ft)
Rannoch Moor
Castle Menzies
Glen Lyon
Aberfeldy
Dewar's
Fortingall
Kenmore
Ben Lawers (3984ft)
Crannog Centre
Loch Tay
A872
BREADALBANE MOUNTAINS
Killin
Glen Almond
A85
Tyndrum
A85
Oban
Ben More (3843ft)
Crianlarich
A85
St Fillans
Glenturret
Lochearnhead
Loch Earn
Comrie
Loch Voil
Ben Vorlich (3201ft)
Balquhidder
Crieff
Drummond Castle Gardens
West Highland Way
Strathearn
Innerpeffray Library
Ardlui
Glengyle
Ben A'an (1520ft)
Loch Lubnaig
Stronachlachar
Loch Katrine
Ben Ledi (2857ft)
A822
Inversnaid
The Trossachs
Callander
Gleneagles
A83
Tarbet
Ben Lomond (3192ft)
Ben Venue (2370ft)
Loch Achray
A821
Loch Venachar
Loch Drunkie
A84
Duke's Pass
Aberfoyle
A873
A9
The
QUEEN ELIZABETH FOREST PARK
Loch Ard
Dunblane
Doune
Lake of Menteith
Blair Drummond Safari Park
Rowardennan
Dumyat (1376ft)
Blairlogie
Alva
A82
Forth
A811
Menstrie
Luss
Kippen
Gargunnock
Cambuskenneth
Loch Lomond
Balmaha
Gargunnock Hills
Stirling
Alloa
Drymen
Fintry Hills
Kincardine Bridge
Arden
The Campsies
Fintry
M80
Grangemouth
Glengoyne
Campsie Fells
Balloch
Denny
Alexandria
Falkirk Wheel
Falkirk
Glasgow

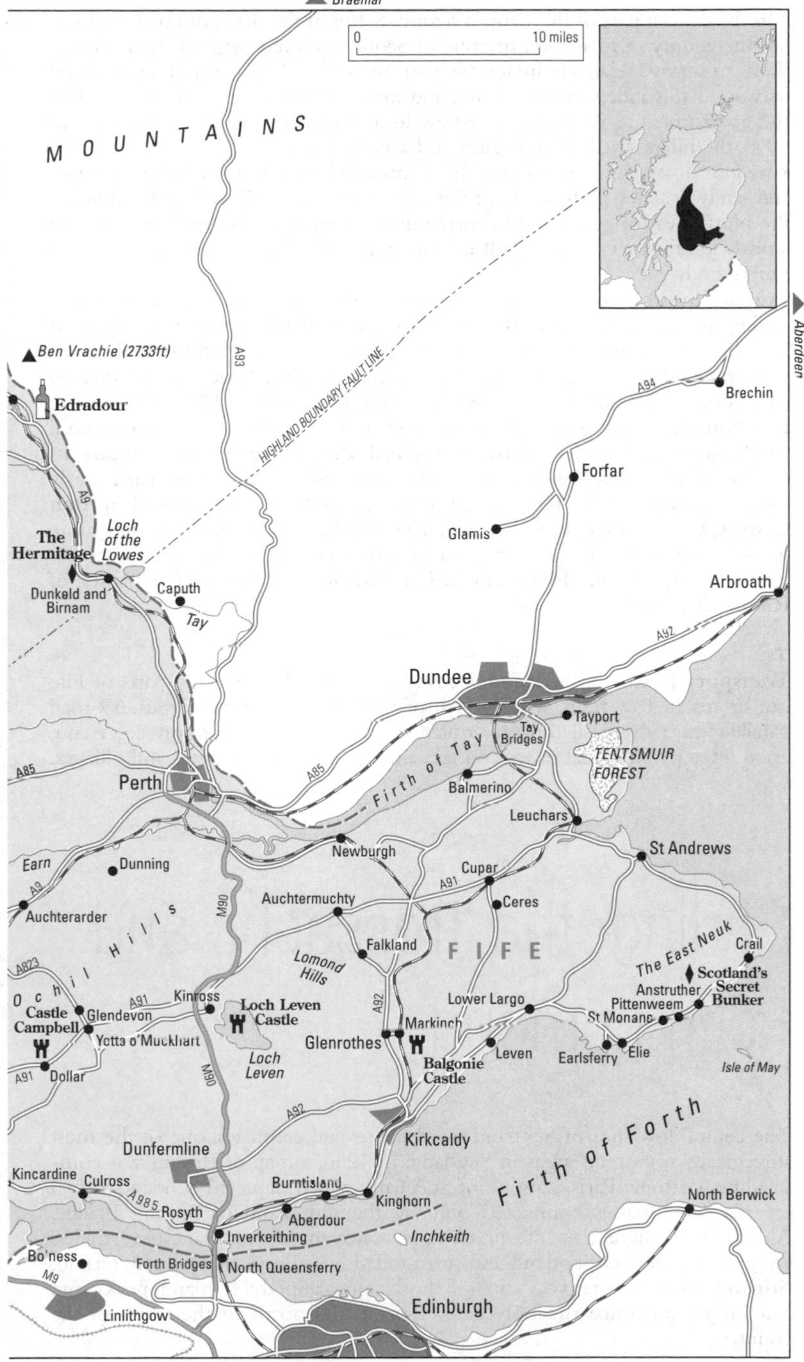
Braemar
0
10 miles
MOUNTAINS
Ben Vrachie (2733ft)
Edradour
A93
HIGHLAND BOUNDARY FAULT LINE
Aberdeen
A94
Brechin
Forfar
Glamis
A9
The Hermitage
Loch of the Lowes
Dunkeld and Birnam
Caputh
Tay
Arbroath
A92
Dundee
Tayport
Tay Bridges
TENTSMUIR FOREST
A85
Perth
A85
Firth of Tay
Balmerino
Leuchars
Newburgh
St Andrews
Earn
Dunning
Cupar
A91
A9
M90
Auchtermuchty
Ceres
Auchterarder
Ochil Hills
Falkland
FIFE
The East Neuk
Crail
Lomond Hills
Scotland's Secret Bunker
A823
Anstruther
Pittenweem
Kinross
Loch Leven Castle
A91
A92
Lower Largo
St Monans
Castle Campbell
Glendevon
Markinch
Yetts o'Muckhart
Glenrothes
Leven
Earlsferry
Elie
Loch Leven
Balgonie Castle
Isle of May
A91
Dollar
M90
A92
Firth of Forth
Kirkcaldy
Dunfermline
Kincardine
Culross
Burntisland
Kinghorn
North Berwick
A985
Rosyth
Aberdour
Inverkeithing
Inchkeith
Bo'ness
Forth Bridges
North Queensferry
M9
Edinburgh
Linlithgow

4 CENTRAL SCOTLAND

In the eastern part of this central region, between the firths of Forth and Tay, lies the county of **Fife**, the only one of Scotland's seven original Pictish kingdoms to survive relatively intact. Neither Norse nor Norman influence found its way to this independent corner, and nine and a half centuries later, when the government at Westminster redrew local boundaries in 1975 and again in 1995, the Fifers stuck to their guns and successfully opposed any changes. The kingdom boasts a fascinating coastline sprinkled with historic fishing villages and sandy beaches, particularly in the area known as the **East Neuk**, while on the North Sea fringe lies the historic university town of **St Andrews**, famous worldwide for its venerable golf courses and as the home of the game's governing body.

Occupying the same strategic position at the mouth of the River Tay as Stirling holds on the Forth, the ancient town of **Perth** has as much claim as anywhere to be the gateway to the Highlands. At nearby **Scone**, Kenneth Macalpine established the capital of the kingdom of the Scots and the Picts in 846. When this settlement was washed away by floods in 1210, William the Lion founded Perth as a royal burgh and it stood as Scotland's capital until 1452. North and west of Perth, **Highland Perthshire** begins to weave its charms: mighty woodlands blend with gorgeously rich scenery, particularly along the banks of the River Tay, leading to **Loch Tay**, overlooked by **Ben Lawers**, the area's tallest peak. Further north, the countryside becomes more sparsely populated and more spectacular, with some wonderful walking country, especially around **Pitlochry**, **Blair Atholl** and the wild expanses of **Rannoch Moor** to the west.

Transport practicalities

Transport in Central Scotland is easy. Stirling, Perth and many parts of Fife can be reached by train, while north of Perth the fast, if dangerous, A9 road parallels the railway all the way north to Inverness. Where trains don't run, good intercity and local buses connect almost all the main towns and villages.

Stirling, the Trossachs and Loch Lomond

The central lowlands of Scotland were, for several centuries, one of the most strategically important areas in Scotland. In 1250, a map of Britain was compiled by Matthew Paris, a monk of St Albans, which depicted Scotland as two separate land masses connected only by the thin band of Stirling Bridge. Although this figurative interpretation was not strictly accurate, nevertheless lying at the heart of Scotland and surrounded by inhospitable marshy terrain, **Stirling**, from where you can see both snowcapped Highland peaks and Edinburgh, was once the only gateway from the north to the south of the country.

Today the town is a tourist attraction in itself, its fine **castle** the perfect vantage point to look far out across the region. The castle rock plunges down to the **Carse of Stirling**, the flat plain extending west, out of which rise the little-visited **Campsie Fells** to the south and the much busier **Trossachs** hills to the north. East, the gentler **Ochil Hills** run towards Loch Leven on the edge of the kingdom of Fife. From the castle's heights in Stirling you can trace the winding course of the once-navigable **Forth River**, which links the industrial towns of Grangemouth and **Falkirk** with the rural west, and identify the great blunt tower of **Cambuskenneth Abbey** and the unmistakable **Wallace Monument**, the nation's most prominent tribute to "Braveheart" William Wallace.

Alongside the beauty of the hills and villages of the region, there's a range of other diversions within an hour's drive of Stirling, from the wonderful island refuges of **Inchmahome** in the Lake of Menteith and **Loch Leven Castle** by Kinross, to the atmospheric **Castle Campbell** in the Ochil Hills. Visits can be combined with a range of outdoor activities; the area is traversed by the **Glasgow–Loch Lomond–Killin cycleway**, well-managed forest tracks are ideal for mountain biking, the hills of the Trossachs provide great walking country, while the **West Highland Way**, Scotland premier long-distance footpath, winds along the length of Loch Lomond up to Fort William in the Highlands.

Stirling

Straddling the River Forth a few miles upstream from the estuary at Kincardine, **STIRLING** appears at first glance like a smaller version of Edinburgh. With its crag-top castle, steep, cobbled streets and mixed community of locals, students and tourists, it's an appealing place, though it lacks the cosmopolitan edge of its near neighbours Edinburgh and Glasgow.

Stirling was the scene of some of the most significant developments in the evolution of the Scottish nation. It was here that the Scots under William Wallace defeated the English at the **Battle of Stirling Bridge** in 1297, only to fight – and win again – under Robert the Bruce just a couple of miles away at the **Battle of Bannockburn** in 1314. Stirling enjoyed its golden age in the fifteenth to seventeenth centuries, most notably when its castle was the favoured residence of the Stuart monarchy and the setting for the coronation in 1543 of the young Mary, future Queen of Scots. By the early eighteenth century the town was again besieged, its location being of strategic importance during the Jacobite rebellions of 1715 and 1745.

Today Stirling is known for its **castle** – as atmospheric and explorable as Edinburgh's – and the lofty **Wallace Monument**, a mammoth Victorian monolith high on Abbey Craig to the northeast which has become a place of pilgrimage for admirers both of William Wallace and of Mel Gibson's Oscar-winning film epic *Braveheart*, based on Wallace.

Arrival and information

The **train station** (☎0845/748 4950) is near the centre of town on Station Road, near the **bus station** (☎01324/613777) on Goosecroft Road. To reach the town centre from the train station, walk up Station Road and turn left at the mini-roundabout; from the bus station cut through the Thistle Shopping Centre opposite to reach the main drag, Port Street.

STIRLING

ACCOMMODATION

Heatherdale	2
Highland Hotel	6
No. 10	9
Park Lodge	10
Portcullis	3
Ravenscroft	8
SYHA Hostel	4
Whitegables	1
Willy Wallace	5
XI Victoria Sq	7

RESTAURANTS & CAFÉS

Darnley Coffee House	D
East India Club	A
Hermann's	B
Olivia's	E
Yill & Kail	C

Stirling's **tourist office** is in the heart of the town centre at 41 Dumbarton Rd (July & Aug Mon–Sat 9am–7.30pm, Sun 9.30am–6.30pm; June & Sept Mon–Sat 9am–6pm, Sun 10am–4pm; rest of year Mon–Sat 10am–5pm; ⓣ01786/475019, ⓦwww.scottish.heartlands.org). This is also the main office for Loch Lomond and the Trossachs, and has a wide range of books, maps and leaflets, as well as an accommodation-booking service. Because of Stirling's compact size – barely five miles from the centre to the outermost fringes – sightseeing is best done **on foot**, though to avoid the steep hills you can take the hop-on hop-off **open-top bus tours** (April–Sept 10am–5pm; £6.50) run by Guide Friday, whose circular route takes in the castle, Wallace Monument, university and the bus and train stations. Actor-led **ghost walks** leave from the Old Town Jail on summer evenings; for details contact the tourist office or the Old Town Jail itself (see opposite).

Accommodation

Between May and October, you'll need to book your **accommodation** as far in advance as possible. A good area to look in is **King's Park**, immediately south of the tourist office, an opulent Victorian suburb built for Glasgow industrialists and merchants and composed of tree-lined avenues and splendid villas, some of them wonderfully Italianate with towers and balconies. There is a high concentration of **B&Bs** on Causewayhead Road which leads to the university north of the centre.

Hotels and B&Bs

Heatherdale 2 Dumyat Rd ⓣ01786/473574, ⓔB&B@heatherdale.f9.co.uk. Small family-run B&B located near the Wallace Monument, castle and university. ❷

Highland Hotel Spittal St ⓣ01786/272727, ⓔandrews@scottishhighlandhotels.co.uk. Upmarket if rather pretentiously genteel hotel in a handsome Victorian Gothic building that once housed Stirling High School. It features comfortable rooms, good leisure facilities – including a pretty pool with saunas – and two restaurants. The location, in the old town just 500 yards from the castle, is excellent. ❼

No. 10 10 Gladstone Place ⓣ01786/472681, ⓦwww.cameron-10.co.uk. Modernized Victorian home providing friendly and pleasant B&B accommodation. ❷

Park Lodge Hotel 32 Park Terrace ⓣ01786/474862, ⓦwww.parklodge.net. Magnificently sited and luxurious, even if the décor is a bit over the top. Overlooks the park and castle and includes the well-established Heritage restaurant. ❺

The Portcullis Castle Wynd ⓣ01786/472290, ⓦwww.theportcullishotel.com. Small, traditional hotel in an imposing two-hundred-year-old building that's recently been refurbished, in a dramatic location adjacent to the castle at the top of the town. ❺

Ravenscroft 21 Clarendon Place ⓣ01786/473815, ⓦwww.ravenscroft.stirling.co.uk. A lovely Victorian house offering B&B with antiques throughout, stripped pine floors and views to the castle. ❷

Whitegables 112 Causewayhead Rd ⓣ01786/479830. A friendly B&B with TVs in all the rooms and excellent breakfasts. ❷

XI Victoria Square 11 Victoria Sq ⓣ01786/475545, ⓦwww.xivictoriasquare.com. A slightly more upmarket B&B with designer rooms, sumptuous breakfasts and great views of the old town. ❹

Hostel, campsite and campus accommodation

Located a hundred yards from the station in an old Victorian building, the liveliest budget option is the **Willy Wallace Independent Hostel**, 77 Murray Place (ⓣ01786/446773, ⓦwww.willywallace.f9.co.uk), a welcoming, friendly place with a big, bright common room, six dorms, a double and a twin. At the top of the town (a strenuous trek with a backpack) is the SYHA **hostel** (ⓣ01786/473442), in a converted church on St John Street with an impressive 1824 Palladian facade. It's modern and a little lacking in character; all rooms have showers and toilets en suite, and continental breakfast is included. The high-season price is £13.75 per person. The pleasant *Witches Craig* **campsite** is at Blairlogie, three miles east off the A91 road to St Andrews (ⓣ01786/474947; April–Oct).

There's **campus accommodation** at Stirling University (ⓣ01786/467140; ❸; June–Aug), a couple of miles north of the town centre, served by regular buses #1, #53 and #58 from Murray Place at the end of the main street (last buses around 10.45pm). Also on campus is the new Stirling Management Centre (ⓣ01786/451712; ❺; all year), with luxurious en-suite rooms looking out at the Wallace Monument.

The Town

Stirling evolved from the top down, starting with its castle and gradually spreading south and east onto the low-lying flood plain. At the centre of the original **Old Town**, Broad Street was the main thoroughfare, with St John Street running more or less parallel, and St Mary's Wynd forming part of the original route to Stirling Bridge below. In the eighteenth and nineteenth centuries, as the threat of attack decreased, the centre of commercial life crept down towards the River Forth, with the modern town growing on the edge of the plain over which the castle has traditionally stood guard.

Stirling Castle

Stirling Castle (daily 9.30am–6.30pm; Oct–March closes 5pm; HS; £6.50, includes entry to Argyll's Lodging) must have presented would-be invaders with a formidable challenge. Its impregnability is most daunting when you approach the town from the west, from where the sheer 250ft drop down the side of the crag is most obvious. The rock was first fortified during the Iron Age, though what you see now dates largely from the fifteenth and sixteenth centuries. Built on many levels, the main buildings are interspersed with delightful gardens and patches of lawn, while endless battlements, cannon ports, hidden staircases and other nooks and crannies make it thoroughly explorable and inspiring.

The **visitor centre**, in a whitewashed cottage on one side of the esplanade car park, shows an introductory film giving a potted history of the castle, but the best place to get an impression of its gradual expansion is the **Outer Close**, the first main courtyard beyond the imposing inner gatehouse to the castle. Here you can join a **guided tour** (free), which leaves every half-hour.

Looming over the courtyard is the magnificent **Great Hall**, dating from 1501–3 and used as a barracks by the British army until 1964. The building stands out not just in the courtyard but across Stirling for its controversially bright, creamy yellow cladding, added after the discovery during renovations of a stretch of the original sixteenth-century limewash behind a bricked-up doorway. Inside, the hall has been restored to its original state as the finest medieval secular building in Scotland, complete with five gaping fireplaces and an impressive hammerbeam ceiling of rough-hewn wood. To one side of the Great Hall, displays in the restored castle **kitchens** make a lively attempt to re-create the preparations for the spectacular Renaissance banquet given by Mary, Queen of Scots for the baptism of the future James VI. Along with an audiovisual display describing how delicacies for the feast were procured, plus an abundance of stuffed animals in various stages of preparation (who, we are assured, died natural deaths), the kitchens feature life-size models fussing over *faux* recipe books with such delights as sugar wineglasses, golden steamed custard and dressed peacock.

The exterior of the **Palace**, the largest building in the castle, dates from 1540–42 and is richly decorated with grotesque carved figures and Renaissance sculpture, including, in the left-hand corner, the glaring bearded figure of James V in the dress of a commoner. Inside in the royal apartments are the **Stirling Heads**, 56 elegantly carved oak medallions which once comprised the ceiling of the Presence Chamber, where visitors were presented to royalty. Otherwise the royal apartments are mostly bare, their emptiness emphasizing the fine dimensions and wonderful views. There's an internal courtyard known as the Lion's Den which had a small garden and was used for outdoor theatre, though the name also indicates that it was the likely exercise area of a lion that James V is known to have received as a gift in 1537.

On the opposite side of the Inner Close, the sloping upper courtyard of the castle, the **Chapel Royal** was built in 1594 by James VI for the baptism of his son, to replace an earlier chapel that was deemed insufficiently impressive. The interior is lovely, with a seventeenth-century fresco of elaborate scrolls and patterns. Alongside, the **King's Old Building**, at the highest point in the castle, now houses the museum of the Argyll and Sutherland Highlanders regiment, with its collection of well-polished silver and memorabilia, including a seemingly endless display of Victoria Crosses. While the regiment has a proud military history, the rooms also make an effort to stay up to date, with material relating to the role of the regiment's soldiers in Northern Ireland and the Gulf War. Go through a narrow passageway between the King's Old Building and the Chapel Royal to get to the **Douglas Gardens**, reputedly the place where the eighth Earl of Douglas, suspected of treachery, was thrown to his death by James II in 1452. It's a lovely, quiet corner of the castle, with mature trees and battlements over which there are splendid views of the rising Highlands beyond, as well as a bird's-eye view down to the **King's Knot**, a series of grassed octagonal mounds which in the seventeenth century were planted with box trees and ornamental hedges.

The Old Town

Leaving the castle, head downhill into the old centre of Stirling, fortified behind the massive, whinstone boulders of the **town walls**, built in the mid-sixteenth century and intended to ward off the advances of Henry VIII, who had set his sights on the young Mary, Queen of Scots as a wife for his son, Edward. The walls now constitute some of the best-preserved town defences in Scotland, and can be traced by following the path known as **Back Walk**. This circular walkway was built in the eighteenth century and in the upper reaches encircles the castle, taut along the edge of the crag, offering panoramic views of the surrounding countryside.

Five minutes' walk down the hill from the castle's visitor centre, you'll find **Argyll's Lodging** (daily: April–Sept 9.30am–6pm; Oct–March 9.30am–5pm; HS; £3), a romantic Renaissance mansion built by Sir William Alexander of Menstrie. Inside, an informative exhibition takes you through the history of the building in its various incarnations, from its period as the home of the first Earl of Stirling, Sir William Alexander, and the ninth Earl of Argyll amongst others, to its later uses as military hospital and youth hostel. The oldest part of the building, marked by low ceilings and tiny windows, is the Great Kitchen, whose enormous fireplace comes complete with a special recess for salt, while the Drawing Room, hung with lavishly decorated purple tapestries, contains the ninth earl's imposing chair of state. An adjoining smaller room for his wife, Anna, contains her personal chamber pot, an ornate affair in purple.

Further down Castle Wynd at the top of Broad Street, a richly decorated facade hides the dilapidated **Mar's Wark**, a would-be palace which the first Earl of Mar, Regent of Scotland and hereditary Keeper of Stirling Castle, started in 1570. His dream house was never to be realized, however, for he died two years later and what had been built was left to ruin, its degeneration speeded up by extensive damage during the 1745 Jacobite Rebellion. Behind here is the **Church of the Holy Rude** (May–Sept Mon–Fri 10am–5pm, Sat times vary, Sunday service), a fine medieval structure, the oldest parts of which, including the impressive oak hammerbeam ceiling, date from the early fifteenth century. It's not hard to imagine the ceremony that was held here in 1567 for the coronation of the infant James VI – later the first monarch of the

United Kingdom; the atmospheric graveyard alongside can conjure up ghosts of a different type if you're here to watch the sun set. Just south of the church on the edge of the crag, the grand E-shaped **John Cowane's Hospital** was built as a 1649 almshouse for "decayed [unsuccessful] members of the Guild of Merchants". Above the entrance, John Cowane, the wealthy merchant who founded the hospital, is commemorated in a statue which, it is said, comes alive at Hogmanay.

A short walk down St John Street, a sweeping driveway leads up to the impressive **Old Town Jail** (April–Sept daily 10am–5pm; Oct–March Mon–Sat 10am–5pm, Sat & Sun 11.30am–3pm; £3.95), a formidable building rescued from dereliction in 1992 and superbly refurbished. Tours are brought to life by enthusiastic actors who change costumes and character a number of times, and there's a working example of the dreaded crank, a lever which prisoners had to turn 14,400 times per day for punishment. Take the glass lift up to the prison roof to admire spectacular views across Stirling and the Forth Valley. Opposite the entrance to the Old Town Jail, look out for the **Boy's Club**, a 1929 conversion of the town's old buttermarket, with its encouraging little mottos engraved above the door such as "Keep Smiling" and "Quarrelling is taboo".

Back on the ground, **Broad Street** was the site of the marketplace and centre of the medieval town. Many of its buildings have been restored in recent years, and preservation work continues, most notably at the Tolbooth, originally built in 1705 and used as both a courthouse and prison, and now destined to become a theatre and arts centre. Just past the **Mercat Cross** (the unicorn on top is known, inexplicably, as "the puggy") is **Darnley's House**, at the bottom of Broad Street, where Mary, Queen of Scots' husband is believed to have lodged while she lorded it up in the castle; it now houses a coffee shop (see below).

The Lower Town

The further downhill you go in Stirling's Lower Town, the more recent the buildings become. By the time the two main streets of the old town merge into King Street, austere Victorian facades block the sun from the cobbled road. Stirling's main **shopping** area is down here, along Port Street and Murray Place. The only other sight of note within the centre is the **Smith Art Gallery and Museum** (Tues–Sat 10am–5pm, Sun 2–5pm; free), a short walk west up Dumbarton Road near the King's Knot. Founded in 1874 with a legacy from local painter and collector Thomas Stuart Smith, it houses "The Stirling Story", a reasonably entertaining whirl through the history of the town, balancing out the stories of kings and queens with more social and domestic history. Among the exhibits is the world's oldest known football, made out of a pig's bladder; it was found in the rafters of the Queen's Chamber in the castle and is thought to date from the 1540s. The small art gallery includes changing displays of arts and crafts, contemporary art and photography.

The fifteenth-century **Old Bridge** over the Forth lies to the north on the edge of the town centre (a 20min walk from Murray Place). Although once the most important river crossing in Scotland – the lowest bridging point on the Forth until the new bridge was built in 1831 – it now stands virtually forgotten, an incidental reminder of Stirling's former importance. An earlier wooden **bridge** nearby, no trace of which survives, was the focus of the Battle of Stirling Bridge in 1297, where William Wallace defeated the English.

Eating

For **eating**, the three-storey *Darnley Coffee House* on Bow Street (the continuation of Broad Street) has plenty of Old Town atmosphere and serves reasonably priced lunches and teas in an impressive barrel-vaulted interior. More upmarket is *Hermann's* in the historic Mar Place House at the top of Broad St (☎01786/450632); its downstairs brasserie is open at lunch time and their Austrian–Scottish evening main courses start around £10. Across the road, the *Yill & Kail*, 39 Broad St, has a relaxed bar downstairs and a restaurant upstairs, seving a broad range of moderately priced Scottish food.

In town, *Olivia's*, 5 Baker St (☎01786/446277), offers modern Scottish cooking in a reasonably smart but informal restaurant. At the *East India Company*, 7 Viewfield Place (☎01786/471330), a five-minute walk from the centre, you can enjoy fabulous Indian food, Raj-style decor, and the friendliest service in town; their buffet (Sun–Thurs) costs around £10 for as much as you can eat.

Nightlife and entertainment

Nightlife in Stirling revolves around **pubs** and **bars** and is dominated by the student population. The lively *Barnton Bar and Bistro*, on Barnton Street, serves a good selection of beers and food in a setting of wrought-iron and marble tables. Try to visit in the morning (from 10.30am) to sample one of their huge breakfasts. Also popular with students is the real ale at the *Settle Inn*, 91 St Mary's Wynd, Stirling's oldest alehouse, built in 1733; nearby at no. 73, *Whistlebinkies* has regular folk music sessions and reasonable bar meals. *Ginger Bar Café* in an old bank at 61 King St is a stylish modern place where you can find bistro snacks, coffees and pre-club drinks.

If you want to carry on after the pubs close, you could try *The Yard*, a mainstream **nightclub** on the Back Walk which gets particularly busy at weekends, or *Fubars* in Murray Place which is known for its lively student nights. The larger Albert Hall is the usual venue for classical and small pop/rock **concerts**, and recently summer rock concerts have been held on the castle esplanade; contact the tourist office for details. The Cowane Theatre on Cowane Street has regular comedy nights mixed in with folk music.

The main venue for **theatre** and **film** is the excellent MacRobert Arts Centre (☎01786/461081) on the university campus (see below), which shows a good selection of drama plus mainstream and art-house films.

Stirling University and around

North of Stirling, a ten-minute walk from the fine Victorian spa town of **BRIDGE OF ALLAN**, lies **Stirling University**, until 1992 (when all British colleges and polytechnics acquired university status), the youngest university in Scotland and once one of the most radical. Its buildings exemplifies successful 1960s architecture, and the landscaped grounds are beautiful – resplendent with daffodils in spring, rhododendrons along the sides of the artificial Airthrey Loch in summer, and the rich colours of the Ochil Hills as a backdrop in autumn. Stranded on the northern edge of the loch, **Airthrey Castle** is a prepossessing late-eighteenth-century affair built by Robert Adam, now housing CELT (the Centre for English Language Teaching). The Pathfoot building displays in its main corridor a rich collection of portraits and landscapes by J.D. Fergusson (see p.351), given to the university by his widow. Frequent **buses** run to the university and Wallace Monument from Murray Place in Stirling, including the Guide Friday tour and local buses #62 and #63.

The National Wallace Monument

Overlooking the university one mile to the southwest is the prominent **National Wallace Monument** (daily: July & Aug 9.30am–6.30pm; June 10am–6pm; March–May, Sept & Oct 10am–5pm; Nov–Feb 10.30am–4pm; £3.95), a freestanding, five-storey tower built in the 1860s as a tribute to Sir William Wallace, the freedom fighter who led Scottish resistance to Edward I, the "Hammer of the Scots", in the late thirteenth century. A hero to generations of Scots, Wallace shot to international fame on the back of his depiction by Mel Gibson in the epic movie *Braveheart*. Though derided by critics for its historical inaccuracies the film was hugely popular not just in Scotland but around the world, and with the general lack of historic buildings closely associated with Wallace, the monument has become a focus for Wallace (and *Braveheart*) fans. The crag on which it is set was the scene of Wallace's greatest victory, when he sent his troops charging down the hillside onto the plain to defeat the English at the Battle of Stirling Bridge in 1297. Exhibits inside the tower include Wallace's long steel sword and the Hall of (Scottish) Heroes, a row of stern white marble busts featuring John Knox and Adam Smith, as well as a life-size "talking" model of Wallace, who tells visitors about his preparations for the battle. If you can manage the climb – up 246 spiral steps – there are superb views across to Fife and Ben Lomond from the top of the 220ft tower.

A shuttle bus runs, for a small charge, every 15 minutes from the base of the hill to the tower. If, however, you use the car park, you can't fail to notice a second, more recent tribute to Wallace: a statue which bears a striking resemblance to Mel Gibson (who, critics record with glee, struggled to match Wallace's towering six-foot-six frame).

Cambuskenneth and Sheriffmuir

A woodland path weaves its way for about a mile south from the Wallace monument to the ruins of **Cambuskenneth Abbey**, located roughly a mile east of Stirling train station (ruins April–Sept; grounds all year; HS; free). Founded in 1147 by David I on the site of an Augustinian settlement, the abbey is distinguished by its early fourteenth-century bell tower, though there's little else to see there now. Its history, however, makes it worth a brief look: the Scots parliament met here in 1326 to pledge allegiance to Robert the Bruce's son David, and James III (1451–88) and his wife, Queen Margaret of Denmark, are both buried in the grounds, their graves marked by a nineteenth-century monument erected at the insistence of Queen Victoria.

Above the university on the edge of the Ochil Hills (see p.311) are the wild moors of **Sheriffmuir**, where the Earl of Mar fought the crown forces in 1715. Access to the area is by car up steep single-track roads, but the splendid hills are worth the effort. In summer you can take "hacks" from the **Drumbrae Farm Riding Centre** (Ⓣ01786/832247), whose ponies are plump and reliable. The 17th-century *Sheriffmuir Inn* (Ⓣ01786/823285, Ⓔres@bouzy-rouge.com; ⑤), sitting in glorious isolation (follow the signs from Dunblane), is unexpectedly funky inside, with the *Bouzy Rouge* restaurant serving interesting modern Scottish food. You can also stay here.

Bannockburn

A couple of miles south of Stirling centre, all but surrounded by suburban housing, the **Bannockburn Heritage Centre** (daily: April–Oct 10am–5.30pm; March, Nov & Dec 11am–4pm; NTS; £2.50) commemorates the most famous battle in Scottish history, when King Robert the Bruce won his mighty victory over the English at the **Battle of Bannockburn** on June 24, 1314. It was this battle, the climax of the Wars of Independence, which united the Scots under Bruce and led to independence under the Declaration of Arbroath (1320) and the Treaty of Northampton (1328).

The centre shows an audiovisual presentation on the battle and the background to it, highlighting the brilliantly innovative tactics Bruce employed in mustering his army to defeat a much larger English force. Outside, a concrete rotunda encloses a cairn which marks the spot said to have been Bruce's command post for the early part of the fight. Of the original bore stone, only a fragment remains, safely on display in the visitor centre. Over-eager visitors used to chip pieces off, and the final straw came when a particularly zealous enthusiast attempted to blast enough of it away to make two curling stones. Pondering the scene is a stirring equestrian **statue** of Bruce, set against the skyline of Stirling Castle, the English army's approach to which he was intentionally blocking. The actual site of the main battle is, oddly, still a matter of debate. Most agree that it didn't take place near the present visitor centre; the most cogent theory argues that it took place on a boggy carse a mile or so to the west. There's nothing to mark the spot here, however, and it may just be a matter of time before the encroaching housing developments spread over the empty green fields. Buses #51 and #52 leave for Bannockburn from Murray Place every half-hour.

Around Stirling

Stirling's strategic position between the Highlands and Lowlands was not only important in medieval times, but as the industrial revolution grew across Scotland's central belt so the town's proximity to the Forth gave it renewed significance. To the north and west of Stirling, the historic aspect of the region is reflected in the cathedral at **Dunblane**, the imposing castle at **Doune** and the unspoilt settlements of the **Carse of Stirling**, while to the east and south, on either side of the Forth, the **Clackmannanshire** mill towns and the area around **Falkirk** tell of a rich industrial heritage. An undoubted highlight of this hinterland is the massive **Falkirk Wheel**, a spectacular feat of engineering which transfers canal boats up and down a 100-foot drop at the interchange of the newly restored Forth & Clyde and Union canals.

Dunblane and Doune

Frequent trains, bus #58 (and bus #358 in school term-time) make the journey four miles north of Stirling to **DUNBLANE**, a small, attractive place which has been an important ecclesiastical centre since the seventh century, when the Celts founded the Church of St Blane here. Despite the length of its history, however it is the more recent past which the town prefers to put gently to one side, Dunblane having witnessed a horrific massacre in March 1996, when one Thomas Hamilton entered a local primary school and shot dead fifteen children and their teacher before turning the gun on himself. Scene of an intensely moving memorial service following the killings, **Dunblane Cathedral** (April–Sept Mon–Sat 9.30am–6.30pm, Sun 1–6.30pm; Oct–March Mon–Sat 9.30am–4.30pm, Sun 2–4.30pm; HS; free) dates mainly from the thirteenth century, and restoration work carried out a century ago has returned it to its Gothic splendour. Inside, note the delicate blue-purple stained

Hotel (ⓣ01360/660245; ⑤) has a restaurant and is prettily sited on the village green, while you can **rent bikes** in order to follow the Loch Lomond cycleway from Lomond Activities, 64 Main St (ⓣ01360/660066; £12 per day). Ten miles southeast of the village in the Blane Valley, Lang Brothers' **Glengoyne Distillery** (Mon–Sat 10am–4pm, Sun noon–4pm; £3.75) offers interesting guided tours of the whisky-making processes.

Falkirk and around

Southeast of Stirling along the south bank of the widening Forth Estuary, farmland gives way to industry, notably BP's gargantuan petrochemical plant nearby at Grangemouth. The lights and fires of the refineries are spectacular at night, and inspired Bertrand Tavernier to make his dour 1979 sci-fi film *Death Watch* in Scotland. Strangely, given its nondescript industrial surroundings, **FALKIRK** – located about halfway between Stirling and Edinburgh on the M9 motorway – has a good deal of visible history, going right back to the remains of the Roman Antonine wall. It was also the site of two major battles, one in 1298, when William Wallace's army fell victim to the English under Edward I, and the other in 1746, when Bonnie Prince Charlie's disintegrating force, retreating northwards, sent the Hanoverians packing in one of its last victories. Traditionally a livestock centre, Falkirk became an industrial node with the development of the now-redundant Carron Ironworks, founded in 1759, which manufactured "carronades" (small cannons) for Nelson's fleet. The town was further transformed later in the eighteenth century by the construction of first the Forth and Clyde Canal, allowing easy access to Glasgow and the west coast, and then the Union Canal, which continued the route through to Edinburgh. Just twenty years later, the trains arrived, and the canals gradually fell into disuse.

Falkirk is now the focal point for the massive £78 million **Millennium Link** project. This has restored the canals to working order in recent years, bringing to life a valuable part of the country's industrial heritage and also encouraging leisure activities, from walking or cycling along the towpaths to canal boat trips (for details of trips on the Union Canal, see p.148). At the interchange of the two canals in Falkirk, in place of an exhausting flight of eleven locks, the Union Canal from Edinburgh has been diverted to a point a mile west of the town centre where the remarkable **Falkirk Wheel**, due to be completed in 2002, is set to become the most impressive engineering spectacle in Scotland since the building of the Forth Rail Bridge. Over 100ft high, the awe-inspiring steel wheel uses two giant caissons to lower up to four boats at a time from the Union Canal down to a holding basin on the Forth and Clyde Canal. Visitors will be able to take a 40-minute trip on a boat which traverses the newly built section of the Union Canal and the Wheel itself, before being dropped off at a high-tech new **visitor's centre** (ⓦwww.millenniumlink.org.uk) by the side of the basin.

The town of Falkirk is a busy local shopping hub, whose only formal attraction, set in Callendar Park, is **Callendar House** (Mon–Sat 10am–5pm; April–Sept also Sun 2–5pm; £1.80), which was owned by the staunchly Jacobite Livingston family. It's now an entertaining local history museum where trained staff in period costume guide you through a printer's and clockmaker's workshop, 1825 kitchens with gleaming utensils and a huge mechanized spit, and a Georgian garden planted with traditional herbs and flowers. In the oak panelled Victorian library of the house, the **Historical Research Centre** (Mon–Fri 10am–12.30pm & 1.30–5pm; free) will gladly help you delve into local family history.

Practicalities

Falkirk's centrally located **bus** station is at Callender Riggs. Regular **trains** run from Edinburgh to Stirling via Falkirk **Grahamston Station**, while Falkirk **High Station**, which is further from the centre, is a stop on the Edinburgh–Glasgow line. From Grahamston Station it's a five-minute walk to the **tourist office**, 2–4 Glebe St (June–Oct daily 9.30am–6pm, Aug until 7pm; April & May daily 9.30am–5pm; Nov–March Mon–Sat 9.30am–12.30pm & 1.30–5pm; ⓣ01324/620244). The best bet for **accommodation** is the elegant *Darroch House* B&B, on Camelon Road at the west end of town (ⓣ01324/623041, ⓔdarroch@amserve.net; ❸), with large and peaceful gardens. Rather different in style, *Beancross* (ⓣ01324/718333, ⓦwww.beancross.co.uk; ❹) is a brightly coloured, modernized farm courtyard off the Laurieston/Polmont bypass near the M9, with a bar, bistro and family area, as well as rooms.

The town has a good selection of decent places to **eat** and **drink**. *Comma Bar Cafe*, 14 Lint Riggs, is a brasserie-style café and trendy bar, while *Quenelles* (ⓣ01324/877411) is a **restaurant** serving pleasant Scottish fare in a whitewashed cottage at 4 Weir St, right in the centre. There's also an upmarket restaurant, *Pierre's* (ⓣ01324/635843), serving classic French cuisine using fresh local produce, near the town centre at 140 Graham's Rd. If you're strolling by the canal, call in at the three-storey *Union Inn* by lock 16, which dates from the days when bargemen and their horses would stop for a drink after a hard day's toil working the locks.

Around Falkirk

In **BONNYBRIDGE**, five miles west of Falkirk by bus #37, is **Rough Castle**, one of the forts which were set up, at two-mile intervals, to defend the entire length of the Roman **Antonine Wall**. The most northerly frontier of the Roman Empire, it was built in 142 AD of turf rather than stone, stretching for 37 miles right across the country from the Forth to the Clyde. Assailed by skirmishing Picts and the grim Scottish weather, it didn't take long for the Romans to abandon the wall and retreat to Hadrian's Wall between the Solway and the Tyne, just south of Scotland's present border with England. The remains at Rough Castle are the best-preserved part of the Antonine Wall, but if you're interested in tracking down further parts of the wall, pick up the factsheet available at Falkirk tourist office.

The **Pineapple**, five miles north of Falkirk (turn off the A905 onto the B9124, or take bus #75), qualifies as one of Scotland's most exotic and eccentric buildings, a 45ft-high stone pineapple built as a garden folly in the 1770s for the fourth Earl of Dunmore. The folly was an elaborate joke on Lord Dunmore's part; returning from a spell as Governor of Virginia, where sailors would put a pineapple on a gatepost to announce their return, he chose to signal his homecoming on a grand scale. The folly is now owned by the NTS, and the outhouse can be rented for holidays through the Landmark Trust (ⓣ01628/825925); it sleeps four, and costs around £550 per week.

The Ochil Hills

The rugged **Ochil Hills** stretch for roughly forty miles northeast of Stirling, forming a steep-faced range which drops down to the flood plain of the Forth Valley and is sliced by a series of deep-cut, richly wooded glens. Tucked up against the southern slopes of the Ochils is a string of settlements known as the **Hillfoot villages**, which have been at the centre of Scotland's wool production for centuries, rivalled only by the Borders. The cottage industry of **Clackmannanshire**, immediately east of Stirling, capitalized on the technological advances of the Industrial Revolution, and by the mid-nineteenth century there were more than thirty mills in a fifteen-mile stretch between the Ochils and the banks of the Forth.

Recent times have seen a change in the industry, with the old family firms and hand-knitters unable to compete with modern technology. Some of the traditions are maintained through the **Mill Trail** that starts in **Alva**, though by and large this has become a little more than a series of shops selling discount woollen products. Clackmannanshire was a convenient base from which the country's powerful families could keep abreast of developments at the Royal Court at Stirling, and a number of fortified tower houses can still be seen, notably at **Alloa** and **Castle Campbell** at Dollar, an atmospheric spot with some great walks nearby. Beyond Dollar the road runs south along the Devon Valley to Kinross, on the shores of Loch Leven, where you can take a boat out to wander round the ruins of a castle in which Mary, Queen of Scots was once imprisoned.

There are no trains to destinations in the Ochils, but regular **buses** shuttle between Stirling and Yetts o'Muckhart northeast of Dollar, and from Alloa to Tillicoultry.

The Hillfoot villages

First of a series of small settlements nestling into the steep south-facing side of the Ochils is the small and appealing village of **BLAIRLOGIE**, three miles or so northeast of Stirling, which sits amidst orchards and gardens below a private castle; it also features an attractive campsite (see p.301). **Logie Old Kirk**, a ruined church and graveyard dating from the late seventeenth century, is beautifully sited by Logie Burn. Immediately to the rear looms **Dumyat** (pronounced "dum-eye-at"), which offers spectacular views from its 1376ft summit.

MENSTRIE, a mile east, is noted for **Menstrie Castle** (May–Sept Sat & Sun 2–4pm; free), a much-restored sixteenth-century stone-built mansion on Castle Road, which is totally at odds with the housing estate that now hems it in. The castle was the birthplace of Sir William Alexander, first Earl of Stirling, who in 1621 set off to found a Scots colony in Nova Scotia. There's little to see now, except an exhibition room displaying the coats of arms of the 109 subsequent baronets of Nova Scotia.

As well as a strong tradition of weaving, **ALVA**, five miles further east, was also known for its silver mining – an industry long since gone. From here you can follow **Alva Glen**, a hearty mile-and-a-half walk dipping down through the hills, which takes in a number of waterfalls. The **Mill Trail** starts from Glentana Mills, on Stirling Street, which doubles as a **tourist office** and **visitor centre** (daily: July–Sept 9am–5pm; rest of year 10am–5pm; ⓣ01259/769696; free), with background on the milling and silver mining industries.

A few miles south of Alva on the A907, the nondescript town of **ALLOA**, once one of the country's main centres of brewing, is home to the beautifully restored **Alloa Tower** (April–Sept daily 1.30–5.30pm; Oct Sat & Sun only; NTS; £3). Ancestral home of the earls of Mar for four centuries, it's now incongruously surrounded by housing estates, though the parapet walk offers lovely views of the Forth.

Dollar and around

Nestling in a fold of the Ochils on the northern bank of the small River Devon, where mountain waters rush off the hills, affluent **DOLLAR** is known for its Academy, founded in 1820 with a substantial bequest from local lad John MacNabb, and now one of Scotland's most respected private schools; its pupils and staff account for around a third of the town's population. Above the town, the dramatic chasm of **Dollar Glen** is commanded by **Castle Campbell** (April–Sept daily 9.30am–6.30pm; Oct–March Mon–Sat 9.30am–4.30pm, Thurs & Fri closes noon, Sun 2–4.30pm; NTS/HS; £2.80), formerly, and still unofficially, known as Castle Gloom – a fine and evocative tag but, prosaically, a derivation of "Gloume", an old Gaelic name. A one-and-a-half-mile road leads up from the main street, but becomes very narrow, very steep, and stops short of the castle, with only limited parking at the top. There is a marked **walk** through the glen to the castle, past mossy crags and rushing streams (see box).

The castle came into the hands of the Campbells in 1481, who changed its name from Castle Gloom in 1489. John Knox preached here in 1556, although probably from within the castle rather than from the curious archway in the garden as is traditionally claimed. In 1654 the castle was burnt by Cromwell's troops; the remains of a graceful seventeenth-century loggia and a roofless hall bear witness to the destruction. However, the oldest part of the castle, the fine fifteenth-century tower built by Sir Colin Campbell, survived the fire; look out for the claustrophobic pit-prison just off the Great Hall and the latrines with their vertiginous views. You can also walk round the roof of the tower, where there's a wonderful vista of the hills behind the castle, and down the glen to Dollar.

The *Lorne Taverna*, 17 Argyll St (☎01259/743423; ❶) is a traditional inn offering simple **B&B** as well as Scottish and Greek food, or there's the comfortable *Castle Campbell Hotel* on Bridge Street (☎01259/742519; ❺). The *Strathallen* hotel on Chapel Road is a good spot for a pub **lunch** with real ale and outside seating, while three miles east of town, on the Tillicoultry road, the *Harvieston Country Inn and Restaurant* offers reasonably priced Scottish food.

Walking above Dollar

Ordnance Survey Landranger map no. 58

The River Devon rises far in the Ochils but does a huge loop round Glendevon and the Crook of Devon before turning to flow along the valley below the Ochil scarp. A three-hour **walk** combining the glen with Castle Campbell and Dollar Hill is highly recommended, while a shorter, two-hour walk is possible if you miss out the hill. Walk up the Burnside from Dollar's town centre (clock tower) and then along a footpath from the top bridge beside the burn to pass an open area and reach the wooded glen. Keep an eye out, as in some places the path is steep and unfenced. Other bridges eventually lead you out near **Castle Campbell**, perched between the Burn of Care and the Burn of Sorrow.

You can return to Dollar by the small tarred road, which stops just short of the castle. But if you want to venture further, **Dollar Hill** (marked as Bank Hill on the OS map) is easily accessible by going up the burn to a bridge over the Sorrow. From here there's a direct descent to Dollar via the golf course. There is also an old drovers' road through to **Glendevon**, but you'll need to arrange transport back to Dollar from there. Leaving the castle, the road dips, then climbs to a cottage (at the start of the track to Glendevon) and a car park with a good view of the keep, before descending steeply to the town below.

The Devon Valley

Beyond Dollar, the A91 leads through the hills to Kinross and runs along the southern edge of the **Devon Valley**, passing through the hamlets of Pool o'Muckhart and Yetts o'Muckhart.

The scenic A823 cuts up from Yetts o'Muckhart through the valley itself, passing through the village of **GLENDEVON**, where there's a simple SYHA **hostel** (Ⓣ01259/781206, Ⓦwww.syha.org.uk; April–Sept), which organizes pony trekking from mid-June to September, and can give advice on walks in the area. The road continues from here to Gleneagles, with its famous hotel and golf course (see p.354).

In the other direction, south of Yetts o'Muckhart, the same road crosses the River Devon at **Rumbling Bridge** – effectively two bridges; the newer one, built in the early nineteenth century, sweeping over the top of the old one, which dates from 1713. The observation point offers breathtaking views of the magnificent, 120ft-deep **gorge**, and you can follow a shady path along the river, through the lush vegetation flourishing in the damp, limestone walls of the chasm.

Kinross and Loch Leven

Although by no means a large place, **KINROSS**, ten miles east of Dollar, has been transformed in the last couple of decades by the construction of the nearby M90 Edinburgh–Perth motorway. The old village is still there, at the southern end of the main street, but apart from the views of Loch Leven its charm has been eroded by amorphous splodges of modern housing, which threaten to nudge it into the loch itself.

Without doubt the most attractive part of Kinross is by the shores of trout-filled **Loch Leven**, signposted from the main street. In recent years the loch has become a National Nature Reserve and as well as some interesting birds, including visiting geese and various types of duck, you'll almost always find a number of fishermen casting from small boats. From the shore a small ferry chugs over to an island on which stands the ruined fourteenth-century **Loch Leven Castle** (April–Sept daily 9.30am–6.30pm; Oct Mon, Wed, Thurs & Sat 9.30am–4.30pm, Sun 2–4.30pm; HS; £3.30), where Mary, Queen of Scots was imprisoned for eleven months in 1567–68. This isn't the only island fortress Mary spent time in, and it's easy to imagine the isolation of the tragic queen, who is believed to have miscarried twins while here. She managed to charm the eighteen-year-old son of Lady Douglas into helping her escape: he stole the castle keys, secured a boat in which to row ashore, locked the castle gates behind them and threw the keys into the loch – from where they were retrieved three centuries later.

The local **visitor centre** (April–Oct Mon–Sat 9.30am–5.30pm, Sun 11am–4pm; Ⓣ01577/863680) is by a filling station on the outskirts of the town, and is most useful if you're heading north towards Perth on the motorway, though it also acts as an orientation point for those travelling west into the Trossachs or east into Fife. Not far from here is Balado Farm, location of the annual **T in the Park**, one of the largest outdoor weekend music events in Britain, where in recent years bands such as Stereophonics, Placebo, Travis and Coldplay have made an appearance.

Loch Lomond

The largest stretch of fresh water in Britain (23 miles long and up to five miles wide), and now at the centre of Scotland's first National Park, **Loch Lomond** is the epitome of Scottish scenic splendour, thanks in large part to the ballad which fondly recalls its "bonnie, bonnie banks". The song was said to be have been written by a Jacobite prisoner captured by the English, who, sure of his fate, wrote that his spirit would return to Scotland on the low road much faster than his living compatriots on the high road. However, all is not so bonnie at the loch nowadays, especially on its overdeveloped western and southern banks, which are mobbed by tour coaches and day-trippers from Glasgow, just twenty or so miles away. The upgraded A82 no longer meanders along the lochside, but speeds traffic past giving only the occasional glimpse across the water. On the loch itself, speedboats tear up and down on summer weekends, destroying the tranquillity which so impressed Queen Victoria, the Wordsworths and Sir Walter Scott. The only place to find any peace and quiet now is on the eastern banks, large sections of which are only accessible on foot.

Balloch and around

The main settlement on Loch Lomond-side is **BALLOCH**, at the southwestern corner of the loch, where the water channels into the River Leven for its short journey south to the sea in the Firth of Clyde. Surrounded by housing estates and overstuffed with undistinguished guesthouses, Balloch has few redeeming features, and is little more than a suburb of the much larger factory town of **ALEXANDRIA**, to the south. Balloch has big plans for a new marina and pier development to the north of the town, which will include a visitor centre showing a film entitled "The Legend of the Loch", as well as numerous shopping outlets, due to be completed in 2002 (Ⓦwww.lomondshores.com). For a more edifying view over the loch, walk over the river and then into

Climbs around Loch Lomond

Ordnance Survey Outdoor Leisure map no. 39

Ben Lomond (3192ft), the most southerly of the "Munros", is one of the most frequently climbed hills in Scotland, its commanding position above Loch Lomond affording amazing views of both the Highlands and Lowlands. You should allow five to six hours for the climb. The tourist route starts in Rowardennan, at the car park at the rear end of the public road just beyond *Rowardennan Hotel*. The route rises through forest and crosses open moors to gain the southern ridge, which leads to the final pyramid. The path zigzags up, then rims the crags of the northeast corrie to reach the summit. You can return the same way or start off westwards, then south, to traverse the subsidiary top of Ptarmigan down to the hostel in Rowardennan and then along the track to the start.

If you're looking for an easier climb, but an equally impressive view over Loch Lomond, consider climbing **Conic Hill** (1175ft) instead. Start from the car park at Balmaha and walk up through the woods. The views open up as soon as you leave the trees behind, so you don't even need to make it all the way to the top. You should allow two to three hours for the walk.

Finally, for an even easier overview of Loch Lomond, climb **Duncryne** (470ft), a small conical hill to the southeast of Gartocharn, on the south side of the loch. The climb, which starts from the woods to the south of the village, is easy but the view is wonderfully rewarding.

extensive mature grounds of **Balloch Castle Country Park**, to the northeast. Formerly a Lennox stronghold, the present mock-Gothic castle dates from 1808 and was built by local capitalist and one-time Tory MP John Buchanan. It's now a **visitor centre** (Easter–Oct daily 10am–6pm; free), and really only of use as a wet-weather refuge; the views from its terrace over the loch, however, are lovely.

Practicalities

Balloch has a direct **train** connection with Glasgow Queen Street, and opposite the train station stands the area's main **tourist office** (daily: July & Aug 9.30am–6.30pm; June & Sept 9.30am–6pm; April, May & Oct 10am–5pm; ⓣ01389/753533). There's really little point in basing yourself in Balloch, though it's worth mentioning that Scotland's most beautiful SYHA **hostel**, a turreted building complete with ghost (ⓣ01389/850226, ⓦwww.syha.org.uk; April–Oct), lies two miles northwest of Balloch train station, just off the A82; you can either walk there from Balloch, or if you're travelling by bus, ask the driver to drop you off close by. On the other side of the main road is *Cameron House* (ⓣ01389/755565, ⓦwww.cameronhouse.co.uk; ⑨), an exclusive lochside **hotel**, with its own health club and nine-hole golf course. In Balloch itself there's the year-round *Lomond Woods Holiday Park*, in Tullichewan (ⓣ01389/759475, ⓦwww.holiday-parks.co.uk), an excellent campsite which also rents out **bikes**.

Various operators offer **boat cruises** from beside the bridge over the River Leven, taking you around the 33 islands scattered across the loch: Mullens Cruises (ⓣ01389/751481) operates daily trips on the *Lomond Duchess* and the *Lomond Maid* (£5); Sweeney's Cruises (ⓣ01389/752376, ⓦwww.sweeney.uk.com) runs one-hour trips departing hourly (starting at around £5), while their daily Balloch–Luss cruise leaves at 2.30pm (£7.50), and ninety-minute evening cruises operate daily during July and August only, leaving at 7.30pm (£6.50).

The eastern shore of Loch Lomond

The tranquil **eastern shore** is far better for walking and appreciating the loch's natural beauty than the western. The dead-end B837 from Drymen (see p.309) will take you halfway up the east bank, while the West Highland Way sticks close to the shores for the entire length of the loch, beginning at the tiny lochside settlement of **BALMAHA**, which stands on the Highland Boundary Fault, the geological fault that separates the Highlands from the Lowlands. If you stand on the viewpoint above the pier, you can see the fault line clearly marked by the series of woody islands that form giant stepping stones across the loch. You can visit the islands on the post boat, or cruise round them on one of the boat trips that leaves from the jetties – try those run by MacFarlane & Son (ⓣ01360/870214). Balmaha has a **Loch Lomond Park Centre** (Easter–Oct daily 10am–6pm; ⓣ01360/870470), one of two principal **information** points on the shores of the loch (the other is in Luss). You can **stay** at purpose-built *Oak Tree Inn* (ⓣ01360/870357, ⓦwww.oaktreeinn.co.uk; ③). opposite the big car park, either in one of their double rooms or in their cheaper bunk-bed quads.

Public transport stops at Balamaha, but a couple of miles or so further up the road, at Cashel, is a lovely secluded Forestry Commission **campsite** (ⓣ01360/870234, ⓦwww.forestholidays.co.uk; April–Oct). Another three miles north through the woods brings you to **ROWARDENNAN**, a scattered

The West Highland Way

Opened in 1980, the spectacular **West Highland Way** was Scotland's first long-distance footpath, stretching some 95 miles from Milngavie (pronounced "mill-guy"; see p.280), six miles north of central Glasgow, to Fort William, where it reaches the foot of Ben Nevis, Britain's highest mountain. Today, it is by far the most popular footpath in Scotland, and while for many the range of scenery, relative ease of walking and nearby facilities make it a classic route, others find it a little too busy in high season, particularly in comparison with the relative isolation which can be found in many other parts of the Highlands.

The route follows ancient **drove roads**, along which Highlanders herded their cattle and sheep to market in the lowlands, as well as military roads built by troops to control the Jacobite insurgence in the eighteenth century, old coaching roads and even disused railway lines. In addition to the stunning scenery, which is increasingly dramatic as the path heads north, walkers may see some of Scotland's rarer **wildlife**, including red deer, feral goats – ancestors of those left behind after the Highland clearances – and, soaring over the highest peaks, golden eagles.

Passing through the lowlands north of Glasgow, the route runs along the eastern shores of Loch Lomond, over the Highland Boundary Fault Line, then round Crianlarich, crossing open heather moorland across the **Rannoch Moor** wilderness area. It passes close to **Glen Coe**, notorious for the massacre of the MacDonald clan, before reaching **Fort William.** Apart from a stretch between Loch Lomond and Bridge of Orchy, when the path is within earshot of the main road, this is wild, remote country: north of Rowardennan on Loch Lomond, the landscape is increasingly exposed, and you should be well prepared for sudden and extreme weather changes.

Though this is emphatically not the most strenuous of Britain's long-distance walks – it passes between lofty mountain peaks, rather than over them – a moderate degree of fitness is required as there are some steep ascents. If you're looking for an added challenge, you could work a climb of Ben Lomond or Ben Nevis into your schedule. You might choose to walk individual sections of the Way (the eight-mile climb from Glen Coe up the Devil's Staircase is particularly spectacular), but to tackle the whole thing you need to set aside at least **seven days**; avoid a Saturday start from Milngavie and you'll be less likely to be walking with hordes of people, and there'll be less pressure on accommodation. Most walkers tackle the route from south to north, and manage between ten and fourteen miles a day, staying at hotels, B&Bs and bunkhouses en route. Camping is permitted at recognized sites.

Although the path is clearly waymarked, you may want to check the **official guide**, published by Mercat Press (£14.99), which includes Ordnance Survey maps as well as descriptions of the route, with detailed cultural, historical, archeological and wildlife information. Further details about the Way, including an accommodation list, can be had from the West Highland Way ranger at Balmaha (ⓣ01389/870470). The very useful **website** ⓦwww.west-highland-way.co.uk has comprehensive accommodation listings as well as links to tour companies and transport providers, who can take your luggage from one stopping point to the next.

settlement which sits below Ben Lomond (see box on p.315); the mountain is the subject of the Scottish proverb "Leave Ben Lomond where it stands", or let things be. Passenger ferries (Easter–Sept 3 daily) cross between Inverbeg and Rowardennan, where **accommodation** is available at the *Rowardennan Hotel* (ⓣ01360/870273; ⑤), whose lawns slope down to the shore, and, half a mile beyond, at a wonderfully situated SYHA **hostel** (ⓣ01360/870259, ⓦwww.syha.org.uk; March–Oct), strategically placed on the West Highland Way. The road peters out between the hotel and the hostel, so only walkers can continue up the loch shore for seven miles to **INVERSNAID**, where the *Inversnaid Lodge* (☎01877/386254; ❻) sits by the shore; it can be reached by road via the B829 from Aberfoyle and also by boat from Inveruglas on the west shore if you phone the hotel. Once the hunting lodge of the Duke of Montrose, it now has a photography centre with instruction and workshops from guest tutors (Ⓦwww.inversnaidphoto.com). From Inversnaid you can take the mile-long lochside walk to **Rob Roy's Cave**, a hide-out which is said to have given shelter to both Rob Roy and Robert the Bruce. The West Highland Way continues through the Inversnaid RSPB reserve to Ardlui (see below) at the head of the loch, five miles north.

The western shore of Loch Lomond

Despite the roar of traffic hurtling along the upgraded A82, the **west bank** of Loch Lomond is an undeniably beautiful stretch of water and gives better views of the loch's wooded islands and surrounding peaks than the heavily wooded east side. The exclusive, US-owned **Loch Lomond golf course**, which obscures the view for part of the way, is the venue for the annual Scottish Open.

LUSS, setting for the Scottish TV soap *High Road*, is without doubt the prettiest village on the west coast, with its prim, identical sandstone and slate cottages garlanded in rambling roses, and its narrow sandy, pebbly strand. However, its charms are no secret, and its streets and beach can become unbearably crowded in summer. If you want to escape the crowds, pop into the parish **church**, which is a haven of peace and has a lovely ceiling made from Scots pine rafters and some good Victorian stained-glass windows. The **Loch Lomond Park Centre** (Easter–Oct 10am–6pm; ☎01436/860601), adjacent to the massive village car park, can help with any enquiries. The *Coach House*, just off the main street towards the church, is the place to grab tea, coffee, cake or a roll.

If you need a place to **stay**, you could worse than hole up in the *Inverbeg Inn* (☎01436/860678, Ⓦwww.scottish-selection.co.uk; ❺), a few miles further north on the A82, which offers very good bar food as well as a few comfortable rooms. A passenger **ferry** (Easter–Sept 3 daily) links Inverbeg with Rowardennan on the east bank (see above). There are plenty of **buses** along the shore from Balloch. Seventeen miles north at **TARBET**, the West Highland **train** – the line from Glasgow to Mallaig, with a branch line to Oban – reaches the shoreline at the point where the A83 heads off west into Argyll; the A82 continues north along the banks of the loch towards Crianlarich. Tarbet has a small **tourist office** (July & Aug 10am–7pm; June & Sept 10am–6pm; April, May & early Oct 10am–5pm; ☎01301/702260), situated opposite the *Tarbet Hotel*, but no other reason for stopping, unless you want to join one of the **loch cruises**, run by *Cruise Loch Lomond* (☎01301/702356) that depart from the pier.

North of Tarbet, the A82 turns back into the narrow, winding road of old, making for slower but much more interesting driving. Again, however, there's little motivation to stop, unless you need to use the toilets or join a loch cruise at **INVERUGLAS**, where, if you ring the *Inversnaid Lodge* (☎01877/386254), a ferry will come and fetch you. There's one more **train station** on Loch Lomond at **ARDLUI**, at the mountain-framed head of the loch, where you can have a pint at the *Ardlui Hotel*. A ferry will take you over to the east bank (on demand in season), and a couple of miles further north at Inverarnan, there's a bridge over the River Falloch beside the *Stagger Inn* (☎01301/

704274; April–Sept only), a top-quality **restaurant** specializing in traditional Scottish fare. Immediately opposite this is the *Drover's Inn* (Ⓣ01301/704234; ❷) one of the most idiosyncratic **hotels** in Scotland: typically, the bar has a roaring fire, barmen dressed in kilts, weary hillwalkers sipping pints and bearded musicians banging out old folk songs. Down the creaking corridors, which are filled with moth-eaten stuffed animals, are a number of haunted and resolutely old-fashioned rooms.

Crianlarich and Tyndrum

At **CRIANLARICH**, some eight miles north of the head of Loch Lomond, the A82 is joined briefly by the A85 Perth–Oban road. Crianlarich is an important staging post on various transport routes, including the West Highland railway which divides here, one branch heading due west towards Oban, the other continuing north over Rannoch Moor to Fort William. The West Highland Way long-distance footpath (see box) also trogs past. Otherwise there's little reason to stop here, unless you're keen on tackling some of the steep-sided hills that rise up from the glen.

Five miles further north from here on the A82/A85, the village of **TYNDRUM** owes its existence to a minor (and very short-lived) nineteenth-century gold rush, but today is dotted with some rather ugly hotels and filling stations. Tyndrum is also home to the famous **Green Welly Shop** (Ⓣ01838/400271, Ⓦwww.greenwellyshop.co.uk), where you can purchase a pair of the old dependables from the vast selection of clothing, boots and other outdoor gear on display, or stop for a bite to eat at the inexpensive *Green Welly Stop* **restaurant** next door. At Tyndrum the road divides, with the A85 heading west to Oban, and the A82 heading for Fort William via Glen Coe. The railway divides further south at Crianlarich, though the two branches run in parallel to Tyndrum: it's only a short walk from Tyndrum Lower station (on the Oban line) to Tyndrum Upper (on the Fort William line).

The Trossachs

Often described as the Highlands in miniature, the **Trossachs** area boasts a magnificent diversity of scenery, with dramatic peaks and mysterious, forest-covered slopes that live up to all the images ever produced of Scotland's wild land. It is country ripe for stirring tales of brave kilted clansmen, a role fulfilled by Rob Roy Macgregor, the seventeenth-century outlaw whose name seems to attach to every second waterfall, cave and barely discernible path. Strictly speaking, the name "Trossachs", normally translated as either "bristly country" or "crossing place", originally referred only to the wooded glen between **Loch Katrine** and Loch Achray, but today it is usually taken as being the whole area from **Callander** in the east to Queen Elizabeth Forest Park in the west, right up to the eastern banks of Loch Lomond.

The Trossachs' high tourist profile was largely attributable in the early days to Sir Walter Scott, whose novels *Lady of the Lake* and *Rob Roy* were set in and around the area. According to one contemporaneous account, after Scott's *Lady of the Lake* was published in 1810, the number of carriages passing Loch Katrine rose from 50 the previous year to 270. Since then, neither the popularity nor beauty of the region have waned, and in high season the place is jam-packed with coaches full of tourists as well as walkers and mountain-bikers taking advantage of the easily accessed richness of the scenery. Autumn is a better

Rob Roy

A member of the outlawed Macgregor clan, **Rob Roy** (meaning "Red Robert" in Gaelic) was born in 1671 in Glengyle, just north of Loch Katrine, and lived for some time as a respectable cattle farmer and trader, supported by the powerful Duke of Montrose. In 1712, finding himself in a tight spot when a cattle deal fell through, Rob Roy absconded with £1000, some of it belonging to the duke. He took to the hills to live as a brigand, his feud with Montrose escalating after the duke repossessed Rob Roy's land and drove his wife from their house. He was present at the Battle of Sheriffmuir during the earlier Jacobite uprising of 1715, ostensibly supporting the Jacobites but probably as an opportunist: the chaos would have made cattle-raiding easier. Eventually captured and sentenced to transportation, Rob Roy was pardoned and returned to **Balquhidder**, where he remained until his death in 1734.

Rob Roy's status as a local hero in the mould of Robin Hood should be tempered with the fact that he was without doubt a notorious bandit and blackmailer. His life has been much romanticized, from Sir Walter Scott's 1818 novel *Rob Roy* to the 1995 film starring Liam Neeson, although the tale does serve well to dramatize the clash between the doomed clan culture of the Gaelic-speaking Highlanders and the organized feudal culture of lowland Scots, which effectively ended with the defeat of the Jacobites at Culloden in 1746. His **grave** in Balquhidder, a simple affair behind the ruined church, is one of the principal sights on the unofficial Rob Roy trail, though the peaceful graveyard is mercifully underdeveloped and free of the tourist trappings which has seen the Trossachs dubbed "Rob Roy Country".

time to come, when the hills are blanketed in rich, rusty colours and the crowds are thinner. In terms of where to stay, **Aberfoyle** has a rather dowdy air while **Callander** feels rather overrun, and you're often better seeking out one of the guesthouses or B&Bs tucked away in secluded corners of the region.

The **Trossachs Trundler** is a minibus which loops usefully round Callander, Loch Katrine and Aberfoyle four times a day from July to mid-Sept (not Wed), stopping at various points en route; contact any tourist office for details. The bus is timed to connect with sailings of the SS *Sir Walter Scott* on Loch Katrine (see p.324), and costs £4 for a day pass or £8 including the bus fare from Stirling to Callander.

Aberfoyle and the Lake of Menteith

Each summer the sleepy little town of **ABERFOYLE**, twenty miles west of Stirling, dusts itself down for its annual influx of tourists. Though of little appeal itself, Aberfoyle's position in the heart of the Trossachs is ideal, with **Loch Ard Forest** and **Queen Elizabeth Forest Park** stretching across to Ben Lomond and Loch Lomond to the west, the long curve of Loch Katrine and Ben Venue to the northwest, and Ben Ledi to the northeast.

Don't come here for lively nightlife or entertainment, but for a good, healthy blast of the outdoors. From Aberfoyle you might like to wander north of the village to **Doon Hill**: cross the bridge over the Forth, continue past the cemetery and then follow signs to the **Fairy Knowe** (knoll). A toadstool marker points you through oak and holly trees to the summit of the Knowe where there is a pine tree, said to contain the unquiet spirit of the Reverend Robert Kirk, who studied local fairy lore and published his inquiries in *The Secret Commonwealth* (1691). Legend has it that, as punishment for disclosing supernatural secrets, he was forcibly removed to fairyland where he has languished

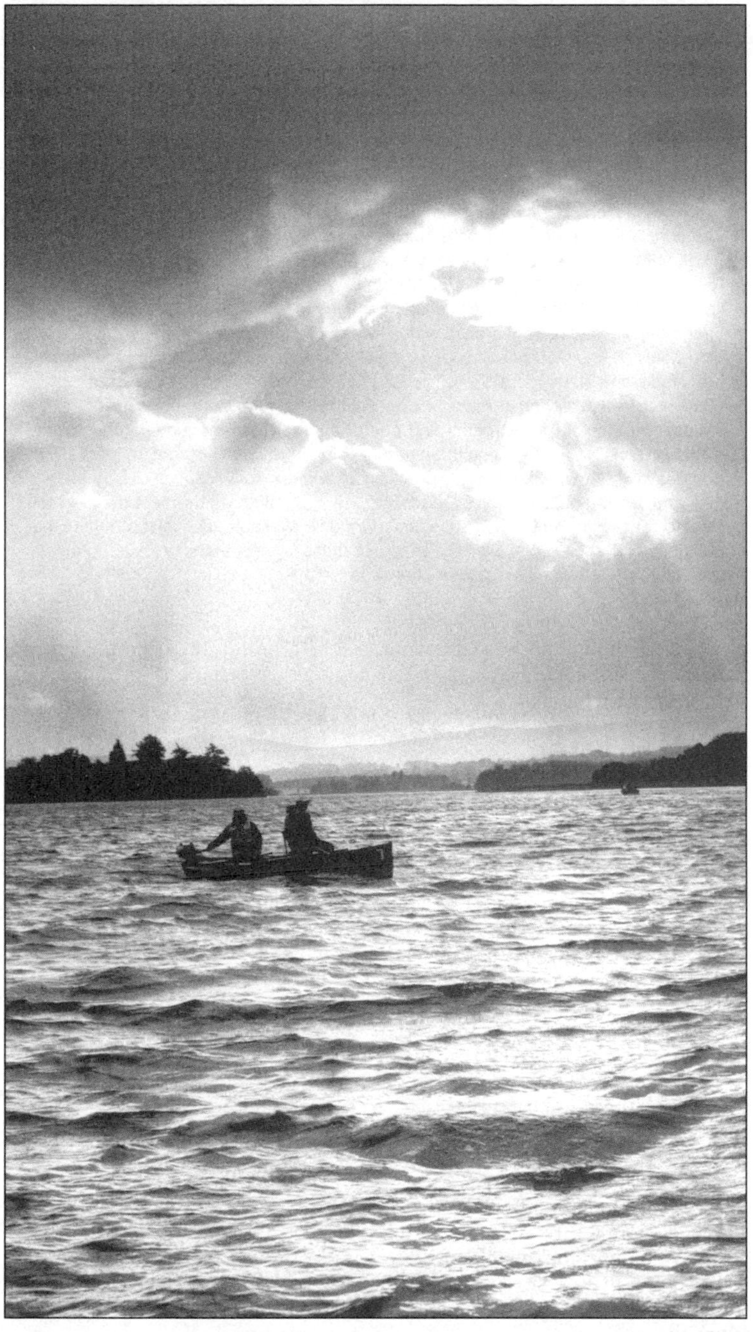

△ Lake of Menteith

Hiking and biking in the Trossachs

Despite the steady flow of coach tours taking in the scenic highlights of the area, the Trossachs is at its best when you take to it **on foot** or on a **mountain bike**. This is partly because the terrain is slightly more benign that the Highlands proper, but much is due to the excellent management of the **Queen Elizabeth Forest Park**, which covers 75,000 acres of land between Loch Lomond and Loch Lubnaig. The park's visitor centre just outside Aberfoyle is well worth a visit if you want to get some orientation on the region and learn about the local trees, geology and wildlife, which includes roe deer and birds of prey.

For **hillwalkers**, the prize peak is Ben Lomond (3192ft), best accessed from Rowardennan (see p.316). Other highlights include Ben Venue and Ben A'an on the shores of Loch Katrine, as well as Ben Ledi, just northwest of Callander, which all offer relatively straightforward but very rewarding climbs and, on clear days, stunning views. Walkers can also choose from any number of waymarked routes through the forests and along lochsides; pick up a map of these at the visitor centre.

The area is also a popular spot for **mountain biking**, with a number of useful rental shops, a network of forest paths and one of the more impressive stretches of the National Cycle Network cutting through the region from Loch Lomond to Killin. If you don't have your own bike, Wheels Cycling Centre, next to *Trossachs Backpackers* a mile and a half southwest of Callander (ⓣ01877/331200), is the best place in the area to **rent**, with front or full suspension models available, as well as baby seats and children's cycles. Also well set up is Trossachs Cycles, at the *Trossachs Holiday Park* on the A81 two miles south of Aberfoyle (ⓣ01877/382614).

ever since, although his mortal remains can be found in the nearby graveyard. This short walk should preferably be made at dusk, when it is at its most atmospheric.

Practicalities

Regular **buses** from Stirling pull into the car park on Aberfoyle's Main Street. The **tourist office** next door (daily: July & Aug 9.30pm–6pm; March–June, Sept & Oct 10am–5pm; ⓣ01877/382352) has full details of local accommodation, sights and outdoor activities. The nearby **Scottish Wool Centre** (daily: May–Sept 9.30am–6pm; Oct–April 10am–5pm) – a popular stopoff point with tour buses – is a glorified country knitwear shop selling all the usual jumpers and woolly toys as well as featuring shows of sheep-shearing and sheep-dog trials.

Accommodation options in Aberfoyle aren't all that inspiring. Best of the B&Bs is *Creag-Ard House* (ⓣ01877/382297; ❸; March–Oct) in the pretty village of Milton, two miles west of Aberfoyle. It looks out on Ben Lomond and Loch Ard, to which it has fishing and boating rights. At **KINLOCHARD**, five miles west of Aberfoyle, is the deluxe *Forest Hills Hotel* (ⓣ01877/387277; ❼), set in 25 acres of woodland, with excellent food and a leisure centre. The **Lake of Menteith** is a beautiful place to stay: the *Lake Hotel and Restaurant* (ⓣ01877/385258, ⓦwww.lake-of-menteith-hotel.com; ❻) at Port of Menteith has a lovely waterfront setting next to the Victorian Gothic parish church, as well as a classy restaurant.

For **camping**, a couple of miles south of Aberfoyle on the edge of Queen Elizabeth Forest Park is *Cobleland* (ⓣ01877/382392; April–Oct), run by the Forestry Commission, which covers five acres of woodland by the River Forth (little more than a stream here). Further south, the excellent family-run *Trossachs Holiday Park* (ⓣ01877/382614; March–Oct), is twice the size and has **bikes** for rent.

For **food** in Aberfoyle, your best bet is to stick with the local hotels: the *Forth Inn* (☎01877/382372) on the main street or the *Covenanters Inn* at the large, turreted *Inchrie Castle Hotel*, five minutes' walk from the centre; both serve bar food and smarter restaurant meals.

The Lake of Menteith

About four miles east of Aberfoyle towards Doune, the **Lake of Menteith** is a superb fly-fishing centre and Scotland's only lake (as opposed to loch), so named due to a historic mix-up with the word *laigh*, Scots for "low-lying ground", which applied to the whole area. To rent a **fishing boat**, contact the Lake of Menteith Fisheries (☎01877/385664; April–Oct).

From the northern shore of the lake, you can take a little ferry (April–Sept daily 9.30am–5.15pm; HS; £3.30) out to the **Island of Inchmahome** in order to explore the lovely Augustine abbey. Founded in 1238, the ruined **Inchmahome Priory** is the most beautiful island monastery in Scotland, its remains rising tall and graceful above the trees. The masons employed to build the priory are thought to be those who built Dunblane Cathedral (see p.307); certainly the western entrance there resembles that at Inchmahome. The nave of the church is roofless, but in the choir are preserved the graves of important families from the surrounding area. Most touching is a late thirteenth-century double effigy depicting Walter, the first Stewart Earl of Menteith, and his Countess Mary who, feet resting on lion-like animals, turn towards each other and embrace.

Also buried here is the adventurer and scholar Robert Bontine Cunninghame Graham, once a pal of Buffalo Bill's in Mexico, an intimate friend of the novelist Joseph Conrad, and first president of the National Party of Scotland. Five-year-old Mary, Queen of Scots was hidden at Inchmahome in 1547 before being taken to France, and there's a formal garden in the west of the island, known as Queen Mary's bower, where legend has it she played. Traces remain of an orchard planted by the monks, but the island is thick now with oak, ash and Spanish chestnut. Visible on an nearby but inaccessible islet is the ruined castle of **Inchtalla**, the home of the earls of Menteith in the sixteenth and seventeenth centuries.

Duke's Pass and around

North of Aberfoyle, the A821 road to Loch Katrine plunges into the Queen Elizabeth forest, winding its way up **Duke's Pass** (so called because it once belonged to the Duke of Montrose). You can walk or drive the short distance to the park's excellent **visitor centre** (daily 10am–6pm; Nov–March closes 4pm; ☎01877/382258; car park fee £1), where you can pick up maps of the walks and cycle routes in the forest, find out background information on the flora and fauna of the area (there's a video relay to a peregrine falcon's nest), or settle into the café with its splendid views out over the tree tops. From the centre, various marked paths wind through the forest, giving glimpses of the lowlands and surrounding hills. The only road in the forest open to cars is the **Achray Forest Drive**, just under two miles further on, which leads through the forest and along the western shore of **Loch Drunkie** before rejoining the main road.

Loch Katrine

Heading down the northern side of the Duke's Pass you come first to **Loch Achray**, tucked under Ben A'an. Look out across the loch for the small

Callander Kirk in a lovely setting alone on a promontory. At the head of the loch a road branches the short distance through to the southern end of **Loch Katrine** at the foot of Ben Venue (2370ft), from where the elegant Victorian passenger **steamer**, the SS *Sir Walter Scott*, has been plying the waters since 1900, chugging up the loch to the wild country of Glengyle. It does two runs from the pier each day, the first departing at 11am and stopping off at Stronachlachar before returning (April–Oct daily except Wed; £4.40 single, £6.50 return), the afternoon cruise departing at 1.45pm but not making any stops (April–Oct daily; £5.40). A popular combination is to rent a bike from the *Katrinewheels* hut by the pier, take the steamer up to Stronachlachar, then cycle back by way of the road around the north side of the loch.

From Loch Katrine the A821 heads due east along the shores of Loch Venacher to Kilmahog, where it meets the A84 a short distance from Callander.

Callander and around

CALLANDER, on the eastern edge of the Trossachs, sits quietly on the banks of the River Teith roughly ten miles north of Doune, at the southern end of the **Pass of Leny**, one of the key routes into the Highlands. Significantly larger than Aberfoyle, it is a popular summer holiday base and suffers in high season for being right on the main tourist trail from Stirling through to the west Highlands. Callander first came to fame during the "Scottish Enlightenment" of the eighteenth and nineteenth centuries, when the glowing reports of the Trossachs given by Sir Walter Scott and William Wordsworth prompted the first tourists to venture into the wilds by horse-drawn carriage. Development was given a boost when Queen Victoria chose to visit, and then by the arrival of the train line – long since closed – in the 1860s.

The present community has not been slow to respond to the onslaught of tourists, establishing a plethora of restaurants and tearooms, antique shops, secondhand bookstores and shops selling local woollens and crafts. As a result, a typical day in summer sees visitors thronging the pavements and traffic crawling down the long main street; you'd be forgiven the desire to move on swiftly to more tranquil countryside beyond. The chief attraction in town is the **Rob Roy and Trossachs Visitor Centre** in a converted church at Ancaster Square on the main street (July & Aug daily 9.30am–8pm; June daily 9.30am–6pm; Sept 10am–6pm; March–May & Oct–Dec daily 10am–5pm; Jan & Feb Sat & Sun 11am–4.30pm; £3.25). Downstairs is the tourist office and bookshop; upstairs a hammed-up audiovisual display offers an entertaining and partisan account of the life and times of Rob Roy and those who have portrayed him in film and fiction.

Practicalities

Callander's **tourist office** is in the Rob Roy and Trossachs Visitor Centre (same times as above; ⓣ01877/330342), and can book **accommodation**. The best options include *The Priory*, on Bracklinn Road (ⓣ01877/330001, ⓔjudith@bracklinnroad.fsnet.co.uk; ❹), a highly recommended Victorian house in its own gardens with good views; and *Arden House*, also on Bracklinn Road (ⓣ01877/330235; ❸). For even more luxury, try the *Roman Camp Country House Hotel*, signposted off the main street (ⓣ01877/330003; ❼), a romantic, turreted seventeenth-century hunting lodge in twenty-acre gardens on the River Teith, or the *Invertrossachs Country House* (ⓣ01877/331126, ⓦwww.invertrossachs.co.uk; ❻), west of Callander on the southern shores of Loch Venachar, a plush Edwardian mansion offering superior B&B.

Budget travellers are also well served: a couple of miles southwest of town down a turn-off from the A81 to Port of Menteith you'll find *Trossachs Backpackers* (ⓣ01877 331200, ⓦwwww.scottish-hostel.co.uk), a friendly and comfortable 32-bed **hostel** and activity centre with self-catering dorms, family rooms and excellent **bike rental** (ⓣ01877/331100).

Despite Callander's popularity, it has few **restaurants** worth recommending. The smartest place is in the *Roman Camp Hotel*, which serves splendid Scottish produce in refined surroundings. For good pub food, try the *Bridgend Hotel* just off the main street in the centre of Callander, or the *Lade Inn* in Kilmahog, just over a mile west of the town.

North of Callander

On each side of Callander, pleasant and untaxing walks wind west for a couple of miles through a wooded gorge to the **Falls of Leny** and north for a mile or so through forest to the **Bracklinn Falls**. Longer walks of varying degrees of exertion thread their way through the surrounding countryside, the most challenging being that to the summit of **Ben Ledi** (2857ft); set off from the car park at the turn-off marked "Strathyre Forest Cabins".

North of town, you can walk or ride the scenic six-mile **Callander to Strathyre Cycleway**, which forms part of the network of cycleways between the Highlands and Glasgow. The route is based on the old Caledonian train line to Oban, which closed in 1965, and runs along the western side of **Loch Lubnaig**. At the head of the loch, the main road runs straight through **STRATHYRE**, though if you're looking for somewhere to stay it's worth turning off to *Creagan House* (ⓣ01877/384638; ❺), an old farm steading with a great restaurant and five cosy rooms.

Just north of here is tiny **BALQUHIDDER**, most famous as the site of the grave of Rob Roy, which you can find in the small yard behind the ruined church. Refreshingly, considering the Rob Roy fever that plagues the region, his grave – marked by a rough stone carved with a sword, cross and a man with a dog – is remarkably underplayed. Avoid the plethora of Rob Roy-themed **accommodation** in Balquhidder, and try instead the award-winning *Monachyle Mhor* hotel (ⓣ01877/384622, ⓦwww.monachylemhor.com; ❼), an eighteenth-century farmhouse which has a terrific restaurant specializing in local game and the added bonus of lovely views out to Loch Voil.

North of Balquhidder the A84 slides past the head of lochs Earn and Tay, both of which stretch eastwards into Perthshire (see p.348), before swinging west towards Crianlarich and the coast.

Fife

The ancient Kingdom of **Fife**, designated as such by the Picts in the fourth century, is a small area barely fifty miles at its widest point, but one which has a definite identity, inextricably linked with the waters which surround it on three sides – the Tay to the north, the Forth to the south, and the cold North Sea to the east. That the Fifers managed to retain their "kingdom" when local government was reorganized in 1975 and 1995 is perhaps testimony to their will.

Despite its small size, Fife encompasses several different regions, with a marked difference between the semi-industrial south and the rural north. In the **south**, the closure of the coal mines over the last twenty years has left local communities floundering to regain a foothold, and the squeeze on the fishing industry may well lead to further decline. In the meantime, a number of the villages have capitalized on their unpretentious appeal and welcomed tourism in a way that has enhanced rather than degraded their natural assets; the perfectly preserved town of **Culross** is the most notable of these with its cobbled streets and collection of historic buildings.

Southern Fife is dominated by the town of **Dunfermline**, a former capital of Scotland, and industralized **Kirkcaldy**, with the **Forth Rail Bridge** and Road Bridge the most memorable sights of this stretch of coastline. North of Kirkcaldy in Central Fife the unremarkable new town of **Glenrothes** is overshadowed by the absorbing village of **Falkland** with its impressive ruined palace and the country town of **Cupar**, a charming market town set in rolling countryside.

Tourism and agriculture are the economic mainstays of the **northeast** corner of Fife, where the landscape varies from the gentle hills in the rural hinterland to the windswept cliffs, rocky bays and sandy beaches on which scenes from the film *Chariots of Fire* were shot. Fishing still has a role, but ultimately it is to **St Andrews**, Scotland's oldest university town and the home of the world-famous Royal and Ancient golf club, that most visitors are drawn. Development here has been cautious, and both the town itself and the hills and hamlets of the surrounding area retain an appealing and old-fashioned feel. South of St Andrews, the tiny stone harbours of the fishing villages of the **East Neuk** are an undeniably appealing extension to any visit to this part of Fife.

Transport practicalities

The main **transport route** through the region is the M90 from Edinburgh to Perth, which edges Fife's western boundary. The coastal route is more attractive, however, and also affords relatively easy access into the centre of Fife. The train line follows the coast as far north as Kirkcaldy and then cuts inland towards Dundee, stopping on the way at Cupar and Leuchars (from where buses run to St Andrews). Exploration by public transport of the eastern and western fringes requires some planning as there is no train service and buses are few and far between. However, if you're planning on tackling a large swathe of Fife in one day, ask for a **Fife Rover** ticket from any bus driver; this costs £10 for a day and is valid on all Stagecoach Fife buses (ⓣ01592/416060), including those connecting with Glasgow, Edinburgh, Dundee and Stirling.

Southern Fife

Although the coast of **southern Fife** is predominantly industrial – with everything from cottage industries to the refitting of nuclear submarines – thankfully only a small part has been blighted by insensitive development. Even in the old coal-mining areas, disused pits and left-over slag heaps have either been well camouflaged through landscaping or put to alternative use as recreation areas. **Culross** was once a lively port which enjoyed a thriving trade with Holland, the Dutch influence obvious in its lovely gabled houses. It was from nearby **Dunfermline** that Queen Margaret ousted the Celtic Church from Scotland in the eleventh century; her son, David I, founded an abbey here in the twelfth century, and Dunfermline remains the chief town and focus of the area. Fife is linked to Edinburgh by the two **Forth bridges**, the red-painted girders of the Rail Bridge representing one of Britain's great engineering spectacles. East of the bridges are a string of historic coastal settlements dominated by the ancient royal burgh of **Kirkcaldy**, familiarly known as "The Lang Toun" for its four-mile-long esplanade which stretches the length of the waterfront. Still largely industrial, it's unlikely to hold you for long; from here you can either head east for the picturesque villages of the East Neuk (see p.345), or turn north along the main A92 road towards Central Fife (see p.334). Trains link the towns and villages of southern Fife, complemented by a good local bus service.

Culross

The A985 crosses the Forth Road Bridge, with unattractive views of the shipyard at Inverkeithing and the naval dock at Rosyth (newly commissioned as a port for ferry crossings to Zeebrugge in Belgium), before heading west along the river to **CULROSS** (pronounced "coorus"), one of Scotland's most picturesque settlements. The town's development began in the fifth century with the arrival of St Serf on the northern side of the Forth at Cuileann Ros ("point where holly grows"), and is also said to have been the birthplace of St Mungo, founder of Glasgow cathedral. Culross today is in excellent condition, thanks to the work of the NTS, which has been renovating its whitewashed, red-tiled buildings since 1932. **Buses** from Glasgow via Stirling and Alloa stop here, along with buses from Dunfermline and Falkirk. To the west, roads continue to Kincardine, where the **Kincardine Bridge** provides a second crossing point over the Forth before the Old Bridge at Stirling.

For an excellent introduction to the burgh's history, make your first stop in Culross the **National Trust Visitor Centre** (Easter week & June–Aug daily 10am–5pm; April, May & Sept daily 12.30–4.30pm; Oct Sat & Sun 12.30–4.30pm; joint ticket for Town House, Palace and Study £5), located in the **Town House** on the main road in the centre. On the upper floor of the house, some of the four thousand witches executed in Scotland between 1560 and 1707 were tried and held while awaiting execution in Edinburgh. Behind the ticket office is a tiny prison with built-in manacles. The focal point of the community is the nearby ochre-coloured **Culross Palace** (same hours), built by wealthy coal merchant George Bruce in the late sixteenth century; it's not a palace at all – its name comes from the Latin *palatium*, or "hall" – but a grand and impressive house, with lots of small rooms and connecting passageways. Inside, well-informed staff point out the wonderful painted ceilings, pine panelling, antique furniture and curios; outside, dormer windows and crow-stepped gables dominate the walled court in which the house stands. The garden is planted with grasses, herbs and vegetables of the period, carefully grown from seed. The **café** (11am–4.30pm) serves home-made food.

A cobbled alleyway known as **Back Causeway**, complete with a raised central aisle formerly used by noblemen to separate them from the commoners, leads up behind the Town House to the **Study**, a restored house that takes its name from the small room at the top of the corbelled projecting tower, reached by a turnpike stair. Built in 1610, its oak panelling in Dutch Renaissance style dates from around twenty years later.

Culross Abbey

Further up the hill from the Study lie the remains of **Culross Abbey**, founded by Cistercian monks on land given to the church in 1217 by the Earl of Fife. The nave of the original building is a ruin, a lawn studded with great stumps of columns. Although it is difficult to get a sense of what the abbey would have looked like, the overall effect is of grace and grandeur. A ladder leads to a vaulted chamber, now exposed to the elements on one side, which feels as if it is suspended in mid-air. This adjoins the fine seventeenth-century **manse**, hung with clematis, and the choir of the abbey, which became the **Parish Church** in 1633. Inside, wooden panels detail the donations given by eighteenth-century worthies to the parish poor, and a tenth-century Celtic cross in the north transept is a reminder of the origins of the abbey (a Celtic church stood here in 450). Alabaster figures of Sir George Bruce, his lady, three sons and five daughters decorate the splendid family tomb, the parents lying in state and the children lined up and kneeling in devotion. A brass plaque tells the story of Edward, Lord Bruce of Kinloss, who was defeated by Sir Edward Sackville in a duel fought in Bergen in Holland in 1613. The luckless lord had been buried in Holland, but a persistent rumour that his heart had been taken back to Scotland was proved true when it was found during building work in the church in 1808, embalmed in a silver casket of foreign workmanship.

The **graveyard** of the church is fascinating. Many of the graves are eighteenth-century, with symbols depicting the occupation of the person who is buried; the gravestone of a gardener has a crossed spade and rake and an hourglass with the sand run out – the latter a symbol of mortality used on many of the graves. Note the Scottish custom, still continued, of marking women's graves with maiden names, even when they are buried with their husbands.

Dunfermline

Scotland's capital until the Union of the Crowns in 1603, **DUNFERMLINE** lies inland seven miles east of Culross, north of the Forth bridges. This "auld, grey toun" is built on a hill, dominated by the **abbey** and ruined **palace** at the top. In the eleventh century, Malcolm III (Malcolm Canmore) offered refuge here to Edgar Atheling, heir to the English throne, and his family, who were shipwrecked in the Forth while fleeing the Norman Conquest. Malcolm married Edgar's Catholic sister Margaret in 1067, and in so doing started a process of reformation that ultimately supplanted the Celtic Church. Until the late nineteenth century, Dunfermline was one of Scotland's foremost linen producers, as well as a major coal-mining centre, and today the town is a busy place, its ever-increasing sprawl attesting to a growing economy.

The Town

Dunfermline's **centre**, at the top of the hill around the abbey and palace, holds an appeal of its own, with its narrow, cobbled streets, pedestrianized shopping areas and gargoyle-adorned buildings. One of the best of these, the **city chambers** on the corner of Bridge and Bruce streets, is a fine example of late nineteenth-century Gothic Revival style. Among the ornate porticoes and grotesques of dragons and winged serpents which adorn the exterior are the sculpted heads of Robert the Bruce, Malcolm Canmore, Queen Margaret and Elizabeth I.

The abbey and palace

The oldest part of **Dunfermline Abbey** (April–Sept Mon–Sat 9.30am–6.30pm, Sun 2–4.30pm; Oct–March Mon–Wed & Sat 9.30am–4.30pm, Thurs

9.30am–12.30pm, Fri & Sun 2–4.30pm; HS; £2) is attributable to Queen Margaret, who began building a Benedictine priory in 1072, the remains of which can still be seen beneath the nave of the present church; her son, **David I**, raised the priory to the rank of abbey in the following century. In 1303, during the first of the **Wars of Independence**, the English king Edward I occupied the palace, had the church roof stripped of lead to provide ammunition for his army's catapults, and also appears to have ordered the destruction of most of the monastery buildings. **Robert the Bruce** helped rebuild the abbey, and when he died of leprosy was buried here 25 years later, although his body went undiscovered until building began on a new parish church in 1821. The enormous stonework graffiti, "King Robert the Bruce", at the top of the tower is attributable to an overexcited architect thrilled by the discovery of Bruce's remains. A plaque beneath the pulpit marks the spot where Robert the Bruce's remains were laid to rest for the second time, while Malcolm and his queen, Margaret, who died of grief three days after her husband in 1093, have a shrine outside.

The guesthouse of Margaret's Benedictine monastery, south of the abbey, became the **palace** in the sixteenth century under James VI, who gave both it and the abbey to his consort, Queen Anne of Denmark. Charles I, the last monarch to be born in Scotland, entered the world here in 1600. All that is left of it today is a long, sandstone facade, especially impressive when silhouetted against the evening sky. The four redundant walls next to the palace are those of the refectory, connected via the gatehouse to the kitchen, which was tacked on at the palace's eastern end.

Near the entrance to the abbey, pink-harled **Abbot House** (daily 10am–5pm; £3), possibly fourteenth-century, is bright from the outside and, some would argue, just as light and frivolous on the inside. This building, variously used as an iron foundry, an art school and a doctor's surgery, now houses a rather haphazard array of exhibits and experiences designed to bring different parts of Dunfermline's past to life, from an audiovisual ghost to a 1960s living room. You can visit the witches'-coven-style café with a patio garden first to decide if you are willing to pay the entrance fee to see more.

Pittencrieff Park and around

Pittencrieff Park, known to locals as "the Glen", covers a huge area in the centre of Dunfermline. Bordering the ruined palace, the 76-acre park used to be owned by the Lairds of Pittencrieff, whose 1610 estate house, built of stone pillaged from the palace, still stands within the grounds. In 1902, however, the entire plot was purchased by the local rags-to-riches industrialist and philanthropist Andrew Carnegie, who donated it to his home town. This was just as much sweet revenge as beneficent public-spiritedness: the young Carnegie had been banned from the estate, according to a former laird's edict that no Morrison would pass through the gates. Since his mother had been a Morrison, Carnegie could do little but gaze through the bars on the one day a year that the estate was open to the rest of the public. Today, **Pittencrieff House** (daily 11am–5pm; Oct–March closes 4pm; free) displays exhibits on local history, the glasshouses are filled with exotic blooms, and the Pavilion coffee shop offers refreshment. In the centre of the park by a small stream are the remains – little more than the foundations – of **Malcolm Canmore's Tower**, which may be the location of Malcolm's residence, known to have been somewhere to the west of the abbey. Dunfermline, meaning "fort by the crooked pool", takes its name from the tower's location: *dun* meaning hill or fort; *fearum* bent or crooked; and *lin* (or *lyne/line*) a pool or running water.

Just beyond the southeast corner of the park, the modest little cottage at the bottom of St Margaret Street is **Andrew Carnegie's Birthplace** (April–Oct Mon–Sat 11am–5pm, Sun 2–5pm; £2). The son of a weaver, Carnegie (1835–1919) lived as a child upstairs with his family, while the room below housed his father's loom shop. After the family emigrated to America in 1848, Carnegie worked first on the railroads and then in the iron and steel industries; he began acquiring steel-production firms in the 1870s and was so successful that by the time he retired in 1901 he was a multimillionaire and one of the richest men in the world. For the next 18 years he devoted himself to giving the money away, endowing educational establishments and free libraries around the world, including some 600 in Britain. Dunfermline's local theatre is Carnegie Hall, though not quite on the scale of its New York namesake. His house has been preserved as it was at the end of the nineteenth century, and the adjacent Memorial Hall details his life and work.

Just north of the park, the holy shrine of **St Margaret's Cave** (Easter–Sept daily 11am–4pm; free) lies incongruously buried beneath the Glen Bridge car park. A dimly lit passageway descends deep into the ground, past displays and information panels that document the pious life of Margaret, who prayed here every day. At the bottom, the sparse stone praying area is small and damp, though in Margaret's day it would have been decorated with crosses and candles.

Practicalities

Trains from Edinburgh stop at Dunfermline's **train station**, halfway down the long hill of St Margaret's Drive, southeast of the centre. It's a fifteen-minute walk up the hill from here to the **tourist office** at 1 High St, immediately opposite the City Chambers (April–Sept Mon–Sat 10am–5pm; Aug also Sun 11.30am–3.30pm; phone for winter hours; ⓣ01383/720999). An hourly bus from Edinburgh and two-hourly services from Glasgow, Perth and Dundee come in at the **bus station**, in the Kingsgate Centre, on the north side of town. For **accommodation**, try the comfortable *Davaar House Hotel*, 126 Grieve St (ⓣ01383/721886; ❺), in a tastefully furnished Victorian town house, or *Hillview House*, 9 Aberdour Rd (ⓣ01383/726278; ❷). There are some good, well-priced **places to eat**, including the stylish modern *Bar Café Brio* on the corner of Canmore and Guildhall streets, *Blossom's*, 6–8 Chalmers St (ⓣ01383 623092), for Chinese food, or you can get bar meals at the *Old Inn*, just down Kirkgate, which has *The Creepy Wee Pub* right next door. For great traditional Italian food, there's *Il Pescatore* (ⓣ01383/872999; ❺) on the coast at Limekilns (about five miles south of the town on the B9156), which also offers reasonable accommodation and boasts of patronage in the past from Prince Andrew and his naval chums.

The Forth bridges and the coast

Fife's **south coast** curves sharply north at the mouth of the Forth, exposing the towns and villages to an icy east wind that somewhat undermines the sunshine image of their beaches. For a pleasant, but time-consuming alternative route to St Andrews, you can head east along the A921 after crossing the **Forth Road Bridge**, following the train line as it clings to the northern shore of the mouth of the Forth. Here you'll find a straggle of Fife fishing communities which have depended on the sea for centuries, and now make popular, although not especially attractive, holiday spots. The **train** line from Inverkeithing and twice-hourly **buses** #7 and #7a from Dunfermline run along this coast, stopping at all towns. The most interesting route is the **Fife**

Coastal Path, a waymarked walking trail which picks its way for over fifty miles along the coast all the way from North Queensferry to Crail.

North Queensferry

Cowering beneath the Forth bridges is **NORTH QUEENSFERRY**, a small fishing village, which, until the opening of the road bridge, was the northern landing point of the ferry from South Queensferry (see p.150) and a nineteenth-century bathing resort. Built on a rocky outcrop, the place is comparatively well preserved for somewhere which takes such a battering from the elements. Everything in North Queensferry is, however, quite literally overshadowed by the two great bridges, each about a mile and a half in length, which traverse the Firth of Forth at its narrowest point. The cantilevered **Forth Rail Bridge**, built from 1883 to 1890 by Sir John Fowler and Benjamin Baker, ranks among the supreme achievements of Victorian engineering. Some 50,000 tons of steel were used in the construction of a design that manages to express grace as well as might. The bridge is renowned for the fact that it takes so long to paint, that as soon as workers reach the end they must go back to the beginning to start repainting. However, an ambitious programme has now been put forward to strip the old paint and replace it with a high-tech, long-lasting coating that will render the continuous painting process redundant.

Derived from American models, the suspension format chosen for the **Forth Road Bridge** alongside makes an interesting modern complement to the older structure. Erected between 1958 and 1964, it finally killed off the 900-year-old ferry, and now attracts a heavy volume of traffic.

While the geometric girders of the rail bridge are one of the most spectacular sights in Scotland, particularly after dark now that they are **floodlit**, the road bridge which parallels it is grand but comparatively dull. The only way to cross the rail bridge is aboard a train heading to or from Edinburgh, though inevitably this doesn't allow much of a perspective of the spectacle itself. For the best **panorama** of the rail bridge, make use of the pedestrian and cycle lane on the east side of the parallel road bridge. For some background to the construction of the bridges, head to the **Forth Bridges Exhibition** (daily 9am–9pm; free), occupying a couple of rooms tacked onto the modern *Queensferry Lodge Hotel*, which has a series of storyboards, photographs, models and displays. Here you can contemplate various mind-boggling statistics such as the fact that there are six and a half million rivets in the rail bridge, and that a shower of rain adds around 100 tons to its weight.

Tucked underneath the mighty geometry of the rail bridge is **Deep-Sea World** (July & Aug daily 10am–6.30pm; April–June, Sept & Oct daily 10am–6pm; Nov–March Mon–Fri 11am–5pm; £6.50), one of Scotland's most popular family attractions. Full of weird and wonderful creatures from sea horses to piranhas, the highlight is a huge aquarium that boasts the world's largest underwater viewing tunnel, through which you glide on a moving walkway while sharks, conger eels and all manner of fish from the deep swim nonchalantly past.

Inverkeithing

The North Queensferry peninsula gives way to Inverkeithing Bay and **INVERKEITHING**, a medieval watering place established by David I in the twelfth century and granted a charter by William I around 1165, thanks to its strategic location and safe harbour. Modern Inverkeithing is unprepossessing, with housing estates sprawling around the more attractive old town centre. The **Parish Church of St Peter**, on Church Street near the train station, began as a wooden Celtic church before Queen Margaret set to work, and ended up as a Norman stone structure bequeathed to Dunfermline Abbey in 1139. The oldest part of it today is the fifteenth-century tower, the rest having been razed by fire in 1825.

Aberdour

Four miles east of Inverkeithing, **ABERDOUR** clings tight to the walls of its **castle** (April–Sept daily 9.30am–6pm; Oct–March Mon–Wed & Sat 9.30am–4pm, Thurs 9.30am–12.30pm; Fri & Sun 2–4pm; HS; £2) at the southern end of the main street. Once a Douglas stronghold, the castle is on a comparatively modest scale, with gently sloping lawns, a large enclosed seventeenth-century garden and terraces. The fourteenth-century tower is the oldest part of the castle, the other buildings having been added in the sixteenth and seventeenth centuries, including the well-preserved dovecote. Worth more perusal is **St Fillan's Church**, also in the castle grounds, which dates from the twelfth century, with a few sixteenth-century additions, such as the porch restored from total dereliction in the last century. There's little else to see here apart from the town's popular **silver sands** beach, which, along with its water-sports, golf and sailing, has earned Aberdour the rather optimistic tourist board soubriquet the "Fife Riviera". From Aberdour you can take a **ferry** (Ⓣ01383/823332) to Inchcolm Island to see its ruined medieval abbey (April–Sept daily 9.30am–6.30pm; HS; £2.80, ferry extra).

For **accommodation**, the real gem is *Hawkcraig House*, Hawkcraig Point (Ⓣ01383/860335; ❸), a guesthouse with a good **restaurant** in an old ferry-man's house overlooking the harbour. Alternatively, you could try the friendly *Aberdour Hotel* on High Street (Ⓣ01383/860325, Ⓦwww.aberdourhotel.co.uk; ❹), which also has an inexpensive restaurant downstairs.

Burntisland

Three miles east of Aberdour is the large holiday resort of **BURNTISLAND** with its fine stretch of sandy beach. The busy High Street runs the length of the waterfront, hemmed in by buildings at the western end, where you'll find the unkempt **train station**. Offices now occupy **Rossend Castle**, a fifteenth-century tower beyond the west end of High Street with sixteenth-century additions, sadly not open to the public. In 1563, Pierre de Chastelard, an eager French poet, was discovered in the bedchamber of the visiting Mary, Queen of Scots. Chastelard, having been warned once already about hiding in the young queen's private rooms at Holyrood Palace, was whisked off to St Andrews where, proclaiming "Adieu, thou most beautiful and most cruel Princess in the world", he was executed.

Although almost every house along the Links, just beyond High Street, sports a B&B sign, Burntisland isn't the most inspiring place to **stay**, particularly given the riches of the East Neuk further along the road. The *Kingswood Hotel*, Kinghorn Road (Ⓣ01592/872329, Ⓦwww.kingswoodhotel.co.uk; ❺), set in its own grounds with views across the Forth, is the most comfortable hotel, while for B&B *Gruinard*, 148 Kinghorn Rd (Ⓣ01592/873877; ❷) is a comfortable place offering a log fire, conservatory and pancakes for breakfast. **Eating** options include *The Smugglers Inn*, 14 Harbour Place, which does snacks and bar meals and has a good vegetarian selection.

Kinghorn

Shortly before reaching **KINGHORN**, the coastal road from Burntisland passes a **Celtic cross** commemorating Alexander III, the last of the Celtic kings, who plunged over the cliff near here one night in 1286 when his horse stumbled. The event was more than unfortunate for Scotland, as it threw the country from relative stability into a crisis of succession in which the English king Edward I was only too happy to play a role. The Wars of Independence followed, during which time Wallace and Bruce enjoyed their famous battlefield victories, but Scotland suffered greatly. The ancient settlement of Kinghorn is today a popular but not too crowded holiday centre, with few formal attractions, but a good beach. The ugly brown pebble-dashed **parish church**, looking over the beach and whipped by wintry winds at the land's edge, dates from 1894, though the site has been used as a church for centuries and the small graveyard is filled with lichen-covered, semi-legible tombstones from the eighteenth century. At the opposite (southern) end of town, a hill lined with Spanish-style villas leads down to the waterfront and the beach at **Pettycur Bay**, where fishing boats cluster round the small harbour and brightly coloured lobster nets dot the sands.

Kirkcaldy

KIRKCALDY (pronounced "kir-coddy") doesn't hold a great deal of interest for the visitor, its charms largely obliterated by overdevelopment. However, a stroll along the promenade is pleasant on a sunny day and there's a good range of the major chain stores in the town centre. The esplanade was built in 1923 – not just to hold back the sea, but also to alleviate unemployment – and runs parallel for part of the way with the shorter High Street. If you're here in mid-April, you'll see the historic **Links Market**, a week-long funfair that dates back to 1305 and is possibly the largest street fair in Britain. The town's history is chronicled in its **Museum and Art Gallery** (Mon–Sat 10.30am–5pm, Sun 2–5pm; free) in the colourful War Memorial Gardens between the train and bus stations. The museum covers everything from archeological discoveries to the tradition of the local Wemyss Ware pottery and the evolution of the present town. Since its inception in 1925, the gallery has built up its collection to around three hundred works by some of Scotland's finest painters from the late eighteenth century onwards, including works by the fine portraitist Sir Henry Raeburn, the historical painter Sir David Wilkie, the Scottish "Colourists", the "Glasgow Boys" and William McTaggart. For a town which is known primarily for linoleum production and whose reputation is firmly rooted in the prosaic, the art gallery is an unexpected boon.

Just beyond the northern end of the waterfront, Ravenscraig Park is the site of the substantial ruin of **Ravenscraig Castle** (free access), a thick-walled, fifteenth-century defence post, which (as long as you're looking out to sea) occupies a lovely spot above a beach. The castle looks out over the Forth, and is flanked on either side by a flight of steps – the inspiration, apparently, for the title of John Buchan's novel, *The Thirty-Nine Steps*. Sir Walter Scott also found this a place worthy of comment, using it as a setting for the story of "lovely Rosabella" in *The Lay of the Last Minstrel*.

On the eastern edge of Kirkcaldy lies the old suburb of **Dysart**, where tall ships once arrived bringing cargo from the Netherlands, setting off again with coal, beer, salt and fish. Well restored, and retaining historic street names such as Hot Pot Wynd (after the hot pans used for salt evaporation), it's an atmospheric place of narrow alleyways and picturesque old buildings. In Rectory Lane, the birthplace of John McDouall Stuart (who in 1862 became the first man to cross Australia from south to north) now holds the **John McDouall Stuart Museum** (June–Aug daily 2–5pm; NTS; free), giving an account of his emigration to Australia in 1838 and his subsequent adventures.

Incidentally, though there's little to show for it today, architect brothers Robert and James Adam were born in Kirkcaldy, as was the eighteenth-century scholar, philosopher and political economist Adam Smith, whose great 1776 work *The Wealth of Nations* established political economy as a separate science and is credited (or blamed) as having a significant influence on the free-market policies pursued by Margaret Thatcher and her acolytes in the 1980s.

Practicalities

Kirkcaldy's **train** and **bus stations** are in the upper part of town – keep heading downhill to get to the centre. For the **tourist office**, 19 Whytescauseway (Mon–Sat 10am–5pm; ⓣ01592/267775), follow the road for about ten minutes round to the right from the bus station. The tourist office's accommodation booking service is a life-saver; there are few places **to stay** in the centre, and the layout of the rest of the town is not easy to follow because of the way it falls across the hillside. In the town centre the refined *Dunnikier House Hotel*, Dunnikier Park, Dunnikier Way (ⓣ01592/268393, ⓦwww.dunnikier-house-hotel.co.uk; ❹), serves fine local food and is set in pleasant grounds. Otherwise, the *Bennochy Bank Guest House* (ⓣ01592/200733; ❷) offers decent B&B in a relatively central location, while along the road in Dysart the *Royal Hotel*, Townhead (ⓣ01592/654112; ❷), occupies one of the village's historic buildings.

The *Royal Hotel* is a good place for **eating**, as is the *Old Rectory Inn*, West Quality Street, also in Dysart. In Kirkcaldy itself, try *Giovanni's*, 66 Dunnikier Rd (ⓣ01592/200659), for traditional Italian food. *Valente's*, 73 Overton Rd, is an unprepossessing, hard-to-find but award-winning fish and chip shop much treasured by locals. (Overton Road is east of the centre, roughly parallel to St Claire Street which leads down to the front.)

There's a good **arts cinema** with a restaurant and bar housed in the Adam Smith Theatre on Bennochy Road in the town centre (ⓣ01592/412929).

Central Fife

The main A92 road cuts right through **Central Fife**, ultimately connecting the Forth Road Bridge on the southern coast of Fife with the Tay Road Bridge on the northern coast. The main settlement of this inland region is **Glenrothes**, a new town created after World War II in old coal mining territory. Generally the scenery in this part of the county is pleasant rather than startling, though it is worth diverting off the road, however, to seek out **Falkland** and its magnificent ruined palace, and **Cupar**, the county town on the road to St Andrews.

Glenrothes and around

Inland from Kirkcaldy, the old **mining towns** of Cowdenbeath, Kelty, Lochgelly and Cardenden huddle together, their fires virtually extinguished by a blanket of economic depression. These are neglected places, and indeed are rarely even seen by visitors shooting up to St Andrews on the coastal route or zooming along the M90 to Perth. Take the train, however, and you'll weave through this forlorn stretch as the line leaves the coast and heads inland.

Ten miles inland from Kirkcaldy, **GLENROTHES** is a largely generic new town. Stark, concrete and utilitarian, it is the European headquarters of the American company Raytheon Systems, who, along with similar microelectronics operations in "Silicon Glen" (Scotland's version of Silicon Valley), have given parts of the region much-needed wealth and self-confidence. Until recently, a sign at Markinch train station (the nearest one to Glenrothes, a little to the east) boldly announced, "Welcome to Glenrothes, the Capital of Fife". So outraged at this audacity were the residents of Cupar, Fife's real capital for centuries, that the sign had to be removed.

If you have even a passing interest in castles and their construction, try to visit **Balgonie Castle**, two miles east of Glenrothes on the B921 off the A911. Set above the River Leven, this splendid castle with its fourteenth-century keep and fine open courtyard has a somewhat unkempt appearance from the outside; only a small plaque stating that it is home to the Laird and Lady of Balgonie suggests it's inhabited. Don't be put off by the huge, but docile, Scottish deerhounds, or by the fact that you may have to wait some time at the door of the keep before anyone hears your knock. Once inside, you are guaranteed a uniquely personal tour from the laird or a member of his family; the castle has the distinction of being open every day of the year (roughly 10am–5pm; £3) except when the fourteenth-century chapel is being used for candlelit weddings. The tour gives in-depth information on the architecture of the castle and its owners and occupiers, including Rob Roy who stayed here with 200 clansmen in 1716. Balgonie was partly restored in 1971 and the present laird, who hails from the West Midlands but is always attired in a kilt, has continued the process.

Falkland

The **Howe of Fife**, north of Glenrothes, is a low-lying stretch of ground (or "howe") at the foot of the twin peaks of the heather-swathed **Lomond Hills** – West Lomond (1696ft) and East Lomond (1378ft). Nestling in the lower slopes of East Lomond, the narrow streets of **FALKLAND** are lined with fine and well-preserved seventeenth- and eighteenth-century buildings. The village grew up around **Falkland Palace** (June–Aug Mon–Sat 10am–5.30pm, Sun 1.30–5.30pm; April, May, Sept & Oct Mon–Sat 11am–5.30pm, Sun 1.30–5.30pm; NTS; £5, gardens only £2.50), which stands on the site of an earlier castle, home to the Macduffs, the Earls of Fife. James IV began the construction of the present palace in 1500; it was completed and embellished by James V, and became a favoured royal residence. Charles II stayed here in 1650, when he was in Scotland for his coronation, but after the Jacobite rising of 1715 and temporary occupation by Rob Roy the palace was abandoned, remaining so until the late nineteenth century when the keepership was acquired by the third Marquess of Bute. He completely restored the palace, and today it is a stunning example of Early Renaissance architecture, complete with corbelled parapet, mullioned windows, round towers and massive walls. A **guided tour** (40min) takes in a cross section of public and private rooms in the south and east wings. The former is better preserved and includes the stately drawing room, the Chapel Royal (still used for Mass) and the Tapestry Gallery, swathed with splendid seventeenth-century Flemish hangings. Outside, the **gardens** are also worth a look, their well-stocked herbaceous borders lining a pristine lawn, and they feature the oldest tennis court in Britain – built in 1539 for James V and still used.

Falkland is also a good base for **walks**, with several leading from the village; but for the more serious hikes to the summits of East and West Lomond, you have to start from Craigmead car park about two miles west of the village (follow the usual safety precautions; see p.46).

Accommodation includes the *Burgh Lodge*, a newly renovated independent **hostel** on Back Wynd (☎01337/857710) which has facilities for families and people with disabilities. Both the *Hunting Lodge Hotel*, on High Street, directly opposite the palace (Ⓣ01337/857226, Ⓦwww.huntinglodgehotel.com; ❸), and the *Covenanter Hotel* (Ⓣ01337/857224, Ⓦwww.covenanterhotel.com; ❸), just up the road, are comfortable traditional inns, with great pubs as well as a couple of rooms upstairs. *The Greenhouse* (Ⓣ01337/858400; closed Mon & Tues), also on the High Street, is a small modern restaurant serving organic food.

Cupar and around

Straddling the small River Eden and surrounded by gentle hills, **CUPAR**, the capital of Fife, has retained much of its medieval character – and its self-confident air – from the days when it was a bustling market centre. A livestock auction still takes place here every week. In 1276 Alexander III held an assembly in the town, bringing together the church, aristocracy and local burgesses in an early form of Scottish parliament. For his troubles he subsequently became the butt of Sir David Lindsay's *Ane Pleasant Satyre of the Thrie Estaitis* (1535), one of the first great Scottish dramas.

Situated at the centre of Fife's road network, Cupar's main street, part of the main road from Edinburgh to St Andrews, is plagued with thundering traffic. The **Mercat Cross**, stranded in the midst of the lorries and cars which speed through the centre, now consists of salvaged sections of the seventeenth-century original, following its destruction by an errant lorry some years ago.

One of the best reasons for stopping off at Cupar is to visit the **Hill of Tarvit** (July & Aug daily 11am–5.30pm; Easter, May, June & Sept daily 1.30–5.30pm; Oct Sat & Sun 1.30–5.30pm; NTS; £5; gardens daily 9.30am–sunset), an Edwardian mansion two miles south of town remodelled by Sir Robert Lorimer from a late seventeenth-century building. The estate, formerly the home of the geographer and cartographer Sir John Scott, includes the five-storey, late sixteenth-century **Scotstarvit Tower**, three-quarters of a mile west of the present house (keys available from the house during season only). Set on a little mound, Scotstarvit is a fine example of a Scots tower house, providing both fortification and comfort. The entire estate was bequeathed to the NTS in 1949, and the house contains an impressive collection of eighteenth-century Chippendale and French furniture, Dutch paintings, Chinese porcelain and a restored Edwardian laundry.

Practicalities

Cupar's **train station** is immediately south of the centre; **bus** #23 from Stirling to St Andrews stops outside. If you want to **stay**, try the friendly *Eden House Hotel*, 2 Pitscottie Rd (Ⓣ01334/652510, Ⓦwww.eden-group.com; ❻), which also serves good Scottish food, or *Westfield House* on Westfield Road (Ⓣ01334/655699; ❸), a smart B&B set in a landscaped garden. There is no shortage of good **restaurants** in the area; try the excellent *Ostler's Close*, 25 Bonnygate (Ⓣ01334/655574), or follow the B940 east to the renowned *Peat Inn* (see p.344). For drinks and bar food, try *Watts* on Coal Road.

Around Cupar

West of Cupar are a couple of attractions particularly suitable for children. The **Scottish Deer Centre** (daily 10am–6pm; Nov–Easter closes 5pm; £4.50), three miles from Cupar on the A91, specializes in the rearing of red deer, and is also home to species of sika, fallow and reindeer. The tamer animals can be approached and there are falconry displays three times a day, as well as play and picnic areas and guided nature trails. A couple of miles further west along the A91, more creatures are on show at the **Fife Animal Park** (April- Oct daily

10am–5pm; £3.50), next to Birnie Loch Nature Reserve. Children will enjoy watching ostriches cavort, and looking at chickens, goats and pot-bellied pigs in the children's farm.

A couple of miles southeast of Cupar, **CERES**, set around a village green, is home to the **Fife Folk Museum** (Easter & mid-May to Oct daily 2–5pm; £2.50). Occupying several well-preserved seventeenth- to nineteenth-century buildings, it exhibits all manner of historical farming and agricultural paraphernalia. The pillory that used to restrain miscreants on market days still stands at the entrance of the old burgh tollbooth, and at the village crossroads is an unusual seventeenth-century stone carving of a man in a three-cornered hat with a toothy grin and a beer glass on his knee, said to be a depiction of a former provost.

Continuing east on the B939, you soon come to **Magnus Muir**, halfway between Cupar and St Andrews, site of the murder of the controversial and oppressive Episcopalian Archbishop of St Andrews by a band of Covenanters in 1679. During the struggle, Archbishop Sharp's daughter, Isabella, was wounded trying to protect him. One of the culprits, Hackston of Rathillet, was captured in Edinburgh and gruesomely executed, his hands being buried in Cupar's graveyard.

The Tay coast

North of Cupar, Fife's **Tay coast** is a peaceful wedge of rural hinterland on the edge of the River Tay looking across to Dundee and Perthshire. It offers little in the way of specific attractions, but a lot of undiscovered hideaways. Gentle hills fringe the shore, sheltering the villages – several of which only acquired running water and streetlights in the past decade or two – that lie in the dips and hollows along the coast.

LEUCHARS, five miles north of St Andrews, is known for its RAF base, from where low-flying jets screech over the hills, appearing out of nowhere and sending sheep, cows and horses galloping for shelter. There is a beautiful twelfth-century church in the village, with fine Norman stonework. Romantic **Earlshall Castle** (no public access), just east of Leuchars, is the home of the Baron and Baroness of Earlshall, whose ancestor, Sir William Bruce, built the castle in 1546.

Northeast of Leuchars, **Tentsmuir Forest** occupies the northeasternmost point of the Fife headland, and is also a nature reserve with a good beach and peaceful woodland walks – so peaceful that you would never guess it's only five miles or so from the **Tay bridges** (80p toll charge on the road bridge), with Dundee just the other side. The current Tay **rail bridge** is the second to span the river on this spot, the first having collapsed in a terrifying disaster during a storm on December 28, 1879, which claimed the lives of around a hundred people in a train crossing the bridge at the time. The event was recorded by the poet William McGonagall, who has gone down in history as being responsible for some of the most banal verse ever written, including a memorably trite rhyme about the disaster:

So the train mov'd slowly along the Bridge of Tay,
Until it was about midway,
Then the central girders with a crash gave way,
And down went the train and passengers into the Tay!
The storm Fiend did loudly bray,
Because ninety lives had been taken away,
On the last Sabbath day of 1879,
Which will be remember'd for a very long time.

There's a **camping** and **caravan** site at **TAYPORT** (☎01382/552334), a popular resort a couple of miles east of the bridge, from where one of Scotland's oldest ferries once ran across the river. Here the "silvery Tay" more than justifies its traditional description, shimmering in the light whatever the season. There are good views across the river from the shingly cove at **BALMERINO**, a quaint hamlet five miles further west, just below the ruin of **Balmerino Abbey** (daily dawn–dusk; NTS; £1), surrounded by venerable old trees, including an enormous gnarled Spanish chestnut, which has stood here for four centuries. The Cistercian abbey was founded in 1229 by Alexander II and his mother Ermengarde, who is buried here, and built by monks from the abbey at Melrose in the Borders. Destroyed by the English in 1547, reconstruction work was halted for good by the Reformation. Unfortunately, the only substantial part remaining is unsafe and inaccessible.

Lindores Abbey, seven miles or so further west along the coast, dates from the century before and was a Benedictine settlement. The west tower still stands, silhouetted against the sky, and there are views down to nearby **NEWBURGH**, stunning on a summer evening, with the setting sun lighting up the mud flats below and skimming across the Tay. Newburgh itself is a fairly quiet, slightly rough-edged place. Originally a fishing village, it evolved due to its proximity to the abbey, and is now known for the admirable **Laing Museum** (April–Sept Mon–Fri 10am–5pm, Sat & Sun 2–5pm; Oct–March Wed & Fri noon–4pm, Sun 2–5pm; free). The collection, donated by the banker and historian Dr Alexander Laing in 1892, includes a fine array of antiques and geological specimens gathered in the area.

St Andrews and the East Neuk

Confident, poised and well groomed, if a little snooty, **ST ANDREWS**, Scotland's oldest **university town** and a pilgrimage centre for **golfers** from all over the world, is situated on a wide bay on the northeastern coast of Fife. Of all Scotland's universities, St Andrews is most often compared to Oxford or Cambridge both for the dominance of gown over town, and for the intimate, collegiate feel of the place. Accentuating the comparison is the fact that the student population has a significant proportion of English undergraduates, among them, famously, Prince William, rather to the chagrin of townsfolk who imagine there to be a tabloid photographer lurking round every street corner.

According to legend, the town was founded, pretty much by accident, in the fourth century. **St Rule** – or Regulus – a custodian of the bones of St Andrew in Patras in southern Greece, had a vision in which an angel ordered him to carry five of the saint's bones to the western edge of the world, where he was to build a city in his honour. The conscientious courier set off, but was shipwrecked on the rocks close to the present harbour. Struggling ashore with his precious burden, he built a shrine to the saint on what subsequently became the site of the **cathedral**; St Andrew became Scotland's patron saint and the town its ecclesiastical capital.

St Andrews isn't a large place, with only three main streets and an open, airy feel encouraged by the long stretches of sand on either side of town and the acreage of golf links all around. Local residents are proud of their town, with its refined old-fashioned ambience. Thanks to a strong and well-informed local conservation lobby, many of the original buildings have survived. Almost the entire centre consists of listed buildings, while the ruined castle and cathedral have all but been rebuilt in the efforts to preserve their remains.

From St Andrews the attractive beaches and little fishing villages of the **East Neuk** (*neuk* is Scots for "corner") are within easy reach, although the area can also be approached from the Kirkcaldy side. Though golf and coastal walks are a shared characteristic, the East Neuk villages have few of the grand buildings and important bustle of St Andrews, with old cottages and merchants' houses huddling round stone-built harbours in scenes fallen upon with joy by artists and photographers.

Arrival and information

St Andrews is not on the train line. The nearest **train station** is on the Edinburgh–Dundee line at Leuchars, five miles northwest across the River Eden, from where regular buses make the fifteen-minute trip into town. (When you buy your rail ticket to Leuchars, ask for a St Andrews rail-bus ticket which includes the bus fare.) Frequent **buses** from Edinburgh and Dundee terminate at the bus station on City Road at the west end of Market Street. The **tourist office**, 70 Market St (July & Aug Mon–Sat 9.30am–7pm, Sun 10am–5pm; May & June Mon–Sat 9.30am–5.30pm, Sun 11am–4pm; Sept Mon–Sat 9.30am–6pm, Sun 11am–4pm; April Mon–Sat 9.30am–5pm, Sun 11am–4pm; Oct–March Mon–Sat 9.30am–5pm; ⓣ01334/472021, ⓦwww.standrews.com), holds comprehensive information about St Andrews and northeast Fife. If you're **driving**, the town's fiendish **parking** system requires vouchers (Mon–Sat 9am–5pm; 40p/hr) which you can get from the tourist office and some local shops.

An open-topped bus (July & Aug daily; June & Sept Fri–Mon; £5.50) takes a one-hour **tour** around town. Audio headsets with a historical tour of the main sights are available from the tourist office. In summer, a **witches tour** seeks out the spooky spots around town (get details on ⓣ01334/655057).

If you're here in early August, don't miss the two-day **Lammas Fair**, Scotland's oldest surviving medieval market, complete with town crier. The other main event in the St Andrews calendar is the **Kate Kennedy Pageant**, usually held on the third Saturday in April, which involves an all-male procession of students taking to the streets dressed as characters associated with the university, from Kate Kennedy herself, niece of one of the university founders, to Mary, Queen of Scots.

Accommodation

With St Andrews' wide ranging appeal to visitors there's no shortage of **accommodation** both in town and around. Upmarket **hotels** are thick on the ground, notably around the golf courses, though what many take to be the finest hotel location, the red sandstone building immediately behind the R&A clubhouse and 18th green of the Old Course, is in fact Hamilton Hall, a student residence. There are plenty of **guesthouses** in a central location, notably huddled together around Murray Place and Murray Park, though rooms often get booked up in the summer, when you should definitely book in advance. **Campus** rooms are no cheaper than many B&Bs, though for **budget** accommodation there is a backpacker hostel in a lively location close to the student union.

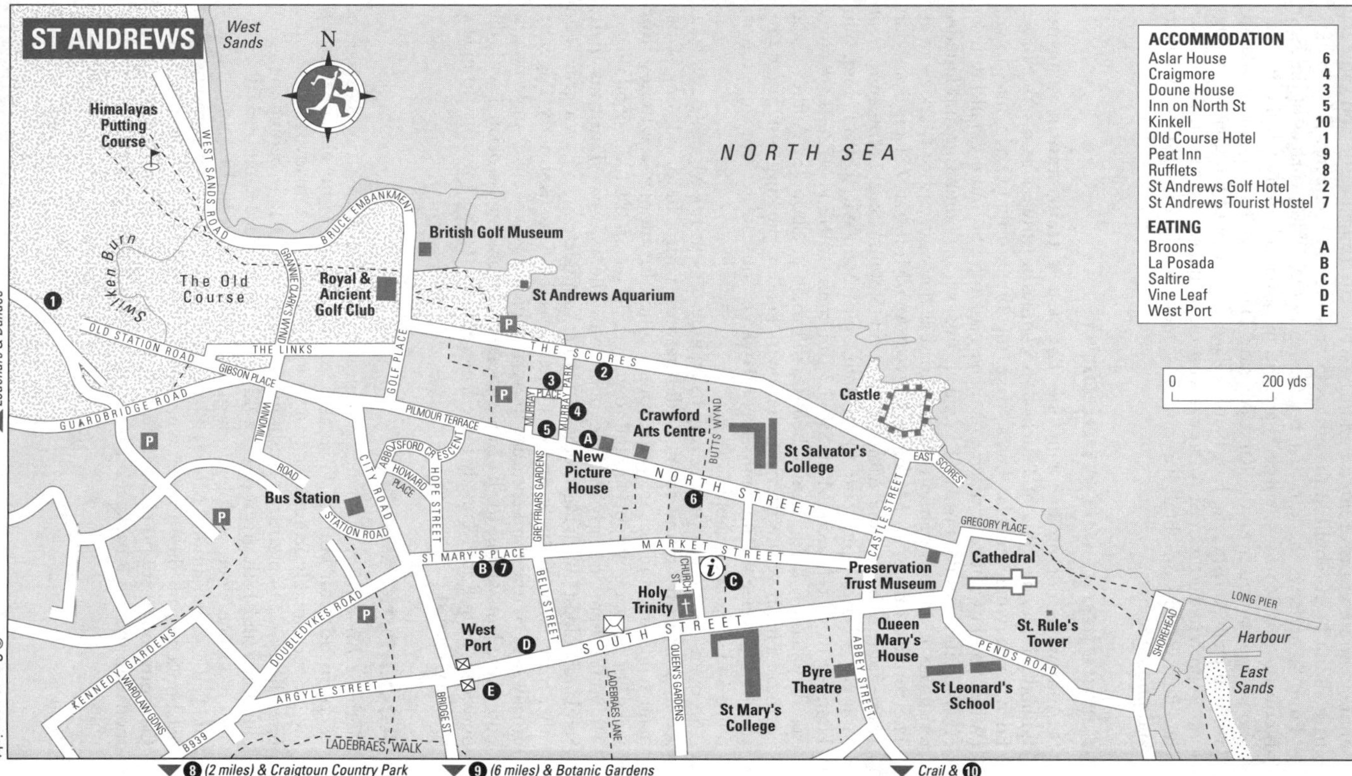
ST ANDREWS
ACCOMMODATION
Aslar House 6
Craigmore 4
Doune House 3
Inn on North St 5
Kinkell 10
Old Course Hotel 1
Peat Inn 9
Rufflets 8
St Andrews Golf Hotel 2
St Andrews Tourist Hostel 7
EATING
Broons A
La Posada B
Saltire C
Vine Leaf D
West Port E
0 200 yds
N
NORTH SEA
West Sands
Himalayas Putting Course
The Old Course
Swilken Burn
West Sands Road
Bruce Embankment
British Golf Museum
St Andrews Aquarium
Royal & Ancient Golf Club
Grannie Clark's Wynd
The Links
Old Station Road
Gibson Place
Guardbridge Road
Golf Place
The Scores
Murray Park
Murray Place
Pilmour Terrace
Crawford Arts Centre
New Picture House
Butts Wynd
St Salvator's College
Castle
East Scores
North Street
Castle Street
Gregory Place
Cathedral
St. Rule's Tower
Long Pier
Shorehead
Harbour
East Sands
Pends Road
St Leonard's School
Queen Mary's House
Preservation Trust Museum
Abbey Street
Byre Theatre
St Mary's College
Market Street
Church St
Holy Trinity
Queen's Gardens
Ladebraes Lane
South Street
Bell Street
Greyfriars Gardens
St Mary's Place
Hope Street
Abbotsford Crescent
Howard Place
City Road
Station Road
Bus Station
Windmill Road
West Port
Bridge St
Argyle Street
Doubledykes Road
Ladebraes Walk
Kennedy Gardens
Wardlaw Gdns
B939
Leuchars & Dundee
8 (2 miles) & Craigtoun Country Park
9 (6 miles) & Botanic Gardens
Crail & 10

In-town accommodation

Hotels

Inn on North Street 127 North St ⓣ01334/473387, ⓦwww.theinnonnorthstreet.com. Appealing mid-range option with a youthful feel, full of tasteful rooms, wooden floors, modern Gaelic twists and a lively bar and restaurant area. ❺

Old Course Hotel ⓣ01334 474371, ⓦwww.oldcoursehotel.co.uk. The best-known hotel in St Andrews, located but a sliced two-iron from the 17th tee. A large, luxurious modern complex with all the facilities including a spa. ❾

St Andrews Golf Hotel 40 The Scores ⓣ01334/472611, ⓦwww.standrews-golf.co.uk. Located just beyond the eastern end of the Old Course in a terrace of three-storey town houses. Chintzy, comfortable bedrooms – those at the front have great views. ❼

B&Bs, campus and hostels

Aslar House 120 North St ⓣ01334/473460, ⓦwww.aslar.com. A smarter guesthouse in a three-storey town house with an unusual round tower at the back. ❸

Craigmore 3 Murray Park ⓣ01334/472142, ⓦwww.standrewscraigmore.com. A neat, non-smoking guesthouse with seven rooms in a very central location. ❷

Doune House 5 Murray Place ⓣ01334/472195, ⓔdounehouse@aol.com. Warm, cosy, family-run guesthouse with six rooms. ❷

St Andrews Tourist Hostel St Mary's Place ⓣ01334/479911, ⓦwww.hostelsaccommodation.com. Recently established backpacker hostel in a pleasantly converted town house right above *La Posada* Mexican restaurant with plenty of dorm beds but no doubles.

University of St Andrews ⓣ01334/462000, ⓔholidays@st-andrews.ac.uk. Rents out rooms in various student residences between June and September, all on a B&B basis with dinner optional. Self-catering houses also available. ❸

Out-of-town accommodation

Kinkell By Brownhills ⓣ01334/472003, ⓦwww.kinkell.com. Rather more affordable is the B&B at a lovely family farmhouse near the beach about two miles south of town off the A917. ❹

The Peat Inn Peat Inn ⓣ01334/840206, ⓦwww.thepeatinn.co.uk. Five miles south of town on the A915 and then one mile west on the B940 in a village named after it, this old coaching inn has eight plush suites in a modern building tucked behind, and is renowned for its wonderful restaurant (see p.344). ❼

Rufflets Strathkinness Low Road ⓣ01334/472594, ⓦwww.rufflets.co.uk. A couple of miles west of St Andrews on the B939 to Ceres, an elegant 1920s country house whose garden provides much of the produce for the hotel's restaurant. ❽

The Town

The centre of St Andrews still follows its medieval layout. On the three main thoroughfares, North Street, South Street and Market Street, which run west to east towards the ruined Gothic cathedral, are several of the original university buildings from the fifteenth century. Narrow alleys connect the cobbled streets, attic windows and gable ends shape the rooftops, and here and there you'll see old wooden doors with heavy knockers and black iron hinges.

St Andrews Cathedral and around

The ruin of the great **cathedral** (visitor centre: April–Sept daily 9.30am–6.30pm; Oct–March Mon–Sat 9.30am–4.30pm, Sun 2–4.30pm; £2, joint ticket with castle £4; grounds: year-round Sun 9am–6.30pm; HS; free), at the east end of town, gives only an idea of the former importance of what was once the largest cathedral in Scotland. Though founded in 1160, it was not finished and consecrated until 1318, in the presence of Robert the Bruce. On June 5, 1559, the Reformation took its toll, and supporters of John Knox, fresh from a rousing meeting, plundered the cathedral and left it to ruin. Stone was still being taken from the cathedral for various local building projects as late as the 1820s.

Golf in St Andrews

St Andrews **Royal and Ancient Golf Club** (or "R&A") is the international governing body for golf, and dates back to a meeting of 22 of the local gentry in 1754, who founded the Society of St Andrews Golfers, being "admirers of the ancient and healthful exercise of golf". The game itself has been played here since the fifteenth century. Those early days were instrumental in establishing Scotland as the home of golf, for the rules were distinguished from those of the French game by the fact that participants had to manoeuvre the ball into a hole, rather than hit an above-ground target. It was not without its opponents, however – particularly James II who, in 1457, banned his subjects from playing since it was distracting them from archery practice.

The approach to St Andrews from the west runs adjacent to the famous **Old Course**, one of seven courses in the immediate vicinity of the town. The Old Course's strictly private **clubhouse**, a stolid, square building dating from 1854, is at the eastern end of the course overlooking both the eighteenth green and the long beach made famous in the film *Chariots of Fire*. The British Open Championship was first held here in 1873, having been inaugurated in 1860 at Prestwick in Ayrshire, and since then it has been held at St Andrews regularly, pulling in enormous crowds. Pictures of golfing greats from Tom Morris to Tiger Woods, along with clubs and a variety of memorabilia donated by famous players, are displayed in the admirable **British Golf Museum** on Bruce Embankment, along the waterfront below the clubhouse (April to mid-Oct daily 9.30am–5.30pm; rest of year Thurs–Mon 11am–3pm; £3.75). There are also plenty of hands-on exhibits, including computers, video screens and footage of British Open championships, tracing the development of golf through the centuries.

Where to play

It is possible to **play** any of the town's courses, ranging from the nine-hole Balgove course (£10 per round) to the venerated Old Course itself – though for the latter you'll need a valid handicap certificate and must enter a daily ballot for tee times; if you're successful the green fees are £85 in summer. All this and more is explained at the clubhouse of the **St Andrews Links Trust** (Ⓦwww.standrews.org.uk), the organization which looks after all the courses in town, located alongside the fairway of the first hole of the Old Course. If you feel the need to sharpen up your game, or the weather is inclement, head to the **Scottish National Golf Centre** (Ⓣ01382/541144), five miles north of St Andrews at Drumoig, where you'll find a driving range, putting area and even an indoor practice area complete with green, bunker and water hazard.

Arguably the best golfing experience in St Andrews, even if you can't tell a birdie from a bogey, is the **Himalayas**, a fantastically lumpy eighteen-hole putting course in an ideal setting right next to the Old Course and the sea. Officially the Ladies Putting Club, founded in 1867, with its own clubhouse, the grass is as perfectly manicured as the championship course, and you can have all the thrill of sinking a six-footer in the most famous location in golf, all for just 80p per round.

The cathedral site, above the harbour where the land drops to the sea, can be a blustery place, with the wind whistling through the great east window and down the stretch of turf that was once the central aisle. In front of the window a slab is all that remains of the high altar, where the relics of St Andrew were once enshrined. Previously, it is believed that they were kept in **St Rule's Tower**, the austere Romanesque monolith next to the cathedral, which was built as part of an abbey in 1130. From the top of the tower (a climb of 157 steps), there's a good view of the town and surroundings, and of the remains of the monastic buildings which made up the priory. Around the entire complex is a sturdy wall dating from the sixteenth century, over half a mile long and with three gateways.

Southwest of the cathedral enclosure lies **the Pends**, a huge fourteenth-century vaulted gatehouse which marked the main entrance to the priory, and from where the road leads down to the harbour, passing prim **St Leonard's**, one of Scotland's leading private schools for girls. The sixteenth-century, rubble-stonework building on the right as you go through the Pends is **Queen Mary's House**, where she is believed to have stayed in 1563. The house was restored in 1927 and is now used as the school library.

Down at the **harbour**, gulls screech above the fishing boats, keeping an eye on the lobster nets strewn along the quay. If you come here on a Sunday morning, you'll see students parading down the long pier, red gowns billowing in the wind, in a time-honoured after-church walk. The beach, **East Sands**, is a popular stretch, although it's cool in summer and bitterly cold in winter. A path leads south from the far end of the beach, climbing up the hill past the caravan site and cutting through the gorse; this makes a pleasant walk on a sunny day, taking in hidden coves and caves.

St Andrews Castle

North of the beach, the rocky coastline curves inland to the ruined **castle** (same hours as cathedral; HS; £2.80, joint ticket with cathedral £4), with a drop to the sea on two sides and a moat on the inland side. Founded around 1200 and extended over the centuries, it was built as part of the Palace of the Bishops and Archbishops of St Andrews and was consequently the scene of some fairly grim incidents at the time of the Reformation. There's not a great deal left of the castle, since it fell into ruin in the seventeenth century, and most of what can be seen dates from the sixteenth century, apart from the fourteenth-century Fore Tower.

Protestant reformer George Wishart was burnt at the stake in front of the castle in 1546, as an incumbent Cardinal Beaton looked on. Wishart had been a friend of John Knox's, and it wasn't long before fellow reformers sought vengeance for his death. Less than three months later, Cardinal Beaton was stabbed to death and his body displayed from the battlements before being dropped into the "bottle dungeon", a 24ft pit hewn out of solid rock which can still be seen in the Sea Tower. The perpetrators then held the castle for over a year, and during that time dug the secret passage which can be entered from the ditch in front. Outside the castle, the initials "GW" are carved in stone.

Around the university

A little way down North Street from the cathedral, housed in a rather cute little sixteenth-century cottage with a low wooden door, the **St Andrews Preservation Trust Museum and Garden** (June–Sept daily 2–5pm; free) presents a cosy picture of the town's history often forgotten in its towering ruins and glamorous golf connections. As you progress towards the centre of town, it's clear that you're in amongst the buildings of St Andrews University, the oldest in Scotland, founded in 1410 by Bishop Henry Wardlaw, although James I, to whom the bishop was tutor, is the nominal founder (and was a great benefactor of the university). The first building was on the site of the Old University Library and by the end of the Middle Ages three colleges had been built: **St Salvator's** (1450) on North Street, **St Leonard's** (1512) on The Pens, and **St Mary's** (1538) on South Street. At the time of the Reformation, St Mary's became a seminary of Protestant theology, and today it houses the university's Faculty of Divinity. Its **quad** has beautiful gardens and some magnificent old trees, perfect for flopping under on a warm day. A **guided tour** of the university buildings starts from the International Office, Butts Wynd, near St Salvator's Chapel (June–Aug Mon–Fri 11.30am & 2pm; £4), or you can wander freely around the buildings at your own pace.

If you've got children in tow you may want to visit the huge **St Andrews Aquarium** (daily 10am–6pm; July & Aug closes 7pm; £4.50), on The Scores, at the west end of town close to the golf museum (see box on p.342). Here you can see marine life of all shapes and sizes with displays, observation pools and underwater walkways.

The Craigtoun Country Park and Botanic Gardens

The fifty-acre **Craigtoun Country Park** (May–Aug daily 10.30am–6.30pm; April & Sept weekends only; £3) lies a couple of miles southwest of town on the B939. As well as several landscaped gardens, you'll find a miniature train, trampolines, adventure playground, crazy golf and picnic areas, plus a country fair each May with craft stalls, wildlife exhibits and showjumping displays.

Another way to escape the bustle of the town is to head to the **Botanic Gardens** on Canongate (daily 10am–7pm; Oct–April closes 4pm; £1.50: glasshouses year-round Mon–Fri 10am–4pm; £2), a peaceful retreat just ten minutes' walk south of South Street.

Eating and drinking

St Andrews has no shortage of **restaurants** and **cafés**. Given the local student population, there's plenty of choice at the cheaper end of the market, and lots of good **pubs**.

Restaurants

La Posada Inchcape House, St Mary's Place. Located opposite the student union, this is a lively Mexican place with a bit more originality in its design and menu than many Tex-Mex efforts. Moderate.

Peat Inn Five miles southwest of town ☎01334/840206, Ⓦwww.thepeatinn.co.uk (see p.341). One of Britain's top restaurants, serving a varied menu of local specialities. The dining area is intimate without being cramped, and a three-course meal – perhaps featuring lobster broth, venison or roast monkfish – will set you back at least £40 per head. Very expensive.

Saltire Scottish Restaurant 11 Crails Lane ☎01334/474084. This place is pure new generation Scottish kitsch – tartan loo seats, folk-rock soundtrack, heather ale and salmon steaks. Moderate.

Vine Leaf 131 South St ☎01334/477497. Upbeat and contemporary, serving gourmet dishes including a good range of seafood and vegetarian. Closed Sun & Mon. Expensive.

West Port 170–172 South St ☎01334/473186. Designer restaurant serving ambitious modern Scottish fare, though they also have simpler, well-priced set menus. Can attract a few too many rich, loud students in term-time. Moderate–expensive.

Pubs and bars

Broons Bistro and Bar North Street. Right beside the classic New Picture House cinema, quickly established as a young and fun café-bar-bistro with regular live music sessions.

The Central Market Street. Serves huge pies and a powerful beer brewed by Trappist monks.

Inn on North Street 127 North St. Tends to attract slightly older students, but houses the happening *Lizard* basement nightclub at weekends.

Ma Belle's 40 The Scores. In the basement of the *St Andrews Golf Hotel*, a lively pub serving cheap food which is often thronged with students.

The Raisin St Mary's Place. A popular student watering hole near the student union.

Rusacks Lounge Bar 16 Pilmour Links. Hotel bar with the best views of the Old Course. Settle into one of their comfy chairs and watch golfers through huge windows as you sip pricey drinks.

The East Neuk

Extending south of St Andrews as far as Largo Bay, the **East Neuk** is famous for its series of quaint fishing villages, all crow-stepped gables and tiled roofs, the Flemish influence in the architecture indicating a history of strong trading links with the Low Countries. Inland, gently rolling hills provide some of the best farmland in Scotland, with quiet country lanes more redolent of parts of southern England than north of the border. Not surprisingly the area is dotted with windy **golf courses**, though if you prefer your walk unspoilt there are plenty of bracing coastal paths, including one out to Fife Ness, the "nose" of Fife sticking out into the North Sea, or along the waymarked **Fife Coastal Path**, which traces the shore from Crail southwest to the Forth Rail Bridge, and is at its most scenic in the East Neuk stretch. **Bus** #95 runs from Leven around the coast to Dundee.

Well patronized by holiday-makers and weekenders from the Central Belt, the various **restaurants** of the East Neuk are one of the highlights of the area, with freshly landed seafood a speciality, but often complemented by produce gleaned from the fertile Fife farmland which rolls off pleasantly into the hinterland.

Crail

CRAIL is the archetypal cute East Neuk fishing village, its maze of rough cobbled streets leading down to a tiny stone-built harbour surrounded by piles of lobster creels and fishermen's cottages tucked into every nook and cranny in the cliff. Though often populated by artists at their easels and camera-toting tourists, it is still a working harbour, and if the boats have been out you can often buy fresh lobster cooked to order from a small shack right on the harbour edge. Above the harbour are perched the grander merchant's houses, as well as the twelfth-century **St Mary's Church**, where legend has it that the large blue stone by the gate was tossed there by the Devil, all the way from the offshore Isle of May. You can trace the history of the town at the fascinating **Crail Museum and Heritage Centre**, 62 Marketgate (Easter–Sept daily 10am–1pm & 2pm–5pm, Sun 2–5pm; free), which also doubles up as the town's **tourist office**. The **Crail Pottery**, 75 Nethergate (Mon–Fri 9am–5pm, weekends 10am–5pm), is worth a visit for its wide range of locally made pottery, while the **Crail Gallery**, 22 High St, has an attractive selection of linocuts, prints and photographs on display and for sale.

Accommodation choices include the *Hazelton Guest House*, 29 Marketgate (Ⓣ01333/450250; ❷), a small establishment with comfortable rooms and excellent breakfasts, and *Selcraig House*, 47 Nethergate (Ⓣ01333/450697; ❷), a non-smoking establishment nearby. Across the road from this, the *Marine Hotel*, 54 Nethergate South (Ⓣ01333/450207; ❷) is a traditional inn with sea views and a welcoming attitude. Also well worth considering is the upmarket B&B on offer at *Cambo House* (Ⓣ01333/450313; ❺) a grand house set among some stunning parkland and beautifully tended gardens near the small village of Kingsbarns, between Crail and St Andrews. The *Sauchope Links* (Ⓣ01337/450460) is a very pleasant **campsite**, a few miles north of Crail. Other than the various hotels in town, however, there's nowhere notable to **eat**, particularly in comparison with what's on offer elsewhere in the East Neuk.

Anstruther and around

ANSTRUTHER, the largest settlement and least attractive fishing harbour in the East Neuk, is home to the wonderfully unpretentious **Scottish Fisheries**

Museum (April–Oct Mon–Sat 10am–5.30pm, Sun 11am–5pm; Nov–March Mon–Sat 10am–4.30pm, Sun noon–4.30pm; £3.50), quite in keeping with the no-frills integrity of the area in general. Set in an atmospheric complex of sixteenth- to nineteenth-century buildings with timber ceilings and wooden floors, it chronicles the history of the Scottish fishing and whaling industries with ingenious displays, including a whole series of exquisite ships models built on site by a resident model maker. The museum incorporates the old Smith & Hutton boat builder's yard, where you can see a number of complete old craft, including the last full-scale "Zulu", a stylish and practical wooden sailing ship which once dominated the Scottish herring industry. Anstruther's helpful **tourist office** (Easter–Sept Mon, Fri & Sat 10am–5pm, Tues–Thurs 10am–1pm & 2–5pm, Sun 11am–4pm; ⓣ01333/311073) is next to the museum.

Located on the rugged **Isle of May**, several miles offshore from Anstruther, is a lighthouse, erected in 1816 by Robert Louis Stevenson's grandfather, as well as the remains of Scotland's first lighthouse, built in 1636, which burnt coals as a beacon. The island is now a nature reserve and bird sanctuary, and can be reached by boat from Anstruther (May–Sept one sailing daily; ⓣ01333/310103; £13). Between April and July the dramatic sea cliffs are covered with breeding kittiwakes, razorbills, guillemots and shags, while inland there are thousands of puffins and eider duck. Grey seals also make the occasional appearance. Check in advance for departure times, as crossings vary according to weather and tide, and allow between four and five hours for a round-trip: an hour each way, and a couple of hours on the island. You'll also need plenty of warm, waterproof clothing.

Anstruther has a decent choice of places to stay and eat. For **B&B**, try the lovely *Hermitage Guest House* on Ladywalk (ⓣ01333/310909, ⓔb&b@thehermitage.co.uk; ❷); or the *Beaumont Lodge Guest House* (ⓣ01333/310315, ⓔreservations@beau-lodge.demon.co.uk; ❷) or *The Spindrift* (ⓣ01333/310573, ⓦwww.thespindrift.co.uk; ❸), both on Pittenweem Road. There is a fine fish **restaurant**, the *Cellar*, at 24 East Green (ⓣ01333/310378), in one of the village's oldest buildings, once a cooperage and smokehouse. For fish and chips that is reputed to be the best in Fife, head for the *Anstruther Fish Bar*, 44 The Shore.

Scotland's Secret Bunker

Four miles inland from Anstruther on the B940 towards St Andrews is **Scotland's Secret Bunker** (April–Oct daily 10am–5pm; £6.95), as idiosyncratic a tourist attraction as you are likely to find. The rather infrequent bus #61 takes you to within two miles, from where you must walk. Long a top-secret part of the military establishment, the bunker was opened to the public in 1994 following its decommission at the end of the Cold War. Above ground, all you can see is an innocent-looking farmhouse, although the various pieces of military hardware now parked outside and the rows of barbed wire fencing hint that something more sinister is afoot. From the farmhouse, you walk down a vast ramp to the bunker, which comprises a vast subterranean complex of corridors and operations rooms 100ft below ground and encased in 15ft of reinforced concrete. In the event of a nuclear war this was to have become Scotland's new administrative centre, from where government and military commanders would have coordinated firefighting and medical help for Scotland. The bunker, which could house 300 people, has not been spruced up for tourists, and remains uncompromisingly spartan, with various rooms showing dormitories, radio rooms and control centres. The best of 1950s technology, today it has a rather kitsch James Bond feel about it, with stiff mannequins sitting beside banks of switches and typewriters. In a cinema room you can see

1950s newsreel giving painfully inadequate instructions to civilians in the event of nuclear war, while there's an attempt to offset the rather sinister militaristic atmosphere with an exhibition gallery devoted to CND (the Campaign for Nuclear Disarmament).

Pittenweem, St Monans and Elie

West of Anstruther are more fishing villages, all undeniable attractive and rewarding if you have the time to stroll around, take in some of the coastline, or seek out one or two of the fine places to eat and drink. Two miles from Anstruther, **PITTENWEEM** has a busy harbour and fish market, as well as a number of small art galleries. At the end of a graceful avenue of trees, **Kellie Castle** (May–Oct daily 1.30–5.30pm; £5; grounds year-round daily 9.30am–sunset; NTS; £2), a couple of miles north of Pittenweem on the B9171, has an unusual but harmonious mix of twin sixteenth-century towers linked by a seventeenth-century building. Abandoned in the early nineteenth century, the castle was discovered in 1878 by Professor James Lorimer, a distinguished political philosopher, who took on the castle as an "improving tenant". The wonderful **gardens**, where space is broken up by arches, alcoves and paths which weave between profuse herbaceous borders, were designed by the professor's son Robert, aged just sixteen. Later Sir Robert Lorimer, he became a well-known architect specializing in restorations and war memorials; among his restoration works is the Hill of Tarvit in Cupar (see p.336).

Pittenweem almost merges into **ST MONANS**, smallest of the East Neuk fishing villages, though if you take the coastal path between the two you'll encounter a reconstructed stone windmill – a reminder of the area's link with the Low Countries – standing above some old saltpans. St Monans is worth a visit for its splendid *Seafood Restaurant*, at the far end of the harbour (ⓣ01333/730327), where you can **eat** or drink in the dignified old bar or eat in the smarter restaurant with its panoramic views over the coastline. The meals, while expensive, make imaginative use of the freshest local fish and crustaceans.

Three miles on from St Monans is **ELIE**, gatherered round a curve of golden brown sand twelve miles south of St Andrews, a popular escape for middle-class Edinburgh families who come for the bracing air and golf courses. Once known as a popular bathing spot, east of Elie bay stands a tower built for Lady Janet Anstruther in the late eighteenth century as a summerhouse, with a changing room to allow her to bathe in a pool in the rocks below. The top local **restaurant** is the *Bouquet Garni* (ⓣ01333/330374), which specializes in fresh seafood and game, though a lot more relaxed and convivial is *The Ship Inn*, located behind the beach near the harbour, where you'll find great bar food and, come summer, lots of lively local banter in the beer garden. You can stay beside the pub at *Rockview Guesthouse* (ⓣ01333/330246; ❸).

Lower Largo

There's not a great deal to **LOWER LARGO**, which clings to the shore of sandy Largo Bay halfway between Elie and Leven, the point where less glamorous, industrial Fife reappears. Largo also has nothing much notable in its history other than the fact that it was the birthplace in 1676 of one **Alexander Selkirk**, the "real" Robinson Crusoe. A navigator on a ship called *Cinque Ports*, he judged the ship unseaworthy and asked to be dropped off at the next island, Juan Fernandez, 400 miles west of Chile. He led a solitary life on the island for over four years before being rescued, returning to Largo for some years and then going to sea again. His adventures were first published in 1713, but were immortalized by Daniel Defoe when he used them as the basis for his famous

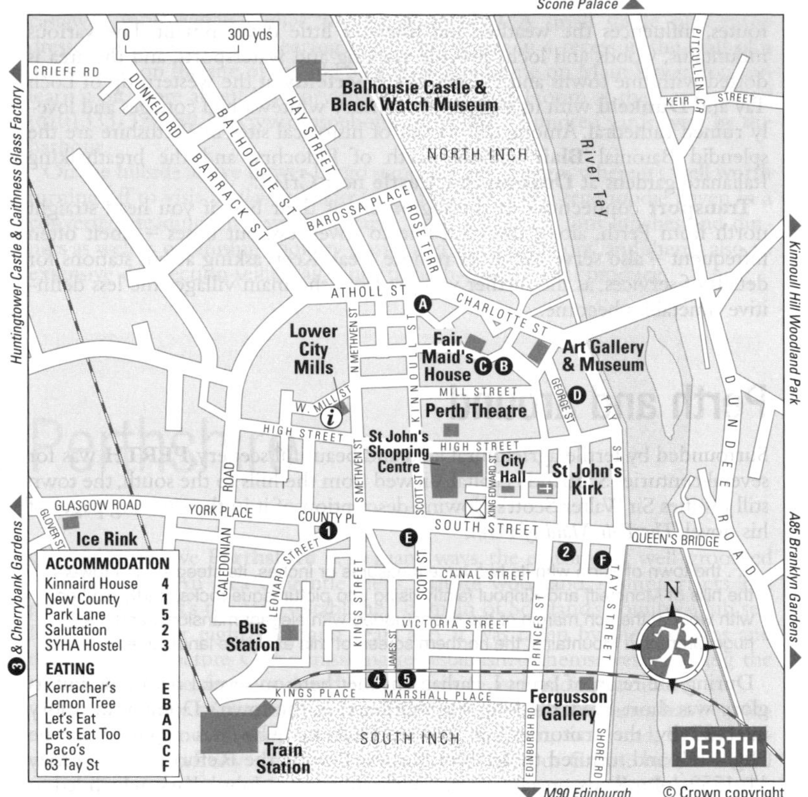

Of the numerous central **hotels**, aim for the freshly refurbished *New County Hotel* on County Place (Ⓣ01738/623355, Ⓦwww.newcountyhotel.com; ❻), or the determinedly old-fashioned *Salutation Hotel*, 34 South St (Ⓣ01738/630066; ❺), which claims to be one of Scotland's oldest hotels and has statues of Highlander soldiers adorning its wonderfully unconventional facade. There are **B&Bs** and guesthouses all over town, notably on the approach roads from Crieff and Stirling. In the centre, Marshall Place, overlooking the South Inch, is the place to look; of the many possibilities along here *Kinnaird House*, 5 Marshall Place (Ⓣ01738/628021, Ⓦwww.kinnaird-guesthouse.co.uk; ❷), offers a warm welcome in a lovely town house with well-equipped en-suite rooms. In an elegant Georgian terrace nearby is the *Park Lane Guest House*, 17 Marshall Place (Ⓣ01738/637218, Ⓦwww.parklane-uk.com; ❷). An SYHA **hostel** is housed in an impressive old 64-room mansion beyond the west end of York Place at 107 Glasgow Rd (Ⓣ01738/623658, Ⓦwww.syha.org.uk; reception closed 10.30am–5pm; March–Oct). It's a fair walk from the bus station; if you've got a heavy rucksack you might want to take bus #7. You can **camp** in pleasant surrounding by Scone Palace (Ⓣ01738/552323) on the outskirts of town, from where there are regular bus connections to Perth town centre.

The Town

Perth's compact **centre** occupies a small area on the west bank of the Tay. Two large areas of green parkland, known as the North and South Inch, flank the centre. The **North Inch** was the site of the Battle of the Clans in 1396, in which thirty men from each of the clans Chattan and Quhele (pronounced "kay") clashed, while the **South Inch** was the public meeting-place for witch-burning in the seventeenth century. Both are now used for more civilized public recreation, with sports matches to the north, and boating and putting to the south.

A good variety of shops line **High Street** and **South Street**, as well as filling St John's shopping centre on King Edward Street. Opposite the entrance to the centre, the imposing **City Hall** is used by Scotland's politicians for party conferences. Behind here lies the solid and attractive **St John's Kirk** (Mon–Sat 10am–4pm, Sun 12.30–2pm, except during services; free), surrounded by cobbled lanes and cafes. It founded by David I in 1126, although the present building dates from the fifteenth century and was restored to house a war memorial chapel designed by Robert Lorimer in 1923–28. Perth was once known as "St John's Town", which is why the local football team took the name St Johnstone.

A couple of minutes' walk north of here, the **Fair Maid's House**, a stone cottage on North Port, stands on the site of a thirteenth-century monastery (and is viewable only from the outside). Its fame is due to Sir Walter Scott, who used it as the house of Simon Glover, father of the virginal Catherine Glover, in his novel *The Fair Maid of Perth*. Set in turbulent times at the close of the fourteenth century, the novel tells a traditional story of love, war and revenge, centring on the attempts by various worthies to win the hand of Catherine.

The **Art Gallery and Museum**, 78 George St (Mon–Sat 10am–5pm; free), another of Perth's grand buildings, has exhibits on local history, art, natural history, archeology and whisky, and gives a good overview of local life through the centuries. From here, a five-minute stroll south along the paved path between Tay Street and the river brings you to the corner of Marshall Place and a round Victorian water tower with ornate Neoclassical flourishes. This is the unlikely setting for the excellent **Fergusson Gallery** (Mon–Sat 10am–5pm; free), which holds a collection of the paintings, drawings and sculpture of J.D. Fergusson, the foremost artist of the Scottish Colourist movement. Imaginative temporary exhibitions explore the artist's preoccupation with light and the sea, and his relationships with fellow modernists. Fergusson's lifelong companion was the dancer and painter Margaret Morris; her summer schools, held annually for forty years, provided him with models and inspired his monumental paintings of bathers, done in pure, bright colours.

North of the town centre, and adjacent to the North Inch, the elegantly restored Georgian terraces beyond the Fair Maid's House give way to newer buildings, which have gradually encroached on the former territory of the fifteenth-century Balhousie Castle, off Hay Street, home of the headquarters and **museum of the Black Watch** regiment (May–Sept Mon–Sat 10am–4.30pm; Oct–April Mon–Fri 10am–3.30pm; free). Originally the home of the earls of Kinnoull, the castle sits incongruously in a peaceful residential area and has been restored in Scots Baronial style with turrets and crow-stepped gables. The Black Watch – whose name refers to the dark colour of their tartan – is the local regiment and one of the oldest in Scotland, having been formed in 1739. The museum chronicles its history through a good display of paintings, uniforms, documents, weapons and photographs.

Perth Ice Rink, in the Dewar's Centre, Glasgow Road, is one of the best places in the country to watch a game of **curling**, a winter sport popular in Scotland, Canada and northern Europe but little-known elsewhere (see p.44).

Eating and drinking

There are lots of reasonable **coffee shops** in town. *Willows*, 12 St John's Place, and *Café Biba* are in amongst the core of pubs and cafés in the streets around St John's Kirk and City Hall. Perth also has an excellent collection of quality **restaurants**. For truly delicious wholefood lunches and home baking through the day head to *The Lemon Tree*, 29–41 Skinnergate, while nearby *Paco's* at 3–5 Mill Street with its outside dining tables is big with locals munching pizza, pasta and the like. At the top end of the market are places such as *63, Tay Street* (ⓣ01738/441451), in a designer setting serving classy and expensive modern Scottish fare; *Kerracher's*, 168 South St (ⓣ01738/449777), a lovely fish restaurant with a downstairs wine bar and coffee shop; and the two award-winning *Let's Eat* restaurants – the original at 77 Kinnoull St (ⓣ01738/643377) has a lighter, livelier atmosphere but both this and *Let's Eat Too* at 33 George St (ⓣ01738/633771) serve innovative, top-notch and reasonably priced food. An Irish **pub** in the town centre, *Mucky Mulligans*, 97 Canal St, claims to be the first "Dublin cottage-style" pub in Scotland and serves specialities like Irish stew all day, with regular live Irish folk music. *Twa Tams*, on Scott Street, has a good beer garden as well as live music, while *Ring O'Bells* is a pleasant, civilized locals' pub right by St John's Kirk.

Around Perth

Almost as well known as Perth itself is **Scone**, one-time home of the Stone of Destiny and the first capital of a united Scotland. The present palace at Scone exudes graceful Scottish country life, and there are some pleasant walks in the grounds – hints of the grander Perthshire countryside you can also find at **Branklyn Gardens** and **Kinnoull Hill** nearby. To the west of Perth, a much trimmer version of Scottish plant life can be found at the **Bell's Cherrybank Gardens**, a showcase home for heather; beyond this **Huntingtower Castle** is the best of the relatively few fortified buildings on view in the Perthshire hinterland.

Scone Palace and around

Just a couple of miles north of Perth on the A93 (catch the Guide Friday tour bus, or bus #58 from South Street) is **Scone Palace** (pronounced "skoon"; April–Oct daily 9.30am–5.15pm; £6.20, grounds only £3.10), one of Scotland's finest historical country homes. Owned and occupied by the Earl and Countess of Mansfield, whose family has owned it for almost four centuries, the two-storey building on the eastern side of the Tay is stately but not overpowering, far more a home than an untouchable monument: the rooms, although full of priceless antiques and lavish furnishings, feel lived-in and used.

Restored in the nineteenth century, the palace today consists of a sixteenth-century core surrounded by earlier buildings, most built of red sandstone, complete with battlements and the original gateway. The abbey that stood here in the sixteenth century, where all Scottish kings until James I were crowned, was one of those destroyed following John Knox's sermon in Perth. Long before that, Scone was the capital of Pictavia, and it was here that Kenneth MacAlpine brought the famous Coronation **Stone of Destiny** (see p.79) and ruled as the first king of a united Scotland.

Inside the palace, a good selection of sumptuous rooms are open to visitors, including the library, which now houses one of the foremost collections of porcelain in the world, with items by Meissen, Sèvres, Chelsea, Derby and Worcester. Look out too for the beautiful papier-mâché dishes, Marie Antoinette's writing desk, and John Zoffany's exquisite eighteenth-century portrait, the *Lady Elizabeth Murray* [daughter of the second earl] *with Dido*. Just as appealing are the **grounds**, where you'll find peacocks strutting in the gardens, Highland cattle roaming, a children's adventure playground, and a maze in the pattern of the heraldic family crest. Scone was the birthplace of botanist **David Douglas**, and following the trail named after him you'll encounter a fragrant pinetum planted in 1848 with many of the exotics discovered by him in California and elsewhere, as well as the country's original Douglas fir, planted from a seed sent home by the intrepid plant hunter.

Branklyn Gardens and Kinnoull Hill

On the same side of the Tay, the **Branklyn Gardens**, 116 Dundee Rd (March–Oct daily 9.30am–sunset; NTS; £3), comprise an astonishing collection of alpine plants and dwarf rhododendrons, spread across a compact two acres of hillside. Looking over the gardens from the north is **Kinnoull Hill**, which also offers splendid views of Perth, the Tay and the surrounding area from its 783ft summit (a 20min walk from the car park on Braes Road). Pick up a leaflet from Perth's tourist office for details of the hill's various woodland walks.

Bell's Cherrybank Gardens

A popular destination for coach tours is **Bell's Cherrybank Gardens** (April–Oct Mon–Sat 9am–5pm, Sun noon–4pm; Nov–March Mon–Fri 10am–4pm; £3), a mile west of Perth town centre by bus #7. Here, among eighteen acres of well-kept gardens, you'll find the largest collection of heathers in Britain, interspersed with a waterfall, pools, aviary and children's play area. The gardens are those of Arthur Bell & Sons, blenders of Bell's whisky, and in the reception area for the gardens is a small exhibition giving their famous brand the hard sell.

Huntingtower Castle

Nothing like as grand as Scone, but intriguing for its historical connections, is **Huntingtower Castle** (April–Sept daily 9.30am–6.30pm; Oct–March Mon–Wed & Sat 9.30am–4.30pm, Thurs 9.30am–1pm; Fri & Sun 2–4.30pm; HS; £2), three miles northwest of Perth on the A85 (bus #14, #15 or #155 from Scott Street). Two three-storey towers formed the original fifteenth- and sixteenth-century tower house, and these were linked in the seventeenth century by a range to provide more room. Formerly known as Ruthven Castle, it was here that the Raid of Ruthven took place in 1582, when the sixteen-year-old James VI, at the request of William, fourth Earl of Ruthven, came to the castle only to be held captive by a group of conspirators demanding the dismissal of favoured royal advisers. The plot failed and the young James was released ten months later. Today the castle's chief attractions are its splendid sixteenth-century painted walls and ceilings – you'll see them in the main hall in the east tower.

The Perthshire Visitor Centre

Eight miles north of Perth along the A9, the **Perthshire Visitor Centre** at Bankfoot (daily 9am–8pm; Oct–March Mon–Thurs closes 7pm; £2) is intended as a tourist trap with its restaurant and gift shop, offering the talking dummies of "The Macbeth Experience" as a slightly dubious sideline. Shakespeare set elements of the Scottish play nearby – Birnam wood is just up the road, while Dunsinane Hill isn't far to the east, though many of the real event concerning Macbeth, who in real life was quite the opposite of the Bard's scheming villain, took place in Aberdeenshire.

Strathearn

Strathearn – the valley of the River Earn – stretches west of Perth for some forty miles to **Loch Earn**, a popular watersports centre located just to the north of the Trossachs. Agricola was here around two thousand years ago, trying to establish a foothold in the Highlands; later the area was frequented by Bonnie Prince Charlie and Rob Roy, both bound up in the north–south struggle between Highlands and Lowlands. Today the main settlement in the valley is the well-heeled town of **Crieff**, which despite its prosperous air has some hints of wilder Highland countryside close by, notably around the popular **Glenturret Distillery**. The two main approaches to the region are to head due west from Perth or north from Stirling and Dunblane.

Auchterarder and Dunning

At the southern edge of Strathearn, twelve miles southwest of Perth on the A9, the large village of **AUCHTERARDER** sees its fair share of visitors, many of whom come to play golf at the swanky five-star **Gleneagles Hotel** nearby (Ⓣ01764/662231, Ⓦwww.gleneagles.com; ❾). There's not much to detain you here, but a **tourist office** on High Street (July & Aug Mon–Sat 9.30am–6pm, Sun noon–4pm; April–June, Sept & Oct Mon–Sat 9.30am–5.30pm; Nov–March phone for opening times; Ⓣ01764/663450) can point you in the right direction for transport links, accommodation or things to do in the area.

It is worth taking a detour from the busy A9 to the quiet village of **DUNNING**, five miles east of Auchterarder on the B8062, which has an impressive history. The village was once the capital of the Picts and was the place where Kenneth I, King of the Picts and Scots, died in 860. Dunning was destroyed by the Jacobites and subsequently rebuilt, which accounts for its homogeneous appearance, the houses all being late eighteenth and early nineteenth century. Only **St Serf's** survived, a rugged church with a Norman tower and arch. Just west of the village is an extraordinary monument, a pile of stones surmounted by a cross, and scrawled with the words: "Maggie Wall, Burnt here, 1657". Maggie Wall was burnt as a witch, and rumour has it that local women replenish the white writing on the monument every year.

Crieff

At the heart of Strathearn is the old spa town of **CRIEFF**, in a lovely position on a south-facing slope of the Grampian foothills. Cattle traders used to come here in the eighteenth century, since this was a good location – between the Highlands and the Lowlands – for buying and selling livestock, but Crieff really came into its own with the arrival of the railway in 1856. Shortly after that Morrison's Academy, a local private school, took in its first pupils, and in 1868 the grand *Crieff Hydro*, then known as the *Strathearn Hydropathic*, opened its doors. These days, Crieff values its respectability and has an array of fine Edwardian and Victorian houses, with a busy little centre which retains something of the atmosphere of the former spa town. The **Crieff Visitor Centre** (daily 9am–5pm), at the bottom of the hill, is a modern place crammed with pottery and paperweights. The **tourist office** is in the town hall on High Street (July & Aug Mon–Sat 9am–7pm, Sun 11am–6pm; April–June, Sept & Oct Mon–Sat 9.30am–5.30pm, Sun 11am–4pm; Nov–March Mon–Fri 9.30am–5pm, Sat 9.30am–1.30pm; ⓣ01764/652578), with, downstairs, a small exhibition of "Stones, Stocks & Stories", including the old town burgh cross, wooden stocks and other artefacts from the town's history.

The *Crieff Hydro* (ⓣ01764/655555, ⓦwww.crieffhydro.com; ❽) is still the nicest place to **stay** in town, despite the institutional atmosphere, and has splendid facilities for families. Cheaper **B&B** options include the *Comely Bank Guest House*, 32 Burrell St (ⓣ01764/653409, ⓦwww.comelybank.demon.co.uk; ❶), and *Galvelmore House* on Galvelmore Street (ⓣ01764/655721, ⓔgalvelmorehse@quista.net; ❶), with a lovely oak-panelled lounge. The one **hostel** in the area is *Braincroft Lodge* (ⓣ01764/670140, ⓔbraincroft@scottishlodge.com), a largeish bunkhouse set on a working sheep farm halfway between Crieff and Comrie, with its own private fishing loch and mountain bike rental. Your best bet for fine **food** in Crieff is the *Bank Restaurant* (ⓣ01764/656575), immediately opposite the tourist office, serving relaxed bistro lunches and more upmarket dinners. Less formal is *Tullybannocher Farm Restaurant* (ⓣ01764/670827), along the A85 towards Comrie, where you'll find a decent range of home-made meals and regular jazz evenings through summer.

Around Crieff

From Crieff, it's a short drive or a twenty-minute walk north to the **Glenturret Distillery** (March–Dec Mon–Sat 9.30am–6pm, Sun noon–6pm, last tour 4.30pm; Jan & Feb Mon–Fri 11.30am–4pm, last tour 2.30pm; free; guided tour £3.50, tasting tour £7.50), just off the A85 to Comrie. To get there on public transport, catch any bus going to Crieff, Comrie or St Fillans and ask the driver to drop you at the bottom of the Glenturret Distillery road, from where it's a five-minute walk. This is Scotland's **oldest distillery**, established in 1775, and a good one to visit, if only for its splendid isolation. Recently, the distillery has also been designated by its large corporate owners as the home of the Famous Grouse blend, Scotland's best-selling whisky. At the "House of Grouse", visitors will be given the opportunity to learn about more about the arts of blending and nosing – unlike wine, the nose of a whisky is ultimately a more reliable guide for an expert to its quality and flavour than tasting.

A complete contrast, certainly in terms of visitor numbers, is the delightfully hidden **Innerpeffray Library** (Feb–Nov Mon–Wed, Fri & Sat 10am–12.45pm & 2–4.45pm, Sun 2–4pm; £2), four miles southeast of Crieff on the B8062 (take the Crieff–Auchterarder bus). Situated right by the River Earn, beside an old stone chapel and schoolhouse, the library, founded in 1680, is the oldest in Scotland, and is a must for bibliophiles, stocking mainly theological and classical books.

The most visually impressive of the attractions around Crieff are the magnificent **Drummond Castle Gardens** (May–Oct daily 2–6pm; £3) near Muthill, two miles south of Crieff on the A822 (bus #47 from Crieff towards Muthill, then a mile and a half walk up the castle drive). The approach to the garden is extraordinary, up a dark avenue of trees; crossing the courtyard of the castle to the grand terrace, you can view the garden in all its symmetrical glory. It was laid out by John Drummond, second Earl of Perth, in 1630, and shows clear French and Italian influence, although the central structural feature of the parterre is a St Andrew's cross. Italian marble statues punctuate the long lines of the cross, and the overall effect is of exceptional harmony and grace. Beyond the formal garden, everything from corn to figs and grapes grows in the Victorian greenhouse and kitchen garden. The castle itself (no public access) is a wonderful mixture of architectural styles, a blunt fifteenth-century keep on a rocky crag adjoining a much-modified Renaissance mansion house.

Comrie

COMRIE, a pretty conservation village another five miles from the turn-off to Glenturret along the River Earn, has the dubious distinction of being the location where more seismic tremors have been recorded than anywhere else in Britain, due to its position on the Highland Boundary Fault. Earthquake readings are still taken at the curious **Earthquake House**, a tiny building set atop a mound all on its own in the middle of a field. If you walk up to the building you can read information panels outside, or peer through the windows at a model of the world's first seismometer, set up here in 1874, as well as some rather more up-to-date equipment. To find the house, follow the signs to Dalrannoch over the hump-backed stone bridge towards the western end of Comrie, then head 600 yards or so along the road.

Loch Earn

At the western edge of Strathearn is **Loch Earn**, a gently lapping Highland loch dramatically edged by mountains. The A85 runs north along the loch shore from the village of **St Fillans**, at the eastern tip, to the slightly larger settlement, **LOCHEARNHEAD**, at the western edge of the loch, where it meets the A84 linking the Trossachs to Crianlarich (see p.319). The wide tranquil expanse of Loch Earn is ideal for **watersports**, and particularly good for beginners. Lochearnhead Watersports (Ⓣ01567/830330) organizes and teaches water-skiing, wake-boarding and the like (including water-skiing for the disabled), as well as renting out Canadian canoes and kayaks. They also run the *Lochside Café*, serving light snacks, teas and coffee. For **accommodation**, try the *Clachan Cottage Hotel* (Ⓣ01567/830247; ❸), or the cheaper and very friendly *Earnknowe* B&B (Ⓣ01567/830238; ❷), both on Lochside. Perhaps the best choice for the area as a whole, though, is the chalet-like *Four Seasons Hotel* (Ⓣ01764/685333, Ⓦwww.thefourseasonshotel.co.uk; ❹) in St Fillans, with its wonderful waterside location. It's also the best choice for **eating**; indeed, there are few other options in the area.

Strath Tay to Loch Tay

From Perth both the railway and main A9 trunk road carry much of the traffic heading into the Highlands, often speeding straight through some of Perthshire's most attractive countryside in its eagerness to get to the bleaker country to the north. Perthshire has been dubbed "**Big Tree Country**" by the tourist board in recognition of some magnificent woodland in the area, including a number of individual trees which rank among Europe's oldest, tallest, and certainly most handsome specimens. Many of these are found around the valley – or "strath" – of the River Tay as it heads towards the sea from attractive Loch Tay, set up among the high Breadalbane mountains. Near the eastern end of the loch is the prosperous small town of **Aberfeldy**; from here the Tay drifts southeast between the unspoilt twin villages of **Dunkeld** and **Birnam** before meandering its way past Perth.

Dunkeld and Birnam

DUNKELD, twelve miles north of Perth on the A9, also served by trains between Perth and Inverness and buses #23 and #27 (bus #22 on Sun), was proclaimed Scotland's ecclesiastical capital by Kenneth MacAlpine in 850. Its position at the southern boundary of the Grampian Mountains made it a favoured meeting place for Highland and Lowland cultures, but in 1689 it was burned to the ground by the Cameronians – fighting for William of Orange – in an effort to flush out troops of the Stuart monarch, James VII. Subsequent rebuilding, however, didn't intrude into the modern era, and as a result the town is one of the area's most pleasant communities, with handsome white-washed houses, appealing arts and crafts shops and a lovely cathedral. The **tourist office** is at The Cross in the town centre (July & Aug Mon–Sat 9am–6.30pm, Sun 11am–5pm; April–June, Sept & Oct Mon–Sat 9.30am–5pm, Sun 11am–4pm; Nov–March Wed—Sun 9.30am–5pm; ⓣ01350/727688).

Dunkeld's partly ruined **cathedral** is on the northern side of town, in an idyllic setting amid lawns and trees on the east bank of the Tay. Construction began in the early twelfth century and continued throughout the next two hundred years, but the building was more or less ruined at the time of the Reformation. The present structure, in Gothic and Norman style, consists of the fourteenth-century choir and the fifteenth-century nave. The choir, restored in 1600 (and several times since), now serves as the parish church, while the nave remains roofless apart from the clock tower. Inside, note the leper's peep near the pulpit in the north wall, through which lepers could receive the sacrament without contact with the congregation. Also look out for the great effigy of "The Wolf of Badenoch", Robert II's son, born in 1343. The Wolf acquired his name and notoriety when, after being excommunicated for leaving his wife, he took his revenge by burning the towns of Forres and Elgin and sacking Elgin cathedral. He eventually repented, did public penance for his crimes and was absolved by his brother Robert III.

Birnam

Dunkeld is linked to its sister community, **BIRNAM**, by Thomas Telford's seven-arched bridge of 1809. This little village has a place in history thanks to Shakespeare, for it was on Dunsinane Hill, to the southeast of the village, that Macbeth declared: "I will not be afraid of death and bane/Till Birnam Forest come to Dunsinane", only to be told later by a messenger:

> As I did stand my watch upon the Hill,
> I look'd toward Birnam, and anon me thought
> The Wood began to move . . .

The **Birnam Oak**, a gnarly old character propped up by crutches just on the edge of the village, is inevitably claimed to be a survivor of the infamous mobile forest. Several centuries after Shakespeare another literary personality, Beatrix Potter, drew inspiration from the area, recalling her childhood holidays here when penning the Peter Rabbit stories. An exhibition on Potter, directed both at children and parents, can be found in the impressive barrel-fronted **Birnam Institute** on the main road, an Arts Lottery-funded theatre and community centre. It incorporates the **Beatrix Potter Garden** (Mon–Sat 10am–4pm, Sun 2–4pm; free), where various characters from the books are hidden amongst the bushes.

Practicalities

There are several large **hotels** in Dunkeld and Birnam, including the *Royal Dunkeld*, Atholl Street (ⓣ01350/727322; ❹), and the Victorian Gothic *Birnam House Hotel* on Perth Road (ⓣ01350/727462; ❹). Much less grand, but full of personality is the *Taybank Hotel* (ⓣ01350/727340, ⓦwww.taybank.com; ❶), owned by popular Scottish folk singer Dougie MacLean – it's a real beacon for music fans and at *MacLean's Real Music Bar* in the hotel there are live sessions at least three times each week. The rooms are simple and inexpensive, and the rate includes a continental breakfast. Local **B&Bs** include *Waterbury Guest House* (ⓣ01350/727324, ⓔbrian@waterburyguesthouse.co.uk; ❷) on Murthly Terrace in Birnam, or the more luxurious *The Pend* (ⓣ01350/727586, ⓦwww.thepend.com; ❹). If you're looking for **food**, any of the hotels, including the *Taybank*, can satisfy; during the day try the café in the Birnam Institute, the *Chattan Tearoom*, just along the road, or pick up some lovely picnic food at the Robert Menzies deli in Dunkeld.

Around Dunkeld

Dunkeld and Birnam are surrounded by some lovely countryside, both along the banks of the Tay and into the deep forests which seem to close in on the settlement. A good way to explore the area is by **bike** – you can rent good-quality mountain bikes, as well as tandems, child seats and maps of local routes, from Dunkeld Bike Hire (ⓣ01350/728744), based in the Old Police Station on the Perth Road in Birnam.

On the other side of the busy A9 from Birnam, paths lead the mile and a half to **The Hermitage**, set in a grandly wooded gorge of the plunging River Braan. Here you'll find a pretty eighteenth-century folly, also known as Ossian's Hall, which was once mirrored to reflect the water, but the mirrors were smashed by Victorian vandals and the folly more tamely restored. The hall, appealing yet incongruous in its splendid setting, neatly frames a dramatic waterfall. Nearby you can crane your neck up a Douglas fir which claims the title as the tallest tree in Britain – measuring these behemoths isn't easy, but last time the tape was out it managed 212ft.

Two miles east of Dunkeld, the **Loch of the Lowes** is a nature reserve which offers a rare chance to see breeding ospreys and other wildfowl; the visitor centre (April–Sept 10am–5pm; £1) has video relay screens and will point you in the direction of the best vantage points. If the surroundings seem appealing enough to warrant lingering a day or two, the mellow *Wester Caputh Independent Hostel* (ⓣ01738/710617), four miles downstream along the Tay from Dunkeld, is a great base; to complement the relaxing and welcoming atmosphere, musical evenings and poetry readings are regular events. They have small dorms and doubles, and good food is often available if you book in advance. For details about how to reach Wester Caputh village, phone the hostel direct.

Aberfeldy and around

From Dunkeld the A9 runs north alongside the Tay for eight miles before the road leaves the river near Ballinluig, a small settlement which marks the turn-off along the A827 to **ABERFELDY**, a prosperous settlement of large stone houses and four-wheel-drive vehicles which acts as a service centre for the wider Loch Tay area. The **tourist office** at The Square in the town centre (July & Aug Mon–Sat 9.30am–6.30pm, Sun 11am–5pm; April–June, Sept & Oct Mon–Sat 9.30am–5.30pm, Sun 11am–4pm; Nov–March Mon–Fri 9.30am–5pm, Sat 10am–2pm; ⓣ01887/820276) gives details of local trails to take in all the main sights.

Aberfeldy sits at the point where the Urlar Burn – lined by the silver birch trees celebrated by Robert Burns in his poem *The Birks of Aberfeldy* – flows into the River Tay. The Tay is spanned by the humpbacked, four-arch **Wade's Bridge**, built by General Wade in 1733 during his efforts to control the unrest in the Highlands, and one of the general's more impressive pieces of work. Overlooking the bridge from the south end is the **Black Watch Monument**, depicting a pensive, kilted soldier, erected in 1887 to commemorate the first muster of the peacekeeping troops of Highlanders gathered together by Wade in 1739.

The small town centre is a busy mixture of craft and tourist shops, with its main attraction the superbly restored early nineteenth-century **Aberfeldy Water Mill** (Easter–Oct Mon–Sat 10am–4.30pm, Sun 11am–4.30pm; £2.50), which harnesses the water of the Urlar to turn the wheel that stone-grinds oatmeal in the traditional Scottish way. **Dewar's World of Whisky** at the Aberfeldy Distillery (April–Oct Mon–Sat 10am–6pm, Sun noon–4pm; Nov–March Mon–Fri 10am–4pm; £3.95) puts on an impressive show describing the making of whisky – worthwhile if you haven't been given a similar lowdown at distilleries elsewhere.

Accommodation includes *Guinach House*, by the Birks (Ⓣ01887/820251, Ⓔ100127.222@compuserve.com; ❺), a tastefully decorated guesthouse in pleasant grounds near the famous silver birches, with a good dining room. For B&B, try *Novar*, 2 Home St (Ⓣ01887/820779; ❶), or *Mavisbank*, Taybridge Drive (Ⓣ01887/820223; ❶; March–Oct), both attractive stone cottages. Up on the hillside above Weem, about two and a half miles from the centre of Aberfeldy, *Glassie Farm* (Ⓣ01887/820265, Ⓦwww.thebunkhouse.co.uk) has a **bunkhouse** which is popular with those taking part in outdoor activities locally.

Decent bar **meals** can be found just over the Wade Bridge in Weem at the *Ailean Chraggan Inn* (Ⓣ01887/820346; ❹); in town, you can get tasty home-made food at *7 The Square Café & Bistro* (Ⓣ01887/829120; closed Sun & Mon).

Castle Menzies

One mile west of Aberfeldy, across Wade's Bridge, **Castle Menzies** (April to mid-Oct Mon–Sat 10.30am–5pm, Sun 2–5pm; £3) is an imposing, Z-shaped, sixteenth-century tower house, which until the middle of the last century was the chief seat of the Clan Menzies. With the demise of the line, the castle was taken over by the Menzies Clan Society, which since 1971 has been involved in the lengthy process of restoring it. Now the interior, with its wide stone staircase, is refreshingly free of fixtures and fittings, restored to authentic austerity.

Even if you pass the castle by, it's well worth stopping at **Castle Menzies Farm** next door, where an imaginative and impressive conversion has turned an old cow byre into the *House of Menzies* (May–Oct daily 10am–5pm; Oct–Dec closed Mon), which combines a specialist wine shop, a tasteful modern café, a deli and an arts and crafts showroom. The antithesis of tacky tourist souvenir shops the length and breadth of Scotland, the emphasis here is on taste, quality and originality, and as such it's fast attracting admirers from near and far.

The road from here carries on either deep into the hills of Glen Lyon, or connects north past the striking mountain Schiehallion to Loch Tummel (see p.363).

Loch Tay

Aberfeldy grew up around a crossing point on the River Tay, which leaves it slightly oddly six miles adrift of Loch Tay, a fourteen-mile-long stretch of fresh water which all but hooks together the western and eastern Highlands. Guarding over the northern end of the loch is **KENMORE**, where white-washed estate houses and well-tended gardens cluster around the gate to the grounds of **Taymouth Castle**, built by the Campbells of Glenorchy in the early nineteenth century, now a private golf club. The main attraction here is the **Scottish Crannog Centre** (April–Oct daily 10am–4.30pm; £3.50), one of the most effective reconstruction-style heritage museums in the country. Crannogs are houses on stilts built by Bronze Age inhabitants of Scotland a short distance from the shore of a freshwater loch, essentially as a defensive measure – the walkway leading to the house could be demolished at a moment's notice to defy an intruder. Following extensive underwater archeological excavations, the team here has reconstructed a crannog in the traditional fashion, and visitors can now walk out over the loch to the thatched wooden dwelling, complete with sheepskin rugs, wooden bowls and other evidence of the way life was lived 2500 years ago.

Kenmore is a popular holidaying spot, and as a result there are a number of activity-based operations here. Best of the lot is Croft-na-Caber (Ⓣ01887/830588), an impressive **outdoor pursuits** complex on the southern bank of the loch, where you can try water-skiing, fishing, river sledging, rafting and jet biking. The nicest place to **stay** is the pleasant and well-run *Kenmore Hotel*, in the village square (Ⓣ01887/830205, Ⓦwww.kenmorehotel.com; ❺), a descendant of Scotland's oldest inn (established here in 1572), where you can eat in a large dining room overlooking the river. On the other side of the river, the *Byre Bistro* by the Kenmore golf course also serves up tasty, well-priced meals.

Dominating the northern side of Loch Tay is moody **Ben Lawers** (3984ft), Perthshire's highest mountain; from the top there are incredible views towards both the Atlantic and the North Sea. The ascent – which should not be tackled without all the right equipment (see p.46) – takes around three hours from the NTS visitor centre (mid-April to Sept daily 10am–5pm; Ⓣ01567/820397), located at 1300ft and reached by a track off the A827. The centre has an audio-visual show, slides of the mountain flowers – including the rare alpine flora found here – and a nature trail with accompanying descriptive booklet.

Killin

The **mountains of Breadalbane**, named after the earls of Breadalbane, loom over the southern end of Loch Tay. Glens Lochay and Dochart curve north and south respectively from the small town of **KILLIN**, where the River Dochart comes rushing out of the hills and down the frothy **Falls of Dochart** before disgorging into Loch Tay. A short distance west of Killin the A827 meets the A85, which links the Trossachs (see p.319) with Crianlarich (see p.319), an important waypoint on the roads to Oban, Fort William and the west coast.

There's little to do in Killin itself, but it makes a convenient base for some of the area's best walks. The **tourist office** is located by the falls (July & Aug daily 9.30am–6.30pm; June & Sept daily 10am–6pm; March–May & Oct daily 10am–5pm; Ⓣ01567/820254), next to the **Breadalbane Folklore Centre** (same times; £2). The centre explores the history and mythology of Breadalbane and holds the thirteen-hundred-year-old "healing stones" of St Fillan, an early Christian missionary who settled in Glen Dochart.

Killin is littered with B&Bs, but one of the more unusual places to **stay** is the *Dall Lodge Hotel*, Main Street (Ⓣ01567/820217, Ⓦwww.dalllodgehotel.co.uk; ❻), which is filled with all manner of exotic Far Eastern bits and pieces, and has a dining room serving fine local produce. Less pricey, and a welcoming place if you're here to do some walking or cycling, is *Drumfinn Guest House* (Ⓣ01567/820900; ❶), on Main Street. There's also an SYHA **hostel** (Ⓣ01567/820546, Ⓦwww.syha.org.uk; Nov–March Fri & Sat only), in a fine old country house just beyond the northern end of the village, with views out over the loch. **Bike rental** is available at the Killin Outdoor Centre and Mountain Shop, on Main Street (Ⓣ01567/820116).

Glen Lyon

North of Breadalbane, the mountains tumble down into **Glen Lyon** – at 34 miles long, the longest enclosed glen in Scotland – where, legend has it, the Celtic warrior Fingal built twelve castles. The narrow single track road down the glen starts at **Keltneyburn**, near Kenmore at the northern end of the loch, although a road does struggle over the hills past the Ben Lawers Visitors Centre to **Bridge of Balgie**, halfway down the glen, where the post office has an art gallery and does good tea and scones. Either way, it's a long, winding journey, much more the place for flights of imagination than tight deadlines. A few miles on from Keltneyburn, the village of **FORTINGALL** is little more than a handful of pretty thatched cottages, although locals make much of their 5000-year-old yew tree – believed (by them at least) to be the oldest living thing in Europe. The venerable tree can be found in the churchyard, showing its age a little but well looked after, with a timeline built into the pathway leading to it suggesting some of the events the yew has lived through. One of these, bizarrely, is the birth of Pontius Pilate, reputedly the son of a Roman officer stationed near Fortingall in the last years BC. If you're taken by the peace and remoteness of Glen Lyon, you might like to **stay** on a working sheep farm nearby, *Kinnighallen* (Ⓣ01887/830619, Ⓦwww.heartlander.scotland.net/home/kinninghallen; ❶), on Duneaves Road not far outside Fortingall.

Highland Perthshire

North of the Tay valley, Perthshire doesn't discard its lush richness immediately, but there are clear indications of the more rugged, barren influences of the Highlands proper. The principal settlements of **Pitlochry** and **Blair Atholl**, both just off the A9, are separated by the narrow gorge of Killiecrankie, a crucial strategic spot in times past for anyone seeking to control movement of cattle or armies from the Highlands to the Lowlands. Though there are reasons to stop in both places, inevitably the greater rewards are to be found further from the main drag, and are often best explored on foot.

Pitlochry

PITLOCHRY has, on the face of it, a lot going for it, not least the backdrop of Ben Vrackie (see box on p.362) and the River Tummel slipping by. However, there's little charm to be found on the main street, filled with crawling traffic and seemingly endless shops selling cut-price woollens, knobbly walking sticks and glass baubles. The town has grown comfortable in its utilitarian, mass-market role and, given its self-appointed role as a "gateway to the Highlands", you'd be perfectly excused if you carried straight on through.

Walks around Pitlochry

Ordnance Survey Landranger maps Nos. 43 & 52

Pitlochry is surrounded by good walking country. The biggest lure has to be **Ben Vrackie** (2733ft), which provides a stunning backdrop for the town and deserves better than a straight up-and-down walk; however, the climb should only be attempted in settled weather conditions, with the right equipment and following the necessary safety precautions (see p.46).

The direct route up the hill follows the course of the Moulin burn past the inn of the same name. Alternatively, a longer but much more rewarding circular route heads north out of Pitlochry, along the edge of attractive Loch Faskally, then up the River Garry to go through the **Pass of Killiecrankie.** This is looked after by the NTS, which has a visitor centre detailing the famous battle here as well as the abundant natural history of the gorge. From the NTS centre walk north up the old A9 and branch off on the small tarred road signposted **Old Faskally**, which twists up under the new A9. The route from here is signposted: continue up the hillside until you finally leave the cultivated land and join a track which zigzags up heathery pasture and then heads across open hillside to reach a saddle by **Loch a'Choire**. Here you join the track from Pitlochry/Moulin which crosses below the dam on the loch and heads directly up the peak. To get back to Pitlochry take the Moulin path back from the loch.

Other worthwhile walks in the area include the trip right round **Loch Faskally**, or you could follow the walk above but turn back from Killiecrankie. A lovely short hill walk from the south end of Pitlochry follows a path through oak forests along the banks of the **Black Spout** burn; when you emerge from the woods it's a few hundred yards further uphill to the lovely Edradour Distillery (see below).

The one attraction with some distinction in the immediate vicinity is the **Edradour Distillery** (March–Oct Mon–Sat 9.30am–5pm, Sun noon–5pm; Nov & Dec Mon–Sat 10am–4pm; free), Scotland's smallest, set in an idyllic position tucked into the hills a couple of miles east of Pitlochry on the A924. Although the whistle-stop audiovisual presentation and tour of the distillery itself isn't out of the ordinary, the lack of industralization and the fact that the whole traditional process is done on site gives Edradour more personality than many of its rivals.

It's hard to say the same for Bells' **Blair Atholl Distillery**, Perth Road (Easter–Oct Mon–Sat 9am–5pm, Sun noon–5pm; Nov–Easter Mon–Fri 10am–4pm; tours every 10min; £3 including tastings), at the southern end of the main street (Atholl Road leading to Perth Road) in Pitlochry, where a more modern visitor centre illustrates the process involved in making the Blair Atholl Malt, one of the key ingredients of the Bell's blend.

On the western edge of Pitlochry, just across the river, lies Scotland's renowned "Theatre in the Hills", the **Pitlochry Festival Theatre** (☎01796/472626; Easter to early Oct). Set up in 1951, the theatre started in a tent on the site of what is now the town curling rink, before moving to the banks of the river in 1981. A variety of productions – mostly mainstream theatre from the resident company, along with regular music events – are staged in the evening. By day it's worth coming here to wander around the **Scottish Plant Collectors Garden** (due to open in 2002), an extended garden and forest area set up in association with the Royal Botanic Garden in Edinburgh to pay tribute to the local botanists and collectors who roamed the world in search of new plant species.

A short stroll upstream from the theatre is the **Pitlochry Power Station and Dam**, a massive concrete wall which harnesses the water of the artificial

Loch Faskally, just north of the town, for hydroelectric power. Although the visitor centre (April–Oct daily 10am–5.30pm; £2) explains the ins and outs of it all, the main attraction here, apart from the views up the loch, is the **salmon ladder**, a staircase of rather murky glass boxes through which you might see some rather nonplussed fish making their way upstream past the dam.

Practicalities

Pitlochry is on the main **train** line to Inverness, and has regular **buses** running from Perth which stop near the train station on Station Road, at the north end of town, ten minutes' walk from the centre and the **tourist office**, 22 Atholl Rd (mid-May to Sept daily 9am–7pm, Sun closes 6pm; Easter to mid-May & Oct Mon–Sat 9am–6pm, Sun 11am–5pm; Nov–Easter Mon–Fri 9am–5pm, Sat 10am–2pm; ⓣ01796/472215). The office can sell you a guide to walks in the surrounding area (50p), and also offers an accommodation booking service.

As a well-established holiday town, Pitlochry is packed with grand houses converted into large- and medium-sized **hotels**. Small but still up-market is *Dunfallandy House* on Logierait Road (ⓣ01796/472648, ⓔdunfalhse@aol.com; ❺), while the *Moulin Hotel* (ⓣ01796/472196, ⓦwww.moulin.u-net.com; ❸), at Moulin on the outskirts of Pitlochry, is a welcoming travellers' inn with a great bar and its own brewery. Also worth considering is the *Port-na-Craig Inn & Restaurant* (ⓣ01796/472777; ❸), on the banks of the River Tummel. Of the many guesthouses and **B&Bs**, try *Kinnaird House*, Kirkmichael Road (ⓣ01796/472843, ⓦwww.kinnaird-house.co.uk; ❸) or *Ferryman's Cottage*, Port-na-Craig (ⓣ01796/473681; ❷), also in a beautiful position next to the River Tummel. The SYHA **hostel** (ⓣ01796/472308, ⓦwww.syha.org.uk) is in a fine stone mansion on Knockard Road at the top of town, while right in the centre *Pitlochry Backpackers Hotel*, 134 Atholl Rd (ⓣ01796/470044, ⓦwww.scotlands-top-hostels.com), is based in a former hotel and offers mainly twin and double rooms. Just along from this is *The Old Bank House Lodge* (ⓣ01796/470022, ⓦwww.scottishlodge.com), a friendly place with some en-suite rooms as well as bunkrooms and good facilities for walkers and cyclists.

Pitlochry is the domain of the tearoom and is pitifully short of **restaurants** and pubs; in town, try the popular restaurant at the Festival Theatre, or the nearby *Port-na-craig Inn & Restaurant*, both of which have beautiful riverside locations. *The Old Mill* at Mill Lane right in the centre makes an effort to serve interesting contemporary bistro food, while the best bet for good **pub grub** is the *Moulin Inn*, handily placed at the foot of Ben Vrackie. Also worth considering is the smart *Killiecrankie Hotel* (ⓣ01796/473220; ❼) at Killiecrankie, three miles north of Pitlochry on the old A9, which serves impressive, upmarket Scottish cuisine.

Loch Tummel and Loch Rannoch

West of Pitlochry, the B8019/B846 makes a memorably scenic traverse of the shores of **Loch Tummel** and then **Loch Rannoch**. These two lochs, celebrated by Harry Lauder in his famous song *The Road to the Isles*, are joined by Dunalastair Water, which narrows to become the River Tummel at the western end of the loch of the same name. This is a spectacular stretch of countryside and one which deserves leisurely exploration. **Queen's View** at the eastern end of Loch Tummel is a fabulous vantage point, looking down the loch across the hills to the misty peak of **Schiehallion** (3520ft) or the "Fairy Mountain", one of the few free-standing hills in Scotland. It's a popular and inspiring mountain to climb, with views on a good day to both sides of Scotland; the path up starts at Braes of Foss, just off the B846 which links

Aberfeldy with Kinloch Rannoch. At Queen's View, the Forestry Commission's **visitor centre** (April–Oct daily 10am–6pm) interprets the fauna and flora of the area, and also has a café. A few miles further on, the *Loch Tummel Inn* (Ⓣ01882/634272; ❹), halfway along Loch Tummel, has a pleasant bar and restaurant and enjoys fine views out across the water.

Beyond Loch Tummel, marking the eastern end of Loch Rannoch, the small community of **KINLOCH RANNOCH** doesn't see a lot of passing trade – fishermen and hill-walkers are the most common visitors. Otherwise, the only real destination here is Rannoch Station, a lonely outpost on the Glasgow–Fort William West Highland train (see p.578), six miles or so beyond the western end of Loch Rannoch. The road goes no further. Here you can contemplate the bleakness of **Rannoch Moor**, a wide expanse of bog, heather and wind-blown pine tree which stretches right across to the imposing entrance to Glen Coe (see p.612). There is a tearoom and hotel here, but even these struggle to diminish the feeling of isolation.

In Kinloch Rannoch the *Bunrannoch House* (Ⓣ01882/632407, Ⓦwww.bunrannoch.co.uk; ❷), a Victorian former shooting lodge with lovely views, is a good bet for **accommodation**; otherwise, in the main square of the village, the huntin', fishin' and shootin' *Dunalastair Hotel* (Ⓣ01882/632323, Ⓦwww.dunalastair.co.uk; ❻) has rooms, and is the place to pull in for a pint or a **meal**. The *Loch Rannoch Hotel* (Ⓣ01882/632201) is a timeshare complex with leisure facilities – you can **rent bikes** here should you fancy tackling the 35-mile round trip around the loch.

North of Pitlochry

Four miles north of Pitlochry, the A9 cuts through the **Pass of Killiecrankie**, a breathtaking wooded gorge which falls away to the River Garry below. This dramatic setting was the site of the **Battle of Killiecrankie** in 1689, when the Jacobites quashed the forces of General Mackay. Legend has it that one soldier of the Crown, fleeing for his life, made a miraculous jump across the 18ft **Soldier's Leap**, an impossibly wide chasm halfway up the gorge. Queen Victoria, visiting here 160 years later, contented herself with recording the beauty of the area in her diary. Exhibits at the slick NTS **visitor centre** (April–Oct daily 10am–5.30pm; Ⓣ01796/473233; parking £1) recall the battle and examine the gorge in detail. The surroundings here are thick, mature forest, full of interesting plants and creatures – the local ranger often sets off on **guided walks** which are well worth joining if you're around at the right time. Walks leave from the visitor centre and they'll let you know what's scheduled when.

Blair Atholl

Three miles north of Killiecrankie, the village of **BLAIR ATHOLL** makes for a much quieter and more idiosyncratic stop than Pitlochry. At the **Atholl Estates Information Centre** (April–Oct daily 9am–4.45pm; Ⓣ01796/481464) you can get details of the extensive network of local walks and bike rides; alongside is Atholl Mountain Bike Hire. The *Atholl Arms Hotel* (Ⓣ01796/481205; ❷) is the best place in town for a drink or a bar meal; alongside it, in the old petrol station, is a secondhand bookshop called Atholl Browse (a pun on "Atholl Brose", a sickly sweet, whisky-laced dessert). Nearby, you can wander round the **Water Mill** on Ford Road (Easter–Oct Mon–Sat 10am–5.30pm, Sun noon–5.30pm; £1.50), which dates back to 1613, and witness flour being milled; better still, you can enjoy the home-baked scones and other treats in its pleasant timber-beamed tearoom.

Blair Castle

Before leading the Jacobites into battle, Graham of Claverhouse, Viscount ("Bonnie") Dundee, had seized **Blair Castle** (April–Oct daily 10am–6pm; £6.25, grounds only £2), reached by a driveway leading from the centre of Blair Atholl village. Seat of the Atholl dukedom, this whitewashed, turreted castle, surrounded by parkland and dating from 1269, presents an impressive sight as you approach up the drive. A piper may be playing in front of the castle, one of the Atholl Highlanders, a select group retained by the duke as his private army – a unique privilege afforded to him by Queen Victoria, who stayed here in 1844.

Thirty or so rooms are open for inspection, and display a selection of paintings, antique furniture and plasterwork that is sumptuous in the extreme. Highlights are the soaring **entrance hall**, with every spare inch of wood panelling covered in weapons of some description; the **Tapestry Room**, on the top floor of the original Cumming's Tower, which is hung with Brussels tapestries and contains an ostentatious four-poster bed, topped with vases of ostrich feathers which originally came from the first duke's suite at Holyrood Palace in Edinburgh; and the vast **ballroom**, with its timber roof, antlers and mixture of portraits.

As impressive as the castle's interior are its surroundings: Highland cows graze the ancient landscaped grounds and peacocks strut in front of the castle. There is a **riding stable** from where you can take treks, and formal woodland walks have been laid out – don't miss the neglected, walled "Hercules" water garden, or the towering giant conifers of Diana's Grove. There is also a well-equipped caravan and **camping** park (☎01796/481263) in the grounds.

Drumochter and Dalwhinnie

A few miles north of Blair Atholl, insistent signs point the way to the *House of Bruar*, an emporium of tweeds, waxed jackets and overpriced foodstuffs which acts as the final outpost of the Perthshire country set before the A9 sweeps northward over the barren **Pass of Drumochter**, often affected by snow falls in winter. Beyond this the bleak little village of **Dalwhinnie** lies at the northern end of **Loch Ericht**, around which are some of the most remote high hills in Scotland, including spooky Ben Alder. The scenery all the way is inspiring and desolate, in equal measure. Not far beyond Dalwhinnie you encounter the neighbouring villages of Kingussie and Newtonmore, the start of the Strathspey region (see p.600).

Travel details

Trains

Balloch to: Glasgow (every 30min; 40min).
Crianlarich to: Fort William (3 daily; 2hr); Glasgow (3 daily; 2hr); Oban (3 daily; 1hr 10min).
Dunfermline to: Edinburgh (every 30min; 30min); Kirkcaldy (hourly; 40min).
Falkirk Grahamston to: Edinburgh (every 30min; 35min); Glasgow Queen Street (every 30min; 25min); Stirling (every 30min; 15min).
Glasgow Queen Street to: Ardlui (2–4 daily; 1hr 35min); Arrochar & Tarbet (2–4 daily; 1hr 15min); Balloch (every 30min; 45min); Crianlarich (2–4 daily; 1hr 50min).
Kirkcaldy to: Aberdeen (hourly; 2hr); Dundee (hourly; 40min–1hr); Edinburgh (every 30min; 50min); Perth (7 daily; 40min).
Leuchars (for St Andrews) to: Dundee (5 daily; 20min); Edinburgh (5 daily; 1hr 45min).
Perth to: Aberdeen (hourly; 1hr 40min); Dundee (hourly; 25min); Edinburgh (9 daily; 1hr 25min); Glasgow Queen Street (hourly; 1hr 5min); Inverness (5 daily; 2hr); Stirling (hourly; 30min).
Stirling to: Aberdeen (hourly; 2hr 15min); Dundee (hourly; 1hr); Edinburgh (hourly; 1hr); Falkirk Grahamston (hourly; 30min); Glasgow Queen Street (hourly; 30min); Inverness (3–5 daily; 2hr 30min); Linlithgow (hourly; 35min); Perth (hourly; 30min).

Buses

Balloch to: Balmaha (every 2hr; 30min); Luss (Mon–Sat 9 daily, 7 on Sun; 15min); Stirling (1 daily; 1hr 25min).

Dunfermline to: Dundee (every 30min; 1hr 30min); Edinburgh (every 30min; 40min); Glasgow (hourly; 1hr 20min); Glenrothes (every 30min; 30min); Kirkcaldy (every 30min; 25min); St Andrews (hourly; 2hr); Stirling (hourly; 40min).

Glenrothes to: Dundee (every 30min; 1hr); Dunfermline (every 30min; 30min); Kirkcaldy (hourly; 20min); St Andrews (hourly; 45min).

Kirkcaldy to: Dundee (10 daily; 1hr 30min); Dunfermline (every 30min; 25min); Glenrothes (hourly; 20min); St Andrews (16 daily; 1hr).

Luss to: Tarbet (Mon–Sat 2–3 daily; 10min).

Perth to: Aberfeldy (6 daily; 1hr 45min); Dunblane (every 30min; 35min); Dunfermline (every 30min; 50min); Edinburgh (hourly; 1hr 20min); Glasgow (hourly; 1hr 35min); Gleneagles (hourly; 25min); Inverness (10 daily; 2hr 30min); London (4 daily; 9hr); Stirling (20 daily; 50min).

St Andrews to: Dundee (every 20min; 40min); Dunfermline (hourly; 1hr 30min); Edinburgh (hourly; 2hr); Glasgow (6 daily; 2hr 50min); Glenrothes (hourly; 45min); Kirkcaldy (16 daily; 1hr); Stirling (6 daily; 2hr).

Stirling to: Aberfoyle (4 daily; 45min); Bo'ness (3 daily; 35min); Callander (11 daily; 45min); Dollar (13 daily; 35min); Doune (14 daily; 30min); Dunblane (20 daily; 1hr 15min); Dundee (12 daily; 1hr 30min); Dunfermline (13 daily; 50min); Edinburgh (hourly; 1hr 35min); Falkirk (every 45min; 30min); Glasgow (hourly; 1hr 10min); Gleneagles (16 daily; 30min); Inverness (12 daily; 3hr 30min); Killin (2 daily; 2hr); Lochearnhead (2 daily; 1hr 40min); Perth (20 daily; 50min); Pitlochry (2 daily; 1hr 30min); St Andrews (6 daily; 2hr).

5

Argyll

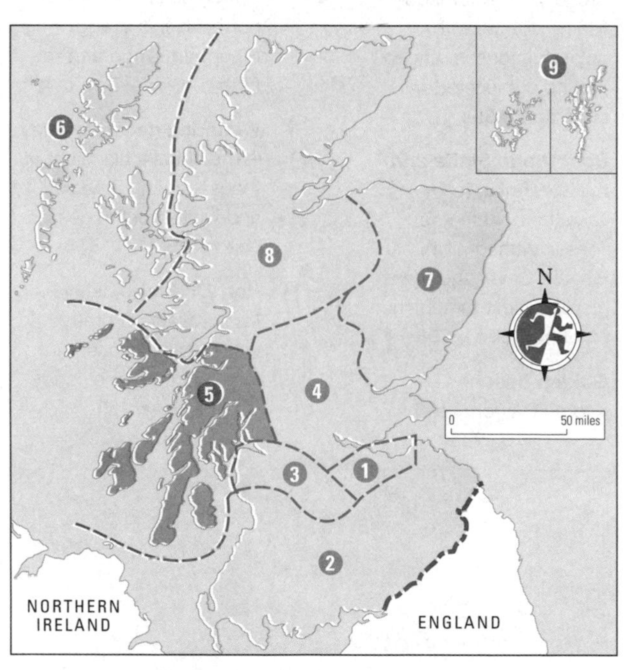

CHAPTER 5 Highlights

* **Loch Fyne Oyster Bar, Cairndow** – Scotland's finest smokehouse and seafood outlet. See p.374
* **Mount Stuart, Bute** – Architecturally overblown mansion with beautiful grounds. See p.379
* **Tobermory, Mull** – Archetypal picturesque fishing village, with colourful houses ranged around a sheltered harbour. See p.394
* **Boat trip to Staffa and the Treshnish Isles** – Take the boat to see "basalt cathedral" of Fingal's Cave, and then picnic amidst the puffins on Lunga. See p.398
* **Golden beaches** – Kiloran Bay on Colonsay is a perfect west-facing sandy beach, and there are plenty more on Islay, Coll and Tiree. See p.408
* **Isle of Gigha** – The ideal island escape: sandy beaches, friendly folk and a decent hotel. See p.418
* **Goat Fell, Arran** – Spectacular views over north Arran's craggy mountain range and the Firth of Clyde. See p.428
* **Wintering geese on Islay** – The spectacular sight of thousands of barnacle and white-fronted geese. See p.435.
* **Port Charlotte, Islay** – Idyllic village of pretty whitewashed houses, looking out over a sandy beach. See p.435.

5

Argyll

Cut off for centuries from the rest of Scotland by the mountains and sea lochs that characterize the region, Argyll remains remote, its scatter of offshore islands forming part of the Inner Hebridean archipelago (the remaining Hebrides are dealt with in Chapter 6). Geographically as well as culturally, this is a transitional area between Highland and Lowland, boasting a rich variety of scenery, from lush, subtropical gardens warmed by the Gulf Stream to flat and treeless islands on the edge of the Atlantic. It's in the folds and twists of the countryside, the interplay of land and water and the views out to the islands that the strengths and beauties of mainland Argyll lie. The one area of man-made sights you shouldn't miss, however, is the cluster of Celtic and prehistoric sites near Kilmartin. Overall, the population is tiny; even Oban, Argyll's chief ferry port, has just seven thousand inhabitants, while the prettiest, Inveraray, boasts a mere four hundred.

The eastern duo of **Bute** and **Arran** are the most popular of Scotland's more southerly islands, the latter – now strictly speaking part of North Ayrshire – justifiably so, with spectacular scenery ranging from the granite peaks of the north to the Lowland pasture of the south. Of the Hebridean islands covered in this chapter, mountainous **Mull** is the most visited, though it is large enough to absorb the crowds, many of whom are only passing through en route to the tiny isle of **Iona**, a centre of Christian culture since the sixth century. **Islay**, best known for its distinctive malt whiskies, is fairly quiet even in the height of summer, as is neighbouring **Jura**, which offers excellent walking opportunities. And, for those seeking further solitude, there's the island of **Colonsay**, with its golden sands, and the more remote islands of **Tiree** and **Coll**, which, although swept with fierce winds, boast more sunny days than anywhere else in Scotland.

Accommodation price codes

Throughout this book, accommodation **prices** have been graded with the codes below, corresponding to the cost of the least expensive double room in high season. Price codes are not given for **campsites**, most of which charge less than £10 per person. Almost all **hostels** and **bunkhouses** charge between £8 and £12 per person per night; the few exceptions to this rule have the prices quoted in the text. For a full account of these codes, see p.28.

- ❶ under £40
- ❷ £40–50
- ❸ £50–60
- ❹ £60–70
- ❺ £70–90
- ❻ £90–110
- ❼ £110–150
- ❽ £150–200
- ❾ £200 and over

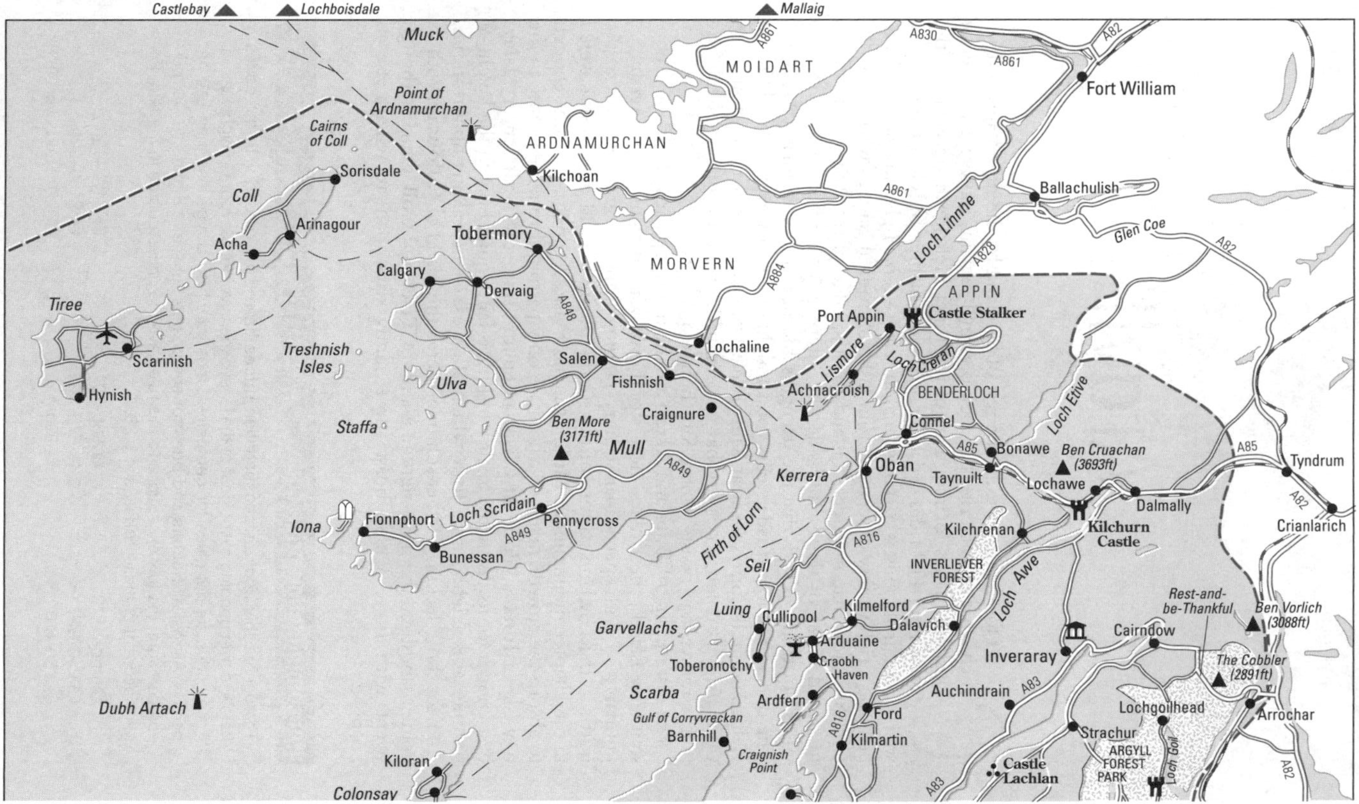

Castlebay
Lochboisdale
Mallaig
Muck
Point of Ardnamurchan
Cairns of Coll
ARDNAMURCHAN
Kilchoan
MOIDART
A861
A830
A82
Fort William
Ballachulish
Glen Coe
A82
Sorisdale
Coll
Arinagour
Acha
Tobermory
MORVERN
A884
Loch Linnhe
A828
APPIN
Calgary
Dervaig
A848
Port Appin
Castle Stalker
Tiree
Scarinish
Hynish
Treshnish Isles
Salen
Lochaline
Lismore
Loch Creran
Ulva
Fishnish
Achnacroish
BENDERLOCH
Loch Etive
Staffa
Ben More (3171ft)
Craignure
Connel
Mull
A85
Bonawe
Ben Cruachan (3693ft)
A85
Tyndrum
A849
Oban
Kerrera
Taynuilt
Lochawe
Dalmally
A82
Crianlarich
Iona
Fionnphort
Loch Scridain
Pennycross
A849
Kilchrenan
Kilchurn Castle
Bunessan
Firth of Lorn
A816
Seil
INVERLIEVER FOREST
Loch Awe
Rest-and-be-Thankful
Ben Vorlich (3088ft)
Luing
Cullipool
Kilmelford
Dalavich
Garvellachs
Arduaine
Cairndow
Inveraray
Toberonochy
Craobh Haven
The Cobbler (2891ft)
Scarba
Ardfern
Auchindrain
A83
Dubh Artach
Gulf of Corryvreckan
Ford
Lochgoilhead
Arrochar
Barnhill
A816
Kilmartin
Strachur
Craignish Point
Castle Lachlan
ARGYLL FOREST PARK
Loch Goil
A82
Kiloran
A83
Colonsay

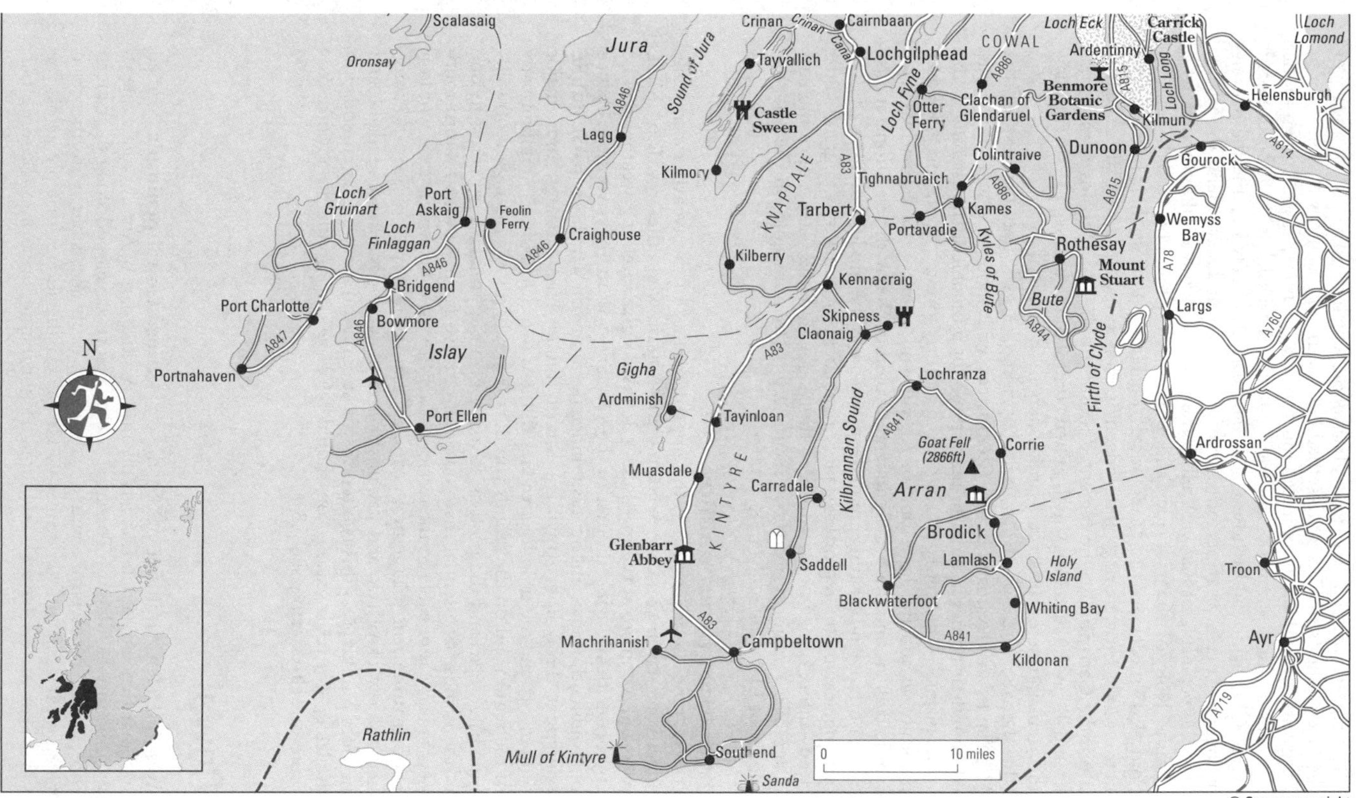

Scalasaig
Oronsay
Jura
Sound of Jura
Crinan
Crinan Canal
Cairnbaan
Lochgilphead
COWAL
Loch Eck
Carrick Castle
Loch Lomond
Ardentinny
Benmore Botanic Gardens
Loch Long
Helensburgh
Tayvallich
Castle Sween
Loch Fyne
Otter Ferry
Clachan of Glendaruel
Kilmun
Lagg
Dunoon
Gourock
A814
A815
A886
A846
A83
Kilmory
KNAPDALE
Tighnabruaich
Colintraive
Loch Gruinart
Port Askaig
Feolin Ferry
Loch Finlaggan
Craighouse
Tarbert
Kames
Portavadie
Kyles of Bute
Rothesay
Mount Stuart
Wemyss Bay
A78
Kilberry
Bridgend
Kennacraig
Bute
A844
Largs
A760
Port Charlotte
Bowmore
Skipness
Claonaig
A847
Islay
Firth of Clyde
N
Portnahaven
Gigha
Lochranza
Ardminish
Tayinloan
Port Ellen
Kilbrannan Sound
A841
Goat Fell (2866ft)
Corrie
Ardrossan
Muasdale
KINTYRE
Carradale
Arran
Brodick
Glenbarr Abbey
Lamlash
Holy Island
Saddell
Troon
Blackwaterfoot
Whiting Bay
Machrihanish
Campbeltown
Ayr
Kildonan
A719
Rathlin
Mull of Kintyre
Southend
0
10 miles
Sanda
© Crown copyright

The region's name derives from *Aragaidheal*, which translates as "Boundary of the Gaels", the Irish Celts who settled here in the fifth century AD, and whose **kingdom of Dalriada** embraced much of what is now Argyll. Known to the Romans as *Scotti* – hence "Scotland" – it was the Irish Celts who promoted Celtic Christianity, and whose Gaelic language eventually became the national tongue. After a brief period of Norse invasion and settlement, the islands (and the peninsula of Kintyre) fell to the immensely powerful Somerled, who became King of the Hebrides and Lord of Argyll in the twelfth century. Somerled's successors, the MacDonalds, established Islay as their headquarters in the 1200s, but were in turn dislodged by Robert the Bruce. Of Bruce's allies, it was the **Campbells** who benefited most from the MacDonalds' demise and, eventually, as the dukes of Argyll, gained control of the entire area – even today, they remain one of the largest landowners in the region.

In the aftermath of the Jacobite uprisings, Argyll, like the rest of the Highlands, was devastated by the **Clearances**, with thousands of crofters evicted from their homes in order to make room for profitable sheep farming – "the white plague" – and cattle-rearing. More recently forestry plantations have dramatically altered the landscape of Argyll, while purpose-built marinas have sprouted all around the heavily indented coastline. Today the traditional industries of fishing and farming are in deep crisis, as is the modern industry of fish-farming, leaving the region ever more dependent on tourism, EU grants and a steady influx of new settlers to keep things going, while Gaelic, once the language of the majority in Argyll, retains only a tenuous hold on the outlying islands of Islay, Coll and Tiree.

Transport practicalities

It's on Argyll's west coast that the unpredictability of the **weather** can really affect your stay. If you can, avoid July and August, when the crowds on Mull, Iona and Arran are at their densest – there's no guarantee the weather will be any better than during the rest of the year, and you might have more chance of avoiding the persistent Scottish midge (for more on which, see p.45). **Public transport** throughout Argyll is minimal, though buses do serve most major settlements, and the train line reaches all the way to Oban. In the remoter parts of the region and on the islands you'll have to rely on a combination of walking, shared taxis and the postbus. If you're planning to take a car across to one of the islands, it's essential that you book both your outward and return journeys as early as possible, as the ferries get very booked up. And lastly, a word on **accommodation**: a large proportion of visitors to this part of Scotland come here for a week or two and stay in self-catering cottages. On some islands and in more remote areas this is often the most common form of accommodation available – in peak season, you should book several months in advance (for more on self-catering, see p.31).

Cowal

West of Helensburgh (see p.285), the claw-shaped **Cowal peninsula**, formed by Loch Fyne and Loch Long, is the most-visited part of Argyll, largely due to its proximity to Glasgow. The area's seaside resorts developed along the eastern shores in the nineteenth century, as they were easily accessible by steamer from Glasgow. It's still quicker to get to Cowal via the ferries that ply across the Clyde; car drivers have a long, though exhilarating, drive through some rich

Highland scenery in order to reach the same spot. The Cowal landscape is extremely varied, ranging from the Munros of the **Argyll Forest Park** in the north (now part of the new Loch Lomond and the Trossachs National Park), to the gentle low-lying coastline of the southwest, but most visitors – and the majority of the population – confine themselves to the area around **Dunoon** (which has Cowal's chief tourist office) in the east, leaving the rest of the countryside relatively undisturbed.

Argyll Forest Park

The **Argyll Forest Park** stretches from the western shores of Loch Lomond south as far as Holy Loch, providing the most grandiose scenery on the peninsula. The park includes the **Arrochar Alps**, north of Glen Croe and Glen Kinglas, whose Munros offer some of the best climbing in Argyll: Ben Ime (3318ft) is the tallest of the range, and Ben Arthur or "The Cobbler" (2891ft) easily the most distinctive. All are for experienced walkers only. Less threatening are the peaks south of Glen Croe, between Loch Long and Loch Goil (branching off Loch Long), known as **Argyll's Bowling Green** – no ironic nickname, but an English corruption of the Gaelic *Baile na Greine* (Sunny Hamlet). At the other end of the scale, there are several gentle forest walks clearly laid out by the Forestry Commission and helpful leaflets available from tourist offices.

Arrochar and around

Approaching from Glasgow along the A82, followed by the A83, you enter the park from **ARROCHAR**, at the head of Loch Long. The village itself is ordinary enough, but the setting is dramatic, and it makes a convenient base for exploring the northern section of the park. There's a **train station** a mile or so east, just off the A83 to Tarbet (see p.417), and numerous **hotels** and **B&Bs**; try the very friendly *Lochside Guest House* on the main road (Ⓣ01301/702467, Ⓔlochsidegh@aol.com; ❷), or the *Fascadail* (Ⓣ01301/702344, Ⓦwww.vacations-scotland.co.uk/fascadail.html; ❷), a guesthouse with a glorious garden, situated a little to the south on the quieter A814 to Garelochhead. If you want a bite **to eat**, head for the nearby *Village Inn*, which has tables outside overlooking the loch. The local **nightlife** revolves around *Callum's Bar*, two doors down from *Lochside Guest House*.

Two miles west of Arrochar at **ARDGARTAN**, there's a well-maintained lochside Forestry Commission **campsite** (Ⓣ01301/702293, Ⓦwww.forestholidays.co.uk; March–Oct), an SYHA **hostel** (Ⓣ01301/702362, Ⓦwww.syha.org.uk; April–Nov) and, a little further down the road, a **tourist office** (daily July & Aug 10am–6pm; April–June, Sept & Oct 10am–5pm; Ⓣ01301/702432), which doubles as a forestry office and has occasional organized walks. There are also waymarked **walks** starting from the tourist office, and a bike rental place called South Park (Ⓣ01301/702288).

If you're heading west, or even south to Cowal, from Arrochar, you're forced to climb **Glen Croe**, a strategic hill pass whose saddle is called – for obvious reasons – **Rest-and-be-Thankful**. Here the road forks, with the single-track B828 heading down to **LOCHGOILHEAD**, overlooking Loch Goil. The setting is difficult to beat, but the village has been upstaged by the *Drimsynie Holiday Resort*, whose triangular chalets pockmark the landscape for a mile to the west. A road tracks the west side of the loch, petering out after five miles at the ruins of **Carrick Castle**, a classic tower-house castle built around 1400 and used as a hunting lodge by James IV.

Cairndow and around

If you'd rather skip Lochgoilhead, continue west along the A83 from Rest-and-be-Thankful down the grand Highland sweep of Glen Kinglas to **CAIRNDOW**, at the head of Loch Fyne. Just behind the village, off the main road, you'll find the **Ardkinglas Woodland Garden** (daily during daylight hours; Ⓦwww.ardkinglas.com; £2), which contains exotic rhododendrons, azaleas and a superb collection of conifers, some of which rise to over 200ft. The *Cairndow Inn*, in the village itself, is good for a pint and inexpensive pub food, with views over the head of Loch Fyne, but for something a bit special continue a mile or so further along on the A83 to the famous **Loch Fyne Oyster Bar** (Ⓣ01499/600264, Ⓦwww.loch-fyne.com), which sells more oysters than anywhere else in the country, plus lots of other fish and seafood treats. You can easily assemble a gourmet picnic here or stock up on provisions for the week, and the moderately expensive **restaurant** is excellent, though booking is advisable at busy times. Inveraray (see p.380) is only six miles along the western shores of Loch Fyne shore on the A83.

Alternative fuelling points on Loch Fyne include the attractive *Old Ferry Inn* at **ST CATHERINES**, four miles down the eastern shoreline from Cairndow, a pub which offers good bar snacks with a view across to Inveraray, or the famous *Creggans Inn* (Ⓣ01369/860279, Ⓦwww.creggans-inn.co.uk; ❻), another four miles south in **STRACHUR**. The inn, which belongs to the son of Sir Fitzroy Maclean, stands just to the north of the village and, even if the rooms and restaurant are too pricey, you can pop into the bar or the all-day coffee shop; they also have self-catering cottages on the estate. Tucked away in Clachan, a kind of suburb of Strachur, is a church with medieval grave slabs set into its walls and the **Strachur Smiddy** (Easter–Sept daily 1–4pm; £1) an old restored blacksmith's which has live shoeing once a year.

Loch Eck and Holy Loch

The road divides at Strachur, with the A815 heading inland to **Loch Eck**. This exceptionally narrow freshwater loch, squeezed between steeply banked woods, is a favourite spot for trout fishing. At the loch's southern tip are the beautifully laid-out **Benmore Botanic Gardens** (March–Oct daily 9.30am–6pm; £3), an offshoot of Edinburgh's Royal Botanic Gardens, famed for their rhododendrons and especially striking for their avenue of Great Redwoods, planted in 1863 and now over 100ft high. There's an excellent, inexpensive **café** by the entrance, open in season, with an imaginative menu; you can eat there without visiting the gardens if trees aren't your thing. It's easy to combine a visit here with one of the most popular of the local **forest walks**, a leisurely stroll up the rocky ravine of **Puck's Glen**; the walk (1hr 30min round-trip) begins from the car park a mile south of the gardens. The family-orientated *Stratheck Country Park* **campsite** at the southern end of Loch Eck (Ⓣ01369/840472; March–Oct) enjoys a good location, surrounded by wooded slopes, and has caravans for rent.

Before heading south to Dunoon, it's worth taking a trip down the north shores of nearby **Holy Loch**, the former site of a US nuclear submarine base which closed in 1992, to **KILMUN**, where there's a fascinating church with a mausoleum – alas closed to the public – where many a Duke of Argyll is buried, several good stained-glass windows and an organ driven by tap water (the church holds teas and tours in the summer). There's also an **arboretum** at Kilmun, through which the Forestry Commission has laid out several pleasant walks. On the banks of the River Eachaig is the *Cot House Caravan and Campsite* (Ⓣ01369/840351; April–Oct) where you can always get bar **food** at the adjacent inn.

Dunoon

In the nineteenth century, **DUNOON**, Cowal's capital, grew from a mere village to a major Clyde seaside resort and favourite holiday spot for Glaswegians. Nowadays, tourists tend to arrive by ferry from Gourock and, though their numbers are smaller, Dunoon remains by far the largest town in Argyll, with 13,000 inhabitants. Apart from its practical uses and its fine pier, however, there's little to tempt you to linger.

The centre of town is dominated by a grassy lump of rock known as **Castle Hill**, crowned by Castle House, built in the 1820s by a wealthy Glaswegian and the subject of a bitter dispute with the local populace over closure of the common land around his house. The people eventually won, and the grounds remain open to the public to this day, as does the house, which is now home to the **Castle House Museum** (Easter–Oct Mon–Sat 10.30am–4.30pm, Sun 2–4.30pm; Ⓦwww.castlehousemuseum.org.uk; £1.50). There's some good hands-on nature stuff for kids, an excellent section on the Clyde steamers as well as details of "Highland Mary", betrothed to Robbie Burns (despite the fact that he already had a pregnant wife), who nursed the poet through typhus while they planned to elope to the West Indies only to die from the disease herself. A statue of her is in the grounds. Another more violent scene in local history is commemorated by a memorial on a nearby rock: at least 36 men of the Lamont clan were executed in 1646 by their rivals, the Campbells, who hanged them from "a lively, fresh-growing ash tree". The tree couldn't take the strain, and had to be cut down two years later; tradition has it that blood gushed from the roots when it was felled.

With an hour or so to spare, you could visit the **Cowal Bird Garden** (April–Oct daily 10.30am–6pm; £3.25), one mile northwest along the A885 to Sandbank, and wander through their woodland amid exotic caged birds as well as free-roaming peacocks, macaws and pot-bellied pigs. If the weather's fine, take the **Ardnadam Heritage Trail**, a mile further up the road, to the wonderful Dunan viewpoint looking out to the Firth of Clyde; if the weather's bad, you could head for Dunoon Ceramics, on Hamilton Street, which produces various styles of high-quality porcelain and bone china, and offers tours around the factory (Mon–Fri 9am–12.30pm & 1–4.30pm).

Practicalities

It's a good idea to take advantage of Dunoon's **tourist office**, the principal one in Cowal, located on Alexandra Parade (May–Sept Mon–Fri 9am–6pm, Sat & Sun 10am–5pm; April & Oct Mon–Fri 9am–5.30pm, Sat 10am–5pm, Sun 11am–3pm; Nov–March Mon–Thurs 9am–5.30pm, Fri 9am–5pm; Ⓣ01369/703785). There are two **ferry crossings** across the Clyde from Gourock to Dunoon; the shorter, more frequent service is half-hourly on Western Ferries to Hunter's Quay, a mile north of the town centre; CalMac's boats, though, arrive at the main pier, and have better transport connections if you're on foot.

There's an enormous choice of **B&Bs**, none of them outstanding. You're better off heading out of town or persuading the tourist office to help you out, since availability is the biggest problem. For real quality, head for the highly reputable *Ardfillayne House*, West Bay (Ⓣ01369/702267, wwww.ardfillayne.activebooking.com; ❹); its welcoming next-door neighbour *Abbot's Brae* (Ⓣ01369/705021, Ⓦwww.abbotsbrae.co.uk; ❹); or, topping the lot, the luxurious *Enmore Hotel* (Ⓣ01369/702230, Ⓦwww.enmorehotel.co.uk; ❺), an eighteenth-century villa on Marine Parade near Hunter's Quay. A **hostel**, run by the Baptist Church, is due to open on Alexandra Parade (for the latest, call the church on ⓣ01369/706665).

Chatters, 58 John St (Wed–Sat only; closed Jan & Feb), is Dunoon's best **restaurant**, offering delicious Loch Fyne seafood and Scottish beef. For something a bit less pricey, the *Argyll* does decent, filling bar snacks, and there's a vast Italian menu at *Di Marco's Café Bar* in Argyll Street (closed Mon). For **bike rental**, head for the Highland Stores on Argyll Street, or the *Argyll Hotel*; for **pony trekking**, contact the Velvet Path Riding and Trekking Centre (ⓣ01369/830580) at Inellan, four miles south of town. Dunoon boasts a two-screen **cinema** (a rarity in Argyll) on John Street, but the town's most famous entertainment is the **Cowal Highland Gathering** (ⓦwww.cowalgathering.com), the largest of its kind in the world, held here on the last weekend in August, and culminating in the awesome spectacle of the massed pipes and drums of more than 150 bands marching through the streets.

Southwest Cowal

The mellower landscape of **southwest Cowal**, which stands in complete contrast to the bustle of Dunoon or the Highland grandeur of the Argyll Forest Park, becomes immediate as soon as you head west along the scenic B836 from Benmore to Loch Striven, and then on to Loch Riddon, where, from either side, there are few more beautiful sights than the **Kyles of Bute**, the slivers of water that separate Cowal from the bleak bulk of the Isle of Bute, and constitute some of the best sailing territory in Scotland.

COLINTRAIVE, on the eastern Kyle, marks the narrowest point in the Kyles – barely more than a couple of hundred yards – and is the place from which the small CalMac car ferry departs to Bute. The most popular spot from which to appreciate the Kyles is the A8003 as it rises dramatically above the sea lochs before descending to the peaceful, lochside village of **TIGHNABRUAICH**, best known for its excellent **sailing school** (ⓣ01700/811717, ⓦwww.tssargyll.co.uk), which offers week-long courses from beginners to advanced. Boat trips still call at the pier and the village is thriving, boasting a bank, a post office and several shops as well as a good inexpensive place to eat – the *Burnside Bistro*. The *Royal Hotel* (ⓣ01700/811239, ⓦwww.royalhotel.org.uk; ❺), by the waterside, serves exceptionally good bar meals, and has wonderful views over the Kyles, but it's a lot cheaper to stay in neighbouring **KAMES** at the *Kames Hotel* (ⓣ01700/811489, ⓔtccandrew@aol.com; ❷), which also has the views. Close by Kames pier, which was originally used for exporting the gunpowder manufactured at nearby Millhouse, is the tank landing site where troops practised for the D-Day landings in World War II. If you're driving to Kintyre, Islay or Jura, you can avoid the long haul around Loch Fyne – some seventy miles or so – by using the **ferry** to Tarbert from **Portavadie**, three miles southwest of Kames.

The Kyles can get busy in July and August, but you can escape the crowds by heading for Cowal's deserted west coast, overlooking Loch Fyne. The one brief glimpse of habitation en route is the luxurious, whitewashed *Kilfinan Hotel* (ⓣ01700/821201; ❺; closed Feb), set back from a sandy bay seven miles along the B8000 west of Tighnabruaich. The road meets the loch shore at **OTTER FERRY**, which has a small sandy beach, a wonderful pub and an oyster restaurant, *The Oystercatcher*, with outside tables in good weather. There was once a ferry link to Lochgilphead from here, though the "otter" part is not derived from the furry beast but from the Gaelic *an oitir* (sandbank), which juts out a mile or so into Loch Fyne. If you're continuing north, you'll pass the romantic ruin of **Castle Lachlan** and then the enchanting road through the wooded glen of Strathlachlan.

The faster road north from Portavadie and the Kyles is the A886, which runs through the lovely forested Glendaruel. En route, you'll pass the pretty village of **CLACHAN OF GLENDARUEL**, whose Georgian, riverside Kilmodan Church was once the place of worship of three Campbell lairds and whose churchyard preserves several medieval grave slabs. **Accommodation** is available at the homely *Glendaruel Hotel* (Ⓣ01369/820274; ❸), which does unusual bar snacks, and there's an award-winning **campsite** in the forest just up the road at *Glendaruel Caravan Park* (Ⓣ01369/820267, Ⓦwww.glendaruelcaravanpark.co.uk; April–Oct), which also rents caravans.

The Isle of Bute

The island of **Bute** is in many ways simply an extension of the Cowal peninsula, from which it is separated by the narrow Kyles of Bute. Until 1975, it formed its own county, along with the Isle of Arran to the south, but it's since been thrown in with Argyll. Thanks to its consistently mild climate and its ferry link with Wemyss Bay (see p.284), Bute has been a popular holiday and convalescence spot for Clydesiders – particularly the elderly – for over a century. Its chief town, **Rothesay**, rivals Dunoon as the major seaside resort on the Clyde, easily surpassing it thanks to the two superb castles nearby. Most of Bute's inhabitants live around the two wide bays on the east coast of the island, which resembles one long seaside promenade. Consequently, it's easy enough to escape the crowds by heading for the sparsely populated west coast, which, in any case, has much the sandiest beaches.

Rothesay

Bute's only town, **ROTHESAY** is a handsome Victorian resort, set in a wide sweeping bay, backed by green hills, with a classic palm-tree promenade and 1920s pagoda-style Winter Gardens. It creates a much better general impression than Dunoon, with its period architecture and the occasional flourishes of wrought-ironwork. Even if you're just passing through, you should pay a visit to the ornate **Victorian toilets** (daily: Easter–Oct 8am–9pm; Nov–Easter 9am–5pm; 10p) on the pier, which were built by Twyfords in 1899 and have since been declared a national treasure. Men have the best time, since the porcelain urinals steal the show, but women can ask for a guided tour, if the coast is clear, and learn about the haunted cubicle. While you're on the harbourfront, look out for the wrought-iron arch marking the **Highland Boundary Fault**, which cuts the island (and Rothesay) in two: the view looks out on the Highlands in one direction and the Lowlands in the other.

Rothesay also boasts the militarily useless, but architecturally impressive, moated ruins of **Rothesay Castle** (April–Sept daily 9.30am–6.30pm; Oct–March Mon–Wed 9.30am–4.30pm, Thurs 9.30am–noon, Sat 9.30am–4.30pm, Sun 2–4.30pm; HS; £2), hidden amid the town's backstreets but signposted from the pier. Built around the twelfth century, it was twice captured by the Vikings in the 1200s; such vulnerability was the reasoning behind the unusual, almost circular, curtain wall, with its four big drum towers, only one of which remains fully intact.

In rainy weather you could hide inside the **Bute Museum** (April–Sept Mon–Sat 10.30am–4.30pm, Sun 2.30–4.30pm; Oct–March Tues–Sat

2.30–4.30pm; £2) behind the castle, whose local history section has some shining imperial weights and measures and a triple mousetrap. More interesting, though, is the fourteenth-century **St Mary's Chapel**, beside the High Kirk on the outskirts of town up the High Street; it houses a couple of impressive canopied medieval tombs and, in the churchyard, the mausoleum of the Marquesses of Bute and the grave of Napoleon's niece, who married a Sheriff of Lancaster.

A real little gem in summer is **Ardencraig Gardens** (May–Sept Mon–Fri 10am–4.30pm, Sat & Sun 1–4.30pm; free), up the hill opposite Craigmore Pier, where the Victorian hothouses and garden are a riot of blooms, with flowers in the midst of aviaries full of exotic birds; there is even a decent tearoom with mouthwatering home-made cakes. More horticultural delights are to be found out along the road to Mount Stuart (see opposite) at the **Ascog Fernery and Garden** (April to mid-Oct Wed–Sun 10am–5pm; £2.50), an unusual Victorian fernery that has been lovingly restored and boasts an ancient fern, reputed to be a thousand years old.

Practicalities

Rothesay's **tourist office** is opposite the pier at 15 Victoria St (July & Aug Mon–Fri 9am–7pm, Sat 10am–7pm, Sun 10am–5pm; May, June & Sept Mon–Fri 9am–5.30pm, Sat & Sun 10am–5pm; April & Oct Mon–Fri 9am–5.30pm, Sat & Sun 9.30am–5pm; Nov–March Mon–Thurs 9am–5.30pm, Fri 9am–5pm; ⓣ01700/502151). Staff can help with **accommodation**, though there's no shortage of B&Bs all along the seafront from Rothesay north to Port Bannatyne. One of the most attractive hotels on the bay is *Cannon House* (ⓣ01700/502819; ❺), a Georgian house close to the pier on Battery Place, while the nearby *Commodore* (ⓣ01700/502178, ⓔspearcommodore @aol.com; ❶) is a more modest guesthouse, but equally accommodating. Another excellent option, set in its own grounds a mile to the north in **ARDBEG**, is *Ardmory House* (ⓣ01700/502346, ⓔardmory.house.hotel@dial.pipex .com; ❺), which is also one of the area's best places to eat. Further out in **ASCOG**, the B&B at *Ascog Farm* (ⓣ01700/503372; ❶) is exceptionally good value, while *New Farm* (ⓣ01700/831646; ❷), just one mile north of Mount Stuart, has a few rooms in a lovely converted farmhouse, above a moderately expensive **restaurant** which uses local ingredients and produces its own delicious bread; it's popular, so be sure to reserve. A good **self-catering** option at Port Ballantyne is the six Victorian cottages in the grounds of *Kames Castle* (ⓣ01700/504500, ⓦwww.kames-castle.co.uk).

The best **food** options in Rothesay itself are *Oliver's*, on Victoria Street, which serves pasta dishes, steak and decent local seafood specials; and the waterfront bistro *Fowlers* (closed Mon & Tues), in the Winter Gardens, which offers a good-value menu and a superb view of the bay. For Rothesay's finest fish and chips, head for the *West End Café* on Gallowgate. You can't miss the town's many Zavaroni cafés, part of the subculture of Italian cafés in the Clyde area; the most famous member of the family was, of course, Lena, a teenage pop star in the 1970s. The *Harbour Café* on the seafront combines coffee, cakes and **internet** surfing.

Rothesay's **cinema** is in the Winter Gardens. Bute holds its own **Highland Games** on the second-to-last weekend in August – Prince Charles, the Duke of Rothesay, occasionally attends – plus an international **folk festival** on the third weekend in July, and a (mainly trad) **jazz festival** over May Bank Holiday. There are several golf courses, **pony trekking** at Kingarth Trekking Centre near Kilchattan Bay (ⓣ01700/831673), and **bike rental** from Rob Cycles on East Princess Street (ⓣ01700/502333).

Mount Stuart

One very good reason for coming to Bute is to visit **Mount Stuart** (May–Sept Mon, Wed & Fri–Sun 11am–5pm; £6.50, gardens only £3), a fantasy Gothic house set amidst acres of lush woodland gardens overlooking the Firth of Clyde three miles south of Rothesay. Today the home of the obscenely wealthy seventh Marquess of Bute, the building was created by the marvellously eccentric third Marquess after a fire in 1877 had destroyed the family seat. With little regard for expense, the marquess shipped in tons of Italian marble, building a railway line to transport it down the coast and employing craftsmen who had worked with the great William Burges on the marquess's earlier medieval concoctions at Cardiff Castle. The building was by no means finished when the third Marquess died in 1900, and work continues even today, though subsequent family members haven't quite had the inspirational taste of their predecessor.

A **bus** runs from Rothesay approximately every 45 minutes to the gates of Mount Stuart, while the house itself is a pleasant fifteen-minute walk through the gardens from the ticket office; if it's raining it might be worth taking the shuttle service provided. You can join a **guided tour** for an extra £2, but it's really not necessary as the guides in each room are just as informative. Inside the building, the showpiece is the columned **Marble Hall**, its vaulted ceiling and stained-glass windows decorated with the signs of the zodiac, reflecting the marquess's taste for mysticism. The marquess was equally fond of animal and plant imagery, hence you'll find birds feeding on berries in the dining-room frieze and monkeys reading (and tearing up) books and scrolls in the library. Look out also for the unusual heraldic plaster ceiling in the drawing room. After all the heavy furnishings, seek aesthetic relief in the **Marble Chapel**, built entirely out of dazzling white Carrara marble, with a magnificent Cosmati floor pattern. Upstairs is less interesting, with the notable exception of the **Horoscope Room**, where you can see a fine astrological ceiling and adjacent observatory.

Although the sumptuous interior of Mount Stuart is not to everyone's taste, it's worth a visit to explore the wonderfully mature **gardens** (open 1hr earlier), established in the eighteenth century by the third Earl of Bute, who had a hand in London's Kew Gardens. If you haven't packed a picnic you can eat at the castle café. Before you leave Mount Stuart, take a look at the planned village of **Kerrycroy**, just beyond the main exit, built by the second Marquess in the early nineteenth century for the estate workers. Semidetached houses – alternately mock-Tudor and whitewashed stone – form a crescent that overlooks a pristine village green and, beyond, the sea.

Around Bute

The Highland–Lowland dividing line passes through the middle of Bute, which is all but sliced in two by the freshwater Loch Fad. As a result, the northern half of the island is hilly, uninhabited and little visited, while the southern half is made up of Lowland-style farmland. The two highest peaks on the island are **Windy Hill** (913ft) and **Torran Turach** (746ft), both in the north; from the latter, there are fine views of the Kyles, but for a gentler overview of the island you can simply walk up to the **viewpoint**, on a hill a few miles east of Rothesay.

A site well worth visiting, which recalls Bute's early monastic history, is **St Blane's Chapel**, a twelfth-century ruin beautifully situated in open countryside six miles south of Rothesay on the west coast, close to the island's southernmost tip. The medieval church stands amidst the foundations of an earlier Christian settlement established in the sixth century by St Catan, uncle to the local-born St Blane. In a rather peculiar arrangement, the upper graveyard was reserved for the men of the parish while the women were consigned to the lower one.

Four miles up the west coast is the sandy strand of **Scalpsie Bay** while, further on, beyond the village of Straad, lies **St Ninian's Point**, where the ruins of a sixth-century chapel overlook another fine sandy strand and the uninhabited island of **Inchmarnock** – to which, according to tradition, alcoholics were banished in the nineteenth century. Bute's finest sandy beach is a little further north at **Ettrick Bay**, with an excellent tearoom (April–Oct) at its north end. On the road from Ettrick Bay east to Rothesay, you can still see traces of the tramlines which used to bring visitors to the beach in its heyday.

Inveraray and around

A classic example of an eighteenth-century planned town, **INVERARAY** was built on the site of a ruined fishing village in 1745 by the third Duke of Argyll, head of the powerful Campbell clan, in order to distance his newly rebuilt castle from the hoi polloi in the town and to establish a commercial and legal centre for the region. Today Inveraray, an absolute set piece of Scottish Georgian architecture, has a truly memorable setting, the brilliant white arches of Front Street reflected in the still waters of **Loch Fyne**, which separate it from the Cowal peninsula.

The Town

Squeezed onto a promontory some distance from the duke's new castle, there's not much more to Inveraray's "New Town" than its distinctive **Main Street** (set at a right angle to Front Street), flanked by whitewashed terraces, whose window casements are picked out in black. At the top of the street, the road divides to circumnavigate the town's Neoclassical church, originally built in two parts: the southern half served the Gaelic-speaking community, while the northern half – still in use and worth a peek for its period wood-panelled interior – served those who spoke English.

East of the church is **Inveraray Jail** (daily: April–Oct 9.30am–6pm; Nov–March 10am–5pm; £4.90), whose attractive Georgian courthouse and grim prison blocks ceased to function in the 1930s. The jail is now an imaginative and thoroughly enjoyable museum, which graphically recounts prison conditions from medieval times up until the nineteenth century – and even brings it up to date by including a picture of life in Barlinnie Prison. You can also sit in the beautiful semicircular courthouse and listen to the trial of a farmer accused of fraud.

Moored at the town pier is the **Arctic Penguin** (daily: April–Sept 9.30am–6pm; Oct–March 10am–5pm; £3), a handsome, triple-masted schooner built in Dublin in 1911 – it has some nautical knick-knacks and displays on the maritime history of the Clyde, but is only really worth exploring if you're a naval enthusiast or wet weather inhibits town wanderings. During the replanning of the town, the fifteenth-century **Inveraray Cross** was moved to its present position on Front Street by the loch; a more interesting example from the island of Tiree can be found in the castle gardens (see opposite), featuring a crucifixion scene on one side, and a stag-hunting scene on the reverse.

For a panoramic view of the town, castle and loch, you can climb the **Bell Tower** (May–Sept daily 10am–1pm & 2–5pm; £2) of All Saints' Church, accessible via the peaceful avenue of trees through the screen arches on Front Street. Built after World War I as a memorial to the fallen Campbells by the tenth Duke of Argyll, the tower houses ten bells, which are the second heaviest set in the world. It takes four hours to ring a complete peal – that is, every musical sequence possible with the ten bells.

Inveraray Castle

A ten-minute walk north of the New Town, the neo-Gothic **Inveraray Castle** (July & Aug Mon–Sat 10am–5.45pm, Sun 1–5.45pm; April–June, Sept & Oct Mon–Thurs & Sat 10am–1pm & 2–5.45pm, Sun 1–5.45pm; £5.50) remains the family home of the Duke of Argyll. Built in 1745 by the third duke, it was given a touch of the Loire in the nineteenth century with the addition of dormer windows and conical roofs. Inside, the most startling feature is the armoury hall, whose displays of weaponry – supplied to the Campbells by the British government to put down the Jacobites – rise through several storeys; look out for Rob Roy's rather sad-looking sporran and dirk handle (a dirk being a dagger, traditionally worn in Highland dress).

Gracing the extensive **castle grounds** (daily during daylight hours; free) is the aforementioned Celtic cross from Tiree, and one of three elegant bridges built during the re-landscaping of Inveraray (the other two are on the road from Cairndow). Of the walks marked out in the grounds, the most strenuous takes you to the tower atop **Dùn na Cuaiche** (813ft), from where there's a spectacular view over the castle, town and loch.

Around Inveraray

If you've got children in tow, the **Argyll Wildlife Park** (April–Oct daily 10am–5pm; £3.50), two miles south of Inveraray, along the A83 towards Campbeltown, provides some light relief, allowing children to come face to face with Scotland's indigenous fauna, from sika deer to owls, waterfowl and wildcats.

Three miles further on, the **Auchindrain Folk Museum** (April–Sept daily 10am–5pm; £3.80) is a fascinating old township of around twenty thatched buildings, which give an idea of life here before the Clearances, and before the planning of towns like Inveraray. Original furniture, straw on the floors and hens wandering in and out of the houses give the place a lived-in feel, and the informative visitor centre has a good bookshop and a **tearoom**, whose water comes from the same spring that served the original township.

Practicalities

Inveraray's **tourist office** is on Front Street (July & Aug daily 9am–6pm; May & June Mon–Sat 9am–5pm, Sun 11am–5pm; April, Sept & Oct Mon–Sat 9am–5pm, Sun noon–5pm; Feb, March & Nov Mon–Fri 11am–4pm, Sat & Sun noon–4pm; Jan & Dec Mon–Fri 10am–3pm, Sat & Sun 11am–3pm; ⓣ01499/302063), as is the town's chief **hotel**, the historic *Argyll* (ⓣ01499/302466; ❹), now run by Best Western but formerly the *Great Inn*, where Dr Johnson and Boswell once stayed. A cheaper, but equally well-appointed alternative is the Georgian *Fernpoint Hotel* (ⓣ01499/302170, ⓔfernpoint.hotel@virgin.net; ❶), round by the pier, which has a nice pub garden; otherwise there's the **B&B** *Creag Dhubh* (ⓣ01499/302430, ⓦwww.creagdhubh.freeuk.com; March–Nov; ❶), in a large garden overlooking Loch

Fyne down the A83 to Lochgilphead. The SYHA **hostel** (ⓣ01499/302454, ⓦwww.syha.org.uk; mid-March to Oct) is in a modern building a short distance north on the A819 Dalmally road, while the old Royal Navy base, two miles down the A83 to Lochgilphead, has been converted into the excellent, fully equipped *Argyll Caravan Park* (ⓣ01499/302285; April–Oct). The **bar** of the central *George Hotel* is the town's liveliest spot, while for tea and cakes head for *The Poacher* round by the *Fernpoint Hotel*. The best place to sample Loch Fyne's delicious fresh fish and seafood is the superb, moderately priced restaurant of the *Loch Fyne Oyster Bar* (see p.374), six miles northeast back up the A83 towards Glasgow.

Loch Awe and Taynuilt

Legend has it that **Loch Awe** – at more than 25 miles in length, the longest stretch of fresh water in the country – was created by a witch and inhabited by a monster even more gruesome than the one at Loch Ness. The northwestern shores of the loch are the most peaceful, with gentle hills and the magnificent **Inverliever Forest**, where the Forestry Commission has laid out a series of none-too-strenuous **forest walks** around Dalavich. The most spectacular of these is the hour-long circular walk from Inverinan up to the Royal Engineers' wooden footbridge, which takes you over a pretty waterfall.

Dotted around the north of the loch, where it's joined by the A819 from Inveraray, the A85 from Tyndrum and the railway from Glasgow, are several tiny islands sporting picturesque ruins. On **Inishail** you can see a crumbling thirteenth-century chapel which once served as a burial ground for the MacArthur clan; the ruined castle on **Fraoch Eilean** dates from the same period. Fifteenth-century **Kilchurn Castle**, strategically situated on a rocky spit – once an island – at the head of the loch and once a Campbell stronghold, has been abandoned to the elements since being struck by lightning in the 1760s, and is now one of Argyll's most photogenic lochside ruins.

During the summer you can sail around Kilchurn Castle as part of an hour-long steamboat cruise that sets off from the pier at **LOCHAWE**, right by the village's train station. A mile further along the A85, it's worth pausing at **St Conan's Kirk**, an unusual building fashioned in a sort of home-made Norman–Gothic style. The original church was built in the 1880s, but the version you see now was begun in 1907 by Walter Campbell and completed by his sister Helen. The church contains a fair amount of historical bric-a-brac, from a piece of Robert the Bruce to fragments from Iona Abbey and Eton College, but by far the finest sections are the ambulatory, with its tall, clear windows overlooking Loch Awe, and the dinky lead-roofed cloisters.

A couple of miles further west, gorged into the giant granite bulk of Ben Cruachan (3695ft), is the underground **Cruachan Power Station** (daily: Easter–June & Sept–Nov 9.30am–5pm; July & Aug 9.30am–6pm; £3), built in 1965. Half-hour guided tours set off every hour from the newly refurbished **visitor centre** by the loch, taking you to a viewing platform above the generating room deep inside the "hollow mountain". Using the water from an artificial loch high up on Ben Cruachan to drive the turbines, the power station can become fully operational in less than two minutes, supplying electricity during surges on the National Grid. Sadly it takes ten percent more electricity to pump the water back up into the artificial loch, so the station only manages to make a profit by buying cheap off-peak power and selling during daytime peak demand. The whole experience of visiting an industrial complex hidden within a mountain is very James Bond, and it certainly pulls in the tour coaches, so if you're keen to go, make sure you get there before the queues start to form, particularly in summer.

In order to maintain the right level of water in Loch Awe itself, a dam was built at the mouth of the loch, which then had to be fitted with a special lift to transport the salmon – for which the loch is justly famous – upriver to spawn. From the dam, the River Awe squeezes through the mountains via the gloomy rock-walled **Pass of Brander** (which means "ambush" in Gaelic), where Robert the Bruce put to flight the MacDougall clan in 1308, cutting them down as they fought with one another to cross the river and escape.

There are two particularly luxurious **hotels** on the northwestern shores of Loch Awe: the wonderfully relaxing *Taychreggan Hotel* (ⓣ01866/833211, ⓔtaycreggan@btinternet.com; ❼), an old drovers' inn by the loch, to the southeast of Kilchrenan, and the *Ardanaiseig Hotel* (ⓣ01866/833333, ⓦwww.ardanaiseig-hotel.com; ❼; closed Jan), a palatial Scottish Baronial pile four miles to the northeast down a dead-end track. Both these hotels have superb, though expensive, restaurants, and the *Ardanaiseig* also has its own glorious gardens (daily 9.30am–dusk), worth visiting even if you're not staying here. Considerably easier to reach is the *Loch Awe Hotel* (ⓣ01838/200261; ❺; closed Jan), another Scots Baronial hotel, on the busy A85, along the north shore of the loch. The nicest **B&Bs** are on the more peaceful western shores: try the comfortable *Thistle-Doo* (ⓣ01866/833339; ❷) at Kilchrenan. Further south, at Dalavich, there are Forestry Commission **chalets** for rent by the loch; you must stay a minimum of three nights (summer rate £179), and book through Forest Holidays (ⓣ0131/334 0303, ⓦwww.forestholidays.co.uk). Loch Awe is stocked full of trout, pike and salmon, and there are **boats to rent** (and fishing tackle) from Donald Wilson (ⓣ01866/833256), based at Ardbrecknish, southwest of Cladich on the east shore, though he will deliver boats to any other point on the loch for a fee.

Taynuilt and Loch Etive

TAYNUILT, six miles west of the Cruachan power station, where the River Awe flows into **Loch Etive**, is a small but sprawling village, best known for its iron-smelting works. To reach this industrial heritage site, follow the signpost off the A85 to **Bonawe Iron Furnace** (April–Sept Mon–Sat 9.30am–6.30pm, Sun 2–6.30pm; HS; £2.50), which was originally founded by Cumbrian ironworkers in 1753. It was clearly cheaper, in those days, to import iron ore from south of the border, rather than transport charcoal to the Lake District, since several iron furnaces were established in the area, of which Bonawe was the most successful. A whole series of buildings in various states of repair are scattered across the factory site, which employed 600 people at its height, and eventually closed down in 1876.

From the pier beyond the iron furnace, **boat cruises** (April & Oct daily 2pm; May–Sept Mon–Fri 10am, noon & 2pm, Sat & Sun 2pm; £5) check out the local seals and explore the otherwise inaccessible reaches of Loch Etive; phone Loch Etive Cruises (ⓣ01866/822430) for more details. A mile or so east up the A85 from Taynuilt, a sign invites you to visit the **Inverawe Fisheries and Smokery** (Easter–Christmas daily 8am–dusk; ⓦwww.smokedsalmon.co.uk), where you can buy traditionally smoked local fish and mussels, learn how to fly-fish, check out the exhibition on traditional smoking techniques (Mon–Fri 9am–4pm; 50p), or go for a stroll down to nearby Loch Etive with your picnic.

Oban and around

The solidly Victorian resort of **OBAN** enjoys a superb setting – the island of Kerrera providing its bay with a natural shelter – distinguished by a bizarre granite amphitheatre, dramatically lit at night, on the hilltop above the town. Despite a population of just 8000, it's by far the largest port in northwest Scotland, the second-largest town in Argyll, and the main departure point for ferries to the Hebrides. If you arrive late, or are catching an early boat, you may have to spend the night here (there's no real need otherwise); if you're staying

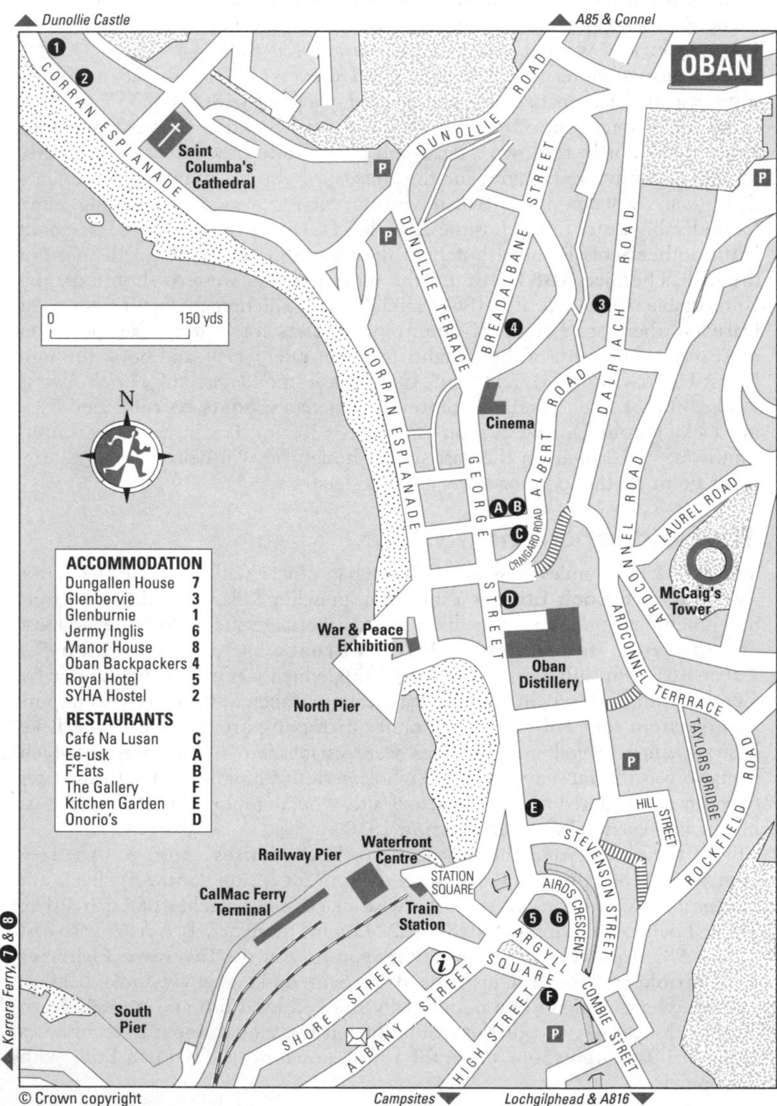

elsewhere, it's a useful base for wet-weather activities and shopping, although it does get uncomfortably crowded in the summer.

Oban lies at the centre of the coastal region known as Lorn, named after the Irish Celt Loarn, who, along with his brothers Fergus and Oengus, settled here around 500 AD. Given the number of tourists that pass through or stay in the area, it's hardly surprising that a few out-and-out tourist attractions have developed, which can be handy to know about if it's raining and/or you have children with you. The mainland is very picturesque, although its beauty is no secret – to escape the crowds, head off and explore the islands, like **Lismore** or **Kerrera**, just offshore.

Arrival, information and accommodation

Arriving in Oban **by car** can be a bit of a nightmare in the summer. If you're heading straight for the ferry, either make sure you leave an extra hour to allow for sitting in the tailbacks, which can stretch for more than a mile back along the A85, or try and approach the town from the south along the A816. If you're just coming in to town to look around, use one of the park-and-ride or supermarket car parks. The CalMac **ferry terminal** (ⓣ01631/566688, ⓦwww.calmac.co.uk) for the islands is on Railway Pier, is a stone's throw from the train station, which is itself adjacent to the bus stops on Station Square. The **tourist office** (April Mon–Fri 9am–5pm, Sat & Sun 10am–5pm; May to mid-June Mon–Sat 9am–5.30pm, Sun 10am–5pm; mid- to late June, early to late Sept Mon–Sat 9am–6.30pm, Sun 10am–5pm; July & Aug Mon–Sat 9am–8pm, Sun 9am–7pm; late Sept to Oct Mon–Sat 9am–5.30pm, Sun 10am–4pm; Nov–March Mon–Fri 9.30am–5pm, Sat & Sun noon–4pm; ⓣ01631/563122, ⓦwww.oban.org.uk) is housed in a converted church on Argyll Square, and has a visually attractive, interactive exhibition where the altar used to be, useful for whiling away half an hour in wet weather.

Oban is positively heaving with **hotels** and **B&Bs**, most of them very reasonably priced and many of them on or near the quayside. Although it's easy enough to search out a vacancy, in high season it might be wise to pay the small fee charged by the tourist office for finding you a room.

Hotels and B&Bs

Dungallen House Hotel Gallanach Road ⓣ01631/563799, ⓦwww.dungallenhotel-oban.co.uk. Solid Victorian villa hotel set in its own woodland grounds, hidden away on the Gallanach Road, with great views across the Sound of Kerrera. Closed Feb & Nov. ❺

Glenbervie Guest House Dalriach Road ⓣ01631/564770. Superior Victorian guesthouse set slightly above the town on a quiet road heaving with accommodation. ❶

Glenburnie Hotel Corran Esplanade ⓣ01631/562089. Efficiently run medium-sized Victorian hotel on the quieter section of the Esplanade, beyond the Cathedral. April–Oct. ❸

Manor House Hotel Gallanach Road ⓣ01631/562087. Beautiful eighteenth-century manor house, peacefully located by the shores of the Sound of Kerrera, with a topnotch restaurant attached. ❻

Royal Hotel Argyll Square ⓣ01631/563021. The best of Oban's big central hotels, the *Royal* is pleasantly plush and has been recently refurbished; all rooms are en suite. ❺

Hostels and campsites

Jeremy Inglis 21 Airds Crescent ⓣ01631/565065 or 563064. Halfway between a hostel and a B&B, with an eccentric proprietor who also runs *McTavish's Kitchens*. Shared rooms, doubles or family rooms available, plus kitchen facilities; breakfast included.

Oban Backpackers Breadalbane Street ⓣ01631/562107, ⓔoban@scotlands-top-hostels

.com. Friendliest, cheapest and most central of Oban's hostels, with a pool table, real fire and a communal kitchen.

Oban Caravan & Camping Park Gallanachmore Farm, Gallanach Road ⓣ01631/562425. Big site, with caravans to rent plus ten pitches, situated two miles southwest of Oban along the Gallanach Road beside the Sound of Kerrera. Open April to mid-Oct.

SYHA hostel Corran Esplanade ⓣ01631/562025, ⓦwww.syha.org.uk. Converted Victorian house, with the purpose-built *Oban Lodge* annexe behind, both a fair trek from the ferry terminal along the Corran Esplanade, just beyond the Catholic Cathedral. Breakfast included.

The Town

The only truly remarkable sight in Oban is the town's landmark, **McCaig's Tower**, a stiff ten-minute climb from the quayside. Built in imitation of Rome's Colosseum, it was the brainchild of a local businessman a century ago, who had the twin aims of alleviating off-season unemployment among the local stonemasons and creating a museum, art gallery and chapel. Originally, the plan was to add a 95-foot central tower, but work never progressed further than the exterior granite walls before McCaig died. In his will, McCaig gave instructions for the lancet windows to be filled with bronze statues of the family, though no such work was ever undertaken. Instead, the folly has been turned into a sort of walled garden, and simply provides a wonderful seaward panorama, particularly at sunset.

Down in the centre of town, you can pass a few hours admiring the boats in the harbour and looking out for scavenging seals in the bay. If the weather's bad, the best option is to sign up for one of the excellent guided tours around **Oban Distillery** (Mon–Fri 9.30am–5pm; Easter–Oct also Sat; July–Sept Mon–Fri until 8.30pm, Sun noon–5pm; ⓦwww.scotch.com; £3.50), in the centre of town off George Street. The tour ends with a generous dram of Oban's lightly peaty malt (and a refund of the admission fee if you buy a bottle). Another welcome refuge in foul weather is the **War and Peace Exhibition** (Mon–Sat 10am–4pm; ⓦwww.obanwarandpeace.fsnet.co.uk; free) on the North Pier. A tiny room stuffed full of memorabilia and staffed by enthusiasts, it tells the story of the intriguing wartime role of the west of Scotland as a training centre for the D-day landings, during which over half a million troops practised secret amphibious manoeuvres around Loch Fyne.

A pleasant half-hour evening stroll can be had by walking north along the Corran Esplanade, past the modern, Roman Catholic **Cathedral of St Columba** – built in the 1920s by Sir Giles Gilbert Scott, architect of Battersea Power Station – to the rocky ruins of **Dunollie Castle**, a MacDougall stronghold on a very ancient site, successfully defended by the laird's Jacobite wife during the 1715 uprising but abandoned after 1745. Folks with kids should consider heading just a couple of miles out of Oban, east along Glencruitten Road, to the popular **Oban Rare Breeds Farm Park** (daily: late March to Oct 10am–5.30pm; mid-June to Aug 10am–7.30pm; £5), which displays rare but indigenous species of deer, cattle, sheep and so forth – they can meet the baby animals at the children's corner.

A host of private tour operators can be found around the harbour, on the North, South and Railway piers: their all-inclusive ferry, coach and/or boat **trips and tours** – to Mull, Iona, Staffa, Seal Island and the Treshnish Isles – are worth considering, particularly if you're pushed for time, or have no transport. Gordon Grant Tours (ⓣ01681/562842), on Oban's Railway Pier, offers a whole range of trips, including an entire day's cruise around the Treshnish Isles. Other operators include the Mull Experience (May–Sept; book through CalMac ⓣ01631/566688), who give you a day-trip minibus tour on Mull taking in Mull Rail, plus Torosay and Duart castles. Those with a bit more stami-

△ Tobermory harbour, Mull

na can take one of the circular day tours from Oban offered by Bowman's, 3 Stafford St (Ⓣ01631/563221, Ⓦwww.bowmanscoaches.com), either taking in Iona and a boat trip to Staffa, or Tobermory and a bit of Mull scenery.

Boat rental is available from Borro Boats, on the Gallanach Road (Ⓣ01631/563292), **bike rental** from Oban Cycles, 9 Craigard Rd (Ⓣ01631/566996), and **car rental** from Practical Car & Van Rental, off the road to Lochgilphead at Lochavullin Industrial Estate (Ⓣ01631/570900). If you fancy taking the plunge and trying your hand at some **diving**, head for the Puffin Dive Centre, a mile south of Oban at Port Gallanach (Ⓣ01631/566088, Ⓦwww.puffin.org.uk).

Eating, drinking and nightlife

If you're only here to catch a ferry, you might as well grab a quick bite to eat at the excellent **takeaway** seafood counter by the side of the CalMac terminal. For sit-down snacks, there's the nearby *Kitchen Garden* deli's mezzanine **café**, on George Street, or *F'Eats*, a modern café on John Street offering delicious toasted panini and good cappuccino. On the corner of George and John Street is Oban's swankiest new designer **restaurant**, *Ee-usk*, which serves up superb fish and seafood dishes. Vegetarians might prefer to head for *Café Na Lusan,* in Craigard Road (closed Mon), an internet café serving inexpensive veggie food. *The Gallery* restaurant (closed Sun), by the pedestrian entrance to Tesco, is another inexpensive but decent option, and, of course, there's always fish and chips from *Onorio's*, 86 George St (closed Sun).

Oban's only half-decent **pub** is the *Oban Inn* opposite the North Pier, with a classic dark-wood-flagstone-and-brass bar downstairs and lounge bar with stained glass upstairs. The town's nightlife doesn't bear thinking about (though you can read all about it in the *Oban Times*). It's worth noting, however, that Oban is one of the few places in Argyll with a **cinema**, confusingly known as The Highland Theatre (Ⓣ01631/562444), at the north end of George Street. You should be able to catch some **live music** at the weekend at *O'Donnell's* Irish pub, underneath *The Gathering*, on Breadalbane Street, or in the bar of the *Royal Hotel*, on Argyll Square, and occasionally (concert-style) at the Corran Halls, along the Esplanade. The annual **Argyllshire Gathering** takes place on the last Thursday in August, featuring piping competitions and Highland Games.

The Isle of Kerrera

One of the best places to escape from the crowds that plague Oban is the low-lying island of **Kerrera**, which shelters Oban Bay from the worst of the westerly winds. Measuring just five miles by two, the island is easily explored on foot and often crawling with geology students in the holidays. The island's most prominent landmark is the **Hutcheson's Monument**, best viewed, appropriately enough, from the ferries heading out of Oban, as it commemorates David Hutcheson, one of the Victorian founders of what is now Caledonian MacBrayne. The best views, however, are from Kerrera's highest point, **Càrn Breugach** (620ft), over to Mull, the Slate Islands, Lismore, Jura and beyond.

The ferry lands roughly halfway down the east coast, at the north end of **Horseshoe Bay**, where King Alexander II died in 1249. If the weather's fine and you feel like lazing by the sea, head for the island's finest sandy beach, **Slatrach Bay**, on the west coast, one mile northwest of the ferry jetty. Otherwise, the most rewarding trail is down to **Gylen Castle**, a clifftop ruin enjoying a majestic setting on the south coast, built in 1582 by the MacDougalls and burnt to the ground by the Covenanter General Leslie in

1647. You can head back to the ferry via the Drove Road, where cattle from Mull and other islands were once herded to be swum across the sound to the market in Oban.

The passenger and bicycle **ferry** departs daily from the mainland two miles down the Gallanach road from Oban (phone ⓣ01631/563665 for the latest schedule; £3 return). Kerrera has a total population of fewer than thirty – and no shop – so if you're day-tripping make sure you bring enough supplies with you. Alternatively, you can eat home-made, often organic, veggie snacks at the *Kerrera Teagarden* (April–Sept daily 10am–5pm), located in a nice spot at Lower Gylen, a 45-minute walk from the ferry. You can also stay there at the *Kerrera Bunkhouse* (ⓣ01631/570223, ⓔkerrerabunkhouse@talk21.com; book ahead Oct–March), a converted eighteenth-century stable building – ring ahead if you need transport from the ferry. For B&B, enquire at *Ardentrive Farm* (ⓣ01631/567180; ❶).

Dunstaffnage Castle and Connel

Just beyond the northern satellite suburbs of Oban, on a strategic promontory overlooking the important water crossroads at the mouth of Loch Etive, lie the ruins of **Dunstaffnage Castle** (April–Sept daily 9.30am–6.30pm; Oct–March Mon–Sat 9.30am–4.30pm, Sun 2–4.30pm; HS; £2). Originally built as a thirteenth-century MacDougall fort, the castle was captured by Robert the Bruce in 1309, and remained in royal hands until it was handed over to the Campbells in 1470. Garrisoned by government forces during the 1745 rebellion, it served as a temporary prison for Flora MacDonald, and was eventually destroyed by fire in 1810. The approach, through a housing estate, is a bit unsettling, but, with the castle's substantial curtain wall battlements partially intact, Dunstaffnage makes for a fun and safe place to explore, and gives great views across to Lismore and Morvern.

The *Wide-Mouthed Frog*, at the nearby marina, is popular with "yotties", serves pub grub and has tables outside with views over to the castle. If you want to take to the water, Alba Sailing, at the marina, offers **yacht rental** and RYA training courses (ⓣ01631/565630).

A couple of miles further up the A85, at **CONNEL**, you can't fail to admire the majestic steel cantilever **Connel Bridge**, built in 1903 to take the old branch railway line across the sea cataract at the mouth of Loch Etive, north to Fort William. The name "Connel" comes from the Gaelic *conghail* (tumultuous flood), which refers to the rapids, clearly visible from the bridge, and caused by the water at low ebb rushing over a ledge of rock between the two shores of the loch. The A828 now crosses Connel Bridge to take you onto Benderloch. If you want to stay out here in Connel, look no further than the non-smoking *Ards House* (ⓣ01631/710255, ⓦwww.ardshouse.demon.co.uk; ❺), a whitewashed Victorian villa overlooking the water.

Benderloch

On the north side of the Connel Bridge lies the hammerhead peninsula of **Benderloch** (from *beinn eadar da loch*, "hill between two lochs"), on whose northern shores you'll find **Barcaldine Castle** (July & Aug daily 11am–5pm; £3.25), an early seventeenth-century Campbell tower house. The house was abandoned by the Campbells in favour of Barcaldine House, three miles north-east, and eventually sold in 1842. Bought back by the family as a ruin in 1896 and restored, it is now run as a tourist attraction by the current heir, London-born and bred Roderick, and his wife Caroline. There are no real treasures here, but the castle is fun to explore, with dungeons and hidden staircases and they offer B&B (Ⓣ01631/720219, Ⓦwww.countrymansions.com; ❻). Those with an unlimited budget might like to stay at Argyll's most exclusive hotel, the *Isle of Eriska*, a luxury, turreted, Scottish Baronial place, run by the Buchanan-Smiths on their own 300-acre island, off the northern point of Benderloch (Ⓣ01631/720371, Ⓦwww.eriska-hotel.co.uk; March–Dec; ❾), with an acclaimed and very expensive dining room (open to non-residents in the evening).

Since the weather in this part of Scotland can be bad at almost any time of the year, it's as well to know about the **Scottish Sea Life & Marine Sanctuary** (April–June daily 10am–5pm; July & Aug daily 9am–7pm; call Ⓣ01631/720386 for winter opening times; £6.50), which is to be found on the A828, along the southern shores of Loch Creran. Here you can see loads of sea creatures at close quarters, touch the (non-) stingrays, do a bit of rock pool dipping, and learn about how common seal orphan pups are rescued and returned to the wild.

Appin

With the new Creagan Bridge in place – the old wrought-iron railway bridge sadly having been demolished – there's no need to circumnavigate Loch Creran in order to reach the district of **Appin**, best known as the setting for Robert Louis Stevenson's *Kidnapped*, a fictionalized account of the "Appin Murder" of 1752, when Colin Campbell was shot in the back, allegedly by one of the disenfranchised Stewart clan. However, the new bridge also means than the eastern reaches of the loch, and **Glen Creran** itself, are now even more peaceful and secluded. The lovely dead-end single-track road through the woods to Fasnacloich shelters several wonderful B&B retreats such as *Lochside Cottage* (Ⓣ01631/730216, Ⓔbroadbent@lochsidecottage.fsnet.co.uk; ❷), a large white house with a garden sloping down to a freshwater loch. At the end of the road there's a seven-mile forest walk over to Ballachulish (see p.614).

The name "Appin" derives from the Gaelic *abthaine*, meaning "Lands belonging to the Abbey", in this case the one on the island of Lismore (see below), which is linked to the peninsula by passenger ferry from **PORT APPIN**, a pretty little fishing village at the westernmost tip of the peninsula. Overlooking a host of tiny little islands dotted around Loch Linnhe, with Lismore and the mountains Morvern and Mull in the background, this is, without doubt, one of Argyll's most picturesque spots. The *Pierhouse Hotel* (Ⓣ01631/730302; ❼), nicely situated right by the ferry, has a popular bar, and an expensive, but excellent and very popular seafood restaurant (prices are slightly lower at lunch times). Alternatively, you could eat at the *Pierhouse*, but stay in the friendly *Rhugarbh Croft* (Ⓣ01631/730309, Ⓔwelcome@cheesemaking.co.uk; closed Feb; ❸), up the road to North Shian, and enjoy home-made bread and free-range eggs for breakfast.

One of Argyll's most romantic ruined castles, the much-photographed **Castle Stalker**, occupies a tiny rock island to the north of Port Appin. Built by the Stewarts of Appin in the sixteenth century and gifted to King James IV as a hunting lodge, it inevitably fell into the hands of the Campbells after 1745. The current owners open the castle to the public for a very short period only each year; ring Ⓣ01631/730234 or ask at Oban tourist office for this year's opening times. **Bike rental** is available from Port Appin Bikes (Ⓣ01631/730391 or 730235) and it's worth noting that bicycles travel for free on the passenger ferry to Lismore (see opposite). For other **outdoor pursuits** head for the

Linnhe Marine Water Sports Centre (☎01631/730401; May–Sept) in Lettershuna (just north of Castle Stalker), which rents out boats of all shapes and sizes, offers sailing and windsurfing lessons, not to mention waterskiing, clay-pigeon shooting and even pony trekking.

The Isle of Lismore

Lying in the middle of Loch Linnhe, to the north of Oban, and barely rising above a hillock, the narrow island of **Lismore** offers wonderful gentle walking or cycling opportunities, with unrivalled views, in fine weather, across to the mountains of Morvern, Lochaber and Mull. Legend has it that saints Columba and Moluag both fancied the skinny island as a missionary base, but as they raced towards it Moluag cut off his finger and threw it ashore ahead of Columba, claiming the land for himself. Of Moluag's sixth-century foundation nothing remains, but from 1236 until 1507 the island served as the seat of the Bishop of Argyll. It was a judicious choice, as Lismore is undoubtedly one of the most fertile of the Inner Hebrides – its name, coined by Moluag himself, derives from the Gaelic *lios mór*, meaning "great garden" – and before the Clearances (see p.768) it supported nearly 1400 inhabitants; the population today is around a tenth of that figure.

Lismore is about eight miles long and one mile wide, and the ferry from Oban lands at **ACHNACROISH**, roughly halfway along the eastern coastline. To get to grips with the history of the island and its Gaelic culture (and have a cup of tea), follow the signs for the nearby **Comann Eachdraidh Lios Mór**, or Lismore Historical Society (Easter & May–Sept Mon–Sat 10am–5pm; £1). The island post office and shop are along the main road between Achnacroish and **CLACHAN**, a couple of miles northeast, where the diminutive, whitewashed former **Cathedral of St Moluag** stands. All that remains of the fourteenth-century cathedral is the choir, which was reduced in height and converted into the parish church in 1749; inside you can see a few of the original seats for the upper clergy, a stone basin in the south wall, and several medieval doorways. Due east of the church – head north up the road and take the turning signposted on the right – the circular **Tirefour Broch**, over two thousand years old, occupies a commanding position and boasts walls almost ten feet thick in places. West of Clachan are the much more recent ruins of **Castle Coeffin**, a twelfth-century MacDougall fortress once believed to have been haunted by the ghost of Beothail, sister of the Norse prince Caiffen. A few other places worth exploring are **Sailean**, an abandoned quarry village further south along the west coast, with its disused kilns and cottages; the ruins of **Achanduin Castle**, in the southwest, where the bishops are thought to have resided; and Barr Mór (416ft), the island's highest point.

Two **ferries** serve Lismore: a small CalMac car ferry from Oban to Achnacroish (Mon–Sat 2–4 daily; 50min), and a shorter passenger- and bicycle-only crossing from Port Appin to the island's north point (daily every 2hr; 5min). There's a **postbus** round the island (Mon–Sat; pick up a timetable from Oban tourist office). **Accommodation** on the island is extremely limited: try the budget B&B at the *Schoolhouse* (☎01631/760262; ❶), north of Clachan, which also serves evening meals. **Bike rental** is available from Island Bike Hire (☎01631/760213) for around £10 a day.

The Isle of Mull

The second largest of the Inner Hebrides, **Mull** (Ⓦwww.holidaymull.org.uk) is by far the most accessible: just forty minutes from Oban by ferry. As so often, first impressions largely depend on the weather – it is the wettest of the Hebrides (and that's saying something) – for without the sun the large tracts of moorland, particularly around the island's highest peak, Ben More (3196ft), can appear bleak and unwelcoming. There are, however, areas of more gentle pastoral scenery around **Dervaig** in the north and **Salen** on the east coast, and the indented west coast varies from the sandy beaches around **Calgary** to the cliffs of Loch na Keal. The most common mistake is to try and "do" the island in a day or two: flogging up the main road to the picturesque capital of **Tobermory**, then covering the fifty-odd miles between there and Fionnphort, in order to visit **Iona**. Mull is a place that will grow on you only if you have the time and patience to explore.

Historically, crofting, whisky distilling and fishing supported the islanders (*Muileachs*), but the population – which peaked at 10,000 – decreased dramatically in the late nineteenth century due to the Clearances and the 1846 potato famine. On Mull, it is a trend that has been reversed, mostly due to the large influx of settlers from elsewhere in the country which has brought the current population up to over 2500. One of the main reasons for this resurgence is, of course, tourism – more than half a million visitors come here each year – although, oddly enough, there are very few large hotels or campsites.

Craignure is the main entry point to Mull, with a frequent daily **car ferry** link to Oban; if you're taking a car over, it's advisable to book ahead for this

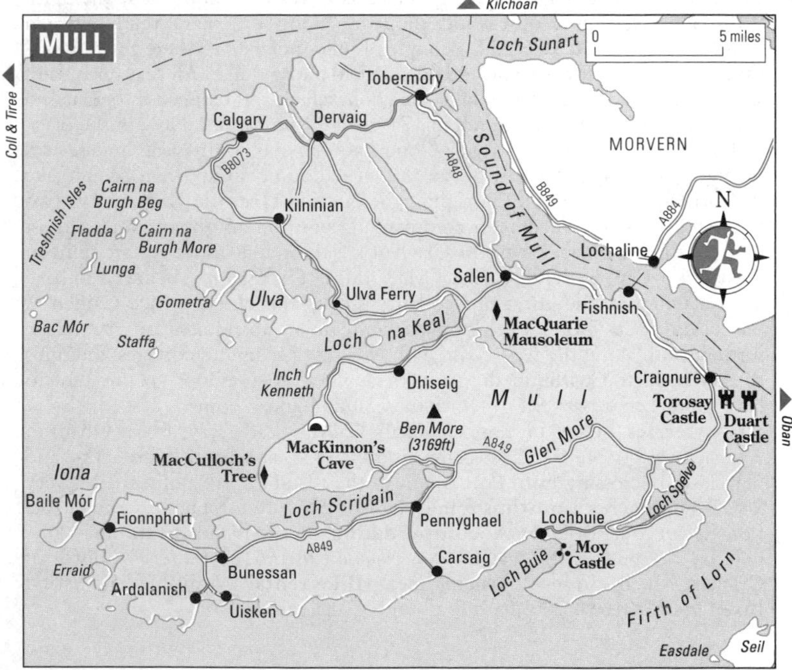

© Crown copyright

service. A much smaller car ferry crosses daily from Lochaline on the Morvern peninsula (see p.617) to the slipway at Fishnish, six miles northwest of Craignure; another even smaller car ferry connects Kilchoan on the Ardnamurchan peninsula (see p.619) with Tobermory, 24 miles northwest of Craignure. Both of these two smaller ferries run on a first-come, first-served basis. **Public transport** on Mull is not too bad on the main A849, but there's more or less no service along the west coast (for more information, visit Ⓦwww.mict.co.uk/travel). Those with **cars** should note that the roads are still predominantly single-track, with passing places, which can cause serious congestion on the main road in summer.

Craignure and around

CRAIGNURE is little more than a scattering of cottages, though there is a small shop, a bar, some toilets and a CalMac and **tourist office** – the only one on the island open all year round – situated opposite the pier (April to mid-June Mon–Fri 8.30am–5.15pm, Sat 9am–6.30pm, Sun 10.30am–5.30pm; mid-June to mid-Sept Mon–Thurs 8.30am–7pm, Fri 8.30am–5.15pm, Sat 9am–6.30pm, Sun 10am–5.30pm; mid-Sept to mid-Oct Mon–Fri 8.30am–5.15pm, Sat 9am–5pm, Sun 10.30am–5.30pm; mid-Oct to mid-April Mon–Sat 10am–5pm, Sun 10.30am–noon & 3.30–5pm; Ⓣ01680/812377). The *Craignure Inn* (Ⓣ01680/812305, Ⓦwww.craignure-inn.co.uk; ❸), just a minute's stroll up the road towards Fionnphort, is a snug **pub** to hole up in, if you need one. There's also a well-equipped **campsite** (Ⓣ01680/812496, Ⓦwww.sheilingholidays.co.uk; April–Oct) on the south side of Craignure Bay, behind the new village hall, run by Sheiling Holidays. The campsite offers the usual pitches, plus hostel or private accommodation in "carpeted cottage tents", purpose-built cottages, bike rental and other outdoor activities. A more picturesque alternative is the well-equipped *Balmeanach Park* site (Ⓣ01680/300342; March–Oct), five miles up the A849 at Fishnish. There are several B&Bs in the area, but the best **guesthouse** is the *Old Mill Cottage* (Ⓣ01680/812442, Ⓦwww.oldmill.mull.com; ❸), a sensitively converted mill, three miles south on the A849 in Lochdon; it also has a small and highly recommended restaurant attached.

Bus connections with Fionnphort (Mon–Sat 3–4 daily, Sun 1 daily; 1hr 10min) and Tobermory (Mon–Sat 4–5 daily, Sun 2 daily; 50min) are infrequent, so check with Oban tourist office before you catch the ferry. The other method of transport available at Craignure is the diminutive, narrow-gauge Mull & West Highland Railway, commonly known as **Mull Rail** (Easter to mid-Oct; Ⓣ01680/812494, Ⓦwww.holidaymull.org.uk/rail; £3.50 return), built in the 1980s and the only working railway in the Scottish Islands. The Craignure station is situated beyond the Sheiling Holidays campsite, and the line stretches southeast for about a mile and a half to Torosay Castle (see below). If you prefer to take the train one-way only, it's a lovely half-hour walk along the coast (with the possibility of spotting an otter). The company uses diesel and steam locomotives, so ring ahead if you want to be sure of a steam-driven train.

Torosay and Duart castles

Two castles lie immediately southeast of Craignure. The first, **Torosay Castle** (Easter to mid-Oct daily 10.30am–5.30pm; £4.50), is a full-blown Scottish Baronial creation. The house itself is stuffed with memorabilia relating to the present owners, the Guthries, all of it amusingly captioned but of no great import, with the possible exception of the belongings of the late David Guthrie-James, who made a daring escape from a POW camp in Germany during World War II. Torosay's real highlight, however, is the magnificent **gardens** (open all year daily 10.30am–5.30pm; gardens only £3.50) with their avenue of eighteenth-century Venetian statues, Japanese section, and views over to neighbouring Duart. If the admission price puts you off Torosay, head for the gold and silversmiths or the workshop of the **Isle of Mull Weavers** (Mon–Sat 9am–5pm; April–Oct also Sun; free), in the castle grounds, where you can watch the old-fashioned dobby loom in the workshop weave tartan.

Lacking the gardens, but perched on a picturesque spit of rock a couple of miles east of Torosay, **Duart Castle** (May to mid-Oct daily 10.30am–6pm; Ⓦwww.duartcastle.com; £3.80) is clearly visible from the Oban–Craignure ferry. Headquarters of the once-powerful MacLean clan from the thirteenth century, it was burnt down by the Campbells and confiscated after the 1745 rebellion. Finally, in 1911 the 26th clan chief, Fitzroy MacLean (1835–1936) – not to be confused with the Scottish writer of the same name – managed to buy it back and restore it. You can peek at the dungeons, climb up to the ramparts, study the family photos, and learn about the world scout movement – the 27th clan chief became Chief Scout in 1959. After your visit, you can enjoy home-made cakes and tea at the castle's excellent tearoom.

Tobermory

Mull's chief town, **TOBERMORY**, at the northern tip of the islands, is easily the most attractive fishing port on the west coast of Scotland, its clusters of brightly coloured houses and boats sheltering in a bay backed by a steep bluff. Founded in 1788 by the British Society for Encouraging Fisheries, it never really took off as a fishing port and only survived due to the steady influx of crofters evicted from other parts of the island during the Clearances. With a population of more than 800, it is, without doubt, the capital of Mull, and if you're staying any length of time on the island you're bound to end up here, not least because it has a Womble named after it.

Information and accommodation

The **tourist office** (April Mon–Fri 10am–5pm, Sat & Sun noon–5pm; May & June Mon–Sat 10am–5pm, Sun 11am–5pm; July & Aug Mon–Sat 9.30am–6pm, Sun 10am–5pm; Sept & Oct Mon–Sat 10am–5pm, Sun noon–5pm; Ⓣ01688/302182) is in the same building as the CalMac ticket office at the far end of Main Street. If you want to rent a **bike**, head for the youth hostel (see below), Archibald Brown the ironmongers on Main Street (Ⓣ01688/302020, Ⓦwww.browns-tobermory.co.uk), or Tom-a'Mhuillin (Ⓣ01688/302164) on the Salen road. The island's only permanent **bank**, the Clydesdale, is on Main Street and has an ATM; a mobile bank tours the island – ask at the tourist office for details.

The tourist office can book you into a **B&B** for a small fee – not a bad idea in high season, when the places on Main Street tend to get booked up fast, and the rest are a stiff climb from the harbour. The small, friendly SYHA **hostel** is on Main Street (Ⓣ01688/302481, Ⓦwww.syha.org.uk; March–Oct) and has laundry facilities. The nearest **campsite** is *Newdale* (Ⓣ01688/302525; April–Oct), nicely situated one and a half miles outside Tobermory on the B8073 to Dervaig.

Baliscate Guest House Salen Road ⓣ01688/302048, ⓦwww.baliscate.com. Imposing whitewashed Victorian guesthouse, with a large garden, set back from the road to Salen, just outside Tobermory. ❷
Failte Guest House Main Street ⓣ01688/302495. Very comfortably and pleasantly furnished en-suite rooms, some of which have views out over the harbour. Open March–Oct. ❷
Glengorm Castle near Tobermory ⓣ01688/302321, ⓦwww.glengormcastle.co.uk. Rambling Baronial mansion in a superb, secluded setting, four miles northwest of Tobermory, overlooking the sea. Guests get use of the castle's huge public rooms; self-catering cottages are available, too (those sleeping four cost £235 per week). ❺
Harbour Guest House Main Street ⓣ01688/302209. Spacious, clean rooms, some great views and big breakfasts. ❶
Highland Cottage Breadalbane Street ⓣ01688/302030, ⓦwww.highlandcottage.co.uk. Superior guesthouse, plushly furnished, fully en suite and boasting excellent home cooking. ❺
Western Isles Hotel ⓣ01688/302012. Tobermory's most distinguished hotel, a grandiose Scottish Baronial building high above the harbour, with terrific views. ❺

The Town

The harbour – known as **Main Street** – is one long parade of multicoloured hotels, guesthouses, restaurants and shops, and you could happily spend an hour or so pottering around: Mull Pottery and the Mull Silver Company are both worth a browse, as is The Gallery, a converted church more of interest for its architecture than the tartan and shortbread on sale. One of Tobermory's endearing features is the incessant chiming of its diminutive **Clock Tower**, erected by the author Isabella Bird in 1905 in memory of her sister, who died of typhoid on the island in 1880. Close by is a polychrome watery cherub, donated by the local water-supply contractors in 1883.

A recent arrival on Main Street is the **Hebridean Whale and Dolphin Trust** (April–Oct daily 10am–5pm; Nov–March Mon–Fri 11am–5pm; ⓦwww.hwdt.org; free), run by a welcoming bunch of enthusiasts. The small office has lots of information on how to identify marine mammals, and on recent sightings. They're very child-friendly, too, and will keep kids amused for an hour or so with computer marine games, word searches and a bit of artwork. Sea Life Surveys (ⓣ01688/302787, ⓦwww.sealifesurveys.co.uk), who offer a variety of whale- and dolphin-watching **tours**, are run from the same office. Another good wet-weather retreat is the **Mull Museum** (Easter to mid-Oct Mon–Fri 10.30am–4pm, Sat 10am–1pm; £1), further along Main Street, which packs a great deal of information and artefacts – including a few objects salvaged from the *San Juan* (see the box on p.396) – into one tiny room. Alternatively, there's the minuscule **Tobermory Distillery** (Easter–Oct Mon–Fri 10am–5pm; £2.50) at the south end of the bay, founded in 1795 but closed down three times since then. Today, it's back in business and offers a pretty desultory guided tour, rounded off with a dram.

A stiff climb up Back Brae will bring you to the island's main arts centre, **An Tobar** (Tues–Sat 10am–4pm; free), housed in a converted Victorian schoolhouse. The centre hosts exhibitions, a variety of live events, and contains a café with comfy sofas set before a real fire. The rest of the upper town is laid out on a classic grid-plan, and merits a stroll, if only for the great views over the bay.

Eating and drinking

Main Street is heaving with **places to eat**. You can get inexpensive fry-ups and fish and chips at *Gannets* or huge bar meals in the lounge bar at the *Mishnish*. For more imaginative local seafood and meat dishes, however, you need to go to *Back Brae* (evenings only), which does moderately expensive set menus and à la carte, or to the *Western Isles Hotel*, which serves superior bar food in the

The Tobermory treasure

The most dramatic event in Tobermory's history was in 1588, when a ship from the **Spanish Armada** sank in mysterious circumstances while having repairs done to its sails and rigging in the town harbour. The story goes that one of the MacLeans of Duart was taken prisoner, but when the ship weighed anchor he made his way to the powder magazine and blew it up. However, several versions of the story exist, and even the identity of the ship has been hotly disputed: for many years it was thought to be the treasure-laden Spanish galleon *Almirante di Florencia*, but it now seems more likely that it was the rather more prosaic troop carrier *San Juan de Sicilia*. Nevertheless, the possibility of precious sunken booty at the bottom of Tobermory harbour has fired the greed of numerous lairds and kings – in the 1950s Royal Navy divers were engaged by the Duke of Argyll in the seemingly futile activity of diving for treasure, and in 1982 another unsuccessful attempt was made.

conservatory overlooking the Sound of Mull, as well as more expensive à la carte dishes in the dining room. Fresh fish and seafood is available from the Tobermory Fish Mart shop, on Main Street, and would do for **picnic** fodder, supplemented, perhaps, by bread and goodies from the excellent Island Bakery, also on the harbour front.

If you want to know what there is in the way of **entertainment** in Tobermory (or anywhere else on Mull), be sure to pick up the free monthly newsletter *Round & About*, and/or buy a copy of *Am Muileach*, the monthly island newspaper. The lively bar of the *Mishnish Hotel* has been the most popular local drinking hole for many years, and features live music at the weekend, It's also the focus of Mull's annual **Traditional Music Festival**, a feast of Gaelic folk music held on the last weekend in April. Unfortunately, the *Mishnish* lost much of its character (and some of its custom) after a facelift, no doubt prompted by the arrival of *MacGochan's*, a purpose-built, though pleasant enough, pub, which also offers occasional live music, on the opposite side of the harbour near the distillery. Mull's other major musical event, after the folk festival, is the annual **Mendelssohn on Mull Festival**, held over ten days in early July, which commemorates the composer's visit here in 1829.

Dervaig and Calgary

The gently undulating countryside west of Tobermory, beyond the freshwater Mishnish lochs, provides some of the most beguiling scenery on the island. Added to this, the road out west, the B8073, is exceptionally dramatic, with fiendish switchbacks much appreciated during the annual Mull Rally, which takes place each October.

The only village of any size is **DERVAIG**, which nestles beside narrow Loch Chumhainn, just eight miles southwest of Tobermory, distinguished by its unusual pencil-shaped church spire and dinky whitewashed cottages set in twos along its main street. Dervaig is best known as the home of **Mull Theatre**, one of the smallest professional theatres in the world, which puts on an adventurous season of plays adapted for a handful of resident actors (April–Sept; ⓣ01688/302828, ⓦwww.mulltheatre.org.uk); booking is recommended. The box office is in the main street, while the theatre itself lies within the grounds of the Victorian *Druimard Country House* (ⓣ01688/400345, ⓦwww.druimard.co.uk; ❼; late March–Oct), which has a decent bar, and offers top-class, expensive pre-theatre dinners. A cheaper spot of refreshment is available from *Coffee and Books*, which offers just that (and a few provisions) from its premises opposite the *Bellacroy Hotel*, whose bar is a great place to shelter for the day in bad weather.

Dervaig has a wide choice of **places to stay**. A reasonable alternative to the aforementioned *Druimard* is the *Druimnacroish Hotel* (Ⓣ01688/400274, Ⓦwww.drumnacroish.co.uk; ❺), a lovely country house two miles out on the Salen road. There are several good B&Bs ranging from the vegetarian-friendly *Glen Bellart House* (Ⓣ01688/400282; ❶; Easter–Oct), in one of the white-washed houses on the main street; *Glenview* (Ⓣ01688/400239; ❷; April–Oct), a really lovely 1890s house on the edge of the village; the excellent *Cuin Lodge* (Ⓣ01688/400346, Ⓦwww.cuin-lodge.mull.com; ❷), an old shooting lodge overlooking the loch, to the northwest of the village; or *Balmacara* (Ⓣ01688/400363; ❸), a modern and extremely luxurious hillside house.

Signposted off the main road, a little beyond Dervaig, the **Old Byre Heritage Centre** (Easter–Oct daily 10.30am–6.30pm; £3) is better than many of its kind, with a video on the island's history, and a passable tearoom. **Boat trips** to Staffa and the Treshnish Isles are operated by Inter-Island Cruises (Ⓣ01688/400264, Ⓦwww.jenny.mull.com) from Croig pier, two miles to the northwest, off the road to Calgary.

The road continues cross-country to **CALGARY**, once a thriving crofting community, now an idyllic holiday spot boasting Mull's finest sandy bay, backed by low-lying dunes and machair, with wonderful views over to Coll and Tiree. There's just one hotel, the delightful *Calgary Farmhouse* (Ⓣ01688/400256, Ⓦwww.calgary.co.uk; ❹; April–Oct), whose excellent, moderately priced *Dovecote* restaurant (closed Mon) is (unsurprisingly) housed in a converted dovecote. The south side of the beach is a favourite spot for **camping** rough, though the only facilities are the public toilets. For the record: the city of Calgary in Canada does indeed take its name from this little village, though it was not so named by Mull emigrants, but by one Colonel McLeod of the North West Mounted Police, who once holidayed here.

Salen and around

SALEN, on the east coast halfway between Craignure and Tobermory, lies at the narrowest point on Mull. As such it makes a good central base for exploring Mull, though it has none of Tobermory's charm. There are, however, several decent places to stay in the vicinity, ranging from the **hostel** accommodation of *Arle Farm Lodge* (Ⓣ01680/300343), a well-equipped modern lodge on a working farm, four miles up the A848, to the pretty, Victorian *Gruline Home Farm* **B&B** (Ⓣ01680/300581, Ⓦwww.gruline.com; ❸), a non-working farmhouse four miles to the southwest, which serves up extra special dinners (non-residents must reserve). Those with even more substantial means should head three miles west to the shores of the Loch na Keal, where the award-winning *Killiechronan Hotel* (Ⓣ01680/300403; ❻; March–Oct) offers a set-menu dinner for around £25 a head. Salen itself has only a couple of very ordinary eating options, though it does have **bike rental** from *On Yer Bike* (Ⓣ01680/300501), who also have child trailers to rent. The nearest **campsite** is the well-equipped site at *Balmeanach Park* (Ⓣ01680/300342; March–Oct), five miles southeast by the Sound of Mull at Fishnish.

The most unusual sight near Salen is the **MacQuarie Mausoleum**, a simple buttressed tomb, set within a walled clearing surrounded by pine trees and rhododendrons, and lovingly maintained by the National Trust for Scotland, on behalf of the National Trust of Australia. Within lies the body of Lachlan MacQuarie (1761–1824), the "Father of Australia", who, as the effusive epitaph explains, was appointed by the British as Governor of New South Wales in 1809, to replace the unpopular William Bligh, formerly of the *Bounty*. However, the enlightened MacQuarie was equally unpopular with the Aussie settlers, primarily for instituting liberal penal reforms, and also had to be recalled in 1820.

The Isle of Ulva

A chieftain to the Highlands bound
Cries "Boatman, do not tarry!
And I'll give thee a silver pound
To row us o'er the ferry!"
"Now who be ye, would cross Lochgyle
This dark and stormy water?"
"O I'm the chief of Ulva's isle,
An this, Lord Ullin's daughter."

Lord Ullin's Daughter by Thomas Campbell (1777–1844)

Around the time poet laureate Campbell penned this tragic poem, **Ulva**'s population was a staggering 850, sustained by the huge quantities of kelp which were exported for glass and soap production. That was before the market for kelp collapsed and the 1846 potato famine hit, after which the remaining population was brutally evicted. Nowadays barely thirty people live here, and the island is littered with ruined crofts, not to mention a church, designed by Thomas Telford, which would once have seated over three hundred parishioners. It's great walking country, however, with several clearly marked paths crisscrossing the native woodland and the rocky heather moorland interior – and you're almost guaranteed to spot some of the abundant wildlife: at the very least deer, if not buzzards, golden eagles and even sea eagles, with seals and divers offshore. Those who like to have a focus for their wanderings should head for the ruined crofting villages, and basalt columns similar to those on Staffa; along the island's southern coastline, for the island's highest point, Beinn Chreagach (1027ft); or along the north coast to Ulva's tidal neighbour, Gometra, off the west coast.

To **get to Ulva** (from the Norse *ulv øy*, or "wolf island") which lies just a hundred yards or so off the west coast of Mull, follow the signs for "Ulva Ferry" from Salen – if you've no transport, a postbus can get you there, but you'll have to make your own way back. From **Ulva Ferry**, a small bicycle-passenger-only ferry is available on demand (Mon–Fri 9am–5pm; June–Aug also Sun; at other times by arrangement on ⓣ01688 500226; £4 return). *The Boathouse*, near the ferry slip on Ulva, serves as a licensed **tearoom** selling soup, cakes, snacks, Guinness and Ulva oysters. You can learn more about the history of the island from the **Heritage Centre** exhibition upstairs, and pop into the newly restored thatched smiddy nearby, which contains **Sheila's Cottage**, which has been restored to something like the state it was in when Sheila MacFadyen used to live there in the first half of the last century. There's no accommodation, but with permission from the present owners (ⓣ01688/500264, ⓔulva@mull.com) you can **camp** rough overnight.

The Isle of Staffa and the Treshnish Isles

Five miles southwest of Ulva, **Staffa** is the most romantic and dramatic of Scotland's many uninhabited islands. On its south side, the perpendicular rock-face features an imposing series of black basalt columns, known as the

Colonnade, which have been cut by the sea into cathedralesque caverns, most notably **Fingal's Cave**. The Vikings knew about the island – the name derives from their word for "Island of Pillars" – but it wasn't until 1772 that it was "discovered" by the world. Turner painted it, Wordsworth explored it, but Mendelssohn's *Die Fingalshöhle*, inspired by the sounds of the sea-wracked caves he heard on a visit here in 1829, did most to popularize the place – after which Queen Victoria gave her blessing, too. The geological explanation for these polygonal basalt organ pipes is that they were created by a massive subterranean explosion some sixty million years ago. A huge mass of molten basalt burst forth onto land and, as it cooled, solidified into what are, essentially, crystals. Of course, confronted with such artistry, most visitors have found it difficult to believe that their origin is entirely natural – indeed, the various Celtic folk tales, which link the phenomenon with the Giant's Causeway in Ireland, are certainly more appealing.

To **get to Staffa**, you can join one of the many boat trips from Fionnphort, Iona, Ulva Ferry, Dervaig or even Oban. Staffa-only trips run from April to October and cost £12.50 per person on the *Iolaire* (Ⓣ01681/700358), which sails out of Fionnphort and Iona twice daily; you get to sail into the cave and land weather permitting. Turus Mara (Ⓣ0800/085 8786, Ⓦwww.turusmara.com), operates out of Ulva Ferry, costs a bit more and also does trips to the Treshnish Isles and whale and dolphin searches. Inter-Island Cruises (Ⓣ01688/400264, Ⓦwww.jenny.mull.com), which run from Dervaig, are also worth the extra money.

Several outfits, such as Turus Mara and Inter-Island Cruises, offer **boat trips** around the archipelago of uninhabited volcanic islets that make up the **Treshnish Isles** northwest of Staffa. None of the islands are more than a mile or two across, the most distinctive being **Bac Mór**, shaped like a Puritan's hat and popularly dubbed the Dutchman's Cap. Most trips include a stopover on **Lunga**, the largest island, and a nesting place for hundreds of seabirds, in particular guillemots, razorbills (mid-May to July) and puffins (late April to mid-Aug), as well as a breeding ground for common seals (June) and Atlantic greys (early Sept). The two most northerly islands, **Cairn na Burgh More** and **Cairn na Burgh Beag**, have the remains of ruined castles, the first of which served as a lookout post for the Lords of the Isles and was last garrisoned in the Civil War; Cairn na Burgh Beag hasn't been occupied since the 1715 Jacobite uprising.

Ben More and the Ardmeanach peninsula

From the southern shores of Loch na Keal, which almost splits Mull in two, rise the terraced slopes of **Ben More** (3169ft) – literally "big mountain" – a mighty extinct volcano, and the only Munro in the Hebrides outside of Skye. It's most easily climbed from Dhiseig, halfway along the loch's southern shores, though an alternative route is to climb up to the col between Beinn Fhada and A'Chioch, and approach via the mountain's eastern ridge. Further west along the shore the road carves through spectacular overhanging cliffs before heading south past the Gribun rocks which face the tiny island of **Inch Kenneth**, where Unity Mitford lived until her death in 1948. There are great views out to Staffa and the Treshnish Isles as the road leaves the coast behind, climbing over the pass to Loch Scribain, where it eventually joins the equally dramatic Glen More road (A849) from Craignure.

If you're properly equipped for walking, however, you can explore the **Ardmeanach peninsula**, to the west of the road, on foot. On the north coast, a mile or so from the road, is **Mackinnon's Cave** – at 100ft high, one of the largest caves in the Hebrides, and accessible only at low tide. As so often, there's a legend attached to the cave, which tells of an entire party, led by a lone piper, who were once devoured here by evil spirits. Starting from the south coast, it's a longer, rougher six-mile hike from the road to **MacCulloch's Tree**, a 40-foot-high conifer that was engulfed by a lava flow some fifty million years ago and is now embedded in the cliffs at Rubha na h-Uambha at the western tip of the peninsula. You'll need a good map, good boots and, again, you need to time your arrival with a falling tide. The area is NTS-owned and there is a car park just before *Tiroran House* (☎01681/705232; ❹; April–Oct), a beautiful secluded **hotel**, with a lovely south-facing garden.

The Ross of Mull

Stretching for twenty miles west as far as Iona is Mull's rocky southernmost peninsula, the **Ross of Mull**, which, like much of Scotland, appears blissfully tranquil in good weather, and desolate and bleak in bad climes. Most visitors simply drive through the Ross en route to Iona, but if you have the time it's definitely worth considering exploring, or even staying, in this little-visited part of Mull.

The most scenic spots on the Ross are hidden away on the south coast. If you're approaching the Ross from Craignure, the first of these (to Lochbuie) is signposted even before you've negotiated the splendid Highland pass of Glen More, which brings you to the Ross itself. The road to **LOCHBUIE** skirts Loch Spelve, a sheltered sea loch, followed by the freshwater Loch Uisg, which is tinged by woodland, before emerging, after eight miles, on a fertile plain beside the sea. The bay here is rugged and wide, and overlooked by the handsome peak of Ben Buie (2352ft), to the northwest. Hidden behind a patch of Scots pine are the ivy-strewn ruins of **Moy Castle**, an old MacLean stronghold; in the fields to the north is one of the few **stone circles** in the west of Scotland, dating from the second century BC, the highest of its stones about 6ft high. The best-value **accommodation** in the vicinity is at *Barrachandroman* (☎01680/814220, ⓔspelve@aol.com; ❷), a converted stone barn in Kinlochspelve, overlooking the sea loch. A popular and fairly easy **walk** is the five-mile hike west along the coastal path to Carsaig (see below).

The main A849 road, single-track (for the most part) and plagued by the large number of coaches that steam down it en route to Iona, hugs the northern coastline of the Ross. The first sign of civilization after Glen More is the small pub, the *Kinloch Hotel*, with an adjoining shop, followed a mile or so later by the tiny settlement of **PENNYGHAEL**, home to the *Pennyghael Hotel* (☎01681/704288; ❹; March–Oct), which has a good restaurant and a decent bar (no under-12s), and overlooks Loch Scridain and Ben More.

A rickety single-track road heads south for four miles from Pennygael to **CARSAIG**, which enjoys an idyllic setting, looking south out to Colonsay, Islay and Jura. Carsaig is home to the Inniemore School of Painting, but most folk come here either to walk east to Lochbuie (see above), or west under the cliffs, to the **Nuns' Cave**, where nuns from Iona are alleged to have hidden during the Reformation, and then, after four miles or so, at Malcolm's Point, the spectacular **Carsaig Arches**, formed by eroded sea caves, which are linked to basalt cliffs.

Meanwhile, the main road continues for another eleven miles to **BUNESSAN**, the largest village on the peninsula, roughly two-thirds of the way along the Ross. Bunessan has a few useful shops, and a pub and a tearoom, but is otherwise pretty undistinguished. Just east of the town, on the A849, however, is the remarkable **Angora Rabbit Farm** (Easter–Oct daily except Sat 11am–5pm; £2). Here, an eccentric couple keep comical, long-haired bunnies in order to harvest their incredibly soft fleeces as yarn. Whatever time you arrive, you'll get a guided tour, and the kids will get to stroke the rabbits, but if you arrive at noon you can watch their fur being clipped, and at 3pm you can observe a spinning demonstration. There are also goats and hens to meet, and a short woodland walk.

If the weather's good, it might be worth heading off from Bunessan to the sandy bays of the south coast. There's a car park near the *Ardachy House Hotel* (Ⓣ01681/700505; ④; March–Sept), which overlooks the wide expanse of **Ardalanish Bay**, or you can continue to the more sheltered bay of sand and granite outcrops at neighbouring **UISKEN**, a mile to the east. Overlooking the latter is *Uisken Croft* (Ⓣ01681/700307; ①; April–Oct), a welcoming, modern B&B, a stone's throw from the beach, which also allows camping.

The road ends at **FIONNPHORT**, facing Iona, probably the least attractive place to stay on the Ross, though it has a nice sandy bay backed by pink granite rocks to the north of the ferry slipway. Partly to ease congestion on Iona, and to give their neighbours a slice of the tourist pound, Fionnphort was chosen as the site for the **St Columba Centre** (Easter–Sept daily 10.30am–1pm & 2–5.30pm; free); inside, a small exhibition outlines Iona's history, tells a little of Columba's life (for more on which, see p.402), and has a few facsimiles of the illuminated manuscripts produced by the islands's monks.

If you're in need of a **B&B** in Fionnphort, try the granite *Seaview* (Ⓣ01681/700235, Ⓦwww.holidaymull.org/seaview; ①), or the whitewashed *Staffa House* (Ⓣ01681/700677; ②; March–Oct), both of which are close to the ferry, and have views over to Iona. Just out of Fionnphort (no bad thing), there's also *Achaban House* (Ⓣ01681/700205, Ⓦwww.achabanhouse.co.uk; ②), an old manse with some character overlooking Loch Pottie. The basic *Fidden Farm* campsite (Ⓣ01681/700427; April–Sept), a mile south along the Knockvologan road by Fidden beach, is the nearest to Iona. Fidden beach looks out to the **Isle of Erraid**, accessible across the sands at low tide. Robert Louis Stevenson is believed to have written *Kidnapped* (its hero, David Balfour, gets shipwrecked here) in one of the island's cottages, overlooking the **Torran Rocks**, out to sea to the south, beyond which lies the remarkable, stripey **Dubh Artach lighthouse**, built by his father in 1862. The island is now in Dutch ownership, and cared for by the Findhorn Community.

The Isle of Iona

Ross: Where is Duncan's body?
Macduff: Carried to Colme-kill,
The sacred storehouse of his predecessors,
And guardian of their bones.

Macbeth (Act II, Scene 4), by William Shakespeare

Less than a mile off the southwest tip of Mull, **IONA** – just three miles long and not much more than a mile wide – has been a place of pilgrimage for several centuries, and a place of Christian worship for more than 1400 years. For it was to this flat Hebridean island that St Columba fled from Ireland in 563 and established a monastery which was responsible for the conversion of more or less all of pagan Scotland as well as much of northern England. This history and the island's splendid isolation have lent it a peculiar religiosity; in the much-quoted words of Dr Johnson, who visited in 1773, "that man is little to be envied . . . whose piety would not grow warmer among the ruins of Iona". Today, however, the island can barely cope with the constant flood of day-trippers, and charges visitors entry to its abbey, so to appreciate the special atmosphere and to have time to see the whole island, including the often over-looked west coast, you should plan on staying at least one night.

Some history

Legend has it that **St Columba** (Colum Cille), born in Donegal some time around 521, was a direct descendant of the semi-legendary Irish king, Niall of the Nine Hostages. A scholar and soldier priest, who founded numerous monasteries in Ireland, he is thought to have become involved in a bloody dispute with the king when he refused to hand over a copy *St Jerome's Psalter* copied illegally from the original owned by St Finian of Moville. This, in turn, provoked the Battle of Cúl Drebene (Cooldrumman) – also known as the **Battle of the Book** – at which Columba's forces won, though with the loss of over 3000 lives. The story goes that, repenting this bloodshed, Columba went into exile with twelve other monks, eventually settling on Iona in 563, allegedly because it was the first island he encountered from which he couldn't see his homeland. The bottom line, however, is that we know very little about Columba, though he undoubtedly became something of a cult figure after his death in 597. He was posthumously credited with miraculous feats such as defeating the Loch Ness monster – it only had to hear his voice and it recoiled in terror – and banishing snakes (and, some say, frogs) from the island. He is also famously alleged to have banned women and cows from Iona, banishing them to Eilean nam Ban (Woman's Island), just north of Fionnphort, for, as he believed, "where there is a cow there is a woman, and where there is a woman there is mischief".

Whatever the truth about Columba's life, in the sixth and seventh centuries, Iona enjoyed a great deal of autonomy from Rome, establishing a specifically **Celtic Christian** tradition. Missionaries were sent out to the rest of Scotland and parts of England, and Iona quickly became a respected seat of learning and artistry; the monks compiled a vast library of intricately **illuminated manuscripts** – most famously the *Book of Kells* (now on display in Trinity College, Dublin) – while the masons excelled in carving peculiarly intricate crosses. Two factors were instrumental in the demise of the Celtic tradition: a series of Viking raids, the worst of which was the massacre of 68 monks on the sands of Martyrs' Bay in 806; and relentless pressure from the established Church, beginning with the Synod of Whitby in 664, which chose Rome over the Celtic Church, and culminated in the suppression of the Celtic Church by King David I in 1144.

In 1203, Iona became part of the mainstream church with the establishment of an **Augustinian nunnery** and a **Benedictine monastery** by Reginald, son of Somerled, Lord of the Isles. During the Reformation, the entire complex was ransacked, the contents of the library burnt and all but three of the island's 360 crosses destroyed. Although plans were drawn up at various times to turn the abbey into a Cathedral of the Isles, nothing came of them until in 1899, when the (then) owner, the eighth duke of Argyll, donated the abbey buildings to the **Church of Scotland**, who restored the abbey church for worship over the course of the next decade. Iona's modern resurgence began in 1938, when **George MacLeod**, a minister from Glasgow, established a group of ministers, students and artisans to begin rebuilding the remainder of the monastic buildings. What began as a mostly male, Gaelic-speaking, strictly Presbyterian community is today a lay, mixed and ecumenical retreat. The entire abbey complex has been successfully restored, and is now looked after by Historic Scotland, while the island, apart from the church land and a few crofts, is in the care of the NTS.

Baile Mór

The passenger ferry from Fionnphort drops you off at the island's main village, **BAILE MÓR** (literally "large village"), which is in fact little more than a single terrace of cottages facing the sea. Just inland lie the extensive pink granite ruins of the **Augustinian nunnery**, disused since the Reformation. A beautifully maintained garden now occupies the cloisters, and if nothing else the complex gives you an idea of the state of the present-day abbey before it was restored. Across the road to the north, housed in a manse built, like the nearby parish church, by the ubiquitous Thomas Telford, is the **Iona Heritage Centre** (April–Oct Mon–Sat 10.30am–4.30pm; £1.50), with displays on the social history of the island over the last 200 years, including the Clearances, which nearly halved the island's population of 500 in the mid-nineteenth century. At a bend in the road, just south of the manse and church, stands the fifteenth-century **MacLean's Cross**, a fine late medieval example of the distinctive, flowing, three-leaved foliage of the Iona school.

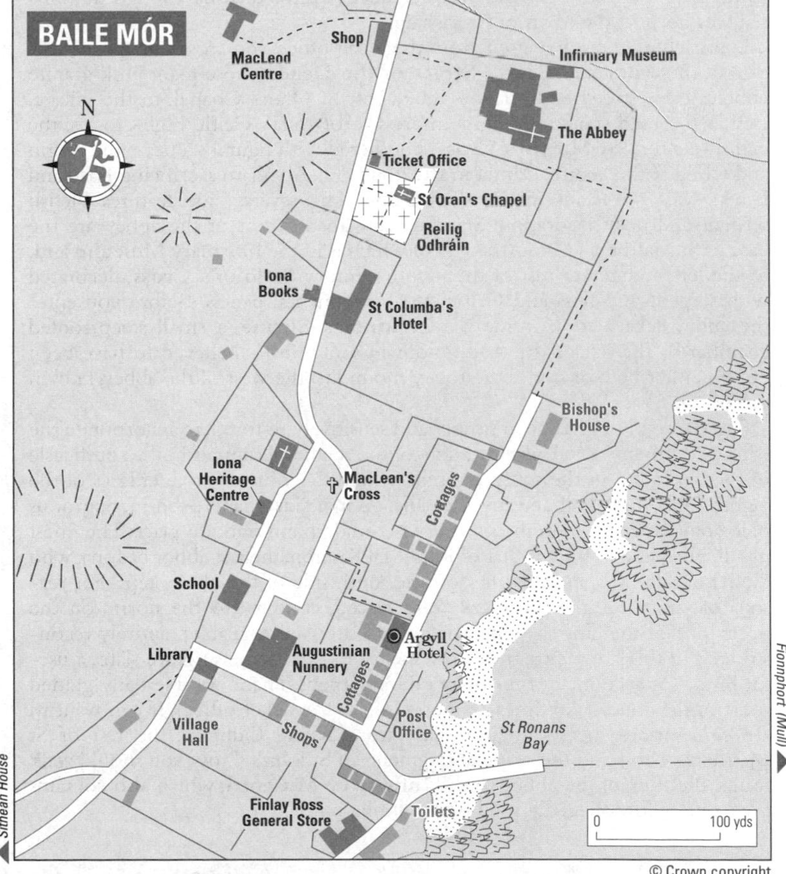

© Crown copyright

Iona Abbey

No buildings remain from Columba's time: the present **abbey** (daily: April–Sept 9.30am–6.30pm; Oct–March 9.30am–4.30pm; HS; £2.80) dates from the arrival of the Benedictines in around 1200; it was extensively rebuilt in the fifteenth and sixteenth centuries, and restored virtually wholesale last century. Iona's oldest building, the plain-looking **St Oran's Chapel**, lies south of the abbey, to your right, and boasts an eleventh-century door. Legend has it that the original chapel could only be completed through human sacrifice. Oran apparently volunteered to be buried alive, and was found to have survived the ordeal when the grave was opened a few days later. Declaring that he had seen hell and it wasn't all bad, he was promptly reinterred for blasphemy.

Oran's Chapel stands at the centre of Iona's sacred burial ground, **Reilig Odhráin** (Oran's Cemetery), which is said to contain the graves of sixty kings of Norway, Ireland, France and Scotland, including Duncan and Macbeth. The best of the early Christian gravestones and medieval effigies which once lay in the Reilig Odhráin have unfortunately been removed to the Infirmary Museum, behind the abbey (see opposite), and to various other locations within the complex. The graveyard is still used as a cemetery by the island, however, and also contains the grave of the short-lived leader of the Labour Party, **John Smith** (1938–94), who was a frequent visitor to Iona, though he himself was born in the town of Ardrishaig.

Approaching the abbey itself, from the ticket office, you cross an exposed section of the evocative medieval **Street of the Dead**, whose giant pink granite cobbles once stretched from the abbey, past St Oran's Chapel, to the village. Beside the road stands the most impressive of Iona's Celtic high crosses, the eighth-century **St Martin's Cross**, smothered with figural scenes – the Virgin and Child at the centre, Daniel in the lion's den, Abraham sacrificing Isaac and David with musicians in the shaft below. The reverse side features Pictish serpent-and-boss decoration. Standing directly in front of the abbey are the base of St Matthew's Cross (the rest of which is in the Infirmary Museum) and, to the left, a concrete cast of the eighth-century **St John's Cross**, decorated with serpent-and-boss and Celtic spiral ornamental panels. Before you enter the abbey, take a look inside **St Columba's Shrine**, a small steep-roofed chamber to the left of the main entrance. Columba is believed to have been buried either here or under the rocky mound to the west of the abbey, known as Tórr an Aba.

The **Abbey** itself has been simply and sensitively restored, to incorporate the original elements. You can spot many of the medieval capitals in the south aisle of the choir and in the south transept, where the white marble effigies of the eighth Duke of Argyll and his wife, Ina, lie in a side chapel – an incongruous piece of Victorian pomp in an otherwise modest and tranquil place. The finest pre-Reformation effigy is that of John MacKinnon, the last abbot of Iona, who died around 1500, and now lies on the south side of the choir steps. For reasons of sanitation, the **cloisters** were placed, contrary to the norm, on the north side of the church (where running water was available); entirely reconstructed in the late 1950s, they now shelter lots of medieval grave slabs, a useful historical account of the abbey's development. There are free daily guided tours of the abbey (the times are posted up at the ticket office). If you want to see some more medieval grave slabs from Reilig Odhráin, the rest of St Matthew's Cross and the original fragments of St John's Cross, you should walk round the back of the abbey to the **Infirmary Museum**, which also contains the stone pillow allegedly used by Columba himself.

Practicalities

There's no **tourist office** on Iona, and as demand far exceeds supply you should organize **accommodation** well in advance. Of the island's two **hotels**, the stone-built *Argyll* (ⓣ01681/700334, ⓦwww.argyllhoteliona.co.uk; ❷–❻; April–Oct), in the terrace of cottages overlooking the Sound of Iona, is by far the nicest. As for **B&Bs**, try the secluded *Sithean House* (ⓣ01681/700331; ❶), a mile from the ferry, on the peaceful west side of the island. **Camping** is not permitted on Iona, but there is a **hostel** (ⓣ01681/700642) . If you want to stay with the **Iona Community**, contact the *MacLeod Centre* (ⓣ01681/700404, ⓦwww.iona.org.uk), popularly known as the "Mac". Hostel accommodation is provided and you must be prepared to participate fully in the daily activities, prayers and religious services.

Visitors are not allowed to bring cars onto the island, but **bikes** can be rented from the Finlay Ross general store (ⓣ01681/700357). **Food** options are limited: the eclectic bar menu of the *Argyll* is probably your best option or, for something lighter, head for the tearoom, beside the Heritage Centre, which serves home-made soup and delicious cakes.

Coll and Tiree

Coll and **Tiree** are among the most isolated of the Inner Hebrides, and if anything have more in common with the outlying Western Isles than with their closest neighbour, Mull. Each is roughly twelve miles long and three miles wide, both are low-lying, treeless and exceptionally windy, with white sandy beaches and the highest sunshine records in Scotland. Like most of the Hebrides, they were once ruled by Vikings, and didn't pass into Scottish hands until the thirteenth century. Coll's population peaked at 1440, Tiree's at a staggering 4450, but both were badly affected by the Clearances, which virtually halved their populations in a generation. Coll was fortunate to be in the hands of the enlightened MacLeans, but they were forced to sell in 1856 to the Stewart family, who sold two-thirds of the island to a Dutch millionaire in the 1960s. Tiree was ruthlessly cleared by its owner, the Duke of Argyll, who sent in the marines in 1885 to evict the crofters. After the passing of the Crofters' Act the following year, the island was divided into crofts, though it remains a part of the Duke of Argyll's estate. Both islands have strong Gaelic roots, but the percentage of English-speaking newcomers is rising steadily.

The CalMac **ferry** from Oban calls at Coll (2hr 40min) and Tiree (3hr 40min) every day except Thursdays and Sundays throughout the year. Tiree also has an **airport** with daily flights (Mon–Sat) to and from Glasgow. The majority of visitors on both islands stay for at least a week in self-catering accommodation (see p.31), though there are B&Bs and hotels on the islands. However, choice is limited, so it's as well to book as far in advance as possible (and that goes for the ferry crossing, too). The only **public transport** is on Tiree, which has an infrequent postbus service (Mon–Sat only), plus a shared taxi system (ⓣ01879/220311 or 220419).

The Isle of Coll

The fish-shaped rocky island of **Coll** (population 180) lies less than seven miles off the coast of Mull. The CalMac ferry drops off at Coll's only real village, **ARINAGOUR**, whose whitewashed cottages line the western shore of Loch Eatharna, a popular safe anchorage for boats. Half the island's population lives

ground. The highlights of this gently undulating scenery lie along the sharply indented west coast, in particular the rich Bronze Age and Neolithic remains in the Kilmartin valley, one of the most important prehistoric sites in Scotland.

The Slate Islands and the Garvellachs

Just eight miles south of Oban, a road heads off the A816 west to a small group of islands commonly called the **Slate Islands**, which at their peak in the mid-nineteenth century quarried over nine million slates annually. Today many of the old slate villages are sparsely populated, and an inevitable air of melancholy hangs over them, but their dramatic setting amid crashing waves makes for a rewarding day-trip.

The Isle of Seil

The most northerly of the Slate Islands is **Seil**, a lush island, now something of an exclusive enclave (Princess Diana's mother, Mrs Shand-Kydd, is a resident). It's separated from the mainland only by the thinnest of sea channels and spanned by an elegant humpback **Clachan Bridge**, built in 1793 and popularly known as the "Bridge over the Atlantic". The pub next door to the bridge is the *Tigh na Truish* (House of the Trousers), where kilt-wearing islanders would change into trousers to conform to the post-1745 ban on Highland dress. The nearby *Willowburn Hotel* (Ⓣ01852/300276, Ⓦwww.willowburn.co.uk; ❻; March–Dec) is the **accommodation** of choice on Seil; a peaceful and very comfortable hotel overlooking Seil Sound, with an excellent restaurant to boot.

The main village on Seil is **ELLENABEICH**, its neat white terraces of workers' cottages – featured in the film *Ring of Bright Water* – crouching below black cliffs on the westernmost tip of the island. This was once the tiny island of Eilean a'Beithich (hence "Ellenabeich") separated from the mainland by a slim sea channel until the intensive slate quarrying succeeded in silting it up. Confusingly, the village is often referred to by the same name as the nearby island of Easdale, since they formed an interdependent community based exclusively around the slate industry.

As you enter the village, be sure to take a stroll round the gardens of **An Cala** (April–Oct daily dawn–dusk; £1.50), best visited in early summer for the glorious azaleas and Japanese flowering cherries. In the village itself is the **Scottish Slate Islands Heritage Centre** (April–Oct daily 10.30am–5pm; £1.50), which is housed in one of the little white cottages. The best feature of the exhibition is the model of the slate quarry as it would have been at the height of its fame in the nineteenth century. Note that, if you're heading over to Easdale, you can buy a combined ticket covering both museums and the ferry for £3.30.

For a good range of snacks and locally caught **fish and seafood**, pop inside the *Seafood & Oyster Bar* (April–Oct only) on the way to the ferry. High adrenalin **boat trips** are offered by Seafari Adventures (Ⓣ01852/300003), who are based at the Ellenabeich jetty; the boats are rigid inflatables and travel at some speed round the offshore islands and through the Corryvreckan Whirlpool.

The Isle of Easdale

Easdale remains an island, though the few hundred yards that separate it from Ellenabeich have to be dredged to keep the channel open. On the eve of a great storm on November 23, 1881, Easdale, less than a mile across at any one point, supported an incredible 452 inhabitants. That night, waves engulfed the island

and flooded the quarries. The island never really recovered, slate quarrying stopped in 1914, and by the 1960s the population was reduced to single figures.

Recently many of the old workers' cottages have been restored: some as holiday homes, others sold to new families (the present population stands at over thirty). One of the cottages now houses the interesting **Easdale Folk Museum** (April–Oct daily 10.30am–5.30pm; £2), near the main square, selling a useful historical map of the island, which you can walk round in about half an hour. The **ferry** from Ellenabeich runs partly to schedule, partly on demand (April–Sept Mon–Sat 7.15am–8.50pm, Sun 9.30am–5.50pm; Oct–March check at Oban tourist office, see p.385), and there's *The Puffer* **bar/restaurant** if you've failed to put together a picnic.

The Isle of Luing

To the south of Seil, across the narrow, treacherous Cuan Sound, lies **Luing** (pronounced "ling"), a long, thin, fertile island which once supported more than 600 people. During the Clearances, the population was drastically reduced to make way for cattle; Luing is still renowned for its beef and for the chocolate-brown crossbreed named after it. A car **ferry** (Mon–Sat 8am–6pm; mid-June to Aug also Fri & Sat 7.30–10.30pm) crosses the Cuan Sound every half-hour or so, though foot passengers can cross until later in the evening (Mon–Thurs 8am–10pm, Fri & Sat 8am–11.30pm, Sun 11am–6pm). There's a **postbus** service on Luing itself (Mon–Sat only).

CULLIPOOL, the pretty main village with its post office and general store, lies a mile or so southwest; quarrying ceased here in 1965, and the place now relies on tourism and lobster fishing. Luing's only other village, **TOBERONOCHY**, lies on the more sheltered east coast, three miles southeast of Cullipool. Its distinctive white cottages, built by the slate company in 1805, nestle below a ruined church, which contains a memorial to fifteen Latvian seamen who drowned off the nearby abandoned slate island of **Belnahua** during a hurricane in 1936. The only **accommodation** available on the island is self-catering cottages, or one of the static caravans at the tiny *Sunnybrae Caravan Park* (Ⓣ01852/314274; March–Oct) close to the ferry. For **bike rental**, phone Luing Bike Hire (Ⓣ01852/314256).

The Isle of Scarba and the Garvellachs

Scarba is the largest of the islands around Luing, a brooding 1500-foot hulk of slate, not much more than a couple of miles across, inhospitable and wild – most of the fifty or so inhabitants who once lived here had left by the mid-nineteenth century. To the south, between Scarba and Jura, the raging **Gulf of Corrievrechan** is the site of one of the world's most spectacular whirlpools, thought to be caused by a rocky pinnacle below the sea. It remains calm only for an hour or two at high and low tide; between flood and half-flood tide, accompanied by a southerly or westerly wind, water shoots deafeningly some 20ft up in the air. Inevitably there are numerous legends about the place – known as *coire bhreacain* (speckled cauldron) in Gaelic – concerning *Cailleach* (Hag), the Celtic storm goddess. The best place from which to view it is the northern tip of Jura (see p.437).

The string of uninhabited islands visible west of Luing are known collectively as the **Garvellachs**, after the largest of the group, **Garbh Eileach** (Rough Rock), which was inhabited as recently as fifty years ago. The most northerly, **Dún Chonnuill**, contains the remains of an old fort thought to have belonged to Conal of Dalriada, and **Eileach an Naoimh** (Holy Isle), the most southerly of the group, is where the Celtic missionary Brendan the Navigator founded a community in 542, some twenty years before Columba landed on Iona (see p.402). Nothing survives from Brendan's day, but there are a few ninth-century remains, among them a double-beehive cell and a grave enclosure. One school of thought has it that the island is Hinba, Columba's legendary secret retreat, where he founded a monastery before settling on Iona.

If you're interested in taking a **boat trip** to Corrievrechan or the Garvellachs, contact Gemini Cruises (Ⓣ01546/830238, Ⓦwww.gemini-crinan.co.uk), who operate from Crinan (see p.415), or Porpoise Charters (Ⓣ01852/300203), who are based at Balvicar, just south of the Clachan Bridge.

Arduaine and Craignish

Probably the finest spot at which to stop and have a bite to eat on the main road from Oban to Lochgilphead is the well-situated *Loch Melfort Hotel* (Ⓣ01852/200233, Ⓦwww.loch-melfort.co.uk; ❺), in **ARDUAINE**, where you can have a pint and a bite to eat, sitting out on the hotel lawn, with views over Asknish Bay and out to the islands of Shuna, Luing, Scarba and Jura. Beside the hotel are the **Arduaine Gardens** (daily 9.30am–dusk; £3; NTS), which enjoy the same idyllic lochside location. Gifted as recently as 1992, the gardens are stupendous, particularly in May and June, and have the feel of a intimate private garden, with pristine lawns, lily-strewn ponds, mature woods and spectacular rhododendrons and azaleas. The gardens' disgruntled former owners, the Wright brothers, still live next door and have an equally lovely adjacent garden. Below the hotel and gardens, *Arduaine Caravan and Camping Park* is a lovely lochside **campsite** (Ⓣ01852/200331, Ⓔcamping@larochfoods.co.uk; Easter–Oct).

A couple of miles south, on the far side of Asknish Bay is the slightly surreal **CRAOBH HAVEN**, a purpose-built holiday village and marina that are reminiscent of a bad film set. There's a fine walk to be had, however, from Craobh Haven along the spine of the **Craignish peninsula** to the southernmost tip some five miles away. Heading back up the single-track road that runs along the shores of Loch Craignish, stop off at the *Galley of Lorne* in yachty **ARDFERN**, a real pub and a great place to quench your thirst, with a rather more upmarket restaurant attached. Opposite the pub is *The Crafty Kitchen* (closed Mon), a small popular restaurant (and craftshop) specialising in inexpensive locally sourced and additive-free food. There's **accommodation** close to Craobh Haven, either in the log-cabin-style *Buidhe Lodge* (Ⓣ01852/500291, Ⓦwww.buidhelodge.com; ❷), or in the rambling Baronial pile of *Lunga* (Ⓣ01852/500237, Ⓔcolin@lunga.demon.co.uk; ❶), run by an eccentric laird.

Kilmartin Glen

The chief sight on the road from Oban to Lochgilphead is the **Kilmartin Glen**, the most important prehistoric site on the Scottish mainland. The most remarkable relic is the **linear cemetery**, where several cairns are aligned for more than two miles, to the south of the village Kilmartin. These are thought to represent the successive burials of a ruling family or chieftains, but nobody can be sure. The best view of the cemetery's configuration is from the Bronze Age **Mid-Cairn**, but the Neolithic **South Cairn**, dating from around 3000 BC, is by far the oldest and the most impressive, with its large chambered tomb roofed by giant slabs.

Close to the Mid-Cairn, the two **Temple Wood stone circles** appear to have been the architectural focus of burials in the area from Neolithic times to the Bronze Age. Visible to the south are the impressively cup-marked **Nether**

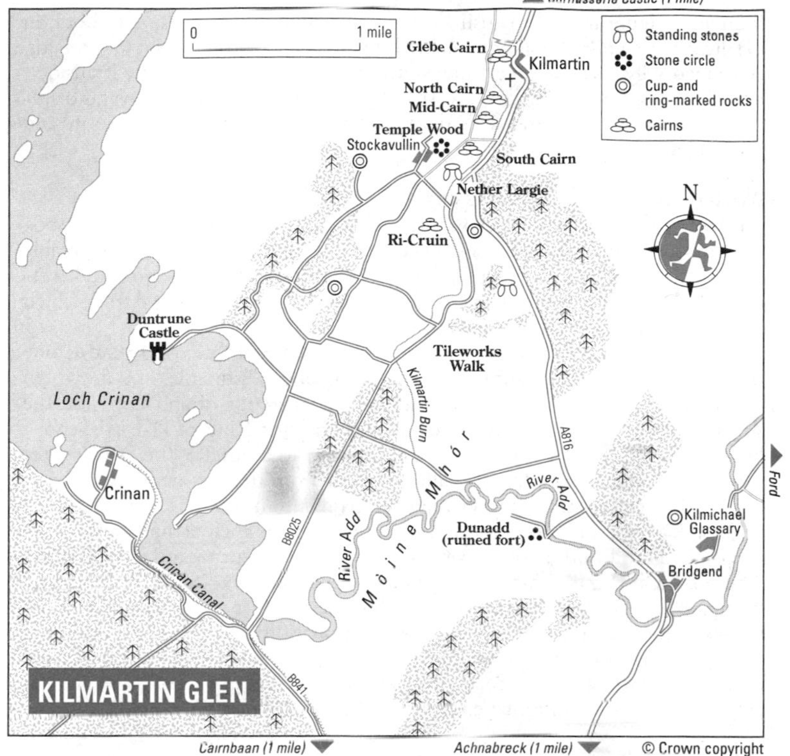

Largie standing stones (no public access), the largest of which looms over 10ft high. **Cup- and ring-marked rocks** are a recurrent feature of prehistoric sites in the Kilmartin Glen and elsewhere in Argyll. There are many theories as to their origin: some see them as Pictish symbols, others as primitive solar calendars. The most extensive markings in the entire country are at **Achnabreck**, off the A816 towards Lochgilphead.

Kilmartin

Situated on high ground to the north of the cairns is the tiny village of **KILMARTIN**, where the old manse adjacent to the village church now houses a **Museum of Ancient Culture** (daily 10am–5.30pm; Ⓦwww.kilmartin.org; £3.90), which is both enlightening and entertaining. Not only can you learn about the various theories concerning prehistoric crannogs, henges and cairns, but you can practise polishing an axe, examine different types of wood and fur, and listen to a variety of weird and wonderful sounds (check out the Gaelic bird imitations). The **café** is equally enticing, with local (often wild) produce on offer, which you can wash down with heather beer.

The nearby church is worth a brief reconnoitre, as it shelters the badly damaged and weathered **Kilmartin crosses**, while a separate enclosure in the graveyard houses a large collection of medieval grave slabs of the Malcolms of Poltalloch. Kilmartin's own castle is ruined beyond recognition; head instead for the much-less-ruined **Carnasserie Castle**, on a high ridge a mile up the road towards Oban. The castle was built in the 1560s by John Carswell, an influential figure in the Scottish church, who published the first ever book in Gaelic, *Knox's Liturgy*, which contained the doctrines of the Presbyterian faith. Architecturally, the castle is interesting, too, as it represents the transition between fully fortified castles and later mansion houses, and has several original finely carved stone fireplaces, doorways, as well as numerous gun-loops and shot holes.

Mòine Mhór and Dunadd

To the south of Kilmartin, beyond the linear cemetery, lies the raised peat bog of **Mòine Mhór** (Great Moss), now a nature reserve and home to remarkable plant, insect and birdlife. To get a close look at the sphagnum moss and wetlands, head for the newly laid-out Tileworks Walk, just off the A816, which includes a short boardwalk over the bog.

Mòine Mhór is best known as home to the Iron Age fort of **Dunadd**, one of Scotland's most important Celtic sites, occupying a distinctive 176-foot-high rocky knoll once surrounded by the sea but currently stranded beside the winding River Add. It was here that Fergus, the first King of Dalriada, established his royal seat, having arrived from Ireland in around 500 AD. Its strategic position, the craggy defences and the view from the top are all impressive, but it's the **stone carvings** between the twin summits which make Dunadd so remarkable: several lines of inscription in ogam (an ancient alphabet of Irish origin), the faint outline of a boar, a hollowed-out footprint and a small basin. The boar and the inscriptions are probably Pictish, since the fort was clearly occupied long before Fergus got there, but the footprint and basin have been interpreted as being part of the royal coronation rituals of the kings of Dalriada. It is thought that the Stone of Destiny was used at Dunadd before being moved to Scone Palace, then to Westminster Abbey in London, where it languished until it was returned to Edinburgh in 1996.

Practicalities

Great-value **B&B** is available at *Tibertich* (ⓣ01546/810281, ⓦwww.tibertich.com; ❶; March–Oct), a working sheep farm in the hills to the north of Kilmartin, off the A816, and also in the supremely isolated *Ardifuir* (ⓣ01546/510271, ⓔduntrune@msn.com; ❷), a farmhouse in the grounds of Duntrune Castle, very close to the sea. Alternatively, you could hole up in Crinan or Cairnbaan (see below). The aforementioned café/restaurant at Kilmartin House is a great lunch-time **eating** option; alternatively, *The Cairn* (ⓣ01546/510254; March–Oct), opposite the church in Kilmartin, is open in the evening, and features moderately expensive Scottish and Mediterranean dishes.

Lochgilphead

The unlikely administrative centre of Argyll & Bute, **LOCHGILPHEAD**, as the name suggests, lies at the head of Loch Gilp, an arm of Loch Fyne. It's a planned town in the same vein as Inveraray, though nothing like as picturesque. If you're staying in the area, however, you're bound to find yourself here at some point, as Lochgilphead has the only bank and supermarket (not to mention swimming pool) for miles. In fine weather, you're best off going for a stroll round **Kilmory Woodland Park**, a couple of miles up the A83 to Inveraray, with its Iron Age fort, bird hide and lochside views, and take in the gardens laid out in 1830 around Kilmory Castle (now headquarters of the Argyll & Bute District Council). Another fine-weather option is **Castle Riding Centre** (ⓣ01546/603274, ⓦwww.brenfield.co.uk) at Brenfield Farm, three miles south, which runs highly enjoyable riding courses lasting from a day to a week, plus trekking and pub rides, and even has golf equipment and **bike rental**.

The **tourist office**, 27 Lochnell St (April Mon–Fri 10am–5pm, Sat & Sun noon–5pm; May & June Mon–Sat 10am–5pm, Sun 11am–5pm; July & Aug Mon–Sat 9.30am–6pm, Sun 10am–5pm; Sept & Oct Mon–Sat 10am–5pm, Sun noon–5pm; ⓣ01546/602344), can help find you **accommodation**, though really you'd be better off either in *Fascadale House* (ⓣ01546/603845, ⓦwww.fascadale.com; ❸), a handsome Victorian guesthouse set back from the road to Adrishaig, or in Kilmartin Glen or Crinan (see below). You can also **camp** at the pristinely maintained *Lochgilphead Caravan Park*, a short distance west of town in Bank Park (ⓣ01546/602003; April–Oct); bike rental is available, too. As for **food**, the *Smiddy*, on Smithy Lane (closed Sun), does simple well-cooked grub – for high-class picnic fare, call in at *Cockles*, a smart deli on the main street that also sells fresh fish and home-made bread.

Knapdale

Forested **Knapdale** – from the Gaelic *cnap* (hill) and *dall* (field) – forms a buffer zone between the Kintyre peninsula and the rest of Argyll, bounded to the north by the Crinan Canal and to the south by West Loch Tarbert and consisting of three fingers of land, separated by Loch Sween and Loch Caolisport.

The Crinan Canal

In 1801 the nine-mile-long **Crinan Canal** opened, linking Loch Fyne, at Ardrishaig south of Lochgilphead, with the Sound of Jura, thus cutting out the long and treacherous journey around the Mull of Kintyre. John Rennie's original design, although an impressive engineering feat, had numerous faults, and by 1816 Thomas Telford was called in to take charge of the renovations. The canal runs parallel to the sea for quite some way before cutting across the bottom of Mòine Mhór and hitting a flight of locks either side of **CAIRNBAAN** (there are fifteen in total); a walk along the towpath is both picturesque and pleasantly unstrenuous. A useful pit stop can be made at the *Cairnbaan Hotel* (ⓣ01546/603668; ❻), an eighteenth-century coaching inn overlooking the canal; it has a decent restaurant and bar meals featuring locally caught seafood – to whip up an appetite you can nip up to the cup- and ring-marked stone behind the hotel

There are usually one or two yachts passing through the locks, but the most relaxing place from which to view the canal in action is **CRINAN**, the pretty little fishing port at the western end of the canal. Crinan's tiny harbour is, for the moment at least, still home to a small fishing fleet; a quick burst up through Crinan Wood to the hill above Crinan will give you a bird's-eye view of the sea lock and its setting. Every room in the *Crinan Hotel* (ⓣ01546/830261, ⓦwww.crinanhotel.com; ❾) looks across Loch Crinan to the Sound of Jura – one of the most beautiful (and expensive) views in Scotland, especially at sunset when the myriad islets and the distinctive Paps of Jura are reflected in the waters of the loch. If the *Crinan* is beyond your means, try the secluded **B&B** *Tigh-na-Glaic* (ⓣ01546/830261; ❸), perched above the harbour, also with views out to sea. Bar **meals** at the *Crinan* are expensive, but utterly delicious, as is the hotel's even more expensive seafood restaurant, *Lock 16*, on the top floor, which commands a panoramic view; there's only one sitting, at 8pm, so booking is advisable. Down on the lockside there is a cheaper, cheerful **café** called the *Coffee Shop* (Easter–Oct), serving mouthwatering home-made cakes and wonderful clootie dumplings. If you want to go on one of the **boat trips** organized by Gemini Cruises (ⓣ01546/830238,

Ⓦwww.gemini-crinan.co.uk), however, you need to go to Crinan's other harbour, half a mile further along the coast; from here the waymarked three-mile **Crinan Walk** takes you through the nearby Forestry Commission plantation, with excellent views out to sea.

Knapdale Forest and Loch Sween

South of the canal, **Knapdale Forest**, planted in the 1930s, stretches virtually uninterrupted from coast to coast, across hills sprinkled with tiny lochs. The Forestry Commission has set out several lovely **walks**, the easiest of which is the circular, mile-long path which takes you deep into the forest just past **Achanamara** (five miles south of Crinan). The three-mile route around **Loch Coille-Bharr**, which begins from a bend in the B8025, to Tayvallich, is fairly gentle; the other walk, although half a mile shorter, is more strenuous, starting from the B841 (halfway between Crinan and Lochgilphead), which runs along the canal, and ascending the peak of **Dunardry** (702ft). There are several good cycle routes, from easy to tough, in this area – all clearly waymarked.

Continuing down the western finger of Knapdale you come to the village of **TAYVALLICH**, with its attractive horseshoe bay, after which the peninsula splits again. The western arm leads eventually to the medieval **Chapel of Keills**, newly roofed, with a display of late-medieval carved stones, and the remains of a small port where cattle used to be landed from Ireland. There is also a fine view of the **MacCormaig Islands**, the largest of which, Eilean Mór (currently owned by the Scottish National Party), was previously a retreat of the seventh-century St Cormac, but is now a breeding ground for seabirds. The other arm, the **Taynish peninsula**, is a National Nature Reserve and has one of the largest remaining oak forests in Britain, boasting over twenty species of butterfly. If you want to eat or drink round here, head for the *Tayvallich Inn* (Ⓣ01546/870282), in the village of the same name, for very good local food.

Six miles south of Achanamara, on the eastern shores of **Loch Sween**, is the "Key of Knapdale", the eleventh-century **Castle Sween**, the earliest stone castle in Scotland, but in ruins since 1647. The tranquillity and beauty of the setting is spoilt by the nearby caravan park, an eyesore which makes a visit pretty depressing. You're better off continuing south to the thirteenth-century **Kilmory Chapel**, also ruined but with a new roof protecting the medieval grave slabs and the well-preserved MacMillan's Cross, an eight-foot fifteenth-century Celtic cross showing the crucifixion on one side and a hunting scene on the other.

The easternmost finger of Knapdale is isolated and fairly impenetrable, but it's worth persevering the twenty miles of single-track road in order to reach **KILBERRY**, where you can **stay** at the *Kilberry Inn* (Ⓣ01880/770223; ❹; Easter–Oct) or **camp** at the *Port Ban Caravan Park* (Ⓣ01880/770224, Ⓦwww.argyllweb.com/portban; April–Oct). There's also a church worth viewing in Kilberry and a small collection of carved medieval graveslabs, while the western shores of West Loch Tarbert are usually replete with birdlife.

Kintyre

But for the mile-long isthmus between West Loch Tarbert and the much smaller East Loch Tarbert, the little-visited peninsula of **KINTYRE** (Ⓦwww.kintyre.org) – from the Gaelic *ceann tire*, "land's end" – would be an island. Indeed, in the eleventh century, when the Scottish king, Malcolm Canmore, allowed Magnus Barefoot, King of Norway, to lay claim to any island he could circumnavigate by boat, Magnus succeeded in dragging his boat across the Tarbert isthmus and added the peninsula to his Hebridean kingdom. During the Wars of the Covenant, the vast majority of the population and property was wiped out by a combination of the 1646 potato blight and the destructive attentions of the Earl of Argyll. Kintyre remained a virtual desert until the earl began his policy of transplanting Gaelic-speaking Lowlanders to the region. They probably felt quite at home here, as the southern half of the peninsula lies on the Lowland side of the Highland Boundary Fault.

Getting around Kintyre without your own transport is a slow business, though services have improved. There are regular daily **buses** from Glasgow to Campbeltown, via Tarbert and the west coast, and even a skeleton service down the east coast. Bear in mind, though, if you're **driving**, that the new west coast road is extremely fast, whereas the single-track east coast road takes more than twice as long. There's a **ferry** service to Tarbert from Portavadie on the Cowal peninsula, and Campbeltown has an airport, with daily **flights** from Glasgow, which is only forty miles away by air, compared to over 120 miles by road.

Tarbert

A distinctive rocket-like church steeple heralds the fishing village of **TARBERT** (in Gaelic *An Tairbeart*, meaning "isthmus"), sheltering an attractive little bay backed by rugged hills. Tarbert's herring industry was mentioned in the Annals of Ulster as far back as 836 AD, though right now the local fishing industry is down to its lowest level ever, due to the strict EU quota system. Ironically, it was local Tarbert fishermen, who, in the 1830s, pioneered the method of herring fishing known as trawling, seining or ring-netting, which eventually wiped out the Loch Fyne herring stocks. Tourism is now an increasingly important source of income, as is the money that flows through the town during the last week in May, when the yacht races of the famous Scottish Series take place.

Tarbert's harbourfront is pretty, and is best appreciated from Robert the Bruce's fourteenth-century **castle** above the town to the south. Only the ivy-strewn ruins of the keep remain, though the view from the overgrown rubble makes the stroll up here worthwhile. There are steps up to the castle and a red waymarked path from beside the excellent Ann Thomas bookshop and gallery on the harbourfront. Longer walks are also marked out, including a hike all the wayover to Skipness (see p.423). The shortest stroll of all, though, is to the far end of Pier Road, where there's a tiny, but very lovely, shell beach.

Tarbert's **tourist office** (April Mon–Fri 10am–5pm, Sat & Sun noon–5pm; May & June Mon–Sat 10am–5pm, Sun 11am–5pm; July & Aug Mon–Sat 9.30am–6pm, Sun 10am–5pm; Sept & Oct Mon–Sat 10am–5pm, Sun noon–5pm; ⓣ01880/820429) is on the harbour. If you need to **stay**, there's no shortage of B&Bs, though none are outstanding – try *Springside* B&B on Pier Road (ⓣ01880/820413, ⓔmarshall.springside@virgin.net; ❶), which overlooks the harbour. Highly recommended, however, are the wonderful *Columba Hotel* a detached Victorian town house further along Tarbert waterfront (ⓣ01880/820808, ⓦwww.columbahotel.com; ❺), and the *Victoria Hotel* (ⓣ01880/820236; ❹), the comfortable bright yellow pub on the opposite side of the harbour. Tarbert's luxury option is *Stonefield Castle Hotel* (ⓣ01880/820836; ❼), two miles up the A83 to Lochgilphead, a handsome

Ferry connections in and around Tarbert

One reason you might find yourself staying in Tarbert is its proximity to no fewer than four **ferry terminals**. The small CalMac ferry, which connects Kintyre with **Portavadie** on the Cowal peninsula, leaves from Tarbert's Pier Road; the busiest terminal, however, is at **Kennacraig**, five miles south along the A83, which runs daily sailings to Islay and a once-weekly service to Colonsay. From Kennacraig, the B8001 cuts across the peninsula to **Claonaig**, where a summer car ferry (April to mid-Oct) runs to Lochranza on Arran; and finally, south of Kennacraig on the A83, the Gigha ferry departs from **Tayinloan**.

grandiose Scots Baronial mansion set in magnificent grounds overlooking Loch Fyne.

The best bar **food** is to be had at the *Victoria*, where you can sit in the conservatory and look out across the harbour. For some excellent local meat, fish and seafood dishes, head for the moderately expensive *Anchorage* (ⓣ01880/820881; Wed–Sat eves only), on the opposite side of the harbour.

The Isle of Gigha

Gigha (ⓦwww.isle-of-gigha.co.uk) – pronounced "geeya", with a hard "g" – is a low-lying, fertile island, just three miles off the west coast of Kintyre, reputedly occupied for 5000 years. The island's Ayrshire cattle produce over a quarter of a million gallons of milk a year, though since the closure of Gigha's creamery in the 1980s, the island's distinctive fruit-shaped cheese has been produced on the mainland. Like many of the smaller Hebrides, Gigha was sold by its original lairds, the MacNeils, and has been put on the market numerous times in recent years, causing great uncertainty amongst the 140 or so inhabitants. In 2001, it was finally bought by the islanders.

The ferry from Tayinloan, 23 miles south of Tarbert, deposits you at the island's only village, **ARDMINISH**, where you'll find the post office and shop and the all-denominations island church with some interesting stained-glass windows, including one to Kenneth Macleod, composer of the well-known ditty *Road to the Isles*. The main attraction on the island is the **Achamore Gardens** (daily 9am–dusk; £2), a mile and a half south of Ardminish. Established by the first postwar owner, Sir James Horlick of hot drink fame, their spectacularly colourful display of azaleas are best seen in early summer. To the southwest of the gardens, the ruins of the thirteenth-century **St Catan's Chapel** are floored with weathered medieval gravestones; the ogam stone nearby is the only one of its kind in the west of Scotland. The real draw of Gigha, however, apart from the peace and quiet, are the white sandy beaches – including one at Ardminish itself – that dot the coastline.

Gigha is so small – six miles by one mile – that most visitors come here just for the day. It is, however, possible **to stay** either at the *Post Office House* (ⓣ01583/505251; ❷) or the *Gigha Hotel* (ⓣ01583/505254; ❻; March–Oct), the very pleasant social centre of the island; if you're interested in self-catering, you should contact the hotel. The *Gigha Hotel* is also the place to go for tea and cakes, and for bar meals (with tables outside should the weather be fine). **Bike rental** is available from the shop (open daily), and there's a nine-hole **golf course**.

The west coast

Kintyre's bleak **west coast** ranks among the most exposed stretches of coastline in Argyll. Atlantic breakers pound the shoreline, while the persistent westerly wind forces the trees against the hillside. However, when the weather's fine and the wind not too fierce there are numerous deserted sandy beaches to enjoy, with great views over to Gigha, Islay, Jura and even Ireland.

There are several **campsites** to choose from along the stretch of coast around **TAYINLOAN**, ranging from the big *Point Sands Caravan Park* (Ⓣ01583/441263; April–Oct), two miles to the north, set back a long way from the main road near a long stretch of sandy beach, or the smaller, more informal *Muasdale Holiday Park*, three miles to the south (Ⓣ01583/421207; April–Oct), squeezed between the main road and the beach. **Accommodation** along the coast includes the *Balinakill Country House* (Ⓣ01880/740206, Ⓦwww.balinakill.com; ❸), a capacious late-Victorian hotel with lots of period touches, set in its own grounds near Clachan north of Tayinloan; the kitchen produces decent bar food until 7pm, and much more expensive à la carte after that. Further south at Bellochantuy, the *Argyll Hotel* (Ⓣ01583/421212, Ⓦwww.argyllhotel.co.uk; ❸) is a welcoming roadside pub serving pub food in its conservatory or on outside tables overlooking the sand and sea – you can also camp next door. Another **food** option along the coast is *North Beachmore*, signposted off the A83, just south of Tayinloan, a restaurant boasting panoramic views out to Gigha, and serving straightforward snacks, lunches and evening meals (reservations advisable at the weekend; Ⓣ01583/421328).

Two-thirds of the way down the coast you can visit **Glenbarr Abbey** (Easter–Oct daily except Tues 10am–5.30pm; £2.50), an eighteenth-century laird's house filled with tedious memorabilia about the once-powerful MacAlister clan, who now augment their income by giving personal guided tours of their house to the trickle of tourists that pass this way. There are plenty of musty old sofas to lounge around in, a tearoom, and attractive grounds which can provide a brief respite from the Atlantic winds. If you're up for a spot of **horse riding**, get in touch with the nearby Barrglen Equitation Centre, based at Arnicle Farm (Ⓣ01583/421397), which offers lessons and longer rides for "the good, the bad and the wobbly".

The only major development along the entire west coast is **MACHRIHANISH**, at the southern end of Machrihanish Bay, the longest continuous stretch of sand in Argyll. There are two approaches to the **beach**: from Machrihanish itself, or from Westport, at the north end of the bay, where the A83 swings east towards Campbeltown; either way, the sea here is too dangerous for swimming. Machrihanish itself was once a thriving salt-producing and coal-mining centre – you can still see the miners' cottages at neighbouring Drumlemble – but now survives solely on tourism. The main draw, apart from the beach, is the exposed championship **golf links** between the beach and Campbeltown airport on the nearby flat and fertile swath of land known as the Laggan. There's also a tiny **seabird observatory** at Uisaed Point, ten minutes' walk west of the village, though it's best visited in the migration periods, when it provides a welcome shelter for ornithologists trying to spot a rare bird blown off course.

Several of the imposing, detached Victorian town houses overlooking the bay in Machrihanish, such as *Ardell House* (Ⓣ01586/810235; ❺; March–Oct), offer **accommodation**; there's also a large, fully equipped and very exposed **campsite** (Ⓣ01586/810366; March–Sept) overlooking the golf links. For **nightlife**, *The Beachcomber* bar is the liveliest place in Machrihanish.

Campbeltown

CAMPBELTOWN's best feature is its setting, in a deep bay sheltered by Davaar Island and the surrounding hills. With a population of 6500, it is also one of the largest towns in Argyll and, if you're staying in the southern half of Kintyre, its shops are by far the best place to stock up on supplies. Originally known as Kinlochkilkerran (*Ceann Loch Cill Chiaran*), the town was renamed in the seventeenth century by the Earl of Argyll – a Campbell – when it became one of the main points for immigration from the Lowlands. As is evident from the architecture, Campbeltown's heyday was the Victorian era, when shipbuilding was going strong, coal was shipped by canal from Drumlemble, the fishing fleet was vast and Campbeltown Loch was said to be made of whisky. The decline of all its old industries has left the town permanently depressed, and unemployment and under-employment remain a persistent problem.

The Town

Nineteenth-century visitors to Campbeltown frequently found the place engulfed in a thick fog of pungent peat smoke from the town's 34 **whisky distilleries**. Today, only Glen Scotia and Springbank are left to maintain this regional subgroup of single malt whiskies (see p.34 for more on whisky), but you can buy a guide to Campbeltown's former distilleries from the tourist office. The deeply traditional, family-owned **Springbank**, off Longrow, is the only distillery in Scotland that does absolutely everything from malting to bottling, on its own premises. There are regular no-nonsense guided tours but it's best to phone ahead just to check (Easter–Sept Mon–Thurs 2pm; ⓣ01586/552085; £3). At the end, you get a voucher to exchange for a miniature at Eaglesomes, on Longrow South, whose range of whiskies is awesome.

The town's one major sight is the **Campbeltown Cross**, a fourteenth-century blue-green cross with figural scenes and spirals of Celtic knotting, which presides over the main roundabout on the quayside. Until the last war, it used to be rather more impressive in the middle of the main street outside the **Town Hall**, with its distinctive eighteenth-century octagonal clocktower. Back on the palm-tree-dotted waterfront is the "**Wee Picture House**", a dinky little Art Deco cinema on Hall Street, built in 1913 and still going strong (daily except Fri). Next door is the equally delightful **Campbeltown Museum and Library** (Tues–Sat 10am–1pm & 2–5pm, Tues & Thurs 5.30–7.30pm; free), built in 1897 in the local sandstone, crowned by a distinctive lantern, and decorated on its harbourside wall with four relief panels depicting each of the town's main industries at the time. Inside, there's a timber-framed ceiling and etched glass partitions to admire, not to mention a rather unusual brass model of the Temple of Solomon (as it might have looked). The museum itself, which you enter through the library, provides a less remarkable rundown on local history; for a more enlightening version, head to the Heritage Centre (described below).

It used to be said that Campbeltown had almost as many churches as it did distilleries, and even today the townscape is dominated by its church spires – in particular, the top-heavy crown spire of **Longrow Church**, on the road to Machrihanish. The former Lorne Street Church, known locally as the "Tartan Kirk", partly due to its Gaelic associations and partly due to its stripy bell-cote and pinnacles, has now become the **Campbeltown Heritage Centre** (April–Oct Mon–Sat 11am–5pm, Sun 2–5pm; £2). A beautiful wooden skiff from 1906 stands where the main altar once was, and there's plenty on the local whisky industry and St Kieran, the sixth-century "Apostle of Kintyre", who lived in a cave – which you can get to at low tide – not far from Campbeltown. A dedicated ascetic, he would only eat bread made of one-third sand and a few herbs; he wore chains, had a stone pillow and slept out in the snow – unsurprisingly, at the age of 33, he died of jaundice.

One of the most popular day-trips is to **Davaar Island**, linked to the peninsula at low tide by a mile-long shoal, or *dóirlinn* as it's known in Gaelic. Check the times of the tides from the tourist office before setting out; you have around six hours in which to make the return journey from Kildalloig Point, two miles or so east of town. Davaar is uninhabited and used for grazing (hence no dogs are allowed); its main claim to fame is the cave painting of the crucifixion executed in secret by local artist Archibald MacKinnon, in 1887, and touched up by him after he'd owned up in 1934; a year later, aged 85, he died. The cave, on the south side of the island, is easy enough to find, but the story is better than the end product, and you're better off walking up to the island's high point (378ft) and enjoying the view.

Practicalities

Campbeltown's **tourist office** is currently on the Old Quay (April Mon–Sat 10am–5pm; May & June Mon–Sat 9am–5pm, Sun noon–5pm; July & Aug Mon–Sat 9am–6pm, Sun 11am–5pm; Sept & Oct Mon–Fri 10am–5pm, Sun 10am–4pm; Nov–March Mon–Fri 9am–4pm; ⓣ01586/552056), and will happily hand out a free map of the town. The **airport** (ⓣ01586/552571) lies three miles west, towards Machrihanish (there's a bus connection); it's hoped that the **ferry** connection with Ballycastle will be resumed in the near future.

The best centrally located **accommodation** is the delightful family-run *Ardshiel Hotel*, on Kilkerran Road (ⓣ01586/552133; ❸), situated on a lovely leafy square, just a block or so back from the ferry terminal, with a cosy bar, and a more expensive à la carte restaurant. On the north side of the bay, *Craigard House* (ⓣ01586/554242, ⓦwww.craigard-house.co.uk; ❻), a former whisky distiller's sandstone mansion with a hint of the Italian Renaissance, is even more palatial and serves moderately expensive meals in its dining room overlooking the loch. Another excellent choice is the *Balegreggan Country House Hotel* (ⓣ01586/552062, ⓔbruce@belegreggan.fsnet.co.uk; ❹), a fine detached no-smoking Victorian villa, in the hills to the north of town, off the A83. For an inexpensive, central B&B, head for *Westbank Guest House*, on Dell Road (ⓣ01586/553660).

As for **places to eat**, the *Locarno Café* on Longrow South is a period-piece greasy spoon, one of many in Campbeltown. The best bar meals are to be found at the aforementioned *Ardshiel Hotel*, while the *Commercial Inn* on Cross Street is a good drinking hole. You can **rent bikes** at The Bike Shop, Longrow (ⓣ01586/554443). If you're here in the middle of August, be sure to check out the **Mull of Kintyre Music & Arts Festival**, which features some great traditional Irish and Scottish bands.

Southend and the Mull of Kintyre

The bulbous, hilly end of Kintyre, to the south of Campbeltown, features some of the most spectacular scenery on the whole peninsula, mixed with large swaths of Lowland-style farmland. **SOUTHEND** itself, a bleak, blustery spot, comes as something of a disappointment, though it does have a golden sandy beach. Below the cliffs to the west of the beach, a ruined thirteenth-century chapel marks the alleged arrival point of St Columba prior to his trip to Iona, and on a rocky knoll nearby a pair of footprints carved into the rock are known as **Columba's footprints**, though only one is actually of ancient origin. Jutting out into the sea at the east end of the bay is **Dunaverty Rock**, where a force of 300 Royalists was massacred by the Covenanting army of the Earl of Argyll in 1647, despite having surrendered voluntarily. A couple of miles out to sea from Dunaverty lies **Sanda Island**, which contains the remains of St Ninian's chapel, plus two ancient crosses, a holy well, an unusual lighthouse and lots of seabirds, including puffins; it's now a holiday retreat with self-catering cottages available (☎01586/553134; April–Sept). Back on the mainland, there are even nicer beaches further west at Carskiey Bay, and at Macharioch Bay, three miles east, looking out to distant Ailsa Craig in the Firth of Clyde.

Most people venture south of Campbeltown to make a pilgrimage to the **Mull of Kintyre** – the nearest Britain gets to Ireland, whose coastline, just twelve miles away, appears remarkably close on fine days. Although the Mull was made famous by the mawkish number-one hit by sometime local resident Paul McCartney, with the help of the Campbeltown Pipe Band, there's nothing specifically to see in this godforsaken storm-racked spot but the view. The roads up to the "**Gap**" (1150ft) – where you must leave your car – and particularly down to the lighthouse, itself 300ft above the ocean waves, are terrifyingly tortuous. It's about a mile from the "Gap" to the lighthouse (and a long haul back up), though there's a strategic viewpoint just ten minutes' walk from the car park; the principal lightkeeper's cottage, known as *Hector's House*, is now a remote **self-catering** option (phone the NTS; ☎0131/243 9331).

Southend still has a **pub**, the *Argyll Arms*, unremarkable except for the fact that it has a post office inside it. The only hotel has been closed for a long time now and cuts a forlorn figure, set back from the bay, but there are a couple of excellent **B&Bs**; *Ormsary Farm* (☎01586/830665; ❶; April–Sept), a small dairy farm up Glen Breakerie, and the nearby picturesque croft of *Low Cattadale* (☎01586/830205; ❶; March–Nov). **Camping** is possible right in the field right by the beach, run by *Machribeg Farm* (☎01586/830249; Easter–Sept). If you're interested in **horse riding**, call the Mull of Kintyre Equestrian Centre at Homeston Farm (☎01586/552437; April–Oct), signposted off the B842 to Southend.

The east coast

The **east coast** of Kintyre is gentler than the west, sheltered from the Atlantic winds and in parts strikingly beautiful, with stunning views across to Arran. However, be warned that bus services are very limited up the east coast and, if you're driving the thirty or so miles up to Skipness on the slow, winding, single-track B842, you'll need a fair amount of time.

The ruins of **Saddell Abbey**, a Cistercian foundation thought to have been founded by Somerled in 1160, lie ten miles up the coast from Campbeltown, set at the lush, wooded entrance to Saddell Glen. The abbey fell into disrepair in the sixteenth century, and, though the remains are not exactly impressive, they do shelter a collection of medieval grave slabs decorated with full-scale relief figures of knights. Standing by the privately owned shoreline there's a splendid memorial to the last Campbell laird to live at Saddell Castle, which he built in 1774.

Further north lies the fishing village of **CARRADALE**, the only place of any size on the east coast and "popular with those who like unsophisticated resorts", as one 1930s guide put it. The village itself is rather drab, but the tiny, very pretty harbour with its small fishing fleet, and the wide, sandy beach to the south, make up for it. On the east side of the beach is **Carradale Point**, a wildlife reserve with feral goats and a good example of a **vitrified fort** built more than two thousand years ago on a small tidal island off the headland (best approached from the beach). There are several pleasant walks with good views across to Arran laid out in the woods around Carradale, for which the best starting point is the car park at Port na Storm on the road into the village. The best wet-weather option is **Network Carradale Heritage Centre** on the outskirts of the village (Easter to mid-Oct Mon–Sat 10am–5pm, Sun 12.30–5pm; £1), which traces the demise of the local herring fleet; it's small in scale but informative, and there's good home baking to be had in the tearoom.

Accommodation is available at the *Carradale Hotel* (Ⓣ01583/431223, Ⓔcarradaleh@aol.com; ❸), whose bar is the hub of village social life (and whose food is good). There are several **B&Bs**, the best of which is the big Victorian *Dunvalanree Guest House* (Ⓣ01583/431226, Ⓦwww.dunvalanree.com; ❷), overlooking the sheltered little bay of Port Righ, towards Carradale Point. There's also a well-equipped *Carradale Bay Caravan Park* **campsite** (Ⓣ01583/431665, Ⓔenquiries@carradalebay.abelgratis.com; Easter–Sept), right by the sandy beach. Carradale also boasts a real baker – try the treacle scones or cookie pudding (bread and butter pudding south of the border). Close by, a little to the south, above a seal-strewn soft shingle beach, the imposing Victorian pile, *Torrisdale Castle*, offers **self-catering** in castle or cottage (Ⓣ01583/431233, Ⓦwww.torrisdale.co.uk).

Five miles further up the coast road is **Grogport Tannery** (daily 9am–6pm; free), which produces naturally coloured, organically tanned, fully washable sheepskins (gloves and slippers, too). The B842 ends seven miles north of Grogport at **CLAONAIG**, little more than a slipway for the small summer car ferry to Arran. Beyond here, a dead-end road winds its way along the shore a few miles further north to the tiny village of **SKIPNESS**, where the considerable ruins of the enormous thirteenth-century **Skipness Castle** and a chapel look out across the Kilbrannan Sound to Arran. You can sit outside and admire both, whilst enjoying fresh oysters, delicious queenies, mussels and home-baked cakes from the excellent **seafood cabin** (late May to Sept) at the Victorian *Skipness Castle*, which also offers **accommodation** in a family home (Ⓣ01880/760207, Ⓔsophie@skipness.freeserve.co.uk; ❺). There are several gentle walks laid out in the nearby mixed woodland, up the nearby glen.

The Isle of Arran

Shaped like a kidney bean, **Arran** (Ⓦwww.arran.net) is the most southerly (and therefore the most accessible) of all the Scottish islands. The Highland–Lowland dividing line passes right through its centre – hence the tourist board's aphorism about it being like "Scotland in miniature" – leaving the northern half sparsely populated, mountainous and bleak, while the lush southern half enjoys a much milder climate. Despite its immense popularity, the tourists, like the population of around 4500 – many of whom are incomers – tend to stick to the southeastern quarter of the island, leaving the west and the north relatively undisturbed.

There are two big crowd-pullers on Arran: geology and golf. The former has fascinated rock-obsessed students since Sir James Hutton came here in the late eighteenth century to confirm his theories of igneous geology. A hundred years later, Sir Archibald Geikie's investigations were a landmark in the study of Arran's geology, and the island remains a popular destination for university and

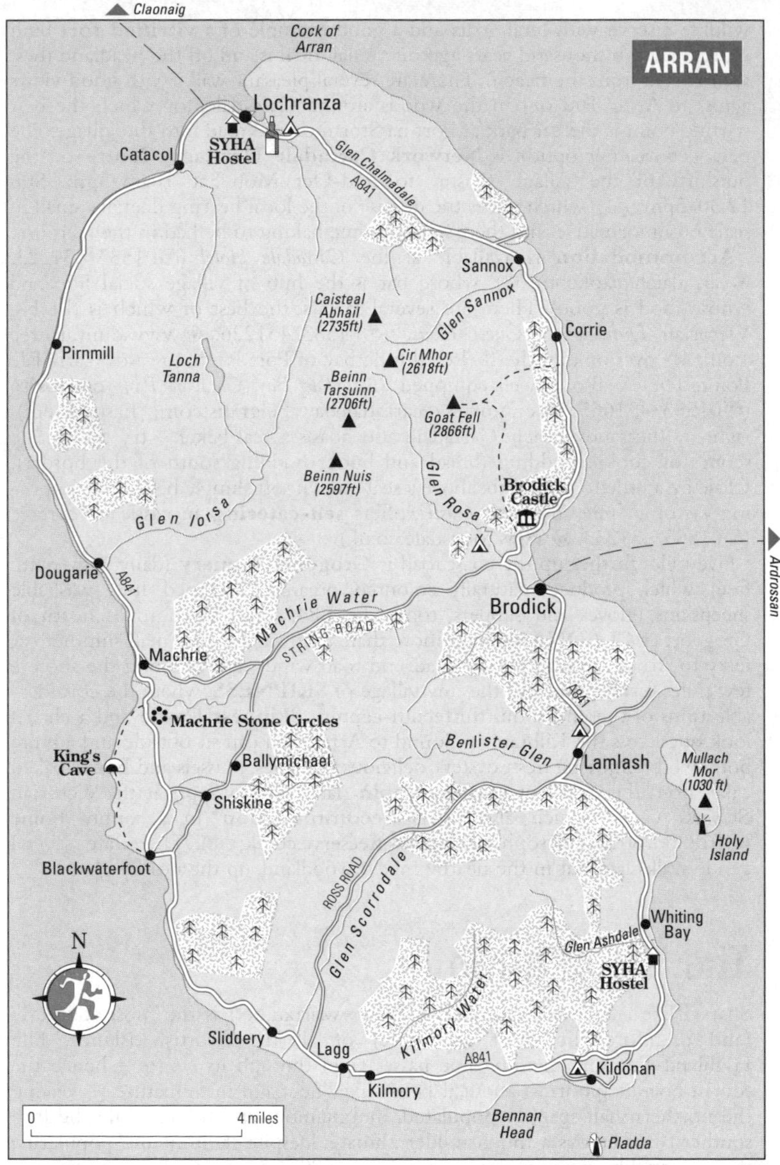

school field trips. As for golf, Arran boasts seven courses, including three of the eighteen-hole variety at Brodick, Lamlash and Whiting Bay, and a unique twelve-hole course at Shiskine, near Blackwaterfoot.

Although tourism is now by far its most important industry, Arran, at twenty miles in length, is large enough to have a life of its own. While the island's post-1745 history and the Clearances (set in motion by the local lairds, the dukes of Hamilton) are as depressing as elsewhere in the Highlands, in recent years Arran has not suffered from the depopulation which has plagued other, more remote islands. Once a county in its own right (along with Bute), Arran has been left out of the new Argyll and Bute district in the latest county boundary shake-up, and is coupled instead with mainland North Ayrshire, with which it enjoys year-round transport links, but little else.

Transport on Arran itself is pretty good: daily **buses** circle the island (Brodick tourist office has timetables) and link in with the two **ferry services**: a year-round one from Ardrossan in Ayrshire to **Brodick**, and a smaller ferry from Claonaig on the Kintyre peninsula to **Lochranza** in the north (April to mid-Oct).

Brodick

Although the resort of **BRODICK** (from the Norse *breidr vik*, "broad bay") is a place of only moderate charm, it does at least have a grand setting in a wide, sandy bay set against a backdrop of granite mountains. Its development as a tourist resort was held back for a long time by its elitist owners, the dukes of Hamilton, though nowadays, as the island's capital and main communication hub, Brodick is by far the busiest town on Arran.

Brodick's shops and guesthouses are clustered along the south side of the bay, along with the tourist office and the CalMac pier. However, Brodick's tourist sights, such as they are, are clustered on the west and north side of the bay, a couple of miles from the ferry terminal. First off, on the road to the castle, there's the **Arran Heritage Museum** (April–Oct daily 10.30am–4.30pm; £2.25), housed in a whitewashed eighteenth-century crofter's farm, and containing an old smiddy, a Victorian cottage with box bed and range. In the old stables there are lots of agricultural bits and bobs, plus material on Arran's wartime role, its intriguing geology, and a Neolithic skull found on the island. Other wet-weather options in the Arran Visitor Centre in neighbouring **Home Farm**, include the Island Cheese Company, where you can see the soft, round crotins of goat's cheese being made and taste Brodick and Glenshant blues; Arran Aromatics (Ⓦ www.arran-aromatics.co.uk) lets you try your hand at natural-soapmaking and *Creelers* smokehouse offers succulent seafood. Round the corner in Cladach, right by the castle, you can also visit the new Arran Brewery (Ⓦ www.arranbrewery.com), buy some of their award-winning beers, and eat outside at the nearby *Wineport*.

Brodick Castle

Even if you're not based in Brodick, it's worth coming here in order to visit **Brodick Castle** (daily: April–June, Sept & Oct 11am–4.30pm; July & Aug 11am–5pm; £6; NTS), former seat of the dukes of Hamilton on a steep bank on the north side of the bay. Just before the entrance, there's a little sandstone jetty where the duke's wine and ice from Canada was landed. It used to serve the village, but the eleventh duke thought the tenants unsightly and had them moved out of sight round the bay. He also closed the barytes mine at Sannox, a vital source of employment for the islanders, on the grounds that it "spoilt the solemn grandeur of the scene".

The bulk of the castle was built in the nineteenth century, giving it a domestic rather than military look, and the **interior** – once you've fought your way past the 87 stags' heads on the stairs – is comfortable but undistinguished. Don't miss the portrait of the eleventh duke's faithful piper, who injured his throat on a grouse bone, was warned never to pipe again, but did so and died. Probably the most atmospheric room is the copper-filled Victorian kitchen, which conjures up a vision of the sweated and sweating labour required to feed the folk upstairs.

Much more attractive, however, are the walled **gardens** (daily 9.30am–dusk; gardens and country park only £2.50) and extensive grounds, a treasury of exotic plants and trees enjoying the favourable climate (including one of Europe's finest collections of rhododendrons), and commanding a superb view across the bay. There is an adventure playground for kids, but the whole area is a natural playground with waterfalls, a giant pitcher plant that swallows thousands of midges daily, and a maze of paths. Buried in the grounds there is a bizarre Bavarian-style **summerhouse** lined entirely with pine cones, one of three built by the eleventh duke to make his wife, Princess Marie of Baden, feel at home. For the energetic there is also a **country park** with eleven miles of scenic trails, starting from a small informative, hands-on nature centre. In summer there are guided walks with the rangers, but at any time you can be surprised by red squirrels, nightjars and the abundance of fungi. The excellent castle **tearoom** serves traditional food with a local flavour and is highly recommended.

Practicalities

Brodick's **tourist office** (May–Sept Mon–Sat 9am–7.30pm, Sun 10am–5pm; Oct–April Mon–Sat 9am–5pm; ⓣ01770/302401) is by the CalMac pier, and has reams of information on every activity from pony trekking to paragliding. Unless you've got to catch an early-morning ferry, however, there's little reason to stay in Brodick, though there's a decent choice should you need to. The best **rooms** close to the ferry terminal are at the excellent *Dunvegan House Hotel* (ⓣ01770/302811; ❹), the Art Deco *Invercloy Hotel* (ⓣ01770/302225, ⓔinvercloyhotel@sol.co.uk; ❹; March–Oct) or *Carrick Lodge* (ⓣ01770/302550; ❷), a sandstone manse, south of the pier on the Lamlash road. Closer to the castle is the peaceful sandstone farmhouse of *Glen Cloy* (ⓣ01770/302351, ⓔmvpglencloy@compuserve.com; ❷), which has real fires and a warm welcome. For those in search of leisure facilities, the *Auchrannie Country House Hotel* (ⓣ01770/302234, ⓦwww.auchrannie.co.uk; ❹), former home of the dowager Duchess of Hamilton, has the lot, including a huge indoor pool, sauna, steam room and gym, all of which are open to non-residents, too. Offering nothing so vulgar as a swimming pool is the tasteful *Kilmichael Country House Hotel* (ⓣ01770/302219, ⓦwww.kilmichael.com; ❼), originally built in the seventeenth century and still retaining lots of period features; dinner here is very expensive and very formal, but it's one of the best you'll get on the island. The nearest **campsite** is *Glenrosa* (ⓣ01770/302380), a lovely, but very basic, farm site (cold water only and no showers), two miles from town off the B880 to Blackwaterfoot.

For **food**, apart from dinner at the aforementioned *Kilmichael*, the only place that really stands out is the moderately expensive seafood restaurant *Creelers* (ⓣ01770/302810; mid-March to Oct), by the museum on the road to the castle. The *Wineport*, near the castle, does above-average bar meals, offering panini, pizzas and more substantial fare from the bar-bistro and the moderately expensive restaurant. Nearer to the ferry terminal, the bar snacks (lunch time only) at *Duncan's Bar* in the *Kingsley Hotel* make a cheaper option and there's real ale too; while the *Douglas Hotel* features regular **live music** sessions on Sundays. If you want to find out about any other events taking place on Arran, pick up a copy of the island's **weekly newspaper**, the *Arran Banner*.

The south

The **southern half of Arran** is less spectacular, and less forbidding than the north; it's more heavily forested and the land is more fertile, and for that reason the vast majority of the population lives here. The tourist industry has followed them, though with considerably less justification.

Lamlash, Holy Island and Whiting Bay

With its distinctive Edwardian architecture and mild climate, **LAMLASH** epitomizes the sedate charm of southeast Arran. Lamlash Bay has in its time sheltered King Haakon's fleet in 1263 before the Battle of Largs and, more recently, served as a naval base in both world wars. Its major drawback for the visitor, however, is that it is made not of sand but of boulder-strewn mud flats. The monument on the village green marks the spot on which a farewell sermon was given to the eleven families, victims of the Clearances, who, in 1829, sailed from here to Canada.

The best reason for coming to Lamlash is to visit the slug-shaped hump of **Holy Island**, which shelters the bay, and is now owned by a group of Tibetan Buddhists who have set up a meditation centre – providing you don't dawdle, it's possible to scramble up to the top of Mullach Mór (1030ft), the island's highest point, and still catch the last ferry back. En route, you might well bump into the island's most numerous residents: feral goats, Highland cattle and rabbits. The Holy Island ferry runs more or less hourly (ⓣ01770/600998; £8 return); alternatively, you might prefer to go **mackerel fishing** – booking essential, from the Lamlash Boat Hire on the pier (ⓣ01770/600349).

If you want to **stay** in style in Lamlash, head for the comfortable *Lilybank* (ⓣ01770/600230, ⓦwww.smoothhound.co.uk/hotels/lilybank; ❸), which does good home-made food. You can **camp** at the fully equipped *Middleton Camping Park* (ⓣ01770/600255; April–Oct), just five minutes' walk south of the centre. Food options in Lamlash are limited to the **bar meals** at the *Pier Head Tavern*, or at the friendly *Drift Inn* by the shore; there's even a Chinese takeaway behind the post office. On the subject of eating, it was a Lamlash man, Donald McKelvie, who made Arran potatoes world-famous, breeding in the rich soil of the island, Arran Pilot, Arran Chief and Arran Victory, of which Maris Piper is a modern descendant.

An established Clydeside resort for over a century now, **WHITING BAY**, four miles south of Lamlash, is spread out along a very pleasant bay, though it doesn't have quite the distinctive architecture of Lamlash. It's a good base for walking, with the gentle hike up to the **Glenashdale Falls** probably the most popular excursion; the waterfall can be reached via a pretty woodland walk that sets off from beside the SYHA hostel (2hr return). Whiting Bay also has some excellent **places to stay**, including the *Royal* (ⓣ01770/700286, ⓦwww.royalarran.co.uk; March–Oct; ❸), the *Argentine House Hotel*, run (confusingly) by a multilingual Swiss couple (ⓣ01770/700662, ⓦwww.argentinearran.co.uk; closed Feb; ❷), both on Shore Road, and the beautiful, whitewashed *Swan's Guest House* (ⓣ01770/700729, ⓦwww.rowallanbb.co.uk; ❷; Feb–Nov), up the hill on School Road. Whiting Bay also boasts an SYHA **hostel** (ⓣ01770/700339, ⓦwww.syha.org.uk; March–Oct), at the southern end of the bay. The **food** is good at the *Burlington Hotel* on Shore Road, and at the *Argentine House Hotel*, though the latter's more expensive. Otherwise, you're limited to the snacks at the *Coffee Pot* on the seafront, or the eclectic menu at the *Pantry* (closed Sun) opposite the post office. For **bike rental**, go to the jetty.

Kildonan to Lagg

Access to the sea is tricky along the south coast, but worth the effort, as the sandy beaches here are among the island's finest. One place you can get down to the sea is at **KILDONAN**, an attractive small village south of Lamlash, set slightly off the main road, with a good sandy beach, which you share with the local wildlife, and views out to the tiny flat island of Pladda, with its distinctive lighthouse, and, in the distance, the great hump of Ailsa Craig (see p.223). Those with kids might like to drop in at the nearby **South Bank Farm Park** (April–Oct daily 10am–5pm; £2), to see rare breeds and the occasional sheep-dog demonstration (phone for details ⓣ01770/820221). There are two good places to camp in Kildonan: either at the **campsite** beside the *Breadalbane Hotel* (ⓣ01770/820284), or right on the shore beside the *Kildonan Hotel* (ⓣ01770/820320).

KILMORY, four miles west of Kildonan, is the home of the prizewinning **Torrylinn Creamery** (daily 10am–4pm), which produces a cheddary cheese called Arran Dunlop, and where you can watch the whole process from a viewing window. Next door to Kilmory is the picturesque village of **LAGG**, nestling in a tree-filled hollow by Kilmory Water. The friendly village stores has an excellent **tearoom**; those feeling flush should **stay** at the comfortable *Lagg Inn* (ⓣ01770/870255, ⓦwww.arran.uk.com/lagg; ❸), an eighteenth-century inn beside the main road, with plenty of woodland out the back. Scotland's only naturist beach is half a mile west of Lagg, down a rough track at Cleat shore.

Blackwaterfoot and Machrie

BLACKWATERFOOT, on the western end of the String Road, which bisects the island, is dominated, not to say somewhat spoilt, by the presence of the island's largest hotel, the *Kinloch Hotel*. In every other way, Blackwaterfoot is a beguiling little place, which boasts the only twelve-hole golf course in the world. A gentle two-mile walk north along the coast will bring you to the **King's Cave**, one of several where Robert the Bruce is said to have encountered the famously patient arachnid, while hiding during his final bid to free Scotland in 1306. If you want **to stay**, the diminutive Victorian *Blackwaterfoot Hotel* (ⓣ01770/860202; ❺; closed Feb) is a good place to hole up, though there's an even better B&B, *Lochside Guest House* (ⓣ01770/860276; ❷), just half a mile south along the main road, set beside its very own trout loch.

North of Blackwaterfoot, the wide expanse of **Machrie Moor** boasts a wealth of Bronze Age sites. No fewer than six **stone circles** sit east of the main road, and, although many of them barely break the peat's surface, the tallest surviving monolith is over eighteen feet high. The most striking configuration is at Fingal's Cauldron Seat, with two concentric circles of granite boulders; legend has it that Fingal tied his dog to one of them while cooking at his cauldron. If you're feeling peckish, the Machrie golf course **tearoom** (April to mid-Oct) is a welcome oasis in this sparsely populated area.

The north

The desolate **north half of Arran** – effectively the Highland part – features bare granite peaks, the occasional golden eagle and miles of unspoilt scenery, within reach only to those prepared to do some serious hiking. Arran's most accessible peak is also the island's highest, **Goat Fell** (2866ft) – take your pick from the Gaelic, *goath*, meaning "windy", or the Norse, *geit-fjall*, "goat mountain" – which can be ascended in just three hours from Brodick or from Corrie (return journey 5hr), though it's a strenuous hike (for the usual safety precautions, see p.46).

Corrie and Sannox

Another good base for hiking is the pretty little seaside village of **CORRIE**, six miles north of Brodick, where a procession of pristine cottages lines the road to Lochranza and wraps itself around an exquisite little harbour and pier. The top choice for **accommodation** is *Blackrock* (ⓣ01770/810282, ⓦwww.arran.net/corrie/blackrock; ❷), a large, traditional seafront guesthouse on the edge of the village. A good budget option is the *North High Corrie Croft*, a **bunkhouse** (ⓣ01770/302203), ten minutes' steep climb above the village on a raised beach; it has one large room for group bookings, and an annexe with eight beds (advance booking advisable). Corrie Golf Club, confusingly in Sannox, offers good-value **meals** all day in summer.

At **SANNOX**, two miles north, the road leaves the shoreline and climbs steeply, giving breathtaking views over to the scree-strewn slopes around Caisteal Abhail (2735ft). If you make this journey around dusk, be sure to pause in **Glen Chalmadale**, on the other northern side of the pass, to catch a glimpse of the red deer that come down to pasture by the water. Another possibility is to turn off to North Sannox, where you can park and walk along the shore to the **Fallen Rocks**, a major rock-fall of Devonian sandstone.

Lochranza

On fair Lochranza streamed the early day,
Thin wreaths of cottage smoke are upward curl'd
From the lone hamlet, which her inland bay
And circling mountains sever from the world.

The Lord of the Isles by Sir Walter Scott

The ruined castle which occupies the mud flats of the bay, and the brooding north-facing slopes of the mountains which frame it, make for one of the most spectacular settings on the island – yet **LOCHRANZA**, despite being the only place of any size in this sparsely populated area, attracts far fewer visitors than Arran's southern resorts. The castle is worth a brief look inside (get the key from the post office), but Lochranza's main sight now is the island's brand new whisky **distillery** (April–Oct daily 10am–5pm; Nov–March phone ⓣ01770/830264, ⓦwww.arranwhisky.com; £3.50), a pristine complex distinguished by its pagoda-style roofs at the south end of the village. The tours are entertaining and slick, and end with a free sample of the island's newly emerging single malt.

The finest **accommodation** is to be had at the superb *Apple Lodge* (ⓣ01770/830229, ⓔapplelodge@easicom.com; ❹), the old village manse where you'll get excellent home cooking, or at *Butt Lodge* (ⓣ01770/830240, ⓦwww.buttlodge.co.uk; ❹; March–Oct), another hotel with character (and real log fires). Cheaper than the above two, but equally welcoming, is the *Lochranza Hotel* (ⓣ01770/830223, ⓦwww.lochranza.co.uk; ❷), whose bar is the centre of the local social scene. Lochranza also has an SYHA **hostel** (ⓣ01770/830631, ⓦwww.syha.org.uk; closed Jan), situated halfway between the distillery and the castle, and a well-equipped **campsite** (ⓣ01770/830273, ⓦwww.arran.net/lochranza; April-Oct) beautifully placed by the golf course on the Brodick Road, where deer come to graze in the early evening.

The best place to eat is the inexpensive but excellent *Harold's* **restaurant**, a state-of-the-art place in the distillery (ⓣ01770/830264; closed Mon eve). If you're just passing through, you can also get decent food at the *Pier Tearoom*, situated opposite the CalMac terminal, which doubles as a licensed restaurant, with good views across to Kintyre.

Catacol and Pirnmill

An alternative to staying or drinking in Lochranza is to continue a mile or so southwest along the coast to **CATACOL**, and stay or drink at the friendly *Catacol Bay Hotel* (ⓣ01770/830231, ⓦwww.catacol.co.uk; ❷). It takes the prize as the island's best pub by far, serving good, basic food (with several veggie options) and great beer on tap (including Arran's own brew); there's a small adjoining **campsite**, and seals and shags to view on the nearby shingle. The pub also puts on live music most weeks, and hosts a week-long **folk festival** in early June.

Just past the pub there is a row of striking black-and-white cottages, known as the **Twelve Apostles**, built by the eleventh Duke of Hamilton, and intended to house tenants displaced to make way, not for sheep, but for deer (thanks to Queen Victoria's passion for stalking them), though no one could be persuaded to live in them for two years. You can stay close by at *Fairhaven Guest House* (ⓣ01770/830237; ❷; March–Oct), a **B&B** with a homely air at the start of the path up Glen Catacol.

From here to the String Road it's very bleak, but ideal for spotting wildlife, on hillside and at sea. The next village of any size is neat and tidy **PIRNMILL**, so called because they used to make "pirns" or bobbins for the mills of Paisley here (until they ran out of trees). In summer you can get a snack in the *Anvil Tearoom*.

The Isle of Islay

The fertile, largely treeless island of **ISLAY** (pronounced "eye-la") is famous for one thing – single malt **whisky**. The smoky, peaty, pungent quality of Islay whisky is unique, recognizable even to the untutored palate, and all seven of the island's distilleries will happily take visitors on a guided tour, ending with the customary complimentary tipple. Yet, despite the fame of its whiskies, Islay remains relatively undiscovered, much as Skye and Mull were some twenty years ago. Part of the reason may be the expense of the two-hour ferry journey from Kennacraig on Kintyre, or perhaps the relative paucity of luxury hotels or fancy restaurants. If you do make the effort, however, you'll be rewarded with a genuinely friendly welcome from islanders proud of their history, landscape and Gaelic culture.

In medieval times, Islay was the political centre of the Hebrides, with **Finlaggan**, near Port Askaig, the seat of the MacDonalds, Lords of the Isles. The picturesque, whitewashed villages you see on Islay today, however, date from the planned settlements founded by the Campbells in the late eighteenth and early nineteenth centuries. Apart from whisky and solitude, the other great draw is the **birdlife** – there's a real possibility of spotting a golden eagle, or the rare crow-like chough, and no possibility at all of missing the scores of white-fronted and barnacle geese who winter here in their thousands. A good time to visit is in late May/early June, when the **Islay Festival** (*Feis Ile*; ⓦwww.ileach.co.uk/festival), takes place, with whisky tasting, piping recitals, folk dancing and other events celebrating the island's Gaelic roots.

Public transport, in the form of buses and postbuses, will get you from one end of the island to the other, but it's as well to know that there is one solitary bus on a Sunday; pick up an island transport guide from the Islay tourist office in **Bowmore**. The **airport**, which lies between Port Ellen and Bowmore, has regular flights to and from Glasgow, and the local bus or postbus will get you to either of the above villages. For a local point of view and news of up-coming

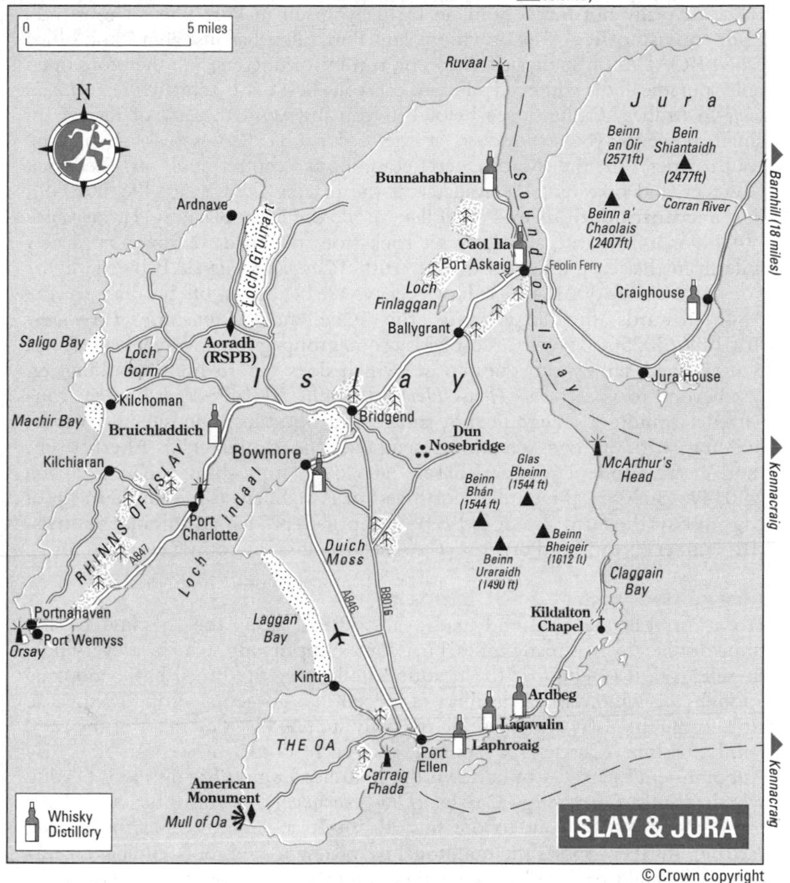

events, pick up a copy of the fortnightly *Ileach* or visit their website (Ⓦwww.ileach.co.uk). The island itself also has its own website at Ⓦwww.isle-of-islay.com.

Port Ellen and around

Laid out as a planned village in 1821 by Walter Frederick Campbell, and named after his wife, **PORT ELLEN** is the chief port on Islay, with the island's largest fishing fleet, and main CalMac ferry terminal. The neat whitewashed terraces of Frederick Crescent, which overlook the town's bay of golden sand, are pretty enough, but the strand to the north, up Charlotte Street, is dominated by the modern maltings, on the Bowmore road, whose powerful odours waft across the town. Arriving at Port Ellen by boat, it's impossible to miss the unusual, square-shaped **Carraig Fhada lighthouse**, at the western entrance to the bay, erected in 1832, in memory of Walter Frederick Campbell's aforementioned wife. Just beyond the lighthouse is the prettiest bay on the island's south coast, Traigh Bhán, or the "**Singing Sands**", a perfect sandy beach, peppered with jagged rocky extrusions.

There's really not much point in basing yourself in Port Ellen. The island's main **tourist office** is in Bowmore, and Port Ellen has just an ad hoc office called KOADA, on Frederick Crescent, run by volunteers, and therefore open only sporadically. If you need a bite to eat, your best bet is actually the *Old Kiln Café* in Ardbeg distillery (see below). If you just want to send or receive an email, however, you can do so at the *Cyber Café* (Ⓦwww.islay-jura.com/youth/cyber) in the MacTaggert community centre, just off Frederick Crescent, and bike rental is available at the playing fields (Ⓣ01496/302349). For **accommodation** in Port Ellen itself, the best place is *Tighcargaman* (Ⓣ01496/302345; ❶), a pottery set back from the road to Bowmore, half a mile from the ferry, followed by the artistic *Carraig Fhada* B&B by the lighthouse (Ⓣ01496/302114; ❶). However, you'd be better off heading up the A846 towards the airport, to the excellent *Glenmachrie Farmhouse* (Ⓣ01496/302560, Ⓦwww.isle-of-islay.com/group/guest/glenmachrie; ❹), a whitewashed, family-run guesthouse, which does superb home cooking, or, just beyond to *Glenegedale House Hotel* (Ⓣ01496/302147; ❸), a homely converted farmhouse, gallery, florists, garage and opticians, opposite the airport building, with its own tearoom-restaurant, *The Heather Hen*. Alternatively, there's an independent **hostel** at the stone-built *Kintra Farm* (Ⓣ01496/302051), three miles northwest of Port Ellen, at the southern tip of Laggan Bay; the farm also does B&B (❶; April–Sept), has an adjoining **campsite**, and serves food and drink at *The Granary* (late May to Aug evenings only).

Along the coast to Kildalton

From Port Ellen, a dead-end road heads off east along the coastline, passing three distilleries in as many miles. First comes **Laphroaig**, which, as every bottle tells you, is Gaelic for "the beautiful hollow by the broad bay", and, true enough, the whitewashed distillery is indeed in a gorgeous setting by the sea. It's also the first Islay whisky to be officially supplied to a member of the royal family (Prince Charles, of course) and each bottle now bears the "By Appointment" stamp. A mile down the road lies **Lagavulin** distillery, beyond which stands **Dunyvaig Castle** (*Dún Naomhaig*), a romantic ruin on a promontory looking out to the tiny isle of Texa. Another mile further on, **Ardbeg** distillery sports the traditional pagoda-style kiln roofs, and has recently been brought back to life by Glenmorangie. In common with all Islay's distilleries, the above three offer guided tours (for more on which, see opposite).

There are a few **B&Bs** along the rapidly deteriorating road – *Tigh-na-Suil* (Ⓣ01496/302483; ❷) has a lovely secluded position. A mile beyond this, slightly off the road, the simple thirteenth-century **Kildalton Chapel** boasts a wonderful eighth-century Celtic ringed cross made from the local "bluestone", which is a rich blue-grey. The quality of the scenes matches any to be found on the crosses carved by the monks in Iona: the Virgin and Child are on the east face, with Cain murdering Abel to the left, David fighting the lion on the top, and Abraham sacrificing Isaac on the right; on the west side amidst the serpent-and-boss work are four elephant-like beasts.

The Oa

The most dramatic landscape on Islay is to be found in the nub of land to the southwest of Port Ellen known as **The Oa** (pronounced "o"), a windswept and inhospitable landscape, much loved by illicit whisky distillers and smugglers over the centuries. Halfway along road, a ruined church is visible to the south, testament to the area's once large population dispersed during the Clearances – several abandoned villages in the north of the peninsula, near Kintra. The

Islay whisky

Islay has only recently woken up to the fact that its **whisky** distilleries are a major tourist attraction. Nowadays, each distillery offers guided tours, traditionally ending with a generous dram, and a refund for your entrance fee if you buy a bottle in the shop – be warned, however, that a bottle of the stuff is no cheaper at source, so expect to pay over £20 for the privilege. Pick up the tourist board's "Islay and Jura Whisky Trail" leaflet, and phone ahead to make sure there's a tour running, as times do change frequently.

Ardbeg ⓣ01496/302244, ⓦwww.ardbeg.com. The ten-year-old Ardbeg is traditionally considered the saltiest, peatiest malt on Islay (and that's saying something). Bought by Glenmorangie in 1997, the distillery has been thoroughly overhauled and restored, yet it still has bags of character inside. The Old Kiln Café is excellent (Mon–Fri 10am–4pm; June-Aug daily 10am–5pm). Guided tours regularly 10.30am–3.30pm; £2.

Bowmore ⓣ01496/810441, ⓦwww.morrisonbowmore.com. Bowmore is probably the best place to head if this is your first distillery tour as it is by far the most central on Islay (with unrivalled disabled access). Bowmore is also one of the few distilleries still doing its own malting and kilning. The standard twelve-year-old Bowmore you get at the end is smooth, with just a hint of Islay peat. Guided tours: Easter–Sept Mon–Fri 10.30am, 11.30am, 2pm & 3pm, Sat 10.30am; Oct–Easter Mon–Fri 10.30am & 2pm; £2.

Bruichladdich ⓣ01496/850221. Bruichladdich only came back into production in 2001, and is the only independent distillery left on Islay. Regular guided tours have only just started again (Mon–Fri 10.30am, 11.30am & 2.30pm, Sat 10.30am & 2.30pm; £3), so it's best to phone ahead.

Bunnahabhainn ⓣ01496/840646. A visit to Bunnahabhainn (pronounced "bunna-have-in") is really only for whisky obsessives. The road from Port Askaig is windy, the whisky is the least characteristically Islay, and the distillery itself is only in production for a few months each year. Guided tours are by appointment (Mon–Fri only; free).

Caol Ila ⓣ01496/3027600. Caol Ila (pronounced "cul-eela"), just north of Port Askaig, is a modern distillery, the majority of whose lightly peaty malt goes into blended whiskies. No-frills guided tours are by appointment (Mon–Fri only; £3).

Lagavulin ⓣ01496/302400, ⓦwww.scotch.com. Lagavulin probably is the classic, all-round Islay malt, with lots of smoke and peat. The distillery enjoys a fabulous setting and is extremely busy all year round. Phone ahead for details of the guided tours (Mon–Fri only; £3), at the end of which you'll get a taste of the best-selling sixteen-year-old.

Laphroaig ⓣ01496/302418, ⓦwww.laphroaig.com. Another classic smokey, peaty Islay malt, and another great setting. One bonus at Laphroaig is that you get to see the malting and see and smell the peat kilns. There are regular guided tours (Mon–Fri 10.15am & 2.15pm; free), but phone ahead to make sure they are running.

chief target for most visitors to the Oa, however, is the gargantuan **American Monument**, built in the shape of a lighthouse on the clifftop above the Mull of Oa. It was erected by the American National Red Cross in memory of those who died in two naval disasters that took place in 1918. The first occurred when the troop transporter, SS *Tuscania*, carrying over 2000 American army personnel, was torpedoed by a German U-boat seven miles offshore in February 1918. As the lifeboats were being lowered, several ropes broke and threw the occupants into the sea, drowning 266 of those on board. The monument also commemorates those who drowned when the *Otranto* was shipwrecked off Kilchoman (see opposite) in October of the same year. The memorial is inscribed with the unusual sustained metaphor: "On Fame's eternal camping ground, their silent tents are spread, while glory keeps with solemn round, the bivouac of the dead." If you're driving, you can park in a car park, just before Upper Killeyan farm, and follow the duckboards across the soggy peat. En route, look out for choughs, golden eagles and other birds of prey, not to mention feral goats and, down on the shore, basking seals; for a longer walk, follow the coast round to or from Kintra (see above).

Bowmore

At the northern end of the seven-mile-long Laggan Bay, across the monotonous peat bog of Duich Moss, lies **BOWMORE**, Islay's administrative capital, with a population of around 800. It was founded in 1768 to replace the village of Kilarrow, which was deemed by the local laird to be too close to his own residence. It's a striking place, laid out in a grid plan rather like Inveraray, with the whitewashed terraces of Main Street climbing up the hill in a straight line from the pier on Loch Indaal to the town's crowning landmark, the **Round Church**, whose central tower looks uncannily like a lighthouse. Built in the round, so that the devil would have no corners in which to hide, it has a plain, wood-panelled interior, with a lovely tiered balcony and a big central mushroom pillar. A little to the west of Main Street is **Bowmore distillery** (see box on p.433), the first of the legal Islay distilleries, founded in 1779, and still occupying its original whitewashed buildings by the loch. One of the distillery's former bonded warehouses is now the **MacTaggart Leisure Centre** (closed Mon), whose pool is partially heated by waste heat from the distillery; if you're camping or self-catering, it's as well to know that it has a very useful, minuscule laundrette.

Islay's only official **tourist office** is in Bowmore (April, Sept & Oct Mon–Sat 10am–5pm; May & June Mon–Sat 9.30am–5pm, Sun 2–5pm; July–Aug Mon–Sat 9.30am–5.30pm, Sun 2–5pm; Nov–March Mon–Fri noon–4pm; ⓣ01496/810254); it can help you find **accommodation** anywhere on Islay or Jura. Like Port Ellen, Bowmore itself is, in fact, not necessarily the best place to stay on the island. If you must, stay in the *Harbour Inn* (ⓣ01496/810330, ⓔharbour@harbour-inn.co.uk; ❹) on Main Street, Bowmore's cosiest and most central pub, or in one of the town's better B&Bs, such as *Lambeth House* (ⓣ01496/810597; ❶), centrally located on Jamieson Street. If you're looking for more character and comfort, head out to the *Bridgend Hotel* (ⓣ01496/810960; ❺), a couple of miles up the road, positioned by the main road junction, but also close to the island's finest patch of deciduous woodland. **Bike rental** is available from the craft shop beside the post office on Main Street.

The *Lochside Hotel*, on Shore Street, has probably the most stupendous array of single malts on the island, while at the *Harbour Inn* on Main Street, you can warm yourself by a peat fire in the **pub**, or eat upstairs at the inn's outstanding **restaurant**: they make award-winning porridge for breakfast, offer reasonably priced lunch-time menu, and serve relatively expensive evening meals. At the other end of the scale, there's *The Cottage* (closed Sun), a cheap and friendly greasy spoon, further up on the same side of the street. Somewhat incredibly there's no permanent fish-and-chip shop in Bowmore, only the mobile *Nippy Chippy*, though there is an excellent **bakery**, again on Main Street.

Loch Gruinart and Kilchoman

If you're visiting Islay between mid-September and the third week of April, it's impossible to miss the island's staggeringly large wintering population of **barnacle** and **white-fronted geese**. During this period, the geese dominate the landscape, feeding incessantly off the rich pasture, strolling by the shores, and flying in formation across the winter skies. In the spring, the geese hang around just long enough to snap up the first shoots of new grass, in order to give themselves enough energy to make the 2000-mile journey to Greenland, where they breed in the summer. Understandably, many local farmers are not exactly very happy about the geese feeding off their land, and they now receive compensation for the inconvenience.

You can see the geese just about anywhere on the island – there are an estimated 15,000 white-fronted and 40,000 barnacles here (and rising) – though they are usually at their most concentrated in the fields between Bridgend and Ballygrant. In the evening, they tend to congregate in the tidal mud flats and fields around **Loch Gruinart**, which is now an **RSPB nature reserve**. The nearby farm of Aoradh (pronounced "oorig") is run by the RSPB, and one of its outbuildings contains a **visitor centre** (daily 10am–5pm; free), housing an observation point with telescopes and a CCTV link with the mud flats; there's also a hide across the road looking north over the salt flats at the head of the loch. From the hide, you're more likely to see pintail, wigeon, teal and other waterfowl than geese.

The road along the western shores of Loch Gruinart to Ardnave is a good place to spot **choughs**, members of the crow family, distinguished by their curved red beaks and matching legs. Halfway along the road, there's a path off to the ruins of **Kilnave Chapel**, whose working graveyard contains a very weathered, eighth-century Celtic cross. The road ends at Ardnave Loch, beyond which lie numerous sand dunes, where seals often sun themselves, while otters sometimes fish offshore. Nature-lovers and twitchers should hole themselves up in *Loch Gruinart House* (Ⓣ01496/850212; ❷), by the reserve.

Without doubt the best sandy beaches on Islay are to be found on the isolated northwest coast, in particular, the lovely golden beach of **Machir Bay**, which is backed by great white sand dunes. The sea here has dangerous undercurrents, however, and is not safe to swim in (the same goes for the much smaller Saligo Bay, to the north). At the nearby settlement of **KILCHOMAN**, set back from Machir Bay, beneath low rocky cliffs, where fulmars nest inland, the church is in a sorry state of disrepair. Its churchyard, however, contains a beautiful fifteenth-century cross, decorated with interlacing on one side and the Crucifixion on the other; at its base there's a wishing stone that should be turned sunwise when wishing. Across a nearby field towards the bay lies the **sailors' cemetery**, containing just 75 graves of the 400 or so who were drowned when the armed merchant cruiser SS *Otranto*, collided with another ship in its convoy in a storm in October 1918. The ship was carrying 1000 army personnel (including 665 Americans), the majority of whom made it safely to a ship which came to their aid; of the 400 who had to try and swim ashore, only 16 survived. The sailors' graves lie in three neat rows, from the cook to the captain, who has his own much larger gravestone.

Port Charlotte and the Rhinns of Islay

PORT CHARLOTTE, founded in 1828 by Walter Frederick Campbell and named after his mother, is generally agreed to be Islay's prettiest village. Known as the "Queen of the Rhinns" (derived from the Gaelic word for a promontory), its immaculate whitewashed cottages cluster around a sandy cove overlooking Loch Indaal. On the northern fringe of the village, in a white-washed former chapel, the imaginative **Museum of Islay Life** (Easter–Oct Mon–Sat 10am–5pm, Sun 2–5pm; £2), has a children's corner, quizzes, a good library of books about the island, and tantalizing snippets about eighteenth-century illegal whisky distillers. The **Wildlife Information Centre** (Easter–Oct Mon, Tues, Thurs & Fri 10am–3pm, Sun 2–5pm; June–Aug Mon, Tues, Thurs & Fri until 5pm; £2), housed in the former distillery warehouse, is also worth a visit for anyone interested in the island's fauna and flora. As well as an extensive library to browse in, there's lots of hands-on stuff for kids: microscopes, a touch table full of natural goodies, a seawater aquarium, a bug-world, and owl pellets to examine. Tickets are valid for a week, allowing you to go back and identify things that you've seen on your travels.

Port Charlotte is the perfect place in which to base yourself on Islay. The welcoming *Port Charlotte Hotel* (Ⓣ01496/850360, Ⓔcarl@portcharlottehot.demon.co.uk; ④) has the best **accommodation** – the seafood lunches served in the bar are very popular, and there's a good (moderately expensive) restaurant. For B&B, you're actually better off going for *Octofad Farm* (Ⓣ01496/850225; ①; April–Oct), a dairy farm a few miles down the road beyond Nerabus. Port Charlotte itself is also home to Islay's SYHA **hostel** (Ⓣ01496/850385, Ⓦwww.syha.org.uk; May–Sept), housed in an old bonded warehouse next door to the Wildlife Information Centre. The *Croft Kitchen* (Ⓣ01496/850230; mid-March to mid-Oct), opposite the museum, serves simple **food**, such as sandwiches and cakes, as well as inexpensive seafood, during the day, and more adventurous fare in the evenings (except Wed). The **bar** of the *Port Charlotte* is very easy-going, while the local crack (and occasional live music) goes on at the *Lochindaal Inn*, down the road, where you can also tuck into a very good local-bred steak. **Bike rental** is available from a house on Main Street (Ⓣ01496/850488).

The main coastal road culminates seven miles south of Port Charlotte at **PORTNAHAVEN**, a fishing and crofting community since the early nineteenth century. The familiar whitewashed cottages wrap themselves prettily around the steep banks of a deep bay, where seals bask on the rocks in considerable numbers; in the distance, you can see Portnahaven's twin settlement, **PORT WEMYSS**, a mile south. The communities share a little whitewashed church, located above the bay in Portnahaven, with separate doors for each village. A short way out to sea are two islands, the largest of which, Orsay, sports the **Rhinns of Islay Lighthouse**, built by Robert Louis Stevenson's father in 1825; ask around locally if you're keen to visit the island. Also worth a mention, just north of Portnahaven, is the island's ground-breaking wave energy generator, **Limpet 500** (Ⓦwww.wavegen.co.uk), which harnesses the power of the sea and turns it into electricity.

Loch Finlaggan and Port Askaig

Just beyond Ballygrant, on the road to Port Askaig, a narrow road leads off north to **Loch Finlaggan**, site of a number of prehistoric crannogs (artificial islands) and, for four hundred years from the twelfth century, headquarters of the Lords of the Isles, semi-autonomous rulers over the Hebrides and Kintyre. The site is evocative enough, but there are, in truth, very few remains beyond the foundations. Remarkably, the palace that stood here appears to have been unfortified, a testament perhaps to the prosperity and stability of the islands in those days. Unless you need shelter from the rain, or are desperate to see the head of the commemorative medieval cross found here, you can happily skip the **visitor centre** (Easter & Oct Tues, Thurs & Sun 2–4pm; May–Sept daily except Sat 2.30–5pm; £2), to the northeast of the loch, and simply head on down to the site itself (access at any time), which is dotted with interpretive panels. Duckboards allow you to walk out across the reed beds of the loch and explore the main crannog, **Eilean Mor**, where several carved gravestones can be seen among the ruins, which seem to support the theory that the Lords of the Isles buried their wives and children, while having themselves interred on Iona. Further out into the loch is another smaller crannog, **Eilean na Comhairle**, originally connected to Eilean Mor by a causeway, where the Lords of the Isles are thought to have held meetings of the Council of the Isles.

Islay's other ferry connection with the mainland, and its sole link with Colonsay and Jura, is from **PORT ASKAIG**, a scattering of buildings which tumble down a little cove by the narrowest section of the Sound of Islay (*Caol Ila*). The only real reason to come here is to catch one of the ferries or go to the hotel bar; if you've time to kill, you can wander round the island's RNLI **lifeboat station** or through the nearby woods of Dunlossit House. Whisky fanatics might want to head half a mile north of Port Askaig to the **Caol Ila distillery** or the **Bunnahabhainn distillery**, a couple of miles further on; both enjoy idyllic settings, overlooking the Sound of Islay, though they are no beauties in themselves (see box on p.433 for details of their tours).

Easily the most comfortable **place to stay** is the lovely whitewashed *Kilmeny Farmhouse* (Ⓣ01496/840668, Ⓦwww.kilmeny.com; ❺), southwest of Ballygrant, a place which richly deserves all the superlatives it regularly receives. The *Ballygrant Inn* is a good **pub** in which to grab a pint, as is the bar of the *Port Askaig Hotel*, which enjoys a wonderful position by the pier at Port Askaig, with views over to the Paps of Jura.

The Isle of Jura

Twenty-eight miles long and eight miles wide, the long whale-shaped island of **Jura** is one of the wildest and most mountainous of the Inner Hebrides, its entire west coast uninhabited and inaccessible except to the dedicated walker. The distinctive **Paps of Jura** – so called because of their smooth breast-like shape, though there are in fact three of them – seem to dominate every view off the west coast of Argyll, their glacial rounded tops covered in a light dusting of quartzite scree. The island's name is commonly thought to derive from the Norse *dyr-oe* (deer island) and, appropriately enough, the current deer population of 6000 outnumbers the 180 humans 33:1. With just one road, which sticks to the more sheltered eastern coast of the island, and only one hotel and a smattering of B&Bs, Jura is an ideal place to go for peace and quiet and some great walking.

If you're just coming over for the day from Islay, and don't fancy climbing the Paps, you could happily spend the day in the lovely wooded grounds of **Jura House** (daily 9am–5pm; £2), five miles up the road from Feolin Ferry, where the car ferry from Port Askaig arrives. Pick up a booklet at the entrance to the grounds, and follow the path which takes you down to the sandy shore, a perfect picnic spot in fine weather. Closer to the house itself, there's an idyllic **walled garden**, divided in two by a natural rushing burn that tumbles down in steps. The garden specializes in Antipodean plants, which flourish in the frost-free climate; in season, you can buy some of the garden's organic produce or take tea in the tea tent.

△ Whisky barrels, Lagavulin, Islay

George Orwell on Jura

In April 1946, Eric Blair (better known by his pen name of **George Orwell**) intending to give himself "six months' quiet" in which to complete his latest novel, moved to a remote farmhouse called **Barnhill**, at the northern end of Jura, which he had visited for the first time the previous year. He appears to have relished the challenge of living in Barnhill, fishing almost every night, shooting rabbits, laying lobster pots, and even attempting a little farming. Along with his adopted 3-year-old son Richard, and later his sister Avril, he clearly enjoyed his spartan existence. The book Orwell was writing, under the working title *The Last Man in Europe*, was to become *1984* (the title was arrived at by simply reversing the last two digits of the year in which it was finished – 1948). During his time on Jura, however, Orwell was suffering badly from tuberculosis, and eventually he was forced to return to London, where he died in January 1950.

Barnhill, 23 miles north of Craighouse, is as remote today as it was in Orwell's day. The road deteriorates rapidly beyond Lealt, where you should park your vehicle, leaving pilgrims a four-mile walk to the house itself. Alternatively, the hotel can organise tranport for you all the way there and back should you so wish. Orwell wrote most of the book in the bedroom (top left window as you look at the house) – at present, there is no public access. If you're keen on making the journey out to Barnhill, you might as well combine it with a trip to the nearby Gulf of Corrievrechan (see p.411), which lies between Jura and Scarba, to the north. Orwell nearly drowned in the whirlpool during a fishing trip in August 1947, along with his three companions (including Richard): the outboard motor was washed away, and they had to row to a nearby island and wait for several hours before being rescued by a passing fisherman. The best time to see the water whirling is between flood and half-flood tide, with a southerly or westerly wind, and the best place to view it from is Carraig Mhor, seven miles from Lealt.

Anything that happens on Jura happens in the island's only real village, **CRAIGHOUSE**, eight miles up the road from Feolin Ferry. The village enjoys a sheltered setting, overlooking Knapdale on the mainland – so sheltered, in fact, that there are even a few palm trees thriving on the seafront. There's a shop/post office, the island hotel and a tearoom, plus the tiny **Isle of Jura distillery** (Ⓣ01496/820240; tours by appointment), which welcomes visitors.

The family-run *Jura Hotel* in Craighouse is the island's one and only **hotel** (Ⓣ01496/820243, Ⓦmembers.aol.com/jurahotel; ❹), not much to look at from the outside, but warm and friendly within, and centre of the island's social scene. The hotel does moderately expensive bar meals, and has a shower block and laundry facilities round the back for those who wish to camp in the hotel gardens. For **B&B**, look no further than Mrs Boardman at 7 Woodside (Ⓣ01496/820379; ❶; April–Sept). There's an infrequent **minibus service** on the island (phone Ⓣ01496/820314 to find out when it's running). The **ferry** from Port Askaig occasionally fails to run if there's a strong northerly or southerly wind, so bring your toothbrush if you're coming for a day-trip. Look out for the *Jura Jottings*, the island's "newspaper".

Travel details

Trains

Glasgow (Queen St) to: Arrochar & Tarbert (2–4 daily; 1hr 15min); Dalmally (2–4 daily; 2hr 15min); Oban (2–4 daily; 3hr).

Mainland buses (excluding postbuses)

Arrochar to: Carrick Castle (Mon–Sat 3 daily; 1hr); Garelochhead (Mon–Fri 2 daily; 20min); Inveraray (Mon–Sat 5 daily, Sun 2 daily; 35min); Lochgilphead (Mon–Sat 3 daily, Sun 2 daily; 1hr 30min); Lochgoilhead (Mon–Sat 3 daily; 40min).
Campbeltown to: Campbeltown airport (Mon–Fri 2 daily; 10min); Carradale (Mon–Sat 3–4 daily, Sun 2 daily; 45min); Machrihanish (Mon–Sat 9–11 daily, Sun 3 daily; 15min); Saddell (Mon–Sat 3–4 daily, Sun 2 daily; 25min); Southend (Mon–Sat 5–6 daily, Sun 2 daily; 23min).
Colintraive to: Dunoon (Mon–Fri 1–3 daily, Sat 3 daily; 40min); Tighnabruaich (Mon–Thurs 1–2 daily; 35min).
Dunoon to: Colintraive (Mon–Fri 1–3 daily, Sat 3 daily; 40min); Inveraray (Mon–Fri 5 daily, Sat 3 daily; 1hr 15min); Lochgoilhead (Mon–Fri 0–3 daily; 1hr 15min).
Glasgow to: Arrochar (Mon–Sat 6 daily, Sun 3 daily; 1hr 10min); Campbeltown (Mon–Sat 3 daily, Sun 2 daily; 4hr 25min); Dalmally (Mon–Sat 4 daily, Sun 2 daily; 2hr 20min); Inveraray (Mon–Sat 6 daily, Sun 3 daily; 1hr 45min); Kennacraig (Mon–Sat 2 daily, Sun 1 daily; 3hr 30min); Lochgilphead (Mon–Sat 3 daily, Sun 2 daily; 2hr 40min); Oban (Mon–Sat 4 daily, Sun 2 daily; 3hr); Tarbert (Mon–Sat 3 daily, Sun 2 daily; 3hr 15min); Taynuilt (Mon–Sat 4 daily, Sun 2 daily; 2hr 45min).
Inveraray to: Dalmally (Mon–Sat 3 daily, Sun 1 daily; 25min); Dunoon (Mon–Fri 5 daily, Sat 3 daily; 1hr 15min); Lochgilphead (Mon–Sat 3 daily, Sun 2 daily; 40min); Oban (Mon–Sat 3 daily, Sun 1 daily; 1hr 5min); Tarbert (Mon–Sat 3 daily, Sun 2 daily; 1hr 30min); Taynuilt (Mon–Sat 3 daily, Sun 1 daily; 45min).
Kennacraig to: Claonaig (Mon–Sat 3 daily; 15min); Skipness (Mon–Sat 3 daily; 20min).
Lochgilphead to: Campbeltown (Mon–Sat 4 daily, Sun 2 daily; 1hr 25min); Crinan (Mon–Fri 1–3 daily, Sat 2 daily; 20min); Inveraray (Mon–Sat 3 daily, Sun 2 daily; 40min); Kilmartin (Mon–Sat 1–5 daily; 15–40min); Oban (Mon–Sat 1 daily; 1hr 30min); Tarbert (2–4 daily; 30min).
Oban to: Appin (Mon–Sat 4 daily, Sun 1 daily; 30min); Benderloch (Mon–Sat 10–14 daily, Sun 6 daily; 20min); Ellenabeich (Mon–Sat 2–4 daily; 45min); Kilmartin (Mon–Sat 1 daily; 1hr 10min); Lochgilphead (Mon–Sat 1 daily; 1hr 30min).
Tarbert to: Campbeltown (Mon–Sat 4 daily, Sun 2 daily; 1hr 10min); Claonaig (Mon–Sat 3 daily; 30min); Kennacraig (Mon–Sat 5 daily, Sun 1 daily; 15min); Skipness (Mon–Sat 3 daily; 35min).
Tighnabruaich to: Portavadie (Mon–Sat 3–4 daily; 25min); Rothesay (Mon–Thurs 1–2 daily; 1hr).

Island buses

Arran

Brodick to: Blackwaterfoot (Mon–Sat 16–19 daily, Sun 5 daily; 30min–1hr 20min); Corrie (Mon–Sat 5–6 daily, Sun 4 daily; 20min); Kildonan (Mon–Sat 4–5 daily, Sun 4 daily; 40min); Lagg (Mon–Sat 4–5 daily, Sun 4 daily; 55min); Lamlash (Mon–Sat 12–13 daily, Sun 4 daily; 10min); Lochranza (Mon–Sat 5–6 daily, Sun 4 daily; 45min); Pirnmill (Mon–Sat 5–6 daily, Sun 4 daily; 1hr); Whiting Bay (Mon–Sat 12–13 daily, Sun 4 daily; 25min).

Bute

Rothesay to: Kilchattan Bay (Mon–Sat 4 daily, Sun 3 daily; 30min); Mount Stuart (1 daily except Tues & Thurs every 45min; 15min); Rhubodach (Mon–Sat 1–2 daily; 20min).

Colonsay

Scalasaig to: Kilchattan (Mon–Fri 2–4 daily; 30min); Kiloran Bay (Mon–Fri 2–3 daily; 12min); The Strand (Mon–Fri 1 daily).

Islay

Bowmore to: Port Askaig (Mon–Sat 8–10 daily, Sun 1 daily; 30–40min); Port Charlotte (Mon–Sat 5–6 daily; 25min); Port Ellen (Mon–Sat 9–12 daily, Sun 1 daily; 20–30min); Portnahaven (Mon–Sat 5–7 daily; 50min).

Mull

Craignure to: Fionnphort (Mon–Sat 3–4 daily, Sun 1 daily; 1hr 10min); Fishnish (Mon–Sat 4 daily, Sun 3 daily; 10min); Salen (Mon–Sat 4 daily, Sun 2 daily; 25min); Tobermory (Mon–Sat 4–5 daily, Sun 2 daily; 50min).
Tobermory to: Calgary (Mon–Fri 3–6 daily, Sat 2 daily; 45min); Dervaig (Mon–Fri 3–6 daily, Sat 2 daily; 30min); Fishnish (Mon–Sat 4 daily, Sun 3 daily; 40min).

Car ferries (summer timetable)

To Arran: Ardrossan–Brodick (Mon–Sat 5–6 daily, Sun 4 daily; 55min); Claonaig–Lochranza (10 daily; 30min).
To Bute: Colintraive–Rhubodach (frequently; 5min); Wemyss Bay–Rothesay (every 45min; 30min).
To Campbeltown: Ballycastle (Northern Ireland)–Campbeltown (2 daily; 3hr).
To Coll: Oban–Coll (1 daily except Thurs & Sun; 2hr 40min).
To Colonsay: Kennacraig–Colonsay (Wed 1 daily; 3hr 40min); Oban–Colonsay (Wed, Fri & Sun 1 daily; 2hr 10min); Port Askaig–Colonsay (Wed 1 daily; 1hr 20min).
To Dunoon: Gourock–Dunoon (hourly; 20min); McInroy's Point–Hunter's Quay (every 30min; 20min).
To Gigha: Tayinloan–Gigha (hourly; 20min).
To Islay: Colonsay–Port Askaig (Wed 1 daily; 1hr 20min); Kennacraig–Port Askaig (Mon–Sat 1–2 daily; 2hr); Kennacraig–Port Ellen (1–2 daily except Wed; 2hr 10min); Oban–Port Askaig (Wed 1 daily; 4hr).
To Jura: Port Askaig–Feolin Ferry (Mon–Sat 14–16 daily, Sun 6 daily; 10min).
To Kintyre: Portavadie–Tarbert (hourly; 25min).
To Lismore: Oban–Lismore (Mon–Sat 2–4 daily; 50min).
To Luing: Cuan Ferry (Seil)–Luing (every 30min; 5min).
To Mull: Kilchoan–Tobermory (Mon–Sat 7–8 daily; July & Aug also Sun 5 daily; 35min); Lochaline–Fishnish (Mon–Sat every 50min, Sun hourly; 15min); Oban–Craignure (Mon–Sat 6 daily, Sun 4–5 daily; 40min).
To Tiree: Oban–Tiree (1 daily except Thurs & Sun; 3hr 40min).

Passenger-only ferries (summer timetable)

To Iona: Fionnphort–Iona (Mon–Sat frequently, Sun hourly; 5min).
To Lismore: Port Appin–Lismore (daily every 2hr; 5min).

Flights

Glasgow to: Campbeltown (Mon–Fri 2 daily; 35min); Islay (Mon–Fri 2 daily, Sat 1 daily; 40min); Tiree (Mon–Sat 1 daily; 45min).

6

Skye and the Western Isles

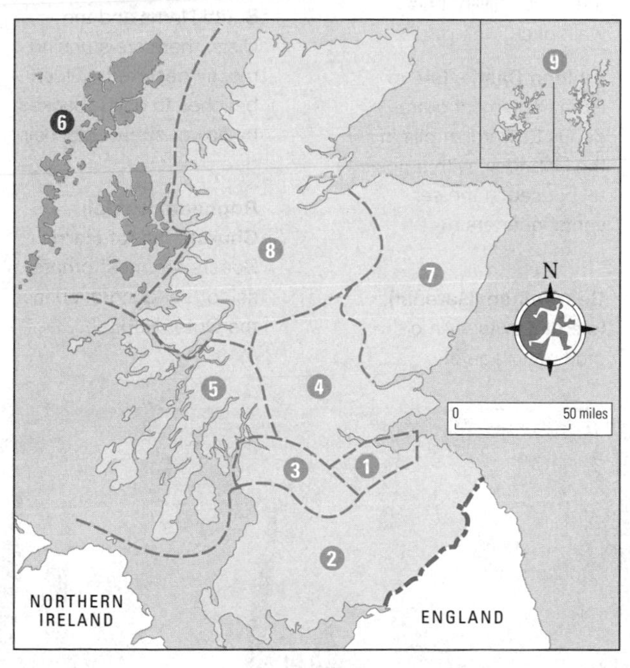

CHAPTER 6 Highlights

* **Skye Cuillin, Isle of Skye** – The jagged peaks of the Skye Cuillin are the real reason why Skye is a great place to visit. See p.454
* **Loch Coruisk boat trip, Isle of Skye** – Take the boat from Elgol to the remote glacial Loch Coruisk in the midst of the Skye Cuillin, and walk back. See p.455
* **Kinloch Castle, Isle of Rùm** –The most outrageous Edwardian pile in the Hebrides, with a hostel housed in the servants' quarters. See p.466
* **Gearrannan (Garenin), Isle of Lewis** – An old crofting village of thatched blackhouses that has been painstakingly restored. See p.481
* **Calanais (Callanish)** – Scotland's finest standing stones are in a serene lochside setting on Lewis. See p.482
* **The golden sandy beaches of the Western Isles** – Particularly in South Harris and the Uists, there are stunning, mostly deserted, golden beaches to enjoy, backed by flower-strewn machair. See p.487
* **Roghadal (Rodel) Church, Isle of Harris** – Boasts the most ornate sculptural decoration in the Outer Hebrides. See p.488

Skye and the Western Isles

A procession of Hebridean islands, islets and reefs off the northwest shore of Scotland, **Skye and the Western Isles** between them boast some of the country's most alluring scenery. It's here that the turbulent seas of the Atlantic smash up against an extravagant shoreline hundreds of miles long, a geologically complex terrain whose rough rocks and mighty sea cliffs are interrupted by a thousand sheltered bays and, in the far west, a long line of sweeping sandy beaches. The islands' interiors are equally dramatic, a series of formidable mountain ranges soaring high above great chunks of boggy peat moor, a barren wilderness enclosing a host of tiny lakes, or lochans.

Skye and the Western Isles were first settled by Neolithic farming peoples in around 4000 BC. They lived along the coast, where they are remembered by scores of remains, from passage graves through to stone circles – most famously at **Calanais** (Callanish) on Lewis. Viking colonization gathered pace from 700 AD onwards – on Lewis four out of every five place names is of Norse origin – and it was only in 1266 that the islands were returned to the Scottish crown. James VI (and I of England), a Stuart and a Scot, though no Gaelic-speaker, was the first to put forward the idea of clearing the Hebrides, though it wasn't until after the Jacobite uprisings, in which many Highland clans disastrously backed the wrong side, that the **Clearances** began in earnest.

The isolation of the Hebrides exposed them to the whims and fancies of the various merchants and aristocrats who caught "island fever" and bought them

Accommodation price codes

Throughout this book, accommodation **prices** have been graded with the codes below, corresponding to the cost of the least expensive double room in high season. Price codes are not given for **campsites**, most of which charge less than £10 per person. Almost all **hostels** and **bunkhouses** charge between £8 and £12 per person per night; the few exceptions to this rule have the prices quoted in the text. For a full account of these codes, see p.28.

❶ under £40	❹ £60–70	❼ £110–150
❷ £40–50	❺ £70–90	❽ £150–200
❸ £50–60	❻ £90–110	❾ £200 and over

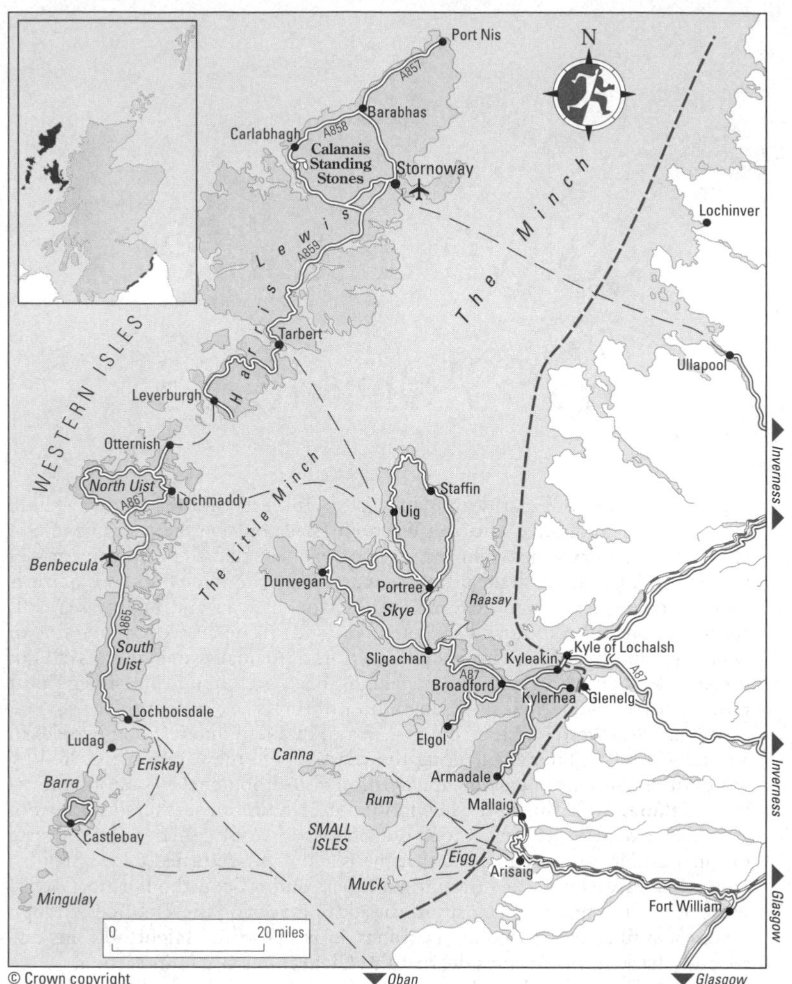

up. Time and again, from the mid-eighteenth century to the present day, both the land and its people were sold to the highest bidder. Some proprietors were well meaning, but insensitive – like **Lord Leverhulme**, who had no time for crofting and wanted to turn Lewis into a centre of the fishing industry in the 1920s – while others were simply autocratic – such as **Colonel Gordon of Cluny**, who bought Benbecula, South Uist, Eriskay and Barra, and forced the inhabitants onto ships bound for North America at gunpoint – but always the islanders were powerless and almost everywhere they were driven from their ancestral homes, robbing them of their particular sense of place. However, their language survived, ensuring a degree of cultural continuity, especially in the Western Isles, where even today the mother tongue of the vast majority is **Gaelic**.

Each island has its own distinct character, though you can split the grouping quite neatly into two. **Skye** and the so-called **Small Isles** – the improbably named **Rùm**, **Eigg**, **Muck** and **Canna** – are part of the Inner Hebrides, which also include the islands of Argyll (see p.367). Beyond Skye, across the unpredictable waters of the Minch, lie the Outer Hebrides or Outer Isles, nowadays known as the **Western Isles**, a 130-mile-long archipelago stretching from **Lewis** and **Harris** in the north to **Barra** in the south.

Although this area is one of the most popular holiday spots in Scotland, the crowds only become oppressive on Skye, and even here most visitors stick to a well-trodden sequence of roadside sights that leaves the rest of the island unaffected. The main attraction, the spectacular scenery, is best explored on **foot**, following the scores of paths that range from the simplest of cross-country strolls to arduous treks. There are four obvious areas of outstanding natural beauty to aim for: on Skye, the harsh peaks of the **Cuillin** and the bizarre rock formations of the **Trotternish** peninsula, both of which attract hundreds of walkers and mountaineers; on the Western Isles, the mountains of **North Harris** and the splendid sandy beaches that string along the Atlantic seaboard of **South Harris** and the **Uists**.

The tourist world and that of the islanders tend to be mutually exclusive, especially in the Western Isles. There are, however, ways to meet people – not so much by sitting in the pubs (they are few and far between in these parts), as by staying in the B&Bs and getting to know the owners. You could, too, join the locals at church, where visitors are generally welcome. This is a highly **religious region**, dotted with numerous tiny churches, whose denominations differ from island to island. In general terms, the south is predominantly Roman Catholic, while the Calvinist north is a stronghold of the strict Free Church of Scotland – more familiarly known as the "Wee Frees" (see p.474). Another good way to get acquainted with local life is to read the weekly *West Highland Free Press*, a refreshingly vociferous campaigning paper published in Broadford on Skye.

Transport practicalities

Travelling around Skye and the Western Isles requires some degree of forethought. The CalMac **ferries** run to a complicated timetable, and the **bus** services are patchy to say the least. It's worth reserving space on the ferries as far in advance as possible, as they get very booked up. Also, in accordance with Calvinist dogma, the entire public transport system of Lewis and Harris closes down on **Sunday**; elsewhere, only a skeleton service remains. You should consider visiting the islands (particularly Skye) in the spring or early autumn, rather than the height of the summer, both to avoid the crowds and to elude the attentions of the pesky **midge** (see p.45).

Skye

Justifiably **Skye** was named after the Norse word for "cloud" (*skuy*), earning itself the Gaelic moniker, *Eilean a Cheo* (Island of Mist). Yet, despite the unpredictability of the weather, tourism has been an important part of the island's economy for almost a hundred years now, since the train line pushed through to Kyle of Lochalsh in the western Highlands in 1897. From here, it was the briefest of boat trips across to Skye, and the Edwardian bourgeoisie was soon swarming over to walk its mountains, whose beauty had been proclaimed by an earlier generation of Victorian climbers.

Most visitors still reach Skye from **Kyle of Lochalsh**, linked with Inverness by train via the controversial Skye Bridge on one of the frequent buses over to **Kyleakin**, on the western tip of the island. However, this part of Skye is relatively dull, and the more scenic approach is from the **ferry** port of **Mallaig**, further south on the Morar peninsula (see p.623). Linked by **train** with Glasgow, the Mallaig boat (up to 7 daily) takes thirty minutes to cross to **Armadale**, on the gentle southern slopes of the **Sleat peninsula**. A third option is the privately operated car **ferry** which leaves the mainland at Glenelg, south of Kyle of Lochalsh, to arrive at **Kylerhea**, from where the road heads inland towards **Portree**. If you're carrying on to the Western Isles, it's 57 miles from Armadale to the opposite end of Skye, where **ferries** leave **Uig** for Tarbert on Harris and Lochmaddy on North Uist.

Skye has several substantial **campsites**, and numerous **hostels** or bunkhouses – all of which recommend advance bookings, particularly in July and August – plenty of B&Bs and a string of pricey, but excellent **hotels**. Most visitors arrive by car, as the **bus** services, while adequate between the villages, peter out in the more remote areas, and virtually close down on Sundays.

The Isle of Skye

Jutting out from the mainland like a giant wing, the bare and bony promontories of the **Isle of Skye** (An t-Eilean Sgiathanach) fringe a deeply indented coastline that makes the island never more than twenty-five, and sometimes as little as seven, miles wide. This causes problems at the height of the tourist season, when the main road system begins to bottleneck with coach tours and minibuses and caravans. Yet Skye is a deceptively large island, and you'll get most out of it – and escape the worst of the crowds – if you take the time to explore the more remote parts of the island.

Though some estimate that only half the island's population are *Sgiathanachs* (pronounced "ski-anaks"), Skye remains the most important centre for **Gaelic culture** and language outside of the Western Isles. Despite the Clearances, which saw an estimated 30,000 emigrate in the mid-nineteenth century, around forty percent of the population is fluent in Gaelic, the Gaelic college on Sleat is the most important in Scotland, and the Free Church (see box on p.474) maintains a strong presence. As an English-speaking visitor, it's as well to be aware of the tensions that exist within this idyllic island, even if you never experience them first-hand. For a taste of the resurgence of Gaelic culture, try and get here in time for the Skye and Lochalsh Festival, *Feis an Eilean*, which takes place over two weeks in mid-July.

The most popular destination on Skye is the **Cuillin** ridge, whose jagged peaks dominate the island during clear weather; to explore them at close quarters you'll need to be a fairly experienced and determined walker. Equally dramatic in their own way are the rock formations of the **Trotternish** peninsula, in the north, from which there are inspirational views across to the Western Isles. If you want to escape the summer crush, shuffle off to **Glendale** and the cliffs of Neist Point or head for the island of **Raasay**, off Skye's east coast. Of the two main settlements, **Broadford** and **Portree**, only the latter has any

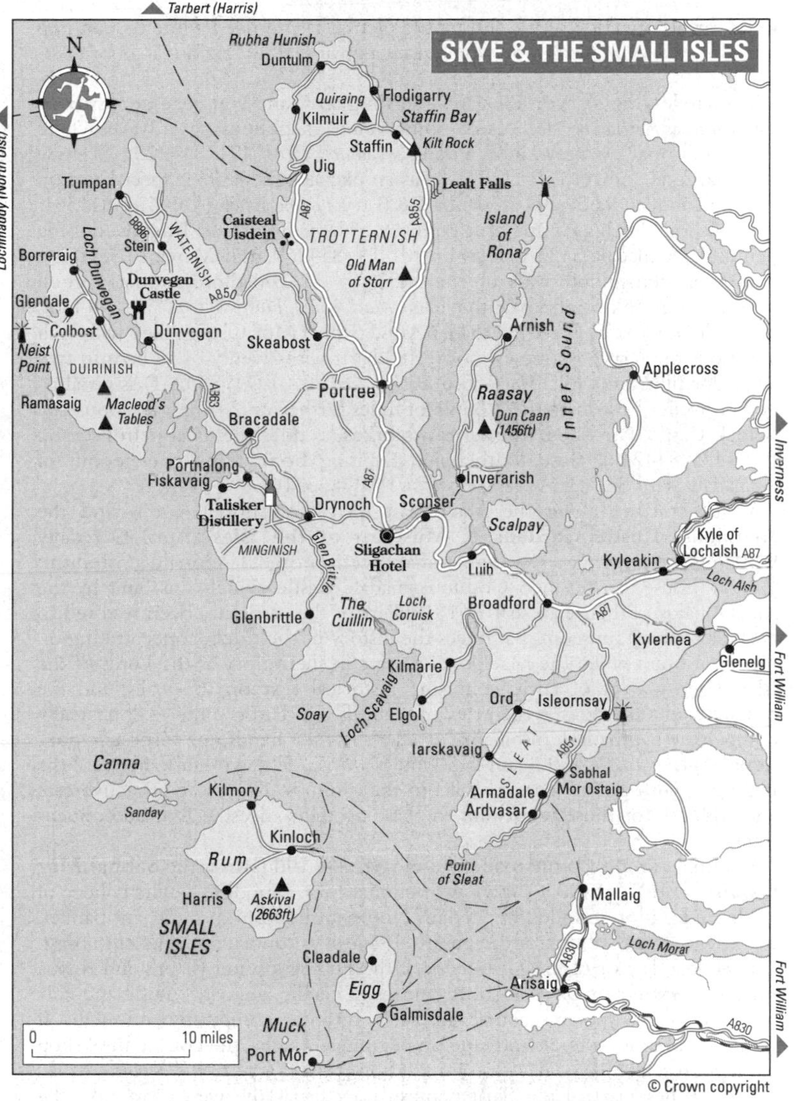

charm attached to it, though both have tourist offices, and make useful bases, especially for those without their own transport.

Sleat

Ferry services (Mon–Sat 6–7 daily; June to mid-Sept also Sun; 30min) from Mallaig connect with the **Sleat** (pronounced "slate") **peninsula**, Skye's southern tip, an uncharacteristically fertile area that has earned it the sobriquet "The Garden of Skye". The CalMac ferry terminal is at **ARMADALE** (Armadal), an elongated hamlet stretching along the wooded shoreline. If you've time to kill waiting for the ferry, take a look at the huge variety of Scottish and Irish knitwear on offer at Ragamuffin by the pier or, if you need a bite **to eat**, pop into the *Pasta Shed* next door, which does a great seafood pizza (eat-in or take-away).

If you're leaving Skye on the early-morning ferry and you need **accommodation** near Armadale, head a mile southwest to neighbouring Ardvasar, where the traditional, whitewashed *Ardvasar Hotel* (Ⓣ01471/844223, Ⓦwww.ardvasarhotel.com; ❺; March–Dec) has an excellent restaurant specializing in local seafood, and a lively bar; or for **B&B** try *Holme Leigh* (Ⓣ01471/844361, Ⓦwww.homeleigh@compuserve.com; ❶). There are three **hostels** on the peninsula: Armadale SYHA **hostel** (Ⓣ01471/844260; mid-March to Sept) is a convenient ten-minute walk up the A851 towards Broadford and has a good position overlooking the bay; the *Flora MacDonald Hostel* (Ⓣ01471/844440), two miles further up the same road, beyond Sabhal Mòr Ostaig (they will fetch you from the ferry), is a newly converted barn with twenty or so beds in two large dormitories; while *Hairy Coo Backpackers* (Ⓣ01471/833231) is an altogether livelier hostel, another couple of miles further on, in Toravaig House by Knock Castle. The SYHA hostel **rents bikes**, as does the local petrol station (Ⓣ01471/844249), close to the pier. Exciting **boat trips** operate out of Armadale with Sea.fari Adventures (Ⓣ01471/833316).

A little further along the A851, past the youth hostel, you'll find the **Armadale Castle Gardens & Museum of the Isles** (April–Oct daily 9.30am–5.30pm; Ⓦwww.highlandconnection.org/clandonaldcentre.htm; £3.90), housed in the neo-Gothic Armadale Castle, which was built by the MacDonalds as their clan seat in 1815. Part of the castle has been restored to create a touristy museum that traces the history of the Gaels, concentrating on medieval times when the MacDonalds were in their glory as the Lords of the Isles. There's a lot of fairly confusing historical text on the walls, and the romantic sound effects – the cries of seabirds and battle songs – don't really compensate for the lack of original artefacts, but the handsome forty-acre **gardens** (April–Oct daily 9.30am–5.30pm; Nov–March dawn–dusk; free) are the highlight, with guided nature walks in the grounds. There's an attractive café and a library for those who want to chase up their ancestral Donald connections.

A couple of miles up the road in an old MacDonald farm is the **Sabhal Mòr Ostaig** (Ⓣ01471/844373, Ⓦwww.smo.uhi.ac.uk), a modern Gaelic college of further education founded by Sir Iain Noble, an Edinburgh merchant banker, who owns a large chunk of the peninsula and is an untiring Gaelic enthusiast. The college is part of the University of the Highlands and Islands and runs a variety of extremely popular short courses in Gaelic language, music and culture, and longer full-time courses in Gaelic business, computing and media. If you're looking for a book and tape on beginners' Gaelic, the college bookshop has a good selection.

The loveliest part of the Sleat peninsula, by far, is the west coast: take the fiercely winding single-track road over to the scattered settlement of **TARSKAVAIG**, with its little sandy beach looking out over to the Small Isles. Further along the coast, through some ancient deciduous woods, you come to **Tokavaig**, where a stony, seaweedy beach overlooked by the ruined Dunscaith Castle boasts views over the entire Cuillin range – this, and neighbouring **ORD**, with a pleasant sandy beach, are the two best places on the whole of Skye from which to view the mountains in fine weather. There are very few places to stay in this area, but there is a B&B with great views in Ord, *Fiordhem* (Ⓣ01471/855226, Ⓦwww.fiordhem.co.uk; ❺; Easter–Oct) which also as a couple of self-catering cottages (4 people; £575 per week in summer).

Continuing northeast, it's another six miles to **ISLEORNSAY** (Eilean Iarmain), a secluded little village of whitewashed cottages that was once Skye's main fishing port. With the mountains of the mainland on the horizon, the views out across the bay are wonderful, overlooking a necklace of seaweed-encrusted rocks and the tidal **Isle of Ornsay**, which sports a trim lighthouse built by Robert Louis Stevenson's father. You can **stay** at another of Sir Iain Noble's enterprises, the mid-nineteenth-century *Isleornsay Hotel* – also known by its Gaelic name *Hotel Eilean Iarmain* – a pricey place with excellent service, whose **restaurant** serves great seafood (Ⓣ01471/833332, Ⓦwww.eilean-iarmain.com; ❻). Also based in Isleornsay is Sir Iain's Gaelic whisky company, Prabann na Linne, which markets a number of unpronounceable Gaelic-named blended and single malt whiskies; the company offers tastings at its head office (phone Ⓣ01471/833266 for opening hours). Another couple of miles brings you to the turning for *Kinloch Lodge Hotel* (Ⓣ01471/833333, Ⓦwww.kinloch-lodge.co.uk; ❼), centred on an old hunting lodge still in the possession of Lord Macdonald of Macdonald with excellent food guaranteed by wife Claire whose cookery books are internationally famous.

Kyleakin and Kylerhea

The aforementioned Sir Iain Noble is also one of the leading advocates of (and investors in) the privately financed **Skye Bridge**, which now links the tidy hamlet of **KYLEAKIN** (Caol Acain – pronounced "ka*la*kin", with the stress on the second syllable) with the Kyle of Lochalsh (see p.625), just half a mile away on the mainland. The bridge, welcomed by the vast majority of islanders, was built entirely by Anglo-German contractors for a cool £30 million. The investors are currently trying to recoup their money by charging around £5 each way for cars and £30 for lorries and coaches, making it the most expensive toll bridge in Europe, and no cheaper than the ferry it replaced. The well-orchestrated campaign by SKAT (Skye & Kyle Against Tolls), 350 of whose members have refused to pay the tolls, provides fierce opposition to the current system and may yet succeed in either reducing or abolishing the fee. Frequent user tickets are available if you are whizzing to and fro: 20 car tickets for £26.80. Strictly speaking there are two bridges which rest on an island in the middle, **Eilean Ban**, once the home of author and naturalist Gavin Maxwell, and now a wildlife sanctuary with the emphasis on otters. Visitors, limited to twelve, arrive by boat and must book through the **Bright Water Visitor Centre** in Kyleakin (Ⓣ01599/530040; £8) for a guided tour. The Centre itself is well worth a visit as it's full of hands-on things for kids of all ages and it's free.

There's really nothing else to see or do in Kyleakin, though you could have a quick look at the scant remains of **Castle Moil**, a fourteenth-century keep poking out into the straits on top of a diminutive rocky knoll, which looks romantic when floodlit. One of its earliest inhabitants, an entrepreneurial Norwegian princess, married to a MacDonald chief, hung a chain across the water and exacted a toll from every passing boat. With its ferry now defunct, Kyleakin has reinvented itself as something of a backpackers' paradise – to the consternation of many villagers – in summer, the population more than doubles. If you're intent on joining the throng, the SYHA **hostel** (Ⓣ01599/534585, Ⓦwww.syha.org.uk; open all year) is an ugly, modern building a couple of hundred yards from the old pier; nearby *Skye Backpackers* (Ⓣ01599/534510, Ⓦwww.scotlands-top-hostels.com; open all year) is a more laid-back option, as is *Dun Caan Hostel* (Ⓣ01599/534087, Ⓔleisureplus@supernet.com; open all year). **Bike rental** is available from *Dun Caan* and Skye Bikes

(Ⓣ01599/534795) on the pier. On the road to Broadford there's the cheery *Crofters Kitchen*, providing homely **food** with a local flavour all day.

You can still avoid crossing the Skye Bridge by taking the ferry service (mid-March to mid-May & Sept to mid-Oct Mon–Sat 9am–6pm; mid-May to Aug Mon–Sat 9am–8.30pm, Sun 10am–6pm; 15min) from Glenelg to **KYLERHEA** (pronounced "kile-ray"), a peaceful little place some four miles down the coast from Kyleakin. From here you can walk half an hour up the coast to the Forestry Commission **Otter Hide**, where, if you're lucky, you may be able to spot one of these elusive creatures.

Broadford

Heading west out of Kyleakin or Kylerhea brings you eventually to the island's second-largest village, charmless **BROADFORD** (An t-Ath Leathann), whose mile-long main street curves round a wide bay. Despite its rather unlovely appearance, Broadford makes a useful base for exploring the southern half of Skye, and is something of a wet-weather retreat, with the unusual **Skye Serpentarium** (Easter–June, Sept & Oct Mon–Sat 10am–5pm; July & Aug also Sun; £2.50), full of snakes, lizards and frogs to amuse bored children. You can also go for trips in a glass-bottomed boat from the pier (check the times on Ⓣ01471/822037). For **mountain climbing and walking**, contact Skye Highs Mountain Guiding (Ⓣ01471/822116, Ⓦwww.skyeguides.co.uk).

More pragmatically, Broadford has a **tourist office** (April & May Mon–Sat 9.30am–5.30pm; June–Sept Mon–Sat 9am–6pm; Sun 10am–2pm; Oct Mon–Sat 9.30am–5pm; Ⓣ01471/822361), next to the Esso garage on the main road, which also contains a laundry, small shop and bureau de change, all open 24 hours. At the west end of the village there's a bank, a bakery, a tearoom and a post office. The SYHA **hostel** is on the west shore of Broadford Bay (Ⓣ01471/822442, Ⓦwww.syha.org.uk; Feb–Dec), or there's the much smaller, more beautiful and primitive *Fossil Bothy* hostel (Ⓣ01471/822644 or 822297, Ⓔfiona-mandeville@talk21.com; open all year, but essential to book), a mile or so east of the bay, in Lower Breakish, off the road to Kyleakin. Two **B&Bs** which stand out are the delightful old croft-house *Lime Stone Cottage*, 4 Lime Park (Ⓣ01471/822142, Ⓔkathielimepark@btinternet.com; ❷), and the modern, comfortable *Ptarmigan* (Ⓣ01471/822744; ❷), on the main road, with views over the bay. If you want a bite to eat, try *Creelers Seafood Restaurant* at the south end of the bay which has a more standard takeaway at the back (daily noon–2pm, 5pm–10pm). Close to the *Fossil Bothy*, the pleasant *Seagull* **restaurant** (Easter–Oct eves & Sun lunch only) serves inexpensive local meat and seafood dishes, while you can **rent bikes** from the SYHA hostel or from *Fairwinds*, another good place to stay (Ⓣ01471/822270; ❷; March–Oct), just past the *Broadford Hotel*.

Scalpay, Luib and The Braes

The A87 from Broadford to Portree continues to hug the coast for the next ten miles, giving out views across Loch na Cairidh to the **Isle of Scalpay**, a huge heather-backed lump that looks something like a giant scone, rising to 1298ft at the peak of Mullach na Carn. The island is part red-deer farm, part forestry plantation, and is currently owned by a merchant banker. Close by the boat slip in Ard Dorch that serves Scalpay is *The Picture House* (Ⓣ01471/822531, Ⓦwww.skyepicturehouse.co.uk; ❶), a **B&B** with stunning views of the Inner Sound, which doubles as a photographic gallery.

As the road twists round into Loch Ainort, there's a turn-off to **Luib Folk**

Museum (daily 9am–6pm; £1), a restored **blackhouse**, with a coffee shop next door. Built low against the wind, the house's thick walls are made up of an inner and outer layer of loose stone on either side of a central core of earth, a traditional type of construction which attracted the soubriquet "black house" (*tigh dubh*) around 1850, when buildings with single-thickness walls, known as "white houses" (*tigh geal*), were introduced from the mainland. The Luib museum is run by local museum magnate and restorer, Peter MacAskill, who's also responsible for two other museums in restored blackhouses on the island.

From the head of Loch Ainort, the main road takes a steep short cut across a pass to Loch Sligachan, while a prettier, minor road meanders round the coast – either way, you'll reach **SCONSER**, departure point for the car ferry to Raasay (see oppposite), and home to a nine-hole **golf course**, with superb views. There's a good **B&B** here by the shore in a croft house, *Loch Aluinn* (☎01478/650288; ❷; March–Oct) or *The Old Schoolhouse* (☎01478/650313; ❶; March–Dec).

On the opposite side of Loch Sligachan are the crofting communities of **The Braes**, whose inhabitants staged a successful rent strike in 1881 against their landlords, the MacDonalds. After eviction summonses were burnt by the crofters, a detachment of fifty Glasgow policemen were drafted in and took part in a "battle", which aroused a great deal of publicity for the crofters' cause (for more on which, see p.457).

The Isle of Raasay

Though it takes only fifteen minutes to reach from Skye, the lovely island of **Raasay**, a nature conservancy area with great walks across its bleak and barren hills, remains well off the tourist trail. For much of its history, Raasay was the property of a branch of the Jacobite MacLeods of Lewis, and the island sent 100 men and 26 pipers to Culloden, as a consequence of which it was practically destroyed by government troops in the aftermath of the 1745 uprising. Bonnie Prince Charlie spent a miserable night in a "mean low hut" on Raasay during his flight and swore to replace the burnt turf cottages with proper stone houses (he never did). Not long after the MacLeods were forced to sell up in 1843, the Clearances started in earnest, a period of the island's history immortalized in verse by Raasay poet, Sorley MacLean (Somhairle MacGill Eathain). In 1921, seven ex-servicemen and their families from the neighbouring isle of Rona illegally squatted crofts on Raasay, and were imprisoned, causing a public outcry. As a result, both islands were bought by the government the following year. Rona, ancestral home of the family of Billy Graham, the American evangelist, is now uninhabited, and Raasay's population stands at around 160, most of them members of the Free Presbyterian Church (see box on p.474). Strict observance of the Sabbath – no work or play on Sundays – is the most obvious manifestation for visitors, who should respect the islanders' feelings.

The ferry docks at the southern tip of the island, an easy fifteen-minute walk from **INVERARISH**, a tiny village set within thick woods on the island's southwest coast. If your time is limited there are several walks in these woods: you can follow the miners' trail which traces the route of the railway constructed to carry iron ore to the jetty, built by German POWs in 1914, most of whom died in the influenza epidemic in 1918. The grand Georgian mansion of **Raasay House** (now an outdoor centre) was built by the MacLeods in the late 1740s, to be all but ruined by government troops a few years later. The grounds slope down to a tiny **harbour**, overlooked by two weathered stone mermaids stuck on top of the remains of a battery armed in the Napoleonic era with several cannons. The house's stable clock stopped on the day in 1914 when 36 men of Raasay went to war – only 14 returned; also in the grounds, there are Pictish symbol stones and the charming ruined thirteenth-century Chapel of St Moluag.

The interior of Raasay is starkly barren, a rugged and rocky terrain of sandstone in the south and gneiss in the north, with the most obvious feature being the curiously truncated basalt cap on top of **Dun Caan** (1456ft), where Boswell "danced a Highland dance" on his visit to the island with Dr Johnson in 1773 – you may feel like doing the same if you're rewarded with a clear view over to the Cuillin and the Outer Hebrides. The trail to the top of the peak is fairly easy to follow, a splendid five-mile trek up through the forest and along the burn behind Inverarish. The quickest return is made down the northwest slope of Dun Caan, but – by going a couple of miles further – you can get back to the ferry along the path by the southeast shore, passing the abandoned crofters' village of Hallaig, whose steep incline led mothers to tether their children to stakes to prevent them rolling onto the shore.

If you want to explore the north of the island you really need your own transport and a fine day to appreciate the views across to the Skye Cuillin, Portree and the Trotternish peninsula. Where the road dips to the east coast the stark remains of fifteenth-century **Brochel Castle** stand overlooking the shore. The last two miles of the road to Arnish is known as **Calum's Road**: in the 1960s the council refused to extend the road to the village, so Calum MacLeod decided to build it himself; it took him ten years and by the time he'd finished he and his wife were the only people left in the village. You can walk on a boggy path to the north end and onto **Eilean Tigh** at low tide, or there's a shorter walk onto **Eilean Fladday**, which is also tidal. Raasay is rich in flora and fauna and it's at the north end that you're more likely to see a golden eagle, snipe, orchids and perhaps the unique Raasay vole. Rather than walking, you could always book a guided tour with Heavy Horses Tours (ⓣ01478/660233; Easter–Oct).

Practicalities

The CalMac **car ferry** departs for Raasay from Sconser (Mon–Sat 9–10 daily; 15min). Many visitors go for the day, since there's plenty to do within walking distance of the pier – if you do take a car, be warned there's no petrol on the island. Comfortable **accommodation** in tastefully Bohemian rooms is available at the *Raasay Outdoor Centre* (ⓣ01478/660266, ⓔraasay.house@virgin.net; ❶; March to mid-Oct), where Boswell and Johnson stayed; there is also a café, open to all. You can **camp** in the grounds and, for a daily cost of around £25, join in the centre's activity programme: anything from sailing, windsurfing and canoeing, to climbing and hill-walking. Close by is the likeably old-fashioned *Isle of Raasay Hotel* (ⓣ01478/660222; ❸), which serves delicious traditional Scottish food and where the view of the Cuillin surpasses any other (bunkroom accommodation is also provided at £10 per person); in the village is a pleasant Victorian guesthouse, *Churchton House* (ⓣ01478/660260; ❶). A rough track cuts up the steep hillside from the village to Raasay's isolated but beautifully placed SYHA **hostel** (ⓣ01478/660240, ⓦwww.syha.org.uk; mid-May to Sept).

The Cuillin and the Red Hills

For many people, the **Cuillin**, whose sharp snowcapped peaks rise mirage-like from the flatness of the surrounding terrain, are Skye's *raison d'être*. When the clouds finally disperse, they are the dominating feature of the island, visible from every other peninsula on Skye. There are basically three approaches to the Cuillin: from the south, by foot or by boat from Elgol; from the *Sligachan Hotel* to the north; or from Glen Brittle to the west of the mountains. Glen Sligachan is one of the most popular routes, dividing as it does the granite of the round-topped **Red Hills** (sometimes known as the Red Cuillin) to the east from the dark, coarse-grained jagged-edged gabbro of the real Cuillin (also known as the Black Cuillin), to the west. With some twenty Munros between them, these are mountains to be taken seriously, and many routes through the Cuillin are for experienced climbers only (for more on safety, see p.46).

Elgol and Loch Coruisk

The road to **ELGOL** (Ealaghol), fourteen miles southwest of Broadford at the tip of the Strathaird peninsula, is one of the most dramatic on the island, leading right into the heart of the Red Hills and then down a precipitous slope, with a stunning view from the top down to Elgol pier. On the way you pass the ruins of a pre-Reformation church and graveyard at Kilchrist, where there are also traces of marble quarries which flourished for a while, employing Belgian experts and running the marble on a small railway to Broadford pier. Further down the road at Torrin you'll see the modern quarry with its white gleaming gash in the hillside; the brilliance of the stone has been compared favourably with Carrara but it is too hard to work and mostly graces local driveways as chippings. In summer there's a busy stall at Elgol pier, serving burgers and seafood because the chief reason for visiting Elgol is, weather permitting, to take a boat across Loch Scavaig (March–Sept 2–4 daily), past a seal colony, to a jetty near the entrance of **Loch Coruisk** (from *coire uish*, "cauldron of water"). An isolated, glacial loch, this needle-like shaft of water, nearly two miles long but only a couple of hundred yards wide, lies in the shadow of the highest peaks of the Black Cuillin, a wonderfully overpowering landscape.

The journey by sea takes 45 minutes and passengers are dropped to spend about one and a half hours ashore; for booking (essential) and details of sailing times, ring the *Bella Jane* (Ⓣ0800/731 3089 before 10am and after 7.30pm). Walkers can use the boat on a one-way trip simply to get to Loch Coruisk, from where there are numerous possibilities for hiking amidst the Red Hills, the most popular (and gentle) of which is the eight-mile trek north over the pass into **Glen Sligachan**. Alternatively, you could walk round the coast to the sandy bay of **Camasunary**, over two miles to the east – a difficult walk that involves a tricky river crossing and negotiating "The Bad Step", an overhanging rock with a thirty-foot drop to the sea – and either head north to Glen Sligachan, continue south three miles along the coast to Elgol, or continue east to the Am Mam shoulder, for a stunning view of mountains and the islands of Soay, Rùm and Canna. From Am Mam, the path leads down to the Elgol road, joining it at Kilmarie.

The only public transport is the **postbus** from Broadford (Mon–Fri 2 daily, Sat 1 daily), which takes two hours to reach Elgol in the morning (check with the tourist office in Broadford about connections). Rather than stay in Elgol, head for *Rowan Cottage* (Ⓣ01471/866287, Ⓔrowan@rowancott.demon.co.uk; ❷; March–Nov), a lovely **B&B** a mile or so east in Glasnakille, or the larger, more luxurious *Strathaird House* (Ⓣ01471/866269, Ⓦwww.strathairdhouse.skye.co.uk; ❸; April–Sept) just beyond Kilmarie, three miles up the road to Broadford. By far the most popular place to stay, though, is the **campsite** (April–Oct) by the *Sligachan Hotel* (Ⓣ01478/650204, Ⓦwww.sligachan.co.uk; ❷) on the A87, at the northern end of Glen Sligachan. The hotel's huge *Seamus Bar* serves food for weary walkers until 10pm, and quenches their thirst with the full range of real ales produced by Skye's very own microbrewery in Uig; there's also a more formal restaurant with splendid food.

Glen Brittle

Six miles along the A863 to Dunvegan from the *Sligachan Hotel*, a turning signed "Carbost and Portnalong" quickly leads to the entrance to stony **Glen Brittle**, edging the most spectacular peaks of the Cuillin; at the end of the glen, idyllically situated by the sea, is the village of **GLENBRITTLE**. Climbers and serious walkers tend to congregate at the SYHA **hostel** (ⓣ01478/640278, ⓦwww.syha.org.uk; March–Sept) or the fairly basic **campsite** (ⓣ01478/640404; April–Oct), a mile or so further south behind the wide sandy beach at the foot of the glen. During the summer, two buses a day (not Sun) from Portree will drop you at the top of the glen, but you'll have to walk the last seven miles; both the youth hostel and the campsite have grocery stores, the only ones for miles.

From the valley a score of difficult and strenuous trails lead east into the **Black Cuillin**, a rough semicircle of peaks rising to about 3000ft, which surround Loch Coruisk. One of the easiest walks is the five-mile round-trip from the campsite up **Coire Lagan**, to a crystal-cold lochan squeezed in among the sternest of rockfaces. Above the lochan is Skye's highest peak, **Sgurr Alasdair** (3258ft), one of the more difficult Munros, while Sgurr na Banachdich (3166ft) is considered the most easily accessible Munro in the Cuillin (for the usual walking safety precautions, see p.46). The Mountain Rescue Service has produced a book of walks for those who are not climbers, available locally.

Minginish

If the Cuillin have disappeared into the mist for the day, you could while away an afternoon exploring the nearby **Minginish** peninsula, to the north of Glen Brittle. One wet-weather activity is to visit the **Talisker whisky distillery** (April–June & Oct Mon–Fri 9am–4.30pm; July–Sept Mon–Sat 9am–4.30pm; Nov–March Mon–Fri 2–4.30pm; by appointment ⓣ01478/640314), which produces a very smoky, peaty single malt. Talisker is the island's only distillery, situated on the shores of Loch Harport at **CARBOST** (and not, confusingly, at the village of Talisker itself, which lies on the west coast of Minginish). Hostellers might like to know that there are three year-round **bunkhouses** in Carbost and **PORTNALONG**: the *Waterfront Bunkhouse* (ⓣ01478/640205) is next to the *Old Inn* in Carbost; the *Croft Bunkhouse and Bothies* (ⓣ01478/640254), with good family accommodation, where you can also **camp**, is signposted just before you get to Portnalong; while the *Skyewalker Independent Hostel* (ⓣ01478/640250, ⓔskyewalker.hostel@virgin.net) is a converted school building beyond Portnalong, en route to Fiskavaig – it also has a campsite, shop and an excellent café which welcomes passers-by. There's also the friendly *Taigh Ailean Hotel* which serves good meals in the evening.

Dunvegan, Duirinish and Waternish

After the Portnalong and Glen Brittle turning, the A863 slips across bare rounded hills to skirt the bony sea cliffs and stacks of the west coast twenty miles or so north to **DUNVEGAN** (Dùn Bheagain). It's an unimpressive place, strung out along the east shore of the sea loch of the same name, though it does make quite a good base for exploring two interesting peninsulas: Duirinish and Waternish.

The main tourist trap in the village is **Dunvegan Castle** (April to Oct daily 10am–5.30pm; Nov to March daily 11am–4pm; £5.50, gardens only £4) which sprawls on top of a rocky outcrop, sandwiched between the sea and several acres of beautifully maintained gardens. It's been the seat of the Clan

MacLeod since the thirteenth century, but the present greying, rectangular fortress, with its uniform battlements and dummy pepper pots, dates from the 1840s. Inside, you don't get a lot of castle for your money and the contents are far from stunning, but there are three famous items: **Rory Mor's Horn**, a drinking vessel made from the horn of a mad bull which each new chief still has to drain at one draught "without setting down or falling down"; the **Dunvegan Cup**, made of bog oak covered in medieval silver filigree believed to have been given to Rory Mor by the O'Neils of Ulster in return for his help against England; and, most intriguing of all, the battered remnants of the **Fairy Flag** in the drawing room. This yellow silken flag from the Middle East may have been the battle standard of the Norwegian king, Harald Hardrada, who had been the commander of the imperial guard in Constantinople. Hardrada died trying to seize the English throne at the Battle of Stamford Bridge in 1066, after which his flag was allegedly carried back to Skye by his Gaelic boatmen. More fancifully, MacLeod family tradition asserts that the flag was the gift of the fairies, blessed with the power to protect the clan in times of danger – as late as World War II MacLeod pilots carried pictures of it for luck. Among the Jacobite mementoes are a lock of hair from the head of Bonnie Prince Charlie (whom the MacLeods, in fact, fought against) and Flora MacDonald's corsets. Elsewhere there's a "virtual" consumptive in the dungeon and an interesting display on the remote archipelago of St Kilda (see box on p.479), long the fiefdom of the MacLeods.

From the jetty outside the castle there are regular seal-spotting **boat trips** out along Loch Dunvegan, as well as longer and less frequent sea cruises to the small islands of Mingay, Islay and Clett, which were cleared of the last crofters in 1860. Outside in the car park you can buy sandwiches from a kiosk or have a more substantial snack in the castle restaurant which also offers a surprisingly good dinner menu with the emphasis on seafood. The estate also has a number of **holiday cottages** (ⓣ01470/521206). On a wet day you might scrape up some enthusiasm for Dunvegan's newest tourist attraction, the **Giant Angus MacAskill Museum** (daily 10am–6pm; £1), the weakest of Peter MacAskill's three museums on Skye, housed in a restored thatched smithy. The museum's eponymous hero was, in fact, born in the Outer Hebrides in 1825 and emigrated to Nova Scotia when he was just 6. Before his untimely death of a fever at the age of just 38, he toured with the midget, Tom Thumb, who, it is said, used to dance on his outstretched hand.

Duirinish and Glendale

The hammerhead **Duirinish peninsula** lies to the west of Dunvegan, much of it inaccessible to all except walkers prepared to scale or skirt the area's twin flat-topped basalt peaks: Healabhal Bheag (1600ft) and Healabhal Mhor (1538ft). The mountains are better known as **MacLeod's Tables**, for legend has it that the MacLeod chief held an open-air royal feast on the lower of the two for James V. The main areas of habitation lie to the north, along the western shores of Loch Dungeon, and in the broad green sweep of **Glen Dale**, attractively dotted with white farmhouses and dubbed "Little England" by the locals, due to its high percentage of "white settlers", English incomers searching for a better life. Glen Dale's current predicament is doubly ironic given its history, for it was here in 1882 that local crofters, following the example of their brethren in The Braes (see p.453), staged a rent strike against their landlords, the MacLeods. Five locals – who became known as the "Glen Dale Martyrs" – were given two-month prison sentences, and eventually, in 1904, the crofters became the first owner-occupiers in the Highlands.

All this, and a great deal more about nineteenth-century crofting, is told through fascinating contemporary news cuttings at **Colbost Folk Museum** (Easter–Oct daily 10am–6.30pm; £1), the oldest of Peter MacAskill's three Skye museums, situated in a restored blackhouse, four miles up the road from Dunvegan. A guide is usually on hand to answer questions, the peat fire smokes all day, and there's a restored illegal whisky still round the back. A little further up the shores of the loch is **Borreraig Park** (daily 9am–7pm; £1.50), an eccentric mix of a huge open-air museum of traditional horse-drawn farm machinery and a retail outlet for Skye-made crafts.

At **BORRERAIG** itself, where there was a famous piping college, is the **MacCrimmon Piping Heritage Centre** (Easter to late May Tues–Sun 11am–5.30pm; late May to early Oct daily same times; £1.50), on the ancestral holdings of the MacCrimmons, hereditary pipers to the MacLeod chiefs for three centuries, until they were sent packing in the 1770s. The plaintive sounds of the *piobaireachd* of the MacCrimmons, the founding family of Scottish piping, fill this illuminating museum – to hear the real thing, go to the annual recital held in Dunvegan Castle early in August.

In the village of **GLENDALE**, at Holmisdale House, an English settler has gathered together mountains of childhood toys and games from the last hundred years, and opened a **Toy Museum** (Mon–Sat 10am–6pm; £2.50), whose hands-on approach manages to appeal to all ages; it's open on Sundays, too, if they're wet. Beyond Glendale, a bumpy road leads to **RAMASAIG**, and beyond for another five miles to the deserted village of Lorgill where, on August 4, 1830, life came to an end when every crofter was ordered to board the *Midlothian* in Loch Snizort to go to Nova Scotia or go to prison (those over the age of seventy were sent to the poorhouse). As a result of such Clearances, the west coast of Duirinish is mostly uninhabited now. For walkers, though, it's a great area to explore, with blustery but easy footpaths leading to the dramatically sited lighthouse on **Neist Point**, Skye's most westerly spot, which features some fearsome sea cliffs, and wonderful views across the sea to the Western Isles – you can even stay at the lighthouse, in one of the three **self-catering** cottages (Ⓣ01470/511200; 6–8 people; £495 per week). Alternatively, head north for the sheer 1000-foot cliffs of **Biod an Athair** near Dunvegan Head, though there's no path, and it's a bit of a slog.

Waternish

Waternish is a thin and little-visited peninsula to the north of Dunvegan. It's not as spectacular as either Duirinish or Trotternish, but it provides equally great views over to the Western Isles on a good day. Before you can explore the peninsula, however, you have to cross the **Fairy Bridge**, at the junction of the B886, where legend has it that a MacLeod chief, foolishly married to a fairy, was forced to say farewell when she decided to go home to her mother. More likely its significance lies in the fact that it's at the meeting of three roads and was the scene of religious assemblies of the Free Church and, later, of rebellious crofters led by John MacPherson, one of the "Glen Dale Martyrs".

Waternish's prettiest village is **STEIN**, on the west coast overlooking Loch Bay. Its row of whitewashed cottages was built in 1787 by the British Fisheries Society, but never saw success, and by 1837 the village was more or less abandoned. Today, however, it seems to be coming back to life, particularly the pub, the sixteenth-century *Stein Inn*, which is well worth a visit.

At the end of the road is **Trumpan Church**, a medieval ruin on a clifftop looking out to the Western Isles. This peaceful site was the scene of one of the bloodiest episodes in Skye history, when, in 1578, the MacDonalds of Uist set fire to the church, while numerous MacLeods were attending a service inside. Everyone perished except one young girl who escaped by squeezing through a window, severing one of her breasts in the process. She raised the alarm, and the rest of the MacLeods quickly rallied and, bearing their famous Fairy Flag (see p.457), attacked the MacDonalds as they were launching their galleys. Every MacDonald was slaughtered and their bodies were thrown in a nearby dyke. In the churchyard, along with two medieval gravestones, you can also see the **Trial Stone**, a four-foot-high pillar with a hole drilled in it. Anyone accused of a crime was blindfolded and had to attempt to put their finger in it: success meant innocence; failure, death. Back on the A850, heading for Portree, Edinbane **pottery** (established 1971) is well worth a visit and a couple of miles before the junction with the A87 in **Bernisdale** there are daily sheepdog demonstrations by a past finalist in the BBC TV series *One Man and his Dog*; they're very popular, so booking is essential (Ⓣ01470/532331).

Practicalities

Dunvegan is by no means the most picturesque place on Skye, but it's a useful alternative base to Portree. It has a new **tourist office** (Mon–Sat 9am–5.30pm; Ⓣ01470/521581) and boasts several excellent **hotels** and **B&Bs** dotted along the main road, such as the converted traditional croft *Roskhill House* (Ⓣ01470/521317, Ⓔstay@roskhill.demon.co.uk; ❸). Other possibilities include the beautifully situated *Silverdale* (Ⓣ01470/521251; ❶), just before you get to Colbost, or the luxurious *Harlosh House* (Ⓣ01470/521367; ❻; April–Oct), four miles south of Dunvegan. There's an excellent lochside **campsite** at Loch Greshornish, 8 miles east of Dunvegan on the A850, (Ⓣ01470/582230, Ⓔinfo@greshcamp.co.uk; April–Sept).

The culinary mecca in the area is the expensive *Three Chimneys* **restaurant** (Ⓣ01470/511258; Mon–Sat), located beside Colbost Folk Museum, which serves sublime meals and is renowned for its marmalade pudding; if you want to stay for bed and breakfast as well, there are six fabulous rooms at the adjacent *House Over-By* (Ⓣ01470/511258, Ⓦwww.threechimneys.co.uk; ❽). More reasonably priced meals can be had at *An Strupag* in Lephin (Ⓣ01470/511204), deeper into Glen Dale. There are welcoming fires and good food at the sixteenth-century *Stein Inn* (Ⓣ01470/592362, Ⓦwww.steininn.co.uk; ❷), in Stein, and outstanding seafood at the *Lochbay Seafood Restaurant* (Ⓣ01470/592235; closed Sat & Sun); you can also stay for bed and breakfast (Easter–October; ❸) or in their attractive self-catering cottage (4 people; £365; Ⓦwww.lochbay-seafood-restaurant.co.uk). Eating in Dunvegan is a little problematic, apart from obvious hotel choices, of which *Atholl House Hotel* (Ⓣ01470/521219) is probably the best for dinner. However, there is a snug **café** attached to *Dunvegan Bakery* (closed Sat afternoon & Sun) where you can also pick up sandwich components and home-made carrot cake. If you want to add fruit to your picnic, there's fresh fare at *The Fruit and Nut Place* in the main street.

Portree

Although referred to by the locals as "the village", **PORTREE** is the only real town on Skye. It's also one of the most attractive fishing ports in northwest Scotland, its deep cliff-edged harbour filled with fishing boats and circled by multicoloured restaurants and guesthouses. Originally known as *Kiltragleann* (The Church at the Foot of the Glen), it takes its current name – some say – from *Portrigh* (Port of the King), after the state visit James V made in 1540 to assert his authority over the chieftains of Skye.

Information and accommodation

Hours vary enormously at Portree's **tourist office**, just off Bridge Street, so the ones here are just a guideline (April–Oct Mon–Sat 9am–8pm, Sun 10am–4pm; Nov–March 9am–5.30pm, closed Sun; ⓣ01478/612137). The office will, for a small fee, book **accommodation** for you – especially useful at the height of the season, when things can get very busy. Accommodation prices tend to be higher in Portree than elsewhere on the island, especially in the town itself, though B&Bs on the outskirts are usually cheaper. Of Portree's year-round **hostels**, the smartest is the *Portree Independent Hostel* (ⓣ01478/613737, ⓔportreeindhostel@hotmail.co.uk) housed in the Old Post Office on the Green, though the *Portree Backpackers Hostel* (ⓣ01478/613641), ten minutes' walk up the Dunvegan road, enjoys a more secluded location (and will pick you up from town if you ring ahead). Torvaig **campsite** (ⓣ01478/612209; April–Oct) lies a mile and a half north of town off the A855 Staffin road.

Probably the best **hotel** is the comfortable *Cuillin Hills* (ⓣ01478/612003, ⓦwww.cuillinhills.demon.co.uk; ❺), ten minutes' walk out of town along the northern shore of the bay; if the rooms are too pricey, try the reasonably priced bar snacks with a splendid view over the harbour or afternoon tea after a walk round the nearby headland. *Viewfield House Hotel* (ⓣ01478/612217; ❺), on the southern outskirts of town, in the possession of the Macdonalds for over 200 years, is worth it for the Victorian atmosphere, stuffed polecats and antiques. The *Bosville Hotel* (ⓣ01478/612846, ⓔbosville@macleodhotels.co.uk; ❺), on Bosville Terrace, commands a good view of the harbour, and has a gourmet seafood restaurant. In the lower price range, try *Conusg*, a B&B in a quiet spot by the *Cuillin Hills Hotel*, originally built for the coachman in the 1880s (ⓣ01478/612426; ❶; Easter–Sept) or *Balloch* in Viewfield Road (ⓣ01478/612093; ❷; Easter–Oct). Further still out of Portree, five miles northwest in Skeabost, is the late Victorian *Skeabost House Hotel* (ⓣ01470/532202, ⓔskeabost@sol.co.uk; ❺; March–Oct), which offers golf, fishing and landscaped gardens, as well as original billiard room and bags of atmosphere.

The Town

The **harbour** is well worth a stroll, with its attractive pier built by Thomas Telford in the early nineteenth century. Fishing boats still land a modest catch, some of which is sold through Anchor Seafoods (Tues–Fri only) at the end of the pier. The harbour is overlooked by **The Lump**, a steep and stumpy peninsula with a flagpole on it that was once the site of public hangings on the island, attracting crowds of up to 5000; it also sports a folly built by the celebrated Dr Ban, a visionary who wanted to make Portree into a second Oban. Up above the harbour is the spick-and-span town centre, spreading out from **Somerled Square**, built in the late eighteenth century as the island's administrative and commercial centre, and now housing the bus station and car park. The **Royal Hotel** on Bank Street occupies the site of the *McNab's Inn* where Bonnie Prince Charlie took leave of Flora MacDonald (see p.463), and where, 27 years later, Boswell and Johnson had "a very good dinner, porter, port and punch".

A mile or so out of town on the Sligachan road is one of Skye's most successful tourist attractions, the **Aros Centre** (daily 9am–6pm; open later in summer). Here, you can enjoy the dramatic Aros Experience (£3), an unsentimental presentation of episodes of the island's history, with stunning life-size figures and special effects, ending with an audiovisual show. There's also an

RSPB live webcam exhibition of sea eagles, but it's overpriced at an extra £2. The centre also contains a modern exhibition space, a licensed coffee bar and a popular restaurant, and there's a special play area for small kids. If it's fine, there are waymarked forest walks and a Gaelic alphabet trail starting just outside.

For a view of the contemporary visual art scene, it's well worth seeking out **An Tuireann Arts Centre**, housed in a converted fever hospital on the Struan road (Mon–Sat 10am–5pm; free), which puts on exhibitions, stages concerts, and has an excellent small café where even the counter is a work of art, with an imaginative range of food on offer (Easter–Oct)

Eating, drinking and nightlife

The best **food** in town is on Bosville Terrace, but it's pricey: the *Bosville Hotel's Chandlery* restaurant serves excellent meals, with its sister *Bosville* restaurant being much cheaper; *Harbour View* has a seafood **restaurant** with candlelit ambience. The popular *Lower Deck Seafood Restaurant* on the harbour has a wood-panelled warmth to it, and is reasonably priced at lunchtime (less so in the evenings); for good **fish and chips**, pop next door to their excellent chippy. For a cuppa and a cake, there's the *Granary* bakery's **teashop** on Somerled Square. The *Café*, an ice-cream parlour on Wentworth Street, serves real cappuccino and espresso, plus a selection of cakes and snacks. As for **pubs**, the bar of the *Pier Hotel* on the quayside is the fishermen's drinking hole, and the *Tongadale* on Wentworth Street is lively. Currently the most popular evening venue by far is the *Isles Inn* on Somerled Square which also has excellent bar meals.

The aforementioned Aros Centre has a striking new **theatre**, which shows films and hosts Gaelic **concerts** (for more details phone ⓣ01471/613649); concerts and events also go on at An Tuireann (see above), and it's also worth checking out what's on at the Portree Community Centre (ⓣ01478/613736), which hosts ceilidhs and so forth. For **bike rental**, go to Island Cycles (closed Sun; ⓣ01478/613121) below the Green; for **horse riding**, head for Skye Riding Centre (ⓣ01470/582419), four miles along the Uig road at Borve, or the Portree Riding and Trekking Centre off the B885 to Struan, signposted "Peiness" (open all year; ⓣ01478/612945). Day or half-day **boat trips** leave the pier for daily excursions to Raasay and Rona (ⓣ01478/613718); **diving** can be organized through Hebridean Diving Services in Lochbay, towards Dunvegan (ⓣ01470/592219). You can check the **internet** or collect your email at Gael Net Ltd on the Dunvegan road (closed Sun; ⓣ01478/613300).

Trotternish

Protruding twenty miles north from Portree, the **Trotternish peninsula** boasts some of the island's most bizarre scenery, particularly on the east coast, where volcanic basalt has pressed down on the softer sandstone and limestone underneath, causing massive landslides. These, in turn, have created sheer cliffs, peppered with outcrops of hard, wizened basalt, which run the full length of the peninsula. These pinnacles and pillars are at their most eccentric in the Quiraing, above Staffin Bay, on the east coast. Trotternish is best explored with your own transport, but an occasional bus service (Mon–Sat 2–4 daily) along the road encircling the peninsula gives access to almost all the coast.

The east coast

The first geological eccentricity on the **Trotternish** peninsula, six miles north of Portree along the A855, is the **Old Man of Storr**, a distinctive column of rock, shaped like a willow leaf, which, along with its neighbours, is part of a massive land-slip. Huge blocks of stone still occasionally break off the cliff face of the Storr (2358ft) above and slide downhill. At 165ft, the Old Man is a real challenge for climbers; less difficult is the half-hour trek up the new footpath to the foot of the column from the woods beside the car park.

Five miles further north, there's another turn-off to the **Lealt Falls**, at the head of a gorge which spends most of its day in shadow (and is home to a fiendish collection of midges). Walking all the way down to the falls is fairly pointless, but the views across to Wester Ross from the first stage of the path are spectacular (weather permitting). The coast here is worth exploring, however, especially the track leading to **Rubha nam Brathairean** (Brothers' Point), where the Glasgow provision boat used to put in, and where fossil hunters can also follow the road that turns off at Dunans down to the end and try their luck on the beach at low tide.

Another car park a few miles up the road gives access to **Kilt Rock**, whose tubelike, basaltic columns rise precipitously from the sea, set amongst sea cliffs dotted with nests for fulmars and kittiwakes. There is a spectacular waterfall which drops 300ft to the sea, and a small loch by the car park alive with wildlife. Close by, near the turn off to Elishader, is the slate-roofed **Staffin Museum** (sporadic opening hours; £1.25), which contains fossil finds from the area, and a dinosaur bone discovered here in 1994.

Over the brow of the next hill, **Staffin Bay**, where several fossilized dinosaur footprints were discovered in 1996, is spread out before you, dotted with whitewashed and "spotty" houses; **STAFFIN** itself is a lively, largely Gaelic-speaking community where crofts have been handed down the generations. A single-track road cuts across the peninsula from the north end of the bay, allowing access to the **Quiraing**, a spectacular forest of mighty pinnacles and savage rock formations. There are two car parks: from the first, beside a cemetery, it's a steep half-hour climb to the rocks; from the second, on the saddle it's a longer but more gentle traverse. Once you're in the midst of the rocks, you should be able to make out the Prison to your right, and the 120-foot Needle, to your left; the Table, a great sunken platform where locals used to play shinty, lies above and beyond the Needle, another fifteen-minute scramble up the rocks; legend also maintains that a local warrior named Fraing hid his cattle there from the invading Norsemen.

The **accommodation** on the east coast is among the best on Skye, with most places enjoying fantastic views out over the sea. Just beyond the Lealt Falls there's the very welcoming and comfortable *Glenview Inn* (Ⓣ01470/562248, Ⓔvaltos@lineone.net; ❸; March–Oct), with an excellent adjoining restaurant, and a **campsite** (Ⓣ01470/562213; April–Sept) south of Staffin Bay. In fine weather, you can enjoy good bar snacks on the castellated terrace of the stylish, award-winning *Flodigarry Country House Hotel* (Ⓣ01470/552203, Ⓦwww.flodigarry.co.uk; ❻), three miles up the coast from Staffin. Behind the hotel (and now part of it) is the cottage where local heroine Flora MacDonald lived, and had six of her seven children, from 1751 to 1759. If the hotel's rooms are beyond your means, try the neat and attractive *Dun Flodigarry Backpackers' Hostel* (Ⓣ01470/552212), a couple of minutes' walk away – you can ring the hostel to arrange transport or catch the local bus. For **boat trips** up the coast ring Ⓣ01470/562217.

Bonnie Prince Charlie

Prince Charles Edward Stewart – better known as **Bonnie Prince Charlie** or "The Young Pretender" – was born in Rome in 1720, where his father, "The Old Pretender", claimant to the British throne, was living in exile. At the age of 25, having little military experience, no knowledge of Gaelic, an imperfect grasp of English and a strong attachment to the Catholic faith, the prince set out for Scotland on a French ship, disguised as a seminarist from the Scots College in Paris. He arrived on the Outer Hebridean island of Eriskay on July 23, 1745, and was immediately implored to return to France by the clan chiefs, who were singularly unimpressed by his lack of army. Charles was unmoved and went on to raise the royal standard at Glenfinnan, gather together a Highland army, win the Battle of Prestonpans, march on London and reach Derby before finally (and foolishly) agreeing to retreat. Back in Scotland, he won one last victory, at Falkirk, before the final disaster at Culloden in April 1746.

The prince spent the following five months in hiding, with a price of £30,000 on his head, and literally thousands of government troops searching for him. He certainly endured his fair share of cold and hunger whilst on the run, but the real price was paid by the Highlanders themselves, who risked their lives (and often paid for it with them) by aiding and abetting the prince. The most famous of these was, of course, 23-year-old **Flora MacDonald**, whom Charles met on South Uist in June 1746. Flora was persuaded – either by his beauty or her relatives, depending on which account you believe – to convey Charles "over the sea to Skye", disguised as an Irish servant girl by the name of Betty Burke. She was arrested just seven days after parting with the prince in Portree, and held in the Tower of London until July 1747. She went on to marry a local man, had seven children, and in 1774 emigrated to America, where her husband was taken prisoner during the American War of Independence. Flora returned to Scotland and was reunited with her husband on his release; they resettled in Skye and she died at the age of 68.

Charles eventually boarded a ship back to France in September 1746, but despite his promises – "for all that has happened, Madam, I hope we shall meet in St James's yet" – never returned to Scotland, nor did he ever see Flora again. After mistreating a string of mistresses, he eventually got married at the age of 52 to the 19-year-old Princess of Stolberg, in an effort to produce a Stewart heir. They had no children, and she eventually fled from his violent drunkenness; in 1788, a none-too-"bonnie" Prince Charles died in the arms of his illegitimate daughter in Rome. Bonnie Prince Charlie became a legend in his own lifetime, but it was the Victorians who really milked the myth for all its sentimentality, conveniently overlooking the fact that the real consequence of 1745 was the virtual annihilation of the Highland way of life.

Duntulm and Kilmuir

Beyond Flodigarry, at the tip of the Trotternish peninsula, by the road to Shulista, a public footpath leads past the ruins of a cleared hamlet to the spectacular sea stacks of **Rubha Hunish**, the most northerly point on Skye. A couple of miles further along the A855 lies **DUNTULM** (Duntuilm), whose heyday as a major MacDonald power base is recalled by the shattered remains of a headland fortress abandoned by the clan in 1732 after a clumsy nurse dropped the baby son and heir from a window onto the rocks below; on these same rocks, it is said, can be seen the keel marks of Viking longships. The imposing *Duntulm Castle Hotel* (☎01470/552213; ❷; March–Nov) is close by, and provides good bar meals as well as wonderful views across the Minch to the Western Isles; the hotel also has **self-catering** cottages, including three former coastguard houses (4–12 people; £625 per week).

Heading down the west shore of the Trotternish, it's two miles to the **Skye Museum of Island Life** (Easter–Oct Mon–Sat 9.30am–5.30pm; £1.75), an impressive cluster of thatched blackhouses on an exposed hill overlooking Harris. The museum, run by locals, gives a fascinating insight into a way of life that was commonplace on Skye a hundred years ago. The blackhouse, now home to the ticket office, is much as it was when it was last inhabited in 1957, while the two houses to the east contain interesting snippets of local history. Behind the museum in the cemetery up the hill are the graves of **Flora MacDonald** and her husband. Thousands turned out for her funeral in 1790, creating a funeral procession a mile long – indeed, so widespread was her fame that the original family mausoleum fell victim to souvenir hunters and had to be replaced. The Celtic cross headstone is inscribed with a simple tribute by Dr Johnson, who visited her in 1773: "Her name will be mentioned in history, if courage and fidelity be virtues, mentioned with honour."

If you want an antidote to folk history and have a liking for puns, don't miss **Macurdie's Exhibition** just off the road in **KILMUIR**. It's unattended, open most of the time, and full of spoof artefacts and pseudo-proverbs such as "it's easier to extract a Mars bar from the gullet of a seagull than to clean your shoes with a blade of grass" – the visitors' book proves people will pay an optional 50p for anything on a wet day. The land around Kilmuir used to be called the "Granary of Skye", since every inch was cultivated; even St Columba's Loch, where there are still indistinct remains of beehive cells and a chapel, was drained and the land eagerly reclaimed by crofters. **Accommodation** is available in the attractive *Kilmuir House*, previously the old manse (ⓣ01470/542262, ⓔphelpskilmuirhouseskye@btinternet.com; ❶), and at the warm and friendly *Whitewave Activities* B&B (ⓣ01470/542414; ❶), in Linicro; they also organize **windsurfing**, **archery** and **sea kayaking**, and run a cosy café in season.

Uig

A further four miles south of Kilmuir is the ferry port of **UIG** (Uige), which curves its way round a dramatic, horseshoe-shaped bay, and is the arrival point for CalMac ferries from Tarbet (Harris) and Lochmaddy (North Uist); if you've time to spare while waiting for a ferry, pop into Uig Pottery. The **tourist office** (April–Oct Mon–Sat 8.45am–6.30pm; mid-July to mid-Sept also Sun 8.45am–2pm; ⓣ01470/542404) is inside the CalMac office on the pier. Most folk come to Uig to take the ferry to the Western Isles, but if you need to stay near the ferry terminal, try the inexpensive **B&B**, *Orasay*, 14 Idrigill (ⓣ01470/542316; ❶), or one of the static *Orasay* **caravans** (ⓣ01470/542316). By contrast, the SYHA **hostel** (ⓣ01470/542211, ⓦwww.syha.org.uk; April–Oct) is high up on the south side of the village, with exhilarating views over the bay. The *Pub at the Pier* offers filling meals, and serves the local Skye beers, which are also on sale in the shop of the nearby brewery (Mon–Fri tours by appointment; ⓣ01470/542477). **Bike rental** is available from Skye Bicycle Hire on the pier (ⓣ01470/542316); **pony trekking**, from the *Uig Hotel* (ⓣ01470/542205).

The prettiest place for a fair-weather stroll and picnic around Uig is the **Fairy Glen**, reached by taking the minor road up to Balnaknock. Another good walk is to the intriguing ruined castle with no door called **Caisteal Uisdein**, built by Hugh MacDonald of Sleat in the seventeenth century. Take the turning to Cuidrach and continue to the end of the road; walk through the village and then follow the posts, but you'll have to climb in through a window – in spring, the castle is filled with primroses. When Hugh's clan chief found he'd been plotting against him, he walled him up in here with a piece of salt beef and an empty water jug. Just after this, there's a signpost to the small *Glen Hinnisdal* **bunkhouse** (Ⓣ01470/542293; Ⓔrlyddon@aol.com).

The Small Isles

The history of the **Small Isles**, which lie to the south of Skye, is typical of the Hebrides: early Christianization, followed by a period of Norwegian rule that ended in 1266 when the islands fell into Scottish hands. Their support for the Jacobite cause resulted in hard times after the failed rebellion of 1745, but the biggest problems came with the introduction of the **potato** in the mid-eighteenth century. The consequences were as dramatic as they were unforeseen: the success of the crop and its nutritional value – when grown in conjunction with traditional cereals – eliminated famine at a stroke, prompting a population explosion. In 1750, there were just a thousand islanders, but by 1800 their numbers had almost doubled.

At first, the problem of overcrowding was camouflaged by the **kelp** boom, in which the islanders were employed, and the islands' owners made a fortune, gathering and burning local seaweed to sell for use in the manufacture of gunpowder, soap and glass. But the economic bubble burst with the end of the Napoleonic Wars and, to maintain their profit margins, the owners resorted to drastic action. The first to sell up was Alexander Maclean, who sold Rùm as grazing land for **sheep**, got quotations for shipping its people to Nova Scotia, and gave them a year's notice to quit. He also cleared Muck to graze cattle, as did the MacNeills on Canna. Only on Eigg was some compassion shown:

Getting to the Small Isles

CalMac run passenger-only ferries to the Small Isles every day except Sunday from Mallaig (Ⓣ01687/462403, Ⓦwww.calmac.co.uk). Day-trips are possible to each of the islands on certain days, and to all four islands on Saturdays, if you catch the 6.30am ferry. The CalMac ferry only docks at Canna; on the other three islands, you (and all the island supplies) have to be transferred to an island tender or "flit boat". However, new piers are currently being constructed, and a new car ferry should be in operation by 2003 at the latest.

From Easter to September, you can also reach Rùm, Eigg and Muck seven days a week from Arisaig with **Arisaig Marine**, run by Murdo Grant (Ⓣ01687/450224, Ⓦwww.arisaig.co.uk). This is a much more pleasant way to get there, as the boat is licensed and, if any marine mammals are spotted en route, the boat will pause for a bit of whale-watching. Day-trips are possible to Eigg on most days, allowing four to five hours ashore, and to Rùm and Muck on a few days, allowing two to three hours ashore. With careful studying of both CalMac and Murdo Grant timetables, you should be able to organize a visit to suit you, especially as Arisaig and Mallaig are linked by railway.

Be warned, however, that boats to the Small Isles are frequently cancelled in bad weather, so be prepared to holiday for longer than you planned.

the new owner, a certain Hugh MacPherson, who bought the island from the Clanranalds in 1827, actually gave some of his tenants extended leases.

Since the Clearances, each of the islands has been bought and sold several times, though only **Muck** is now privately owned by the benevolent laird, Lawrence MacEwen. **Eigg** hit the headlines in 1997, when the islanders finally managed to buy the island themselves and put an end to more than 150 years of property speculation. The other islands were bequeathed to national agencies: **Rùm**, by far the largest and most-visited of the group, possessing a cluster of formidable volcanic peaks and the architecturally remarkable Kinloch Castle, passed to the Nature Conservancy Council (now Scottish Natural Heritage) in 1957; and **Canna**, in many ways the prettiest of the isles with its high basalt cliffs, has been in the hands of the NTS since 1981.

Accommodation on the Small Isles is limited and requires **forward planning** at all times of year; formal public transport is nonexistent, but the locals will usually oblige if you have heavy baggage to shift.

Rùm

Like Skye, **Rùm** is dominated by its Cuillin, which, though only reaching a height of 2663ft at the summit of Askival, rises up with comparable drama straight up from the sea in the south of the island. The majority of the island's thirty or so inhabitants now live in **KINLOCH**, on the sheltered east coast, and most are employed by Scottish Natural Heritage (SNH), who run the island as a National Nature Reserve. SNH have been reintroducing native woodland to the island, and overseeing a long-term study of the vast red deer population. However, the organization's most notable achievement to date is the successful reintroduction of **white-tailed (sea) eagles**, whose wingspan is even greater than that of the golden eagle. These magnificent birds of prey were last known to have bred on the island of Skye in 1916. After a caesura of some seventy years, the eagles are back, and have mostly abandoned Rùm in favour of neighbouring islands.

Rùm's chief formal attraction is **Kinloch Castle** (guided tours most days at 2pm; £3), a squat red sandstone edifice fronted by colonnades and topped by crenellations and turrets, that dominates the village of Kinloch. Completed at enormous expense in 1900 – the red sandstone was shipped in from Arran and the soil for the gardens from Ayrshire – its interior is a perfectly preserved example of Edwardian decadence, "a living memorial of the stalking, the fishing and the sailing, the tenantry and plenty of the days before 1914". From the galleried hall, with its tiger rugs, stags' heads and giant Japanese incense burners, to the "Extra Low Fast Cushion" of the Soho snooker table in the Billiard Room, the interior is packed with knick-knacks and technical gismos accumulated by **Sir George Bullough** (1870–1939), the spendthrift son of self-made millionaire, Sir John Bullough, who bought the island as a sporting estate in 1888. As such, it was only really used for a few weeks each autumn, during the "season", yet employed an island workforce of one hundred all year round. Bullough's guests were woken at eight each morning by a piper; later on, an orchestrion, an electrically driven barrel organ (originally destined for Balmoral), crammed in under the stairs, would grind out an eccentric mixture of pre-dinner tunes: *The Ride of the Valkyries* and *Ma Blushin' Rosie* among others (a demo is included in the tour). The ballroom has a sprung floor, the library features a gruesome photographic collection from the Bulloughs' world tours, but the *pièce de résistance* has to be Bullough's **Edwardian bathrooms**, whose baths have hooded walnut shower cabinets, fitted with two taps and four dials, which allow the bather to fire high-pressure water at their body from every angle.

For those with limited time or energy, there are two gentle waymarked **heritage trails**, both of which start from Kinloch, and take around two hours to complete. For longer walks, you must fill in route cards and pop them into the White House (Mon–Fri 9am–12.30pm), where the reserve manager can give useful advice. *Rum Wild* (ⓣ01687/462942) offers **guided walks** around the island from a short stroll along the shore to a nighttime hike to see the shearwaters.

The island's best beach is at **KILMORY**, to the north (5hr return), though this part of the island is only open to the public on the weekend as it's given over to the study of red deer; it's also closed completely in June, during calving, and October, during rutting. When the island's human head count peaked at 450 in 1791, the hamlet of **HARRIS** on the southwest coast (6hr return) housed a large crofting community – all that remains now are several ruined blackhouses and the extravagant **Bullough Mausoleum**, built by Sir George to house the remains of his father in the style of a Greek Doric temple, overlooking the sea. This is, in fact, the second one to be constructed here: the first was lined with Italian marble mosaics, but when a friend remarked that it looked like a public lavatory Bullough had it dynamited and the current Neoclassical one erected.

Practicalities

Until Rùm passed into the hands of the SNH, it was known as the "Forbidden Isle" because of its exclusive use as a sporting estate for the rich – nowadays, visitors are made very welcome by the SNH staff. Day-trips are possible more or less daily in the summer, either via CalMac or Murdo Grant (see above). If you plan to stay the night, you do need to book in advance, as **accommodation** is fairly limited. There's just one **B&B** on the island, *Ferry Cottage* (ⓣ01687/462767; ❶; Easter–Oct), in Kinloch, with only one twin room with shared facilities. Kinloch Castle was a luxury hotel until the early 1990s, and still lets a few of its four-poster rooms (❺), but it's basically run as an independent **hostel** (ⓣ01687/462037), with dormitories in the old servants' quarters and a farmhouse bothy (March–Oct). SNH also run two simple mountain **bothies** (three nights maximum stay), in Dibidil and Guirdil, and basic **camping** on the foreshore near the jetty. You need to book ahead for both by contacting the reserve manager at the *White House* (ⓣ01687/462026).

Wherever you're staying, you can either do self catering – hostellers can use the hostel kitchen – or eat the unpretentious **food** offered in the hostel's licensed bistro, which serves full breakfasts, offers packed lunches, and charges just over £10 a head for a three-course evening meal. There is also a small shop/off-licence/post office in Kinloch. Bear in mind that Rùm is the wettest of the Small Isles, and is known for having some of the worst **midges** (see p.45) in Scotland – come prepared for both. Finally, note that overnight visitors cannot bring dogs, but day-trippers can.

Eigg

Eigg (Ⓦwww.isleofeigg.org) is without doubt the most easily distinguishable of the Small Isles from a distance, since the island is mostly made up of a basalt plateau 1000ft above sea level, and a great stump of columnar pitchstone lava, known as An Sgurr, rising out of the plateau another 290ft. It's also by far the most vibrant, populous and welcoming of the Small Isles, with a real strong sense of community. This has been given an enormous boost by the 1997 buy-out by the seventy-odd islanders (along with the local council and the Scottish Wildlife Trust), which ended Eigg's unhappy history of private ownership, most notoriously with the Olympic bobsleigher and gelatine heir Keith Schellenberg. The anniversary of the buy out is celebrated every year with an all-night ceilidh on the weekend nearest June 12.

Visitors arrive in the southeast corner of the island – which measures just five miles by three – at **GALMISDALE**, where **An Laimhrig** (The Anchorage), the island's community centre stands, housing a shop, post office, tearoom and information centre. The island minibus meets incoming ferries, and will take you to wherever you need to go on the island. If time is limited, you could simply head for the nearby **Lodge**, the former laird's house and gardens which the islanders plan to renovate in the future. With the island's great landmark, **An Sgurr** (1292ft), watching over you wherever you go, many folk feel duty bound to climb it, and enjoy the wonderful views over to Muck and Rùm. The easiest approach is to take the path that skirts the summit to the north, and ascend from the saddle to the west; the return trip takes between three and four hours.

Many visitors head off to **CLEADALE**, the main crofting settlement in the north of the island, where the beach, known as Camas Sgiotaig or the "**Singing Sands**", is comprised of quartz, which squeaks underfoot when dry (hence the name). If you're up for it, the steep climb up to the ridge of **Ben Bhuidhe**, to the east, is worth it for the views across to Rùm and Skye. A large colony of **Manx shearwater** nests in burrows around the base of Ben Bhuidhe; to view the birds, you need to be there just after dusk.

The nicest place **to stay** on Eigg is *Kildonnan House* (Ⓣ01687/482446; full board ④), a beautiful eighteenth-century wood-panelled house where the cooking is superb. Eigg's other B&B is *Laig Farm* (Ⓣ01687/482412; full board ④), friendly enough, but a bit little basic. There are several **self-catering** options, which you can get off the island's website at Ⓦwww.isleofeigg.org, plus the *Glebe Barn* (Ⓣ01687/482417), a comfortable new **bunkhouse** where you must book ahead, and several **bothies**, including one, run by Sue Holland (Ⓣ01687/482480), where **camping** is also possible; wild camping is restricted to the beach by the pier. **Bike rental** is available from the craftshop by the pier. In season, there are **guided walks** on Thursdays, run by the Scottish Wildlife Trust warden (Ⓣ01687/482477), and live music on a Saturday evening in the tearoom. You'll probably notice, as you walk around the island, that Eigg has no mains electricity, so many of the houses run off noisy diesel generators.

Muck

Smallest and most southerly of the Small Isles, **Muck** is low-lying, mostly treeless and extremely fertile, and as such shares more characteristics with the likes of Coll and Tiree than its nearest neighbours. Its name derives from *muc*, the

Gaelic for "pig" – or, as some would have it, *muc mara*, "sea pig" or porpoise, which abound in the surrounding water – and has long caused much embarrassment to generations of lairds who preferred to call it the "Isle of Monk", because it had briefly belonged to the medieval church.

PORT MÓR, the village on the southeast corner of the island, is where visitors arrive. The prominent memorial in the local graveyard commemorates two islanders and a visiting student who were drowned shooting shags near Eilean nan Each (Horse Island). A road, just over a mile in length, connects Port Mór with the island's main farm, **GALLANACH**, which overlooks the rocky seal-strewn skerries on the north side of the island. The nicest sandy beach is Camas na Cairidh, to the east of Gallanach. Despite being only 452ft above sea level, it really is worth climbing **Beinn Airein**, in the southwest corner of the island, for the 360-degree panoramic view of the surrounding islands; the return journey from Port Mór takes around two hours.

You can **stay** with one of the MacEwen family, who have owned the island since 1896, at *Port Mór House* (Ⓣ01687/462365; full board ❹); the rooms are pine-clad and enjoy great views, and the food is delicious. Alternatively, you can stay at the island's **bunkhouse** (Ⓣ01687/462042), a characterful, wood-panelled bothy heated by a Rayburn stove – it's a seven-bed hostel, with three rooms, but can be booked exclusively as a self-catering unit. With permission from the landowner you may also **camp rough**, but bring supplies with you as there is no shop. For more **self-catering** options, contact Barbara Graves (Ⓣ01687/462814).

The craftshop in Port Mór springs into life when day-trippers arrive, and doubles as a licensed **restaurant**. Willow basketmaking courses are an island speciality (contact *Port Mór House* for more details). The island currently runs on wind power, which means electricity can be scarce in the middle of the day if there isn't enough wind.

Canna

Measuring a mere five miles by one, and with a population of just twenty, **Canna** is run as a single farm by the National Trust of Scotland. The island enjoys the best harbour in the Small Isles, a horn-shaped haven at its south-eastern corner protected by the tidal island of Sanday, now linked to Canna by a footbridge. For visitors, the chief pastime is walking: from the dock it's about a mile across a grassy basalt plateau to the bony sea cliffs of the north shore, which rise to a peak around Compass Hill (458ft) – so called because its high metal content distorts compasses – in the northeastern corner of the island, from where you get great views across to Rùm and Skye. The cliffs of the buffeted western half of the island are a breeding ground for both Manx shearwater and puffin. Some seven miles offshore, stands the **Heiskeir of Canna**, a curious mass of stone columns sticking up thirty feet above the water.

Accommodation is extremely limited. With permission from the National Trust for Scotland (NTS), you may **camp rough** on Canna; otherwise, the only other option is **B&B** with Wendy MacKinnon (Ⓣ01687/462465; full board ❺). The NTS runs two **self-catering** cottages: *Tighard*, a Victorian house half a mile from the jetty, which sleeps a maximum of ten people, and *Kate's Cottage*, a much simpler (and cheaper) bothy, which sleeps eight. Both of the above can be booked through the NTS regional office in Oban (Ⓣ01631/570000, Ⓦwww.nts.org.uk). The NTS rep on Canna is Winnie

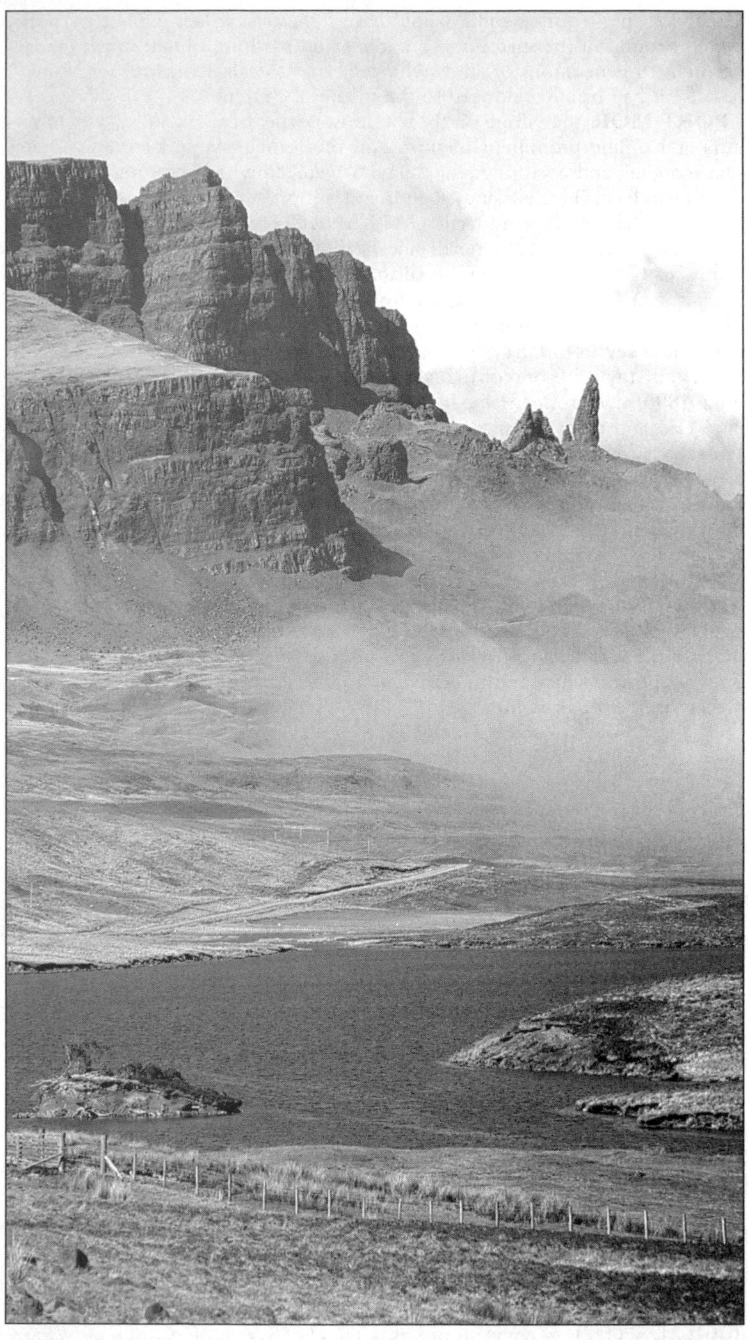

△ Quiraing, Skye

MacKinnon, who can help answer most queries (Ⓣ01687/462466). Remember, however, that there are no shops on Canna (bar the post office), so you must bring your own supplies, or order them to be delivered from Mallaig.

The Western Isles

The wild and windy **Western Isles** (Ⓦwww.witb.co.uk) – also known as the Outer Hebrides or the Long Isle – vaunt a strikingly hostile mix of landscapes from windswept golden sands to harsh, heather-backed mountains and peat bogs. An elemental beauty pervades each of the more than two hundred islands that make up the archipelago, only a handful of which are actually inhabited by a total of just over 30,000 people. The influence of the Atlantic Gulf Stream ensures a mild but moist climate, though you can expect the strong Atlantic winds to blow in rain on two out of every three days even in summer. Weather fronts, however, come and go at such dramatic speed in these parts that there's little chance of mist or fog settling and few problems with midges.

The most significant difference between Skye and the Western Isles is that here tourism is much less important to the islands' fragile economy, still mainly concentrated around crofting, fishing and weaving, and the percentage of "white settlers" is a lot lower. The Outer Hebrides remain the heartland of **Gaelic** culture, with the language spoken by the vast majority of islanders, though its everyday usage remains under constant threat from the national dominance of English. Its survival is, in no small part, due to the all-pervading influence of the Free Church and its offshoots, whose strict Calvinism is the creed of the vast majority of the population, with the sparsely populated South Uist, Barra and parts of Benbecula adhering to the more relaxed demands of Catholicism.

The interior of the northernmost island, **Lewis**, is mostly peat moor, a barren and marshy tract that gives way abruptly to the bare peaks of **North Harris**. Across a narrow isthmus lies **South Harris**, presenting some of the finest scenery in Scotland, with wide beaches of golden sand trimming the Atlantic in full view of the mountains and a rough boulder-strewn interior lying to the east. Further south still, a string of tiny, flatter islets, mainly **North**

Gaelic in the Western Isles

Except in Stornoway, and Balivanich on North Uist, **road signs** are now almost exclusively in **Gaelic**, a difficult language to the English-speaker's eye, with complex pronunciation (see p.835), though as a (very) general rule, the English names can often provide a rough pronunciation guide. Particularly if you're driving, it's essential to buy the bilingual Western Isles **map**, produced by the local tourist board, Bord Turasachd nan Eilean, and available at most tourist offices. To reflect the signposting, we've put the Gaelic first in the text, with the English equivalent in brackets. Thereafter we've stuck to the Gaelic names, to try to familiarize readers with their (albeit variable) spellings – the only exceptions are in the names of islands and ferry terminals, where we've stuck to the English names (with the Gaelic in brackets) partly to reflect CalMac's own policy.

Uist, **Benbecula**, **South Uist** and **Barra**, offer breezy beaches, whose fine sands front a narrow band of boggy farmland, which, in turn, is mostly bordered by a lower range of hills to the east.

In direct contrast to their wonderful landscapes, villages in the Western Isles are rarely picturesque in themselves, and are usually made up of scattered, relatively modern croft houses strung out along the elementary road system. **Stornoway**, the only real town in the Outer Hebrides, is eminently unappealing. Many visitors, walkers and nature watchers forsake the settlements altogether and retreat to secluded cottages and B&Bs, though for this you really need your own transport.

Transport practicalities

British Regional Airlines and Loganair operate fast and frequent **flights** (Mon–Sat only) from Glasgow and Inverness to Stornoway on Lewis, and Barra and Benbecula on North Uist. But be warned: the weather conditions on the islands are notoriously changeable, making flights prone to both delay and stomach-churning bumpiness. On Barra, the other complication is that you land on the beach, so the timetable is adjusted with the tides. CalMac **car ferries** run from Ullapool in the Highlands to Stornoway (Mon–Sat only); from Uig, on Skye, to Tarbert and Lochmaddy (Mon–Sat only); and from Oban and Mallaig to South Uist and Barra (daily). There's also an **inter-island ferry** from Leverburgh, on Harris, to Otternish, on North Uist, and between South Uist and Barra (for more on ferry services, see "Travel details" on p.501).

Although travelling around the islands is time-consuming, for many people this is part of their charm. A series of inter-island causeways makes it possible to drive from one end of the Western Isles to the other with just two interruptions – the CalMac **ferry** trip from Harris to North Uist, and the one from South Uist to Barra. The islands boast a distinctly low-key **bus** service, with no buses on Sundays. Note, however, that several local companies offer very reasonable **car rental** – around £125 a week – though you're not permitted to take their vehicles off the Western Isles.

The islands' **hostels** are geared up for the outdoor life, occupying remote locations on or near the coast. Several of them are run by the Gatliff Hebridean Hostels Trust (GHHT), who have renovated some isolated crofters' cottages. None of these has phones, so you can't book in advance, and you really need to bring your own bedding; each has a simple kitchen, so take your own food. If you're after a little more comfort, then the islands have a generous sprinkling of reasonably priced **B&Bs** and **guesthouses** – many of which are a lot more inviting than the hotels and can be easily booked over the phone, or through the tourist offices for a small fee.

Lewis (Leodhas)

Shaped rather like the top of an ice-cream cone, **Lewis** is the largest and by far the most populous of the Western Isles and the northernmost island in the Hebridean archipelago. Most of the island's 20,000 inhabitants – two-thirds of the Western Isles' total population – now live in the crofting and fishing villages strung out along the northwest coast, between **Calanais** and **Port Nis**, in one of the most densely populated rural areas in the country. On this coast you'll also find the islands' best-preserved **prehistoric remains** – Dùn Charlabhaigh broch and Calanais standing stones – as well as a smattering of ancient crofters'

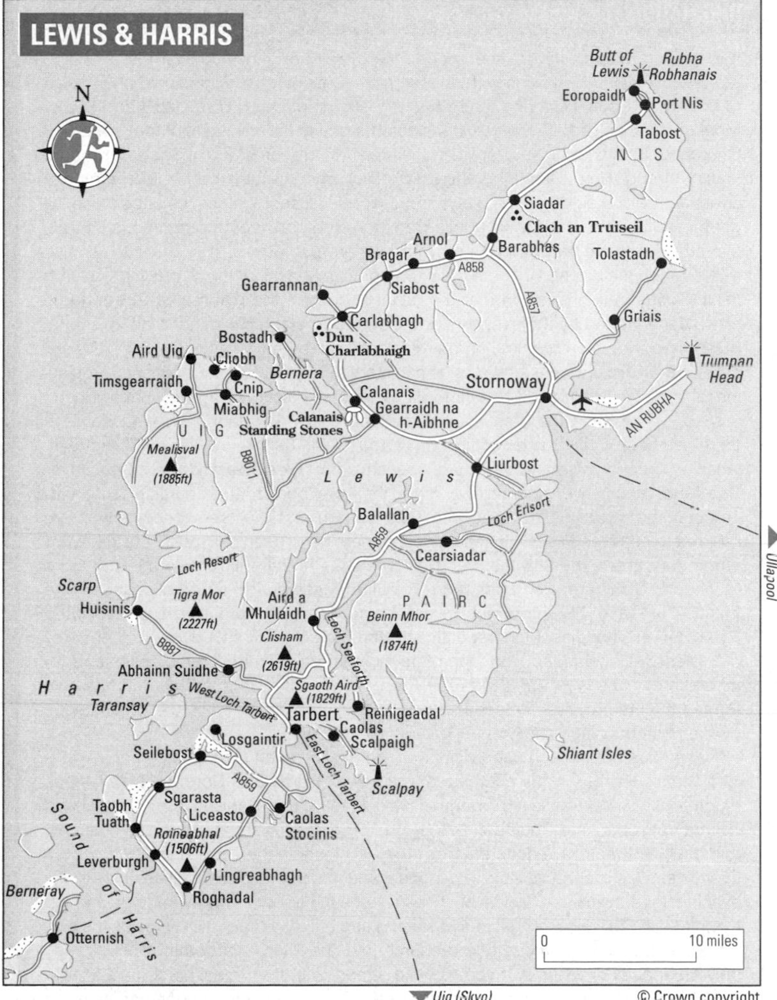

houses in various stages of abandonment. The landscape is mostly flat peat bog – hence the island's name, derived from the Gaelic *leogach* (marshy) – with a gentle shoreline that only fulfils its dramatic potential around Rubha Robhanais (Butt of Lewis), a group of rough rocks on the island's northernmost tip, near Port Nis. To the south, where Lewis is physically joined with Harris, the land rises to just over 1800ft, providing a more exhilarating backdrop for the excellent beaches that pepper the isolated coastline of **Uig**, to the west of Calanais.

Most visitors use **Stornoway**, on the east coast, as a base for exploring the island, though this presents problems if you're travelling by **bus**. There's a regular service to Port Nis and Tarbert, and although the most obvious excursion – the 45-mile round trip from Stornoway to Calanais, Carlabhagh, Arnol and back – is difficult to complete by public transport, minibus tours make the trip on most days from April to October (see p.475).

Religion in the Western Isles

It is difficult to overestimate the importance of **religion** in the Western Isles, which are sharply divided – though with little enmity – between the Catholic southern isles of Barra and South Uist, and the Protestant islands of North Uist, Harris and Lewis. Most conflicts arise from the very considerable power the ministers of the Protestant Church, or Kirk, wield in secular life in the north, where the creed of **Sabbatarianism** is very strong. Here, Sunday is the Lord's Day, and virtually the whole community (irrespective of their degree of piety) stops work – all shops close, all pubs close, all garages close and there's no public transport and, perhaps most famously of all, even the swings in the children's playgrounds are padlocked.

The other main area of division is, paradoxically, within the Protestant Church itself. Scotland is unusual in that the national church, the **Church of Scotland**, is presbyterian (ruled by the ministers and elders of the church) rather than episcopal (ruled by bishops). At the time of the main split in the Presbyterian Church – the so-called **1843 Disruption** – a third of its ministers left the Church of Scotland, protesting at the law which allowed landlords to impose ministers against parishioners' wishes, and formed the breakaway **Free Church of Scotland**. Since those days there has been a gradual reconciliation although, in 1893, there was another break, when a minority of the Free Church became the **Free Presbyterian Church of Scotland**; meanwhile, others slowly made their way back to the Church of Scotland. To confuse matters further, both the Free Church and the Free Presbyterians are referred to as "**Wee Frees**". In recent years, there have been still more schisms within the Wee Frees: in 1988 the Free Presbyterian Church split over a minister, Lord Mackay of Clashfern, who attended a Requiem Mass during a Catholic funeral of a friend – he and his supporters went on to form the break-away Associated Presbyterian Churches. More recently still, the Free Church split over the "heresies" of Professor Donald MacLeod, one of its more liberal members, who writes a regular column in the *West Highland Free Press*. A minority within the church has now formed the Free Church of Scotland (Continuing), accompanied by the usual battles over church buildings and congregations.

The various brands and subdivisions of the Presbyterian Church may appear trivial to outsiders, but to the churchgoers of Lewis, Harris and North Uist (as well as much of Skye and Raasay) they are still keenly felt. In part, this is due to social and cultural reasons: Free Church elders helped organize resistance to the Clearances, and the Wee Frees have done the most to help preserve the Gaelic language. A Free Church service is a memorable experience, and in some villages it takes place every evening (and twice on Sundays): there's no set service or prayer book and no hymns, only Biblical readings, psalm singing and a fiery sermon all in Gaelic; the pulpit is the architectural focus of the church, not the altar; and communion is taken only on special occasions. If you want to attend one, the Free Church on Kenneth Street in Stornoway has reputedly the largest Sunday-evening congregation in the UK, of up to 1500 people.

Some history

After Viking rule ended in 1266, Lewis became a virtually independent state, ruled over by the **MacLeod clan** for several centuries. King James VI, however, had other ideas: he declared the folk of Lewis to be "void of religion", and attempted to establish a colony, as in Ulster, by sending Fife Adventurers to attack Lewis. They were met with armed resistance by the MacLeods so, in retaliation, James VI granted the lands to their arch rivals, the MacKenzies of Kintail. In 1844, the MacKenzies sold Lewis to **Sir James Matheson**, who'd made a fortune from the Chinese opium trade. Matheson invested heavily in the island's infrastructure, though, as his critics point out, he made sure he recouped his money through tax or rent. He was relatively benevolent when the island was hit by potato famine in the mid-1840s, but ultimately opted for solving the problem through eviction and emigration. His chief factor, Donald Munro, was utterly ruthless, and was only removed after the celebrated Bernera Riot of 1874 (see p.483). The 1886 Crofters Act greatly curtailed the power of the Mathesons; it did not, however, right any of the wrongs of the past. Protests, such as the Pairc Deer Raid of 1887, in which starving crofters killed 200 deer from one of the sporting estates, and the Aignish land raids of the following year, continued against the Clearances of earlier that century.

When **Lord Leverhulme**, founder of the soap empire Unilever, acquired the island (along with Harris) in 1918, he was determined to drag Lewis out of its cycle of poverty by establishing an integrated fishing industry. To this end he founded MacFisheries, a nationwide chain of retail outlets for the fish which would be caught and processed on the islands: he built a cannery, an ice factory, roads, bridges and a light railway; he bought boats, and planned to use spotter planes to locate the shoals of herring. But the dream never came to fruition. Unfortunately, Leverhulme was implacably opposed to the island's centuries-old tradition of crofting, which he regarded as inefficient and "an entirely impossible way of life". He became involved in a long, drawn-out dispute over the distribution of land to returning ex-servicemen, the "land fit for heroes" promised by the Board of Agriculture. In the end, however, it was actually financial difficulties which prompted Leverhulme to pull out of Lewis in 1923, and concentrate on Harris. He generously gifted Lews Castle and Stornoway to its inhabitants and offered free crofts to those islanders who had not been involved in land raids. In the event, few crofters took up the offer – all they wanted was security of tenure, not ownership. Whatever the merits of Leverhulme's plans, his departure left a huge gap in the non-crofting economy, and between the wars thousands more emigrated.

Stornoway (Steornabhagh)

In these parts, **STORNOWAY** is a buzzing metropolis, with some 8000 inhabitants, a one-way system, pedestrian precinct with CCTV and all the trappings of a large town. It's a centre for employment, a social hub for the island and, perhaps most importantly of all, home to the **Comhairle nan Eilean Siar** (Western Isles Council), set up in 1974, which has done so much to promote Gaelic language and culture, and try to stem the tide of anglicization. For the visitor, however, the town is unlikely to win any great praise – aesthetics are not its strong point, and the urban pleasures on offer are limited.

Information and accommodation

The best thing about Stornoway is the convenience of its services. The island's **airport** is four miles east of the town centre, a £5 taxi ride away; the swanky new octagonal CalMac **ferry terminal** is on South Beach, close to the **bus station**. You can get bus timetables, a map of the town and other useful information from the **tourist office**, near North Beach at 26 Cromwell St (April–May & Sept to mid-Oct Mon–Fri 9am–6pm, Sat 9am–5pm; June–Aug Mon, Tues, Thurs & Sat 9am–6pm & 8–9pm, Wed & Fri 9am–8pm; mid-Oct to March Mon–Fri 9am–5pm; ⓣ01851/703088); they also sell tickets for **minibus tours** to Calanais (Mon–Fri) and for Out and About **wildlife trips** round Lewis and Harris.

Of the **hotels**, the *Royal Hotel* on Cromwell Street (ⓣ01851/702109; ❺) is your best bet. Otherwise try the modern and rather pretentious *Caberfeidh* on Macauley Road, north of the town centre, (ⓣ01851/702604, ⓦwww.calahotels.com; ❻); or the more reliable choice of the *Park Guest House* (ⓣ01851/702485; ❷) on James Street where the public areas have bags of lugubrious late Victorian character; the bedrooms significantly less. Of the **B&Bs** along leafy Matheson Road, try *Fernlea*, a listed Victorian house, at no. 9 (ⓣ01851/702125; ❷). The *Stornoway Backpackers'* **hostel** is a basic affair about five minutes' walk from the ferry at 47 Keith St (ⓣ01851/703628, ⓦwww.stornoway-hostel.co.uk). The nearest **campsite**, *Laxdale Holiday Park* (ⓣ01851/703234, ⓦwww.laxdaleholidaypark.force9.co.uk; open all year), lies a mile or so along the road to Barabhas, on Laxdale Lane; the campsite has holiday caravans (short breaks available), a self-catering bungalow and a purpose-built **bunkhouse**. *Fairhaven* in Keith Street (ⓣ01851/705862, ⓦwww.hebrideansurf.co.uk; ❶) is primarily a centre for surfers, but welcomes all; accommodation consists of bunkhouse, family rooms and single rooms.

The Town

For centuries, life in Stornoway has focused on its **harbour**, whose quayside was filled with barrels of pickled herring, and whose deep and sheltered waters were thronged with coastal steamers and fishing boats in their nineteenth-century heyday, when more than a thousand boats were based at the port. Today, most of the catch is landed on the mainland and, despite the daily comings and goings of the CalMac ferry from Ullapool, the harbour is a shadow of its former commercial self. The nicest section of the harbour is Cromwell Street Quay, by the tourist office, where the remaining fishing fleet ties up for the night.

Stornoway's commercial centre, to the east, is little more than a string of unprepossessing shops and bars. The one exception is the old **Town Hall** on South Beach, a splendid Scots Baronial building, its rooftop peppered with conical towers, above which a central clock tower rises. On the first floor you'll find the **An Lanntair Art Gallery** (Mon–Sat 10am–5.30pm; free), whose exhibitions feature the work of local artists, plus a very pleasant cafe. Anyone remotely interested in Harris Tweed should head for the **Lewis Loom Centre** (Mon–Sat 9am–6pm; £1), run by an eccentric and engaging man and located at the far end of Cromwell Street, in the Old Grainstore off Bayhead. There's an exhibition on the cloth, a shop, and three looms, one of which is a Hattersley, which you may catch going through its paces.

Continuing up the pedestrian precinct into Francis Street, you'll eventually reach the **Museum nan Eilean** (April–Sept Mon–Sat 10am–5.30pm; Oct–March Tues–Fri 10am–5pm, Sat 10am–1pm; free), housed in the old Victorian Nicolson Institute school. The ground-floor gallery explores the island's history until the MacKenzie takeover, and is full of artefacts found during peat cutting, including a lovely Viking dish made from alderwood. There's also a chance to view a Gaelic/English CD-ROM on the Lewis Chessmen (see p.484). The first-floor gallery includes lots of information about the herring and weaving industries, and houses an old loom shed with one of the semi-automatic looms introduced by Lord Leverhulme in the 1920s.

To the northwest of the town centre stands **Lews Castle**, a nineteenth-century Gothic pomposity built by Sir James Matheson in 1863. As the former laird's pad, it is seen as a symbol of old oppression by many: it was here, in the house's now defunct conservatory, that Lady Matheson famously gave tea to the Bernera protesters when they marched on Stornoway prior to the riot (see p.483); when the eccentric Lord Leverhulme took up residence, he had unglazed bedroom windows which allowed the wind and rain to enter, and gutters in the floor to carry off the residue. The current plan is to make it part of the new University of the Highlands and Islands. For the moment, however, its chief attraction is its mature wooded grounds, a unique sight on the Western Isles, for which Matheson had to import thousands of tons of soil from the mainland. If you enter or exit Stornoway via Willowglen Road (A858), you'll see the town **War Memorial**, a castle tower set high above the town amidst gorse bushes, and a good place to take in the sprawl that is Stornoway.

Eating, drinking and nightlife

Decent **food** options are disappointingly limited in Stornoway, especially in the evening. The best hotel food is served in the *Boatshed* restaurant at the *Royal Hotel*. Another good place is the *Thai Café* at 27 Church St (☎01851/701811), which serves inexpensive but authentic **Thai** food – as a consequence it's very popular, so book ahead. There are excellent light lunches to be had from the *An Lanntair* tearoom, and good value snacks from *An Leabharlann*, the coffee shop in the new library on Cromwell Street. The *Golden Ocean* **Chinese** restaurant opposite is not a bad choice for lunch, early evening or takeaway, but is otherwise quite expensive. Your best bet for local food is the restaurant of the *Park Guest House*, on James Street (closed Sun & Mon), but it's expensive, unless you go for the "early bird" option. The *Coffee Pot* near the pier is a cheap option for chips with everything. The biggest problem is that all the above places are closed on Sunday. The expensive *Caberfeidh Hotel*, on Macauley Road, is one of the few hotels to serve Sunday lunch, although the *Royal* opens on Sundays in the summer, while the *Stornoway Balti House*, near the bus station on South Beach, opens on Sunday evenings.

As for **pubs**, *MacNeills* on Cromwell Street is the liveliest central pub, with a mixed clientele of keen drinkers. *The Criterion*, a tiny wee pub on Point Street, is another option, as is the very pleasant bar of the *Royal Hotel*. There's sometimes live music as well as pub grub at the *Whaler's Rest* in Francis Street. Needless to say, all pubs are closed on Sundays, while hotel bars are open for residents only.

Listings

Bakery Stag Bakery, Cromwell St; next door is Nature's Store, a health-food shop.
Banks The following banks all have ATMs: Bank of Scotland, Cromwell Street; Clydesdale, South Beach; Lloyds TSB, Francis Street; Royal Bank of Scotland, North Beach.
Bike rental Alex Dan's, 67 Kenneth St (☎01851/704025; closed Sun).
Bookshops Baltic Bookshop, Cromwell Street.
Car rental Lewis Car Rental, 52 Bayhead (☎01851/703760); Mackinnon Self-Drive, south-east of the town centre, at 18 Inaclete Rd (☎01851/702984).
Internet Stornoway Library, 19 Cromwell St (☎01851/703064; closed Sun).
Fishing Fishing trips for wild brown trout (☎01851/706939).
Laundry Erica's Laundrette, Macauley Road (closed Wed & Sun; last wash 1.40pm). It's situated beyond the second roundabout out of town, and is therefore not central.
Pharmacy Boots is on the corner of Cromwell Street and Point Street.
Taxis Central Cabs, 20 MacMillan Brae (☎01851/706900).

The road to Tolastadh (Tolsta)

Given the relative paucity of attractions in Stornoway, the dead-end B895 to **TOLASTADH**, twelve miles north along the east coast, is a good road to head out on. It boasts several excellent golden beaches and marks the starting point of a lovely coastal walk to Nis.

The legacy of Lord Leverhulme's brief ownership of Lewis is recalled by the striking **Griais Memorial** to the Lewis land-raiders, situated by Griais Bridge, above Gress Sands. It was here that Leverhulme's plans came unstuck: he wanted to turn the surrounding crofting land into three big farms, which would provide milk for the workers of his fish-canning factory; the local crofters just wanted to return to their traditional way of life. Such was Leverhulme's fury at the Griais (Gress) and Col (Coll) land-raiders that, when he offered to gift the crofts of Lewis to their owners, he made sure the offer didn't include Griais and Col. The stone-built memorial is a symbolic croft split asunder by Leverhulme's interventions.

Further north, beyond Tolastadh, is probably the finest of the coast's sandy beaches, Gheardha (Garry), and the beginning of the footpath to Nis. Shortly after leaving the bay, the path crosses the "**Bridge to Nowhere**", built by Leverhulme as part of an unrealized plan to forge a new road right along the east coast. A little further along the track, there's a fine waterfall on the Abhainn na Cloich (River of Stones). The makeshift road peters out, but a path continues for another ten miles via the old sheiling village of Diobadail, to Nis (see below). If you're in search of a cuppa, try the **pottery** back in Col.

The road to Barabhas (Barvas) and Nis (Ness)

Northwest of Stornoway, the A857 crosses the vast, barren **peat bog** of the interior, an empty, undulating wilderness riddled with stretchmarks formed by peat cuttings and pockmarked with freshwater lochans. The whole area was once covered by forests, but these disappeared long ago, leaving a smothering deposit of peat that is, on average, six feet thick, and is still being formed in certain places. Tourists tend to cross this barren landscape at speed, while ecologists have identified these natural wetlands as important "carbon sinks", whose erosion should be protected. For the people of Lewis, the peat represents a valuable energy resource, with each crofter being assigned a slice of the bog. The islanders spend several very sociable weeks each spring cutting the peat, turning it over and leaving it neatly laid out in the open air to dry, returning in summer to collect the dried sods and stack them outside their houses. Though tempting to take home as souvenirs, these piles are the fruits of hard labour, and remain the island's main source of domestic fuel, its pungent smoke one of the most characteristic smells of the Western Isles.

Twelve miles across the peat bog the road approaches the west coast of Lewis and divides, heading southwest towards Calanais (see p.482), or northeast through **BARABHAS** (Barvas), and a whole string of bleak and fervently Free Church crofting and weaving villages. These scattered settlements have none of the photogenic qualities of Skye's whitewashed villages: the churches are plain and unadorned; the crofters' houses relatively modern and smothered in grey, pebble-dash rendering or harling; the stone cottages and enclosures of their forebears often lie half-abandoned in the front garden; while a rusting assortment of discarded cars and vans store peat bags and the like. Just beyond Barabhas, a signpost points to the pleasant **Morven Gallery** (Easter–Oct Mon–Sat 11am–5pm; free), which hosts exhibitions and has a handy café to hole up in during bad weather. Three miles further up the road, you pass the twenty-foot monolith of **Clach an Truiseil**, the first of a series of prehistoric sights between the crofting and weaving settlements of **BAILE AN TRUISEIL** (Ballantrushal) and **SIADAR** (Shader). Beyond Siadar, anyone with a passing interest in pottery should visit **Borgh Pottery** (Mon–Sat 9.30am–6pm; free), where you can watch the husband-and-wife team creating hand-thrown pots.

Offshore islands

Though three men dwell on Flannan Isle
To keep the lamp alight,
As we steer'd under the lee, we caught
No glimmer through the night.

Flannan Isle by Wilfred Wilson Gibson

On December 15, 1900, a passing ship reported that the lighthouse on the **Flannan Isles,** built the previous year by the Stevensons some 21 miles west of the Butt of Lewis, was not working. Gibson's poem goes on to recount the arrival of the relief boat from Oban on Boxing Day, whose crew found no trace of the three keepers. More mysteriously still, a full meal lay untouched on the table, one chair was knocked over, and only two oilskins were missing. Subsequent lightkeepers doubtless spent many lonely nights trying in vain to figure out what happened, until the lighthouse went automatic in 1971.

Equally famous, but for different reasons, is the tiny island of **Sula Sgeir**, 41 miles due north of the Butt of Lewis. Every August since anyone can remember, the young men of Nis have set sail from Port Nis to harvest the young gannet or guga that nest in their thousands high up on the islet's sea cliffs. It's a dangerous activity, and one that the RSPB has tried its best to stop, but for some unknown reason boiled gannet and potato continues to be a popular Lewis delicacy, and there's never any shortage of eager volunteers for the annual cull.

Somewhat incredibly, the island of **Rona**, less than a mile across and ten miles east of Sula Sgeir, was inhabited on and off until the mid-nineteenth century. The island's St Ronan's Chapel is one of the oldest Celtic Christian ruins in the country. St Ronan was, according to legend, the first inhabitant, moving here in the eighth century with his two sisters, Miriceal and Brianuil, until one day he turned to Brianuil and said, "My dear sister, it is yourself that is handsome, what beautiful legs you have." She apparently replied that it was time for her to leave the island, and made her way to neighbouring Sula Sgeir. Rona is now in the care of Scottish Natural Heritage (Ⓣ01870/705258), from whom you must get permission before landing.

The largest of all the offshore islands is the NTS-owned **St Kilda** archipelago, roughly a hundred miles west southwest of the Butt of Lewis and over forty miles from its nearest landfall, Griminish Point on North Uist. The last 36 Gaelic-speaking inhabitants of Hirta, St Kilda's main island, were evacuated at their own request in 1930, ending several hundred years of harsh existence – well recorded in Tom Steel's book *The Life and Death of St Kilda*. Today, the island is partly occupied by the army, who have a missile-tracking radar station here linked to South Uist. The NTS (Ⓣ01870/620238) organizes week-long volunteer groups, which you can apply to join, though be prepared for a rough, fourteen-hour crossing from Oban. With a calm sea and permission from the NTS – even tour operators have to negotiate long and hard – you may go ashore to visit the museum in the old village, restored by volunteers, and struggle up the massive cliffs, where the islanders once caught puffins, young fulmars and gannets.

Nis (Ness)

The main road continues through a string of straggling villages, until you reach the various densely populated settlements that make up the parish of **NIS** (Ness), at the northern tip of Lewis. The folk of Nis are perhaps best known for their annual culling of young gannets on Sula Sgeir (see box). For an insight into the social history of the area, take a look inside **Comunn Eachdriadh Nis** (Ness Historical Society; Mon–Fri 10.30am–5pm; donations welcome), on the left as you pass through **TABOST** (Habost). The museum, housed in an unlikely looking building, contains a huge collection of photographs, but its prize possession is a diminutive sixth- or seventh-century cross from the Isle of Rona (see box), decorated with a much-eroded nude male figure, and thought by some to have been St Ronan's gravestone; you can have tea and coffee there too. The road terminates at the fishing village of **PORT NIS** (Port of Ness), with a tiny harbour and lovely golden beach.

Shortly before you reach Port Nis, a minor road heads two miles northwest to the hamlet of **EOROPAIDH** (Europie) – pronounced "Yor-erpee". Here, by the road junction that leads to the Butt of Lewis, the simple stone structure of **Teampull Mholuaidh** (St Moluag's Church) stands amidst the runrig fields. Thought to date from the twelfth century, when the islands were still under Norse rule, but restored in 1912 (and now used once a month by the Scottish Episcopal Church for sung Communion), the church features a strange south chapel with only a squint window connecting it to the nave. In the late seventeenth century, the traveller Martin Martin noted: "they all went to church . . . and then standing silent for a little time, one of them gave a signal . . . and immediately all of them went into the fields, where they fell a drinking their ale and spent the remainder of the night in dancing and singing, etc". Church services aren't what they used to be.

From Eoropaidh, a narrow road twists to the bleak and blustery northern tip of the island, **Rubha Robhanais** – well known to devotees of the BBC shipping forecast as the **Butt of Lewis** – where a lighthouse sticks up above a series of sheer cliffs and stacks, alive with kittiwakes, fulmars and cormorants, with skuas and gannets feeding offshore, and a great place for marine mammal-spotting. The lighthouse is closed to the public, though a shop and tearoom are planned for the near future. In the meantime, you're better off backtracking half a mile or so, where there's a path down to the tiny sandy bay of **Port Sto**, a more sheltered spot for a picnic than the Butt itself. From Europaidh, you can also gain access to the dunes and machair of the nearby coastline that stretches for two or three miles to the southwest.

Practicalities

There are between four and six buses a day from Stornoway to Port Nis, Sundays excepted, and one or two **accommodation** possibilities. The best place to stay is *Galson Farm Guest House* (Ⓣ01851/850492, Ⓦwww.galsonfarm.freeserve.co.uk; ❺), an eighteenth-century farmhouse in Gabhsann Bho Dheas (South Galson), halfway between Barabhas and Port Nis, with a **bunkhouse** close by (phone number as above). Another, more modest, option is the modern croft of *Eisdean* (Ⓣ01851/810240; ❶), in Coig Peighinnean (Five Penny Borve), near Port Nis, or *Cross Inn* (Ⓣ01851/810378; ❶), remarkable primarily for being the only pub in the entire parish. There's no handy tearoom and very few shops (other than mobile ones) in these parts, so it's as well to stock up in Stornoway before you set out.

Bru (Brue), Arnol and Siabost (Shawbost)

Heading southwest from the crossroads near Barabhas brings you to several villages that meander down towards the sea. The first is **BRU** (Brue), where you'll find the **Oiseval Gallery** (Mon–Sat 10.30am–5.30pm; free), a photographic gallery that's worth a look. In the neighbouring village of **ARNOL**, the remains of numerous blackhouses lie abandoned in the village, one of which, at the far end of the village, has been restored as a **Black House Museum** (May–Sept Mon–Sat 9.30am–6.30pm; Oct–March 9.30am–4.30pm; £2.80; HS). Dating from the 1870s and inhabited until 1964, its chimneyless roof is overlaid with grassy sods and oat-straw thatch, lashed down with fishnets and ropes. Beneath, a simple system of wooden tie beams supports the roof, which covers both the living quarters and the attached byre and barn. The postwar wallpaper inside has been removed to reveal sooty rafters above the living room, where, in the centre of the stone and clay floor, the peat fire was the focal point of the house. Today, many visitors look back with nostalgia at the old abandoned blackhouses, but it's as well to remember that they were a breeding ground for disease, and that, essentially, life in the blackhouse was pretty grim. Across the road is an example of a white house, built around 1920.

Returning to the main road, it's about a mile or so to **BRAGAR**, where you'll spot a stark arch formed by the jawbone of a blue whale, washed up on the nearby coast in 1920. The spear sticking through the bone is the harpoon, which only went off when the local blacksmith was trying to remove it, badly injuring him. Another two miles on at **SIABOST** (Shawbost), local schoolchildren created the appealingly amateurish **Shawbost School Museum** (Mon–Sat 9am–6pm; free) in 1970. The converted church contains a real hotchpotch of stuff – most of it donated by locals – including a rare Lewis brick from the short-lived factory set up by Lord Leverhulme, an old hand-driven loom and a reconstructed living room with a traditional box bed. There's a great **B&B** in Siabost Bho Deas (South Shawbost) at *Airigh* (Ⓣ01851/710478, Ⓔeileenmaclean@lineone.net; ❷; March–Nov) and behind the church is the *Eilean Fraoich* **campsite** (Ⓣ01851/710504; May–Oct). You can grab a bite to eat at the *Shawbost Inn*.

Just outside Siabost, to the west, there's a sign to the newly restored **Norse Mill and Kiln**. It's a ten-minute walk over a small hill to the two thatched bothies beside a little stream; the nearer one's the kiln, the further one's the horizontal mill. Mills and kilns of this kind were common in Lewis up until the 1930s, and despite the name are thought to have been introduced here from Ireland as early as the sixth century. To the east beyond Siabost is lovely Dalbeg Bay where there is a **tearoom,** *The Copper Kettle*, with a terrace for sunny days.

Carlabhagh (Carloway) and Calanais (Callanish)

Five miles on, the landscape becomes less monotonous, with boulders and hillocks rising out of the peat moor, as you approach the parish of **CARLABHAGH** (Carloway), with its scattering of croft houses. A mile-long road leads off north to the beautifully remote coastal settlement of **GEARRANNAN** (Garenin), where nine thatched crofters' houses – the last of which was abandoned in 1973 – have been restored. There's a visitor centre with a **café** serving soup and sandwiches, and also offering guided tours of the village (£1.75). One blackhouse now serves as the GHHT **hostel** where there are four **self-catering** houses, sleeping from 2 to 16 people, (Ⓣ01851/643416, Ⓦwww.gearrannan.com; weekly/nightly rates and winter packages) while another contains public toilets. A night here is unforgettable, and there's a beautiful stony beach from which to view the sunset.

Just beyond Carlabhagh, about 400 yards from the road, Dùn Charlabhaigh Broch perches on top of a conspicuous rocky outcrop overlooking the sea. Scotland's Atlantic coast is strewn with the remains of over 500 brochs, or fortified towers, but this is one of the best preserved, its drystone circular walls reaching a height of more than 30ft on the seaward side. The broch consists of two concentric walls, the inner one perpendicular, the outer one slanting inwards, the two originally fastened together by roughly hewn flagstones, which also served as lookout galleries reached via a narrow stairwell. The only entrance to the roofless inner yard is through a low doorway set beside a crude and cramped guard cell. As at Calanais (see below), there have been all sorts of theories about the purpose of the brochs, which date from between 100 BC and 100 AD; the most likely explanation is that they were built to provide protection from Roman slave-traders.

Dùn Charlabhaigh now has its very own **Doune Broch Centre** (April–Oct Mon–Sat 10am–6pm; free), situated at a discreet distance, stone-built and sporting a turf roof. It's a good wet-weather retreat, and fun for kids, who can walk through the hay-strewn mock-up of the broch as it might have been. A mile or so beyond the broch, beside a lochan, is the *Doune Braes Hotel* (Ⓣ01851/643252, Ⓔhebrides@doune_braes.co.uk; ❹), a friendly, unpretentious place whose bar serves up the same tasty seafood dishes as its restaurant, only cheaper.

Calanais

Five miles south of Carlabhagh lies the village of **CALANAIS** (Callanish), site of the islands' most dramatic prehistoric ruins, the **Calanais Standing Stones**, whose monoliths – nearly fifty of them – occupy a serene lochside setting. There have been years of heated debate about the origin and function of the stones – slabs of gnarled and finely grained gneiss up to 15ft high – though almost everyone agrees that they were lugged here by Neolithic peoples between 3000 and 1500 BC. It's also obvious that the planning and construction of the site – as well as several other lesser circles nearby – was spread over many generations. Such an endeavour could, it's been argued, only be prompted by the desire to predict the seasonal cycle upon which these early farmers were entirely dependent, and indeed many of the stones are aligned with the position of the sun and the stars. This rational explanation, based on clear evidence that this part of Lewis was once a fertile farming area, dismisses as coincidence the ground plan of the site, which resembles a colossal Celtic cross, and explains away the central burial chamber as a later addition of no special significance. These two features have, however, fuelled all sorts of theories ranging from alien intervention to human sacrifice.

A blackhouse adjacent to the main stone circle has been refurbished as a **tearoom** and shop, and it's to this you should head for refreshment rather than the superfluous **Calanais Visitor Centre** (Mon–Sat: April–Sept 10am–7pm; Oct–March 10am–4pm; museum £1.75) on the other side of the stones (and thankfully out of view), to which all the signs direct you from the road. The centre runs a decent restaurant and a small museum on the site, but with so much information on the panels beside the stones there's little reason to visit it. You're politely asked not to walk between the stones, only along the path that surrounds them, so if you want to commune with standing stones in solitude, head for the smaller circles in more natural surroundings a mile or two southeast of Calanais, around Gearraidh na h-Aibhne (Garynahine).

If you need a place to stay, there are several inexpensive **B&Bs** in Calanais itself: try Mrs Catherine Morrison, 27 Calanais (Ⓣ01851/621392; ❶; March–Sept), or an excellent B&B, which caters well for veggies and is run by Debbie Nash (Ⓣ01851/621321; ❶) in neighbouring Tolastadh a Chaolais (Tolsta Chaolais), three miles north. Calanais also has a modern *Eschol Guest House* (Ⓣ01851/621357; ❸), no beauty from the outside, but very comfortable within. If it's just **food** you want, *Tigh Mealros* (closed Sun), in Gearraidh na h-Aibhne, serves good, inexpensive lunches and evening meals, featuring local seafood.

Bernera (Bearnaraigh)

From Gearraidh na h-Aibhne, the main road leads back to Stornoway, while the B8011 heads off west to Uig (see below), and, a few miles on, the B8059 sets off north to the island of Great Bernera, usually referred to simply as **Bernera**. Joined to the mainland via a narrow bridge that spans a small sea channel, Bernera is a rocky island, dotted with lochans, fringed by a few small lobster-fishing settlements and currently owned by Comte Robin de la Lanne Mirrlees, the Queen's former herald.

Bernera has an important place in Lewis history due to the **Bernera Riot** of 1872, when local crofters successfully defied the eviction orders delivered to them by the landlord, Sir James Matheson. In truth, there wasn't much of riot, but three Bernera men were arrested and charged with assault. The crofters marched on the laird's house, Lews Castle in Stornoway, and demanded an audience with Matheson, who claimed to have no knowledge of what his factor, Donald Munro, was doing. In the subsequent trial, Munro was exposed as a ruthless tyrant, and the crofters were acquitted. A stone-built cairn now stands as a memorial to the riot, at the crossroads beyond the central settlement of **BREACLEIT** (Breaclete), which sits beside one of the island's many lochs. Here, you'll find the **Bernera Museum** (April–Sept Mon–Sat 11am–6pm; £1.50), housed in the local community centre. There's a small exhibition on lobster fishing, a St Kilda mailboat, and a mysterious 5000-year-old Neolithic stone tennis ball, but it's hardly worth the entrance fee, unless you're tracing your ancestry.

Much more interesting is the replica **Iron Age House** (Tues–Sat noon–4pm; £1) that has been built above a precious little bay of golden sand beyond the cemetery at **BOSTADH** (Bosta), three miles north of Breacleit – follow the signs "to the shore". In 1992, gale-force winds revealed an entire late Iron Age or Pictish settlement hidden under the sand; due to its exposed position, the site has been refilled with sand, and a full-scale mock-up built instead, based on the "jelly baby" houses – after the shape – that were excavated. Inside, the house is incredibly spacious, and very dark, illuminated only by a central hearth and a few chinks of sunlight. If the weather's fine and you climb to the top of the nearby hills, you should get a good view over the forty or so islands in Loch Roag, and maybe even the Flannan Isles (see p.479) on the horizon.

If you want to stay, there are a couple of comfortable, modern **B&Bs** on the island: *Kelvindale* (Ⓣ01851/612347; ❶; April–Oct) in Tobson, a couple of miles northwest of Breacleit, and *Garymilis* (Ⓣ01851/612341, Ⓔailtenis@globalnet.co.uk; ❶; Feb–Nov), in **Circebost** (Kirkibost).

Uig

It's a long drive along the partially upgraded B8011 to the remote parish of **Uig**, one of the areas of Lewis that suffered very badly from the Clearances, The landscape here is hillier and more dramatic than elsewhere, a combination of myriad islets, wild cliff scenery and patches of pristine golden sand.

At the crossroads to **MIABHAIG** (Miavaig), you have a choice of either heading straight for the Uig Sands (see opposite), or veering off the main road, and heading along a dramatic little road northeast to **CLIOBH** (Cliff). The Atlantic breakers that roll onto the beach below the village are often spectacular, but make it unsafe for swimmers, who should continue another mile to **CNÌP** (Kneep), to the southeast of which is **Tràigh na Beirghe**, a glorious strand of shell sand, backed by dunes and machair, in which there's a small, primitive **campsite** (Ⓣ01851/672265; mid-April to mid-Sept).

The other route choice from Miabhaig is to continue along the main road through the narrow canyon of Glen Valtos (Glèann Bhaltois) to **TIMSGEARRAIDH** (Timsgarry), which overlooks **Uig Sands** (Tràigh Uuige), the largest and most prized of all the golden strands on Lewis. It was in the nearby village of Eadar dha Fhadhail (Ardroil) in 1831 that a local cow stumbled across the **Lewis Chessmen**, twelfth-century Viking chesspieces carved from walrus ivory that now reside in Edinburgh's Museum of Antiquities and the British Museum in London. You can see replicas of the chessmen in the **Uig Heritage Centre** (Mon–Sat noon–5pm; £1), housed in Uig School in Timsgearraidh. As well as putting on some excellent temporary exhibitions, the museum has bits and bobs from blackhouses, and is staffed by locals, who are happy to answer any queries you have; there's also a welcome **tearoom** in the adjacent nursery during the holidays.

The most intriguing **place to stay** is *Baile na Cille* (ⓣ01851/672241, ⓔrandjgollin@compuserve.com; ❹; April–Sept), in an idyllic setting overlooking the Uig Sands in Timsgearraidh; they also have a couple of **self-catering** cottages (6 people; £350 per week). It's an easy-going place, run by an eccentric couple, who are very welcoming to families – the Blairs have stayed here – and dish up wonderful, though expensive, set-menu dinners. An entirely different (but equally unusual) experience is to stay at the old RAF station in **AIRD UIG**, three miles north of Timsgearraidh, which is slowly being transformed by an enterprising Breton. The concrete buildings themselves are something of an eyesore, but the position, overlooking a rocky inlet beside Gallan Head, is superb. The whole complex includes **B&B** (ⓣ01851/672474; ❶), **self-catering** (5 people; £250 per week), a **hostel**, and the popular *Bonaventure* **restaurant** (closed Mon & Sun; booking advisable), which serves up outstanding French–Scottish food at bargain prices. Boat trips to Bernera and Calanais and elsewhere along the west coast are available from Sea Trek (ⓣ01851/672464, ⓦwww.seatrel.co.uk), run by Murray MacLeod from **Uigean** (Uigen), near Miabhaig.

Harris (Na Hearadh)

Lewis and **Harris** are, in fact, one island, the "division" between the two embedded in a historical split in the MacLeod clan, lost in the mists of time. The border between the two was a county boundary until 1975, with Harris lying in Inverness-shire, and Lewis belonging to Ross and Cromarty. Nowadays, the dividing line is rarely marked even on maps; for the record, it comprises Loch Resort in the west, Loch Seaforth in the east, and the six miles in between. Harris itself is more clearly divided by a minuscule isthmus, into the wild, inhospitable mountains of **North Harris** and the gentler landscape and sandy shores of **South Harris**.

Along with Lewis, Harris was purchased in 1918 by **Lord Leverhulme**, and after 1923, when he pulled out of Lewis, all his efforts were concentrated here. In contrast to Lewis, though, Leverhulme and his ambitious projects were broadly welcomed by the people of Harris. His most grandiose plans were drawn up for Leverburgh (see p.489), but he also purchased an old Norwegian whaling station in Bun Abhain Eadara in 1922, built a spinning mill at Geocrab and began the construction of four roads. Financial difficulties, a slump in the tweed industry and the lack of market for whale products meant that none of the schemes was a wholehearted success, and when Leverhulme died in 1925 the plug was pulled on all of them by his executors.

Harris Tweed

Far from being a picturesque cottage industry, as it's sometimes presented, the production of **Harris Tweed** is vital to the local economy, with a well-organized and unionized workforce. Traditionally the tweed was made by women, from the wool of their own sheep, to provide clothing for their families, using a 2500-year-old process. Each woman was responsible for plucking the wool by hand, washing and scouring it, dyeing it with lichen, heather flowers or ragwort, carding (smoothing and straightening the wool, often adding butter to grease it), spinning and weaving. Finally the cloth was dipped in sheep's urine and "waulked" by a group of women, who beat the cloth on a table to soften and shrink it whilst singing Gaelic waulking songs. Harris Tweed was originally made all over the islands, and was known simply as *clò mór* (big cloth).

In the mid-nineteenth century, the Countess of Dunmore, who owned a large part of Harris, started to sell surplus cloth to her aristocratic friends, thus forming the genesis of the modern industry, which serves as a vital source of employment, though demand (and therefore employment levels) can fluctuate wildly as fashions change. To earn the official Harris Tweed Association trademark of the Orb and the Maltese Cross – taken from the Countess of Dunmore's coat of arms – the fabric has to be hand-woven on the Outer Hebrides from 100 percent pure new Scottish wool, while the other parts of the manufacturing process must take place only in the local mills.

The main centre of production is now Lewis, where the wool is dyed, carded and spun; you can see all these processes by visiting the **Lewis Loom Centre** in Stornoway (see p.476). In recent years there has been a revival of traditional tweed-making techniques, with several small producers, like Anne Campbell at **Clò Mór** in Liceasto (Mon–Fri 9am–5pm; ⓣ01859/530364), religiously following old methods. One of the more interesting aspects of the process is the use of indigenous plants and bushes to dye the cloth: yellow comes from rocket and broom, green from heather, grey and black from iris and oak and, most popular of all, reddish brown from crotal, a flat grey lichen scraped off rocks.

Since the Leverhulme era, unemployment has been a constant problem in Harris. Crofting continues on a small scale, supplemented by the Harris Tweed industry, though the main focus of this has shifted to Lewis. Shellfish fishing continues on **Scalpay**, while the rest of the population gets by on whatever employment is available: roadworks, crafts and, of course, tourism. There's a regular **bus** connection between Stornoway and **Tarbert**, and an occasional service which circumnavigates South Harris (see also "Travel details" on p.500).

Tarbert (Tairbeart)

The largest place on Harris is the ferry port of **TARBERT**, sheltered in a green valley on the narrow isthmus that marks the border between North and South Harris. The town's mountainous backdrop is impressive, and the town is attractively laid out on steep terraces sloping up from the dock. However, it does boast the only **tourist office** (April–Oct Mon–Sat 9am–1pm & 2pm–5pm; also open to greet the ferry; winter hours variable; ⓣ01859/502011) on Harris, close to the ferry terminal. The office can arrange modest, inexpensive B&B **accommodation** and has a full set of bus timetables, but its real value is as a source of information on local walks.

If you wish to base yourself in Tarbert there's an excellent new **hostel** called the *Rockview Bunkhouse* (ⓣ01859/502626), on Main Street, which also offers **bike rental**. Close to the ferry terminal, there's a very good B&B, *Tigh na Mara* (ⓣ01859/502270, ⓔtighnamara@tarbert-harris.freeserve.co.uk; ❶), or the easy-going old-fashioned *Harris Hotel* (ⓣ01859/502154, ⓔcameronharris@btinternet.com; ❹), five minutes' walk away. You'll need to book ahead to stay in Tarbert's two most popular **guesthouses**: *Allan Cottage* (ⓣ01859/502146; ❸; May–Sept), in the old telephone exchange, and *Leachin House* (ⓣ01859/502157, ⓦwww.leachin-house.com; ❺), further up the Stornoway road; another good option is the Victorian B&B *Dunard* (ⓣ01859/502340; ❸). The purpose-built hotel **bar** acts as the local social centre and serves excellent bar meals; the adjacent *Crofters* **restaurant** serves moderately expensive standard fare. During the day, you're best off heading for the very pleasant *First Fruits* **tearoom** (April–Sept; closed Sun), behind the tourist office, housed in an old stone-built cottage and serving real coffee, home-made cakes, toasties and so forth. The only alternative is the **fish and chip shop** (April–Oct; closed Sun), next to the hostel.

North Harris (Ceann a Tuath na Hearadh)

The A859 north to Stornoway takes you over a boulder-strewn saddle between mighty **Sgaoth Aird** (1829ft) and An Cliseam or the **Clisham** (2619ft), the highest peak in the Western Isles. This bitter terrain, littered with debris left behind by retreating glaciers, offers but the barest of vegetation, with an occasional cluster of crofters' houses sitting in the shadow of a host of pointed peaks, anywhere between 1000ft and 2500ft high. These bulging, pyramidal mountains reach their climax around the dramatic shores of the fjord-like **Loch Seaforth**. Just beyond **Aird a' Mhulaidh** (Ardvourlie), at the border between Lewis and Harris, is a rare patch of woodland, much of it blighted. If you're planning on walking in North Harris, and can afford it, consider using the spectacular *Ardvourlie Castle* (ⓣ01859/502307; ❼; April–Oct), ten miles north of Tarbert by the shores of Loch Seaforth, as a launch pad. In nearby **Bogha Glas** (Bowglass), there's also a thatched **self-catering** cottage, *Tigh na Seileach* (4 people; £250 per week; ⓣ01859/502411, ⓔtighnaseileach@bigfoot.com).

A cheaper, but equally idyllic spot is the GHHT **hostel** (no phone; open all year) in the lonely coastal hamlet of **REINIGEADAL** (Rhenigdale), until recently only accessible by foot or boat. To reach the hostel without your own transport, walk east five miles from Tarbert along the road to **Caolas Scalpaigh** (Kyles Scalpay). After another mile or so, watch for the sign marking the start of the path which threads its way through the peaks of the craggy promontory that lies trapped between Loch Seaforth and East Loch Tarbert. It's a magnificent hike, with superb views out along the coast and over the mountains, but you'll need to be properly equipped (see p.46) and should allow three hours for the one-way trip.

Scalpay (Scalpaigh)

Caolas Scalpaigh looks out across East Loch Tarbert to the former island of **Scalpay** (Scalpaigh) – from the Norse *skalp-ray* (the island shaped like a boat) – now accessible via the brand-new £6-million single-track bridge. Traditionally, Scalpay is the place where Bonnie Prince Charlie tried unsuccessfully to get a boat to take him back to France after the defeat at Culloden. Today this tightly knit prawn-fishing community is surprisingly buoyant, maintaining a relatively large population of around 400. On a good day, it's a pleasant and fairly easy three-mile hike across the island to the **Eilean Glas** lighthouse, which looks out over the sea to Skye. The first lighthouse to be erected in Scotland, in 1788, the current tower was Stevenson-designed and is built out of Aberdeen granite.

Alternatively, you can drive to the end of the road and walk over the headland; both paths are waymarked. There are several B&Bs on the island: try the well-situated *Hirta House* (Ⓣ01859/540394, Ⓔmmackenzie@lineone.net; ❶) or *New Haven* (Ⓣ01859/540325, ⒺNewhaven@madasafish.com; ❶), both with sea views. If you're interested in **diving**, contact Scalpay Diving Services (Ⓣ01859/540328).

The road to Huisinis (Hushinish)

The only other road on North Harris is the winding, single-track B887, which clings to the northern shores of West Loch Tarbert, and gives easy access to the awesome mountain range of the (treeless) Forest of Harris to the north. Immediately as you turn down the B887, you pass through **BUN ABHÀINN EADARRA** (Bunavoneadar), where some Norwegians established a short-lived whaling station – the slipways and distinctive red-brick chimney can still be seen. Seven miles further on, the road takes you through the gates of **Amhuinnsuidhe Castle** (pronounced "avan-soo-ee"), built in Scottish Baronial style in 1868 by the Earl of Dunmore, and right past the front door, much to the annoyance of the castle's owners, who have tried in vain to have the road rerouted. As it is, you have time to admire the lovely salmon-leap waterfalls and pristine castle grounds.

It's another five miles to the end of the road at the small crofting community of **HUISINIS** (Hushinish), where you are rewarded with a south-facing beach of shell sand that looks across to South Harris. A slipway to the north of the bay serves the nearby island of **Scarp**, a hulking mass of rock rising to over 1000ft, once home to more than two hundred people and abandoned as recently as 1971 (it's now just a private holiday hideaway). The most bizarre moment in its history was undoubtedly in 1934, when the German scientist Gerhardt Zucher conducted an experiment with rocket mail, but the letter-laden missile exploded before it even got off the ground, and the idea was shelved.

South Harris (Ceann a Deas na Hearadh)

The mountains of **South Harris** are less dramatic than in the north, but the scenery is equally breathtaking. There's a choice of routes from Tarbert to the ferry port of **Leverburgh**, which connects with North Uist: the east coast, known as **Na Baigh** (The Bays), is rugged and seemingly inhospitable, while the **west coast** is endowed with some of the finest stretches of golden sand in the whole of the archipelago, buffeted by the Atlantic winds. Several buses set off from Tarbert, Sundays excepted, travelling out along the east coast, and returning via all points along the west coast – for more information, see "Travel details" (p.500) or contact Tarbert tourist office.

Na Baigh (The Bays)

Paradoxically, most people on South Harris live along the harsh eastern coastline of **Bays** rather than the more fertile west side. But not by choice – they were evicted from their original crofts to make way for sheep-grazing. Despite the uncompromising lunar-esque terrain – mostly bare grey gneiss and heather – the crofters managed to establish "lazybeds" (small labour-intensive raised plots between the rocks fertilized by seaweed and peat), a few of which are still in use even today. The narrow sea lochs provide shelter for fishing boats, while the interior is speckled with freshwater lochans, and the whole coast is now served by the endlessly meandering **Golden Road** (so called because of the expense of constructing it).

There are just a few places to stay along the coast, the most obvious being the independent **hostel** (ⓣ01859/511255) three miles south of Tarbert in **DRINISIADAR** (Drinishader); alternatively, there's *Hillhead* (ⓣ01859/511226; April–Oct), a good tweed-making B&B in **SCADABHAGH** (Scadabay).

Six miles beyond Liceasto at **LINGREABHAGH** (Lingarabay), the road skirts the foot of **Roineabhal** (1508ft), the southernmost mountain of the island and known as *An Aite Boidheach* (The Beautiful Place). The majority of the locals are currently fighting to prevent the building one of Europe's largest superquarries here, which would demolish virtually the entire mountain over the next seventy years. Environmentalists charge that local fishing grounds would be badly affected, while the devout are up in arms over the possibility of Sunday working. After the longest public enquiry in British legal history, the final outcome of this dispute was still undecided at the time of going to print.

Roghadal (Rodel)

A mile or so from Rubha Reanais (Renish Point), the southern tip of Harris, is the old port of **ROGHADAL** (Rodel), where a smattering of ancient stone houses lies among the hillocks surrounding the dilapidated harbour where the ferry from Skye used to arrive. On top of one of these grassy humps, with sheep grazing in the graveyard, is **St Clement's Church** (Tur Chliamainn), burial place of the MacLeods of Harris and Dunvegan in Skye. Dating from the 1520s – in other words pre-Reformation, hence the big castellated tower – the church was saved from ruination in the eighteenth century, and fully restored in 1873 by the Countess of Dunmore. The bare interior is distinguished by its wall tombs, notably that of the founder, Alasdair Crotach (also known as Alexander MacLeod), whose heavily weathered effigy lies beneath an intriguing backdrop and canopy of sculpted reliefs depicting vernacular and religious scenes – elemental representations of, among others, a stag hunt, the Holy Trinity, St Michael, and the devil and an angel weighing the souls of the dead. Look out, too, for the *sheila-na-gig* halfway up the south side of the church tower; unusually, she has a brother displaying his genitalia, below a carving of St Clement on the west face. Beyond the church, tucked away by a quiet harbour, the *Rodel Hotel* is being completely restored and should be excellent when it opens; you can check on progress on its website Ⓦwww.rodelhotel.co.uk or ring the tourist office in Tarbert.

The west coast

The main road from Tarbert into South Harris snakes its way west for ten miles across the boulder-strewn interior to reach the coast. Once there, you get a view of the most stunning **beach**, the vast golden strand of **Tràigh Losgaintir**. The road continues to ride above a chain of sweeping sands, backed by rich **machair**, that stretches for nine miles along the Atlantic coast. In good weather, the scenery is particularly impressive, foaming breakers rolling along the golden sands set against the rounded peaks of the mountains to the north and the islet-studded turquoise sea to the west – and even on the dullest day the sand manages to glow beneath the waves. A short distance out to sea is the large island of **Taransay** (Tarasaigh), which once held a population of nearly a hundred, but was abandoned as recently as 1974. In 2000 it was the scene of the BBC series *Castaway*, in which thirty-odd contestants were filmed living on the island for the best part of a year; you can now take day-trips to the island (ⓣ07747/842218 or ⓣ07769/908672) and self-catering accommodation is planned (Ⓦwww.visit-taransay.com).

Nobody bothers much if you **camp** or park beside the dune-edged beach, as long as you're careful not to churn up the machair, and there are two very good B&Bs, *Moravia* (Ⓣ01859/550262; ❶; March–Oct), overlooking the sands at **LOSGAINTIR** (Luskentyre) and *Beul na Mara* at **SEILEBOST** (Ⓣ01859/550205, Ⓔmorrisoncl@talk21.com; ❷). Just south of **BORGH** (Borve), there's a newly built **self-catering** thatched house by the beach (Ⓣ01859/550222, Ⓦwww.borvemor.zetnet.co.uk; 4 people; £365 per week), and two stone-built renovated steadings (6–8 people; £325 per week); the *Borvemor* gallery/café (closed Mon, Sat & Sun) serving home-made cakes and real coffee, is attached. The most luxurious accommodation, though, is five miles further south in **SGARASTA** (Scarista), where one of the first of the Hebridean Clearances took place in 1828, when thirty families were evicted and their homes burnt. Here, the Georgian former manse of *Scarista House* (Ⓣ01859/550238, Ⓦwww.scaristahouse.com; ❼; May–Sept) overlooks the nearby golden sands; if you can't afford to stay, it's worth splashing out and booking for dinner, as the meat and seafood served here is among the freshest and finest on the Western Isles.

If you're intrigued by the local machair, you can go on guided walks (mid-May to mid-Sept Mon 2.30pm, or by arrangement Ⓣ01859/520258; £2.50) across a particularly magnificent stretch by the golden sands close to the village of **TAOBH TUATH** (Northton), a lovely spot overlooked by the round-topped hill of Chaipabhal at the southwesternmost tip of the island. Taobh Tuath itself is no picture postcard, with the exception of the award-winning **MacGillivray Centre** (open all year at any time), whose design was inspired by the Hebridean blackhouse. However, it's the building that clearly won the accolades and not the centre, which contains precious little information on the naturalist, William MacGillivray (1796–1852), after whom it's named, and only a little on crofting and machair. There's more information on geology, flora and fauna to be found in **Seallam**, on the main road, primarily a centre for eager ancestor hunters, but also providing interest for kids, literally at their level; there's a permanent exhibition (£2.50) as well as temporary ones.

Leverburgh (An t-Ob)

From Taobh Tuath the road veers to the southeast to trim the island's south shore, eventually reaching the sprawling settlement of **LEVERBURGH** (An t-Ob), where a series of brown clapperboard houses strikes an odd Scandinavian note. Named after Lord Leverhulme, who planned to turn the place into the largest fishing port on the west coast of Scotland, it's a place that has languished for some time, but has picked up quite a bit since the establishment of the CalMac **car ferry** service to Otternish on North Uist. The seventy-minute journey across the skerry-strewn Sound of Harris is one of Scotland's most tortuous ferry routes, with the ship taking part in a virtual slalom race to avoid numerous hidden rocks – it's also a great crossing from which to spot seabirds and sea mammals.

There are several **B&Bs** strung out within a two-mile radius of Leverburgh: try *Caberfeidh House* (Ⓣ01859/520276; ❶), a lovely stone-built Victorian building by the turn-off to the ferry, or *Sorrel Cottage* (Ⓣ01859/520319, Ⓔsorrelcottage@talk21.com; ❶), which specializes in vegetarian and seafood cooking. A cheaper alternative is the welcoming purpose-built timber-clad *An Bothan* **bunkhouse** (Ⓣ01859/520251), which has great facilities, and is only a few minutes' walk from the ferry. On the north side of the bay, *An Clachan* co-op store has a **café** (closed Sun) upstairs, and hosts temporary local history exhibitions, while *The Anchorage* (closed Sun), overlooking the ferry slipway, is a good basic café, open from first to last ferry.

North Uist (Uibhist a Tuath)

Compared to the mountainous scenery of Harris, **North Uist** – seventeen miles long and thirteen miles wide – is much flatter and for some comes as something of an anticlimax. Over half the surface area is covered by water, creating a distinctive peaty-brown lochan-studded "drowned landscape". Most visitors come here for the trout and salmon fishing and the deerstalking, both of which (along with poaching) are critical to the survival of the island's economy. Others come for the smattering of prehistoric sites and sheer peace of this windy isle, and the solitude of North Uist's vast sandy beaches, which extend – almost without interruption – along the north and west coast.

There are two **car ferry** services to North Uist: the first is from Leverburgh on Harris to Otternish (Mon–Sat 4 daily; 1hr 10min), from where there are regular **buses** to Lochmaddy, the principal village on the east coast; the second is from Tarbert on Harris, via Uig on Skye (Mon–Sat 1–2 daily; 4hr), which docks at Lochmaddy itself. Five or six daily buses leave for Lochboisdale in South Uist along the main road, and several buses travel some way round the coastal road. There is no public transport on Sundays.

Loch nam Madadh (Lochmaddy) and around

Despite being situated on the east coast, some distance away from any beach, the ferry port of **LOCH NAM MADADH (LOCHMADDY)** – "Loch of the Dogs" – makes a good base for exploring the island. Occupying a narrow, bumpy promontory, overlooked by the brooding mountains of North Lee and South Lee to the southeast, it's difficult to believe that this sleepy settlement was a large herring port as far back as the seventeenth century. Its most salient feature now is the sixteen incongruous brown weatherboarded houses, which arrived from Sweden in 1948. The loch itself has been declared a European Marine Special Area of Conservation because of the richness and diversity of its marine life.

One place that's well worth visiting is **Taigh Chearsabhagh** (Mon–Sat 10am–5pm), a converted eighteenth-century merchant's house, now home to an arts centre, airy café, shop and excellent museum (£1) which is a replica Norse house where children can dress up in costume and touch everything. There's a **sculpture trail** starting outside the arts centre on the shore; to see the highlight, take a walk out past the Uist Outdoor Centre, and across the footbridge that leads to the derelict Sponish House. From here a path leads east to Lochmaddy's most intriguing sight, **Both nam Faileas** (Hut of the Shadow), an ingenious drystone, turf-roofed camera obscura built by sculptor Chris Drury that projects the nearby land, sea and skyscape onto its back wall – take time to allow your eyes to adjust to the light, and on the way back look out for otters, who love the tidal rapids hereabouts.

The **tourist office** (mid-April to mid-Oct Mon–Fri 9am–5pm, Sat 9.30am–5.30pm; also open to greet the evening ferry; ⓣ01876/500321), near the quayside, has local bus and ferry timetables, and can help with **accommodation**. There are a couple of nice Victorian B&Bs, north off the main road: try the *Old Courthouse* (ⓣ01876/500358, ⓔmjohnson@oldcourthouse.fsnet.co.uk; ❷). A little further north lies the *Uist Outdoor Centre* (ⓣ01876/500480, ⓦwww.uistoutdoorcentre.co.uk), which has **hostel** accommodation in four-person bunk rooms, and offers a wide range of outdoor activities, from canoeing round the indented coastline to "rubber tubing".

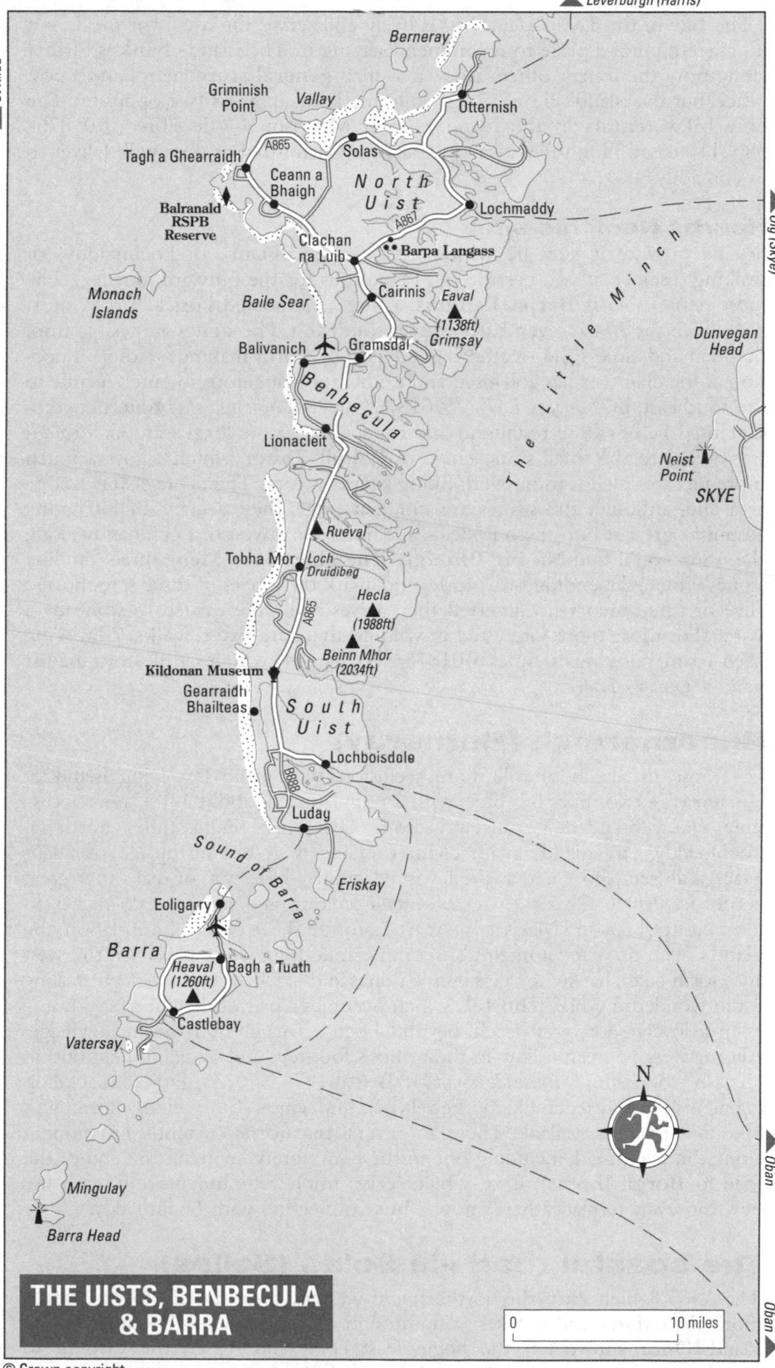
Leverburgh (Harris)
St Kilda
Berneray
Griminish Point
Vallay
Otternish
A865
Solas
Tagh a Ghearraidh
Ceann a Bhaigh
North Uist
Balranald RSPB Reserve
Lochmaddy
A867
Uig (Skye)
Clachan na Luib
Barpa Langass
Monach Islands
Baile Sear
Cairinis
Eaval (1138ft)
Grimsay
Balivanich
Gramsdal
Benbecula
Dunvegan Head
The Little Minch
Lionacleit
Neist Point
SKYE
Rueval
Tobha Mor
Loch Druidibeg
Hecla (1988ft)
A865
Beinn Mhor (2034ft)
Kildonan Museum
Gearraidh Bhailteas
South Uist
Lochboisdale
B888
Ludag
Sound of Barra
Eriskay
Eoligarry
Barra
Heaval (1260ft)
Bagh a Tuath
Castlebay
Vatersay
N
Oban
Mingulay
Barra Head
THE UISTS, BENBECULA & BARRA
0
10 miles
Oban

The **bar** in the *Lochmaddy Hotel* is lively and serves the usual bar meals, but it's currently not a place to recommend staying in. The island's **bank** is further along from the tourist office. There is a small **general store**, petrol and a post office, but the island's nearest large supermarket is in Solas (see opposite). The only **bike rental** on the island is from Morrison Cycle Hire (ⓣ01876/580211), based nine miles away in Cairinis (Carinish), but they will deliver to Lochmaddy.

Nearby Neolithic sites

Several prehistoric sites lie within easy cycling distance of Lochmaddy (or walking distance, if you use the bus or postbus for the outward journey). The most remarkable is **Barpa Langass**, a huge chambered burial cairn a short walk from the A867, seven barren miles southwest. The stones are visible from the road and, unless the weather's good, it's not worth making a closer inspection as the chamber has collapsed and is now too dangerous to enter. A mile to the southeast, by *Langass Lodge* (ⓣ01876/500285, ⓔlangass@btinternet.com; ❹; closed Feb), whose restaurant and bar snacks feature local seafood, a rough track leads to the small stone circle of **Pobull Fhinn**, which enjoys a much more picturesque location overlooking a narrow loch. The circle covers a large area and, although the stones are not that huge, they occupy an intriguing amphitheatre cut into the hillside. Three miles northwest of Lochmaddy along the A865 you'll find **Na Fir Bhreige** (The Three False Men), three standing stones which, depending on your legend, mark the graves of three spies buried alive or three men who deserted their wives and were turned to stone by a witch. For those more interested in wildlife, there are **otter walks** (May–Aug Wed 10am; booking essential ⓣ01876/560284; £4) which set off from the car park at *Langass Lodge*.

Bhearnaraigh (Berneray)

For those in search of still more seclusion, there's the low-lying island of **Berneray** – two miles by three, with a population of about 140 – now accessible via a brand-new causeway from **Otternish**, eight miles north of Lochmaddy. The island's main claim to fame is as the birthplace of Giant MacAskill (see p.457) and as the favoured holiday hideaway of that other great eccentric, Prince Charles, lover of Gaelic culture and royal potato-picker to local crofter, "Splash" MacKillop. Apart from the sheer peace and isolation, the island's main draw for non-royals is a three-mile-long sandy beach on the west and north coast, backed by rabbit-free dunes and machair. The other great draw is the wonderful GHHT **hostel**, which occupies a pair of thatched blackhouses in a lovely spot by a beach, beyond Loch a Bhàigh and the main village. Alternatively you can follow in the prince's footsteps and stay (and help out) at "Splash" MacKillop's *Burnside Croft* **B&B** (ⓣ01876/540235, ⓔsplashmackillop@burnsidecroft.fsnet.co.uk; ❷; Feb–Nov), and enjoy "storytelling evenings"; bike rental is also available. There are several **tearooms** currently functioning along the main road, including one in the community centre at the end of the road to **Borgh** (Borve), all of which serve simple refreshments and, with the new causeway in place, there's now a **bus** connection with Lochmaddy.

The coastal road via Solas (Sollas)

The A865, which skirts the northern and western shoreline of North Uist for more than thirty miles, takes you through the most scenic sections of the island. Once you've left the boggy east coast and passed the turning to

Otternish, the road reaches the parish of **SOLAS** (Sollas), which stands at the centre of a couple of superb tidal strands – sea green at high tide, golden sand at low tide – backed by large tracts of machair that are blanketed with wild flowers in summer. A new memorial opposite the local co-op recalls the appallingly brutal Clearances undertaken by Lord MacDonald of Sleat in Solas. The current laird, Lord Granville, who owns much of North Uist, occupies the large house on the tidal island of **Vallay** (Bhalaigh), which is connected by a road that crosses the largest of the two strands. For a comfortable, friendly **B&B** with great views across Vallay Strand, head for *Struan House* (ⓣ01876/560282; ❶; April–Sept), or the hospitable *Daisy Bank* in An Ceathramh Meadhanach (Middlequarter) (ⓣ01876/560208; ❶; March–Oct).

Beyond Solas, the rolling hills that occupy the centre of North Uist slope down to the sea. Here, in the northwest corner of the island, you'll find **Scolpaig Tower**, a castellated folly on an islet in Loch Scolpaig, erected as a famine relief project in the nineteenth century – you can reach it, with some difficulty, across stepping stones. A tarmac track leads down past the loch and tower to Scolpaig Bay, beyond which lies the rocky shoreline of **Griminish Point**, the closest landfall to St Kilda (see box on p.479), which is clearly visible on the horizon in fine weather, looming like some giant dinosaur's skeleton emerging from the sea.

Roughly three miles south of Scolpaig Tower, through the sand dunes, is the **Balranald RSPB Reserve**, one of the last breeding grounds of the corncrake, among Europe's most endangered birds. Sightings are rare, partly because the birds are very good at hiding in long grass, but the males' loud "craking" is relatively easy to hear from May to July. From the excellent new **visitor centre** there's a two-hour walk along the headland, marked by posts, giving you ample opportunity for appreciating the wonderful carpet of flowers that covers the machair in summer, and for spotting corn buntings and arctic terns inland, and gannets and Manx shearwaters out to sea – guided walks take place throughout the summer (May–Aug Tues & Thurs 2pm; ⓣ01878/602188). On a clear day you can see the unmistakable shape of St Kilda, seeming miraculously near.

Children might enjoy a visit to the **Uist Animal Visitor Centre** (daily 10am–10pm; £2), a farm that lies just off the main road, beyond Paible School, in **CEANN A BHAIGH** (Bayhead). Here, you can see Eriskay ponies, Highland cattle, Scottish wildcats and other rare Scottish breeds at close quarters; the centre also has a café, and **horse-drawn Romany caravans** to rent (ⓣ01876/510706). Adults may prefer to continue a couple of miles down the main road and pop into the new Cladach Kirkibost Centre at **Claddach Chirceboist**; it has an excellent café in a conservatory with sea views, uses local produce and has internet facilities (Tues–Sat 11am–4pm). Half a mile further on, you can get peat-smoked salmon and other seafood delights by the roadside from Mermaid Fish Supplies (Mon–Sat 9am–6pm).

Clachan to Griomasaigh (Grimsay)

At **CLACHAN NA LUIB**, by the crossroads with the A867 from Lochmaddy, there's a post office and general store. There's also the *Carinish Inn* (ⓣ01876/580673); it's a bit starkly new, but the food's good and it sometimes has live music. Offshore, to the south, lie two tidal dune and machair islands, the largest of which is **Baleshare** (Baile Sear), with its fantastic three-mile-long beach, connected by causeway to North Uist. In Gaelic the island's name means "east village", its twin "west village" having disappeared under the sea during a freak storm in the fifteenth or sixteenth century. This also isolated the

Monach Islands (sometimes known by their old Norse name of Heisgeir or Heisker), once connected to North Uist at low tide, now eight miles out to sea. The islands, which are connected with each other at low tide, were inhabited until the 1930s when the last remaining families moved to North Uist. In an isolated position, overlooking Baleshare, is *Taigh mo Sheanair* (Ⓣ01876/580246), a very welcoming, family-run **hostel**, where you can also **camp**. The hostel is clearly signposted from the main road, from which it's a good fifteen-minute walk.

On leaving North Uist the main road squeezes along a series of single-track causeways, built by the military in 1960, that cross the tidal rapids separating North Uist from Benbecula. The causeways trim the west edge of **Griomasaigh** (Grimsay), a peaceful, little-visited, rocky island that's really quite pretty, especially around **BAGH MOR** (Baymore). The main source of employment is lobster fishing, which takes place at the modern pier in **NA CEALLAN** (Kallin), where there's also an excellent little B&B, *Glendale* (Ⓣ01870/602029, Ⓔglendale@ecosse.net; ❶).

Benbecula (Beinn na Faoghla)

Blink and you could miss the pancake-flat island of **Benbecula** (put the stress on the second syllable), sandwiched between Protestant North Uist and Catholic South Uist. Most visitors simply trundle along the main road that cuts across the middle of the island in less than five miles – not such a bad idea, since the island is scarred from the postwar present of the Royal Artillery, who until recently made up half the local population. Economically, of course, the area benefited enormously from the military presence, though the impact on the environment and Gaelic culture (with so many English-speakers around) has been less positive.

The legacy of Benbecula's military past is only too evident in **BALIVANICH** (Baile a Mhanaich), the grim, grey capital of Benbecula in the northwest. The only reason to come here at all is if you happen to be flying into or out of **Benbecula airport** (direct flights to Glasgow, Barra and Stornoway), need to take money out of the Bank of Scotland ATM (the only one on the Uists), or stock up on provisions, best done at the old NAAFI store (now a Spar supermarket; open daily), to the west of the post office. There's no tourist office and, if you've got your own transport, there's no need to **stay** here, but if you're reliant on public transport try the modern **hostel** *Taigh-na-Cille* (Ⓣ01870/602522), within easy walking distance of the airport, on the road to North Uist. The best thing about Balivanich is *Stepping Stone*, the purpose-built **café/restaurant** situated opposite the post office, a place with an ambivalent character: the lunchtime café is cheap and cheerful, offering filled rolls and chips with everything, while in the evening it's home to *Sinteag* restaurant, where the à la carte menu is around £20 per head. **Car rental** is available at the airport from Ask Car Hire (Ⓣ01870/602818), who are based in neighbouring Uachdar, half a mile east of Balivanich, where you'll also find *MacLean's Bakery* (closed Sun), useful for amassing a picnic. If you want to stay in the area, there is an attractive thatched self-catering cottage a mile or so east of Balivanich in **GRAMSDAL** (Gramsdale) (Ⓣ01870/602536; sleeps 2–4; £300). Also at Gramsdal, on the causeway, the West Minch Salmon Company sell fresh local fish (Mon–Fri 10am–5pm, Sat 10am–2pm).

The nearest **campsite**, *Shell Bay* (ⓣ01870/602447; April–Oct), is in the south of the island at **LIONACLEIT** (Liniclate). Adjacent is the modern **Sgoil Lionacleit**, the only secondary school (and public swimming pool) on the Uists and Benbecula, and home to a small **museum**, which acts as a temporary exhibition space for Museum nan Eilean (Mon, Wed & Thurs 9am–4pm, Tues & Fri 9am–8pm, Sat 11am–1pm & 2–4pm). The island's most comfortable **hotel**, *Dark Island Hotel* (ⓣ01870/602414, ⓔdarkislandhotel@msn.com; ❺), is also next door, though it's no charmer from the outside. It serves bar meals and has a moderately expensive restaurant, featuring local specialities such as Grimsay lobsters, but you'll get better value for money at the *Orasay Inn*, just across the water in South Uist (see p.496).

South Uist (Uibhist a Deas)

To the south of Benbecula, the island of **South Uist** is arguably the most appealing of the southern chain of islands. The west coast boasts some of the region's finest machair and beaches – a necklace of gold and grey sand strung twenty miles from one end to the other – while the east coast features a ridge of high mountains rising to 2034ft at the summit of Beinn Mhor. Whatever you do, don't make the mistake of simply driving down the main A865 road, which runs down the centre of the island like a backbone. To reach the beaches (or even see them), you have to get off the main road and pass through the old crofters' villages that straggle along the west coast; to climb the mountains in the east, you need a detailed 1:25,000 map, in order to negotiate the island's maze of lochans. The only blot on South Uist's landscape is the old Royal Artillery missile range, which occupies the northwest corner of the island.

Loch Druidibeg, Tobha Mòr (Howmore) and Kildonan Museum

The Reformation never took a strong hold in South Uist (or Barra), and the island remains Roman Catholic, as is evident from the various roadside shrines and the slender modern statue of *Our Lady of the Isles* that stands by the main road below the small hill of **Rueval**, known to the locals as "Space City" for its forest of aerials and golf balls, which help track the missiles heading out into the Atlantic. To the south of Rueval is the freshwater **Loch Druidibeg**, a breeding ground for greylag geese and a favourite spot for mute swans. The area around the loch is made up of such diverse habitats, from brackish lagoons and peaty moorland to dune and machair, that Scottish National Heritage now manages the place as a National Nature Reserve. At first glance it may not seem to be teeming with wildlife, but it's lovely countryside, and there's the chance of seeing some raptors hunting over the moorland, including hen harriers; there's a waymarked path through the reserve that begins just by the telephone box on the main road in **Stadhlaigearraidh** (Stilligarry) (map available from Tourist Office).

One of the best places to gain access to the sandy shoreline is at **TOBHA MÒR** (Howmore), a pretty little crofting settlement with a fair number of restored houses, many still thatched, including one distinctively roofed in brown heather. A GHHT **hostel** (no phone) occupies one such house near the village church, from where it's an easy walk across the flower-infested machair to the gorgeous beach. Close by the hostel are the shattered, lichen-encrusted remains of no fewer than four medieval churches and chapels, and a burial ground now harbouring just a few scattered graves. The sixteenth-century **Clanranald Stone**, carved with the arms of the clan who ruled over South Uist from 1370 until 1839, used to lie here. It's now displayed in the nearby Kildonan Museum (see below), after it was stolen in 1990 and removed to London by a Canadian artist, Lawren Maben. It took three months before anyone noticed it had disappeared. Five years later, it was discovered by the artist's father in a bedsit near Euston Station, as he sorted out his son's belongings, following his "death by misadventure".

There's much more besides the aforementioned stone at the **Kildonan Museum** (Mon–Sat 10am–5pm, Sun 2–5pm; £1.80), on the main road five miles south of Tobha Mòr. Mock-ups of Hebridean kitchens through the ages, two lovely box beds and an impressive selection of old photos are accompanied by a firmly unsentimental yet poetic written text on crofting life in the last two centuries. Among the more unusual exhibits is a pair of ornamental shoes made of deer hooves. The museum also runs a café serving sandwiches and home-made cakes, and has a choice of historical videos for those really wet and windy days. A little to the south of the museum, the road passes a cairn that sits amongst the foundations of **Flora MacDonald**'s childhood home (see p.463); she was born nearby, but the house no longer stands.

Without doubt, the best **hotel** on the Uists is the *Orasay Inn* (Ⓣ01870/610298, Ⓔorasayinn@btinternet.com; ❸), located in a peaceful spot off the road to Loch a Charnain (Lochcarnan), in the northeastern corner of the island. It's nothing to look at from the outside, but ask for a room looking east out towards the Minch and you can enjoy a bit of bird-watching from your balcony. The bar meals are good value, the restaurant fairly expensive, and the breakfasts huge. If you're just passing along the main road and need a bit to eat, pop into the *Crofters Kitchen*, an inexpensive **café** near the causeway to Benbecula, serving not only herring in oatmeal, toasted sarnies, tatties and neaps, but also "flaky smoked salmon". This is a speciality you can also buy straight from its source, *Salar* (closed Sat & Sun), further along the road to Loch a Charnain, beyond the *Orasay Inn* turn-off.

Lochboisdale (Loch Baghasdail)

Although South Uist's chief settlement and ferry port, **LOCHBOISDALE**, occupying a narrow, bumpy promontory on the east coast, has, if anything, even less to offer than Lochmaddy, with just the *Lochboisdale Hotel* for somewhere to have a drink and a proper meal, but its lounge bar is comfortable. It is, however, a favourite with the **fishing** fraternity – there's even a set of scales in the hotel foyer – and rents out boats and sells permits for brown trout, sea trout and salmon. There's a small café by the pier *Past & Present Tea House,* which in spite of its name is more chips with everything and a takeaway (daily 10am–9.30pm). If you're arriving here late at night on the seven-hour boat trip from Oban (or from Castlebay on Barra; 1hr 50min), you should try to book accommodation in advance; otherwise, head for the **tourist office** (Easter to mid-Oct Mon–Sat 9am–5pm; also open to meet the night ferry; Ⓣ01878/700286). Next door to the tourist office is a useful coin-operated shower and toilet block (daily 9am–6pm). There are several small, perfectly ordinary **B&Bs** within comfortable walking distance of the dock, one of the nearest being *Brae Lea House* (Ⓣ01878/700497; ❷); or try *Lochside Cottage* (Ⓣ01878/700472; ❷), and a few more luxurious ones slightly further afield, such as *The Sheiling* (☎01878/700504; ❶), in Gearraidh Sheile (Garryhallie), near Dalabrog (Daliburgh). There's a bank, but the shops in Lochboisdale are pretty limited; the nearest supermarket is in Dalabrog.

Perhaps the best place to hole up in this part of South Uist is the *Polochar Inn* (☎01878/700215; ❹), eight miles from Lochboisdale, right on the south coast overlooking the Sound of Barra, with its own sandy beach close by. If you're heading for Barra you could take the passenger ferry which also takes bikes, 3–4 times daily, from **Ludag jetty**, two miles east of the *Polochar Inn*, and lands at Eoligarry on Barra's north coast (book through ☎01851/701702 as sailing depends on tides) – and now the causeway to Eriskay is complete, there are plans to institute a car ferry service to Barra.

Eriskay (Eiriosgaigh)

To the south of South Uist lies the barren, hilly island of **Eriskay**, famous for its patterned jerseys (on sale at the community centre), and a peculiar breed of pony, originally used for carrying peat and seaweed. The island, which measures just over two miles by one, shelters a small fishing community of about 150, and makes a great day-trip from South Uist, as long as the weather's fine. It's now connected by a newly built and impressive causeway, which misleadingly signposts you at the other end to the car ferry to Barra: this, however, does not yet exist since Barra has only just got the funding.

For a small island, Eriskay has had more than its fair share of historical headlines. The island's main beach on the west coast, Coilleag a Phrionnsa (Prince's Cockle Strand), was where **Bonnie Prince Charlie** landed on Scottish soil on July 23, 1745 – the sea bindweed that grows there to this day is said to have sprung from the seeds Charles brought with him from France. The prince, as yet unaccustomed to hardship, spent his first night in a local blackhouse, and ate a couple of flounders, though he apparently couldn't take the peat smoke and chose to sleep sitting up rather than endure the damp bed.

Eriskay's other claim to fame came in 1941 when the 8000-ton **SS Politician** or *"Polly"* as it's fondly known, sank on its way from Liverpool to Jamaica, along with its cargo of bicycle parts, £3 million in Jamaican currency and 264,000 bottles of whisky, inspiring Compton MacKenzie's book, and the Ealing comedy (filmed on Barra in 1948), *Whisky Galore!* (released as *Tight Little Island* in the US). The real story was somewhat less romantic, especially for the 36 islanders who were charged with illegal possession by the Customs and Excise officers, nineteen of whom were found guilty and imprisoned in Inverness. The ship's stern can still be seen at low tide northwest of Calvay Island in the Sound of Eriskay, and one of the original bottles (and lots of other related memorabilia) is on show in *Am Politician*, the island's purpose-built pub near the two cemeteries on the west coast where you can get something to eat when the bar's open (open daily – times vary).

If you're here for the day, it's best to park the car in the village and head for **St Michael's Church**, built in 1903 in a vaguely Spanish style on raised ground above the harbour. The most striking features of the church are the bell, which comes from the World War I battlecruiser *Derfflinger*, the last of the scuttled German fleet to be salvaged from Scapa Flow, and the altar, which is made from the bow of a lifeboat. From here, it's a short walk to the **community centre** (Mon–Sat 11am–3pm), which serves tea and snacks in summer, sells jumpers, and occasionally hosts exhibitions. The village shop is open daily. The walk up to the island's highest point, **Ben Scrien** (607ft), is well worth the effort on a clear day, as you can see the whole island, plus Barra, South Uist, and across the sea to Skye, Rùm, Coll and Tiree (2–3hr return from the village). On the way up or down, look out for the diminutive Eriskay ponies, who roam free on the hills but tend to graze around Loch Crakavaig, the island's freshwater source.

You can **camp rough** with permission, or stay at the **self-catering** apartment run by Mrs Campbell (☎01878/720274; 4 people; £180 per week).

Barra (Barraigh)

Just four miles wide and eight miles long, **Barra** has a well-deserved reputation for being the Western Isles in miniature. It has sandy beaches, backed by machair, glacial mountains, prehistoric ruins, Gaelic culture, and a laid-back, welcoming Catholic population of just over 1300. Like some miniature feudal island state, it was ruled over for centuries, with relative benevolence, by the MacNeils. Unfortunately, however, the family sold the island in 1838 to Colonel Gordon of Cluny, who had also bought Benbecula, South Uist and Eriskay. The colonel deemed the starving crofters "redundant", and offered to turn Barra into a state penal colony. The government declined, so the colonel called in the police and proceeded with some of the most cruel forced Clearances in the Hebrides. In 1937, the 45th chief of the MacNeil clan bought back most of the island, and the island returned with relief to its more familiar, feudal roots.

Castlebay (Bagh a Chaisteil)

The only settlement of any size is **CASTLEBAY** (Bagh a Chaisteil), which curves around the barren rocky hills of a wide bay on the south side of the island. It's difficult to imagine it now, but Castlebay was a herring port of some significance back in the nineteenth century, with up to 400 boats in the harbour and curing and packing factories ashore. Barra's religious allegiance is immediately announced by the large Catholic church, Our Lady, Star of the Sea, which overlooks the bay; to underline the point, there's a Madonna and Child on the slopes of **Heaval** (1260ft), the largest peak on Barra, and a fairly easy hike from the bay.

As its name suggests, Castlebay has a castle in its bay, the medieval islet-fortress of **Kisimul Castle** (April–Sept daily 9.30am–6.30pm; Oct Mon–Wed & Sat 9.30am–4.30pm, Thurs 9.30am–12.30pm, Sun 2–4.30pm; HS; £3), ancestral home of the MacNeil clan. The castle burnt down in the eighteenth century, but when the 45th MacNeil chief – conveniently enough an architect by training – bought the island back in 1937, he set about restoring the castle. You can take a stroll round it by heading down to the slipway at the bottom of Main Street, where you can signal to the HS ferryman to come over and get you (weather permitting; ☎01871/810313).

To learn more about the history of the island, and about the postal system of the Western Isles, it's worth paying a visit to **Barra Heritage Centre** (Mon–Fri 11am–5pm; £1), housed in an unprepossessing block on the road that leads west out of town.

North to Cockle Strand and Eoligarry

Following the west coast round will bring you to the island's finest sandy beaches, particularly those at Halaman Bay and near the village of **ALLATHASDAL** (Allasdale). At **BAILE NA CREIGE** (Craigston), between the two, a dead-end road leads inland to the **Black House Museum** (June–Oct Mon–Fri 11am–5pm; £1), an isolated thatched croft house, half a mile's walk from the end of the metalled road, which remains much as it was when last inhabited in the 1970s.

One of Barra's most fascinating sights is, in fact, its **airport**, on the north side of the island, where planes land and take off from the crunchy shell sands of Tràigh Mhór, better known as **Cockle Strand**; the exact timing of the flights depends on the tides, since at high tide the beach (and therefore the runway) is covered in water. As its name suggests, the strand is also famous for its cockles and cockleshells, the latter being used to make harling (the rendering used on most Scottish houses). In 1994, mechanical cockle extraction using tractors was introduced, and quickly began to decimate the cockle stocks and threaten the beach's use as an airport – as a result it has now been banned, in favour of traditional hand-raking.

To the north of the airport, connected by a thin strip of land, is the coastal village of **EOLIGARRY** (Eolaigearraidh), with a passenger ferry link to Ludag on South Uist and several sheltered sandy bays close by. To the west of the village is **Cille-Bharra**, burial ground of the MacNeils (and Compton MacKenzie). The ground lies beside the ruins of a medieval church and two chapels, one of which has been reroofed to provide shelter for several carved gravestones, some rather bizarre religious and secular objects, and a replica of an eleventh-century rune-inscribed cross, the original of which is in the National Museum of Scotland in Edinburgh.

Vatersay (Bhatarsaigh)

To the south of Barra, the island of **Vatersay** (Bhatarsaigh), shaped rather like an apple core, is now linked to the main island by a causeway – a mile or so southwest of Castlebay – to try and stem the depopulation which has brought the current head count down to just over seventy. The main settlement (also known as Vatersay) is on the south coast, and to get to it you must cross a narrow isthmus, with the golden sands of Vatersay Bay to the east, and the stones and sands of Bàgh Siar a few hundred yards to the west. Above, on the dunes of the latter, is the **Annie Jane Monument**, a granite needle erected to commemorate the 350 emigrants who lost their lives when the *Annie Jane* ran aground off Vatersay in 1853 en route to Canada.

Practicalities

If you're arriving at Eoligarry, on the passenger **ferry** from South Uist, you can rent **bikes** from Barra Cycle Hire (Ⓣ01871/810284), who will meet you at the ferry. There's also a fairly decent **bus/postbus** service which does the rounds of the island (Mon–Sat). Arriving in Castlebay by **car ferry** from Lochboisdale, Oban or Mallaig is more straightforward, and you can rent **bikes** from Castlebay Cycle Hire (Ⓣ01871/810284), half a mile east of the town centre. **Car rental** is available from Barra Car Hire (Ⓣ01871/810243), who will deliver vehicles to the airport or either ferry terminal. Barra's **tourist office** (April to mid-Oct Mon–Sat 9am–5pm; also open to greet the ferry; Ⓣ01871/810336) is situated on Main Street in Castlebay just round from the pier, and can help book accommodation, though it's as well to book in advance for B&Bs and hotels. Those interested in a **boat trip** to the sea cliffs on the island of **Mingulay**, south of Barra, whose last two inhabitants were evacuated in 1934, should phone Mr MacLeod (Ⓣ01871/810223) or enquire at the *Castlebay Hotel*.

In Castlebay itself, the *Castlebay Hotel* (Ⓣ01871/810223; ❹) is the most comfortable **place to stay**, followed by *Tigh-na-Mara* (Ⓣ01871/810304; ❷; April–Oct), a guesthouse a couple of minutes' walk from the pier by the sea; another good choice is *Grianamul* (Ⓣ01871/810416, Ⓔronnie.macneil@virgin.net; ❸; April–Oct). Although architecturally something of a 1970s monstrosity, the *Isle of Barra Hotel* (Ⓣ01871/810383, Ⓦwww.isleofbarra.com/iob.html; ❻; late April to early Sept) enjoys a classic location overlooking Halaman Bay. The best option outside Castlebay is *Northbay House* (Ⓣ01871/890255; ❷), which is a converted school in Buaile nam Bodach (Balnabodach) or *Aros Cottage* near the airport (01871/890355, Ⓔarosbarra@aol.com; ❷). There's a GHHT **hostel** (no phone) in Breibhig (Brevig), a couple of miles east of Castlebay, where you can also **camp**; if you're camping rough you can use the toilets and shower in the CalMac office on the pier.

In contrast to the rest of the Western Isles, Castlebay is positively buzzing on a Sunday morning, when all the shops open for the folk coming out of Mass. The *Kisimul Galley* **café** serves breakfast all day every day, and specializes in cheap-and-cheerful Scottish fry-ups – try the stovies and the bridies. For more fancy fare, head to the *Castlebay Hotel*'s cosy **bar**, which regularly has cockles, crabs and scallops on its menu, and good views out over the bay. If the *Castlebay* isn't serving food, try the bar at the neighbouring *Craigard Hotel*, which serves food whenever it's open. There are two bars at the *Isle of Barra Hotel*, one of which is the locals' pub, while the other lies within the hotel itself; the food here also features excellent local fish and seafood and the hotel runs an Oriental takeaway. The only two watering holes in the north of the island are the airport terminal café and the lively bar of the *Heathbank Hotel* in **Bagh a Tuath** (Northbay). **Films** are occasionally shown on Saturday evenings at the local school – look out for the posters – where there is also a swimming pool, library and sports centre, all of which are open to the general public.

In Vatersay, the friendly community centre is open daily in season for soups, snacks, tea and cakes.

Travel details

Trains

Aberdeen to: Kyle of Lochalsh (Mon–Sat 1 daily; 5hr).

Fort William to: Mallaig (4–5 daily; 1hr 25min).
Glasgow (Queen St) to: Mallaig (Mon–Sat 3 daily, Sun 1 daily; 5hr 20min); Oban (2–4 daily; 3hr).

Inverness to: Kyle of Lochalsh (Mon–Sat 3 daily, Sun 1 daily; 2hr 30min).

Buses

Mainland

Edinburgh to: Broadford (2 daily; 6hr 30min); Oban (1 daily; 4hr); Portree (2 daily; 7hr 40min).
Glasgow to: Broadford (3 daily; 5hr 25min); Oban (Mon–Sat 4 daily, Sun 2 daily; 3hr); Portree (3 daily; 6hr–6hr 30min); Uig (Mon–Sat 2 daily; 7hr 40min).

Inverness to: Broadford (2 daily; 2hr 50min); Portree (2 daily; 3hr 15min); Ullapool (Mon–Sat 2–3 daily; 1hr 20min).
Kyle of Lochalsh to: Broadford (7 daily; 30min); Portree (7 daily; 1hr).

Skye

Armadale to: Broadford (Mon–Sat 4–5 daily; 45min); Portree (Mon–Sat 3–4 daily; 1hr 20min); Sligachan (Mon–Sat 3–4 daily; 1hr 10min).

Broadford to: Portree (Mon–Sat 5–6 daily; 40min).

Dunvegan to: Glendale (Mon–Sat 1–4 daily; 30min).

Kyleakin to: Broadford (Mon–Sat 12–14 daily, Sun 7 daily; 15min); Portree (Mon–Sat 6–7 daily, Sun 5 daily; 1hr); Sligachan (Mon–Sat 7–8 daily, Sun 5 daily; 45min); Uig (Mon–Sat 2 daily; 1hr 20min).

Portree to: Carbost (Mon–Fri 2–3 daily, Sat 1 daily; 35min); Duntulm (Mon–Sat 2–3 daily; 1hr); Dunvegan (Mon–Sat 4 daily; 50min); Fiskavaig (Mon–Fri 2 daily, Sat 1 daily; 50min); Staffin (Mon–Sat 3 daily; 40min); Uig (Mon–Sat 4–5 daily; 30min).

Lewis/Harris

Ⓦ www.witb.co.uk/services/bus.htm

Stornoway to: Barabhas (Mon–Sat 8–12 daily; 25min); Calanais (Mon–Sat 4–6 daily; 40min); Carlabhagh (Mon–Sat 4–6 daily; 1hr); Great Bernera (Mon–Sat 4 daily; 1hr); Leverburgh (Mon–Sat 4–5 daily; 2hr); Point (Mon–Sat hourly; 40min); Port Nis (Mon–Sat 4–6 daily; 1hr); Siabost (Mon–Sat 4–6 daily; 45min); Tarbert (Mon–Sat 4–5 daily; 1hr 10min); Tolsta (Mon–Sat every 90min; 40min); Uig (Mon–Sat 3–4 daily; 1hr–1hr 30min).

Tarbert to: Huisinis (Mon–Fri schooldays only 3–4 daily; 45min); Leverburgh (Mon–Sat 8 daily; 50min); Leverburgh via the Bays (Mon–Sat 3–4 daily; 1hr 10min); Scalpay (Mon–Sat 3–5 daily; 20min).

Uists/Benbecula

Lochboisdale to: Eriskay (Mon–Sat 5 daily; 30–45min).

Lochmaddy to: Balivanich (Mon–Sat 5–6 daily; 45min–2hr); Balranald (Mon–Sat 3 daily; 50min); Berneray (Mon–Sat 6–7 daily; 30min); Lochboisdale (Mon–Sat 5–6 daily; 2hr).

Otternish to: Balivanich (Mon–Sat 3–4 daily; 1hr–2hr 20min); Lochmaddy (Mon–Sat 6–7 daily; 20–50min).

Barra

Castlebay to: Airport/Eoligarry (Mon–Sat 6–7 daily; 35min/45min); Vatersay (Mon–Sat 3–4 daily; 20min).

Ferries (summer timetable)

To Barra: Lochboisdale–Castlebay (Tues, Thurs, Fri & Sun; 1hr 35min); Mallaig–Castlebay (Sun; 3hr 45min); Oban–Castlebay (Mon, Wed, Thurs & Sat; 5hr).

To Canna: Eigg–Canna (Mon & Sat; 2hr 45min–3hr); Mallaig–Canna (Mon, Wed, Fri & Sat; 2hr 30min–4hr 15min); Muck–Canna (Sat; 2hr 15min); Rùm–Canna (Mon, Wed, Fri & Sat; 1hr–1hr 15min).

To Eigg: Canna–Eigg (Mon & Sat; 2hr 15min–3hr); Mallaig–Eigg (Mon, Tues & Thurs–Sat; 1hr 30–1hr 50min); Muck–Eigg (Tues & Thurs–Sat; 45–50min); Rùm–Eigg (Mon & Sat; 1hr 15min–2hr).

To Harris: Lochmaddy–Tarbert via Uig (Mon–Sat 1–2 daily; 4hr); Otternish–Leverburgh (Mon–Sat 4 daily; 1hr 10min); Uig–Tarbert (Mon–Sat 1–2 daily; 1hr 45min).

To Lewis: Ullapool–Stornoway (Mon–Sat 2–3 daily; 2hr 40min).

To Muck: Canna–Muck (Sat; 2hr 15min); Eigg–Muck (Tues, Thurs & Sat; 1hr); Mallaig–Muck (Tues, Thurs, Fri & Sat; 2hr 40min–4hr 45min); Rùm–Muck (Sat; 1hr 15min).

To North Uist: Leverburgh–Otternish (Mon–Sat 4 daily; 1hr 10min); Tarbert–Lochmaddy via Uig (Mon–Sat 1–2 daily; 4hr); Uig–Lochmaddy (1–2 daily; 1hr 50min).

To Raasay: Sconser–Raasay (Mon–Sat 9–11 daily; 15min).

To Rùm: Canna–Rùm (Mon, Wed, Fri & Sat; 1hr–1hr 15min); Eigg–Rùm (Mon & Sat; 1hr 30min–2hr); Mallaig–Rùm (Mon, Wed, Fri & Sat; 1hr 45min–3hr 30min); Muck–Rùm (Sat; 1hr 15min).

To Skye: Glenelg–Kylerhea (daily frequently; 15min); Mallaig–Armadale (Mon–Sat 6–7 daily; June–Aug also Sun; 30min).

To South Uist: Castlebay–Lochboisdale (Mon, Wed, Thurs & Sat; 1hr 40min); Mallaig–Lochboisdale (Tues; 3hr 30min); Oban–Lochboisdale (daily except Tues & Sun; 5hr–6hr 50min).

Flights

Benbecula to: Barra (Mon–Fri 1 daily; 20min); Stornoway (Mon–Fri 1 daily; 35min).

Glasgow to: Barra (Mon–Sat 1 daily; 1hr 5min); Benbecula (Mon–Sat 2 daily; 1hr); Stornoway (Mon–Sat 2 daily; 1hr).

Inverness to: Stornoway (Mon–Fri 2 daily, Sat 1 daily; 20min).

7

Northeast Scotland

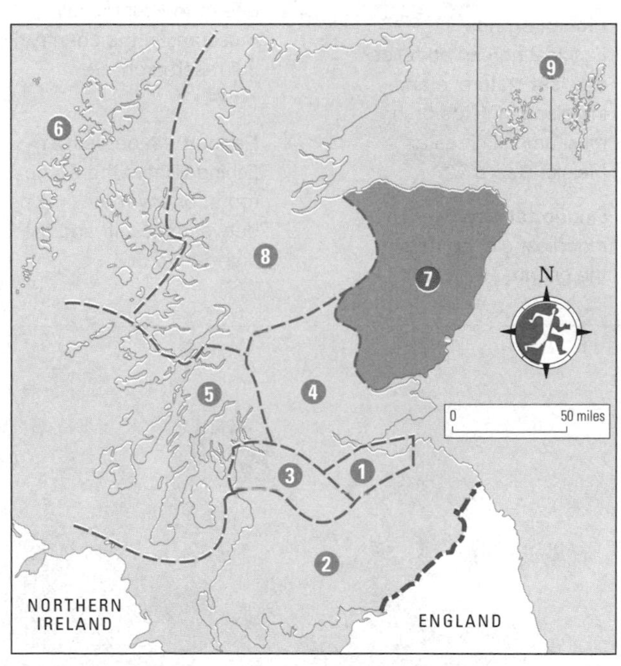

CHAPTER 7

Highlights

* **DCA** – Arts centre/cinema/café at the hip new heart of Dundee's up-and-coming cultural scene. See p.513
* **Arbroath smokie** – A true Scottish delicacy: succulent haddock still warm from the oak smoker. See p.517
* **Pictish stones** – Fascinating carved relics of a lost culture, standing alone in fields or in museums such as at Meigle. See p.523
* **Dunnottar Castle** – The moodiest clifftop ruin in the country. See p.546
* **Speyside Way** – Walking route taking in Glenfiddich, Glenlivet and Glen Grant, with the chance to drop in and taste their whiskies too. See p.558
* **Museum of Scottish Lighthouses** – Lights, lenses and legends at one of the best small museums in the country, in Fraserburgh. See p.564
* **Pennan** – A one-street fishing village: there's no room for any more between the cliff and the sea. See p.565

7

Northeast Scotland

A large triangle of land thrusting into the North Sea, northeast Scotland comprises the area east of a line drawn roughly from Perth north to the fringe of the Moray Firth at Forres. The area takes in the county of Angus and the city of Dundee to the south and, beyond the Grampian Mountains, the counties of Aberdeenshire and Moray and the city of Aberdeen. Geographically diverse, the landscape in the south of the region is made up predominantly of undulating farmland, but, as you get further north of the Firth of Tay, this gives way to wooded glens, mountains and increasingly harsh land fringed by a dramatic coast of cliffs and long sandy beaches.

The northeast was the southern kingdom of the **Picts**, reminders of whom are scattered throughout the region in the form of numerous symbolic and beautifully carved stones found in fields, churchyards and museums (such as the one at **Meigle**). Remote, self-contained and cut off from the centres of major power in the south, the area never grew particularly prosperous, and a handful of feuding and intermarrying families, such as the Gordons, the Keiths and the Irvines, grew to wield disproportionate influence, building many of the region's **castles** and religious buildings, and developing and planning its towns.

Many of the most appealing settlements are along the coast, but while the fishing industry is but a fondly held memory in many parts, a number of the northeast's ports have been transformed by the discovery of **oil** in the North Sea in the 1960s – particularly **Aberdeen**, Scotland's third-largest city. Despite its relative isolation in the Scottish context, Aberdeen remains a sophisticated city which, for the time being, still rides a diminishing wave of oil-based prosperity. At the same time, **Dundee**, the northeast's next-largest metropolis, is fast losing its depressed post-industrial image with an reinvigorated cultural scene

Accommodation price codes

Throughout this book, accommodation prices have been graded with the codes below, corresponding to the cost of the least expensive double room in high season. Price codes are not given for campsites, most of which charge less than £10 per person. Almost all hostels and bunkhouses charge between £8 and £12 per person per night; the few exceptions to this rule have the prices quoted in the text. For a full account of these codes, see p.28.

❶ under £40	❹ £60–70	❼ £110–150
❷ £40–50	❺ £70–90	❽ £150–200
❸ £50–60	❻ £90–110	❾ £200 and over

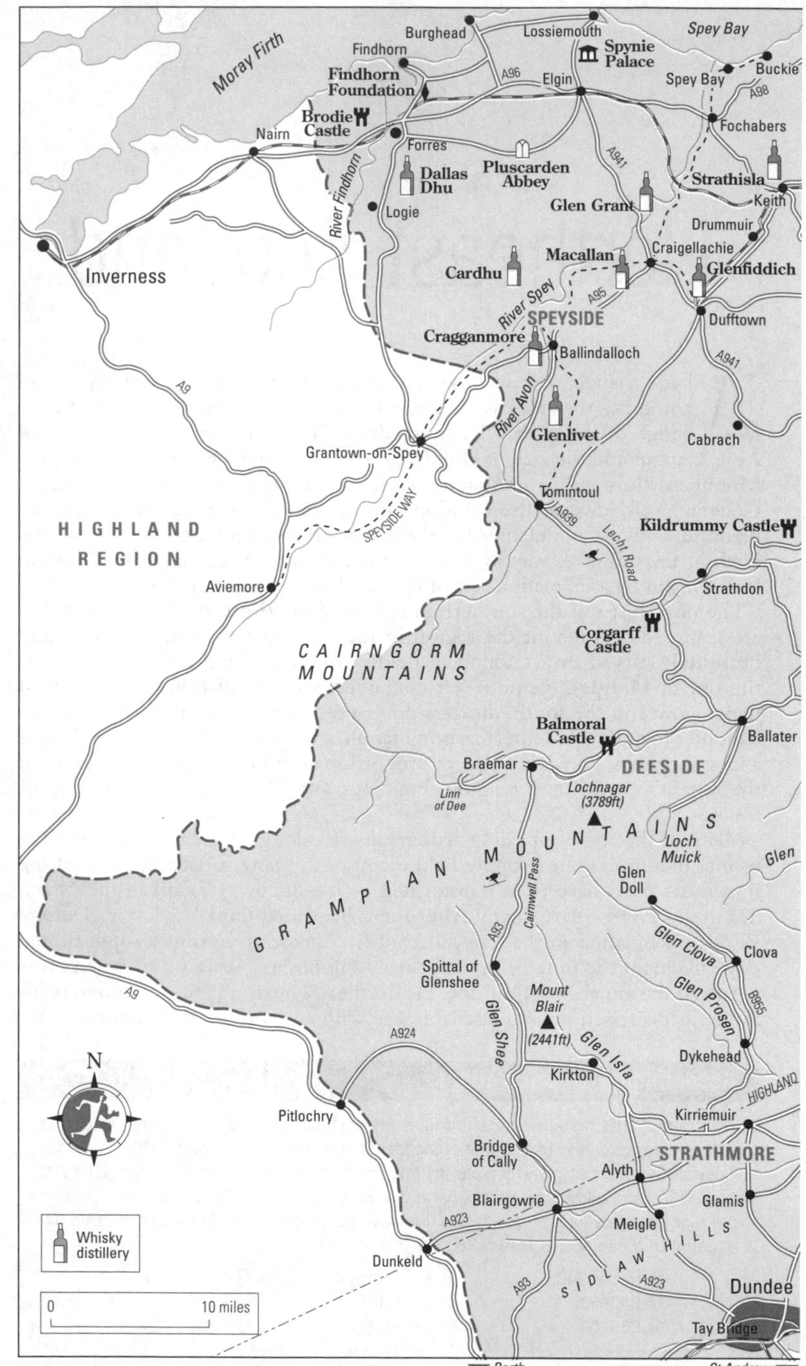
Moray Firth
Burghead
Lossiemouth
Spey Bay
Findhorn
Spynie Palace
Findhorn Foundation
A96
Elgin
Spey Bay
Buckie
A98
Brodie Castle
Nairn
Forres
Fochabers
Dallas Dhu
Pluscarden Abbey
A941
Strathisla
River Findhorn
Logie
Glen Grant
Keith
Drummuir
Craigellachie
Inverness
Cardhu
Macallan
Glenfiddich
River Spey
A95
SPEYSIDE
Dufftown
Cragganmore
Ballindalloch
A941
A9
River Avon
Glenlivet
Cabrach
Grantown-on-Spey
Tomintoul
A939
SPEYSIDE WAY
HIGHLAND REGION
Kildrummy Castle
Lecht Road
Strathdon
Aviemore
Corgarff Castle
CAIRNGORM MOUNTAINS
Balmoral Castle
Ballater
Braemar
DEESIDE
Linn of Dee
Lochnagar (3789ft)
GRAMPIAN MOUNTAINS
Loch Muick
Glen
Cairnwell Pass
Glen Doll
A93
Glen Clova
Clova
Spittal of Glenshee
Glen Prosen
A9
Mount Blair (2441ft)
B955
Glen Shee
A924
Glen Isla
Dykehead
Kirkton
N
HIGHLAND
Kirriemuir
Pitlochry
Bridge of Cally
STRATHMORE
Alyth
Glamis
Blairgowrie
A923
Meigle
Whisky distillery
SIDLAW HILLS
Dunkeld
A93
A923
Dundee
0
10 miles
Tay Bridge
Perth
St Andrews

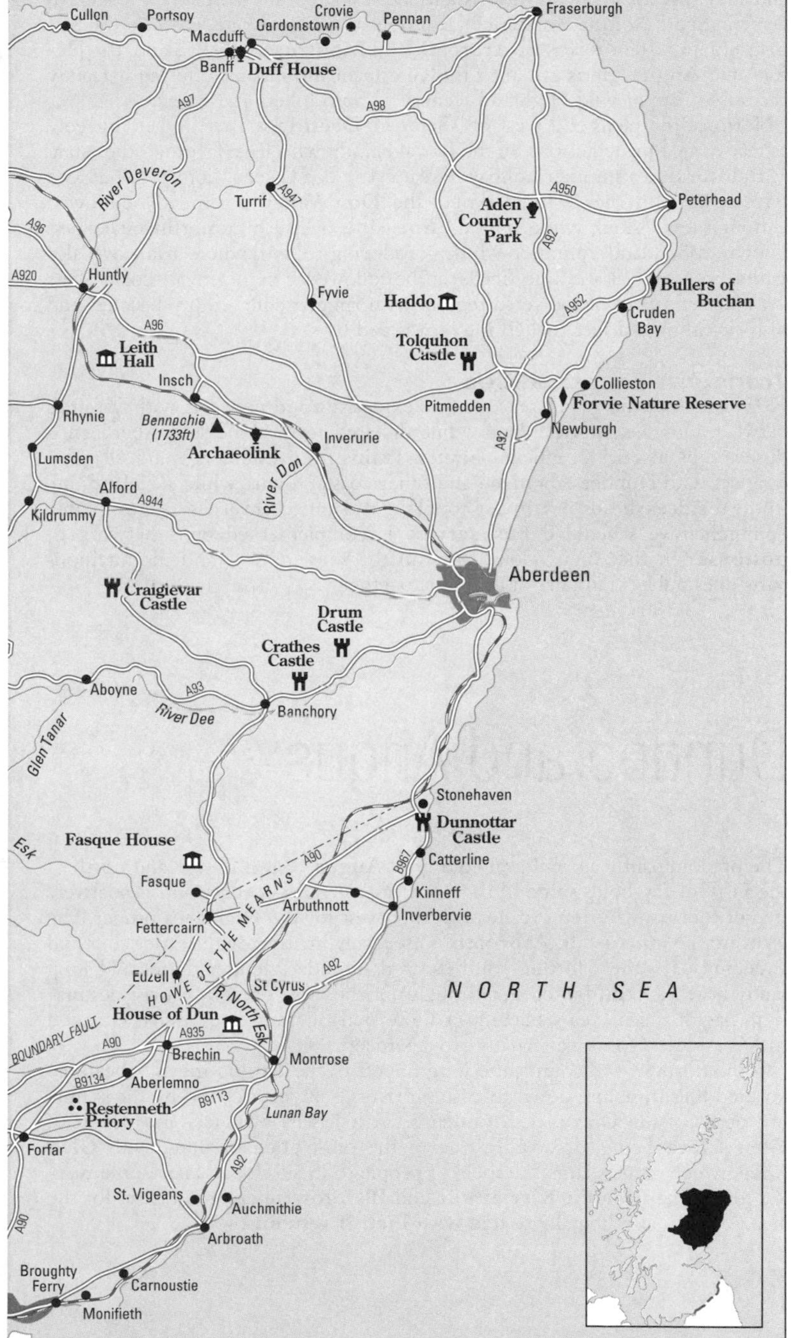

Cullen
Portsoy
Crovie
Pennan
Fraserburgh
Gardonstown
Macduff
Banff
Duff House
A97
A98
River Deveron
Turrif
A947
A950
Aden
Country
Park
Peterhead
A96
A92
A920
Huntly
Fyvie
Haddo
Bullers of
Buchan
A952
Cruden
Bay
A96
Leith
Hall
Tolquhon
Castle
Insch
Collieston
Forvie Nature Reserve
Pitmedden
Rhynie
Bennachie
(1733ft)
Newburgh
Archaeolink
Inverurie
A92
Lumsden
River Don
Alford
A944
Kildrummy
Aberdeen
Craigievar
Castle
Drum
Castle
Crathes
Castle
Aboyne
A93
River Dee
Banchory
Glen Tanar
Stonehaven
Dunnottar
Castle
Esk
Fasque House
A90
Catterline
B967
Fasque
HOWE OF THE MEARNS
Kinneff
Arbuthnott
Inverbervie
Fettercairn
A92
Edzell
St Cyrus
NORTH SEA
R. North Esk
House of Dun
BOUNDARY FAULT
A90
A935
Brechin
Montrose
B9134
Aberlemno
B9113
Restenneth
Priory
Lunan Bay
Forfar
A92
St. Vigeans
Auchmithie
A90
Arbroath
Broughty
Ferry
Carnoustie
Monifieth

and some heavily marketed tourist attractions, including *Discovery*, the ship of Captain Scott ("of the Antarctic"). A little way up the Angus coast lie the historically important towns of **Arbroath** and **Montrose** while, inland, the picturesque **Angus glens** cut into the Grampian mountains, offering a readily accessible taste of wild Highland scenery to both hikers and skiers.

North of the glens and west of Aberdeen, **Deeside** is a fertile yet ruggedly attractive area made famous by the Royal Family, who have favoured the estate at **Balmoral** as a summer holiday retreat ever since Queen Victoria fell in love with it back in the 1840s. Beyond, the **Don Valley** is similarly endowed although less visited, while tranquil **Speyside**, a little way northwest, is best known as Scotland's premier whisky-producing region, where **malt whisky trails**, both official and unofficial, can be followed. The northeast coast offers yet another aspect of a diverse region, with rugged cliffs, empty beaches and historic fishing villages tucked into coves and bays.

Transport practicalities

Northeast Scotland is well served by an extensive **road** network, with fast links between Dundee and Aberdeen, while the area north and east of Aberdeen is dissected by a series of efficient routes. **Trains** from Edinburgh and Glasgow connect with Dundee, Aberdeen and other coastal towns, while an inland line from Aberdeen heads northwest to Elgin and on to Inverness. A reasonably comprehensive scheduled **bus service** is complemented by a network of **postbuses** in the Angus glens. Only in the most remote and mountainous parts does public transport disappear altogether.

Dundee and Angus

The predominantly agricultural county of **Angus**, east of the A9 and north of the Firth of Tay, holds some of the northeast's greatest scenery and is relatively free of tourists, who tend to head further west for the Highlands proper. The coast from **Montrose** to **Arbroath** is especially inviting, with scarlet cliffs and sweeping bays, then, further south towards Dundee, gentler dunes and long sandy beaches. **Dundee** itself, although not the most obvious tourist destination, has in recent years become a more dynamic and progressive city, and makes for a less snooty alternative to Aberdeen.

In the north of the county, the long fingers of the **Angus glens** – heather-covered hills tumbling down to rushing rivers – are overlooked by the southern peaks of the Grampian Mountains. Each has its own feel and devotees, **Glen Clova** being, deservedly, one of the most popular, along with **Glen Shee**, which attracts large numbers of people to its ski slopes. Handsome market towns like **Brechin**, **Kirriemuir** and **Blairgowrie** are good bases for the area. Angus is also liberally dotted with **Pictish remains**.

Dundee

At first sight, **DUNDEE** can seem a grim place. In the nineteenth century it was Britain's main processor of jute, the world's most important vegetable fibre after cotton, which earned the city the tag "Juteopolis". The decline of manufacturing wasn't kind to Dundee, but regeneration is very much the buzz word today, with some commentators drawing comparisons to Glasgow's reinvention of itself as a city of culture in the 1980s and 1990s. Less apparent is the city's international reputation as a centre of biotechnology and cancer research, a theme soon to be given a notable monument in the construction of a cancer care centre, the first public commission in the UK of Frank O. Gehry, the world-famous US architect responsible for Bilbao's Guggenheim.

Even prior to its Victorian heyday, Dundee was a town of considerable importance. It was here in 1309 that **Robert the Bruce** was proclaimed the lawful King of Scots, and during the Reformation it earned itself a reputation for tolerance, sheltering leading figures such as **George Wishart** and **John Knox**. During the Civil War, the town was destroyed by the Royalists and Cromwell's army. Later, prior to the Battle of Killiecrankie, the city was razed to the ground once more by Jacobite **Viscount Dundee**, known in song and folklore as "Bonnie Dundee", who had been granted the place for his services to the Crown by James II. The city picked itself up in the 1800s, its train and harbour links making it a major centre for shipbuilding, whaling and the manufacture of **jute**. This, along with jam and journalism – the three Js which famously defined the city – has all but disappeared, with only local publishing giant D.C. Thomson, publisher of the timelessly popular *Beano* and *Dandy* comics, as well as a spread of other comics and newspapers, still playing a meaningful role in the city. As factories shut the planners moved in, hardly helping Dundee's self-image with the imposition of a couple of garish central shopping malls and the seemingly endless spread of 1970s housing estates around the city edges, a legacy which is only now being pushed aside by the development of the cultural quarter and waterfront areas.

The major sight is Captain Scott's Antarctic explorer ship, **RRS Discovery**, docked underneath the Tay Road Bridge. **Verdant Works** is a re-created jute mill which has picked up tourism awards for its take on the city's distinctive industrial heritage, while the suburb of **Broughty Ferry** offers a distinct change of tone, particularly if you're looking for somewhere to eat or drink. You should also try to spend some time at the upbeat **DCA** (Dundee Contemporary Arts), the totemic building of the developing cultural quarter around which most of the city's lively artistic and social life revolves.

Arrival, information and city transport

Dundee's **airport** (ⓣ01382/643242; see p.572 for flight details) is five minutes' drive west of the city centre. There are no buses, but a taxi into the centre will only set you back £2–3. By **train**, you'll arrive at Taybridge Station on South Union Street (enquiries ⓣ0845/748 4950), about 300 yards south of the city centre near the river. Long-distance **buses** arrive at the Seagate bus station (enquiries ⓣ0870/608 2608), a couple of hundred yards east of the centre.

The very helpful **tourist office** is right in the centre of things at 21 Castle St (June–Sept Mon–Sat 9am–6pm, Sun noon–4pm; Oct–May Mon–Sat 9am–5pm; ⓣ01382/527527, ⓦwww.angusanddundee.co.uk or ⓦwww.dundeecity.gov.uk), and sells bus tickets as well as booking accommodation. You can also pick up the free *Accent* listings magazine here, which details local

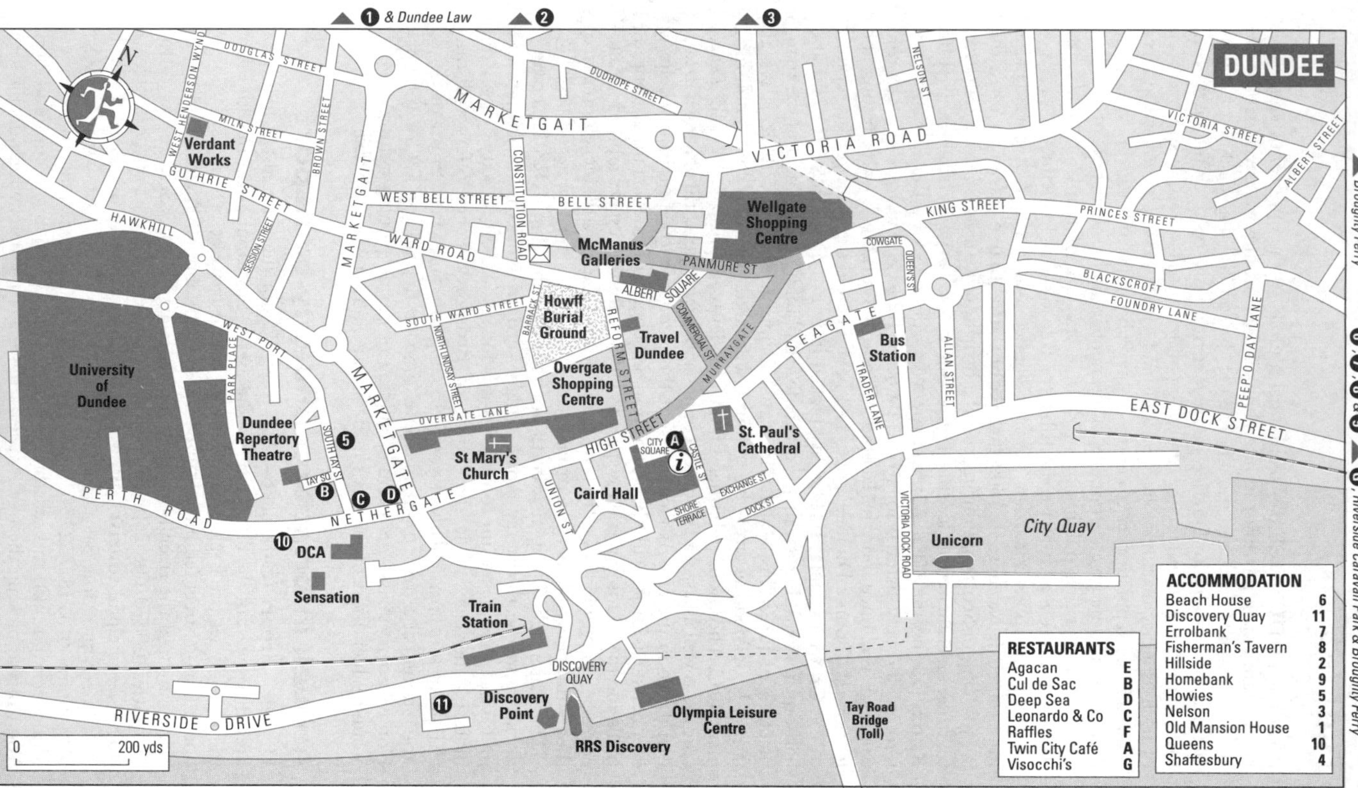
DUNDEE
1 & Dundee Law
2
3
4
E & F
Broughty Ferry
6, 7, 8 & 9
G, Riverside Caravan Park & Broughty Ferry
Leuchars
ACCOMMODATION
Beach House 6
Discovery Quay 11
Errolbank 7
Fisherman's Tavern 8
Hillside 2
Homebank 9
Howies 5
Nelson 3
Old Mansion House 1
Queens 10
Shaftesbury 4
RESTAURANTS
Agacan E
Cul de Sac B
Deep Sea D
Leonardo & Co C
Raffles F
Twin City Café A
Visocchi's G
Verdant Works
University of Dundee
Dundee Repertory Theatre
DCA
Sensation
Train Station
Discovery Point
Discovery Quay
RRS Discovery
Olympia Leisure Centre
Tay Road Bridge (Toll)
City Quay
Unicorn
St Mary's Church
Caird Hall
City Square
St. Paul's Cathedral
Overgate Shopping Centre
Howff Burial Ground
Travel Dundee
McManus Galleries
Wellgate Shopping Centre
Bus Station
Douglas Street
West Henderson Wynd
Miln Street
Brown Street
Guthrie Street
Hawkhill
Session Street
Marketgait
Dudhope Street
Constitution Road
West Bell Street
Bell Street
Ward Road
Victoria Road
Nelson St
Victoria Street
Albert Street
King Street
Princes Street
Cowgate
Queen's St
Panmure St
Albert Square
Blackscroft
Foundry Lane
Peep O' Day Lane
Barrack St
South Ward Street
North Lindsay Street
Reform Street
Commercial St
Murraygate
Seagate
Trader Lane
Allan Street
East Dock Street
West Port
Park Place
Overgate Lane
Marketgate
South Tay St
Tay Sq
High Street
Castle St
Exchange St
Dock St
Shore Terrace
Union St
Nethergate
Perth Road
Victoria Dock Road
Riverside Drive
0 200 yds
N
© Crown copyright

theatre, music and exhibitions. The city's two daily newspapers are the morning *Courier & Advertiser* and the *Evening Telegraph & Post*.

Dundee's centre is reasonably compact and you can walk to most sights; **local buses** leave from the High Street or from Albert Square, one block to the north; for bus information, call ⓣ01382/201121 or go to the Travel Dundee Travel Centre, 95 Commercial St. A Daysaver ticket, with unlimited bus travel for a day, costs £2.

Accommodation

In a city that's only just getting used to tourists, **accommodation** isn't plentiful, but it is comparatively inexpensive and there are some decent guesthouses out from the city centre. There isn't any recommended hostel or backpacker accommodation – the cheaper B&Bs on the fringes of the city centre are the most reasonable alternative. You'll find plenty of rooms out by the suburb of Broughty Ferry, a twenty-minute bus ride (90p) into the city on Travel Dundee buses #7, #8 or #9X, or Strathtay buses #73 and #76 (all leave from either Commercial St or Seagate in the town centre). The **tourist office** charges a £1 fee plus a deposit of ten percent of the first night's tariff for booking accommodation.

Hotels

Discovery Quay Travel Inn Riverside Drive ⓣ01382/203240, ⓦwww.travelinn.co.uk. Bland, modern chain hotel well positioned right beside Discovery Point and the railway station. ❸

Howies 25 Tay St ⓣ01382/322999, ⓦwww.howies.co.uk. Four designer rooms above the restaurant right beside the action in the Cultural Quarter. ❹

Old Mansion House Auchterhouse ⓣ01382/320366. Historic, high-luxury country house hotel on the outskirts of Dundee, with a growing reputation for food and service. ❼

Queens 160 Nethergate ⓣ01382/322515, ⓦwww.queenshotel-dundee.com. Grand old hotel with refurbished rooms and a friendly welcome. Its location is good too, right in the heart of the action between the city and the university, and it has discount rates at the weekend. ❹

Shaftesbury 1 Hyndford St ⓣ01382/669216, ⓦwww.shaftesbury-hotel.co.uk. A converted jute merchant's house with a dozen comfortable rooms in a residential area not far west of the centre. ❺

Guesthouses and B&Bs

Beach House 22 Esplanade, Broughty Ferry ⓣ01382/776614. Well-presented if slightly over-elaborate guesthouse fronting the Tay. ❷

Errolbank 9 Dalgleish Rd ⓣ01382/462118. No-smoking Victorian villa with good views of the Tay; all rooms en suite. ❷

Fisherman's Tavern 12 Fort St, Broughty Ferry ⓣ01382/775941, ⓦwww.fishermans-tavern-hotel.co.uk. Creaky rooms above a cosy pub with decent food, great real ales and malt whiskies. ❷

Hillside 43 Constitution St ⓣ01382/223443, ⓔinfo@tildab.co.uk. Homely, central B&B with four comfortable, no-smoking rooms. ❷

Homebank 9 Ellleslea Rd, Broughty Ferry ⓣ01382/477481. B&B in an elegant mansion house set in walled gardens, a good example of why Broughty Ferry was the suburb of choice for the wealthy. ❸

Nelson Guest House 8 Nelson Terrace ⓣ01382/225354. Inexpensive B&B with three twin rooms, located up the hill from the downtown area. ❶

Campus accommodation and camping

Riverview Caravan Park Marine Drive, Monifieth ⓣ01382/535471. Well-run camping park in a suburb beyond Broughty Ferry, with an easy train link to Dundee. March–Oct.

University of Dundee ⓣ01382/344039, ⓦwww.dundee.ac.uk/residences. Self-catering flats for weekly rental (from £315 a week for four-bedroom flat), including use of the university swimming pool and sports centre. Short-term B&B is also available in student residences at 319 Perth Rd (ⓣ01382/647171; ❶). July to mid-Sept.

The City and around

The best approach to Dundee is across the mile-and-a-half-long **Tay Road Bridge** from Fife. While the Tay bridges aren't nearly as spectacular as the bridges over the Forth near Edinburgh, they do offer a magnificent panorama of the city on the northern bank of the firth. The bridge, opened in 1966, has a central walkway for pedestrians. An 80p toll is levied on cars leaving the city, but you can enter from the south for free. Running parallel half a mile upstream is the **Tay Rail Bridge**, opened in 1887 to replace the spindly structure which collapsed in a storm in May 1878 only eighteen months after it was built, killing the crew and 75 passengers on a train passing over the bridge at the time.

Dundee's city centre is focused on **City Square**, a couple of hundred yards north of the Tay. The attractive square, set in front of the city's imposing Caird Hall, has been much spruced up in recent years, with fountains, benches and extensive pedestrianization making for a relaxing environment, though the grand old buildings and churches close to the centre have been rather overwhelmed by large shopping malls filled with a mundane mass of chain stores.

The main street, which is pedestrianized as it passes City Square, starts as Nethergate in the west, becomes High Street in the centre, then divides into Murraygate (which is also pedestrianized) and Seagate. Opposite this junction is the mottled spire of **St Paul's Episcopal Cathedral** (open to the public, though hours vary; free), a rather gaudy Gothic Revival structure by George Gilbert Scott, notable for its vividly sentimental stained glass and floridly gilded high altar. Immediately in front of the cathedral is a recently erected statue to one of the city's heroes, **Admiral Duncan of Camperdown**, who defeated a Dutch fleet not far off the coast from here during the Napoleonic wars in one of the more critical naval encounters of the period not involving Nelson.

At the other old church in the centre, St Mary's, now engulfed by the vast Overgate Shopping Centre, is an attraction called **The Old Steeple** (April–Sept Mon–Sat 10am–5pm, Sun noon–4pm; Oct–March Mon–Sat 11am–4pm, Sun noon–4pm; £2; joint ticket with Verdant Works and Discovery Point £12.15). Led by a guide, you'll have to tackle a lot of steps, encountering along the way the belfry and the church's massive, seven-ton bells, followed by the mechanism for the steeple's clock. At the top you step out onto a parapet for great views over the city and the Tay with its bridges.

A hundred yards north of City Square, at the top of Reform Street, is the attractive **Albert Square**, home of the imposing D.C. Thomson building, Dundee High School and, on its eastern side, the **McManus Art Galleries and Museum** (Mon–Sat 10.30am–5pm, Thurs until 7pm, Sun 12.30–4pm; free). Designed by Gilbert Scott, the museum is Dundee's most impressive Victorian structure, with a delightful sweep of outside curved stone staircases and elaborate Gothic touches. Inside, the museum gives an excellent overview of the city's past, with displays ranging from Pictish stones to the Tay Bridge disaster. On the ground floor, the most impressive exhibit is the skeleton of a whale, washed up on a nearby beach in 1883 and eulogized in a poem by William McGonagall, a strong contender for the title of the world's worst poet ("'Twas in the month of December, and in the year 1883,/That a monster whale came to Dundee"). Upstairs, the magnificent **Albert Hall** – crowned by a roof of 480 pitch-pine panels in a Gothic arch – houses antique musical instruments, decorative glass, gold, silver, sculpture and some exquisite furniture. Don't miss the table at which the Duke of Cumberland signed the death warrants of captured Jacobites after the Battle of Culloden. On the same floor, the barrel-roofed **Victoria Gallery**'s red walls are packed with nineteenth- and twentieth-century paintings, including some notable Pre-Raphaelite and Scottish collections, William McTaggart's seascapes being a particular highlight.

Across Ward Road from the museum, the **Howff Burial Ground** on Meadowside (daily 9am to dusk) has some great carved tombstones dating from the sixteenth to nineteenth centuries. Originally gardens belonging to a monastery, the land was given to Dundee for burials in 1564 by Mary, Queen of Scots. Five minutes' walk west of here, on West Henderson Wynd in Blackness, an award-winning museum, **Verdant Works**, tells the story of jute from its harvesting in India to its arrival in Dundee on clipper ships (opening hours under review – check on ⓣ01382/225282; £5.95, joint ticket with Discovery Point and Old Steeple £12.15). In the nineteenth century, Dundee's jute mills employed fifty thousand people and were responsible for the rapid industrialization and development of the city as a trading port. The museum, set in an old jute mill, makes a lively attempt to recreate the turn-of-the-century factory floor, the highlight being the chance to watch jute being processed on fully operational quarter-size machines originally used for training workers.

The Cultural Quarter

Immediately west of the city centre, High Street becomes Nethergate and passes into what is now being dubbed, with a fair amount of justification, Dundee's "**Cultural Quarter**". As well as the university and the highly respected Rep theatre, the area is also home to the best concentration of pubs and cafés in the city. Principal among the area's many arts venues is the hip and exciting **DCA**, or Dundee Contemporary Arts, at 152 Nethergate (Mon–Sat 10.30am–midnight, Sun 10.30am–11pm; galleries Tues–Sun 11.30am–5.30pm; ⓣ01382/432000, ⓦwww.dca.org.uk), a stunningly designed centre which incorporates galleries, a print studio and an airy café-bar. The centre, opened in 1999, was designed by Richard Murphy, who converted an old brick building which had been a garage and car showroom into an inspiring new space, given energy and confidence by its bright, sleek interior and distinctive ship-like exterior. It's worth visiting for its stimulating temporary and touring exhibitions of contemporary art and eclectic programme of art-house films and cult classics.

Tucked in behind DCA is another new building, **Sensation** (daily 10am–6pm; Nov–March closes 5pm; ⓦwww.sensation.org.uk; £5), best approached from Greenmarket, off Marketgate. Aimed squarely at families and schoolchildren, it's a fun-packed exploration of science, using sixty different interactive exhibits and participatory experiments.

The waterfront

Just south of the city centre, at the water's edge alongside the Tay Road Bridge, the domed **Discovery Point** is an impressive development centring on the Royal Research Ship *Discovery* (April–Oct Mon–Sat 10am–5pm, Sun 11am–5pm; Nov–March Mon–Sat 10am–4pm, Sun 11am–4pm; £5.95, joint ticket with Verdant Works and Old Steeple £12.15). Something of an icon for Dundee's renaissance, *Discovery* is a three-mast steam-assisted vessel built in Dundee in 1901 to take Captain Robert Falcon Scott on his polar expeditions. A combination of brute strength and elegance, she has been beautifully restored, with polished wood panels and brass trimmings giving scant indication of the privations suffered by the crew. Temperatures on board would plummet to -28°C in the Antarctic, and turns at having a bath came round every 47 days. As an introduction before stepping aboard you're led through a series of displays about the construction of the ship and Scott's journeys, including the chill-inducing "Polarama" about life in Antarctica and a compelling, if overhyped, audiovisual spectacular involving a model ship bursting through the screen and lots of dry ice.

In total contrast is the endearingly simple wooden frigate **Unicorn** (April–Oct daily except Tues 10am–5pm; Nov–March Wed–Sun 10am–4pm; £3.50), moored in Victoria Dock on the other side of the road bridge (a footpath connects the two ships). Built in 1824, it's the oldest British warship still afloat and was in active service up until 1968. During its service years, over three hundred men would have lived and worked aboard. The fact that its 46 guns – eighteen-pounder cannons are still on display – were never fired in aggression probably accounts for its survival. Although the interior is sparse, the cannons, the splendid figureheads and the wonderful model of the ship in its fully rigged glory (the real thing would have featured over 23 miles of rope) are fascinating.

Out from the centre

A mile or so north of town, **Dundee Law** is the plug of an extinct volcano and, at 571ft, the city's highest point. Once the site of a seventh-century defensive hillfort, it is now an impressive lookout, with great views across the whole city and the Tay; the climb is steep and often windy. It takes thirty minutes to walk to the foot of the Law from the city centre, or you can take bus #3 or #4 from Albert Square.

The city's other volcanic plug of rock sits a mile to the west of Dundee Law. **Balgay Hill** is skirted by the wooded **Lochee Park**, while on its summit sits the **Mills Observatory** (April–Sept Tues–Fri 11am–5pm, Sat & Sun 12.30–4pm; Oct–March Mon–Fri 4–10pm, Sat & Sun 12.30–4pm; free), Britain's only full-time public observatory with a resident astronomer. The best time to go is after dark on winter nights; in summer there's little to be seen through the telescope, but well-explained, quirky exhibits and displays chart the history of space exploration and astronomy, and on sunny days you can play at being a human sundial and take in the fantastic views over the city through little telescopes. A **planetarium** has shows on the last Friday of every month (£1), while the observatory also has special opening times to coincide with eclipses and other astronomic events. Bus #2, #36 or #37 drops you in Balgay Road, at the entrance to the park.

In the north of the city, at 34 Mains Loan between Clepington Road and the A90 ringroad, is the cheery **Shaws Dundee Sweet Factory** (June–Aug except last week in July & first week in Aug Mon–Fri 11am–4pm; March–May & Sept–Dec Wed only 1.30–4pm; free), situated in one part of the old Keiller's marmalade factory. It's nothing glamorous, but you'll find yourself rapt with child-like wonder at someone grappling with a five-foot slab of toffee in the small factory on the other side of a large viewing window. Bus #55 goes to the factory gate.

Broughty Ferry and around

Four miles east of Dundee's city centre lies the seaside settlement of **BROUGHTY FERRY**, now engulfed by the city as a reluctant suburb. Comprising an eclectic mix of big villas built by jute barons up the hillside and small fishermen's cottages along the shoreline, "The Ferry", as it's known, has experienced a recent resurgence in popularity. Now a pleasant and relaxing spot with some good restaurants and pubs, it has none of Dundee's industrialization, though the pollution level on the beach itself is pretty dire: all the city's sewage seems to end up here. The striking **Broughty Castle and Museum**, right by the seashore (Mon–Sat 10am–4pm, Sun 12.30–4pm; Oct–March closed Mon; free), is worth a look. Built in the fifteenth century to protect the estuary, its four floors now house local-history exhibits, covering the story of Broughty Ferry as a fishing village and the history of whaling, as well as details of local geology and wildlife.

Just north of Broughty Ferry, at the junction of the A92 and B978, the chunky bricks of **Claypotts Castle** (limited opening hours; details on ⓣ01786/431324) constitute one of Scotland's most complete Z-shaped tower houses. Built between 1569 and 1588, its two round towers have stepped projections to support extra rooms, a sixteenth-century architectural practice that makes Claypotts look like it's about to topple.

Eating, drinking and nightlife

The West End of Dundee, around the main university campus and Perth Road, is the best area for **eating and drinking**, while the city centre, though good for a few pubs, is a bit of a non-starter for decent food. The suburb of Broughty Ferry is a pleasant spot with a good selection of pubs and restaurants, which get particularly busy on summer evenings.

Restaurants and cafés

Agacan 113 Perth Rd ⓣ01382/644227. Tiny Turkish restaurant with an unmistakeable colourful exterior and rough-hewn walls inside; they serve up decent kebabs and stuffed pittas, and also do takeaways. Moderate. Closed lunchtimes & all day Mon.

Cul de Sac 10 South Tay St ⓣ01382/202070. A branch of the successful Glasgow chain, well located between the Rep and DCA, serving pasta and crêpe dishes in the restaurant, and lunch snacks in the bar area. Inexpensive.

Deep Sea 81 Nethergate ⓣ01382/224449. The best of Dundee's fish-and-chips restaurants and takeaways, serving huge and tasty portions, but closes early (6.40pm). Inexpensive.

Howies 25 Tay St ⓣ01382/322999. Large restaurant serving modern Scottish dishes, with *The Lounge* café-bar on the lower ground floor for cocktails and light snacks. Moderate.

Jute In DCA (Dundee Contemporary Arts), 152 Nethergate. Trendy spot occupying a large open-plan space on the lower level of the new arts centre, with large windows looking out over the industrial wasteland and railway tracks which line the Tay. Has table service and a decent range of sandwiches and light meals, served until 11pm. Inexpensive.

Leonardo & Co 107–113 Nethergate ⓣ01382/606555. Prominently located in the Cultural Quarter, this modern-style Italian chain has done away with Chianti-bottle candles, but pizza and pasta are still *numero uno*. Moderate.

Raffles 18 Perth Rd ⓣ01382/226344. Stylish bar-café serving wraps, steaks and vegetarian meals until 7pm. Inexpensive.

Twin City Café 4 City Sq ⓣ01382/223662. Almost achieves a continental feel, with tables and chairs spilling out onto City Square. The menu ranges through light dishes and snacks associated with all the different cities twinned with Dundee, from the US to Croatia. Inexpensive. Closes Mon–Thurs 7pm, Fri & Sat 9pm.

Visocchi's 40 Gray St, Broughty Ferry. Authentic Italian fare served in an informal, popular ice-cream café. Inexpensive.

Pubs

Drouthie Neebours 142–146 Perth Rd. A cheerful bar with a Robbie Burns theme, lavish painted murals and a lively student clientele.

Laing's 8 Roseangle, off Perth Road. Usually packed on warm summer nights, thanks to its beer garden and great river views.

Mercantile 100 Commercial St. Popular with the grey-suit brigade, but worth persevering with, for its excellent range of beers and quality pub snacks.

Nosey Parkers 160 Nethergate. Recently smartened-up bar and bistro on the ground floor of the *Queen's Hotel*, between the DCA and the university.

Ship Inn 121 Fisher St, Broughty Ferry. A narrow pub with a warm atmosphere right on the waterfront. The bistro upstairs has views over the Tay and serves great food.

Nightlife

When it comes to post-pub **nightlife**, Dundee is muted, to say the least. There's a handful of **nightclubs** beside each other along South Ward Road, midway between the centre and the university precincts; *Fat Sam's* and *Mardi Gras* in particular have a regular student following. Another place which might be worth checking out – keep an eye on posters or flyers for details – is *The Cooler* on Session Street.

Right at the heart of the Cultural Quarter on Tay Square, north of Nethergate, is the prodigious Dundee Repertory Theatre (ⓣ01382/223530, ⓦwww.dundeereptheatre.co.uk), an excellent place for indigenously produced contemporary **theatre** and the home of the only permanent repertory company in Scotland. The best venue for **classical** music, including visits by the Royal Scottish Orchestra and other bigwigs, is Caird Hall (ⓣ01382/434451), whose bulky frontage dominates City Square. For **movies**, DCA (ⓣ01382/606220, ⓦwww.dca.org.uk) has two comfy auditoriums showing an appealing range of foreign and art movies alongside the more challenging mainstream releases; otherwise you have to head a fair way out of the centre to the UGC multiplex at Camperdown Leisure park (ⓣ0870/902 0407; bus #4/4a).

Listings

Airport ⓣ01382/643242.

Banks Bank of Scotland, 2 West Marketgate (ⓣ01382/317500); Clydesdale Bank, 96 High St (ⓣ0845/782 4404); Lloyds TSB, Meadowside (ⓣ01382/228801); Royal Bank of Scotland, 3 High St (ⓣ01382/228111).

Bike rental Just Bikes, 57 Grey St, Broughty Ferry (ⓣ01382/732100).

Books James Thin, 7 High St; Waterstone's, 34 Commercial St.

Bus information Scottish Citylink (ⓣ0870/550 5050); Strathtay Scottish for regional buses (ⓣ01382/228345); Travel Dundee (ⓣ0870/608 2608).

Car rental Arnold Clark, East Dock St (ⓣ01382/225382); Alamo National, 45–53 Gellatly St (ⓣ01382/224037); Hertz, 18 West Marketgate (ⓣ01382/223711).

Gay, lesbian and bisexual Switchboard ⓣ01382/202620 (Mon 7–10pm; ⓦwww.dundeelgb.freeserve.co.uk).

Genealogical research Tay Valley History Society, 179 Princes St (ⓣ1382/461845).

Internet Webgate Internet (ⓣ01382/434332) at the Central Library in the Wellgate Shopping Centre (Mon–Fri 9.30am–8.30pm, Sat 9.30am–4.30pm). The tourist office also has internet access.

Library The Central Library is in the Wellgate Shopping Centre.

Medical facilities Ninewells Hospital in the west of the city has an Accident and Emergency department (ⓣ01382/660111). Boots pharmacy is at 49–53 High St (Mon–Sat 8.30am–5.45pm, Thurs until 7pm, Sun 12.30–5pm).

Police Tayside Police HQ, West Bell St (ⓣ01382/223200).

Post office 4 Meadowside (Mon–Fri 9am–5.30pm, Sat 9am–12.30pm; ⓣ0845/722 3344).

Sport The city has two leading football clubs, Dundee (ⓣ01382/889966) and Dundee United (ⓣ01382/833166), whose stadiums face each other across Tannadice Street in the north of the city. Fortunes fluctuate for the teams, but one or the other is usually playing in the Premier League. There are public golf courses at Ashludie, Golf Avenue, Monifieth (ⓣ01382/535553); Caird Park (ⓣ01382/438871); and Camperdown Country Park (ⓣ01382/432688). Other courses along the Angus coast include Carnoustie (ⓣ01241/853789), a British Open venue. The Olympia leisure complex, beside Discovery Point, has a swimming pool (Mon–Fri 10am–8pm, Sat & Sun 10am–5pm; ⓣ01382/434888).

Taxis There are taxi ranks on Nethergate, or call City Cabs (ⓣ01382/566666), Handy Taxis (ⓣ01382/225825) or, in nearby Broughty Ferry, Discovery Taxis (ⓣ01382/732111).

The Angus coast

Two roads link Dundee to Aberdeen and the northeast coast of Scotland. By far the more pleasant option is the slightly longer A92 coast road which joins the inland A90 at Stonehaven, just south of Aberdeen. Intercity **buses** follow both roads, while the coast-hugging train line from Dundee is one of the most picturesque in Scotland, passing attractive beaches and impressive cliffs, and stopping in the old seaports of **Arbroath** and **Montrose**.

Arbroath and around

Since it was settled in the twelfth century, local fishermen have been landing their catches at **ARBROATH**, situated on the Angus coast where it starts to curve in from the North Sea towards the Firth of Tay, about fifteen miles northeast of Dundee. The name of the town stems from Aber Brothock, the burn which runs into the sea here, and although it has a great location, with long sandy beaches and stunning sandstone cliffs on either side of town as well as an attractive old working harbour, Arbroath – like Dundee – has suffered from short-sighted development, its historical associations all but subsumed by pedestrian walkways, a mess of one-way systems and ugly shopping centres.

The town's most famous product is the **Arbroath smokie** – line-caught haddock, smoke-cured over smouldering oak chips, and still made here in a number of family-run smokehouses tucked in around the harbour. One of the most approachable and atmospheric is M&M Spink's tiny whitewashed premises at 10 Marketgate; chef and cookery writer Rick Stein described the fish here, warm from the smoke, as "a world-class delicacy".

Down by the harbour, the elegant Regency **Signal House Museum** (Mon–Sat 10am–5pm, July & Aug also Sun 2–5pm; free) stands sentinel as it has since 1813 when it was built as the shore station for the Bell Rock lighthouse, improbably erected on a reef eleven miles offshore by Robert Stevenson. The interior is now given over to some excellent local-history displays: a school room, fisherman's cottage and lighthouse kitchen have all been carefully re-created, with the addition of realistic smells.

Arbroath Abbey

By the late eighteenth century, chiefly due to its harbour, Arbroath had become a trading and manufacturing centre, famed for boot-making and sail-making

Walks around Arbroath

There's not much to see in Arbroath besides the abbey and the smokehouses, but there are some great walks in the vicinity. From the Signal House, you can wander through the huddled cottages of the Fit o'the Toon, the harbour district where the smell of Arbroath smokies usually hangs heavy in the air. Beyond it, the seafront road heads into Victoria Park; at the far end of the road, a path climbs up over the red sandstone cliffs of Whiting Ness, stretching endlessly onto the horizon and eroded into a multitude of inlets, caves and arches that warrant hours of leisurely exploration. The Arbroath Cliffs Nature Trail Guide, free from the tourist office, picks out twenty good viewing points along the first mile and a half, and also gives details on the local flora and fauna; you may even see puffins. After four miles the path comes to the foot of the neat little fishing village of Auchmithie; a further four (very windy) miles north is the crest of Lunan Bay, a classic sweep of glorious sand crowned by the eerie ruins of Red Castle at the mouth of the Lunan Water.

(the *Cutty Sark's* sails were made here). The town's real glory days, however, came much earlier in the thirteenth century with the completion in 1233 of **Arbroath Abbey** (April–Sept daily 9.30am–6.30pm; Oct–March Mon–Wed & Sat 9.30am–4.30pm, Thurs 9.30am–12.30pm, Sun 2–4.30pm; HS; £2.50), whose rose-pink sandstone ruins, described by Dr Johnson as "fragments of magnificence", stand on Abbey Street. Founded in 1178 but not granted abbey status until 1285, it was the scene of one of the most significant events in Scotland's history when, on April 6, 1320, a group of Scottish barons drew up the **Declaration of Arbroath**, asking the Pope to reverse his excommunication of Robert the Bruce and recognize him as king of a Scottish nation independent from England. The wonderfully resonant language of the document still makes for a stirring expression of Scottish nationhood: "For so long as one hundred of us remain alive, we will never in any degree be subject to the dominion of the English, since it is not for glory, riches or honour that we do fight, but for freedom alone, which no honest man loses but with his life." It was duly despatched to Pope John XXII in Avignon, who in 1324 agreed to Robert's claim.

The abbey was dissolved during the Reformation, and by the eighteenth century it was little more than a source of red sandstone for local houses. However, there's enough left to get a good idea of how vast the place must have been: the semicircular **west doorway** is more or less intact, complete with medieval mouldings, and the **south transept** has a beautiful round window, once lit with a beacon to guide ships. In the early 1950s, the Stone of Destiny had a brief sojourn here when it was stolen from London by a group of Scottish nationalists and appeared, wrapped in a Scottish flag, at the High Altar. It was duly returned to Westminster Abbey, where it stayed until its recent move to Edinburgh Castle (see p.79). A new **visitors' centre** at the Abbey Street entrance offers some in-depth background on these events and other aspects of the history of the building.

St Vigeans and Auchmithie

Although now little more than a northwestern dormitory of Arbroath, the pristine and peaceful hamlet of **ST VIGEANS** is a fine example of a Pictish site colonized by Christians: the church is set defiantly on a pre-Christian mound at the centre of the village. Many Pictish and earlier remains are housed in the wonderful little **museum** (only on request; collect the key from Arbroath Abbey; free), including the Drosten Stone, presumed to be a memorial. One side depicts a hunt, laced with an abundance of Pictish symbolism, while the other side bears a cross, which dates it to around 850 AD.

Four miles north of Arbroath by road or coastal footpath, the clifftop village of **AUCHMITHIE** is the true home of the Arbroath smokie. However, the village didn't have a proper harbour until the nineteenth century – local fishermen, apparently, were carried to their boats by their wives to avoid getting wet feet – so Arbroath became the more important port and laid claim to the delicacy. Now an attractive little fishing village, Auchmithie's main attraction is the *But'n'Ben* restaurant (☎01241/877223; closed Tues), one of the best along this coast, which specializes in delicious, moderately priced Scottish dishes and seafood.

Practicalities

Arbroath's helpful **tourist office** is at Market Place right in the middle of town (June–Aug Mon–Sat 9.30am–5.30pm, Sun 10am–3pm; April, May & Sept Mon–Fri 9am–5pm, Sat 10am–5pm; Oct–March Mon–Fri 9am–5pm, Sat 10am–3pm; ☎01241/872609). Staff can recommend local walks and book accommodation. The **bus** station is on Catherine Street (Ⓣ01241/870646), about a five minute walk south of the tourist office, while **trains** (Ⓣ0845/748 4950) arrive at the station just across the road on Keptie Street.

For somewhere **to stay**, it's hard to beat the clifftop isolation of the *Auchmithie Hotel* (Ⓣ01241/873010; ❸), perched on a clifftop in tiny Auchmithie with a bar and restaurant staring out over the North Sea. The *Five Gables Guest House* (Ⓣ01241/871632; ❶) is a mile south of Arbroath on the A92; formerly a golf clubhouse, it too has a great position overlooking the sea. Alternatively, try the *Harbour House Guest House*, 4 The Shore (Ⓣ01241/878047; ❶), down by the harbour, which is also where you'll find the best **restaurants** and **pubs**. The best place to sample Arbroath smokies is while they're still warm, straight from one of the smokehouses. *The Old Brewhouse* (Ⓣ01241/879945) is a convivial and moderately priced restaurant-cum-pub by the harbour wall at the end of High Street. For more conventional fish and chips, the local's favourite is *Peppo's* by the harbour at 51 Ladybridge St.

Montrose and around

"Here's the Basin, there's Montrose, shut your een and haud your nose." As the old rhyme indicates, **MONTROSE**, a seaport and market town since the thirteenth century, can sometimes smell a little rich, mostly because of its position on the edge of a virtually landlocked two-mile-square lagoon of mud known as the Basin. But with the wind in the right direction, Montrose is a great little town to visit, with a pleasant old centre and an interesting museum. The Basin too is of interest: flooded and emptied twice daily by the tides, it is a nature reserve for the host of geese, swans and wading birds who frequent the ooze. On the south side of the Basin, a mile out of Montrose along the A92, the **Montrose Basin Wildlife Centre** (redevelopment is planned during 2002; call Ⓣ01674/676336 to confirm opening times and admission charges; previously daily 10.30am–5pm, Nov–March closes 4pm) has binoculars, high-powered telescopes, bird hides and remote-control video cameras. In addition, the centre's resident ranger leads regular guided walks around the reserve.

Montrose locals are known as "Gable Endies", because of the unusual way in which the town's eighteenth- and nineteenth-century merchants, influenced by architectural styles they had seen on the continent, built their houses gable-end to the street. The few remaining original gabled houses line the wide **High Street**, off which are numerous tiny alleyways and quiet courtyards.

Two blocks behind the soaring kirk steeple at the lower end of High Street, the **Montrose Museum and Art Gallery** (Mon–Sat 10am–5pm; free) in Panmure Place on the western side of Mid Links park, is one of Scotland's oldest museums, dating from 1842. For a small-town museum, it has some particularly unusual exhibits, among them the so-called Samson Stone, a Pictish relic dating from 900 AD bearing a carving of Samson slaying the Philistines. In the local history section, look out for the mechanical paper sculpture of the town of Montrose, with a green train running along the top and yachts sailing by. On the upper floor, the maritime history exhibits include a cast of Napoleon's death mask and a model of a British man-of-war, sculpted out of bone by Napoleonic prisoners at Portsmouth. Most intriguing, however, is the message on a scrap of paper found in a bottle at nearby Ferryden beach in 1857, written by the chief mate of a brigantine eighty years earlier: "Blowing a hurricane lying to with close-reefed main topsails ship waterlogged. Cargo of wood from Quebec. No water on board, provisions all gone. Ate the dog yesterday, three men left alive. Lord have mercy on our souls. Amen."

Outside the museum entrance stands a winsome study of a boy by local sculptor William Lamb (1893–1951). More of his work can be seen in the moving **William Lamb Memorial Studio** on Market Street (July to mid-Sept daily 2–5pm; at other times, ask at the museum; free), including bronze heads of the Queen, Princess Margaret and the Queen Mother. The earnings from these pieces enabled him to buy the studio in the 1930s, which he donated to the town of Montrose on his death. A superbly talented but largely unheralded artist, Lamb's work is made the more impressive by the fact that he taught himself to sculpt with his left hand, having suffered a war wound in his right. You can see another Lamb sculpture, *Whisper*, outside the library on the High Street. Opposite this, the castellated building which now houses the Job Centre has a long history: built on the site of Montrose Castle after it was demolished by William Wallace, it became the home of the Graham family, whose most famous scion, James Graham, **Marquis of Montrose**, was one of Scotland's most brilliant military strategists, commemorated by a statue outside.

Finally, don't ignore the town's fabulous golden **seashore**. The beach road, Marine Avenue, across from the town museum, heads down through sand dunes and golf links to car parks fringing the fine, wide beach overlooked by a slender white lighthouse.

Around Montrose: the House of Dun

Across the Basin, four miles west of Montrose, is the Palladian **House of Dun** (July & Aug daily 11am–5.30pm; Easter weekend, May, June & Sept daily 1.30–5.30pm; Oct Sat & Sun 1.30–5.30pm; NTS; £6, grounds only £1), accessible on the regular Montrose–Brechin bus #30 – ask the driver to let you off outside. Built in 1730 for David Erskine, Laird of Dun, to designs by William Adam, the house was opened to the public in 1989 after extensive restoration, and is crammed full of period furniture and *objets d'art*. Inside, the ornate relief plasterwork is the most impressive feature, extravagantly emblazoned with Jacobite symbolism. You can also see some gorgeous pieces of intricate needlework, stitched by the illegitimate child of King William IV, Lady Augusta, who married into the Dun family in 1827.

The buildings in the courtyard – a hen house, gamekeeper's workshop and potting shed – have been renovated, and include a tearoom and a shop where local weavers give displays of their traditional skills.

Practicalities

Montrose **tourist office** is squeezed into a former public toilet next to the library, at the point where Bridge Street merges into the lower end of High Street (July & Aug Mon–Sat 9.30am–5.30pm; April–June & Sept Mon–Sat 10am–5pm; ⓣ01674/672000). Most **buses** stop in the High Street, while the **train** station lies a block back on Western Road. For B&B **accommodation**, try *Oaklands*, over the river bridge at 10 Rossie Island Rd (ⓣ01674/672018, ⓦwww.nebsnow.com/oaklands; ❶), or the friendly *Murray Lodge Hotel*, 2–8 Murray St, the northern continuation of High Street (ⓣ01674/678880; ❸). *Kirkside* (ⓣ01674/830780; ❷) is an isolated converted fishing bothy situated on the edge of the sand dunes by St Cyrus Nature Reserve, just over two miles north of Montrose at the mouth of the North Esk River.

For **eating**, the liveliest place in town is unquestionably *Roo's Leap*, a sports bar and restaurant by the golf club off the northern end of Traill Drive, with an unlikely, but excellent, mix of Scottish, American and Australian cuisine. If you want a **drink**, the vitality of *Roo's Leap* is matched by *Sharky's*, a cavernous venue close to the centre of town at 21 George St, which also serves pastas, burgers and the like, while on High Street the more traditional *Cornerhouse Hotel* hosts **folk music** nights on Tuesdays. The *Salutation Inn*, 69–71 Bridge St, serves good, cheap food and has a beer garden.

Strathmore and the Angus glens

Immediately north of Dundee, the low-lying Sidlaw Hills divide the city from the rich agricultural region of **Strathmore**, whose string of tidy market towns lies on a fertile strip along the southernmost edge of the heather-covered lower slopes of the Grampian Mountains. These towns act as gateways to the **Angus glens**, a series of tranquil valleys penetrated by single-track roads and offering some of the most rugged and majestic landscapes of northeast Scotland. It's a rain-swept, wind-blown, sparsely populated area, whose roads become impassable with the first snows, sometimes as early as October, and in the summer there are ferocious midges to contend with. Nevertheless, most of the glens, particularly **Glen Clova**, are well and truly on the tourist circuit, with the rolling hills and dales attracting hikers, birdwatchers and botanists in the summer, grouse shooters and deerhunters in autumn and a growing number of skiers in winter. The most useful road through the glens is the A93, which cuts through **Glen Shee** to Braemar on Deeside (see p.551). It's pretty dramatic stuff, threading its way over Britain's highest main-road pass, the **Cairnwell Pass** (2199ft). Public transport in the region is limited: to get up the glens you'll have to rely on the **postbuses** from Blairgowrie (for Glen Shee) and Kirriemuir (for glens Clova and Prosen).

Blairgowrie and Glen Shee

The upper reaches of **Glen Shee**, the most dramatic and best known of the Angus glens, are dominated by its ski fields, ranged over four mountains above the Cairnwell mountain pass. During the season (December to March), ski lifts and tows give access to gentle beginners' slopes, while experienced skiers can try the more intimidating Tiger run. In summer it's all a bit sad, with lifeless chairlifts and bare, scree-covered slopes, although hang-gliders take advantage of the crosswinds between the mountains and there are some excellent hiking and mountain-biking routes.

To get to Glen Shee from the south you'll pass through the well-heeled town of **BLAIRGOWRIE**, little more than one main road set among raspberry

Skiing at Glenshee

Glenshee is the most accessible of Scotland's **ski** areas, just over two hours from both Glasgow and Edinburgh; for information, contact Ski Glenshee (ⓣ013397/41320, ⓦwww.ski-glenshee.co.uk), who also offer ski rental and lessons. In addition, lessons, skis and boards are available from Cairnwell Mountain Sports (ⓣ01250/885255), at the Spittal of Glenshee. **Ski rental** starts at around £12 a day, while lessons are around £10 for two hours. **Lift passes** cost £18 per day or £72 for a five-day (Mon–Fri) ticket. For the latest snow and **weather conditions**, phone the Ski Hotline (ⓣ0900/165 4656) or check out the Ski Scotland website (ⓦwww.ski.scotland.net). Should you be more interested in **cross-country** skiing, there are some good touring areas in the vicinity; contact Cairnwell Mountain Sports (see above) or Braemar Mountain Sports (ⓣ013397/41242) for information and equipment rental.

fields on the glen's southernmost tip, but a good place to pick up information and plan your activities. Set right on the river Ericht, the town's modest claim to fame is that St Ninian once camped at Wellmeadow, a pleasant grassy triangle in the town centre. If you've time to kill here, wander up the leafy river bank to **Keathbank Mill** (daily May–Oct 10.30am–5pm; £4.25), a huge old jute mill with an 1862 steam turbine driven by the largest working waterwheel in Scotland. Also housed within the complex are some absorbing workshops where the country's largest heraldic crests are carved. Altogether more ambitious is the sixty-mile **Cateran Trail**, a long-distance footpath which starts in Blairgowrie then heads off on a long loop into the glens to the north following some of the drove roads used by caterans, or cattle thieves. If you're interested in tackling the five-day trail, which has a well-organized network of B&Bs, luggage transfers and guides, contact the trail office in Blairgowrie (Ⓣ0800/027 7200).

Blairgowrie **tourist office** (July & Aug Mon–Sat 9.30am–6.30pm, Sun 11am–5pm; April–June, Sept & Oct Mon–Sat 9.30am–5.30pm, Sun 11am–4pm; Nov–March Mon–Fri 9.30am–5pm, Sat 10am–2pm; Ⓣ01250/872960, Ⓦwww.perthshire.co.uk), on the high side of the Wellmeadow, can help with **accommodation**. Over the bridge spanning the fast-flowing River Ericht, Blairgowrie melts into its twin community of **RATTRAY**, where, on the main street (Boat Brae) is the B&B *Ivy Bank House* (Ⓣ01250/873056, Ⓦwww.ivybankhouse.com; ❶), in a central location and offering sweeping views of the river and surrounding hills. There are some lovely places to stay in the surrounding Perthshire countryside, including the charming and hospitable *Marlee House* (Ⓣ01250/884216; ❹), at **KINLOCH** on the A923 to Dunkeld, and *Heathpark House* (Ⓣ01250/870700, Ⓦwww.heathparkhouse.com; ❹) at **ROSEMOUNT** on the Coupar Angus Road. **Camping** is available at the year-round *Blairgowrie Holiday Park* on Rattray's Hatton Road (Ⓣ01250/876666). Blairgowrie boasts plenty of places to **eat**: *Cargills* by the river on Lower Mill Street (Ⓣ01250/876735; closed Mon) is the best bet for a formal meal or civilized coffee and cakes, while, for less elaborate meals and takeaways, there's the *Dome Restaurant*, just behind the tourist office, which has been run by two local Italian families since the 1920s. For good **pub** grub try the youthful *Driftwood*, just off the Wellmeadow, which has a terrace overlooking the river, or head six miles north of town on the A93 to the delightfully situated *Bridge of Cally Hotel* (Ⓣ01250/886231; ❸). You can rent **bikes** from *Crichton's Cycle Hire*, 87 Perth Rd (Ⓣ01250/876100).

Nearly twenty miles north of Blairgowrie, the **SPITTAL OF GLENSHEE**, though ideally situated for skiing, is little more than a tacky service area, only worth stopping at for a quick drink or bite to eat. However, it does boast the excellent *Gulabin Bunkhouse* on the A93, run by Cairnwell Mountain Sports (Ⓣ01250/885255), which rents out skis and bikes and offers hang-gliding lessons. Tucked away among the hills behind Spittal, the smart *Dalmunzie House* (Ⓣ01250/885224, Ⓔdalmunzie@aol.com; ❺) is a turreted traditional Highland sporting lodge, reflecting the peace and tranquillity of the rugged scenery. From Spittal the road climbs another five miles or so to the ski centre at the crest of the Cairnwell Pass.

Blairgowrie is well linked by hourly **bus** #57 to both Perth and Dundee. To travel up Glen Shee, you'll have to rely on the **postbus**, which leaves town at 7.30am (not Sun) and returns from the Spittal of Glenshee at 12.30pm (confirm on Ⓣ01250/872766).

Meigle and Glen Isla

Fifteen miles north of Dundee on the B954 lies the tiny settlement of **MEIGLE**, home to Scotland's most important collection of early Christian and Pictish inscribed stones. Housed in a modest former schoolhouse, the **Meigle Museum** (April–Nov daily 9.30am–6pm; HS; £2) displays some thirty pieces dating from the seventh to the tenth centuries, all found in and around the nearby churchyard. The majority are either gravestones that would have lain flat, or cross slabs inscribed with the sign of the cross, usually standing. Most impressive is the 7ft-tall great cross slab, said to be the gravestone of Guinevere, wife of King Arthur, carved on one side with a portrayal of Daniel surrounded by lions, a beautifully executed equestrian group, and mythological creatures including a dragon and a centaur. On the other side various beasts are surmounted by the "ring of glory", a wheel containing a cross carved and decorated in high relief. The exact meaning and purpose of the stones and their enigmatic symbols is obscure, as is the reason why so many of the stones were found at Meigle. The most likely theory suggests that Meigle was once an important ecclesiastical centre which attracted secular burials of prominent Picts.

Glen Isla

Three miles north of Meigle is **Alyth**, near which, legend has it, Guinevere was held captive by Mordred. The sleepy village lies at the south end of **Glen Isla**, which runs parallel to Glen Shee and is linked to it by the A926. Dominated by Mount Blair (2441ft), Glen Isla is a lot less dramatic than its sister glens, and suffers from an excess of angular conifers alongside great bald chunks of hillside waiting to be planted. Heading north along the B954, the River Isla narrows and then plunges some 60ft into a deep gorge to produce the classically pretty waterfall of **Reekie Linn**, or "smoking fall", so called because of the water mist produced when the fall hits a ledge and bounces a further 20ft into a deep pool known as the Black Dub. Just after this, a sideroad leads east to the pleasant Loch of Lintrathen, beside which is the *Lochside Lodge* (Ⓣ01575/560340, Ⓦwww.lochsidelodge.com; ❸), a cosy bar set in a converted steading full of old pews and farming implements, with a noted restaurant alongside and four bedrooms in the old hay loft. Heading back into the glen proper, you'll come on the tiny hamlet of **KIRKTON OF GLENISLA** ten miles or so up the glen. Here, the cosy *Glenisla Hotel* (Ⓣ01575/582223, Ⓦwww.glenisla-hotel.co.uk; ❹) is great for classy bar meals and convivial drinking. In the nearby Glenisla forest there are some **hiking** trails, while just before Kirkton, a turn-off on the right-hand side leads northeast up a long bumpy road to the unexpected Glenmarkie Farmhouse Health Spa and Equestrian Centre (Ⓣ01575/582295; ❷) which offers pedicures and pony trekking.

Transport connections into the glen are limited: Alyth is on the main bus routes linking Blairgowrie with Dundee and Kirriemuir, while hourly bus #57 from Dundee to Perth passes through Meigle. Transport up to Kirkton is limited to a postbus which leaves Blairgowrie at 7am (not Sun) and travels via Alyth (confirm on Ⓣ01250/872766).

Forfar and around

Around fifteen miles north of Dundee on the main A90 lies **FORFAR**, Angus's county town and the ancient capital of the Picts. Old Pictish connections are still evident in Forfar's strong support for the Scottish National Party (SNP), with a profusion of Scottish flags and stirring messages on civic buildings. The wide High Street is framed by some impressive Victorian architecture and small old-fashioned shops. Midway along, at 20 West High St, the **Meffen Institute Museum and Art Gallery** (Mon–Sat 10am–5pm; free) exhibits Neolithic, Pictish and Celtic remains and a thoroughly enjoyable collection of re-created historical street scenes. The most disturbing examines the town's seventeenth-century passion for witch-hunting, with a taped re-creation of locals baying for blood. There is also a comprehensive interactive computer catalogue of all the Pictish stones in Angus, and an excellent art gallery.

A series of glacial lochs peters out in the west of the town at **Forfar Loch**, now surrounded by a pleasant country park with a visitors' centre and three-mile nature trail. Two miles east, high above the wooded Loch Fithie, are the impressive remains of **Restenneth Priory** (free access), approached along a hard-to-spot side road off the B9113. Built by King Nechtan of the Picts in about the eighth century, it was adapted as an Augustinian priory in the twelfth century. Still something of a Pictish shrine, it's common to find mementoes and flowers left by pilgrims. The splayed foot spire, first seen beckoning from the road, was added in the fifteenth century. A little way south of this, off the B9128, a cairn in the village of **Dunnichen** commemorates a battle at nearby Nechtansmere in 685 in which the Picts unexpectedly defeated a Northumbrian army, thus preventing the Angles from extending their kingdom northwards.

Forfar's small **tourist office** (July & Aug Mon–Sat 9.30am–5.30pm; April–June & Sept Mon–Sat 10am–5pm; ⓣ01307/467876) is at 45 East High St, opposite the soaring steeple of the parish church. Numerous shops and bakers stock the famous **Forfar Bridie**, a semicircular folded pastry-case of mince, onion and seasonings, including Saddlers, a few doors down from the tourist office, and McLarens (the locals' favourite), at 8 West High St. Otherwise, all-day **food** and **drink** can be found at the *Royal Hotel* on Castle Street, by the Town Hall.

Glamis Castle

Bus #125 from Forfar runs regularly to Dundee via the pink-sandstone **Glamis Castle** (April–Oct daily 10.30am–4.45pm; £6.20, grounds only £3.10), located a mile north of the picturesque village of **GLAMIS** (pronounced "glahms"). A wondrously over-the-top, L-shaped five-storey pile set in an extensive landscaped park complete with deer and pheasants, this is one of the most famous Scottish castles. Shakespeare chose it as a central location in *Macbeth* and its royal connections (as the childhood home of the Queen Mother and birthplace of Princess Margaret) make it one of the essential stops on every coach tour of Scotland, though for many visitors the Queen Mum gloss is laid on rather thick.

Approaching the castle down the long main drive, a riot of turrets, towers and conical roofs appears fantastically at the end of the sweeping avenue of trees, framed by the Grampian Mountains. The bulk of the current building dates from the fifteenth century, although many of the later additions (particularly from the seventeenth century) give it its startling Disneyesque appearance. Glamis began life as a comparatively humble hunting lodge, used in the eleventh century by the kings of Scotland. In 1372, King Robert II gave the property to his son-in-law, Sir John Lyon, who built the core of the present building. His descendants, the earls of Kinghorne and Strathmore – the fourteenth of which was the Queen Mother's father – have lived here ever since.

The guided tour starts upstairs in the Victorian **Dining Room**, notable for its fine rose-and-thistle ceiling. The garish silver ship that forms the centrepiece of the table display was a golden wedding gift to the thirteenth earl from his estate workers in 1903. Another present – the grandfather clock in the corner – came from their 27 grandchildren, including a three-year-old Elizabeth Bowes-Lyon, now the Queen Mother. The atmosphere changes dramatically in the fifteenth-century **Crypt**, more properly the Lower Hall of the original tower house, which you enter through a door in the wood panelling of the Dining Room. The crypt's 12ft-thick walls enclose a haunted "lost" room, reputed to be have been sealed with the red-bearded Lord of Glamis and Crawford (also known as Beardie Crawford) inside, after he dared to play cards with the Devil one Sabbath. From here, the tour passes up a seventeenth-century staircase, whose hollow central pillar provided a primitive system of central heating.

Next is the arch-roofed **Drawing Room**, with delightful wedding-cake plasterwork (dated 1621). Classical portraits line the walls, the most notable being the vast family grouping of the third earl, who was responsible for many of the castle's seventeenth-century alterations, by Jacob de Wet. The artist painted the earl in classical armour that, unfortunately, looks like a flimsy negligee. The highlight of the tour is the family **Chapel**, completed in 1688. De Wet was commissioned to produce the frescoes from the family Bible, although his depictions of Christ wearing a hat and St Peter in a pair of glasses have raised eyebrows ever since. The chapel is said to be haunted by the spectre of a grey lady, the ghost of the sixth Lady Glamis who was burnt as a witch on the order of James V. The **Billiard Room**, complete with full-sized table and a beautiful polished walnut piano that cost £199 when it was commissioned in 1866, is decorated with various species of stuffed bird and lined with paintings and tapestries, of which the vast and colourful *Fruit Market* by Flemish artist Frans Snyders draws the most attention. **King Malcolm's Room**, so called because it is believed he died nearby in 1034, is most notable for its carved wooden chimneypiece, on which many of its most decorative panels are, in fact, highly polished leather.

From here, the tour passes into the **Royal Apartments**, where you can see the Queen Mother's delicate gilt four-poster bed which was a wedding present from her mother, who embroidered the names and dates of birth of her ten children into its panels. **Duncan's Hall**, a fifteenth-century guardroom, is the traditional – but inaccurate – setting for Duncan's murder by Macbeth (it actually took place near Elgin). Finally, the tour concludes with a random display of family artefacts that include the Queen Mother's old doll's house.

Glamis' **grounds** are worth a few hours in their own right, holding lead statues of James VI and Charles I at the top of the main drive, a seventeenth-century Baroque sundial, a formal Italian Garden and verdant walks out to Earl John's Bridge and through the woodland. In Glamis village the humble **Angus Folk Museum** (July & Aug daily 10am–5pm; April–June & Sept daily 11am–5pm; Oct Sat & Sun 11am–5pm; NTS; £3), housed in six low-slung cottages in Kirk Wynd, has a bewildering array of local ephemera, including bizarrely named agricultural implements, a nineteenth-century horse-drawn hearse and a section on local bothies.

Aberlemno

Five miles east of Forfar, straddling the ridge-topping B9134, the hamlet of **ABERLEMNO** is home to a superb collection of open-air Pictish stones, unfortunately boxed out of sight in winter (Oct–April) in weatherproofed wood. In the churchyard, just off the main road, an eighth-century cross slab combines a swirling Christian Celtic cross with Pictish beasts on one side and an elaborate Pictish battle scene on the other, thought to commemorate victory over the Northumbrians in 685. Three other stones, bristling with Pictish and early Christian symbols, sit by the main road, overlooking huge sweeps of valley and mountain, though plans are afoot to move all the stones to a nearby indoor location to prevent further erosion. The Forfar–Brechin **bus** #21a stops in Aberlemno.

Kirriemuir and glens Prosen, Clova and Doll

The sandstone town of **KIRRIEMUIR**, known locally as Kirrie, is set on a hill six miles northwest of Forfar on the cusp of glens Clova and Prosen. Despite the influx of hunters up for the "season", it's still a pretty special place, a haphazard confection of narrow closes, twisting wynds and steep braes. The main cluster of streets have all the appeal of an old film set, with their old-fashioned bars, tiled butcher's shop, tartan outlets and haberdasheries somehow managing to avoid being contrived and quaint – although the recent recobbling of the town centre around a twee statue of Peter Pan undermines this somewhat.

Peter Pan's presence is justified, however, since Kirrie was the birthplace of his creator, **J.M. Barrie**. A local handloom-weaver's son, Barrie first came to notice with his series of novels about "Thrums", a village based on his hometown, in particular *A Window in Thrums* and his third novel, *The Little Minister*. The story of Peter Pan, the little boy who never grew up, was penned by Barrie in 1904 – some say as a response to a strange upbringing dominated by the memory of his older brother, who died as a child. **Barrie's birthplace**, a plain little whitewashed cottage at 9 Brechin Rd (April–Sept Mon–Sat 11am–5.30pm, Sun 1.30–5.30pm; Oct Sat 11am–5.30pm, Sun 1.30–5.30pm; NTS; £3), displays his writing desk, photos and newspaper clippings. The wash house outside – romantically billed as Barrie's first "theatre" – was apparently the model for the house built by the Lost Boys for Wendy in Never-Never Land. Barrie chose to be buried at the nearby St Mary's Episcopal Church in Kirrie, despite being offered a more prestigious plot at London's Westminster Abbey. Another local son who attracts a handful of rather different pilgrims is **Bon Scott** of the rock band AC/DC, who was born and lived here before emigrating to Australia.

More on Scott, as well as other notable residents of the town, can be found in the **Kirriemuir Museum** (Mon–Wed, Fri & Sat 10am–5pm, Thurs 1–5pm; free), in the old Town House on the main square. The oldest building in Kirrie, it has seen service as a tolbooth, court, jail, post office, police station and chemist; these days you can find two floors of information and exhibits on the town and the Angus Glens, including scale models of the town in 1604, the year the tolbooth was erected, and one of Glen Clova, showing the relief of the hills. Other attractions in Kirrie include the **Aviation Museum** (April–Sept Mon–Thurs & Sat 10am–5pm, Fri & Sun 11am–5pm; free), a jumble of military uniforms, photos, World War II memorabilia and Airfix models, and a **camera obscura** (April–Sept daily 1–4pm; £1.50) in an old cricket pavilion above town. This unexpected treasure was donated to the town in 1930 by Barrie, and offers splendid views of Strathmore and the glens.

Kirrie's helpful **tourist office** is in Cumberland Close (July & Aug Mon–Sat 9.30am–5.30pm; April–June & Sept Mon–Sat 10am–5pm; ⓣ01575/574097), in the new development behind *Visocchi's* in the main square. **Accommodation** is available at *Crepto B&B*, Kinnordy Place (ⓣ01575/572746; ❷), or the respectable *Airlie Arms*, St Malcolm's Wynd

(Ⓣ01575/572487, Ⓦwww.airliearms-hotel.co.uk; ❸). More rustic and very pleasant are the farm cottages of *Littleton of Airlie* (Ⓣ01575/530422; ❸), three miles out of town on the A926 to Alyth. *Visocchi's* is great for daytime **snacks** and ice cream, while the *Airlie* and *Hook's Hotel* on Bank Street both serve good food in the evening. Of the **pubs**, *Hook's Hotel* or, opposite the museum, *Three, Bellies Brae*, are the most lively.

Postbuses into glens Clova and Prosen leave from the main post office on Reform Street at 8.30am (not Sun). A second Glen Clova bus leaves at around 3pm (Mon–Fri), but only goes as far as Clova village before returning to Kirriemuir. Hourly buses run to Forfar.

Glen Prosen

Five miles north of Kirrie, the low-key hamlet of **DYKEHEAD** marks the point where **Glen Prosen** and Glen Clova divide. A mile or so up Glen Prosen, you'll find the house where Captain Scott and fellow explorer Doctor Wilson planned their ill-fated trip to Antarctica in 1910–11, with a roadside **stone cairn** commemorating the expedition. From here, Glen Prosen proper unfolds before you. Little has changed since Scott's time, and it remains essentially a quiet wooded backwater, with all the wild and rugged splendour of the other glens but without the crowds. To explore the area thoroughly you need to go on foot, but a good road circuit can be made by crossing the river at the tiny village of **GLENPROSEN** and returning to Kirriemuir along the western side of the glen via Pearsie.

The best walk in the area is the reasonably easy four-mile **Minister's Path** connecting Prosen and Clova (so called because the local minister would walk this way twice every Sunday to conduct services in both glens). Take the footpath between the kirk and the bridge in Glenprosen village, then the right fork where the track splits and continue over the colourful burnt moorland down into Clova. As there is no afternoon return service by postbus from Prosen to Kirriemuir, you either have to stay the night or follow the path to its end, **Wester Eggie**, and pick up the Clova village postbus (Mon–Fri 3.30pm).

Glen Clova and Glen Doll

Of all the Angus glens, **Glen Clova** – which in the north becomes **Glen Doll** – with its stunning cliffs, heather slopes and valley meadows, is the firm favourite of many. Although it can get unpleasantly congested in peak season, the area is still remote enough so that you can leave the crowds with little effort. Wildlife is abundant, with deer on the mountains, wild hares and even grouse and the occasional buzzard. The meadow flowers on the valley floor and arctic plants (including great splashes of white and purple saxifrage) on the rocks also make it something of a botanist's paradise.

The B955 from Dykehead and Kirriemuir divides at the Gella bridge over the swift-coursing River South Esk (unofficially, road traffic is encouraged to use the western branch of the road for travel up the glen, and the eastern side going down). Six miles north of Gella, the two branches of the road join up once more at the hamlet of **CLOVA**, little more than the hearty *Glen Clova Hotel* (Ⓣ01575/550350, Ⓦwww.clova.com; ❸), which also has a refurbished bunkhouse (£9.50 per night). Meals and real ale are available in the lively *Climbers' Bar* at the side of the hotel. Also pleasant, though slightly less susceptible to the high jinks of university climbing clubs, is *Brandy Burn House* (Ⓣ01575/550203, Ⓦwww.glenclova.co.uk; ❷), with a bar and coffee shop in its stables, a beer garden and comfortable B&B. An excellent, if fairly strenuous, four-hour walk from behind the old school at the back of the hotel leads up

Walks from Glen Doll

Ordnance Survey Landranger maps nos. 43 & 44.

These walks are some of the main routes across the Grampians from the Angus glens to Deeside, many of which follow well-established old drovers' roads. A number of them cross the royal estate of Balmoral, and Prince Charles's favourite mountain – Lochnagar – can be seen from all angles. The walks should always be approached with care; make sure to follow the usual safety precautions.

Capel Mounth to Ballater (15 miles; 7hr). Head across the bridge from the car park, turning right after a mile when the track crosses the Cald Burn. Out of the wood, the path zigzags its way up fierce slopes before levelling out on the moorland plateau. Soon descending, the path crosses a scree near the eastern end of Loch Muick. With the loch to your left, walk down along the scree till you reach the River Muick, crossing the bridge to take the quiet track along the river's northern shore to Ballater.

Capel Mounth round-trip (15 miles; 8hr). Follow the above route to Loch Muick, then take the path down to loch level and double back on yourself along the loch's southern shore. When the track crosses the Black Burn, either take the steep left fork or continue along the shore for another mile, heading up the dramatic Streak of Lightning path that follows Corrie Chash. Both paths meet at the ruined stables below Sandy Hillock. Just beyond, take the path to the left, descending rapidly to the waterfall by the bridge at Bachnagairn, where a gentle burn-side track leads the three miles back to Glen Doll car park.

Jock's Road to Braemar (14 miles; 7hr). Take the road north from the car park past the hostel. After almost a mile, follow the signposted Jock's Road to the right, keeping on the northern bank of the burn. Pass a barn, Davey's Shelter, below Cairn Lunkhard and continue onto a wide ridge towards the path's summit at Crow Craigies (3018ft). From here, the path bumps down over scree slopes to the head of Loch Callater. Go either way round the loch, and follow the Callater Burn at the other end, eventually hitting the main A93 two miles short of Braemar.

into the mountains and around the lip of **Loch Brandy**, which legend predicts will one day flood and drown the valley below.

North from Clova village, the road turns into a rabbit-infested lane coursing along the riverside for four miles to the car park and informal **campsite** in Glen Doll, a useful starting point for numerous superb **walks** (see box). From the car park, it's only a few hundred yards further to the SYHA **hostel** (Ⓣ01575/550236, Ⓦwww.syha.org.uk; May–Sept), a restored hunting lodge that boasts a squash court along with the usual facilities and is typically busy with climbers and youth groups.

Brechin

Twelve miles or so east of Kirriemuir, **BRECHIN** is an attractive, confident town whose red sandstone buildings give it a warm, welcoming feel. The chief attraction is the old **Cathedral** on Bishop's Close, off the High Street. There's been a religious building of sorts here since the arrival of evangelizing Irish missionaries in 900 AD, and the red sandstone structure has become something of a hotchpotch of architectural styles. What you see today chiefly dates from an extensive rebuilding in 1900, with the oldest surviving part of the cathedral being the 106ft round tower, one of only two in Scotland. The cathedral's doorway, built 6ft above the ground for protection against Viking raids, has some notable carvings, while inside you can see various Pictish stones, illuminated by the jewel-coloured stained-glass windows. A mile from the town centre along the Forfar road in the Brechin Castle Park is **Pictavia** (Mon–Sat 9am–6pm, Sun 10am–6pm; Nov–March Mon–Fri closes 5pm; £3.25), a custom-built tourist attraction rather incongruously integrated into a garden centre. Based on the history and heritage of the Picts, you'll find the increasingly familiar blend of sound-and-light entertainments and distinctively designed displays, along with a handful of Pictish stones and fibreglass casts of stones. Overall, it's a bit lacking in substance, and is missing the slightly mystical atmosphere you can find at stones out in the wild in places such as nearby Aberlemno (see p.525) and throughout the northeast.

The library on St Ninian Square, to the north of the cathedral, houses Brechin's **museum** (Mon & Wed 9.30am–8pm, Tues 10am–6pm, Thurs 9.30am–6pm, Fri & Sat 9.30am–5pm; free), a one-room jumble of history, civic memorabilia, geology and painting. Just off the square is the train station of the **Caledonian Railway** (talking timetable ⓣ01356/622992; information line ⓣ01561/377760), operating steam trains on summer Sundays and bank holidays along four miles of track from Brechin to the Bridge of Dun.

There is a **tourist office** desk at Pictavia (April–Sept Mon–Sat 9.30am–5.30pm, Sun 10am–5.30pm; ⓣ01356/623050), as well as an information office in town near the cathedral on High Street (June–Sept Mon–Sat 10am–4pm, Wed closes 1pm; ⓣ01356/622292). Both can help you find accommodation locally or offer information on hiking in Glen Esk. Brechin is on main **transport** routes: bus #30 runs hourly to Montrose, nine miles east, and it's also served by regular Citylink coaches between Dundee and Aberdeen.

Edzell and Glen Esk

Travelling around Angus, you can hardly fail to notice the difference between organic settlements and planned towns built by landowners who forcibly rehoused local people in order to keep them under control, especially after the Jacobite uprisings. One of the better examples of the latter, **EDZELL**, five miles north of Brechin on the B966 (and linked to it by buses #21, #29 and #30), was cleared and rebuilt with Victorian rectitude a mile to the west of its original site in the 1840s. Through the Dalhousie Arch at the entrance to the village the long, wide and ruler-straight main street is lined with prim nineteenth-century buildings, now doing a roaring trade as genteel teashops and antique emporia.

The original village (identifiable from the cemetery and surrounding grassy mounds) lay immediately to the west of the wonderfully explorable red sandstone ruins of **Edzell Castle** (April–Sept daily 9.30am–6.30pm; Oct–March Mon–Wed & Sat 9.30am–4.30pm, Thurs 9.30am–noon, Sun 2–4.30pm; HS; £2.80), itself a mile west of the planned village. The main part of the old castle is a good example of a comfortable tower house, whose main priority became luxurious living rather than defence, with some intricate decorative corbelling on the roof, a vast fireplace in the first-floor hall and numerous telltale signs of building from different ages.

It is, however, the **pleasance garden** overlooked by the castle tower that makes a visit to Edzell essential, especially in late spring and early to midsummer. The garden was built in 1604, at the height of the optimistic Renaissance, by Sir David Lindsay, and its refinement and extravagance are evident. The walls contain sculpted images of erudition: the Planetary Deities on the east side, the Liberal Arts (including a decapitated figure of Music) on the south and, under floods of lobelia, the Cardinal Virtues on the west wall. In the centre of the garden, low-cut box hedges spell out the family mottoes and enclose voluminous beds of roses.

Four miles southwest of Edzell, lying either side of the lane to Bridgend which can be reached either by carrying on along the road past the castle, or by taking the narrow road at the southern end of Edzell village, are the **Caterthuns**, twin Iron Age hill forts that were probably occupied at different times. The surviving ramparts on the White Caterthun (978ft) – easily reached from the small car park below – are the most impressive, and this is thought to be the later fort, occupied by the Picts in the first few centuries AD. Views from both, over the mountains to the north and the plains and foothills to the south, are stunning.

Just north of Edzell, a fifteen-mile road climbs alongside the River North Esk to form **Glen Esk**, the most easterly of the Angus glens and, like the others, sparsely populated. Ten miles along the Glen, the excellent **Glenesk Folk Museum** (June to mid-Oct daily noon–6pm; Easter–May Sat & Sun noon–6pm; £2), brings together records, costumes, photographs, maps and tools from the Angus glens, depicting the often harsh way of life for the inhabitants. The museum is housed in a lovely old shooting lodge known as The Retreat, and is run independently and enthusiastically by the local community. Inside there's also a craft shop and a noted tearoom – due reward for those who have endured the winding glen road. There are some excellent **hiking** routes further up the glen, including one to Queen Victoria's Well in Glen Mark and another up Mount Keen, Scotland's most easterly Munro.

There's decent **B&B** in Edzell at *Elmgrove*, Inveriscandye Road (ⓣ01356/648266, ⓦwww.elmgrove.edzell.org.uk; ❶), while the most attractive of the hotels in town, the *Panmure Arms* (ⓣ01356/648950, ⓦwww.panmurearmshotel.co.uk; ❹) at the far end of the main street near the turn-off to the castle, has recently been smartened up and offers rooms and meals. Further up the glen, you can **camp** one and a half miles north of the village at the *Glenesk Caravan Park* (ⓣ01356/648565; April–Oct), while at **INVERMARK**, near the head of the Glen and a good jumping-off point for various hiking routes, is *The House of Mark* (ⓣ01356/670315, ⓦwww.houseofmark.com; ❷), a former manse in a lovely setting, which can arrange evening meals featuring local game and home baking.

Aberdeenshire and Moray

Aberdeenshire and Moray cover some 3500 square miles of open and varied country dotted with historic and archeological sights, from neat NTS properties and eerie prehistoric rings of standing stones to quiet kirkyards, serene abbeys and a rash of dramatic castles. Geographically, the counties break down into two distinct areas: the **hinterland**, once barren and now a patchwork of fertile farms, rising towards high mountains, sparkling rivers and gentle valleys; and the **coast**, a classic stretch of rocky cliff, remote fishing villages and long, sandy beaches.

For visitors, the large city of **Aberdeen** is the obvious focal point of the region, and while it's not a place to keep you engrossed for long, it does boast some intriguing architecture, attractive museums and a lively social scene. From here, it's a short hop west to **Deeside**, annually visited by the Royal Family and an easily accessed gateway to some spectacular mountain scenery. To the north lies the **Don Valley**, a quiet area which leads into the Cairngorms at the Lecht, a remote mountain pass where there's a skiing centre in winter, and **Speyside**, the heart of Scotland's malt whisky industry. Further north, the **coast** offers some dramatic scenery, punctuated by picturesque villages left almost unchanged by the centuries.

Aberdeen has an **airport**, and **trains** to Inverness and major points further south. **Buses** in the hinterland can be few and far between, often running on schooldays only, but the main centres are well served. By car, signposted **trails** set up by the tourist board make navigation around the Speyside whisky distilleries and visiting the northeast coast and castles a bit easier.

Aberdeen

The third-largest city in Scotland, **ABERDEEN**, commonly known as the Granite City, lies 120 miles northeast of Edinburgh, on the banks of the rivers Dee and Don smack in the middle of the northeast coast. Based around a working harbour, it's a place that people either love or hate. Lewis Grassic Gibbon, one of the northeast's most eminent novelists, summed it up: "One detests Aberdeen with the detestation of a thwarted lover. It is the one hauntingly and exasperatingly lovable city of Scotland." Certainly, while some extol the many tones and colours of Aberdeen's **granite** buildings, others see only uniform grey and find the city grim, cold and unwelcoming. The weather doesn't help: Aberdeen lies on a latitude north of Moscow and the cutting wind and driving rain (even if it does transform the buildings into sparkling silver) can be tiresome.

Since the 1970s, **oil** has made Aberdeen a hugely wealthy and self-confident place: only four percent of Scotland's population live in the city, yet it has eight percent of the country's spending power. Despite (or perhaps because of) this, it can seem a soulless city; there's a feeling of corporate sterility and sometimes, despite its long history, Aberdeen seems to exist only as a departure point and service station for the transient population of some ten to fifteen thousand who live on the 130 oil platforms out to sea.

That said, Aberdeen's **architecture** is undeniably striking – a granite cityscape created in the nineteenth century by three fine architects: Archibald Simpson and John Smith in the early years of the century and, subsequently, A. Marshall Mackenzie. Classical inspiration and Gothic Revival styles predominate, giving grace to a material once thought of as only good enough for tombs and paving stones. In addition, it sometimes seems like every spare inch of ground has been turned into **flower gardens**, the urban parks being some of the most beautiful in Britain. This positive floral explosion – Aberdeen has been barred from "Britain in Bloom" competitions because it kept winning – has certainly cheered up the general greyness.

Staying in such a prosperous place has its advantages. There are plenty of good restaurants and hotels, local transport is efficient and certain sights, including Aberdeen's splendid **Art Gallery** and the excellent **Maritime Museum**, are free. Furthermore, the the fact that the city is the bright light in a wide hinterland helps it to sustain a lively nightlife with some decent pubs and a colourful arts and cultural scene.

Some history

In the twelfth century, Alexander I noted "Aberdon" as one of his principal towns, and by the thirteenth century it had become a centre for **trade and fishing**, a jumble of timber and wattle houses perched on three small hills, with the castle to the east and St Nicholas's kirk outside the gates to the west.

It was here that **Robert the Bruce** sought refuge during the Scottish Wars of Independence, leading to the garrison of the castle by Edward I and Balliol's supporters. In a night-time raid in 1306, the townspeople attacked the garrison and killed them all, an event commemorated by the city's motto "Bon Accord", the watchword for the night. The victory was not to last, however, and in 1337 Edward III stormed the city, forcing its rebuilding on a grander scale. A century later Bishop Elphinstane founded the Catholic university in the area north of town known today as **Old Aberdeen**, while the rest of the city developed as a mercantile centre and important port.

Industrial and economic expansion led to the Aberdeen New Streets Act in 1800, setting off a hectic half-century of development that almost led to financial disaster. Luckily, the city was rescued by a boom in trade: in the **shipyards** the construction of Aberdeen Clippers revolutionized sea transport, giving Britain supremacy in the China tea trade, and in 1882 a group of local businessmen acquired a **steam** tugboat for trawl fishing. Sail gave way to steam, and fisher families flooded in.

By the mid-twentieth century, Aberdeen's traditional industries were in decline, but the discovery of **oil** in the North Sea transformed the place from a depressed port into a boom town (see box). The oil-borne prosperity may have served to mask the thinness of the region's other wealth creators, but it

Oil and Aberdeen

When **oil** was discovered in BP's Forties Field in 1970, Aberdonians rightly viewed it as a massive financial opportunity, and – despite fierce competition from other east coast British ports, Scandinavia and Germany – the city succeeded in persuading the oil companies to base their headquarters here. Land was made available for housing and industry, millions were invested in the harbour and offshore developments, new schools opened and the airport expanded to include a heliport, which has since become the busiest in the world.

The city's **population** swelled by sixty thousand, and earnings escalated from fifteen percent below the national average to a figure well above it. Wealthy oil companies built prestigious offices, swish new restaurants, upmarket bars and shops. At the peak of production in the **mid-1980s**, 2.6 million barrels a day were being turned out, and the price had reached $80 a barrel. The effect of the slump of 1986 – when oil prices dropped to $10 a barrel – was devastating: jobs vanished at the rate of a thousand a month, house prices dropped and Aberdeen soon discovered just how dependent on oil it was. The moment oil prices began to rise, crisis struck again with the loss of 167 lives when the **Piper Alpha oilrig** exploded, precipitating an array of much-needed but very expensive safety measures.

In recent years production levels have steadily risen back up to those of the early 1980s, though with assurances that this time the dangers of boom-and-bust policies have been heeded. Oil remains the cornerstone of Aberdeen's economy, keeping unemployment down to one of the lowest levels in Britain and driving up house prices not just in the city itself but in an increasingly wide area of its rural hinterland. Predictions of the imminent decline in oil reserves and the end of Aberdeen's economic boom are heard frequently, as they have been since 1970, but reliable indicators suggest that the black gold will be flowing well into the new millennium.

has nonetheless allowed Aberdeen to hold its own as a cultural and academic centre and as a focus of the northeast's identity into the new century.

Arrival, information and city transport

Aberdeen's Dyce **airport**, seven miles northwest of town, is served by flights from most parts of the UK and a few European cities. The airport bus #27 and Aberdeen–Inverness bus #10 run to the city centre; a taxi costs approximately £10. The main **train station** is on Guild Street, in the centre of the city (ⓣ0845/748 4950), with the **bus** terminal for intercity and regional services right beside it (regional buses ⓣ0870/608 2608; intercity buses ⓣ0870/550 5050).

Aberdeen is also linked to Lerwick in Shetland and Stromness in Orkney by P&O Scottish **ferry**, with regular crossings from Jamieson's Quay in the harbour. Note that from October 2002, a new operator, Northlink, will be taking over this service; see p.683 for details.

Information

From the train and bus station it's a two-minute walk up the hill to Union Street, Aberdeen's main thoroughfare, and an even shorter stroll to the **tourist office** in Old Provost Ross's House, next door to the Maritime Museum on Ship Row (July & Aug Mon–Sat 9.30am–7pm, Sun 10am–4pm; June & Sept Mon–Sat 9.30am–5pm; rest of year Mon–Fri 9.30am–5pm, Sat 10am–2pm; ⓣ01224/288828, ⓦwww.agtb.org). They'll book accommodation for you, charging ten percent of the first night's room rate, redeemable at your hotel.

At the tourist office you can pick up a *What's On* leaflet, with details of upcoming events and scheduled art exhibitions and theatre. The local newspapers, the morning *Press and Journal* and the *Evening Express*, are both good for cinema and what's on that day. More esoteric information – anything from t'ai chi workshops to festivals and ceilidhs – is given in the glossy bimonthly programme produced by the Lemon Tree Arts Centre, 5 West North St (ⓣ01224/642230, ⓦwww.lemontree.org), a vibrant place which fills a role as the city's cultural hub. For details of local gigs and live music sessions, consult ⓦwww.cellarscene.co.uk.

City transport and tours

The centre of Aberdeen is best explored by foot, but you might need to use **local buses**, almost all of which pass along Union Street, to reach some of the sights. There is no all-inclusive day ticket, but you can get a weekly bus pass for £12. If you plan to use the buses a lot, you should buy a **Farecard** (in £2, £5 or £10 denominations) from the main **transport office**, 395 King St, or the busy city-centre kiosk outside Marks & Spencer on Union Street, which also hands out transport **maps**; each time you travel the fare is deducted from the card. For information on local bus services, call Grampian Busline (ⓣ01224/650065).

Taxis, which operate from ranks throughout the city centre, are rarely necessary, except late at night. If you don't manage to hail one, call Mairs Taxis (ⓣ01224/353535).

An open-topped **bus tour** passing by the main sights runs regularly throughout the summer (July–Sept). It leaves from outside the Town House on Union Street and costs £4 for a standard ticket or £6 for an "explorer" ticket which gets you on the tour and all other local buses for the rest of the day.

ABERDEEN

RESTAURANTS	
Ashvale	M
Big Cheese	E
Howies	J
Inversnecky	C
Lemon Tree	A
Martha's Vineyard	L
Nargile	D
Owlies	B
Poldino's	G
Silver Darling	I
Soul & Spice	H
Wild Boar	F
Yu	K

ACCOMMODATION	
Allan Guest House	19
Braeside Guest House	15
Brentwood Hotel	13
Campbell's Guest House	2
Crombie Johnstone Halls	1
Ferryhill House	20
Fourways Guest House	17
Globe Inn	6
Jay's Guest House	3
King George VI Memorial Hostel	9
Mannofield Hotel	16
The Marcliffe at Pitfodels	18
Patio Hotel	4
Queen's Hotel	10
Royal Crown Guest House	14
Simpson's Hotel	11
Skene House Rosemount	5
Speedbird Inn	12
Thistle Aberdeen Caledonian	7
Travelodge	8

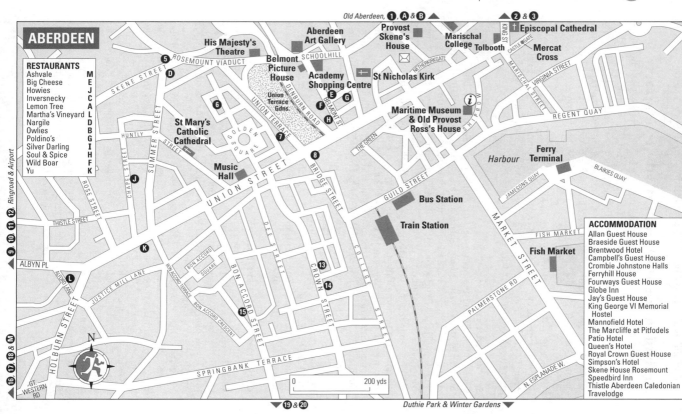

Old Aberdeen, 1, A & B
2 & 3
Beach, 4 & C
Footdee & I
Duthie Park & Winter Gardens
19 & 20
16, 17, 18 & M
9, 10, 11, 12, Ringroad & Airport

His Majesty's Theatre
Aberdeen Art Gallery
Provost Skene's House
Marischal College
Tolbooth
Episcopal Cathedral
Mercat Cross
Belmont Picture House
Academy Shopping Centre
St Nicholas Kirk
Maritime Museum & Old Provost Ross's House
St Mary's Catholic Cathedral
Music Hall
Union Terrace Gdns.
Harbour
Ferry Terminal
Bus Station
Train Station
Fish Market

ROSEMOUNT VIADUCT
SCHOOLHILL
SKENE STREET
KING ST
CASTLEGATE
NETHERKIRKGATE
MARISCHAL STREET
VIRGINIA STREET
REGENT QUAY
SHIPROW
DENBURN ROAD
BELMONT ST
UNION TERRACE
GOLDEN SQUARE
HUNTLY STREET
SUMMER STREET
CHAPEL STREET
ROSE STREET
THISTLE STREET
UNION STREET
BRIDGE STREET
THE GREEN
GUILD STREET
JAMESONS QUAY
BLAIKIES QUAY
MARKET STREET
FISH MARKET
DEE STREET
CROWN STREET
COLLEGE STREET
PALMERSTONE RD
ALBYN PL
ALFORD LANE
JUSTICE MILL LANE
BON ACCORD SQUARE
BON ACCORD TERRACE
BON ACCORD CRESCENT
BON ACCORD STREET
HOLBURN STREET
SPRINGBANK TERRACE
GT. WESTERN RD
N. ESPLANADE W.

N

0 200 yds

Accommodation

As befits a high-flying business city, Aberdeen has a large choice of **accommodation** – much of it is characterless and expensive, although you can almost always find cheaper weekend deals even at the smarter hotels. Predictably, the best budget options are the **B&Bs** and **guesthouses**, many of which are strung along Bon Accord and Crown streets (served by buses #6 and #17 to and from Union Street), and the Great Western Road (buses #18, #19 and #24). Cheapest of all are the **hostel** and **student halls** left vacant for visitors in the summer.

Hotels

Brentwood 101 Crown St ⓣ01224/595440, ⓦwww.brentwood-hotel.demon.co.uk. Spick-and-span refurbished old hotel south of Union Street. Popular with business people and often full during the week. ❹

Ferryhill House 169 Bon Accord St ⓣ01224/590867. A mansion set apart in its own grounds within walking distance of Union St. Its historic pub has real ale, a beer garden and decent food. ❺

Mannofield 447 Great Western Rd ⓣ01224/315888, ⓦwww.procona.co.uk. Charming old granite building, once a posh private house, a mile west of town on a busy road. Excellent-value three-course dinners. ❹

The Marcliffe at Pitfodels North Deeside Road, Pitfodels ⓣ01224/861000, ⓦwww.marcliffe.com. By far the most luxurious and tasteful option in the area. A forty-room, family-run small hotel in its own grounds four miles west of the city centre, with two fine restaurants and some exquisite touches. ❼

Patio Beach Boulevard ⓣ01224/633339, ⓦwww.patiohotels.com. Business hotel with pool and gym, as well as all the familiar trappings of a chain hotel, but in a decent setting not far from the beach. ❻

Queen's 51–53 Queen's Rd ⓣ01224/209999, ⓦwww.vagabond-hotels.com. Cheerful medium-sized city-centre hotel, recently refurbished, with a good culinary reputation. ❹

Simpson's 59 Queen's Rd ⓣ01224/327777, ⓔaddress@simpsonshotel.com. Highly style-conscious, terracotta-coloured modern interior to this large granite terrace house, with an excellent brasserie and good weekend rates. ❼

Speedbird Inn Argyll Road, Dyce ⓣ01224/772884, ⓦwww.speedbirdinns.co.uk. Large, modern chain hotel at the airport. ❷

Thistle Aberdeen Caledonian 10–14 Union Terrace ⓣ01224/640233. The best of the posh hotels, in an impressive Victorian edifice just off Union Street. ❼

Travelodge 9 Bridge St ⓣ01224/584555, ⓦwww.travelodge.co.uk. Typically bland budget hotel – but you can't beat it for convenience, right on Union Street and minutes from the station. ❷–❸

Guesthouses and B&Bs

Allan Guest House 56 Polmuir Rd ⓣ01224/584484, ⓦwww.camtay.co.uk. Unexpectedly tasteful and enthusiastically run guesthouse not far from Duthie Park. Good meals or supper available if arranged in advance. ❸

Braeside Guest House 68 Bon Accord St ⓣ01224/571471. Standard but inexpensive B&B within easy walking distance of the station and city centre. ❶

Campbell's Guest House 444 King St ⓣ01224/625444, ⓔcam444@zetnet.co.uk. Highly recommended breakfasts. One mile from the city centre and handy for the beach and Old Aberdeen. ❷

Fourways Guest House 435 Great Western Rd ⓣ01224/310218. A converted manse in the West End of town, usefully positioned near the main roads to the west of the city. ❷

Globe Inn 13–15 North Silver St ⓣ01224/624258. Easy-going, traditional-style city centre inn with seven en-suite rooms above a bar which regularly features live jazz. Rate includes continental breakfast. ❷

Jay's Guest House 422 King St ⓣ01224/638295, ⓦwww.jaysguesthouse.co.uk. Well-run, non-smoking house located in Old Aberdeen, near the university. ❸

Royal Crown Guest House 111 Crown St ⓣ01224/586461, ⓦwww.royalcrown.co.uk. Comfortable, family-run guesthouse within walking distance of station and Union Street. Non-smoking. ❷

Hostel, campus and self-catering accommodation

Crombie Johnstone Halls College Bounds, Old Aberdeen ⓣ01224/272664. Private rooms in the best of the student halls, located in one of the most interesting parts of the city. Available from late June to Sept. ❶

King George VI Memorial Hostel 8 Queen's Rd ⓣ01224/646988, ⓦwww.syha.org.uk. Rather soulless SYHA hostel with rooms for four to six, and a 2am curfew. Bus #15 from the train station. Breakfast is included in high season.

Skene House Rosemount 96 Rosemount Viaduct ⓣ01224/645971, ⓦwww.skene-house.co.uk. Serviced apartments with 1–3 rooms, all with TVs and microwaves. Good central location. ❹

The City

Aberdeen divides neatly into five main areas. The **city centre**, roughly bounded by Broad Street, Union Street, Schoolhill and Union Terrace, features the opulent **Marischal College**, the colonnaded **Art Gallery** with its fine collection, and homes that predate Aberdeen's nineteenth-century town planning and have been preserved as **museums**. Union Street continues west to the comparatively cosmopolitan **West End**, where much of the city's decent nightlife can be found amid the tall grey town houses. To the south, the **harbour** still heaves with boats serving the fishing and oil industries, while north of the centre lies attractive **Old Aberdeen**, a village neighbourhood presided over by **King's College** and **St Machar's Cathedral** and influenced by the large student population. The long sandy **beach** with its esplanade development, only a mile or so from the heart of the city, marks Aberdeen's eastern border.

The city centre

The centre of Aberdeen is dominated by mile-long **Union Street**, whose impressive architecture, sometimes lost among the shoppers and chain stores, is still the grandest and most ambitious single thoroughfare in Scotland. The key to the early nineteenth-century city planners who conceived the street was the building of the ambitious **Union Street bridge**, spanning two hills and the Denburn gorge. The first attempt, a triple-span design by Glasgow architect David Hamilton, bankrupted the city and collapsed during construction. The famous Thomas Telford, called in as an adviser, proposed a single-arch structure which, when completed, became one of the engineering wonders of its age. Since completion in 1805 the bridge has been widened twice, the second time, in 1963, adding a row of shops to the southern side which rather hides the dramatic impact of the structure.

Castlegate and around

Any exploration of the **city centre** should begin at the open, cobbled **Castlegate**, where Aberdeen's long-gone castle once stood. At its centre is the late seventeenth-century **Mercat Cross**, carved with a unique gallery of Stewart sovereigns alongside some fierce gargoyles. Castlegate was once the focus of city life but nowadays is rather lifeless, with litter swirling around and pigeons easily outnumbering shoppers. However, the view up gently rising Union Street – a jumble of grey spires, turrets and jostling double-decker buses – is quintessential Aberdeen and well worth taking a moment or two to savour.

As Union Street begins you have to crane your neck to get a good view of the towering, turreted spire of the granite **Town House**, though the steely-grey nineteenth-century exterior is in fact simply a facade behind which lurks the early seventeenth-century **Tolbooth**, one of the city's oldest buildings. Used as a jail for many centuries, the Tolbooth presently houses a mothballed museum on the theme of crime and imprisonment.

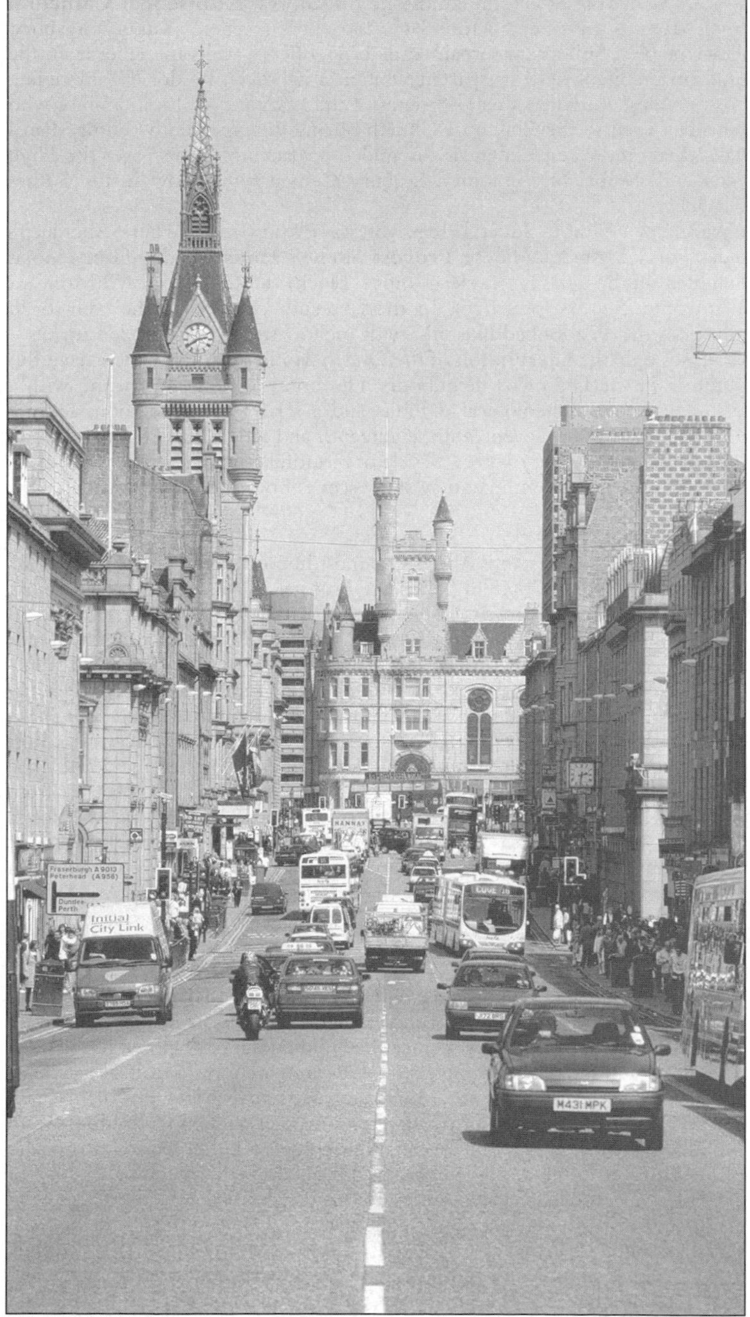

△ Union Street, Aberdeen

Nearby, on King Street, the sandstone **St Andrew's Episcopal Cathedral** (mid-May to mid-Sept Mon–Sat 11am–4pm), where Samuel Seabury, America's first bishop, was ordained in 1784, offers a welcome relief from the uniform granite. Inside, its spartan whiteness is broken by florid gold ceiling bosses representing the (then) 48 states of the USA and 48 local families who remained loyal to the Episcopal Church during the eighteenth-century Penal Laws. Even more resplendent is the gilded baldachino canopy over the High Altar and the brightly coloured Seabury Centenary window in the Suther Chapel.

West down Union Street brings you to Broad Street, where Aberdeen's oldest-surviving private house, **Provost Skene's House**, dating from 1545, is hemmed in by ghastly modern office blocks at 45 Guestrow (Mon–Sat 10am–5pm, Sun 1–4pm; free). In the sixteenth century all the well-to-do houses in the area looked like this, with mellow stone and rounded turrets – yet it was only the intervention of the Queen Mother in 1938 which saved this house from the fate of its neighbours. The house is now a museum, with a costume gallery, archeological exhibits and a series of period room settings illustrating life in the seventeenth, eighteenth and nineteenth centuries. Don't miss the Painted Gallery, where a cycle of beautiful religious tempera paintings from the mid-seventeenth century show scenes from the life of Christ.

The Marischal College and museum

On Broad Street itself stands Aberdeen's most imposing edifice and the world's second-largest granite building after the Escorial in Madrid – the exuberant **Marischal College**, whose tall, steely-grey pinnacled neo-Gothic facade is in absolute contrast to the hideously utilitarian concrete office blocks which face it. This spectacular architecture with all its soaring, surging lines has been painted and sketched more than any other in Aberdeen, and though not to everyone's taste – it was once described by a minor art historian as "a wedding cake covered in indigestible grey icing" – there's no escaping the fact that it is a most extraordinary feat of sculpture. The college itself was founded in 1593 by the fourth Earl Marischal, and coexisted as a separate Protestant university from Catholic King's, just up the road, for over two centuries. It was long Aberdeen's boast that their city had as many universities as the whole of England, and it wasn't until 1860 that the two were united as the University of Aberdeen. In 1893, the central tower was more than doubled in height by A. Marshall Mackenzie and the profusion of spirelets added, though the facade, which fronts an earlier quadrangle designed by Archibald Simpson in 1837–41, was not completed until 1906.

Behind the tower, through the college entrance, the Mitchell Hall's east window illustrates the history of the university in stained glass. You're unlikely to get a good view of this, however, since the building is mostly closed to the public as more and more of the university's functions are moved from the college. What you can get to see is the **Marischal Museum** (Mon–Fri 10am–5pm, Sun 2–5pm; free), made up of two large rooms that contain a wealth of weird exhibits, many gathered by Victorian anthropologists and other collectors who roamed the world filling their luggage with objects. The museum, sensitive to the cultural crassness this represents to the modern world, concentrates as much on the phenomenon of these collectors as the objects they brought back. But that's not to say that many of the exhibits – from a high-relief mummy case of a five-year-old Egyptian girl to a stomach-churning human foot, unbound and preserved in brine – aren't intriguing. Look out too for a kayak, discovered off the coast of Aberdeen around 1700 with the preserved body of an Inuit fisherman inside. The "Encyclopaedia of the Northeast" exhibition – running alphabetically from Aberdeen through to Whisky – is an amusing and lively display pulling together the nature and character of this corner of Scotland.

St Nicholas Kirk

Between Upperkirkgate and Union Street stands the long **St Nicholas Kirk** (May–Sept Mon–Fri noon–4pm, Sat 1–3pm, Oct–April Mon–Fri 10am–1pm; free), actually two churches in one, with a solid, central bell tower rising from the middle, from where the 48-bell carillon, the largest in Britain, regularly chimes across the city. There's been a church here since at least 1157, but as the largest kirk in Scotland it was severely damaged during the Reformation and divided into the West and the East Church, separated today by the transepts and crossing; only the north transept, known as Collinson's aisle, survives from the twelfth century. The Renaissance-style **West Church**, formerly the nave of St Nicholas, was designed in the mid-eighteenth century by James Gibbs, architect of St Martin in the Fields in London. The **East Church** was rebuilt over the groin-vaulted crypt of the restored fifteenth-century St Mary's Chapel (entered from Correction Wynd), which back in the 1600s was a place to imprison witches: you can still see the iron rings to which they were chained. Take time to explore the large peaceful churchyard, which with its green marble tombs and Baroque monuments seems a million miles from the bustling main street.

The Aberdeen Art Gallery and around

A little further west up Schoolhill, Aberdeen's engrossing **Art Gallery** (Mon–Sat 10am–5pm, Sun 2–5pm; free) was purpose-built in 1884 to a Neoclassical design by Mackenzie. You enter via the airy **Centre Court**, dominated by Barbara Hepworth's central fountain and the thick pillars running down from the upper balcony, each hewn from a different local marble. The walls here highlight the gallery's policy of acquiring contemporary art, with British work to the fore, including one of Francis Bacon's *Pope* paintings – the artist was obsessed with this subject for some thirty years and the series is considered his most important work. From here, the **Side Court** contains selected work by YBAs (Young British Artists) gifted by the Saatchi Collection in 2000, including Jordan Baseman's extraordinary *I Love You Still*, made from tree limbs and human hair. The ground-floor **Applied Art Gallery** includes changing displays of historical and contemporary ceramics, glass, metalwork and jewellery. Beyond this is the **Memorial Court**, a calming, white-walled circular room under a skylit dome that serves as the city's principal war memorial. It also houses the Lord Provost's book of condolence for the 167 people who died in the 1988 Piper Alpha oil rig disaster in the North Sea.

The **upstairs** rooms house the main body of the gallery's painting collection. The permanent collection is occasionally moved around, and some of the rooms are given over to temporary and touring exhibitions: you'll find these advertised downstairs as well as in the local press.

Starting at the top of the staircase, the sheer number of landscapes crowding the walls of **Room One** can be disconcerting at first, but closer inspection reveals a superb collection of Victorian narrative art. Pre-Raphaelite canvases by Rossetti and William Waterhouse are on display beside Queen Victoria's favourite painter, Aberdeen-born John Phillip (1817–67), so heavily influenced by Velázquez and Murillo that he became known as "Spanish Phillip"; look out for his anecdotal scenes of everyday Scottish life such as *The Scotch Fair* (1848) and *Baptism in Scotland* (1850). **Room Two** takes a step back in history, concentrating on eighteenth-century painters such as landscape artist Alexander Nasmyth and Scotland's famous portraitists, Henry Raeburn and Alan Ramsay.

Room Three is predictably popular for its Impressionist collection, including works by Boudin, Courbet, Sisley, Monet, Pissarro and a deliciously bright Renoir, *La Roche Guyon*. A fabulous, sinewy cast of a Rodin male torso is the room's sculptural highlight. The strong connections between the French schools and the development of modernism in Scottish painting saw the emergence of the "Glasgow Boys" in the 1880s (see p.260), exemplified here by John Lavery's *The Tennis Party*. Inheritors of the Glasgow Boys' mantle, the now much in vogue Scottish Colourists, can be found in **Room Four**. Here, Peploe's *Landscape, Cassis* shows off his instinct for colour, with daringly angled foreground tree trunks in rich blue, chocolate and purple shadows. In **Room Six** and on the balcony overlooking the Central Court you'll find some superb works by British Impressionists and Modernists: look out for Stanley Spencer's joyful portrait of the British seaside, *Southwold*, as well as Robert Brough's half-dazed *View of Elgin* and Duncan Grant's haunting *Self-Portrait*. You'll also find a good selection of modern Scottish artists here, including Peter Howson, Alan Davie and Joan Eardley, who captured the landscape around Catterline, a coastal village just to the south of Aberdeen, so memorably.

Immediately opposite the gallery is a designer shopping arcade called **The Academy**, which acts as a gateway to Aberdeen's answer to a Bohemian quarter. Though still a little unsure of itself, the area is developing something of a cultured feel, with cobbled Belmont and Little Belmont streets the home of a number of the city's more interesting bars, shops and restaurants. West of Belmont Street, across the Denburn gorge which is spanned by the Union Bridge and Schoolhill viaduct, the sunken **Union Terrace Gardens**, bordered by the sparkling light-grey granite buildings of Union Terrace, are a welcome relief from the hubbub of heavy traffic on Union Street. In summer, free brass-band concerts and orchestral performances make it a great place to have a picnic. From here there are views across to the three domes of the Central Library, St Mark's Church and His Majesty's Theatre, traditionally referred to as "Education, Salvation and Damnation". Outside the theatre stands a hulking great statue of William "Braveheart" Wallace, erected in 1888.

The West End

Tatty gentility characterizes much of the **West End**, the area around the westernmost part of Union Street, which begins more or less at the great granite columns of the city's **Music Hall**. A block north is **Golden Square** – a misnomer, as the trim houses, pubs and restaurants surrounding the statue of the Duke of Gordon are uniformly grey. The city has invested much in gentrifying the area north of Union Street, resulting in neat cobbles, old-fashioned lamps and mushrooming designer boutiques. Huntly Street, west of Golden Square, heads off towards the curiously thin spire of **St Mary's Catholic Cathedral** (daily 8.30am–5pm; Nov–March closes 4pm), a typical example of Victorian Gothic church architecture.

On the southern side of Union Street, wedged between Bon Accord Street and Bon Accord Terrace, **Bon Accord Square** is a typical, charming Aberdeen square. In the middle, a grassy centre surrounds a huge solid block of granite, commemorating **Alexander Sampson**, architect of much of nineteenth-century Aberdeen. West of Bon Accord Terrace is Justice Mill Lane, a slightly seedy area where a collection of bars and nightclubs see a fair amount of action on Friday and Saturday nights.

The harbour

The old cobbled road of Ship Row winds down from Castlegate at the east end of Union Street to the north side of the **harbour**. Just off this steep road, peering out at the harbour through a striking modern glass facade, is the **Maritime Museum** (Mon–Sat 10am–5pm, Sun noon–3pm; free), which combines a thoroughly modern, airy museum with Aberdeen's oldest-surviving building, **Old Provost Ross's House**, laced with labyrinthine corridors, low doorways and small rooms, one of which houses the tourist office. The marriage has been successful, and the museum is a thoroughly engrossing, imaginatively designed tribute to Aberdeen's maritime traditions.

As you walk in the front entrance, you'll see a series of blackboards, computer readouts and barometers showing everything from the time of high tide to the up-to-the-minute price of a barrel of crude oil. Suspended above the foyer and visible from five different levels is a spectacular 27ft-high model of an oil rig, which, along with terrific views over the bustling harbour, serves as a constant reminder that Aberdeen's maritime links are very much alive today. While large sections of the museum are devoted to telling the story of North Sea oil and gas production, the older industries of herring-fishing, whaling, shipbuilding and lighthouses also have their place, with well-designed displays and audiovisual presentations, many of which draw heavily on personal reminiscences. Passages lead from various levels of the museum into Provost Ross's House, where intricate ship's models and a variety of nautical paintings and drawings are on display.

At the bottom of Ship Row, the cobbles meet Market Street, which runs the length of the **harbour**. Here, brightly painted oil-supply ships, sleek cruise ships and peeling fishing boats jostle for position to an ever-constant clatter and the screech of well-fed seagulls. With high fences, rushing traffic and a series of drab office blocks, it's not the most attractive part of the city, but you'll encounter plenty of life and colour if you follow your nose down the road to the **fish market**, best visited early (7–8am) when the place is in full swing. The current market building dates from 1982, but fish has been traded here for centuries: the earliest record dates back to 1281 when an envoy of Edward I was charged for 1000 barrels of sturgeon and 5000 salt fish.

Back at the north end of Market Street, Trinity Quay runs to the shipbuilding yards and down York Street to the east corner of the harbour. Here you'll come to Aberdeen's **Footdee** or "fitee"(an easy walk or bus #14 from Union Street), a quaint nineteenth-century fishermen's village of higgledy-piggledy cottages which back onto the sea, their windows and doors facing inwards to protect from storms but also, so they say, to prevent the devil from sneaking in the back door. Here, in a great setting beside the lighthouse which marks the channel into the harbour, you'll find the *Silver Darling*, one of the finest seafood restaurants in the Northeast.

From Market Street it's a twenty-minute walk or ten-minute bus ride (#6 from Market Street or #16 or #17 from Union Street) to **Duthie Park** (daily 9.30am–dusk; free), situated on the banks of the Dee at the end of Polmuir Road. The rose garden here, known as Rose Mountain due to its profusion of blooms, can be stunning in summer, but the real treat is the Winter Gardens (daily: May–Sept 9.30am–7.30pm; Oct–March 9.30am–4.30pm; April 9.30am–5.30pm; free), a steamy jungle paradise of enormous cacti, exotic plants and tropical birds, jokingly held to be a favourite haunt with Aberdonians saving on their heating bills. From the northwestern corner of Duthie Park, a great cycle and walkway, the **Old Deeside Railway Line**, heads west out of the city past numerous disused train stations.

Old Aberdeen

An independent burgh until 1891, the tranquil district of **Old Aberdeen**, a twenty-minute ride north of the city centre on bus #20, has always maintained a separate village-like identity. Dominated by King's College and St Machar's Cathedral, its medieval cobbled streets, tiny wynds and little lanes are beautifully preserved.

The southern half of High Street is overlooked by **King's College Chapel** (Mon–Fri 9am–5pm; free), the first and finest of the college buildings, completed in 1495, with a chunky Renaissance spire. Named in honour of James IV, the chapel's west door is flanked by his coat of arms and those of his queen. It stands on the quadrangle, whose gracious buildings retain a medieval plan but were built much later; those immediately north were designed by Mackenzie early last century, with the exception of Cromwell Tower at the northeast corner, which was completed in 1658. The first thing you notice inside the chapel is that, unusually, there is no aisle. The screen, the stalls (each unique) and the ribbed arched wooden ceiling are rare and beautiful examples of medieval Scottish woodcarving. The remains of Bishop Elphinstone's tomb and the carved pulpit from nearby St Machar's are also here. A **visitor centre** (Mon–Sat 10am–5pm, Sun noon–5pm; free) in the main college buildings tells the tempestuous tale of the establishment of the University of Aberdeen, which came about finally in 1860 when Protestant Marischal College and sceptical King's College were merged, well over two hundred years after the first attempt. Rivalry between the two establishments (which led to well-charted brawls in the streets) has always been intense.

From the college, the cobbled High Street leads a short way north to **St Machar's Cathedral** on the leafy Chanonry (daily 9am–5pm, except during services; free), overlooking Seaton Park and the River Don. The site was reputedly founded in 580 by Machar, a follower of Columba, when he was sent by the latter to find a grassy platform near the sea, overlooking a river shaped like the crook on a bishop's crozier. This setting fitted the bill perfectly, and the cathedral, a huge fifteenth-century fortified building, became one of the city's first great granite edifices. Inside, the stained-glass windows are a dazzling blaze of colour, and above the nave the heraldic oak ceiling from 1520 is illustrated with nearly fifty different coats of arms from Europe's royal houses and Scotland's bishops and nobles.

Next door to the cathedral, the **Cruickshank Botanic Gardens** (May–Sept Mon–Fri 9am–4.30pm, Sat & Sun 2–5pm; Oct–April Mon–Fri 9am–4.30pm; free), laid out in 1898, offer lovely glimpses of the cathedral through the trees. In spring and summer it's worth checking out the flowerbeds, but don't bother with the dreary zoological museum.

A wander through Seaton Park will bring you to the thirteenth-century **Brig o'Balgownie**, which gracefully spans the River Don nearly a mile north of the cathedral. Still standing (despite Thomas the Rhymer's prediction that it would fall were it ever to be crossed by an only son riding a mare's only foal), the bridge is best visited at sunset; Byron, who spent much of his childhood in Aberdeen, remembered it as one of his favourite places. Across the bridge, at 79 Balgownie Road, is a small museum (Tues–Sat 10.30am–4.30pm, Sun 1.30–4.30pm; £3) celebrating the life of **Thomas Blake Glover**, the "Scottish Samurai" who introduced railway locomotives to Japan and helped establish the Mitsubishi business empire. It's also claimed that his relationship with a Japanese woman inspired Puccini's opera *Madame Butterfly*. The museum, worth checking out if you know something of Japan, is set in the family house, and examines Glover's life with a collection of artefacts and images.

The beach

Aberdeen can surely claim to have the best **beach** of all Britain's large cities. Less than a mile east of Union Street is a great two-mile sweep of clean sand, broken by groynes and lined all along with an esplanade, where most of the city's population seems to gather on a sunny day. Towards the southern end of the beach is a burgeoning concrete expanse of cinemas and fast-food outlets, a couple of fairly tatty amusement parks and a vast leisure centre. As you head further north, most of the beach's hinterland is devoted to successive golf links. Bus #14 goes along the southern esplanade.

A few hundred yards inland, the city's old tram depot at 179 Constitution Street, just across from the *Patio Hotel*, houses **Satrosphere** (Mon–Sat 10am–5pm, Sun 1.30–5pm; Ⓦwww.satrosphere.net; £5), Aberdeen's thoroughly entertaining hands-on science exhibition.

Eating, drinking and nightlife

Aberdeen is certainly not short of good places to **eat**, though you will find it more pricey than elsewhere in northeast Scotland. Union Street and the surrounding area has a glut of attractive **cafés** and **restaurants**. Like most ports Aberdeen caters for a transient population with a lot of disposable income and a desire to get drunk as quickly as possible. Although you'll find no shortage of loud, flashy **bars** catering to such needs, there are still a number of more traditional old **pubs** which, though usually packed, are well worth a visit.

Cafés and restaurants

Ashvale 46 Great Western Rd. One of Scotland's finest, and biggest, fish-and-chip shops, with seating for 300. Restaurant open daily until 11pm; takeaway until 1am. Inexpensive.

Big Cheese 22 Belmont St. Specialist cheese shop with a mini-café through the back for lunchtime cheese platters.

Howies 50 Chapel St ⓣ01224/639500. Aberdeen outpost of an Edinburgh institution, serving modern Scottish cooking in a very accessible environment. Good price set meal deals and cheap house wine. Moderate.

Inversnecky Beach Esplanade. Still the best of the beach cafés despite the imposing chains which have set up nearby; great for big hangover breakfasts and ice-cream specials. Inexpensive.

Lemon Tree 5 West North St. Easy-going café inside the arts centre; serves good vegetarian and vegan snacks and meals. Inexpensive.

Martha's Vineyard 1 Alford Lane ⓣ01224/213795. Highly regarded West End bistro with an excellent daily-changing menu of European/Scottish cuisine. There's a more formal restaurant, The Courtyard, upstairs. Moderate. Closed all day Sun & Mon evenings.

Nargile Corner of Skene & Summer streets ⓣ01224/636093. Much loved and highly regarded family-run Turkish restaurant. Not to be mistaken for *Nargile Meze Bar*, a new chain restaurant on Rose St. Moderate.

Owlies Unit C, Littlejohn Street ⓣ01224/649267. A long-standing favourite serving French brasserie food upstairs and tapas downstairs. Known for its decent vegetarian selection. Moderate. Closed Sun & Mon.

Poldino's 7 Little Belmont St ⓣ01224/647777. Lively, authentic Italian restaurant in a happening area of the city. Moderate. Closed Sun.

Silver Darling Pocra Quay, North Pier ⓣ01224/576229. Attractively located right at the mouth of the Dee in Footdee, this pricey restaurant serves the best seafood in town. Expensive. Closed Sat lunch & Sun.

Soul & Spice 15–17 Belmont St ⓣ01224/645200. Entertaining and colourful café serving up fantastic African and Caribbean dishes. Moderate. Open evenings only Tues–Fri, all day Sat & Sun.

Wild Boar 19 Belmont St ⓣ01224/625357. Upbeat gallery/coffee shop/brasserie with well-priced vegetarian food, soups, salads and oriental-style noodles, as well as great cake and coffee through the day. Food served until 9pm (Fri & Sat 8pm), after which DJs move in. Moderate.

Yu 347 Union St ⓣ01224/580318. Decent, central Chinese with good fish dishes. Moderate.

Pubs and bars

Archibald Simpson 5 Castle St. A J.D. Wetherspoon chain-pub on the corner of Union Street, named after one of the architects of the

Granite City, in typically ornate style with tiles floors and an extravagant interior.
Café Continental Esplanade. Large designer conservatory with windswept, rain-battered or sun-drenched views; about the best spot for a drink on the seafront.
Carriages In *Brentwood Hotel*, 101 Crown St. Unusually lively hotel cellar bar with the city's largest range of real ales and ciders. Also serves excellent bar food.
Frankenstein Pub 504 Union St. The full horror theme, with monsters and test tubes lining the walls. DJs play at weekends; food served from 9am until closing time.
The Lounge 39 Summer St. Associated with *Howies* restaurant, a stylish café-bar filled with ambient music and cocktail menus.
Ma Cameron's Inn Little Belmont Street. Aberdeen's oldest pub, though only a section remains of the original. Serves food.
Prince of Wales 7 St Nicholas Lane. The quintessenial Aberdeen pub with a long bar and flagstone floor. Serves fine pub grub, is renowned for its real ales and has a Sunday evening folk session; little wonder that it's often crowded.
RSVP Academy Shopping Centre, Schoolhill ⓣ01224/625590. Stylish and busy venue with designer furniture and live jazz on a Sunday afternoon.
St Machar Bar 97 High St, Old Aberdeen. The medieval quarter's only pub, a pokey, old-fashioned bar inevitably full of King's College students.

Nightlife

A number of **nightlife** venues have regular jazz or folk **music sessions**, while the Lemon Tree Arts Centre has as good a selection of touring threatre groups, bands and workshops as anywhere of its size in Scotland. You can buy tickets for events at most of Aberdeen's **theatres** and **concert halls** from the box office beside the Music Hall on Union Street (Mon–Sat 9.30am–6pm; ⓣ01224/641122).

Clubs and live music venues

Amadeus Queen's Links Centre, Beach Esplanade. Huge nightclub – the largest in Scotland – with all the mainstream sounds; the crowd tends to be young and raucous.
The Blue Lamp 121 Gallowgate. A big bar featuring live bands (Fri & Sat) and a folk session (Mon); there's also a much smaller snug for relative peace and quiet.
Franklyn's 44 Justice Mill Lane. Contains three very different rooms: a piano bar; a club bar with live bands (Fri & Sat); and crowd-pleasing chart music pumping out in the main dance area.
The Globe Inn 13–15 North Silver St. Pleasant city-centre inn with jazz and blues on Tues, Fri, Sat & Sun.
Lemon Tree 5 West North St. The fulcrum of the city's arts scene, with a great buzz and regular live music, comedy and folk.
Ministry of Sin 16 Dee St. The hottest dance club for miles; Sunday nights are legendary. Occasionally has big-name guest DJs.
O'Donnaghue's 16 Justice Mill Lane. Aberdeen's most popular Irish bar, with a large venue upstairs hosting touring tribute bands.

Theatres, cinemas and concert halls

Aberdeen Arts Centre 33 King St ⓣ01224/635208. Hosts a variety of theatrical productions alongside a programme of lectures and exhibitions.
Aberdeen Exhibition and Conference Centre Off Ellon Road at Bridge of Don. Huge hall hosting the biggest rock and pop acts.
Belmont Picture House 9 Belmont St ⓣ01224/343536, ⓦwww.picturehouse-cinema.co.uk/ab. Art-house cinema showing the more cultured new releases and a back-list of classic, cult and foreign-language films. There's a decent café inside and some good places nearby for a bite before or after.
Cowdray Hall Schoolhill ⓣ01224/523700. Classical music, often with visiting orchestras.
His Majesty's Rosemount Viaduct ⓣ01224/637788. Aberdeen's main theatre, in a beautifully restored Edwardian building, with a programme that ranges from highbrow drama and opera to pantomime.
Lemon Tree 5 West North St ⓣ01224/642230, ⓦwww.lemontree.org. Avant-garde events with off-the-wall comedians and plays, many coming hotfoot from the Edinburgh festivals.
Music Hall Union Street ⓣ01224/632080. Big-name comedy and music acts.
UGC Beach Esplanade ⓣ0870/155 0502. Huge multiplex cinema in a beach-side development showing all the mainstream releases.

Listings

Airport ⓣ01224/722331.
Banks Bank of Scotland, 201 Union St; Clydesdale Bank, 238 Union St; Royal Bank of Scotland, 12 Golden Sq.
Bike rental Alpine Bikes, 66–70 Holburn St ⓣ01224/211455; Cycling World, 460 George St ⓣ01224/632994.
Bookshops The largest are Waterstone's, 269–271 Union St, and Ottakar's, in Trinity Shopping Centre, Union Bridge. Bon Accord Books, 69–75 Spittal, is the best for secondhand.
Bus information Grampian Transport Busline (ⓣ01224/650065).
Car rental Arnold Clark, Girdleness Rd (ⓣ01224/249159), and at the airport (ⓣ01224/663723); Budget, Wellheads Drive (ⓣ01224/793333), and at the airport (ⓣ01224/771777); National, 46 Summer St and at the airport (both ⓣ0870/400 4502).
Exchange Thomas Cook in the Bon Accord Centre (Mon–Sat 9.30am–5.30pm, Sun noon–5pm; ⓣ01224/807100).
Ferry information P&O Scottish Ferries ⓣ01224/572615, ⓦwww.posf.co.uk.
Genealogical research Aberdeen & North-East Family History Society, 164 King St (ⓣ01224/646323; ⓦwww.anesfhs.org.uk).
Internet There's free access in the Reference section of the main library on Rosemount Viaduct (Mon–Thurs 9am–8pm, Fri & Sat 9am–5pm). Costa Coffee on Loch Street, at the back of the Bon Accord Centre, also offers access.
Left luggage Small 24hr lockers at the train station cost £2.
Lesbian and Gay Switchboard (Wed & Fri 7.30–9.30pm; ⓣ01224/212600; ⓦwww.glgbs.org.uk).
Libraries Main Library, Rosemount Viaduct (ⓣ01224/652500).
Medical facilities The Royal Infirmary, on Foresterhill, northeast of the town centre, has a 24hr casualty department (ⓣ01224/681818). Boots pharmacy is at 161 Union St (Mon–Sat 8am–6pm; ⓣ01224/211592). Late-night pharmacies are listed each day in the *Evening Express*.
Outdoor supplies Tiso, 26 Netherkirkgate, and Marshall's Mountain and Ski Equipment, 186 George St, have all you'll need for hiking and outdoor pursuits, including maps and tips on where to go.
Police Main station is on Queen Street (ⓣ01224/386000).
Post office The central post office is in the St Nicholas Centre, between Union Street and Upperkirkgate (Mon–Sat 9am–5.30pm), with a branch at 489 Union St (Mon–Fri 9am–5.30pm, Sat 9am–12.30pm).
Sports The local football team, Aberdeen, these days struggles to live up its the golden era of the 1980s when then-manager Alex Ferguson brought home league titles and European trophies. Home fixtures take place at Pittodrie Stadium (ⓣ01224/632328), located between King's Road and the beach. There are golf courses dotted all over the northeast; those in Aberdeen include the municipal King's Links (ⓣ01224/641577) skirting the beach, and Murcar Golf Club (ⓣ01224/704354) a testing links course five miles north of Aberdeen at Bridge of Don, which has an attractive nine-hole course, Strabathie, beside it. Bon Accord Baths and Leisure Centre, Justice Mill Lane (ⓣ01224/587920), has a 36-metre swimming pool; Beach Leisure Centre on the Esplanade has a fun pool with flumes and slides.
Taxis Mairs Taxis (ⓣ01224/353535).
Travel agents STA, 30 Upperkirkgate (ⓣ01224/658222); Usit Campus, 110 High St (ⓣ01224/273559).

Stonehaven and the Mearns

South of Aberdeen, the A92 and the main train line follow the coast to **Stonehaven**, a pretty harbour town and base for nearby **Dunnottar Castle**, a stunningly romantic ruin perched on the cliffs. The area to the south and west is known as the **Mearns**, an agricultural district of scattered population and gathering hills famous for its links to Scots author Lewis Grassic Gibbon. On the edge of the hills which rise up into the Angus glens, the village of **Fettercairn** is a focal point for its proximity to **Fasque House**, family home of the former prime minister Gladstone.

Stonehaven is easily reached by **bus** or **train** from Aberdeen or Montrose, although public transport inland into the Mearns is virtually nonexistent.

Stonehaven and around

A busy, pebble-dashed town, **STONEHAVEN** attracts hordes of holiday-makers in the summer due to its sheltered Kincardine coastline, and in mid-July in particular because of its respected **folk festival**. The town itself is split into two parts, the picturesque working harbour area being most likely to detain you. On one side of the harbour, Stonehaven's oldest building, the **Tolbooth** (June–Sept daily except Tues 1.30–4.30pm; free), built as a storehouse during the construction of Dunnottar Castle (see below) is now a museum of local history and fishing. On calm summer evenings, you can also take **boat trips** from the harbour to the RSPB reserve at Fowlsheugh (June & July Tues, Thurs & Fri 6pm & 7.30pm; booking necessary on ⓣ01224/624824).

The old High Street, lined with some fine town houses and civic buildings, connects the harbour and its surrounding old town with the late eighteenth-century planned centre on the other side of the River Carron. On New Year's Eve, High Street is the location for the ancient ceremony of **Fireballs**, when locals parade its length, swinging metal cages full of burning debris around their heads to ward off evil spirits for the year ahead. The **new town** focuses on the market square, overlooked by the dusky-pink granite market hall with its impressive steeple. From here, Evan Street heads inland before swinging right into Arduthie Road, which climbs up to the train station, a good fifteen-minute walk from the centre.

Practicalities

The **tourist office** is at 66 Allardice St, the main street past the square (July & Aug Mon–Sat 10am–7pm, Sun noon–6pm; April–June, Sept & Oct Mon–Sat 10am–5pm; ⓣ01569/762806). For **B&B** accommodation, *Arduthie House* on Ann Street (ⓣ01569/762381, ⓔarduthie@talk21.com; ❸) and the non-smoking *Sirdhana* at 11 Urie Crescent (ⓣ01569/763011; ❷) are both good bets, while, a few miles south of town on the A92, *Dunnottar Mains Farm* (ⓣ01569/762621; ❷) is a decent farmhouse B&B beautifully situated right beside Dunnottar Castle. For **food**, the *Tolbooth Seafood Restaurant* (ⓣ01569/762287; closed Mon), above the museum on the harbour, is the place to go – it's pricey but worth it. Another excellent option, four miles north of town at Netherley, *Lairhillock Inn* (ⓣ01569/730001, ⓦwww.lairhillock.co.uk) serves imaginative, if expensive, modern Scottish food in at atmospheric old coaching inn. For cheaper **pub** food or just a drink, try the entertaining *Marine Hotel* or the attractive *Ship Inn*, both on the harbour. For moving on, **buses** #107 and #117 ply the coast road between Montrose and Aberdeen.

Dunnottar Castle, Kinneff and Arbuthnott

Two miles south of Stonehaven (the tourist office sells a walking guide for the scenic amble), **Dunnottar Castle** (Easter–Oct Mon–Sat 9am–6pm, Sun 2–5pm; rest of year Mon–Fri 9am–4pm; Dec & Jan closes 3pm; £3.50) is one of the finest of Scotland's ruined castles, a huge ninth-century fortress set on a three-sided sheer cliff jutting into the sea – a setting striking enough to be chosen as the backdrop for Zeffirelli's movie version of *Hamlet*. Once the principal fortress of the northeast, the ruins are worth a good root around, and there are any number of dramatic views out to the crashing sea. Siege and blood-stained drama splatter the castle's past: in 1297 William Wallace burnt alive the whole English Plantagenet garrison here, while one of the more gruesome tales from the castle's history tells of the imprisonment and torture of 122 men and 45 women Covenanters in 1685 – an event, as it says on the Covenanters'

Stone in the churchyard, "whose dark shadow is for evermore flung athwart the Castled Rock".

Four miles south of Dunnottar Castle, **CATTERLINE** is a clifftop hamlet typical of those along this stretch of coast – worth a visit for the views and the delicious, well-priced shellfish at the cosy *Creel Inn*, which also offers **B&B** (☎01569/750254; ❸).

Four miles further south, the tiny village of **KINNEFF** lies among fields tumbling down to the sea. Its church, for the most part eighteenth-century, is a successor to the one in which the Scottish crown jewels were hidden as Cromwell marched on Scotland in 1651. Popular tradition has it that the wives of the Dunnottar garrison commander and the Kinneff parish minister hid the crown under an apron and carried the state sceptre, disguised as a distaff, with bundles of flax. The state's most precious assets were successfully hidden here for nine years. Memorials and interpretive boards inside the beautifully light and simple old church tell the story.

Some five miles inland, the straggling village of **ARBUTHNOTT** was the home of prolific local author, **Lewis Grassic Gibbon** (1901–35), whose romanticized realism perfectly encapsulates the spirit of the agricultural Mearns area. His descriptions were often quite awesome: Glasgow, for example, he neatly summed up as "the vomit of a cataleptic commercialism". *Sunset Song*, his most famous work, is an essential read for those travelling in this area (for an extract, see p.813). The community-run **Grassic Gibbon Centre** (April–Oct daily 10am–4.30pm; £2), on the B967 through the village, is a great introduction to this fascinating and self-assured man who died so young. He is buried (under his real name of James Leslie Mitchell) in the corner of the little village graveyard, overlooking the forested banks of the Bervie Water off the main road. The parish church itself, one of the few surviving intact in Scotland that predate the Reformation, is interesting for its Norman arch, unusual fifteenth-century circular bell tower and glorious thirteenth-century chancel.

Fettercairn and Fasque House

Eight miles southeast of Arbuthnott on the tiny B9120 (and served by buses from Montrose), the village of **FETTERCAIRN** is renowned for its handsome arch, which was erected in 1861 after Queen Victoria stayed at the local pub, the *Ramsay Arms* (☎01561/340334; ❸), which is still a good place to stay or to stop for a drink. One mile west, and well signposted, the **Fettercairn distillery** (May–Sept Mon–Sat 10am–4pm; free) is one of Scotland's oldest, with free tours and the customary free taster.

A short drive north on the Edzell–Banchory road, the once-beautiful, but now somewhat neglected **Fasque House** (May–Sept daily 11am–5.30pm; £3.50) is set in grounds filled with deer, pheasants and rabbits. Sometimes a little misleadingly called the home of Victorian prime minister William Ewart Gladstone – it only became the family home when he was a student – Fasque was built between 1789 and 1809 and passed into the Gladstone family in 1829 when Sir John, William's father and a rich grain broker, bought the estate, on which members of the family still live. Sir John added various extensions to the house, developing the gardens and building roads and bridges. Today, in all its intriguing decrepitude, Fasque House offers a great insight into how the affluent Victorian landowner lived. Downstairs, domestic implements litter the place in a refreshingly haphazard manner, while the upstairs appears equally untouched, with a library crammed full of the Gladstones' books, a splendid Victorian bathroom complete with shower, and bedrooms looking much as the nineteenth-century maids would have left them.

Deeside

More commonly known as **Royal Deeside**, the land stretching west from Aberdeen along the River Dee revels in its connections with the Royal Family, who have regularly holidayed here, at **Balmoral**, since Queen Victoria bought the estate. Eighty thousand Scots turned out to welcome her on her first visit in 1848, but some weren't so charmed: one local journalist remarked that the area was about to be "desolated by cockneys and other horrible reptiles". Today, most locals are fiercely protective of the royal connection.

Many of Victoria's guests weren't as enthusiastic about Deeside as she was: Count von Moltke, then aide-de-camp to Prince Frederick William of Prussia, observed, "It is very astonishing that the Royal Power of England should reside amid this lonesome, desolate, cold mountain scenery", while Tsar Nicholas II whined, "The weather is awful, rain and wind every day and on top of it no luck at all – I haven't killed a stag yet." However, Victoria adored the place, and the woods were said to remind Prince Albert of Thuringia, his homeland.

Deeside is undoubtedly handsome in a fierce, craggy, Scottish way, and the royal presence has helped keep a lid on any unattractive mass development. The villages strung along the A93, the main route through the area, are well heeled and the facilities for visitors first-class, with a number of bunkhouses and hostels, some outstanding hotels and plenty of castles and grounds to snoop around. It's also an excellent area for **outdoor activities**, with hiking routes into both the Grampian and Cairngorm mountains, and good mountain biking, horse riding and skiing.

Bluebird **bus** #201 from Aberdeen regularly chugs along the A93, serving most of the towns on the way to Braemar.

West of Aberdeen

West of Aberdeen, you'll pass through low-lying land of mixed farming, forestry and suburbs. Easily reached from the main road are the castles of **Drum** and **Crathes**, both interesting fortified houses with pleasant gardens, while the uneventful town of **Banchory** serves as gateway to the heart of Royal Deeside. Further west, **Glen Tanar** is a great example of the area's attractive blend of forest, river and mountain scenery.

Drum Castle and Crathes Castle

Ten miles west of Aberdeen on the A93, **Drum Castle** (June–Aug daily 11am–5.30pm; April, May & Sept daily 1.30–5.30pm; Oct Sat & Sun 1.30–5.30pm; grounds same days 10am–6pm; NTS; £6, grounds only £1) stands in a clearing in the ancient **woods of Drum**, made up of the splendid pines and oaks that once covered this whole area before the shipbuilding industry precipitated mass forest clearance. The castle itself combines a 1619 Jacobean mansion with Victorian extensions and the original, huge thirteenth-century keep which has recently been restored and reopened. Given by Robert the Bruce to his armour-bearer, William de Irvine, in 1323 for services rendered at Bannockburn, the castle remained in Irvine hands for 24 generations until the NTS stepped in in 1976. To get a sense of the medieval atmosphere of the place, ascend the Turnpike Stair, above the Laigh Hall where a 700-year-old window seat gives views of the ancient forest.

Further along the A93, four miles west of Drum Castle, **Crathes Castle** (daily: April–Sept 10.30am–5.30pm; Oct 10.30am–4.30pm; NTS; £3.50, or £7 including grounds and walled garden) is a splendid sixteenth-century granite tower house adorned with flourishes such as overhanging turrets, gargoyles and conical roofs. Its thick walls, narrow windows and tiny rooms loaded with heavy old furniture make Crathes rather claustrophobic, but it is saved by some wonderfully painted ceilings, either still in their original form or sensitively restored; the earliest dates from 1602. Don't miss the Room of the Nine Nobles, where great heroes of the past, among them Julius Caesar, King David and King Arthur, are skilfully painted on the beams. More intriguing still is the Green Lady's Room, where a mysterious child's skeleton was found beneath the floor and the ghost of a young girl, sometimes carrying a child, is said to have been spotted – most recently in the 1980s. The Muses Room, with portrayals of the nine muses and seven virtues, is also impressive. Beware the "trip stair", originally designed to foil seventeenth-century burglars.

By the entrance to Crathes, a cluster of restored stone cottages houses an interesting **crafts shop**, an **art gallery** and the *Milton* (Ⓣ01330/844566, Ⓦwww.themilton.co.uk; closed Mon), an unexpectedly up-market **restaurant** serving ambitious, expensive meals as well as lighter brunch, lunch and supper menus. Proud of its reputation that is able to draw out discerning diners from Aberdeen, it even boasts a helipad for oil executives unimpressed with oil-rig fare. Booking is advised for evening meals and Sunday lunch times.

Banchory

BANCHORY, meaning "fair hollow", is really just a one-street town, and there's not much to see, though it can be a useful place to stay. The small local **museum** on Bridge Street, behind High Street (May–Sept Mon–Sat 11am–1pm & 2–4.30pm, Sun 2–4.30pm; April & Oct Sat only 11am–1pm & 2–4.30pm; free), may warrant half an hour or so if you're a fan of local boy James Scott Skinner, renowned fiddler and composer of such tunes as *The Bonnie Lass o'Bon Accord*. Alternatively, you can watch salmon leap at the little footbridge where the Dee joins the Feugh River to the south of town.

The **tourist office** in the museum (July Mon–Sat 9.30am–1pm & 2–6pm, Sun 1–6pm; April–June & Aug–Oct Mon–Sat 10am–1pm & 2–5pm; Ⓣ01330/822000), can provide information on walking and fishing in the area. There are several reasonable places **to stay** here and in the surrounding countryside. In town, the *Burnett Arms Hotel*, 25 High St (Ⓣ01330/824944, Ⓔtheburnett@email.msn.com; ❺), a friendly former coaching inn, does Banchory's best pub grub, while *Primrose Hill*, on North Deeside Road on the eastern outskirts of town (Ⓣ01330/823007; ❷), is a decent B&B. Outside Banchory on the Inchmarlo road, the smart *Tor-Na-Collie Hotel* (Ⓣ01330/822242, Ⓔtornacoille@btinternet.com; ❻) was once a retreat for Charlie Chaplin and his family, and serves splendid Scottish salmon, venison and malt whisky in its upscale **restaurant**.

Aboyne and Glen Tanar

Twelve miles west of Banchory on the A93, **ABOYNE** is a typically well-mannered Deeside village at the mouth of **Glen Tanar**, which runs southwest from here for ten miles or so deep into the Grampian hills. The glen, with few steep gradients and some glorious stands of mature Caledonian pine, is ideal for walking, mountain biking or horse riding; the ranger information point two miles into the glen off the B976 has details of suitable routes, while the Glen Tanar Equestrian Centre (Ⓣ013398/86448) offers one- and two-hour horse trails. Aboyne has some handy retreats for **food** after a day's activity: the excellent *Black Faced Sheep* coffee shop just off the main road serves home baking and light lunches, the *Boat Inn* on Charlestown Road right beside the bridge over the Dee does good quality pub grub, and the *White Cottage* restaurant (Ⓣ013398/86265), a couple of miles before Aboyne on the Banchory side, specializes in high-quality Scottish cooking made with fresh local produce. Smart **B&B** is available too, notably at *Lys-na-Greyne House* (Ⓣ013398/87397, Ⓔdwhite7301@aol.com; ❹), on Rhu-na-Haven Road, just to the south of the Dee.

Ballater

Ten miles west of Aboyne is the neat and ordered town of **BALLATER**, attractively hemmed in by the river and fir-covered mountains. The town was dragged from obscurity in the nineteenth century when it was discovered that the local waters were useful in curing scrofula, and these days Ballater spring water is back in fashion and on sale around town.

It was in Ballater that Queen Victoria first arrived in Deeside by train from Aberdeen back in 1848; she wouldn't allow a station to be built any closer to Balmoral, eight miles further west. Although the line has long been closed, the town's rather self-important royalism is much in evidence at the restored **train station** in the centre of town (same hours as the tourist office), where various video presentations and life-sized models relive the comings and goings of generations of royals. The local shops, having provided Balmoral with groceries and household basics, also flaunt their connections, with oversized "By Appointment" crests sported above the doorways of most businesses from the butcher to the newsagent.

If you prefer to discover the fresh air and natural beauty that Victoria came to love so much, Ballater is an excellent base for local **walks and outdoor activities**. There are numerous hikes from Loch Muik (pronounced "mick"), nine miles southwest of town, including the Capel Mounth drovers' route over the mountains to Glen Doll (see p.527), and a well-worn but strenuous all-day trek up and around Lochnagar (3789ft), the mountain much painted and written about by the current Prince of Wales. The starting point for all these walks is the Balmoral Rangers' **visitors' centre**, on the shores of the loch (call Ⓣ013397/55059 for opening hours), which also offers a series of free guided nature walks. Good-quality **bikes** can be rented from Wheels and Reels (Ⓣ013397/55864) at 2 Braemar Rd, just over the railway bridge from Station Square. Other outdoor equipment, as well as local guidebooks, a full range of OS maps and good advice about heading to the local hills, is available at the friendly Lochnagar Leisure outdoor shop on Station Square (daily 9am–5.30pm).

Practicalities

The **tourist office** is in the disused, renovated train station (July & Aug Mon–Sat 9.30am–7pm, Sun 1–7pm; June & Sept Mon–Sat 10am–1pm & 2–6pm, Sun 1–6pm; April, May, Oct & Nov Mon–Sat 10am–1pm & 2–5pm, Sun 1–5pm; Dec–March Sat & Sun 10am–5pm; Ⓣ013397/55306). **Bunkhouse** accommodation is available for groups or backpackers at the *Schoolhouse*, Ferndean, Anderson Road (Ⓣ013397/56333, Ⓔschoolhouseballater@btinternet.com; ❶), while there are plenty of reasonable **B&Bs** in town, including the no-smoking *Inverdeen House*, on Bridge Square (Ⓣ013397/55759, Ⓦwww.inverdeen.com; ❷), which offers a wide choice of breakfasts, most involving local produce and home baking. Other places to try include the welcoming *Deeside Hotel* (Ⓣ013397/55420; ❸), or the small and upmarket *Green Inn Restaurant*, 9 Victoria Rd (Ⓣ013397/55701; ❻), which has three very comfortable rooms at half-board rates. A few miles north of town on the road to Tomintoul (see p.556) is *Gairnshiel Lodge* (☎013397/55582;❶). In a remote but beautiful setting, it's a particularly child-friendly place and a great base for walking or cycling. For **camping**, the *Anderson Road Caravan Park* (☎013397/55727; Easter–Oct) down towards the river, has around sixty tent pitches.

There are numerous **places to eat**, from smart hotel restaurants to bakers and coffee shops: the award-winning *Green Inn* is pricey but excellent quality, while *La Mangiatoia* (☎013397/55999), on Bridge Square opposite the *Monaltrie Hotel*, is a family pizza/pasta place. The *Station Restaurant* (☎013397/55050), next door to the tourist office in the Victorian station, serves home-made bakery, lunches and smarter evening fare. For **drinking** with locals and the opportunity to tuck into some real ales, try the back bar (entrance down Golf Street) of the *Prince of Wales*, which faces the main square.

Balmoral Estate and Crathie Church

Originally a sixteenth-century tower house built for the powerful Gordon family, **Balmoral Castle** (mid-April to July daily 10am–5pm; £4.50) has been a royal residence since 1852, when it was converted to the Scottish Baronial mansion that stands today. The Royal Family traditionally spend their summer holidays here, but despite its fame it can be something of a disappointment even for a dedicated royalist. For the three months when the doors are nudged open, the general riffraff are permitted to view only the ballroom and the grounds; for the rest of the year it is not even visible to the paparazzi who converge en masse when the royals are in residence here in August. With so little of the castle on view, it's worth making the most of the grounds and larger estate by following some of the country walks or joining a two-hour **pony trek** (daily except Thurs 10am & 2pm; call for details ☎013397/42334; £25).

Opposite the castle's gates on the main road, the otherwise dull granite church of **CRATHIE**, built in 1895 with the proceeds of a bazaar held at Balmoral, is the royals' local church. A small **tourist office** operates in the car park by the church on the main road in Crathie (daily: July & Aug 9.30am–6pm; April–June, Sept & Oct 9.30am–5pm; ☎013397/42414).

Braemar

Continuing for another few miles, the road rises to 1100ft above sea level in the upper part of Deeside and the village of **BRAEMAR**, situated where three passes meet and overlooked by an unremarkable **castle** (July & Aug daily 9.30am–5.30pm; Easter–June, Sept & Oct closed Fri; £3). Signs as you enter Braemar boast that it's an "Award-Winning Tourist Village", which just about sums it up, as everything seems either to have been prettified to within an inch of its life, or to have a price tag on it. That said, it's an invigorating, outdoor kind of place, well patronized by committed hikers, but probably best known for its Highland Games, the annual **Braemar Gathering**, on the first Saturday of September (Ⓦwww.braemargathering.org). Games were first held here in the eleventh century, when Malcolm Canmore set contests for the local clans in order to pick the bravest and strongest for his army. Since Queen Victoria's day, successive generations of royals have attended, and the world's most famous Highland Games have become rather an overcrowded, overblown event. You're not guaranteed to get in if you just turn up; the website has details of how to book tickets in advance.

A pleasant diversion from Braemar is to head six miles west to the end of the road and the **Linn of Dee**, where the river plummets savagely through a

Climbing Morrone

Ordnance Survey Landranger map No. 43.
Late August and through autumn is the best time to ascend **Morrone** (allow 4hr for the return trip), when the mountain is plush with extravagant colours. In winter, it can be a spectacular viewpoint but very exposed. Make your way up Chapel Brae at the west end of Braemar, passing a car park and pond, then Mountain Cottage, and swinging left up through fine birch woods (a nature reserve). Keep right of the fences and house. The track bears right (west), and at a fork take the left branch up to the Deeside Field Club view indicator. Skirt the crags above this to the left and the path is obvious thereafter. The summit provides a fantastic sweeping view of the Cairngorms. You can descend by the same route, but an easy continuation is to head down by the Mountain Rescue post's access path, which twists along and then down into Glen Clunie. Turn left along the minor road back to Braemar; the walk finishes by heading through the local golf course.

narrow rock gorge. From here there are countless walks into the surrounding countryside or up into the heart of the Cairngorms (see p.594), including the awesome Lairig Ghru pass which cuts all the way through to Strathspey. There's a very basic SYHA hostel just before the falls at Inverey (book through the Braemar hostel on ⓣ013397/41659, ⓦwww.syha.org.uk; mid-May to early Sept). A postbus runs from Braemar to the Linn of Dee every weekday at 12.30pm.

Practicalities

Braemar's **tourist office** is in the modern building known as the Mews in the middle of the village on Mar Road (July & Aug daily 9am–7pm; June & Sept daily 10am–6pm; rest of year Mon–Sat 10am–1pm & 2–5pm, Sun noon–5pm; ⓣ013397/41600). **Accommodation** is scarce in Braemar in the lead-up to the Games, but at other times there's a wide choice. *Clunie Lodge Guest House*, Clunie Bank Road (ⓣ013397/41330, ⓔclunielodge@msn.com; ❷), on the edge of town, is a good **B&B** with lovely views up Clunie Glen, and there's a large SYHA **hostel** at Corrie Feragie, 21 Glenshee Rd (ⓣ013397/41659, ⓦwww.syha.org.uk; Jan-Oct). The cheery *Rucksacks*, an easy-going bunkhouse well equipped for walkers and backpackers, is just behind the Mews complex (ⓣ013397/41517). The *Invercauld Caravan Club Park* (ⓣ013397/41373), just south of the village off Glenshee Road, has fifteen **camping** pitches.

Standard and fairly pricey hotel **food** is available from the bars of the various large hotels, or for some cheap stodge there's the *Braemar Takeaway* by the river bridge. For a better pub meal head for the *Inver Hotel* (ⓣ013397/42345), six miles east along the A96 towards Balmoral, an old coaching inn which also has rooms (❷). For advice on **outdoor activities**, as well as ski, mountain-bike and climbing equipment rental, head to Braemar Mountain Sports (daily 8.30am–6pm), opposite the *Takeaway*.

The Don Valley and the Lecht

The quiet countryside around the **Don Valley**, once renowned for its illegal whisky distilleries and smugglers, used also to be a prosperous agricultural area. As the region industrialized, however, the population drifted towards Dundee and Aberdeen, and nowadays little remains of the old farming communities except the odd deserted crofter's cottage. From Aberdeen, the River Don winds northwest through **Inverurie**, where it takes a sharp turn west to **Alford**, then continues past ruined castles through the **Upper Don Valley** and the heather moorlands of the eastern Highlands. This remote and undervisited area is positively littered with ruined castles, Pictish sites, stones and hillforts. Excellent free leaflets in the Grampian Archeology series (available from all tourist offices) give full detail, while the well-signposted "Castle Trail" takes in the area's main castles. The Lecht Road, crossing the area of bleak high country known as **The Lecht** from Corgarff to the remote mountain village of **Tomintoul**, passes the Lecht ski centre at 2090ft above sea level, but is frequently impassable in winter due to snow.

Inverurie is served by the regular Aberdeen to Inverness **train** and various **bus** services up the A96. Bluebird buses #215 and #220 link Aberdeen with Alford, but getting as far as Strathdon is much harder, and public transport links with Tomintoul are all but nonexistent.

Inverurie and around

Some seventeen miles northwest of Aberdeen, the prosperous granite farming town of **INVERURIE** makes a convenient base for visiting the numerous relics and castles in the area. The **tourist office** (Mon–Sat 9.30am–6pm; Oct–May closes 5pm; ⓣ01467/625800) shares space with a bookshop at 18 High St, not far from the station, and is a good place to stop before setting off to find the local sites, many of which are tucked away and confusingly signposted. While you're in Inverurie, don't miss the **Thainstone Mart**, just off the A96 south of town, one of Europe's largest and most impressive livestock sales (Mon & Wed–Fri around 10am).

Bennachie and Archaeolink

The granite hill **Bennachie**, five miles west of Inverurie, is possibly the site of Mons Graupius, Scotland's first-ever recorded battle, when the Romans defeated the Picts in 84 AD. At 1733ft, this is one of the most prominent tors in the region, with tremendous views, and makes for a stiff two-hour walk. The best route starts from the **Bennachie Centre** (Tues–Sun: April–Oct 10am–5pm; Nov–March 9.30am–4.30pm), located two miles south of **Chapel of Garioch** (pronounced "geery"). A mile immediately west of Chapel of Garioch is one of the most notable Pictish standing stones in the region, the **Maiden Stone**, a 10ft slab inscribed with marine monsters, an elephant-like beast, and the mirror and comb for which the stone is named.

A further four miles northwest of Chapel of Garioch, the **Archaeolink Prehistory Park**, on the B9002 at Oyne (April–Oct daily 11am–5pm; £4), gives an insight into the area's Pictish heritage. An ambitious modern attraction, it includes a reconstructed Iron Age farm, a hillside archeological site, and an innovative grass-roofed building containing lively audiovisual displays and hands-on exhibits. Although it's a clear attempt to capture the imagination of young people, adults will be just as enthralled, partly because the park is spread across forty acres of hillside, with short walks, impressive views and interesting archeological projects. A coffee shop, play area and various re-enactments and demonstrations of ancient crafts are all part of the experience.

Fyvie Castle

Some thirteen miles north of Inverurie stands the huge, ochre mansion of **Fyvie Castle** (June–Aug daily 11am–5.30pm; Easter–May & Sept daily 1.30–5.30pm; Oct Sat & Sun 1.30–5.30pm; NTS; £6). Scottish Baronial to the hilt, Fyvie's fascinating roofscape sprouts five curious steeples, one for each of the families who lived here from the thirteenth to the twentieth century. Beginning life as a typical courtyard castle, with a protective wall more than 6ft thick, over the ensuing centuries the place met with considerable architectural expansion. The Chancellor of Scotland bought Fyvie in 1596 and was probably responsible for the elaborate south front with its gables and turrets; his grandson sympathized with the Jacobites and, following his exile, the estate was confiscated and handed over to the Gordons. In 1889 the castle was sold to the Forbes-Leiths, a local family who had made a fortune in America and were responsible for the grand Edwardian interior. The exquisite dining room is nowadays rented out for corporate entertaining by oil companies who hobnob among the Flemish tapestries, Delft tiles and the fine collection of paintings that includes feathery Gainsborough portraits and twelve works by Sir Henry Raeburn.

Alford and around

ALFORD (pronounced "af-ford"), 25 miles west of Aberdeen, only exists at all because it was chosen, in 1859, as the terminus for the Great North Scotland Railway. A fairly grey little town now firmly within the Aberdeen commuter belt, it's still well worth making the trip here for the **Grampian Transport Museum** on Main Street (April–Oct daily 10am–5pm; Ⓣ019755/62292, Ⓦwww.gtm.org.uk; £3.80). Here you'll find a large, diverse display of transport through the ages from tramcars to sleek designs which have won endurance events for eco friendly designs. Mixing the bizarre with nostalgic, exhibits include the Craigevar Express, a strange, three-wheeled steam-driven vehicle developed by the local postman for his rounds before petrol-driven transport came in vogue; various generations of cars; and that famous monument to British eccentricity and ingenuity, the Sinclair C5 motorized tricycle. A steam engine runs outside the museum each weekend and there are regular events through the summer (call or check the website for details).

Practically next door is the terminus for the **Alford Valley Railway** (June–Aug daily 1–4.30pm; April, May & Sept Sat & Sun 1–4.30pm; Ⓣ019755/62811), a narrow-gauge train that runs for about a mile from Alford Station through wooded vales to the wide open space of **Murray Park**; the return journey takes an hour. The station is also home to the neat **tourist office** (July & Aug Mon–Sat 10am–5pm, Sun 1–5pm; April–June, Sept & Oct Mon–Sat 10am–5pm, Sun 1–5pm; Ⓣ019755/62052).

Craigievar Castle

Six miles south of Alford on the A980, **Craigievar Castle** (guided tours only: Easter–Sept daily 1.30–5.30pm; Ⓣ013398/83635; NTS; £7) is a fantastic pink confection of turrets, gables, balustrades and cupolas bubbling over from its top three storeys. It was built in 1626 by a Baltic trader known as Willy the Merchant, who evidently allowed his whimsy to run riot. The castle's massive popularity, however – it features on everything from shortbread tins to tea towels all over Scotland – has been its undoing, and the sheer number of visitors has caused interior damage. The NTS is currently limiting the number of visitors by keeping the guided tours small, but in any case the best part of the castle is its external appearance, which you can see from the well-kept **grounds** (all year 9.30am to sunset; £1).

Lumsden and Rhynie

The A944 heads west from Alford, meeting the A97 just south of the tiny village of **LUMSDEN**, an unexpected hot spot of Scottish sculpture. A contemporary **Sculpture Walk** – heralded by a fabulous skeletal black horse at its southern end – runs parallel to the main road, coming out near the premises of the widely respected **Scottish Sculpture Workshop** (Mon–Fri 9am–5pm or by arrangement; ⓣ01464/861372), very much an active workshop rather than a gallery, at the northern end of village. Immediately after the workshop there's a turning to **Lumsden Bothy**, which sells local crafts including scarfs and socks knitted with mohair from the farm's angora goats, and serves tea and home baking.

The village of **RHYNIE**, folded beautifully into the hills three miles further north up the A97, is forever associated with one of the greatest Pictish memorials, the **Rhynie Man**, a remarkable 6ft boulder discovered in 1978, depicting a rare whole figure, clad in a tunic and holding what is thought to be a ceremonial axe. The original can be seen in the foyer of the regional council's headquarters at Woodhill House in Aberdeen, but there's a cast on display at the school in Rhynie, across the road from the church; if you want to see it, contact Bill Inglis on ⓣ01464/861398. A further claim to fame for the village is that the bedrock lying deep beneath it, known as **Rhynie Chert**, contains plant and insect fossils up to 400 million years old, making them some of the earth's oldest fossils. A mile or so from the village, along the A941 to Dufftown, a car park gives access to a path up the looming **Tap O'Noth**, Scotland's second-highest Pictish hillfort (1847ft), where substantial remnants of the wall around the lip of the summit show evidence of vitrification (fierce burning), probably to fuse the rocks together.

Rhynie is a reasonable – if very quiet – place **to stay**. The cheapest and the best choice is the simple *Gordon Arms Hotel*, on Main Street (ⓣ01464/861615; ❶).

The Upper Don Valley

Ten miles west of Alford stand the impressive ruins of the thirteenth-century **Kildrummy Castle** (April–Sept daily 9.30am–6.30pm; HS; £2), site of some particularly hideous moments of conflict. During the Wars of Independence, Robert the Bruce sent his wife and children here for their own protection, but the castle blacksmith, bribed with as much gold as he could carry, set fire to the place and it fell into English hands. Bruce's immediate family survived, but his brother was executed and the entire garrison hung, drawn and quartered. Meanwhile, the duplicitous blacksmith was rewarded for his help by having molten gold poured down his throat. Other sieges took place during the subsequent centuries: Balliol's forces attacked in 1335, Cromwell took over in 1654 and the sixth Earl of Mar used the castle as the headquarters of the ill-fated Jacobite risings in 1715. Following John Erskine's withdrawal, Kildrummy became redundant and it was abandoned as a fortress and residence and fell into ruin. Beside the ruins is a Scottish Baronial-style castle built in 1901, now the grand *Kildrummy Castle Hotel* (ⓣ019755/71288, ⓦwww.kildrummycastlehotel.co.uk; ❼), superbly endowed with wood-panelled rooms, Victorian furniture and a raised terrace on which you can enjoy afternoon tea overlooking the castle.

Ten miles further west, the A944 sweeps round into the parish of **STRATHDON**, little more than a succession of occasional buildings by the roadside. However, four miles north of here, up a rough track leading into Glen Nochty, lies the unexpected **Lost Gallery** (daily except Tues 11am–5pm; ⓣ019756/51287, ⓦwww.lostgallery.co.uk), which shows work by some of Scotland's leading modern artists in a wonderfully remote and tranquil setting. Heading west again on the A944, past the much-photographed signs to the village of Lost, you'll come to **Candacraig Gardens** (May–Sept daily

10am–5pm; free), the walled grounds of Candacraig House, Highland retreat of comedian Billy Connolly, who starred alongside Dame Judi Dench in the 1990s film *Mrs Brown*, set at nearby Balmoral Castle (see p.551). The house is private, but the gardens, an exuberant display of colour and energy, are open to the public, as is an art gallery housed in the Gothic summerhouse built into the garden wall. In the old laundry on the other side of the main house, *No. 3 Candacraig Square* (Ⓣ019756/51472, Ⓦwww.candacraig.com; ❸) is a stylish **B&B** with wooden floors, piles of books and a promise of fresh fish for breakfast.

A further eight miles west, just beyond the junction of the Ballater road, lies **Corgarff Castle** (April–Sept daily 9.30am–6.30pm; Oct–March Sat 9.30am–4.30pm, Sun 2–4.30pm; HS; £2.80), an austere tower house with an unusual star-shaped curtain wall and an eventful history. Built in 1537 – the wall was added in 1748 – it was first attacked in 1571, during a religious feud between the Forbes, family of the laird of the castle, and the Gordons, who torched the place, killing the laird's wife, family and servants. In 1748, in the aftermath of Culloden, the Hanoverian government turned Corgarff into a barracks in order to track down local Jacobite rebels, and finally, in the mid-nineteenth century, the English Redcoats were stationed here with the unpopular task of trying to control whisky smuggling. Today there's little to see inside, but the place has been restored to resemble its days as a barracks, with stark rooms and rows of hard, uncomfortable beds – authentic touches which extend to graffiti on the walls and peat smoke permeating the building from a fire on the upper floor. One unexpected bonus here if you're from far-flung parts is the chance to hear the history of the castle in one of the nineteen languages the keeper has recorded it in over the years, ranging from Thai to Icelandic.

Leading to the castle from the south is the old military road, which, unusually, hasn't been covered over by the present road and is fairly clear for about three miles. A mile or so along this from the castle, approached from the main road by the track beside Rowan Tree Cottage, is *Jenny's Bothy* at Dellachuper (Ⓣ019756/51449), a beautifully remote and simple **bunkhouse**, surrounded by empty scenery and wild animals. You'll have to bring your own supplies if you're coming here, but it's a great base for hiking, cycling or skiing, or just detaching yourself from the madding crowd for a day or two. Another bunkhouse, along with standard **B&B** accommodation can be found at the *Allargue Arms Hotel* (Ⓣ019756/51410, Ⓦwww.allargue.demon.co.uk; ❶), an old wayside inn overlooking Corgarff Castle and a cosy base for skiing, fishing or hiking trips.

Tomintoul

Just past Corgarff, at Cock Bridge, the road leaps up towards the ski slopes of the Lecht (see box) and, four miles further on, **TOMINTOUL** (pronounced "*tom*-in-towel"), at 1150ft the highest village in the Scottish Highlands. Tomintoul owes its existence to the post-1745 landowners' panic when, as in other parts of the north, isolated inhabitants were forcibly moved to new, planted villages, where a firm eye could be kept on everybody. Its long, thin layout is reminiscent of a Wild West frontier town; Queen Victoria, passing through, wrote that it was "the most tumble-down, poor looking place I ever saw". That said, it makes a good base for **skiing** the Lecht area in winter, and there's some terrific **walking** hereabouts, including a spur of the long-distance Speyside Way (see p.558).

In the central square, the **tourist office** (July & Aug Mon–Sat 9.30am–6pm, Sun 1–6pm; April–June, Sept & Oct Mon–Sat 10am–1pm & 2–5pm; Ⓣ01807/580285) also acts as the local **museum** (same times; free), with

Skiing the Lecht

The Lecht is the most remote of Scotland's ski areas, but it works hard to make itself appealing with a range of winter and summer activities. While its twenty runs include some gentle beginners' slopes there's little really challenging for experienced skiers other than a Snowboard Fun Park, with specially built jumps and ramps. Snow-making equipment helps extend the snow season beyond January and February, while there are also various summer activities, including a dry ski-slope and "Devalkarts", go-karts with balloon tyres imported from the Alps which you can use to speed down the slopes from the top of the chairlift. Day passes (summer and winter) start at around £12; ski and boot rental costs £12.50 a day from the ski school at the base station, which also provides tuition for £6 an hour.

For **information** on skiing and road conditions here, call the base station on ⓣ01975/651440 or check ⓦwww.lecht.co.uk or ⓦwww.ski-scotland.net.

mock-ups of an old farm kitchen and a smithie. Information about the extensive Glenlivet Crown Estate, its wildlife (including reindeer) and numerous paths and bike trails is available from the **ranger's office** at the far end of the long main street (call ⓣ01807/580283 for opening hours). It is possible to **camp** here, though there are no facilities.

For **accommodation**, the *Tomintoul Bunkhouse*, immediately beside the tourist office, is plain but friendly; contact the neighbouring *Gordon Hotel* (ⓣ01807/580206) to make bookings or call in at the hotel reception. There's also a basic SYHA **hostel** on Main Street (ⓣ01807/580282, ⓦwww.syha.org.uk; mid-May to Sept). Of the **B&Bs**, try *Bracam House*, 32 Main St (ⓣ01807/580278; ❶), or *Findron Farm*, half a mile south of town on the Braemar road (ⓣ01807/580382; ❶). Of the **hotels** gathered around the main square, the *Glenavon* (ⓣ01807/580218; ❶) is the most convivial for a drink, and serves ale made in the nearby Aviemore Brewery, while the best bet for something to **eat** is a pub meal here or at the *Gordon Hotel*.

Speyside

Strictly speaking, **Speyside** is the region surrounding the Spey River, but to most people the name is synonymous with the **whisky triangle**, stretching from just north of Craigellachie down towards Tomintoul in the south, and west to Huntly. Indeed, there are more whisky distilleries and famous brands concentrated in this small area (including Glenfiddich and Glenlivet) than in any other part of the country. Running through the heart of the region is the River Spey, whose clean clear waters play such a vital part in the whisky industry and are home to thousands of salmon. At the centre of Speyside is the quiet market town of **Dufftown**, which along with nearby **Craigellachie** makes the best base for a tour of the distilleries. The only other settlement of note is **Huntly**, well served by road (A96) and rail links with Aberdeen and Elgin.

Dufftown and Craigellachie

The cheery community of **DUFFTOWN**, founded in 1817 by James Duff, the fourth Earl of Fife, proudly proclaims itself "Malt Whisky Capital of the World", and indeed it exports more of the stuff than anywhere else in Britain. There isn't a great deal to do in the town, but it's a useful starting point for

The Speyside Way

The **Speyside Way**, with its beguiling mix of mountain, river, wildlife and whisky, is fast establishing itself as an appealing alternative to the popular West Highland and Southern Upland long distance footpaths. Starting at **Buckie** on the Moray Firth coast, it follows the fast-flowing River Spey from its mouth at Spey Bay south to **Aviemore** (see p.595), with branches linking it to **Dufftown**, Scotland's malt whisky capital, and **Tomintoul** on the remote edge of the Cairngorm mountains. Some 65 miles long without taking on the branch routes, the whole thing is a five- to seven-day expedition, but its proximity to main roads and small villages means that it is excellent for shorter walks or even bicycle trips, especially in the heart of **distillery** country between Craigellachie and Glenlivet: Glenfiddich, Glenlivet, Macallan and Cardhu distilleries, as well as the Speyside Cooperage, lie directly on or a short distance off the route. Other highlights include the chance to encounter an array of **wildlife**, from dolphins at Spey Bey to ospreys at Loch Garten, as well as the restored **railway** trips on offer at Dufftown and Aviemore. The path uses disused railway lines for much of its length, and there are simple campsites and good B&Bs at strategic points along the route. For more details contact the Speyside Way Visitor Centre at Craigellachie (Ⓣ01340/881266, Ⓦwww.moray.org/area/speyway/webpages/index.htm).

orienting yourself towards the whisky trail, and if you're keen to immerse yourself in some of the local history and lore relating to the precious liquid, the small **museum** at 24 Fife St (Mon–Fri 2–7pm, Sat & Sun 10am–5pm) has a collection of illicit distilling equipment, books and old photographs.

On the edge of town along the A941 is the town's largest working distillery, **Glenfiddich** (see opposite), as well as the old Dufftown train station, which has been restored by enthusiasts in recent years and is now the departure point for the **Keith & Dufftown Railway** (April–Oct Sat & Sun; call Ⓣ01340/821181 for journey times), which chugs for 45 minutes through whisky country to Keith, home of the Strathisla distillery (see opposite). Behind Glenfiddich distillery, the ruin of the thirteenth-century **Balvenie Castle** (April–Sept daily 9.30am–6.30pm; HS; £1.50) sits on a mound overlooking vast piles of whisky barrels. The castle was a Stewart stronghold, which was abandoned after the 1745 uprising, when it was last used as a government garrison. There are more atmospheric remains to be seen if you're approaching Dufftown from the south along the A941; look out for the gaunt hilltop ruins of **Auchindoun Castle** about three miles before you reach town. Although you can't go inside, it's enjoyable to wander along the track from the main road to this three-storey keep encircled by Pictish earthworks.

Four miles north of Dufftown, the small settlement of **CRAIGELLACHIE** sits above the confluence of the sparkling waters of the Fiddich and the Spey. From the village, you can look down on a beautiful iron bridge over the Spey built by Thomas Telford in 1815. By the River Fiddich on the A95 Huntly road, there's a **visitor centre** for the Speyside Way (Easter–Oct generally daily 9am–5pm; Ⓣ01340/881266), which sells maps of the route and gives advice on what to look for along the way.

Practicalities

Dufftown's four main streets converge on Main Square. The official **tourist office** is located inside the handsome clocktower at the centre of the square (July & Aug Mon–Sat 10am–6pm, Sun 1–6pm; April–June, Sept & Oct Mon–Sat 10am–1pm & 2–5pm; Ⓣ01340/820501), though an informal information and accommodation booking service has developed at *The Whisky Shop*

The Malt Whisky Trail

Speyside's **Malt Whisky Trail** is a clearly signposted seventy-mile meander around the region via eight distilleries. Unless you're seriously interested in whisky, it's best to just pick out a couple that appeal, perhaps choosing one because you know the whisky and another for its setting. All the distilleries offer a guided **tour** (some are free, others charge but then give you a voucher which is redeemable against a bottle of whisky from the distillery shop) with a tasting to round it off; if you're driving you'll be offered a miniature to take away with you. Most people travel the route by car, though you could cycle parts of it, or even walk using the Speyside Way (see box opposite). The following are selected highlights.

- **Cardhu**, on the B9102 at Knockando (July–Sept Mon–Fri 10am–6pm, Sat 10am–4.30pm & Sun 11am–4pm; March–June & Oct Mon–Fri 10am–4.30pm; Nov–Feb Mon–Fri 11am–3pm; £3 including voucher). This distillery was established over a century ago when the founder's wife was nice enough to raise a red flag to warn local crofters if the authorities were on the lookout for their illegal stills. Sells rich, full-bodied whisky which has distinctive peaty flavours and comes in an attractive bulbous bottle.
- **Glen Grant**, Rothes (April–Oct Mon–Sat 10am–4pm, Sun 12.30–4pm; £3). A well-known, floral whisky which you can sample in a heather-thatched tasting pavilion. It's well worth taking time to wander through the attractive Victorian gardens.
- **Glenfiddich**, on the A941 just north of Dufftown (April to mid-Oct Mon–Sat 9.30am–4.30pm, Sun noon–4.30pm; rest of year Mon–Fri 9.30am–4.30pm; free). Probably the best known of the malt whiskies, and the biggest and slickest of all the distilleries. It's a light, sweet whisky which comes in triangular-shaped bottles. Uniquely, the whisky is bottled on the premises – an interesting process to watch. The tours are informative, though the place is thronged with tourists.
- **Glenlivet**, on the B9008, ten miles north of Tomintoul (April–Oct Mon–Sat 10am–4pm, Sun 12.30–4pm; £3 including voucher). A famous name in a lonely hillside setting. This was the first licensed distillery in the Highlands, following the 1823 Act of Parliament which aimed to reduce illicit distilling and smuggling. The Glenlivet twelve-year-old malt is a floral, fragrant medium-bodied whisky.
- **Speyside Cooperage**, Craigellachie (Mon–Fri 9.30am–4.30pm; £2.95). Not a distillery, but a fascinating adjunct to the industry. After a short exhibition explaining the ancient and skilled art of cooperage, you're shown onto a balcony overlooking the large workshop where the oak casks for whisky are made and repaired by fast-working, highly skilled coopers.
- **Strathisla**, Keith (April–Oct Mon–Sat 10am–4pm, Sun 12.30–4pm; £4, including a voucher worth £2). A small old-fashioned distillery claiming to be Scotland's oldest (1786); it's certainly one of the most attractive, situated in a highly evocative highland location on the strath of the Isla River. The malt itself has a rich almost fruity taste and is pretty rare, but is used as the heart of the better-known Chivas Regal blend.

There are also **other distilleries** not on the official trail that you can visit: the **Macallan** distillery near Craigellachie (Mon–Sat 10am–3.30pm; booking advised ⓣ01340/871471; free) has in-depth tours limited to a maximum of ten people, and **Cragganmore** at Ballindalloch (tours June–Sept Mon–Fri 10am, 1pm & 3pm; booking essential ⓣ01479/874700; £5) also offers a personalized, exclusive tour.

(ⓣ01340/821097) across the road. You'll certainly need to look no further than this for a vast array of whiskies produced not just on Speyside but all over Scotland; nosings and other special events are organised regularly here, most notably the twice-yearly **Spirit of Speyside Whisky Festival** (Ⓦwww.spiritofspeyside.com), which draws whisky experts and enthusiasts to the area in early May and late September.

There's a good range of places **to stay** in Dufftown itself, as well as in the surrounding countryside. In town, *Morven*, on Main Square (Ⓣ01340/820507; ❶), offers good, cheap B&B, and although the only hostel accommodation is the small self-catering *Swan Bunkhouse* (Ⓣ01542/810334) located at Drummuir, three miles northeast of Dufftown, it's a pleasant spot and the owners will arrange pick-ups from Dufftown or Keith. In Craigellachie there's the extremely welcoming and tasteful B&B attached to the *Green Hall Gallery* on Victoria Street (Ⓣ01340/871010, Ⓦwww.greenhall-gallery.co.uk; ❷). For unquestionable style and luxury, head to *Minmore House* (Ⓣ01807/590378, Ⓔminmorehouse@ukonline.co.uk; limited opening Nov–March; ❺), the former home of Glenlivet owner George Smith, which sits right beside the Glenlivet distillery on a quiet hillside above the Livet Water. In Archiestown, a few miles west of Craigellachie, the pleasant *Archiestown Hotel* (Ⓣ01340/810218; ❺) caters for fishermen and outdoor types; it's filled with an eclectic collection of odd artefacts and serves impressive meals in a flagstone-floored dining room.

The smartest of Dufftown's **restaurants** are the expensive *La Faisanderie*, on the corner of the square and Balvenie Street (Ⓣ01340/821273), which serves local produce such as trout and game in a French style and puts on a special whisky-tasting dinner on Fridays; and *Taste of Speyside*, 10 Balverie St (Ⓣ01340/820860), just off the square, which is moderately priced and manages to be even more Scottish in its presentation. For more down-to-earth pub grub you're better off heading to the busy *Highlander Inn* (Ⓣ01340/881446; ❷) on Victoria Street in Craigellachie, which serves decent meals, has frequent folk **music sessions** in its bar, and five guest rooms. There are one or two unique **drinking** spots in the area, including the *Grouse Inn* at Cabrach, tucked away among the hills ten miles out along the A941 to Rhynie, which boasts the largest collection of whiskies for miles. The tiny *Fiddichside Inn*, on the A95 just outside Craigellachie, is a wonderfully original and convivial pub with a garden by the river; quite unfazed by the demands of fashion, it has been in the hands of just two landladies (mother and daughter) for the last seventy years or so.

You can rent **bikes** from Clarke's Cycle Hire (Ⓣ01340/881525), beside the *Fiddichside Inn* at Craigellachie.

Huntly and around

A small town set in attractive rolling farmland, the ancient burgh of **HUNTLY**, ten miles east of Dufftown and on the main train route from Aberdeen to Inverness, has little to offer other than its proximity to the Whisky Trail. It does boast, however, one of the smallest and prettiest castles in the area (albeit rather skeletal). **Huntly Castle**, power centre of the Gordon family (April–Sept daily 9.30am–6.30pm; Oct–March Mon–Sat 9.30am–4.30pm, Thurs closes noon, Sun 2–4.30pm; HS; £2.80), sits in a peaceful clearing on the banks of the Deveron River, a ten-minute walk from the town centre down Castle Street and through an elegant arch. Built over a period of five centuries, it has sheltered the likes of Robert the Bruce and James IV (who attended a wedding here), and in 1562 became the headquarters of the Counter-Reformation in Scotland. After the Battle of Corrichie, brought about by the wish of the fourth earl's third son to marry Mary, Queen of Scots, and which effectively ended the Gordons' 250-year rule, the castle was pillaged and its treasures sent to St Machar's Cathedral in Aberdeen. During the Civil War the Earl of Huntly, who had supported Charles

I and declared, "you can take my head off my shoulders, but not my heart from my sovereign", was shot against his castle's walls with his escort, after which the place was left to fall into ruin.

Today you can still make out the twelfth-century **motte**, a grassy mound on the west side of the complex, while the main castle ruin, with its splendid **doorway** fronted by an elaborate coat of arms, dates from the mid-fifteenth century. In the basement, a narrow passage leads to the **prisons**, where medieval graffiti of tents, animals and people adorn the walls.

Huntly was also the birthplace of the much-loved children's author George MacDonald, whose writing influenced Lewis Carroll, J.R.R. Tolkien and C.S. Lewis, among others. A plaque commemorates his birthplace on Duke Street, and you can get more information from a pamphlet available at the tourist office.

Seven miles south of Huntly and served by the occasional bus, the modest chateau-style **Leith Hall** (Easter weekend & May–Sept daily 1.30–5.30pm; Oct Sat & Sun 1.30–5.30pm; NTS; £6) is worth visiting, even when closed, for a wander around its 113-acre grounds (daily 9.30am to dusk; £2). Home to the Leith and Leith-Hay family since 1650, the vast estate of varied farm and woodlands includes ponds, eighteenth-century stables, a bird-observation hide and signposted countryside walks. Inside, you can see personal memorabilia of the successive Leith lairds, a number of whom were in the armed services overseas.

Huntly is on the fringe of whisky country, and at **Glendronach Distillery**, eight miles northeast of Huntly (tours Mon–Fri 10am & 2pm; free), many of the traditional methods such as malting and heating the stills by coal fires are still used. Meanwhile, three miles northwest of Huntly, between the A920 to Dufftown and the A96 to Keith (signposted from both), the **North East Falconry Centre** (March–Oct daily 10.30am–5.30pm; £3.75) is home to about fifty fabulous falcons, owls and eagles, with flying demonstrations four times a day.

Practicalities

Huntly's **tourist office**, 9a The Square (July & Aug Mon–Sat 9.30am–6pm, Sun 10am–3pm; April–June, Sept & Oct Mon–Sat 10am–5pm; ⓣ01466/792255), will book accommodation for a ten percent deposit, redeemable on the first night's stay. For luxurious **accommodation**, head for the former home of the Duke of Gordon, the *Castle Hotel* (ⓣ01466/792696, ⓔcastlehot@enterprise.net; ➎), which stands at the end of a long driveway behind the castle ruins. At the other end of the scale, there's a simple bunkhouse (➊) attached to the *Gordon Arms Hotel* (ⓣ01466/792288; ➋) in the main square, while you'll find decent, inexpensive B&B at *Kirklea*, 10 Church St (ⓣ01466/792324, ⓦwww.kirklea-huntly.co.uk; ➊). The *Auld Pit* on Duke Street is a decent **pub** with regular folk music, and serves pub meals, as does the *Gordon Arms*. **Bikes** can be rented from Changing Gear (ⓣ01466/793508), or from the Nordic Ski Centre near the castle (ⓣ01466/794428), where you can also brush up your cross-country skiing skills on all-weather tracks if there's no snow.

The coast

The **coast** of northeast Scotland from Aberdeen to Inverness is a rugged, often bleak, landscape. Still, if the weather is good, it's well worth spending a couple of days meandering through the various little fishing villages and along the miles of deserted, unspoilt beaches. Keen walkers have the best run of the area: some of the cliffs are so steep that you have to hike considerable distances to get the best views of the coast.

The largest towns along the coast are **Peterhead** and **Fraserburgh**, both dominated by sizeable fishing fleets and, while neither has much to offer, the latter's Museum of Scottish Lighthouses is one of the most attractive small museums in Scotland. More appealing to most visitors are the quieter spots along the Moray coast, including the idyllic villages of **Pennan**, **Portsoy** and nearby **Cullen**. The other main attractions are **Duff House**, a branch of the National Gallery of Scotland, in Banff; the working abbey at **Pluscarden** by Elgin; and the **Findhorn Foundation**, near Forres.

The main towns and larger villages are fairly well served by **buses**, while **trains** from Aberdeen and Inverness stop at Elgin, Forres and Nairn. Even so, it's preferable to have your own transport for reaching some of the far-flung places.

Pitmedden and around

Fourteen miles north of Aberdeen, on the outskirts of Pitmedden village, **Pitmedden Gardens** (May–Sept daily 10am–5.30pm; NTS; £5) are the creation of Alexander Seton – formerly Lord Pitmedden, before James VII removed his title as punishment for opposing his Catholicism. Seton spent his enforced retirement on perfecting an elaborate garden project he had begun in 1675, and today the utterly ordered gardens have been restored to their seventeenth-century pattern, with neat box hedges, pavilions, fountains and sundials. In the lower garden (best viewed from the terrace), the layout of three of the flowerbeds mimics those of Holyrood Abbey in Edinburgh, while the fourth flowerbed – with its crest and a weather vane, surmounted by soldiers – are tributes to Seton's father who died fighting against the Covenanters in Aberdeen. Admission to the gardens also takes in the **Museum of Farming Life**, where you'll see old tools and a chilly, dark bothy that was once home to the workers of the 100-acre Pitmedden estate.

Set amidst rolling green hills, the atmospheric pink granite ruins of **Tolquhon Castle** (pronounced "tal-worn"; April–Sept daily 9.30am–6.30pm; Oct–March Sat 9.30am–4.30pm, Sun 2–4.30pm; HS; £2), are tucked away off a sideroad a mile or so northwest of Pitmedden. Of the medieval remains, the gatehouse facade is the most impressive, with its handsome arched portal protected by drum towers and enriched with all manner of sculpted figures and coats of arms. You can still make out what each room was used for: the kitchen has two huge ovens gouged out of the wall, and one of the bedrooms has its own dungeon with an ominous trapdoor – at any one time there could have been eight or nine prisoners below.

Four miles north of Pitmedden, the huge Palladian mansion of **Haddo House** (Easter weekend & May–Sept daily 1.30–5.30pm; call ⓣ01651/851440 for winter opening times; NTS; £6), completed to a design by William Adam in 1735, is set in 177 acres of woodland, lakes and ponds. Since 1731 Haddo has been the seat of the Gordons and several earls and marquesses of Aberdeen; the gardens, now home to otters, red squirrels, pheasants and deer, were created from a wasteland by the fourth earl in the early years of the nineteenth century. The house is now renowned for staging local music, drama and arts; check with the Haddo Arts Trust (ⓣ01651/851770) for details of forthcoming productions.

Forvie Nature Reserve and around

Fifteen miles north of Aberdeen, a sideroad (signposted to Collieston) leads off the A92 past **Forvie National Nature Reserve**. This area incorporates the Sands of Forvie, one of Britain's largest and least disturbed dune systems, and boasts a rich array of birdlife. There's a small but informative **visitors' centre** (April–Sept daily 9am–5pm; call for winter hours; ⓣ01358/751330) from which a network of trails winds along the coast and through the dunes, with one leading to a fifteenth-century village, buried by the shifting sands. Local legend has it that the village suffered its fate after three local sisters were cast adrift in a boat to deny them their rightful inheritance. They cursed the village – and shortly thereafter, a nine-day storm buried it.

COLLIESTON itself is a pleasant hamlet with a harbour but little else; for somewhere to eat or stay it's worth making for **NEWBURGH**, a rather unattractive satellite town of Aberdeen. Here you'll find the comfy *Udny Arms Hotel* on Main Street (ⓣ01358/789444, ⓦwww.udny.co.uk; ❺) which has a superb **restaurant** overlooking the mouth of the Ythan River, a very popular spot with Aberdonians at the weekends.

Cruden Bay

Pleasant sandy beaches can also be found eight miles north of Forvie at **CRUDEN BAY**, from where a pleasant fifteen-minute walk leads to the huge pink-granite ruin of **Slains Castle**. The ruin itself is not especially interesting – it was over-modernized in the nineteenth century – though its stark clifftop beauty is striking and it claims notoriety as the place which inspired Bram Stoker to write *Dracula*. Stoker used to holiday here and another of his stories, *Mystery of the Sea*, is directly related to a local ghost story. The castle is surprisingly badly signposted: from the car park on the left at the end of Cruden Bay's Main Street, head for the sea, then along the cliffs.

A precarious three-mile walk north from Slains Castle along the cliffs brings you to the **Bullers of Buchan**, a splendid 245ft-deep sea chasm, where the ocean gushes in through a natural archway eroded by the sea. This is some of the finest cliff scenery in the country and attracts a huge number of (smelly) nesting seabirds. An alternative access point is the signposted car park just off the A975, from where a short footpath leads past some old cottages to the very edge of the chasm.

Peterhead and around

PETERHEAD, the easternmost mainland town in Scotland, stands in sharp contrast to the picturesque fishing villages on this stretch of coast. As notable for its high-security prison and ugly power station as its busy harbour, it's an unashamedly functional place. Although in recent years the oil industry has created a surge in wealth and population, Peterhead's *raison d'être* is **fishing**, and it was for many years the busiest white-fish port in Europe. The boom is now over and Peterhead has felt the consequences of the overfishing of the North Sea. Although the town itself is unappealing, it's a friendly spot and the locals are quick to point out its benefits.

The oldest building in town is the 400-year-old **Ugie Salmon Fish House** on Golf Road at the mouth of the River Ugie, at the north end of town (Mon–Fri 9am–5pm, Sat 9am–noon; free), where you can watch the traditional methods of oak-smoking salmon and trout in Scotland's oldest smokehouse; the finished product is for sale at reasonable prices. One of the town's newest buildings houses the **Peterhead Maritime Heritage Museum** (April–Oct daily 10.30am–5pm; call ⓣ01779/473000 for winter opening; £2.60), on the beach just off the main road. It's an airy, pleasant place with a café, and the helpful staff are happy to help with tourist **information**. The museum tells the story of the town's fishing industry from the old herring fleet to the modern day, with a live relay of the harbourmaster's radio channel. Listen out too for the recordings of old fishermen and women, who still speak the distinctive Doric dialect.

Peterhead has no official tourist office, but you should be able to find somewhere **to stay**; the spick, span and welcoming *Invernettie Guest House* on South Road (Ⓣ01779/473530, Ⓦwww.btinternet.com/~invernettie; ❷) is very good value, while the *Carrick Guest House* (Ⓣ01779/470610, Ⓔcarrickhouse@ukonline.co.uk; ❸) is situated in the faded but interesting old town. For **food**, the *Dolphin* serves good fish and chips from right next to the fish market in the harbour area, while the *Copper Kettle* on Union St has a tasty lunch-time menu.

Aden Country Park

Nine miles west of Peterhead is the 230-acre **Aden Country Park** (daily 7am to dusk; free), just beyond the town of Mintlaw. In addition to woodlands, a lake and a huge variety of wildlife, the park is home to the atmospheric and well-conceived **Aberdeenshire Farming Museum** (May–Sept daily 11am–4.30pm; April daily noon–4.30pm; Oct Sat & Sun noon–4.30pm; free), the highlight of which is a unique semicircular farmstead built early in the nineteenth century.

Fraserburgh and the north coast

Ten miles or so north of Aden Park, **FRASERBURGH** is a large and fairly severe-looking town in the same vein as Peterhead, although its economy still relies on fishing alone. At the northern tip of the town, an eighteenth-century lighthouse protrudes from the top of sixteenth-century **Fraserburgh Castle**, where the highest wind speeds on mainland Britain were recorded in 1989 (they reached 140mph). The lighthouse was one of the first to be built in Scotland and is now part of the excellent **Museum of Scottish Lighthouses** (April–Oct Mon–Sat 10am–6pm, Sun noon–6pm; Nov–March closes 4pm; £3.50), where you can see a collection of huge lenses and prisms gathered from decommissioned lighthouses, and a display on various members of the famous "Lighthouse" Stevenson family, who designed many of them (including the father and grandfather of author Robert Louis Stevenson). Highlight of the museum is the tour of Kinnaird Head light itself, preserved as it was when the last keeper left in 1991, with its century-old equipment still in perfect working order.

Next door, and also well worth a visit, is the recently opened **Fraserburgh Heritage Centre** (April–Oct Mon–Sat 11am–5pm, Sun 1–5pm; call Ⓣ01346/512888 for winter opening; £2.50), a wide-ranging exhibition on the history of the town with small boats, audiovisual presentations, and details of some experiments in wireless communication performed by Marconi in Fraserburgh in 1904.

Fraserbugh's **tourist office**, in Saltoun Square (July & Aug Mon–Sat 10am–1pm & 2–6pm, Sun 1–6pm; April–June, Sept & Oct Mon–Sat 10am–1pm & 2–5pm; Ⓣ01346/518315), gives out information about the surrounding area, while *Jim's Plaice* opposite does decent fish and chips. The friendly *Vine Coffee Shop*, on Cross St, serves great sandwiches, soup and cakes.

West of Fraserburgh

The coast road between Fraserburgh and Pennan, twelve miles west, is particularly attractive: it's lined with pretty churches and cottages, while countless paths lead off it to ruined castles, clifftop walks and lonely beaches. **PENNAN** itself, a tiny fishing hamlet, lies just off the road, down a steep and hazardous hill. Consisting of little more than a single row of whitewashed stone cottages tucked between a cliff and the sea, the village leapt into the limelight when the British movie *Local Hero* was filmed here in 1982. You can stay at one of the identifiable landmarks from the film, the *Pennan Inn* (Ⓣ01346/561201; ❷), a convivial, lively spot with an excellent seafood **restaurant** and a cosy bar, whose customers spill out onto the sea wall on summer evenings. The tiny village of **CROVIE** (pronounced "crivie"), whose residents frequently have their doorsteps washed by the sea, is just as appealing. Tucked against the steep cliffs, it's so narrow that its residents have to park at one end of the village and continue to their houses on foot. **GARDENSTOWN**, another village of the same style on the other side of Troup Head from Pennan, is a little larger and slightly down-at-heel, but has a nice beach.

Macduff and Banff

Heading west along the coast from Pennan brings you, after ten miles, to **MACDUFF**, a famous spa town during the nineteenth century and now with a thriving and pleasant harbour. The superb **Macduff Marine Aquarium**, 11 High Shore (daily 10am–5pm; Ⓦwww.marine-aquarium.com; £3.90), is an intriguing display of local aquatic life with its huge centrepiece aquarium tank open to the air.

Macduff and its neighbour **BANFF** are separated by little more than the beautiful seven-arch bridge over the River Deveron. Banff's **tourist office** (July & Aug Mon–Sat 10am–1pm & 2–6pm, Sun 1–6pm; April–June & Sept Mon–Sat closes 5pm; Ⓣ01261/812419) is housed in the old gatehouse of Duff House in St Mary Square. Here, for a £1 deposit, you can collect a thoroughly enjoyable **Walkman tour** of the town, which introduces both the grand Georgian upper town and, down by the harbour, the older, scruffier Scotstown.

A mile southwest of Banff along the A97, the intriguing **Colleonard Sculpture Park** (visits by arrangement only; Ⓣ01261/818284) is the world's only garden of archetypal abstractionism. Sculptor Frank Bruce began his outdoor collection here in 1965; a man of immense talent, he carves figures and scenes of vitality and intensity from tree trunks, which he then places around the wonderfully peaceful site.

Duff House

Banff's undoubted highlight is the extravagant **Duff House** (generally April–Oct daily 11am–5pm, Nov–March Thurs–Sun 11am–4pm, though hours can be irregular; call Ⓣ01261/818181 to check; HS; £4). Built to William Adam's design in 1730, this elegant four-floor Georgian Baroque house was originally intended for one of the northeast's richest men, William Braco, who became Earl of Fife in 1759. It was clearly built to impress, and could have been even more splendid had Adam been allowed to build curving colonnades either side; Braco's refusal to pay for carved Corinthian columns to be shipped in from Queensferry caused such bitter argument that the laird never actually came to live here and even went so far as to pull down his coach curtains whenever he passed by.

The house has been painstakingly restored and reopened as an outpost of the **National Gallery of Scotland**'s extensive collection, although the emphasis is to display period artwork rather than any broader selection of the Gallery's paintings. The downstairs rooms set the tone, principally the Rococo vestibule and the **dining room**, hung with ponderous eighteenth-century portraits, among which Allan Ramsay's *Elizabeth, Mrs Daniel Cunyngham* leaps out for its delightfully cool composition. To the left is the **Private Drawing Room**, containing a bust of William Adam and the sweeping canvases of Welsh landscapist Richard Wilson (1714–82). On the other side of the ground floor, Countess Agnes' Boudoir, formerly Lord Macduff's dressing room, contains a riotous gilded Rococo mirror and El Greco's heartfelt *St Jerome in Penitence*, which dominates a wall of mainly religious art.

Ascending the **Great Staircase**, all eyes are drawn to the enormous copy of Raphael's *Transfiguration* by Inverness's Grigor Urquhart (1797–1846). Most of the accompanying portraits are also Scottish. Upstairs, the **North Drawing Room** contains the only piece of furniture original to the house, a 1760s mirror, but more obvious is the bewilderingly bold gold and cherry-red ceiling, a not entirely successful Victorian pastiche of Adam's style. In the **Great Drawing Room**, William's son Robert Adam's symmetrical classicism meets French opulence head on, and somehow it works. The best example of this is the 1764 furniture suite of two gilded sofas and two chairs originally designed by the younger Adam and built by Chippendale, combining the Classical reference of lion's-paw feet and the Rococo influence of florid gold shells. Two chairs from the same collection recently sold at auction for £1.7 million – twice the amount previously paid for a piece of Chippendale furniture. Beyond the house there are extensive grounds with some pleasant parkland walks, notably along the River Deveron to a local beauty spot, the **Bridge of Alvah**, a couple of miles south.

Practicalities

There are numerous **B&B**s nearby. The *Orchard* (Ⓣ01261/812146, Ⓦwww.strathdee.com/orchard.html; ❸) is superbly set in the grounds of Duff House, on the edge of woodland, while the *St Helens Guest House* (Ⓣ01261/818241, Ⓦwww.sthelensbanff.demon.co.uk; ❷) on Bellevue Rd in Banff is a good option, as is Mrs Grieg's in the heart of Macduff at 11 Gellymill St (Ⓣ01261/833314; ❶). **Camping** is best to the west of Banff near the beach at the windy *Banff Links Caravan Park* (Ⓣ01261/812228; April–Oct). Various pubs serve **food and drink**: the *Aul' Fife*, 12 Low St in Banff, just along from the tourist office, serves reasonable pub grub, and the *Highland Haven* overlooking the water in Macduff, although busy with coach parties, does good value meals. More upmarket is the French restaurant in the *County Hotel* in Banff (Ⓣ01261/815353), while in Whitehills, an unremarkable town just to the west, *Fagin's* (Wed–Sat evenings & Sun lunch; Ⓣ01261/861321) serves good seafood that belies the restaurant's plain outward appearance.

Cullen and around

Twelve miles west of Banff is **CULLEN**, served by bus from Aberdeen. The town, strikingly situated beneath a superb series of arched rail viaducts, is made up of two sections: Seatown, by the harbour, and the new town on the hillside. There's a lovely stretch of sheltered sand by Seatown, where the colourful houses – confusingly numbered according to the order in which they were built – huddle end-on to the sea. Cullen's attractive old **kirk**, dating from the 1300s, lies a twenty-minute stroll south of the centre.

The town's independent and enthusiastic **tourist office** (June–Aug daily 11am–5pm) is on the main square of the new town, and while the hotels are found in the new town, the most appealing **B&Bs** are down in Seatown; no. 53 is friendly and comfortable (Ⓣ01542/840819; ❶). The local delicacy, Cullen skink – a soup made from cream, potato and smoked haddock – is best at the friendly *Three Kings* **pub** on North Castle Street, though most of the smarter hotels around town also serve it, including the grand *Seafield Hotel* (Ⓣ01542/840791, Ⓦwww.theseafieldhotel.com; ❹), a seventeenth-century coaching inn which also produces expensive but delicious meals.

Six miles east is the quiet village of **PORTSOY**, renowned for its green marble once shipped to Versailles, and its annual traditional boat festival in early July. The *Shore Inn* by its atmospheric old stone harbour is a top spot for a beer or a meal on a sunny day.

Buckie and around

West of Cullen, the dull fishing and service town of **BUCKIE** is home to the **Buckie Drifter** heritage museum (April–Oct Mon–Sat 10am–5pm, Sun noon–5pm; £2.75), a hands-on exhibition telling the history of the area's fishing industry. It's well geared to families, though inevitably given the dominance of fishing a century and more ago, it's only one of half-a-dozen maritime heritage museums found up and down this coast.

Buckie also marks the terminus of the **Speyside Way** long distance footpath (see p.558). This follows the coast west for five miles to to windy **Spey Bay**, also reached by a small coastal road from Buckie, at the mouth of the river of the same name. It's a remote spot bounded by sea and river and sky; interpretation is offered by a small **wildlife centre** (daily July & Aug 10.30am–7pm; April–June, Sept & Oct closes 5.30pm; Ⓦwww.mfwc.co.uk; £1.50), whose main mission is research of the Moray Firth dolphin population (for more on which, see p.589). It houses an exhibition and a busy tearoom. Look out too for the **ice house** at Tugnet, a partially subterranean, thick-walled house with a turf roof used by fishermen in the days before electric refrigeration to store their ice and catches.

Five miles south along the Speyside Way, and also on the main A96 road between Buckie and Elgin, the small village of **FOCHABERS** is dominated by **Baxters Highland Village** (daily 9am–6pm; Oct–March closes 5pm; free), an over-the-top mock village celebrating the company Baxters of Speyside, an old-fashioned culinary institution most famous (in Scotland at least) for its tinned soups and beetroot pickle. The friendly family-grocer image has been exploited to the full, and you'll find the series of shops and restaurants in the village brimming with slick marketing and crowded with adoring coach parties.

Elgin and around

The lively market town of **ELGIN**, just inland about fifteen miles west of Cullen, grew up in the thirteenth century around the River Lossie. It's an appealing place, still largely sticking to its medieval street plan, with a busy main street opening out onto an old cobbled marketplace and a tangle of wynds and pends.

On North College Street, just round the corner from the tourist office and clearly signposted, is the lovely ruin of **Elgin Cathedral** (April–Sept daily 9.30am–6.30pm; Oct–March Mon–Sat 9.30am–4.30pm, Thurs closes noon, Sun 2–4.30pm; HS; £2.80, joint ticket with Spynie Palace £3.30). Once considered Scotland's most beautiful cathedral, rivalling St Andrews in importance, today it is little more than a shell, though it does retain its original facade. Founded in 1224, the three-towered building was extensively rebuilt after a fire in 1270, and stood as the region's highest religious house until 1390 when the inimical Wolf of Badenoch (Alexander Stewart, Earl of Buchan and illegitimate son of Robert II) burned the place down, along with the rest of the town, in retaliation for having been excommunicated by the Bishop of Moray when he left his wife. The cathedral suffered further during the post-Reformation, when all its valuables were stripped and the building was reduced to common quarry for the locals. Unusual features include the Pictish cross slab in the middle of the ruins and the cracked gravestones with their *memento mori* of skulls and crossbones.

At the very top of High Street is one of Britain's oldest museums, the **Elgin Museum** (April–Oct Mon–Fri 10am–5pm, Sat 11am–4pm, Sun 2–5pm; £2), housed in this building since 1843. Along with the usual local exhibits, there's a weird anthropological collection including reptilian skulls, a shrunken head from Ecuador and a grinning mummy from Peru. In addition, you can see an excellent collection of fossils and well-explained Pictish relics.

Practicalities

Elgin is well served by public transport, with the Aberdeen–Inverness train stopping here several times a day. The **bus station** is on Alexandra Road (ⓣ01343/544222), a block from St Giles Church, while the **train station** is slightly less convenient, on the south side of town on Station Road (turn right out of the station, left at the island and up Moss Street to reach the centre).

The **tourist office**, 17 High St (July & Aug Mon–Sat 10am–6pm, Sun 11am–6pm; April–June & Sept Mon–Sat 10am–5pm, Sun 11am–3pm; Oct–March Mon–Sat 10am–4pm; ⓣ01343/542666), will book **accommodation**. Central *Belleville B&B*, 14 South College St (ⓣ01343/541515, ⓔbelleville@talk21.com; ❶) is good value; *Lodge*, 20 Duff Ave (ⓣ01343/549981, ⓔmarilynspence5@hotmail.com; ❷), is a good-quality B&B in a house built for a former tea-plantation owner; while the castle-like *Mansion House Hotel*, The Haugh (ⓣ01343/548811, ⓦwww.mhelgin.co.uk; ❼), is one of the most exclusive in the region, and overlooks the river. Five miles east of town in Urquhart, *The Old Church of Urquhart* (ⓣ01343/843063; ❷) is an unusual and comfortable B&B in a striking converted church on Meft Road.

For **food**, the *Abbey Court* restaurant (ⓣ01343/552849) on Greyfriars St offers good food at low prices, while the *Emperor* (ⓣ01343/551133), next to the Elgin Museum on North College St, serves commendable Thai and Chinese dishes. Otherwise there's *Littlejohn's Brasserie*, 193 High St, a Tex-Mex and Cajun chain restaurant, or the *Ashvale* on Moss Street for fish and chips. The best **pubs** include *Thunderton House* on Thunderton Place, off High Street, which incorporates the seventeenth-century Great Lodge of Scottish kings, and *High Spirits*, in an old church on Moss Street. For great **picnic** foods, head to the old-fashioned high-street store Gordon & McPhail, 58–60 South St, an Aladdin's cave of aromas, colours and delicacies, which sells one of the widest range of malt whiskies in the world.

Pluscarden Abbey

Set in attractive countryside in a verdant valley seven miles southwest of Elgin, **Pluscarden Abbey** (daily 4.30am–8.45pm; ⓦwww.geocities.com/athens/thebes/2553; free), looms impressively large in a peaceful clearing off an unmarked road. One of only two abbeys in Scotland with a permanent community of monks, it was founded in 1230 for a French order and, in 1390, became another of the properties burnt by the Wolf of Badenoch (see above); recovering from this, it became a priory of the Benedictine Abbey of Dunfermline in 1454 and continued as such until monastic life was suppressed in Scotland in 1560. The abbey's revival began in 1897 when the Catholic antiquarian, John, third Marquis of Bute, started to repair the building. In 1948 his son donated it to a small group of Benedictine monks from Gloucester, who established the present community. They are an active bunch, running stained-glass workshops, making honey and even recording Gregorian chants on CDs, all of which is detailed on their website. The abbey itself is airy and tranquil, with the monks' singing often eerily floating through from the connecting chapel. It is possible to **stay** here on retreat for a few days; see the website for details.

Lossiemouth, Spynie Palace and Duffus

Elgin's nearest seaside town, **LOSSIEMOUTH**, five miles north across the flat land of the Laich of Moray, is generally known as Lossie, a cheery golf-oriented resort blessed with two lovely sandy beaches. The glorious duney spit of the East Beach is reached over a footbridge across the River Lossie from the town park. In the easternmost part of the older harbour's grid of stone streets, Pitgaveny Street has the tiny **Fisheries Museum** (May–Sept Mon–Sat 10.30am–5pm; £1), which includes some interesting scale models of fishing boats and a re-creation of the study of local-lad-made-good James Ramsay Macdonald (1866–1937), Britain's first Labour prime minister. The town's only blight is the is frequent sky-tearing noise of military aircraft from the nearby RAF base.

Lossiemouth's development as a port came when the nearby waterways of **SPYNIE**, three miles inland, silted up and became useless to the traders of Elgin. Little remains of the settlement, although the hulking shape of **Spynie Palace** (April–Sept daily 9.30am–6.30pm; Oct–March Sat 9.30am-4.30pm, Sun 2–4pm; HS; £2, joint ticket with Elgin Cathedral £3.30) indicates its former significance. Until 1224, Holy Trinity Church, which was part of the palace, was the cathedral of the Bishopric of Moray before the honour passed to Elgin. Although there's no evidence of the church today, the palace remained an integral part of the local ecclesiastical setup, primarily as the bishop's residence, right through until that office was abolished in the Scottish Church in 1689. The enormous rectangular David's Tower – visible for miles around – is the largest tower house in Scotland, and the views from the top over the Spynie Canal, the much-diminished sea loch, and the Moray Firth, are stunning. Under the tower is a beautiful fourteenth-century beehive-roofed storage cellar. Next door, a slightly later cellar contains the wide-mouthed gun holes installed by Bishop Patrick Hepburn (1538–73), who, as a Catholic, survived the Reformation at Spynie for a full thirteen years.

Straight roads and water ditches crisscross the flat land west of Spynie. Past the sinister shapes of the planes and hangars of RAF Lossiemouth is the spread-eagled settlement of **DUFFUS**, five miles west of Lossie. Old Duffus is no more than a farm or two and a motte and bailey **castle** (free access), part of which leans at a rakish angle. New Duffus, two miles northwest, is best known as the gateway to **Gordonstoun School**, the spartan (but hugely expensive) public school favoured by royalty, although Prince Charles reportedly despised its fresh-air-and-cold-showers puritanism. A quarter of a mile down the lane to Gordonstoun lie the remains of the **Duffus old kirk**, dating from at least 1226. A fine fourteenth-century parish cross, some beautifully inscribed graves and an 1830 watch house against grave-diggers are the highlights. Judging by the number of discarded cigarette packets, you're also likely to see a few Gordonstoun pupils at leisure.

Burghead

Windswept **BURGHEAD** (served by bus #331 from Elgin) was, before the imposition of the town in 1805–09 – a tightly packed grid of streets on the natural promontory – the site of an important Iron Age fort and the ancient Pictish capital of Moray. The **Burghead Bulls** were crafted here, a series of at least 25 unique Pictish stone carvings, all but six of which were destroyed when the town was built. One of these is on display in the window of the library on the main Grant Street; others can be seen in Elgin Museum, the National Museum in Edinburgh and the British Museum in London. A **well**, tucked away down King Street (key and interpretative boards are in the porch at 69 King St), is the most remarkable surviving feature. Under a barrel roof, an impressive underground chamber fed by springs is believed to have been the water supply for the Iron Age and Pictish strongholds. The headland tip of the town is still pocked with the scant remains of early defences, including two earth ramparts just off Bath Street, upon which an eerie burnt-out pillar sits. This is where the **Clavie** – a burning tar barrel still carried around the town on January 11, to mark the old calendar's new year – ends its annual journey. From the harbour, a wide sweep of sandy beach stretches five miles around Burghead Bay to Findhorn.

The *Red Craig* **hotel**, on the B9040 above the headland on the east side of town (Ⓣ01343/835663, Ⓦwww.redcraig-hotel.co.uk; ❶), has B&B and camping, serves **food and drink**, and hosts occasional live music and dances.

Findhorn

A mile beyond the controversial **Findhorn Foundation** (see box) is the tidy village of **FINDHORN**, which has a magnificent beach, a delightful harbour, a small **Heritage Centre** (June–Aug daily except Tues 2–5pm; May & Sept Sat & Sun 2–5pm; free) and a couple of good pubs: on a sunny day, a pint on the terrace at the *Kimberbey Inn* is hard to beat.

Forres

FORRES, one of Scotland's oldest agricultural towns, is of little note except for its pretty flower-filled parks, and the 20ft **Sueno's Stone**, on the eastern outskirts of town, one of the most remarkable Pictish stones in Scotland. Now housed in what looks like a huge glass telephone box as protection against further erosion, the stone was found buried in 1726 and mistakenly named after Swein Forkbeard, King of Denmark, though it more probably commemorates a battle between the people of Moray and the Norse settlers in Orkney. Carvings on the east face can be read as one of the earliest examples of war reportage, with the story told from the arrival of the leader at the top to the decapitated corpses of the vanquished at the bottom.

Forres is on the main Inverness–Aberdeen **train** line; the train station is half a mile west of the tourist office near the north end of Market Street. **Bus** #10 between Elgin and Inverness stops outside St Leonard's Church on High Street, a little way along from Forres' friendly **tourist office** at no. 116 (April–Oct Mon–Sat 10am–1pm & 2–5pm; Ⓣ01309/672938). The Bluebird bus company also runs other local services (call Ⓣ01343/544222 for details). **Accommodation** includes the *Tormhor* B&B, 11 High St (Ⓣ01309/673837; ❶), which has large, comfortable rooms in a Victorian house overlooking some colourful gardens.

A mile of so south of Forres on the A940, the **Dallas Dhu Historic Distillery** (April–Sept daily 9.30am–6.30pm; Oct–March Mon–Wed & Sat 9.30am–4.30pm, Thurs 9.30am–12.30pm, Sun 2–4.30pm; HS; £3) is an outpost

The Findhorn Foundation

In 1962, with little money and no employment, Eileen and Peter Caddy, their three children and friend Dorothy Maclean, settled on a caravan site at **Findhorn**. Dorothy believed she had a special relationship with what she called the "devas... the archetypal formative forces of light or energy that underlie all forms in nature – plants, trees, rivers", and from the uncompromising sandy soil they built a remarkable garden filled with plants and vegetables, far larger than had ever been seen in the area.

Today, the **Findhorn Foundation** (Mon–Sat 9am–noon & 2–5pm, Sun 2–5pm; free) has blossomed from its early core of three adults and three children into a full-blown community of a couple of hundred people, with classes and facilities for around eight thousand visitors a year. The Original Caravan – as it is marked on the site's map – still stands, surrounded by a whole host of newer timber buildings and other caravans employing solar power, earth roofs and other green initiatives, such as an ecological sewage treatment centre. **Guided tours** (Mon, Wed & Fri–Sun 2pm; £1) allow visitors a more informed look at the different activities of the foundation, as well as some of the site's more interesting buildings, while residential workshops and short-term stays are also available.

As can be expected, the foundation is not without controversy: one community leader declared that "behind the benign and apparently religious front lies a hard core of New Agers experimenting with hallucinatory techniques marketed as spirituality". Findhorn, now a public company, is also accused of being overly well heeled: a glance into the shop or a tally of the large cars parked outside the houses does give some substance to such ideas. However, most people here, although honest about the downsides of community living, are extremely positive about its benefits. The reputation of the place is such that it attracts visitors both sympathetic and cynical – and both find something to feed their impressions.

Bizarrely enough, despite its enormous growth, the foundation is still situated on Findhorn's caravan and **camping park** (☎01309/690203; April–Oct), located on the B9011 about ten miles west of Elgin and served by bus #310 from Forres – which creates an intriguing combination of people onsite. For details of all activities contact the **visitor centre** (Mon–Fri 9am–5pm, Sat & Sun 2–5pm; ☎01309/690311, ®www.findhorn.org), which is clearly signposted from the entrance. There's a smart **café** and richly stocked **delicatessen** and general **shop** on site.

of the Malt Whisky trail. Unlike most distilleries, this one isn't in production and there aren't guided tours: you're free to wander through the buildings at your own pace, making use of a free personal audioguide if you choose. Further south, the River Findhorn winds through an area of great natural beauty with a couple of appealing picnic spots. Five miles or so south along the A940, a short walk from the car park leads to **Sluie Gorge**, while a couple of miles further, off the B9007 (take the Carrbridge road) is **Randolph's Leap**, a beautiful riverside glade in beech forests. It's not marked, but there is a small parking area – the path to the river is opposite. Between the two, at **Logie Steading**, there's a small craft community with a good secondhand bookshop.

Brodie Castle

Four miles west of Forres and eight miles east of Nairn (see p.592), just off the A96, is **Brodie Castle** (April–Sept Mon–Sat 11am–5.30pm, Sun 1–5.30pm; Oct Sat 11am–5.30pm, Sun 1–5.30pm; NTS; £5). Dating from 1567, this is a classic Z-shaped Scottish tower house set in lovely grounds (open all year; free) with drifts of daffodils in spring. Although it's now the property of the NTS, the 25th Earl of Brodie still lives here, and his presence very much contributes to the country-house atmosphere. Inside, there are all the rooms you'd expect: a panelled dining room with fabulous plasterwork, several bedrooms complete with four-posters, and a massive Victorian kitchen and servants' quarters, all linked by winding passages. The collections of furniture, porcelain and especially paintings are outstanding, with works by Jacob Cuyp and Edwin Landseer, among others. To end your trip there's a **tearoom**, where the staff dish out splendid home-baked cakes.

Travel details

Trains

Aberdeen to: Arbroath (every 30min; 1hr); Dundee (every 30min; 1hr 15min); Edinburgh (1–2 hourly; 2hr 35min); Elgin (hourly; 1hr 30min); Forres (hourly; 1hr 45min); Glasgow (1–2 hourly; 2hr 35min); Huntly (hourly; 50min); Insch (hourly; 35min); Inverurie (hourly; 20min); Keith (hourly; 1hr 5min); Montrose (every 30min; 45min); Nairn (hourly; 2hr); Stonehaven (every 30min; 15min).
Dundee to: Aberdeen (every 30min; 1hr 15min); Arbroath (hourly; 20min); Montrose (hourly; 15min).
Elgin to: Forres (hourly; 15min); Nairn (hourly; 25min).

Buses

Aberdeen to: Arbroath (hourly; 1hr 20min); Ballater (hourly; 1hr 45min); Banchory (hourly; 55min); Banff (hourly; 1hr 55min); Braemar (4–6 daily; 2hr 10min); Crathie (for Balmoral) (4–6 daily; 1hr 55min); Cruden Bay (hourly; 50min); Cullen (hourly; 1hr 50min–2hr 30min); Dufftown (2 weekly; 2hr 10min); Dundee (hourly; 2hr); Elgin (hourly; 2hr 35min–3hr 40min); Forfar (2 daily; 1hr 20min); Forres (hourly; 2hr 35min); Fraserburgh (hourly; 1hr 20min); Fyvie (hourly; 1hr); Huntly (hourly; 1hr 35min); Inverurie (hourly; 45min); Macduff (hourly; 1hr 50min); Mintlaw (for Aden Park) (hourly; 50min); Montrose (hourly; 1hr); Nairn (hourly; 2hr 50min); Peterhead (every 30min; 1hr 15min); Pitmedden (hourly; 50min); Stonehaven (every 30min; 25–45min).
Ballater to: Crathie (June–Sept 1 daily; 15min).
Banchory to: Ballater (June–Sept 1 daily; 45min); Braemar (June–Sept 1 daily; 1hr 20min); Crathie (June–Sept 1 daily; 1hr); Spittal of Glenshee (June–Sept 1 daily; 2hr).
Dufftown to: Elgin (hourly; 1hr).
Dundee to: Aberdeen (hourly; 2hr); Arbroath (every 15min; 40min–1hr); Blairgowrie (every 30min; 50min–1hr); Forfar (every 30min; 30min); Glamis (2 daily; 40min); Kirriemuir (hourly; 1hr 10min); Meigle (hourly; 40min); Montrose (hourly; 1hr 15min).
Elgin to: Aberdeen (hourly; 2hr 35min–3hr 40min); Burghead (Mon–Sat hourly; 30min); Duffus (Mon–Sat hourly; 15min); Forres (hourly; 25min); Huntly (3 daily; 50min); Inverurie (3 daily; 1hr 45min); Lossiemouth (every 30min; 20min); Nairn (hourly; 40min); Pluscarden (1 daily; 20min).
Forres to: Elgin (hourly; 25min); Findhorn (Mon–Sat 8 daily; 20min).
Fraserburgh to: Banff (2 daily; 55min); Macduff (2 daily; 45min).
Montrose to: Brechin (hourly; 20min).
Peterhead to: Cruden Bay (every 30min; 20min).

Ferries

Aberdeen to: Lerwick, Shetland (summer only: 4–5 weekly; 14hr); Stromness, Orkney (summer only: 2 weekly; 8–10hr).

Flights

Aberdeen to: Belfast (Mon–Fri 1 daily; 2hr 45min); Birmingham (Mon–Fri 3 daily; 1hr 30min); Glasgow (1 daily; 45min); London Gatwick (5 daily; 1hr 30min); London Heathrow (7 daily; 1hr 30min); London Luton (2 daily; 1hr 30min); London Stansted (4 daily; 1hr 30min); Manchester (Mon–Fri 9 daily, Sat 3 daily, Sun 4 daily; 1hr 20min); Newcastle (Mon–Fri 5 daily; Sat & Sun 2 daily; 1hr); Sumburgh, Shetland (Mon–Fri 4 daily, Sat & Sun 2 daily; 1hr).
Dundee to: London City (Mon–Fri 2 daily; 1hr 15min).

8

The Highland region

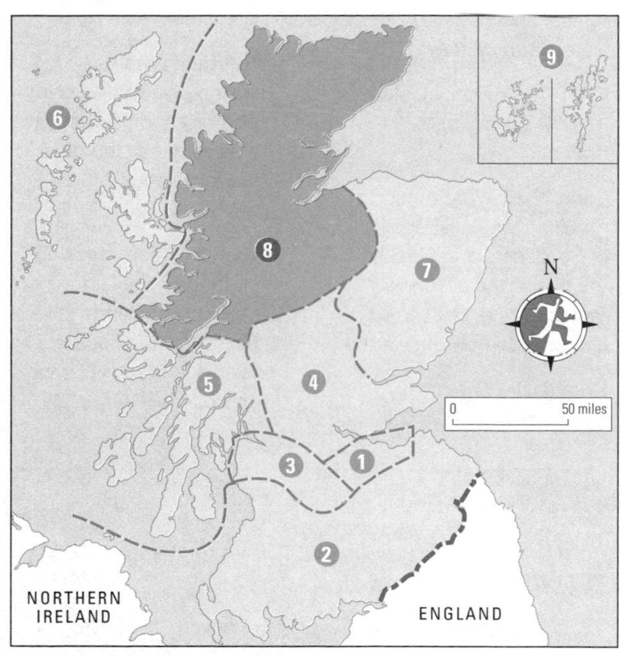

CHAPTER 8 Highlights

* **West Highland Railway** – From Glasgow to Mallaig via Fort William; the further north it travels, the more spectacular it gets. See p.578

* **The Cairngorms** – Scotland's unique mountain massif, a place of wild animals, ancient forests and inspiring vistas. See p.594

* **Glen Coe** – Spectacular, moody, poignant, dramatic. See p.612

* **Loch Shiel** – The most romantic and least spoilt of Scotland's great lochs, the place where Bonnie Prince Charlie first raised an army. See p.621

* **Knoydart** – The most remote peninsula in the Highlands: you can only reach it by boat or a two-day hike over the mountains. See p.624

* **Wester Ross** – Scotland's finest scenery, a heady mix of dramatic mountains, rugged sea lochs, sweeping bays and scattered islands. See p.630

* **Gairloch whale-watching trips** – Seals, porpoises, dolphins and whales are all found in the local waters. See p.633

* **Ceilidh Place, Ullapool** – The best venue for modern Highlands culture, regularly hosting evenings of music, song and dance. See p.638

8

The Highland region

The Highland region of Scotland, covering the northern two-thirds of the country, holds much of the mainland's most spectacular scenery: a classic combination of mountains, glens, lochs and rivers surrounded on three sides by a magnificently pitted and rugged coastline. The inspiring landscape and the tranquillity and space which it offers are without doubt the main attractions of the region. You may be surprised at just how remote much of it still is: the vast peat bogs in the north, for example, are among the most extensive and unspoilt wilderness areas in Europe, while a handful of the west coast's isolated crofting villages can still be reached only by boat.

Capital of the Highlands and the only major urban centre in the region, **Inverness** is an obvious springboard for more remote areas, with its good transport links and facilities, and while there are some engaging historic sites nearby, the city itself is of limited appeal. South of Inverness, the **Strathspey** region, with a string of villages lying along the River Spey, is dominated by the dramatic **Cairngorm mountains**, an area brimming with attractive scenery and opportunities for outdoor activity.

The Monadhliath mountains lie between Strathspey and **Loch Ness**, the largest and most famous of the necklace of lochs which make up the **Great Glen**, an ancient geologic faultline which cuts southwest across the region from Inverness to the town of **Fort William**. From Fort William, located beneath Scotland's highest peak, Ben Nevis, it's possible to branch out to some fine scenery – most conveniently the beautiful expanses of **Glen Coe**, but also in the direction of the appealing **west coast**, notably the remote and tranquil **Ardnamurchan peninsula**, the "Road to the Isles" to **Mallaig**, and the lochs and glens that lead to **Kyle of Lochalsh** on the most direct route to Skye (see p.448). Between Kyle of Lochalsh and **Ullapool**, the main settlement in

Accommodation price codes

Throughout this book, accommodation prices have been graded with the codes below, corresponding to the cost of the least expensive double room in high season. Price codes are not given for campsites, most of which charge less than £10 per person. Almost all hostels and bunkhouses charge between £8 and £12 per person per night; the few exceptions to this rule have the prices quoted in the text. For a full account of these codes, see p.28.

❶ under £40	❹ £60–70	❼ £110–150
❷ £40–50	❺ £70–90	❽ £150–200
❸ £50–60	❻ £90–110	❾ £200 and over

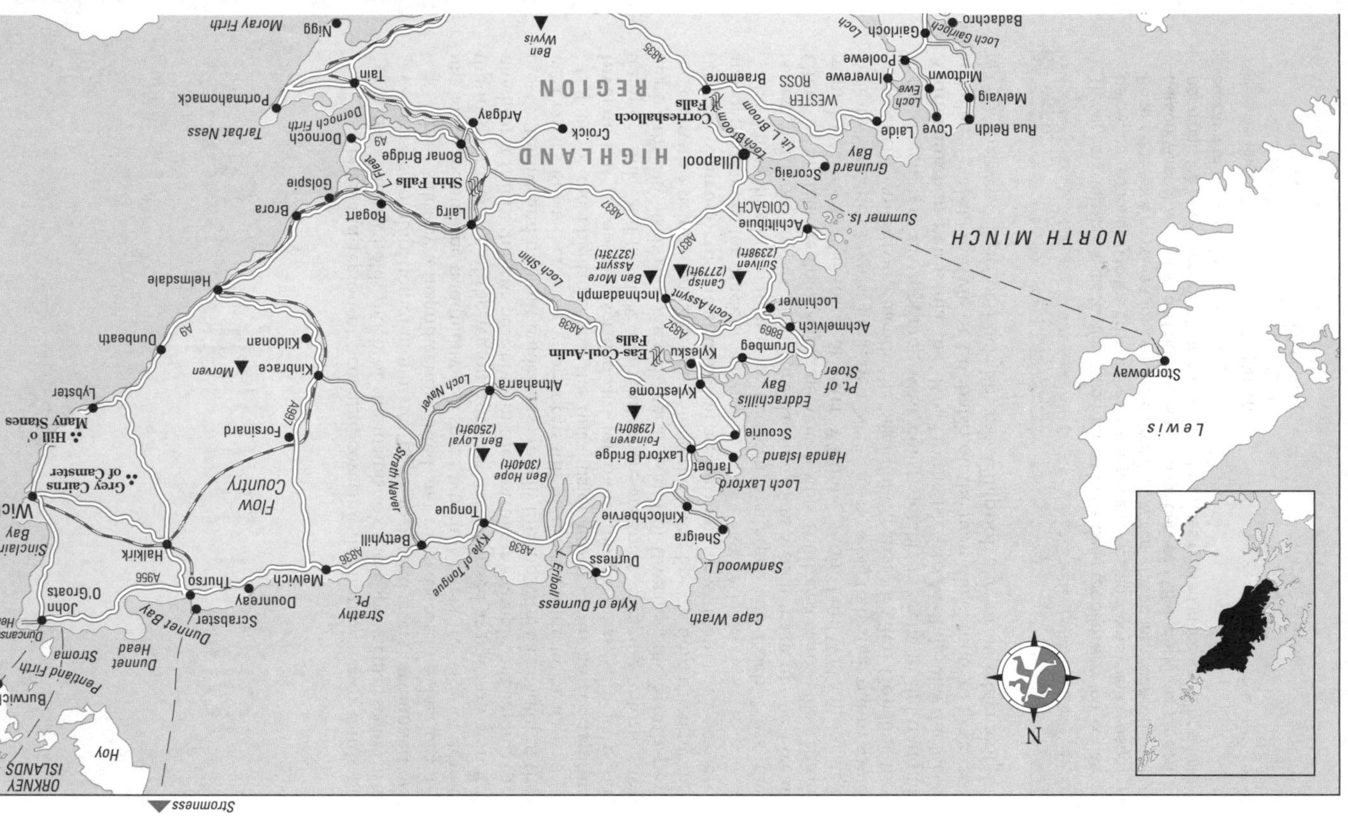
St Margaret's Hope
Stromness
ORKNEY ISLANDS
Hoy
Burwick
Pentland Firth
Stroma
Duncansby Head
Dunnet Head
Dunnet Bay
John O'Groats
Sinclair's Bay
Wick
Hill o' Many Stanes
Grey Cairns of Camster
Lybster
Dunbeath
Halkirk
A956
Thurso
Scrabster
Dounreay
Melvich
Flow Country
Forsinard
Morven
Helmsdale
A9
A997
Kinbrace
Kildonan
Brora
Golspie
Strathy Pt.
A836
Bettyhill
Strath Naver
Loch Naver
Tongue
Kyle of Tongue
Ben Loyal (2509ft)
Ben Hope (3040ft)
A838
Altnaharra
L. Eriboll
Kyle of Durness
Durness
Kinlochbervie
Sheigra
Cape Wrath
Sandwood L.
Foinaven (2980ft)
Laxford Bridge
Tarbet
Loch Laxford
Handa Island
Scourie
Kylestrome
Eas-Coul-Aulin Falls
Kylesku
Eddrachillis Bay
Drumbeg
B869
Pt. of Stoer
Achmelvich
Lochinver
Inchnadamph
Ben More Assynt (3273ft)
Canisp (2779ft)
Suilven (2398ft)
Loch Assynt
A832
A837
Loch Shin
Lairg
Rogart
Shin Falls
L. Fleet
Bonar Bridge
Dornoch
Dornoch Firth
Tarbat Ness
Portmahomack
Tain
Nigg
Moray Firth
Ardgay
Croick
Ben Wyvis
HIGHLAND REGION
Achiltibuie
COIGACH
Summer Is.
Ullapool
Loch Broom
Lit. L. Broom
Corrieshalloch Falls
Braemore
A835
Scoraig
Gruinard Bay
WESTER ROSS
Laide
Cove
Rua Reidh
Melvaig
Inverewe
Loch Ewe
Poolewe
Midtown
Gairloch
Loch Gairloch
Loch
Badachro
NORTH MINCH
Stornoway
Lewis
N

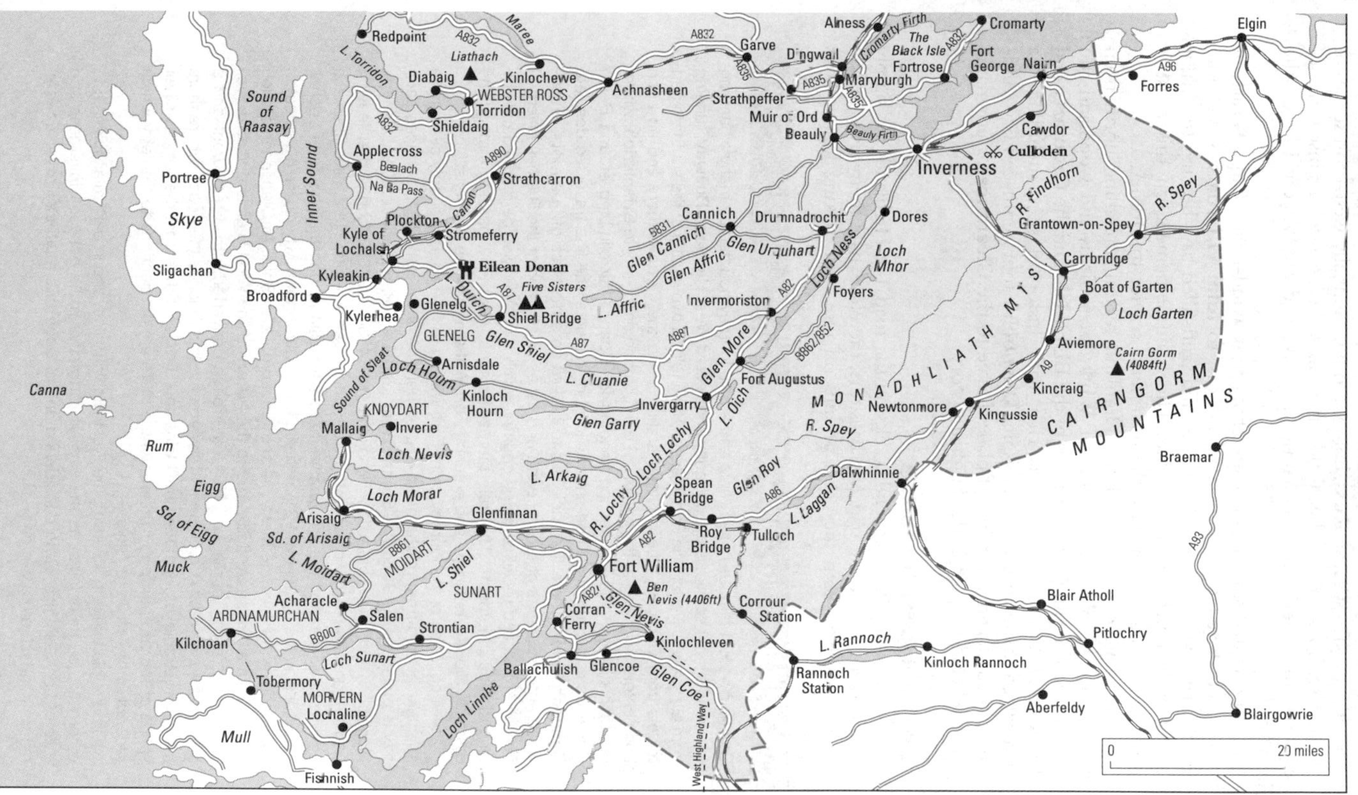
Redpoint
L. Torridon
A832
Maree
Liathach
Diabaig
Kinlochewe
WEBSTER ROSS
Torridon
Shieldaig
Sound of Raasay
Applecross
Bealach
Na Ba Pass
A890
Strathcarron
Portree
Inner Sound
Skye
Plockton
L. Carron
Stromeferry
Kyle of Lochalsh
Sligachan
Kyleakin
Eilean Donan
Broadford
Kylerhea
Glenelg
L. Duich
A87
Five Sisters
Shiel Bridge
GLENELG
Glen Shiel
Arnisdale
Sound of Sleat
Loch Hourn
Kinloch Hourn
Canna
KNOYDART
Mallaig
Inverie
Loch Nevis
Rum
Loch Morar
Eigg
Sd. of Eigg
Arisaig
Sd. of Arisaig
Glenfinnan
Muck
L. Moidart
B861
MOIDART
L. Shiel
SUNART
Acharacle
ARDNAMURCHAN
Salen
B8007
Strontian
Kilchoan
Loch Sunart
Tobermory
MORVERN
Lochaline
Mull
Fishnish
Loch Linnhe
Alness
Cromarty Firth
A832
Garve
A835
Dingwall
Achnasheen
Strathpeffer
Maryburgh
Muir of Ord
Beauly
Beauly Firth
The Black Isle
Fortrose
Cromarty
Fort George
Nairn
Elgin
A96
Forres
Cawdor
Culloden
Inverness
R. Findhorn
R. Spey
Grantown-on-Spey
Carrbridge
Boat of Garten
Loch Garten
Aviemore
Cairn Gorm (4084ft)
A9
Kincraig
Kingussie
Newtonmore
CAIRNGORM MOUNTAINS
MONADHLIATH MTS
B831
Cannich
Glen Cannich
Glen Affric
Drumnadrochit
Glen Urquhart
Loch Ness
Dores
Loch Mhor
Foyers
L. Affric
Invermoriston
A82
A887
B862/852
Glen More
Fort Augustus
L. Cluanie
Invergarry
L. Oich
Glen Garry
R. Spey
Loch Lochy
L. Arkaig
Spean Bridge
Glen Roy
A86
Dalwhinnie
L. Laggan
R. Lochy
Roy Bridge
Tulloch
Fort William
Ben Nevis (4406ft)
A82
Glen Nevis
Corran Ferry
Corrour Station
Kinlochleven
Ballachulish
Glencoe
Glen Coe
West Highland Way
L. Rannoch
Rannoch Station
Kinloch Rannoch
Braemar
A93
Blair Atholl
Pitlochry
Aberfeldy
Blairgowrie
0
20 miles

the northwest, lies **Wester Ross**, home to quintessentially west-coast scenes of sparkling sea lochs, rocky headlands and sandy beaches set against some of Scotland's most dramatic mountains, with Skye and the Western Isles on the horizon.

The little-visited **north coast** stretching from wind-lashed **Cape Wrath**, at the very northwest tip of the mainland, east to **John O'Groats** is yet more rugged than the west, with sheer cliffs and sand-filled bays bearing the brunt of frequently fierce Atlantic storms. The main settlement on this coast is **Thurso**, jumping-off point for the main ferry service to Orkney.

On the fertile **east coast** of the Highland region, stretching north from Inverness to the old herring port of **Wick**, green fields and woodland run down to the sweeping sandy beaches of the **Black Isle** and the **Cromarty** and **Dornoch firths**. This region is rich with historical sites, including the **Sutherland Monument** by Golspie, **Dornoch**'s fourteenth-century sandstone cathedral, and a number of places linked to the **Clearances**, a poignantly remembered chapter in the Highland story.

Transport practicalities

Unless you're prepared to spend weeks on the road, the Highlands are simply too vast to see in a single trip. Most visitors, therefore, base themselves in one or two areas, exploring the coast or hills on foot, and making longer hops

The West Highland Railway

Scotland's most famous railway line, and a train journey counted by many as among the world's most scenic, is the brilliantly engineered **West Highland Railway**, running from Glasgow to Mallaig via Fort William. The line is in two sections: the southern part travels from **Glasgow** Queen Street station along the Clyde estuary and up Loch Long before switching to the banks of Loch Lomond on its way to **Crianlarich**, where the train divides with one section heading for Oban. After climbing around Beinn Odhar on a unique horseshoe-shaped loop of viaducts, the line traverses desolate **Rannoch Moor**, where the track had to be laid on a mattress of tree roots, brushwood and thousands of tons of earth and ashes. By this point the line has diverged from the road, and travels through country which can otherwise be reached only by long-distance footpaths. The train then swings into Glen Roy, passing through the dramatic **Monessie Gorge** and entering **Fort William** from the northeast.

The second leg of the journey, from Fort William to Mallaig, is arguably even more spectacular, and from mid-June to September one of the scheduled services each day is pulled by the **Jacobite Steam Train** (departs Fort William 10.20am, departs Mallaig 2.10pm; day return £22; book on ⓣ01463/239026). Shortly after leaving Fort William the railway crosses the Caledonian Canal beside Neptune's Staircase by way of a swing bridge at **Banavie**, before travelling along the shores of Locheil and crossing the magnificent 21-arch viaduct at **Glenfinnan**, where you'll also catch a glimpse of the Jacobite Memorial at the head of Loch Shiel. At Glenfinnan station there's a small **museum** dedicated to the history of the West Highland line, as well as two old railway carriages which have been converted into a restaurant and a bunkhouse (see p.621). Not long afterwards the line reaches the coast, where there are unforgettable views of the Small Isles and Skye as it runs past the famous silver sands of **Morar** and up to **Mallaig**, where there are connections to the ferry which crosses to Armadale on Skye.

If you're planning on travelling the West Highland line, and in particular linking it to other train journeys (such as the similarly attractive route between Inverness and Kyle of Lochalsh), it's worth considering one of ScotRail's multi-day **rover tickets**, details of which are given on p.24.

across the interior by car, bus or train. Getting around the Highlands, particularly the remoter parts, is obviously easiest if you've got your own transport, but with a little forward planning you can see a surprising amount using **buses** and **trains**, especially if you fill in with **postbuses** (for which you can get timetables at most post offices). It is worth remembering, however, that much of the Highlands comes to a halt on Sundays, when bus services are sporadic at best and you may well find most shops and restaurants closed.

Inverness and around

Inverness, 105 miles northwest of Aberdeen by the A96, and 114 miles north of Perth by the A9, is the only "city" in the Highlands – a status it attained in 2000 as a millennium gesture by the government. A good base for day-trips and a jumping-off point for many of the more remote parts of the region, it is not a compelling place to stay for long and inevitably you are drawn to the attractions of sea and mountains beyond. The approach to the city on the A9 over the barren Monadhliath Mountains from Perth and Aviemore provides a spectacular introduction to the district, with the **Great Glen** to the left, stretching southwestwards towards Fort William and, beyond, the massed peaks of Glen Affric. To the north is the huge, rounded form of Ben Wyvis, whilst to the east lies the **Moray Firth**, to some extent a commuter belt for Inverness, but also boasting a lovely coastline and some of the region's best castles and historic sites. The gentle, undulating green landscape is well tended and tranquil, a fertile contrast to the windswept moorland and mountains that almost surround it.

A string of worthwhile sights punctuates the approaches to Inverness along the main route from Aberdeen. The low-key holiday resort of **Nairn**, with its long white-sand beaches and championship golf course, stands within striking distance of several monuments, including the whimsical **Cawdor Castle**, featured in Shakespeare's *Macbeth*, and **Fort George**, one of several impressive Hanoverian bastions erected in the wake of the Jacobite rebellion. The infamous battle and ensuing massacre that ended Bonnie Prince Charlie's uprising took place on the outskirts of Inverness at **Culloden**, where a small visitor centre and memorial stones beside a heather-clad moor recall the gruesome events of 1746.

Inverness

Straddling a nexus of major road and rail routes, **INVERNESS** is the busy and prosperous hub of the Highlands, and an inevitable port of call if you're exploring the region by public transport. **Buses** and **trains** leave for communities right across the far north of Scotland, and it isn't uncommon for people from as far afield as Thurso, Durness and Kyle of Lochalsh to travel down for a day's shopping here – Britain's most northerly chain-store centre. Though boasting few conventional sights, the city's setting on the banks of the River Ness is appealing. Crowned by a pink crenellated **castle** and lavishly decorated with flowers, the compact centre still has some hints of its medieval street layout, although pedestrianization and some unsightly concrete blocks do a fairly efficient job of masking it. Within walking distance of the centre are peaceful spots along by the Ness, leafy parks and friendly B&Bs located in prosperous-looking stone houses.

Some history

Inverness's sheltered **harbour** and proximity to the open sea made it an important entrepôt and shipbuilding centre during medieval times. David I, who first imposed a feudal system on Scotland, erected a **castle** on the banks of the Ness to oversee maritime trade in the early twelfth century, promoting it to royal burgh status soon after. Bolstered by receipts from the lucrative export of leather, salmon and timber, the town grew to become the kingdom's most prosperous northern outpost, and an obvious target for the marauding Highlanders who plagued this remote border area.

A second wave of growth occurred during the eighteenth century as the Highland cattle trade flourished. The arrival of the **Caledonian Canal** and **rail** links with the east and south brought further prosperity, heralding a tourist boom that reached a fashionable zenith in the Victorian era, fostered by the Royal Family's enthusiasm for all things Scottish. Over the last thirty years, the town has become one of the fastest-expanding in Britain, with its population virtually doubling due to the growing tourist industry and improved communications.

Arrival and information

Inverness **airport** (ⓣ01667/464000) is at Dalcross, seven miles east of the city; from here, **bus** #11 (Mon–Sat every 1hr–1hr 30min; 20min; £2.50) goes into town, while a **taxi** costs around £10. The **bus station** (ⓣ01463/233371) and **train station** (ⓣ0845/748 4950) both lie just off Academy Street to the east of the centre. The **tourist office** (June–Aug Mon–Fri 9am–6pm, Sat & Sun 9.30am–5pm; mid-July to Aug Mon–Fri until 8pm; rest of year Mon–Fri 9am–5pm, Sat 10am–4pm; ⓣ01463/234353) is in a 1960s block on Castle Wynd, just five minutes' walk from the station. It stocks a wide range of literature on the area, including useful free maps of the city and environs, and the friendly staff can book local accommodation for a £3 fee.

Accommodation

Inverness is one of the few places in the Highlands where you're unlikely to have problems finding **accommodation**, although in July and August you'll have to book ahead. You can reserve a bed through the tourist office, or in the train station concourse at the Thomas Cook booth, but bear in mind that both places levy a booking fee and also charge the hotel or guesthouse owner a hefty commission which is then passed on to you in your room tariff. Inverness boasts several good **hotels**, and nearly every street in the older residential areas of town has a sprinkling of **B&Bs**. Good places to look include both banks of the river south of the Ness Bridge, and Kenneth Street and its offshoots on the west side of the river. There are several **hostels** in town, all reasonably central, and a couple of large **campsites**, one near the Ness Islands and the other farther out to the west.

Tours and cruises

Inverness is the departure point for a range of day **tours** and **cruises** to nearby attractions, including Loch Ness and the Moray Firth.

Guide Friday run an open-topped double-decker tour of **Inverness** itself (May–Sept daily every 45min; 30min; £5.50), which you can hop on and off all day; the bus also goes out to **Culloden** (1hr 20min; £7.50). You can buy tickets on the buses, which leave from Bridge Street near the tourist office, or at Guide Friday's office in the train station (May–Sept daily 9am–6pm). An entertaining if slightly bizarre **Terror Tour** takes groups on foot around Inverness town centre (daily 7pm from the tourist office; £5.50), with grisly tales told along the way of ghosts, torture and witches.

There are various **Loch Ness** tours leaving from the tourist office, such as Guide Friday's three-hour trip which incorporates a short cruise on the loch and visits to the monster exhibition at **Drumnadrochit** and **Urquhart Castle** (£14.50 including admission fees). Far more original and personal are Tony Harmsworth's **Discover Loch Ness** tours (ⓣ01456/450168 or ⓣ0800/731 5564, ⓦwww.discoverlochness.com), which combine an insightful introduction to the monster-hype with visits to places of geological or historical interest. Longer **boat trips** on Loch Ness are run morning and afternoon by Jacobite Cruises (April–Oct; ⓣ01463/233999); a courtesy bus operates from the tourist office down to their dock at Tomnahurich Canal Bridge on Glenurquhart Road, a mile and a half south of Inverness town centre.

Inverness is also about the one place where transport connections allow you to embark on a major **grand tour** of the Highlands. It is possible, cabin fever notwithstanding, to catch the early train to Kyle of Lochalsh, a bus on to Skye and across the island to catch the ferry to Mallaig, which meets the train to Fort William, from where you can take a bus back to Inverness, all in less than twelve hours (£28.90; tickets from the tourist office). To explore the northwest, Dearman Coaches have a daily service to **Ullapool**, **Lochinver**, **Durness**, **Smoo Cave** and back which stops at several hostels en route (June–Sept Mon–Sat; £17.50; or you can buy a £25 rover ticket valid for six days).

Enjoyable trips up to **John O'Groats** and back in a day, with the chance to see puffins and visit prehistoric sites, are run by Puffin Express (ⓣ01463/717181, ⓦwww.puffinexpress.co.uk), who also put together a package which includes an overnight stop on **Orkney**. You can get to the islands and back with a gruelling full-day whistle-stop tour on the Orkney Bus, which leaves Inverness bus station every day during the summer (£44; advance bookings may be made at the tourist office or on ⓣ01955/611353).

See p.589 for details of **dolphin**-spotting cruises on the Moray Firth.

Hotels

Brae Ness Ness Bank ⓣ01463/712266, ⓦwww.braenesshotel.co.uk. A homely Georgian hotel with only ten rooms (all non-smoking) overlooking the river and St Andrews Cathedral. April–Oct. ❹

Dunain Park ⓣ01463/230512, ⓦwww.dunainparkhotel.co.uk. Luxurious country house hotel off the A82 Fort William road, about three miles west of the centre of town. Excellent food (dinner is around £25 per person) and beautiful rooms. ❼

Glenmoriston Town House Hotel 20 Ness Bank ⓣ01463/223777, ⓦwww.glenmoriston.com. Very classy and comfortable hotel slap on the riverside with well-appointed rooms and a top-notch Italian restaurant. ❻

Royal Highland 18 Academy St ⓣ01463/231926, ⓦwww.royalhighlandhotel.co.uk. The old station hotel, dripping with the grandeur of the golden days of Highland travel. Perfect for those en route to their grouse moor. ❺

B&Bs

Brewers House 2 Moray Park, Island Bank Rd ⓣ01463/235557. A welcoming B&B in a characterful old house a little further down the river than some pricier guesthouses, but still an easy stroll from the centre. ❶

Craigside Lodge 4 Gordon Terrace ⓣ01463/231576. Spacious rooms, great views, a friendly welcome and handily placed near the

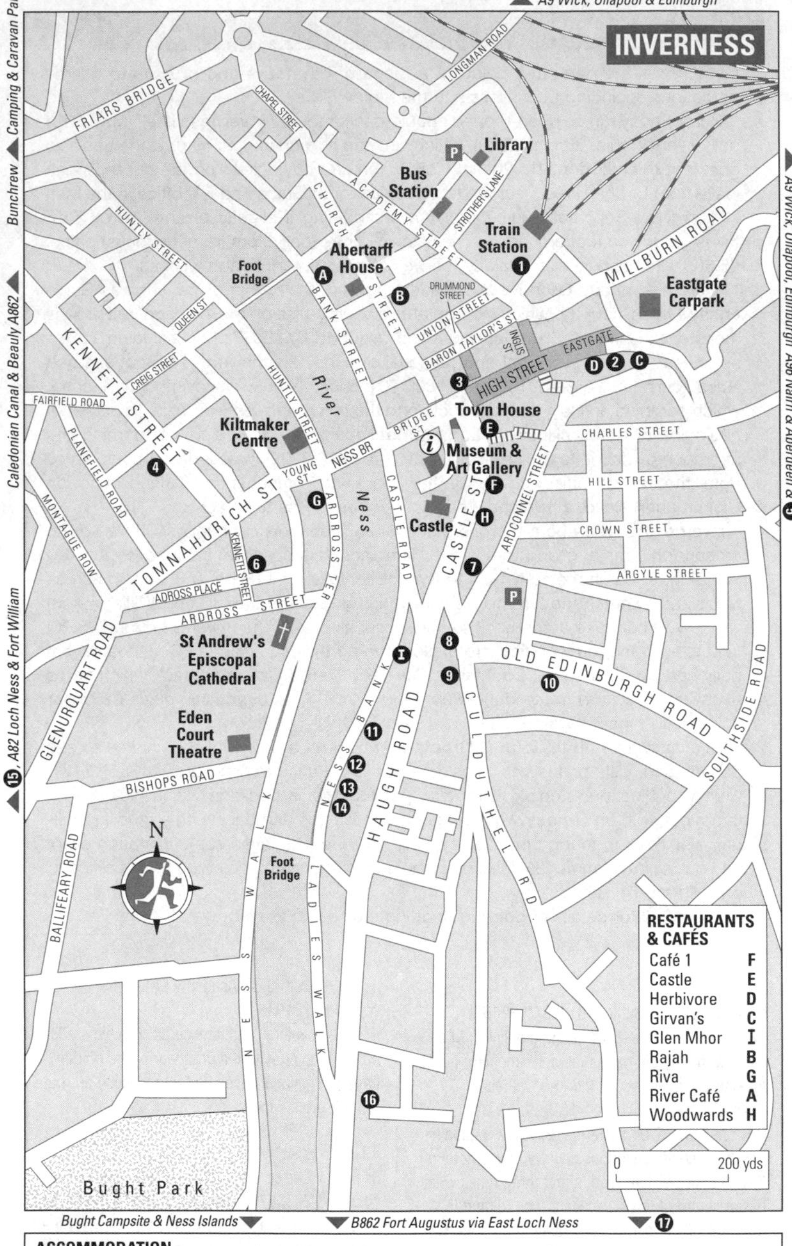

ACCOMMODATION

Bazpackers	8	Eastgate Hostel	2	Ho Ho Hostel	3	Melrose Villa	4
Brae Ness	11	Edenview	14	Inverness Student Hotel	9	Old Drummond House	17
Brewers House	16	Glenmoriston	12	Ivybank	10	Royal Highland	1
Craigside Lodge	7	Heathfield	6	Macrae House	13	SYHA hostel	5
Dunain Park	15						

castle and town centre. ❷

Edenview 26 Ness Bank ⓣ01463/234397. Very pleasant B&B in a riverside location as good as the more expensive hotels, five minutes' walk from the centre. Non-smoking. ❸

Heathfield 2 Kenneth St ⓣ01463/230547. A very comfortable and friendly place at the quiet end of a street packed with B&Bs. All rooms have central heating and some are en suite. Non-smoking. ❶

Ivybank Guest House 28 Old Edinburgh Rd ⓣ01463/232796. A grand Georgian home just up the hill from the castle, with open fires and a lovely wooden interior. ❷

Macrae House 24 Ness Bank ⓣ01463/243658, ⓦwww.macraehouse.co.uk. Right on the river, friendly, and with large, comfortable rooms. Non-smoking. ❷

Melrose Villa 35 Kenneth St ⓣ01463/233745. Very family-friendly, with excellent breakfasts. Three singles as well as doubles and twins, with most rooms en suite. ❶

Old Drummond House Oak Avenue ⓣ01463/226301. Part of a nicely renovated 200-year-old mansion at the quiet end of a suburban avenue, a mile or so south of the centre. ❷

Hostels

Bazpackers Top of Castle Street ⓣ01463/717663. The most cosy and relaxed of the city's hostels, with thirty beds including two double rooms and a twin; some dorms are mixed. Has good views and a garden, which is used for barbecues, as well as the usual cooking facilities. Non-smoking.

Eastgate Hostel Eastgate ⓣ01463/718756, ⓦwww.hostelsaccommodation.com. Well-maintained former hotel above *Herbivore* vegetarian restaurant. Sleeps 38 in six-bed dorms and two twin rooms. Free tea and coffee is provided; no curfew.

Ho Ho Hostel 23a High St ⓣ01463/221225. Formerly the grand Highland Club, a town base for lairds; now a large hostel with big rooms which tends to attract a partying crowd.

Inverness Student Hotel 8 Culduthel Rd ⓣ01463/236556. A busy fifty-bed hostel with the usual facilities and fine views over the river. Part of the Macbackpackers group, so expect minibus tours to pull in most days.

SYHA hostel Victoria Drive, off Millburn Road, about three-quarters of a mile east of the centre ⓣ01463/231771, ⓦwww.syha.org.uk. One of SYHA's flagship hostels, fully equipped with large kitchens and communal areas, ecofriendly facilities and ten four-bed family rooms among the 188-bed total, but all rather soulless.

Camping

Bught Caravan and Camping Site Bught Park ⓣ01463/236920. Inverness's main campsite, on the west bank of the river near the sports centre. Good facilities, but it can get very crowded at the height of the season.

Bunchrew Caravan and Camping Park Bunchrew, three miles west of Inverness on the A862 ⓣ01463/237802. Well-equipped site with lots of space for tents on the shores of the Beauly Firth, with hot water, showers, laundry and a shop. Very popular with families.

The Town

The logical place to begin a tour of Inverness is the central **Town House** on the High Street. Built in 1878, this Gothic pile hosted Prime Minister Lloyd George's emergency meeting to discuss the Irish crisis in September 1921, and now accommodates council offices. There's nothing of note inside, but look out for the old **Mercat Cross** next to the main entrance. The cross stands opposite a small square formerly used by merchants and traders and above the ancient *clach-na-cudainn*, or "**stone of tubs**" – so called because washerwomen used to rest their buckets on it on their way back from the river. A local superstition holds that as long as the stone remains in place, Inverness will continue to prosper.

Looming above the Town House and dominating the horizon is **Inverness Castle** (mid-May to Sept Mon–Sat 10am–5pm; £3), a predominantly nineteenth-century red-sandstone edifice perched picturesquely above the river. The original castle formed the core of the ancient town, which had rapidly developed as a port trading with Europe after its conversion to Christianity by St Columba in the sixth century. Two famous Scots monarchs were associated with the building: **Robert the Bruce** wrested it back from the English during the Wars of Independence, destroying it in the process, and **Mary, Queen**

of Scots had the governor of the second castle hanged from its ramparts after he had refused her entry in 1562. This structure was also destined for destruction, held by the Jacobites in both the 1715 and the 1745 rebellions, and blown up by them to prevent it falling into government hands. Today's edifice houses the Sheriff Court and, in summer, the **Castle Garrison Encounter**, an entertaining and noisy interactive exhibition in which the visitor plays the role of a new recruit in the eighteenth-century Hanoverian army. Around 7pm during the summer, a lone piper clad in full Highland garb performs for tourists on the castle esplanade. The statue of a woman staring south from the terrace is a memorial to **Flora MacDonald**, the clanswoman who helped Bonnie Prince Charlie escape to Skye in the wake of Culloden (see p.588).

Below the castle, the **Inverness Museum and Art Gallery** on Castle Wynd (Mon–Sat 9am–5pm; free) gives a good general overview of the development of the Highlands. Informative sections on geology, geography and history cover the ground floor, while upstairs you'll find a muddled selection of silver, taxidermy, weapons and bagpipes, alongside a mediocre art gallery.

Leading north from the Town House, medieval **Church Street** is home to the town's oldest-surviving buildings. On the corner with Bridge Street stands the **Steeple** (1791), whose spire had to be straightened after an earth tremor in 1816. Farther down Church Street is **Abertarff House**, reputedly the oldest complete building in Inverness and distinguished by its stepped gables and circular stair tower. It was erected in 1593 and is now owned by the National Trust for Scotland. The **Old High Church** (Fri noon–2pm & during services; tour at 12.30pm), founded by St Columba in 1171 and rebuilt on several occasions since, stands just along the street, hemmed in by a walled graveyard. Any Jacobites who survived the massacre of Culloden were brought here and incarcerated prior to their execution in the cemetery. If you take the guided tour, you'll be shown bullet holes left on gravestones by the firing squads.

Along the River Ness

Just across Ness Bridge from Bridge Street is the **Kiltmaker Centre** in the Hector Russell shop (mid-May to Sept Mon–Sat 9am–10pm, Sun 10am–5pm; rest of year Mon–Sat 9am–5.30pm; £2). Entered through the factory shop, a visitor centre sets out everything you ever wanted to know about tartan, and on weekdays you can watch various tartan products being made in the workshop. The finished products are, of course, on sale in the showroom downstairs, along with all manner of Highland knitwear, woven woollies and Harris tweed.

Rising from the west bank directly opposite the castle, **St Andrew's Episcopal Cathedral** was intended by its architects to be one of the grandest buildings in Scotland. However, funds ran out before the giant twin spires of the original design could be completed. The interior is pretty ordinary, too, though it does claim an unusual octagonal chapterhouse. Alongside the cathedral is **Eden Court Theatre**, an awkward-looking 1970s construction. The main auditorium in Inverness, it has a reasonably busy programme of touring plays, musicals and concerts.

From here, you can wander a mile or so upriver to the peaceful **Ness Islands**, an attractive, informal public park reached and linked by footbridges. Laid out with mature trees and shrubs, the islands are the favourite haunt of local anglers. Further upstream still, the river runs close to the **Caledonian Canal**, designed by Thomas Telford in the early nineteenth century as a link between the east and west coasts, joining lochs Ness, Oich, Lochy and Linnhe. Today its main use is recreational, and there are cruises through part of it to Loch Ness (see p.602), while the towpath provides relaxing walks with good views.

The truth about tartan

To much of the world, **tartan** is synonymous with Scotland. It's the natural choice of packaging for Scottish exports from shortbread to Sean Connery, and when the Scottish football team travels abroad to play a fixture, the high-spirited "Tartan Army" of fans are never far behind. Not surprisingly, tartan is big business for the tourist industry and every year hundreds of visitors return home from Scotland clutching tartan souvenirs (often manufactured overseas) tied with tartan ribbon, or lengths of cloth inspiringly named Loch This, Ben That or Glen Something-Else. Yet the truth is that romantic fiction and commercial interest have enclosed this ancient Highland art form within an almost insurmountable wall of myth.

The original form of tartan, the kind that long ago was called "**Helande**", was a fine, hard and almost showerproof cloth spun in Highland villages from the wool of the native sheep, dyed with preparations of local plants and with patterns woven by artist-weavers. It was worn as a huge single piece of cloth, or **plaid**, which was belted around the waist and draped over the upper body, rather like a knee-length toga. The natural colours of old tartans were clear but soft, and the broken pattern gave superb camouflage, unlike modern versions, where garish, clashing colours are often used to create impact.

The myth-makers were about four centuries ahead of themselves in dressing up the warriors of the film *Braveheart* in plaid: in fact tartan did not become popular in the Lowlands until the beginning of the eighteenth century, when it was adopted as the anti-Union badge of the **Jacobites**. After Culloden, a ban on the wearing of tartan in the Highlands lasted some 25 years; in that time it became a fondly held emblem for emigrant Highlanders in the colonies and was incorporated into the uniforms of the new Highland regiments in the British Army. Then Sir Walter Scott set to work glamourizing the clans, dressing George IV in a kilt (and, just as controversially, flesh-coloured tights) for his visit to Edinburgh in 1822. By the time Queen Victoria set the royal seal of approval on both the Highlands and tartan with her extended annual holidays at Balmoral, the concept of tartan as formal dress rather than rough Highland wear was assured.

Hand-in-hand with the gentrification of the kilt came "rules" about the correct form of attire and the idea that every clan had its own distinguishing tartan. To have the right to wear tartan, one had to belong, albeit remotely, to a clan, and so the way was paved for the "what's-my-tartan?" lists that appear in tartan picture books and souvenir shops. Great feats of genealogical gymnastics were performed in the concoction of these lists; where these left gaps, a more recent marketing phenomenon of themed tartans developed, with new patterns for different districts, companies and even football teams being produced.

Scotsmen today will commonly wear the **kilt** for weddings and other formal occasions; properly made kilts, however – comprising some four yards of 100-percent wool – are likely to set you back £300 or more, with the rest of the regalia at least doubling that figure. If the contents of your sporran don't stretch that far, most places selling kilts will rent outfits by the day. The best place to find better quality material is a recognized Highland outfitter rather than a souvenir shop: in Inverness, try the Scottish Kiltmaker Centre at Hector Russell's (see opposite) or Chisholms Kiltmakers at 47–51 Castle St.

Three miles to the west of the town, on the top of **Craig Phadrig** hill, there's a vitrified **Iron Age fort**, reputed to be where the Pictish King Brude received St Columba in the sixth century. The walls of the fort were built of stone laced with timber and, when the timber was set alight, some of the stone fused to glass – hence the term "vitrified". Waymarked forest trails start from the car parks at the bottom of the hill and lead up to the fort, though only the outline of its perimeter defences are now visible and recent tree planting is beginning to block some of the views. Bus #14 from Church Street (Mon–Sat every 30min) drops you at the foot of Craig Dunain, right beside Craig Phadrig.

Eating and drinking

Inverness has lots of **eating** places, including a few excellent-quality gourmet options, while for the budget-conscious there's no shortage of **pubs**, **cafés** and **restaurants** around the town centre. **Takeaways** cluster on Young Street, just across the river, and at the ends of Eastgate and Academy Street. Good places for **picnic food** include The Gourmet's Lair, 8 Union St, and Lettuce Eat on Drummond Street.

Restaurants

Café 1 75 Castle St ⓣ01463/226200. Impressive contemporary Scottish cooking using good local ingredients in a bistro-style setting. Closed Sun. Moderate to expensive.

Castle Restaurant 41 Castle St. Classic, long-established café that does a roaring trade in down-to-earth Scottish food – meat pies, chicken and fish, dished up with piles of chips. Open at 8am for breakfast; closed Sun. Inexpensive.

Herbivore 38 Eastgate ⓣ01463/231075. Laid-back, modern vegetarian restaurant open right through the day and for decent evening meals. Moderate.

Dunain Park Hotel Restaurant Dunain Park ⓣ01463/230512. Award-winning Scots–French restaurant in a country-house hotel set in lovely gardens just southwest of town; a good choice for a leisurely dinner. Expensive.

Girvan's 2–4 Stephen's Brae ⓣ01463/711900. Uncomplicated but decent restaurant serving Scottish meat and fish dishes, that doubles as a daytime patisserie.

Glen Mhor Hotel 9 Ness Bank ⓣ01463/234308. Fairly lavish Scottish cuisine (mainly local salmon, beef and game) at moderate prices, either in *Nico's Bistro* or the *Riverview Restaurant* at the front.

Rajah Post Office Avenue ⓣ01463/237190. An excellent Indian restaurant, tucked away in a backstreet basement. Moderate.

Riva 4–6 Ness Walk ⓣ01463/237377. Reasonably authentic modern Italian bistro/café beside the river with antipasta, decent mains and good coffee and cakes. Moderate. Upstairs, inexpensive pasta dishes can be had at *Pazzo's Pasta Bar* (evenings only; closed Sun & Mon).

River Café and Restaurant 10 Bank St ⓣ01463/714884. Healthy wholefood lunches and evening meals, with a great selection of freshly baked cakes and good coffee. Inexpensive to moderate.

Woodwards 99 Castle St ⓣ01463/709809. Classy and interesting modern Scottish cuisine; reasonably formal and upmarket. Expensive.

Nightlife and entertainment

The liveliest **nightlife** in Inverness revolves around the pubs and, on Friday and Saturday nights, the city's main nightclub. The far end of Academy Street has a cluster of good **pubs**; the public bar of the *Phoenix* is the most original town-centre place, though *Blackfriars* across the street has a bit more going for it with entertainment seven nights a week, including ceilidhs popular with Australian backpackers searching for their roots. In a basement beside the river on the corner of Bank and Bridge streets, *Johnny Foxes* drapes itself in shamrocks but draws eager crowds to its regular live music sessions. Over on Bridge Street, the *Gellions* is a legendary local watering hole with several other congenial places in between.

The town's liveliest **nightclub** is *G's* on Castle Street, which has queues of the town's youth forming outside at weekends. The local **folk music** scene, always lively and authentic, is still recovering from the closure of the widely respected Balnain House. There are normally gigs happening somewhere in

Inverness during the week, and particularly at weekends: look out for local adverts or check with the tourist office to find out what's going on.

Listings

Airport ☎01667/464000.
Bike rental Barney's, 35 Castle St ☎01463/232249.
Bookshops Leakey's, Greyfriars' Hall on Church Street, is a great spot to browse for secondhand books, with a café inside and a warming wood stove in winter; James Thin, 29 Union St, has an excellent range of Scottish books and maps; and Waterstone's is at 50–52 High St.
Car rental Budget is on Railway Terrace, behind the train station (☎01463/713333); Europcar has an office on Telfer St (☎01463/235337); Arnold Clark is at 47–49 Harbour Rd (☎01463/236200); Thrifty is at 33 Harbour Rd (☎01463/224466); and Sharps Reliable Wrecks is based at Station Square (☎01463/236684) as well as the airport.
Cinemas The Eden Court Theatre and the attached Riverside Screen, on the banks of the Ness, host touring theatre productions, concerts and films; La Scala (☎01463/233302) on Strother's Lane, just off Academy Street, has two screens; Warner Village (☎01463/711175), on the A96 Nairn road about two miles from the town centre, boasts seven screens.
Dentist Contact the Scotland-wide National Health Service Line (☎0800/224488) for local and emergency dentists.
Exchange American Express agents Alba Travel are at 43 Church St (Mon–Sat 9am–5pm; ☎01463/239188). The tourist office's *bureau de change* changes cash and currency for a small commission.
Hospital Raigmore Hospital (☎01463/704000) on the southeastern outskirts of town close to the A9.
Internet MTC, 2 Grant St (Mon–Thurs 9am–5pm, Fri 9am–4.30pm). There are also two terminals in the tourist office.
Laundry Young Street Laundrette, 17 Young St (☎01463/242507).
Left luggage Train station lockers cost from £2 to £4 for 24hr; the left-luggage room in the bus station costs £1 per item (Mon–Sat 8.30am–6pm, Sun 10am–6pm).
Library Inverness library (☎01463/236463), housed in the Neoclassical building on the north-east side of the bus station, has an excellent genealogical research unit (Mon–Fri 10am–1pm & 2–5pm; ext. 9). Consultations with the resident genealogist cost £12 per hour, but are free if shorter than ten minutes. An appointment is advisable.
Outdoor supplies Clive Rowland Outdoor Sports, 9 Bridge St (☎01463/238746); Graham Tiso, 41 High St (☎01463/716617).
Pharmacy Boots, Eastgate Shopping Centre (Mon–Fri 9am–5.30pm, Thurs 9am–7pm, Sun noon–5pm; ☎01463/225167).
Post office 14–16 Queensgate (Mon–Thurs 9am–5.30pm, Fri 9.30am–5.30pm, Sat 9am–6pm; ☎0845/722 3344).
Public toilets Usually immaculate ones in Mealmarket Close, north side of High Street.
Radio The local radio station is Moray Firth Radio on 97.4FM and 1107AM.
Sports centre Inverness sports centre and Aquadome leisure pool (Mon–Fri 7.30am–10pm, Sat & Sun 7.30am–9pm; ☎01463/667500), a mile or so south of the town centre off the A82, has a large pool, gym and other indoor sports facilities.
Taxis Culloden Taxis (☎01463/790000); Rank Radio Taxis (☎01463/221111).

East of Inverness

East of Inverness lies the fertile, sheltered coastal strip of the **Moray Firth** and its hinterland, the pastoral countryside contrasting with the scenic splendours you'll encounter once you head further north into the Highlands. Primary among the sites is **Culloden**, the most poignant battlefield site in Scotland, where Bonnie Prince Charlie's Jacobites were routed in 1746. Further east are **Cawdor Castle** and **Fort George**, two of the best-preserved fortified structures in the Highlands. **Nairn**, the main town of the district, has a pretty harbour as well as appealing walks and cycle routes.

The overloaded A96 traverses this stretch and the region is well served by public transport, with all the historic sites and castles accessible on day-trips from

Inverness, or en route to Aberdeen. To get to Fort George, Cawdor Castle and Culloden you can juggle the Highland County Tourist Trail buses (#11, #12 and #13; £6 for a day rover ticket) which depart from Queens Gate in Inverness.

Culloden

The windswept moorland of **CULLODEN** (site open all year; free), five miles east of Inverness, witnessed the last-ever battle on British soil when, on April 16, 1746, the Jacobite cause was finally subdued – a turning point in the history of the Scottish nation.

The second Jacobite rebellion had begun on August 19, 1745, with the raising of the Stuarts' standard at **Glenfinnan** on the west coast (see 621). Shortly after, Edinburgh fell into Jacobite hands, and Bonnie Prince Charlie began his march on London. The English had appointed the ambitious young Duke of Cumberland to command their forces, and his pursuit, together with bad weather and lack of funds, eventually forced the Jacobites to retreat north. They ended up at Culloden, where, ill-fed and exhausted after a pointless night march, they were hopelessly outnumbered by the English. The open, flat ground of Culloden Moor was totally unsuitable for the Highlanders' style of courageous but undisciplined fighting, which needed steep hills and lots of cover to provide the element of surprise, and they were routed. After the battle, in which 1500 Highlanders were slaughtered (many of them as they lay wounded on the battlefield), Bonnie Prince Charlie fled west to the hills and islands, where loyal Highlanders sheltered and protected him. He eventually escaped to France, leaving his erstwhile supporters to their fate – and, in effect, ushering in the end of the clan system. The clans were disarmed, the wearing of tartan and playing of bagpipes forbidden, and the chiefs became landlords greedy for higher and higher rents. The battle also unleashed an orgy of violent reprisals on Scotland, as unruly English troops raped and pillaged their way across the region; within a century, the Highland way of life had changed out of all recognition.

The battle site

Today you can walk freely around the battle site; flags show the positions of the two armies, and **clan graves** are marked by simple headstones. The **Field of the English**, for many years unmarked, is a mass grave for the fifty or so English soldiers who died. Half a mile east of the battlefield, just beyond the crossroads on the main road, is the **Cumberland Stone**, thought for many years to have been the point from where the Duke watched the battle. It is more likely, however, that he was much further forward and simply used the stone for shelter. Thirty Jacobites were burnt alive outside the old **Leanach cottage** next to the visitor centre; inside, it has been restored to its eighteenth-century appearance.

The **visitor centre** itself (daily: April–Oct 9am–6pm; Nov–March 10am–4pm; closed early to mid-Jan; NTS; £4) provides background information through detailed displays and a film show, as well as a short play set on the day of the battle presented by local actors (June–Sept only; included in admission fee), or you can take the evocative hour-long guided **walking tour** (June–Sept daily; £3). In April, on the Saturday closest to the date of the battle, there's a small commemorative service. The visitor centre has a reference library, and will check for you if you think you have an ancestor who died here.

The site is served by Guide Friday **buses** from Bridge Street in Inverness (May–Sept; 10 daily from 10am; last return bus leaves Culloden at 5.45pm) and Highland Country bus #12 from Inverness post office (Mon–Sat 8 daily).

The dolphins of the Moray Firth

The **Moray Firth**, a great wedge-shaped bay forming the eastern coastline of the Highlands, is one of only three areas of UK waters that supports a resident population of **dolphins**. Over a hundred of these beautiful, intelligent marine mammals live in the estuary, the most northerly breeding ground for this particular species – the bottle-nosed dolphin (*Tursiops truncatus*) – in Europe, and you stand a good chance of spotting a few, either from the shore or a boat. Both adults and calves frequently leap out of the water, "bow riding" in front of boats and performing elegant synchronized swimming routines.

Bottle-nosed dolphins are the largest in the world, typically growing to a length of around 13ft and weighing between 400 and 650 pounds. The adults sport a tall, sickle-shaped dorsal fin and a distinctive beak-like "nose", and usually live for around 25 years, although a number of fifty-year-old animals have been recorded. During the summer, herds of thirty to forty have been known to congregate in the Moray Firth; no one is exactly sure why, although experts believe the annual gatherings, which take place between late June and August, may be connected to the breeding cycle. In the past, the local dolphins have been known to toss dead or dying porpoises around in the waves as if for fun; several porpoise corpses with serrated tooth marks have been washed ashore in the area.

Dolphin-spotting has become something of a craze in the Moray Firth area. One of the best places in Scotland, if not in Europe, to look for them is **Chanonry Point**, on the Black Isle (see p.657) – a spit of sand protruding into a narrow, deep channel, where converging currents bring fish close to the surface, and thus the dolphins close to shore; the hour or so before high tide is the most likely time to see them. **Kessock Bridge**, one mile north of Inverness, is another prime dolphin-spotting location. You can go all the way down to the beach at the small village of North Kessock, underneath the road bridge, where there's a decent place to have a drink at the pub in the *North Kessock Hotel*, or you can stop above the village in a car park just off the A9 at the visitor centre and listening post (see p.657) set up by a team of zoologists from Aberdeen University studying the dolphins, where hydrophones allow you to eavesdrop on the clicks and whistles of underwater conversations.

In addition, several companies run dolphin-spotting **boat trips** around the Moray Firth. However, researchers claim that the increased traffic is causing the dolphins unnecessary stress, particularly during the all-important breeding period, when passing vessels are thought to force calves underwater for uncomfortably long periods. They have therefore devised a code of conduct for boat operators, based on the experiences of other countries where dolphin-watching has become disruptive. So, if you decide to go on a spotting cruise, make sure the operator is a member of the Dolphin Space Programme's Accreditation Scheme. Operators currently accredited include Majestic Cruises, Inverness (☎01463/731661); Benbola Tours, 21 Great Eastern Rd, Portessie, Buckie (☎01542/832289); Macaulay Charters, Inverness (☎01463/751263); Moray Firth Cruises, Shore Street, Inverness (☎01463/717900); and Dolphin Écosse, Bank House, High Street, Cromarty (☎01381/600323). Half-day trips cost around £20.

The Clava Cairns

If you're visiting Culloden with your own transport, a short detour is worthwhile to the **CLAVA CAIRNS**, an impressive collection of prehistoric burial chambers clustered around the south bank of the River Nairn, a mile south-east of the battlefield. Erected some time before 2000 BC, the cairns, which are encircled by standing stones in a spinney of mature beech trees, are of two different kinds: one large and one very small **ring-cairn**, and two **passage**

graves, which have a narrow passageway from edge to centre. Though cremated remains have been found in both types of structure, and unburnt remains in the passage graves, little is known about the nomadic herdsmen who are thought to have built them.

Cawdor Castle

The pretty, if slightly self-satisfied village of **CAWDOR**, eight miles east of Culloden, is the site of **Cawdor Castle** (May to mid-Oct daily 10am–5.30pm; £5.90; gardens only £3), a setting intimately linked to Shakespeare's *Macbeth*: the fulfilment of the witches' prediction that Macbeth was to become Thane of Cawdor sets off his tragic desire to be king. Though visitors arrive here in their droves each summer because of the site's literary associations, the castle, which dates from the early fourteenth century, could not possibly have witnessed the grisly historical events on which the Bard's drama was based. However, the immaculately restored monument – a fairy-tale affair of towers, turrets, hidden passageways, dungeons, gargoyles and crenellations whimsically shooting off from the original keep – is still well worth a visit.

Six centuries on, the Campbells of Cawdor still spend their winters here, and the castle feels like a family home, albeit one with tapestries, pictures and opulent furniture (all catalogued with mischievous humour). As you explore, look out for the **Thorn Tree Room**, a vaulted chamber complete with the remains of an ancient holly tree carbon-dated to 1372 – an ancient pagan fertility symbol believed to ward off fairies and evil spirits. According to Cawdor family legend, the fourteenth-century Thane of Cawdor dreamed he should build on the spot where his donkey lay down to sleep after a day's wandering; the animal chose this tree and construction began immediately.

The **grounds** of the castle are impressive, with an attractive walled garden, a topiarian maze, a small golf course, a putting green and nature trails. It's also worth visiting the village for a drink or meal at the traditional *Cawdor Tavern*, an old inn serving beautifully prepared local food. Highland **bus** #12 (Mon–Sat 8 daily; 35min) runs to Cawdor from Inverness post office, with the last bus back departing from the castle just after 6pm.

Fort George

Eight miles of undulating coastal farmland separate Cawdor Castle from **Fort George** (April–Sept daily 9.30am–6.30pm; Oct–March Mon–Sat 9.30am–4.30pm, Sun 2–4.30pm; HS; £4.50), an old Hanoverian bastion with walls a mile long, considered by military architectural historians to be one of the finest fortifications in Europe. Crowning a sandy spit that juts into the middle of the Moray Firth, it was built between 1747 and 1769 as a base for George II's army, in case the Highlanders should attempt to rekindle the Jacobite flame. By the time of its completion, however, the uprising had been firmly quashed and the fort has been used ever since as a barracks; note the armed sentries at the main entrance and the periodic crack of live gunfire from the nearby firing ranges.

Apart from the sweeping panoramic **views** across the Firth from its ramparts, the main incentive to visit Fort George is the **Regimental Museum** of the Queen's Own Highlanders. Displayed in polished glass cases is a predictable array of regimental silver, coins, moth-eaten uniforms and medals, along with some macabre war trophies, ranging from blood-stained nineteenth-century Sudanese battle robes to Iraqi gas masks gleaned in the Gulf War. The heroic deeds performed by various recipients of Victoria Crosses make compelling

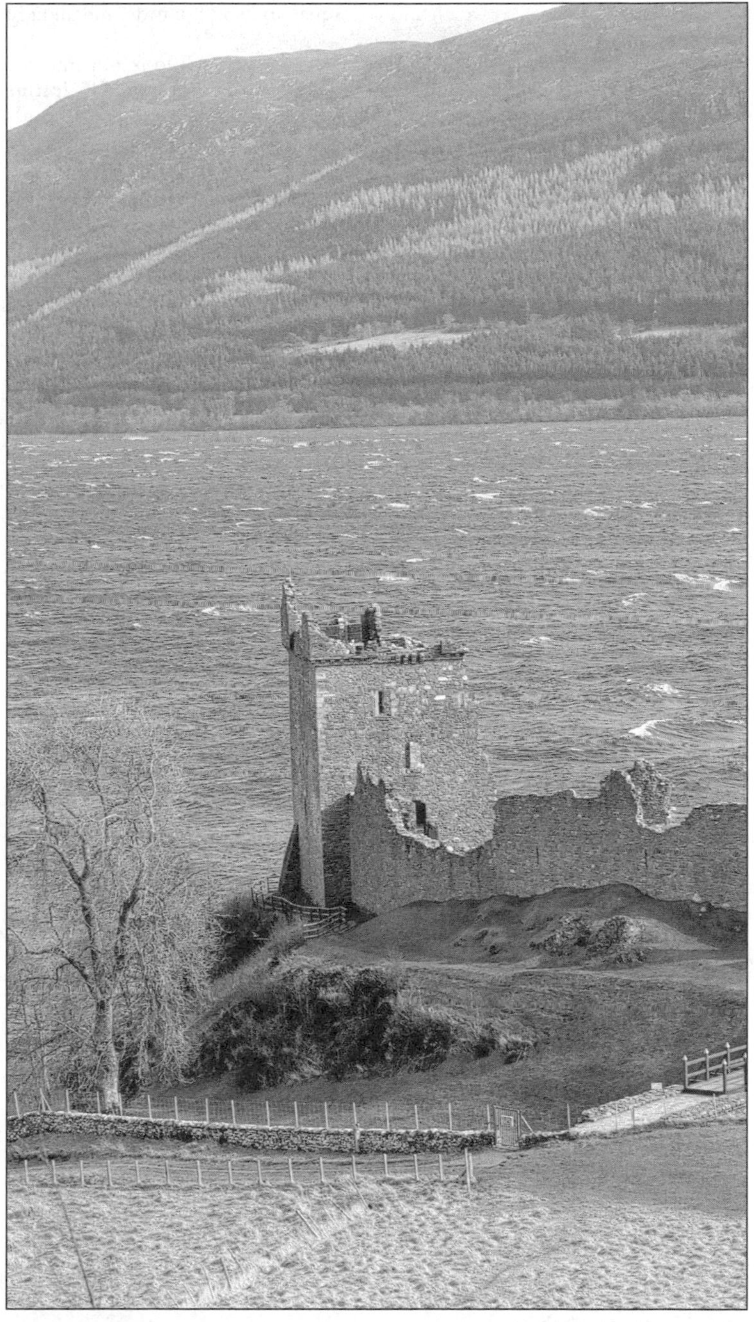

△ Castle Urquhart, Loch Ness

reading. The **chapel** is also worth a look – squat and solid outside, and all light and grace within.

Walking on the northern, grass-covered casemates, which look out into the estuary, you may be lucky enough to see the school of bottle-nosed **dolphins** (see box on p.589) swimming in with the tide. This is also a good spot for bird-watching: a colony of kittiwakes occupies the fort's slate rooftops, while the white-sand beach and mud flats below teem with waders and seabirds.

Highland **bus** #11 from Inverness post office serves the fort (Mon–Sat 9 daily; 25min).

Nairn and around

One of the driest and sunniest places in the whole of Scotland, **NAIRN**, sixteen miles east of Inverness, began its days as a peaceful community of fishermen and farmers. The former spoke Gaelic, the latter English, allowing James VI to boast that a town in his kingdom was so large that people at one end of the main street could not understand those at the other end. Nairn became popular in Victorian times, when the train line offered a convenient link to its revitalizing sea air and mild climate, and today it still relies on tourism, with all the ingredients for a traditional seaside holiday – a sandy beach, ice-cream shops and fish-and-chip stalls. It boasts two championship golf courses, and Thomas Telford's **harbour** is filled with leisure craft rather than fishing boats. Nearby, amid the huddled streets of old Fishertown – the town centre is known as new Fishertown – is the tiny **Fishertown Museum** (June–Sept Mon–Sat 10.30am–12.30pm; free), signposted from the town centre and the harbour. The more interesting exhibits focus on the parsimonious and puritanical life of the fishing families. The larger **Nairn Museum** (May–Sept Mon–Sat 10am–4.30pm; £1) at Viewfield House, up Viewfield Drive from the tourist office, gives a more general insight into the history and prehistory of the area.

With a good map to help navigate the maze of minor roads, you can explore some pleasant countryside south of Nairn, particularly in the valley of the **River Findhorn**, with **Dulsie Bridge**, on the old military road linking Perth and Fort George, being a favourite local picnic spot. A few miles farther south, the waters of **Lochindorb** surround a ruined thirteenth-century castle. The relative flatness of the land makes these roads ideal for cycling; a bike is also a great way to explore **Culbin Forest**, an unusual area of coastal forest north-east of Nairn where the trees were planted to stabilize an extensive area of sand dune. The forest, a Site of Special Scientific Interest, has a network of paths and information boards, along with picnic spots and plenty of wildlife, including an array of migrating water fowl at the adjacent RSPB reserve of Culbin Sands.

Nairn's helpful **tourist office** is at 62 King St (June–Aug daily 9am–6pm; Easter–May, Sept & Oct Mon–Sat 10am–5pm; ⓣ01667/452753). For **accommodation**, try Ben & Iris Murray at 53 King St in Old Fishertown (ⓣ01667/453798; ❶), whose small B&B is welcoming and refreshingly kitsch-free. *Greenlawns*, 13 Seafield St (ⓣ01667/452738, ⓦwww.greenlawns.uk.com; ❷), is a spacious and friendly B&B with most rooms en suite. The *Golf View Hotel* (ⓣ01667/452301, ⓦwww.morton-hotels.com; ❽), overlooks the sea (and, unsurprisingly, the golf course) and serves meals in its restaurant and conservatory. The more down-to-earth *Longhouse Restaurant* (ⓣ01667/455532) on the corner of Harbour Street and Watson's Place, serves big portions of appetizing seafood and many other dishes. **Bike rental** is available from Nairn Watersports (ⓣ01667/455416) down by the harbour, and there's an **internet café**, Nexus, on High St.

West of Inverness

West of Inverness, the Moray Firth becomes the **Beauly Firth**, a sheltered sea loch bounded by the Black Isle in the north and the wooded hills of the Aird to the south. At the head of the firth is the medieval village of **Beauly**, seat of the colourful Lovat clan, with the small settlement of **Muir of Ord**, known for its whisky, close by. Most northbound traffic uses Kessock Bridge to cross the Moray Firth from Inverness, so this whole area is quieter, and the A862, which skirts the shoreline and the mud flats, offers a more scenic alternative to the faster A9.

Beauly and around

The sleepy stone-built village of **BEAULY** lies ten miles west of Inverness, at the point where the Beauly River – one of Scotland's most renowned salmon-fishing streams – flows into the Firth. It's ranged around a single main street that widens into a spacious marketplace, at the north end of which stand the skeletal red sandstone remains of **Beauly Priory** (daily 9.30am–6pm; HS; £1.20). Founded in 1230 by the Bisset family for the Valliscaulian order, and later becoming Cistercian, it was destroyed during the Reformation and is now in ruins.

The locals will tell you the name Beauly was bestowed on the village by Mary, Queen of Scots, who, when staying at the priory in the summer of 1564, allegedly cried, *"Ah, que beau lieu!"* ("What a beautiful place!"). In fact, the description "beau lieu" was bestowed by the Lovat family, who came to the region from France with the Normans in the eleventh century. Among the more notorious members of this dynasty was Lord Simon Lovat, whose legendary misadventures included a kidnap attempt on a nine-year-old girl, followed by forced marriage to her mother. He was outlawed for this, but went on to play an active role in the Jacobite uprisings, expediently swapping sides whenever the one he was spying for looked likely to lose. Such chicanery earned him the nickname "The Old Fox of '45", but failed to save him from the chop: Lovat was eventually beheaded in London (ironically enough for backing the wrong side at Culloden). The Victorian **monument** in the square, opposite the Priory, commemorates the more illustrious career of one of Simon Lovat's descendants, Simon Joseph, the sixteenth Lord Lovat, who founded a fighting unit during the Boer War.

Beauly has a surprising number of **places to stay**. The most comfortable is the modern *Priory Hotel* (Ⓣ01463/782309, Ⓦwww.priory-hotel.com; ❺) at the top of town, which also has a good restaurant. The *Lovat Arms Hotel* (Ⓣ01463/782313, Ⓔlovat.arms@cali.co.uk; ❹), at the opposite end of the main street, is a more traditional option and hosts occasional ceilidhs. If you're looking for something cheaper, try the *Heathmount Guest House* (Ⓣ01463/782411; ❷), one of several pleasant **B&Bs** in a row of large Victorian houses just south of the *Lovat* on the main road.

Finding somewhere to **eat** isn't a problem. Both of the town's hotels sport pricey à la carte restaurants, while the *Archdale Hotel's* cosy café, at the bottom of the square, serves a range of inexpensive snacks and main meals, including several vegetarian specialities. Otherwise, head for the *Beauly Tandoori*, which dishes up moderately priced Indian food, or the *Friary* chippy; both are on the main square.

Around Beauly

Muir of Ord, a sprawling village four miles north of Beauly, is visited in huge numbers for the **Glen Ord Distillery** (March–Oct Mon–Fri 9.30am–5pm; July–Sept also Sat 9.30am–5pm & Sun 12.30–5pm; £3), on its northern outskirts. Its well-laid-out visitor centre explains the mysteries of whisky production with a tour that winds up in the cellars, where you get to sample a selection of the famously peaty Glen Ord malts, most of which find their way into well-known blends on sale in the distillery shop. To get to Ord take the Stagecoach Inverness **bus** #19 from Union Street in Inverness, which travels via Beauly (Mon–Sat hourly); more helpfully, the **train** from Inverness stops at Muir of Ord station (Mon–Sat 6–7 daily; June–Sept also Sun, 4 daily; 15min).

If you want to find out more about the colourful Lovats and other scions of the Fraser clan, head to the restored **Wardlaw Mausoleum** at **Kirkhill**, about four miles east of Beauly signposted off the main A862 Inverness road (May–Sept Wed & Sat 2–4pm; free), which was built in 1634 but includes a fourteenth-century window from a church previously built on the site.

As a change from distilleries, you can visit a **winery** at **Moniack Castle** (March–Oct Mon–Sat 10am–5pm; Nov–Feb Mon–Sat 11am–4pm; £2), also four miles east of Beauly, just off the A862, where you can taste and buy over 25 different home-made products, including silver-birch or meadowsweet wine, sloeberry liqueur, juniper chutney and rosehip jam.

Strathspey and the Cairngorms

Rising high in the heather-clad hills above remote Loch Laggan, forty miles due south of Inverness, the **River Spey**, Scotland's second longest river, drains northeast towards the Moray Firth through one of the Highlands' most spellbinding valleys. Famous for its **ancient forests**, **salmon fishing** and **ospreys**, Strathspey describes the broad river valley between the rolling Monadhliath mountains and the ice-sculpted **Cairngorm** massif. The Cairngorm range, Britain's most extensive mountainous massif, unique in supporting subarctic tundra on its high plateau, is scheduled to become Scotland's second **national park** some time in 2002. Note that Strathspey is distinct from Speyside, located further downstream to the north and famous for its whiskies, which is described on p.557.

Outdoor enthusiasts flock to Strathspey year-round to take advantage of the superb hiking, watersports and winter snows, aided by the fact that the area is easily accessible from both the Central Belt and Inverness by road and rail. Of Strathspey's scattered settlements, **Aviemore** absorbs the largest number of visitors, particularly in midwinter when it metamorphoses into the UK's busiest ski resort. The village itself isn't up to much, but the 4000ft summit plateau of the Cairngorm is often snowcapped, providing stunning mountain scenery on a grand scale. The planned Georgian town of **Grantown-on-Spey** makes a good alternative base for summer visitors, with similar facilities and more charm than Aviemore. Further upriver, the sedate towns of **Kingussie** and **Newtonmore** are older-established holiday centres, popular more with anglers and grouse hunters than canoeists and climbers. Rather unusually for Scotland, the area boasts a wide choice of good-quality accommodation, particularly in the budget market, with various easygoing hostels run by and for outdoor enthusiasts.

Aviemore and around

The once-sleepy village of **AVIEMORE** was first developed as a ski and tourism resort in the mid-1960s and, over the years, it fell victim to profiteering developers with scant regard for the needs of the local community. Although a large-scale facelift has removed some of the architectural eyesores of that era, the settlement remains dominated by a string of soulless shopping centres and fairly tacky shops surrounding an attractive Victorian railway station. That said,

Walks around Aviemore

Ordnance Survey Landranger Map No. 36.

Walking of all grades is a highlight of the Aviemore area, though before setting out you should heed the usual safety guidelines (see p.46). These are particularly important if you want to climb to the high tops, which include a number of Scotland's loftiest peaks. However, as well as the high mountain trails, there are some lovely and well-signposted **low-level walks** in the area. It takes an hour or so to complete the gentle circular walk around pretty **Loch an Eilean** (with its ruined castle) in the Rothiemurchus Estate, beginning at the end of the back road that turns east off the B970 two miles south of Aviemore. The helpful estate **visitor centres** at the loch-side and by the roadside at Inverdruie provide more information on the many woodland trails that crisscross this area. A longer walk through this estate, famous for its atmospheric native woodland of gnarled Caledonian pines and shimmering birch trees, starts at the near end of **Loch Morlich**. Cross the river by the bridge and follow the dirt road, turning off after about twenty minutes to follow the signs to Aviemore. The path goes through beautiful pine woods and past tumbling burns, and you can branch off to Coylumbridge and Loch an Eilean. Unless you're properly prepared for a 25-mile hike, don't take the track to the **Lairig Ghru**, a famous old cattle drovers' route through a dramatic cleft in the mountain range which eventually brings you out near Braemar on the far side of the Cairngorm range.

Another good shortish (half-day) walk leads along a well-surfaced forestry track from *Glenmore Lodge* up towards the **Ryvoan Pass**, taking in An Lochan Uaine, known as the "Green Loch" and living up to its name, with amazing colours that range from turquoise to slate grey depending on the weather. The track narrows once past the loch and leads east towards Deeside, so retrace your steps if you don't want a major trek. The **Glenmore Forest Park Visitor Centre** by the roadside at the turn-off to *Glenmore Lodge* is the starting point for the 3-hour round-trip climb of Meall a' Bhuachallie (2654ft), which offers excellent views and is usually accessible year-round. The centre has information on other trails in this section of the forest.

The **Speyside Way** (see p.558), the long-distance footpath which begins on the Moray Firth coast at Buckie and follows the course of the Spey through the heart of whisky country, has recently been extended to Aviemore. A pleasant day-trip involves walking from Aviemore to Boat of Garten, on to the RSPB osprey sanctuary at Loch Garten, and return on the Strathspey Steam Railway.

Aviemore is well equipped with services and facilities for visitors to the area and is the most convenient base for the Cairngorms, benefits which for most folk far outweigh its lack of aesthetic appeal

The main attractions of Aviemore are its outdoor pursuits, though train enthusiasts are drawn to the restored **Strathspey Steam Railway**, which chugs the short distance between Aviemore and Boat of Garten village five times daily through the summer (June–Sept; less regular service at other times; call ⓣ01479/810725 for details). Another unusual form of transportation is the **Cairngorm funicular railway** (every 10–20min; £7.50), which in 2001 replaced the main chairlift as the principal means of transportation to the top of the ski area. A highly controversial £15 million scheme, it whisks skiers in winter, and tourists in summer, from the Coire Cas car park up to an altitude of 3600 feet. At the top is an exhibition/interpretation area and restaurant from which spectacular views can be had on clear days, though you should note that there is no access beyond the confines of the centre and its open-air viewing terrace unless you're embarking on winter skiing; anyone wanting to walk on the subarctic Cairngorm plateau will have to trudge up from the car park at the bottom.

Summer activities

In summer, the main activities around Aviemore are **walking** (see box on p.595) and **watersports**, though there are great opportunities to do most things from mountain biking to fly-fishing. There are two centres that offer sailing, windsurfing and canoeing: the Loch Morlich Watersports Centre (ⓣ01479/861221, ⓦwww.aviemore.co.uk/lochmorlich), at the east end of the loch five miles or so east of Aviemore, rents equipment and offers tuition in a lovely setting with a sandy beach, while six miles up-valley near Kincraig, the Loch Insh Watersports Centre (see p.599) offers the same facilities in equally beautiful surroundings. It also rents mountain bikes, boats for loch fishing, and gives ski instruction on a 164ft dry slope.

Riding and **pony trekking** are on offer up and down the valley: try Ingrid at Alvie Stables near Kincraig (ⓣ01540/651409), or the Carrbridge Trekking Centre, Station Road, Carrbridge, a few miles north of Aviemore (ⓣ01479/841602).

Fishing is very much part of the local scene; you can fish for trout and salmon on the River Spey, and the Rothiemurchus Estate has a stocked trout-fishing loch at **Inverdruie**, where success is virtually guaranteed. Instruction and rod rental is available from the centre beside the loch. Fishing permits cost around £5–15 per day to fish a stocked loch and £25 on the Spey itself, and are sold at Speyside Sports in Aviemore and at Loch Morlich Watersports Centre (see above), which also rents rods and tackle. The Aviemore tourist office has a helpful brochure on the complex series of permits required for the different lochs and waters in the Strathspey area.

The area is also great for **mountain biking**, with both Rothiemurchus and Glenmore estates more progressive in their attitude to the sport than many. The Rothiemurchus visitor centre at Inverdruie has route maps, and you can also rent bikes here, while Bothy Bikes (ⓣ01479/810111), in the Aviemore Shopping Centre beside the train station on Grampian Road, rents out good-quality mountain bikes with front suspension, as well as offering advice and guided bike tours. For other outdoor equipment, in particular **climbing** and **hill-walking** gear, try Mountain Supplies in Aviemore (ⓣ01479/810903).

Winter activities

Scottish **skiing** on a commercial level first really took off in Aviemore. By continental European and North American standards it's all on a tiny scale, but occasionally snow, sun and lack of crowds coincide and you can have a great day. February and March are usually the best times, but there's a chance of decent snow at any time between mid-November and April. Lots of places – not just in Aviemore itself – sell or rent equipment; for a rundown of ski schools and rental facilities in the area, check out the tourist office's *Ski Scotland* brochure or Ⓦwww.ski.scotland.net.

The **Cairngorm Ski Area**, about eight miles southeast of Aviemore, above Loch Morlich in Glen More Forest Park, is well served during winter by buses from Aviemore. You can rent skis, boards and other equipment from the Day Lodge at the foot of the ski area (Ⓣ01479/861261, Ⓦwww.cairngormmountain.com), which also has a shop, a bar and restaurant, and the base station for the **funicular railway**, the principal means of getting to the top of the ski slopes. Various types of ski pass are available from here – in person, by phone or online. If there's lots of snow, the area around **Loch Morlich** and into the **Rothiemurchus Estate** provides enjoyable cross-country skiing through lovely woods, beside rushing burns and even over frozen lochs.

For a crash-course in surviving Scottish winters, you could do worse than try a week at the National Outdoor Training Centre at *Glenmore Lodge* (see below) in the heart of the Glenmore Forest Park at the east end of Loch Morlich. This superbly equipped and organized centre offers winter and summer courses in hill-walking, mountaineering, alpine ski-mountaineering, avalanche awareness and much besides, including an array of more recreational courses in kayaking, abseiling and the like. To add to the winter scene, there's a herd of **reindeer** at The Reindeer Centre by Loch Morlich (daily 10am–5pm; £1.50), and the Siberian Husky Club holds its races in the area.

Practicalities

Aviemore's businesslike **tourist office** is just south of the train station on the main drag, Grampian Road (April–Oct Mon–Fri 9am–5.30pm, Sat 10am–5pm, Sun 10am–4pm; Nov–March Mon–Fri 9am–5pm, Sat 10am–5pm; Ⓣ01479/810363). It offers an accommodation booking service and reams of leaflets on local attractions. The cheapest **internet access** in town is at Chill, close to the tourist office, while Baztex computer shop, the *Cairngorm Hotel* and the SYHA hostel also offer public facilities.

Accommodation

There's no shortage of **accommodation** locally. On Grampian Road in Aviemore, *MacKenzies Hotel* (Ⓣ01479/810672, Ⓔmackhotel@aol.com; ❷) is welcoming and family-friendly, while *Ravenscraig* (Ⓣ01479/810278, Ⓔravenscraig@aol.com; ❷) offers similarly good value. The grandest place in the area is *Corrour House Hotel* at Inverdruie, two miles southeast of Aviemore (Ⓣ01479/810220, Ⓦwww.corrourhousehotel.com; ❺).

Aviemore's large SYHA **hostel** (Ⓣ01479/810345, Ⓦwww.syha.org.uk; £13.25), is close to the tourist office, while the bunkhouse above Mountain Supplies in the centre of Aviemore (Ⓣ01479/810903, Ⓦwww.mountainman.co.uk) has good facilities and no curfew. Towards the Cairngorms, there's another SYHA hostel at Loch Morlich (Ⓣ01479/861238, Ⓦwww.syha.org.uk), as well as excellent accommodation in twin rooms (with shared facilities) at *Glenmore Lodge* (Ⓣ01479/861276, Ⓦwww.glenmorelodge.org.uk; ❶) – full use of their superb facilities, which include a pool, weights room and indoor climbing wall is included. There's no shortage of **campsites** either: two of the best are the Campgrounds of Scotland site at Coylumbridge (☎01479/812800) and the Forestry Enterprise site at Glenmore (☎01479/861271).

Eating and drinking

All Aviemore's hotels serve run-of-the-mill bar **food**, but for a more interesting option head to *The Old Bridge Inn* on the east side of the railway, below the bridge, which serves delicious meals and real ales in a mellow, cosy setting, or *Café Mambo*, in Aviemore Shopping Centre on Grampian Road, with its bright, funky decor and cheerful burger'n'chips-style menu. Also on the main road, the *Winking Owl* has a beer garden that's a pleasant spot for a **drink** on a summer evening.

Carrbridge

Worth considering as an alternative to Aviemore – particularly as a skiing base – **CARRBRIDGE** is a pleasant, quiet village about seven miles north. Its main attraction is the **Landmark Forest Heritage Park** (daily: April to mid-July 10am–6pm; mid-July to Aug 10am–7pm; Sept–March 10am–5pm; £6.85), which combines interactive exhibitions with forest walks, nature trails, a maze and fun rides; it's more tastefully done than some similar places and an excellent place for children to let off steam. Carrbridge has some decent **accommodation** options, including *Carrmoor* B&B (☎01479/841244, ⓔcarrmoor.gh@lineone.net; ❶) and the friendly *Cairn Hotel* (☎01479/841212; ❷). The cosy, basic *Carrbridge Bunkhouse* (☎01479/841250, ⓔjonesbunk@aol.com), which has its own sauna, is a good base for walkers half a mile or so north of the village on the Inverness road.

Loch Garten and around

The **Abernethy Forest RSPB Reserve** on the shore of **LOCH GARTEN**, seven miles northeast of Aviemore and eight miles south of Grantown-on-Spey, is famous as the nesting site of one of Britain's rarest birds. A little over fifty years ago, the **osprey**, known in North America as the fish hawk, had completely disappeared from the British Isles. Then, in 1954, a single pair of these exquisite white-and-brown raptors mysteriously reappeared and built a nest in a tree half a mile or so from the loch. Although efforts were made to keep the exact location secret, one year's eggs fell victim to a gang of thieves, and thereafter the area became the centre of an effective high-security operation. Now the birds are well established not only here but elsewhere, and there are believed to be up to 150 pairs nesting across the Highlands. The best time to visit is between late April and August, when the ospreys return from West Africa to nest and the RSPB opens an **observation centre** (daily 10am–6pm; £2.50), complete with powerful telescopes and CCTV monitoring of the nest. This is the place to come to get a glimpse of osprey chicks in their nest; you'll be luckier to see the birds perform their trademark swoop over water to pluck a fish out with their talons, though nearby Loch Garten, as well as Loch Morlich and Loch Insh, are good places to stake out in the hope of a sighting, while one of the best spots is the Rothiemurchus trout loch at Inverdruie. The reserve is also home to several other species of rare birds and animals, including the Scottish crossbill, capercaillie, whooper swan and red squirrel; once-weekly **guided walks** leave from the observation centre (Wed 9.30am).

Loch Garten is about a mile and a half west of **BOAT OF GARTEN** village: from the village, if you cross the Spey then take the Grantown road, the reserve is signposted to the right. Boat of Garten has a couple of good **accommodation** options: *Fraoch Lodge*, 15 Deshar Rd (Ⓣ01479/831331, Ⓦwww.scotmountain.co.uk) is an excellent hostel with bunkhouse and twin rooms (❶), and provides high quality home-cooked meals along with good facilities. It is enthusiastically run by experienced mountaineers, who also offer tailor-made tours of the Highlands that combine self-drive and guided options in your own rental car. Alternatively, *Craigard House Hotel* (Ⓣ01479/831423; ❸) offers stylish accommodation in an old hunting lodge, and includes a restaurant serving local game and fish which is open to non-residents.

Kincraig

At **KINCRAIG**, six miles southwest of Aviemore on the B9152 towards Kingussie, there are a couple of unusual encounters with animals which offer a memorable diversion if you're not setting off on outdoor pursuits. While the style of the **Highland Wildlife Park** (daily: June–Aug 10am–7pm; April, May, Sept & Oct closes 6pm; Nov–March closes 4pm; last entry 2hr before closing; in snowy conditions call in advance; Ⓣ01540/651270; £6.50), with its various captive animals, may not appeal to everyone, it is accredited to the Royal Zoological Society of Scotland and offers a chance to see exotic foreigners such as wolves and bison, as well as many rarely seen natives, including pine martens, capercaillie, wildcat and eagles. Nearby, the engrossing **Working Sheepdogs** show at Leault Farm (open daily; call Ⓣ01540/651310 for the schedule of demonstrations; £3.50) offers the rare opportunity to see a champion shepherd demonstrate how to herd a flock of sheep with up to eight dogs, using whistles and other commands. The fascinating hour-long display also includes geese-herding, a chance to see traditional hand-shearing, and displays on how collie pups are trained.

There are some good low-price **accommodation** options nearby. The Loch Insh Watersports Centre (Ⓣ01540/651272, Ⓦwww.lochinsh.com), beautifully sited beside the loch, has en-suite B&B and self-catering chalets (❶) as well as a handy waterfront café. At the *Glen Feshie Hostel* at Balachroick on the hillside above Loch Insh (Ⓣ01540/651323), the all-in price includes bed linen and as much porridge as you like for breakfast.

Grantown-on-Spey

Buses run from Aviemore and Inverness to the small town of **GRANTOWN-ON-SPEY**, about fifteen miles northeast of Aviemore, which makes a relaxing alternative base for exploring the Strathspey area. Life is concentrated around the central square, with its attractive Georgian architecture, including a small **museum** and resource centre on Burnfield Avenue (Mon–Fri 10am–4pm; £2; Ⓦwww.grantown-on-spey.co.uk) which tells the story of the town; it also offers **internet access** and maintains a useful local website. The **tourist office** is on the High Street (April–Oct Mon–Fri 9am–5pm, Sat 10am–5pm, Sun 10am–4pm; Ⓣ01479/872773). Logan's Bike Hire is on High St (Ⓣ01479/872197), while, for courses in hillwalking, climbing, canoeing and cycling, contact the Ardenbeg Outdoor Centre (Ⓣ01479/872824, Ⓦwww.ardenbeg.co.uk), on Grant Road, parallel to the High Street.

As with much of Speyside, there's a decent choice of **accommodation**. For B&B, *Parkburn Guest House* (Ⓣ01479/873116; ❷) is welcoming, while, if you're after something more upmarket, head for the large seventeenth-century *Garth Hotel*, at the north end of the square (Ⓣ01479/872836; ❸) or the smart

Auchendean Lodge Hotel (☎01479/851347; ❺), three miles southeast of Grantown near Dulnain Bridge, best known for its gourmet meals. In the budget range, *Speyside Backpackers* at The Stopover, 16 The Square (☎01479/873514, ⓦwww.scotpackers-hostels.co.uk) has dorms and doubles (❶) with excellent facilities, while a mile or two south of town at Nethy Bridge, between Grantown and Boat of Garten, is the *Lazy Duck Hostel* (☎01479/821642, ⓦwww.lazyduck.co.uk), a peaceful and comfortable retreat with great moorland walking on its doorstep.

Both the *Garth* and *Tyree House* hotels have good **restaurants** that serve Scottish-style menus. To eat out in style, head for the *Auchendean Lodge Hotel* (see above) near Dulnain Bridge, where the highly rated meals sometimes include locally collected mushrooms.

Newtonmore and Kingussie

Twelve miles south of Aviemore, close neighbours **NEWTONMORE** and **KINGUSSIE** (pronounced "king-*yoos*-ee") are pleasant towns at the head of the Strathspey Valley separated by a couple of miles of farmland. On the **shinty** field, however, their peaceful coexistence is forgotten and the two become bitter rivals; in recent years Kingussie have been the dominant force in the game, a fierce, home-grown relative of hockey (see p.44; ⓦwww.kingussie.co.uk/shinty).

The chief attraction here is the excellent **Highland Folk Museum** (☎01540/661307), split between complementary sites in the two towns. The Kingussie section (April–Sept Mon–Sat 9.30am–5.30pm; winter by appointment; £1 admission covers both sites) contains an absorbing collection of artefacts typical to traditional Highland ways of life, as well as a farming museum, an old smokehouse, a mill, a Hebridean "blackhouse", and a traditional herb and flower garden; most days in summer there's a demonstration of various traditional crafts. The larger outdoor site at Newtonmore (April–Aug daily 10.30am–5.30pm; Sept & Oct Mon–Fri 11am–4.30pm; call for details of weekend opening at other times), tries to create more of a living history museum, with reconstructions of a working croft, a church where recitals on traditional Highland instruments are given through the summer months, and a small village of blackhouses constructed using only authentic tools and materials.

Kingussie is also notable for the ruins of **Ruthven Barracks** (free access), standing east across the river on a hillock. The best-preserved garrison built to pacify the Highlands after the 1715 rebellion, it makes for great exploring by day and is impressively floodlit at night. Taken by the Jacobites in 1744, Ruthven was blown up in the wake of Culloden to prevent it from falling into enemy hands. It was also the place from where clan leader Lord George Murray dispatched his acrimonious letter to Bonnie Prince Charlie, holding him personally responsible for the string of blunders that had precipitated their defeat. Of a rather different tone is Newtonmore's **Waltzing Waters** aqua theatre (daily 10am–4pm; £4), a "water, light and music spectacular" which is popular with coach parties but definitely not for the weak-bladdered.

Practicalities

Kingussie's friendly **tourist office** is in the same building as the entrance to the Highland Folk Museum, on Duke Street (same hours as museum; ☎01540/661297). The Wildcat Centre in Newtonmore (Mon–Fri 9.30am–12.30pm & 2.15–5.15pm, Sat 9.30am–12.30pm) also offers local information and details of walking trails in the area. Bike rental is available at

Cairngorm Mountain Tours in Newtonmore. *Dunmhor House* (ⓣ01540/661809; ❶) is a good-value **B&B** on the main street in Kingussie, while the *Auld Poor House* (ⓣ01540/661558, ⓦwww.yates128.freeserve.co.uk), on the road to Kincraig, is a comfortable B&B with a resident qualified masseuse. The best of the local **hostels** are the *Newtonmore Independent Hostel* (ⓣ01540/673360, ⓦwww.highlandhostel.co.uk), a welcoming and well-equipped place, and the *Strathspey Mountain Hostel* (ⓣ01540/673694), just up the road, which is also of high standard. Of the **hotels**, the *Scot House* in Kingussie (ⓣ01540/661351, ⓦwww.scothouse.com; ❹) is known for its hospitality and restaurant.

The most ambitious **food** in the area is served at *The Cross* restaurant, in a converted tweed mill on Tweed Mill Brae in Kingussie (ⓣ01540/661166, ⓦwww.thecross.co.uk; closed Tues & Dec–Feb). Its pricey meals make interesting use of local ingredients and there's a vast wine list; they also have several rooms for half board (❾). Cheaper food is available at several cafés and pubs in both towns – *The Glen* or the *Brae Riach* in Newtonmore, or the *Royal Hotel* or *Tipsy Laird* in Kingussie. The *Capercaillie* restaurant on the main street in Newtonmore serves tasty Italian and Scottish cuisine. *La Cafetière* in Kingussie has excellent coffee, with good home baking, soup, toasties and baked potatoes, while *The Pantry* serves similarly comforting fare on the main road in Newtonmore.

The Great Glen

The **Great Glen**, cutting diagonally across the Highlands from Fort William to Inverness, follows a major geological fault line. This huge rift valley was formed when the northwestern and southeastern sides slid against each other along the fault for more than sixty miles, and were later smoothed by glaciers that only retreated around 8000 BC. The glen is impressive more for its sheer scale than its great beauty, but is an obvious and rewarding route between the east and west coast.

Of the Great Glen's four elongated lochs, the most famous is **Loch Ness**, home to the mythical monster; lochs **Oich**, **Lochy** and **Linnhe** (the last of these a sea loch) are less renowned though no less attractive. All four are linked by the **Caledonian Canal**, surveyed by James Watt in 1773 and completed in the early 1800s by Thomas Telford to enable ships to pass between the North Sea and the Atlantic without having to navigate Scotland's treacherous northern coast. Only 22 miles of it are *bona fide* canal – the remaining 38 exploit the glen's natural lochs and west-flowing rivers.

The traditional and most rewarding way to travel through the glen is by **boat**. A flotilla of kayaks, small yachts and pleasure vessels take advantage of the canal and its old wooden locks during the summer, among them Jacobite Cruises (see p.581 for details). Forest Enterprise (ⓣ01320/366322) has also established an excellent **cycle path** through the glen, divided into twelve manageable stages that follow winding timber trails, towpaths and stretches of minor roads, making a tranquil alternative to the traffic-choked A82; a leaflet outlining the route is available at most tourist offices or direct from Forest Enterprise. Following a broadly similar route is a long-distance footpath, the seventy-mile **Great Glen Way**, which takes between five and seven days to walk in full, details of which can be had from tourist offices or Scottish Natural Heritage (ⓣ01463/712221). In addition, the Great Glen is reasonably well served by **buses**, with several daily services between Inverness and Fort William, and a couple of extra buses covering the section between Fort William and Invergarry during school terms.

Loch Ness and around

Twenty-three miles long, unfathomably deep, cold and often moody, **Loch Ness** is bounded by rugged heather-clad mountains rising steeply from a wooded shoreline and attractive valleys opening up on either side. Its fame, however, is based overwhelmingly on its legendary inhabitant Nessie, the "Loch Ness monster", whose fame ensures a steady flow of hopeful visitors to the settlements dotted along the loch, in particular **Drumnadrochit**. Nearby, the impressive ruins of **Castle Urquhart** – a favourite monster-spotting location – perch atop a rock on the loch-side and attract a deluge of bus parties during the summer. Almost as busy in high season is the village of **Fort Augustus**, at the more scenic southwest tip of Loch Ness, where you can watch queues of boats tackling one of the Caledonian Canal's longest flight of locks.

Away from the lochside, and seeing a fraction of Loch Ness's visitor numbers, the remote **glens** of **Urquhart** and **Affric** make an appealing contrast, with Affric in particular boasting narrow, winding roads, gushing streams and hillsides dotted in ancient Caledonian pine forests. More commonly encountered is the often bleak high country of **Glen Moriston**, a little to the southwest of Glen Affric, which holds the main road between Inverness and Skye.

Although most visitors use the tree-lined A82 road, which runs along the western shore of Loch Ness, the sinuous single-track B862/B852 (originally a military road built to link Fort Augustus and Fort George) that skirts the eastern shore is quieter and affords far more spectacular views. However, buses from Inverness along this road only run as far south as **Foyers**, so you'll need your own transport to complete the whole loop around the loch, a journey which includes a most impressive stretch between Fort Augustus and the high, hidden **Loch Mhor**, overlooked by the imposing Monadhliath range to the south.

Drumnadrochit and around

Situated above a verdant, sheltered bay of Loch Ness fifteen miles southwest of Inverness, **DRUMNADROCHIT** is the epicentre of Nessie hype, sporting a rash of tacky souvenir shops and two rival monster exhibitions whose head-to-head scramble for punters occasionally erupts into acrimonious exchanges, detailed with relish by the local press. Of the pair, the **Loch Ness 2000 Exhibition**, formerly the Official Loch Ness Monster Exhibition (daily: July & Aug 9am–8pm; June & Sept 9am–6pm; Easter–May 9.30am–5pm; Oct–Easter 10am–4pm; £5.95), though more expensive, is the better bet, offering an in-depth rundown of eyewitness accounts through the ages and mock-ups of the various research projects carried out in the loch. A recent upgrade has attempted to offer something to sceptics as well as believers by outlining more of the scientific background to set against the various myths.

Nessie

The world-famous **Loch Ness monster**, affectionately known as "**Nessie**" (and by serious aficionados as *Nessiteras rhombopteryx*), has been a local celebrity for some time. The first mention of a mystery creature crops up in St Adamnan's seventh-century biography of **St Columba**, who allegedly calmed an aquatic animal which had attacked one of his monks. Present-day interest, however, is probably greater outside Scotland than within the country, and dates from the building of the road along the loch's western shore in the early 1930s. In 1934, the *Daily Mail* published London surgeon R.K. Wilson's sensational photograph of the head and neck of the monster peering up out of the loch, and the hype has hardly diminished since. Recent encounters range from glimpses of ripples by anglers to the famous occasion in 1961 when thirty hotel guests saw a pair of humps break the water's surface and cruise for about half a mile before submerging.

Photographic evidence is showcased in the two "Monster Exhibitions" at Drumnadrochit, but the most impressive of these exhibits – including the renowned black-and-white movie footage of Nessie's humps moving across the water, and Wilson's original head and shoulders shot – have now been exposed as fakes. Indeed, in few other places on earth has watching a rather lifeless and often grey expanse of water seemed so compelling, or have floating logs, otters and boat wakes been photographed so often and with such excitement. Yet while even hi-tech sonar surveys carried out over the past two decades have failed to come up with conclusive evidence, it's hard to dismiss Nessie as pure myth. After all, no one yet knows where the unknown layers of silt and mud at the bottom of the loch begin and end: best estimates say the loch is over 750 feet deep, deeper than much of the North Sea, while others point to the possibilities of underwater caves and undiscovered channels connected to the sea. What scientists have found in the cold, murky depths, including pure white eels and rare Arctic char, offer fertile grounds for speculation, with different theories declaring Nessie to be a remnant from the dinosaur age, a giant newt or a huge visiting Baltic sturgeon. With the possibility of a definitive answer sending shivers through the local tourist industry, monster-hunters are these days recruited over the web, with the site ®www.lochness.scotland.net offering a list of the latest sightings as well as round-the-clock **web-cams** offering views both across the loch and underwater.

The **Original Loch Ness Monster Exhibition** (daily: July & Aug 9am–9pm; rest of year 10am–6pm; Dec–March closes 4pm; £3.50) is less worthwhile – basically a gift shop with a shoddy audiovisual show tacked on the side.

Cruises on the loch aboard the *Nessie Hunter* (Easter–Oct hourly 9.30am–6pm; 50min; £8) can be booked at the Original Loch Ness Visitor Centre, though a more relaxing alternative is to head out **fishing** with a local gillie – the boat can take 5–8 people and costs around £30 for two hours; contact Bruce on ®01456/450279 to book. If you want to turn your back on all the hype and enjoy the surrounding scenery, you could opt for the well-run **pony trekking** available at the Highland Riding Centre (®01456/450220), at Borlum Farm, just before you get to Castle Urquhart.

Castle Urquhart

Most photographs allegedly showing the monster have been taken a couple of miles east of Drumnadrochit, around the fourteenth-century ruined lochside **Castle Urquhart** (daily: July & Aug 9.30am–8.30pm; April–June & Sept 9.30am–6.30pm; Oct–March 9.30am–4.30pm; HS; £3.80). Built as a strategic base to guard the Great Glen, the castle played an important role in the Wars of Independence. It was taken by Edward I of England and later held by Robert the Bruce against Edward III, only to be blown up in 1692 to prevent it from falling to the Jacobites. Today it's one of Scotland's classic picture-postcard ruins, crawling with tourists by day but particularly splendid floodlit at night when all the crowds have gone. The castle receives more visitors each year than any other historic site in the Highlands, and to cope with the numbers a new **visitor centre** has been built into the hillside, ostensibly to create sufficient parking above the castle. There's a footpath alongside the A82 road between Drumnadrochit and the castle, though the constant stream of cars, caravans and tour buses doesn't make it a particularly pleasant stroll.

Practicalities

Drumnadrochit's **tourist office** (April–Oct daily 9am–5.30pm; Nov–March Mon–Sat 9am–12.30pm; ⓣ01456/459076) shares space with a Highland Council service point in the middle of the main car park in the village. There's a good range of **accommodation** around Drumnadrochit and in the adjoining village of Lewiston. Two very welcoming **B&Bs** are *Gilliflowers* (ⓣ01456/450641, ⓔgillyflowers@cali.co.uk; ❶), a renovated farmhouse tucked away down a country lane in Lewiston, or the modern *Drumbuie* (ⓣ01456/450634, ⓔdrumbuie@amserve.net; ❶), on the northern approach to Drumnadrochit, which has great views and a resident herd of Highland cattle. **Hotels** include the pleasant and secluded *Benleva* (ⓣ01456/450288; ❸) between Lewiston and the loch. Two miles west of Drumnadrochit along the Cannich road is a particularly relaxed country-house hotel, *Polmaily House* (ⓣ01456/450343, ⓦwww.polmaily.co.uk; ❼); it's very family-friendly and there's acres of space, a swimming pool, sauna, riding, and sailing on Loch Ness. For **hostel** beds, head to the immaculate and friendly *Loch Ness Backpackers Lodge* (ⓣ01456/450807, ⓦwww.lochness-backpackers.com), at Coiltie Farmhouse in Lewiston; follow the signs to the left when coming from Drumnadrochit. As well as dorm beds, it has one double room (❶), and excellent facilities, including boat trips and recommended walks.

Most of the hotels in the area – the *Benleva* in particular – serve good bar **food**; in Drumnadrochit the *Glen Café* has a short and simple menu with basic grills, while the slightly more upmarket *Fiddlers' Café Bar*, next door to the *Glen* on the village green, offers local steaks, salmon and appetizing home-baked pizza; it also rents good-quality **mountain bikes** (ⓣ01456/450223), and provides maps and rain capes. The *Blairmore Bar*, just opposite the supermarket, also serves inexpensive pub grub and has live entertainment at weekends.

Glen Affric

Due west of Drumnadrochit is a vast area of high peaks, remote glens and few roads. The reason most folk head this way is to explore the native forests and grand mountains of **Glen Affric**, generally held as one of Scotland's most beautiful landscapes. The approach to the glen is through the small settlement of **CANNICH**, 14 miles west of Drumnadrochit on the A831 through **Glen Urquhart**, and also accessible on a direct road from Beauly near Inverness. Cannich doesn't have a great deal going for it, but you should manage to find room at either the SYHA **hostel** (ⓣ01456/415244, ⓦwww.syha.org.uk; May–Oct) or next door at the *Glen Affric Backpackers Hostel* (ⓣ01456/415263; year-round), which offers inexpensive twin or four-bed rooms. On weekdays there's a **bus** three times a day from Inverness to Cannich, but to get right into the heart of Glen Affric you'll need a car or a bike.

Glen Affric itself is an inspiring place, with a rushing river and Caledonian pine and birch woods opening out onto an island-studded loch that was considerably enlarged after the building of a **dam**, one of many hydroelectric schemes hereabouts. Hemmed in by a string of Munros, the glen is great for picnics and pottering, particularly on a calm and sunny day, when the still water reflects the islands and surrounding hills. From the car park at the head of the single-track road along the glen, 10 miles southwest of Cannich, there's a selection of **walks**: the trip round Loch Affric will take you a good five hours but captures the glen and its wildlife and woodlands in all their remote splendour.

You could also do some serious **hiking**. Munro-baggers are normally much in evidence, and it is possible to tramp 25 miles all the way through Glen Affric to Shiel Bridge, on the west coast near Kyle of Lochalsh, which takes at least two full days. The trail is easy to follow, but can get horrendously boggy if there's been a lot of rain, so allow plenty of time and take adequate wet-weather gear, as well as the relevant Ordnance Survey map. The remote but recently revamped Allt Beithe SYHA **hostel** (Ⓣ0870/155 3255, Ⓦwww.syha.org.uk; May–Oct) near the head of Glen Affric makes a convenient if primitive stopover halfway.

Invermoriston and west

Heading south along Loch Ness from Castle Urquhart, **INVERMORISTON** is a tiny, attractive village just above the loch, from where you can follow well-marked woodland trails past a series of grand waterfalls. Dr Johnson and Boswell spent a couple of nights here in 1773 planning their journey to the Hebrides; you, too, could stay at the *Glenmoriston Arms Hotel* (Ⓣ01320/351206, Ⓦwww.lochness-glenmoriston.co.uk; ❺), an old-fashioned inn with more than a hundred malt whiskies at the bar. Alternatively, the SYHA *Loch Ness Hostel* (Ⓣ01320/351274, Ⓦwww.syha.org.uk; April–Oct), three and a half miles north of Invermoriston and overlooking the loch, is a more economical base.

The A887 leads west from Invermoriston to the **west coast** (via the A87) on the main commercial route to the Skye Bridge. Rugged and somewhat awesome, the stretch through **Glen Moriston**, beside **Loch Cluanie**, has serious peaks at either side and little sign of human habitation as the road climbs. At the western end of the loch, you'll find the isolated *Cluanie Inn* (Ⓣ01463/340238; ❺), once a cosy wayfarer's refuge but now more concerned with welcoming coach parties to their adjoining craft centre. From here, the road drops gradually down **Glen Shiel** into the superb mountainscape of Kintail (see box on p.627).

Fort Augustus

FORT AUGUSTUS, a tiny village at the scenic southwestern tip of Loch Ness, was named after George II's son, the chubby lad who later became the "Butcher" Duke of Cumberland of Culloden fame; it was built as a barracks after the 1715 Jacobite rebellion. Today, it's dominated by comings and goings along the Caledonian Canal, which leaves Loch Ness here, and by its large former **Benedictine Abbey**, a campus of grey Victorian buildings founded on the site of the original fort in 1876. The abbey formerly housed a Catholic boys school and was subsequently home to a small but active community of monks. These days, there are plans to re-establish it as a visitor attraction, but for the meantime visitors can once again wander round the cloisters and grounds of the peaceful lochside building (daily 10am–4pm; £3.50).

Traditional Highland culture is the subject of the lively and informative exhibition at the **Clansmen Centre** (Easter to mid-Oct daily 10am–6pm; £3), on the banks of the canal. Guides sporting sporrans and rough woollen plaids talk you through the daily life of the region's seventeenth-century inhabitants inside a mock-up of a turf-roofed stone croft, followed by demonstrations of weaponry in the back garden. Most of the young staff work here for fun, donning kilts on their free weekends to fight mock battles with enthusiasts from other parts of the Highlands, which must be why they're so unnervingly adept at wielding broadswords. Rather more sedate is the small **Caledonian Canal Heritage Centre** (July–Sept daily 10am–5pm; Easter–June & Oct Mon–Thurs & Sun 10am–5pm; free), in Ardchattan House on the northern bank of the canal, where you can view old photographs and records about the history of the canal and watch a black-and-white film of the days when paddle boats and large barges passed through the locks every day.

Practicalities

Fort Augustus's small **tourist office** (daily: July & Aug 9am–7pm; April–June, Sept & Oct 9am–5pm; ☎01320/366367) hands out useful free maps detailing popular walks in the area. They'll also help sort out fishing permits for the loch or nearby river. The only **hostel** accommodation is at *Morag's Lodge* (☎01320/366289) above the petrol station on the Loch Ness side of town, where the atmosphere livens up with the daily arrival of backpackers' minibus tours. The *Old Pier* (☎01320/366418; ❸) is a particularly appealing B&B right on the loch at the north side of the village; there are log fires in the evenings – often very welcome even in summer – and boats and horse riding are available to guests. Of the **hotels**, try the small, friendly *Caledonian* (☎01320/366256; ❸), overlooking the abbey.

For **food**, your best bet is to head to the lively local pub, the *Lock Inn*, which has regular music and draws a mixed clientele of locals, yachties and backpackers, as does *Poachers* on the main road. The *Bothy Bite* beside the canal serves Scottish specialities, including a good range of moderately priced fish, steak and pies. There's some good **cycling** routes locally, along the Great Glen cycle route and elsewhere; the only place to rent bikes nearby is at South Laggan, eight miles or so southwest at the head of Loch Lochy, where Monster Activities (☎01809/501340) rents bikes, boats and canoes.

The east side of Loch Ness

The tranquil and scenic **east side of Loch Ness** is skirted by General Wade's old military highway, now the B862/B852. While we've described the route here from south to north, it's just as easy to follow it in the opposite direction, heading south from Inverness following signs to Dores.

From Fort Augustus, the narrow single-track road swings up, away from the lochside through the near-deserted **Stratherrick** valley, dotted with tiny lochans and flocks of shaggy sheep, before dropping down to rejoin the shores of Loch Ness at **FOYERS**, where there are numerous marked forest trails and an impressive waterfall. In the village, the friendly *Foyers House* (☎01456/486405; ❸) has B&B **accommodation**, a terrace with great views and a **restaurant** serving up local salmon, venison, rabbit and vegetarian options. Adjoining is a bunkhouse (☎01456/486623; ❶) offering dorms and doubles.

Three miles further north at **INVERFARIGAIG** – where a road up a beautiful, steep-sided river valley leads east over to Loch Mhor – stands **Boleskine House**. This was formerly the residence of the self-styled "Great Beast" of black magic, the infamous Satanist and occultist Aleister Crowley, who lived here between 1900 and 1918 amid rumours of devil worship and human sacrifice. In the 1970s, rock guitarist Jimmy Page bought the place, but sold it after the tragic death of his daughter some years later. Set back in its own grounds, the house still has a gloomy air about it, and is not open to the public.

A much warmer welcome awaits visitors at the sleepy village of **DORES**, nestled at the northeastern end of Loch Ness, where the *Dores Inn* makes a pleasant pit stop. Only nine miles southwest of Inverness, the old pub, which serves an excellent pint of "80 shilling" and inexpensive bar food, is popular with Invernessians, who trickle out here on summer evenings for a stroll along the grey-pebble beach and some monster-spotting.

Fort William and around

With its stunning position on Loch Linnhe, tucked in below the snow-streaked bulk of Ben Nevis, **FORT WILLIAM** (known by the many walkers and climbers that come here as "Fort Bill"), should be a gem. Sadly, the same lack of taste that nearly saw the town renamed "Abernevis" in the 1950s is evident in the ribbon bungalow development and ill-advised dual carriageway – complete with grubby pedestrian underpass – which have wrecked the waterfront. The main street and the little squares off it are more appealing, though occupied by some decidedly tacky tourist gift shops.

The countryside around the town is a blend of rugged mountain terrain and tranquil sea loch. Dominating the scene to the south is **Ben Nevis** – Britain's highest peak, best approached from scenic Glen Nevis. Some of the best views of "the Ben", as it's sometimes called, can be found at the Commando Memorial by **Spean Bridge**, a small village which marks the junction of the Great Glen with **Glen Roy**, which stetches east into some remote high country in the centre of Scotland. The most famous glen of all, **Glen Coe**, lies on the main A82 road half an hour's drive south of Fort William, the two separated by the coastal inlet of **Loch Leven**. Nowadays the whole area is unashamedly given over to tourism, and Fort William is swamped by bus tours throughout the summer, but, as ever in the Highlands, within a thirty-minute drive you can be totally alone.

The Nevis Range

Seven miles northeast of Fort William by the A82, on the slopes of **Aonach Mhor**, one of the high mountains abutting Ben Nevis, the **Nevis Range** (☎01397/705825, ⓦwww.nevis-range.co.uk) is, in winter, Scotland's highest ski area. All year round, however, Highland County bus #41 runs from Fort William four times a day (June–Oct) to the base station of the country's only **gondola** system (July & Aug daily 9.30am–6pm, Thurs & Fri until 8.30pm; Sept to mid-Nov & mid-Dec to June daily 10am–5pm; £6.90 return). The one-and-a-half mile gondola trip (15min), rising 2000ft, gives an easy approach to some high-level walking as well as spectacular views from the terrace of the self-service restaurant at the top station. Active Highs (☎01397/712188, ⓦwww.active-highs.co.uk) offer dual **paragliding** flights off the mountain, while Britain's only championship-grade **downhill mountain bike course**, a hair-raising 3-km route, starts at the gondola top station. There's also 25 miles of waymarked off-road bike routes on the mountainside and in the Leanachan Forest, ranging from gentle paths to cross-country scrambles. Off Beat Bikes (☎01397/704008, ⓦwww.offbeatbikes.co.uk) rent general mountain bikes as well as full-suspension bikes for the downhill course from their shops in Fort William and at the gondola base station (June–Sept).

The area has a turbulent and bloody **history**. Founded in 1655 and named in honour of William III, the town was successfully held by government troops during both of the Jacobite risings; the country to the southwest is inextricably associated with Bonnie Prince Charlie's flight after Culloden. Glen Coe is another historic site with a violent past, renowned as much for the infamous massacre of 1692 as for its magnificent scenery.

Arrival, information and accommodation

Next to each other at the north end of the High Street are the **bus station** (with services from Inverness) and the **train station** (a stop on the scenic West Highland Railway direct from Glasgow; see p.578). The busy **tourist office** is on Cameron Square, just off High Street (July & Aug Mon–Sat 9am–7pm, Sun 10am–6pm; June, Sept & Oct Mon–Sat 9am–5.30pm, Sun 10am–4pm; April & May Mon–Sat 9am–5pm, Sun 10am–4pm; Nov–March Mon–Fri 9am–5pm, Sat 10am–4pm; ☎01397/703781). They can book accommodation around the Fort William area for a £3 fee. **Mountain bikes** are available for rent at Off Beat Bikes (☎01397/704008) at 117 High St; they also have a branch open at the Nevis Range gondola base station (June–Sept) – useful should you want to explore forest tracks in that area.

Fort William's plentiful **accommodation** ranges from large luxury hotels to budget hostels and bunkhouses. Numerous B&Bs are also scattered across the town, many of them in the suburb of Corpach on the other side of Loch Linnhe, three miles along the Mallaig road (served by regular buses), where you'll also find a couple of good hostels.

Hotels and B&Bs

In town

Alexandra Milton Hotel The Parade ☎01397/702241, ⓦwww.miltonhotels.com. Established hotel right in the town centre, with well-appointed rooms and a restaurant. ❺

Bank Street Lodge Bank Street ☎01397/700070. New and slightly characterless lodge with neat doubles, twin and family rooms, all with TVs, and a very central location. Also has a couple of rooms used as four- or eight-bed dorms (£11 per person). ❶

Distillery House North Road, just north of the town centre near the junction for Glen Nevis ☎01397/700103. Very comfortable and well-equipped upper-range B&B. ❸

The Grange Grange Road ☎01397/705516. Top-grade accommodation in a striking old stone house, with four luxurious en-suite doubles and a spacious garden. Vegetarian breakfasts on request. Non-smoking. April–Oct. ❺

Rhu Mhor 42 Alma Rd ☎01397/702213, ⓦwww.rhumhor.co.uk. Congenial B&B ten minutes' walk from the town centre, offering good breakfasts; vegetarians and vegans are catered for by arrangement. ❶

St Andrews West Fassifern Road ☎01397/703038, ⓦwww.standrewsguesthouse.co.uk. Comfortable and extremely central B&B in an attractive converted granite choir school featuring various inscriptions and stained-glass windows. ❶

Out of town

Glenloy Lodge Hotel About six miles north of town on the minor road running north from Banavie ☎01397/712700. Comfortable, friendly and secluded small hotel with views across to Ben Nevis. ❹

Inverlochy Castle Two miles north of town on the A82 ☎01397/702177. A grand country house hotel set in wooded parkland; exceptional levels of service and outstanding food – but at a price. ❾

Rhiw Goch Beside Neptune's Staircase, Banavie ☎01397/772373. Modern, non-smoking villa with three twin rooms in a great situation beside the canal looking over to Ben Nevis. ❷

Hostels and campsites

In town

Calluna Heathcroft ☎01397/700451, ⓦwww.guide.u-net.com. Family-run budget self-catering flats with twin and four-person rooms and standard facilities. It can be tricky to find – though a free pick-up from town is available. The owner is

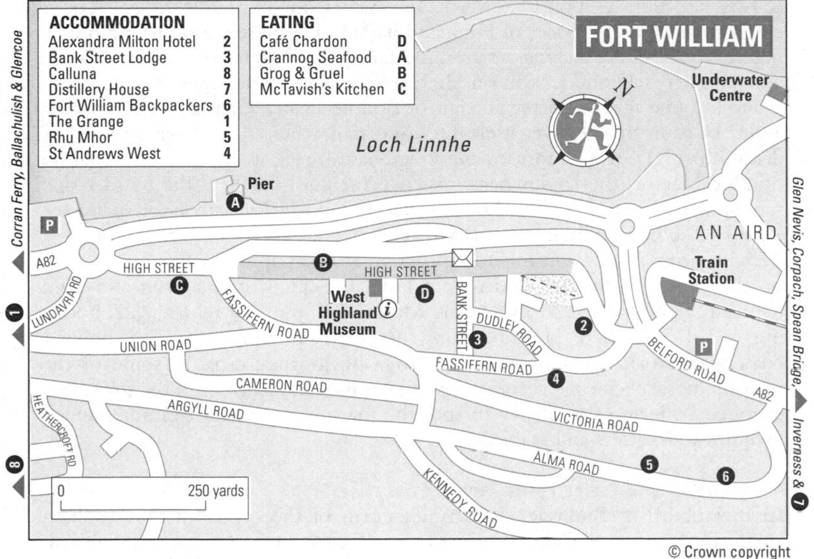

one of the area's top mountain guides, so there's plenty of good outdoor advice available.

Fort William Backpackers Alma Road ☎01397/700711. A big, rambling, archetypal backpacker hostel five minutes' walk up the hill from town, with great views and large communal areas. Part of the Macbackpackers chain, so minibus tours pull in at regular intervals.

Out of town

Ben Nevis Bunkhouse Achintee Farm, Glen Nevis ☎01397/702240, @www.glennevis.com. A more civilized option than the nearby SYHA place, with hot showers, self-catering kitchen and a small licensed restaurant. Located just over the river from the Ben Nevis Visitor Centre – get to it by following the Ben path across the river or by taking Achintee Road along the north side of the river Nevis from Claggan.

Farr Cottage On the main A830 in Corpach ☎01397/772315, @www.farrcottage.co.uk. One of the liveliest of the local backpacker hostels, with everything from pizza feasts to whisky tastings going on in the evenings. Accommodation, in medium-sized dorms, is slightly more expensive than others locally.

Glen Nevis Caravan and Camping Park Two miles up the Glen Nevis road ☎01397/702191. Good facilities include hot showers, a shop and restaurant.

Glen Nevis SYHA hostel Two and a half miles up the Glen Nevis road ☎01397/702336, @www.syha.org.uk. Large, but best avoided in mid-summer, when it's chock-full of teenagers. Handy for the Ben Nevis path but a long walk from town.

Smiddy Bunkhouse Station Road ☎01397/772467, @www.highland-mountain-guides.co.uk. A cosy fourteen-bed hostel and simpler bunkhouse right next to Corpach train station at the entrance to the Caledonian Canal. Part of the Snowgoose Mountain Centre, offering year-round mountaineering, kayaking and other outdoor activities, including family-oriented action activities.

The town and around

Fort William's downfall started in the nineteenth century, when the original fort, which gave the town its name, was demolished to make way for the train line. Today, the town is a sprawl of dual carriageways, and there's little to detain you except the splendid and idiosyncratic **West Highland Museum**, on Cameron Square, just off the High Street (June–Sept Mon–Sat 10am–5pm; July

& Aug also Sun 2–5pm; Oct–May Mon–Sat 10am–4pm; £2). Its collections cover virtually every aspect of Highland life and the presentation is traditional, but very well done, making a refreshing change from state-of-the-art heritage centres. There's a good section on Highland clans and tartans and, among interesting Jacobite relics, a secret portrait of Bonnie Prince Charlie, seemingly just a blur of paint that resolves itself into a portrait when viewed against a cylindrical mirror. Look out, too, for the long Spanish rifle used in the assassination of a local factor (the landowner's tax-collector-cum-bailiff) – the murder that subsequently inspired Robert Louis Stevenson's novel *Kidnapped*. You'll also see a 550kg slab of aluminium, the stuff that's processed locally into silver foil.

Excursions from town include the popular day-trip to Mallaig (see p.623) on the **Jacobite Steam Train** (mid-June to Sept Mon–Fri; Aug also Sun; depart Fort William 10.20am, depart Mallaig 2.10pm; day return £22; bookings ⓣ01463/239026). Heading along the north shore of Loch Eil to the west coast via historic Glenfinnan (see p.621), the journey takes in some of the region's most spectacular scenery. Several **cruises** also leave from the town pier every day, offering the chance to spot the marine life of Loch Linnhe, which includes seals, otters and seabirds.

Neptune's Staircase and Corpach

At the suburb of **Banavie**, three miles north of the centre of Fort William along the A830 to Mallaig, the Caledonian Canal climbs 64ft in less than half a mile via a punishing but picturesque series of eight locks known as **Neptune's Staircase**. There are stunning views from here of Ben Nevis and its neighbours, and it's a popular point from which to walk or cycle along the canal towpath. Bikes and Canadian canoes can be rented from Caledonian Activity Breaks (ⓣ01397/772373), based at Rhiw Goch, one of the cottages backing onto the canal at the top of the sequence of locks.

Another mile west along the road is the suburb of **Corpach**, the point where the canal enters from Loch Linnhe. The site of a mothballed paper mill, the main event here is the **Treasures of the Earth** exhibition (daily: July–Sept 9.30am–7pm, Feb–June & Oct–Dec 10am–5pm; £3), a useful rainy-day option for families, which has a dazzling array of rocks, crystals, gemstones and fossils and detailed explanations about where they come from and how they get their different colours. The displays include a recreated mine showing how the stones are discovered and a chamber lit with ultraviolet light to reveal the psychedelic colours hidden inside different gemstones.

Eating

Fort William has a reasonable range of places **to eat**. On the High Street, the *Grog and Gruel* serves an eclectic mix of pizzas, pasta and Mexican dishes with real ale, while *McTavish's Kitchen*, an American/Scottish restaurant, has a predictable menu of moderately priced steaks and seafood with several vegetarian options; in summer, it also hosts nightly Scottish entertainment sessions (8.30–11.30pm). The pick of the bunch is the *Crannog Seafood Restaurant*, an elegantly converted bait store on the pier, where oysters, langoustines, prawns and salmon are cooked with flair. The wine list is also excellent, although the prices make it best kept for a treat. There are also a number of places out of town well worth seeking out: the *Old Pines* near Spean Bridge (see p.612) is superb, while *An Crann* at Seangan Bridge, a little north of Banavie (ⓣ01497/772077) is a highly regarded place serving tasty Scottish dishes. A good place for **picnic food** as well as a snack is the *Café Chardon*, up a lane off High Street next to A.T. Mays; they do excellent baguettes, croissants and pastries to eat in or take away.

Glen Nevis

A ten-minute drive south of town, **Glen Nevis** is indisputably among the Highlands' most impressive glens: a classic U-shaped glacial valley hemmed in by steep bracken-covered slopes and swaths of blue-grey scree. Herds of shaggy Highland cattle graze the valley floor, where a sparkling river gushes through glades of trees. With the forbidding mass of Ben Nevis rising steeply to the north, it's not surprising this valley has been chosen as the location for scenes in several films, such as *Rob Roy* and *Braveheart*. Apart from its natural beauty, Glen Nevis is also the starting point for the ascent of Britain's highest peak, Ben Nevis, and you can rent **mountain equipment** and **mountain bikes** at the trailhead. The best map is "Harvey's Ben Nevis Walkers Map and Guide", available from the tourist office and most local bookshops and outdoor stores. Highland County **bus** #42 runs from An Aird, beside the Safeway supermarket and the railway station, Fort William (roughly hourly) as far as the SYHA hostel, two and a half miles up the Glen Nevis road; some buses carry on another two and a half miles up the glen to the car park by the Lower Falls (mid May to Sept only; 10–20min beyond the hostel).

A great **low-level walk** runs from the end of the road at the top of Glen Nevis. The good but very rocky path leads through a dramatic gorge with impressive falls and rapids, then opens out into a secret hanging valley, carpeted with wild flowers, with a high waterfall at the far end. It's a pretty place for a picnic and if you're really energetic you can walk on over Rannoch Moor to **Corrour Station**, where you can pick up one of four daily trains to take you back to Fort William.

Ben Nevis

Of all the walks in and around **Glen Nevis**, the ascent of **Ben Nevis** (4406ft), Britain's highest summit, inevitably attracts the most attention. Despite the fact that it's quite a slog up to the summit, and that it is by no means the most attractive mountain in Scotland, in high summer the trail is teeming with hikers, whatever the weather. However, this doesn't mean the mountain should be treated casually. It can snow round the summit any day of the year and more people perish here annually than on Everest, so take the necessary precautions (see p.46); in winter, of course, the mountain should be left to the experts.

The most obvious **route** to the summit, a Victorian pony path up the whaleback south side of of the mountain, built to service the observatory that once stood on the top, starts from the helpful Glen Nevis visitor centre (daily June–Sept 9am–6pm; Easter–May & Oct 9am–5pm), a mile and a half south-east of Fort William along the Glen Nevis road (bus #42 from An Aird in Fort William). From the centre, cross the footbridge over the River Nevis, then follow the path (20min) which connects with the path down to the SYHA hostel. Continue upwards over two aluminium footbridges, swinging onto a wide saddle with a small loch before veering right to cross the Red Burn. A series of seemingly endless zigzags rises from here over boulderfields on to a plateau, which you cross to reach the summit, marked by cairns, a shelter and a trig point. Return via the same route or, if the weather is settled and you're confident enough, make a side trip from the wide saddle into the **Allt a'Mhuilinn glen** for spectacular views of the great cliffs on Ben Nevis's north face. The Allt a'Mhuilinn may be followed right down to valley level as an alternative route off the mountain, reaching the distillery on the A82 a mile north of Fort William. Allow a full day for the climb (8hr).

Spean Bridge and Glen Spean

Ten miles northeast of Fort William, the village of **Spean Bridge** marks the junction of the A82 with the A86 from Dalwhinnie (see p.365) and Kingussie (see p.600). If you're here, its well worth heading a mile out of the village on the A82 towards Inverness to the **Commando Memorial**, a group of bronze soldiers sculpted in 1952 by Scott Sutherland in memory of the men who trained in the area and lost their lives during World War II. The statue stands on a raised promontory overlooking an awesome sweep of moor and mountain that takes in Lochaber and the Ben Nevis massif.

A few hundred yards from the memorial, on the minor B8004 which heads towards **Gairlochy**, is one of the Highland's great foodie havens, the *Old Pines* "restaurant with rooms" (ⓣ01397/712324, ⓦwww.oldpines.co.uk; half board ❼). With their own smokehouse, kitchen garden and a phalanx of top-notch local suppliers, owners Sukie and Bill Barber serve up original, fine-tasting food in relaxed, cultured surroundings. The house and rooms are welcoming and comfortable, as well as being well set up for guests with disabilities and families with children.

At **ROY BRIDGE**, three miles east of Spean Bridge, a minor road turns off up **Glen Roy**. A couple of miles along the glen, you'll see the so-called "parallel roads": not roads at all, but ancient beaches at various levels along the valley sides which mark the shorelines of a loch confined here by a glacial dam in the last Ice Age. Back on the A86, two miles east of Roy Bridge, *Aite Cruinnichidh*, 1 Achluachrach (ⓣ01397/712315, ⓔinfo@highlandbunkhouses.co.uk), is a comfortable **bunkhouse** in a beautiful setting, with good facilities (including a sauna) and local advice for climbers, walkers and cyclists. The West Highland Railway line runs right past the hostel, fringing the River Spean and the spectacular Monassie Gorge, which you can view from a footpath leading down from the roadside.

The railway line and road part company at **TULLOCH**, a few miles further east, where trains swing south to pass Loch Treig and cross Rannoch Moor (see p.364). The station building at Tulloch is now a **bunkhouse**, *Station Lodge* (ⓣ01397/732333, ⓦwww.stationlodge.co.uk), again with good facilities for walkers and climbers. Further east, the A86 runs alongside the artificial **Loch Laggan**, raised in 1934 to provide water for the aluminium works at Fort William; the water travels in tunnels of up to 15ft in diameter carved through miles of solid rock. Fans of the BBC TV series *Monarch of the Glen* may well recognize the loch, and in particular picturesque Ardverikie Castle on its southern shore. To the north of the loch is the **Creag Meagaidh National Nature Reserve**, where a hill track leads up through changing bands of mountain vegetation to **Lochan a Choire**. Right by the nature reserve car park, you can see several small herds of red deer, kept here for scientific study.

Glen Coe

Breathtakingly beautiful **Glen Coe** (literally "Valley of Weeping"), sixteen miles south of Fort William on the A82, is one of the best-known Highland glens: a spectacular mountain valley between velvety-green conical peaks, their tops often wreathed in cloud, and cascades of rock and scree. In 1692 it was the site of a notorious massacre, in which the MacDonalds were victims of a longstanding government desire to suppress the clans. Fed up with what they regarded as unacceptable lawlessness, and a groundswell of Jacobitism and Catholicism, the government offered a general pardon to all those who signed an oath of allegiance to William III by January 1, 1692. When clan chief **Alastair MacDonald** missed the deadline, a plot was hatched to make an example of "that damnable sept", and **Campbell of Glenlyon** was ordered to billet his soldiers in the homes of the MacDonalds, who for ten days entertained them with traditional Highland hospitality. In the early morning of February 13, the soldiers turned on their hosts, slaying between 38 and 45 and causing more than 300 to flee in a blizzard, some to die of exposure.

Beyond the small village of **GLENCOE** at the western end of the glen on the shore of Loch Leven, an inlet of Loch Linnhe, the glen itself, a property of the National Trust for Scotland since the 1930s, is virtually uninhabited, and provides outstanding climbing and walking. The emptiness of the glen, and the poignancy that reflects, has been at the heart of a furious local row in recent years as the NTS struggle to reconcile local opinion with their plans to build a new **visitor centre**, dubbed by some "as similar to building a supermarket in the middle of the glen". The rather dated present construction (April–Oct 9.30am–5.30pm; 50p), near Clachaig, shows a short video about the massacre, and has a gift shop selling the usual books, postcards and Highland kitsch; for information about the area, the tourist office at Ballachulish (see p.614) is more useful. There is a shortish **walk** from the centre through the forest to **Signal Rock**, which offers good views up and down the glen. More substantial are the informative ranger-led **guided walks** (June–Aug): on different days of the week a high-level hike and a low-level walk set off from the visitor centre.

At the eastern end of Glen Coe beyond the demanding Buachaille Etive Mhor, the landscape opens out onto the vast Rannoch Moor, dotted with small lochs and crossed by the West Highland Way, the A82 and, farther east, the West Highland Railway. From the **Glen Coe Ski Centre** (ⓣ01855/851226), a chairlift climbs 2400ft to Meall a Bhuiridh, giving spectacular views over Rannoch Moor and to Ben Nevis (lift open in ski season and July & Aug; 15min; £4 return). At the base station, there's a simple but pleasant café.

Practicalities

To get to the heart of Glen Coe from Fort William by **public transport** either hop on the Glasgow-bound Scottish Citylink coach service, or catch the daily postbus from Fort William post office (Mon–Fri 9.30am, Sat 9am). The Highland County bus #44 from Fort William to Kinlochleven also stops at Glencoe village.

There's a good selection of **accommodation** in Glen Coe and the surrounding area. Basic options include an SYHA **hostel** (ⓣ01855/811219, ⓦwww.syha.org.uk) on a back road halfway between Glencoe village and the *Clachaig Inn*; the year-round *Red Squirrel* **campsite** (ⓣ01855/811256) nearby; and a grassier NTS campsite (ⓣ01855/811397; April–Oct) on the main road. Glencoe village has a few comfortable **B&Bs**, such as the secluded *Scorry Breac* (ⓣ01855/811354, ⓔjohn@scorrybreac.freeserve.co.uk; ❶), and the *Glen Coe Guest House* (ⓣ01855/811244; ❶), while the best-known **hotel** in the area is the stark *Clachaig Inn* (ⓣ01855/811252, ⓦwww.glencoe-scotland.co.uk; ❸), a great place to swap stories with fellow climbers and to reward your exertions with pints of beer and heaped platefuls of food; it's three miles up Glen Coe, on the minor road from Glencoe village. At the other, eastern end of the glen, close to the Glen Coe ski area, is another well-established climber's watering hole, the *Kingshouse Hotel* (ⓣ01855/851259; ❷ excludes breakfast), a classic

Walks around Glen Coe

Ordnance Survey Landranger Map No. 41.

Flanked by sheer-sided Munros, Glen Coe offers some of the Highlands' most challenging **hiking** routes, with long, steep ascents over rough trails and notoriously unpredictable weather conditions that claim lives every year. The walks outlined below number among the glen's less ambitious routes, but still require a map. It's essential that you take the proper precautions (see p.46), and stick to the paths, both for your own safety and the sake of the soil, which has become badly eroded in places.

A good introduction to the splendours of Glen Coe is the half-day hike over the **Devil's Staircase**, which follows part of the old military road that once ran between Fort William and Stirling. The trail, part of the West Highland Way and a good option for families and less experienced hikers, starts at the village of **Kinlochleven**, due north across the mountains from Glen Coe at the far eastern tip of Loch Leven (take the B863): head along the single-track road from the British Aluminium Heritage Centre to a wooden bridge, from where a gradual climb on a dirt jeep track winds up to Penstock Farm. The path is marked from here onwards by thistle signs, and is therefore easy to follow uphill to the 1804ft pass and down the other side into Glen Coe. The Devil's Staircase was named by 400 soldiers who endured severe hardship to build it in the seventeenth century, but in fine settled weather the trail is safe and affords stunning views of Loch Eilde and Buachaille Etive Mhor. A more detailed account of this hike features in the leaflet *Great Walks: Kinlochleven* (no. 4), on sale at most tourist offices in the area.

Leaflet no. 5 in the Great Walks series (*Glen Coe*) gives a good description of the **Allt Coire Gabhail** hike, another old favourite. The trailhead for this half-day route is in Glen Coe itself, at the car park opposite the distinctive Three Sisters massif on the main A82 (look for the giant boulder). From the road, drop down to the floor of the glen and cross the River Coe via the wooden bridge, where you have a choice of two onward paths; the easier route, the less worn one, peels off to the right. Follow this straight up the Allt Coire Gabhail for a couple of miles until you rejoin the other

wayfarers' inn which always proves a welcome sight after the wide emptiness of Rannoch Moor. You can rent **mountain bikes** and **tandems** from the *Clachaig Inn*.

Ballachulish and Kinlochleven

Two miles west of Glencoe village, **BALLACHULISH** was, from 1693 to 1955, a major centre for the production of roofing slates, while another mile further west the name is also given to the terminals for the ferry across the mouth of Loch Leven, now crossed by a bridge. One of the better local sightseeing opportunities are the **boat trips** (call ⓣ01855/811658 for details) which leave from the West Pier at Ballachulish and take you round Eilean Munde, an island in Loch Leven where clan chiefs are buried.

At the eastern end of Loch Leven, at the foot of the spectacular mountains known as the Mamores, is the rather lifeless settlement of **KINLOCHLEVEN**, which has felt rather ignored ever since the bridge at Ballachulish ended the flow of northbound traffic detouring around the loch in preference to waiting in long queues for the ferry. Kinlochleven was the site of a huge aluminium smelter, established in 1904 and powered by a hydro-electric scheme that dammed the Blackwater valley above the village and which at the time it was built was the largest in Europe. The tale is told in **The Aluminium Story** (April–Oct Mon–Fri 10am–1pm & 2–5pm; free), a small (lower) path, which has ascended the valley beside the burn via a series of rock pools and lively scrambles. Cross the river here via the stepping stones and press on to the false summit directly ahead – actually the rim of the so-called "Lost Valley" which the Clan MacDonald used to flee to and hide their cattle in when attacked. Once in the valley, there are superb views of Bidean, Gearr Aonach and Beinn Fhada, which improve as you continue on to its head, another twenty- to thirty-minute walk. Unless you're well equipped and experienced, turn around at this point, as the trail climbs to some of the glen's high ridges and peaks.

Undoubtedly one of the finest walks in the Glen Coe area not entailing the ascent of a Munro is the **Buachaille Etive Beag** (BEB) circuit, for which you should check out the Ordnance Survey Pathfinder Guide: *Fort William and Glen Coe Walks*. Following the textbook glacial valleys of Lairig Eilde and Lairig Gartain, the route entails a 1968ft climb in only nine miles of rough trail. Park near the waterfall at **The Study** – the gorge part of the A82 through Glen Coe – and walk up the road until you see a sign pointing south to "Loch Etiveside". The path angles up from here, criss-crossing the Allt Lairig Eilde before the final pull to the top of the pass, a rise of 787ft from the road. The burn flowing through Glen Etive to Dalness is, confusingly, also called the Allt Lairig Eilde; follow its west bank path until you reach a fenced-off area, and then cross the stream, using the trail that then ascends Stob Dubh (the "black peat") directly from Glen Etive to gain some height. Next, pick a traverse line across the side of the valley to the col of the Lairig Gartain, and onwards to the top of the pass – a haul of around 984ft that is the last steep ascent of this circuit. The drop down the other side towards the estate lodge of Dalness is easy. When you reach the single-track road, follow the path signposted as the "Lairig Gartain", northeast to a second pass, from where an intermittent trail descends the west (left) side of the River Coupall valley, eventually rejoining the A82. Much the most enjoyable path back northeast down the glen from here is the roughly parallel route of the old military road, which offers a gentler and safer return with superb views of the Three Sisters – finer than those ever seen by drivers.

series of displays in the same building as the town library; the final chapter of the tale is that the factory is now all but closed, and despite various attempts to revive the town it is largely being left to fade slowly. The one sign of life in Kinlochleven comes from climbers heading into the Mamores, and from walkers strolling in on the **West Highland Way**, for whom the town is a convenient overnight stop a day's walk from Fort William.

Practicalities

Ballachulish has a useful **tourist office**, on Albert Road (June–Aug Mon–Sat 10am–6pm, Sun 10am–5pm; April, May, Sept & Oct Mon–Sat 10am–5pm; ⓣ01855/811296), though most of the best accommodation is across the bridge in North Ballachulish and nearby Onich. For a cheap bed, head to the inexpensive *Inchree Centre* (ⓣ01855/821287, ⓦwww.inchreecentre-scotland.com) at Onich, where accommodation is available in a bunkhouse or chalets and there's a decent real-ale pub and bistro called *The Four Seasons*. In Ballachulish village, *Fern Villa* (ⓣ01855/811393, ⓦwww.fernvilla.com; ❷) is a welcoming **B&B**, while *Cuildorag House* (ⓣ01855/821529, ⓦwww.cuildoraghouse.com; ❷) in Onich is a particularly pleasant vegetarian and vegan B&B, renowned for its great breakfasts. **Hotels** include the *Ballachulish* (ⓣ01855/821582, ⓦwww.freedomglen.co.uk; ❻) just below the southern end of the bridge, a grand but welcoming old place where residents have use of the pool and leisure centre at the nearby *Isles of Glencoe Hotel*, while the *Onich Hotel* on the north

Sound of Mull, from where a small ferry chugs to **Fishnish** – the shortest crossing from the mainland. Lochaline village, little more than a scattering of houses around a small pier, with a diving centre specializing in underwater archeology (①01967/421627), is a popular anchorage for yachts cruising the west coast, but holds little else to detain you. However, the easy stroll to the nearby fourteenth-century ruins of **Ardtornish Castle**, reached via a track that turns east off the main road one and a half miles north of Lochaline, makes an enjoyable detour. A further walk takes you to the **Loch Tearnait crannog**, a defensive island dating back about 1500 years; this walk and others are detailed in the "Great Walks" series available from tourist offices in the area. For **accommodation**, try the tiny *Lochaline Hotel* (①01967/421657; ❶), which serves reasonable bar food and has a couple of small but comfortable rooms.

Sunart and Ardgour

North of Morvern, the predominantly roadless regions of **Sunart** and **Ardgour** make up the country between Loch Shiel, Loch Sunart and Loch Linnhe: the heart of Jacobite support in the mid-eighteenth century and a Catholic stronghold to this day. The area's only real village is sleepy **STRONTIAN**, grouped around a green on an inlet of Loch Sunart. In 1722, lead mines here yielded the first-ever traces of the element **strontium**, named after the village. Worked by French POWs, the same mines also furnished shot for the Napoleonic wars. Strontian's other claim to fame is the "**Floating Church**", which was moored nearby in Loch Sunart in 1843. After being refused permission by the local laird to found their own "kirk", or chapel, on the estate, members of the Free Presbyterian Church (see p.474) bought an old boat on the River Clyde, converted it into a church and then had it towed up the west coast to Loch Sunart.

You can get to Strontian on the 7.55am **bus** (Mon–Sat) from Kilchoan (see below), or on a bus that leaves Fort William at 12.25pm and Ardgour at 12.50pm. Strontian's **tourist office** (Easter–Oct Mon–Sat 9am–5pm, Sun 10am–4pm; ①01967/402381) will book accommodation for a small fee. The modern *Kinloch House* (①01967/402138; ❷) is a very comfortable B&B, with stunning views down the loch. Strontian also has a couple of good **hotels**, including the *Strontian Hotel* (①01967/402029; ❷), in a splendid position near the water, and the luxurious *Kilcamb Lodge* (①01967/402257, Ⓦwww.kilcamblodge.co.uk; ❺ room only; March–Nov), a restored country house set in its own grounds on the lochside, whose **restaurant** serves excellent, if pricey, food. Six miles west of Strontian, only two miles before Salen, *Resipole Farm* (①01967/431235, Ⓦwww.resipole.co.uk) has a great set-up, with a **camping** and caravan park, self-catering accommodation and the *Farm Bar*, serving snacks and unexpectedly good meals.

The Ardnamurchan peninsula

The tortuous single-track B8007 road winds west from Salen along the northern shore of Loch Sunart to the wild **Ardnamurchan peninsula**, the most westerly point on the British mainland. The unspoilt landscape is relatively gentle and wooded at the eastern end, with much of the coastline of long Loch Sunart fringed by ancient oakwoods, protected as among the last remnants of the extensive temperate rainforests once common along the Atlantic coast of Europe. The further west you travel, however, the trees disappear and are replaced by a wild, salt-sprayed moorland. The peninsula, which lost most of its inhabitants during the infamous Clearances (see p.768), has only a handful of tiny crofting settlements clinging to its jagged coastline and is sparsely populated – all the more so when you realize that many of the houses are seldom-used holiday cottages. Ardnamurchan, however, can be an inspiring place for its pristine, empty beaches, wonderful vistas of sea and island, and the sense of nature all around. With its variety of undisturbed habitats the peninsula harbours a huge variety of birds, animals and wildflowers such as thrift and wild iris, making **walking** an obvious attraction. A variety of routes, from hill-climbs to coastal scrambles, are detailed in a comprehensive guide to the peninsula produced annually by the local community (available from tourist offices and most shops on the peninsula, priced around £4), while **guided walks** are also available at most of the nature reserves dotted along the Loch Sunart shoreline; these are run under the auspices of the Highland Council Ranger Service (Ⓣ01967/402232).

The Glenmore Natural History Centre

An inspiring introduction to the diverse flora, fauna and geology of Ardnamurchan is the superb **Glenmore Natural History Centre** (April–Oct Mon–Sat 10.30am–5.30pm, Sun noon–5.30pm; £2.50), nestled near the shore just west of the hamlet of **GLENBORRODALE**. Brainchild of local photographer Michael MacGregor (whose stunning work enlivens postcard stands along the west coast), the centre is housed in a sensitively designed timber building called "The Living Building", complete with turf roof and wildlife ponds. CCTV cameras relay live pictures of the comings and goings of the surrounding wildlife, from a pine marten's nest, a heronry and from underwater pools in the nearby river, while an excellent audiovisual show features MacGregor's photographs of the area accompanied by specially composed music. The small **café** serves sandwiches and good home-baked cakes and there's a useful bookshop. The nearby **RSPB reserve**, a mile to the east, is rich in wildlife too, being home to tree creepers, golden eagles, otters and seals, while for coastal wildlife-spotting – or trips to Tobermory on Mull or Fingal's Cave – contact Ardnamurchan Charters at Glenborrodale (Ⓣ01972/500208).

Kilchoan and Ardnamurchan Point

KILCHOAN, nine miles west of the Glenmore Centre, is Ardnamurchan's main village – a straggling but appealing crofting township overlooking the Sound of Mull. In summer, a **car ferry** runs from here to Tobermory (Easter to mid-Oct 7 daily; 35min), while in the winter a passenger ferry plies the route for schoolchildren and shoppers. The new community centre in the village houses a **tourist office** (Easter–Oct daily 10am–6pm; Ⓣ01972/510222, Ⓦwww.ardnamurchan.com), who will help with and book accommodation, though year-round the community centre will act as an informal source of local advice and assistance. For **boat trips** out of Kilchoan – either wildlife-spotting or fishing – contact Nick Peake (Ⓣ01972/510212), who also leads guided walks to look for land-based wildlife such as eagles, pine martens and badgers. The only direct **bus** to Kilchoan leaves from Corran Ferry at 12.40pm (Mon–Sat), arriving two hours later.

The road continues beyond Kilchoan to the rocky, windy **Ardnamurchan Point**, with its famous **lighthouse** and spectacular views of the Hebrides north and south. The lighthouse buildings house a decent café and an enthusiastically run **visitor centre** (April–Oct 10am–5.30pm; £2.50; Ⓣ01972/510210), with well-assembled displays about lighthouses in general, their construction and the people who lived in them. Best of all is the chance to admire the Egyptian-style lighthouse tower, and find a sheltered spot on the nearby cliff to sit peering out to sea. Whales are sometimes seen here – indeed, the Hebridean Whale and Dolphin Trust, based in Tobermory, often send volunteers over to the lighthouse to sit by the massive old Fog Horn and peer out through binoculars counting sightings.

Also worth exploring around the peninsula are the myriad coves, beaches and headlands along the long coastline. The finest of the sandy beaches is about three miles north of the lighthouse at **Sanna Bay**, a shell-strewn strand and series of dunes which offers truly unforgettable vistas of the Small Isles to the north, circled by gulls, terns and guillemots.

Practicalities

Accommodation isn't plentiful in Kilchoan, and in summer you're well advised to book well ahead. In Kilchoan itself, *Far View Cottage* (ⓣ01972/510357; ❻ half board), just along from the ferry pier, is a good bet, while *Water's Edge* (ⓣ01972/510261; ❻ half board) has one double room in a house in the village. *Doirlinn House* (ⓣ01972/510209; ❷; March–Oct) is a simpler B&B, again with great views. The only budget accommodation on the peninsula is *Bruach na Fearna* (ⓣ01972/500208; ❶), an excellent self-catering wooden chalet above the beach at Laga, just east of Glenborrodale. Nearby is an exquisite upmarket guesthouse, *Feorag House* (ⓣ01972/500248, ⓦwww.feorag.demon.co.uk; ❼ half board), which has three tasteful, modest rooms in a beautifully secluded house at Glenborrodale.

Many of these guesthouses offer only half-board (dinner, bed and breakfast) packages, but should you be looking for places to **eat** both the *Salen Inn* (ⓣ01967/431661; ❸) and the *Kilchoan House Hotel* (ⓣ01972/510200; ❸) do decent bar meals, and you should be able to get pub grub at the *Sonachan Hotel* (ⓣ01972/510211; ❷), which despite being hailed as the most westerly hotel on the British mainland is tucked inland away from the coast, halfway between Kilchoan and Ardnamurchan Point. The Ferry Stores in Kilchoan, the only **shop** west of Salen, makes an impressive effort to carry fresh food and local produce when it's available.

Acharacle and around

At the eastern end of Ardnamurchan, just north of Salen where the A861 heads north towards the district of Moidart, the main settlement is **ACHARACLE**, an ancient crofting village lying at the seaward end of freshwater **Loch Shiel**. Surrounded by gentle hills, it's an attractive place whose scattered houses form a real community, with several shops, a post office, and plenty of places to **stay**. The pleasant *Loch Shiel House Hotel* (ⓣ01967/431224; ❸) is set back from the loch and has a hospitable feel, serving good meals. *Belmont* (ⓣ01967/431266; ❷) is a simple and comfortable B&B, as is Mrs Crisp's (ⓣ01967/431318; ❶) just across the road. Best of the lot is *Dalilea House* (ⓣ01967/431253; ❷; March–Oct), three miles west along the shores of Loch Shiel, an attractive historic house where modest, secluded B&B is complemented by imaginative modern Scottish cooking.

You can get to Acharacle by **boat** from Glenfinnan at the head of Loch Shiel (Wed only) with Loch Shiel Cruises (ⓣ01397/722235), or on infrequent **buses** from Mallaig or Fort William. There are plenty of untaxing and attractive **walks** in the local area; the local shop, just behind the hotel, stocks a book detailing these. Beside the shop is the *Upper Crust*, a takeaway and bakery with good picnic fodder, though for a much classier feast pay a visit to the tiny

Moidart Smoke House, at Dalnabreac on the western edge of Acharacle. For evening **entertainment** your best bet is the *Clanranald Hotel* at Mingarry, again just west of Archaracle, which is run by a well-known local accordianist and band leader, Fergie Macdonald.

Castle Tioram

A mile north of Acharacle, a sideroad running north off the A861 winds for three miles or so past a secluded estuary lined with rhododendron thickets and fishing platforms to **Loch Moidart**, a calm and sheltered sea loch. Perched atop a rocky promontory in the middle of the loch is **Castle Tioram** (pronounced "cheerum"), one of Scotland's most atmospheric historic monuments. Reached via a sandy causeway, the thirteenth-century fortress, whose Gaelic name means "dry land", was the seat of the MacDonalds of Clanranald until it was destroyed by their chief in 1715 to prevent it from falling into Hanoverian hands while he was away fighting for the Jacobites. Today, a certain amount of controversy surrounds the castle: while the setting and approach to the castle are undoubtedly stunning, large notices and fences keep you from getting too close to the castle due to the danger of falling masonry.

The Road to the Isles

The "**Road to the Isles**" from Fort William to Mallaig, followed by the West Highland Railway and the narrow, winding A830, traverses the mountains and glens of the Rough Bounds before breaking out near **Arisaig** onto a spectacularly scenic coast of sheltered inlets, stunning white beaches and wonderful views to the islands of Rùm, Eigg, Muck and Skye. This is country commonly associated with **Bonnie Prince Charlie**, whose adventures of 1745–46 began and ended on this stretch of coast, with his first, defiant raising of the standard at **Glenfinnan** at the head of lovely **Loch Shiel**.

Glenfinnan

GLENFINNAN, 19 miles west of Fort William at the head of Loch Shiel, was where Bonnie Prince Charlie raised his standard to signal the start of the Jacobite uprising of 1745. Surrounded by no more than 200 loyal clansmen, the young rebel prince waited to see if the Cameron of Loch Shiel would join his army. The drone of this powerful chief's pipers drifting up the glen was eagerly awaited, for without him the Stuarts' attempt to claim the English throne would have been sheer folly. Despite strong misgivings, Cameron did decide to support the uprising, and arrived at Glenfinnan on a sunny August 19 with 800 men, thereby encouraging other, wavering clan leaders to follow suit. Assured of adequate backing, the prince raised his red-and-white silk colour, proclaimed his father King James III of England, and set off on the long march to London – from which only a handful of the soldiers gathered at Glenfinnan would return. The spot is marked by a column (now a little lopsided, Pisa-like), crowned with a clansman in full battle dress, erected as a tribute by Alexander Macdonald of Glenaladale in 1815.

Glenfinnan is a poignant place, a beautiful stage for the opening scene in a brutal drama which was to change the Highlands for ever. The **visitor centre** and café (daily: June–Aug 9.30am–6pm; April, May, Sept & Oct 10am–5pm; NTS; £1.50), opposite the monument, gives an account of the '45 uprising through to the rout at **Culloden** eight months later (see p.588). A **boat trip** on the loch with Loch Shiel Cruises (April–Oct; ⓣ01397/722235) is highly recommended.

Glenfinnan is one of the most spectacular parts of the **West Highland Railway** line (see p.578), not only for the glimpse it offers of the monument and graceful Loch Shiel, but also the mighty 21-arched **viaduct** built in 1901 and one of the first-ever large constructions made out of concrete. You can learn more of the history of this section of the railway at the **Glenfinnan Station Museum** (June–Sept daily 9.30am–4.30pm; 50p), set in the old booking office of the station. Right beside the station, two old railway carriages have been pressed into use as a highly original **restaurant** and **bunkhouse**; the *Dining Car* (June–Sept daily 10am–5pm; ⓣ01397/722300) is open for light lunches, home baking and evening meals (Fri–Sun until 8.30pm), while the *Sleeping Car* (ⓣ01397/722295; year-round), a converted 1958 camping coach, sleeps ten in bunkbeds.

Arisaig

West of Glenfinnan, the A830 runs alongside captivating Loch Eilt in the district of **Morar**, through Lochailort – where it meets the road from Acharacle – and onto a coast marked by acres of white sands, turquoise seas and rocky islets draped with orange seaweed. **ARISAIG**, scattered round a sandy bay at the west end of the Morar peninsula, makes a good base for exploring this area. The only specific attraction is the **Land, Sea and Islands Centre** (call ⓣ01687/450263 for opening hours), a small community project relating the social and natural history of the area, with some intriguing detail on local events, including secret operations during World War II and the filming of various movies in the area, along with background on local characters such as the person who inspired Robert Louis Stevenson's fictional pirate Long John Silver. If the weather's fine you could spend hours wandering along the beaches and quiet backroads, and there's a small seal colony at nearby **Rhumach**, reached via the single-track lane leading west out of Arisaig village along the headland. A **boat** also leaves from here daily during the summer for the Small Isles (see p.465), operated by Arisaig Marine (ⓣ01687/450224). **Accommodation** in the village is plentiful. *Kinloid Farm House* (ⓣ01687/450366; ❸; March–Oct) is one of several pleasant B&Bs with sea views, while the more upmarket *Old Library Lodge* (ⓣ01687/450651, ⓦwww.oldlibrary.co.uk; ❺; April–Oct) has a handful of well-appointed rooms, though only two overlook the seafront. The **restaurant** downstairs, serving moderately priced lunches and decent à la carte dinners (reservations recommended), is renowned for adding an exotic twist to fresh local ingredients: try Mallaig cod with Moroccan marinade.

Morar

Stretching for eight miles or so north of Arisaig is a string of stunning white-sand **beaches** backed by flowery machair, with barren granite hills and moorland rising up behind and wonderful seaward views of Eigg and Rùm. The next settlement of any significance is **MORAR**, where the famous beach scenes from *Local Hero* were shot. Since then, however, a bypass has been built around the village, and the white sands, plagued by the rumble of frozen-cod lorries, are no longer an unspoilt idyll. Of the string of **campsites** try *Camusdarach* (ⓣ01687/450221, ⓦwww.road-to-the-isles.org.uk/camusdarach), which isn't quite on the beach but is quieter and less officious than others nearby. **B&B** is also available in the converted billiard room of their attractive main house (❶). **Loch Morar** – rumoured to be the home of a monster called Morag, a lesser-known rival to Nessie – runs east of Morar village into the heart of a huge wilderness area, linked to the sea by what must be one of the shortest rivers in

Scotland. Hemmed in by heather-decked mountains, it featured in the movie *Rob Roy*: the cattle-rustling clansman's cottage was sited on its roadless northern shore.

Mallaig

A cluttered, noisy port whose pebble-dashed houses struggle for space with great lumps of granite tumbling down to the sea, **MALLAIG**, 47 miles west of Fort William along the A830 (regular buses and trains run this route), is not pretty. Before the railway reached here in 1901, it consisted of only a few cottages, but now it's a busy, bustling place and, as the main ferry stop for Skye and the Small Isles (see p.448), is always full of visitors. The continuing source of the village's wealth is its thriving **fishing** industry: on the quayside, piles of nets, tackle and ice crates lie scattered around a bustling modern market. When the fleet is in, trawlers encircled by flocks of raucous gulls choke the harbour, and the pubs, among the liveliest on the west coast, host bouts of serious drinking. The stretch of coast to the north encompasses the lonely **Knoydart** and **Glenelg** peninsulas, two of Britain's last true wilderness areas. This whole region is also popular with Munro baggers, harbouring a string of summits over 3000ft. The famous Five Sisters massif and Kintail Ridge, flanking the A87 well northeast of Mallaig, offer some of the Highlands' most challenging **hikes** and are easily accessible by road; by way of contrast, the high peaks of Knoydart are prized for their inaccessibility.

Apart from the daily bustle of Mallaig's harbour, the main attraction in town is **Mallaig Marine World**, north of the train station near the harbour (June–Sept Mon–Sat 9am–6pm, Sun 10am–6pm; July & Aug Mon–Sat until 7pm; Oct–May Mon–Sat 9am–5.30pm, Sun 11am–5pm; £2.75), where tanks of local sea creatures and informative exhibits about the port provide an unpretentious introduction to the local waters. Alongside the train station, the **Mallaig Heritage Centre** (June–Sept Mon–Sat 9.30am–4.30pm, Sun 1.30–4.30pm; April, May & Oct Mon–Sat 11am–4pm; phone for winter hours; ⓣ01687/462085; £1.80), displaying old photographs of the town and its environs, is worth a browse. The walking trail to **Mallaigmore**, a small cove with a white-sand beach and isolated croft, begins at the top of the harbour on East Bay; follow the road north past the tourist office and turn off right when you see the signpost between two houses. The round trip takes about an hour.

Practicalities

Mallaig is a compact place, concentrated around the harbour, where you'll find the **tourist office** (April–Oct Mon–Sat 10am–6pm; Nov–March Mon, Wed & Fri 11am–3pm; ⓣ01687/462170), which will book accommodation for you, and the **bus** and **train stations**. The CalMac ticket office (ⓣ01687/462403), serving passengers for Skye and the Small Isles, is also nearby, and you can arrange transport to Knoydart by calling Bruce Watt Cruises (ⓣ01687/462320 or 462233), which sails to Inverie, on the Knoydart peninsula, every morning and afternoon (June to mid-Sept Mon–Fri; otherwise Mon, Wed & Fri), the later cruise continuing east along Loch Nevis to Tarbet; the loch is sheltered, so crossings are rarely cancelled.

There are plenty of places **to stay**; the *West Highland Hotel* (ⓣ01687/462210; ❸) is pleasantly old-fashioned, if a little shabby in places, and some rooms have excellent sea views, while the *Marine* (ⓣ01687/462217; ❸) is much smarter inside than first impressions suggest. For **B&B**, head around the harbour to East Bay, where you'll find the immaculate *Western Isles Guest House* (ⓣ01687/462320, ⓔwestrnisles@aol.com; ❶). *Sheena's Backpackers' Lodge*

(☎01687/462764), a refreshingly laid-back independent **hostel** overlooking the harbour, has mixed dorms, self-catering facilities and a sitting room. For **eating**, the *Marine Hotel* serves good-value bar meals featuring fresh seafood which are well above average, while the nearby *Seafood Restaurant* (also known as the *Cabin*) has a more ambitious menu but is very popular, so booking is wise. During the day, the *Tea Garden* at *Sheena's Lodge* is a great place to watch the world go by while you tuck into a bowl of cullen skink (soup made from smoked haddock), a pint of prawns, or home-made scones. Also worth seeking out are the freshest of fish and chips, served at the *Cornerstone*, just across the road from the tourist office.

The Knoydart peninsula

Many people regard the **Knoydart peninsula** as Britain's most dramatic and unspoilt wilderness area. Flanked by **Loch Nevis** ("Loch of Heaven") in the south and the fjord-like inlet of **Loch Hourn** ("Loch of Hell") to the north, Knoydart's knobbly green peaks – three of them Munros – sweep straight out of the sea, shrouded for much of the time in a pall of grey mist. To get to the heart of the peninsula, you must catch a **boat** from Mallaig or Glenelg, or else **hike** for a couple of days across rugged moorland and mountains and sleep rough in old stone bothies (most of which are marked on Ordnance Survey maps). Unsurprisingly, the peninsula tends to attract walkers, lured by the network of well-maintained trails that wind east into the wild interior, where Bonnie Prince Charlie is rumoured to have hidden out after Culloden.

At the end of the eighteenth century, around a thousand people eked out a living from this inhospitable terrain through crofting and fishing. Evictions in 1853 began a dramatic decrease in the population, which continued to dwindle through the twentieth century as a succession of landowners ran the estate as a hunting and shooting playground, prompting a famous land raid in 1948 by a group of crofters known as the "Seven Men of Knoydart", who staked out and claimed ownership of portions of the estate. Although their bid failed, the memory of their cause was invoked when the crofters of Knoydart finally achieved control over the land they lived on in a community buy-out in 1998. These days the peninsula supports around seventy people, most of whom live in the hamlet of **INVERIE**. Nestled beside a sheltered bay on the south side of the peninsula, it has a pint-sized post office, a shop and mainland Britain's most remote pub, the *Old Forge*.

Practicalities

Bruce Watt Cruises' **boat** chugs into Inverie from Mallaig (see p.623). To arrange for a boat crossing from Arnisdale on the Glenelg peninsula to the north coast of Knoydart or Kinloch Hourn, contact Len Morrison (☎01599/522352; £8–25, depending on passenger numbers).

There are two main **hiking routes** into Knoydart: the trailhead for the first is **KINLOCH HOURN**, a crofting hamlet at the far east end of Loch Hourn which you can get to by road (turn south off the A87 six miles west of Invergarry). From Kinloch Hourn, a well-marked path winds around the coast to Barrisdale and on to Inverie. The second path into Knoydart starts at the west side of **Loch Arkaig**, approaching the peninsula via Glen Dessary. These are both long hard slogs over rough, desolate country, so take wet-weather gear, plenty of food, warm clothes and a good sleeping bag, and leave your name and expected time of arrival with someone when you set off.

Most of Knoydart's **accommodation** is concentrated in and around Inverie.

Torrie Shieling (☎01687/462669, ⓔtorrreidh@aol.com; £15 per person), an upmarket independent **hostel** located three-quarters of a mile east of the village on the side of the mountain, is popular with hikers and families, offering top-notch self-catering facilities, comfortable wooden beds in four-person rooms, and superb views across the bay. They also have a Land Rover and boat for ferrying guests around the peninsula, and to neighbouring lochs and islands. In Inverie itself, *Pier House* (☎01687/462347, ⓦwww.thepierhouse.co.uk; ⑤ half board), is a great place to stay, and has its own licensed **restaurant** serving à la carte evening meals, including some good veggie options. Dinner is available to non-residents (three courses for around £15). If you want total isolation and all the creature comforts book into the beautiful *Doune Stone Lodges* (☎01687/462667; ⑥ full board), on the remote north side of the peninsula. Rebuilt from ruined crofts, this place has pine-fitted en-suite double rooms right on the shore, near the ruins of an ancient Pictish fort. They'll pick you up by boat from Mallaig if you book ahead. The *Old Forge's* has generous bar meals, served indoors beside an open fire, and often live music of an evening. You can rent **mountain bikes** from *Pier House*; they've established various mountain-bike trails in the area, and offer mountain walks for groups of four or more.

Kyle of Lochalsh and around

As the main gateway to Skye, **Kyle of Lochalsh** is an important transit point for tourists, locals and services. However, despite the through traffic and the fact that it is the terminus for the train route from Inverness, the town itself has little to show off. Of much more interest to most visitors is nearby **Eilean Donan Castle**, one of Scotland's most famous and popular sights, perched at the end of a stone causeway on the shores of **Loch Duich**. It's not hard, however, to step off the tourist trail, with the **Glenelg** peninsula on the south side of Loch Duich testimony to how quickly the west coast can seem remote and undiscovered. A few miles north of Kyle of Lochalsh, the delightful village of **Plockton** is a refreshing alternative to its utilitarian neighbour, with cottages grouped around a yacht-filled bay and Highland cattle wandering the streets. Plockton lies on the southern shore of **Loch Carron**, a long inlet which, together with **Strathcarron** at the head of the loch, acts as a dividing line between the Kyle of Lochalsh district and the scenic splendours of Wester Ross to the north.

Kyle of Lochalsh

KYLE OF LOCHALSH is not particularly attractive – concrete buildings, rail junk and myriad signs of the fishing industry abound – and is ideally somewhere to pass through rather than linger in. Since the **Skye road bridge** was opened in 1995, traffic has little reason to stop before rumbling over the channel a mile to the west, leaving Kyle's shopkeepers bereft of the passing trade they used to enjoy. The bridge, built with private-sector money, has also sparked controversy over its high tolls.

Buses run to Kyle of Lochalsh's harbour from Glasgow via Fort William and Invergarry (3 daily; 5hr 30min–6hr 15min), and from Inverness via Invermoriston (2 daily; 2hr); there's also a summer service from Edinburgh (1 daily; 7hr 15min). Book in advance for all of them (☎0870/550 5050). All continue at least as far as Portree on Skye. Buses also shuttle across the bridge to Kyleakin on Skye every thirty minutes or so. **Trains** run to Kyle of Lochalsh from Inverness (Mon–Sat 3–4; summer Sun 1–2; 2hr 30min); curving north through Achnasheen and Glen Carron, the train line is a rail enthusiast's dream, even if scenically it doesn't quite match the West Highland line to Mallaig.

Kyle's **tourist office** (July & Aug Mon–Sat 9am–6pm, Sun 10am–4pm; April–June, Sept & Oct Mon–Sat 9am–5pm; ⓣ01599/534276), on top of the small hill near the old ferry jetty, can book **accommodation** – a useful service as there are surprisingly few options. One of the most pleasant in the area is the *Old Schoolhouse* at Erbusaig, between Kyle and Plockton (ⓣ01599/534369; ❸), a good-quality guesthouse with three reasonably priced and comfortable rooms. For B&B, try *Crowlin View* (ⓣ01599/534286; ❶), a traditional house one and a half miles north of Kyle on the Plockton road with views to Skye. There's a simple, clean hostel in town, *Cúchulainn's* (ⓣ01599/534492), above a pub across the main street from the tourist office. To **eat**, head for the *Seagreen Restaurant and Bookshop* (ⓣ01599/534388), on the Plockton road on the edge of town, which has a pleasant, unfussy atmosphere and serves excellent fresh seafood and vegetarian meals. The *Seafood Restaurant* at the train station is also recommended, if a little pricier.

Loch Duich

Skirted on its northern shore by the A87, **Loch Duich**, the boot-shaped inlet just to the south of Kyle of Lochalsh, features prominently on the tourist trail, with buses from all over Europe thundering down the sixteen miles from **SHIEL BRIDGE** to Kyle of Lochalsh on their way to Skye. The main road, which connects to the Great Glen at Invermoriston (see p.605), makes for a dramatic approach to the loch out of Glen Shiel, where the much-photographed mountains known as the Five Sisters of Kintail surge impressively up to heights of 3000ft. With steep-sided hills hemming in both sides of the loch, it's sometimes hard to remember that this is, in fact, the sea. There's a congenial SYHA **hostel** just outside Shiel Bridge at **RATAGAN** (ⓣ01599/511243, ⓦwww.syha.org.uk; April–Oct), popular with walkers newly arrived off the Glen Affric trek from Cannich (see p.604).

Eilean Donan Castle

After Edinburgh's hilltop fortress, **Eilean Donan Castle** (April–Oct daily 10am–5.30pm; £3.75), ten miles north of Shiel Bridge on the A87, has to be Scotland's most photographed monument. Presiding over the once strategically important confluence of lochs Alsh, Long and Duich, the forbidding crenellated tower rises from the water's edge, joined to the shore by a narrow stone bridge and with sheer mountains as a backdrop.

The original castle was established in 1230 by Alexander II to protect the area from the Vikings. Later, during a Jacobite uprising in 1719, it was occupied by troops dispatched by the King of Spain to help the "**Old Pretender**", James Stuart. However, when King George heard of their whereabouts, he sent frigates to weed the Spaniards out, and the castle was blown up with their stocks of gunpowder. Thereafter, it lay in ruins until John Macrae-Gilstrap had it rebuilt between 1912 and 1932. Eilean Donan has also been the setting of several major **films**, including *Highlander* and the James Bond adventure *The World is Not Enough*. Three floors, including the banqueting hall, the bedrooms and the troops' quarters are open to the public, with various Jacobite and clan relics also on display, though like many of the region's most popular castles, the large numbers of people passing through make it hard to appreciate the real charm of the place.

Hiking in Glen Shiel

Ordnance Survey Map No. 33.

The mountains of **Glen Shiel**, sweeping southeast from Loch Duich, offer some of the best hiking routes in Scotland. Rising dramatically from sea level to over 3000ft in less than a couple of miles, they are also exposed to the worst of the west coast's notoriously fickle weather. Don't underestimate either of these two routes. Tracing the paths on a map, they can appear short and easy to follow; nonetheless, unwary walkers die here every year, often because they failed to allow enough time to get off the mountain by nightfall, or because of a sudden change in the weather. Only attempt these routes if you're confident in your walking experience, and have a map, a compass and a detailed trekking guide – the *SMC's Hill Walks in Northwest Scotland* is recommended. Also make sure to follow the usual safety precautions outlined on p.46.

Taking in a bumper crop of Munros, the **Five Sisters traverse** is deservedly the most popular trek in the area. Allow a full day to complete the whole route, which begins at the first fire break on the left-hand side as you head southeast down the glen on the A87. Strike straight up from here and follow the ridge north along to Scurr na Moraich (2874ft), dropping down the other side to Morvich on the valley floor.

The distinctive chain of mountains across the glen from the Five Sisters is the **Kintail Ridge**, crossed by another famous hiking route that begins at the *Cluanie Inn* (see p.605) on the A87. From here, follow the well-worn path south around the base of the mountain until it meets up with a stalkers' trail, which winds steeply up Creag a' Mhaim (3108ft) and then west along the ridgeway, with breathtaking views south across Knoydart and the Hebridean Sea.

There are several places to **stay** less than a mile away in the hamlet of **DORNIE**, including the *Silver Fir Bunkhouse* (☎01599/555264), little more than a simple hut with two bunkbeds and a woodburning stove, but friendly and characterful. Otherwise, the *Dornie Hotel*, Francis Street (☎01599/555205; ❸), boasts comfortable rooms, while the *Loch Duich Hotel* (☎01599/555213; ❸), has splendid doubles overlooking the loch and a small **restaurant** serving upmarket bar snacks and evening meals. On Sunday nights they have a popular **folk music** session in the bar. Another good place for a bar meal is the popular *Clachan*, just along from the *Dornie Hotel*.

The Glenelg peninsula

South of Loch Duich, the **Glenelg peninsula**, jutting out into the Sound of Sleat, is the isolated and little-known crofting area featured in Gavin Maxwell's otter novel, *Ring of Bright Water*. Maxwell disguised the identity of this pristine stretch of coast by calling it "Camusfearnà", and it has remained a tranquil backwater in spite of the traffic that trickles through during the summer for the Kylerhea ferry to Skye (see p.448 for details of the wildlife sanctuary at Eilean Ban, once Maxwell's home). The landward approach to the peninsula is from the east by turning off the fast A87 at Shiel Bridge on Loch Duich, from where a narrow single-track road climbs a tortuous series of switchbacks to the Mam Ratagan Pass (1115ft), affording spectacular views over the awesome **Five Sisters** massif. Following the route of an old military highway and drovers' trail, the road, covered each morning by the postbus from Kyle of Lochalsh (departs 10am), drops down the other side through Glen More, with the magnificent Kintail Ridge visible to the southeast, towards the peninsula's main settlement, **GLENELG**, strewn along a pebbly bay on the Sound of Sleat. A row of little whitewashed houses surrounded by trees, the village is dominated by the rambling, weed-choked ruins of Fort Bernera, an eighteenth-century garrison for English government troops, but now little more than a shell. The *Glenelg Inn* (Ⓣ01599/522273, Ⓦwww.glenelg-inn.com; ⑤) is a wonderful spot to discover at the end of so remote a road, with its luxurious, cosy rooms overlooking the bay, tasty food served all day and a good chance of live music from any local musicians who happen to be in the pub.

The frequent six-car **Glenelg–Kylerhea ferry** (5min; information Ⓣ01599/511302; April–Oct) shuttles across the Sound of Sleat from a jetty northwest of the village. In former times, this choppy channel used to be an important drovers' crossing: 8000 cattle each year were herded head to tail across from Skye to the mainland.

One and a half miles south of Glenelg village, a left turn up Glen Beag leads to the **Glenelg Brochs**, some of the best-preserved Iron Age monuments in the country. Standing in a sheltered stream valley, the circular towers – Dun Telve and Dun Troddan – are thought to have been erected around 2000 years ago to protect the surrounding settlements from raiders. About a third of each main structure remains, with the curving drystone walls and internal passages still impressively intact.

Arnisdale

A narrow backroad snakes its way southwest beyond Glenelg village through a scattering of old crofting hamlets and timber forests. The views across the Sound of Sleat to Knoydart grow more spectacular at each bend, reaching a high point at a windy pass that takes in a vast sweep of sea, loch and islands. Below the road at **Sandaig** is where Gavin Maxwell and his otters lived in the 1950s: the site of his house is now marked by a cairn. Swinging east, the road winds down to the waterside again, following the north shore of Loch Hourn as far as **ARNISDALE**, departure point for the boat to Knoydart (see p.624). Arnisdale is made up of the two hamlets of **Camusbane** and **Corran**, the former consisting of a single row of old cottages ranged behind a long pebble beach, with a massive scree slope behind, while the latter, a mile along the road, is a minuscule whitewashed fishing hamlet at the water's edge. Aside from the arrival of electricity and a red telephone box, the only major addition to this gorgeous hamlet in the last hundred years has been Mrs Nash's **B&B** and tea hut (Ⓣ01599/522336; ❶), where you can enjoy hot drinks and home-baked cake in a "shell garden", with breathtaking views on all sides. The only other B&B is at *Croftfoot* (Ⓣ01599/522352; ❶), where dinner is also available if you book in advance. You can get to Arnisdale on the **postbus** from Kyle of Lochalsh (daily 10am; 4hr 50min; the return bus leaves Arnisdale at 7.10am), or use the Diversions Glenelg service between Kyle, Ratagan Hostel and Glenelg post office (Mon, Wed & Fri 11.20am; 1hr 5min; Ⓣ01599/522233). On request, the latter can go on to Arnisdale and Corran; similarly, the return bus from Glenelg can make arrangements to meet the Inverness or Glasgow buses at Kyle.

Plockton

A fifteen-minute train ride north of Kyle at the seaward end of islet-studded Loch Carron lies the unbelievably picturesque village of **PLOCKTON**: a chocolate-box row of neatly painted cottages ranged around the curve of a tiny harbour and backed by a craggy landscape of heather and pine. Originally known as Am Ploc, the settlement was a crofting hamlet until the end of the eighteenth century, when a local laird transformed it into a prosperous fishery, renaming it "Plocktown". Its fifteen minutes of fame came in the mid-1990s, when the BBC chose the village as the setting for the TV drama *Hamish Macbeth*. Though the resulting spin-off has quietened down a little, in high season it's still packed full of tourists, yachties and second-home owners. The unique brilliance of Plockton's light has also made it something of an artists' hangout, and during the summer the waterfront, with its row of shaggy palm trees, even shaggier Highland cattle, flower gardens and pleasure boats, is invariably dotted with painters dabbing at their easels.

The friendly, cosy *Haven Hotel*, on Innes Street (☎01599/544223; ❺), is renowned for its excellent food, while the *Plockton Inn*, also on Innes Street (☎01599/544222; ❸), makes an informal and comfortable alternative. The *Plockton Hotel*, Harbour Street (☎01599/544274, ⓦwww.plocktonhotel.com; ❹), overlooking the harbour with some rooms in a nearby cottage, has a friendly bar and serves good seafood. Of the fifteen or so **B&Bs**, *The Shieling* (☎01599/544282; ❷) has a great location on a tiny headland at the top of the harbour, and the nearby *Heron's Flight* (☎01599/544220; ❷) has uninterrupted views across the loch from its upstairs bedrooms. At *An Caladh* (☎01599/544356; ❶) on the main street, guests have the free use of a wooden sailing dinghy. There's also the attractive new *Station Bunkhouse* (☎01599/544235, ⓔgill@ecosse.com), built in the shape of a signal box next to the railway station, which has four- and six-person dorms and a cosy open-plan kitchen and living area. An interesting **self-catering** option is to stay at the *Craig Rare Breeds Farm* (☎01599/544205), midway between Plockton and Stromeferry, where you can rub shoulders with ancient breeds of Scottish farm animals, llamas and peacocks; ask for one of the cottages on the beach (one sleeps two, the other six).

Both the *Haven* and the *Plockton Inn* have excellent seafood **restaurants**, while *Off the Rails*, in the train station, serves good-value, imaginative snacks by day, and evening meals. *The Buttery*, part of Plockton Stores on the seafront, is also open all day for snacks and inexpensive meals. For **fishing** or **seal-spotting** boat trips from Plockton, try Leisure Marine (☎01599/544306) or Plockton Activity Holidays (☎01599/544356).

Strathcarron and around

The sea lochs immediately north of Plockton are the dual inlets of **Loch Kishorn**, so deep it was once used as an oil-rig construction site, and Loch Carron, which cuts inland to **STRATHCARRON**, a useful linking point between the Kyle of Lochalsh and the Torridon area to the north. Strathcarron has a station on the Kyle–Inverness line; both a postbus (9.45am) and a daily lunch-time service (12.30pm) meet trains before heading on to Sheildaig and Torridon. Right by the station is the Strathcarron Centre (☎01520/722882), where you can pick up local **information** and details of walks, while next door, the *Strathcarron Hotel* (☎01520/722227; ❸) uses lots of local produce in its tasty bar **meals** and also serves real ale. A mile along the road to Kyle, the *Carron Restaurant* (☎01520/722488) also serves up good food. The linked Carron Pottery is a good place to see some local crafts.

Another useful connection point is **ACHNASHEEN**, 18 miles northeast of Strathcarron at the head of Glen Carron. Also a stop on the Kyle train line, Achnasheen marks a fork in the road from Inverness: one branch, the A890, follows the railway towards Strathcarron and Kyle, the other, the A832, snakes through the mountains to Kinlochewe, beside the Torridon hills. Here again there are postbus links from the railway through to Torridon.

Wester Ross

Wester Ross, the western seaboard of the old Scottish county of Ross-shire, is widely regarded as the most glamorous stretch of this coast. Here all the classic elements of Scotland's **coastal scenery** – dramatic mountains, sandy beaches, whitewashed crofting cottages and shimmering island views – come together in spectacular fashion. Though popular with generations of adventurous Scottish holiday-makers, only one or two places feel blighted by tourist numbers, with places such as **Applecross** and the peninsulas north and south of **Gairloch** maintaining an endearing simplicity and sense of isolation. There is some tough but wonderful **hiking** to be had in the mountains around **Torridon** and **Coigach**, while **boat trips** out among the islands and the prolific sea- and bird-life of the coast are a common feature. The main settlement is the attractive fishing town of **Ullapool**, port for ferry services to Stornoway in the Western Isles, but a pleasant enough place to use as a base, not least for its active social and cultural scene.

The Applecross peninsula

The most dramatic approach to the **Applecross peninsula** (the English-sounding name is a corruption of the Gaelic *Apor Crosan*, meaning "estuary") is from the south, along the infamous **Bealach na Ba** (literally "Pass of the Cattle"). Crossing the forbidding hills behind Kishorn and rising to 2053ft, with a gradient and switchback bends worthy of the Alps, this route – a popular cycling piste – is hair-raising in places, but the panoramic views across the Minch to Raasay and Skye more than compensate. The other way in is from the north: a beautiful coast road that meanders slowly from Shieldaig on Loch Torridon, with tantalizing glimpses of the Cuillin to the south.

The sheltered, fertile coast around **APPLECROSS** village, where the Irish missionary monk Maelrhuba founded a monastery in 673 AD, comes as a surprise after the bleakness of the moorland approach. It's an idyllic place: you can wander along lanes banked with wild iris and orchids, and explore beaches and rock pools on the shore. It's also quite an adventure to get here by **public transport**. The nearest train station is seventeen miles northeast at Strathcarron (see p.629), which you have to reach by 9.50am in order to catch the postbus to Shieldaig, on Loch Torridon. From here, a second postie leaves for Applecross at 11.30am, arriving around 1pm. No buses run over the Bealach na Ba. The old *Applecross Inn* (Ⓣ01520/744262, Ⓦwww.applecross.net; ❷), right beside the sea, is the focal point of the community, with rooms upstairs and a lively bar serving snacks and tasty platefuls of local seafood. The inn is the first stop for most folk coming here; if their rooms are full they'll happily recommend any houses locally offering B&B. **Camping** (Ⓣ01520/744268) is provided at the *Flowertunnel*, as you come into the village from the pass. There are a number of short waymarked trails along the shore – great for walking off a pub lunch. If you're interested in something more exerting, contact the local experts Applecross Mountain & Sea (Ⓣ01520/744393), who organize mountain expeditions and kayaking around the coast.

Loch Torridon

Loch Torridon marks the northern boundary of the Applecross peninsula, its awe-inspiring setting backed by the appealingly rugged mountains of **Liathach** and **Beinn Eighe**, tipped by streaks of white quartzite. The greater part of this area is composed of the reddish 750-million-year-old Torridonian sandstone, and some 15,000 acres of the massif are under the protection of the National Trust for Scotland. They run a **Countryside Centre** (May–Sept Mon–Sat 10am–5pm, Sun 2–5pm) at Torridon village at the east end of the loch, where you can call in and learn a bit more about the local geology, flora and fauna. The trust also look after **Shieldaig Island**, which lies off the pretty village of **SHIELDAIG** on the southern shore of Loch Torridon, where a heronry has been established among the tall Scots pines which cover the island; you might also have a chance of spotting a kestrel or an otter. There's an attractive small **hotel** by the shore in the village, *Tigh-an-Eilean* (☎01520/755251; April–Oct; ❻), and also a simple campsite a little way up the hill. Out of the village at Doireaonor, on the southwest side of Loch Shieldaig, west of Shieldaig across the inlet, is a good B&B, *Tigh Fada* (☎01520/755248; ❶; Feb–Nov), while *Kinloch* (☎01520/755206; ❷), just outside Shieldaig, is a great place for outdoor types and families. Loch Torridon prides itself on its **seafood**, either caught or farmed locally. *Tigh an Eilean* at Shieldaig serves impressive meals, while the much simpler *Loch Torridon Smoke House* on the back road behind Shieldaig sells various kinds of smoked fish as well as serving tea and home baking.

At **TORRIDON** village the main road heads inland through Glen Torridon, while the minor road which runs along the northern shore of the loch is scenic and dramatic, winding first along the shore then climbing and twisting past lochans, cliffs and gorges to the green wooded slopes of **Diabaig**. At Torridon

Walks around Torridon

Ordnance Survey Outdoor Leisure map No. 8.

There can be difficult conditions on virtually all hiking routes around Torridon, and the weather can change very rapidly. If you're relatively inexperienced but want to do the magnificent ridge walk along the **Liathach** (pronounced "*lee*-ach") massif, or the strenuous traverse of **Beinn Eighe** (pronounced "ben *ay*"), you can join a National Trust Ranger Service guided hike (details from the Torridon Countryside Centre; ☎01445/791221).

For those confident to go it alone, one of many possible routes takes you behind Liathach and down the pass, **Coire Dubh**, to the main road in Glen Torridon. This is a great, straightforward walk if you're properly equipped (see p.46), covering thirteen miles and taking in superb landscapes. Allow yourself the whole day. Start at the stone bridge on the Diabaig road along the north side of Loch Torridon. Follow the Abhainn Coire Mhic Nobuil burn up to the fork at the wooden bridge and take the track east to the pass (a rather indistinct watershed) between Liathach and Beinn Eighe. The path becomes a little lost in the boggy area studded with lochans at the top of the pass, but the route is clear and, once over the watershed, the path is easy to follow. At this point you can, weather permitting, make the rewarding diversion up to the **Coire Mhic Fhearchair**, widely regarded as the most spectacular corrie in Scotland; otherwise continue down the Coire Dubh stream, ford the burn and follow its west bank down to the Torridon road, from where it's about four miles back to Loch Torridon.

A rewarding walk even in rough weather is the seven-mile hike up the coast from **Lower Diabaig**, ten miles northwest of Torridon village, to **Redpoint**. On a clear day, the views across to Raasay and Applecross from this gentle undulating path are superlative, but you'll have to return along the same trail, or else make your way back via Loch Maree on the A832. If you're staying in Shieldaig, the track that winds up the peninsula running north from the village makes a pleasant ninety-minute round walk.

itself, near the NTS visitors centre, there's a modern SYHA **hostel** (ⓣ01445/791284, ⓦwww.syha.org.uk; April–Oct), as well as one of the area's grandest **hotels**, the rambling Victorian *Loch Torridon Hotel* (ⓣ01445/791242; ❽), set amid well-tended loch-side grounds. Next door, *Ben Damph Lodge* (ⓣ01445/791242, ⓦwww.bendamph.lochtorridonhotel.com; ❸) is a modern conversion of an old farmstead, with neat if characterless rooms and a large climber's bar. Along at Diabaig, Miss Ross (ⓣ01445/790240; ❶) has comfortable accommodation overlooking the rocky bay. There's no road to the tiny, spartan *Craig* hostel (no phone; May–Aug), a stone cottage by the shore three miles beyond Diabeg.

Loch Maree

About eight miles north of Loch Torridon, **Loch Maree**, dotted with Caledonian pine-covered islands, is one of the west's scenic highlights, best viewed from the A832 road that drops down to its southeastern tip through Glen Docherty. It's also surrounded by some of Scotland's finest **deerstalking** country: the remote, privately owned *Letterewe Lodge* on the north shore, accessible only by helicopter or boat, lies at the heart of a famous deer forest. Queen Victoria stayed a few days here in 1877 at the wonderfully sited *Loch Maree Hotel* (ⓣ01445/760288, ⓔlochmaree@easynet.co.uk; ❺), which is a bit tumbledown these days but not a bad spot for a bar meal, particularly on a nice day when you can sit outside on the lochside lawn.

At the southeastern end of the loch, the A896 from Torridon meets the A832 from Achnasheen (see p.629) at the small settlement of **KINLOCHEWE**, another good base if you're heading into the hills. There is a plain bunkhouse as well as decent B&B at the *Kinlochewe Hotel* (ⓣ01445/760253; bunkhouse ❶, B&B ❷), but for little extra you're much better off heading a mile southwest along the road towards Torridon to *Cromasaig* B&B (ⓣ01455/760234, ⓔcromasaig@msn.com; ❶), a great place for hill-walkers set in the forest right at the foot of the track up Beinn Eighe. In Kinlochewe itself, MORU outdoor shop at the old petrol station opposite the hotel will furnish you with maps and guidebooks, as well as equipment and sound local advice. The *Kinlochewe Hotel* serves good meals and bar food.

The A832 skirts the southern shore of Loch Maree, passing the **Beinn Eighe Nature Reserve**, the UK's oldest wildlife sanctuary. Parts of the Beinn Eighe reserve are forested with Caledonian pinewood, which once covered the whole of the country, and it is home to pine marten, wildcat, fox, badger, Scottish crossbill, buzzards and golden eagles. There's also a wide range of flora, with the higher rocky slopes producing spectacular natural alpine rock gardens. A mile north of Kinlochewe, the **Beinn Eighe Visitor Centre** (Easter & May–Sept daily 10am–5pm) on the A832, gives details of the area's rare species and sells pamphlets describing two excellent **walks** in the reserve: a woodland trail through loch-side forest, and a more strenuous half-day hike around the base of Beinn Eighe. Both start from the car park a mile north of the visitor centre.

Gairloch and around

Mostly scattered around the sheltered northeastern shore of **Loch Gairloch**, the crofting township of **GAIRLOCH** thrives during the summer as a low-key holiday resort with several tempting sandy beaches and some excellent coastal walks within easy reach. The **Gairloch Heritage Museum** (April–Sept Mon–Sat 10am–5pm; Oct Mon–Fri 10am–1.30pm; call for winter hours; ⓣ01445/712287; £2.50) has eclectic, appealing displays covering geology, archeology, fishing and farming that range from a mock-up of a croft house to an early knitting machine. Probably the most interesting section is the archive made by elderly locals – an array of photographs, maps, genealogies, lists of place names and taped recollections, mostly in Gaelic.

Practicalities

There's a late-afternoon **bus** (Mon–Sat) from Inverness to Gairloch, though the route and arrival time varies. Two postbus services leave from in front of Gairloch post office: one at 8.20am goes northwest to Melvaig, and the other at 10.35am goes southwest to Redpoint.

Gairloch has a good choice of **accommodation**, most of it mid-range; the **tourist office**, right by the museum (July to mid-Sept Mon–Sat 9am–6pm, Sun noon–5pm; June Mon–Fri 9.30am–5.30pm, Sat 10am–5pm; April, May & mid-Sept to Oct Mon–Fri 10am–5pm, Sat 11am–4pm; ⓣ01445/712130) can help you search for possibilities. The secluded *Shieldaig Lodge Hotel* (ⓣ01445/741250, ⓔshieldaigH@aol.com; ❹) is an old Victorian shooting lodge right on the shore along the Badachro road; while along the north side of the loch, a little past the North Erradale junction, is *Little Lodge* (ⓣ01445/771237; half board ❼; minimum stay two nights) an outstanding spot with immaculately furnished rooms, a log-burning stove, cashmere goats and dramatic sea views, as well as superb food. In the heart of the village, the *Mountain Lodge & Restaurant* (ⓣ01445/712316; ❷) offers a refreshingly alternative experience – run by enthusiastic, young outdoor types the ground floor has a shop crammed with wind chimes and travel books, a café serving hearty, wholesome food and a conservatory and deck with great views over the bay, while upstairs are three comfortable rooms. There are good **B&Bs** scattered throughout the area: try Gaelic-speaking Miss Mackenzie's *Duisary* (ⓣ01445/712252; ❶); nearby *Croit Mo Sheanair* (ⓣ01445/712389; ❶); or *Harbour View* (ⓣ01445/741316; ❶) at Badachro. There's an SYHA **hostel** in a spectacular setting on the edge of a cliff at **Carn Dearg** two miles up the Melvaig road (ⓣ01445/712219, ⓦwww.syha.org.uk; mid-May to Sept), as well as accommodation at Rua Rheidh lighthouse (see below). **Camping** is possible at Big Sand or at Redpoint.

For **food**, the fact that the chef at Gairloch's *Scottish Seafood Restaurant* next to the petrol station near the pier is also the harbourmaster means that the fish and shellfish served up will be the pick of the catch. Nearby the *Old Inn* serves bar meals and a decent range of real ales. Another seafood option is *The Steading* beside the Heritage Museum. For **snacks**, the *Mountain Lodge* do a busy trade with their massive (and pricey) muffins and decent cups of coffee; they also serve evening meals in the summer months.

One leisurely way to explore the coast is on a wildlife-spotting **cruise**: Gairloch Marine Life Centre & Cruises (Easter–Oct; ⓣ01445/712636), at the pier, run informative and enjoyable boat trips across the bay in search of dolphins, porpoises, seals and even the odd whale. You can also **rent a boat** for the day through Gairloch's chandlery shop (ⓣ01445/712458).

Rua Reidh and around

The area's real attraction, however, is its beautiful **coastline**. To get to one of the most impressive stretches, head around the north side of the bay and follow the single-track B8021 beyond Big Sand (a cleaner and quieter beach than the one in Gairloch) to the tiny crofting hamlet of **Melvaig** (reachable by the 8.20am Gairloch postbus), from where a narrow surfaced track winds out to **Rua Reidh Point** (pronounced "roo-a-ray"). The converted **lighthouse** here, which looks straight out to Harris in the Outer Hebrides, serves slap-up afternoon teas and home-baked cakes (Easter–Oct Tues & Thurs 11am–5pm; ⓣ01445/771263, ⓦwww.ruareidh.co.uk). You can also stay in its comfortable and relaxed **bunkhouse** or **double rooms** (❶) – popular in high season – or use it as a base for one of the popular walking or activity holidays organized by the folk who run the bunkhouse.

Around the headland from Rua Reidh lies the secluded and beautiful **Camas Mor** beach. For a great half-day walk, follow the marked footpath inland (southeast) from here along the base of a sheer scarp slope, and past a string of lochans, ruined crofts and a remote wood to **Midtown** on the east side of the peninsula, five miles north of Poolewe on the B8057. However, unless you leave a car at the end of the trail or arrange to be picked up, you'll have to walk or hitch back to Gairloch, as the only transport along this road is an early morning post van.

Badachro and Redpoint

Three miles south of Gairloch, a narrow single-track lane (built with the Destitution Funds raised during the nineteenth-century potato famine) winds west from the main A832, past wooded coves and inlets on its way south of the loch to **BADACHRO**, a sleepy former fishing village in a very attractive setting with a wonderful pub, the *Badachro Inn*, right by the water's edge, where you can sit in the beer garden watching the boats come and go and tuck into some lovely food.

Beyond Badachro, the road winds for five more miles along the shore to **Redpoint**, a straggling hamlet with beautiful beaches of peach-coloured sand and great views to Raasay, Skye and the Western Isles. It also marks the trailhead for the wonderful coast walk to Lower Diabaig, described on p.631. Even if you don't fancy a full-blown hike, following the path a mile or so brings you to the exquisite **beach** hidden on the south side of the headland, which you'll probably have all to yourself. Redpoint is served by the Gairloch postbus (see below).

Poolewe and around

It's a fifteen-minute hop by bus over the headland from Gairloch to the trim little village of **POOLEWE** on the sheltered south side of Loch Ewe, at the mouth of the River Ewe as it rushes down from Loch Maree. One of the area's best **walks** begins near here, signposted from the layby-cum-viewpoint on the main A832, a mile south of the village. It takes a couple of hours to follow the easy trail across open craggy moorland to the shores of Loch Maree, and thence to the car park at **Slatterdale**, seven miles southeast of Gairloch. If you reach Slatterdale just before 7pm on a Tuesday, Thursday or Friday, you should be able to pick up the Westerbus from Inverness back to Poolewe or Aultbea (confirm times on ⓣ01445/712255). Also worthwhile is the ten-mile drive along the small sideroad running along the west shore of Loch Ewe to **COVE**. Here you'll find an atmospheric cave that was used by the severe Presbyterian "Wee Frees" as a church into this century; it's quite a perilous scramble up, however, and there's little to see once you're there.

The *Poolewe Hotel* (ⓣ01445/781241; ❹) is on the Cove road; it's old-fashioned but very pleasant and serves straightforward food. From September until April they also have a bunkhouse available for hill-walkers. Rather more upscale is the *Pool House Hotel* (ⓣ01445/781272, ⓦwww.inverewe.co.uk; ❻) which belonged to Osgood Mackenzie (see below); it has lovely views out over the loch and serves tasty, if pricey, bar and restaurant meals. For **B&B** in Poolewe, *The Creagan* (☎01445/781424; ❶), up the track on the village side of the campsite, is a welcoming modern house wreathed with honeysuckle. At Cove, Mrs MacDonald (☎01445/781354; ❷; April–Oct) offers upscale B&B with fine loch views. There's also an excellent **campsite** between the village and Inverewe Gardens (☎01445/781249; April–Oct). *The Bridge Cottage Coffee Shop*, just up the Cove road from the village crossroads, is the best of the local snack stops.

Inverewe Gardens

Half a mile across the bay from Poolewe on the A832, **Inverewe Gardens** (daily: mid-March to Oct 9.30am–9pm; Nov to mid-March 9.30am–5pm; NTS; £5), a verdant oasis of foliage and riotously colourful flower collections, forms a vivid contrast to the wild, heathery crags of the adjoining coast. The gardens were the brainchild of **Osgood Mackenzie**, who inherited the surrounding 12,000-acre estate from his stepfather, the laird of Gairloch, in 1862. Taking advantage of the area's famously temperate climate (a consequence of the Gulf Stream, which draws a warm sea current from Mexico to within a stone's throw of these shores), Mackenzie collected plants from all over the world for his walled garden, which still forms the nucleus of the complex. Protected from Loch Ewe's corrosive salt breezes by a dense brake of Scots pine, rowan, oak, beech and birch trees, the fragile plants flourished on rich soil brought here as ballast on Irish ships to overlay the previously infertile beach gravel and sea grass. By the time Mackenzie died in 1922, his garden sprawled over the whole peninsula, surrounded by 100 acres of woodland. Today the National Trust for Scotland strives to develop the place along the lines envisaged by its founder.

Around 180,000 visitors pour through here annually, but the place rarely feels overcrowded. Interconnected by a labyrinthine network of twisting paths and walkways, more than a dozen gardens feature exotic plant collections from as far afield as Chile, China, Tasmania and the Himalayas. Strolling around the lotus ponds, palm trees, and borders ablaze with exotic blooms, it's amazing to think you're at the same latitude as Hudson's Bay. Mid-May to mid-June is the best time to see the rhododendrons and azaleas, while the herbaceous garden reaches its peak in July and August, as does the wonderful Victorian vegetable and flower garden beside the sea. Look out, too, for the grand old eucalyptus in the Peace Plot, which is the largest in the northern hemisphere, and the nearby Ghost Tree *(Davidia involucrata)*, representing the earliest evolutionary stages of flowering trees. You'll need at least a couple of hours to do the whole lot justice, and leave time for the **visitor centre** (mid-March to Oct daily 9.30am–5.30pm), which houses an informative display on the history of the garden and is the starting-point for **guided walks** (April–Oct Mon–Fri 1.30pm). The **restaurant** at the top of the car park does good snacks and lunches.

Gruinard Bay and Scoraig

Three buses each week (Mon, Wed & Sat; eastwards in the morning, westwards in the evening) run the twenty-mile stretch along the A832 from Poolewe past **Aultbea**, a small NATO naval base, to the head of **Little Loch Broom**, surrounded by a salt marsh that is covered with flowers in early summer. From **LAIDE** (linked by postbus with Braemore and the train station at Achnasheen), the road skirts the shores of **Gruinard Bay**, offering fabulous views and, at the inner end of the bay, some excellent sandy beaches. During World War II, **Gruinard Island**, in the bay, was used as a testing ground for biological warfare, and for years was ringed by huge signs warning the public not to land. The anthrax spores released during the testing can live in the soil for up to a thousand years, but in 1987, after much protest, the Ministry of Defence had the island decontaminated and it was finally declared "safe" in 1990.

The road heads inland before joining the A835 at **Braemore Junction** (three Inverness–Ullapool buses stop here daily) above the head of **Loch Broom**. Just nearby, and easily accessible from the A835, are the spectacular 164ft **Falls of Measach**, which plunge through the mile-long **Corrieshalloch Gorge**. You can overlook the cascades from a special observation platform, or from the impressive suspension bridge that spans the chasm, whose 197ft vertical sides are draped in a rich array of plant life, with thickets of wych elm, goat willow and bird cherry miraculously thriving on the cliffs. North from the head of Loch Broom to Ullapool is one of the so-called **Destitution Roads**, built to give employment to local people during the nineteenth-century potato famines.

As befits the stunning scenery, there are some lovely places to **stay** all along this stretch, including the excellent *Old Smiddy* (Ⓣ01445/731425, Ⓔoldsmiddy@aol.com; ❹; April–Oct) on the main road in Laide. Crammed with travel trophies, family memorabilia, books and paintings by local artists (some on sale), the hotel has fine mountain views to the east, and serves outstanding food. Another option is *Cul-na-Mara* (Ⓣ01445/731295, Ⓦwww.culnamara-guesthouse.co.uk; ❷), up the turning just past the *Sand Hotel*. At the head of Little Loch Broom, the *Dundonnell Hotel* (Ⓣ01854/633204, Ⓦwww.dundonnellhotel.com; ❻) is smart and comfortable and serves bar meals, while *Sail Mhor Croft* (Ⓣ01854/633224, Ⓔsailmhor@btinternet.com) is a small independent **hostel** in a lovely location on the lochside a couple of miles before the *Dundonnell Hotel*.

The Scoraig peninsula

The outer part of the rugged **Scoraig peninsula**, dividing Little Loch Broom and Loch Broom, is one of the remotest places on the British mainland, accessible only by boat or on foot. Formerly dotted with crofting townships, it is now deserted apart from tiny **SCORAIG** village, where a mostly self-sufficient community has established itself, complete with windmills, organic vegetable gardens and a thriving primary school. Understandably, Scoraig's inhabitants would rather not be regarded as tourist curiosities, so you should only venture out here if you're sympathetic to such a community. To reach Scoraig, you have two main options: you can drive to Badrallach and walk from there, or phone the Scoraig **boat** operator (Ⓣ01854/633392), who'll make the run by appointment. Accommodation is limited to a small but particularly pleasant **campsite** at Badrallach, on the northeast shore of Little Loch Broom where there's also a good bothy available (Ⓣ01854/633281).

Ullapool

ULLAPOOL, the northwest's principal centre of population, was founded at the height of the herring boom in 1788 by the British Fisheries Society, on a sheltered arm of land jutting into Loch Broom. The grid-plan town is still an important fishing centre, though the **ferry** link to Stornoway on Lewis (see p.475) means that in high season its personality is practically swamped by visitors. Even so, it's still a hugely appealing place and a good base for exploring the northwest Highlands. Regular **buses** run from here to Inverness and

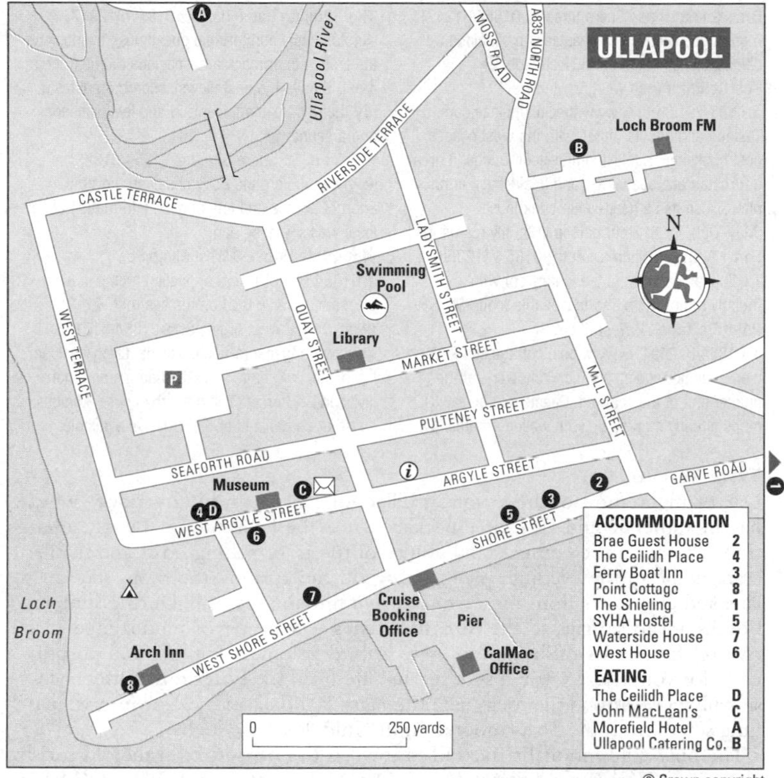

Durness, while there's an early morning run through to the remote train station at Lairg. Accommodation is plentiful and Ullapool is an obvious hideaway if the weather is bad, with cosy pubs, a new swimming pool and a lively arts centre, the *Ceilidh Place*.

Arrival and information

Forming the backbone of its grid plan, Ullapool's two main arteries are the loch-side **Shore Street** and, parallel to it, **Argyle Street**, further inland. **Buses** stop at the pier, in the town centre near the ferry dock, from where it's easy to get your bearings. The well-run **tourist office** (June–Aug Mon–Sat 9am–5.30pm, Sun noon–5pm; April, May, Sept & Oct Mon–Sat 9am–5pm, Sun noon–4pm; Oct Mon–Fri 10am–5pm, Sat noon–4pm; Nov & Dec Mon–Fri 2–5.30pm; ⓣ01854/612135), on Argyle Street, offers an accommodation booking service. There are two or three daily **ferries** to the Outer Hebrides (Mon–Sat; 2hr 30min) run by CalMac (ⓣ0870/565 0000, ⓦwww.calmac.co.uk).

Accommodation

Ullapool has all kinds of **accommodation**, including a couple of welcoming hostels and some decent guesthouses and B&Bs, plus a well-situated **campsite** near the tip of the peninsuala between town and the sea.

Brae Guest House Shore Street ⓣ01854/612421. A great guesthouse in a beautifully maintained traditional building right on the loch-side. ❷

The Ceilidh Place West Argyle Street ⓣ01854/612103, ⓦwww.theceilidhplace.com. Tasteful and popular hotel, with the west coast's best bookshop, a relaxing first-floor lounge, a great bar/restaurant, sea views, and a laid-back atmosphere. Also has a good-value bunkhouse (May–Oct), for £12 per person in family rooms. ❻

Ferry Boat Inn Shore Street ⓣ01854/612366. Traditional inn right on the waterfront with a friendly atmosphere and reasonable food. ❸

Point Cottage 22 West Shore St ⓣ01854/612494, ⓦwww.pointcottage.co.uk. Very well-equipped rooms and good showers, at the quieter end of the seafront. Guests can borrow OS maps already marked up with walking routes. ❷

The Shieling Garve Road ⓣ01854/612947. Outstandingly comfortable guesthouse overlooking the loch with immaculate, spacious rooms (rooms 4 and 5 have the best views), superb breakfasts (try their home-made venison and leek sausages) and a sauna. ❷

SYHA hostel Shore Street ⓣ01854/612254, ⓦwww.syha.org.uk. Busy hostel on the front, with internet access and lots of good information about local walks. Closed Jan.

Waterside House 6 West Shore St ⓣ01854/612140. Very appealing rooms in a very pleasant, friendly B&B on the seafront. ❷

West House West Argyle St ⓣ01854/613126, ⓦwww.scotpackers-hostels.co.uk. Lively, welcoming hostel with four- to six-bed dorms and more civilized B&B on offer in a nearby house. Minibus day-tours organized and bike rental available.

The Town

Day or night, most of the action in Ullapool centres on the **harbour**, which has an authentic and salty air, especially when the boats are in. By day, attention focuses on the comings and goings of the ferry, fishing boats and smaller craft, while in the evening, yachts swing on the current, the shops stay open late, and customers from the *Ferry Boat Inn* line the sea wall. During summer, booths advertise trips to the **Summer Isles** – a cluster of uninhabited islets two to three miles offshore – to view seabird colonies, dolphins and porpoises, but if you're lucky you'll spot marine life from the waterfront. Otters occasionally nose around the rocks near the *Ferry Boat Inn*, and seals swim past begging scraps from the boats moored in the middle of the loch.

The only conventional attraction in town is the **museum**, in the old parish church on West Argyle Street (April–Oct Mon–Sat 9.30am–5.30pm; March Mon–Sat 11am–3pm; Nov–Feb Wed, Thurs & Sat 11am–3pm; £2), with displays on crofting, fishing, local religion and emigration. During the Clearances, Ullapool was one of the ports through which evicted crofters left to start new lives in Canada, Australia and New Zealand.

Eating, drinking and entertainment

The two best **pubs** in Ullapool are the *Arch Inn*, home of the Ullapool football team, and the *Ferry Boat Inn* (known as the "FBI"), where you can enjoy a pint of real ale at the lochside – midges permitting. The slightly less characterful *Seaforth* by the pier is the place to catch middle-of-the-road live **music**, while live folk music is a regular occurrence at *The Ceilidh Place* or on Thursday nights at the *FBI*. *The Ceilidh Place* is one of the happening places in the Highlands, with a decent-quality line-up of touring plays, music festivals, poetry-readings and live entertainment.

The *Ceilidh Place* is also one of the best places in town to find something to **eat**, with a coffee shop, a pleasant bar serving filling snacks and a spacious restaurant offering a selection of imaginative seafood and vegetarian dishes. The other main restaurant in town is in the *Morefield Hotel*, on Morefield Lane off North Road (ⓣ01854/612161), which despite the rather uninspiring motel setting is a long-standing locals' favourite for seafood, big on portions and rich, creamy sauces. It's not so great for vegetarians, and is hard to find, being improbably hidden in a modern housing estate beyond the bridge on the north

Walks, hikes and cycle rides around Ullapool

Ordnance Survey maps nos. 15, 19 & 20.

Ullapool lies at the start of several excellent **hiking trails**, ranging from sedate shoreside ambles to long and strenuous ascents of Munros. However, the weather here can change very quickly, so take the necessary precautions (see p.46). More detailed descriptions of the routes outlined below are available from the hostel on Shore Street (30p); hostellers can also rent the relevant up-to-date OS maps – essential for the hill walks.

An easy **half-day ramble** begins at the north end of Quay Street: cross the walkway/footbridge here and follow the riverbank on the far side left towards the sea. Walk past the golf course and follow the shore line as best you can for around two miles until you reach a hilltop lighthouse from where you gain fine views across the sea to the Summer Isles. Return the same way or via the main A835 road.

For a harder **half-day hike**, head north along Mill Street on the east edge of town to Broom Court retirement home, trailhead for the Ullapool hill walk (look for the sign next to the electricity substation). A rocky path zigzags steeply up from the roadside to the summit of **Meall Mor**, where there are great views of the area's major peaks. This is also a prime spot for botanists, with a rich array of plants and flowers, including two insect-eating species: sundew and butterwort. The path then drops sharply down the heather-clad north side of Meall Mor into **Glen Achall**, where you turn left onto the surfaced road running past the limestone quarry; the main road back to Ullapool lies a further thirty minutes' walk west. A right turn where the path meets the road will take you up to Loch Achall and the start of an old drovers' trail across the middle of the Highlands to **Croick** (see p.664). A well-maintained bothy at **Knockdamph**, eleven miles further on, marks the midway point of this long-distance hike, which should not be undertaken alone or without proper gear.

If you're reasonably experienced and can use a map and compass, a day-walk well worth tackling is the rock path to **Achininver**, near Achiltibuie. The route, which winds along one of the region's most beautiful and unspoilt stretches of coastline to a small **hostel** (book ahead on ⓣ01854/622254, ⓦwww.syha.org.uk; mid-May to Sept), is easy to follow in good weather, but gets very boggy and slippery when wet. Sound footwear, a light pack and a route guide are essential.

The warden and assistants at Ullapool hostel can also give advice on more serious mountain hikes in the area. Among the most popular is the walk to **Scoraig** (see p.636), following the old coast route over the pass to Badrallach, and then northwest to Scoraig village itself. The only drawback with this rewarding route is that you'll need to make use of one of the local ferry services to get back to Ullapool. If you have a **mountain bike**, the return trip to Scoraig via Badrallach can be completed in a single day.

Alternatively, try the **Rhidorroch** estate track, which turns right off the A835 just past the *Glenfield Hotel* (two miles west of Ullapool), and then heads past the limestone quarry mentioned earlier to Loch Achall and beyond. At the East Rhidorroch Lodge, ignore the suspension bridge and strike up the steep hill ahead onto open moorland and secluded **Loch Damph**, where there's a small bothy.

A much easier but no less scenic cycle route is the tour of Loch Broom, taking in the hamlets of **Letters** and **Loggie** on the tranquil western shore, which you can get to via a quiet single-track road (off the A832 once you've cycled south and round the loch from Ullapool). At the end of this, a jeep track heads for the vitrified Iron Age fort at **Dun Lagaidh**; you have to return by the same route.

side of the town. All three pubs also serve bar meals – the FBI is probably the pick of the bunch. If you're looking for **picnic** or **self-catering fare**, try John MacLean's wholefood shop and deli on West Argyle Street, or the Ullapool Catering Company at Unit 3, West Morefield Industrial Estate

(☎01854/612969) where you can pick up organic vegetables, fresh seafood and sandwiches.

The Coigach peninsula

North of Ullapool, the landscape changes to consist not of mountain ranges but of extraordinary peaks rising individually from the moorland. As you head further north, the peaks become more widely spaced and settlements smaller and fewer, linked by twisting single-track roads and shore-side footpaths that make excellent hiking trails. You can easily sidestep what little tourist traffic there is by heading down the peaceful backroads, which, after twisting through idyllic crofts, invariably end up at a deserted beach or windswept headland with superb clear-day views west to the Outer Hebrides.

Ten miles north of Ullapool, a single-track road winds west off the A835 to squeeze between the northern shore of Loch Lurgainn and the lower slopes of **Cul Beag** (2523ft) and craggy Stac Pollaidh (2012ft) to reach the **Coigach peninsula**. To the southeast, the awesome bulk of **Ben More Coigach** (2439ft) presides over the district, which contains some spectacular coastal scenery including a string of sandy beaches and the Summer Isles, scattered just offshore.

Achiltibuie

Coigach's main settlement is **ACHILTIBUIE**, an old crofting village stretched across the hillside above a series of white-sand coves and rocks tapering into the Atlantic, from where a fleet of small fishing boats carries sheep, and tourists, to the enticing pastures of the **Summer Isles** which lie a little way offshore. The village also attracts gardening enthusiasts, thanks to the unlikely presence of the **Hydroponicum** (late May to Sept daily 10am–5pm; £4.75; tours on the hour), a cross between a giant greenhouse and a futuristic scientific research station. Dubbed "The Garden of the Future", all kinds of flowers, fruits and vegetables are grown without using soil in conditions that concentrate the sun's heat while protecting the plants from winter (and summer) chill. Bumper crops of strawberries, salad leaves, figs and even bananas result – guided tours explain how it's all done and show you round the different "climate zones". You can taste whatever's being harvested in the subtropical setting of the *Lily Pond Café*, which serves meals, desserts and snacks and is open in the evening (Thurs–Sun only). Also worth a visit is the **Achiltibuie Smokehouse** (April–Sept Mon–Sat 9.30am–5pm; free), five miles north of the Hydroponicum at **Altandhu**, where you can see meat, fish and game being cured in the traditional way and can buy some afterwards. Next to this, the *Am Fuaran* bar serves evening meals and, like everywhere else along this stretch, enjoys terrific views over to the Summer Isles. For **boat** trips round these attractive islets, including some time ashore on the largest, Tanera Mor, Ian Macleod's boat *Hectoria* (☎01854/622200) runs twice a day from the pier by Achiltibuie.

For **accommodation**, the wonderfully understated *Summer Isles Hotel* (☎01854/622282, Ⓔsummerisleshotel@aol.com; ❻; April–Oct), just up the road from the Hydroponicum, enjoys a near-perfect setting with views over the islands, and is virtually self-sufficient. The hotel buys in Hydroponicum fruit and vegetables, but has its own dairy, poultry, and even runs a small smokehouse, so the food in its excellent **restaurant** (open to non-residents) is about as fresh as it comes. A set dinner costs about £40, although superb bar snacks and lunches feature crab, langoustines and smoked mackerel starting from £5. Of Achiltibuie's several **B&Bs**, *Dornie House* (☎01854/622271; ❶), halfway to

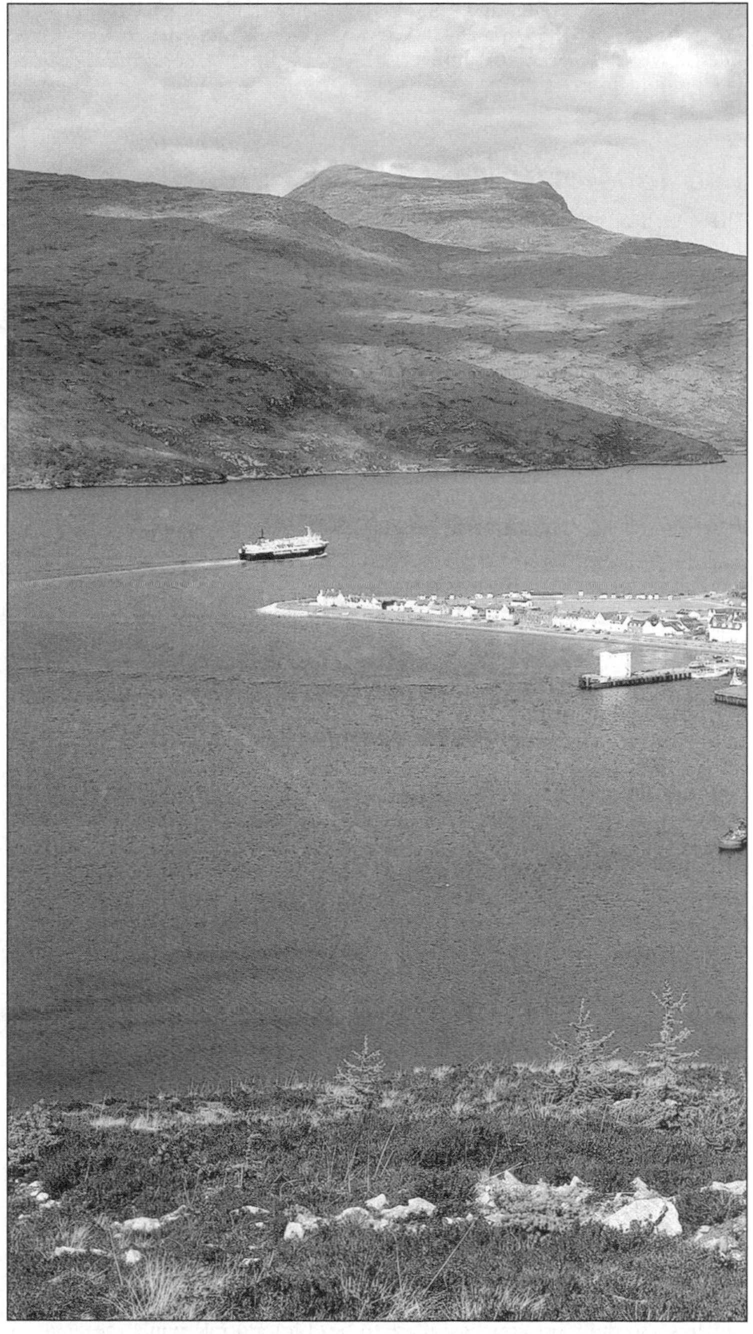

△ Ullapool

Altandhu, is welcoming, and there's also a beautifully situated twenty-bed SYHA **hostel** (Ⓣ01854/622254, Ⓦwww.syha.org.uk; mid-May to Sept), three miles down the coast at Achininver, which is handy for accessing Coigach's many mountain hikes.

The far northwest coast

The stretch of coast north of Wester Ross is sometimes ignored in favour of the rich pickings around places such as Ullapool and Gairloch, yet for many the stark, elemental beauty of the Highlands is to be found on the **far northwest coast** as nowhere else. Certainly the hills of **Assynt**, the area immediately north of Coigach gathered around the port of **Lochinver**, are among the most distinctive in the country, and the features of the ragged coastline, from the towering rock stack **The Old Man of Stoer** to the beautiful strip of sand at **Sandwood Bay**, retain an essence of wildness. Elsewhere, those inspired to explore can discover hidden **waterfalls** and secret **trout lochs**, while a simple ferry can take you to see the puffins of the island wildlife reserve of **Handa**. Places to stay and eat can be thin on the ground, particularly out of season, but the very lack of infrastructure is testimony to the isolation which this corner of Scotland delivers in such sweeping style.

Lochinver and around

The potholed and narrow road north from Achiltibuie through Inverkirkaig is unremittingly spectacular, threading its way through a tumultuous landscape of secret valleys, moorland and bare rock, past the startling shapes of **Cul Beag** (2523ft), **Cul Mor** (2785ft) and the distinctive sugar-loaf **Suilven** (2398ft). A scattering of pebble-dashed bungalows around a sheltered bay heralds your arrival at **LOCHINVER**, 16 miles due north of Ullapool (although more than twice that by road) and the only sizeable village between there and Thurso – with the only cash machine too. It's a workaday place, with a huge fish market, from where large trucks head off around Britain. There's a better-than-average **tourist office** (April–Oct Mon–Sat 10am–5pm; July & Aug also Sun 10am–5pm; Ⓣ01571/844330), whose visitor centre gives an interesting rundown on the area's geology, wildlife and history; a countryside ranger is available to advise on walks. The area is popular with **fishing** enthusiasts; the place to go for information or to rent equipment is *Ardglas House* (see below). You can get hold of permits at the tourist office or post office, while for boat trips for sea fishing contact Badnaban Cruises (Ⓣ01571/844358).

Lochinver has a range of good **B&Bs**: on the north side of the harbour, *Ardglas* (Ⓣ01571/844257, Ⓔardglas@btinternet.com; ❶) has superb views, though no en-suite rooms, while nearby *Davar* (Ⓣ01571/844501; ❷; March–Oct) is better equipped. More central, just above the tourist office, the comfortable *Polcraig* (Ⓣ01571/844429, Ⓔcathelmac@aol.com; ❷) can arrange fishing. A pleasant and relaxing upmarket option is the small *Albannach Hotel* (Ⓣ01571/844407; ❼ half board; March–Dec) at Baddidarroch, an attractive nineteenth-century building set in a walled garden and renowned for its excellent seafood, caught locally and served in a lovely wood-panelled dining room. Lochinver's most imaginative **food** can be found in the *Larder Riverside Bistro* on the main street: it has local seafood, venison and several vegetarian choices at reasonable prices. Decent bar meals are available at the *Caberfeidh* next door, which is also the most convivial place to head for a drink, while the *Seamen's*

Mission, down at the harbour, is a good option for filling meals (some vegetarian) if you're on a tight budget.

Inverkirkaig Falls

Approaching Lochinver from the south, the road bends sharply through a wooded valley where a signpost for **Inverkirkaig Falls** marks the start of a long but gentle **walk** to the base of **Suilven** – the most distinctive mountain in Scotland, its huge sandstone dome rising above the heather boglands of Assynt. Serious hikers use the path to approach the mighty peak, but you can follow it for an easy three-to-four-hour ramble, taking in a waterfall and a tour of a secluded loch. Just by the start of the trail but tucked away among the dark pine trees, **Achins Bookshop** must rate as the Highland's best-hidden nooks. Though slightly surreal – particularly as there are unlikely to be many other folk around – you can browse the shelves of heavyweight classics and local interest titles, then shuffle into the adjoining **coffee shop** for a bowl of soup or some home baking.

The coast road north of Lochinver

Heading **north** from Lochinver, there are two possible routes: the fast A837, which runs eastwards along the shore of Loch Assynt (see below) to join the northbound A894, or the narrow, more scenic B869 **coast road** that locals dub "The Breakdown Zone", because its ups and downs claim so many victims during summer. Hugging the indented shoreline, this route offers superb views of the Summer Isles, as well as a number of rewarding side-trips to beaches and dramatic cliffs. Post- and schoolbuses from Lochinver cover the route as far as Ardvar or Drumbeg (Mon–Sat).

Unusually, most of the land and lochs around here are owned by local crofters rather than wealthy landlords. Helped by grants and private donations, the **Assynt Crofters' Trust** made history in 1993 when it pulled off the first-ever community buyout of estate land in Scotland, and it's now pursuing a number of projects aimed at strengthening the local economy and conserving the environment. The Trust owns the lucrative fishing rights to the area, too, selling permits for £5 per day (£25 per week) through local post offices and the Lochinver tourist office. An alternative outdoor activity is **pony trekking**, which is available through Clachtoll Trekking Centre (Ⓣ01571/855364, Ⓦwww.normist.co.uk), at Clachtoll on the road between Achmelvich and Stoer.

The first village worthy of a detour is **ACHMELVICH**, a couple of miles along a side road, whose tiny bay cradles a stunning white-sand beach lapped by startlingly turquoise water. There's a noisy **campsite** and a basic forty-bed SYHA **hostel** (Ⓣ01571/844480, Ⓦwww.syha.org.uk; May–Sept) just behind the largest beach. However, for total peace and quiet, head to other, equally seductive beaches beyond the headlands.

The sideroad that branches north off the B869 between **Stoer** and **Clashnessie**, both of which have sandy beaches, ends abruptly by the automatic lighthouse at **Raffin**, built in 1870 by the Stevenson brothers (one of whom was the author Robert Louis Stevenson's dad). You can continue for two miles along a well-worn track to the Point of Stoer, named after the colossal rock pillar that stands offshore known as **"The Old Man of Stoer"**, surrounded by sheer cliffs and splashed with guano from the seabird colonies that nest on its 200ft sides.

East of Lochinver

The area **east of Lochinver**, traversed by the A837 and bounded by the gnarled peaks of the **Ben More Assynt** massif, is a wilderness of mountains, moorland, mist and scree. Dotted with lochs and lochans, it's also an angler's paradise, home to the only non-migratory fish in northern Scotland, the brown trout, and numerous other sought-after species, including the Atlantic salmon, sea trout, Arctic char and a massive prize strain of cannibal ferox. **Fishing** permits for the rivers in this area are like gold dust during the summer, snapped up months in advance by exclusive hunting-lodge hotels, but you can sometimes obtain last-minute cancellations (try the *Inver Lodge* on ⓣ01571/844496); permits to fish lochs are easier to get hold of.

Although most of the land here is privately owned, nearly 27,000 acres are managed as the **Inverpolly National Nature Reserve**, whose grass-roofed, unmanned visitor centre (free access), just up from the roadside at Knockan Crag, twelve miles north of Ullapool on the A835, gives a thorough overview of the diverse flora and wildlife in the surrounding habitats. The theory of thrust faults was developed here in 1859 by eminent geologist James Nicol, and two interpretive **trails** (one 15min, the other 1hr) shows you how to detect the movement of rock plates in the nearby cliffs. A few miles further on in the village of **KNOCKAN**, the *Birchbank Holiday Lodge* (ⓣ01854/666215; ❷) is an excellent base if you're planning to hike or fish in the area; it's on a working sheep farm run by one of the area's top outdoor guides, who has a wealth of information on the best routes and places to explore. They've also got a small campsite with facilities if you'd prefer to pitch your tent.

The *Inchnadamph Hotel* (ⓣ01571/822202; ❺), ten miles further north on **Loch Assynt**, is a wonderfully traditional Highland retreat; inside, the walls are covered with the stuffed catches of its past guests. The hotel offers fine old-fashioned cooking, usually with good vegetarian options, in its moderately priced restaurant and bar. It's popular with anglers, who get free fishing rights to Loch Assynt, as well as several hill lochs backing onto Ben More, haunts of the infamous ferox trout. Just along the road, the **Assynt Field Centre** at *Inchnadamph Lodge* (ⓣ01571/822218, ⓦwww.highland-hostels.co.uk; ❶) has basic but comfortable bunk rooms, some twins as well as more spacious B&B accommodation. Through the year, the centre offers a variety of outdoor activity breaks and holidays, ranging from hill-walking to dry-stone dyke building and cookery courses focusing on local products.

On a rocky promontory pushing out into Loch Assynt stand the jagged remnants of **Ardveck Castle** (free access), a MacLeod stronghold from 1597 that fell to the Seaforth Mackenzies after a siege in 1691. Previously, the Marquis of Montrose had been imprisoned here after his defeat at Carbisdale in 1650. The rebel duke, whom the local laird had betrayed to the government for £20,000 and 400 bowls of sour meal, was eventually led away to be executed in Edinburgh, lashed back to front on his horse.

Kylesku to Sandwood Bay

KYLESKU, 33 miles north of Ullapool on the main A894 road, is the point where a graceful, award-winning road bridge sweeps over the mouth of lochs Glencoul and Glendhu. Opened in 1994, it replaced a ferry connection – and a 100 mile detour via Lairg if you missed the last ferry. There's very little to the place, though the congenial *Kylesku Hotel* (ⓣ01971/502231; ❹; March–Oct) by the water's edge above the old ferry slipway has en-suite rooms, a welcoming bar popular with locals, and an excellent **restaurant** serving outstanding fresh seafood, including lobster, crab, mussels and local salmon (you can watch the fish being landed on the pier). Alternatively, *Newton Lodge* (ⓣ01971/502070; ❹; mid-March to mid-Oct) is a modern, friendly and comfortable small hotel a mile or so up the road towards Ullapool. Cheaper accommodation is available at *Kylesku Lodges and Backpackers* (ⓣ01971/502003, ⓦwww.kyleskulodges.co.uk), with twin rooms in a series of reasonable A-frame lodges with great views to Quinaig mountain and out to sea.

Statesman Cruises runs entertaining **boat trips** (March–Oct daily 11am, Sun–Thurs also 3pm, Fri & Sat also 2pm; round trip 2hr; £10; ⓣ01571/844446) from the jetty below the *Kylesku Hotel* to the 650ft **Eas-Coul-Aulin**, Britain's highest waterfall, located at the head of Loch Glencoul; otters, seals, porpoises and minke whales can occasionally be spotted along the way. The boat also makes regular trips out to **Kerracher Gardens** (mid-May to mid-Sept Tues–Thurs & Sun; boat departs 1pm; £10), only accessible from the sea, another of the remarkable west-coast gardens which harnesses the Gulf Stream weather to create a riot of colour and exotic vegetation in the rugged Highland scenery.

It's also possible to reach Eas-Coul-Aulin on foot: a rough trail (3hr) leaves the A894 three miles south of Kylesku, skirting the south shore of **Loch na Gainmhich** (known locally as the "sandy loch") to approach the falls from above. Great care should be taken here as the path above the cliffs can get very slippery when wet; the rest of the route is also difficult to follow, particularly in bad weather, and should only be attempted by experienced, properly equipped and compass-literate hikers.

There are several less demanding walks around Kylesku; one of the most popular is the half-day low-level route along the north side of Loch Glendhu, beginning at **Kylestrome**, on the opposite side of the bridge from the *Kylesku Hotel*. Follow the surfaced jeep track east from the trailhead and turn left onto a footpath that leads through the woods. This eventually emerges onto the open mountainside, dropping down to cross a burn from where it then winds to a boarded-up old house called Glendhu, where there's a picturesque pebble beach. Several interesting side-trips and variations to this walk may be undertaken with the help of the detailed *Ordnance Survey Landranger Map No. 15*, but you'll need a compass and wet-weather gear.

Scourie and around

Ten miles north of Kylesku, the widely scattered crofting community of **SCOURIE**, on a bluff above the main road, surrounds a beautiful sandy beach whose safe bathing has made it a popular holiday destination for families; there's plenty to do for walkers and trout anglers, too. Scourie itself has some good **accommodation**: try the charming *Scourie Lodge* (ⓣ01971/502248; ❷; March–Oct), an old shooting retreat with a lovely garden; the welcoming owners also do great evening meals. **UPPER BADCALL** village, three miles south of Scourie and even more remote, has a couple of **B&Bs**, including *Stoer View* (ⓣ01971/502411; ❶), whose clean and comfortable rooms look over Eddrachillis Bay to Stoer Point. For a little more luxury, try the nearby long-established *Eddrachillis Hotel* (ⓣ01971/502080; ❺), which enjoys a spectacular situation on the bay, and serves reasonable bar food. There's also a good **campsite**, the *Scourie Caravan and Camping Park* (ⓣ01971/502060) near the centre of the village.

Handa Island

Visible just offshore to the north of Scourie is **Handa Island**, a huge chunk of red Torridon sandstone surrounded by sheer cliffs, carpeted with machair and purple-tinged moorland, and teeming with seabirds. It's private property, but is administered as an internationally important **wildlife reserve** by the Scottish Wildlife Trust and is a real treat for ornithologists, with vast colonies of razorbills and guillemots breeding on its guano-splashed cliffs during summer. From late May to mid-July, large numbers of puffins waddle comically over the turf-covered clifftops where they dig their burrows.

Apart from a solitary warden, Handa is deserted. Until midway through the nineteenth century, however, it supported a thriving, if somewhat eccentric, community of crofters. Surviving on a diet of fish, potatoes and seabirds, the islanders, whose ruined cottages still cling to the slopes by the jetty, devised their own system of government, with a "queen" (Handa's oldest widow) and "parliament" (a council of men who met each morning to discuss the day's business). Uprooted by the 1846 potato famine, most of the villagers eventually emigrated to Canada's Cape Breton.

You'll need about three hours to follow the **footpath** around the island – an easy and enjoyable walk taking in the north shore's Great Stack rock pillar and some fine views across the Minch: a detailed route guide is featured in the SWT's free leaflet, available from the warden's office when you arrive.

Practicalities

Weather permitting, **boats** (ⓣ01971/502347) leave for Handa throughout the day (April–Sept daily 9.30am–2pm; last return 5pm; £7) from the tiny cove of **TARBET**, three miles northwest of the main road and accessible by postbus from Scourie (Mon–Sat 1 daily; 1.50pm), where there's a small car park and jetty.You're encouraged to make a **donation** of around £1.50 towards Handa's upkeep.

Camping is not allowed on the island, but the SWT maintains a **bothy** for bird-watchers (reservations essential on ⓣ0131/312 7765 or with the warden). In Tarbet, the *Croft House* (ⓣ01971/502098; ❶) is a comfortable little **B&B** overlooking the bay. For **food**, Tarbet's unexpected *Seafood Restaurant* (Mon–Sat noon–7pm) serves delicious, moderately priced fish and vegetarian dishes, and a good selection of home-made cakes and desserts, in its airy conservatory just above the jetty.

Kinlochbervie and around

North of Scourie, the road sweeps inland through the starkest part of the Highlands; rocks piled on rocks, bog and water create an almost alien landscape, and the astonishingly bare, stony coastline looks increasingly inhospitable. Just before you reach **Rhichonich**, little more than a hotel tucked under the shadow of another of the northwest's memorable mountains, Foinaven, you'll come to the splendidly remote settlement of **ARDMORE**, located on the peninsula between lochs Inchard and Laxford and reachable only by footpath or boat. An outdoor school was established here in the 1960s by adventurer John Ridgway; now his daughter, Rebecca, and husband Will have set up **Cape Adventure International** (ⓣ01971/521006, ⓦwww.capeventure.com; June–Sept), where you can get stuck into all sorts of outdoor thrills and spills including sea kayaking, rock climbing and land yachting. While they run residential course and "castaway" weekends, if you're only in the area for a short period you can also join in any of the activities as a day course.

At Rhiconich, you can branch off the main road to **KINLOCHBERVIE**, which for all the world seems to be a typical, straggling West Highland crofting community until you turn a corner and encounter an incongrously huge fish-processing plant and modern concrete harbour. Trucks from all over

Europe pick up cod and shellfish from the trawlers here, crewed mainly by east coast fishermen. Don't miss the fish and chips at the Fisherman's Mission (Mon–Thurs 10am–8pm, Fri 10am–4pm). Further sustenance can be found at *The Old Schoolhouse Restaurant and Guest House* (☎01971/521383; ❸), a couple of miles before Kinlochbervie, which provides comfortable accommodation and home-cooked meals.

Sandwood Bay

A single-track road takes you northwest of Kinlochbervie through isolated **Oldshoremore**, a working crofters' village scattered above a stunning white-sand beach, to **BLAIRMORE**, where you can park for the four-mile walk across peaty moorland to deserted **Sandwood Bay**. Few visitors make this half-day detour north, but the **beach** at the end of the rough track is one of the most beautiful in Scotland. Flanked by rolling dunes and lashed by fierce gales for much of the year, the shell-white sands and its dramatic leaning rock stack are said to be haunted by a bearded mariner – one of many sailors to have perished on this notoriously dangerous stretch of coast since the Vikings first navigated it over a millennium ago. Around the turn of the twentieth century, the beach, whose treacherous undercurrents make it unsuitable for swimming, also witnessed Britain's most recent recorded sighting of a **mermaid**. Plans are afoot to bulldoze a motorable road up here, so enjoy the tranquillity while you can. Cape Wrath, the most northwesterly point in mainland Britain (see p.649), lies a day's hike north, but if you're planning to meet the Cape Wrath minibus (see below) to Durness, contact them first since it won't run if the weather turns bad, leaving you stranded. There's a well equipped **campsite** at Oldshoremore (☎01971/521281), or you can continue through Blairmore to **Sheigra**, where the road ends, for informal camping behind the beach.

The north coast

Though a constant stream of sponsored walkers, caravans and tour groups makes it to **John O'Groats**, surprisingly few visitors travel the whole length of the Highlands' wild **north coast**. Those that do, however, rarely return disappointed. Pounded by one of the world's most ferocious seaways, Scotland's rugged northern shore is backed by barren mountains in the west, and in the east by lochs and open rolling grasslands. Between its far ends, mile upon mile of crumbling cliffs and sheer rocky headlands shelter bays whose perfect white beaches are nearly always deserted, even in the height of summer – though, somewhat incongruously, they're also home to Scotland's best **surfing** waves (see p.51). This is a great area for **bird-watching**, with huge seabird colonies clustered in clefts and on remote stacks at regular intervals along the coast; **seals** also bob around in the surf offshore, and in winter **whales** put in the odd appearance in the more sheltered estuaries of the northwest.

Public transport around this stretch of coast can be a slow and frustrating business: **Thurso**, the area's main town and springboard for Orkney, is well connected by bus and train with Inverness, but further west, after the main

A836 peters into a single-track road, you have to rely on **postbus** connections or, in peak season, the single Highland Country bus #387.

Durness and around

Scattered around a string of sheltered sandy coves and grassy clifftops, **DURNESS**, the most northwesterly village on the British mainland, straddles the turning point on the main A838 road as it swings east from the inland peat bogs of the interior to the north coast's fertile strip of limestone machair. First settled by the Picts around 400 BC, the area has been farmed ever since, its crofters being among the few not cleared off estate land during the nineteenth century. Today, Durness is the centre for several crofting communities and an unexpectedly pleasant base for a couple of days, with some good walks. Even if you're only passing through, it's worth pausing here to see the **Smoo Cave**, a gaping hole in a sheer limestone cliff, and to visit beautiful **Balnakiel beach**, to the west. In addition, Durness is the jumping-off point for rugged **Cape Wrath**, the windswept promontory at the Scotland's northwest tip, which has retained an end-of-the-world mystique lost long ago by John O'Groats.

Practicalities

Public transport is sparse; the key service is the Highland Country bus #387 (June to mid-Sept Mon–Sat) leaving Thurso for Durness at 11.30am, and departing Durness on the return journey at 3pm. Durness is also served by the daily Dearman Coaches link (June–Sept) from Inverness via Ullapool and Lochinver. Postbuses provide a more complicated year-round alternative and meet trains at Lairg; check schedules at the post office or tourist office.

Durness's officious **tourist office** (April–Oct Mon–Sat 10am–5pm; July & Aug also Sun 11am–4pm; Oct–March Mon–Fri 10am–1.30pm; ⓣ01971/511259), can help with accommodation and arranges ranger-guided walks; its small visitor centre also features excellent interpretive panels detailing the area's history, geology, flora and fauna, with some good insights into the day-to-day life of the community. There is some good **accommodation**. The excellent *Lazy Crofter Bunkhouse* (ⓣ01971/511209, ⓦwww.durnesshostel.co.uk) is open all year and has good facilities including a drying room. The basic SYHA **hostel** (ⓣ01971/511244, ⓦwww.syha.org.uk; April–Sept), beside the Smoo Cave car park half a mile east of the village, also rents out mountain bikes. Durness's most picturesque **hotel** is the *Cape Wrath Hotel* (ⓣ01971/511212; main hotel ❺, annexe ❸), which has a beautiful setting near the ferry jetty at Keoldale. Popular with walkers and fishermen, its rather austere character is offset by friendly service and a stunning view from the dining room. Of the **B&Bs**, *Puffin Cottage* (ⓣ01971/511208; April–Oct; ❶) is small but very pleasant. There's **camping** at *Sango Sands*, Harbour Road (ⓣ01971/511222), adjoining the comfortable village pub, which also serves unremarkable evening meals. Better eating options are at the bookshop at Balnakeil or the restaurant at Loch Eriboll's *Port-Na-Con* guesthouse (see p.650; book in advance). Opposite the tourist office is Balnakeil Wines, who make an incredible array of wines and spirits from flowers, fruit, and herbs; some of them are outstanding.

The Smoo Cave

Half a mile east of Durness village lies the 200ft-long **Smoo Cave**, formed partly by the action of the sea and partly by the small burn that flows through it. Tucked away at the end of a narrow sheer-sided sea cove, guides will show you the illuminated interior (£2.50), although the much-hyped rock formations are less memorable than the short rubber-dinghy trip you have to make in the second of three caverns, where the whole experience is enlivened after wet weather by a waterfall that crashes through the middle of the cavern. A **boat trip** (May–Sept daily; 1hr 30min; £7; call ☎01971/511365 or 511284 for schedule) leaves from Smoo Cave on a wildlife tour of the coast around Durness, taking in seabird colonies and stretches of the shoreline that are only accessible by sea; sightings of seals, puffins and porpoises are common. A couple of miles east of Smoo Cave is the spectacular sandy bay of **Ceannabeinne** – worth the walk on a sunny day.

Balnakiel

A narrow road winds northwest of Durness to tiny **BALNAKIEL**, whose name derives from the Gaelic *Baile ne Cille* (Village of the Church). The ruined **chapel** that today overlooks this remote hamlet was built in the seventeenth century, but a church has stood here for at least 1200 years. A skull-and-crossbones stone set in the south wall marks the grave of Donald MacMurchow, a seventeenth-century highwayman and contract killer who murdered eighteen people for his clan chief (allegedly by throwing them from the top of the Smoo Cave). The "half-in, half-out" position of his grave was apparently a compromise between his grateful employer and the local clergy, who initially refused to allow such an evil man to be buried on church ground. Balnakiel is also known for its **golf course**, whose ninth and final hole involves a well-judged drive over the Atlantic; you can rent equipment from the clubhouse. The **Balnakiel Craft Village** back towards Durness, is worth a visit. Housed in an imaginatively converted 1940s military base, the campus consists of a dozen or so workshops where you can watch painters, potters, leather workers, candle makers, woodworkers, stone carvers, knitters and weavers in action – there's also a friendly bookshop with an excellent **café-restaurant** (☎01971/511777; daily 10am–6pm, plus evening meals Fri–Mon).

The white-sand beach on the east side of Balnakiel Bay is a stunning sight in any weather, but most spectacular on sunny days when the water turns to brilliant turquoise. For the best views, walk along the path that winds north through the dunes (pockmarked from occasional naval bombing exercises) behind it; this eventually leads to **Faraid Head** – from the Gaelic *Fear Ard* (High Fellow) – where you stand a good chance of spotting puffins from late May until mid-July. The fine views over the mouth of Loch Eriboll and west to Cape Wrath make this round walk (3–4hr) the best in the Durness area.

Cape Wrath

An excellent day trip from Durness begins three miles southwest of the village at **Keoldale**, where a foot-passenger ferry (June–Aug hourly 9.30am–4.30pm; May & Sept approximately 4 daily; no motorcycles; no service in bad weather; ☎01971/511376) crosses the Kyle of Durness estuary to link up with a minibus (☎01971/511287; May–Sept) that runs the eleven miles out to **Cape Wrath**, the British mainland's most northwesterly point. The headland takes its name not from the stormy seas that crash against it for most of the year, but from the Norse word *hvarf*, meaning "turning place" – a throwback to the days when Viking warships used it as a navigation point during raids on the Scottish coast. These days, a lighthouse (another of those built by Robert Louis Stevenson's father) warns ships away from the treacherous rocks. Looking east to Orkney and west to the Outer Hebrides, it stands above the famous **Clo Mor cliffs**, the highest sea cliffs in Britain and a prime breeding site for seabirds. You can walk from here to remote Sandwood Bay (see p.647), visible to the south, although the route, which cuts inland across lochan-dotted moorland, is hard to follow in places. Hikers generally continue south from Sandwood to the trail end at Blairmore; if you hitch or walk the six miles from here to Kinlochbervie you can, with careful planning, catch a bus back to Durness. Note that much of the land bordering the headland is a military firing range and the area is sometimes closed; check with Durness tourist office before you set off.

Loch Eriboll

Ringed by ghost-like limestone mountains, deep and sheltered **Loch Eriboll**, six miles east of Durness, is the north coast's most spectacular sea loch. Servicemen stationed here during World War II to protect passing Russian convoys nicknamed it "Loch 'Orrible", but if you're looking for somewhere wild and unspoilt, you'll find this a perfect spot. Porpoises and otters are a common sight along the rocky shore, and minke whales occasionally swim in from the open sea.

Overlooking its own landing stage at the water's edge, *Port-Na-Con* (Ⓣ01971/511367, Ⓔportnacon70@hotmail.com; ❶; March–Oct), seven miles from Durness on the west side of the loch, is a wonderful **B&B**, popular with anglers and divers (it'll refill air tanks for £2.50). Top-notch food is served in its small **restaurant** (open all year, including Christmas), with a choice of vegetarian haggis, local kippers, fruit compôte and home-made croissants for breakfast, and adventurous three-course evening meals for around £12; the menu always includes a gourmet vegetarian dish. Non-residents are welcome, although you'll need to book. A further half a mile south, *Choraidh Croft* (Ⓣ01971/511235; ❶; Easter–Nov), offers B&B and has a collection of rare farm animal breeds (£2), as well as a good café.

Tongue

It's a long slog around Loch Eriboll and east over the top of A Mhùine moor to the pretty crofting township of **TONGUE**. Dominated by the ruins of **Varick Castle**, the village, an eleventh-century Norse stronghold, is strewn over the east shore of the **Kyle of Tongue**, which you can either cross via a new causeway, or by following the longer and more scenic single-track road around its southern side. When the tide recedes, this shallow estuary becomes a mass of golden sand flats, superb on sunny days, with the sharp profiles of **Ben Hope** (3040ft) and **Ben Loyal** (2509ft) looming large to the south. Tongue's relatively temperate maritime climate even allows it to claim Britain's most northerly palm tree.

In 1746, the Kyle of Tongue was the scene of a naval engagement reputed to have sealed the fate of Bonnie Prince Charlie's **Jacobite rebellion**. In response to a plea for help from the prince, the king of France dispatched a sloop and £13,600 in gold coins to Scotland. However, the Jacobite ship *Hazard* was spotted by the English frigate *Sheerness*, and fled into the Kyle, hoping that the larger enemy vessel would not be able to follow. It did, though, and soon forced the *Hazard* aground. Pounded by English cannon fire, its Jacobite crew slipped ashore under cover of darkness in an attempt to smuggle the treasure to Inverness, but they were followed by scouts of the local Mackay clan, who were not of the Jacobite persuasion. The next morning, a larger platoon of Mackays waylaid the rebels, who, hopelessly outnumbered and outgunned, began throwing the gold into **Lochan Hakel**, southwest of Tongue (most of it was recovered later). The prince, meanwhile, had sent 1500 of his men north to rescue the treasure, but these too were defeated en route; historians debate whether the missing men might have altered the outcome of the Battle of Culloden three weeks later. Locals maintain that cows still occasionally wander out of the loch's shallows with gold pieces stuck in their hooves.

Accommodation in Tongue includes *Rhian Cottage* (Ⓣ01847/611257, Ⓔjenny.anderson@tesco.net; ❷), a pretty whitewashed house with an attractive garden about a mile down the road past the post office. *Cloisters* (Ⓣ01847/601286, Ⓦwww.cloistertal.demon.co.uk; ❷), two miles out of town at Talmire on the west side of the Kyle, has great views out towards the Orkney Islands and is well worth heading out of town for. The *Ben Loyal Hotel* (Ⓣ01847/611216, Ⓔthebenloyalhotel@btinternet.com; ❺ room only) is comfortable, while the *Tongue Hotel* (Ⓣ01847/611206; ❺; March–Oct), former hunting lodge of the Duke of Sutherland, does excellent food, and has a cosy downstairs bar. There's also a well-situated SYHA **hostel** with rather inconvenient opening hours (Ⓣ01847/611301, Ⓦwww.syha.org.uk; April–Sept; lockout 10.30am–5pm), right beside the causeway a mile north of the village centre on the east shore of the Kyle, and two **campsites** – *Kincraig* (Ⓣ01847/611218) just south of Tongue post office, and *Talmine* (Ⓣ01847/601225), just behind a sandy beach at Talmine, five miles north of Tongue on the western side of the Kyle. Seven miles east of town, at Borgie, the *Borgie Lodge Hotel* (Ⓣ01641/521332, Ⓦwww.borgielodgehotel.co.uk; ❺) is dominated by shooting and fishing types, but it does boast an award-winning restaurant.

Bettyhill and around

BETTYHILL, a major crofting village set among rocky green hills, straggles along the side of a narrow tidal estuary, and down the coast to two splendid beaches. Forming an unbroken arc of pure white sand between the Naver and Borgie rivers, **Farr Beach**, on the east side of the village, is safer for swimming, and more sheltered, while **Torrisdale beach** (access off the road to Borgie five miles west of Bettyhill) is the more visually impressive of the pair, ending in a smooth white spit that forms part of the **Invernaver Nature Reserve**. During summer, arctic terns nest here on the river banks, dotted with clumps of rare Scottish primroses, and you stand a good chance of spotting an otter or two. The delightful and loyally maintained **Strathnaver Museum** (April–Oct Mon–Sat 10am–1pm & 2–5pm; £2), housed in the old church set apart from the village near the sea, is full of locally donated bits and pieces, and includes panels by local schoolchildren telling the story of the Strathnaver Clearances. You can also see some Pictish stones and a 3800-year-old, early Bronze Age beaker found in Strathnaver, the river valley south of the village, whose numerous prehistoric sites are mapped on an excellent pamphlet sold at the entrance desk.

Bettyhill's small **tourist office** (July & Aug Mon–Sat 10.30am–5.30pm, Sun noon–5.30pm; April–June & Sept Mon–Sat noon–5pm; Ⓣ01641/521342) can book **accommodation**; there's also a pleasant café in the same building. The *Bettyhill Hotel* (Ⓣ01641/521230; ❶), at the top of the hill, has character and does good bar food. There are also several good-value B&Bs, including *Shenley* (Ⓣ01641/521421; ❶; April–Oct), a grand but cosy detached house with good views from its elevated spot in the middle of the village, and *Bruachmhor* (Ⓣ01641/521265; ❶; April–Sept), a small but comfortable croft house facing south over the village.

Melvich and Dounreay

As you move east from Bettyhill, the north coast changes dramatically as the hills on the horizon recede to be replaced by fields fringed with flagstone walls. At the hamlet of **MELVICH**, twelve miles east of Bettyhill, the A897 cuts south through Strath Halladale, the Flow Country (see below) and the Strath of Kildonan to Helmsdale on the east coast (see p.668). Melvich has some good **accommodation**, including the wonderfully hospitable *Sheiling Guesthouse* (☎01641/531256, ⓔthesheiling@btinternet.com; ❷; April–Oct) by the main road, whose impressive breakfasts feature locally smoked haddock and fresh herring. The *Melvich Hotel* is the best option for an evening meal.

Five miles further east, **Dounreay Nuclear Power Station**, a surreal collection of stark domes and chimney stacks marooned in the middle of nowhere, was the first reactor in the world to provide mains electricity. It's still a major local employer, though the reactors themselves were decommissioned in 1994 and the site is now being gradually detoxified, an operation estimated to take forty years or so. A permanent **exhibition** (May–Oct daily 10am–4pm; free) in the old aircraft control tower details the processes (and, unsurprisingly, the benefits) of nuclear power, and does at least make an attempt to address issues such as the area's "leukaemia cluster", and the high levels of radiation reported over the years on the nearby beaches. **Free tours** of the site are run from the centre (June–Sept Tues & Thurs), though you're not allowed out of the bus. This section of coast is accustomed to the unusual: during World War II the reactor site was a dummy airfield designed to draw German bombing raids, while until the mid-1990s the Americans operated a surveillance station a short distance to the east. Set up to monitor the USSR, it was in turn watched closely – Soviet trawlers bristling with antennae were a common sight offshore.

South from Melvich: the Flow Country

From Melvich, you can head forty miles or so south towards Helmsdale on the A897, through the **Flow Country**. This huge expanse of bog land came into the news a few years ago when ecology experts, responding to plans to transform the area into forest, drew attention to the threat to this fragile landscape, described by one contemporary commentator as of "unique and global importance, equivalent to the African Serengeti or Brazil's rainforest". Some forest was planted, but the environmentalists won the day, and the forestry syndicates have had to pull out. There's an excellent RSPB Flow Country **visitor centre** (April–Oct daily 9am–6pm; ☎01641/571225), based in the train station at Forsinard, fifteen miles south of Melvich, which is easily accessible from Thurso, Wick and the south by train. Guided walks through the RSPB **nature reserve** leave from the visitor centre (May–Aug Tues & Thurs) and illuminate the importance of the area and its wildlife.

Thurso

Approached from the isolation of the west, **THURSO** feels like a metropolis. In reality, it's a relatively small service centre visited mostly by people passing through to the adjoining port of **Scrabster** to catch the ferry to Stromness in Orkney. The town's name derives from the Norse word *Thorsa*, literally "River of the God Thor", and in Viking times this was a major gateway to the mainland. Later, ships set sail from here for the Baltic and Scandinavian ports loaded with meal, beef, hides and fish. Much of the town, however, dates from the 1790s, when Sir John Sinclair built a large new extension to the old fishing port. The nearby Dounreay Nuclear Power Station ensured continuing prosperity after World War II, when workers from the plant (dubbed "Atomics" by the locals) settled in Thurso in large numbers. Its gradual rundown over recent years has cast a shadow over the local economy, but investment in new industries such as telecommunications has improved matters.

Traill Street is the main drag, turning into the pedestrianized Rotterdam Street and High Street precinct at its northern end. However, the shops are uninspiring, and you're better off heading to the old part of town near the harbour, to see **Old St Peter's Church**, a substantial ruin with origins in the thirteenth century, but which has been much altered over the years. There's a long sandy beach nearby. Alternatively, you could visit the **Thurso Heritage Museum**, High Street (Mon–Sat 10am–1pm, 2–5pm; £1) whose most intriguing exhibit is the Pictish Skinnet Stone, intricately carved with enigmatic symbols and a runic cross.

Practicalities

From Thurso **train station**, with services to Inverness and Wick, it's a ten-minute walk down Princes Street and Sir George Street to the **tourist office** on Riverside Road (April–Oct Mon–Sat 10am–5pm; also Sun: June & July 10am–5pm, Aug 10am–6pm, Sept & Oct 11am–4pm; ⓣ01847/892371). The bus station, close by, runs regular **buses** to John O'Groats, Wick and Inverness and a summer service to Durness. Postbuses run as far as Tongue. **Ferries** operate daily from adjoining Scrabster to Orkney, which has less frequent links to Shetland and Aberdeen; you can book ahead through CalMac (ⓣ0870/565 0000, ⓦwww.calmac.co.uk) or through any local tourist office. Scrabster is a mile west of town; a **taxi** (ⓣ01847/892868) will set you back £3.

Thurso is well stocked with **accommodation**, including the cramped but very welcoming **hostel** *Sandra's*, 24 Princes St (ⓣ01847/894575, ⓔsandras-backpackers@ukf.net), with four-bed bunkrooms and drying and self-catering facilities above the lively local chippie; they also offer ferry transfers and **internet** access. Inexpensive if institutional dorms and doubles are also available at *Ormlie Lodge* (ⓣ01847/896888), a block of student accommodation on Ormlie Road, close to the station; the *Thurso Youth Club* on Millbank Rd also offer dorms in July and August (ⓣ01847/892964). Of the **B&Bs**, *Murray House*, 1 Campbell St (ⓣ01847/895759; ❷), is central, comfortable and friendly; there's also *Tigh Na Abhainn* on the river at 21 Millers Lane (ⓣ01847/893443; ❶), or the long-established *Orcadia*, 27 Olrig St (ⓣ01847/894395; ❶). The nearest **campsite** (ⓣ01847/805503) is out towards Scrabster alongside the main road, though there's a much nicer one at Dunnet Bay, a few miles east (see below).

Food options include *Le Bistro*, 2 Traill St (ⓣ01847/893737; Tues–Sat), with a reasonable-value menu of lunchtime snacks and more ambitious evening meals, and *Upper Deck*, by the harbour at Scrabster, serving large, moderately priced steaks and seafood dishes. There are several **cafés** in the town centre which offer standard, filling snacks, including *Sandra's* on Princes Street. There are a couple of good **restaurants** out of town; the *Bower Inn* (ⓣ01955/661292) on the road to Castletown is popular with locals, as is the *Forss Country House Hotel* (ⓣ01847/861201) to the west of town. The most enjoyably rowdy **pub** is the *Central*, on Traill Street; party on at *Skinandi's Nightclub* on Sir Georges Street.

You can **rent bikes** at *Sandra's* or at Wheels Cycle Shop on the extension of the High Street, beyond its junction with Couper Street, while Harper's fishing shop, a little further along at 57 High St (ⓣ01847/893179) is the place to rent wetsuits or boards, or get hold of other **surfing** supplies, before you take on the mighty north-coast breaks. If you fancy a **boat trip** to spot wildlife or go fishing, contact Pentland Firth Charters (Ⓣ01847/892849, Ⓦwelcome.to/pentlandfirthcharters). There's a **cinema** at the All-Star Factory centre and a decent secondhand bookshop, Tall Tales, on Olrig St.

East of Thurso

Despite the publicity that John O'Groats customarily receives, Britain's northernmost mainland point is in fact **Dunnet Head**. The headland is at the far side of Dunnet Bay, a vast sandy beach backed by huge dunes about six miles east of Thurso. The bay is popular with surfers, and even in the winter you can usually spot intrepid figures far out in the Pentland Firth's breakers. There's a **Ranger Centre** (April–Sept Tues–Fri 2–5pm, Sat & Sun 2–6pm) beside the excellent campsite at the east end of the bay, where you can pick up information on good local history and nature walks, including a short self-guided trail into Dunnet Forest, a failed plantation which has been left to go – literally – to seed, allowing a rich range of plant and animal life to thrive. Nearby is the small village of **DUNNET**, where it's worth stopping in at **Mary-Ann's Cottage** (June–Sept Tues–Sun 2–4.30pm; £1), a farming croft vacated in 1990 by 93-year-old Mary-Ann Calder, whose grandfather had built the cottage, and maintained just as she left it, full of reminders of the three generations who lived and worked there over the last 150 years.

For Dunnet Head, turn off at Dunnet onto the B855, which runs for four miles over windy heather and bog to the tip of the headland, crowned with a Victorian lighthouse. The red cliffs below are startling, with weirdly eroded rock stacks and a huge variety of seabirds; on a clear day you can see the whole northern coastline from Cape Wrath to Duncansby Head, and across the Pentland Firth to Orkney. It's worth stopping off at the *Dunnet Head Tearoom* (Ⓣ01847/851774, Ⓦwww.dunnethead.co.uk; ❶), halfway along the road to the headland. It serves snacks and filling meals, has **internet** access, views, and does good-value **B&B**.

John O'Groats

Romantics expecting to find a magical meeting of land and water at **JOHN O'GROATS** are invariably disappointed – sadly, but all too predictably, it's a seedy little tourist trap. The views north to Orkney are fine enough, but the village is little more than a string of overpriced souvenir shops thronged with coach parties. The village gets its name from the Dutchman, Jan de Groot, who obtained the ferry contract for the hazardous crossing to Orkney in 1496. The eight-sided house he built for his eight quarrelling sons (so that each one could enter by his own door) is echoed in the octagonal tower of the much-photographed *John O'Groats Hotel*, which is fast falling into disrepair but remains a good stop-off for a drink.

Aside from the frequent if irregular links with Land's End (the far southwest tip of England), maintained by a succession of walkers, cyclists, vintage-car drivers and pushers of baths, John O'Groats is connected by regular **buses** to Wick (7 daily Mon–Sat; 50min) and Thurso (Mon–Fri 5 daily, 2 on Sat; 1hr).

The **tourist office** (April–Oct Mon–Sat 9am–5pm; Ⓣ01955/611373) by the car park can help sort out **accommodation**: alternatively, try *Swona View* B&B (Ⓣ01955/611297; ❶; April–Sept) on the road to Duncansby Head, or *Bencorragh House* (Ⓣ01955/611449; ❷; March–Oct), which has very pleasant farmhouse accommodation and spectacular views at Upper Gills in Canisbay.

The small SYHA **hostel** (Ⓣ01955/611424, Ⓦwww.syha.org.uk; April–Sept) is at Canisbay, while there are two local **campsites**; *Stroma View* (Ⓣ01955/611313), one mile along the Thurso road, is far more pleasant than the windswept site at John O'Groats itself (Ⓣ01955/611329).

Ferries to Orkney

John O'Groats Ferries (Ⓣ01955/611353, Ⓦwww.jogferry.co.uk) operates a daily passenger **ferry** across to Burwick (with a connecting bus to Kirkwall) in the Orkney Islands (May & Sept 2 daily; June–Aug 4 daily; 40min; £26 return): officially this is a foot-passenger service, but it will take bicycles and motorbikes if it isn't too busy. The company also offers a couple of whistle-stop **day-tours** of Orkney, as well as a more leisurely afternoon **wildlife cruise** round the Stacks of Duncansby and the seabird colonies of nearby Stroma Island (1hr 30min; £12), as do North Coast Marine Adventures (Ⓣ0786/766 6273, Ⓦwww.northcoast-marine-adventures.co.uk). Mr Simpson (Ⓣ01955/611252) periodically takes groups across to **Stroma Island** in his boat.

From **Gills Bay**, five miles west of John O'Groats, Pentland Ferries runs a car and passenger ferry over to St Margaret's Hope (Ⓣ01856/831226, Ⓦwww.pentlandferries.co.uk; 3 daily year-round; 1hr 45min; £10 one-way, plus £25 for a car).

Duncansby Head

If you're disappointed by John O' Groats, press on a couple of miles further east to **Duncansby Head**, which, with its lighthouse, dramatic cliffs and well-worn coastal path, has a lot more to offer. The birdlife here is prolific, and south of the headland lie some spectacular 200ft cliffs, cut by sheer-sided clefts known locally as *geos*. This is also a good place from which to view Orkney. Dividing the islands from the mainland is the infamous **Pentland Firth**, one of the world's most treacherous waterways. Only seven miles across, it forms a narrow channel between the Atlantic Ocean and North Sea, and for fourteen hours each day the tide rips through here from west to east at a rate of ten knots or more, flooding back in the opposite direction for the remaining ten hours. Combined with the rocky sea bed and a high wind, this can cause deep whirlpools and terrifying 30ft or 40ft towers of water when the ebbing tide crashes across the reefs offshore. The latter, known as the "Bores of Duncansby", are the subject of many old mariners' myths from the time of the Vikings onwards. Ever-increasing numbers of oil tankers are braving the Pentland Firth to save time on the longer passage north of the Orkneys – an environmental catastrophe waiting to happen, according to locals.

The east coast

The **east coast** of the Highlands, between Inverness and Wick, is nowhere near as spectacular as the west, with gently undulating moors, grassland and low cliffs where you might otherwise expect to find sea lochs and mountains.

Washed by the cold waters of the North Sea, it's markedly cooler, too, although less prone to spells of permadrizzle and midges. Although the Inverness–Thurso train line is twice forced by topography to head inland, the region's main transport artery, the A9 road – slower here than in the south – follows the coast, which veers sharply northeast exactly parallel with the Great Glen and formed by the same geological fault.

While many visitors bypass this region in a headlong rush to the Orkneys, those who choose to dally will find equally impressive prehistoric and historic sites and reminders here. The area around the Black Isle and the Tain Peninsula was a Pictish heartland, and has yielded many important finds. Further north, from around the ninth century AD onwards, the **Norse** influence was more keenly felt than in any other part of mainland Britain, and dozens of Scandinavian-sounding names recall the era when this was a Viking kingdom. The whole area is studded with prehistoric brochs, cairns and standing stones, many in remarkable condition.

Culturally and scenically, much of the east coast is more lowland than highland, and Caithness in particular evolved more or less separately from the Highlands, avoiding the bloody tribal feuds that wrought such havoc further south and west. Later, however, the nineteenth-century **Clearances** hit the region hard, as countless ruined cottages and empty glens show. Hundreds of thousands of crofters were evicted and forced to emigrate to New Zealand, Canada and Australia, or else take up fishing in one of the numerous herring ports established on the coast. The oil boom has brought a transient prosperity to one or two places over the past two decades, but this has been countered by the downturn in the North Sea fishing industry, and the area remains one of the country's poorest, reliant on sheep farming, fishing and tourism.

The one stretch of the east coast that's always been relatively rich is the **Black Isle** just over the Kessock Bridge heading north out of Inverness, whose main village, **Cromarty**, is the region's undisputed highlight, with a crop of elegant mansions and appealing fishermen's cottages clustered near the entrance to the Cromarty Firth. In late medieval times, pilgrims including James IV of Scotland poured through here en route to the red-sandstone town of **Tain** to worship at the shrine of St Duthus, where the former sacred enclave has now been converted into one of the many "heritage centres" that punctuate the route north. Beyond **Dornoch**, a famous golfing resort recently famous as the site of Madonna's wedding, the ersatz-Loire château **Dunrobin Castle** is the main tourist attraction, a monument as much to the iniquities of the Clearances as to the eccentricity of Victorian taste. The award-winning **Timespan Heritage Centre** further north at Helmsdale recounts the human cost of the landlords' greed, while the area around the port of **Lybster** is littered with the remains of more ancient civilizations. **Wick**, the largest town on this section of coast, has an interesting past inevitably entwined with the fishing industry, whose story is told in another good heritage centre, but is otherwise uninspiring. The relatively flat landscapes of this northeast corner – windswept peat bog and farmland dotted with lochans and grey and white crofts – are a surprising contrast to the more rugged country south and west of here.

The Black Isle and around

Sandwiched between the Cromarty Firth to the north and, to the south, the Moray and Beauly firths which separate it from Inverness, the **Black Isle** is not an island at all, but a fertile peninsula whose rolling hills, prosperous farms and stands of deciduous woodland make it more reminiscent of Dorset or Sussex than the Highlands. It probably gained its name because of its mild climate: there's rarely frost, which leaves the fields "black" all winter; another explanation is that the name derives from the Gaelic word for black, *dubh* – a possible corruption of St Duthus (see p.662).

The Black Isle is littered with dozens of **prehistoric sites**, but the main incentive to make the detour east from the A9 is to visit the picturesque eighteenth-century town of **Cromarty**, huddled at the northeast tip of the peninsula. A string of villages along the south coast is also worth stopping off in en route, and one of them, Rosemarkie, has an outstanding small **museum** devoted to Pictish culture. Nearby Chanonry Point is among the best **dolphin-spotting** sites in Europe.

The southern Black Isle

Just across the Kessock Bridge from Inverness is a roadside complex with a **tourist office** (Easter–Oct Mon–Sat 10am–5pm, Sun 11am–4pm; July & Aug Mon–Sat until 6pm; ☎01463/731505), as well as two wildlife centres. The **dolphin and seal centre** (May–Oct daily 10am–5pm; £1) offers the chance to see (and listen to) these popular creatures, while the RSPB have set up an observation post for the **red kite**, a bird of prey successfully reintroduced to Scotland in 1992.

The most rewarding approach to Cromarty is along the south side of the Black Isle, on the A832 past a **clootie well**, just north of Munlochy, where a colourful, if somewhat motley, collection of rags has been hung on overhanging branches to bring luck and health. Ailing children used to be left here alone overnight in hopes of a miracle cure. Just south of here, kids not yet abandoned by their parents will enjoy the Black Isle Wildlife and Country Park (March–Nov daily 10am–6pm; £4), while the nearby **Black Isle Brewery** produces tasty organic ales and lager (tours Mon–Sat 10am–6pm; July & Aug also Sun; free). Nearby is the attractive harbourside fishing village of **AVOCH** (pronounced "och"), where the *Station Hotel* serves good bar meals and real ale; there's a tiny heritage centre in the basement at the back (June–Sept Mon–Sat).

Fortrose and Rosemarkie

FORTROSE, a few miles east of Avoch, is a quietly elegant village dominated by the beautiful ruins of an early thirteenth-century **cathedral** (daily 8am–8pm). Founded by King David I, it now languishes on a lovely green bordered by red-sandstone and colourwashed houses, where a horde of gold coins dating from the time of Robert III was unearthed in 1880. There's also a memorial to the Seaforth family, whose demise the Brahan Seer famously predicted (see box on p.658).

There's a memorial plaque to the seer at nearby **Chanonry Point**, reached by a back road from the north end of Fortrose; the thirteenth hole of the golf course here marks the spot where he met his death. Jutting into a narrow channel in the Moray Firth (deepened to allow warships into the estuary during World War II), the point, fringed on one side by a beach of golden sand and shingle, is an excellent place to look for **dolphins** (see p.589). Come here around high tide, and you stand a good chance of spotting a couple leaping through the surf in search of fish brought to the surface by converging currents.

ROSEMARKIE, a lovely one-street village a mile north of Fortrose at the opposite (northwest) end of the beach, is thought to have been evangelized by St Boniface in the early eighth century. The cosy **Groam House Museum**

The Brahan Seer

A memorial plaque in Fortrose remembers the seventeenth-century visionary **Cùinneach Odhar** (Kenneth Mackenzie), known as the Brahan Seer, who was born at Uig on Skye and lived and worked on the estate of the Count and Countess of Seaforth. Legend has it that he derived his powers of second sight from a small white divination stone passed on to him, through his mother, from a Viking princess. With the pebble pressed against his eye, Cùinneach foretold everything from outbreaks of measles in the village to the building of the Caledonian Canal, the Clearances and World War II. His visions brought him widespread fame, but also resulted in his untimely death. In 1660, Countess Seaforth, wife of the local laird, summoned the seer after her husband was late home from a trip to France. Reluctantly – when pressurized – he told the Countess that he had seen the earl "on his knees before a fair lady, his arm round her waist and her hand pressed to his lips". At this, she flew into a rage, accused him of sullying the family name and ordered him to be thrown head first into a barrel of boiling tar. However, just before the gruesome execution, which took place near Brahan Castle on Chanonry Point, Cùinneach made his last prediction: when a deaf and dumb earl inherited the estate, the Seaforth line would end. His prediction finally came true in 1815 when the last earl died.

(May–Sept Mon–Sat 10am–5pm, Sun 2–4.30pm; Oct–April Sat & Sun 2–4pm; £1.50), at the bottom of the village, displays a bumper crop of intricately carved Pictish standing stones (among them the famous Rosemarkie Cross Slab), and shows an informative video highlighting Pictish sites in the region. A lovely mile-and-a-half **woodland walk**, along the banks of a sparkling burn to Fairy Glen, begins at the car park just beyond the village on the road to Cromarty. Quality bar food is available at the wonderfully old-fashioned *Plough Inn*, just down the main street from the museum. It's owned by the local Black Isle Brewery and is a good spot to try their range.

Cromarty

An ancient legend recalls that the twin headlands flanking the entrance to the **Cromarty Firth**, known as The Sutors (from the Gaelic word for shoemaker), were once a pair of giant cobblers who used to protect the Black Isle from pirates. Nowadays, however, the only giants in the area are Nigg and Invergordon's colossal oil rigs, marooned in the estuary like metal monsters marching out to sea. Built and serviced here for the Forties oil field in the North Sea, they form a surreal counterpoint to the web of tiny streets and chocolate-box workers' cottages of **CROMARTY**, the Black Isle's main settlement. Sheltered by The Sutors at the northeast corner of the peninsula, the town, an ancient ferry crossing-point on the pilgrimage trail to St Duthus's shrine in Tain, lost much of its trade during the nineteenth century to places served by the railway; a branch line to the town was begun but never completed. Although a royal burgh since the fourth century, Cromarty didn't became a prominent port until 1772 when the entrepreneurial local landlord, George Ross, founded a hemp mill here. Imported Baltic hemp was spun into cloth and rope in the mill, fuelling a period of prosperity during which Cromarty acquired some of Scotland's finest Georgian houses; these, together with the terraced fishers' cottages of the nineteenth-century herring boom, have left the town with a wonderfully well-preserved concentration of Scottish domestic architecture.

To get a sense of Cromarty's past, head straight for the award-winning **museum** housed in the old **Courthouse** on Church Street (daily: April–Oct

10am–5pm; Nov–Dec & March noon–4pm; £3), which tells the history of the town using audiovisuals and animated figures, including one of Sir Thomas Urquhart, an eccentric local laird who traced his ancestry back to Adam and Eve, and reportedly died laughing on hearing of the restoration of Charles II. You are also issued with a personal stereo, a tape and a map for a walking tour around the town. **Hugh Miller**, a nineteenth-century stonemason turned author, geologist, folklorist and Free Church campaigner, was born in Cromarty, and his **birthplace** (May–Sept Mon–Sat 11am–1pm & 2–5pm, Sun 2–5pm; NTS; £2.50), a modest thatched cottage on Church Street, has been restored to give an idea of what Cromarty must have been like in his day.

Aside from any formal sights, Cromarty is a pleasant place just to wander around, and there's an excellent **walk** out to the south Sutor stacks. You can pick up the path by leaving town on Miller Road, and turning right when the lane becomes "The Causeway"; follow this through the woods and past eighteenth-century Cromarty House until you reach the junction at Mains Farm; a left turn here takes you across open fields and through woods to the top of the headland, from where there are superb views across the Moray Firth. You can return via the beach and along Shore Street.

The widely respected Dolphin Écosse (Ⓣ01381/600323, Ⓦwww.dolphinecosse.co.uk) runs half- or full-day **boat trips** to see seals, porpoises, bottle-nosed dolphins and occasionally minke whales from their Dolphin Centre by the harbour behind the *Royal Hotel*. At the centre is background information on dolphins and whales, along with some spectacular photographs of the animals taken by clients while out on the boat. The tiny two-car Nigg–Cromarty **ferry** (May–Sept daily 9am–6pm), Scotland's smallest, also doubles up as a cruiser on summer evenings; you can catch it from the jetty near the lighthouse.

Practicalities

Nine **buses** a day run to Cromarty from Inverness (55min), returning from the car park at the bottom of Forsyth Place. During summer, **accommodation** is in short supply. Most upmarket is the traditional *Royal Hotel* (Ⓣ01381/600217; ❺), down at the harbour, which has rather small but richly furnished rooms overlooking the Firth. For **B&B**, try one of the attractive old houses on Church Street, such as Mrs Robertson's at no. 7 (Ⓣ01381/600488; ❶), where you can also **rent bikes**. Above the town, *Beechfield House* (Ⓣ01381/600308; ❷) offers modern rooms and good views.

The most down-to-earth place **to eat** is the *Cromarty Arms*, which has a beer garden and serves basic, inexpensive bar meals – it also has occasional live music. The *Royal Hotel*'s restaurant features Scottish specialities, while cheaper meals are available in the cosy public bar or, on fine nights, on the terrace outside with great views over the firth.

Dingwall and the Cromarty Firth

Most traffic nowadays takes the upgraded A9 north from Inverness, bypassing the small market town of **DINGWALL** (from the Norse *thing*, "parliament", and *vollr*, "field"), a royal burgh since 1226 and former port that was left high and dry when the river receded during the nineteenth century. Today, it has succumbed to the curse of British provincial towns and acquired an ugly business park and characterless pedestrian shopping street. Dingwall's only real claim to fame is that it was the birthplace of Macbeth, whose family occupied the now ruined castle on Castle Street. There's a small **museum** in the centre of town (May–Sept Mon–Sat 10am–5pm; £1.50), and it's worth checking out The Casbah on Tulloch St for a small but quirky collection of secondhand books, vinyl and curios.

Castle Street is a good place to look for **B&Bs**: try *The Croft* at no. 25 (☎01349/863319; ❶), or *St Clements* at no. 17 (☎01349/862172; ❷). The smartest **hotel** is the stylish *Tulloch Castle*, Castle Drive (☎01349/861325; ❻), a former Highland clan headquarters. The jaded but central *Royal Hotel*, High Street (☎01349/862130; ❶) does B&B and inexpensive bar meals.

Northeast of Dingwall, the **Cromarty Firth** has always been recognized as a perfect natural harbour. During World War I it was a major **naval base**, and today its sheltered waters are used as a centre for repairing North Sea oil rigs. The A862 road from Dingwall rejoins the A9 just after the main road crosses the firth on a long causeway; a few miles further along, look out for the extraordinary edifice on the hill behind **EVANTON**. This is the **Fyrish Monument**, built by a certain Sir Hector Munro, partly to give employment to the area and partly to commemorate his own capture of the Indian town of Seringapatam in 1781 – hence the design, resembling an Indian gateway. If you want to get a close-up look, it's a tough two-hour walk through pine woods to the top. An easier, but no less dramatic, walk from the village is to follow the Allt Graad river to the mile-long **Black Rock** gorge, an unexpected chasm formed when glacial meltwaters cut a deep furrow in a band of softer sandstone. The gorge, a giddy 100ft deep in places but only 12–15ft wide, was reputedly once jumped by a local man, but the proximity of the surrounding wood, as well as the curtain of damp ferns and mosses which cling to the rocks, would make a repeat of this pretty dangerous. The best approach to the gorge is a half-hour walk along a track which leaves from *Black Rock Caravan Park*, set in a peaceful grassy glen, where there's also a simple but neat bunkhouse (☎01349/830917, ©mlb@blackrockscot.freeserve.co.uk).

Strathpeffer

STRATHPEFFER, a mannered and leafy Victorian spa town surrounded by wooded hills four miles west of Dingwall, is pleasant enough but does suffer from a high density of coach parties. During its heyday, this was a renowned European **health resort** reached by the tongue-twisting Strathpeffer Spa Express train from Aviemore. A recent facelift is redeveloping the grand pavilion as a performing arts centre and has recently restored the **Pump Room** (April–Oct), where visitors drank the water from five different wells which were supposed to treat all manner of ailments. They can still be sampled, but drinking the foul sulphurous liquid is more masochistic than medicinal. The water can also be tasted at the small pavilion in the main square, dwarfed by the old Highland Hotel looming on the hillside.

Also making the most of the Victorian theme is the **Highland Museum of Childhood** (April–Oct Mon–Sat 10am–5pm, Sun 2–5pm; £1.50), located at the restored Victorian train station half a mile east of the main square. An attraction aimed at families, the museum looks at growing up in the Highlands, from home- and school-life to folklore and festivals, with some well-displayed photographs, display cabinets with toys and games, and a colourful series of commissioned murals. In other parts of the station are a pleasant café and craft workshops.

Strathpeffer is within striking distance of the bleak **Ben Wyvis**, and so is also a popular base for walkers. One of the best hikes in the area begins from the SYHA hostel, at the west end of the village, from where a forestry track leads through dense woodland towards the hill of Cnoc Mor. Rather less than a mile farther on, you can turn up onto the ridge on the right and follow it to reach the vitrified Iron Age hillfort of **Knock Farril**, which affords superb panoramic views to the Cromarty Firth and the surrounding mountains. From here, you can pick up a minor road and continue along the ridge to Dingwall, from where there are buses back to Strathpeffer. A shorter route drops back down from Knock Farril to the main road and then on to the village. Allow a full day for the longer route, a half-day for the shorter. Another good walk is through Ord Wood to picturesque Loch Kinellan, where a small island bears the ruin of a fort.

Practicalities

Buses run regularly between Dingwall and Strathpeffer (11 daily Mon–Sat), dropping passengers in the square, where you'll find a small **tourist office** (July & Aug Mon–Sat 9am–5.30pm, Sun 10am–5.30pm; June to mid-Oct Mon–Sat 10am–5pm, Sun 11am–4pm; April & May Mon–Sat 10am–5pm; ⓣ01997/421415) with information on points west as well as local areas. The **hotels** in the village are very popular with bus tours, but often have room: the vast *Ben Wyvis* (ⓣ01997/421323, ⓦwww.british-trust-hotels.co.uk; ❺) is adequate, with good views and nice grounds, while north of the main square a converted Victorian villa, complete with turrets, houses the *Holly Lodge Hotel* (ⓣ01997/421254; ❸). The *Inver Lodge*, west of the main square (ⓣ01997/421392; ❶; March–Dec), and *Francisville*, just past the church (ⓣ01997/421345; ❶; April–Oct), both offer good **B&B**. The rambling fifty-bed SYHA **hostel** (ⓣ01997/421532, ⓦwww.syha.org.uk; May–Sept) is a mile southwest of the main square up the hill towards Jameston. Those keen on tackling a broader range of outdoor pursuits, including canoeing, mountain biking and assault courses, should head to the excellent Fairburn Activity Centre (ⓣ01997/433397; ❷), set in the grounds of a magnificent country estate about three miles outside the village of Marybank, south of Strathpeffer and northwest of Muir of Ord. For **food**, cheap bar meals can be had at the *Strathpeffer Hotel*, while the *Richmond Hotel* offers similar fare.

The Dornoch Firth and around

North of the Cromarty Firth, the hammer-shaped **Tain peninsula** can still be approached from the south by the ancient ferry crossing from Cromarty to Nigg, though to the north the link is a more recent causeway over the **Dornoch Firth**, the inlet which marks the northern boundary of the peninsula. On the southern edge of the Dornoch Firth the A9 bypasses the quiet town of **Tain**, probably best known as the home of Glenmorangie whisky. Inland, at the head of the firth, there's not much to the village of **Bonar Bridge**, but fans of unusual hostels travel from far and wide to spend a night with the ghosts at the Duchess of Sutherland's imposing former home, **Carbisdale Castle**. Further inland, the rather lonely village of **Lairg** is a connection point between west and east coasts, with roads spearing through the glens from northwest Sutherland and the railway making a laboured detour in from the east coast. Back on the coast, on the north side of the Dornoch Firth, the neat town of **Dornoch** itself, long known for its impressive cathedral and well-manicured golf courses, found renewed fame in 2000 as the venue for an outbreak of Madonna-mania, when it hosted the pop star's wedding.

Tain

The peninsula's largest settlement is **TAIN**, an attractive and pleasant small town of grand whisky-coloured sandstone buildings that was the birthplace of **St Duthus**, an eleventh-century missionary who inspired great devotion in the Middle Ages. His miracle-working relics were enshrined in a sanctuary here in the eleventh century, and in 1360 St Duthus Collegiate Church was built, visited annually by James IV, who usually arrived here fresh from the arms of his mistress, Janet Kennedy, whom he had conveniently installed in nearby Moray. A good place to get to grips with the peninsula's past is the **Tain Through Time** exhibition (April–Oct daily 10am–6pm; call for winter opening hours; ⓣ01862/894089; £3.50), which makes creative use of three old buildings around the church and graveyard, leading you round using an audioguide. The ticket price also includes a walking tour of the town and neighbouring **museum** on Castle Brae (just off the High Street), housing an interesting display of the much sought-after work of the Tain silversmiths, along with mediocre archeological finds and clan memorabilia. There's not a great deal more to see, but check out High Street's castellated eighteenth-century **Tolbooth**, with its stone turrets and old curfew bell. Tain's other main attraction is the **whisky distillery** where the highly rated Glenmorangie malt is produced (ⓣ01862/892477; shop Mon–Fri 9am–5pm, June–Aug also Sat 10am–4pm, Sun noon-4pm; tours Mon–Fri 10am–3.30pm, Sat & Sun 10.30am–2.30pm; £2); it lies just off the A9 on the north side of town. Booking is recommended for the tours.

Practicalities

For **accommodation**, the *Mansfield House Hotel* (ⓣ01862/892052, ⓦwww.mansfield-house.co.uk; ❻), a modernized mansion-hotel in the Scots-Baronial mould, is renowned for its cooking, while the more modest *Golf View House* (ⓣ01862/892856; ❸), three minutes' drive south of the town centre on Knockbreck Road, offers comfortable B&B, as does *Northfield House*, 23 Moss Rd (ⓣ01862/894087; ❶). Good-quality, moderately priced **food** is available at the *Morangie House Hotel* to the north of town, while the *Royal Hotel* (ⓣ01862/892013; ❺), a lovely sandstone building at the western end of the main street, has an excellent menu. *Harry Gow* on the High Street (open all day) serves typical Scottish food, and classic Italian is dished up at *Café Volante*, also on High Street, beside the post office.

Portmahomack

Although few people bother to explore the Tain area as far east as **Tarbat Ness** on the tip of the peninsula, if you're driving it's well worth setting aside a couple of hours to make the detour. The green, windswept village of **PORTMAHOMACK** sprawls downhill to a sandy beach and tidal harbour with wide views around the bay. On top of the hill, the **Tarbat Discovery Centre** (daily: May–Sept 10am–5.30pm; March, April & Oct–Dec 2–5pm; £3.50) is housed in the pretty whitewashed old kirk. It deals with the archeology of the Picts in the area, and has many original and replica examples of sculpture. There's also a **lighthouse** – one of the highest in Britain – at the gorse-covered point, reached along narrow roads running through fertile farmland. A good seven-mile **walk** starts here (2–3hr round trip): head south from Tarbat Ness for three miles, following the narrow passage between the foot of the cliffs and the foreshore, until you get to the hamlet of Rockfield. A path leads past a row of fishermen's cottages from here to Portmahomack, then joins the tarmac road running northeast back to the lighthouse. Further south on the Tain peninsula, there are impressive Pictish **standing stones** at Hilton and at Shandwick, erected as powerful symbols of the new Christian faith in the late eighth or early ninth centuries. Close by, at Fearn, there's a scenic ruined abbey.

In Portmahomack, the *Oystercatcher* on Main Street (☎01862/871560) is one of the **restaurant** highlights of this stretch of the east coast, serving delicious seafood, home-made soups and salads. For **accommodation**, try the *Caledonian Hotel* (☎01862/871345; ❸) further along Main Street in a stately old building on the beach, looking over the Dornoch Firth.

Bonar Bridge and around

Before the causeway was built across the Dornoch Firth, traffic heading along the coast used to skirt west around the estuary, crossing the Kyle of Sutherland at the village of **BONAR BRIDGE**. In the fourteenth and fifteenth centuries, the village harboured a large iron foundry. Ore was brought across the peat moors of the central Highlands from the west coast on sledges, and fuel for smelting came from the oak forest draped over the northern shores of the nearby kyle. However, James IV, passing through here on his way to Tain, was shocked to find the forest virtually clear-felled and ordered that oak saplings be planted in the gaps. Although now hemmed in by spruce plantations, the beautiful ancient woodland east of Bonar Bridge dates from this era.

Bonar Bridge has struggled since it was bypassed: there's little of note here other than the **bridge** itself, which has had three incarnations up to the present steel construction of 1973, all recalled on a stone plinth on the north side. You may want to check out the unusual **airboat** trips (book on ☎01863/766839; 1hr; £20), run from the *Trading Post Hotel*. The unlikely looking craft, with a huge fan mounted on the back of a flat-bottomed launch, previously saw service in the Everglade swamps of Florida, and is used in similar fashion on the kyle to skim over shallow water and mud flats to get a closer look at the local wildlife and scenery.

Carbisdale Castle

Towering high above the River Shin, three miles northwest of Bonar Bridge, the daunting neo-Gothic profile of **Carbisdale Castle** overlooks the Kyle of Sutherland, as well as the battlefield where the gallant Marquis of Montrose was defeated in 1650, finally forcing Charles II – if he wanted to be received as king (see p.765) – to accede to the Scots' demand for Presbyterianism. The castle was erected between 1906 and 1917 for the dowager Duchess of Sutherland, following a protracted family feud. After the death of her husband, the late Duke of Sutherland, the will leaving her the lion's share of the vast estate was contested by his stepchildren from his first marriage. In the course of the ensuing legal battle, the Duchess was found in contempt of court for destroying important documents pertinent to the case, and locked up in London's Holloway prison for six weeks. However, the Sutherlands eventually recanted (although there was no personal reconciliation) and, by way of compensation, built their stepmother a castle worthy of her rank. Designed in three distinct styles (to give the impression it was added to over a long period of time), Carbisdale was eventually acquired by a Norwegian shipping magnate in 1933, and finally gifted, along with its entire contents and estate, to the Scottish Youth Hostels Association, which has turned it into what must be one of the most opulent **hostels** in the world, full of white Italian marble sculptures, huge gilt-framed portraits, sweeping staircases and magnificent drawing rooms alongside standard facilities such as self-catering kitchens, games rooms, TV rooms and thirty dorms, including some recently upgraded four-bed family rooms (☎01549/421232; March–Oct; £13.50), often booked out by groups. The best way to get here by public transport is to take a **train** to nearby Culrain station, which lies within easy walking distance of the castle. **Buses** from Inverness (3 daily; 1hr 30min) and Tain (4 daily; 25min) only stop at **Ardgay**, three miles south.

Croick Church

A mile or so southwest of Bonar Bridge, the scattered village of **ARDGAY** stands at the mouth of Strath Carron, a wooded river valley winding west into the heart of the Highlands. It's worth heading ten miles up the strath to **Croick Church**, which harbours one of Scotland's most poignant and emotive reminders of the Clearances. Huddled behind a brake of wind-bent trees, the graveyard surrounding the tiny grey chapel sheltered eighteen families (92 individuals) evicted from nearby Glen Calvie during the spring of 1845 to make way for flocks of Cheviot sheep, introduced by the Duke of Sutherland as a money earner. An evocative written record of the event is preserved on the diamond-shaped panes of the chapel windows, where the villagers scratched **graffiti memorials** still legible today: "Glen Calvie people was in the churchyard May 24th 1845", "Glen Calvie people the wicked generation", and "This place needs cleaning".

Lairg and around

North of Bonar Bridge, the A836 parallels the River Shin for eleven miles to **LAIRG**, a bleak and scattered place at the eastern end of lonely **Loch Shin**. On fine days, the vast wastes of heather and deergrass surrounding the village can be beautiful, but in the rain it can be a deeply depressing landscape. Lairg is predominantly a transport hub and the railhead for a huge area to the northwest; there's nothing much to see in town. However, a mile southeast on the A839, there are signs of early settlement at nearby **Ord Hill**, where archeological digs have recently yielded traces of human habitation dating back to Neolithic times. The Ferrycroft Countryside Centre and **tourist office**, on the west side of the river (April–Oct daily 10am–5pm; mid-July to mid-Aug Mon–Sat 9am–6pm, Sun 10am–5pm; ☎01549/402160), is friendly and helpful, and has a good free display on the woodlands and history of the area; it's also the starting-point for forest walks and an archeological trail to Ord Hill. Four miles south of Lairg, on the opposite side of the river – along the A836, then the B864 – the **Falls of Shin** is one of the best places in Scotland to see **salmon** leaping on their upstream migration; there's a viewing platform, and an overpriced café/shop by the car park catering to bus parties. The season for salmon returning to spawn is from June to September. Every August, Lairg hosts an annual lamb sale, the biggest one-day livestock market in Europe, when sheep from all over the north of Scotland are bought and sold.

Practicalities

Lairg, at the centre of the region's **road system**, is distinctly hard to avoid: the A838, traversing some of the loneliest country in the Highlands, is the quickest route for Cape Wrath; the A836 heads up to Tongue on the north coast; and the A839 links up to the A837 to push west through lovely Strath Oykel to Lochinver on the west coast. Lairg is also on the **train** line connecting

Inverness to Wick and Thurso and is the nexus of several **postbus** routes around the northwest Highlands, including one which links Lairg with Ledmore, on the Ullapool–Durness road. The train station is a mile south of town on the road to Bonar Bridge; buses stop right on the loch. Should you want to **stay**, *Carnbren* (☎01549/402259; ❶), just south of the bridge on the Bonar Bridge road, is comfortable, as is the *Old Coach House* (☎01549/402378; ❶; Easter–Oct), three miles south of Lairg on the B864 at Achany. The *Lochside* B&B (01549/402130; ❶) offers good views, as does *Park House* (☎01549/402208, ⓔdwalkerparkhouse@tinyworld.co.uk; ❸) on Station Road, overlooking Loch Shin, which is a welcoming spot if you're planning on doing some walking, fishing or cycling in the area. Ten miles towards the east coast, at Rogart, is the excellent *Sleeperzzz.com* railway-carriage hostel (see p.668). In Lairg, good bar **food** can be had at the *Nip Inn*, next to the post office.

Dornoch

DORNOCH, a genteel and appealing town eight miles north of Tain, lies on a flattish headland overlooking the **Dornoch Firth**. Surrounded by sand dunes and blessed with an exceptionally sunny climate by Scottish standards, it's something of a middle-class holiday resort, with solid Edwardian hotels, trees and flowers in profusion, and miles of sandy beaches giving good views across the estuary to the Tain peninsula. The town is also renowned for its championship **golf course**, ranked eleventh in the world and the most northerly first-class course. Dornoch was the scene for 2000's most prestigious rock'n'roll wedding, when Madonna married Guy Ritchie at nearby Skibo Castle and had her son baptized in Dornoch cathedral.

Dating from the twelfth century, Dornoch became a royal burgh in 1628. Among its oldest buildings, which are all grouped round the spacious square, the exquisite **cathedral** was founded in 1224 and built of local sandstone. The original building was horribly damaged by marauding Mackays in 1570, and much of what you see today was restored by the Countess of Sutherland in 1835, though her worst Victorian excesses were removed last century, when the interior stonework was returned to its original state. The vaulted roof is particularly appealing; the stained-glass windows in the north wall were later additions, endowed by the expat Andrew Carnegie (see p.330). Opposite, the fortified sixteenth-century **Bishop's Palace**, a fine example of vernacular architecture with stepped gables and towers, has been refurbished as an upmarket hotel (see below). Next door, the castellated **Old Town Jail** is home to a series of galleries and craft shops.

In 1722, Dornoch saw the last burning of a **witch** in Scotland. The unfortunate old woman, accused of turning her daughter into a pony and riding her around town, ruined her chances of acquittal by misquoting the Gaelic version of the Lord's Prayer during the trial, and was sentenced to burn alive in a barrel of boiling tar – an event commemorated by the **Witch's Stone**, just south of the Square on Carnaig Street. Another memorial stone, at Proncy Croy, a mile northwest, remembers the 99 victims of the Meikle Ferry disaster: the boat foundered in Dornoch Firth in 1809.

Practicalities

Buses from Tain and Inverness stop in the Square, where you'll also find a **tourist office** (May–Oct Mon–Fri 9am–5pm; ☎01862/810400). There's no shortage of **accommodation**: *Tordarroch B&B* (☎01862/810855; March-Oct; ❷), has a great location opposite the cathedral, as does the *Trevose* (☎01862/

810269; ❶; March–Sept) which is swathed in roses. The *Trentham Hotel* (Ⓣ01862/810551;❶) is less central but open all year. The characterful *Dornoch Castle Hotel* (Ⓣ01862/810216, Ⓦwww.dornochcastlehotel.com; ❺; April–Oct), in the Bishop's Palace on the Square, has a cosy old-style bar and relaxing tea garden. The *Caravan Park* (Ⓣ01862/810423; April–Oct) is attractively set between the manicured golf course and the uncombed vegetation of the sand dunes which fringe the beach; it offers **camping** although the site does get busy with caravans in July and August. Expensive gourmet **meals** are available at the *2 Quail* restaurant (Ⓣ01862/811811; Tues–Sat) on Castle Street, which also has tasteful rooms (❹), while both the hotels do good bar and restaurant meals. In addition, *Mallin House Hotel* (Ⓣ01862/810355) is famous for seafood, and *Luigi's*, on Castle St, is a good spot for snacks and lunches.

The immaculate Skibo Castle, a favourite hideaway of the world's rich and powerful, is an exclusive, private hotel not open to the public: Madonna fans will have to stump up around £800 per night for a double room.

North to Wick

North of Dornoch, the A9 hugs the coastline for most of the sixty or so miles to **Wick**, the principal settlement in the far north of the mainland. Perhaps the most important landmark in the whole stretch is the **Sutherland Monument** near Golspie, erected in memory of the first Duke of Sutherland, known as the landowner who oversaw the eviction of thousands of his tenants in a process known as the Clearances. The bitter memory of those times resonates through most of the small towns and villages on this stretch, including **Brora**, the gold-prospecting village of **Helmsdale**, **Dunbeath** and **Lybster**. With sites dotted around recalling Iron-Age settlers and Viking rule, many of these settlements also hark back to the days of a thriving fishing trade, none more so than the main town of Wick, once the busiest herring port in Europe.

Golspie and around

Ten miles north of Dornoch on the A9 lies the straggling red-sandstone town of **GOLSPIE**, whose status as an administrative centre does little to relieve its dullness. It does, however, boast an eighteen-hole golf course and a sandy beach, while half a mile further up the coast, the **Big Burn** has several rapids and waterfalls that can be seen from an attractive **woodland trail** beginning at the *Sutherland Arms Hotel.*

Dunrobin Castle

The main reason to stop in Golspie is to look around **Dunrobin Castle** (April to mid-Oct Mon–Sat 10.30am–4.30pm, Sun noon–4.30pm; June–Sept daily until 5.30pm; £6), overlooking the sea a mile north of town. Approached via a long tree-lined drive, this fairy-tale confection of turrets and pointed roofs – modelled by the architect Sir Charles Barry (designer of the Houses of Parliament) on a Loire château – is the seat of the infamous Sutherland family, at one time Europe's biggest landowners, with a staggering 1.3 million acres, and the principal driving force behind the Clearances in this area. The castle is on a correspondingly vast scale, boasting 189 furnished rooms, of which the tour takes in only seventeen. Staring up at the pile from the midst of its elaborate **formal gardens**, it's worth remembering that such extravagance was paid for by uprooting literally thousands of crofters from the surrounding glens. Much of the extra income generated by the evictions was lavished on the castle's opulent **interior**, which is crammed full of fine furniture, paintings (including works by Landseer, Allan Ramsay and Sir Joshua Reynolds), tapestries and *objets d'art*.

Set aside at least an hour for Dunrobin's amazing **museum**, housed in an eighteenth-century building at the edge of the garden. Inside, hundreds of disembodied animals' heads and horns peer down from the walls, alongside other more macabre appendages, from elephants' toes to rhinos' tails. Bagged mainly by the fifth Duke and Duchess of Sutherland, the trophies vie for space with other fascinating family memorabilia, including one of John O'Groat's bones, Chinese opium pipes, and such curiosities as a "picnic gong from the South Pacific". There's also an impressive collection of ethnographic artefacts acquired by the Sutherlands on their frequent hunting jaunts, ranging from an Egyptian sarcophagus to some finely carved Pictish stones. The admission price to the castle includes a falconry display (3 daily).

Conveniently, the castle has its own **train** station on the main Inverness–Wick line; this is no surprise, really, as the duke built the railway.

The Sutherland Monument

A mile northwest of Golspie, you can't miss the 100ft **monument** to the first Duke of Sutherland, which peers proprietorially down from the summit of the 1293ft **Beinn a'Bhragaidh** (Ben Bhraggie). An inscription cut into its base recalls that the statue was erected in 1834 by "a mourning and grateful tenantry [to] a judicious, kind and liberal landlord [who would] open his hands to the distress of the widow, the sick and the traveller". Unsurprisingly, there's no reference to the fact that the duke, widely regarded as Scotland's own Josef Stalin, forcibly evicted 15,000 crofters from his million-acre estate – a fact which, in the words of one local historian, makes the monument "a grotesque representation of the many forces that destroyed the Highlands". The campaign to have the statue smashed and scattered over the hillside has largely died down; the general attitude now seems to be that the statue stands as a useful reminder of the duke's infamy as much as his achievements.

It's worth the wet, rocky **climb** to the top of the hill (round trip 1hr 30min) for the wonderful views south along the coast past Dornoch to the Moray Firth and west towards Lairg and Loch Shin. It's steep and strenuous, however, and there's no view until you're out of the trees, about ten minutes from the top. Take the road opposite Munro's TV Rentals in Golspie's main street, which leads up the hill, past a fountain, under the railway and through a farmyard; from here, follow the Beinn a'Bhragaidh footpath (BBFP) signs along the path into the woods. You can go back the way you came, or follow a clear track which initially goes north from the monument and then winds down through Benvraggie Wood to meet a tarred road; turn left here to link into the path of the Big Burn Glen walk (see above).

Loch Fleet

Just to the south of Golspie, the A9 fringes a tidal estuary on a causeway that was constructed in 1816 by Thomas Telford. The inlet, **Loch Fleet**, is part of a large nature reserve (open access) harbouring some delicate coastal and woodland vegetation, including Britain's greatest concentration of one-flowered wintergreen, also known as St Olaf's candlestick, as well as a range of birdlife including greylag geese and arctic terns, and sealife such as seals and otters. You can walk in the reserve by following the minor road south out of Golspie for three miles; from Balblair Bay a path leads into pine-forested

Balblair Wood, while from Littleferry there are walks along the coastal heathland to the Moray Firth beaches.

Four miles northwest of Loch Fleet on the A839 to Lairg is one of Scotland's most unusual and imaginative **hostels**, *Sleeperzzz.com* (ⓣ01408/641343, ⓦwww.sleeperzzz.com), where you can stay in one of two first-class railway carriages parked in a siding beside the station on the Inverness–Thurso line in the tiny settlement of **ROGART**. Each of the comfortable compartments has a bunk bed on one side and the original seats on the other, while the two end compartments are used as a kitchen and common room. The owners have free **mountain bikes** available to let you explore the local countryside, and the place stands 100 yards from a convivial local **pub**, the *Pittentrail Inn*, that serves warming evening meals. A small reduction is even offered to those arriving by train or bicycle.

Brora

BRORA, on the coast six miles north of Golspie, once boasted the only bridge in the region – thus the name, which means "River of the Bridge" in Norse. Until the 1960s, it was the only coal-mining village in the Highlands, having played host to the industry for four hundred years. These days, however, the small grey town harbours little of interest, although it's friendly, accessible by bus and train, and does have *Capaldi's* on High Street, which sells acclaimed home-made ice cream. Three miles south of the town is the remarkably well-preserved Iron Age broch of **Carn Liath**, with great twelve-foot thick walls and a number of obvious features intact, such as a staircase and entrance passage. The car park for the site is on the inland side of the A9, just before the broch if you're travelling north. A more interesting way to reach it is by walking along the coastal path which links Golspie and Brora. A mile or so north of town, the **Clynelish Distillery** (April–Oct Mon–Fri 9.30am–5pm; Nov-March by appointment; ⓣ01408/623000; £2), will give you a guided tour and a sample dram.

There are a couple of good **B&Bs** in the area. The *Selkie* (ⓣ01408/621717; ❶), on Harbour Road, is superbly located where the river meets the sea – otters and seals are frequent sights from the garden. *Clynelish Farm* (ⓣ01408/621265; ❷; March-Oct) – turn left after the petrol station – is a working Victorian stone farmhouse with en-suite rooms, built to provide employment for dispossessed crofters after the Clearances. The rooms here are spacious, with views over the fields to the Moray Firth, and evening meals are available by arrangement.

Helmsdale and around

Eleven scenic miles north along the A9 from Golspie, **HELMSDALE** is an old herring port, founded in the nineteenth century to house the evicted inhabitants of Strath Kildonan, which lies behind it. Today, the sleepy-looking grey village attracts thousands of tourists, most of them coming to see the attractively designed **Timespan Heritage Centre** beside the river (April to mid-Oct Mon–Sat 9.30am–5pm, Sun 2–5pm; July & Aug until 6pm; £3.50). It's a remarkable venture for a place of this size, telling the local story of Viking raids, witch-burning, Clearances, fishing and gold-prospecting through hi-tech displays, sound effects and an audiovisual programme. The centre also has an art gallery, which often has a decent show of works by Scottish artists.

Helmsdale's devoted **tourist office** (April–Sept Mon–Sat 10.30am–4pm; ⓣ01431/821482, ⓔvmgdesigns@amserve.net) is currently housed in the library/community centre. There are several good-value **B&Bs**: the *Customs House* (☎01431/821648; ❶) is on the harbour on Shore St, while *Broomhill House* on Navidale Road (☎01431/821259; ❷), has bedrooms in a turret added to the former croft by a miner who struck it lucky in the Kildonan gold rush (see below). Alternatively, try *Torbuie* (☎01431/821424; ❶), in Navidale, on the A9 less than a mile north of the village; Mrs Sutherland, on Golf Road, (☎01431/821334; ❶); or the *Bayview* (☎01431/821679; ❶), just south of Helmsdale at Portgower, all three of which offer comfortable rooms. There's also a small **hostel** (☎01431/821577; mid-May to Sept), on the A9 north of the harbour.

Eating options abound in Helmsdale. On the main street, local fish wars are taking place between the *Mirage* restaurant and the *Bunillidh* opposite: the proprietor of the *Mirage* has become something of a Scottish celebrity, modelling herself on the romantic novelist Barbara Cartland, whose shooting lodge is nearby. The fittings and furnishings reflect her predilection for all things pink and frilly, with fish tanks, fake-straw parasols and plastic seagulls set off by the country-and-western soundtrack. There's obviously no love lost between her and the kitsch-free *Bunillidh* – opposing billboards and identical take-away outlets fight for the tourists emerging from the Timespan Centre. The aggressive marketing conceals the happy fact that both serve excellent meals (especially seafood) at rock-bottom prices. Meals are also served at the friendly *Belgrave Arms* pub, as well as the *Bannockburn* opposite.

Baile an Or

From Helmsdale the single-track A897 runs up Strath Kildonan and across the Flow Country (see p.652) to the north coast, at first following the River Helmsdale, a strictly controlled and exclusive salmon river frequented by the Royal Family. Some eight miles up the Strath at **BAILE AN OR** (Gaelic for "goldfield"), gold was discovered in the bed of the Kildonan Burn in 1869; a **gold rush** ensued, hardly on the scale of the Yukon, but quite bizarre in the Scottish Highlands. A tiny amount of gold is still found by some hardy prospectors every year: should you fancy **gold-panning** yourself, you can rent the relevant equipment for £2.50 from Helmsdale's gift and fishing-tackle shop, Strath Ullie, on the harbour, which also sells a booklet with a few basic tips.

Dunbeath and around

Just north of Helmsdale, the A9 begins its long haul up the **Ord of Caithness**. This steep hill used to form a pretty impregnable obstacle, and the desolate road still gets blocked during winter snowstorms. Once over the pass, the landscape changes dramatically as heather-clad moors give way to miles of treeless green grazing lands, peppered with derelict crofts and latticed by long drystone walls. This whole area was devastated during the Clearances; the ruined village of **Badbea**, reached via a footpath running east off the main road a short way after the pass, is a poignant monument to this cruel era. Built by tenants evicted from nearby Ousdale, the settlement now lies deserted, although its ruined hovels show what hardship the crofters had to endure: the cottages stood so near the windy cliff edge that children had to be tethered to prevent them from being blown into the sea.

DUNBEATH, hidden at the mouth of a small strath, twelve miles north of Ord of Caithness, was another village founded to provide work in the wake of the Clearances. The local landlord built a harbour here in 1800, at the start of the herring boom, and the settlement briefly flourished. Today it's a sleepy place, with lobster pots stacked at the quayside and views of windswept

Dunbeath Castle (no public access) on the opposite side of the bay. The novelist Neil Gunn was born here, in one of the terraced houses under the flyover that now swoops above the village; you can find out more about him at the **Dunbeath Heritage Centre** (Easter–Oct daily 10am–5pm; £1.50), signposted from the road. The staff can advise you on several good walks along the *Highland River* of Gunn's novel; his other most famous book, *The Silver Darlings*, was also set on this coastline. Up the strath are several archeological remains, as well as the lonely but lovely cemetery of Tutnaguail. The best of the handful of modest **B&Bs** here is *Tormore Farm* (Ⓣ01593/731240; ❶), a large farmhouse with four comfortable rooms, half a mile north of the harbour on the A9.

Just north of Dunbeath is the simple but moving **Laidhay Croft Museum** (Easter to mid-Nov daily 10am–6pm; £1), which offers a useful perspective on the sometimes over-romanced life of the Highlander before the Clearances. A little further up the coast, obvious from the A9 between the villages of Latheron and Lybster, is the **Clan Gunn Heritage Centre and Museum** (June–Sept Mon–Sat 11am–1pm, 2–4pm; July & Aug also Sun 2–4pm; £2), housed in an old white church surrounded by a graveyard, set against green fields and the precipitous coastline. It's mainly a place for members of the Clan Gunn and its septs – which include the more common surnames of Johnson, Thomson and Wilson, although it also doles out a bit more local history and a few tidbits for those on the trail of Neil Gunn.

Lybster and around

The final stretch of road before Wick gives great views out to sea to the oil rigs perched on the horizon. The spectacular series of green-topped cliffs and churning bays are gorgeous in the sun and impressively bleak in bad weather. The planned village of **LYBSTER** (pronounced "libe-ster"), established at the height of the nineteenth-century herring boom, once had 200-odd boats working out of its harbour. The new **Water Lines** heritage centre on the harbour (April–Sept daily 11am–5pm; £2) is an attractive modern display about the "silver darlings" and the fishermen that pursued them; there's a snug café downstairs. There's not much else to see here apart from the harbour area; the upper town is a grim collection of grey pebble-dashed bungalows centred on a broad main street.

The **Grey Cairns of Camster**, seven miles due north and one of the most memorable sights on the northeast coast, are a different story. Surrounded by bleak moorland, these two enormous reconstructed prehistoric burial chambers, originally built four or five thousand years ago, were immaculately designed, with corbelled drystone roofs in their hidden chambers, which you can crawl into through narrow passageways. More extraordinary ancient remains lie at **East Clyth**, two miles north of Lybster on the A99, where a path leads to the "**Hill o'Many Stanes**". Some 200 boulders stand in the ground here, forming 22 parallel rows that run north to south; no one has yet worked out what they were used for, although archeological studies have shown there were once 600 stones in place. A fourteen-mile track waymarked as a cycle path leads between the two sites, entering the forest at a car park half a mile south of the Camster Cairns and emerging near the single-track road which passes the Hill o'Many Stanes and connects with the A99.

Another relatively unknown historic site in the area is the **Whaligoe staircase**, ten miles north of Lybster on the A99 at the north end of the village of Ulbster. The stairway, which has 365 steps constructed out of the distinctive local slab stone, leads steeply down from the side of the house beside the car park to a natural harbour surrounded by cliffs. At the bottom you'll see a few remnants of the harbour used by herring fishermen in the last century, as well as vast numbers of seabirds, including cormorants, skuas and puffins; the daunting climb back up is made a little bit easier by the thought that, unlike the women of Ulbster, you don't have a creel full of herring to carry all the way to the top. The stairway is steep and uneven for much of the way down, so be particularly careful if the steps are wet. To get to the stairway, turn off towards the sea at the junction signposted on its landward side to the "Cairn o'Get".

Wick and around

Originally a Viking settlement named *Vik* (meaning "bay"), **WICK** has been a royal burgh since 1589. It's actually two towns: Wick proper, and **Pultneytown**, immediately south across the river, a messy, rather run-down community planned by Thomas Telford in 1806 for the British Fisheries Society, to encourage evicted crofters to take up fishing.

Wick's heyday was in the mid-nineteenth century, when it was the busiest herring port in Europe, with a fleet of over 1100 boats, exporting tons of fish to Russia, Scandinavia and the West Indian slave plantations. Although Robert Louis Stevenson described it as "the meanest of man's towns, situated on the baldest of God's bays", it's by no means a bad place, although there's no doubt it has a down-at-heel atmosphere. Pultneytown, lined with rows of fishermen's cottages, is the area most worth a wander, with the acres of largely derelict net-mending sheds, stores and cooperages around the harbour giving some idea of the former scale of the fishing trade. The town's story is told in the excellent **Wick Heritage Centre** in Bank Row, Pultneytown (June–Sept Mon–Sat 10am–5pm; £2), which contains a fascinating array of artefacts from the old fishing days, including fully rigged boats, original boat models, the old Noss Head lighthouse light and a great photographic collection dating from the 1880s. Interestingly, Wick was a dry town for quarter of a century until 1947, although that didn't stop some of the locals heading off to Lybster or Thurso for a quiet beer or two.

Rising steeply from a needle-thin promontory three miles north of Wick are the dramatic fifteenth- to seventeenth-century ruins of **Sinclair** and **Girnigoe castles**, which functioned as a single stronghold for the earls of Caithness. In 1570 the fourth earl, suspecting his son of trying to murder him, imprisoned him in the dungeon here until he died of starvation. There's a good clifftop walk (2hr 30min) to the castles from the tiny fishing village of **Staxigoe**: head north from the harbour to Field of Noss farm and follow the line of the cliffs, where you'll encounter all sorts of seabirds, including puffins; you will have to negotiate various gates and stiles along the way. When you reach Noss Head lighthouse, head along the access road to a car park, where a path leads out to the castles on the north-facing coastline. To the left is the beautiful Sinclair Bay beach, popular for windsurfing and sand-yachting.

Three miles south of Wick, at Altimarlach, the last clan battle on Scottish soil took place in 1680 when the Sinclairs of Kriss came off second-best to the Campbells of Glenorchy.

Practicalities

The **train** station and **bus** stops are next to each other behind the hospital. Frequent local buses run to Thurso and up the coast to John O'Groats (7 daily). Wick also has an **airport** (☎01955/602215), a couple of miles north of the town, with direct flights from Edinburgh and Aberdeen, and connections further south. From the train station, head across the river down Bridge Street to the cheerful **tourist office**, just off the High Street (April–Oct Mon–Sat 10am–5pm; July–Oct also Sun 11am–4pm; Nov–March Mon–Fri 11am–2.30pm; ⓣ01955/602596), which can organize local **accommodation**. On Louisburgh St, the *Nethercliffe Hotel* (ⓣ01955/602044; ❷) is good value, while the best of the hotels is *Mackay's*, by the river in the town centre (ⓣ01955/602323, ⓦwww.mackayshotel.co.uk; ❺). Among the **B&B** options are the central *MacMillan House*, on Tolbooth Lane (ⓣ01955/602120, ⓔsammy.777@btinternet.com; ❷), the low-priced *Quayside*, 25 Harbour Quay (ⓣ01955/603229, ⓔquaysidewick@compuserve.com; ❶), and *Mt Pleasant House*, North Road (ⓣ01955/605716; ❶), on the north side of town. Five miles towards Thurso is the lovely *Bilbster House* (ⓣ01955/621212; April-Oct; in winter by arrangement; ❶).

The north bank of the river, at the east end of High Street, is the best spot for eating and drinking. On Market Street, the *Bord de l'Eau* (ⓣ01955/604400; Tues–Sun) produces gourmet French cuisine at excellent prices, while round the corner *Cabrelli's* may be trapped in a time warp but it serves piles of fish and chips, along with authentic pizza. A few doors further on, *Carter's* has unremarkable pub grub, while the adjoining *Silver Darling* is among the liveliest of the **pubs** in the evenings, with occasional live music. At the other end of High St, the good-value *Lamplighter Restaurant* (ⓣ01955/603287; Wed–Sat) serves enormous helpings of imaginative food; downstairs in the same building, *Houston's Café* cheerfully churns out good burgers.

North of Wick

The road to John O'Groats (see p.654), seventeen miles north of Wick, is bleak and windswept. At Auckengill the **Northlands Viking Centre** (June–Sept daily 10am–4pm; £1.50) is a small archeological museum rather than a horned-helmets Valhallarama. A long but worthwhile video gives a good account of the prehistory of the Highlands, while the small exhibition focuses on Norse settlement in the Auckengill area, including Sweyn Aslafson (1120–71), so-called "last of the Vikings" and a notorious pirate and reveller. Keen for one last escapade before age overtook him, he sailed to Dublin with his men and held the town to ransom. According to legend, the Dubliners pleaded that they needed a day to collect the money but, during the night, as Sweyn and his men celebrated their success on his ship, the townfolk dug a series of concealed pits. When Sweyn realized the townsfolk weren't going to stump up the next day he attacked, but the pits proved his downfall, his force was soundly defeated, and he himself killed.

Travel details

Trains

Aviemore to: Edinburgh (Mon–Sat 5 daily, 3 on Sun; 3hr); Inverness (Mon–Sat 5 daily, 4 on Sun; 40min); Newtonmore (Mon–Sat 5 daily, 3 on Sun; 20min).

Dingwall to: Helmsdale (Mon–Sat 3 daily, plus 2 on Sun in summer; 2hr); Inverness (Mon–Sat 6–7 daily, plus 4 on Sun in summer; 25min); Kyle of Lochalsh (Mon–Sat 3–4 daily, plus 2 on Sun in summer; 2hr); Lairg (Mon–Sat 3 daily, plus 2 on Sun in summer; 1hr); Thurso (Mon–Sat 3 daily, plus 2 on Sun in summer; 3hr); Wick (Mon–Sat 3 daily, plus 2 on Sun in summer; 3hr 20min).

Fort William to: Arisaig (Mon–Sat 4 daily, 1–3 on Sun; 1hr 10min); Crianlarich (Mon–Sat 3–4 daily, 1–2 on Sun; 1hr 40min); Glasgow (Mon–Sat 3 daily, 1–2 on Sun; 4hr); Glenfinnan (4 daily; 35min); London (1 nightly; 12hr); Mallaig (Mon–Sat 4 daily, 1–3 on Sun; 1hr 25min).

Inverness to: Aviemore (Mon–Sat 5 daily, 3 on Sun; 40min); Dingwall (Mon–Sat 6–7 daily, plus 4 on Sun in summer; 25min); Edinburgh (Mon–Sat 5 daily, 3 on Sun; 3hr 30min); Helmsdale (Mon–Sat 3 daily, plus 2 on Sun in summer; 2hr 20min); Kyle of Lochalsh (Mon–Sat 3–4 daily, plus 2 on Sun in summer; 2hr 40min); Lairg (Mon–Sat 3 daily, plus 2 on Sun in summer; 1hr 40min); London (Mon–Fri & Sun 1 nightly; 8hr 35min); Plockton (Mon–Sat 3–4 daily, plus 2 on Sun in summer; 2hr 15min); Thurso (Mon–Sat 3 daily, plus 2 on Sun in summer; 3hr 25min); Wick (Mon–Sat 3 daily, plus 2 on Sun in summer; 3hr 45min).
Kyle of Lochalsh to: Dingwall (Mon–Sat 3–4 daily, plus 2 on Sun in summer; 2hr); Inverness (Mon–Sat 3–4 daily, plus 2 on Sun in summer; 2hr 40min); Plockton (Mon–Sat 3–4 daily, plus 2 on Sun in summer; 20min).
Lairg to: Dingwall (Mon–Sat 3 daily, plus 2 on Sun in summer; 1hr 10min); Inverness (Mon–Sat 3 daily, plus 2 on Sun in summer; 1hr 40min); Thurso (Mon–Sat 3 daily, plus 2 on Sun in summer; 1hr 50min); Wick (Mon–Sat 3 daily, plus 2 on Sun in summer; 2hr 20min).
Mallaig to: Arisaig (Mon–Sat 4 daily, plus 3 on Sun in summer; 15min); Fort William (Mon–Sat 4 daily, plus 3 on Sun in summer; 1hr 25min); Glasgow (Mon–Sat 3 daily, 1–2 on Sun; 5hr 20min); Glenfinnan (Mon–Sat 4 daily, plus 3 on Sun in summer; 35min).
Newtonmore to: Aviemore (Mon–Sat 5 daily, 3 on Sun; 20min); Inverness (Mon–Sat 5 daily, 3 on Sun; 55min).
Thurso to: Dingwall (Mon–Sat 3 daily, plus 2 on Sun in summer; 3hr); Inverness (Mon–Sat 3 daily, plus 2 on Sun in summer; 3hr 20min); Lairg (Mon–Sat 3 daily, plus 2 on Sun in summer; 1hr 50min).
Wick to: Dingwall (Mon–Sat 3 daily, plus 2 on Sun in summer; 3hr 20min); Inverness (Mon–Sat 3 daily, plus 2 on Sun in summer; 3hr 45min); Lairg (Mon–Sat 3 daily, plus 2 on Sun in summer; 2hr 5min).

Buses

Aviemore to: Grantown-on-Spey (6–9 daily; 35min); Inverness (15 daily; 40min); Newtonmore (8 daily; 20min).
Dornoch to: Inverness (10 daily; 1hr 10min); Thurso (4 daily; 2hr 20min).
Fort William to: Acharacle (Mon–Sat 2–4 daily; 1hr 30min); Aviemore (2 daily; 1hr 50min); Drumnadrochit (6 daily; 1hr 30min); Fort Augustus (6 daily; 1hr); Inverness (6 daily; 2hr); Mallaig (1–2 daily; 2hr).
Gairloch to: Dingwall (3 weekly; 2hr); Inverness (3 weekly; 2hr 20min); Redpoint (1–3 daily; 1hr 35min).
Inverness to: Aberdeen (hourly; 3hr 40min); Aviemore (12–15 daily; 40min); Cromarty (8 daily; 45min); Drumnadrochit (6 daily; 25min); Durness (June–Sept 1 daily; 5hr); Fort Augustus (6 daily; 1hr); Fort William (6 daily; 2hr); Gairloch (1 daily; 2hr 20min); Glasgow (10 daily; 3hr 35min–4hr 25min); Kyle of Lochalsh (2 daily; 2hr); Lairg (Mon–Sat 2 daily; 2hr); Lochinver (June–Sept 1 daily; 3hr 10min); Nairn (Mon–Sat hourly; 35min); Newtonmore (8 daily; 1hr 10min); Oban (Mon–Sat 2 daily; 4hr); Perth (12–15 daily; 2hr 35min); Portree (2 daily; 3hr 20min); Tain (hourly; 1hr 15min); Thurso (Mon–Sat 5 daily, Sun 4 daily; 3hr 30min); Ullapool (2–4 daily; 1hr 25min); Wick (Mon–Sat 5 daily, Sun 4 daily; 3hr).
Kyle of Lochalsh to: Fort William (3 daily; 1hr 50min); Glasgow (3 daily; 5hr); Inverness (2 daily; 2hr).
Lochinver to: Inverness (June–Sept 1 daily; 3hr 10min).
Mallaig to: Acharacle (1–3 daily; 1hr 45min); Fort William (1–2 daily; 2hr).
Thurso to: Bettyhill (2 daily; 1hr 20min); Inverness (Mon–Sat 5 daily, Sun 4 daily; 3hr 30min); Wick (Mon–Fri hourly, Sat & Sun 6 daily; 35min).
Wick to: Inverness (Mon–Sat 3 daily, 3hr), Thurso (Mon–Fri hourly, Sat & Sun 6 daily; 35min).

Ferries

To Lewis: Ullapool–Stornoway, see p.501.
To Mull: Kilchoan–Tobermory, see p.441.
To Orkney: Scrabster–Stromness, John O'Groats–Burwick, Gills Bay–St Margaret's Hope, see p.655.
To Skye: Mallaig–Armadale and Glenelg–Kylerhea, see p.501.
To the Small Isles: Mallaig–Eigg, Rum, Muck and Canna, see p.501.

Flights

Inverness to: Edinburgh (Mon–Fri 2 daily, Sat & Sun 1 daily; 50min); Glasgow (Mon–Fri 3 daily, Sat 1 daily; 50min); Kirkwall (Mon–Sat 2 daily; 45min); London (Gatwick 3 daily; Luton 1–2 daily; 1hr 45min); Shetland (Mon–Sat 1 daily; 1hr 45min); Stornoway (Mon–Fri 2 daily, 1 on Sat; 40min).

Orkney and Shetland

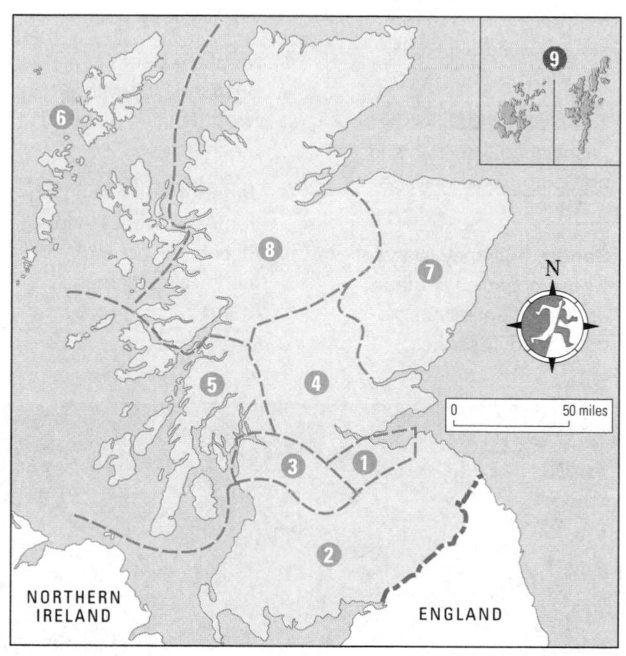

CHAPTER 9

Highlights

* **Maes Howe** – Orkney's, and Europe's, finest Neolithic chambered tomb. See p.687
* **Woodwick House** – Beautiful guesthouse hideaway, producing simple but superb food. See p.692
* **St Magnus Cathedral**, Kirkwall – Beautiful red-stone cathedral built by the Vikings. See p.695
* **Tomb of the Eagles** – Fascinating Neolithic site on South Ronaldsay. See p.701
* **Sanday** – Orkney island whose coastline is made up almost entirely of glorious sandy beaches, backed by sand dunes. See p.716
* **Traditional music** – Weekly sessions in Shetland, plus the annual Shetland Folk Festival. See p.728
* **Isle of Noss** – Guaranteed seals, puffins and dive-bombing "bonxies". See p.729
* **Mousa** – Remote Shetland islet with a two-thousand-year-old broch. See p.731
* **Jarlshof** – Site mingling Iron Age, Bronze Age, Pictish, Viking and medieval settlements. See p.733

Orkney and Shetland

Reaching up towards the Arctic Circle, and totally exposed to turbulent Atlantic weather systems, the Orkney and Shetland islands gather neatly into two distinct and very different clusters. Often referring to themselves first as Orcadians or Shetlanders, and with unofficial but widely displayed flags, their inhabitants regard Scotland as a separate entity; the mainland to them is the one in their own archipelago, not the Scottish mainland. This feeling of detachment arises from their distinctive geography, history and culture, in which they differ not only from Scotland but also from each other.

To the south, just a short step from the Scottish mainland, are the seventy or so **Orkney Islands**. With the major exception of **Hoy**, which is high and rugged, these islands are mostly low-lying, gently sloping and richly fertile, and for centuries have provided a reasonably secure living for their inhabitants from farming and, to a much lesser extent, fishing. In spring and summer the days are long, the skies enormous, the sandy beaches dazzling and the meadows thick with wild flowers. There is a peaceful continuity to Orcadian life reflected not only in the well-preserved treasury of Stone Age settlements, such as **Skara Brae**, and standing stones, most notably the **Stones of Stenness**, but also in the rather conservative nature of society here today.

Another sixty miles north, the Shetland Islands are in nearly all respects a complete contrast. Dramatic cliffs, teeming with thousands of seabirds, rise straight out of the water to rugged, heather-coated hills, while ice-sculpted sea

Accommodation price codes

Throughout this book, accommodation **prices** have been graded with the codes below, corresponding to the cost of the least expensive double room in high season. Price codes are not given for **campsites**, most of which charge less than £10 per person. Almost all **hostels** and **bunkhouses** charge between £8 and £12 per person per night; the few exceptions to this rule have the prices quoted in the text. For a full account of these codes, see p.28.

❶ under £40	❹ £60–70	❼ £110–150
❷ £40–50	❺ £70–90	❽ £150–200
❸ £50–60	❻ £90–110	❾ £200 and over

Island wildlife

Orkney and Shetland support huge numbers of **seabirds**, particularly during the breeding season from April to August, when cliffs and coastal banks are alive with thousands of guillemots, razorbills, puffins, fulmars and, particularly in Shetland, gannets. Arctic terns are often to be found on small offshore islets or gravelly spits. On coastal heathland or moorland you should see arctic skuas, great skuas, curlews and occasionally whimbrel or golden plover, while in remoter meadows in Orkney you may hear a corncrake. Many kinds of wild duck are present, especially in winter, but eiders are particularly common. In spring and autumn, large numbers of migrants drop in on their way north or south and very rare specimens may turn up at any time of year. Fair Isle, in particular, has a long list of rarities, and Shetland's isolation has produced its own distinctive subspecies of wren. We've noted in the guide text some of the best or most accessible bird sites.

The separation of the islands from the mainland has also meant that some species of **land mammal** are absent and others have developed subspecies. For instance, Shetland has no voles but Orkney boasts its own distinctive type. However, both groups have considerable populations of seals, and Shetland is probably the best place in the whole of Europe to see an otter. Further offshore you may well see porpoises, dolphins and several species of whale, including minke, pilot, sperm and killer. Shetland is also home to the famous Shetland pony, now mostly domesticated; you can see the diminutive ponies all over the islands, and there are a few places where they still run wild.

Neither of the island groups supports many **trees**, and very few are native. However, the clifftops and meadows of both Orkney and Shetland are rich with beautiful **wild flowers**, including pink thrift, the pale-pink heather-spotted orchid, red campion and, in wetter areas, golden marsh marigolds, yellow iris and insect-eating sundew. Notable **smaller plants** include the purple Scottish primrose, which grows only in Orkney and the far north of Scotland, and the Shetland (or Edmondston's) mouse-eared chickweed, with its delicate white flower streaked with yellow, which grows only on the island of Unst.

inlets cut deep into the land, offering memorable coastal walks in Shetland's endless summer evenings. With little fertile ground, Shetlanders have traditionally been crofters rather than farmers, often looking to the sea for an uncertain living in fishing and whaling or the naval and merchant services. Today islanders enthusiastically embrace new opportunities such as fish farming and computing. Nevertheless, the past isn't forgotten; the Norse heritage is clear in every roadsign and there are many well-preserved prehistoric sites, such as **Mousa Broch** and **Jarlshof**.

Since people first began to explore the North Atlantic, Orkney and Shetland have been stepping stones on routes between Britain, Ireland and Scandinavia, and both groups have a long history of settlement, certainly from around 3500–4000 BC. The **Norse settlers**, who began to arrive from about 800 AD, with substantial migration from around 900 AD, left the islands with a unique cultural character. Orkney was a powerful Norse earldom, and Shetland (at first part of the same earldom) was ruled directly from Norway for nearly three hundred years after 1195. The Norse legacy is clearly evident today in place names and in dialect words; neither group was ever part of the Gaelic-speaking culture of Highland Scotland, and the later Scottish influence is essentially a Lowland one.

Dialect and place-names

Between the tenth and seventeenth centuries, the chief language of Orkney and Shetland was **Norn**, a Scandinavian tongue close to modern Faroese and Icelandic. After the end of Norse rule, and with the transformation of the church, the law, commerce and education, Norn gradually lost out to Scots and English, eventually petering out completely in the eighteenth century. Today, Orkney and Shetland have their own dialects, and individual islands and communities within each group have local variations. The **dialects** have a Scots base, with some Old Norse words; however, they don't sound strongly Scottish, with the Orkney accent – which has been likened to the Welsh one – especially distinctive. Listed below are some of the words you're most likely to hear, including some birds' names and common elements in place names. In most cases, the Shetland form is given; the Orkney terms are very similar, if not identical.

aak	guillemot
alan	storm petrel
ayre	beach
bister	farm
böd	fisherman's store
bonxie	great skua
bruck	rubbish
burra	heath rush
corbie	raven
crö	sheepfold
du	familiar form of "you"
dunter	eider duck
eela	rod-fishing from small boats
ferrylouper	incomer (Orkney)
fourareen	four-oared boat
foy	party or festival
geo	coastal inlet
haa	laird's house
hap	hand-knitted shawl
howe	mound
kame	ridge of hills
kishie	basket
maa	seagull
mallie (Shetland) or *mallimak* (Orkney)	fulmar petrel
mool	headland
moorit	brown
mootie	tiny
muckle	large
neesick	porpoise
noost	hollow place where a boat is drawn up
norie	puffin (or *tammie-norie*)
noup	steep headland
peerie (often *peedie* in Orkney)	small
plantiecrub (or *plantiecrö*)	small drystone enclosure for growing cabbages
quoy	enclosed, cultivated common land
reestit	cured (as in *reestit* mutton)
roost	tide race
scattald	common grazing land
scootie alan	arctic skua
scord	gap or pass in a ridge of hills
setter	farm
shaela	dark grey
shalder	oystercatcher
simmer dim	summer twilight
sixern	six-oared boat
solan	gannet
soothmoother	incomer (Shetland)
tystie	black guillemot
voe	sea inlet

Transport practicalities

Orkney and Shetland may share a common Norse heritage, but the modern **transport links** between them are surprisingly poor. In the winter, there is just one ferry a week between them, and only two a week in the height of summer. And while it's possible to meet a fellow visitor who's visiting both sets of islands, it's rare to find an Orcadian who's been to Shetland, or vice versa. When leaving their homeland, for whatever reason, Shetlanders tend to go to Aberdeen, while

Orcadians pop over to Caithness on the Scottish mainland. **Public transport** is not bad, and the council-run **inter-island ferries** on Shetland are very cheap; Orkney's inter-island ferries, by contrast, are expensive. If you're thinking of bringing your own vehicle, it might be worth looking into renting one locally instead, given the time and cost of the car ferries from the mainland.

It's impossible to underestimate the influence of the **weather** in these parts. The one thing you can say about it is that it's interesting, frequently dramatic. More often than not, it will be windy and rainy; though, as they say in the nearby Faroes, you can have all four seasons in one day. The wind-chill factor is not to be taken lightly, and there is often a dampness or drizzle in the air, even when it's not actually raining. Even in late spring and summer, when there can be long dry spells with lots of sunshine, you still need to come prepared for wind, rain and, most frustrating of all, the occasional sea fog. The one good thing about the almost constant presence of the wind is that midges are less of a problem, except on Hoy.

Orkney

Just a short step from John O'Groats, the **Orkney Islands** are a unique and fiercely independent archipelago. In spring and summer, the meadows and clifftops are a brilliant green, shining with wild flowers, while long days pour light onto the land and sea. In autumn and winter, the islands are often battered by gale-force winds and daylight is scarce, but the temperature stays remarkably mild thanks to the ameliorating effect of the Gulf Stream. For an Orcadian, the "Mainland" invariably means the largest island in Orkney rather than the rest of Scotland, and throughout their history the Orcadians have been linked to lands much further afield, principally Scandinavia. In the words of the late Orcadian poet George Mackay Brown:

> Orkney lay athwart a great sea-way
> from Viking times onwards, and its lore
> is crowded with sailors, merchants, adventurers,
> pilgrims, smugglers, storms and sea-changes.
> The shores are strewn with wrack, jetsam,
> occasional treasure.

Small communities began to settle in the islands around 4000 BC, and the village at **Skara Brae** on the Mainland is one of the best-preserved Stone Age settlements in Europe. This and many of the other older archeological sites, including the **Stones of Stenness** and **Maes Howe**, are concentrated in the central and western parts of the Mainland. Elsewhere the islands are scattered with chambered tombs and stone circles, a tribute to the well-developed religious and ceremonial practices taking place here from around 2000 BC. More sophisticated **Iron Age** inhabitants built fortified villages incorporating stone towers known as *brochs*, protected by walls and ramparts, many of which are still in place. Later, **Pictish** culture spread to Orkney and the remains of several of

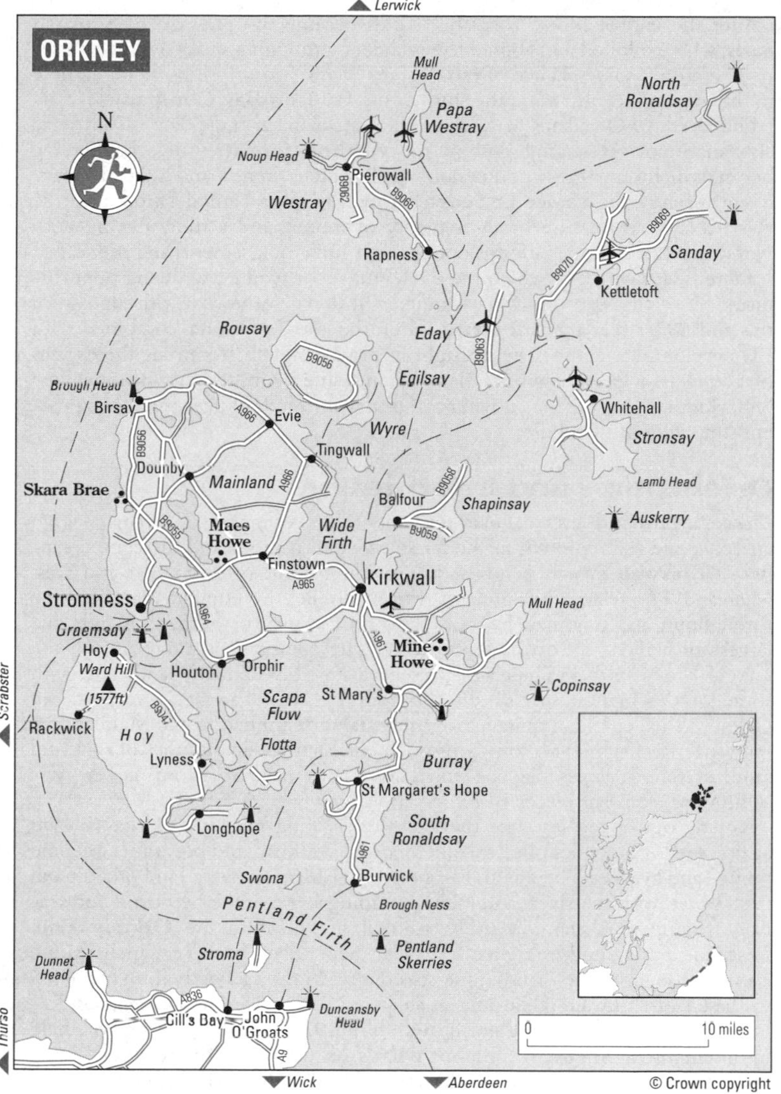

their early Christian settlements can still be seen, the best at the **Brough of Birsay** in the West Mainland, where a group of small houses is clustered around the remains of an early church. In the ninth century or thereabouts, **Norse** settlers from Scandinavia arrived and the islands became Norse earldoms, forming an outpost of a powerful, expansive culture which was gradually forcing its way south. The last of the Norse earls was killed in 1231, but they had an enduring impact on the islands, leaving behind not only their language but also the great **St Magnus Cathedral** in Kirkwall, one of Scotland's outstanding examples of medieval architecture.

After the end of Norse rule, the islands became the preserve of **Scottish earls**, who exploited and abused the islanders, although a steady increase in sea trade did offer some chance of escape. French and Spanish ships sheltered here in the sixteenth century, and the ships of the **Hudson Bay Company** recruited hundreds of Orcadians to work in the Canadian fur trade. The islands were also an important staging post in the **whaling industry** and the herring boom, which drew great numbers of small Dutch, French and Scottish boats. More recently, the choice of **Scapa Flow**, Orkney's natural harbour, as the Royal Navy's main base brought plenty of money and activity during both world wars, and left the clifftops dotted with gun emplacements and the seabed scattered with wrecks – which these days make for wonderful diving opportunities. Since the war, things have quietened down somewhat, although since the mid-1970s the large **oil terminal** on the island of Flotta, combined with EU development grants, have brought surprise windfalls, stemming the exodus of young people. Meanwhile, many disenchanted southerners have become "ferryloupers" (incomers), moving to Orkney in search of peace and the apparent simplicity of island life.

Orientation and information

Orkney **Mainland** has two main settlements: the ferry port of **Stromness**, an attractive old fishing town on the far southwestern shore, and the central capital of **Kirkwall**, which stands at the dividing point between East and West Mainland. The whole of Mainland is relatively heavily populated and farmed throughout, and is joined by causeways to a string of southern islands, the largest of which is **South Ronaldsay**. The southern island of **Hoy**, the second-largest in the archipelago, presents a superbly dramatic landscape, with some of the highest seacliffs in the country. Hoy, however, is atypical of Orkney's smaller, much quieter **northern islands** (linked to the Mainland by regular ferries), which are low-lying, elemental but fertile outcrops of rock and sand, scattered across the ocean. The islands' tourist board at Ⓦwww.visitorkney.com has plenty of information.

Rolling out of the sea "like the backs of sleeping whales" (Mackay Brown again), the Orkney isles offer excellent coastal **walking** and beautiful sweeping white-sand beaches. There is also some good **fishing** to be had in both salt and fresh water, with the rivers and lochs providing some of the best trout and sea-trout fishing in Britain. A lively cultural life includes the **Orkney Folk Festival** in May, and a science festival in September, both of which feature events throughout the islands. June sees the **St Magnus Festival**, an arts festival based in Kirkwall, while July is peppered with several island regattas, followed by numerous agricultural shows, culminating in the County Show held in the middle of August. To find out **what's on** (and what the weather's going to be like), tune in to Radio Orkney on 93.7FM (Mon–Fri 7.30–8am), and buy yourself a copy of *The Orcadian*, the local newspaper, which comes out on a Thursday (Ⓦwww.orcadian.co.uk).

Arrival

Orkney is connected to the Scottish mainland by several **ferry** routes. Until October 2002, P&O Scottish Ferries (Ⓣ01856/850655, Ⓦwww.posf.co.uk) runs car ferries to **Stromness** once a week (June–Aug 2 weekly) from **Aberdeen** (takes 8–10hr) and daily on the much shorter and cheaper crossing from **Scrabster** (takes 2hr), which is very near Thurso (there are plenty of trains and buses from Inverness to Thurso, and a shuttle bus from there to

Scrabster). There's also a weekly (June–Aug 2 weekly) P&O service to Stromness from **Lerwick** in Shetland (takes 2hr). Note that NorthLink take over all the above services as of October 2002, which means timings may well change. Pentland Ferries (Ⓣ01856/831226, Ⓦwww.pentlandferries.co.uk) operates a short car-ferry crossing from **Gills Bay**, on the north coast near John O'Groats to **St Margaret's Hope** on South Ronaldsay (3 daily; takes 1hr).

A passenger ferry runs from **John O'Groats** to **Burwick** on South Ronaldsay (May–Sept 2–4 daily; 40min), its departure timed to connect with the arrival of the Orkney Bus from Inverness; there's also a free bus service from Thurso. A day-trip package is available from Inverness or John O'Groats, including a tour of some of the major sights on Orkney; details of both ferry and bus are available from John O'Groats Ferries (Ⓣ0800/731 7872, Ⓦwww.jogferry.co.uk). The ferry is small and, except in fine weather, is recommended only for those with strong stomachs.

Direct **flights** serve Kirkwall airport from Sumburgh in Shetland, Wick, Inverness and Aberdeen, and there are good connections from Edinburgh, Glasgow, Manchester, Birmingham and London. All can be booked through British Airways (Ⓣ0845/773 3377, Ⓦwww.britishairways.com).

Island transport

Bus services on the Orkney Mainland are very poor, and virtually non-existent on Sundays, with some of the most interesting areas not served at all. On the islands, there's usually a bus service to and from the ferry terminal and that's all, making a Day Rover (£6) or Three-Day Rover (£15) of limited value (see Ⓦwww.rapsons.co.uk for more). However, **cycling** is cheap and, with few steep hills and modest distances, relatively easy, though the wind can make it hard going. You can rent bikes in Kirkwall, Stromness and on most of the smaller islands. Bringing a **car** to Orkney is straightforward, if expensive; alternatively, you can **rent** a car in Kirkwall, Stromness or on several of the islands (details are given in the text). If your time is limited, you may want to consider one of the informative bus or minibus **tours** on offer: Wildabout Orkney Tours (Ⓣ01856/851011, Ⓦwww.orknet.co.uk/wildabout) have good-value tours of the chief sights on the Mainland and Hoy; other tours for specific islands are detailed in the text.

Getting to the other islands from the Mainland isn't difficult, though it is relatively expensive: Orkney Ferries (Ⓣ01856/872044, Ⓦwww.orkneyferries.co.uk) operates several **ferries** daily to Hoy, Shapinsay and Rousay, and between one and three a day, depending on route and season, to all the others except North Ronaldsay, which has a weekly boat on Fridays. If you're taking a car on any of the ferries, it is sensible to book your ticket well in advance. There are also **flights** from Kirkwall to Eday, North Ronaldsay, Westray, Papa Westray, Sanday and Stronsay, operated by Loganair (Ⓣ01856/872420, Ⓦwww.loganair.co.uk), using a tiny eight-seater plane. Loganair also offers **sightseeing flights** over Orkney, which are spectacular in fine weather (but cancelled in bad), as well as a discounted Orkney Adventure Ticket, which allows you to visit three islands.

Travel between individual islands by sea or air isn't so straightforward, but careful study of timetables can sometimes reduce the need to come all the way back to Kirkwall. It's worth enquiring from Orkney Ferries about their additional sailings on summer Sundays that often make useful inter-island connections.

Stromness

STROMNESS has to be one of the most enchanting ports at which to arrive by boat, its picturesque waterfront a procession of tiny sandstone jetties and slate roofs nestling below the green hill of Brinkies Brae. As Orkney's main point of arrival, Stromness is a great introduction, and one that's well worth spending a day exploring, or using as a base in preference to Kirkwall. Its natural sheltered harbour (known as Hamnavoe) must have been used in Viking times, but the town itself only really took off in the eighteenth century. At that time, European conflicts made it safer for ships heading across the Atlantic to travel around the north of Scotland rather than through the English Channel, and many of them called in to Stromness to take on food, water and crew. The Hudson's Bay Company made Stromness its main base from which to make the long journey across the North Atlantic, and crews from Stromness were also hired for herring and whaling expeditions – and, of course, press-ganged into the Royal Navy.

By 1842, the town boasted forty or so pubs, and reports circulated of "outrageous and turbulent proceedings of seamen and others who frequent the harbour". The herring boom brought large numbers of small boats to the town, along with thousands of young women who gutted, pickled and packed the fish in barrels. Things got so rowdy by World War I that the town voted in a referendum to ban the sale of alcohol, leaving Stromness dry from 1920 until 1947. Today Stromness remains an important harbour town and fishing port, serving as Orkney's main ferry terminal and as the headquarters of the Northern Lighthouse Board.

Information and accommodation

Arriving by ferry, you'll disembark at the new ferry terminal, which also houses the **tourist office** (April–Oct Mon–Sat 8am–5pm, Sat 9am–4pm & Sun 10am–3pm; Nov–March Mon–Fri 9am–5pm; ⓣ01856/850716). As far as **hotels** go, the venerable Victorian *Stromness Hotel* (ⓣ01856/850298, ⓦwww.stromnesshotel.com; ❺) – the town's first – is probably your best bet. As for **B&Bs**, there's a traditional end-on waterfront house next to the museum at 2 South End (ⓣ01856/850215; ❷; April–Oct); if you've got your own transport, you might prefer to head to the modern *Thira* (ⓣ01856/851181; ❸), up on the hill above the town, boasting great views overlooking Hoy.

Stromness has an SYHA **hostel** in a converted school on Helliehole Road (ⓣ01856/850589, ⓦwww.syha.org.uk; mid-May to Sept), signposted off the main street; it has a curfew and single-sex dorms. More laid-back is the family-run *Brown's Hostel*, 45–47 Victoria St (ⓣ01856/850661), with bunk beds in shared rooms and kitchen facilities; it's open all year, and there's no daytime closing or late-night curfew. There's also a **campsite** (ⓣ01856/873535; May to mid-Sept) in a superb setting a mile south of the ferry terminal at Point of Ness, with views out to Hoy; it's well equipped and even has its own lounge, but is extremely exposed, especially if a southwesterly is blowing.

The Town

Stromness still has a few reminders of its trading heyday, starting with the **Warehouse**, situated diagonally opposite the new ferry terminal. Though it may not look like it, the building was constructed in the 1760s – just too late to catch the trade in American rice. More eye-catching is the **Stromness Hotel**, a tall and imposing sandstone building behind the Warehouse; during World War II, Gracie Fields sang from its balcony, when it served as the head-

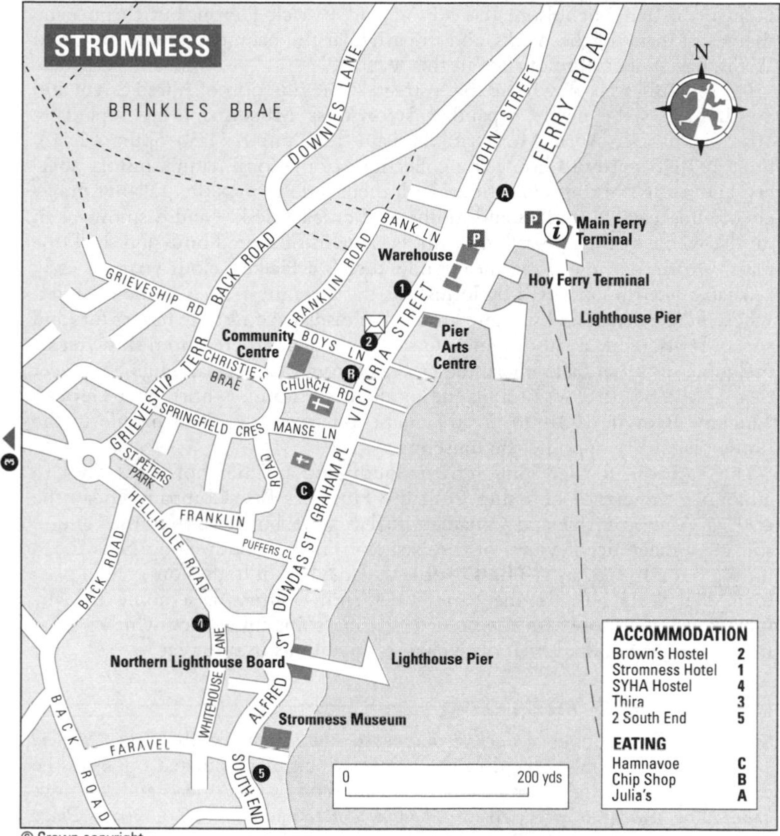

© Crown copyright

quarters of the Orkney and Shetland Defence (OS Def).

Unlike Kirkwall, the old town of Stromness – famously described by Sir Walter Scott as "a dirty, straggling town" – still hugs the shoreline, its one and only street, a narrow winding affair, built long before the advent of the motor car, still paved with great flagstones and fed by a tight network of alleyways or closes. The central section, which begins at the *Stromness Hotel*, is known as **Victoria Street**, though in fact it takes on several other names – Graham Place, Dundas Street, Alfred Street and South End – as it threads its way southwards. On the east side of the street the houses are gable-end-on to the waterfront, and originally each one would have had its own pier, from which merchants would trade with passing ships.

You can visit the first of the old jetties, to the south of the modern harbour, since it now houses the **Pier Arts Centre** (Tues–Sat 10.30am–12.30pm & 1.30–5pm; free). The art gallery is spread over two buildings, divided by a lovely flagstone suntrap courtyard (access is down an alleyway off the main street): the first building hosts temporary exhibitions, often featuring painting and sculpture by local artists, while the warehouse has a remarkable permanent display of twentieth-century British art. At first it comes as a shock to see abstract works executed by members of the Cornish art scene such as Barbara

Hepworth, Ben Nicholson, Terry Frost and Patrick Heron, but the marine themes of many of the works, and in particular the primitive scenes by Alfred Wallis, have a special resonance in this seaport.

Ten minutes' walk down the main street, at the junction of Alfred Street and South End, is the newly expanded **Stromness Museum** (May–Sept daily 10am–5pm; Oct–April Mon–Sat 10.30am–12.30pm & 1.30–5pm; £2.50), built in 1858, partly to house the collections of the local natural history society. The natural history collection is still there – don't miss the pull-out drawers of birds' eggs, butterflies and moths by the ticket desk – and has now taken up the whole of the upper floor with its cabinets of stuffed birds and shell displays. On the ground floor, meanwhile, there's a Halkett cloth boat, an early inflatable like the one used by John Rae, the Stromness-born Arctic explorer, whose fiddle, octant and shotgun are also on display. Amidst the beaver furs and model boats, there are also numerous salty artefacts gathered from shipwrecks, including some barnacle-encrusted crockery from the German High Seas Fleet that sank in Scapa Flow. As a plaque recalls, the Stromness-born poet **George Mackay Brown** (1921–96) lived out the last twenty years of his life in the house diagonally opposite the museum.

The **cannon**, further south down South End by the shore, was fired to announce the arrival of a ship from the Hudson's Bay Company. Today the trade in American rice and Canadian fur has gone, but the site of the cannon still gives magnificent views of the harbour. Further south along Ness Road jutting out into the bay is **The Doubles**, a large pair of houses on a raised platform that were built in the early nineteenth century as a home by Mrs Christian Robertson with the proceeds of her shipping agency, which sent as many as eight hundred men on whaling expeditions in one year.

Eating and drinking

Stromness has a couple of decent **places to eat**, starting with *Julia's Café and Bistro* (lunchtime only except in the height of summer), situated opposite the ferry terminal, a bright lemon-coloured café serving tasty meals and delicious cakes. The moderately expensive *Hamnavoe Restaurant,* at 35 Graham Place (☎01856/850606; Thurs–Sun eves only), offers the town's most ambitious cooking, using local produce including shellfish, fish and beef and offering some delicious vegetarian dishes, in a very pleasant setting. For something less formal, head for the upstairs lounge bar of the *Stromness Hotel*, which does very good bar meals – go for their specials. For **takeaways**, head for the *Chip Shop* on the main street (closed Thurs eve, Sat lunch & Sun). The downstairs *Flattie Bar* of the *Stromness Hotel* is a congenial place to warm yourself by a real fire (or, depending on the season, sit outside) with a **drink**; another popular pub is the *Ferry Inn*, opposite the hotel. *Argo's Bakery*, on Victoria Street, has a wide range of **picnic** basics, while *Orkney Wholefoods*, a few doors down, sells seafood, health food, cheese, local ice cream and delicious made-to-order sandwiches.

Listings

Banks There are branches of the Bank of Scotland and Royal Bank of Scotland on the main street, both with ATMs.
Bike rental Stromness Cycle Hire, opposite the ferry terminal (☎01856/850750).
Bookshops J.L. Broom is the best of the bookshops on the main street, and probably the best in the whole of Orkney.
Car rental Brass's Self Drive, Blue Star Garage, North End Road (☎01856/850850); Stromness Car Hire, 75 John Street (☎01856/850973).
Internet access You can send an email or surf (£5 an hour) from Julia's Café, on the harbour front (☎01856/850904).

West Mainland

Stromness sits in the southwesternmost corner of the **West Mainland** – west of Kirkwall, that is – the great bulk of which is fertile, productive farmland, fenced off into a patchwork of fields used either to produce crops or for cattle-grazing. Fringed by some spectacular coastline, particularly in the west, West Mainland is littered with some of the island's most impressive prehistoric sites, such as the village of **Skara Brae**, the standing **Stones of Stenness** and the chambered tomb of **Maes Howe**. Despite the intensive farming, there are still some areas which are too barren to cultivate, and the high ground and wild coastline are protected by several interesting **wildlife reserves**.

Stenness

The parish of **STENNESS**, northeast of Stromness along the main road to Kirkwall, slopes down from Ward Hill (881ft) to the lochs of Stenness and Harray, the first of which is tidal, the second of which is Orkney's most famous freshwater trout loch. The two lochs are separated by a couple of promontories, now joined by a short causeway that may well have been a narrow isthmus around 3000 BC, when it stood at the heart of Orkney's most important Neolithic ceremonial complex, centred on the burial chamber of **Maes Howe**.

The Stones of Stenness and the Ring of Brodgar

The most visible part of the complex between lochs Stenness and Harray is the **Stones of Stenness**, originally a circle of twelve rock slabs, now just four, the tallest of which is a real monster at over 16ft, though it's more remarkable for its incredible thinness. A broken table-top lies within the circle, which is surrounded by a much-diminished henge (a circular bank of earth and a ditch) with a couple of entrance causeways. A path leads east from the stones to the **Barnhouse Settlement**, where the foundations of a Neolithic village contemporary with the stones are marked out on the ground.

Less than a mile to the northwest, past the awesome **Watch Stone** which stands beside the road at over 18ft in height, you reach another stone circle, the **Ring of Brodgar**, a much wider circle dramatically sited on raised ground. Here there were originally sixty stones, 27 of which now stand; of the henge, only the ditch survives.

Maes Howe

There are several quite large burial mounds visible to the south of the Ring of Brodgar, but these are entirely eclipsed by one of the most impressive Neolithic burial chambers in the whole of Europe, **Maes Howe** (April–Sept daily 9.30am–6.30pm; Oct–March Mon–Sat 9.30am–4.30pm, Sun 2–4.30pm; £2.80; HS), which lies less than a mile northeast of the Stones of Stenness. Dating from around 3000 BC, its excellent state of preservation is partly due to the massive slabs of sandstone it was constructed from, the largest of which weighs over thirty tons. To enter the tomb, you must first buy a ticket from

Orkney's Historic Scotland sights

If you're planning on visiting more than one of Orkney's Historic Scotland sights, it might be worth buying the **joint ticket**, which costs £11 and covers entry to Maes Howe, Skara Brae, the Broch of Gurness, and the Bishop's and Earl's palaces in Kirkwall.

nearby **Tormiston Mill**, a converted nineteenth-century meal mill by the main road, which now houses the **ticket office**, toilets and interpretive display on the ground floor; a shop and some of the original mill machinery on the middle floor; and a café, which calls itself a restaurant but isn't, on the top floor.

Once you've reached the tomb, a guide will lead you into the **central chamber** down a low, long passage, one wall of which is comprised of a single immense stone. Once inside, you can stand upright and admire the superb masonry of the lofty corbelled roof. Perhaps the most remarkable aspect of Maes Howe is that the tomb is aligned so that the rays of the winter solstice sun hit the top of the Barnhouse Stone, half a mile away, and reach right down the passage of Maes Howe to the ledge of one of the three cells built into the walls of the tomb. When Maes Howe was opened in 1861, it was found to be virtually empty, thanks to the work of generations of grave-robbers, who had left behind only a handful of human bones. The Vikings entered in the twelfth century, probably on their way to the Crusades, leaving large amounts of runic graffiti, some of which are cryptographic twig runes, cut into the walls of the main chamber and still clearly visible today. They include phrases such as "many a beautiful woman has stooped in here, however pompous she might be", and "these runes were carved by the man most skilled in runes in the entire western ocean", to the more prosaic "Thor and I bedded Helga".

Practicalities

Given the density of prehistoric sites around Stenness, and its central position on the Mainland, it's not a bad area in which to base yourself. Both the **hotels** in the area attract large numbers of anglers: the *Standing Stones* (Ⓣ01856/850449, Ⓦwww.visitorkney.com/accommodation/standingstones; ❹), on the southern shore of the Loch of Stenness, has been pretty tastelessly modernized, though it's certainly comfortable; the *Merkister* (Ⓣ01856/771515, Ⓦwww.smoothhound.co.uk/hotels/merkister; ❸), on the northeastern shore of the Loch of Harray, has a little more character, and its **bar** is very popular with the locals. A more relaxing place than either of the above, however, is the carefully converted *Mill of Eyrland* (Ⓣ01856/850136, Ⓦwww.orknet.co.uk/mill; ❸), in a delightful setting by a mill stream on the A964 to Orphir; it's filled with wonderful antiques, old mill machinery plus all mod cons, and serves enormous breakfasts.

Skara Brae and around

Around seven miles north of Stromness, the parish of **SANDWICK** contains the best known of Orkney's prehistoric monuments, the Neolithic village of **Skara Brae** (April–Sept daily 9.30am–6.30pm; Oct–March Mon–Sat 9.30am–4.30pm, Sun 2–4.30pm; £4.50 in summer, £3.50 in winter), situated beside the beautiful white curve of the Bay of Skaill. Here, the extensive remains of a small Neolithic fishing and farming village, dating back to 3000 BC, were discovered in 1850 after a fierce storm ripped off the dunes covering them. The village is very well preserved, its houses huddled together and connected by narrow passages which would originally have been covered over with turf. The houses themselves consist of a single, spacious living room, filled with domestic detail, including dressers, fireplaces, built-in cupboards, beds and boxes, all ingeniously constructed from slabs of stone.

Before you reach the site you must buy a ticket from the new **visitor centre**, which houses an excellent **café-restaurant**. After watching a short video, you pass through a small introductory **exhibition**, with a few replica finds, and some hands-on stuff for kids, all of which helps put the site in context.

You then proceed to a full-scale replica of House 7 (the best-preserved house), complete with a fake wood and skin roof. It's all a tad neat and tidy, with fetching up-lighting – rather than dark, smoky and smelly – but it'll give you the general idea. Unfortunately, the sheer numbers now visiting Skara Brae mean that you can no longer explore the site itself properly, but only look down from the outer walls. Sadly, too, House 7 now sports a perspex roof to protect it from the elements; however, House 1, which also contains a dresser, as yet does not.

Skaill House

In the summer months, your ticket to Skara Brae also covers entry to nearby **Skaill House**, an extensive range of buildings 300 yards inland, home of the laird of Skaill. The original house was a simple two-storey block with a small courtyard, built for Bishop George Graham in the 1620s, but it has since been much extended. The house's prize possession is Captain Cook's dinner service from the *Resolution*, which was delivered after Cook's death when the *Resolution* and the *Discovery* sailed into Stromness in 1780. The last occupant of the house was Mrs Kathleen Scarth, who died in 1991; her bedroom has been left as it was, and is filled with old frocks, an ostrich feather fan and a "twist and slim exerciser".

Yesnaby

The other good reason for exploring the area around Skara Brae is the cliffs to the north and south of the Bay of Skaill, which provide some of the most spectacularly rugged **coastal walks** on Orkney's Mainland. The best place to head for is **Yesnaby**, to the south of the Bay of Skaill, where the sandstone cliffs have been savagely eroded into stacks and geos by the force of the Atlantic. Come here during a westerly gale and you'll see the waves sending sea spray shooting over the wartime buildings and the neighbouring fields. As a result, the clifftops support a unique plantlife, which thrives on the salt spray, including the rare and very small Scottish Primrose, which flowers in May and from July to late September. The walk south along the coast from here is exhilarating: the Old Man of Hoy is visible in the distance and, after a mile and a half, you come to West Mainland's own version of the Old Man, known as **Yesnaby Castle**.

Practicalities

With only infrequent bus connections, you really need your own transport to reach Sandwick parish. There's no main settlement as such, though there are a number of inexpensive **B&Bs** around and about: try the Georgian former manse of *Flotterston House* off the B9056 (ⓣ01856/841700; ❶), or *Brettobreck Farm*, a traditional, cosy Orcadian farmhouse on a working dairy farm further south in Kirbister, off the A967 (ⓣ01856/850373; ❶).

Birsay and around

Occupying the northwest corner of the Mainland, the parish of **BIRSAY** was the centre of Norse power in Orkney for several centuries before the earls moved to Kirkwall, some time after the construction of its cathedral. Today a tiny cluster of homes is gathered around the sandstone ruins of the **Earl's Palace**, which was built in the second half of the sixteenth century by Robert Stewart, Earl of Orkney, using the forced labour of the islanders, who weren't even given food and drink for their work. By all accounts, it was a "sumptuous and stately dwelling", built in four wings around a central courtyard, its upper rooms decorated with painted ceilings and rich furnishings; surrounding the palace were flower and herb gardens, a bowling green and archery butts. The palace appears to have lasted barely a century before falling into rack and ruin; the crumbling walls and turrets retain much of their grandeur, although inside there is little remaining domestic detail. However, its vast scale makes the Earl's Palace in Kirkwall seem almost humble in comparison.

Half a mile southeast of the palace, up the burn, is the **Barony Mills** (April–Sept daily 10am–1pm & 2–5pm; £1.50), Orkney's only working nineteenth-century water mill to survive into the modern era. The mill specializes in producing traditional stoneground beremeal, essential for making bere bannocks. Bere is a four-kernel barley crop with a very short growing season perfectly suited for the local climate and was once the staple diet in these parts. The miller on duty will give you a guided tour and show you the machinery going through its paces, though milling only takes place in the autumn.

Brough of Birsay

Just over half a mile northwest of the palace is the **Brough of Birsay**, a substantial Pictish settlement on a small tidal island that is only accessible during the two hours each side of low tide. Stromness and Kirkwall tourist offices have the tide times and Radio Orkney broadcasts them (93.7FM; Mon–Fri 7.30–8am). Once you reach the island, there's a small ticket office where you must pay your **entrance fee** (June–Sept daily; £1.50), and where you can see a few artefacts gathered from the site, including a game made from whalebone and an antler pin. Coastal erosion over the last eight centuries means that some of the site has disappeared off the side of the low cliffs, and concrete sea defences are currently in place to try and stem the tide.

The focus of the village was – and still is – the sandstone-built twelfth-century **St Peter's Church**, which stands higher than the surrounding buildings; the stone seating along the walls is still in place, and there are a couple of semicircular recesses for altars, and a semicircular apse. The church is thought to have stood at the centre of a monastic complex of some sort – the foundations of a courtyard and outer buildings can be made out to the west. Close by is a large complex ofViking-era buildings, including several houses, a sauna and some sophisticated stone drains.

The Brough of Birsay is a popular day-trip, partly due to the fun of dodging the tides, but few folk bother to explore the rest of the island, whose gentle green slopes, when viewed from the mainland, belie the dramatic, rugged cliffs that characterize the rest of the coastline. In winter, sea spray from the waves crashing against the cliffs can envelop the entire island. In summer the cliffs are home to various seabirds, including a fair few puffins, making the half-mile walk to the island's castellated **lighthouse** and back along the northern coastline well worth the effort. If you make it out here, spare a thought for the lighthouse keepers who used to man the **Sule Skerry** lighthouse – the most isolated in Britain – which lies on a piece of bare rock barely visible some 37 miles out to sea, and whose only contact with the outside world was via carrier pigeon.

Marwick Head and The Loons

The best of Birsay's coastal scenery lies to the south of Birsay Bay around **Marwick Head**. The headland itself is clearly visible on the horizon thanks to the huge castellated tower of the **Kitchener Memorial**, raised by the people of Orkney to commemorate the Minister of War, Lord Kitchener, who drowned along with all but twelve of the crew of the 11,000-ton cruiser HMS *Hampshire* when the ship struck a mine just off the coast on June 5, 1916. There has been much speculation about the incident over the years, due to the fact that Kitchener was on a secret mission to Russia to hold talks with the Tsar. As a result, salvage operations were closely controlled by the Admiralty and the findings of the naval court of enquiry kept secret, fanning the rumours that Kitchener had been deliberately sent to his death (he was extremely unpopular at the time). In reality, it appears to have been a simple case of naval incompetence: a weather forecast from the Admiralty warning of severe northwesterly gales was ignored, as were the reports of submarine activity in the area.

Marwick Head is also an **RSPB reserve** and, during the nesting season, there are numerous fulmar, kittiwakes, guillemots and razorbills in residence on the 200-foot cliffs; at that time, the sight and smell is quite overwhelming. A mile or so inland, another RSPB reserve is centred on the wetlands of **The Loons**. There's no public access to the area, but you can watch the waterfowl, snipe, curlews and even the odd short-eared owl from the hide on the northwest side of the reserve on the road to Twatt.

Kirbuster and Corrigall farm museums

Lying between the Loch of Boardhouse and the Loch of Hundland, the **Kirbuster Farm Museum** (March–Oct Mon–Sat 10.30am–1pm & 2–5pm, Sun 2–7pm; free) offers an interesting insight into life on an Orkney farm steading in the mid-nineteenth century. Built in 1723, the farm is made up of a typical collection of flagstone buildings, though Kirbuster is more substantial than most, and boasts its own, very beautiful, garden. Ducks, geese and sheep wander around the grassy open yard, which is entered through a whalebone archway. The most remarkable thing about Kirbuster, however, is that, despite being inhabited until as late as 1961, it has retained its Firehoose, in which the smoke from the central peat fire is used to dry fish fillets, and eventually allowed simply to drift up towards a hole in the ceiling; the room even retains the old neuk-beds, simple recesses in the stone walls, which would have originally been lined with wood.

If you've enjoyed your time at Kirbuster – and kids almost certainly will – then it's definitely worth visiting **Corrigall Farm Museum** (same times), another eighteenth-century farmstead some five miles southeast of Kirbuster, beyond Dounby in the parish of Harray. There are lovely views west and south from the honeysuckle-draped ticket office, as well as hens and sheep scampering around the farmyard. Be sure to check out the well-preserved flagstone byre, and the stable, which has a characteristic beehive-shaped kiln for drying grain at one end.

Evie and the Broch of Gurness

Overshadowed by the great wind turbine on Burgar Hill, the village and parish of **EVIE**, on the north coast, looks out across the turbulent waters of Eynhallow Sound towards the island of Rousay. Its chief draw is the **Broch of Gurness** (April–Sept daily 9.30am–6.30pm; £2.80; HS), the best-preserved broch on an archipelago replete with them, and one which is still surrounded by a remarkable complex of later buildings. As at Birsay, the sea has eaten away half the site, but the broch itself, dating from around 100 BC, still stands, its walls reaching a height of 12ft in places, its inner cells still intact. The compact group of homes clustered around the broch have also survived amazingly well, with much of their original and ingenious stone shelving and fireplaces still in place. The best view of the site is from the east, where you can clearly make out the "main street" leading towards the broch. The **visitor centre** where you buy your ticket is also worth a quick once-over, especially for those with kids, who will enjoy using the quernstone corn grinder. The broch is clearly signposted from Evie, the road skirting the pristinely white **Sands of Evie**, a perfect picnic spot in fine weather.

A large section of the hills to the southwest of Evie now form the **RSPB Birsay Moors Reserve**, whose heather-coated ground provides good hunting for kestrels, merlins and hen harriers. **Lowrie's Water**, on Burgar Hill itself, meanwhile, is regularly used as a nesting site by red-throated divers; there's an RSPB hide from which you can view the loch at the top of the rough track leading to the **aerogenerators**, first built here in the 1980s in order to carry out research into wind power. The moor is also a source of more traditional fuel, and if you take the B9057 towards Dounby you can make out the areas in which peat is cut, with small stacks often drying on the hillside.

Before you reach Dounby itself, a sign points across a field to the turf-roofed **Dounby Click Mill**, the only surviving example of a horizontal watermill in Orkney. With only limited water power available, this type of mill was a simple but effective way of grinding flour for two to three families. The mechanism inside has been fully restored, and you can see the wheel underneath the building.

Practicalities

Evie has the best **accommodation** on the whole of Orkney, *Woodwick House* (Ⓣ01856/751330, Ⓦwww.orknet.co.uk/woodwick; ❸), situated in a secluded position southeast of the main village. The house itself is beautifully decorated, and has two resident lounges, both with real fires. The food is superb, the wooded grounds are delightful (and feature a seventeenth-century doocot), and there are even occasional concerts. Non-residents can eat there for around £20 a head. At the other end of the scale, you can stay in the nicely modernized **bothy and campsite**, run by Dale Farm (Ⓣ01856/751270; April–Oct) and situated in a sheltered spot right by the junction of the road to Dounby (and not to be confused with the much tattier bothy back down the road to Kirkwall). The local shop and post office are close by.

Orphir

The southern shores of the West Mainland, overlooking Scapa Flow, are much gentler than the rest of the coastline, and have fewer of Orkney's premier league sights. However, if you've time to spare, or you're heading for Hoy from the car ferry terminal at Houton, there are a couple of points of interest in the neighbouring parish of **ORPHIR**. Here, beside the parish cemetery, the council have built a new **Orkneyinga Saga Centre** (daily 9am–5pm; free), where a small exhibition and a fifteen-minute audiovisual show attempts to give you a brief rundown of the plot of the *Orkneyinga Saga*, the bloodthirsty Viking tale written around 1200 AD by an unnamed Icelandic author, which described the conquest of the Northern Isles by the Norsemen. The Earl's Bu at Orphir features in the saga as the home of Earl Thorfinn the Mighty, Earl Paul and his son, Haakon, who ordered the murder of Earl (later St) Magnus on Egilsay (see p.709). The foundations of what is presumed to have been the Earl's Bu have been uncovered just outside the cemetery gates, while inside the cemetery is a section of the round church, built by Haakon after his pilgrimage to Jerusalem.

Further east along the A954 towards Kirkwall lies the **Hobbister RSPB reserve**, a mixture of moorland, sea cliffs, salt marsh and sand flats that's great for spotting a wide variety of birdlife and, at the sandy Waulkmill Bay, a relatively warm place in which to swim.

Kirkwall

Initial impressions of **KIRKWALL**, Orkney's capital, are not always favourable. It has nothing to match the picturesque harbour of Stromness, and its residential sprawl is far less appealing. However, it does have one great redeeming feature – its sandstone **cathedral**, without doubt the finest medieval building in the north of Scotland. In any case, if you're staying any length of time in Orkney you're more or less bound to find yourself in Kirkwall at some point, as the town is home to the islands' better-stocked shops, including the only large supermarket, and is the departure point for most of the ferries to Orkney's northern isles.

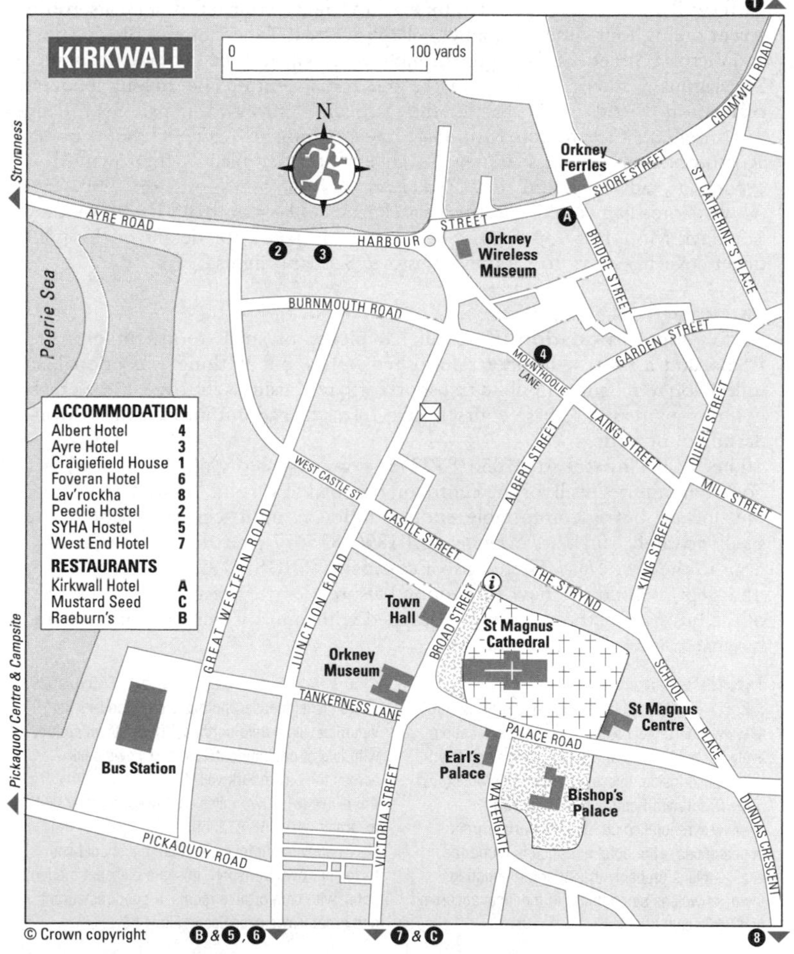

Part of the reason for Kirkwall's disappointing waterfront is that today's harbour is a largely modern invention; in the mid-nineteenth century, the shoreline ran along Junction Road, and before that it was flush with the west side of Broad Street. Nowadays, the town is very much divided into two main focal points: the busy **harbour**, at the north end of the town, where ferries come and go all year round, and where, during the summer, launches offload smartly dressed holidaymakers from the numerous cruise ships that weigh anchor in the Bay of Kirkwall; and the flagstoned **main street**, which changes its name four times as it twists its way south from the harbour past the cathedral.

Arrival, information and accommodation

Buses meet the inter-island car-ferry arrivals at Stromness and passenger-ferry arrivals at Burwick on South Ronaldsay, taking 40–45 minutes to shuttle into Kirkwall. The **bus station** is five minutes' walk west of the town centre. Kirkwall **airport** is about three miles southeast of town on the A960; it's not served by buses, but a taxi into town should only set you back about £6.

Kirkwall is an easy place in which to orientate yourself, despite its **main street** taking four different names – Bridge Street, Albert Street, Broad Street and Victoria Street – as it winds through the town, and the prominent spire of St Magnus Cathedral clearly marks the town centre. The helpful **tourist office**, on Broad Street beside the cathedral graveyard (April–Sept daily 8.30am–8pm; Oct–March Mon–Sat 9.30am–5pm; ⓣ01856/872856), books accommodation, changes money and gives out a free plan of the town. Most events are advertised in *The Orcadian*, which comes out on Thursdays (ⓦwww.orcadian.co.uk), and there's a *What's on Diary* on BBC Radio Orkney (93.7FM; Mon–Fri 7.30–8am). See the box on p.687 for details of the joint ticket covering entry to Orkney's Historic Scotland sights.

Accommodation

As for **accommodation**, Kirkwall has plenty of small rooms in ordinary B&Bs, and a host of blandly refurbished hotels, but nothing exceptional, so unless you're reliant on public transport, or have business in town, there's really no strong reason to base yourself here. Instead, head out into Orkney's wonderful countryside.

The SYHA **hostel** (ⓣ01856/872243, ⓦwww.syha.org.uk; April–Sept) is a good ten minutes' walk of the centre on the road to Orphir. It's no beauty from the outside, but is comfortable enough inside. A more central option is the small privately run *Peedie Hostel* (ⓣ01856/875477), on the waterfront next door to the *Ayre Hotel*. There's also a **campsite** (ⓣ01856/879900; mid-May to mid-Sept) behind the new Pickaquoy Leisure Centre, five minutes' walk west of the bus station; the site is well equipped with laundry facilities, but it's hardly what you'd call picturesque.

Hotels and B&Bs

Albert Hotel Mounthoolie Lane ⓣ01856/876000, ⓦwww.alberthotel.co.uk. Great central location, lively bar (with disco attached), and completely refurbished inside, this is a comfortable option. ❸

Ayre Hotel Ayre Road ⓣ01856/873001, ⓦwww.ayrehotel.co.uk. Despite harbourfront appearances – the hotel entrance is round the back – this is probably the smartest option in town, as well as being home to the local accordion and fiddle club (Wed). ❺

Craigiefield House Craigiefield ⓣ01856/872029, ⓔcraigiefieldhouse@hotmail.com. Good-looking Victorian villa a mile northeast of the town centre, with lots of original features, and views back across the bay to Kirkwall. ❹

Foveran Hotel Two miles southwest on the A964 to Orphir ⓣ01856/872389, ⓦwww.foveranhotel.co.uk. Suitable should you have your own transport, this is a pleasant modern hotel, with comfortable rooms, a good restaurant and great views over Scapa Flow. ❹

Lav'rockha Guest House Inganess Road ☎01856/876103, ⓦwww.norsecom.co.uk/lavrockha. Modern guesthouse near the Highland Park distillery southeast of the centre that's a cut above the rest. ❷

West End Hotel 14 Main St ☎01856/872368, ⓦwww.westendhotel.org.uk. Comfortable and welcoming hotel in an old, characterful building down a quiet side street, a short walk south of the town centre; currently seeking new owners. ❹

The Town and around

Standing at the very heart of Kirkwall, **St Magnus Cathedral** (Mon–Sat 8.30am–6.30pm, Sun 1.30–6.30pm) is the town's most compelling sight. This beautiful red sandstone building was begun in 1137 by the Orkney Earl Rognvald, who decided to make full use of a growing cult surrounding the figure of his uncle Magnus, killed on the orders of his cousin Haakon in 1117 (see p.709). When Magnus's body was buried in Birsay a heavenly light was said to have shone overhead, and his grave soon became a place of pilgrimage attributed with miraculous powers that drew pilgrims from far afield. When Rognvald finally took over the earldom he built the cathedral in his uncle's honour, moving the centre of religious and secular power from Birsay to Kirkwall.

The first version of the cathedral, built using yellow sandstone from Eday and red sandstone from the Mainland, was somewhat smaller than today's structure, which has been added to over the centuries, with a new east window in the thirteenth century, the extension of the nave in the fifteenth century and a new west window to mark the building's 850th anniversary in 1987. Today much of the detail in the soft sandstone has worn away – the capitals around the main doors are reduced to gnarled stumps – but it's still an immensely impressive building, its shape and style echoing the great cathedrals of Europe. Inside, the atmosphere is surprisingly intimate, the bulky sandstone columns drawing your eye up to the exposed brickwork arches, while around the walls is a series of mostly seventeenth-century tombstones, many carved with a skull and crossbones and other emblems of mortality, alongside chilling inscriptions calling on the reader to "remember death waits us all, the hour none knows". In the square pillars on either side of the high altar, the bones of Magnus and Rognvald are buried. In the southeastern corner of the cathedral lies the tomb of the Stromness-born Arctic explorer John Rae, who went off to try and find Sir John Franklin's expedition; he is depicted asleep, dressed in moleskins and furs, his rifle and Bible by his side. Beside Rae's tomb is Orkney's own poets' corner, with memorials to, among others, George Mackay Brown, Eric Linklater, Edwin Muir and Robert Rendall (who was also an eminent conchologist). Another poignant monument is the one to the dead of HMS *Royal Oak*, which was torpedoed in Scapa Flow in 1939 with the loss of 833 men (see p.696).

If you want to learn more about the life of St Magnus, pop into the new **St Magnus Centre** (Mon–Sat 8.30am–6.30pm, Sun 1.30–4.30pm; free), behind the cathedral, where you can watch a short video on his martyrdom and the history of the cathedral, and consult some of the books in the study/library.

To the south of the cathedral are the ruined remains of the **Bishop's Palace** (April–Sept daily 9.30am–6.30pm; Oct & Nov Mon–Sat 9.30am–4.30pm, Sun 2–4.30pm; £2; HS), residence of the Bishop of Orkney since the twelfth century. It was here that the Norwegian King Haakon died in 1263 on his return from defeat at the Battle of Largs. Most of what you see now, however, dates from the time of Bishop Robert Reid, the founder of Edinburgh University, in the mid-sixteenth century. The walls still stand, as does the tall round tower in which the bishop had his private chambers; a narrow spiral staircase takes you to the top for a good view of the cathedral and across Kirkwall's rooftops.

The ticket for the Bishop's Palace also covers entry to the neighbouring **Earl's Palace**, built by the infamous Earl Patrick Stewart around 1600 using forced labour, rather better preserved, and a lot more fun to explore. With its grand entrance, fancy oriel windows, dank dungeons, massive fireplaces and magnificent central hall, it has a confident solidity, and is reckoned to be one of the finest examples of Renaissance architecture in Scotland. The roof may be missing, but many domestic details remain, including a set of toilets and the stone shelves used by the clerk to do his filing. Earl Patrick enjoyed his palace for only a very short time before he was imprisoned. The earl ordered his son, Robert, to organize an insurrection; he held out for four days in the palace against the Earl of Caithness, but eventually shared the same fate as his father (see p.736).

Opposite the cathedral stands the sixteenth-century Tankerness House, a former home for the clergy. It has been renovated countless times over the years, most recently in the 1960s in order to provide a home for the **Orkney Museum** (Mon–Sat 10.30am–5pm; May–Sept also Sun 2–5pm; free). Among the more unusual artefacts to look out for are a witch's spell box, and a lovely whalebone plaque from a Viking boat grave discovered on Sanday. There's also a collection of balls used in a traditional Orkney street game, **The Ba'**, played at Christmas and New Year, which begins at the Mercat Cross outside the cathedral. In addition, there are a couple of rooms which have been restored as they would have been in 1820, when the building was a private home for the Baikie family. On a warm summer afternoon, the **gardens** (which can be entered either from the house itself or from a gate on Tankerness Lane) are thick with the buzz of bees and vibrantly coloured flora.

At the harbour end of Junction Road, at Kiln Corner, you can browse around the tiny **Orkney Wireless Museum** (April–Sept Mon–Sat 10am–4.30pm, Sun 2–4.30pm; £2), a single room packed to the roof with every variety of antique radio equipment you can imagine. The museum is particularly strong on technical flotsam from the two world wars, and there's even a working crystal set which you can listen to.

Out of the centre

Further afield, a mile or so south of the town centre on the A961 to South Ronaldsay, is the **Highland Park distillery** (April–Oct Mon–Fri 10am–5pm; July–Sept also Sat noon–5pm, Sun noon–4pm; Nov–March Mon–Fri tours at 2pm; ⓣ01856/874619, ⓦwww.highlandpark.co.uk; £3), billed as "the most northerly legal distillery in Scotland". It's been in operation for more than two hundred years, and still has its own maltings, although it was closed during World War II when the army used it as a food store and the huge vats served as communal baths. You can decide for yourself whether the taste still lingers by partaking of the customary dram after one of the regular guided tours of the beautiful old buildings.

If the weather happens to be unusually good and you're moved to consider taking the plunge for a dip, do as the locals do and head one mile south of town on the B9148 to **Scapa Bay**, Kirkwall's very own sandy beach. Briefly a naval headquarters at the outbreak of World War I, Scapa's pier is now used by the council tugs and pilot launches servicing the oil tankers out in Scapa Flow. Visible from the beach is the green Admiralty wreck buoy marking the position of HMS *Royal Oak*, which was torpedoed by a German U-boat on October 14, 1939, with the loss of 833 men (out of a total crew of around 1400). A small display shed at the eastern end of the bay tells the full story, and has photos of the wreck (still an official war grave) as it looks today.

If you've time to kill and the weather's not so good, you could search out one of Kirkwall's more unusual sights, the **Grain Earth House**, a food cellar dating back to the first millennium BC, now hidden in the industrial estate northwest of the town centre. Collect the key (and a torch) from Ortak jewellers, at the entrance to the estate, and head round the corner. Steep steps lead down to a long, dark, curving passageway which ends at a stone-clad cellar held up by large stone pillars; now you know what it felt like to be an Iron Age bere bannock.

Eating, drinking and entertainment

Given the quality of Orkney beef, and the quantity of shellfish caught in the vicinity, Kirkwall's **food** options are pretty disappointing. *Trenabies* and the *Pomona Café*, both on Albert Street, are venerable institutions, but the nicest **café** for lunch is the *Mustard Seed*, 86 Victoria St (closed Wed & Sun), which serves home-made soups and imaginative, inexpensive main courses; it also doubles as a Christian bookshop. In the evening, there's nothing for it but to head for one of the town's hotels: the *Kirkwall*, on Harbour Street, is probably the best option, as it offers both **bar meals** and reasonable à la carte, though the bar meals at the *Albert* are okay, too. The best **fish and chips** is from *Raeburn's* at the corner of Union Street and Junction Road.

The **nightlife** scene in Kirkwall is a lot more animated. The liveliest **pub** is the *Torvhaug Inn* at the harbour end of Bridge Street; another good place to try is the *Bothy Bar* in the *Albert Hotel*, which sometimes has live music and is attached to *Matchmakers* **disco** (Thurs–Sat). The *Ayre Hotel* has regular Orkney Accordion & Fiddle Club nights on Wednesdays, and there's sometimes live music at the *Quoyburray Inn*, a couple of miles beyond the airport on the A960, and at other hotels in Kirkwall. Check the *Orcadian* entertainment listings for the latest (Ⓦwww.orcadian.co.uk).

Kirkwall's new **Pickaquoy Leisure Centre** (Ⓦwww.pickaquoy.com) – known locally as the "Picky" – is a short walk west of the town centre, up Pickaquoy Road past Safeway supermarket. It now serves as one of the town's main large-scale venues, and also contains the New Phoenix **cinema** (Ⓣ01856/879900). There's a swimming pool on the other side of town on Thomas Street.

Listings

Airport Ⓣ01856/872421.

Banks The main street has branches of the big Scottish banks, all with ATMs.

Bike rental Bobby's Cycle Hire, Tankerness Lane (Ⓣ01856/875777).

Bookshops Leonard's at the corner of Bridge Street and Albert Street, and The Orcadian Bookshop, 50 Albert Street (Ⓦwww.orcadian.co.uk), are the best stocked.

Camping gear and outdoor sports Eric Kemp, 31–33 Bridge St (Ⓣ01856/872137).

Car rental Peace's Car Hire, Junction Road (Ⓣ01856/872866, Ⓦwww.orkneycarhire.co.uk); Scarth Car Hire, Great Western Road (Ⓣ01856/872125); W.R. Tullock, Castle Street and Kirkwall Airport (Ⓣ01856/876262).

Consulates Denmark and Germany, J. Robertson, Shore Street (Ⓣ01856/872961); Norway, J. Jolly, 21 Bridge St (Ⓣ01856/872268).

Exchange In addition to the banks, the tourist office in Broad Street runs an exchange service (summer daily 8.30am–8pm).

Ferries Orkney Ferries, Shore Street (Mon–Fri 7am–5pm, Sat 7am–noon & 1–3pm; Ⓣ01856/872044, Ⓦwww.orkneyferries.co.uk); P&O Passenger Terminal, Kirkwall Pier (Mon–Fri 9am–1pm & 2–5pm; Ⓣ01856/873330, Ⓦwww.posf.co.uk).

Internet access Orkney College, East Rd (Mon–Thurs 4–9pm; Ⓣ01856/872839).

Laundry Launderama, 47 Albert Street (Mon–Fri 8.30am–5.30pm, Sat 9am–5.30pm).

Medical care Balfour Hospital, Kirkwall Health Centre and Dental Clinic, New Scapa Road (☎01856/885400).

Post office Junction Road (Mon–Fri 9am–5pm, Sat 9.30am–12.30pm).

East Mainland and South Ronaldsay

Southeast from Kirkwall, the narrow spur of the **East Mainland** juts out into the North Sea and is joined, thanks to the remarkable Churchill Barriers, to several smaller islands, the largest of which are **Burray** and **South Ronaldsay**. As with the West Mainland, the land here is relatively densely populated and heavily farmed, but there are none of Orkney's most famous sights. Nevertheless, there are several interesting fishing villages, some good coastal walks to enjoy, an unusual new Iron Age site to explore at **Mine Howe** and, at the **Tomb of the Eagles**, one of the most enjoyable and memorable of Orkney's prehistoric sites.

East Mainland

The northern side of the **East Mainland** consists of three exposed peninsulas that jut out like giant claws. The most intriguing peninsula is the easternmost one of Deerness (see below), but before you reach it, you should pay a quick visit to the recently excavated Iron Age mound of **Mine Howe** (June–Aug daily 11am–5pm; May Wed & Sun 11am–3pm; Sept Wed & Sun 11am–2pm; £2), just off the A960 in the Tankerness peninsula, beyond the airport. Originally Mine Howe would have been a large mound surrounded by a deep ditch, but only a small section has been excavated. At the top of the mound a series of steps leads steeply down to a half-landing, and then plunges down even deeper to a small chamber some twenty feet below the surface. Visitors don a hard hat and grab a torch, before heading underground. The whole layout is totally unique and has left archeologists totally baffled, though, naturally, numerous theories as to its purpose abound, from execution by ritual drowning to a temple to the god of the underground. Likewise, Mine Howe's relationship to the nearby mound and broch of Longhowe has still to be unravelled.

The easternmost peninsula of **Deerness** is joined to the Mainland only by a narrow, sandy isthmus. The northeastern corner around the sea cliffs of **Mull Head** boasts a large colony of nesting seabirds from May to August, including fulmars, kittiwakes, guillemots, razorbills and puffins, plus, inland, arctic terns that swoop and screech threateningly. The only way to reach Mull Head is to walk from the car park, located a mile or so to the south. On a short walk east of the car park you can also view **The Gloup**, an impressive collapsed sea cave, the name of which stems from the Old Norse *gluppa*, or "chasm"; the tide still flows in and out through a natural arch, making strange gurgling noises. Half a mile north of the Gloup is the **Brough of Deerness**, a grassy promontory whose narrow land bridge has collapsed, and which is now accessible only via a precipitous path; the ruins are thought to have once been a Norse or Pictish monastic site.

Visible across the sea to the north are Auskerry and Stronsay and, to the southeast, the uninhabited island of **Copinsay**, with its lighthouse, perched on yet more seabird-infested cliffs. Copinsay is now an **RSPB reserve**, with huge seabird colonies nesting on its cliffs in season; to find out about access, make enquiries with the tourist board or the RSPB ☎01856/850176.

Scapa Flow

Apart from a few oil tankers, there's generally very little activity in the great natural harbour of **Scapa Flow**. Yet for the first half of the twentieth century, the Flow served as the main base of the Royal Navy, with over a hundred warships anchored here at any one time. The coastal defences required to make Scapa Flow safe to use as the country's chief naval headquarters were considerable and many are still visible all over Orkney, ranging from half-sunk blockships to the Churchill Barriers (see p.700) and the gun batteries that pepper the coastline. Unfortunately, these defences weren't sufficient to save **HMS Royal Oak** from being torpedoed by a German U-boat in October 1939 (see p.696), but they withstood several heavy German air raids during the course of 1940. Ironically, the worst disaster the Flow has ever witnessed was self-inflicted, when **HMS Vanguard** sank on July 9, 1917, after suffering an internal explosion, taking over a thousand of her crew with her.

Scapa Flow's most celebrated moment in naval history, however, was when the entire **German High Seas Fleet** was interned here immediately after the end of World War I. A total of 74 ships, manned by several thousand German sailors, was anchored off the island of Cava awaiting the outcome of the Versailles Peace Conference. At around noon on Midsummer's Day, 1919, believing either that the majority of the German fleet was to be handed over, or that hostilities were about to resume, the commanding officer, Admiral von Reuter, ordered the fleet to be scuttled. By 5pm, every ship was beached or had sunk and nine German sailors had lost their lives, shot by outraged British servicemen. The British government was publicly indignant, but privately relieved since the scuttling avoided the diplomatic nightmare of dividing up the fleet between the Allies.

Between the wars, the largest **salvage operation** in history took place in Scapa Flow, with the firm of Cox & Danks alone raising twenty-six destroyers, one light cruiser, four battlecruisers and two battleships. Despite this, seven large German ships – three battleships and four light cruisers – remain on the sea bed of Scapa Flow, along with four destroyers and a U-boat. Although the remaining vessels can only be salvaged on a piecemeal basis, their pre-atomic era steel is still extremely valuable as it is radiation-free and is in great demand in the space and nuclear industries. Scapa Flow is also considered one of the world's greatest dive sites. Scapa Scuba (Ⓣ01856/851218, Ⓦwww.scapascuba.co.uk), based in Stromness, offers one-to-one **scuba diving** tuition for beginners, lasting three hours, diving on one of the blockships sunk by the Churchill Barriers; they also offer wreck diving for those with more experience. If you don't want to get your feet wet, Roving Eye Enterprises (Ⓣ01856/811360, Ⓦwww.orknet.co.uk/rov) runs a boat fitted with an underwater camera, which does the diving for you, while you sit back and watch the video screen; their trip leaves from Houton Pier at 1.20pm, takes three hours, and includes a visit to the Scapa Flow Visitor Centre in Lyness (see p.705).

On the south coast, just before you hit the Churchill Barriers, stands **ST MARY'S**, an old fishing village whose livelihood was destroyed by the building of the causeways. Just east of St Mary's, you'll find the **Norwood Antiques** (June–Sept Tues–Thurs & Sun 2–5pm & 6–8pm; also by arrangement Ⓣ01856/781217; £3), a display of antiques collected by local stonemason Norrie Wood from the age of 13. Only about half of the collection is on display, but it's a fascinating and eccentric selection of bits and pieces from around the world, including pottery, painting, medals, furniture, cutlery, clocks, even a narwhal's tusk, all housed in a grand Orkney home.

The Churchill Barriers

To the south of St Mary's is the first of four causeways known as the **Churchill Barriers**, since they were given the go-ahead by Churchill when he was First Lord of the Admiralty. They were built during World War II as antisubmarine barriers, which would seal the waters between the Mainland and the string of islands to the south, and thus protect the Royal Navy, based in Scapa Flow at the time, from German U-boat attack. However, the Admiralty was only prompted into action by the sinking of the battleship HMS *Royal Oak* on October 14, 1939 (see p.696). Despite the presence of blockships, deliberately sunk during World War I in order to close off the eastern approaches, one German U-boat captain managed to get through and torpedo the *Royal Oak*, before returning to a hero's welcome in Germany. He claimed to have acquired local knowledge while fishing in the islands before the war. As you cross the barriers, you can still see the blockships, rusting away, an eerie reminder of Orkney's important wartime role.

The barriers – an astonishing feat of engineering when you bear in mind the strength of Orkney tides – were an incredibly expensive undertaking, costing an estimated £2.5 million at the time. Special camps were built on the uninhabited island of Lamb Holm, in order to accommodate the 1700 men involved in the project, 1200 of whom were Italian POWs. The camps have long since disappeared, but the Italians left behind the extraordinary **Italian Chapel** (daily: April–Sept 9am–10pm; Oct–March 9am–4.30pm; free) on Lamb Holm. This, the so-called "miracle of Camp 60", must be one of the greatest adaptations ever, made from two Nissen huts, concrete, barbed wire and parts of a rusting blockship. It has a great false facade, and colourful trompe l'oeil decor, lovingly restored by the chapel's principal architect, Domenico Chiocchetti, who returned in 1960. Mass is still said regularly.

Burray

If you're travelling with children, you may like to stop off on the island of **Burray** in order to visit the **Orkney Fossil and Vintage Centre** (daily: April–Sept 10am–6pm; Oct 10.30am–6pm; £2), housed in a converted farm on the main road across the island. Most of the fossils on display downstairs have been found locally, so they tend to be of fish and sea creatures, since Orkney was at the bottom of a tropical sea in Devonian times. The UV room, where the rocks reveal their iridescent colours, is a particular favourite with kids. Upstairs, there's a lot of wartime memorabilia, books to read, a rocking horse to play on and a comfy chair and binoculars with which to spot the birdlife down by the shore. There's also a tearoom attached to the museum.

BURRAY VILLAGE, on the south coast of the island, expanded in the nineteenth century during the boom years of the herring industry, but was badly affected by the sinking of the blockships during World War I. The two-storey warehouse, built in 1860 in order to cure and pack the herring, has recently been converted into the *Sands Motel*, where you can get a **drink** and a bite to **eat**. The best place to stay, though, is out at *Vestlaybanks* (Ⓣ01856/731305, Ⓦwww.vestlaybanks.co.uk; ❷), a very comfortable **B&B** along the road to Littlequoy, which boasts great views over Scapa Flow.

South Ronaldsay

At the southern end of the series of four barriers is low-lying **South Ronaldsay**, the largest of the islands linked to the Mainland and, like the latter, rich farming country. It was traditionally the chief crossing-point to the Scottish mainland, as it's only six miles across the Pentland Firth from Caithness. Nowadays, the car ferries arrive at Stromness, but there is still a small passenger ferry between John O'Groats and Burwick, on the southernmost tip of the island (see p.683 for details).

St Margaret's Hope

The main settlement on South Ronaldsay is **ST MARGARET'S HOPE**, which local tradition says takes its name from Margaret, the Maid of Norway, who is thought to have died here in November 1290 while on her way to marry the English prince Edward (later Edward II). Margaret had already been proclaimed Queen of Scotland, and the marriage was intended to unify the two countries. Today, St Margaret's Hope – or "The Hope", as it's known locally – is a pleasing little gathering of stone-built houses overlooking a sheltered bay, and is by far the best base from which to explore the area. As is obvious from the architecture, and the piers, The Hope was once a thriving port, and locals are backing the new car-ferry link with Caithness, which began in 2001. Until or unless this begins to make serious inroads into Scrabster–Stromness traffic, however, The Hope remains a very peaceful place.

The village smithy on Cromarty Square has been turned into a **Smiddy Museum** (June–Aug Mon–Fri 1.30–4pm, Sat & Sun noon–4pm; May & Sept Mon–Fri 1.30–3.30pm, Sat & Sun 2–4pm; Oct Sun 2–4pm; free), which is particularly fun for kids, who enjoy getting hands-on with the old tools, drills and giant bellows. There's also a small exhibition on the annual **Boys' Ploughing Match**, in which local boys compete with miniature hand-held ploughs. The competition, which is taken extremely seriously by all those involved, happens on the third Saturday in August, at the beautiful golden beach at the **Sands O'Right** in Hoxa, a couple of miles west of The Hope.

St Margaret's Hope has some good **accommodation** options. First choice are the rooms above *The Creel* on the harbourfront (ⓣ01856/831311, ⓦwww.thecreel.co.uk; ❹), one of the best **restaurants** in Scotland and winner of all sorts of awards for its superb food featuring local produce. At £25 for two courses, it's expensive, but also friendly and relaxed, and the rooms are comfortable. More modest bar meals are available from the popular *Galley Inn*, also on the seafront, and the *Murray Arms Hotel* (ⓣ01856/831205, ⓦwww.murrayarmshotel.com; ❷), on Back Road, which has rooms above the pub and a backpackers dorm round the side. The best B&B option is *Bellevue Guest House* (ⓣ01856/831294; ❷), a stone-built Victorian house on a hill just west of the village. For a **hostel** with more character, head for *Wheems Bothy* (ⓣ01856/831537; April–Oct), a mile and a half from the war memorial on the main road outside The Hope. Mattresses and ingredients for a wholesome breakfast are provided, and organic produce from the croft is on sale.

The Tomb of the Eagles

One of the most enjoyable archeological sights on Orkney is the ancient chambered burial cairn at the southeastern corner of South Ronaldsay, known as the **Tomb of the Eagles** (daily: April–Oct 10am–8pm; Nov–March 10am–noon; £3). Discovered, excavated and still owned by a local farmer, Ronald Simpson of Liddle, a visit here makes a refreshing change from the usual interpretative centre. First off, you get to look round the family's private museum of prehistoric artefacts; this is the original hands-on museum, so visitors can actually touch and admire the painstaking craftsmanship of Neolithic folk, and examine a skull. Next you get a brief guided tour of a nearby Bronze

Age **burnt mound**, which is basically a Neolithic rubbish dump, beside which there was a large trough, where joints of meat were boiled by throwing in rocks from the fire. Finally you get to walk out to the **chambered cairn**, by the cliff's edge, where human remains were found alongside talons and carcasses of sea eagles. To enter the cairn, you must lie on a trolley and pull yourself in using an overhead rope – something that's guaranteed to put a smile on every visitor's face. The cairn's clifftop location is spectacular, and walking along the coast in either direction is rewarding: south to the sea inlet of Ham Geo, or north to Halcro Head, and beyond to Wind Wick Bay, where seals and their pups can be seen in the autumn.

Hoy

Hoy, Orkney's second-largest island, rises sharply out of the sea to the southwest of the Mainland. The least typical of the islands, but certainly the most dramatic, its north and west sides are made up of great glacial valleys and mountainous moorland rising to over 1500ft, dropping into the sea off the red sandstone cliffs of St John's Head and, to the south, forming the landmark sea stack known as the **Old Man of Hoy**. The northern half of Hoy, though a huge expanse, is virtually uninhabited, with just the cluster of houses at **Rackwick** nestling dramatically in a bay between the cliffs. Meanwhile, most of Hoy's four hundred or so residents live on the gentler, more fertile land in the southeast, in and around the villages of **Lyness** and **Longhope**. This part of the island is littered with buildings dating from the two world wars, when Scapa Flow served as the main base for the Royal Navy.

Two **ferry services** run to Hoy: a passenger ferry from Stromness to the village of Hoy (2–5 daily; takes 25min; ⓣ01856/850624), which also serves the small island of Graemsay; and the roll-on/roll-off car ferry from Houton on the Mainland to Lyness (Mon–Fri 6 daily, Sat & Sun 2–3 daily; takes 30min–1hr; ⓣ01856/811397), which sometimes calls in at the oil terminal island of Flotta, and begins and ends its daily schedule at Longhope. There's no bus service on Hoy, but those arriving on the passenger ferry from Stromness should find a **minibus** waiting to take them to Rackwick.

North Hoy

Much of Hoy's magnificent landscape is embraced by the **North Hoy RSPB Reserve** (which covers most of the northwest end of the island), in which the rough grasses and heather harbour a cluster of arctic plants and a healthy population of mountain hares, as well as numerous great skuas, plus a few merlins, kestrels and peregrine falcons, while the more sheltered valleys are nesting sites for snipe and arctic skua. Walkers arriving by passenger ferry from Stromness at Moaness Pier, near the tiny village of **HOY**, and heading for Rackwick (four miles southwest), can either catch the minibus or take the well-marked footpath that passes Sandy Loch, and along the large open valley beyond. On the western side of this valley is the narrow gully of **Berriedale**, which supports Britain's most northerly native woodland, a huddle of birch, hazel and honeysuckle.

The minibus route to Rackwick is via the single-track road along another valley to the south. En route, duckboards head across the heather to the **Dwarfie Stane**, Orkney's most unusual chambered tomb, cut from a solid block of sandstone and dating back to 3000 BC. The sheer effort that must

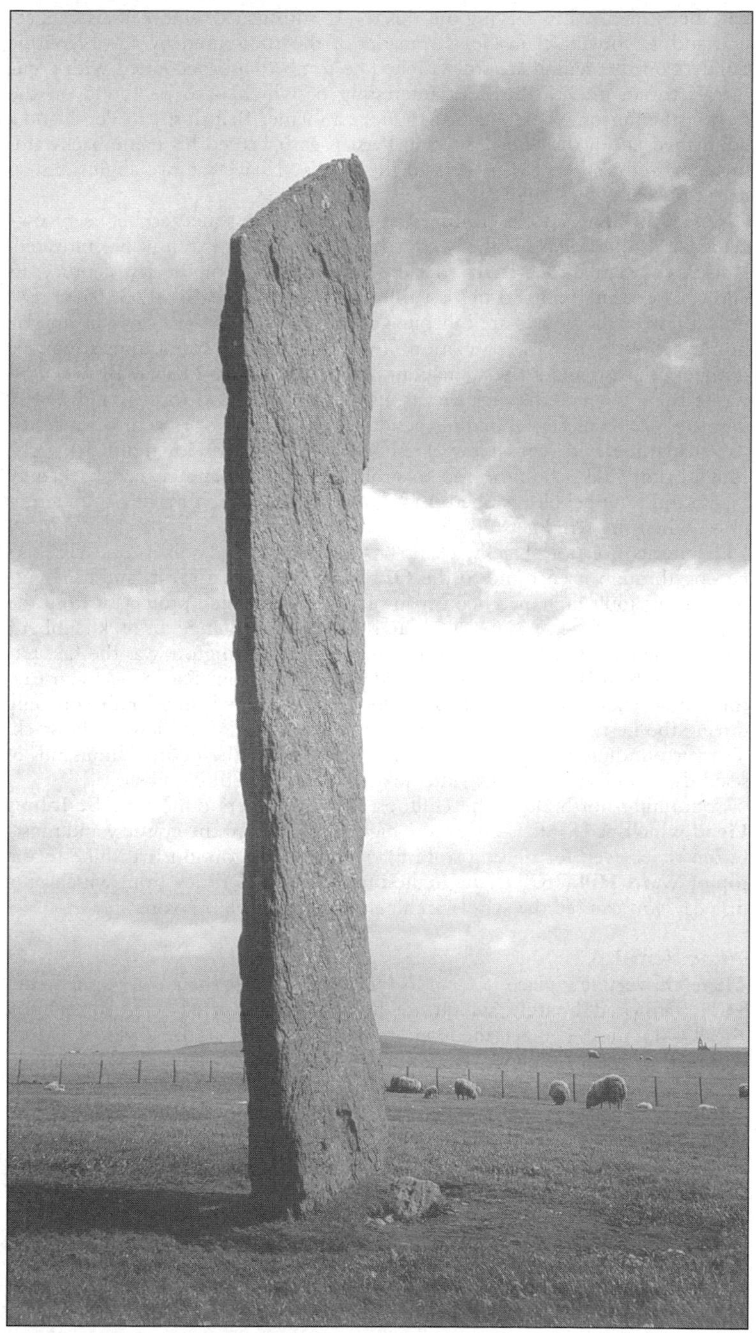

△ Stones of Stenness, Orkney

have been involved in carving out this tomb, with its two side-cells, is staggering, and as you crawl inside, the marks of the tools used by the Neolithic builders on the ceiling are still visible. The tomb is also decorated with copious Victorian graffiti, the most interesting of which is to be found on the northern exterior, where Major Mouncey, a former British spy in Persia and a confirmed eccentric who dressed in Persian garb, carved his name backwards in Latin, and also carved in Persian the words "I have sat two nights and so learnt patience."

RACKWICK is an old crofting and fishing village squeezed between towering sandstone cliffs on the west coast. Once quite extensively cultivated, Rackwick went into a steady decline in the middle of the last century: its school closed in 1953 and the last fishing boat put to sea in 1963. These days only a few of the houses are inhabited all year round (the rest serve as holiday homes), though the savage isolation of the place has provided inspiration to a number of artists and writers, including Orkney's George Mackay Brown, who wrote that "when Rackwick weeps, its grief is long and forlorn and utterly desolate". A small farm building beside the hostel serves as a tiny **museum** (open anytime; free), with a few old photos and a brief rundown of Rackwick's rough history. Take the time, too, to stroll down to the sandy beach, backed by giant sandstone pebbles washed smooth by the sea, which make a thunderous noise when the wind gets up.

Despite its isolation, Rackwick has a steady stream of walkers and climbers passing through it en route to the **Old Man of Hoy**, a great sandstone column some 450ft high, perched on an old lava flow which protects it from the erosive power of the sea. The Old Man is a popular challenge for rock climbers, and a 1966 ascent, led by the mountaineer Chris Bonington, was the first televised climb in Britain. The well-trodden footpath from Rackwick is an easy three-mile walk (3hr round trip) – the great skuas will divebomb you only during the nesting season – and gives the reward of a great view of the stack. The surrounding cliffs provide ideal rocky ledges for the nests of thousands of seabirds, including guillemots, kittiwakes, razorbills, puffins and shags.

Continuing north along the clifftops, the path peters out before **St John's Head** which, at 1136ft, is one of the highest sea cliffs in the country and mostly too sheer even for nesting seabirds. Another, safer, option is to hike to the top of **Ward Hill** (1577ft), the highest mountain in Orkney, from which on a fine day you can see the whole archipelago laid out before you.

Practicalities

There are very few places to stay in North Hoy other than two council-run, SYHA-affiliated **hostels**, which are housed in converted schools; to book ahead, you must contact the education department at the Orkney Islands Council (ⓣ01856/873535). The *North Hoy Hostel* (May to mid-Sept) in Hoy village is the larger of the two, but the *Rackwick Hostel* (mid-March to mid-Sept), with just eight beds, enjoys a better location. You can **camp** in Rackwick, either behind the hostel, down by the unusually attractive public toilets, or beside *Burnside Cottage* (ⓣ01856/791316), the heather-thatched **bothy** in a beautiful setting right by the beach, which has no mattresses or kitchen facilities. **Bike rental** is available from Moaness Pier (ⓣ01856/791225). However, there's no shop in Rackwick, so take all your supplies with you; the post office shop in Hoy only sells chocolate, but the *Hoy Inn* (closed Mon), near the post office, serves very good **bar meals**. Be warned, too, that North Hoy is probably the worst place on Orkney for midges.

Lyness and Longhope

Along the sheltered eastern shore of Hoy, high moorland gives way to a gentler environment similar to that on the rest of Orkney. Hoy defines the western boundary of Scapa Flow, and **LYNESS** played a major role for the Royal Navy during both world wars. Many of the old wartime buildings have been cleared away over the last few decades, but the harbour and hills around Lyness are still scarred with the scattered remains of concrete structures which once served as hangars and storehouses during World War II, and are now used as barns and cowsheds. Among these are the remains of what was – incredibly – the largest cinema in Europe, but perhaps the most unusual remaining building is the monochrome Art Deco facade of the old **Garrison Theatre**, on the main road south of Lyness. Formerly the grandiose facade and foyer of a huge Nissen hut which disappeared long ago, it's now a private home. Lyness also has a large **naval cemetery**, where many of the victims of the various disasters that have occurred in the Flow, such as the sinking of the *Royal Oak* (see p.696) now lie, alongside a handful of German graves.

The old oil pumphouse, which still stands opposite the new Lyness ferry terminal, has been turned into the **Scapa Flow Visitor Centre & Museum** (Mon–Fri 9am–4.30pm; mid-May to Oct also Sat & Sun 10.30am–3.30pm; free), a fascinating insight into wartime Orkney. As well as the usual old photos, torpedoes, flags, guns and propellers, there's a paratrooper's folding bicycle, and a whole section devoted to the scuttling of the German High Seas Fleet and the sinking of the *Royal Oak*. The pump house itself retains much of its old equipment – you can even ask for a working demo of one of the oil-fired boilers – used to pump oil off tankers moored at Lyness into sixteen tanks, and from there into underground reservoirs cut into the neighbouring hillside. Every hour (on the half-hour), an audiovisual show on the history of Scapa Flow is screened in the sole surviving tank, which has incredible acoustics.

Melsetter House

The finest architecture on Hoy is to be found at **Melsetter House** (Thurs, Sat & Sun by appointment; ⓣ01856/791352), four miles southwest of Lyness, overlooking the deep inlet of North Bay. Originally built in 1738, it was bought by Thomas Middlemore, heir to a Birmingham leather tycoon, who commissioned the Arts and Crafts architect William Lethaby to transform the house in 1898. The charming owners will happily take you round a handful of the thoroughly lived-in rooms in the house itself, all of which are simply decorated with white wood panelling, floral plasterwork and William Morris-style fabrics, and leave you to wander freely around the house's very beautiful grounds. Don't miss the little **Chapel of St Margaret and St Colm** that Lethaby fashioned from the Melsetter's outhouses, which features some characteristic symbolic touches, and four tiny, stained-glass windows by, among others, Ford Madox Brown and Burne-Jones. The walk back along the cliffs of the west coast to Rackwick is spectacular and takes about six hours.

Longhope and around

To the east of Melsetter House, a narrow spit of sand connects the rest of Hoy with **South Walls**, a fertile peninsula which is more densely populated with farms and homes. On the north side of South Walls is the main settlement of **LONGHOPE** (ⓦwww.longhope.co.uk), an important safe anchorage during the Napoleonic wars and World War I, but since then overshadowed by Lyness and Flotta. Longhope remains a lifeboat station, and the **Longhope Lifeboat** capsized in strong gale force winds in 1969 on its way to the aid of a Liberian freighter. The entire eight-man crew was killed, leaving seven widows and ten fatherless children; the crew of the freighter, by contrast, survived. There's a moving memorial to the men – six of whom came from just two families – in **Kirkhope Churchyard** on the road to Cantick Head Lighthouse.

Evidence of Longhope's strategic importance during the Napoleonic wars lies to the east of the village at the Point of Hackness, where the **Hackness Martello Tower** stands guard over the entrance to the bay, with a matching tower on the opposite promontory of Crockness. Built in 1815, these two circular sandstone Martello Towers are the northernmost in Britain, and were built to protect merchant ships waiting for a Royal Navy escort from American and French privateers. You can visit Hackness Tower (if it's locked, a sign will tell you where to pick up the key) via a steep ladder connected to the upper floor, where nine men and one officer shared the circular room. Originally a portable ladder would have been used and retracted, making the place pretty much impregnable: the walls are up to 9ft high on the seaward side, and the tower even had its own water supply. Overlooking the bay at the nearby **Hackness Battery**, positioned closer to the shore, yet more cannon were trained on the horizon.

Practicalities

Hoy has a handful of very good, friendly **B&Bs**, including *Stonequoy Farm* (Ⓣ01856/791234, Ⓦwww.visithoy.com; ❶), a lovely 200-acre stone-built farm south of Lyness, overlooking Longhope; and the *Old Custom House* (Ⓣ01856/701358, Ⓦwww.longhope.co.uk; ❶), a historic building situated on the other side of the bay in Longhope, distinguished by the miniature lions that sit atop the columns flanking its doorway. **Self-catering** options include the lighthouse keepers' cottages at Cantick Head (4–6 people; £210 per week; Ⓣ01856/701255). For **food**, there's little choice other than B&Bs, which will often provide an ample and sometimes delicious evening meal. Or the *Scapa Flow Visitor Centre* café which serves tea, coffee and snacks. There are two shops: one round the back of the former *Hoy Hotel in Lyness*, and one by the pier in Longhope. **Car rental** is available from Halyel Car Hire in Lyness (Ⓣ01856/791240), while the couple at *Stonequoy Farm* can organize a day-long minibus tour of Hoy, including lunch at their farm (Ⓦwww.visithoy.com; from £45 per person).

Shapinsay

Just a few miles northeast of Kirkwall, **Shapinsay** is the most accessible of Orkney's northern isles. A gently undulating grid-plan patchwork of rich farmland, it's a bit like an island suburb of Kirkwall, which is clearly visible across the bay. Its chief attraction for visitors is **Balfour Castle** (May–Sept Wed & Sun guided tours 3pm; see below for details of the all-inclusive ticket), the imposing Baronial pile designed by David Bryce and completed in 1848 by the Balfour family of Westray, who had made a small fortune in India the previous century. The Balfours died out in 1960 and the castle was bought by a Polish cavalry officer, Captain Tadeusz Zawadski, whose family now run the place as a hotel. The guided tours are great fun, and go down very well with children too, as they finish off with complimentary tea and home-made cakes in the servants' quarters. Before you enter the castle, you get to walk through the wooded grounds and view the vast kitchen gardens, which are surrounded by 15ft-high walls, and once had coal-fired greenhouses to produce fruit and vegetables out of season. The interior of the castle is not that magnificent, though it has an attractively lived-in ambience and is pretty grand for Orkney; decorative otters crop up all over the place, as they feature prominently in the Balfour family crest.

The Balfours also reformed the island's agricultural system and built **BALFOUR** village, a neat and disciplined cottage development, to house their estate workers. The family's grandiose efforts in estate management have left some appealingly eccentric relics. Melodramatic fortifications around the harbour include the huge and ornate **Gatehouse**, which now serves as the local pub. There's also a stone-built coal-fired **Gasometer**, which once supplied castle and harbour with electricity and, southwest of the pier, the castellated **Dishan Tower**, a seventeenth-century doocot that was converted into a cold, saltwater shower in Victorian times. The old village **Smithy** on the main street (daily noon–4.30pm, Wed & Sun until 5.30pm; free) now serves as a museum of local history, with a tearoom upstairs.

Most folk visit Shapinsay on a day-trip, but if you're staying here for a few days you'd do well to explore one or two points of interest beyond the castle and village. One mile north of Balfour village is the small **Mill Dam RSPB reserve**, with a hide to the west, from which you can look down on the wigeon, teal, shovelers and (if you're really lucky) pintail, all of which breed on the wetlands. The east coast from the Bay of Linton to the Foot of Shapinsay has the most interesting cliffs and sea caves and is backed by the only open moorland on the island. On the far northeastern peninsula is Shapinsay's best-preserved ancient monument, the **Broch of Burroughston**, a well-preserved strongly fortified Iron Age broch with the remains of living quarters within, a bar hole to make fast the door, and a guard-cell. This bit of the coast is also a good spot for watching **seals** sunning themselves on the nearby rocks. The finest stretch of sandy beach is at the sweeping curve of **Sandgarth Bay** in the southeast.

Practicalities

Less than thirty minutes from Kirkwall by **ferry**, Shapinsay is an easy day-trip. If you want to visit the castle, before you set out you must buy an **all-inclusive ticket** from Kirkwall tourist office (£16), which includes a return ferry ticket and castle admission. The ferry for the guided tour leaves at 2.15pm (Wed & Sun only), but you can catch an earlier ferry if you want to have some time to explore the rest of the island. It's also possible **to stay** in opulent style at the *Balfour Castle Hotel* (Ⓣ01856/711282, Ⓦwww.balfourcastle.co.uk; ❺); the rooms are vast and beautifully furnished, and you also get use of the library and the other public rooms. More modest **B&B** is available at *Girnigoe* (Ⓣ01856/711256, Ⓔjean@girnigoe.p9.co.uk; ❷), a very comfortable Orcadian croft close to the north shore of Veantro Bay that offers optional full board. The only non-hotel **eating** option is the café in the old smithy (May–Sept), which serves teas and sandwiches.

Rousay, Egilsay and Wyre

Just over half a mile from the Mainland's northern shore, the hilly island of **Rousay** is home to a number of intriguing prehistoric sites, as well as being one of the more accessible northern isles. The group of a dozen or so houses above the ferry terminal is the only settlement of any size, but a single road runs around the edge of the island, connecting a string of small farms which make use of the more cultivable coastal fringes. Many visitors come on a day-trip, as it's easy enough to reach the main points of archeological interest on the south coast by foot from the ferry terminal.

Rousay's diminutive neighbours, **Egilsay** and **Wyre**, contain a few medieval attractions of their own, which can either be visited on a day-trip from Rousay itself, or from the mainland.

Trumland House to the Knowe of Yarso

Despite its long history of settlement, Rousay is today home to little more than 200 people (many of them incomers), as this was one of the few parts of Orkney to suffer Highland-style clearances, initially by George William Traill at Quandale in the northwest. His successor, Lieutenant General Traill-Burroughs, built the derelict **Trumland House**, a forbidding Jacobean-style pile designed by David Bryce in 1873, hidden in the trees half a mile north-west of the ferry terminal. Continuing to substitute sheep for people, he built a wall to force crofters onto a narrow coastal strip and eventually provoked so much distress and anger that a gunboat had to be sent to restore order. You can learn a little more about the history and wildlife of the island from the well-laid-out display room of the **Trumland Visitors Centre**, housed in the back of the ferry waiting room.

The first trio of archeological sights is spread out over the next couple of miles, on and off the road that leads west from the ferry terminal. **Taversoe Tuick**, the nearest chambered cairn, lies just beyond Trumland House, and was discovered by workers during the building of a Victorian viewpoint. Dating back to 3500 BC, it's unusual in that it exploits its sloping site by having two storeys, one entered from the upper side and one from the lower. A little further west is the **Blackhammar Cairn**, which is more promising inside than it looks from the outside. You enter through the roof via a ladder; the long interior is divided into "stalls" by large flagstones, rather like the more famous cairn at Midhowe (see below). Finally, there's the **Knowe of Yarso**, another stalled cairn dating from the same period that's a stiff climb up the hill from the road, but worth it, if only for the magnificent view. The remains of 29 individuals were found inside, with the skulls neatly arranged around the walls; the bones of 36 deer were also buried here.

A footpath sets off from beside the Taversoe Tuick tomb into the **RSPB reserve** that encompasses a large section of the nearby heather-backed hills, the highest of which is **Blotchnie Fiold** (821ft). This high ground offers good hill-walking, with superb panoramic views of the surrounding islands, as well as excellent birdwatching. If you're lucky, you may well catch a glimpse of merlins, hen harriers, peregrine falcons and red-throated divers, although the latter are more widespread just outside the reserve on one of the island's three freshwater lochs, which also offer good trout fishing.

Midhowe Cairn and Broch

The southwestern side of Rousay is home to the most significant of the island's archeological remains, strung out along the shores of the tide races of Eynhallow Sound, which runs between the island and the Mainland. Most lie on the **Westness Walk**, a mile-long heritage trail that begins at Westness Farm, four miles west of the ferry terminal. **Midhowe Cairn**, about a mile on from the farm, comes as something of a surprise, both for its immense size – it's known as "the great ship of death" and measures nearly 100ft in length – and for the fact that it's now entirely surrounded by a stone-walled barn with a corrugated roof. Unfortunately, you can't actually explore the roofless communal burial chamber, dating back to 3500 BC, but only look down from the overhead walkway. The central corridor is partitioned with slabs of rock, with twelve compartments on each side, where the remains of 25 people were discovered in a crouched position with their backs to the wall.

A couple of hundred yards beyond Midhowe Cairn is Rousay's finest archeological site, **Midhowe Broch**, whose compact layout suggests that it was originally built as a sort of fortified family house, surrounded by a complex series of ditches and ramparts. These are now partially obscured by later houses, many of which have shelving and stairs still intact. The broch itself looks as though it's about to collapse: it was obviously shored up with flagstone buttresses back in the Iron Age, and has more recently been given extra sea defences by Historic Scotland. The interior of the broch is divided into two separate rooms, each with their own hearth, water tank and quernstone, all of which date from the final phase of occupation around the second century AD.

From Midhowe Broch you get a good view of the nearby small island of **Eynhallow**, which is surrounded by the most ferocious tides. The island was cleared in 1851, at which point it was discovered that one of the houses was in fact a converted church, possibly part of a monastery, dating back to at least the twelfth century. Beyond Midhowe, a walk along the coast will take you past the impressive cliff scenery around **Scabra Head**, where numerous seabirds nest in summer. Inland, the heathland of Quandale and Brings provides yet more birdwatching, with arctic terns and arctic skuas in abundance.

Egilsay and Wyre

Egilsay, the largest of the low-lying islands sheltering close to the eastern shore of Rousay, makes for an easy day-trip. The island is dominated by the ruins of **St Magnus Church**, with its distinctive round tower. Built around the twelfth century in a prominent position in the middle of the island, probably on the site of a much earlier version, the roofless church is the only surviving example of the traditional round-towered churches of Orkney and Shetland. It is possible that it was built as a shrine to Earl (later Saint) Magnus, who arranged to meet his cousin Haakon here in 1117, only to be treacherously killed on Haakon's orders by the latter's cook, Lifolf. A cenotaph marks the spot where the murder took place, about a quarter of a mile southeast of the church. Egilsay is almost entirely inhabited by incomers, and a large slice of the island's farmland is managed by the RSPB in an (often vain) attempt to encourage corncrakes. If you're just here for the day, walk due east from the ferry terminal to the coast, where there's a beautiful sandy bay overlooking Eday.

The tiny, neighbouring island of **Wyre**, to the southwest, directly opposite Rousay's ferry terminal, is another possible day-trip, and is best known for **Cubbie Roo's Castle**, the "fine stone fort" and "really solid stronghold" mentioned in the *Orkneyinga Saga*, and built around 1150 by local farmer Kolbein Hruga. The castle gets another mention in *Haakon's Saga*, when those inside successfully withstood all attacks. The outer defences have survived well on three sides of the castle, which has a central keep, with walls to a height of around six feet, its central water tank still intact. Close by the castle stands **St Mary's Chapel**, a roofless twelfth-century church founded either by Kolbein or his son, Bjarni the Poet, who was Bishop of Orkney. Kolbein's permanent residence or Bu is recalled in the name of the nearby farm, the Bu of Wyre, where the poet **Edwin Muir** (1887–1959) spent his childhood, described in detail in his autobiography. To learn more about Muir, Cubbie Roo or any other aspect of Wyre's history, pop into the **Wyre Heritage Centre**, near the chapel. If you walk to very western tip of Wyre, known as **The Taing**, you're pretty much guaranteed to see large numbers of grey and common **seals** basking on the rocks.

Practicalities

Rousay makes a good day-trip from the Mainland, with regular **car ferry** sailings from Tingwall (30min), linked to Kirkwall by buses. Most ferries also call in at Egilsay and Wyre, but some need to be booked the day before at the Tingwall ferry terminal (ⓣ01856/751360). Alternatively, you can join one of the very informative **minibus tours** run by Rousay Traveller (June–Aug Tues–Thurs; ⓣ01856/821234; £15), which connect with ferries and last between two and six hours, the longer ones allowing extended walks. **Bike rental** is available from *Arts, Bikes & Crafts*, near the pier (ⓣ01856/821398).

Accommodation on Rousay is limited to a couple of B&Bs: try the Victorian croft *Blackhamar* (ⓣ01856/821333, ⓦwww.orknet.co.uk/blackhamar; ❶). Another option is the hostel at *Trumland Farm* (ⓣ01856/821252), half a mile or so west of the terminal. As well as a couple of dorms, you can also camp, and there's a self-catering cottage, sleeping four. The *Pier Restaurant* (ⓣ01856/821359), right beside the terminal, serves bar meals at lunchtime and functions as a pub in the evenings; if you phone in advance, they will pack you a delicious **picnic** of crab, cheese, fruit and bannock bread. Don't arrive expecting to be able to buy yourself any provisions, as *Marion's Shop*, the island's main general store, is in the northeastern corner of the island.

Westray

Although exposed to the full force of the Atlantic weather in the far northwest of Orkney, **Westray** shelters one of the most tightly knit and prosperous island communities. It has a fairly stable population of 700 or so, producing superb beef, scallops, shellfish and a large catch of white fish, with its own small fish-processing factory and an organic salmon farm. Old Orcadian families still dominate every aspect of life, giving the island a strong individual character. The landscape is very varied, with sea cliffs and a trio of hills in the west, and rich low-lying pastureland and sandy bays elsewhere. However, given that distances are fairly large – it's about twelve miles from the ferry terminal in the south to the cliffs of Noup Head in the far northwest – and that the boat from Kirkwall takes nearly an hour and a half, Westray is an island that repays a longer stay, especially as the locals are extremely welcoming and genuinely interested in visitors.

The main village and harbour is **PIEROWALL** in the north of the island, a good eight miles from the Rapness ferry terminal on the southernmost tip of the island. Pierowall is a place of some considerable size, relatively speaking, with a school, several shops, a bakery (Orkney's only one off the Mainland), and the excellent **Westray Heritage Centre** (mid-May to mid-Sept Tues–Sat 9.30am–12.30pm & 2–5pm; £2), a tiny building hidden up a lane flanked by fuchsias. This is a very welcoming wet-weather retreat, with a great mock-up of the sea cliffs of Noup Head (see below) and a really imaginative range of hands-on exhibits for kids; it's also the only place on the island where you can get a cup of tea. Pierowall also boasts the **Lady Kirk**, a ruined chapel sporting a diminutive belfry, to the north of the village centre, which contains two very fine seventeenth-century tombstones.

The island's most impressive ruin, however, is the colossal sandstone hulk of **Noltland Castle** (June–Sept daily 9.30am–6.30pm; £1.50; HS), which stands above the village half a mile west up the road to Noup Head. This Z-plan castle, which is pockmarked with over seventy gun loops, was begun around 1560 by Gilbert Balfour, a shady character from Fife, who was Master of the Household to Mary, Queen of Scots, and was implicated in the murder of her husband Lord Darnley in 1567. Mary was deposed before she could make her planned visit to Noltland, and Balfour, having joined an unsuccessful uprising in favour of the exiled queen, was forced to flee to Sweden. There he was found guilty of plotting to murder the Swedish king and was executed in 1576. Somewhat miraculously, the Balfour family managed to hold on to Noltland (and Westray), eventually shifting their seat to Shapinsay (see p.706). To explore the castle, you must first pick up the key, which hangs outside the back door of the nearby farm. The most striking features of the interior are the huge, carved stone newel at the top of the grand, main staircase, and the secret compartments built into the sills of two of the windows.

The northwestern tip of Westray rises up sharply, culminating in the dramatic sea cliffs of **Noup Head**, which are particularly spectacular when a good westerly swell is up. The whole area is an RSPB reserve, and during the summer months the guano-covered rock ledges are packed with over 100,000 nesting seabirds, primarily guillemots, razorbills, kittiwakes and fulmars, with puffins as well: a truly awesome sight, sound and smell. There's a great viewpoint just to the northwest of the lighthouse, and another at Lawrence's Piece, half a mile to the south, where a narrow rocky ledge juts out into the sea. The open ground above the cliffs, which is grazed by sheep, is superb maritime heath and grassland, carpeted with yellow, white and purple flowers, and a favourite breeding ground for arctic terns and arctic skuas.

The coastal walk along the top of Westray's red sandstone cliffs from Noup Head south to Inga Ness is thoroughly recommended, as is a quick ascent of **Fitty Hill** (557ft), Westray's highest point. Also in the south of the island is the tiny **Cross Kirk** which, although ruined, retains an original Romanesque arch, door and window. It's right by the sea, and on a fine day the nearby sandy beach is a lovely spot for a picnic, with views over to the north side of Rousay. The sea cliffs in the southeast of the island around **Stanger Head** are not quite as spectacular as at Noup Head, but it's here that you'll find **Castle o'Burrian**, a sea stack that was once an early Christian hermitage. It's now the best place on Westray at which to see **puffins** nesting; there's even a signpost to the puffins from the main road.

Practicalities

Westray is served by car **ferry** from Kirkwall (2–3 daily; takes 1hr 25min; ☎01856/872044), or you can **fly** on Loganair's tiny eight-seater plane from Kirkwall to Westray (Mon–Sat 1–2 daily; 12min). **Minibus tours** of the island can also be arranged with Island Explorer (☎01857/677355), which connects with ferries. J&M Harcus of Pierowall (☎01857/677450) runs a **bus service** which will take you from Rapness to Pierowall, though you should phone ahead to check it's running. For **bike rental**, contact Sand O'Gill (☎01857/677374), Twiness (☎01857/677319), or Bis Geos hostel (☎01857/677420).

Westray's finest **accommodation** is at the *Cleaton House Hotel*

(Ⓣ01857/677508, Ⓦwww.orknet.co.uk/cleaton; ❹), a whitewashed Victorian manse about two miles southeast of Pierowall, with great views over to Papa Westray. *Cleaton House* is also the only place on the island where you can sample Westray's organic salmon, either in the expensive hotel **restaurant** or in the hotel's congenial **bar**. Somewhat bizarrely, the hotel also has a **pétanque** pitch, which residents and non-residents alike are welcome to use. The *Pierowall Hotel* (Ⓣ01857/677472, Ⓦwww.orknet.co.uk/pierowall; ❷), in Pierowall itself, is less stylish, a lot less expensive, but nevertheless welcoming, with a popular bar and a reputation for excellent fish and chips.

B&B is available at *Sand O'Gill* (Ⓣ01857/677374; ❶), where you can also **camp** or rent the self-catering **caravan**. Of Westray's two brand-new **hostels**, *Bis Geos* (Ⓣ01857/677420, Ⓦwww.bisgeos.co.uk; May–Sept), on the road to Noup Head, has the edge, with unbeatable views along the cliffs and out to sea; inside, it's beautifully furnished, and there are also a couple of very good **self-catering cottages**. *The Barn* (Ⓣ01857/677214, Ⓦwww.orkneyisles.co.uk/thebarn), is situated in an old farm on the south side of Pierowall Bay; it's easier to get to, and has a small **campsite** adjacent to it. You can rent clubs from Tulloch's shop (Ⓣ01857/677373) to play the somewhat eccentric **golf course** on the links northwest of Pierowall. To find out when the local **swimming pool** is available, phone Ⓣ01857/677750.

Papa Westray

Across the short Papa Sound from Westray is the island of **Papa Westray**, known locally as "Papay" (Ⓦwww.papawestray.co.uk). With a population hovering precariously between sixty and seventy, Papay has had to fight hard to keep itself viable over the last couple of decades, helped by a hefty influx of outsiders. With one of Orkney's best-preserved Neolithic settlements, and a large nesting seabird population, Papay is worthy of a stay in its own right or an easy day-trip from its neighbour. As the name suggests – *papøy* is Old Norse for "priest" – the island was once a medieval pilgrimage centre, focused on a chapel dedicated to **St Tredwell**, which is now reduced to a pile of rubble on a promontory on the loch of the same name just inland from the ferry terminal. St Tredwell (Triduana) was a plucky young local girl who gouged out her eyes and handed them to the eighth-century Pictish King Nechtan when he attempted to rape her. By the twelfth century, the chapel had become a place of pilgrimage for those suffering from eye complaints.

The island's visual focus is **Holland House**, occupying the high central point of the island and once seat of the local lairds, the Traill family, who ruled over Papay for three centuries. The main house, with its crow-stepped gables, is still in private hands, but the current owners are perfectly happy for visitors to explore the old buildings of the home farm, on the west side of the road, which include a kiln, a doocot and a horse-powered threshing mill. An old bothy for single male servants, decorated with red horse yokes, has even been restored and made into a small **museum** (open anytime; free), filled with bygone bits and bobs, from a wooden flea trap to a box bed.

A road leads down from Holland House to the western shore, where Papay's prime prehistoric site, the **Knap of Howar**, stands overlooking Westray. Dating from around 3500 BC, this Neolithic farm building makes a fair claim to being the oldest-standing house in Europe. It's made up of two roofless buildings, linked by a little passageway; one has a hearth and copious stone shelves, and is thought to have been some kind of storehouse. Half a mile north along the coast from the Knap of Howar is **St Boniface Kirk**, a pre-Reformation church that has recently been restored. Inside, it's beautifully simple, with a bare flagstone floor, dry-stone walls, a little wooden gallery and just a couple of surviving box pews. The church is known to have seated at least 220, which meant they would have been squashed in, fourteen to a pew. In the surrounding graveyard there's a Viking **hogback grave**, decorated with carvings in imitation of the wooden shingles on the roof of a Viking longhouse.

The northern tip of the island around **North Hill** (157ft) is now an **RSPB reserve**. During the breeding season, you're asked to keep to the coastal fringe, where razorbills, guillemots, fulmar, kittiwakes and puffins nest, particularly around Fowl Craig on the east coast, where you can also view the rare Scottish primrose, which flowers in May and from July to late September. If you want to explore the interior of the reserve, which plays host to one of the largest arctic tern colonies in Europe as well as numerous arctic skuas, contact the warden at Rose Cottage (Ⓣ01857/644240), who conducts regular escorted walks.

If you're here for more than a day, it's worth considering renting a boat to take you over to the **Holm of Papay**, an islet off the east coast. Despite its tiny size, the Holm boasts several Neolithic chambered cairns, one of which, occupying the highest point, is extremely impressive. Descending into the tomb via a ladder, you enter the main rectangular chamber which is nearly 70ft in length, with no fewer than twelve side-cells, each with its own lintelled entrance. To arrange a boat, contact the Community Co-operative (see below).

Practicalities

Papay is an easy day-trip from Westray, with a regular **passenger ferry** service from Pierowall (3–6 daily; takes 25min). However, it's just as easy to stay on Papay and take a day-trip to Westray instead: on Tuesdays and Fridays, the **car ferry** from Kirkwall to Westray continues on to Papa Westray (at other times, you can catch the bus from Rapness to Pierowall to connect with the passenger ferry). Papay is also connected to Westray by the **world's shortest scheduled flight** – two minutes in duration, or less with a following wind. Tickets from Loganair cost around £15 one-way. You can also fly direct from Kirkwall to Papa Westray (Mon–Fri 2 daily, Sat 1 daily).

Papay's Community Co-operative (Ⓣ01857/644267, Ⓔpapaycoop@orkney.com) has a **minibus** which will take you from the pier to wherever you want on the island, and can arrange a "package tour" (mid-May to mid-Sept Tues, Thurs & Sat; £28). It also runs a shop, a sixteen-bed SYHA-affiliated **hostel** (Ⓦwww.syha.org.uk) and the *Beltane House* **hotel** (❷; optional full board), all housed within the old estate workers' cottages at Beltane, east of Holland House, and contactable via the Community Co-op.

Eday

A long, thin island at the centre of Orkney's northern isles, **Eday** shares more characteristics with Rousay and Hoy than with its immediate neighbours, dominated as it is by a great block of heather-covered upland, with farmland confined to a narrow strip of coastal ground. However, Eday's hills have proved useful in their own way, providing huge quantities of peat which has been exported to the other peatless northern isles for fuel, and was even, for a time, exported to various whisky distillers. Eday's yellow sandstone has also been extensively quarried, and was used to build the St Magnus Cathedral in Kirkwall.

The island is very sparsely inhabited, has no real village as such, and is almost divided in two by its thin waist, flanked on either side by sandy bays, between which lies the island's airfield (known as London Airport). Eday has Orkney's only resident population of whimbrels, which nest around Flaughton Hill (328ft), a mile or so to the south, but the chief points of interest are all in the northern half of the island, beyond the post office, petrol pump and community shop on the main road. This marks the beginning of the signposted **Eday Heritage Walk**, which covers all the main sights, and takes about three hours to complete. The walk initially follows the road heading northwest, past the RSPB bird hide overlooking **Mill Loch**, where several pairs of red-throated divers regularly breed.

Clearly visible to the north of the road is the fifteen-foot **Stone of Setter**, Orkney's most distinctive standing stone, weathered into three thick, lichen-encrusted fingers. The stone clearly held centre stage in the Neolithic landscape, and is visible from the other nearby prehistoric sites. From here, passing the less spectacular Braeside and Huntersquoy chambered cairns en route, you can climb the hill to reach Eday's finest, the **Vinquoy Chambered Cairn**, which has a similar structure to that of Maes Howe. You can crawl into the tomb through the narrow entrance: a skylight inside lets light into the main, beehive chamber, now home to some lovely ferns, but not into the four side-cells. From the cairn, you can continue north to the viewpoint on the summit of **Vinquoy Hill** (248ft), and on to the very northernmost tip of the island, where lie the dramatic red sandstone sea cliffs of **Red Head**, where guillemots, razorbills, puffins and other seabirds nest in summer.

Visible on the east coast is **Carrick House**, the grandest home on Eday (mid-June to mid-Sept Sun 2pm; £2; ⓣ01857/622260). Built by the Laird of Eday in 1633, it was extended in the original style by successive owners, but is best known for its associations with the pirate **John Gow** – on whom Sir Walter Scott's novel *The Pirate* is based – whose ship *The Revenge* ran aground on the Calf of Eday in 1725. He asked for help from the local laird, but was taken prisoner in Carrick House, before eventually being sent off to London where he was tortured and executed. Highlight of the languid tour is the blood stain on the floor of the living room, where John Gow was detained, and stabbed whilst trying to escape.

From Carrick House, the uninhabited island of the **Calf of Eday** is only a stone's throw away. If you're keen to visit the island, contact Carrick House (ⓣ01857/622260). The islet features several chambered cairns, and is home to some massive bird colonies along its eastern cliffs, including a large colony of great black-backed gulls and numerous black guillemots, as well as all the usual suspects.

Practicalities

Eday's **ferry** terminal is at Backaland pier in the south, not ideal for visiting the more interesting northern section of the island, although if you haven't got your own transport you should find it fairly easy to get a lift with someone off the ferry (2–3 daily; takes 1hr 15min–2hr). Alternatively, car rental and taxis can be organized through Mr A. Stewart by the pier (ⓣ01857/622206); he also runs tailor-made two-hour minibus tours (mid-May to Aug Mon, Wed & Fri). Orkney Ferries offer an **Eday Heritage Tour** every Sunday (July to mid-Sept), which costs £12 per person; you need your own vehicle, but will be met by a guide, given lunch and have a guided tour of the archeological sights and

Carrick House. It's also possible to do a day-trip on Loganair's Wednesday **flight** from Kirkwall to Eday (Ⓣ01856/872494 or 873457). **Bike rental** is available from Martin Burkett at Hamarr, in the valley below the post office (Ⓣ01857/622331).

Friendly **B&B** with full board is available at *Skaill Farm*, a traditional farmhouse just south of the airport (Ⓣ01857/622271; ❸; closed April & May). The SYHA-affiliated **hostel** (Ⓦwww.syha.org.uk), situated in an exposed spot just north of the airport, is pretty bleak and basic, has no resident warden and is run by Eday Community Association (Ⓣ01857/622206; April–Sept), who will also advise on **camping**.

Stronsay

A low-lying, three-legged island to the southeast of Eday, **Stronsay** is strongly agricultural, its interior an almost uninterrupted patchwork of green pastures. The island features few real sights, but the coastline has enormous appeal: a beguiling combination of sandstone cliffs, home to several seabird colonies, interspersed with wide white sands and (in fine weather) clear turquoise bays. Stronsay has seen two economic booms in the last three hundred years. The first took place in the eighteenth century, and employed as many as three thousand people; it was built on collecting vast quantities of seaweed and exporting the **kelp** for use in the chemical industry, particularly in making iodine, soap and glass. In the following century, **fishing** on a grand scale came to dominate life here, as Whitehall harbour became one of the main Scottish centres for the curing of herring caught by French, Dutch and Scottish boats. By the 1840s, up to four hundred boats were working out of the port, attracting hundreds of women herring-gutters. By the 1930s, however, the herring stocks had been severely depleted and the industry began a long decline.

WHITEHALL, in the north of the island, is the only real village on Stronsay, made up of rows of stone-built fishermen's cottages set between two large piers. Wandering along the tranquil, rather forlorn harbour front today, you'll find it hard to believe that the village once supported five thousand people in the fishing industry during the summer season, as well as a small army of coopers, coal merchants, butchers, bakers, several Italian ice-cream parlours and a cinema. It was said that, on a Sunday, you could walk across the decks of the boats all the way to **Papa Stronsay**, the tiny island that shelters Whitehall from the north, on which a new monastery is currently being built by monks from the Oder of the Transalpine Redemporists. The old fish market by the pier used to house a **museum**, with a few photos and artefacts from the herring days; ask at the small café (closed Tues) to see if it's still open.

If the weather's fine, you can choose which of the island's many arching, dazzlingly white beaches to relax on. The most dramatic section of coastline, featuring great layered slices of sandstone, lies in the southeast corner of the island. Signposts show the way to Orkney's biggest and most dramatic natural arch, the **Vat of Kirbuster**. Before you reach the arch there's a seaweedy, shallow pool in a natural sandstone amphitheatre, where the water is warmed by the sun and kids and adults can safely wallow: close by is a rocky inlet for those who prefer colder, more adventurous swimming. You'll find progressively more nesting seabirds, including a few puffins, as you approach **Burgh Head**, further along down the coast. Meanwhile, at the promontory of **Lamb Head**, there are usually loads of seals, a large colony of arctic terns, and good views out to the lighthouse on the outlying island of **Auskerry**, to the south.

Practicalities

Stronsay is served by a regular car **ferry** service from Kirkwall to Whitehall (2 daily; takes 1hr 40min–2hr), and weekday Loganair **flights**, also from Kirkwall (Mon–Fri 2 daily; takes 25min). There's no bus service, but D.S. Peace (☎01857/616335) operates taxis and **rents cars**. Of the few **accommodation** options, a good choice is the *Stronsay Fish Mart* **hostel** (☎01857/606220) in the old fish market by the pier, with a well-equipped kitchen, washing machine and comfortable bunk-bedded rooms. The pub opposite is the newly refurbished *Stronsay Hotel* (☎01857/616213; ❹), which once boasted the longest bar in the north of Scotland. A cheaper alternative is the *Stronsay Bird Reserve* (☎01857/616363; ❷), a nicely positioned **B&B** in a lovely old croft-house, which also tolerates camping on the shores of Mill Bay; the folk who run it are bird enthusiasts and keep a record of the astonishing number of rare migrants which regularly turn up on the island. The *Stronsay Hotel* does good pub **food** – try the seafood taster – but otherwise, you'll need to bring your own supplies and make use of the island's two shops. There's a **swimming pool** behind the school which is available for public use, but it's operated on a voluntary basis, so check first at the shop in Whitehall.

Sanday

Sanday, though the largest of the northern isles, is also the most insubstantial, a great low-lying, drifting dune strung out between several rocky points. The island's sweeping aquamarine bays and vast stretches of clean white sand are the finest in Orkney, and in dry, clear weather it's a superb place to spend a day or two. The sandy soil is, in fact, very fertile, and the island remains predominantly agricultural even today, holding its very own agricultural show each year at the beginning of August.

The island has a long history as a shipping hazard, with many wrecks smashed against its shores, although the construction of the **Start Point Lighthouse** in 1802 on the island's exposed eastern tip reduced the risk for seafarers. Shipwrecks were, in fact, not an unwelcome sight on Sanday, as the island has no peat, and driftwood was the only source of fuel other than cow dung – it's even said that the locals used to pray for shipwrecks in church. The present Stevenson lighthouse, which dates from 1870, now sports very natty vertical black and white stripes. It actually stands on a tidal island, which is accessible only either side of low tide, so ask locally for the tide times before setting out (it takes an hour to walk there and back); phone the lighthouse keeper (☎01857/600385) in advance if you want to see inside.

The shoreline supports a healthy seal, otter and wading bird population, and behind the splendid sandy beaches are stretches of beautiful open machair and grassland, thick with wild flowers during the spring and summer. The entire coastline presents the opportunity for superb walks, with particularly spectacular sand dunes to the south of Cata Sand. Sanday is also rich in archeology, with hundreds of mostly unexcavated sites including cairns, brochs and burnt mounds. The most impressive is **Quoyness Chambered Cairn**, on the fertile farmland of Els Ness peninsula. The tomb, which dates from before 2000 BC, has been partially reconstructed, and rises to a height of around 13ft. The imposing, narrow entrance, flanked by high drystone walls, would originally have been roofed for the whole of the way into the 13-foot-long main chamber, where bones and skulls were discovered in the six small side-cells.

The island's knitting factory recently closed down, but you can still visit Sanday's unusual **Orkney Angora** craft shop (ⓣ01857/600421, ⓦwww.orkneyangora.co.uk), in Upper Breckan in the parish of Burness. The owner will usually oblige with a quick look and a stroke of one of the comically long-haired albino rabbits who supply the wool. Close by is the stone tower of an old windmill, which belonged to the neighbouring farmstead and house of **Scar**, where you can still see the chimney from the farm's old steam-powered meal mill.

Practicalities

Ferries to Sanday arrive at the new terminal at the southern tip of the island and are met by the **minibus** (book on ⓣ01857/600467), which will take you to most points. The airfield is in the centre of the island and there are regular Loganair **flights** to Kirkwall (Mon–Fri 2 daily, Sat 1 daily; 10–20min). The fishing port of **KETTLETOFT** is where the ferry used to dock, and where you'll find the island's two **hotels**. Of the two, the *Belsair Hotel* (ⓣ01857/600206, ⓔjoy@sanday.quista.net; ❷) is probably the one to stay at, and has the slightly more adventurous restaurant menu; the *Kettletoft Hotel* has a lively bar that's popular with the locals. Of the handful of **B&Bs**, try the plain family-run *Quivals* (ⓣ01857/600467; ❶), who can also organize car and bike rental.

North Ronaldsay

North Ronaldsay – or "North Ron" as it's fondly known – is Orkney's most northerly island. Separated from Sanday by the treacherous waters of the North Ronaldsay Firth, it has a unique outpost atmosphere, brought about by its extreme isolation. Measuring just three miles by one and rising only 66ft above sea level, the island is almost overwhelmed by the enormity of the sky, the strength of wind and the ferocity of the sea – so much so that its very existence seems an act of tenacious defiance. Despite these adverse conditions, North Ronaldsay has been inhabited for centuries, and continues to be heavily farmed, from old-style crofts whose roofs are made from huge local flagstones. With no natural harbours and precious little farmland, the islanders have been forced to make the most of what they have and **seaweed** has played an important role in the local economy. During the eighteenth century, kelp was gathered here, burnt in pits and sent south for use in the chemicals industry.

The island's **sheep** are a unique, tough, goatlike breed, who feed mostly on seaweed, giving their flesh a dark tone and a rich, gamey taste, and making their thick wool highly prized. A high **drystone dyke**, completed in the mid-nineteenth century and running the thirteen miles around the edge of the island, keeps them off the farmland, except during lambing season, when the ewes are allowed onto the pastureland. North Ronaldsay sheep are also unusual in that they can't be rounded up by sheepdogs like ordinary sheep, but scatter far and wide at some considerable speed. Instead, once a year the islanders herd the sheep communally into a series of **drystone "punds"** near Dennis Head, for clipping and dipping, in what is one of the last acts of communal farming practised in Orkney.

There are very few real sights on the island, and the most frequent visitors are ornithologists, who come in considerable numbers to catch a glimpse of the rare migrants who land here briefly on their spring and autumn migrations. The peak times of year for migrants are from late March to early June, and from mid-August to early November, although there are also many breeding species which spend the spring and summer here, including gulls, terns, waders, black guillemots, cormorants and even the odd corncrake. As on Fair Isle (see p.734), there's now a permanent **Bird Observatory**, established in 1987 by adapting a croft situated in the southwest corner of the island to wind and solar power; they can give advice as to what birds have recently been sighted.

Holland House – built by the Traill family who bought the island in 1727 – and the two lighthouses at Dennis Head, are the only features to interrupt the flat horizon. The attractive, stone-built **Old Beacon** was first lit in 1789, but the lantern was replaced by the huge bauble of masonry you now see as long ago as 1809. The **New Lighthouse**, half a mile to the north, is the tallest land-based lighthouse in Britain, rising to a height of over 100ft. On a clear day you can see Fair Isle, and even Sumburgh and Fitful Head on Shetland.

Practicalities

The **ferry** from Kirkwall to North Ronaldsay runs only once a week (usually Fri; takes 2hr 40min–3hr), though day-trips are possible on occasional Sundays between late May and early September (phone ⓣ01856/872044 for details). Your best bet is to catch a Loganair **flight** from Kirkwall (Mon–Sat 2 daily): if you stay the night on the island, you're eligible for a bargain £10 return fare. You can **stay** at the *North Ronaldsay Bird Observatory* (ⓣ01857/633200, ⓦwww.nrbo.f2s.com; ❸), which offers full board either in private guest rooms or in dorms. Full-board accommodation is also available at *Garso*, in the north-east (ⓣ01857/633244, ⓔchristine.muir@virgin.net; ❸), which also has a self-catering cottage. The *Burrian Inn*, to the southeast of the war memorial, is the island's small **pub**, and does hot food. **Camping** is possible; for further information, phone Mr Scott on ⓣ01857/633222.

Shetland

Many maps plonk the **Shetland Islands** in a box somewhere off Aberdeen, but in fact they're a lot closer to Bergen in Norway than Edinburgh, and to the Arctic Circle than Manchester. The Shetland **landscape** is a product of the struggle between rock and the forces of water and ice that have, over millennia, tried to break it to pieces. Smoothed by the last glaciation, the surviving land has been exposed to the most violent weather experienced in the British Isles; it isn't for nothing that Shetlanders call the place "the Old Rock", and the coastline, a crust of cliffs with caves, blowholes and stacks, testifies to the continuing battle. Inland (a relative term, since you're never more than three miles from the sea), the terrain is a barren mix of moorland, often studded with peaty lochs which glitter a brilliant blue when the sun shines, and the occasional patch of green farmland, dotted with hardy, multicoloured sheep and diminutive ponies. In winter, gales are routine and Shetlanders take even the

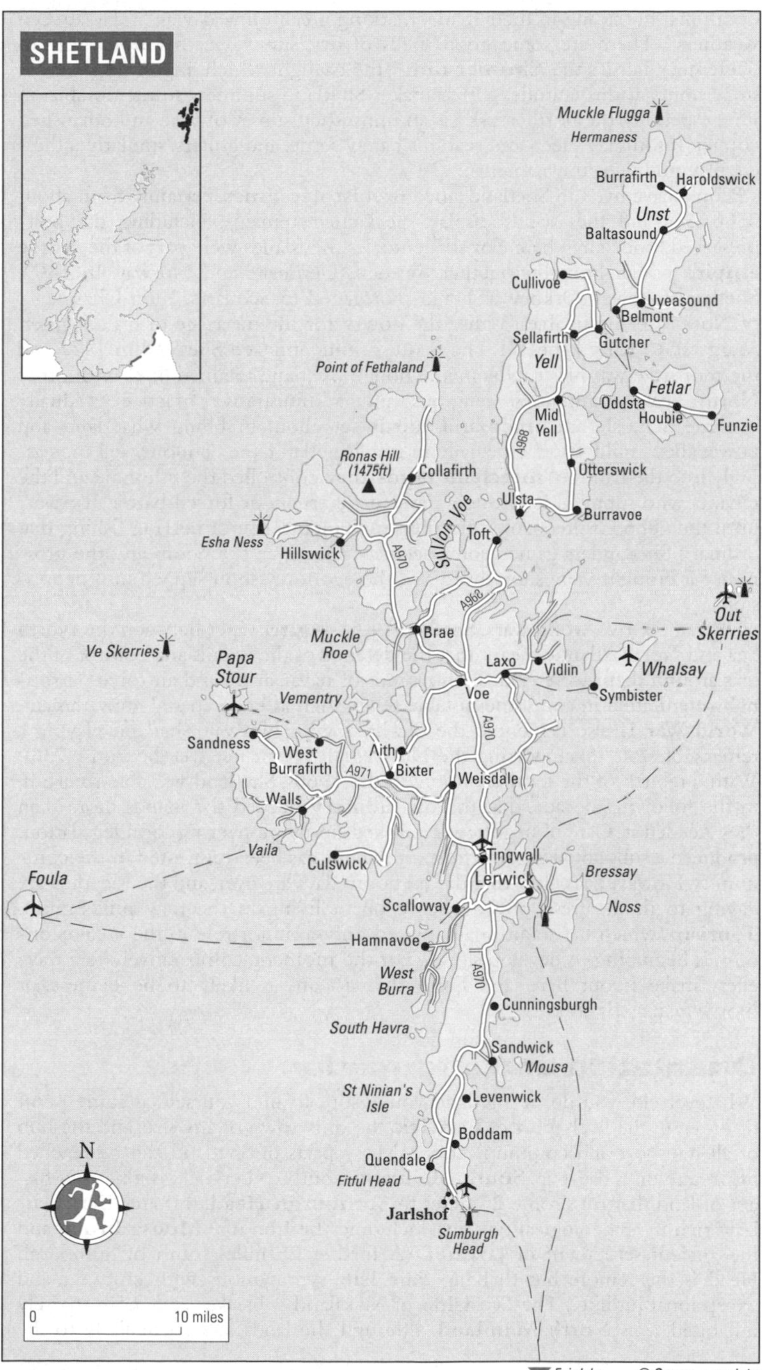
SHETLAND
Muckle Flugga
Hermaness
Burrafirth
Haroldswick
Unst
Baltasound
Cullivoe
Uyeasound
Belmont
Sellafirth
Gutcher
Yell
Point of Fethaland
Fetlar
Oddsta
Houbie
Funzie
Mid Yell
A968
Ronas Hill (1475ft)
Collafirth
Otterswick
Ulsta
Burravoe
Sullom Voe
Toft
Esha Ness
Hillswick
A970
A968
Out Skerries
Brae
Muckle Roe
Ve Skerries
Papa Stour
Laxo
Vidlin
Whalsay
Symbister
Voe
Vementry
A970
Sandness
West Burrafirth
Aith
A971
Bixter
Weisdale
Walls
Vaila
Tingwall
Culswick
Foula
Lerwick
Bressay
Scalloway
Noss
Hamnavoe
A970
West Burra
Cunningsburgh
South Havra
Sandwick
Mousa
St Ninian's Isle
Levenwick
Boddam
N
Quendale
Fitful Head
Jarlshof
Sumburgh Head
0
10 miles
Fair Isle

occasional hurricane in their stride, marking a calm fine day as "a day atween weathers". There are some good spells of dry, sunny weather from May to September, but it's the "**simmer dim**", the twilight which lingers through the small hours at this latitude, which makes Shetland summers so memorable; in June especially, the northern sky is an unfinished sunset of blue and burnished copper. Insomniac sheep and seabirds barely settle, and golfers, similarly afflicted, play midnight tournaments.

People have lived in Shetland since **prehistoric times**, certainly from about 3500 BC, and the islands display spectacular remains, including the best-preserved broch anywhere. For six centuries the islands were part of the **Norse empire** which brought together Sweden, Denmark and Norway. In 1469, Shetland followed Orkney in being mortgaged to Scotland, King Christian I of Norway being unable to raise the dowry for the marriage of his daughter, Margaret, to King James III. The Scottish king annexed Shetland in 1472 and the mortgage was never redeemed. Though Shetland retained links with other North Sea communities, religious and administrative practice gradually become Scottish, and **mainland lairds** set about grabbing what land and power they could. Later, especially in rural Shetland, the economy fell increasingly into the hands of **merchant lairds**; they controlled the fish trade and the tenants who supplied it through a system of truck, or forced barter. It wasn't until the 1886 Crofters' Acts and the simultaneous rise of herring fishing that ordinary Shetlanders gained some security. However, the boom and the prosperity it brought were short-lived and the economy soon slipped into depression.

During the two world wars, Shetland's role as gatekeeper between the North Sea and North Atlantic meant that the defence of the islands and control of the seas around them were critical: thousands of naval, army and air force personnel were drafted in and some notable relics, such as huge coastal guns, remain. **World War II** also cemented the old links with Norway, Shetland playing a remarkable role in supporting the Norwegian Resistance (see box on p.736). With a rebirth of the local economy in the 1960s, Shetland was able to claim, in the following decade, that the **oil industry** needed the islands more than they needed it. Careful negotiation, backed up by pioneering local legislation, produced a substantial income from oil which has been reinvested in the community. However, it's clear that the oil boom days are over, and the islanders are having to think afresh how to carve out a living in the new millennium. **Tourism**, which has traditionally played only a minor role in the local economy, is beginning to develop slowly. For the moment, comparatively few travellers make it out here, and those that do are as likely to be Faroese or Norwegian as British.

Orientation and information

Whatever else you do in Shetland you're sure to find yourself, at some point or other, in the lively port of **Lerwick**, the only town of any size, and the hub of all transport and communications. Many parts of Shetland can be reached from here on a day-trip. **South Mainland**, south of Lerwick, is a narrow finger of land that runs some 25 miles to **Sumburgh Head**; this area is particularly rich in archeological remains, including the Iron Age **Mousa Broch** and the ancient settlement of **Jarlshof**. (A further 25 miles south of Sumburgh Head is the remote but thriving **Fair Isle**, synonymous with knitwear and exceptional birdlife.) The **Westside** of Mainland is bleaker and more sparsely inhabited, as is **North Mainland**, although the landscape, particularly to the north, opens out in scale and grandeur as it comes face to face with the Atlantic. Off the west coast, **Papa Stour** lies just a mile from Sandness and boasts some spectacular caves and stacks; much further out are the distinctive peaks and precipitous cliffs of the remote island of **Foula**. Shetland's three **North Isles** bring Britain to a dramatic, windswept end. Their landscapes and seascapes have been shaped by centuries of fierce storms and have an elemental beauty. Nevertheless, the three islands differ markedly from one another: **Yell** has the largest population of otters in Shetland; **Fetlar** is home to the rare red-necked phalarope; north of **Unst**, there's nothing until you reach the North Pole. The islands' tourist board at Ⓦwww.visitshetland.com has extensive information.

Supporting an impressive array of **birds and wildlife**, the islands offer excellent birdwatching and coastal walking. The **fishing** is good, too, with lochs well stocked with brown trout, sea trout in the voes and the chance to go sea angling for ling, mackerel or even shark and halibut. **Camping** rough isn't discouraged in Shetland if done considerately and the landowner is asked first. However, make sure you're fully equipped to cope with the Shetland wind, which tests the most resilient of tents to the limit: pick a sheltered site, if possible, and use all the guy ropes you have.

Arrival

P&O Scottish Ferries (Ⓣ01224/572615 or Ⓣ01595/695252, Ⓦwww.posf.co.uk) operates a direct overnight **car ferry** from **Aberdeen** to Lerwick four or five times a week (takes 14hr). There's also a once-weekly daytime service from **Stromness** in Orkney (takes 8–10hr), which increases to twice weekly in summer (June–Aug) – one overnight, one daytime. If you're visiting both Orkney and Shetland, be sure to check out the discounted **round-trip fares** advertised by P&O. Note, too, that from October 2002 these services will be run by NorthLink.

There are **flights** on British Airways (Ⓣ0845/733 3377) nonstop to Shetland from **Aberdeen**, **Inverness**, **Kirkwall** and **Wick**, with connections into those airports from Edinburgh, Glasgow, Birmingham, Manchester and London. Shetland's main airport is at **Sumburgh**, from where buses make short work of the 25-mile journey north to Lerwick. Standard fares are high, but various cheaper tickets and special offers are sometimes available, often with booking conditions.

Island transport

Public transport is pretty good in Shetland, with **buses** fanning out from Lerwick to just about every corner of Mainland, and even via ferries across to Yell and Unst: you can buy the full timetable (£1; includes all ferries and flights) from Lerwick tourist office. Various **tours** by bus, minibus or private car are also available; operators include John Leask & Son (Ⓣ01595/693162, Ⓦwww.leaskstravel.co.uk), or the more specialist Shetland Wildlife Tours (Ⓣ01950/460254, Ⓦwww.shetlandwildlife.co.uk). If you want to **rent a car** once on the islands, there are several firms to choose from in Lerwick and Sumburgh, though none is cheap. **Hitching** is viable and pretty safe, but **cycling** is hard-going due to the almost constant wind.

Inter-island travel is very straightforward: the larger islands have frequent **car ferry** services throughout the day; journey times are mostly less than half an hour, and fares are much cheaper than those in Orkney or the Hebrides.

Onwards from Shetland

Thanks to the historical ties and the attraction of a short hop to continental Europe, **Norway** is a popular destination for Shetlanders and Orcadians. Norwegians often think of Shetland and Orkney as their western isles and, particularly in west Norway, old wartime bonds with Shetland are still strong. Norwegian yachts and sail training vessels are frequent visitors to Lerwick and Kirkwall. Shetlanders can also go by ferry to the **Faroe Islands** – steep, angular shapes rising out of the North Atlantic – and on to **Iceland**.

From late May to early September the Smyril Line's large, comfortable and fast Faroese car **ferry** *Norröna* makes weekly return trips from her home port in Faroe to Shetland, Norway, Iceland and Denmark. From Shetland, the voyages to **Bergen** in Norway or **Tórshavn** in Faroe both take thirteen hours; to **Seydisfjördur** in Iceland it takes 33 hours including a brief stop in Faroe; on the way back there's a two-day stopover in Faroe while the ship makes a return trip to **Hanstholm** in Denmark. For information on charter flights between Shetland and Norway, contact Hay & Co (ⓣ01950/460661).

Adults pay around £2.50 return on most routes (around £5 to Foula, Fair Isle, Papa Stour or Out Skerries), and a car plus driver cross for around £9 return. There are also British Airways **flights** linking Tingwall Airport, five miles west of Lerwick, to Fair Isle and less frequent Loganair flights to Whalsay, Out Skerries, Papa Stour and Foula. (Some Fair Isle flights leave from Sumburgh Airport.) Sample one-way fares include £20 Tingwall to Foula, and £38 Tingwall to Fair Isle; be sure to book well in advance, however, as the planes only take eight passengers, and be prepared to be flexible, as flights are often cancelled due to the weather. It's also possible to take **boat trips** for pleasure, to explore the coastline and spot birds, seals, porpoises, dolphins and whales; operators include Shetland Wildlife Tours (see above), and Tom Jamieson from Sandwick (for the Broch of Mousa; ⓣ01950/431367, ⓦwww.mousaboattrips.co.uk). Specialist services for **diving** or **sea angling** can be tracked down through the Lerwick tourist office.

Lerwick

For Shetlanders, there's only one place to stop, meet and do business and that's "da toon", **LERWICK**. Very much the focus of Shetland's commercial life, Lerwick is home to about 7500 people, roughly a third of the islands' population. All year, its sheltered **harbour** at the heart of the town is busy with ferries, fishing boats, oil-rig supply vessels and a variety of more specialized craft including seismic survey and naval vessels from all round the North Sea. In summer, the quaysides come alive with local pleasure craft, visiting yachts, cruise liners, historic vessels such as the restored *Swan*, and the occasional tall sailing ship. Behind the old harbour is the compact town centre, made up of one long main street, Commercial Street; from here, narrow lanes, known as "**closses**", rise westwards to the late-Victorian new town.

Lerwick began life as a temporary settlement, catering to the **Dutch** herring fleet in the seventeenth century, which brought in as many as twenty thousand men. During the nineteenth century, with the presence of ever larger Scottish, English and Scandinavian boats, it became a major **fishing** centre, and whalers called to pick up crews on their way to the northern hunting grounds. In 1839,

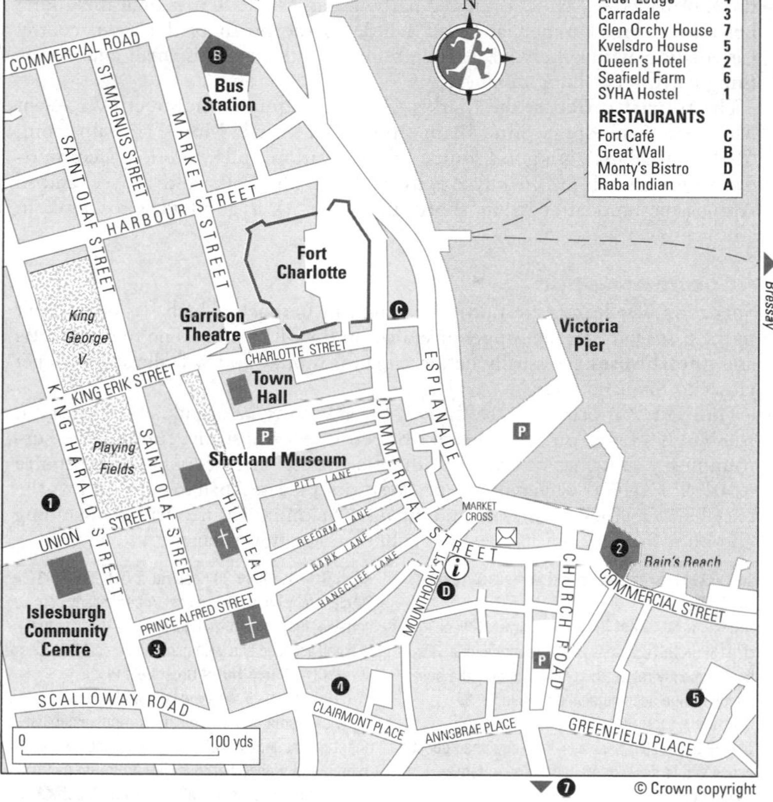

the visiting Danish governor of Faroe declared that "everything made me feel that I had come to the land of opulence". Business was conducted largely from buildings known as **lodberries**, each typically having a store, a house and small yard on a private jetty. **Smuggling** was part of the daily routine, and secret tunnels – some of which still exist – connected the lodberries to illicit stores. During the late nineteenth century, the construction of the Esplanade along the shore isolated several lodberries from the sea, but further south beyond the *Queen's Hotel* are some that still show their original form. Lerwick expanded considerably at this time and the large houses and grand public buildings established then still dominate, notably the **Town Hall**, which remains the most prominent landmark. Another period of rapid growth began during the oil boom of the 1970s, with the farmland to the southwest disappearing under a suburban sprawl, the town's northern approaches becoming an industrial estate.

Arrival, information and accommodation

First impressions of Lerwick are very much dependent on the weather (and, if you arrive by boat, the crossing you've just experienced). The **ferry terminal** is situated in the unprepossessing north harbour, about a mile from the town centre. **Flying** into Sumburgh Airport, you can take one of the regular buses to Lerwick; taxis (around £25) and car rental are also available. Buses stop on the Esplanade, very close to the old harbour and Market Cross, or at the Viking bus station on Commercial Road a little to the north of the town centre. Orientation within Lerwick is straightforward: the town is small and everything is within walking distance.

The **tourist office**, at the Market Cross on Commercial Street (May–Sept Mon–Sat 8am–6pm, Sun 10am–1pm; Oct–April Mon–Fri 9am–5pm; ⓣ01595/693434), is a good source of information, and will book accommodation for a small fee. In July, August and over the Folk Festival weekend in April, accommodation is in short supply, so it's a good idea to book in advance.

Accommodation

Shetland's best **hotels** are not to be found in Lerwick, which has been spoilt in the past by the steady supply of visitors in the oil business. The town's **B&Bs** and **guesthouses** are usually better value for money, and will allow you to get closer to Shetland life.

The SYHA **hostel** (ⓣ01595/692114, ⓦwww.syha.org.uk; April–Sept) at Islesburgh House on King Harald Street, offers unusually comfortable surroundings, and has useful laundry facilities. The *Clickimin* **campsite** (ⓣ01595/741000, ⓔclickimincentre@srt.org.uk; late April to Sept), enjoys the excellent facilities of the neighbouring Clickimin leisure centre, including good hot showers, but its sheltered suburban location is far from idyllic.

Hotels, guesthouses and B&Bs

Alder Lodge Guest House 6 Clairmont Place ⓣ01595/695705. Converted former Victorian bank, recently refurbished, and probably the best middle-range accommodation available. ❸

Carradale Guest House 36 King Harald St ⓣ01595/692251. Spacious, well-equipped guesthouse in a large, comfortable Victorian family home. ❷

Glen Orchy House 20 Knab Rd ⓣ01595/692031, ⓔglenorchy.house@virgin.net. A particularly comfortable, fully modernized guesthouse that's virtually a hotel, licensed and with good home cooking. ❹

Kvelsdro House Hotel Greenfield Place ⓣ01595/692195, ⓦwww.kgqhotels.co.uk. Lerwick's smartest and most luxurious establishment (pronounced "kelro"), with immaculate bedrooms and a good harbour view from the bar. It's hard to find, but locals will usually help out. ❻

Böds

With only one official SYHA hostel in the whole of Shetland, it's worth knowing about the islands' unique network of **camping böds**, which are open from April to September. Traditionally, a böd was a small building beside the shore, where fishermen used to house their gear and occasionally sleep; the word was also applied to trading posts established by merchants of the Hanseatic League. Today, the tourist board uses the term pretty loosely: none of the places they run is strictly speaking a böd, ranging instead from stone-built cottages to weatherboarded sail lofts. In order to stay at a böd, you must **book in advance** through Lerwick tourist office (ⓣ01595/693434), as there are no live-in wardens. All the böds have some form of (primitive) heating system, cold water, toilets, a kitchen (though no stove or cooking utensils), and bunk beds, but (as yet no mattresses), so a sleeping bag and bedding mat are pretty much essential. If you're on a camping trip, they're a great way to escape the wind and rain for a night or two; they're also remarkably good value, at around £5 per person per night. Except in June, July and August, it's even possible to pay for exclusive use of any of the böds; prices range from £35 to £90 per night depending on the size of the böd.

Queen's Hotel Commercial Street ☎01595/692826, Ⓦwww.kgqhotels.co.uk. A beautiful old building right on the waterfront with its feet in the sea and views over Bressay Sound from many of its bedrooms, all of which have recently been upgraded. ❻

Seafield Farm Off Sea Road ☎01595/693853. A very friendly B&B in a huge modern farmhouse overlooking the sea, a mile or so southwest of the town centre and therefore best for those with their own transport. ❷

The Town

Lerwick's attractive, flagstone-clad **Commercial Street**, universally known to locals as "da street", is still very much the core of the town. Its narrow, winding form, set back one block from the Esplanade, provides shelter from the elements even on the worst days, and is where locals meet, shop, exchange news and gossip and bring in the New Year to the sound of a harbourful of ships' sirens. The buildings exhibit a mixed bag of architectural styles, from the powerful neo-Baroque of the Bank of Scotland at no. 117 to the plainer houses and old lodberries at the south end, beyond the *Queen's Hotel*. Here, you'll find **Bain's Beach**, a small, hidden stretch of golden sand that's one of the prettiest spots in Lerwick. Further south lie the Victorian Anderson Homes and the Anderson High School, the latter's ornate, Franco-Scottish towers and dormers now unfortunately rather lost among later additions. Both were the gift of **Arthur Anderson** (1792–1868), cofounder of the Peninsular and Oriental Steam Navigation Company (P&O), for more on whom see p.726.

The Street's northern end is marked by the towering walls of **Fort Charlotte** (daily: June–Sept 9am–10pm; Oct–May 9am–4pm; free), which once stood directly above the beach. Begun for Charles II in 1665 during the wars with the Dutch, the fort was attacked and burnt down by the Dutch fleet in August 1673. In the 1780s it was repaired and given its name in honour of George III's queen. Since then, it's served as a prison and a Royal Navy training centre; it's now open to the public, except on rare occasions when it's used by the Territorial Army. The fort affords good views from its solid battlements, and has four replica eighteenth-century cannons pointing out across Bressay Sound.

Although the narrow lanes or **closses** that connect the Street to Hillhead are now a desirable place to live, it's not so long ago that they were regarded as slumlike dens of iniquity, from which the better-off escaped to the Victorian new town laid out to the west on a grid plan. The steep stone-flagged lanes are now fun to explore, each one lined by tall houses with trees, fuchsia, flowering currant and honeysuckle pouring over the garden walls. If you look at the street signs, you can see that all the closses have two names: their former ones and their current titles, chosen in 1845 by the Police Commissioners – Reform, Fox and Pitt, reflecting the liberal political culture of the period, or derived from the writings of Sir Walter Scott.

Hillhead, up in the Victorian "new town", is dominated by the splendid **Town Hall** (Mon–Thurs 9am–5pm, Fri 9am–4pm; free), a Scottish-Baronial monument to civic pride, built by public subscription. Visitors are free to wander round the building (providing there are no functions going on), to admire the wonderful stained-glass windows in the main hall, which celebrate Shetland's history, and to climb the castellated central tower which occupies the town's highest point. Opposite the town hall, housed on the first floor of the desperately ugly municipal library, the **Shetland Museum** (Mon, Wed & Fri 10am–7pm, Tues, Thurs & Sat 10am–5pm; Ⓦwww.shetland-museum.org.uk; free) is full to the brim with nauticalia. More unusual exhibits include Shetland's oldest telephone, fitted with a ceramic mouthpiece, and a carved head of

Up Helly-Aa

On the last Tuesday in January, whatever the weather, Lerwick's new town is the setting for the most spectacular part of the **Up Helly-Aa**, a huge fire festival, the largest of several held in Shetland from January to March. Around nine hundred torchbearing participants, all male and all in extraordinary costumes, march in procession behind a grand Viking longship. The annually appointed Guizer Jarl and his "squad" appear as Vikings and brandish shields and silver axes; each of the forty or so other squads is dressed for their part in the subsequent entertainment, perhaps as giant insects, space invaders or ballet dancers. Their circuitous route leads to the King George V Playing Field where, after due ceremony, all the torches are thrown into the longship, creating an enormous bonfire. A firework display follows, then the participants, known as "guizers", set off in their squads to do the rounds of more than a dozen "halls" (which usually include at least one hotel and the Town Hall) from around 8.30pm in the evening until 8am the next morning, performing some kind of act – usually a comedy routine – at each.

Up Helly-Aa itself is not that ancient, dating only from Victorian times, when it was introduced to replace the much older Christmas tradition of rolling burning tar barrels through the streets, which was banned in 1874. Seven years later a torchlight procession took place, which eventually developed into a full-blown Viking celebration, known as "Up Helly-Aa". Although this is essentially a community event with entry to halls by invitation only, visitors are welcome at the Town Hall, for which tickets are sold in early January; contact the tourist office well in advance. To catch some of the atmosphere of the event, check out the annual Up Helly-Aa exhibition in the **Galley Shed** on St Sunniva Street (mid-May to mid-Sept Tues 2–4pm & 7–9pm, Fri 7–9pm, Sat 2–4pm; £2.50), where you can see a full-size longship, costumes, shields and photographs.

Goliath by Adam Christie (1869–1950), a Shetlander who spent much of his life in Montrose Asylum, and who is perhaps best known for his application to patent a submarine built of glass, which would thus be invisible to enemies.

Clickimin Broch and the Böd of Gremista

A mile or so southwest of the town centre on the road leading to Sumburgh, the much-restored **Clickimin Broch** stands on what was once a small island in Loch Clickimin. The settlement here began as a small farmstead around 700 BC and was later enclosed by a defensive wall. The main tower served as a castle and probably rose to around 40ft, as at Mousa (see p.731), though the remains are now not much more than 10ft high. There are two small entrances, one at ground level and the other on the first floor, which are carefully protected by outer defences and smaller walls. With the modern housing in the middle distance, it's pretty hard to imagine the original setting or sense the magical atmosphere of the place. Excavation of the site has unearthed an array of domestic goods that suggest international trade, including a Roman glass bowl thought to have been made in Alexandria around 100 AD.

In earlier times the seasonal nature of the Shetland fishing industry led to the establishment of small stores, known as **böds** (see box on p.724), often incorporating sleeping accommodation, beside the beaches where fish were landed and dried. Just beyond Lerwick's main ferry terminal, a mile and a half north of the town centre, stands the **Böd of Gremista** (June to mid-Sept Wed–Sun 10am–1pm & 2–5pm; Ⓦ www.shetland-museum.org.uk; free), the birthplace of **Arthur Anderson** (1792–1868). Though almost lost among the surrounding industrial estate, the building has been completely restored and the displays explore Anderson's life as beach boy (helping to cure and dry fish), naval seaman, businessman, philanthropist, Shetland's first native MP and founder of Shetland's first newspaper, the *Shetland Journal*. Built at the end of the eighteenth century for Anderson's father, the ground floor was originally used as an office and fish-curing station, while the trader and his family resided permanently upstairs.

Eating

Shetland produces a huge harvest of fresh fish from the surrounding seas, including shellfish and salmon, and from the land there's superb lamb and even local tomatoes, cucumbers and peppers, grown under glass. The most celebrated local delicacy is *reestit* mutton: steeped in brine, then air-dried, it's the base for a superb potato soup cooked by locals around New Year. Unfortunately, the **food** on offer in the majority of Lerwick's hotels and pubs doesn't do these ingredients justice. It's not even possible to assemble a decent picnic without resorting to a visit to the Safeway supermarket, situated a mile or so southwest of town, opposite the Clickimin Broch.

Daytime cafés

Faerdie-Maet Commercial Street (by the post office). Cosy café serving generously filled rolls to eat in or take away, as well as cakes, teas, real cappuccino and good ice cream. No smoking. Closed Sun.

Havly Centre 9 Charlotte St. Spacious Norwegian lunchtime café much frequented by locals and tourists, with big comfy sofas and armchairs and a kids' corner; it offers home-made cakes, bread and pizzas. Closed Sun & Mon.

Osla's Café Mounthooly Street. Snug, basement café with outdoor seating, decked out in bright Aztec colours, specializing in savoury and sweet pancakes. Closed Sun.

Peerie Café Esplanade. Funky designer shop/gallery/café in an old lodberry, with imaginative cakes and sandwiches, and what is probably Britain's northernmost latte. Closed Sun.

Restaurants

Fort Café 2 Commercial St. Lerwick's best fish-and-chip shop, situated below Fort Charlotte: take away or eat inside in the small café. Closed Sun.

Great Wall Viking Bus Station ☎01595/693988. A Chinese/Thai restaurant located above the bus station. Highly rated by the locals.

Kvelsdro House Hotel Greenfield Place ☎01595/692195. The traditional bar meals or *table d'hôte*, served in the modern cocktail bar overlooking Bressay Sound, are above average in price and quality.

Monty's Bistro 5 Mounthooly St ☎01595/696555. Unpretentious place serving inexpensive and delicious meals and snacks at lunchtimes, and accomplished contemporary cooking – the best in Lerwick – in the evening, with friendly service. Moderately expensive. Closed Sun & Mon.

Raba Indian Restaurant 26 Commercial Rd ☎01595/695585. A consistently excellent curry house, with cheerful, efficient service and reasonable prices.

Drinking, nightlife and entertainment

The downstairs bar in the *Thule* on the Esplanade is an archetypal rough-and-ready seaport **pub**, usually heaving with serious drinkers. The friendliest place in town is the upstairs bar in the *Lounge*, up Mounthooly Street, where local musicians often do sessions. If you're desperate to keep going until the early hours, the town has two main dance venues: *Posers* (Wed & Fri), a small **nightclub** at the back of the *Grand Hotel* on Commercial Street, or the *North Star* up Harbour Street (Sat only). Better than either of these, though, is *Klub Revolution*, the Friday night sessions at Shetland Country Music Club on Commercial Road. The *Garrison Theatre*, by the Town Hall, shows **films** as well as putting on occasional theatre productions, comedy acts and live gigs. The Islesburgh Community Centre has introduced regular crafts and culture evenings (mid-May to mid-Sept

Wed & Fri), where you can buy local knitwear and listen to traditional music.

Music features very strongly in Shetland life and every style has an enthusiastic following. The emphasis in traditional music is firmly instrumental, not vocal, with substantial numbers of young people learning the fiddle. In late April, musicians from all over the world converge on Shetland for the excellent **Shetland Folk Festival**, which embraces a wider range of musical styles than the title might suggest; there are concerts and dances in every corner of the islands. For details, contact the Folk Festival Society at 5 Burns Lane, Lerwick ZE1 0EL (ⓣ01595/694757, ⓦwww.sffs.shetland.co.uk). In mid-October, there's an **Accordion and Fiddle Festival**: similar format, same co-ordinating office, but a different musical focus. Throughout the year, there are **traditional dances** in local halls all over Shetland; the whole community turns up and you can watch, or join in with, dances like the Boston Two-Step, Quadrilles or the Foula Reel. There are also **gigs** featuring a surprising number of accomplished local groups; rock-tinged folk styles are particularly strong. Legendary local fiddler Aly Bain (see p.792) makes occasional appearances on the islands. For details of **what's on**, listen in to *Good Evening Shetland* on BBC Radio Shetland, 92.7FM (Mon–Fri 5.30pm), buy the *Shetland Times* on Fridays, or consult ⓦwww.shetlandtoday.co.uk. Some events are also advertised on Shetland's independent radio station SIBC, 96.2FM. To pick up a CD or cassette of traditional Shetland music, head for High Level Music, up the steps by the chemist on the Market Cross.

Not surprisingly, another Shetland passion is **boating and yachting**, and regattas take place most summer weekends, in different venues throughout the islands. The sport of **yoal racing** has a big following, too, and teams from different districts compete passionately in large six-oared boats which used to serve as the backbone of Shetland's fishing industry.

Listings

Airports Tingwall Airport ⓣ01595/840246; Sumburgh Airport ⓣ01950/460654.
Banks Clydesdale, Bank of Scotland and Royal Bank of Scotland are all on Commercial Street; Lloyds TSB is the gleaming and locally controversial structure on the Esplanade.
Bike rental Grantfield Garage, Commercial Road (Mon–Sat 8am–5pm, Sun 11am–5pm; ⓣ01595/692709).
Bookshops Shetland Times Bookshop, 73–79 Commercial St (Mon–Sat 9am–6pm, Thurs until 7pm; ⓣ01595/695531, ⓦwww.shetlandtoday.co.uk/shop).
Bus information ⓣ01595/694100.
Car rental Bolts Car Hire, 26 North Rd (ⓣ01595/693636); John Leask & Sons, Esplanade (ⓣ01595/693162); Star Rent-a-Car, 22 Commercial Rd (ⓣ01595/692075). All of these also have offices at Sumburgh Airport.
Consulates Denmark, Iceland, Netherlands and Sweden: Hay & Co., 66 Commercial Rd (ⓣ01595/692533); Finland, France, Germany and Norway: Shearer Shipping Services, Garthspool (ⓣ01595/692556).
Internet access At the tourist office (£2 for 20min).
Laundry There is no self-service laundry in Shetland. Lerwick Laundry, 36 Market St (closed Sat lunch & Sun; ⓣ01595/693043), charges for each item.
Medical care The Gilbert Bain Hospital (ⓣ01595/743000), and the Lerwick Health Centre (ⓣ01595/693201), are opposite each other on Scalloway Road.
Newspapers Daily newspapers arrive in Lerwick around noon (weather permitting); the *Shetland Times* comes out every Friday.
Post office Commercial Street (Mon–Fri 9am–5pm, Sat 9am–12.30pm); there's a sub-post office in the Toll Clock Shopping Centre, 26 North Rd.
Sports centre The large, modern Clickimin Leisure Centre is in Lochside, on the west side of town by Loch Clickimin (ⓣ01595/694555), with a superb leisure pool, café and bar.
Travel agents John Leask & Son, Esplanade (ⓣ01595/693162, ⓦwww.leaskstravel.co.uk); Shetland Travelscope, Toll Clock Shopping Centre, 26 North Rd (ⓣ01595/696644, ⓦwww.shetland-travelscope.co.uk).

Bressay and Noss

Shielding Lerwick from the full force of the North Sea is the island of **Bressay**, dominated at its southern end by the conical Ward Hill (744ft) – "da Wart" – and accessible on an hourly car and passenger ferry from Lerwick (takes 5min). At the end of the nineteenth century, Bressay had a population of around eight hundred, due mostly to the prosperity brought by the Dutch herring fleet; now about 350 people live here. To find out more on the history of the island, visit the **Bressay Heritage Centre** (phone ⓣ01595/820368 for opening times), by the ferry terminal in **MARYFIELD**. A short distance to the north lies **Gardie House**, built in 1724 and, in its Neoclassical detail, one of the finest of Shetland's laird houses, where the likes of Sir Walter Scott and minor royalty once stayed.

In 1917, convoys of merchant ships would gather in Bressay Sound before travelling by naval escort across the Atlantic. Huge World War I gun batteries at Score Hill on Aith Ness in the north, and on Bard Head in the south, were constructed, and now provide a focus for a couple of interesting cliff and coastal walks. Another fine walk can be made to **Bressay Lighthouse**, three miles south of the ferry terminal at Kirkibuster Ness, built by the Stevensons in the 1850s. There are plans to turn the lighthouse and its shore station into a Marine Heritage Centre and camping böd (call Shetland Amenity Trust ⓣ01595/694688 for the latest). Until the camping böd is open, your best bet for **accommodation** is the *Maryfield House Hotel* near the ferry terminal (ⓣ01595/820207; ❸), which is friendly and serves good-value meals in the restaurant and cosy bar.

Noss

The chief reason most visitors pass through Bressay is in order to visit the tiny but spectacular island of **Noss** – the name means "a point of rock" – just off Bressay's eastern shore. Sloping gently into the sea at its western end, and plunging vertically from over 500ft at its eastern end, Noss has the dramatic and distinctive outline of a half-sunk ocean liner. The island was inhabited until World War II but is now a National Nature Reserve and sheep farm, partly managed by Scottish Natural Heritage (ⓣ01595/693345), who operate an inflatable as a **ferry** from Bressay (mid-May to Aug daily except Tues & Fri 10am–5pm; takes 2min; £3 return). The ferry departs from the landing stage below the car park overlooking Noss Sound, two miles from Maryfield – an easy stroll or short journey on bikes rented in Lerwick beforehand. A morning postcar takes over two hours to reach Noss Sound from Mayfield. If the weather is abnormally windy, check with the Lerwick tourist office that the Noss ferry is running before setting off.

A good alternative is to join one of the **boat trips** that set out from Lerwick to see the rock arches and caves of Bressay and the cliffs and nesting seabirds on Noss: try those run by Shetland Wildlife Tours (daily except Wed & Sun; ⓣ01950/460254).

On the island, the old farmhouse or Haa of Gungstie contains a small **visitor centre** (open whenever the ferry is operating), where the warden will give you a quick briefing and a free map and guide. Nearby is a sandy beach, perfect for a picnic in fine weather, while behind the Haa is a **Pony Pund**, a square stone enclosure built for the breeding of Shetland ponies. A stud was established here in the latter years of the nineteenth century, when the Marquis of Londonderry needed ponies to replace the women and children who had been displaced by new laws from his coal mines in County Durham. The animals were specially bred to produce "as much weight as possible and as near the ground as it can be got". The stud only lasted for about twenty years and was closed in 1899, superseded by English studs able to meet the demand at lower cost. There are no ponies on Noss today, but it's said that the influence of the breeding programme can still be seen in those roaming other parts of Shetland.

As Noss is only one mile wide, it's easy enough to make an entire circumference of the island in one day. If you do, make sure you keep close to the coast, since otherwise the great skuas (locally known as "bonxies") will dive-bomb you. The most memorable feature of Noss is its coastline of cliffs, rising to a peak at the massive 500-foot **Noup**, from which can be seen vast colonies of cliff-nesting gannets, puffins, guillemots, shags, razorbills and fulmars: a truly wonderful sight and one of the highlights of Shetland. One of the features on the walk is the **Holm of Noss**; until 1864, it was connected to the main island by an extraordinary device called a cradle, a sort of basket suspended on ropes which was intended to allow access for the grazing of sheep. The Foula man who allegedly installed it in the seventeenth century is said to have died when, preferring to climb back down the cliffs, he fell.

South Mainland

Shetland's **South Mainland** is a long, thin finger of land, only three or four miles wide, but 25 miles long, ending in the cliffs of **Sumburgh Head** and **Fitful Head**. The main road hugs the eastern side of the Clift Hills which form the peninsula's backbone; on the west side, there's no road between Scalloway and Maywick, except for a short spur from Easter to Wester Quarff. It's a beautiful area with wild landscapes but also good farmland, and has yielded some of Shetland's most impressive archeological treasures – in particular, **Jarlshof**.

Cunningsburgh

The view opens up to the south soon after leaving Lerwick, at the shoulder of Shurton Hill above Gulberwick. To appreciate the coastal scenery here, it's best to leave the main road at Fladdabister, a favourite haunt of local artists who come to sketch and paint among the ruins of the old crofts and where, in summer, the meadows are a mass of wild flowers. In **CUNNINGSBURGH**, the first large settlement, the best views are again from the back roads to the east through the hamlets and hay meadows of Aith and Voxter. Hostel **accommodation** is available at the *Cunningsburgh Village Club* (Ⓣ01950/477241; June–Aug), which has dorm beds, good showers and a well-equipped kitchen.

Half a mile or so south of the Mail junction, the main road crosses the Catpund Burn. From the westward loop of the old road at this point, it's possible to scramble up the valley for about 300 yards to a remarkable prehistoric industrial site, the **Catpund Quarries**. In Norse times, this area was the biggest soapstone (steatite) quarry in Britain. Products would have included various types of bowl, weights for fishing nets or for looms, and possibly items of jewellery. It's not difficult to see where vessels were carved directly from the rock. Goods from here almost certainly found their way to Norse communities in Britain, Ireland, Iceland, Faroe and mainland Europe. The small area revealed by the 1988 excavation of the site is fenced off and a board gives more information, but there's similar evidence over much of the valley floor.

Mousa

The island of **Mousa**, which lies off the east coast of South Mainland, about halfway down the peninsula, boasts the most amazingly well-preserved broch in the whole of Scotland. Rising to more than 40ft, and looking rather like a Stone Age cooling tower, **Mousa Broch** has a remarkable presence, and features in both *Egil's Saga* and the *Orkneyinga Saga*, contemporary chronicles of Norse exploration and settlement. In the former, a couple eloping from Norway to Iceland around 900 AD take refuge in it after being shipwrecked, while in the latter the broch is besieged by an Earl Harald Maddadarson when his mother is abducted and brought here from Orkney by Erlend the Young, who wanted to marry her. To get to the broch, simply head south from the jetty along the western coastline for about half a mile. The low entrance passage leads through two concentric walls to a central courtyard, divided into separate beehive chambers. Between the walls, a rough (very dark) staircase leads to the top parapet; a torch is provided for visitors.

To get to Mousa, take the small **passenger ferry** from Leebitton in the district of Sandwick (mid-April to mid-Sept 1–2 daily; takes 15min; £5 return; ⓣ01950/431367, ⓦwww.mousaboattrips.co.uk), though it's best to ring ahead to check the current schedule. Mousa is only a mile wide, but, if the weather's not too bad, it's easy enough to spend the whole day here. For a start, there are usually lots of grey and common **seals** sunning themselves on the rocks by the East and West Pool, at the southeastern corner of the island, plus black guillemots (or "tysties" as they're known in Shetland) breeding along the low-lying coast, and arctic tern colonies inland. Elsewhere, there are the remains of several buildings, some of which were inhabited until the mid-nineteenth century. From late May to late July, a large colony of around five thousand **storm petrels** breeds in and around the broch walls, fishing out at sea during the day, and only returning to the nests after dark. The ferry also runs special late-night trips (Wed & Sat weather permitting), setting off in the "simmer dim" twilight around 11pm. Even if you've no interest in the storm petrels, which appear like bats as they flit about in the half-light, the chance to explore the broch at midnight is worth it alone.

Levenwick and Boddam

In Hoswick, halfway between Sandwick and Levenwick, is **Da Warp and Weft** (May–Sept Mon–Sat 10am–5pm, Sun noon–5pm; free), a visitor centre run alongside Laurence J. Smith's traditional knitwear showroom, offering an introduction to the history of local knitwear as well as teas and snacks. At Channerwick on the main road south, it's possible to cross to the west side of the Mainland for St Ninian's Isle (see p.732). Staying on the east side, the next settlement is **LEVENWICK**, where there's a lovely beach of white sand and another broch site. There's also a small, terraced **campsite** run by the local community (ⓣ01950/422207; May–Sept), which has hot showers, a tennis court and a superb view over the east coast.

Just beyond **BODDAM**, a back road winds around the southern shore of the nearby voe to the **Shetland Crofthouse Museum** (May–Sept daily 10am–1pm & 2–5pm; ⓦwww.shetland-museum.org.uk; £2), housed in a thatched croft built around 1870. The museum portrays nineteenth-century crofting life with traditional furniture and fittings, including spinning wheels, high-backed Shetland chairs and baskets woven from heather fibres.

St Ninian's Isle to Quendale

On the west coast, near **BIGTON** village, a signposted track leads down to a spectacular sandy causeway, or **tombolo**, leading to **St Ninian's Isle**. The tombolo – a concave strip of sand with Atlantic breakers crashing on either side, the best example of its kind in Britain – is usually exposed, letting you can walk over to the island, where there are the ruins of a church probably dating from the twelfth century and built on the site of an earlier, Pictish, one. The site was excavated in the 1950s and **treasure**, a hoard of 28 objects of Pictish silver, was found hidden in a larch box beneath a slab in the earlier building's floor; the larch probably came from the European mainland, as it didn't grow in Britain at that time. The treasure included bowls, a spoon and brooches and probably dates from around 800 AD; it may have been hastily hidden during a Norse raid. Replicas are in the Shetland Museum in Lerwick and the originals can be seen in the Museum of Antiquities in Edinburgh.

South of Bigton, the coast is spectacular: cliffs alternate with beaches and the vivid greens and yellows of the farmland contrast with black rocks and a sea which may be grey, deep blue or turquoise. The **Loch of Spiggie**, which used to be a sea inlet, is an RSPB reserve known particularly for large autumn flocks of almost four hundred whooper swans, but several types of duck as well as greylag geese and waders can be seen, depending on the time of year. Otters also thrive here. There's information about the reserve at the RSPB hide on the northern shore. On the other side of the road, there's a long, reasonably sheltered sandy beach known as the **Scousburgh Sands**.

A few miles south of the loch lies **QUENDALE**, overlooking a sandy south-facing bay. The village contains the beautifully restored full-size **Quendale Watermill** (May–Sept daily 10am–5pm; £1.50), built in the 1860s but not in operation since the early 1970s. You can explore the interior and watch a short video of the mill working, and there's a tearoom attached. Not far from here, near the head of the rocky inlet of Cro Geo, on the other side of Garth's Ness, lies a rusting ship's bow, all that remains of the **Braer oil tanker**, a Liberian-registered, American-owned ship that ran onto the rocks here at 11.13am on January 5, 1993, a wild Tuesday morning etched in the memory of every Shetlander. Although the *Braer* released twice the quantity of oil spilt even by the *Exxon Valdez* in Alaska, the damage was less serious than it might have been, due to the oil being churned and ultimately cleansed by huge waves built by hurricane-force winds which, unusually even for Shetland, blew for most of January.

The best place to **stay** in the South Mainland is, without a doubt, the *Spiggie Hotel* (Ⓣ01950/460563; ❷), overlooking the loch, which has a bar and **restaurant**, both of which share the same inexpensive menu.

Sumburgh

From Boddam southwards, in the area known as **Dunrossness**, the landscape changes to a rolling agricultural one often compared with that of Orkney, but is still dominated from the west by the great brooding mass of Fitful Head, to the southwest. The main road leads to **SUMBURGH**, whose **airport** is busy with helicopters and aircraft shuttling to and from the North Sea oilfields, as well as passenger services.

By the main road, just west of the airport, excavations are currently underway at **Old Scatness** (July to early Aug daily except Fri 10am–5.30pm; £2), where a broch, and possibly the best-preserved Iron Age house in Europe, have recently been discovered. Whilst the dig is in progress (for a month or so in the height of summer), you can get a guided tour of the site, and for kids there's a taste of life in Norse and Pictish times provided by costumed guides.

The Mainland comes to a dramatic end at **Sumburgh Head**, which rises sharply out of the land only to drop vertically into the sea about a mile or so southeast of Jarlshof. The **lighthouse**, on the top of the cliff, was built by Robert Stevenson in 1821, and is not open to the public. However, its grounds offer great views northwards to Noss and south to Fair Isle, as well as being the perfect site for watching nesting seabirds such as kittiwakes, fulmars, shags and guillemots, not to mention gannets diving for fish. This is also the easiest place in Shetland to get close to **puffins**: during the nesting season (May to mid-Aug), you simply need look over the western wall, just before you enter the lighthouse complex, to see them arriving at their burrows a few yards below with beakfuls of sand eels or giving flying lessons to their offspring. However, on no account should you try to climb over the wall.

Jarlshof

Of all the archeological sites in Shetland, **Jarlshof** (April–Sept daily 9.30am–6.30pm; £2.50; HS; Oct–March open access to grounds; free) is the largest and most impressive. What makes Jarlshof so amazing is the fact that you can walk right into a house built 1600 years ago, which is still intact to above head height. The site is big and confusing, scattered with the ruins of buildings dating from the Stone Age to the early seventeenth century. The name, which is misleading as it is not primarily a Viking site, was coined by Sir Walter Scott, who decided to use the ruins of the Old House in his novel *The Pirate*. However, it was only at the end of the nineteenth century that the Bronze Age, Iron Age and Viking settlements you see now were discovered, after a violent storm ripped off the top layer of turf.

The site guidebook, available from the small **visitor centre** where you buy tickets, is very badly designed, and you'd be just as well off using the information panels. The Bronze Age smithy and Iron Age dwellings nearest the entrance, dating from the first and second millennia BC, are as nothing compared with the cells which cluster around the **broch**, close to the sea. Only half of the original broch survives, and its courtyard is now an Iron Age aisled roundhouse, with stone piers. However, it's difficult to distinguish the broch from the later Pictish **wheelhouses** which now surround it. Still, it's all great fun to explore, as, unlike at Skara Brae in Orkney, you're still free to roam around the cells, checking out the in-built stone shelving, water tanks, beds and so on. Inland lies the maze of grass-topped foundations marking out the **Viking longhouses**, dating from the ninth century AD and covering a much larger area than the earlier structures. Towering over the whole complex are the ruins of the laird's house, built by Robert Stewart, Earl of Orkney and Lord of Shetland, in the late sixteenth century, and the **Old House of Sumburgh**, built by his son, Earl Patrick.

Practicalities

The only place to get something to **eat** is the Scottish Baronial *Sumburgh Hotel*, next door to Jarlshof, where the bar meals are surprisingly good. There's also a camping böd in *Betty Mouat's Cottage*, a reconstructed traditional crofthouse that provides basic **accommodation** (book through Lerwick tourist office; April–Oct). Betty Mouat herself was quite a character. In January 1886, at the age of sixty, she set off for Lerwick in the smack *Columbine* crewed by three local men. A storm swept the skipper overboard and the other two jumped in to try to rescue him; they failed, the skipper drowned and the two men, though they survived, lost contact with the smack. Betty and her boat were battered by the storm for nine days and nights, finally running ashore north of Aalesund in Norway. Astonishingly, she survived this experience, existing on some milk which she had with her. She returned to Shetland to become a celebrity, living into her nineties.

Fair Isle

Fair Isle measures just three miles by one-and-a-half, marooned in the sea halfway between Shetland and Orkney and very different from both. The weather reflects its isolated position: you can almost guarantee that it'll be windy, though if you're lucky your visit might coincide with fine weather – what the islanders call "a given day".

At one time Fair Isle's population was not far short of four hundred, but Clearances forced emigration from the middle of the nineteenth century. By the 1950s, the population had shrunk to just 44, a point at which evacuation and abandonment of the island was seriously considered. **George Waterston**, who'd bought the island and set up a bird observatory in 1948, passed it into the care of the NTS in 1954 and rejuvenation began. Since then, islanders, the Trust and the Shetland Islands Council have invested in many improvements to housing, the harbour and basic services, including an advanced electricity system integrating wind and diesel generation. Crafts including boatbuilding, the making of fiddles, felt and stained glass have been developed and today Fair Isle supports a vibrant community of around seventy people.

The north end of the island rises like a wall; the Sheep Rock, a sculpted stack of rock and grass on the east side, is one of its most dramatic features. The croft land and the island's scattered houses are concentrated in the south, but the focus for many visitors is the **Bird Observatory**, built just above the sandy bay of North Haven where the ferry from Shetland Mainland arrives. It's one of the major European centres for ornithology and its work in watching, trapping, recording and ringing birds goes on all year. Fair Isle is a landfall for a huge number and range of migrant birds during the spring and autumn passages. Migration routes converge here and more than 345 species, including many rarities, have been noted. As a result, Fair Isle is a haven for twitchers; for more casual birders, however, there's also plenty of resident birdlife to enjoy. The high-pitched screeching that fills the sky above the airstrip comes from hundreds of arctic terns, and arctic skuas can also be seen here. Those in search of puffins should head for the cliffs around Furse, while to find gannets head to the spectacular Stacks of Scroo.

Fair Isle is, of course, even better known for its **knitting** patterns, still produced with great skill by the local knitwear co-operative, though not in the quantities which you might imagine from a walk around city department stores; from time to time there are displays at the Community Hall, by the island school (usually on a Monday, or when a cruise ship calls by). If the Hall is closed, then you'll have to make do with the samples on display at the island's **museum** (Mon 2–5pm, Wed 10am–noon, Fri 2–4.30pm; ⓣ01595/760244; free), which is named after George Waterston and situated next door to the island's Methodist Chapel. Particularly memorable are stories of shipwrecks; in 1868 the islanders undertook a heroic rescue of all 465 German emigrants aboard the *Lessing*. More famously the *El Gran Grifon*, part of the retreating Spanish Armada, was lost here in 1588 and three hundred Spanish seamen were washed up on the island. Food was in such short supply that fifty died of starvation before help could be summoned from Shetland. The idea that the islanders borrowed all their patterns from the shipwrecked Spanish seamen is nowadays regarded as a patronizing myth.

Fair Isle has two **lighthouses**, one at either end of the island, both designed by the Stevenson family and erected in 1892. Before that, the Vikings used to light beacons to signal an enemy fleet advancing, and in the nineteenth century a semaphore consisting of a tall wooden pole was used; it can still be seen on the hill above South Lighthouse. The North Lighthouse was considered to be on such an exposed spot that the foghorn was operated from within. Both lighthouses were automated in 1998, and the South Lighthouse had the distinction of the being the last manned lighthouse in the country.

Practicalities

For matters of administration and transport, Fair Isle is linked to Shetland. The passenger **ferry** connects Fair Isle with either Lerwick (on alternate Thurs; takes 4hr 30min) or Grutness in Sumburgh (Tues, Sat & alternate Thurs; takes 2hr 40min). For bookings, contact J.W. Stout in advance on ⓣ01595/760222. The crossing can be very rough at times, so if you're at all susceptible to seasickness it might be worth considering catching a **flight** from Tingwall (Mon, Wed, Fri & Sat) or Sumburgh (Sat); a one-way ticket costs £38, and day-trips are possible on Mondays, Wednesdays and Fridays.

Camping is not permitted, but there is full-board **accommodation** at the *Fair Isle Lodge & Bird Observatory* (ⓣ01595/760258, ⓦwww.fairislebirdobs.co.uk; ❹) in twins and singles or hostel-style dorms. To guests and visitors alike, the Bird Observatory offers tea, coffee and good home cooking for lunch and dinner; you might even be able to lend a hand with the Observatory's research programme. A good **B&B** option – with full-board option – is *Upper Leogh* in the south of the island (ⓣ01595/760248, ⓔkathleen.coull@lineone.net; ❷), where you'll be well looked after. There is a shop/post office nearby (closed Thurs & Sun).

Central Mainland

The districts of Tingwall and Weisdale, plus the old capital of **Scalloway**, make up the **Central Mainland**, an area of minor interest in the grand scheme of things, but one which is very easy to reach from Lerwick. In fine weather, it's a captivating mix of farms, moors and lochs, and includes Shetland's only significant woodland; the scale of the scenery ranges from the intimate to the vast, with particularly spectacular views from high points above Whiteness and Weisdale. The area also holds strong historical associations, with the Norse parliament at **Lawting Holm** and unhappy memories of Earl Patrick Stewart's harsh rule at Scalloway, and nineteenth-century Clearances at Weisdale.

Scalloway

Approaching **SCALLOWAY** from the shoulder of the steep hill to the east known as the **Scord**, there's a dramatic view over the town and the islands to the south and west. Once the capital of Shetland, Scalloway's importance waned through the eighteenth century as Lerwick, just six miles to the east, grew in trading success and status. Nowadays, Scalloway is fairly sleepy, though its prosperity, always closely linked to the fluctuations of the fishing industry,

The Shetland Bus

The story of the **Shetland Bus**, the link between Shetland and Norway that helped to sustain the Norwegian resistance through the years of Nazi occupation, is quite extraordinary. Constantly under threat of attack by enemy aircraft or naval action, small Norwegian fishing boats set out from Shetland to run arms and resistance workers into lonely fjords. The trip took at least 24 hours and on the return journey boats brought back Norwegians in danger of arrest by the Gestapo, or those who wanted to join Norwegian forces fighting with the Allies. For three years, through careful planning, the operation was remarkably successful: instructions to boats were passed in cryptic messages in BBC news broadcasts. Although local people knew what was going on, the secret was generally well kept. In total, 350 refugees were evacuated, and more than four hundred tons of arms, large amounts of explosives and sixty radio transmitters were landed in Norway.

Originally established at **Lunna** in the northeast of the Mainland, the service moved to **Scalloway** in 1942, partly because the village could offer good marine engineering facilities at Moore's Shipyard at the west end of Main Street, where a plaque records the morale-boosting visit of the Norwegian Crown Prince Olav. Many buildings in Scalloway were pressed into use to support the work: explosives and weapons were stored in the castle. **Kergord House** in Weisdale was used as a safe house and training centre for intelligence personnel and saboteurs. The hazards, tragedies and elations of the exercise are brilliantly described in David Howarth's book, *The Shetland Bus*; their legacy today is a heartfelt closeness between Shetland and Norway.

has recently been given a boost with investment in new fish-processing factories, and in the impressive North Atlantic Fisheries College on the west side of the busy harbour.

In spite of modern developments nearby, Scalloway is dominated by the imposing shell of **Scalloway Castle**, a classic fortified tower house built with forced labour in 1600 by the infamous Earl Patrick Stewart, and thus seen as a powerful symbol of oppression. Stewart, who'd succeeded his father Robert to the Earldom of Orkney and Lordship of Shetland in 1592, held court in the castle and gained a reputation for enhancing his own power and wealth through the calculated use of harsh justice, frequently including confiscation of assets. He was eventually arrested and imprisoned in 1609, not for his ill-treatment of Shetlanders, but for his aggressive behaviour towards his fellow landowners; his son, Robert, attempted an insurrection and both were executed in Edinburgh in 1615. The castle was used for a time by Cromwell's army, but had fallen into disrepair by 1700 and is nowadays in the hands of Historic Scotland. The castle itself is well preserved and fun to explore; if the door is locked, the key can be borrowed from the Shetland Woollen Company (Mon–Sat 9am–5pm), next door to the castle.

On Main Street, the small **Scalloway Museum** (May–Sept Mon 9am–2pm, Tues–Sat 9am–2pm & 4.30–7pm; free), run by volunteers, holds a few local relics. It explains the importance of fishing and attempts to tell the story of the **Shetland Bus** (see box). West of Scalloway, there's a pleasant if energetic walk up **Gallows Hill** (2–3hr), where alleged witches were put to death, and then on to the hamlet of Burwick, a former fishing settlement.

Scalloway's best **accommodation** is at the very comfortable and welcoming *Hildasay Guest House* (Ⓣ01595/880822; ❷), a Hansel and Gretel weather-boarded house on the top of the hill above Scalloway, behind the swimming pool. For **food**, head for *Da Haaf* (closed Sat & Sun), the unpretentious licensed restaurant in the North Atlantic Fisheries College, which serves fresh fish, simply prepared, with broad harbour views to enjoy as well.

Trondra and Burra

Southwest of Scalloway – and now connected to the Mainland by bridges – is the island of **Trondra** and, further south, the twin islands of East and West **Burra**, which have some beautiful beaches and some fairly gentle coastal walks.

West Burra has the largest settlement in the area, **HAMNAVOE**, a planned fishing settlement unlike any other in Shetland, established mainly in the early 1900s and still very much a working, seagoing community. Just south of Hamnavoe, a small path leads down from the road to the white sandy beach at **Meal**, deservedly popular on warm summer days. At the southern end of West Burra, at **Banna Minn**, there's another fine beach, with excellent walking nearby on the cliffs of Kettla Ness, linked to the rest of West Burra only by a sliver of tombolo.

East Burra, joined to West Burra at the middle like a Siamese twin, ends at the hamlet of **HOUSS**, distinguished by the tall, ruined laird's house or Haa. From the turning place outside the cattle-grid, continue walking southwards, following the track to the left, down the hill and across the beach, and after about a mile you'll reach the deserted settlement of **Symbister**, inhabited until the 1940s. You can now see ancient field boundaries and, just south of the ruins, a **burnt mound** (an overgrown pile of Neolithic cooking stones dumped when no longer usable). Half a mile further south, the island ends in cliffs, caves and wheeling fulmars. From there, the islet of **South Havra**, topped by the ruins of Shetland's only **windmill**, is just to the southwest. Once supporting a small fishing community, the islet was abandoned, except for the grazing of sheep, by the last eight families in 1923; it was such a perilous existence that children as well as animals had to be tethered to prevent them from falling over the cliffs.

Tingwall

TINGWALL, the name for the loch-studded, fertile valley to the north of Scalloway, takes its name from the **Lawting** or Althing (from *thing*, the Old Norse for "parliament"), in existence from the eleventh to the sixteenth century, where local people and officials gathered to make or amend laws and discuss evidence. From the late thirteenth century, Shetland's laws were based on those of the Norwegian king Magnus the Lawmender; after the sixteenth century, judicial affairs were dealt with in Patrick Stewart's new castle at Scalloway. The Lawting was situated at **Law Ting Holm**, the small peninsula at the northern end of Loch Tingwall, that was once an island linked to the shore by a causeway. Although structures on the holm have long since vanished, there's an information board which helps in visualizing the scene. At the southwest corner of the loch, a seven-foot **standing stone** by the roadside is said to mark the spot where, after a dispute at the Lawting in 1389, Earl Henry Sinclair killed his cousin and rival, Marise Sperra, together with seven of his followers.

Just north of the loch is **Tingwall Kirk**, unexceptional from the outside, but preserving its attractive late eighteenth-century interior. In the burial ground, there's a dank, turf-covered **burial aisle** from the old medieval church that was demolished in 1788. Inside are several very old gravestones, including one to a local official called a *Foud* – a representative of the king – who died in 1603. The ornate seventeenth-century sarcophagus in the graveyard was used as a social meeting point and resting place by locals who arrived early for the Sunday service.

Tingwall Airport (Ⓣ01595/840246) is easily accessible by taxi from Lerwick or Scalloway. One of the best places to **stay**, within easy striking distance of the airstrip, is the modern B&B of *South Haven* (Ⓣ01595/840350; ❸), located in Nesbister overlooking Whiteness Voe; the proprietor couldn't be more accommodating and helpful, and the rooms are very spacious. You can **eat**, or enjoy some draught Shetland ale whilst enjoying the view, at the *Westings Hotel*, a short way back up the A971. The distinctive red *Herrislea House Hotel* (Ⓣ01595/840208; ❺) overlooks the airstrip by the main crossroads; its spacious **bar**, the idiosyncratically decorated *Starboard Tack*, doubles as Tingwall's social centre, serves good pub food and regularly features live **traditional music** (currently on Tuesdays).

Weisdale

Weisdale, five miles or so northwest of Tingwall, is notable primarily for **Weisdale Mill** (Wed–Sat 10.30am–4.30pm, Sun noon–4.30pm; free), situated up the B9075 from the head of Weisdale Voe. Built for milling grain in 1855, this is now an attractively converted arts centre, housing the small, beautifully designed **Bonhoga Gallery**, in which touring and local exhibitions of painting, sculpture and other media are shown. Don't miss the small but fascinating **Shetland Textile Working Museum** in the basement (Wed–Sat 10.30am–4pm, Sun noon–4pm; £1), which puts on temporary exhibitions, and has pull-out drawers showing the knitted patterns unique to Shetland and Fair Isle. There's also a very pleasant café, serving soup, scones and snacks in the south-facing conservatory overlooking the stream.

Weisdale is an evocative name in Shetland, for in this valley some of the cruellest Clearances of people in favour of sheep took place in the middle of the nineteenth century. The perpetrator was David Dakers Black, a farmer from the county of Angus who began buying land in 1843. Hundreds of tenants were dispossessed and in 1850 the large **Kergord House**, then called Flemington, was built towards the northern end of the valley from the stones of some of the older houses. The ruined shells of some of the rest still stand on the valley sides; local writers, particularly John J. Graham, have recounted the period in novels (notably his *Shadowed Valley*) and drama.

Around Kergord House and on the upper valley sides there are several **tree plantations** dating mainly from around 1920 but with a later experimental addition by the Forestry Commission. An amazing range of species is present, from the sycamores and willows which thrive in many Shetland gardens to examples of chestnut, copper beech, monkey puzzle and much else besides. Along with the trees comes a woodland ecosystem, with foxgloves, Britain's most northerly rookery and a reliable cuckoo. During the war, Kergord House played a role in the Shetland Bus operation (see box on p.736); the saboteurs who trained here are said to have amused visitors by demonstrating booby traps and incendiary devices in the garden.

South of Kergord House and Weisdale Mill around the head of Weisdale Voe, it's possible to turn southwards along the west shore where, among trees near the voe's narrowest point, is the ruined house once occupied by **John Cluness Ross** (1786–1853). Ross travelled to the Indian Ocean and settled in the Cocos Islands, going into coconut farming and appointing himself king; he was the first in a family dynasty of three which ruled – some would say oppressed – the Cocos islanders for decades.

The Westside

The western Mainland of Shetland – known as the **Westside** – stretches west from Weisdale and Voe to Sandness. Although there are some important archeological remains and wildlife in the area, the area's greatest appeal lies in its outstanding **coastal scenery** and walks. At its heart, the Westside's rolling brown and purple moorland, dotted with patches of bright-green reseeded land, glistens with dozens of small, picturesque blue or silver lochs. On the west coast the rounded form of Sandness Hill (750ft) falls steeply away into the Atlantic. The coastal scenery, cut by several deep voes, is very varied; aside from dramatic cliffs, there are intimate coves and some fine beaches, as well as, just offshore, the stunning island of **Papa Stour**.

Bixter and around

The chief crossroads for the area is **BIXTER**, a place of no particular consequence from where you can travel south to Skeld and Reawick, west to Walls, West Burrafirth and Sandness, or northwest along a scenic winding road towards **AITH** and eventually Voe (see p.742). There isn't a lot at Aith, either, except a shop and school, and an attractive little harbour that serves as the base for the west of Shetland lifeboat. Northwest of Aith, the road ends at the farm of **Vementry**, also, confusingly, the name of the nearby island that boasts the best-preserved **heel-shaped cairn** in Shetland, right on top of the highest hill, Muckle Ward (298ft). There are also two excellently preserved **six-inch guns** from World War I on Swarbucks Head, in the north of the island. To reach the island, enquire locally or through Lerwick tourist office (see p.724).

Southwest of Bixter, on the picturesque Sandsting peninsula, there are two beautiful terracotta-coloured **sandy bays** at Reawick, and excellent **coastal walks** to be had along the coast around Westerwick and Culswick, past red granite cliffs, caves and stacks. Three miles southwest of Bixter lies the finest Neolithic structure in the Westside, dubbed the **Staneydale Temple** by the archeologist who excavated it because it resembled a temple on Malta. Whatever its true function, it was twice as large as the surrounding oval-shaped houses (now in ruins) and was certainly of great importance, perhaps as some kind of community centre. The horseshoe-shaped foundations measure more than 40ft by 20ft internally, with immensely thick walls, still around 4ft high, whose roof would have been supported by spruce posts (two postholes can still be clearly seen). To reach the temple, take the path marked out by black-and-white poles across the moorland for half a mile from the road. There's another significant prehistoric sight, the **Scord of Brouster**, near the Brig of Waas, where the Walls and Sandness roads divide. A helpful information board provides an explanation of the layout of various ruined houses and field boundaries, making it easier to imagine what life might have been like for the people who lived on this hillside between 3000 and 1500 BC.

Walls and Sandness

Once an important fishing port, **WALLS** (pronounced "*waas*"), appealingly set round its harbour, is now a quiet village which comes alive once a year in the middle of August for the Walls Agricultural Show, the biggest farming bash on the island. At other times, you can visit the small **Walls Museum** (Thurs–Sun 2–6pm; free), mostly of knitwear, but also displaying a typical croft interior from the turn of the century, and sundry bits of nauticalia. Walls also boasts by far the best **accommodation** options on the Westside. The beautifully restored *Voe House* (book through Lerwick tourist office; April–Oct) is the largest camping böd on Shetland; the modest price includes peat for the fires. The best B&B around is the wonderfully welcoming *Skeoverick* (Ⓣ01595/809349; ❶), a lovely modern croft house which lies a mile or so north of Walls. The only hotel in the area is *Burrastow House* (Ⓣ01595/809307, Ⓦwww.users.zetnet.co.uk/burrastow-house-hotel; ❼), beautifully situated about three miles southwest of Walls; the house itself dates back to 1759, and has real character, with wood panelling, a traditional Victorian sit-down bathtub, and a conservatory. *Burrastow House* is also one of the best places to **eat** in the whole of Shetland, offering distinguished cooking in idyllic surroundings; meals, though expensive, are superb, and booking ahead is pretty much essential.

A short distance across the sea lies the island of **Vaila**, from where in 1837 Lerwick philanthropist Arthur Anderson operated a fishing station in an unsuccessful attempt to break down the system of fishing tenures under which tenants were forced to fish for the landlords under pain of eviction. The ruins of Anderson's fishing station still stand on the shore, but the most conspicuous monument is **Vaila Hall**, the largest laird's house on Shetland, originally built in 1696, but massively enlarged by a wealthy Yorkshire mill-owner, Herbert Anderton, who bought the island in 1893. Anderton also restored the island's ancient watchtower of Mucklaberry Castle, built a Buddhist temple (now sadly in ruins), and had a cannon fired whenever he arrived on the island. The island is currently owned by an eccentric young Polish woman and her partner; if you wish to visit, enquire at *Burrastow House*.

At the end of a long winding road across an undulating, uninhabited, boulder-strewn landscape, you eventually reach the fertile scattered crofting settlement of **SANDNESS** (pronounced "*saaness*"), which you can also reach by walking along the coast from Walls past the dramatic Deepdale and across Sandness Hill. It's an oasis of green meadows in the peat moorland, with a nice beach, too. The modern **Jamieson's Spinning Mill** at Sandness (Mon–Fri 8am–5pm; free) is the only one on Shetland producing pure Shetland wool; the factory welcomes visitors, and you can watch how workers take the fleece and then wash, card and spin the exceptionally fine Shetland wool into yarn.

Papa Stour

A mile offshore from Sandness is the quintessentially peaceful island of **Papa Stour**, created out of volcanic lava and ash which has subsequently been eroded into some of the most impressive coastal scenery in Shetland. In good weather, it makes for a perfect day-trip, but in foul weather or a sea mist it can certainly appear pretty bleak. Its name, which means "big island of the priests", derives from its early Celtic Christian connections, and the island was home, in the eighteenth century, to people who were mistakenly believed to have been lepers (though in fact they were suffering from a hereditary skin disease caused by severe malnutrition). The land is very fertile, and in the nineteenth century Papa Stour supported around three hundred inhabitants, but by the early 1970s there was a population crisis: the island's school closed, and the remaining sixteen inhabitants were all past child-bearing age; worse still, it looked like the post office would close and the mailboat be withdrawn. The islanders made appeals for new blood to revive the fragile economy and managed to stage a dramatic recovery, releasing croft land to young settlers from Britain and overseas. Papa Stour was briefly dubbed "the hippie isle", but it wasn't long before some newcomers moved on, to other parts of Shetland or elsewhere, making a further appeal necessary in the early 1990s. Today the island supports a community of thirty or so.

Papa Stour's main settlement, **BIGGINGS**, lies in the west near the pier, and it was here that excavation in the early 1980s revealed the remains of a thirteenth-century Norse house, which is thought to have belonged to Duke Haakon, heir to the Norwegian throne. There's an explanatory panel, but nothing much to see – in any case, the chief reason to come to Papa Stour is to go **walking**; to reach the best of the coastal scenery, head for the far west of the island. From **Virda Field** (285ft), the highest point, in the far northwest, you can see the treacherous rocks of Ve Skerries, three miles or so northwest off the coast, where a lighthouse was erected as recently as 1979. The couple of miles of coastline from here southeast to Hamna Voe has some of the island's best stacks, blowholes and natural arches. Probably the most spectacular formation of all is the **Christie's Hole**, a gloup or partly roofed cleft, which extends far inland from the cliff line, and where shags nest on precipitous ledges. Other points of interest include a couple of defunct horizontal click-mills, below Dutch Loch, and the remains of a "meal road", so called because the workmen were paid in oatmeal or flour. Several pairs of red-throated divers breed on inland lochs such as Gorda Water.

Practicalities

In summer, the passenger **ferry** runs from West Burrafirth on the Westside to Papa Stour (Mon, Wed & Fri–Sun). Always book in advance, and reconfirm the day before departure (ⓣ01595/810460); day-trips are only possible on Friday, Saturday and Sunday. There's also a **flight** from Tingwall Airport every Tuesday, and again a day-trip is feasible; tickets cost just £16 one way. Papa Stour's airstrip is southwest of Biggings, by the school. The only accommodation on the island is *North House* **B&B** (ⓣ01595/873238; ❶), with optional full board, who can arrange boat trips around the stacks and sea caves. There's no shop, so even day-trippers should bring their own picnic with them.

Foula

Southwest of Walls, at "the edge of the world", **Foula** is without a doubt the most isolated inhabited island in the British Isles, separated from the nearest point on Mainland Shetland by about fourteen miles of often turbulent ocean. Seen from the Mainland, its distinctive mountainous form changes subtly, depending upon the vantage point, but the outline is unforgettable. Its western **cliffs**, the second highest in Britain after those of St Kilda, rise at **The Kame** to some 1220ft above sea level; a clear day at The Kame offers a magnificent panorama stretching from Unst to Fair Isle. On a bad day, the exposure is complete and the cliffs generate turbulent blasts of wind known in Shetland as "flans", which rip through the hills with tremendous force.

Foula has been inhabited since prehistoric times, and the people here take pride in their separateness from Shetland, cherishing local traditions such as the observance of the **Julian calendar**, officially dropped in Britain in 1752, where Old Yule is celebrated on January 6 and the New Year doesn't arrive until January 13. The folk of Foula were still using Norse **udal law** in the late seventeenth century, seemingly unaware that it had been superseded by Scots law in the rest of the country. Foula was also the last place that **Norn**, the old Norse language of Orkney and Shetland, was spoken as a first language, in the eighteenth century. Likewise, the island's isolation meant that more of the Shetland dialect survived here than elsewhere; in the late nineteenth century, Foula's people provided an enormous amount of information on the dialect and its roots in Norn for a study undertaken by the Faroese philologist Jakob Jakobsen. Foula's population, which peaked at around two hundred at the end of the nineteenth century, has fluctuated wildly over the years, dropping to three in 1720 following an epidemic of "muckle fever" or smallpox. Today, the community numbers around forty.

Arriving on Foula, you can't help but be amazed by the sheer size of the island's immense, bare mountain summits. However, the gentler eastern slopes provide good crofting land and plentiful peat, and it is along this "green belt" that the island's population are scattered. The island, whose name is derived from the Old Norse for "bird island", also provides a home for a quarter of a million **birds**. Arctic terns wheel overhead at the airstrip, red-throated divers can usually be seen on Mill Loch, while fulmars, guillemots and gannets cling to the rock ledges, but it is the island's colony of **great skuas** or "bonxies" whom you can't fail to notice. From the edge of extinction a hundred years ago, the bonxies are now thriving, with an estimated three thousand pairs on Foula, making it the largest colony in Britain. Sadly, the skuas, who eat the eggs and young of other birds, have devastated the puffin population and, during the nesting season, they attack anyone who comes near. Although their dive-bombing antics are primarily meant as a threat, they can make walking across the island's moorland interior fairly stressful: the best advice is to stick to the coast.

Practicalities

A day-trip to Foula by **ferry** isn't possible, as the summer passenger service from Walls only runs on Tuesdays, Thursdays and Saturdays (takes 2hr 30min); it's essential to book and reconfirm (Ⓣ01595/810460). The boat arrives at Ham, in the middle of Foula's east coast, and has to be winched up onto the pier to protect it. Aside from Tuesdays, however, day-trips are possible by **flying** from Tingwall (Mon–Wed & Fri; Ⓣ01595/753226); tickets cost around £22 one-way. Foula's only **B&B** is *Leraback* (Ⓣ01595/753226; ❸), near Ham, which does full board only, though they can also rent out a self-catering cottage on a daily basis. There's no shop, so you'll need to take all your food and supplies with you. There's just one road, which runs along the eastern side of the island, and is used by Foula's remarkable fleet of clapped-out vehicles.

North Mainland

The **North Mainland**, stretching more than thirty miles north from the central belt around Lerwick, is wilder than much of Shetland, with almost relentlessly bleak moorland and some rugged and dramatic coastal scenery. It is all but split in two by the isthmus of Mavis Grind: to the south are the districts of Delting (home to Shetland's oil terminal), Lunnasting (gateway to the islands of Whalsay and Out Skerries), and Nesting; to the north is the remote region of Northmavine, which boasts some of the most scenic cliffs in Shetland.

Voe and around

If you're travelling north, you're bound to pass by **VOE**, as it sits at the main crossroads of the North Mainland: to the east, the road leads to Vidlin and Laxo, ferry terminals for Whalsay and Out Skerries; to the northeast, the road cuts across to Toft, where the ferry departs for Yell; to the northwest, it continues on to Brae and Northmaven. If you stay on the main road, it's easy to miss the picturesque old village, a tight huddle of homes and workshops down below the road around the pier. Set at the head of a deep, sheltered, sea loch, Voe has a Scandinavian appearance, helped by the presence of the **Sail Loft**, painted in a rich, deep red. The building was originally used by fishermen and whalers for storing their gear; later, it became a knitwear workshop, and it was here that woollen jumpers were knitted for the 1953 Mount Everest expedition. Today, the building has been converted into a large **camping böd** (book through Lerwick tourist office; April–Oct); it has hot showers, a kitchen, and a solid-fuel heater in the smaller of the bedrooms. There's a handy bakery across the road, and the *Pierhead Restaurant & Bar*, a cosy wood-panelled **pub** with a real fire and occasional live music, which offers a good bar menu and à la carte including the odd catch from the local fishing boats.

A mile or so beyond Laxo, the ferry terminal for Whalsay (see p.746), you'll pass **The Cabin** (open when the flag flies; ⓣ01806/577243; free), a glorified garden shed packed to the rafters with mostly wartime memorabilia collected over many years by the eccentric, but very welcoming, proprietor. Three miles or so further north past Vidlin, the departure point for the Out Skerries (see p.747), is **Lunna House**, with its distinctive red window surrounds, set above a sheltered harbour nine miles northeast of Voe. The house was originally built in 1660 by the Hunter family, but is best known as the initial headquarters from which the Shetland Bus resistance operation was conducted during World War II (see box on p.736). Down the hill lies the little whitewashed **Lunna Kirk**, built in 1753, with a beautiful tiny interior including a carved hexagonal pulpit. Among its more peculiar features is a "lepers' squint" on the outside wall, through which those believed to have the disease could participate in the service without risk of infecting the congregation; there was, however, no leprosy here, the outcasts in fact suffering from a hereditary, non-infectious skin condition brought on by malnutrition. In the graveyard, several unidentified Norwegian sailors, torpedoed by the Nazis, are buried.

Brae and Sullom Voe

BRAE, a sprawling settlement that still has the feel of a frontier town, was one of four expanded in some haste in the 1970s to accommodate the workforce for the huge **Sullom Voe Oil Terminal**, just to the northeast. Sullom Voe is the longest sea loch in Shetland and has always attracted the interest of outsiders in search of a deep-water harbour. During World War II it was home to the Norwegian Air Force and a base for RAF seaplanes. Although the oil terminal, built between 1975 and 1982, has passed its production peak, it is still the largest of its kind in Europe. Its size, however, isn't obvious from beyond the site boundary and few clues remain to the extraordinary scale of the construction effort, which for several years involved a workforce of six thousand accommodated in two large "construction villages" and two ships. It is still a major source of employment, and has recently been given a boost with the opening up of the new oilfields west of Shetland.

Brae may not, at first sight, appear to be somewhere to spend the night, but it does boast one of Shetland's finest **hotels**, *Busta House* (ⓣ01806/522506, ⓦwww.bustahouse.com; ❻), a lovely laird's house with stepped gables that has been tastefully enlarged over the last four hundred years and which sits across the bay of Busta Voe from the modern sprawl of Brae. Even if you're not staying the night here, it's worth coming for afternoon tea in the Long Room, for a stroll around the lovely wooded grounds, or for a drink and an excellent bar meal in the hotel's pub-like bar. A cheaper alternative is the modern croft house **B&B** of *Westayre* (Ⓣ01806/522368; ❷), beyond Busta, overlooking a red sandy bay on the peaceful island of Muckle Roe, which is linked to the mainland by a bridge.

Northmavine

Northmavine, the northwest peninsula of North Mainland, is unquestionably one of the most picturesque areas of Shetland, with its often rugged scenery, magnificent coastline and wide open spaces. The peninsula begins a mile west of Brae at **Mavis Grind**, a narrow isthmus at which it's said you can throw a stone from the Atlantic to the North Sea, or at least to Sullom Voe. Three miles north of the isthmus, it's worth abandoning the main road to explore the remoter corners; the twisting side road west to Gunnister and Nibon travels through a wonderful tumbled landscape of pink and grey rock where abandoned fields and broken shells of croft houses provide abundant evidence of past human struggles to make a living. Where the road ends, at Nibon, you can view a jigsaw of islands and rocky headlands which, even on a relatively calm day, smash the Atlantic into streams of white foam.

Hillswick

HILLSWICK, the main settlement in the area, was once served by the steamboats of the North of Scotland, Orkney & Shetland Steam Navigation Company, and in the early 1900s the firm built the **St Magnus Hotel** to house their customers, importing it in the form of a timber kit from Norway. Despite various alterations over the years, it still stands overlooking St Magnus Bay, rather magnificently clad in black timber-framing and white weatherboarding. Nearer the shore is the much older Hillswick House and, attached to it, **Da Böd**, once the oldest pub in Shetland, said to have been founded by a German merchant in 1684, now an alternative veggie café and wildlife sanctuary called *The Booth* (Ⓣ01806/503348; May–Sept).

The *St Magnus Hotel* is full to the rafters with contractors working at Sullum Voe, so if you want a decent **B&B** in the vicinity, look to *Almara* (Ⓣ01806/503261, Ⓔalmara@zetnet.co.uk; ❷), a mile or two back down the road in Upper Urafirth, which will present you with good food, a family welcome and excellent views. The nicest, sandiest **beach** to collapse on is on the west side of the Hillswick isthmus, overlooking Dore Holm (see below), a short walk across the fields from the hotel.

Esha Ness

Just outside Hillswick, a sideroad leads west to the exposed headland of **Esha Ness** (pronounced "*Ay*sha Ness"), celebrated for its splendid coastline views. Spectacular red granite **cliffs**, eaten away to form fantastic shapes by the elements, are spread out before you as the road climbs away from Hillswick: in the foreground are the stacks known as **The Drongs** off the Ness of Hillswick, while in the distance the Westside and Papa Stour are visible.

A mile or so south off the main road is the **Tangwick Haa Museum** (May–Sept Mon–Fri 1–5pm, Sat & Sun 11am–7pm; free), which, through photographs, old documents and fishing gear, tells the often moving story of this remote corner of Shetland and its role in the dangerous trade of deep-sea fishing and whaling. Kids and adults alike will also enjoy the shells, the Shetland wool and sand samples, and the prize exhibit, the Gunnister Man, who was found preserved in peat in 1951. Over 250 years old now, he's down to his bones, for the most part, but his clothes are in good condition, as is his knitted purse, which contained three coins: two Dutch and one Swedish.

Just before it finally peters out, the road divides, with the southern branch leading to the remains of **Stenness fishing station**, which was once one of the most important deep-sea or haaf fishing stations in Shetland. The remains of a few of the böds used by the fishermen are still visible along the sloping pebbly beach where they would dry their catch. At the peak of operations in the early nineteenth century, as many as eighteen trips a year were made in up to seventy open, six-oared boats, known as "sixareens", to the fishing grounds thirty or forty miles to the west. A Shetland folk song, *Rowin' Foula Doon*, recalls how the crews rowed so far west that the island of Foula began to sink below the eastern horizon. Visible half a mile offshore to the south is **Dore Holm** or the "Drinking Horse", an impressive island with a natural arch.

The northern branch of the road ends at the **Esha Ness Lighthouse**, a great place to view the red sandstone cliffs, stacks and blowholes of this stretch of coast. A useful information board at the lighthouse details some of the dramatic geological features here and, if the weather's a bit rough, you should be treated to some spectacular crashing waves. One of the features to beware of at Esha Ness are the blowholes, some of which are hidden far inland. The best example is the **Holes of Scraada**, a partly roofed cleft where the sea suddenly appears 300 yards inland from the cliff line. The incredible power of the sea can be seen in the various giant boulder fields above the cliffs: these **storm beaches** are formed by rocks torn from the cliffs in storms and deposited inland.

One of the few places to stay in Esha Ness is *Johnnie Notions* **camping böd** (April–Oct; book through Lerwick tourist office; no electricity), up a turning north off the main road, in the hamlet of **HAMNAVOE**. The house was originally the birthplace of Johnnie "Notions" Williamson (1740–1803), a man of many talents, including blacksmithing and weaving, whose fame rests on his work in protecting several thousand of the population against smallpox using a serum and a method of inoculation he'd invented himself, to the amazement of the medical profession. He used a scalpel to lift a flap of skin without drawing blood, then placed the serum he'd prepared underneath, dressing it with a cabbage leaf and a bandage.

Ronas Hill

North of Ronas Voe, by the shores of Colla Firth, an unmarked road leads up **Collafirth Hill**, at the top of which are the crumbling remains of a NATO radio station. The natural landscape is much more impressive, with tremendous views on a clear day, and a foreground of large, scattered stones with hardly any vegetation. Though the walk isn't quite as straightforward as it looks, scale and distance being hard to judge in this setting, Collafirth Hill is the easiest place from which to approach the rounded contours of **Ronas Hill**, Shetland's highest point (1475ft). The climb, with no obvious path, is exhausting but rewarding (4hr round trip; be aware of the safety precautions on p.46): from the top you can look west to one of the most beautifully sculptured parts of the Shetland coast, as the steep slope of the hill drops down to the arching sand and shingle beach called the **Lang Ayre**, south and east over all of the Mainland, north along the coast of Yell, or out into the daunting expanse of the Atlantic. Also at the summit, among subarctic vegetation and block-fields of granite boulders formed by intense frost and wind, is a Neolithic or Bronze Age **chambered cairn**, one of the best preserved in Shetland and useful as a shelter from the wind.

Whalsay and Out Skerries

The island of **Whalsay**, known in Shetland as the "Bonnie Isle", is a thriving and extremely friendly community of over a thousand, devoted almost entirely to fishing. The islands' crews operate a fleet of immense super-trawlers and have coped with the change and uncertainty that characterize the industry by investing huge sums in fishing further afield and catching a wider range of species, and have thus sustained a remarkable level of prosperity. The island is, in addition, extremely fertile, but crofting takes second place to fishing here; there are also plentiful supplies of peat, which can be seen in spring and summer, stacked neatly to dry out above huge peat banks, ready to be bagged for the winter.

Ferries from the Mainland arrive at the island's chief town, **SYMBISTER**, in the southwest, whose harbour is usually dominated by the presence of several of the island's sophisticated, multi-million-pound purse-netters, some over 180ft long; you'll also see smaller fishing boats and probably a few "fourareens", which the locals race regularly in the summer months. Across the busy harbour from the ferry berth stands the tiny grey-granite **Pier House** (Mon–Sat 9am–1pm & 2–5pm, Sun 2–4pm; 50p), the key for which resides in the shop opposite. This picturesque little building, with a hoist built into one side, is thought to have been a Hanseatic merchants' store, and contains a good display on how the Germans traded salt, tobacco, spirits and cloth for Whalsay's salted, dried fish from medieval times until the eighteenth century. Close by is the Harbour View house that is thought to have been a Hanseatic storehouse or booth (and is now a private house and hairdresser's). On a hill overlooking the town is the imposing Georgian mansion of **Symbister House**, built in grey granite and boasting a Neoclassical portico. It was built in the 1830s at great expense by Robert Bruce, not because he wanted to live on Whalsay but, so the story goes, because he wanted to deprive his heirs of his fortune. Since 1940 it has served as the local school and, in the process, has lost some of its grandeur.

About half a mile east of Symbister at the hamlet of **SODOM** – an anglicized version of Sudheim, meaning "South House" – is **Grieve House** (now a camping böd; see below), the modest former home of celebrated Scots poet, writer and republican **Hugh MacDiarmid** (1892–1978), born Christopher Grieve in the Borders town of Langholm. He stayed here from 1933 until 1942, writing about half of his output, including much of his best work: lonely, contemplative poems honouring fishing and fishermen, with whom he sometimes went out to sea. Estranged from his first wife and family and with a drink problem, MacDiarmid, practically broken, had sought temporary relief in Shetland. At first, he seems to have fallen in love with the islands, but poor physical and mental health, exacerbated (if not caused) by chronic poverty, dogged him. Eventually, unwillingly conscripted to work in a Glasgow munitions factory, he left with his new wife and young son, never to return.

Although the majority of folk live in or around Symbister, the rest of Whalsay – which measures roughly two miles by eight – is quite evenly and fairly densely populated. Of the prehistoric remains, the most notable are the two **Bronze Age houses** on the northeastern coast of the island, half a mile south of Skaw, known respectively as the "Benie Hoose" and "Yoxie Biggins". The latter is also known as the "Standing Stones of Yoxie", due to the use of megaliths to form large sections of the walls, many of which still stand. The houses were clearly used over a very long period, as over 1800 tools were discovered in the Benie Hoose; the community also built the nearby chambered tomb.

Car ferries run regularly to Whalsay from Laxo on the Mainland (every 45min–1hr 15min; takes 30min); if you have a car, it's an idea to book ahead (℡01806/566259). In bad weather, especially southeasterly gales, the service operates from Vidlin instead. There are also regular **flights** from Tingwall (Mon & Wed–Fri), but these are request-only, so you must book ahead (℡01595/840246); day-trips are only possible on Thursdays. A few locals do **B&B** for the odd visitor who turns up: try Mrs Simpson (℡01806/566293; ❶) or enquire at the post office; a different Mrs Simpson also has a few inexpensive self-catering options on the island (℡01806/566429). Alternatively, you can stay at the **camping böd** of *Grieve House* in Sodom (April–Oct; book through Lerwick tourist office; no electricity). The house has lovely views overlooking Linga Sound, but is hidden from the main road, so ask for directions at the shop on the brow of the hill along the road to Huxter Loch. The island also has an eighteen-hole **golf course**, near the airstrip in Skaw, in the northeast, several shops, and a **leisure centre** with an excellent swimming pool close to the school in Symbister.

Out Skerries

Lying four miles out to sea, off the northeast tip of Whalsay, the **Out Skerries** (or plain "Skerries" as the locals call them), consist of three tiny low-lying rocky islands, Housay, Bruray and Grunay, the first two linked by a bridge. That people live here at all is remarkable, and that Out Skerries is one of Shetland's most dynamic communities is astonishing, its affluence based on fishing from a superb, small natural harbour sheltered by all three islands, and on salmon farming in a nearby inlet. There are good, if short, walks, with a few prehistoric remains, but the majority of visitors are divers exploring the wreck-strewn coastline, and ornithologists who come here when the wind is in the east, in the hope of catching a glimpse of rare migrants.

The Skerries' jetty and airstrip are both on the middle island of **Bruray**, which also boasts the Skerries' highest point, Bruray Wart (173ft), an easy climb, and one which brings you up close to the islands' ingenious spiral channel collection system for rainwater, which can become scarce in summer. The easternmost island, **Grunay**, is now uninhabited, though you can clearly see the abandoned lighthouse keepers' cottages on the island's chief hill; despite appearances, the Stevenson-designed lighthouse itself sits on the outlying islet of Bound Skerry. The largest of the Skerries' trio, **Housay**, has the most indented and intriguing coastline, to which you should head if the weather's fine. En route, make sure you wander through the Battle Pund stone circle, a wide ring of boulders in the southeastern corner of the island.

Ferries to and from Skerries leave from Vidlin on the Mainland (Mon & Fri–Sun; takes 1hr 30min) and Lerwick (Tues & Thurs; takes 2hr 30min), but day-trips are only possible from Vidlin on Fridays, Saturdays and Sundays. Make sure you book your journey by 5pm the previous evening (℡01806/515226), or the ferry might not run. You can take your car over, but, with less than a mile of road to drive along, it's hardly worth it. There are also regular **flights** from Tingwall (Mon & Wed–Fri), with day-trips possible on Thursdays. There is a shop, and a shower/toilet block by the pier, and **camping** is permitted, with permission. Alternatively, you can stay in *Rocklea* (℡01806/515228; ❶), a friendly **B&B** on Bruray run by Mrs Johnson, who offers optional full board.

The North Isles

Many visitors never make it out to Shetland's trio of remote **North Isles**, which is a shame, as the ferry links are frequent and inexpensive, and the roads fast. Certainly, there is no dramatic shift in scenery: much of what awaits you is the familiar Shetland landscape of undulating peat moorland, dramatic coastal cliffs and silent glacial voes. However, with Lerwick that much further away, the spirit of independence and self-sufficiency in the North Isles is much more keenly felt. **Yell**, the largest of the three, is best known for its vast otter population, but is otherwise often overlooked. **Fetlar**, the smallest of the trio, is home to the rare red-necked phalarope, but **Unst** has probably the widest appeal, partly as the most northerly land mass in the British Isles, but also for its nesting seabird population.

Yell

Historically, **Yell** hasn't had good write-ups. The writer Eric Linklater described it as "dull and dark", while the Scottish historian Buchanan claimed it was "so uncouth a place that no creature can live therein, except such as are born there". Certainly, if you keep to the fast main road, which links the island's two ferry terminals of Ulsta and Gutcher, you'll pass a lot of uninspiring peat moorland, but the landscape is relieved by several voes which cut deeply into it, providing superb natural harbours used as hiding places by German submarines during World War II. Yell's coastline, too, is gentler and greener than the interior and provides an ideal habitat for a large population of **otters**; locals will point out the best places to watch for them.

At **BURRAVOE**, in the southeastern corner of Yell, there's a lovely whitewashed laird's house dating from 1672, with crow-stepped gables, that now houses the **Old Haa Museum** (late April to Sept Tues–Thurs & Sat 10am–4pm, Sun 2–5pm; free), which is stuffed with artefacts, and has lots of material on the history of the local herring and whaling industry; there's a very pleasant wood-panelled café on the ground floor, too. Back at the crossroads stands **St Colman's Kirk**, a stylish little church completed in 1900, featuring an apsed chancel and several winsome Gothic windows and surmounted by a tiny little spire. From May to August, you'll find thousands of **seabirds** (including puffins) nesting in the cliffs above Ladies Hole, less than a mile to the northeast of the village.

The island's largest village, **MID YELL**, has a couple of shops, a pub and a leisure centre with a good swimming pool. A mile or so to the northwest of the village, on an exposed hill above the main road, stands the spooky, abandoned **Windhouse**, dating in part from the early eighteenth century; skeletons were found under the floor and in its wood-panelled walls, and the house is now believed by many to be haunted (its ghost-free lodge is a camping böd; see below). North of Windhouse, around the Loch of Lumbister, there's an **RSPB reserve** that's home to merlins, whimbrels, golden plover, skuas and red-throated divers, and is scattered with wild flowers in summer. A pleasant walk leads along the nearby narrow gorge known as **Daal of Lumbister**, where you can see a lush growth of honeysuckle, wild thyme and moss campion.

In the north of Yell, the area around **CULLIVOE** has relatively gentle, but attractive, coastal scenery. The **Sands of Brekken** are made from crushed shells, and are beautifully sheltered in a cove a mile or two north of Cullivoe. A couple of miles to the west, the road ends at **GLOUP**, with its secretive,

△ Papa Stour, Shetland

narrow voe. In the nineteenth century, this was one of the largest haaf-fishing stations in Shetland; a memorial commemorates the 58 men who were lost when a great storm overwhelmed six of their "sixerns" (open, six-oared rowing boats) in July 1881. This area provides some excellent walking, as does the coast further west, where there's an Iron Age fort and field system at **Burgi Geos**.

Practicalities

Ferries to Yell from Toft on the Mainland are frequent and inexpensive, and taking a car over is easy, too (1–2 hourly; takes 20min). One of the best **B&Bs** on Yell is *Hillhead* (Ⓣ01957/722274; ❶), a comfortable modern house halfway between Ulsta and Burravoe; you can also stay with the very welcoming Tullochs at *Gutcher Post Office* (Ⓣ01957/744201; ❶) overlooking the ferry terminal. A cheaper alternative is to stay in the **camping böd** at *Windhouse Lodge* (April–Oct; book through Lerwick tourist office), the gatehouse on the main road near Mid Yell; it has a small wood- and peat-fired heater and hot showers. There isn't a great range of **food** options on the island, but the non-smoking café in the *Old Haa Museum* at Burravoe (closed Mon, Fri & Sun lunch) has soup, snacks and delicious home baking. The functional *Hilltop Bar* in Mid Yell offers standard bar meals, while the *Seaview Café*, opposite the post office at Gutcher provides a welcome shelter, as well as snacks and hot drinks.

Fetlar

Fetlar is the most fertile of the North Isles, much of it grassy moorland and lush green meadows with masses of summer flowers. It's known as "the garden of Shetland", though that's pushing it a bit, as it's still, relatively speaking, an unforgiving, treeless landscape. Around nine hundred people once lived here and there might well be more than a hundred now were it not for the activities of **Sir Arthur Nicolson**, who in the first half of the nineteenth century cleared many of the people at forty days' notice to make room for sheep. Nicolson's architectural tastes were rather more eccentric than some other local tyrants; his rotting but still astonishing **Brough Lodge**, a rambling castellated composition built in stone and brick in the 1820s, can be seen a mile or so south of the ferry terminal, and owes something – perhaps an apology – to Gothic, Classical and maybe even Tudor styles. Nicolson is also responsible for the nearby round-tower folly, which was built with stone taken from the abandoned croft houses.

Today Fetlar's population live on the southern and eastern sides of the island. At the main settlement, **HOUBIE**, in the centre of the island on the south coast, there's a rather less adventurously styled laird's house called Leagarth, with an impressive conservatory, built by Fetlar's most famous son, Sir William Watson Cheyne (1852–1932), who with Lord Lister pioneered antiseptic surgery. You can learn more about Cheyne's colourful life from the nearby **Fetlar Interpretive Centre** (May–Sept Tues–Sun noon–5pm; free), a welcoming museum with information on the Fetlar's outstanding birdlife and the island's history. Fetlar also shelters Britain's most northerly religious community, the Society of Our Lady of the Isles, who are based in the modern lodge on the edge of the cliffs at Aith Ness, to the southeast of Houbie.

Much of the northern half of the island around Fetlar's highest point, Vord Hill (522ft), is now the **RSPB North Fetlar Reserve**, which is closed from mid-May to mid-July, during which time visits are only possible with permission from the warden at Baelan, the house signposted off the main road from

Brough Lodge to Houbie (☎01957/733246). As well as harbouring important colonies of arctic skuas and whimbrels, the reserve is perhaps best known for Britain's only breeding pair of **snowy owls**, which bred on Stackaberg, to the southwest of Vord Hill, from 1967 to 1975. Around twenty chicks were raised before the old male died, and since then only the occasional female has been spotted. The warden can advise you on the latest, and occasionally conducts guided walks in search of the snowy owl. Fetlar is also one of very few places in the UK where you'll see graceful **red-necked phalarope** (late May to early Aug): the birds are unusual in that the female does the courting and then leaves the male in charge of incubation. The island boasts ninety percent of the UK's phalarope population, and an RSPB hide has been provided overlooking the marshes (or mires) to the east of the **Loch of Funzie** (pronounced *finny*); the loch itself is also a good place at which to spot the phalaropes, and is a regular haunt of red-throated divers.

If you're just looking for a nice sandy bay in which to relax, then head for **Tresta**, on the south coast, which boasts a beautiful, sheltered beach of golden sand, with the freshwater loch of Papil Water immediately behind it. Of the archeological remains on Fetlar, perhaps the most remarkable is the **Funzie Girt** or Finnigirt, an ancient stone boundary of uncertain date, which divides the island into two. Its southern end has been destroyed, but it is well preserved on the western and northern slopes of **Vord Hill**, within the RSPB reserve (see above). Fetlar also offers some great coastal walks along its jagged shores, which are punctuated by an enormous number of natural arches. The cliffs are particularly impressive on Lamb Hoga, the higher moorland peninsula to the southwest, where storm petrels return to their nests at night.

Practicalities

Ferries to Fetlar (6–8 daily; takes 20min) depart from both Gutcher on Yell and Belmont on Unst, though they are by no means as frequent as the ferries between the Mainland, Yell and Unst. The ferry docks at **ODDSTA**, three miles northwest of Houbie; the only public transport is an infrequent postcar (Mon, Wed & Fri), so if you don't have a car you should try to negotiate a lift while on the ferry. If you do have a car, bear in mind that there's no petrol station on Fetlar, so fill up before you come across. **Accommodation** is in short supply, with just two B&Bs, and booking is advisable: *Gord* (☎01957/733227; ❷) is a comfortable modern house attached to the island shop in Houbie, while *The Glebe* (☎01957/733242; ❶) is an old manse of considerable character near Papil Water, which shelters behind one of the few patches of woodland in Shetland; both places do dinner, bed and breakfast. *The Garths* **campsite** (☎01957/733227; May–Sept) is a simple field just to the west of Houbie, with toilets, showers and drying facilities. The post office, shop and **café** (closed Thurs & Sun) are all in one building in the middle of Houbie.

Unst

Unst has been thrown into something of a crisis by the drastic downsizing of the local RAF radar base at Saxa Vord, which until recently used to employ a third of the island's thousand-strong population. Much of the interior is rolling grassland – a blessed relief after the peaty moorland of Yell – but the coast is more dramatic: a fringe of cliffs relieved by some beautiful sandy beaches. As Britain's most northerly inhabited island, there is a surfeit of "most northerly" sights, which is fair enough, given that many visitors only come here in order to head straight for Hermaness, to see the seabirds and look out over Muckle

Flugga and the northernmost tip of Britain, to the North Pole beyond.

On the south coast of the island, not far from the ferry terminal, is **UYEASOUND**, with Greenwell's Booth, an old Hanseatic merchants' warehouse by the pier, sadly now roofless. The house on the island of Uyea, which protects the harbour, was once the home of Sir Basil Neven-Spence, the local MP (1935–50). Further east lie the ruins of **Muness Castle**, a diminutive defensive structure, with matching bulging bastions and corbelled turrets at opposite corners. The castle was built in 1598 by the Scots incomer, Laurence Bruce, stepbrother and chief bullyboy of the infamous Earl Robert Stewart, and probably designed by Andrew Crawford, who shortly afterwards built Scalloway Castle for Robert's son Patrick. The inscription above the entrance asks visitors "not to hurt this vark aluayis", but the castle was sacked by Danish pirates in 1627 and never really re-roofed. To gain entry, you must get the keys and a torch from the nearby house. A little to the north is a vast sandy beach, backed by the deserted crofting settlement of Sandwick.

Unst's main settlement is **BALTASOUND**, five miles north, whose herring industry used to boost the local population of around five hundred to as much as ten thousand during the fishing season. To learn more about the herring boom and other aspects of Unst's history, head for the excellent new **Unst Heritage Centre** (May–Sept daily 2–5pm; free), housed in the old school building by the main crossroads. Baltasound also boasts Britain's most northerly brewery, the **Valhalla Brewery**, source of the Shetland Ales you see around the islands, which welcomes visits by appointment (Mon–Fri by appointment ⓣ01957/711348; £3). As you leave Baltasound, heading north, be sure to take a look at **Bobby's bus shelter**, an eccentric, fully furnished Shetland bus shelter on the edge of the town.

From Baltasound, the main road crosses a giant boulder field of serpentine, a greyish green, occasionally turquoise rock found widely on Unst, that weathers to a rusty orange. The **Keen of Hamar**, east of Baltasound, and clearly signposted from the main road, is one of the largest expanses of serpentine debris in Europe, and is home to an extraordinary array of plantlife. It's worth taking a walk on this barren, exposed, almost lunar landscape that's thought to resemble what most of northern Europe looked like at the end of the last ice age. With the help of one of the SNH leaflets, you can try and identify some of the area's numerous rare and miniscule plants, including Norwegian sandwort, frog orchid, moonwort, and the mouse-eared Edmondston's chickweed, which flowers in June and July and is found nowhere else in the world.

Beyond the Keen of Hamar, the road drops down into **HAROLDSWICK**, where near the shore you'll find the **Unst Boat Haven** (May–Sept daily 2–5pm; otherwise a key is available from the adjacent shop; free), displaying a beautifully presented collection of historic boats with many tools of the trade and information on fishing; most of the boats are from Shetland, with one from Norway. Less than a mile north of Haroldswick is **SAXA VORD**, the eyesore **RAF base** (also confusingly the name of the nearby hill), beyond which the road continues for another couple of miles before ending at Skaw, with a beautiful beach and the very last house in Britain.

The road that heads off northwest from Haroldswick leads to the head of **Burra Firth**, a north-facing inlet surrounded by cliffs and home to Britain's most northerly golf course. It is guarded to the east by the hills of **Saxa Vord** (936ft), Unst's highest point, topped by several Ministry of Defence installations. It was here that the country's unofficial wind-speed record of 194mph was recorded in 1992. To the west of Burra Firth lies the bleak headland of **Hermaness**, now a National Nature Reserve and home to more than 100,000 nesting seabirds. There's an excellent **visitor centre** in the former lighthouse keepers' shore station, where you can pick up a leaflet showing the marked routes across the heather, which allow you access into the reserve. Whatever you do, stick to the path so as to avoid annoying the vast numbers of nesting great skuas.

From Hermaness Hill, you can look down over the jagged rocks of the wonderfully named Vesta Skerry, Rumblings, Tipta Skerry and **Muckle Flugga**. There are few more dramatic settings for a lighthouse, and few sites could ever have presented as great a challenge to the builders, who erected it in 1858. Beyond the lighthouse is **Out Stack**, the most northerly bit of Britain, where Lady Franklin landed in 1849 in order to pray (in vain, as it turned out) for the safe return for her husband from his expedition to discover the Northwest Passage, undertaken four years previously. The views from here are inevitably marvellous, as is the birdlife; there's a huge gannetry on one of the stacks, and puffins burrow all along the clifftops. The walk down the west side of Unst towards Westing is one of the finest in Shetland: if the wind's blowing hard, the seascape is memorably dramatic.

Practicalities

Ferries shuttle regularly from Gutcher on Yell over to **BELMONT** on Unst (every 15–30min; takes 10min); booking in advance is wise (ⓣ01957/722259). By far the best and most unusual **accommodation** is historic *Buness House* (ⓣ01957/711315, ⓦwww.users.zetnet.co.uk/buness-house; ❹), a seventeenth-century Haa in Baltasound still owned and run by the eccentric Edmondstons (of chickweed fame). Another very good bet is *Prestagaard* (ⓣ01957/755234; ❶), a more modest Victorian B&B in Uyeasound, where there's also the very handy *Gardiesfauld Hostel* (ⓣ01957/755259, ⓔtelecroft2000@talk21.com; April–Sept), a clean and modern hostel near the pier, which allows **camping**, and offers **bike rental**. The *Baltasound Hotel* serves very ordinary **bar food** and drink to non-residents, while snacks and teas can be had at the tearoom in Nornova Knitwear just north of Muness Castle. The largest **shop** around is the NAAFI store within the RAF base at Saxa Vord, which is now open to the public. Shetland Wildlife Tours (ⓣ01950/460254) offers a very popular, though expensive **boat trip** around Muckle Flugga, though you need good sea legs to enjoy it even in calm weather; the boats leave from Mid Yell (May–Aug Wed 10am; £70).

Travel details

Orkney

Ferries to Orkney (summer only)
Aberdeen to: Stromness (2 weekly; 8–10hr).
Gill's Bay to: St Margaret's Hope (3 daily; 1hr).
John O'Groats to: Burwick (passengers only; 2–4 daily; 40min).
Lerwick to: Stromness (2 weekly; 8hr).
Scrabster to: Stromness (1–3 daily; 2hr).

Inter-island ferries (summer only)
To Eday: Kirkwall–Eday (2–3 daily; 1hr 15min–2hr).
To Egilsay: Tingwall–Egilsay (3–4 daily; 50min–1hr 45min).
To Flotta: Houton–Flotta (2–5 daily; 45min).
To Hoy: Houton–Lyness (Mon–Fri 6 daily, Sat & Sun 2–3 daily; 30min–1hr); Stromness–Hoy (passengers only; 2–5 daily; 25min).
To North Ronaldsay: Kirkwall–North Ronaldsay (1 weekly, usually Fri; 2hr 40min–3hr).
To Papa Westray: Kirkwall–Papa Westray (Tues & Fri; 2hr 15min); Pierowall (Westray)–Papa Westray (passengers only; 3–6 daily; 25min).
To Rousay: Tingwall–Rousay (6 daily; 30min).
To Sanday: Kirkwall–Sanday (1–3 daily; 1hr 25min).
To Shapinsay: Kirkwall–Shapinsay (5–6 daily; 45min).
To Stronsay: Kirkwall–Whitehall (2 daily; 1hr 35min–2hr).

To Westray: Kirkwall–Westray (2–3 daily; 1hr 25min).

To Wyre: Rousay–Wyre (4–5 daily; 45min–2hr 5min).

Inter-island flights (Mon–Sat only)

Kirkwall to: Eday (3 on Wed; 8–36min); North Ronaldsay (2 daily; 15min); Papa Westray (Mon–Fri 2 daily; 12min); Sanday (Mon–Fri 2 daily, 1 on Sat; 10–20min); Stronsay (Mon–Fri 2 daily; 25min); Westray (Mon–Sat 1–2 daily; 12min).

Buses on Orkney Mainland

Kirkwall to: Burwick (4 daily; 45min); Deerness via airport (Mon–Sat 2–4 daily; 25min); Evie (Mon–Sat 2–4 daily; 30min); Houton (Mon–Sat 3–5 daily; 30min); St Margaret's Hope (Mon–Sat 3–4 daily; 40min); Stromness (Mon–Sat 10 daily; 30min); Tingwall (Mon–Sat 5–7 daily; 35min).

Stromness to: Houton (Mon–Sat 2–3 daily; 20min).

Shetland

Ferries to Shetland (summer only)

Aberdeen to: Lerwick (4–5 weekly; 14hr).

Stromness (Orkney) to: Lerwick (1–2 weekly; 8–10hr).

Inter-island ferries (summer only)

To Bressay: Lerwick–Bressay (every 30min–1hr; 5min).

To Fair Isle: Lerwick–Fair Isle (1 on alternate Thurs; 4hr 30min); Sumburgh–Fair Isle (1 on Tues, Sat & alternate Thurs; 2hr 40min).

To Fetlar: Belmont (Unst) & Gutcher (Yell)–Oddsta (6–8 daily; 25min).

To Foula: Scalloway–Foula (1 on alternate Thurs; 3hr); Walls–Foula (1 on Tues & alternate Thurs; 2hr 30min).

To Out Skerries: Lerwick–Skerries (Tues & Thurs 1 daily; 2hr 30min); Vidlin–Skerries (1 on Mon, Fri–Sun 3 daily; 1hr 30min).

To Papa Stour: West Burrafirth–Papa Stour (Mon, Wed & Sun 1 daily, Fri & Sat 2 daily; 45min).

To Unst: Gutcher (Yell)–Belmont (every 15–45min; 10min).

To Whalsay: Laxo–Symbister (14–16 daily; 30min).

To Yell: Toft–Ulsta (every 20–40min; 20min).

Inter-island flights (summer only)

Sumburgh to: Fair Isle (1 on Sat; 15min).

Tingwall to: Fair Isle (Mon, Wed & Fri 2 daily, 1 on Sat; 25min); Foula (Mon, Wed & Fri 2 daily, 1 on Tues; 15min); Out Skerries, calling at Whalsay on request (Mon, Wed & Fri 1 daily, 2 on Thurs; 20min); Papa Stour (2 on Tues; 10min).

Buses on Shetland Mainland

Lerwick to: Brae (Mon–Fri 4–5 daily, 2 on Sat; 45min); Hamnavoe (Mon–Sat 1–2 daily; 30min); Hillswick (1 daily except Wed & Sun; 1hr 15min); Laxo (Mon–Sat 1 daily; 40min); Sandwick (Mon–Sat 5–6 daily, Sun 3 daily; 25min); Scalloway (Mon–Sat hourly; 15min); Sumburgh (2–5 daily; 45min); Toft (Mon–Sat 1 daily; 55min); Vidlin (Mon–Sat 2 daily; 45min); Voe (Mon–Fri 5–6 daily, Sat & Sun 2–3 daily; 35min); Walls (Mon–Sat 2–4 daily; 45min).

Buses on Unst

Baltasound to: Haroldswick (2–4 daily; 5–10min).

Belmont to: Baltasound (Mon–Fri school term only 1 daily; 1hr); Uyeasound (Mon–Sat 1–3 daily; 5min).

Buses on Yell

Mid Yell to: Gutcher (Mon–Sat 1–3 daily, 1 on Sun in school term; 25min).

Ulsta to: Burravoe (Mon–Sat 1 daily; 10min); Gutcher (Mon–Sat 1–2 daily, 1 on Sun in school term; 30min).

contexts

contexts

The historical framework

Scotland's colourful and compelling history looms large. Peppered with tragic yet romantic heroes, the country's past has thrown up notable fighters, innovators and politicians. Often the nation's history has been defined either by fierce internecine conflict or epic struggles with its more populous and richer neighbour, England. Yet from earliest times the influences of Ireland, Scandinavia and continental Europe have been as important, particularly in aspects of Scotland's creative and cultural development. The result has been a sophistication and ambition few associate with the land of warring clans and burning castles.

Prehistoric Scotland

Scotland, like the rest of prehistoric Britain, was settled by successive waves of peoples arriving from the east. These first inhabitants were **hunter-gatherers**, whose heaps of animal bones and shells have been excavated, amongst other places, in the caves along the coast near East Wemyss in Fife. Around 4500 BC, **Neolithic farming peoples** from the European mainland began moving into Scotland. To provide themselves with land for their cereal crops and grazing for their livestock, they cleared large areas of upland forest, usually by fire, and in the process created the characteristic moorland landscapes of much of modern Scotland. These early farmers established permanent settlements, some of which, like the well-preserved village of **Skara Brae** on Orkney, were near the sea, enabling them to supplement their diet by fishing and develop their skills as boat-builders. The Neolithic settlements were not as isolated as was once imagined: geological evidence has, for instance, revealed that the stone used to make axe-heads found in the Hebrides was quarried in Northern Ireland.

Settlement spurred the development of more complex forms of religious belief. The Neolithic peoples built large chambered burial mounds or **cairns**, such as Maes Howe in Orkney. This reverence for human remains suggests a belief in some form of afterlife, a concept that the next wave of settlers, the **Beaker people**, certainly believed in. They placed pottery beakers filled with drink in the tombs of their dead to assist the passage of the deceased on their journey to, or their stay in, the next world. The Beaker people also built the mysterious **stone circles**, thirty of which have been discovered in Scotland. Such monuments were a massive commitment in terms of time and energy, with many of the stones carried from miles away, just as they were at Stonehenge in England, the most famous stone circle of all. One of the best-known Scottish circles is that of **Callanish** on the Isle of Lewis, where a dramatic series of monoliths (single standing stones) form avenues leading towards a circle made up of thirteen standing stones. The exact function of the circles is still unknown, but many of the stones are aligned with the position of the sun at certain points in its annual cycle, suggesting that the monuments are related to the changing of the seasons.

The Beaker people also brought the **Bronze Age** to Scotland. Bronze, an alloy of copper and tin, was stronger and more flexible than its predecessor, flint, which had long been used for axe-heads and knives. New materials led directly to the development of more effective weapons, and the sword and the shield made their first appearance around 1000 BC. Agricultural needs plus new weaponry added up to a state of endemic warfare as villagers raided their neighbours to steal livestock and grain. The Bronze Age peoples responded to the danger by developing a range of defences, among them the spectacular **hillforts**, great earthwork defences, many of which are thought to have been occupied from around 1000 BC and remained in use throughout the Iron Age, sometimes far longer. Less spectacular but equally practical were the **crannogs**, smaller settlements built on artificial islands constructed of logs, earth, stones and brush, such as Cherry Island in Loch Ness.

Conflict in Scotland intensified in the first millennium BC as successive waves of **Celtic** settlers, arriving from the south, increased competition for land. Around 400 BC, the Celts brought the technology of **iron** with them and, as Winston Churchill put it, "Men armed with iron entered Britain and killed the men of bronze." These fractious times witnessed the construction of hundreds of **brochs** or fortified towers. Concentrated along the Atlantic coast and in the northern and western isles, the brochs were dry-stone fortifications (that is, built without mortar or cement) often over 40ft in height. Some historians claim they provided protection for small coastal settlements from the attentions of Roman slave traders. Much the best-preserved broch is on the Shetland island of **Mousa**; its double walls rise to about 40ft, only a little short of their original height. The Celts continued to migrate north almost up until Julius Caesar's first incursion into Britain in 55 BC.

At the end of the prehistoric period, immediately prior to the arrival of the Romans, Scotland was divided among a number of warring Iron Age tribes, who, apart from the raiding, were preoccupied with wresting a living from the land, growing barley and oats, rearing sheep, hunting deer and fishing for salmon. The Romans were to write these people into history under the collective name Picti, or **Picts**, meaning painted people, after their body tattoos.

The Romans

The **Roman conquest** of Britain began in 43 AD, almost a century after Caesar's first invasion. By 80 AD the Roman governor, Agricola, felt secure enough in the south of Britain to begin an invasion of the north, building a string of forts across the Clyde–Forth line and defeating a large force of Scottish tribes at Mons Graupius. The long-term effect of his campaign, however, was slight. Work on a major fort – to be the base for 5000 soldiers – at Inchtuthill, on the Tay, was abandoned before it was finished, and the legions withdrew south. In 123 AD the emperor **Hadrian** decided to seal the frontier against the northern tribes and built **Hadrian's Wall**, which stretched from the Solway Firth to the Tyne and was the first formal division of the island of Britain. Twenty years later, the Romans again ventured north and built the **Antonine Wall** between the Clyde and the Forth. This was manned for about forty years, but thereafter the Romans, frustrated by the inhospitable terrain of the Highlands, largely gave up their attempt to subjugate the north, and instead adopted a policy of containment.

It was the Romans who produced the first **written** accounts of the peoples of Scotland. In the second century AD, the Greco–Egyptian geographer Ptolemy drew up the first-known map of Scotland, which identified seventeen tribal territories. Other descriptions were less scientific, compounding the mixture of fear and contempt with which the Romans regarded their Pictish neighbours. Dio Cassius, a Roman commentator writing in 197 AD, informed his readers:

They live in huts, go naked and unshod. They mostly have a democratic government, and are much addicted to robbery. They can bear hunger and cold and all manner of hardship; they will retire into their marshes and hold out for days with only their heads above water, and in the forest they will subsist on barks and roots.

The Dark Ages

In the years following the departure of the Romans, traditionally put at 450 AD, the population of Scotland changed considerably. By 500 the **Picts** occupied the northern isles, and the north and the east as far south as Fife. Today their settlements can be generally identified by place names with a "Pit" prefix, such as Pitlochry, and by the existence of carved symbol stones, like those found at Aberlemno in Angus. To the west, between Dumbarton and Carlisle, was a population of **Britons**. Many of the Briton leaders had Roman names, which suggests that they were a Romanized Celtic people, possibly a combination of tribes maintained by the Romans as a buffer between the Wall and the northern tribes, and peoples pushed west by the Anglo-Saxon invaders landing on the east coast. Both the Britons and the Picts spoke variations of P-Celtic, from which Welsh, Cornish and Breton developed.

On the west coast, to the north and west of the Britons, lived the **Scotti**, Irish–Celtic invaders who would eventually give their name to the whole country. The first Scotti arrived in the Western Isles from Ireland in the fourth century AD, and about a century later their great king, Fergus Mor, moved his base from Antrim to Dunadd, near Lochgilphead, where he founded the kingdom of Dalriada. The Scotti spoke Q-Celtic, the precursor of modern Gaelic. On the east coast, the Germanic **Angles** had sailed north along the coast to carve out an enclave around Dunbar in East Lothian. The final addition to the ethnic mix was also non-Celtic; from around 800 AD, **Norse** invaders began to arrive, settling mainly in the northern isles (see box on p.760) and the northeast of the mainland.

The next few centuries saw almost constant warfare among the different groups. The main issue was land, but this was frequently complicated by the need of the warrior castes, who dominated all of these cultures, to exhibit martial prowess. Military conquests did play their part in bringing the peoples of Scotland together, but the most persuasive force was **Christianity**. Many of the Britons had been Christians since Roman times and it had been a Briton, St Ninian, who conducted the first missionary work among the Picts at the end of the fourth century. Attempts to convert the Picts were resumed in the sixth century by **St Columba**, who, as one of the Gaelic-speaking Scotti, demonstrated that Christianity could provide a bridge between the different tribes.

Christianity proved attractive to pagan kings because it seemed to offer them extra supernatural powers. As St Columba declared, when he inaugurated his cousin Aidan as king of Dalriada in 574, "Believe firmly, O Aidan, that none of your enemies will be able to resist you unless you first deal falsely against me and my successors." This combination of spiritual and political power, when taken with Columba's establishment of the island of **Iona** as a centre of Christian culture, opened the way for many peaceable contacts between the Picts and Scotti. Intermarriage became commonplace, and the Scotti king Kenneth MacAlpine, who united Dalriada and Pictland in 843, was the son of a Pictish princess (the Picts traced succession through the female line). Similarly, MacAlpine's creation of the united kingdom of **Alba**, later known as

The northern isles

With their sophisticated ships and navigational skills, the **Vikings**, who began their expansion in the eighth century, soon gained supremacy over the Pictish peoples in Shetland, Orkney, the extreme northeast corner of the mainland and the Western Isles. In 872, the king of Norway set up an earldom in **Orkney** from which **Shetland** was also governed: for the next six centuries the northern isles took a path distinct from the rest of what is now called Scotland, becoming a base for raiding and colonization in much of the rest of Britain and Ireland, and a link in the chain that connected Faroe, Iceland, Greenland and, more tenuously, North America. Norse culture flourished, and buildings such as St Magnus Cathedral in Kirkwall, Orkney, begun in 1137, give some idea of its energy. However, there were bouts of unrest, and finally Shetland was brought under direct rule from Norway at the end of the twelfth century.

When Norway united with Sweden under the Danish crown in the fourteenth century, Norse power began to wane and Scottish influence to increase. In 1469, a marriage was arranged between Margaret, daughter of the Danish king Christian I, and the future King James III of Scotland. Short of cash for her dowry, Christian mortgaged Orkney to Scotland in 1468, followed by Shetland in 1469; neither pledge was ever successfully redeemed. The laws, religion and administration of the northern isles became Scottish, though their Norse heritage is still very evident in place names, dialect and culture.

Scotia, was part of a process of integration rather than outright conquest. Kenneth and his successors gradually extended the frontiers of their kingdom by marriage and force of arms until, by 1034, almost all of what we now call Scotland was under their rule.

The Middle Ages

By the time of his death in 1034, **Malcolm II** was recognized as the king of Scotia. He was not, though, a national king in the sense that we understand the term, as under the Gaelic system kings were elected from the *derbfine*, a group made up of those whose great-grandfathers had been kings. The chosen successor, supposedly the fittest to rule, was known as the *tanist*. By the eleventh century, however, Scottish kings had become familiar with the principle of heredity, and were often tempted to bend the rules of *tanistry*. Thus, the childless Malcolm secured the succession of his grandson **Duncan** by murdering a potential rival *tanist*. Duncan, in turn, was killed by **Macbeth** in 1040. Macbeth was not, therefore, the villain of Shakespeare's imagination, but simply an ambitious Scot of royal blood acting in a relatively conventional way.

The victory over Macbeth in 1057 of **Malcolm III**, known as Canmore ("Bighead"), marked the beginning of a period of fundamental change in Scottish society. Having avenged his father Duncan, Malcolm III, who had spent the previous seventeen years at the English court, sought to apply to Scotland a range of ideas he had brought back with him. He and his heirs established a secure dynasty based on succession through the male line and introduced **feudalism** into Scotland, a system that was diametrically opposed to the Gaelic system, which rested on blood ties: the followers of a Gaelic king were his kindred, whereas the followers of a feudal king were vassals bought with land. The Canmores successfully feudalized much of southern and eastern Scotland by making grants to their Norman, Breton and Flemish followers but, beyond that, traditional clan-based forms of social relations persisted.

Kings and queens of Scotland

Kenneth I 842–58
Donald I 858–62
Constantine I 862–76
Aed 876–78
Giric 878–89
Donald II 889–900
Constantine II 900–43
Malcolm I 943–54
Indulf 954–62
Duf 962–66
Culén 966–71
Kenneth II 971–95
Constantine III 995–97
Kenneth III 997–1005
Malcolm II 1005–34
Duncan I 1034–40
Macbeth 1040–57
Malcolm III (Canmore) 1057–93
Donald III 1093–94
Duncan II 1094
Donald III 1094–97
Edgar 1097–1107
Alexander I 1107–24
David I 1124–53
Malcolm IV 1153–65
William the Lion 1165–1214
Alexander II 1214–49
Alexander III 1249–86
Margaret 1286–90
John Balliol 1292–96
Robert I (the Bruce) 1306–29
David II 1329–71
Robert II 1371–90
Robert III 1390–1406
James I 1406–37
James II 1437–60
James III 1460–88
James IV 1488–1513
James V 1513–42
Mary (Queen of Scots) 1542–67
James VI 1567–1625

The Canmores, independent of the local nobility, who remained a military threat, also began to reform the **Church**. This development started with the efforts of **Margaret**, Malcolm III's English wife, who brought Scottish religious practices into line with those of the rest of Europe and was eventually canonized. **David I** continued the process by importing monks to found a series of monasteries, principally along the border at Kelso, Melrose, Jedburgh and Dryburgh. By 1200 the entire country was covered by a network of eleven bishoprics, although church organization remained weak within the Highlands. Similarly, the dynasty founded a series of **royal burghs**, towns such as Edinburgh, Stirling and Berwick, and bestowed upon them charters recognizing them as centres of trade. The charters usually granted a measure of self-government, vested in the town corporation or guild, and the monarchy hoped this liberality would both encourage loyalty and increase the prosperity of the kingdom. Scotland's Gaelic-speaking clans had little influence within the burghs and, by 1550, Scots – a northern version of Anglo-Saxon – had become the main **language** throughout the Lowlands.

The policies of the Canmores laid the basis for a **cultural rift** in Scotland between the Highland and Lowland communities. Before that became an issue, however, the Scots had to face a major threat from the south. In 1286 Alexander III died, and a hotly disputed succession gave **Edward I**, King of England, an opportunity to subjugate Scotland. In 1291 Edward presided over a conference where the rival claimants to the Scottish throne presented their cases. Edward chose **John Balliol** in preference to **Robert the Bruce**, his main rival; he also obliged Balliol to pay him homage, thus turning Scotland into a vassal kingdom. Bruce refused to accept the decision, thereby continuing the conflict, and in 1295 Balliol renounced his allegiance to Edward and sided with France – the beginning of what is known as the "Auld Alliance". In the conflict that followed, the Bruce family sided with the English, Balliol was defeated and imprisoned, and Edward seized control of almost all of Scotland.

Edward had shown little mercy during his conquest of Scotland – he had, for example, had most of the population of Berwick massacred – and his cruelty seems to have provoked a truly national resistance. This focused on **William Wallace**, a man of relatively lowly origins who raised an army of peasants, lesser knights and townsmen that was fundamentally different to the armies raised by the nobility. Figures like Balliol, holding lands in England, France and Scotland, were part of an international aristocracy for whom warfare was merely the means by which they struggled for power. Wallace, by contrast, led proto-nationalist forces determined to expel the English from their country. Probably for that very reason Wallace never received the support of the nobility and, after a bitter ten-year campaign, he was betrayed and executed in London in 1305.

With Wallace out of the way, feudal intrigue resumed. In 1306 Robert the Bruce, the erstwhile ally of the English, defied Edward and had himself crowned king of Scotland. Edward died the following year, but the unrest dragged on until 1314, when Bruce decisively defeated a huge English army under Edward II at the battle of **Bannockburn**. At last Bruce was firmly in control of his kingdom, and in 1320 the Scots asserted their right to independence in a successful petition to the pope, now known as the **Declaration of Arbroath**.

In the years following Bruce's death in 1329, the Scottish monarchy gradually declined in influence. The last of the Bruce dynasty died in 1371, to be succeeded by the "Stewards", hence **Stewarts**, but thereafter a succession of Scottish rulers, culminating with James VI in 1567, came to the throne when still children. The power vacuum was filled by the nobility, whose key members exercised control as Scotland's regents while carving out territories where they ruled with the power, if not the title, of kings. At the close of the fifteenth century, the Douglas family alone controlled Galloway, Lothian, Stirlingshire, Clydesdale and Annandale. The more vigorous monarchs of the period, notably **James I**, did their best to curb the power of such dynasties, but their efforts were usually nullified at the next regency. **James IV**, the most talented of the early Stewarts, might have restored the authority of the crown, but his invasion of England ended in a terrible defeat for the Scots – and his own death – at the battle of **Flodden Field**.

The reign of **Mary, Queen of Scots** typified the problems of the Scottish monarchy. Mary came to the throne when just one week old, and immediately caught the attention of the English king, Henry VIII, who sought, first by persuasion and then by military might, to secure her hand in marriage for his five-year-old son, Edward. Beginning in 1544, the English launched a series of devastating attacks on Scotland, an episode Sir Walter Scott later called the "Rough Wooing", until, in the face of another English invasion in 1548, the Scots – or at least those not supporting Henry – turned to the "Auld Alliance". The French king proposed marriage between Mary and the Dauphin Francis, promising in return military assistance against the English. The six-year-old queen sailed for France in 1548, leaving her loyal nobles and their French allies in control, and her husband succeeded to the French throne in 1559. When she returned thirteen years later, following the death of Francis, she had to pick her way through the rival ambitions of her nobility and deal with something entirely new – the religious Reformation.

The Reformation

The **Reformation** in Scotland was a complex social process, whose threads are often hard to unravel. Nevertheless, it is quite clear that, by the end of the sixteenth century, the established Church was held in general contempt. Many members of the higher clergy regarded their relationship with the Church purely in economic terms, and forty percent of known illegitimate births (ie those subsequently legitimized) were the product of the "celibate" clergy's liaisons.

Another spur to the Scottish Reformation was the identification of Protestantism with anti-French feeling. In 1554, Mary of Guise, the French mother of the absent Queen Mary, had become regent, and her habit of appointing Frenchmen to high office was seen as part of an attempt to subordinate Scotland's interests to those of France. There was considerable resentment, and in 1557 a group of nobles banded together to form the **Lords of the Congregation**, whose dual purpose was to oppose French influence and promote the reformed religion. With English military backing, the Protestant lords succeeded in deposing the French regent in 1560, and, when the Scottish Parliament assembled shortly afterwards, it asserted the primacy of Protestantism by forbidding the Mass and abolishing the authority of the pope. The nobility proceeded to confiscate two-thirds of Church lands, a huge prize that did much to bolster their new beliefs.

Even without the economic incentives, Protestantism was a highly charged political doctrine. **Luther** had argued that each individual's conscience was capable of discerning God's will. This meant that a hierarchical priesthood, existing to interpret God's will, was unnecessary and that the people themselves might conclude their rulers were breaking God's laws, in which case the monarch should be opposed or even deposed. This point was made very clearly to Queen Mary by the Protestant reformer **John Knox** at their first meeting in 1561. Subjects, he told her, were not bound to obey an ungodly monarch.

Knox, born in East Lothian, had returned to Scotland in 1559 from exile. He was a follower of the Genevan reformer Calvin, who combined Luther's views on individual conscience with a belief in predestination. Calvinism argued that an omnipotent God must know everything, including the destinies of every human being. Consequently, it was determined before birth who was to be part of the Elect, bound for heavenly glory, and who was not, a doctrine that placed enormous pressure on its adherents to demonstrate by their godly behaviour that they were of the Elect. This was the doctrine that Knox brought back to Scotland and laid out in his Articles of Confession of Faith, better known as the **Scot's Confession**, which was to form the basis of the reformed faith for over seventy years.

Mary ducked and weaved, trying to avoid an open breach with her Protestant subjects. The fires of popular displeasure were kept well stoked by Knox, however, who declared "one Mass was more fearful than if ten thousand enemies were landed in any part of the realm". At the same time, Mary was engaged in a balancing act between the factions of the Scottish nobility. Her difficulties were exacerbated by her disastrous second marriage to **Lord Darnley**, a cruel and politically inept character, whose jealousy led to his involvement in the murder of Mary's favourite, David Rizzio, who was dragged from the queen's supper room at Holyrood and stabbed 56 times. The incident caused the Scottish Protestants more than a little unease, but they were entirely scandalized in 1567, when Darnley himself was murdered and Mary promptly married the **Earl of Bothwell**, widely believed to be the murderer. This was too much to bear, and the Scots rose in rebellion, driving Mary into exile in England at the age of just 25. The queen's illegitimate half-brother, the Earl of Moray, became regent, and her son, the infant James, was left behind to be raised a Protestant prince. Mary, meanwhile, became perceived as such a threat to the English throne that Queen Elizabeth I had her executed in 1587.

Knox could now concentrate on the organization of the reformed Church, or **Kirk**, which he envisaged as a body empowered to intervene in the daily lives of the people. **Andrew Melville**, another leading reformer, wished to push this theocratic vision further. He proposed the abolition of all traces of Episcopacy – the rule of the bishops in the Church – and that the Kirk should adopt a **Presbyterian** structure, administered by a hierarchy of assemblies, part-elected and part-appointed. At the bottom of the chain, beneath the General Assembly, Synod and Presbytery, would be the Kirk session, responsible for church affairs, the performance of the minister and the morals of the parish. In 1592, the Melvillian party achieved a measure of success when presbyteries and synods were accepted as legal church courts and the office of bishop was suspended.

James VI disliked Presbyterianism because its quasi-democratic structure – particularly the lack of royally appointed bishops – appeared to threaten his authority. He was, however, unable to resist the reformers until, strengthened by his installation as James I of England after Elizabeth's death in 1603, he restored the Scottish bishops in 1610. The argument about the nature of Kirk organization would lead to bloody conflict in the years after James's death.

The religious wars

Raised in Episcopalian England, **Charles I** had little understanding of Scottish reformism. He believed in the Divine Right of Kings, an authoritarian creed that claimed the monarch was God's representative on earth and, therefore, his authority had divine sanction, a concept entirely counter to Protestant thought. In 1637, Charles attempted to impose a new prayer book on the Kirk, laying down forms of worship in line with those favoured by the High Anglican Church. The reformers denounced these changes as "popery" and organized the **National Covenant**, a religious pledge that committed the signatories to "labour by all means lawful to recover the purity and liberty of the Gospel as it was established and professed".

Charles declared all the "**Covenanters**" to be rebels, a proclamation endorsed by his Scottish bishops. Consequently, when the king backed down from military action and called a General Assembly of the Kirk, the assembly promptly abolished the Episcopacy. Charles pronounced the proceedings illegal, but lack of finance stopped him from mounting an effective military campaign – whereas the Covenanters, well financed by the Kirk, assembled a proficient army under Alexander Leslie. In desperation, Charles summoned the English Parliament, the first for eleven years, hoping it would pay for an army. But, like the calling of the General Assembly, the decision was a disaster and parliament was much keener to criticize his policies than to raise taxes. In response Charles declared war on parliament in 1642.

Until 1650, Scotland was ruled by the Covenanters, and the power of the Presbyterian Kirk grew considerably. Laws were passed establishing schools in every parish and, less usefully, banning trade with Catholic countries. The only effective opposition to the theocratic state came from the **Marquis of Montrose**, who had initially supported the Covenant but lined up with the king when war broke out. His army was drawn from the Highlands and Islands, where the Kirk's influence was weakest. Montrose was a gifted campaigner who won several notable victories against the Covenanters, but the reluctance of his troops to stay south of the Highland Line made it impossible for him to capitalize on his successes, and he was eventually captured and executed in 1650.

Largely confined to the peripheries of Scotland, Montrose's campaigns were a side show to the **Civil War** being waged further south. Here, the Covenanters and the English Parliamentarians faced the same royal enemy and in 1643 formed an alliance. Indeed, it was the Scots army that captured Charles at Newark in Nottinghamshire, in 1646. There was, however, friction between the allies. Many of the Parliamentarians, including Cromwell, were **Independents**, who favoured a looser form of doctrinal control within the state Church than did the Presbyterians, and were inclined towards religious toleration for the law-abiding sects outside the state Church. In addition, the Scots believed the English were tainted with **Erastianism** – a belief in placing the secular authority of Parliament over the spiritual authority of the Church.

The Parliamentarians in turn suspected the Scots of hankering for the return of the monarchy, a suspicion confirmed when, at the invitation of the Earl of Argyll, the future Charles II came back to Scotland in 1650. To regain his Scottish kingdom, Charles was obliged to renounce his father and sign the Covenant, two bitter pills taken to impress the population. In the event, the "Presbyterian restoration" was short-lived. Cromwell invaded, defeated the Scots at Dunbar and forced Charles into exile. Until the Restoration of 1660, Scotland was united with England and governed by seven commissioners.

Although the restoration of **Charles II** brought bishops back to the Kirk, they were integrated into an essentially Presbyterian structure of Kirk sessions and presbyteries, and the General Assembly, which had been abolished by Cromwell, was not re-established. Over 300 clergymen, a third of the Scottish ministry, refused to accept the reinstatement of the bishops and were edged out of the Church, forced to hold open-air services, called **Conventicles**, which Charles did his best to suppress. Religious opposition inspired military resistance and the Lowlands witnessed scenes of brutal repression as the king's forces struggled to keep control in what was known as "The Killing Time". In the southwest, a particular stronghold of the Covenanters, the government imported Highlanders, the so-called "Highland Host", to root out the opposition, which they did with great barbarity.

Charles II was succeeded by his brother **James VII** (James II of England), whose ardent Catholicism caused a Protestant backlash in England. In 1689, he was forced into exile in France and the throne passed to **Mary**, his Protestant daughter, and her Dutch husband, **William of Orange**. In Scotland, William and Mary restored the full Presbyterian structure and abolished bishops, though they chose not to restore the political and legal functions of the Kirk, which remained subject to parliamentary control. This settlement ended Scotland's religious wars and completed its reformation.

The Union

Although the question of Kirk organization was settled in 1690, the political issue of the relationship between the Crown and the Scottish Parliament was not. From 1689 to 1697, William was at war with France, partly financed by Scottish taxes and partly fought by Scottish soldiers. Yet many Scots, mindful of the Auld Alliance, disapproved of the war and others suffered financially from the disruption to trade with France. There were other economic irritants too, principally the legally sanctioned monopoly that English merchants had over trade with the English colonies. This monopoly inspired the **Darien Scheme**, a plan to establish a Scottish colony in Panama. The colonists set off in 1698, but, thwarted by the opposition of both William and the English merchants, the scheme proved a miserable failure. The colony collapsed with the loss of £200,000 – an amount equal to half the value of the entire coinage in

The Highlands

The country that was united with England in 1707 contained three distinct cultures: in south and east Scotland, they spoke **Scots**; the local dialect in Shetland, Orkney and much of the northeast, though Scots-based, contained elements of **Norn** (Old Norse), while the language of the rest of north and west Scotland, including the Western Isles, was **Gaelic**. These linguistic differences were paralleled by different forms of social organization and customs. The people of north and west Scotland were mostly **pastoralists**, moving their sheep and cattle to Highland pastures in the summer and returning to the glens in the winter. They lived in single-room dwellings, heated by a central peat fire and sometimes shared with livestock, and in hard times they would subsist on cakes made from the blood of their live cattle mixed with oatmeal. **Highlanders** supplemented their meagre income by raiding their clan neighbours and the prosperous Lowlands, whose inhabitants regarded their northern compatriots with a mixture of fear and contempt. In the early seventeenth century, Montgomerie, a Lowland poet, suggested that God had created the first Highlander out of horseshit. When God asked his creation what he would do, the reply was "I will doun to the Lowland, Lord, and thair steill a kow."

It would be a mistake, however, to infer from the primitive nature of Highland life that the institutions of this society had existed from time immemorial. This is especially true of the "**clan**", a term that only appears in its modern usage in the sixteenth century. In theory, the clan bound together blood relatives who shared a common ancestor, a concept clearly derived from the ancient Gaelic notion of kinship. But in practice many of the clans were of non-Gaelic origin – such as the Frasers, Sinclairs and Stewarts, all of Anglo-Norman descent – and it was the mythology of a common ancestor, rather than the actuality, that cemented the clans together. Furthermore, clans were often made up of people with a variety of surnames, and there are documented cases of individuals changing their names when they swapped allegiances.

At the upper end of Highland society was the **clan chief** (who might have been a minor figure, like MacDonald of Glen Coe, or a great lord, like the Duke of Argyll, head of the Campbells), who provided protection for his followers: they would, in turn, fight for him when called upon to do so. Below the clan chief were the **chieftains of the septs**, or subunits of the clan, and then came the **tacksmen**, major tenants of the chief to whom they were frequently related. The tacksmen sublet their land to **tenants**, who were at the bottom of the social scale. The Highlanders wore a simple belted plaid wrapped around the body – rather than the kilt – and not until the late seventeenth century were certain **tartans** roughly associated with particular clans. The detailed codification of the tartan was produced by the Victorians, whose romantic vision of Highland life originated with George IV's visit to Scotland in 1822, when he appeared in an elaborate version of Highland dress, complete with flesh-coloured tights (for more on tartan, see box on p.585).

Scotland – and an angry Scottish Parliament threatened to refuse the king taxes as rioting broke out in the cities.

Meanwhile, in the north, the Highlanders blamed William for the massacre of the **MacDonalds of Glen Coe**. In 1691, William had offered pardons to those Highland chiefs who had opposed his accession, on condition that they took an oath of allegiance by New Year's Day 1692. Alasdair MacDonald of Glen Coe had turned up at the last minute, but his efforts to take the oath were frustrated by the king's officials, who were determined to see his clan, well known for their support of the Stewarts, destroyed. In February 1692, Captain Robert Campbell quartered his men in Glen Coe and, two weeks later, in the middle of the night, his troops acted on their secret orders and slaughtered as many MacDonalds as they could. Thirty-eight died, and the massacre caused a national scandal, especially among the clans, where "Murder under Trust" – killing those offering you shelter – was considered a particularly heinous crime.

The situation in Scotland was further complicated by the question of the succession. Mary died without leaving an heir and, on William's death in 1702, the crown passed to her sister **Anne**, who was also childless. In response, the English Parliament secured the Protestant succession by passing the Act of Settlement, which named the Electress Sophia of Hanover as the next in line to the throne. The Act did not, however, apply in Scotland, and the English feared that the Scots would invite James Edward Stewart back from France to be their king. Consequently, Parliament appointed commissioners charged with the consideration of "proper methods towards attaining a union with Scotland". The project seemed doomed to failure when the Scottish Parliament passed the **Act of Security** in 1703, stating that Scotland would not accept a Hanoverian monarch unless they had first received guarantees protecting their religion and their trade.

Nevertheless, despite the strength of anti-English feeling, the Scottish Parliament passed the **Act of Union** by 110 votes to 69 in January 1707. Some historians have explained the vote in terms of bribery and corruption. This certainly played a part (the Duke of Hamilton, for example, switched sides at a key moment and was subsequently rewarded with an English dukedom), but there were other factors. Scottish politicians were divided between the Cavaliers – Jacobites (supporters of the Stewarts) and Episcopalians – and the Country party, whose Presbyterian members dreaded the return of the Stewarts more than they disliked the Hanoverians. There were commercial considerations too. In 1705, the English Parliament had passed the Alien Act, which threatened to impose severe penalties on cross-border trade, whereas the Union gave merchants of both countries free access to each other's markets. The Act of Union also guaranteed the Scottish legal system and the Presbyterian Kirk, and offered compensation to those who had lost money in the Darien Scheme.

Under the terms of the Act, both parliaments were to be replaced by a new British Parliament based in London, with the Scots apportioned 45 MPs and 16 peers. There were riots when the terms became known, but no sustained opposition.

The Jacobite risings

When James VII/II was deposed he had fled to France, where he planned the reconquest of his kingdom with the support of the French king. In 1702, James's successor, William, died, and the hopes of the Stewarts passed to his cousin James, the "Old Pretender" (Pretender in the sense of having pretensions to the throne; Old to distinguish him from his son Charles, the "Young Pretender"). James's followers became known as **Jacobites**, derived from Jacobus, the Latin equivalent of James. The British crown passed to Anne, however, and after her death and the accession of the Hanoverian George I, the first major **Jacobite uprising** occurred in 1715. Its timing appeared perfect. Scottish opinion was moving against the Union, which had failed to bring Scotland any tangible economic benefits. The English had also been accused of bad faith when, contrary to their pledges, they attempted to impose their legal practices on the Scots. Neither were Jacobite sentiments confined to Scotland. There were many in England who toasted the "king across the water" and showed no enthusiasm for the new German ruler. In September 1715, the fiercely Jacobite John Erskine, Earl of Mar, raised the Stewart standard at Braemar Castle. Just eight days later, he captured Perth, where he gathered an army of over 10,000 men, drawn mostly from the Episcopalians of northeast Scotland and from the Highlands. Mar's rebellion took the government by surprise. They had only 4000 soldiers in Scotland, under the command of the Duke of Argyll, but Mar dithered until he lost the military advantage. There was an indecisive battle at Sheriffmuir in November, but by the time the Old Pretender arrived the following month 6000 veteran Dutch troops had reinforced Argyll. The rebellion disintegrated rapidly and James slunk back to exile in France in February 1716.

The **Jacobite uprising** of 1745, led by James's dashing son, Charles Edward Stewart (known as "**Bonnie Prince Charlie**"), had little chance of success. The Hanoverians had consolidated their hold on the English throne, Lowland society was uniformly loyalist, and even among the Highlanders Charles attracted only just over half of the 20,000 clansmen who could have marched with him. Nevertheless, after a decisive victory over government forces at Prestonpans, Charles made a spectacular advance into England, getting as far as Derby. London was in a state of panic: its shops were closed and the Bank of England, fearing a run on sterling, slowed withdrawals by paying out in sixpences. But Derby was as far south as Charles got. On December 6, threatened by superior forces, the Jacobites decided to retreat to Scotland. The Duke of Cumberland was sent in pursuit and the two armies met on **Culloden Moor**, near Inverness, in April 1746. Outnumbered and outgunned, the Jacobites were swept from the field, losing over 1200 men compared to Cumberland's 300 or so. After the battle, many of the wounded Jacobites were slaughtered, an atrocity that earned Cumberland the nickname "Butcher". Jacobite hopes died at Culloden and the prince lived out the rest of his life in drunken exile.

In the aftermath of the uprising, the wearing of tartan, the bearing of arms and the playing of bagpipes were all banned. Rebel chiefs lost their land and the Highlands were placed under military occupation. Most significantly, the government prohibited the private armies of the chiefs, thereby effectively destroying the clan system.

The Highland Clearances

Once the clan chief was forbidden his own army, he had no need of the large tenantry that had previously been a vital military asset. Conversely, the second half of the eighteenth century saw the Highland population increase dramatically after the introduction of the easy-to-grow and nutritious **potato**. Between 1745 and 1811, the population of the Outer Hebrides, for example, rose from 13,000 to 24,500. The clan chiefs adopted different policies to deal with the new situation. Some encouraged emigration, and as many as 6000 Highlanders left for the Americas between 1800 and 1803 alone. Other landowners developed alternative forms of employment for their tenantry, mainly fishing and kelping. **Kelp** (brown seaweed) was gathered and burnt to produce soda ash, which was used in the manufacture of soap, glass and explosives. There was a rising market for soda ash until the 1810s, with the price increasing from £2 a ton in 1760 to £20 in 1808, making a fortune for some landowners and providing thousands of Highlanders with temporary employment. Other landowners developed **sheep runs** on the Highland pastures, introducing hardy breeds like the black-faced Linton and the Cheviot. But extensive sheep farming proved incompatible with a high peasant population, and many landowners decided to clear their estates of tenants, some of whom were forcibly moved to tiny plots of marginal land, where they were to farm as **crofters**.

The pace of these **Highland Clearances** accelerated after the end of the Napoleonic Wars in 1815, when the market price for kelp, fish and cattle declined, leaving sheep as the only profitable Highland product. The most notorious Clearances took place on the estates of the Countess of Sutherland, who owned a million acres in northern Scotland. Between 1807 and 1821, around 15,000 people were thrown off her land, evictions carried out by Patrick Sellar, the estate factor, with considerable brutality. Those who failed to leave by the appointed time had their homes burnt in front of them, and one elderly woman, who failed to get out of her home after it was torched, subsequently died from her burns. The local sheriff charged Sellar with her death, but a jury of landowners acquitted him – and the sheriff was sacked. As the dispossessed Highlanders scratched a living from the acid soils of tiny crofts, they learnt through bitter experience the limitations of the clan. Famine followed, forcing large-scale emigration to America and Canada and leaving the huge uninhabited areas found in the region today.

The crofters eked out a precarious existence, but they hung on throughout the nineteenth century, often by taking seasonal employment away from home. In the 1880s, however, a sharp downturn in agricultural prices made it difficult for many crofters to pay their rent. This time, inspired by the example of the Irish Land League, they **resisted eviction**, forming the Highland Land Reform Association and the Crofters' Party. In 1886, in response to the social unrest, Gladstone's Liberal government passed the **Crofters' Holdings Act**, which conceded three of the crofters' demands: security of tenure, fair rents to be decided independently, and the right to pass on crofts by inheritance. But Gladstone did not attempt to increase the amount of land available for crofting, and shortage of land remained a major problem until the **Land Settlement Act** of 1919 made provision for the creation of new crofts. Nevertheless, the population of the Highlands has continued to decline since then, with many of the region's young people finding city life more appealing.

Industrialization

Glasgow was the powerhouse of Scotland's **Industrial Revolution**. The passage from Glasgow to the Americas was much shorter than that from rival English ports and a lucrative transatlantic trade in tobacco had developed as early as the seventeenth century. This in turn stimulated Scottish manufacturing, since, under the terms of the Navigation Acts, Americans were not allowed to trade manufactured goods. Scottish-produced linen, paper and wrought iron were exchanged for Virginia tobacco and, when the American War of Independence disrupted the trade in the 1770s and 1780s, the Scots successfully turned to trade with the West Indies and, most important of all, to the production of cotton textiles.

Glasgow's west coast location gave it ready access to the sources of raw cotton in the Americas, while the rapid growth of the British Empire provided an expanding market for its finished cloth. Initially, the city's **cotton industry**, like the earlier linen industry, was organized domestically, with spinners and weavers working in their homes, but increased demand required mass production and a need for factories. In 1787, Scotland had only nineteen mills; by 1840 there were nearly 200.

The growth of the textile industry spurred the development of other industries. In the mid-eighteenth century, the **Carron Ironworks** was founded near Falkirk, specializing in the production of military munitions. Here, the capital and expertise were English, but the location was determined by Scottish coal reserves. By 1800 it was the largest ironworks in Europe. The basis of Scotland's

shipbuilding industry was laid as early as 1802, when the steam vessel *Charlotte Dundas* was launched on the Forth–Clyde canal. Within thirty years, 95 steam vessels had been built in Scotland, most of them on Clydeside. The growth of the iron and shipbuilding industries, plus the extensive use of steam power, created a massive demand for coal, and pit shafts were sunk across the coalfields of southern Scotland.

Industrialization led to a concentration of Scotland's **population** in the central Lowlands. In 1840, one-third of the country's industrial workers lived in Lanarkshire alone, and Glasgow's population grew from 17,000 in the 1740s to over 200,000 a century later. Such sudden growth created urban overcrowding on a massive scale and, as late as 1861, 64 percent of the entire Scottish population lived in one- or two-room houses. For most Clydesiders, "house" meant a couple of small rooms in a grim tenement building, where many of the poorest families were displaced Highlanders and Irish immigrants, with the Irish arriving in Glasgow at the rate of a thousand a week during the potato famine of the 1840s.

By the late nineteenth century a measure of prosperity had emerged from industrialization, and the well-paid Clydeside engineers went to their forges wearing bowler hats and starched collars. They were confident of the future, but their optimism was misplaced. Scotland's industries were very much geared to the export market, and after **World War I** they found conditions much changed. During the war years, when exports had been curtailed by a combination of U-boat activity and war production, new industries had developed in India and Japan, and the eastern market for Scottish goods never recovered. The postwar world also witnessed a contraction of world trade, which hit the shipbuilding industry very hard and, in turn, damaged the steel and coal industries. By 1931, for instance, pig-iron production was at less than 25 percent of its 1920 output.

These difficulties were compounded by the financial collapse of the early 1930s, and by 1932 28 percent of the Scottish workforce was unemployed. Some 400,000 Scots emigrated between 1921 and 1931, and those who stayed endured some of the worst social conditions in the British Isles. By the late 1930s, Scotland had the highest infant mortality rate in Europe, while some thirty percent of homes had no toilet or bath. There was a partial economic recovery in the mid-1930s, but high unemployment remained until the start of **World War II**.

The Labour movement

In the late eighteenth century, conditions for the labouring population varied enormously. At one extreme, the handloom weavers, working from home, were well paid and much in demand, whereas the coal miners remained serfs, bought and sold with the pits they worked in, until 1799. During this period, the working class gave some support to the **radical movement**, loosely connected groups of reformers, led by the lower middle class, who took their inspiration from the French Revolution. One of these groups, the "Friends of the People", campaigned for the extension of the right to vote, and such apparently innocuous activities earned one member, Thomas Muir, a sentence of fourteen years' transportation to Australia.

In 1820, the radicals called for a national strike and an insurrection to "show the world that we are determined to be free". At least 60,000 workers downed tools for a week, and one group set off for the Carron Ironworks to seize arms. The government was, however, well prepared. It slammed radical leaders into prison and a heavy military presence kept control of the streets. The strike fizzled out and three leading radicals, all weavers, were later executed.

The 1832 **Scottish Reform Act** extended the franchise to include a large proportion of the middle class and thereafter political radicalism assumed a more distinctive working-class character, though its ideals still harked back to the American and French revolutions. In the 1840s, the **Chartists** led the campaign for working-class political rights by sending massive petitions to Parliament and organizing huge demonstrations. When Parliament rejected the petitions, the more determined Chartists – the "physical-force men" – urged insurrection. This call to arms was not taken up by the Scottish working class, however, and support for the Chartists fell away. The insurrectionary phase of Scottish labour was over.

During the next thirty years, as Scotland's economy prospered, skilled workers organized themselves into **craft unions**, such as the Amalgamated Society of Engineers, dedicated to negotiating improvements for their members within the status quo. Politically, the trade unions gave their allegiance to the Liberal Party, but the first major crack in the Liberal–union alliance came in 1888, when **Keir Hardie** left the Liberals to form the Scottish Socialist Party, which was later merged with the Independent Labour Party, founded in Bradford in 1893. Scottish socialism as represented by the ILP was ethical rather than Marxist in orientation, owing a great deal to the Kirk background of many of its members. But electoral progress was slow, partly because the Roman Catholic priesthood consistently preached against socialism.

In the early years of the twentieth century, two small Marxist groups established themselves on Clydeside: the **Socialist Labour Party**, which concentrated on workplace militancy, and the party-political **British Socialist Party**, whose most famous member was the Marxist lecturer John MacLean. During World War I, the local organizers of the SLP gained considerable influence by playing on the fears of the skilled workers, who felt their status was being undermined by the employment of unskilled workers. After the war, the influence of the shop stewards culminated in a massive campaign for the forty-hour working week. The strikes and demonstrations of the campaign, including one of 100,000 people in St George's Square in Glasgow, panicked the government into sending in the troops. But this was no Bolshevik Revolution; as Manny Shinwell, the seamen's leader and future Labour Party politician, observed, "[The troops] had nothing much to do but chat to the local people and drink their cups of tea." The rank and file may have had little interest in revolution, but many of the activists did go on to become leaders within the newly formed Communist Party of Great Britain.

The ILP, by then an affiliated part of the socialist **Labour Party**, made its electoral breakthrough in 1922, when it sent 29 Scottish MPs to Westminster. They set out with high hopes of social progress and reform, aspirations that were dashed, like trade union militancy, by the 1930s Depression. At the 1945 general election, Labour won forty seats in Scotland and, in more recent times, the party has dominated Scottish politics with its gradual eclipse of the Scottish Conservatives. In 1955 the Conservatives held 36 Scottish seats; by 1995 they had just ten, and by 1997 none at all.

The ILP MPs of the 1920s combined their socialism with a brand of Scottish nationalism. In 1924, for instance, the MP James Maxton had declared his intentions to "make English-ridden, capitalist-ridden Scotland into the Scottish socialist Commonwealth". The Labour Party maintained an official policy of self-government for Scotland, endorsing home rule in 1945 and 1947, but these endorsements were made with less and less enthusiasm. In 1958, Labour abandoned the commitment altogether and adopted a unionist vision of Scotland, much to the chagrin of many Scottish activists.

In 1971, **Upper Clyde Shipbuilders** stood on the brink of closure, its demise symbolizing the failure of traditional Labour politicians to revive Scotland's industrial base, which had resumed its decline after the end of World War II. In the event, UCS was partly saved by the work-in organized by two Communist shop stewards, Jimmy Reid and Jimmy Airlie. After fourteen months, the work-in finally succeeded in winning government support to keep part of the shipyard open, and Scots saw the broadly based campaign waged on its behalf as a national issue – Scottish industries set against an indifferent London government. Many socialist Scots, like James Jack, General Secretary of the Scottish TUC, moved towards some form of nationalism. Twenty-one years later, the closure of the steelworks at **Ravenscraig** in Motherwell revived many of the same emotions.

Towards devolution

The **National Party of Scotland** was formed in 1928, its membership averaging about 7000 people, mostly drawn from the non-industrial parts of the country. Very much a mixture of practical politicians and left-leaning eccentrics, such as the poet Hugh MacDiarmid, in 1934 it merged with the right-wing Scottish Party to create the **Scottish National Party**. The SNP, after years in the political wilderness, achieved its electoral breakthrough in 1967 when Winnie Ewing won Hamilton from Labour in a by-election. The following year the SNP won 34 percent of the vote in local government elections and gained control of Cumbernauld, successes that had repercussions within both the Labour and Conservative parties. Both parties, wishing to head off the Nationalists, began to work on schemes to give Scotland a measure of self-government, and the term "**devolution**" became common currency in Scottish politics. However, when the Conservatives came to power in 1970, Edward Heath, the prime minister, shelved plans for devolution because the SNP had secured only a twelve percent share of the Scottish vote.

The situation changed dramatically in 1974, when Labour were returned to power with a wafer-thin majority. The SNP held seven seats, which gave them considerable political leverage, and devolution was back on the agenda. The SNP had also run an excellent election campaign, concentrating on North Sea oil, which was now being piped ashore in significant quantities. Their two most popular slogans, "England expects... Scotland's oil" and "Rich Scots or Poor Britons?", seemed to have caught the mood of Scotland.

In 1979, the Labour government, struggling to hold onto office after its "winter of discontent" of strikes had decimated public services, put its devolution proposals before the Scottish people in a **referendum**. The "yes" vote gained 33 percent, the "no" vote 31 percent – but the required 40 percent threshold had not been reached. Not for the first time, Scottish opinion had shifted away from home rule; the reluctance to embrace it was based on uncertainty about what might follow, a concern about too many layers of government and, in some areas, a fear that the resulting assembly might be dominated by the Clydeside conurbation. The incoming Conservative government of **Margaret Thatcher** set its face against any form of devolution. It argued that the majority of Scots had voted for parties committed to the Union – namely Labour, the Liberal Democrats and themselves – and that only a minority supported the separation advocated by the SNP. At the same time, the government asserted that any form of devolution would lead inevitably to the break-up of the

United Kingdom and, therefore, that the devolution solutions put forward by other parties could not be what the Scottish people wanted, because the inescapable result would be separation.

As the Thatcher years rolled on, growing evidence from opinion polls and central and local government elections suggested that few Scottish voters accepted either this reasoning or the implication that Scots did not know what was good for them. The Conservatives' support in Scotland was further eroded by their introduction of the deeply unpopular Community Charge – universally nicknamed the **Poll Tax** – a form of local taxation that was charged per head and took little account of income. The fact that it had been imposed in Scotland a year earlier than in England and Wales was the source of further resentment.

In 1992, having largely rejected Conservative ideology and all but a few of the party's candidates, Scots found themselves still under a Tory government, this time with **John Major** at the helm. Though some Scottish Conservatives quietly supported devolution, their limited influence in the party as a whole was evident in the appointment of Michael Forsyth, one of the most articulate advocates of Thatcherite policy, as Secretary of State for Scotland.

Throughout the 1980s and early 1990s, the case for devolution had been made consistently by both Labour and the Liberal Democrats. In 1989, they, together with a cross-section of Scottish organizations, including local government, churches and trade unions, co-operated in the establishment of the **Scottish Constitutional Convention**, a standing conference which developed detailed proposals for the introduction of a devolved Scottish legislature. Initially, the SNP saw the Convention as a diversion from their aim of an independent Scotland firmly attached to the European Union and did not join. Later, however, nationalists began to argue that devolution might after all offer a stepping stone to independence.

By the mid-1990s the promise of change was in the air, but without their hands directly on the levers of power, none of the main players could make it happen. Scotland's new political era began with the general election of May 1997, won by Tony Blair's **Labour Party**; the Conservatives were routed across the UK, losing every seat in Scotland. Under the stewardship of Scottish Secretary Donald Dewar, the new Labour government moved swiftly to publish its proposals for devolution and a **referendum** was organized for that September. The electorate responded with a clear endorsement: 75 percent of voters were in favour of establishing a separate Scottish Parliament.

The excitement generated in Scotland by the referendum helped imbue the subsequent establishment of the parliament with a palpable sense of destiny, something it had to cling to as many of the fears voiced in 1979 again resurfaced. By and large, however, the optimistic mood was carried through to Scotland's **general election** in May 1999 – the first-ever, given that the last elected Scottish parliament in 1707 had not been under universal suffrage. The form of proportional representation adopted for the election made it unlikely that any one party would achieve an overall majority in the 129-seat assembly, and indeed the final result left Labour needing to enter into a coalition with the Liberal Democrats (or LibDems) to achieve a governing majority. The leader of the Labour group, **Donald Dewar**, became Scotland's First Minister, with **Jim Wallace**, leader of the Scottish LibDems, his deputy. The SNP won just under thirty percent of the vote, making them the second largest party, while proportional representation ensured that the Conservatives regained a presence in Scottish politics once more. Joining the main parties in the assembly were the first Green politician to be elected in a national vote in the UK and a left-wing socialist, Tommy Sheridan, whose vocal and principalled support for Scotland's underclass brought him both attention and admiration. The new MSPs (Members of the Scottish Parliament) voted **Sir David Steel**, former leader of the British Liberal Party and one of the elder statesmen of Scottish politics, to be the Presiding Officer.

In a **ceremony** deliberately mixing pomp with down-to-earth, populist touches, the Queen came to the Parliament's temporary home in the Church of Scotland Assembly Hall in Edinburgh to open the Parliament officially on July 1, 1999. This marked the official transfer of power to the new assembly in matters of education, health, law and order, social work, local government, planning and the environment, economic development, agriculture and fisheries, sport and the arts (Westminster retains control over defence, foreign affairs, major economic and tax issues and social security). The new parliament has the power to initiate new legislation, and to pass bills without the endorsement of Westminster.

The delicate balancing act that the Labour–LibDem coalition faced in the first few years of the parliament was to prove that devolved government could still offer distinctive Scottish solutions without breaking from policies being pursued by the Labour government in Westminster. It made its mark with important decisions abolishing tuition fees for Scottish university students, repealing a law banning the promotion of homosexuality in school classrooms, and granting state support for the elderly in care, all policies notably to the left of the Labour programme elsewhere in the UK. While the parliament has had to work hard to earn respect from a broadly cynical and demanding media, the general consensus is that the increased scrutiny under which Scottish affairs are now being conducted has brought a greater sense of realism and responsibility to the political scene.

A far greater blow to the credibility of the infant project came in October 2000 with the untimely death of First Minister Donald Dewar, widely respected as the one politician of true stature in the parliament. The post of First Minister was taken up by Henry McLeish, another former Westminster MP, but within a year he had resigned over financial irregularities, to be replaced in November 2001 by Jack McConnell, a Labour politician with no experience of the Westminster parliament.

Nor will the parliament be allowed to settle into its role without a handful of recurring irritations. Still unanswered are the consequences of devolution for the British parliament and **constitution**. For years, the outspoken Westminster Labour MP for West Lothian, **Tam Dalyell**, has criticized his own party for its failure to answer what has become known as the West Lothian Question. Simply put, this asks why Scottish MPs at Westminster should continue to have the same amount of influence over the affairs of the rest of Britain now that a Scottish parliament is looking after the same affairs in Scotland. Also controversial is the issue of the **parliament's new home**, with MSPs due to move sometime in 2002 to a custom-built new building in Edinburgh. The death within six months of each other of both Donald Dewar and the building's architect, Enric Miralles, left the project without an identifiable champion, and the inevitable squabbles over spiralling costs have, for the moment, taken the shine off what promises to be one of the more striking emblems of Scotland's new political age.

Prospects

Although Scots have had to readjust to finding the sometimes tawdry business of day-to-day politicking taking place in their own backyard rather than tucked away in London, a degree of idealism remains that the parliament will stimulate a vitality and originality in the way Scottish issues are tackled. Core to this is the realization that, for better or worse, the parliament is here to stay and that it is the proper way for a nation as proud and singular as Scotland to conduct its affairs.

In recent years the Scottish **economy** has benefited from the general prosperity enjoyed in the UK as a whole. There have been hard times, however, particularly in central Scotland, where the decline of **heavy industry**, including deep coal-mining, steelmaking, shipbuilding and engineering, has been all but total, and **unemployment** has produced profound social problems in parts of Glasgow, Edinburgh and smaller towns. Hopes that employment in a broadening range of technology-based industries would underpin the new economy were shaken severely with the closure of factories run by giants such as Motorola and Hyundai; meanwhile another great hope, **tourism**, was struggling to grow as expected even before the disastrous spread of foot and mouth disease to farms in Scotland in 2001. Financial services and insurance, on the other hand, have been a growth area in the Central Belt. In northeast Scotland, particularly around Aberdeen, the **oil industry** – although past its boom – continues to underpin an economy which might otherwise have struggled to cope with the uncertainties of agriculture and, especially, fishing.

Though there have been encouraging signs of recent progress, the **Highlands and Islands** remains an economically fragile area that needs special measures, distance from markets being an obvious and fundamental problem. Prosperity of a temporary sort has been provided in some areas by oil, but the best options for the future are likely to lie in selective, high-quality development in fishing, fish farming and other food-based industries, activities which use the internet and other advanced telecommunications technology, primary industries such as forestry and quarrying and, last but certainly not least, tourism. Increasingly, the local environment is seen as a major asset for the attraction and success of most kinds of employment, and the establishment of a system of National Parks is seen as an important waymark in providing legislative support to those ideals. One of the keys to Highland development is the ownership and control of land. Some of the largest Highland estates continue to be owned and managed from afar, with little regard to local needs or priorities; the success of groups of crofters in buying estates in Assynt and Knoydart, as well as the purchase of the island of Eigg by its inhabitants, hints at a broadening of land ownership which many hope the land reforms that the Scottish Parliament brought in early will do more to promote.

One aspect of Scottish life which has remained upbeat in the last decade or so is its **cultural life**. Writers such as Jim Kelman and A.L. Kennedy, pop groups Travis and Primal Scream, classical composer James Macmillan, and artists Andy Goldsworthy and David Mach, have all given Scotland a substantial presence on the British arts scene. Also notable has been the revival of **Gaelic**, supported by large investments in broadcasting and publishing, and demonstrated by the popularity among young audiences – few of them Gaels – of folk/rock bands like Runrig and Capercaillie. But the transformation goes beyond that: old inhibitions about writing in Scots or in Shetland dialect have been laid to rest too, and much of the revival of cities such as Glasgow and Dundee is attributed to their focus on the arts. Indeed, contemporary culture is one of the healthiest aspects of Scotland today, and artists have often been able to articulate the richness of Scotland's post-devolution future with more ambition and colour than the country's frequently uninspiring politicians.

Flora and fauna

A comprehensive account of Scotland's wildlife would fill a book: what follows is a general overview of the effects of climate and human activity on the country's flora and fauna.

Climate

Scotland's mountains are high enough to impose harsh conditions, especially in the Highlands, and the **Cairngorm plateau** (the largest area of high ground in the whole of Britain) is almost arctic even in summer. Despite this, however, since the easing of the Ice Age about 10,000 years ago, Scotland has developed a rather complex climate, and some areas of the country are quite mild.

The warmish water of the Gulf Stream tempers conditions on the west coast, so that at **Inverewe**, for example, you'll find incongruously lush gardens blooming with subtropical plants. Inland, the weather becomes more extreme, but what restricts plant life on many Scottish hills is not the cold so much as the stress of wind and gloomy cloud cover. **Ben Nevis**, for example, is clouded and whipped by 50mph gales for more than two-thirds of the year, and as a result the tree line – the height to which trees grow up the slopes – may be only 150ft above sea level near the west coast, but over 2000ft on some of the sheltered hillsides inland.

A brief history

After the Ice Age, "arctic" and "alpine" plants abounded, eventually giving way to woody shrubs and trees, notably the **Scots pine**. Oak and other hardwood trees followed in some places, but the Scots pine remained the distinctive tree, spreading expansively to form the great **Caledonian Forest**. Parts of this ancient forest still remain, miraculously surviving centuries of attack, but it is only comparatively recently that positive attempts at conservation have been made.

Early **settlement**, from the Picts to the Norsemen, led to clearance of large areas of forest, and huge areas were burned during the clan wars. When centuries of unrest ended with the Jacobite defeat at Culloden in 1745, the glens were ransacked for timber, which was floated downriver to fuel iron smelting and other industries. The clansmen had had a freebooting cattle economy, but during the infamous **Clearances** both the cattle and the defeated Highlanders were replaced by the more profitable sheep of the new landlords. As also happened on the English downland and moorland, intensive sheep grazing kept the land open, eventually destroying much woodland by preventing natural regeneration.

In Victorian times, **red deer** herds, which also graze heavily, provided stalking, and when rapid-firing breech-loading guns came into general use around the 1850s, **grouse shooting** became a passion. Since grouse graze heather, large areas of forest were burned to encourage fresh green growth and maintenance of open moorland.

The flatter **lowlands** are now dominated by mechanized farming; barley, beef, turnips and potatoes conspire against wildlife, and pollution and development are as damaging here as elsewhere. Even the so-called "**wilderness**" is under threat. Its own popularity obviously holds dangers, and the unique flora of the Cairngorm peaks, for example, is in danger of being stamped out under the feet of the summer visitors using the ski lifts. But even more damaging than tourism is **conifer planting.** In recent decades, boosted (if not caused) by generous grant aid and tax dodges, large areas of open moorland have been planted with tightly packed monocultural ranks of foreign conifers, forbidding to much wildlife. Coniferization is particularly threatening to large areas of bogland in the "Flow Country" of Caithness and elsewhere, areas that are as unique a natural environment as the tropical rainforests. For these and other similar habitats, registration as an **SSSI** – a Site of Special Scientific Interest – has proved barely adequate, and the only real safeguard is for such areas to be owned or managed by organizations such as Scottish Natural Heritage (the national agency) or the Scottish Wildlife Trust, the Royal Society for the Protection of Birds or similar voluntary groups.

Wild flowers

Relic patches of the Scots pine Caledonian Forest, such as the Black Wood of Rannoch and Rothiemurchus Forest below the Cairngorms, are often more open than an oak wood, the pines, interspersed with birch and juniper, spaced out in hilly heather. These woods feature some wonderful wild flowers, such as the **wintergreens** which justify their name, unobtrusive **orchids** in the shape of creeping lady's tresses and lesser twayblade and, in parts of the northeast especially, the rare beauty of the **twinflower**, holding its paired heads over the summer needle litter.

You'll also find old oak woods in some places, especially in the lower coastward lengths of the southern glens. Here the Atlantic influence encourages masses of spring flowers including **wood anemone** and **wild hyacinth**, the Scottish term for what in England is called a bluebell. (In Scotland the name "bluebell" describes the summer-flowering English harebell that grows on more open ground.) Scotland, or at least lowland Scotland, has many flowers found further south in Britain – **maiden pink**, orchids, **cowslip** and others in grassy areas. Roadside flowers, such as **meadowsweet** and **meadow buttercup**, **dog rose, primrose** and **red campion**, extend widely up through Scotland, but others, such as the **white field rose** and **mistletoe**, **red valerian**, **small scabious**, **cuckoo pint** and **traveller's joy** (and the elm tree), reach the end of their range in the Scottish central lowlands.

Scotland's mountains, especially where the rock is limey or basic in character, as on Ben Lawers, for example, are dotted with arctic-alpine plants, such as mountain **avens**, with their white flowers and glossy oak-like leaves, and handsome **purple saxifrage**, both of which favour a soil rich in calcium. Here, as elsewhere, the flowers are to be found on ledges and rock-faces out of reach of the sheep and deer. Other classic mountain plants are **alpine lady's mantle** and **moss campion**, which grows in a tight cushion, set with single pink flowers.

Higher up on the bleak wind-battered mountain tops, there may be nothing much more than a low "heath" of mosses and maybe some tough low grasses or rushes between the scatterings of rubble. Because this environment encourages few insects, such plants are generally self-fertilizing and some even produce small plants or "bulbils" in their flower heads instead of seed.

A variety of ferns shelter in the slopes amid the tumbled rock screes or in cracks in the rock alongside streams. In Scotland's damp climate, you'll also see many ferns on lower ground, but some, the **holly fern** for one, are true mountain species. **Lichens**, too, are common on exposed rocks, and in the woods bushy and bearded lichens can coat the branches and trunks.

Bogs are a natural feature of much of the flatter ground in the Highlands, often extending for miles. Scottish bogland comprises an intricate mosaic of domes of living bog moss (sometimes bright green or a striking orange or yellow), domes of drier, heathery peat, and pools dotted in between. The wettest areas give rise to specialized plants such as **cranberry**, **bearberry** and also the **sundews**, which gain nutrients in these poor surroundings by trapping and absorbing midges with the sticky hairs on their flat leaves.

At sea level, the rivers spawn estuaries; these and some sea lochs are edged with **salt marshes**, which in time dry out into "meadows" colourful with **sea aster** and other flowers. The west coast, especially the cliffs of Galloway, shimmers blue with **spring squill** as soon as the winter eases, while the Galloway shore marks the southernmost limit of **Scots lovage**, a celery-scented member of the cow parsley family. A relic of arctic times, the **oysterplant**, with blue-grey leaves and pink bell flowers, also grows here, as it does on the shores of Iceland and Scandinavia.

Scotland has some wonderful **sand dune** systems, which on the back shores harden into grassy patches often grazed by rabbits to create a fine turf.

Birds

It might seem unusual to find birds nesting at over 3000ft, but in Scotland the wind is strong enough to blow patches of icy ground clear of snow, enabling birds to make their homes on the mountains. The **dotterel**, a small wader with a chestnut stomach, is a rare summer visitor to the Cairngorms and other heights – in the Arctic it nests down to sea level. Even rarer is the **snow bunting**, the male black and white, the female brownish; perhaps only ten pairs nest on Scotland's mountains, although they are seen much more widely around the coasts in winter, when the male also becomes brown. The **snowy owl**, at the southern limit of its range, is a regular visitor to Shetland.

More common on the heights is the **ptarmigan**, shy and almost invisible in its summer coat, as it plays hide and seek amongst the lichen-patched boulders. You're most likely to see it on the Cairngorms, as it ventures out for the sandwich crusts left by the summer visitors using the ski lifts. It is resident up here, and moults from mottled in summer to pure white in winter.

The ptarmigan's camouflage helps protect it from the **golden eagle**. This magnificent bird ranges across many Highland areas: there are perhaps three hundred nesting pairs on Skye, the Outer Hebrides, above Aviemore and Deeside, and in the northwest Highlands, each needing a territory of thousands of acres over which to hunt hares, grouse and ptarmigan. The **raven** also has strong links with the mountains, tumbling in crazy acrobatics past the rock-faces. After nearly seventy years' absence, the **white-tailed (sea) eagle**, whose wing span is even greater than that of the golden eagle, has been successfully reintroduced to Rùm. The resident breeding population is still very small, however, and the exact location of the eyries is kept secret.

Where the slopes lessen to moorland, the domain of the **red grouse** begins. This game bird not only affects the landscape but also, via the persecution of gamekeepers, threatens eagles and other birds of prey, although they are all theoretically protected. The **cuckoo** can be heard as far north as Shetland – one of its favourite dupes, the **meadow pipit**, is fairly widespread on any rough ground up to 3000ft. **Dunlin** and other waders nest on the wet moorlands and boglands, where the soft land allows them to use their delicate bills to probe for insects and other food.

You'll come across many notable birds where pine woods encroach onto open moor. One such is the **black grouse**, with its bizarre courtship rituals, where both sexes come together for aggressive, ritualistic display in a small gathering area known as a "lek". The **capercaillie**, found deeper in the forest and perhaps floundering amongst the branches, is an unexpectedly large, turkey-like bird, about 3ft from bill to end of tail, which also has a flamboyant courting display. A game bird, it was shot to extinction but reintroduced into Scotland from Europe in 1837. Other birds that favour the pine woods are the **long-eared owl**, many of the tit family (including the **crested tit** in the Spey Valley), the **siskin** and the **goldcrest**. The Speyside woods, especially, are a stronghold of the **crossbill**, which uses its overlapping bill to prise open pine cones.

Scottish lochs are as rich in birdlife as the moorlands that embrace them. After fifty years of absence, the **osprey** returned and more than a hundred pairs now breed; the best site to see them is near Loch Garten on Speyside. In addition to common species such as **mallard** and **tufted duck**, you might also see **goosander**, **red-breasted merganser** and other wildfowl. The superbly streamlined fish-eating **red-** and **black-throated divers** nest in the north-west, while the **great northern diver**, with its shivery wailing call, is largely a winter visitor on the coasts, although one or two pairs may occasionally nest.

Scotland is also strong on coastal birds. **Eider duck** gather in their thousands at the mouth of the Tay, and the estuaries are also a magnet for **waders** and **wild geese** in winter: the total population of barnacle geese from the Arctic island of Spitsbergen winters in the Solway estuary and on the farmland alongside. Other notable areas are remote cliffs such as St Abb's Head in the Borders, and the many offshore "**bird islands**", which, although often little more than bare rock, attract vast colonies that fish the sea around them. Some have their own speciality: **Manx shearwaters** have vast colonies on Rùm, for example, while the Shetland isle of Foula has three thousand pairs of **great skuas**, about a third of the total population breeding in the northern hemisphere. Remote St Kilda is also stunning, with snowstorms of **gannets, puffins, guillemots, petrels** and **shearwaters**.

In addition to Scotland's resident bird population, and the winter and spring migrants, the western coasts and islands often see transatlantic "accidentals" blown far off course, which give rise to inbred **subspecies**. St Kilda is of particular interest to specialists, not only for its sheer numbers of resident birds but also for the St Kilda wren, a distinct subspecies. Fair Isle also sees large numbers of migrant and vagrant birds from both sides of the Atlantic. In northern and parts of eastern Scotland, the English all-black carrion crow is replaced by the "hoodie" or **hooded crow**, also found around the Mediterranean, with its distinctive grey back and underparts. Where the ranges of carrion crow and hoodie overlap, they interbreed, producing offspring with some grey patches of plumage.

Mammals

By the mid-eighteenth century, much of Scotland's wild animal life – including the Scottish **wolf**, **beaver**, **wild boar** and **elk** – had already disappeared (though the beaver is now being reintroduced). The indigenous **reindeer** was wiped out in the twelfth century, but more recently a semi-wild herd of Swedish stock was reintroduced to the slopes of the Cairngorms above Aviemore. Of two other semi-wild species, **Highland cattle** and **Shetland ponies**, the former is a classic case of breeding fitting conditions (they can survive in snow for fifty days a year), while the latter, the smallest British native pony, probably arrived in the later stages of the Ice Age when the ice was retreating but still gave a bridge across the salt water. There are feral **goats** in some places, but probably the most interesting of such animals is the **Soay sheep** of St Kilda. This, Britain's only truly wild sheep, notable for its soft brown fleece, can be seen as a farm pet and in wildlife parks – and is even used to graze some nature reserves in the south of Britain.

Although there are **sika** and **fallow deer** in places, and **roe deer** are widespread, Scotland is the stronghold of wild **red deer** herds, which, despite culling, stalking for sport and harsh winters, still number more than quarter of a million head. By origin a woodland animal, they might graze open ground – of necessity when the forest has been cleared – but they also move up to high ground in summer to avoid the biting flies and the tourists, and to graze on heather and lichens. They're most obvious in the snowy depths of winter, when, forced downhill in search of food, large numbers may be seen by road or rail travellers on Rannoch Moor or between Blair Atholl and Drumochter Pass.

The **fox** is widespread, as are the **mole** and **hedgehog**, but the **badger** is rather more rare. The **wild cat** and **pine marten** live in remote areas, hiding away in the moors and forests. The former, despite its initial resemblance to the family pet, is actually quite different – larger, with longer, striped fur, and a blunt-ended bushy tail that is also striped. The agile cat-sized pine marten, although hunted by gamekeepers, is maintaining reduced numbers, preying on squirrels and other small animals.

Native red **squirrels** are predominantly found in the Highlands, where they are still largely free from competition from the greys, which began to establish themselves about a century ago and now have a strong presence in many lowland areas. **Rabbit** and **brown hare** are widespread, as are the **blue** or **mountain hare** in the Highlands, usually adopting a white or patchy white coat in winter. The north Scottish **stoat** also dons a white winter coat, its tail tipped with black, when it is known as **ermine**. Although Scotland is too far north for the dormouse and the harvest mouse, **shrews, voles** and **field mice** abound and, though there are few bats, the related **pipistrelle** is quite widely seen.

You may also be lucky enough to encounter the **otter**, endangered in the rest of Britain. In Scotland, they are found not only in the rushing streams but more often along the west coast and in the northern and western isles, where they hunt the seashore for crabs and inshore fish. The otter is not to be confused with the feral **mink**, escaped from fur farms to take up life in the wild; these mink are a scourge in some areas, destroying birds.

Whales and their kin are frequent visitors to coastal waters and **seals**, including the shy grey seal, are quite common. However, in the hitherto virgin sea lochs of the west coast, both the seals and the coastal otters are under threat from the spread of **fish farms** (for salmon and sea trout). Not only are they poisoned by the chemicals used to keep the trapped fish vermin-free, but they also face the threat of being shot by the fish-farm owners when they raid what is to them simply a natural larder.

Fish, reptiles and insects

Quite apart from the Loch Ness monster, Scotland has a rich water life. The Dee and other rivers are fished when **salmon** swim upstream to breed in their ancestral gravel headwaters. The fish leap waterfalls on the way, and many rivers which have been dammed for hydroelectric power generation have "salmon ladders" to help them – these make great tourist attractions. The **sea trout** is also strongly migratory, the **brown** or **mountain trout** less so, although river or stream dwellers do move upstream and loch dwellers move up the incoming rivers to spawn. Related to these game fish is the **powan** or **freshwater**

herring, found only in the poorer northern basins of Loch Lomond, and possibly a relic from Ice Age arctic conditions. The richer southern waters of Loch Lomond and similar lakes contain **roach**, **perch** and other "coarse" fish.

Although the **adder** is common, the grass snake is not found in Scotland. Both **lizards** and the snake-like **slowworm** (in fact a legless lizard) are widespread, as are the **frog** and **toad**; the natterjack toad, however, is rarely seen this far north.

Scottish boglands are notable for their **dragon flies**, which prefer acid water, and **hawkers, darters** and **damselflies** feature in the south. One Scottish particular is the **blue hawker**, common in parts of the western Highlands. As for **butterflies**, some of the familiar types from further south – common blue, hairstreaks and others – are scattered in areas where conditions are not too harsh. One species with a liking for the heights is the **mountain ringlet**, only seen elsewhere in the English Lake District and in the Alps, which flies above 1500ft in the Grampians. Adapted to quite harsh conditions, it is clearly a relic of early post-glacial times. Another mountain butterfly, the **Scotch argus**, no longer found in England or Wales, is widespread in Scotland, and the **elephant hawk moth** can be seen in the Insh marshes below the Cairngorms.

Architecture

From crofts to castles, the Victorian grand residence to the "new towns", Scotland has a rich legacy of strong, unique buildings. Stonework predominates, from the long, low crofthouses of the Western Isles to the soft red sandstone that fills the streets of Glasgow. Surrounding countries have also had a substantial influence: some settlements in Orkney and Shetland evoke links with the Norse kingdoms, while the ruined church architecture of the Central Belt and Borders is testimony to a long history of battles with the marauding English.

Prehistoric times to the thirteenth century

One morning in 1850, after a ferocious storm, the villagers of Orkney woke to find **Skara Brae** – one of the earliest prehistoric sites in Scotland – revealed beneath the beautiful white sands. This **Neolithic** stone village is so well preserved that you can still see domestic details typical of the age, such as flagstone box beds, built due to the lack of timber on the islands. Small passages unite what must have been quite a large and intricate settlement of stock farmers, who originally came to Scotland from mainland Europe; a turf roof provided insulation from wind and cold. The chambered tombs at **Maes Howe** on Orkney are another great architectural achievement, dating from 2750 BC and complete with Viking graffiti from later raids on the islands. These tombs are remarkably well constructed, incorporating monoliths into the fine masonry that supports the narrow passages and small tomb cells. A fairly large community also existed at the **Jarlshof** prehistoric and Norse settlement on Shetland, where small stone cells grouped around a central hearth provided the main accommodation, with now-ruined outhouses used for bronze work and sheltering cattle. The survival of a number of ritual sites, including many **stone circles**, suggests some form of religious activity in Scotland at this time. One of the most beautiful and well-preserved stands at **Callanish** on Lewis, where a circle of megaliths rise majestically from the ground with radiating lines of stone in a mysteriously symbolic form. The central stone is nearly 16ft high and sits next to a small chambered cairn, which may have once contained human remains.

During the **Bronze Age**, from around 1000 BC, the two predominant types of defensive settlements, made from earth and timber, were spectacular **hillforts**, and artificial islands built in the middle of lochs, called **crannogs**; little now remains of either of these. It wasn't until the **Iron Age** (from around 400 BC) that the next significant architectural development was to occur. For residents of the northwest mainland and the northern islands, the need for protection from attack or invasion and from the harshness of the weather was particularly pressing, and so it's here that most of Scotland's 400 or so **brochs**, the majority in ruins, can be found. Circular, windowless and tall – some over 40ft high – these dry-stone buildings were sturdily built to protect the inhabitants who lived inside, sheltered underneath wooden constructions. Broad at the bottom and narrow at the top, the unusual shape was due to the necessity for a thick base to support the high walls and provide storage and guard rooms. Brochs also had two walls and a spiral staircase leading up to a timber roof – a very useful vantage point. Some were inhabited for several centuries; the finest example is Shetland's **Broch of Mousa** from about 100 BC, which is remarkably well preserved due to its isolated position on a small island, free from the stone-stealing that plagued subsequent settlements.

In 83 AD, the Scottish border came under threat from the **Romans**. Their success was limited, however, and the civilizing influence of Rome was to have barely any effect on the life and tribes of Scotland, who continued to live in brochs and crannogs, or erect primitive buildings of timber, wattle and clay. Of the Roman structures that have survived, the most impressive are the remnants of the **Antonine Wall**, a 36-mile-long construction that stretched from Kilpatrick to Bo'ness. Less substantial than the great Hadrian's Wall, it was originally built as a temporary measure to aid the overthrow of the fierce Pictish tribes, but was soon abandoned.

The subsequent introduction of **Christianity** left a much greater architectural legacy in Scotland. The primitive church of 397 AD at **Whithorn** marks one of the earliest Christian sites in Scotland and, with the arrival of St Columba at Iona in 563, the Celtic Christian community really came to dominate the country's religious matters. Evidence of this can be seen in the characteristic **round towers** at **Brechin** in Angus and **Egilsay** in Orkney. Places of refuge for the monastic fellowship during times of attack, these were well defended, with a raised entrance and few windows. The simple and basic structures of the Irish Celtic church conveyed their ascetic religious beliefs, while artistic and creative energies were poured into the making of sculpted crosses and illuminated manuscripts. Fine carving survives at the monastic foundation on **Iona**, a religious community that still thrives today. Few other such buildings remain, indicating that they were constructed from materials like timber, clay and turf.

The marriage of Malcolm III to the Saxon princess Margaret in 1070 heralded a dramatic upsurge in Scottish architecture. Malcolm created a feudal society based on agriculture and, more importantly, his wife orchestrated the reintroduction of Latin Christianity to the central areas of Scotland, founding many ecclesiastical buildings and finally bringing a European influence to this region – while the Highlands and Islands continued to build in the vernacular tradition. The **Romanesque** (or Norman) style can be seen at its best at **Dalmeny**. This simple, thick-walled three-cell church has narrow window openings and a round arched doorway crowned by typically Romanesque wall arcading. The Anglo-Norman influence also created larger buildings, cruciform in plan with aisled naves and three-storey elevations; these were not actual physical levels but would consist of arches, a middle storey, usually formed by blind arches or decorative wall hangings but sometimes an actual gallery for the local notables and, at the top, stained-glass windows. The thick piers and semicircular arches of **Dunfermline Abbey** in Fife are typically Norman.

The introduction of Gothic

It was the Cistercians who brought the significant pointed arch and lancet window to Scotland and introduced the **Gothic** style to the country's craftsmen. As buildings were either reconstructed or modified in future centuries, the church at **Dunstaffnage** in Argyll, with its simple rectangular plan and lancet windows, is a rare example of Early Gothic design. The twelfth-century abbey at **Jedburgh** in the Borders was just one of the abbeys that housed the religious communities being imported from England and France to southern and central parts of the country. Now in ruins, this church is very much in the transitional style between Romanesque and Gothic, as the west front contains a Romanesque round-arched doorway with a thirteenth-century rose window in the main gable. One of the most complete of the ruined Border Abbeys,

Dryburgh Abbey, in beautiful red sandstone, has an unusual vertical emphasis in the main arcade. **Melrose Abbey** contains examples of High Gothic detail, such as delicate tracery and flying buttresses, while **Kelso Abbey** stands out for its simplicity and massive proportions. These great Scottish abbeys, with the exception of the austere Cistercian communities, would have been richly decorated with tapestries, murals and carved furnishings. Unfortunately, their position in the southeast of Scotland left them vulnerable to attack from the English and they suffered badly as a result.

In the thirteenth century, the Norman kings brought a more settled period, establishing their authority through a network of loyal nobles who controlled parts of the country but recognized the king as overall ruler. This allowed for the building of great cathedrals, notably those of Glasgow and Elgin. **Glasgow Cathedral** is Scotland's only complete medieval cathedral to survive the Reformation; the verticality of the interior and the elegance of the clustered piers are monuments to the power of the Gothic tradition. The building itself is an amalgam of influences, from the Early Pointed style of the east end of the choir to the magnificent Late Gothic vaulting of the lower church, and is a poignant reminder of the wealth of architecture that has been lost to the nation over the years. **Elgin Cathedral**, with its unusual double aisles and rich furnishings, was an extravagant Anglo-Saxon statement of refinement and power, built to impress the Highland clans. It is in ruins, having been destroyed in 1390 by an earl angry at being excommunicated for leaving his wife.

Early castles

The popular image of the great Scottish **castle**, the stuff of myth and legend, perched on a rocky crag and often surrounded by woodlands, heather and deer, is remarkably different from the cold reality of daily castle living. Rising in stone above the small peasant dwellings of turf and timber, the castle was a centre of administrative and judicial control, as well as a secure place in times of conflict. **Castle Sween** on Loch Sween is the earliest stone castle in Scotland, built in the eleventh century with a Norman-style round-arched doorway leading into the centre of the quadrangular building, once roofed with timber. With its origins in the twelfth century, **Edinburgh Castle** stands out as the archetypal royal Scottish castle. Built on an extinct volcano, it commanded a strong strategic position and served throughout much of its history as a resonant symbol of power and protection. The epitome of the romantic Highland castle, on the other hand, is the beautifully picturesque **Eilean Donan** on Loch Duich. Originally a small thirteenth-century castle of enclosure, it was used to garrison Spanish troops as part of the Jacobite Rising, and was destroyed by English warships in 1719. The present building is predominantly a reconstruction, initiated at the beginning of the twentieth century, an immaculate three-storey keep perched on a rocky outcrop with a dramatic arched bridge.

Developments in warfare and architecture marched hand in hand, and thirteenth-century castles employed a number of defensive techniques: the use of catapults and assault towers, the strengthening of outer walls, and construction of round towers to allow for a better view of the base. The tall, thick walls of **Dunstaffnage** are topped with a crenellated wall walk and contain few windows but many well-placed firing slits; an outer defence like the moat at **Rothesay**, which was established around 1204, was also common. Natural defences such as rocky outcrops were particularly impenetrable; **Dirleton Castle** uses one to great advantage, its weaker side protected by three towers forcing outwards in an aggressive manner, and **Stirling Castle** is similarly well defended. Situated on a grassy hilltop, the reinforced tower at **Bothwell Castle** near Blantyre provided an effective last refuge in an attack.

The fourteenth and fifteenth centuries

With the power of the monarch declining and the nobility fighting for territory and power, the **fourteenth century** was a time of great strife and warfare in Scotland; consequently, law and order were overthrown and few buildings constructed. The destruction predominantly affected the Lowlands, the Highlanders being a law unto themselves within their own social system, strategically using the mountains to defend their proud autonomy. Castles continued to be strengthened, often growing in size to accommodate larger buildings. The impressive fourteenth-century castles of **Tantallon** near North Berwick and **Doune** in Perthshire both contain a massive gatehouse employed to protect the entrance, and provide the lord with accommodation. This gave him full control of the castle's defences, necessary at a time when hired mercenaries were commonly used in private armies. For lesser nobles, the **tower house** was the perfect solution to the conflicting problems of comfort and defence. It became a popular high-security residence, being smaller and cheaper than a great castle. Tall and narrow with smooth walls and few windows, these buildings featured a raised entrance and crenellated parapet as the main elements of passive defence – relying on thick walls and great height for effect. Being of a simple yet flexible design, the majority were expanded and decorated in later centuries, and none exist in their original form.

The **fifteenth century**, fluctuating between periods of war and peace, allowed tower houses to retain their popularity among the lesser nobles, being secure, yet comfortable enough for everyday living. High Gothic principles became established in ecclesiastical buildings, and the construction of the great royal residences introduced the spirit of the **Early Renaissance** to Scotland. In the 1420s, James I began to rebuild **Linlithgow Palace**, which by 1500 had become a large and symmetrical structure, in contrast to the random organization of medieval castles. Designed as a quadrangle with an open central court, it was primarily a domestic royal residence with a system of corridors and stairwells and large, regularly placed windows. This hint of Renaissance order and elegance was markedly different from the usual defensive principles of high walls and small window openings. Once considered the finest in the realm, the central chambers would have been luxuriously decorated with painted plaster and wall hangings.

The Gothic style was still favoured in ecclesiastical architecture, most apparent in **Melrose Abbey**. Twice destroyed in the fourteenth century, the rebuilding left excellent examples of High Gothic, the east window being the work of the York school of masons, and the richly carved south transept by a French master mason, which accounts for the lavish use of decoration. The flying buttresses are of particular note, being structural, not merely decorative. Due to an increase in trade with other countries, wealthy landowners could afford to construct small churches, staffed by secular clergy to pray for the soul of the benefactor. Many small collegiate buildings were built at this time, predominantly with a Late Gothic flavour: the most unusual and extreme is the mid-fifteenth-century **Rosslyn Chapel** near Edinburgh, with its elaborate carving and decorative flying buttresses. Also around this time, the castellated features of castles and towers began to creep into church architecture, seen in the use of crow-stepped gables at **St Michael's Church** in Linlithgow, or the crenellated parapet at **King's College Chapel** in Aberdeen.

The sixteenth and seventeenth centuries

The massacre of the Scots at Flodden in 1513 set the tone for unrest in the early part of the **sixteenth century**, leaving little opportunity for new buildings or styles. However, the Stewart dynasty continued to breathe the Renaissance spirit into their opulent palaces. A royal holiday home for the Stewart monarchs, **Falkland Palace** in Fife, with its reconstructed south range, is an excellent example of **French Renaissance** design, the solid buttresses transformed into Classical columns. This courtly look is also apparent at **Stirling Castle**, a true amalgam of styles, perched high up on a rocky outcrop. Here, the Renaissance facade of the Royal Palace, completed in 1540, is merely tacked onto the Gothic structure, with a line of restless statues perched on elegant wall shafts. Ultimately, this fashion did not catch on, as nobles preferred security and comfort over elegance.

The Reformation of 1560 released a wave of wholesale destruction of sculptural and other decorative items in church buildings. The tower house, however, regained popularity, as a considerable amount of church land had been sold off to nobles, who then wanted to create mini-castles as emblems of power and prestige. These buildings developed right through to the seventeenth century, often changing dramatically in plan, for example at **Drum Castle** in Aberdeen. Originally built in the late thirteenth century, the dignified tower was extended to its full Jacobean glory in the seventeenth century, when the desire for greater comfort and space called for a larger building. The **Scottish Baronial** style, characterized by crow-stepped gables and conical roofs, lightened the austerity of the original tower form and took these buildings to their peak. Excellent examples include **Claypotts Castle** near Dundee, where defensive features have been subsumed to the need for extra accommodation, which is corbelled out at the top of the Z-plan towers. Other castles of note are **Crathes** on Deeside, **Fyvie** near Inverurie, and **Glamis Castle** north of Dundee, which was constructed in the early seventeenth century. A later, even more decorative approach can be found at the absurdly pink-hued **Craigievar Castle**, west of Aberdeen, built in 1626 and hailed as the finest tower house in Scotland. Its crenellation serves to enhance the top-heavy accommodation area, but the beautifully preserved interior contains excellent stucco work. In all of these examples, useful defensive elements have been manipulated for effective decorative purposes.

The religious Wars of the Covenant (1639–44) and invasion of Cromwell (1650) initially discouraged contemporary building in the **seventeenth century**. However, the final development of the **Early Scottish Renaissance** emerged, marked by regular, symmetrical plans, the use of pediments and other decorative details of Classical origin, and an ordered dignified facade. Initiated in 1628, the elaborate **George Heriot's Hospital** in Edinburgh, which is now a school, is an excellent example. Here, Renaissance ideas are not merely decorative items tacked onto the front but are incorporated by the architect, **William Wallace**, into the overall design. The quadrangular plan with a tower at each corner is a feast of turrets, chimneys and cupolas that top the symmetrical facade. As the century progressed, the landed classes, having travelled and become more aware of the cultural conditions in England and Europe, began to take a serious interest in the design of their mansions, led by the influential figure of Sir William Bruce, who essentially founded the **Classical** school in Scotland. He undertook the major reconstruction of the **Palace of Holyrood** in Edinburgh in 1671–79, creating a delicate and restrained courtyard frontage of fine proportion and exacting detail. **Drumlanrig Castle** in Dumfries, built between 1679 and 1690, is an extravagant mansion, more obviously Classical with a balanced plan and a sweeping double staircase at the entrance.

The eighteenth century

Immediately after the Act of Union of 1707, the Scottish economy was at a low ebb. Gradually conditions began to improve as trade, encouraged by the union, began to take off, further enhanced by the agricultural revolution. By mid-century, the industrial age had ignited an architectural explosion. The towns of Edinburgh and Glasgow were to receive the best in **Neoclassical** architecture, as steadily increasing industrial production called for more housing, warehouses and municipal buildings. In line with the rationality and order of the Enlightenment, symmetry and proportion in design came into stride with the English Classicism of Sir Christopher Wren and Inigo Jones. Edinburgh's **New Town**, designed by **James Craig** in 1767, is characterized by wide, symmetrical streets and large tree-filled squares, with service lanes that follow the main axis of the roads. Amongst this sandstone glory lies **Charlotte Square**, the north side of which was designed by the renowned Classicist **Robert Adam** in 1791. The Venetian windows and restrained use of decoration create a unified facade, the main rooms clearly defined by angular stonework in comparison to the smooth sandstone of the other storeys. Compared with the medieval **High Street** that descends from the Castle, and the narrow lanes that run from it, these formal squares reflect a new approach to civilized urban living, allowing the upper classes to dwell in their own spacious areas away from the huddle of the Old Town. Adam was the shining light in a talented family of architects, who modified elegant **Hopetoun House** in Edinburgh around 1721–60. Set in an excellent position overlooking the Forth, this delicate and symmetrically designed building makes full use of triangular pediments and round-headed windows to recall the noble spirit of Classical times.

Concurrently, an interest in medieval architecture, encouraged by romantic fiction and the cult of the picturesque, led to **Gothic Revivalism**. Here, the pointed arch took over from the geometric rigours of Classicism. **Inveraray Castle** in Argyll, built between 1745 and 1761, is one of the first Georgian castles to re-create itself in this neo-Gothic style. Although the interior is inspired by Classicism, the exterior makes use of pointed arches and crenellated parapets, the conical roofs being a later addition. Another neo-Gothic building is **Culzean Castle** (1771–92), attractively situated on a clifftop south of Ayr and extensively remodelled by Robert Adam. He designed every detail, from the fine interior plasterwork, complete with swags and urns, to the castellated exterior with mock arrow slits, to give a romantically medieval touch to the dramatic setting.

The nineteenth century

By 1800, Scotland had changed dramatically, climbing from a poor backwater to become one of the Empire's leading industrial centres. Furthermore, after Queen Victoria "discovered" Scotland in 1842, it became highly fashionable, fuelled by the image of wild clans and rugged, lonely landscapes – a far cry from the bitter reality of life within the rapidly industrializing Central Belt, populated increasingly by families left homeless by the Highland Clearances. The major cities of Glasgow, Edinburgh and Dundee were expanding at great speed, filling up with warehouses, municipal buildings and workers' accommodation. This ushered in the **Victorian Age** of architecture. Marked by a continuation of the Romantic and Classical idioms established in the eighteenth century, grand buildings celebrated the pride and self-confidence of the industrial giants. A fusion of historical styles became common, and architects increasingly looked for novel ways to decorate their buildings. For instance, the Tudor–Gothic **Donaldson's Hospital** in Edinburgh, designed by **William Playfair** in 1851, fuses a symmetrical plan with elaborate turrets and a central decorated tower. Playfair was also responsible for creating the rich facade at **Floors Castle** near Kelso in 1838, cloaking the building in a new fashionable guise without changing the basic structural design.

Inspired by simple proportion and logical harmony, the followers of the **Greek Revival** created buildings of massive serenity, using little decoration. In Glasgow, **Alexander "Greek" Thomson** brought a unique interpretation to this style. He created buildings from warehouses to tenements and churches, such as Glasgow's impressive **St Vincent Street Church**, an imposing construction that mixes the massive solidity of Greek design with exotic motifs and decoration. In Edinburgh, it was **William Playfair** who created the city's icons of Greek Revivalism: the **Royal Scottish Academy** of 1836, and the **National Gallery of Scotland** of 1857, are both well proportioned with precise detail, the former making more use of scrolls and wreaths, the latter slightly less ponderous and more elegant. With the Gothic style no longer restricted to ecclesiastical architecture, the majestic **Glasgow University** building of 1870, designed by George Gilbert Scott, dominates the skyline of the West End in pseudo-medieval splendour. Similarly, in Edinburgh, the **Scottish National Portrait Gallery** of 1885–90, designed by Sir R. Rowand Anderson, is richly detailed with pointed arches and turrets.

New materials of the industrial age, such as cast iron, were being used to great effect in buildings such as **Kibble Palace** in the Glasgow's Botanic Gardens and the interior of the **Royal Museum of Scotland** in Edinburgh, which was based on London's Crystal Palace. The industrial age also gave birth to such great figures of **engineering** as **William Telford**, **Sir Benjamin Baker** and **Sir John Fowler**, who constructed roads and bridges throughout Scotland. Baker and Fowler were responsible for the pinnacle of Scottish engineering that straddles the Firth of Forth in cantilevered steel glory, the **Forth Railway Bridge**, which spans more than a mile, took seven years to build and employed more than 5000 men at a time, rivalling the Eiffel Tower in its complexity.

The twentieth century

At the turn of the **twentieth century**, Scotland was riding on the crest of a wave, with a healthy economy and solid industrial base, but a long period of postwar depression was to destroy this security. In any case, while the Victorian well-to-do had been luxuriating in their fine buildings, the workers had lived in slums, a situation that was to result in mass demolition later in the century.

Despite many financial difficulties, Glasgow's **Charles Rennie Mackintosh** (see p.256) began to design exciting new buildings, motivated by the desire for complete organic unity of structure and decoration. Associated with the Art Nouveau school and their push for change after the conservatism of the previous century, he produced some buildings of excellent quality and form. The **Glasgow School of Art** is the archetypal Mackintosh work, fusing the curvilinear shapes of Art Nouveau with the crow-stepped gables and conical roofs of the Scottish Baronial tradition. The interior effectively combines practicality with decorative beauty, and the library in particular promotes his forward-thinking style as it makes use of a strong vertical motif for its columns, lighting and furnishing. Outside bustling Glasgow at **Hill House** in Helensburgh, Mackintosh created a domestic building in 1902 that unites the turrets and chimney stack of the Baronial tradition with a modern interior. In the drawing room he creates two "zones", the wide bay window overlooking the Firth, for summer, and a cosy fireplace with a bookcase as a backdrop for winter evenings.

World War I brought a dramatic shift in scientific and artistic sensibilities; with the old ways undermined, people looked more and more to the future. This new atmosphere was represented in the **Art Deco** style, celebrating speed and technology. Typical features include modern, flat roofs, soaring geometric motifs and the use of reinforced concrete, which allowed semicircular glazed bays to project out from the building. However, due to financial constraints, few buildings were actually being erected; some gems that were include Glasgow's **Baird Hall of Residence** in Sauchiehall Street, built in 1938. The architect W. Beresford Inglis used two soaring projecting towers with bay windows to give a dynamic prominence to the general bulk of the building. In contrast, the large, brick-covered planes of the **Glasgow Film Theatre**, constructed one year later and designed by James McKissack, enhance the squat flat-roofed building. **The Maybury**, on the outskirts of Edinburgh, is a typical "roadhouse" built to cater for the new car-bound tourist, who could gaze up into the regularly spaced windows of the tower, designed to emulate the radiator of a huge limousine.

Despite the innovative ideas for town planning after World War I and the great rehousing plans set in motion after World War II, few public or private buildings of note were produced. Instead, vast **suburban sprawls** were constructed in the most economical manner, resulting in a bland architectural character. More recently, the development of housing associations has allowed residents to have some influence over their living space, and tower blocks have been replaced with small brick buildings laid out in crescents and tree-lined streets. In the public realm, the possibilities of modern technology continued to be explored, for example at the **Exhibition Plant Houses** at Edinburgh's Royal Botanic Garden, built in 1967. Here, a glass skin is held in place by an outside structure of steel and iron to provide the maximum use of interior space. The manipulation of glass to enhance space is also apparent at the **Burrell Collection** in Pollok Park, Glasgow, built in 1983 to house the great collection of Sir William Burrell. The architect Barry Gasson effectively fused nature and art, employing large panes of glass to take advantage of the surrounding woodland light, while the geometric use of red sandstone contrasts well with the wildness of the parkland.

Contemporary architecture

The current trend for conservation and renovation has produced some fine work: the glass-fronted **Festival Theatre** in Edinburgh, the **Maritime Museum** in Aberdeen and **The Lighthouse** in Glasgow, now Scotland's Centre for Architecture, Design and the City, are all successful and dynamic conversions of older buildings. Glasgow's year as UK City of Architecture and Design in 1999, of which The Lighthouse was the showpiece, tended to focus on the city's rich architectural heritage, but it did strive to remind Scots of the importance of the buildings around them. The prominence of work such as Sir Norman Foster's "**Armadillo**" building on the banks of the Clyde, and the titanium-clad **Glasgow Science Centre**, opened immediately opposite the Armadillo in 2001, prove that the city still has an appetite for innovative modern design.

Dundee, too, is expressing its cultural renaissance with some appealing architecture, notably Richard Murphy's inspiring **DCA** (Dundee Contemporary Arts) building, but also a cancer care centre at Ninewells Hospital – the first British work of **Frank Gehry**, the American architect of Bilbao's Guggenheim museum. Edinburgh, meanwhile, waits with baited breath for the new **Scottish Parliament** building, based on designs by the late Catalan architect Enric Miralles, to rise from the building site opposite the Palace of Holyroodhouse at the bottom of the Royal Mile. Encouraged by the enthusiastic reception for the innovative and beautiful **National Museum of Scotland**, which has been described as the finest postwar building in the capital, expectations are high that the new parliament building will offer the Scots an architectural icon to help define their aspirations in a new century.

Music

The new century has found Scottish indigenous music in remarkably fine health. Outstanding young musicians and bands abound, either faithfully recreating the traditions of old or finding bold new ways to interpret and express them. After years of being stifled by the rigidly twee, cliché-ridden images of Scottishness as expressed by the likes of Andy Stewart and Jimmy Shand, the real spirit of Scots music enjoyed a significant rebirth towards the end of the twentieth century with a Celtic upsurge courtesy of bands like Silly Wizard, Tannahill Weavers and the Battlefield Band.

Scotland through the 1980s and 1990s saw an explosion of **roots** and **dance music** and, at the same time, a renewal and revisiting of traditions that had seemed perilously close to destruction. The influx of talent, energy and awareness in the national culture has been such that the scene is as vibrant now as it has been for years – from the thriving venues in Glasgow and the lively sessions in Edinburgh to the young musicians upholding their own tradition all over Shetland and the Orkneys. The revival has its own magazine *Living Tradition* and a selection of specialist record companies championing the music.

Things looked very different thirty years ago, when the stern disciplines and structures involved in effectively mastering Scottish **traditional music**, which allowed little scope for flair – particularly with bagpipe-playing – had seemed very outmoded alongside the poppier approach favoured south of the border. But taking their cue from the great Irish bands of the 1970s like Planxty and the Bothy Band, the young Scots musicians looked for new, more informal ways to express that tradition. Adopting non-traditional influences, they set about shaking the cobwebs off the old music. The virtuosos who've surfaced in their wake are themselves testament to the success of their musical revolution.

The Celtic Folk Band arrives

As in much of northern Europe, the story of Scotland's roots scene begins amid the "**folk revival**" of the 1960s, a time when folk song and traditional music engaged people who did not have strong family links with an ongoing tradition. For many in Scotland, traditional music had skipped a generation and they had to make a conscious effort to learn about it. At first, the main influences were largely American – skiffle music and artists like Pete Seeger – but soon people started to look to their own traditions, taking inspiration from the Gaelic songs of **Cathy-Ann McPhee**, then still current in rural outposts, or the old travelling singers like the **Stewarts of Blairgowrie**, **Isla Cameron**, **Lizzie Higgins** and, the greatest of them all, Lizzie's mother, **Jeannie Robertson**.

On the instrumental front, there were fewer obvious role models despite the continued presence of a great many people playing in **Scottish dance bands**, **pipe bands** and **Strathspey and Reel Societies** (fiddle orchestras). In the 1960s the action was coming out of Ireland and the recorded repertoire of bands like The Chieftains became the core of many a pub session in Scotland. Even in the early 1970s, folk fiddle players were rare, although **Aly Bain** (see box on p.792) made a huge impression when he arrived from Shetland and, soon after, Shetland Reels started to creep into the general folk repertoire.

The "**Celtic Folk Band**" was a creation of the 1960s. Previously the art of a traditional musician was essentially a solo one. These days, however, there is a

Aly Bain and Shetland Magic

Aly Bain has been a minor deity among Scottish musicians for three decades. A fiddle player of exquisite technique and individuality, he has been the driving force throughout that time of one of Scotland's all-time great bands, Boys of the Lough, while latterly diversifying into roles as a TV presenter and author. In these guises, he has been instrumental in spreading the reach of Scottish music. First and foremost, though, Bain is a Shetlander and his greatest legacy is the inspiration he has provided for a revival of Shetland's own characteristic tradition.

Aly was brought up in the capital of Shetland, Lerwick, and was enthused to play the fiddle by **Bob Duncan** – who endlessly played him records by the Strathspey king Scott Skinner – and later the old maestro, **Tom Anderson**. These two were the last of an apparently dying breed, and the youthful Aly was an odd sight dragging his fiddle along to join in with the old guys at the Shetland Fiddlers Society. Players like **Willie Hunter Jnr** and **Snr**, **Willie Pottinger** and **Alex Hughson** were legends locally, but they belonged to another age.

By the time the teenage Aly was persuaded to leave for the mainland, Shetland was changing by the minute, and the discovery of North Sea oil altered it beyond redemption, as the new industrial riches trampled its unique community spirit and sense of tradition. The old fiddlers gradually faded and died, and Shetland music, inflected with the eccentricity of the isolated environment and the influence of nearby Scandinavia, seemed destined to disappear too.

That it didn't was largely down to Aly. After a spell with Billy Connolly (then a folk artist) on the Scottish folk circuit, Aly found himself working with blues iconoclast Mike Whellans, and then the two of them tumbled into a link-up with two Irishmen, Robin Morton and Cathal McConnell, in a group they called **Boys of the Lough**. Aly's joyful artistry, unwavering integrity and unquenchable appetite and commitment to the music of his upbringing has kept Shetland music alive in a manner he could never have imagined. Even more importantly, it stung the imagination of the generation that followed.

These days, Shetland music is buzzing again, with its own annual **festival** a treat of music-making and drinking. There are young musicians pouring out of the place, and a plethora of bands of all styles, including pop-oriented groups such as Rock, Salt & Nails and more recently Red Vans. The pick of the roots players, currently, is **Catriona MacDonald**, who was also taught by Tom Anderson in his last days. She is adept at classical music, and is fast becoming accomplished in Norwegian music; her mum went to school with Aly Bain – which in Shetland counts for an awful lot.

more or less standard formula with a melody lead – usually fiddle or pipes – plus guitar, bouzouki and a singer. The singer is often just another sound in the band whereas before it was the song that was the focus. Instrumental in these developments was a Glasgow folk group, **The Clutha**, who in a folk scene dominated by singers and guitarists, boasted not one but two fiddlers, along with a concertina, and four strong singers – including the superb **Gordeanna McCulloch**.

The Clutha were hugely influential and became even more successful when **Jimmy Anderson** introduced a set of chamber pipes into the line-up. Jimmy was not only a great piper but was also a pipe maker and he "invented" a set of pipes to be played in the key of D which sounded much quieter than the Highland pipes. This was essential at that time, as virtually all the venues were acoustic and sound systems were not up to the job of balancing out the sounds of pipes, fiddle and voices.

Key, too, to developments were the **Boys of the Lough**, a Scots–Irish group led by the Shetland fiddler **Aly Bain** (see box) and **The Whistlebinkies**.

Developing in the Glasgow folk scene alongside The Clutha, both these groups took a strong instrumental line, rather than The Clutha's song-based approach. These two bands were in many ways Scotland's equivalent of Ireland's The Chieftains and through their musical ability and recognition outside the folk clubs, played an important part in breaking down musical barriers.

The Whistlebinkies were notable for employing only traditional instruments, including fine clarsach (Celtic harp) from **Judith Peacock**. However, the most important, and definingly Scottish, element of all three of these bands was the presence of **bagpipes**. Clutha had piper **Jimmy Anderson**, the Whistlebinkies featured **Rab Wallace**, who had a firm background in the Scots piping scene, while The Boys also had an experienced piper in **Robin Morton**. They were pioneers for what was to become a revolution in the late 1970s with bands like Battlefield Band, Tannahill Weavers, Silly Wizard, Boys of the Lough and Ossian.

Pibroch: Scots pipes

Bagpipes are synonymous with Scotland yet they are not a specifically Scots instrument. The pipes were once to be found right across Europe, and pockets remain, across the English border in Northumbria, all over Ireland, in Spain and Italy, and in eastern Europe, where bagpipe festivals are still held in rural areas. In Scotland, bagpipes seem to have made their appearance around the fifteenth century, and over the next hundred years or so they took on several forms, including quieter varieties (small pipes), both bellows and mouth blown, which allowed a diversity of playing styles.

The Highland bagpipe form known as **pibroch** (*piobaireachd* in Gaelic) evolved around this time, created by clan pipers for military, gathering, lamenting and marching purposes. Legendary among the clan pipers of this era were the MacCrimmons (they of the famous *MacCrimmon's Lament*, composed during the Jacobite rebellion), although they were but one of several important piping clans, among which were the MacArthurs, MacKays and MacDonalds, and others. In the seventeenth and eighteenth centuries, through the influence of the British army, reels and strathspeys joined the repertoire and a tradition of military pipe bands emerged. After World War II they were joined by civilian bands, alongside whom developed a network of piping competitions.

The bagpipe tradition has continued uninterrupted, although for much of the last century under the domination of the military and the folklorists Piobaireachd Society. Recently, however, a number of Scottish musicians have revived the pipes in new and innovative forms. Following the lead of The Clutha, Boys of the Lough and Whistlebinkies, a new wave of young bands began to feature pipers, notably **Alba** with the then-teenage Alan McLeod, **Ossian** with Iain MacDonald, and Duncan McGillivray with the **Battlefield Band**. Battlefield have subsequently used a selection of high-quality pipers, most recently the American Mike Katz. These players redefined the boundaries of pipe music using notes and finger movements outside the traditional range. They also showed the influence of Irish Uillean pipe players (particularly Paddy Keenan of the **Bothy Band**) and Cape Breton styles which many claim is the original, pre-military Scottish style.

In 1983 **Robin Morton** released *A Controversy of Pipers* on his Temple Records label, an album featuring six pipers from folk bands who were also top competitive players in the piping world. Up until this point, pipers in a folk band could be considered second-class by some in the piping establishment. This recording made a statement and soon the walls began to crumble.

Alongside all this came a revived interest in traditional piping, and in particular the strathspeys, slow airs and reels, which had tended to get submerged beneath the familiar military territory of marches and laments. The twentieth century's great bagpipe players, notably **John Burgess**, received a belated wider exposure. His legacy includes a masterful album and a renowned teaching career to ensure that the old piping tradition marches proudly into the twenty-first century.

Folk song and the club scene

While the folk bands were starting to catch up on the Irish and integrating bagpipes, **folk song** was also flourishing. The song tradition in Scotland is one of the strongest in Europe and in all areas of the country there are pockets of great singers and characters. In the 1960s the common ground was the folk club network and the various festivals dotted around the country.

The great modern pioneer of Scots folk song, and a man who perhaps rescued the whole British tradition, was the great singer and songwriter **Ewan MacColl**, born in Perthshire in 1915. He recorded the seminal *Scottish Popular Ballads* as early as 1956, and founded the first folk club in Britain. After MacColl, another of the building blocks of the 1960s folk revival were the Aberdeen group, **The Gaugers**. Song was the heart of this group – Tam Speirs, Arthur Watson and Peter Hall were all good singers – though they were also innovative in using instrumentation (fiddle, concertina and whistle) without a guitar or other rhythm instrument to tie the sound together.

Other significant Scots groups on the 1960s scene included the **Ian Campbell Folk Group**, Birmingham-based but largely Scots in character (and including future Fairport Daves, Swarbrick and Pegg, as well as Ian's sons, Ali and Robin, who went on to form UB40). They flirted with commercialism and pop sensibilities – as virtually every folk group of the era was compelled to do – and were too often unfairly bracketed with England's derided Spinners as a result. So too were **The Corries**, although they laced their blandness with enterprise, inventing their own instrumentation and writing the new unofficial national anthem, *Flower of Scotland*.

Other more adventurous experiments grew out of the folk and acoustic club scene in mid-1960s Glasgow and Edinburgh. It was at Clive's Incredible Folk Club in Glasgow that **The Incredible String Band** made their debut, led by **Mike Heron** and **Robin Williamson**. They took an unfashionable glance back into their own past on the one hand, while plunging headlong into psychedelia and other uncharted areas on the other. Their success broke down significant barriers, both in and out of Scotland, and in their wake came a succession of Scottish folk-rock crossover musicians. Glasgow-born **Bert Jansch** launched folk super-group Pentangle with Jacqui McShee, John Renbourn and Danny Thompson, and the flute-playing **Ian Anderson** found rock success with Jethro Tull. Meanwhile, a more traditional Scottish sound was promoted by the likes of **Archie**, **Ray** and **Cilla Fisher**, who sang new and traditional ballads, individually and together.

The great figure, however, along with MacColl, was the singer and guitarist **Dick Gaughan**, whose passionate artistry towers like a colossus above three decades. He started out in the Edinburgh folk club scene with an impenetrable accent, a deep belief in the socialist commitment of traditional song, and a guitar technique that had old masters of the art hanging on to the edge of their seats. For a couple of years in the early 1970s, he played with Aly Bain in the Boys of the Lough, knocking out fiery versions of trad Celtic material.

Gaughan became frustrated, however, by the limitations of a primarily instrumental (and fiddle-dominated) group and subsequently formed **Five Hand Reel.** Again playing Scots–Irish traditional material, they might have been the greatest folk-rock band of them all if they hadn't just missed the Fairport/Steeleye Span boat.

Leaving to pursue an independent career, Gaughan became a fixture on the folk circuit and made a series of albums exploring Scots and Irish traditional music and reinterpreting the material for guitar. His *Handful of Earth* (1981) was perhaps the single best solo folk album of the decade, a record of stunning intensity with enough contemporary relevance and historical belief to grip all generations of music fans. And though sparing in his output, and modest about his value in the genre, he's also become one of the best songwriters of his generation.

Crucial contributions to folk song came, too, from two giants of the Scottish folk scene who were probably more appreciated throughout Europe than at home – the late **Hamish Imlach** and **Alex Campbell** – and from song collectors and academics such as **Norman Buchan**, with his hugely influential songbook *101 Scottish Songs*, and **Peter Hall** with *The Scottish Folksinger*. **Robin Hall** and **Jimmie McGregor**, too, while like The Corries often derided for their high profile and their occasional lapses into opportunist populism, were a formidable presence for many years. There has also been a massive contribution from **Hamish Henderson** both as folklorist and researcher, an immense conduit of songs and tunes. That Henderson has also written some of the most telling songs in modern currency add to his legend.

Gaelic rocking and fusions

Scottish music took an unexpected twist in 1978 with the low-key release of an album called *Play Gaelic*. It was made by a little-known ceilidh group called **Runrig**, who took their name from the old Scottish oil field system of agriculture, and worked primarily in the backwaters of the Highlands and Islands. The thing, though, that stopped people in their tracks was the fact that they were writing original material in Gaelic. This was the first time any serious Scottish working band had achieved any sort of attention with Gaelic material, although Ossian were touching on it around a similar time, as were Nah-Oganaich.

Runrig marched on to unprecedented heights, appearing in front of rock audiences at concert halls around the world where only a partial proportion of the audience were Scots in exile. As their popularity grew the Gaelic content reduced, but they started a whole new ball rolling, chipping away at prejudices, adopting accordions and bagpipes, ever-sharper arrangements, electric instruments, full-blown rock styles, surviving the inevitable personnel changes and the continuous carping of critics accusing them of selling out with every new market conquered. They even made a concept album *Recovery*, which related the history of the Gael in one collection, provoking immense interest in the Gaelic language after years of it being regarded as moribund and defunct. They lost their main man **Donnie Munro** to politics during the 1990s but after an extended break made a powerful comeback in 2000.

Capercaillie, too, rooted in the arrangements of **Manus Lunny** and the gorgeous singing of **Karen Mattheson**, rose from Argyll pub sessions to flirt with mass commercial appeal, reworking Gaelic and traditional songs from the West Highlands and promoting Gaelic language and culture, primarily as a result of the songs learned by Mattheson from her grandmother. They even got into the chart with one ancient Gaelic song, an ironic development considering the fact

Ceilidhs, festivals and contacts

Scottish dances thrived for years under the auspices of the RSCDS, the Royal Scottish Country Dance Society. Their events tended to be fairly formal, with dancers who were largely skilled, but in the 1970s and 1980s more and more Scottish dances, or **ceilidhs** (pronounced "kay-lees"), adopted the English barn-dance practice of a "caller" to call out the moves. Nowadays there are two types of traditional dance events: ceilidh dances, usually with a caller and perhaps a more folky band, and **Scottish Country Dances**, usually with a more traditional Scottish dance band line-up and an expectation that the dancers will know the dance forms.

Scottish **music festivals** range from the Celtic Connections Festival (held in January at the Glasgow Royal Concert Hall) where you can catch many of the top names in the Celtic music world in a comfortable concert setting, to lots of smaller festivals which offer a mix of concert, ceilidh and informal sessions. In recent years there has been an increase in the number of festivals where teaching takes a central role. Many of these are in the Highlands and Islands where the Feisean movement has introduced thousands of people to traditional music-making.

Scottish bands such as Capercaillie and Runrig feed the notion that folk music can be exciting, electric and diverse, without losing sight of its roots. However, the survival of traditional music depends on support from young players: they need to play it, listen to it, and take it forward. In Scotland, change is coming from a grass-roots **Feisean Movement** (*feis* is Gaelic for festival). These festivals, held during summer months and school holidays, involve children receiving tuition in traditional music, drama, art, dance and Gaelic singing, with evening gigs in local venues. The teachers (and performers) are often leading musicians.

The idea began on the island of Barra, in the southern Hebrides, in 1981 and has spread to many parts of the Highlands and Islands. Its results have been remarkable. Beginners on the fiddle, clarsach, guitar, tin whistle or accordion have now begun to form bands and teach others. And the sheer numbers of young people coming through the Feis throughout the Highlands has resulted in more and more communities holding workshops and ceilidhs. In small communities there are great economic spin-offs for instrument makers, music shops and for teachers of traditional music.

Tuition projects have not been limited to the Highlands. In Edinburgh, Stan Reeves has made remarkable progress with the **Scots Music Group** within the Adult Learning Project (ALP), leading to several hundred people learning traditional instruments and an annual festival of fiddle music. In Glasgow, the **Glasgow Fiddle Workshop**, under the guidance of Ian Fraser, has made similar progress and is starting to widen its brief beyond fiddle tuition.

Contacts

ALP Scots Music Group ⓣ0131/337 5442, ⓦwww.alpscotsmusic.org.

Feisean nan Gaidheal ⓣ01478/613355, ⓦwww.feisean.org.

The Living Tradition ⓣ01563/571220, ⓦwww.folkmusic.net. A traditional music magazine covering music from Britain and Ireland, with a focus, obviously, on Scotland. They also run a mail order service for traditional recordings.

The Piping Centre ⓣ0141/353 0220, ⓦwww.thepipingcentre.co.uk. The place to visit for anybody with an interest in piping. They have an exhibition, a teaching programme, concert space, café and even a hotel.

Royal Scottish Country Dance Society ⓣ0131/225 3854, ⓦwww.rscds.org.

that Karen was actively discouraged from learning the language and her grandmother was made to feel ashamed of her Gaelic culture after moving to the Scottish mainland. Others have subsequently come to the fore, like **Margaret**

Bennett, while the culture has remained defiantly intact courtesy of Scottish roots families in Cape Breton, Canada. **Mary Jane Lamond** is just one who's made the triumphant return journey back to Scotland with her repertoire of ancient Gaelic songs.

Of course, not everyone applauds. Critics point out that many singers using the language are not native Gaelic speakers and only learn the words phonetically, while further controversy has been caused by the "sampling" of archive recordings for use in backing tracks. For many people these songs are important and personal, and, in the case of some of the religious singing, they felt very strongly that this use was in bad taste.

Nonetheless, the popularity of Gaelic roots bands undeniably paved the way for "purer" Scots musicians and singers: clarsach player **Alison Kinnaird**, for instance; singers **Savourna Stevenson**, **Christine Primrose**, **Flora McNeill**, **Cathy-Ann MacPhee**, **Heather Heywood**, and **Jock Duncan**; and the **Wrigley sisters** from Orkney – who started out as teenagers playing traditional music with technical accomplishment and attitude and are now the core of the band **Seelyhoo**.

And among the ranks of the roots or fusion bands, each with their own agendas and styles, have passed many – perhaps most – of Scotland's finest contemporary musicians. **Silly Wizard**, especially, featured a singer of cutting quality in **Andy M. Stewart** (and did he need that M.), while **Phil and Johnny Cunningham** have gone on to display a pioneering zeal in their efforts to use their skills on accordion and fiddle to knit Scottish traditional music with other cultures.

Mouth Music, too, were innovative: a Scots-origin (but recently Canadian) duo of **Martin Swan** and **Talitha MacKenzie**, who mixed Gaelic vocals (including the traditional "mouth music" techniques of sung rhythms) with African percussion and dance sounds. MacKenzie later went solo, radically transforming traditional Scottish songs, from which she clears the dust of folklore with wonderful multitracked vocals and the characteristic Mouth Music African rhythms.

Another development was the fusion of traditional music and **jazz** by bands such as **The Easy Club** and the duo of piper **Hamish Moore** and jazz saxophonist **Dick Lee**. Moore has since come full circle, now taking his inspiration from a parallel Scottish culture which has developed in Cape Breton. Scottish interest in Cape Breton music has also led to the more or less lost tradition of Scottish step dancing being reintroduced.

Contemporary Celts

Young Celtic music artists have been leading from the front in the touchy subject of **fusion** and **electronica**. The **Easy Club** pioneered Celtic swing years ago, their example propagated by drummer/composer and Scottish National Jazz Orchestra member John Rae and his band **Celtic Feet**, while **Salsa Celtica** have made a considerable mark lacing their Celtic background with a genuinely deep love and understanding of Latin music. At the other end of the spectrum **Jennifer** and **Hazel Wrigley** and **Catriona MacDonald** have done some stirring conceptual work, even incorporating an almost classical mentality to the complex instrumental pieces they have created. MacDonald's increasing influence is also underlined by her leading role in the band of massed fiddle players, **Blazing Fiddles**, which took the UK by storm in 1999. The likes of **Deaf Shepherd**, **Mad Pudding** and **Tartan Amoebas** have also provided an explosive new edge to old notions of Celtic folk rock, while Cape

Breton's **Natalie McMaster** has produced a succession of brilliant fiddle albums involving daring variants on a Scottish traditional theme.

Perhaps most intriguing – and controversial – are those bending the music to its limits by taking it into the realms of a modern club and dance scene involving an alien world of samples, sequencers, loops, computers and drum machines. Even Capercaillie – and one of their offshoots **Big Sky** – experimented in this area with mixed results, while the likes of **Simon Thoumire** and **Paul Mounsey** have been at the forefront of these technological forays. Multi-talented Mounsey lived in Brazil for a decade and has made it count with a series of alluring electronic experiments. The idea of marrying the common ingredients of Scottish and Latino music has also been explored to good effect by **Mac Umba**, one of several Scots bands who've made their mark abroad.

Shooglenifty, who captured the imagination of a new audience with a style they wryly described as "acid croft", and who played at the 2000 Sydney Olympics, are among those who've embraced technology with the most conviction. While most have treated it with kid gloves, Shooglenifty have gone in with the brashness of youth to utilize all the sounds and equipment around them to enhance the music without any caution or the sense of guilt of older musicians. **Peatbog Faeries**, too – featuring excellent piper Peter Morrison and fiddle player/throat singer Ben Ivitsky – have pushed back the boundaries in stirring futuristic fashion without compromising the tradition in any way. Yet the man who's been most responsible for shifting the goalposts is **Martyn Bennett**, a fiddle and bagpipe player of no mean accomplishment who has driven the music, inspiringly, right to the edge with his albums *Bothy Culture* and *Hardland*. He made his mark as a dreadlocked busker in Edinburgh but proved his credentials with an extraordinary adaptation of Sorley McLean's equally extraordinary poem *Hallaig*, featuring McLean's own reading of it recorded shortly before his death. If any evidence were needed that the old and the new and apparently alien cultures can clash to resounding effect, this is it.

Discography

In addition to the discs reviewed below, see the box opposite for details of the remarkable Scottish Tradition series of CDs and cassettes. For further information, check out www.musicscotland.com – a wonderful site with links to many label and artist pages.

General compilations

The Caledonian Companion (Greentrax, Scotland). A 1975 live recording of four of Scotland's most-respected northeast musicians – Alex Green, Willie Fraser, Charlie Bremner and John Grant – featuring solo fiddle, mouth organ, whistle and diddling.

The Nineties Collection (Greentrax, Scotland). Sixteen artists, including four pipers and well-known names such as Aly Bain and Phil Cunningham play all-new tunes in a traditional style. Also available is a companion book containing over 200 tunes, published by Canongate Books, Scotland.

Rough Guide to Scottish Music (World Music Network, UK). A terrific compilation, this is strongest on the new roots bands – with good selections from Battlefield Band, Capercaillie and Wolfstone, among others – but it also delves into folk (Dick Gaughan) and traditional singing (Catherine-Ann McPhee, Heather Heyward).

Traditional singers

Jock Duncan is an authentic bothy ballad singer from Pitlochry who gets to the heart of any song. He made his recording debut aged seventy, backed by musicians including his son, the piper Gordon Duncan, on *Ye Shine Whar Ye Stan'* (Springthyme, Scotland). Some of the traditional singing on this album is truly remarkable and the production from Battlefield Band founder Brian McNeill is impressive, too, creating an atmosphere that only falls a little short of the experience of a live performance.

Heather Heywood, from Ayrshire, is reckoned by many to be Scotland's foremost traditional singer of her generation. She performs largely core Scottish ballads and songs. *By Yon Castle Wa'* (Greentrax, Scotland) is a 1993 disc of epic ballads and contemporary songs, produced by Battlefield Band founder Brian McNeill. Heywood's forte is traditional song which she usually sings *a cappella*. McNeill makes the

The Scottish Tradition series

Scottish traditional music – in its deepest, darkest manifestations – has been superbly documented in a series of archive recordings produced by Peter Cooke and others at Edinburgh University's School of Scottish Studies. The highlights of this collection have found their way onto the **Scottish Tradition** series, which, if you're seriously interested in the roots of many of the musicians covered in this article, are nothing less than a treasure trove. All titles in the series are available from the Scottish label Greentrax (Ⓦwww.greentrax.com) or from Ⓦwww.musicscotland.com.

The first volume in the series, *Bothy Ballads*, is one of the most important and fascinating. These **narrative songs** were composed, sung and passed around the unmarried farmworkers accommodated in bothies or outhouses in late-Victorian and Edwardian days. The songs were often comic or satirical, such as warnings about skinflint farmers to be avoided at the hiring markets. Under the bothy system, workers would move on from farm to farm after six-month "fees", so the songs were in constant circulation and reinvention. They include some gorgeous ballads and instrumentals.

Volume 2, *Music from the Western Isles*, is another intriguing disc: **Gaelic songs** recorded in the Hebrides, including some great examples of "**mouth music**", the vocal dance music where sung rhythms are employed to take the place of instruments. There are *pibroch* songs on this disc, too – the vocal equivalent of the pipers' airs and laments. On Volume 3, *Waulking Songs from Barra*, you enter another extraordinary domain, that of Gaelic **washing songs**, thumped out by women to the rhythms of their cloth pounding. If you were played this blind, you could imagine yourself to be thousands of miles from Scotland. More amazing vocal traditions are unleashed on Volume 6, *Gaelic Psalms from Barra*, with their slow, fractured unison singing.

An equally compelling vocal tradition is that of the Scottish **Travelling Singers**, showcased on Volume 5, *The Muckle Sangs*. This is a delight, including virtually all the greats, Jeannie Robertson, Lizzie Higgins and the Stewarts of Blairgowrie among them.

Fiddle music is also outstandingly represented in the series, with several volumes devoted to the art. Volume 4, *Shetland Fiddle Music*, features classic players such as Tom Anderson and George Sutherland, who were to exert such influence on the likes of Aly Bain and Catriona MacDonald. Volume 9, *The Fiddler and His Art*, is a fine overall compilation, showing the different styles prevalent around the country.

Finally, as you'd expect, the Scottish Tradition has recordings of some of the finest **pibroch pipers**, among them George Moss (volume 15), and pipe majors William MacLean, Robert Brown and R.B. Nicol (volumes 10, 11 and 12).

album accessible, without compromising the basic style, with the addition of accompaniment, including pipes – something which is difficult to do in live performance. This was a landmark recording in the traditional area.

Catherine-Ann MacPhee, from Barra, has a warm yet strong voice and her Gaelic has the soft pronunciation of the southern islands of the Outer Hebrides. *Canan Nan Gaidheal* (*The Language of the Gael*; Greentrax, Scotland) is a superb 1980s recording, rereleased on CD, showing mature traditional singing from one of the best of the current generation of Gaelic singers.

Gordeanna McCulloch, the lead singer of seminal 1960s band, The Clutha, is another of the great voices of the Scottish Folk revival. On *In Freenship's Name* (Greentrax, Scotland), her voice is a strong, sweet and flexible instrument, capable of a variety of tones. Here she is at home among some great Scots songs, all traditional bar one, and backed by some of Scotland's top musicians.

Jim Reid was, with Arbroath's Foundry Bar band, a well-known face at festivals and ceilidhs throughout Scotland for many years. One of the country's finest singers, whose *I Saw the Wild Geese Flee* (Springthyme, Scotland) is a selection of songs ranging from his own compositions to traditional ballads. Jim's version of *I Saw the Wild Geese Flee* alone makes this reissued album a classic.

Margaret Stewart and Allan MacDonald. Lewis-born Stewart is a talented Gaelic singer; MacDonald is one of the famous piping family from Glenuig – his brother was the piper with Ossian and Battlefield Band. Their *Fhuair Mi Pog* (Greentrax, Scotland) is a fascinating CD of music and Gaelic song that works as terrific entertainment; lovely singing and great tunes, some of the best written by Allan himself.

Jane Turriff is a legendary song carrier. Born into the Aberdeenshire Stewart family in 1915, she grew up in a travelling family. *Singin is Ma Life* (Springthyme, Scotland) is a must for anyone interested in traditional song style. Content ranges from the "big" ballads such as *Dowie Dens of Yarrow* through to the classic C&W song *Empty Saddles*.

Sheena Wellington is a broadcaster and radio presenter, Fife Council's Traditional Arts development officer, and one of Scotland's leading traditional singers. *Strong Women* (Greentrax, Scotland) is a live recording showing off what Sheena does best: communicating traditional song to an audience.

Mick West, well known as a session singer, is now rated at home and abroad as one of the country's finest traditional singers. *Fine Flowers & Foolish Glances* (KRL, Scotland) is one of the most successful albums to use jazz musicians with a strong traditional singer. It may prove to be a classic.

Instrumentalists

Aly Bain, Shetland-born (see box on p.792), is one of the great movers in Scottish music's revival, through his band Boys of the Lough and a panoply of solo and collaborative ventures. *Aly Bain and Friends* (Greentrax, Scotland) is one of the bestselling Scottish albums of modern times, compiled from a TV series Bain produced on traditional Scottish music. The "friends" include Boys of the Lough, Capercaillie, Hamish Moore and Dick Lee, and zydeco star Queen Ida and her Bonne Temps band. *The Silver Bow:*

The Fiddle Music of Shetland (Topic, UK) is a collection of Shetland fiddle tunes notable for bringing together Bain with his old teacher, Tom Anderson. They played both individually and together on the album and the effect is never less than enthralling. On *The Pearl* (Whirlie, Scotland), Bain teams up with Phil Cunningham, Scotland's finest accordion player, for some fabulous tunes from slow airs to Shetland reels, reflecting the incredible range of styles which this duo have mastered. Phil composed almost half of the tracks and he plays five of the six instruments featured.

John Burgess is arguably the twentieth century's greatest exponent of traditional bagpipes. On *King of the Highland Pipers* (Topic, UK), the maestro demonstrates his art to devastating effect through *piobaireachd*, strathspeys, hornpipes, reels and marches. Not for the faint-hearted!

Pete Clarke is a great fiddle player whose skills with slow air playing also makes him in great demand as a song accompanist. *Fiddle Case* (Smiddymade, Scotland) comprises an hour of top-notch traditional music – not all Scottish fiddle though – with tunes from Europe and the US and even a couple of songs. There's a classical feel to some of the pieces which works well, with cello and flute parts.

Gordon Duncan, the son of bothy singer Jock, is one of Scotland's younger generation of pipers who is stretching the boundaries with some breathtaking solo piping. On *The Circular Breath* (Greentrax, Scotland), as well as performing on the Great Highland Bagpipe, Gordon plays the practice chanter and low whistle. He is joined by banjo-player Gerry O'Connor, Ian Carr on guitar, Ronald MacArthur on bass guitar, Jim Sutherland playing clay pots and Andy Cook on Ugandan harp.

Alasdair Fraser is a master fiddler, renowned for his slow airs and now for his leading of The Skyedance Band, whose members provided music for the film *Braveheart*. *Dawn Dance* (Culburnie, Scotland) is an album of completely self-penned tunes in the traditional style which bounces along, defying you to sit still while you listen. Fraser has a rare clarity of playing, without sacrificing the feel and enthusiasm essential to traditional music.

Willie Hunter and Violet Tulloch. Hunter was one of the all-time greats of the Shetland fiddle and Tulloch is one of Shetland's leading piano accompanists. *The Willie Hunter Sessions* (Greentrax, Scotland) is a set of recordings made over several years including Scots and Shetland strathspeys, reels and slow airs. "Traditional chamber music" of the highest order.

William Jackson is one of Scotland's best-known traditional composers. He wrote some – and arranged most – of the music for folk band Ossian, and now works solo. *Inchcolm* (Linn Records, Scotland) brings Billy's harp playing to centre stage. It is a collection of largely unrelated tracks with some orchestral interludes and forays into Early and Eastern musics.

Mac-Talla is a Gaelic supergroup, which in 1994 made a small number of concert appearances and one spectacular recording – *Mairidh Gaol is Ceol* (Temple, Scotland), featuring glorious harmony and solo singing, accordion and harp – before settling back into their own individual paths having "made the statement". Mac-Talla's members included singers Arthur Cormack, Christine Primrose and Eilidh MacKenzie plus Alison Kinnaird on clarsach, and ex-Runrig musician Blair Douglas.

Iain McLachlan is a well-known and respected accordion player who also plays fiddle and melodeon. From the writer of *The Dark Island*, *An Island Heritage* (Springthyme, Scotland) is real traditional music from the Western Isles played on accordion, fiddle, melodeon and pipes.

Hamish Moore is one of Scotland's finest contemporary pipers, playing Border pipes, Scottish Small pipes and the great Highland Bagpipe. Inspired by the Scottish culture he discovered in Cape Breton, on *Stepping on the Bridge* (Greentrax, Scotland) Moore plays Scottish pipes with Cape Breton accompanists to produce a lively glimpse of what piping may have been like before it became regimented.

Scott Skinner was a legendary Victorian-era fiddler, formidably kilted and moustachioed. *Music of Scott Skinner* (Topic, UK) is an essential roots album, featuring rare and authentic recordings by this elusive genius of the fiddle – and the weird strathspey style in particular – dating from 1908. Some of the quality is understandably distorted, though the collection is supplemented by modern interpretations by Bill Hardie.

"New Roots" groups

Battlefield Band have been perhaps the pre-eminent Scottish band of the last thirty years, despite numerous personnel changes. Some great musicians have come and gone – Brian McNeil has developed into one of Scotland's greatest modern songwriters – but Alan Reid remains a constant and the band even survived the death of their hugely popular singer Davey Steele and continue with one of the country's brightest young vocal talents Karine Polwart (also of Malinky and MacAlias). *Rain, Hail or Shine* (Temple, Scotland) features all the Battlefield Band trademarks in force – distinctive keyboard playing, well-chosen pipe tunes, guitar and bouzouki injecting excitement and tension, fine singing – and John McCusker's sharp fiddle-playing is a joy throughout.

Boys of the Lough have been a benchmark of taste for thirty years, with the virtuoso talents of Shetland fiddler Aly Bain and singer/flautist Cathal McConnell at the heart of the band. *The Boys of the Lough* (Shanachie, US) was the group's 1973 debut and remains one of their strongest sets, powered by contributions from Dick Gaughan and piper Robin Morton. *The Day Dawn* (Lough Records, Scotland) is characterized by quality, taste, superb singing and the relaxed easy style that comes from skilled musicians with years of experience. Along with the concertina and mandola of Dave Richardson, Aly on fiddle and Cathal on flute, whistle and vocals, this album features singer and *uillean* piper Christy O'Leary.

Capercaillie is a hugely influential and successful group that has taken Gaelic music to a worldwide audience in a modern contemporary style from a traditional base. They have in Karen Mattheson one of the best singers around today. On *Beautiful Wasteland* (Survival Records, Scotland/GreenLinnet, US), flute, whistle and *uillean* pipes pop up all over the place and a whole host of things are happening with fiddles, bouzoukis, keyboards and percussion.

Ceolbeg were not a full-time band but produced some of the finest albums of the genre, featuring some fabulous songs from their singer, Davy Steele. *An Unfair Dance* (Greentrax, Scotland) is an impressive collection of tunes played on a huge variety of instruments, with a great sense of light and shade.

Deaf Shepherd are a passionate contemporary band following in the footsteps of the Battlefield Band, rooted in the Scottish tradition and getting more skilled all the time. *Synergy* (Greentrax, Scotland) is a really varied album, including traditional and new material, and jumps from reels to jigs and back, involving vigorous fiddle playing and powerful bouzouki. Poignant guitar, fiddle and whistle counter-melodies blend smoothly with the vocals.

The Easy Club, an admirably ambitious and sadly underrated group, took the baton from the more thoughtful Scots bands of the 1970s and ran with it at a pace, injecting traditional rhythms with a jazz sense. *Essential* (Eclectic, Scotland) is undoubtedly essential; MacColl's *First Time Ever I Saw Your Face* never sounded like this before.

Mouth Music – Talitha MacKenzie and Martin Swan – combined Gaelic nonsense songs (*puirt-a-beul*) with ambient dance, funk keyboards and African sampling. MacKenzie has gone on to a solo career but Mouth Music's first disc *Mouth Music* (Cooking Vinyl, UK) remains her finest hour, one of the best Celtic fusions committed to disc, featuring stunning rhythms, funk, Gaelic sea shanties and *puirt-a-beul*.

Ossian, a groundbreaking band, formed in the mid-1970s, that has recently reformed with a new line-up featuring Iain MacInnes on pipes and Stuart Morison on fiddle alongside founder members Billy Jackson on harp and Billy Ross on guitar and dulcimer. *The Carrying Stream* (Greentrax, Scotland) is a fine album, signalling the welcome return of Ossian's quintessentially Scottish sound. This is a collection of terrific tunes – first rate jigs and reels, both traditional and contemporary, blended with songs in English, Scots and Gaelic.

Runrig, a band of Gaelic rock pioneers, was formed in North Uist in 1973 by brothers Rory (bass/vocals) and Calum MacDonald (drums/vocals), with singer Donnie Munro joining the following year. They worked their way up, over fifteen years, from ceilidhs to stadiums, going Top 10 in the UK charts in 1991. They are perhaps at their very best live, with memorable tunes and vocals and well-honed, subtle musicianship. *Alba* (Pinnacle, UK) is an excellent "best of" compilation from this most dynamic Gaelic band.

Seelyhoo feature the Wrigley sisters from Orkney, who have made their own statement with their own recordings. On *Leetera* (Greentrax, Scotland), they're joined by several other musicians in a band which came out of the Edinburgh session scene and exemplify a fresh approach to traditional tunes and Gaelic song using fiddle, guitar, bass guitar, accordion, whistle, keyboard and percussion. Vibrant music from some of Scotland's young rising stars.

Shooglenifty are a brilliant, innovative band who've had an impact well beyond the Scottish roots scene with their grafting of Scottish trad motifs and club culture trance-dance. Live, they are unstoppable. *A Whisky Kiss* (Greentrax, Scotland) is the album that coined the term "acid croft", with elements of traditional music and house. A sound here, a strange sound there, a sequence played in an odd way. There's nothing else like it.

Silly Wizard were a key roots band, featuring Andy M. Stewart (vocals, bouzouki, guitar), Phil (accordion, etc) and Johnny Cunningham (fiddle). Their albums are full of fresh, lively takes on the whole traditional repertoire and *Live Wizardry* (Green Linnet, US) feature the band at their zenith in 1988, playing traditional and self-composed dance tunes and narrative ballads.

Andy M. Stewart, Phil Cunningham and Manus Lunny. Two former members of Silly Wizard combine with an Irishman on *Fire In The Glen* (Shanachie, US), a formidable celebration of Scottish traditional music. Phil Cunningham's brilliance as an accordion player is demonstrated on any number of albums, but it's especially impressive placed against the wonderful singing of Andy M. Stewart.

The Whistlebinkies – often dubbed the "Scottish Chieftains" – are one of the founding folk groups in Scotland and are still playing music with a difference. *A Wanton Fling* (Greentrax, Scotland) has all the freshness of early Binkies recordings, a combination of lowland pipes, clarsach, flute, concertina and fiddle.

Wolfstone play folk-rock from the Highlands – "stadium rock meets village-hall ceilidh" said one reviewer – full of passion and fire. *The Half Tail* (Green Linnet, Scotland) is a more subdued progressive sound than usual for Wolfstone, featuring amongst other tracks, a classic whaling song *Bonnie Ship the Diamond*, *The Last Leviathan* and catchy instrumental sets.

Folk singer-songwriters

Eric Bogle emigrated from Scotland to work in Australia as an accountant but when he returned home he was hailed for writing one of the great modern folk songs, *The Band Played Waltzing Matilda*. Bogle's singing doesn't quite match his songwriting, but he has all-star support on *Something of Value* (Sonet, UK/Philo, US), which includes *Waltzing Matilda*.

Archie and Cilla Fisher. The Fisher family – Archie, Ray and Cilla – were mainstays of the 1960s–70s Scottish folk club scene, reviving old ballads and creating new ones. *The Man With A Rhyme* (Folk Legacy, US) was Archie's finest hour, fourteen tracks from 1976 with the Fisher voice and guitar backed by concertina, banjo, dulcimers, cello, fiddle and flute. *Cilla and Artie* (Greentrax, Scotland), released in 1979 and featuring Cilla Fisher and Artie Trezise, still retains an ease and freshness; Cilla's imperious rendition of the late Stan Rogers' *The Jeannie C* is in itself worth the acquisition.

Dick Gaughan is one of the most charismatic of Scottish performers – a singer/guitarist/songwriter who can make you laugh, cry and explode with anger with every twist and nuance of delivery. His new material is still up there with his classic albums of the 1980s, and in 2001 he forged a hugely successful working partnership with another great Scottish music legend Brian McNeil. *Handful of Earth* (Sonet, UK/Philo, US) is the Gaughan classic: a majestic album of traditional and modern songs, still formidable a decade on. When *Folk Roots* magazine asked its readers to nominate the album of the 1980s, it won by a street – and deservedly so.

Robin Laing is one of the best songwriters and performers to emerge out of the Scottish folk scene in the 1990s. *Walking In Time* (Greentrax, Scotland) includes four reworkings of traditional songs – three by other writers and seven of Laing's own songs, accompanied by his own Spanish guitar. Producer Brian McNeill's multi-instrumental talents are also in evidence on most of the tracks.

Ewan MacColl was, simply, one of the all-time greats of British folk song. *In Black and White* (Cooking Vinyl, UK/Green Linnet, US) is a posthumous compilation, lovingly compiled by his family, showcasing MacColl's superb technique as a singer, his gift for choruses (*Dirty Old Town*), his colourful observation as a lyricist (*The Driver's Song*), and his raging sense of injustice (*Black And White*, written after the Sharpeville Massacre of 1963). A fitting epitaph.

Dougie MacLean, one-time member of The Tannahill Weavers, is now carving out a successful solo career as a singer-songwriter. *The Dougie MacLean Collection* (Putumayo, US) is a good selection from Dougie's extensive recorded output including perhaps his most famous song, *Caledonia*.

Adam McNaughtan has written many songs rich in Glasgow wit including one which has travelled the world, *Oor Hamlet*, a condensed version of Shakespeare's *Hamlet* to the tune of *The Mason's Apron*. He has a deep understanding of the tradition and is one of Scotland's national treasures. Adam's comic songs are masterpieces and on *Last Stand At Mount Florida* (Greentrax, Scotland) he is in excellent voice, accompanied by fellow Stramash members Finlay Allison, Bob Blair and John Eaglesham.

Brian McNeill is a man of amazing talents, the one-time fiddling founder of the Battlefield Band and a multi-instrumentalist and a songwriter of some substance. *No Gods* (Greentrax, Scotland) shows the broadening of McNeill's writing talent both in song and tunes. He is joined by ten backing musicians including masterful guitarist Tony MacManus.

by Pete Heywood and Colin Irwin
(Taken from the *Rough Guide to World Music* and updated for this edition by Colin Irwin)

Scottish rock, pop and dance

Identifying certain **rock and pop** acts as specifically Scottish isn't always an easy – or helpful – task, given the amount of cross-pollination that goes on across the whole of the UK. As late as the end of the 1970s, commercial success was very much dependent upon the London marketing scene – until, in the DIY spirit fomented by punk, a small independent record label, **Postcard**, was set up in Glasgow, a hotbed of burgeoning rock talent. The label was to have a crucial and long-lasting effect on the Scottish music industry, starting out by signing up virtually unknown acts such as Aztec Camera and Orange Juice. The nationwide popularity of these bands gave other independent Scottish labels and bands the confidence to challenge international markets. Signs that this independent spirit is still alive and well in the Scottish music scene are to be found in Glasgow's **Chemikal Underground** label, which signs both local and foreign acts.

The 1950s to the 1970s

The first "rock" star from Scotland was, like many who followed, generally regarded as British rather than specifically Scottish. In the 1950s, London-based

Glaswegian **Lonnie Donegan** gave the world the hugely influential new style of **skiffle** (his version of US blues and country). Britain loved it, and his single *Rock Island Line* (1955) sold three million copies within six months, influencing, among others, a Liverpool group named The Quarrymen, led by one John Lennon. The record was also a hit in the US, quite a feat for the time.

It wasn't until the mid-1960s, long after skiffle had merged into a peculiarly British brand of rock'n'roll (which then mutated into rock), that further serious Scottish talent would be seen. As the "British Invasion" of the US steamed ahead, singer-songwriter **Donovan** (born in Glasgow, raised mostly in Hertfordshire) rolled with the times with *Catch The Wind* (1965), which saw him labelled as a lightweight Bob Dylan – it was released a whole year after *The Times They Are A-Changin*, and it soon became evident that Donovan was a musical chamelon, adapting passing styles from folk to pop, from flower power to rock, always lagging slightly behind the creative leaders. Elsewhere the folk influence also held sway, though with increasingly unorthodox results, as Glaswegian **The Incredible String Band** began fusing multiethnic styles, blues and psychedelia, the results of which produced their classic album *The Hangman's Beautiful Daughter* (1968). And in 1967, down in London, Edinburgh-born **Ian Anderson** began his career as the charismatic frontman for the mighty **Jethro Tull**.

At the close of the 1960s, Paisley boy **Gerry Rafferty** and his folky **Humblebums**, who also numbered future comedian Billy Connolly, were having little impact. When the band split, Rafferty relocated to London and formed **Stealer's Wheel**, whose single *Stuck In The Middle With You* (1973) was made unforgettable by Quentin Tarantino's use of it in *Reservoir Dogs* in the 1990s. The group's success petered out, but in 1978 Rafferty's solo *Baker Street* – classic MOR sheen or banal dirge, according to taste – imprinted its mournful saxophone riff upon pop history, and the album *City to City* (1978) went platinum in the States.

In 1974, a bunch of Glaswegian expats in Australia formed the hard rock/heavy metal beast **AC/DC** that would produce the classic *Back In Black* (1980), while 1975 saw the **Average White Band** – formed in London although hailing from Glasgow and Dundee – with their classic *Pick Up The Pieces*, playing tightly arranged funk to an appreciative, loosened-up audience.

The 1970s also saw phenomenal success for teenybop bands. Between 1974 and 1976, Edinburgh's tartan-draped pin-ups, the **Bay City Rollers**, inspired besotted victims to scream loudly and buy enough records to give them nine Top 10 hits – despite there being a surfeit of cover versions and an admission that the band hadn't played on some tracks. Thankfully for non-fans, they went abroad to crack the US market, at which point home interest began to wane and the posters began to come down from countless bedroom walls.

And then punk arrived. Of Scotland's very own clenched-fist malcontents, Glasgow's **Johnny and the Self Abusers** split up on the release of their first single. Slightly more staying power was provided by Dunfermline's **The Skids**, whose anthemic top-ten *Into The Valley* (1979) posited the group as musical warriors in full charge, an image that slotted in neatly beside the urban guerrilla approach of punk rockers south of the border. And in London itself, new wave group **The Tourists**, with vocals from Aberdeen's Annie Lennox, enjoyed a couple of hits before disbanding in 1980. Although short-lived, all three groups were nurturing rock stars for the 1980s – members of Simple Minds, Big Country and the Eurythmics respectively.

The 1980s

Arty post-punkers **Simple Minds** played grandiose synthesizer-driven rock, such as *Once Upon A Time* (1985), which typified both the best and worst of 1980s stadium rock; tellingly, their only US single to chart well was *Don't You (Forget About Me)* (1985), one of the decade's ultimate arena singalongs. **Big Country's** debut album *The Crossing* (1983) boasted soaring Celtic-sounding guitars, which proved popular both in the UK and the US; their second, *Steeltown* (1984), was bleaker but notable for dealing with Scottish economic and industrial decline. The **Eurythmics** got off to a shaky start, but in 1983 their striking image was adorning many an MTV screen as the pop-video generation embraced *Sweet Dreams (Are Made Of This)*. By 1990 they'd split, with **Annie Lennox** going on to enjoy solo success, though they continue to re-form periodically.

Meanwhile, Glasgow's independent record label Postcard had been kick-starting a Scottish pop revolution. **Orange Juice**'s clean, soulful music reached its largest audience with the finger-clicking *Rip It Up* (1982), and singer-songwriter **Edwyn Collins** maintains an intermittent career as both producer and solo artist (his *A Girl Like You* was a worldwide hit in 1995). Postcard also discovered the **Bluebells** (with Lonnie Donegan's son), whose breezy *Young At Heart* charted in 1980 and again in 1993, and a fifteen-year-old **Roddy Frame**, whose group **Aztec Camera** later achieved success with the sublime acoustic pop of the singles *Oblivious* (1982) and *Somewhere In My Heart* (1988); like Collins, Frame continues to produce sporadic solo material.

Complimenting this poppy exuberance, rather more sedate American influences were evident in the underrated **Love And Money**, who doled out a few biting lyrics plus the neglected torch-song *You're Beautiful*, and also in **Hipsway**, who scored on both sides of the Atlantic with *The Honey Thief* (1986). **Wet Wet Wet**'s *Wishing I Was Lucky* (1987) was superb recession pop mixed with blue-eyed soul; subsequent material was somewhat restrained and slicker – terminally so for some tastes – and the hits continued, though in 1999 singer Marti Pellow left the band to go solo. Slide-guitar slithered all over **Texas**' hit *I Don't Want A Lover* (1989), after which things went quiet for them until the stylistic magpie of an album *White On Blonde* (1997) hauled them onto the international stage. Less successful in the long term were Dundee boys **Danny Wilson**, who briefly dented the Top 30 with *Mary's Prayer* (1987) but reserved their best for *Second Summer of Love* (1989), a pithy ditty about acid house culture. If you wanted political lyrics sung in a broad Scots accent, **The Proclaimers** briefly provided, strumming their way through the hugely enjoyable *Sunshine On Leith* (1986). A more consistent presence has been maintained by **Del Amitri** (and their sideburns) whose easy-going trad-rock began with their 1990 debut *Waking Hours*.

More original were Glasgow's rather mournful **Blue Nile**, who have thus far produced three shimmering albums at a snail's pace: *A Walk Across The Rooftops* (1984), *Hats* (1989) and *Peace At Last* (1996). While the critics continue to lavish praise on the songs – minimalist paeans to love – the public mostly ignore them. Following the success of *Sulk* (1982), a cult following was also to be the largest reward for Dundee's eclectic **Associates** and the solo work of frontman **Billy Mackenzie**. **The Silencers** too, whose second album *A Blues For Buddha* (1988) showcased a knack for cinematic tunes and hypnotic rhythms, managed to garner a small following – though mostly in France. Greater commercial success eventually went to Edinburgh man **Mike Scott**, who gathered together the **Waterboys** in London in 1982 and began the quest for what he termed "the Big Music," which resulted in anthemic singles like *The Whole of the Moon* (1985). Such loftiness was reduced in scope for the excellent *Fisherman's Blues* (1988), and his solo and group work continues to delight.

Throughout the mainstream-dominated mid-1980s, the alternative scene was brewing a heady concoction that would have far-reaching effects. Spearheading this underground movement was Manchester-based label **Creation**, formed by a Scot named Alan McGee, who was, in time, to talent-spot some of the UK's best acts, including Oasis. At the time, his most significant signing was **The Jesus and Mary Chain**, whose hedonistic approach to life – sex, drugs and biker imagery, all interchangeable metaphors for each other – immediately gained a place in disaffected teenagers' record collections with the benchmark debut *Psychocandy* (1984), wherein clanging feedback and West Coast melodies gave a pretty good impression of sonic claustrophobia. Bubblegum pop and Velvet Underground influences would also surface in **The Pastels**, who appeared on *NME*'s seminal *C86* compilation, though they were never to scale the commercial heights of the Mary Chain. Similarly, Bathgate's **Goodbye Mr Mackenzie** featured Shirley Manson on vocals, whose success with Garbage in the 1990s would eclipse the work of her former band and their fine album *The Rattler* (1986). For a while, however, it seemed that the Glasgow suburb of Bellshill was to be alternative music's creative capital. From here came the closely related **Vaselines**, **BMX Bandits** and **Captain America** (who became **Eugenius**), who between them provided several rough gems that would resurface in the grunge years when Kurt Cobain paid them homage, plus several band members for **Teenage Fanclub**, whose own *Bandwagonesque* (1991) is every bit as essential as Nirvana's *Nevermind*.

The 1990s to the present

Until the late 1980s, Scotland's most obvious contribution to dance music had been the hi-NRG disco of **Bronski Beat**, formed in London, whose album *Age of Consent* (1984), armed with the falsetto of Glaswegian **Jimmy Somerville**, addressed gay issues. But as the house scene became difficult to ignore and the Ecstasy-fuelled dance-rock crossover of "Madchester" stormed the charts with a vengeance, Scottish outfits were present and correct. As **The JAMMS**, Jimmy Cauty and Bill Drummond had already scored a major hit with *Doctorin' The Tardis* (1988), but as **The KLF**, their 1990 "Stadium House Trilogy" brought the cash rolling in; they capitalized on the image by later burning £1 million cash, in what was variously described as an act of art-terrorism or a publicity stunt. The KLF were also a huge influence on ambient music when their classic *Chill Out* (1990) became the scene's very own *Dark Side Of The Moon*, and when Jimmy Cauty cofounded the influential **Orb**.

Initially an indie guitar band, **The Shamen** got clubbers chanting "E's are good!" to the chorus of *Ebeneezer Goode* (1992), while the **Soup Dragons** adopted the Rolling Stones' *I'm Free* and gave it a baggy beat. And, grand masters of being high as a kite, **Primal Scream** (formed by Bobby Gillespie, ex-drummer for the Jesus and Mary Chain) floated around in yet more Stonesy, dubbed-out bliss with the timeless *Screamadelica* (1989).

Scotland's own dance scene has since flowered to become one of the liveliest in Europe. Independent labels such as **Soma** – who signed French dance-groovers Daft Punk – **Bellboy Records** and **Hook Records** have all released top-quality dance tracks. DJs **Stuart MacMillan** and **Orde Meikle**, creators of Slam, perform globally, returning with world-class DJs to pack out Glasgow clubs. DJ **Howie B** helped break the boundaries of performance by mixing

U2 live on their 1997 tour, while the camera-shy **Blue Boy** is a club favourite with his fusion of dance and funky soul, and the **Glasgow Underground** label ensures that deep house maintains a presence worthy of its influence. Treading the middle ground between dance and rock, Edinburgh-raised **Finlay Quaye** produced his laid-back and summery *Maverick A Strike* (1997), mixing up reggae, rock and soul, for which he received a Brit award in 1998. **The Beta Band**, meanwhile, pilfer various elements of dance music and match them to folk and rock influences, a hypnotic sound best exemplified by their collection *The Three EPs* (1998).

The strong independent tradition carries on apace, with Glasgow still apparently full of musos, many of them signed to guitar group **The Delgados**' label Chemikal Underground. If there's a particular theme to the moment, lo-fi might just about encapsulate the folk-tinged wispiness of **Belle and Sebastian**, the minimalism of **Arab Strap** and the sonic experimentalism of **Mogwai**. Punk too resurfaces in various guises, from **Idlewild** to **Bis** (who, in 1996, were the first unsigned band to appear on *Top of the Pops*), and is funked up a little by **Urusei Yatsura**. Alan McGee also continues to maintain his Scottish connections with his latest label Poptones, to which are signed Glaswegians **The Cosmic Rough Riders**, a group every bit as inspired by the US West Coast bands of the 1960s as their name implies; their *Enjoy the Melodic Sunshine* (2000) is well worth investing in, if only to wonder how such great pop music can go largely unoticed. To prove that Scottish acts aren't just watching from the commercial sidelines, however, **Travis** moved on from their early glam-rock style to produce the best-selling *The Man Who* (1999), brimming with tasteful angst, which they followed up in 2001 with *The Invisible Band*.

by Geoff Howard

Scotland's writers

Robert Burns

Scotland's national poet, ***Robert Burns*** *(1759–96) is celebrated not just for the lyrical genius in his prodigious output of poetry and song, but also for the fact that he was the ploughman-poet, a son of the soil who could give voice to Scottish nationalism and universal ideals of love and socialism.* To a Mouse *is one of his early poems, expressing both his intimacy with nature and a philosophical world view. Though written in Scots, its second-to-last stanza originates a phrase which is widely known in its anglicized form but which few attribute to Burns. We've added a boxed glossary explaining some unfamiliar Scots words.* *For a profile of Burns, see p.218.*

To a Mouse, On turning her up in her Nest, with the Plough, November 1785

Wee, sleeket, cowran, tim'rous beastie,
O, what a panic 's in thy breastie!
Thou need na start awa sae hasty,
Wi' bickering brattle!
I wad be laith to rin an' chase thee,
Wi' murd'ring pattle!

I'm truly sorry Man's dominion
Has broken Nature's social union,
An' justifies that ill opinion,
Which makes thee startle,
At me, thy poor, earth-born companion,
An' fellow-mortal!

I doubt na, whyles, but thou may thieve;
What then? poor beastie, thou maun live!
A daimen-icker in a thrave
'S a sma' request.
I'll get a blessin wi' the lave,
An' never miss't!

They wee-bit housie, too, in ruin!
Its silly wa's the win's are strewin!
An' naething, now, to big a new ane,
O' foggage green!
An' bleak December's winds ensuin,
Baith snell an' keen!

Thou saw the fields laid bare an' wast,
An' weary Winter comin fast,
An' cozie here, beneath the blast,
Thou thought to dwell,
Till crash! the cruel coulter past
Out thro' thy cell.

That wee-bit heap o' leaves an' stibble
Has cost thee monie a weary nibble!
Now thou 's turn'd out, for a' thy trouble,
But house or hald,
To thole the Winter's sleety dribble
An' cranreuch cauld!

But Mousie, thou art no thy lane,
In proving foresight may be vain;
The best-laid schemes o' Mice an' Men
Gang aft agley,
An' lea'e us nought but grief an' pain,
For promis'd joy!

Still thou art blest, compar'd wi' me!
The present only toucheth thee:
But Och! I backward cast me e'e
On prospects drear!
An' forward, tho' I canna see,
I guess an' fear!

Glossary

Sleeket Glossy
Cowran Cowering
Na Not
Sae So
Wi' With
Brattle Clatter, hurry
Wad Would
Laith Loath, unwilling
Rin Run
Pattle Type of spade
Whyles Sometimes
Thieve Steal
Maun Must
Daimen-icker Occasional ear of corn
Thrave A measure of corn
Sma' Small
Lave Remainder
Silly Feeble
Wa's Walls
Win's Winds
Foggage Moss
Baith Both
Snell Bitter
Coulter Cutting blade of plough
Stibble Stubble
Monie Many
Hald Hold, dwelling
Cranreuch Hoar-frost
Cauld Cold
Lane Alone
Gang Go, depart
Aft Often
Agley Awry
Lea'e Leave
E'e Eye

Robert Louis Stevenson

The son of a lighthouse engineer who grew up in Edinburgh's New Town, ***Robert Louis Stevenson*** *(1850–94) is most famous worldwide for* Treasure Island *and* The Strange Case of Dr Jekyll and Mr Hyde. *An enduring favourite in* Scotland is Kidnapped, *in which the hero David Balfour crosses Scotland in a series of lively scrapes. Its sequel,* Catriona, *was written when Stevenson was living in Samoa, but as this extract from the opening chapter of the book shows, he was able to re-create vividly the feel and flavour of his home town.* *For more on Stevenson, see p.139.*

From *Catriona*

Here I was in this old, black city, which was for all the world like a rabbit-warren, not only by the number of its indwellers, but the complication of its passages and holes. It was, indeed, a place where no stranger had a chance to find a friend, let be another stranger. Suppose him even to hit on the right close, people dwelt so thronged in these tall houses, he might very well seek a day before he chanced on the right door. The ordinary course was to hire a lad they called a *caddie*, who was like a guide or pilot, led you where you had occasion, and (your errands being done) brought you again where you were lodging. But these caddies, being always employed in the same sort of services, and leaving it for obligation to be well informed of every house and person in the city, had grown to form a brotherhood of spies: and I knew from tales of Mr Campbell's how they communicated one with another, what a rage of curiosity they conceived as to their employer's business, and how they were like eyes and fingers to the police. It would be a piece of little wisdom, the way I was now placed, to take such a ferret to my tails. I had three visits to make, all immediately needful: to my kinsman Mr Balfour of Pilrig, to Stewart the Writer that was Appin's agent, and to William Grant Esquire of Prestongrange, Lord Advocate of Scotland. Mr Balfour was a non-committal visit; and besides (Pilrig being in the country) I made bold to find the way to it myself, with the help of my two legs and a Scots tongue. But the rest were in a different case. Not only was the visit to Appin's agent, in the midst of the cry about the Appin murder, dangerous in itself, but it was highly inconsistent with the other. I was like to have a bad enough time of it with my Lord Advocate Grant, the best of ways; but to go to him hot-foot from Appin's agent, was little likely to mend my own affairs, and might prove the mere ruin of friend Alan's. The whole thing, besides, gave me a look of running with the hare and hunting with the hounds that was little to my fancy. I determined, therefore, to be done at once with Mr Stewart and the whole Jacobitical side of my business, and to profit for that purpose by the guidance of the porter at my side. But it chanced I had scarce given him the address, when there came a sprinkle of rain – nothing to hurt, only for my new clothes – and we took shelter under a pend at the head of a close or alley.

Being strange to what I saw, I stepped a little farther in. The narrow paved way descended swiftly. Prodigious tall houses sprang upon each side and bulged out, one storey beyond another, as they rose. At the top only a ribbon of sky showed in. By what I could spy in the windows, and by the respectable persons that passed out and in, I saw the houses to be very well occupied; and the whole appearance of the place interested me like a tale.

I was still gazing, when there came a sudden brisk tramp of feet in time and a clash of steel behind me. Turning quickly, I was aware of a party of armed soldiers, and in their midst, a tall man in a great coat. He walked with a stoop that was like a piece of courtesy, genteel and insinuating: he waved his hands plausibly as he went, and his face was sly and handsome. I thought his eye took me in, but could not meet it. This procession went by to a door in the close, which a serving-man in a fine livery set open; and two of the soldier-lads carried the prisoner within, the rest lingering with their firelocks by the door.

There can nothing pass in the streets of a city without some following of idle folk and children. It was so now; but the more part melted away incontinent until but three were left. One was a girl; she was dressed like a lady, and had a screen of the Drummond colours on her head; but her comrades or (I should say) followers were ragged gillies, such as I have seen the matches of by the dozen in my Highland journey. They all spoke together earnestly in Gaelic, the sound of which was pleasant in my ears for the sake of Alan; and, though the rain was by again, and my porter plucked at me to be going, I even drew nearer where they were, to listen. The lady scolded sharply, the others making apologies and cringeing before her, so that I made sure she was come of a chief's house. All the while the three of them sought in their pockets, and by what I could make out, they had the matter of half a farthing among the party: which made me smile a little to see all Highland folk alike for fine obeisances and empty sporrans.

It chanced the girl turned suddenly about, so that I saw her face for the first time. There is no greater wonder than the way the face of a young woman fits in a man's mind, and stays there, and he could never tell you why; it just seems it was the thing he wanted. She had wonderful bright eyes like stars, and I daresay the eyes had a part in it; but what I remember the most clearly was the way her lips were a trifle open as she turned. And, whatever was the cause, I stood there staring like a fool. On her side, as she had not known there was anyone so near, she looked at me a little longer, and perhaps with more surprise, than was entirely civil.

Glossary

Close Narrow passageway leading to a block of flats

Pend A vaulted entranceway to a close or passageway

Gillies Most commonly attendants while hunting or fishing; used here simply to indicate lads or youths

Lewis Grassic Gibbon

***Lewis Grassic Gibbon** was the pen name of James Leslie Mitchell (1901–35), and though Mitchell achieved moderate success writing non-fiction in the early part of his career, recognition only really came when he adopted his pseudonym and re-created in fiction the language and life of the farming community known as the Mearns in northeast Scotland where he had grown up* *(see p.547).* Sunset Song, *the first of a trilogy known as* A Scots Quair, *is now widely regarded as the finest Scottish work of fiction in the twentieth century. In it, Gibbon introduces the spirited but tragic heroine Chris Guthrie, who after her mother's death and the departure of her brother Will overseas, is left to nurse her hard, unflinching father John through an illness at their farm Blawearie in the village of Kinraddie. This extract comes shortly after John Guthrie has died and Chris is left to battle with her own lack of emotion and uncertainty about the future. A glossary explains some of the distinctive north-east dialect used.*

From *Sunset Song*

And the next forenoon the lawyer man came down from Stonehaven, it was Peter Semple, folk called him Simple Simon but swore that he was a swick. Father had trusted him, though, and faith! you'd be fell straight in your gait ere John Guthrie trusted you. Not that he'd listened to advice, father, he'd directed a will be made and the things to be set in that will; and when Mr Semple had said he was being fell sore on some of his family father had told him to mind his own business, and that was a clerk's. So Mr Semple drew up the will, it had been just after Will went off to the Argentine, and father had signed it; and now the Blawearie folk sat down in the parlour, with whisky and biscuits for Mr Semple, to hear it read. It was short and plain as you please, Chris watched the face of her uncle as the lawyer read and saw it go white in the gills, he'd expected something far different from that. And the will told that John Guthrie left all his possessions, in silver and belongings, to his daughter Christine, to be hers without let or condition, Mr Semple her guardian in such law matters as needed one, but Chris to control the goods and gear as she pleased. And folk were to say, soon as Kinraddie heard of the will, and faith! they seemed to have heard it all before it was well out of the envelope, that it was an unco will, old Guthrie had been fair spiteful to his sons, maybe Will would dispute his sister's tocher.

The money was over three hundred pounds in the bank, it was hard to believe that father could have saved all that. But he had; and Chris sat and stared at the lawyer, hearing him explain and explain this, that, and the next, in the way of lawyers: they presume you're a fool and double their fees. Three hundred pounds! And now she could do as she'd planned, she'd go up to the College again and pass her exams and go on to Aberdeen and get her degrees, come out as a teacher and finish with the filthy soss of a farm. She'd sell up the gear at Blawearie, the lease was dead, it had died with father, oh! she was free and free to do as she liked and dream as she liked at last!

And it was pity now that she'd all she wanted she felt no longer that fine thrill that had been with her while she made her secret plans. It was as though she'd lost it down in Kinraddie kirkyard; and she sat and stared so still and white at the lawyer man that he closed up his case with a snap. *So think it well over, Christine*, he said and she roused and said *Oh, I'll do that*; and off he went, Uncle Tam drew a long, deep breath, as though fair near choked he'd been *Not a word of his two poor, motherless boys!*

It seemed he'd expected Alec and Dod would be left their share, maybe that was why he'd been so eager to adopt them the year before. But Auntie cried *For shame, Tam, how are they motherless now that I've got them? And you'll come up and live with us when you've sold Blawearie's furnishings, Chris?* And her voice was kind but eyes were keen, Chris looked at her with her own eyes hard, *Ay, maybe* and got up and slipped from the room, *I'll go down and bring home the kye*.

And out she went, though it wasn't near kye-time yet, and wandered away over the fields; it was a cold and louring day, the sound of the sea came plain to her, as though heard in a shell, Kinraddie wilted under the greyness. In the ley field old Bob stood with his tail to the wind, his hair ruffled up by the wind, his head bent away from the smore of it. He heard her pass and give a bit neigh, but he didn't try to follow her, poor brute, he'd soon be over old for work. The wet fields squelched below her feet, oozing up their smell of red clay from under the sodden grasses, and up in the hills she saw the trail of the mist, great sailing shapes of it, going south on the wind into Forfar, past Laurencekirk they would sail, down the wide Howe with its sheltered glens and its late, drenched harvests, past Brechin smoking against its hill, with its ancient tower that the Pictish folk had reared, out of the Mearns, sailing and passing, sailing and passing, she minded Greek words of forgotten lessons, Παντα ρει, *Nothing endures*. And then a queer thought came to her there in the drookèd fields, that nothing endured at all, nothing but the land she passed across, tossed and turned and perpetually changed below the hands of the crofter folk since the oldest of them had set the Standing Stones by the loch of Blawearie and climbed there on their hold days and saw their terraced crops ride brave in the wind and sun. Sea and sky and the folk who wrote and fought and were learnéd, teaching and saying and praying, they lasted but as a breath, a mist of fog in the hills, but the land was forever, it moved and changed below you, but was forever, you were close to it and to you, not at a bleak remove it held you and hurted you. And she had thought to leave it all!

She walked weeping then, stricken and frightened because of that knowledge that had come on her, she could never leave it, this life of toiling days and the needs of beasts and the smoke of wood fires and the air that stung your throat so acrid, Autumn and Spring, she was bound and held as though they had prisoned her here. And her fine bit plannings! – they'd been just the dreamings of a child over toys it lacked, toys that would never content it when it heard the smore of a storm or the cry of sheep on the moors or smelt the pringling smell of a new-ploughed park under the drive of a coulter. She could no more teach a school than fly, night and day she'd want to be back, for all the fine clothes and gear she might get and hold, the books and the light and the learning.

The kye were in sight then, they stood in the lithe of the freestone dyke that ebbed and flowed over the shoulder of the long ley field, and they hugged to it close from the drive of the wind, not heeding her as she came among them, the smell of their bodies foul in her face – foul and known and enduring as the land itself. Oh, she hated and loved in a breath! Even her lover might hardly endure, but beside it the hate was no more than the whimpering and fear of a child that cowered from the wind in the lithe of its mother's skirts.

Glossary

Swick Sly cheat
Fell Cruel, exceedingly
Unco Unusual, very
Tocher Inheritance
Soss Mess
Kye Cattle
Louring Overcast, threatening
Ley Fallow
Smore lit. smother; a wind thick with fine rain
Drookèd Drenched
Crofter Smallholder farmers
Pringling Prickling, tingling
Coulter Cutting blade of a plough
Lithe Shelter

Alan Warner

*Born in Oban in 1964, **Alan Warner** was, along with the likes of Irvine Welsh, one of the writers to emerge from the Rebel Inc. group in the early 1990s, who portrayed the drug culture and street life of working-class urban Scotland with a vividness verging on glamour. Warner's first novel,* Morvern Callar, *tells the story of a headstrong and independent supermarket assistant in a Scottish west-coast town who takes off to the rave clubs of Ibiza. In this extract she is returning to her home in "the Port", a thinly disguised Oban.*

From *Morvern Callar*

We moved east to the Back Settlement then in west till we came in behind The Complex and down into the port through the long cutting by the signal box. With both hands I pulled down the cab window; the port looked same as ever round the bay. The cab swayed a little and a hiss came from the brake handle as Coll nudged it over. As we ran along the platform edge I swung the seat round and bent down to pick up the bag. Woofit was up, circling and wagging his tail. The engine stopped moving and there was a dying honk of air as Coll snapped down the worn reddish-painted handle on the cab wall behind him. I opened the cab door and Woofit was out the train engine and sniffing around the passengers who were crowded up against the gate with Zipper checking tickets. I jumped down onto the platform.

Coll stood up in the cab doorway shouting Woofit away from the passengers. Coll sniffed and says, Mmm the only time these machines smell good is after youve been in them Morvern Callar.

I laughed and goes, I'd best be shooting, thanks for the hurl.

Aye no bother, no bother, you'd best away and find that man.

He'll be on the sesh.

No surprised. You take care you crazy thing.

You too, bye Woofit, I goes, kneeling and giving the dog a good clapping round the ears.

I crossed the square then looked up. There was still time to make it to the superstore.

Once across the carpark I moved through the sliding door and past the signing book. You saw The Seacow who was alone on tills turn and stare. I took the door up to the ladies' staffroom and Creeping Jesus's office. The staffroom was empty so I used the key on my locker then pushed aside the nylon uniform and the tights in a ball. I took out the schoolish shoes then rummaged through the shelf. I took a few things: make-up, a bottle paracetamol and vitamins, then put them in my bag.

I walked through, knocked on Creeping Jesus's door then stepped in.

Well, well, look whos arrived, our own suntanned supermodel, Creeping Jesus says.

There was a long bit of silentness.

Going to tell me why youre two weeks late for work then? Creeping Jesus says.

Thirteen days, I goes.

It's not just me suffers you know Morvern, the whole section suffers, working a man short.

I'm not a man.

Dont get smart.

Well, I'm not, I went then coughed.

Where've you been?

Thats none of your business just tell me where I stand, have I got a job? Cause if I dont then why should I be stood in your office like this?

What do you think Morvern?

Fine I goes.

It was the orangey plastic chair that always sat by the door I threw across his office at him. A back leg hit the front of the desk so the chair made a wobbling noise and shot off into the corner of the room. Creeping Jesus had got crouched down behind the desk, shouting about police.

Away crawl under the stone you came from, Creeping Jesus, I says. I wrenched the door open so bad-temperedly it crashed into the filing cabinets.

I walked out into the carpark, used the goldish lighter on a Silk Cut under one of the lights then crossed The Black Lynn that flows under the port.

In the night, rain was spotting down from the light's haloes. I walked into Haddows, asked for a half bottle voddy and counted out more of the money yon Tom and Susan subbed me. I walked quick up past Video Rental, St John's then the Phoenix. Cars were circling the port roads with elbows out windows. I dug my house keys from the bag.

On the mat were seven catalogues from model shops in the south and the letter with a queer postmark addressed to me. I picked them all up and dropped them on His desk. I put De Devil Dead by Lee Perry on the CD then I towelled my hair and twisted it up into a French roll. I put on the heater and immerser.

I'd forgot to get something for diluting the voddy and of course the fridge was bare so I opened this bottle of sweet wine and used that to dilute it. There was a can tinned potatoes so I opened it, drained the can then popped the potatoes in my mouth one after the other. While chewing I was just staring at the black window.

When that immerser had heated I gulped some more of the bogging-tasting drink then stripped in front of the fire, standing on one leg of the wet jeans to tug the other foot out.

After shaving my legs and having a good bath I used every clean towel on me and put SDI on the DC. In the scud with that religious music going I got down on the polished floorboards and tried hard with a wee prayer. I suddenly jumped up and paraded about all agitated. I took out De Devil Dead and put in From the Secret Laboratory by Lee Perry. I flicked forward to tracks 6 and 7. This time the praying went an awful lot better and when I'd finished I was shivering with perished coldness. I got dressed then put on the steerhide jacket from the wardrobe. I drank some more voddy then got the brolly and headed outside.

The wind tugged at the brolly and drops vibrated off of the edge as I hunched under.

I walked towards the phonebox, took the brolly down and got in. There was no answer at The Complex. I phoned V the D's out the Back Settlement.

Hello 206, she goes.

It's Morvern.

Morvern where are you? Your father's worried sick about you as if he doesn't have enough of his own problems.

I'm home.

We thought you'd been kidnapped or something.

Where is he then?

He's there in the port tonight. I've told him not to worry, I mean we'll get by, might have to put off the extension. Have you been to work?

Aye. Sacked.

Oh Morvern, she sighed and laughed. What are we going to do with the Callars? Surely you'll get a bit hotel work before the end of the season?

The pips started and I looked up at the ceiling.

Morvern . . .?

I put the phone down softly and listened to the rain on the roof of the box. I pushed out the door.

I used the shortcut up to the circular folly trying no to go skiteing in the runny mud. From the top of Jacob's Ladder I looked down on the port and the fishing boats tied up at the pier. I tried to look behind The Complex towards the mountains where the pass goes west to the village beyond the power station but there were only the moving clouds above orangey street light.

Going down Jacob's Ladder I tried to miss the puddles. Water was splattering over from the cliff above. No couples kissed on the benches of each platform. I looked down on the dark street under the cliff and the dull lights of Red Hanna's local: The Politician Hotel.

I pushed open the door and shook water off the steerhide jacket's arms. All heads turned and followed me as I walked to the fridge where not only was Povie the butcher's extra meat kept but the Politician had placed the pool table cause it wouldnt fit anywhere else. I stuck my head in: five men were round the table, two were playing. A big hunk of meat was hung from one of the hooks and a man was holding it aside so the player could take a good shot. The other men were puffing into their hands.

Look it's one of the strippers, says a guy in a boilersuit.

Shh, thats yon engine driver's girl, another went as I turned round, stepped up to the bar and goes, Has Red Hanna been in the night?

A week past Friday, goes a voice behind me. I turned round.

An old greyhead was sat with tears coming from his eyes that he kept dabbing with a hanky. He was far from greeting though and it was a double he had in front him.

I'd Tod the Post, youre Morvern, Red Hanna's girl, you work in the superstore, eh?

Not any more I dont. Have you seen him then?

Not since he was in yon time, no like him to neglect us for so long.

Any inkling where he'll be?

Havent the foggiest. You'd be best parking yourself here and making an old fool happy; whats your pleasure?

Nah, I couldnt get you back.

Ah, sit yourself down. Red Hanna would skin me if he hears youve been in and no treated well. It's The Weekday Club the night, a'bhailaich, get the girl with the smashing suntan a drink.

A Southern Comfort and lemonade please, I goes.

A what says the barman.

Southern Comfort?

We dont have that here.

I looked at the bottles and says, A Sweetheart Stout please.

Extract from MORVERN CALLAR by Alan Warner,
published by Jonathan Cape. Used by permission of
The Random House Group Limited.

Glossary

Hurl Lift
Sesh lit. "session"; drinking bout
Bogging Foul
Scud Naked
Skiteing Slipping
A'bhailaich (Gaelic) O boy, or My boy

Books

Wherever a book is in print, the UK publisher is given first in each listing, separated, where applicable, from the US publisher by an oblique slash. Where books are published in only one of these countries we have specified which one; when the same company publishes the book in both, its name appears just once. Out-of-print titles are indicated as o/p; these should be easy to track down in secondhand bookshops. Titles marked with ★ are particularly recommended.

Fiction

★ **Iain Banks** *The Bridge* (Abacus/HarperCollins); *Complicity* (Abacus/Bantam); *The Crow Road* (Abacus/Bantam); *Espedair Street* (UK Abacus); *A Song of Stone* (Abacus/Touchstone); *The Wasp Factory* (Abacus/Simon and Schuster); *Whit* (UK Abacus). Just a few titles by this astonishingly prolific author, who also writes sci-fi as Iain M. Banks. His work can be funny, pacy, thought-provoking, imaginative and downright disgusting. It is never dull.

J.M. Barrie *Peter Pan*. Born and educated in Scotland, Barrie moved to London to work as a journalist. Aside from *Peter Pan*, his best-known work, he wrote a series of short stories and other works set in Kirriemuir where he was born.

M.C. Beaton *Death of a Dustman* and *Death of an Addict* (Warner Brothers/Mysterious Press). Crime novels with Hamish Macbeth as the unlikely offbeat policeman in a small Highland town.

Christopher Brookmyre *One Fine Day In the Middle of the Night*, *Not the End of the World*, *Country of the Blind* (all UK Abacus). All very funny, racy novels that refuse to be categorized. You'll probably find them in the crime section, but they're as much politico-satirical.

George Mackay Brown *Beside the Ocean of Time* (UK Flamingo). A child's journey through the history of an Orkney island, and an adult's effort to make sense of the place's secrets in the late twentieth century. *Magnus* (Canongate/Interlink) is his retelling of the death of St Magnus with parallels for modern times.

John Buchan *The Complete Richard Hannay* (Penguin/Godine). This single volume includes *The 39 Steps*, *Greenmantle*, *Mr Standfast*, *The Three Hostages* and *The Island of Sheep*. Good gung-ho stories with a great feel for the Scottish landscape. In the US, both Oxford University Press and Godine publish various editions of the Hannay stories. Less well-known, but better, are Buchan's historical romances such as *Midwinter* (UK B&W Publishing), a Jacobite thriller, and *Witchwood* (Canongate), a tale of religious strife in the seventeenth century.

Isla Dewar *Women Talking Dirty* (UK Headline Review). Set in Edinburgh suburbia, the outrageous, funny and poignant soul-bearing of two women who become fast friends over a bottle of vodka and detailed post-match analysis. *Keeping up with Magda* (Review/Trafalgar Square) and *Giving up on Ordinary* (UK Headline Review) are in a similar style.

Dorothy Dunnett *Gemini* (Penguin/Vintage). The latest from the pen of this popular historical novelist has a Scottish hero and is set in 1477. A good read.

Christine Marion Fraser *Kinvara* (HarperCollins). Glasgow-born Fraser's family saga is centred on a lighthouse keeper on the west coast of Scotland. Her latest novel *Children of Rhanna* (Coronet) traces the lives of four people who were brought up as children in a close-knit community on the island of Rhanna.

George MacDonald Fraser *The General Danced at Dawn* (Fontana/HarperCollins); *McAuslain Entire* (Akadine Press); *The Sheikh and the Dustbin* (HarperCollins). Touching and very funny collections of short stories detailing life in a Highland regiment after World War II by the author of the Flashman novels.

Janice Galloway *The Trick is to Keep Breathing* (Minerva/Dalkey Archive). The story of a woman's mind as she slowly spirals into depressive madness. Almost unwittingly readers are drawn into the vortex and suddenly find themselves empathizing with the heroine's confusion. A brilliantly written, intense book. Her much acclaimed novel *Foreign Parts* (Vintage/Dalkey Archive) explores the friendship of two women.

★ **Lewis Grassic Gibbon** *A Scots Quair* (Penguin/Canongate). A landmark trilogy set in northeast Scotland during and after World War I, the events seen through the eyes of Chris Guthrie, torn between her love for the land and her desire to escape a peasant culture. Strong, seminal work.

Alasdair Gray *Lanark: A Life in Four Books* (Picador/Harvest). A postmodern blend of social realism and labyrinthine fantasy. Gray's extraordinary debut as a novelist, featuring his own allegorical illustrations, takes invention and comprehension to their limits.

Andrew Greig *When They Lay Bare* (Faber). A disturbing mystery where ancient Border family feuds catch up with contemporary violence and sexual intrigue.

★ **Neil M. Gunn** *The Silver Darlings* (UK Faber). Probably Gunn's most representative and best-known book, evocatively set on the northeast coast and telling the story of herring fishermen during the great years of the industry.

James Hogg *The Private Memoirs and Confessions of a Justified Sinner* (Penguin/Broadview). Complex, dark mid-nineteenth-century novel dealing with possession, myth and folklore, as it looks at the confession of an Edinburgh murderer from three different points of view.

Quintin Jardine *Thursday Legends* (UK Headline) is the latest of these popular thrillers where crime is always mixed with power politics in Edinburgh.

Jackie Kay *Trumpet* (Picador/Vintage). Joss Moody, the protagonist of this novel, Kay's first, is dead before the story begins. He was a black Scottish jazz trumpeter, who has left a wife in mourning and a son in deep shock, for the posthumous medical report revealed Moody, revered in the jazz world, to be a woman. A humane and multi-layered work.

James Kelman *The Busconductor Hines* (UK Phoenix). The wildly funny story of a young Glasgow bus conductor with an intensely boring job and a limitless imagination. *How Late it Was, How Late* (UK Minerva) is Kelman's Booker Prize-winning and disturbing look at life as seen through the eyes of a foul-mouthed, blind Glaswegian drunk.

★ **A.L. Kennedy** *Looking for the Possible Dance* (UK Minerva). Young Scottish writer dissects the difficulties of human relationships on a personal and wider social level. More recent novels *So I Am Glad* and *Original Bliss* (both UK Minerva) have the same deft touch.

Eric Linklater *The Dark of Summer* (Canongate). Set on the Faroes, Shetland, Orkney (where the author was born) and in theatres of war, this novel exhibits the best of Linklater's compelling narrative style, although his comic *Private Angelo* (Canongate) is better known.

Alexander MacArthur and Kingsley Long *No Mean City* (UK Corgi). Classic story of razor gangs in 1935 Glasgow.

William McIlvanney *Docherty* (UK Sceptre). Tale of a hard, poverty-wracked Scottish coal-mining community by one of the country's most-respected contemporary authors.

Compton Mackenzie *Whisky Galore* (UK Penguin). Comic novel based on a true story of the wartime wreck of a cargo of whisky on a Hebridean island. Full of predictable stereotypes but still funny.

Naomi Mitchison *Lobster on the Agenda* (UK House of Lochar). Recently republished, Mitchison's novel written in 1952 about contemporary life in the West Highlands precisely captures a community which, shaken by the war, is trying to look forward while hampered by the prejudices of the past.

Neil Munro *Para Handy* (UK Birlinn). Engaging and witty stories relating the adventures of a Clyde puffer captain as he more or less legally steers his grubby ship up and down the west coast. Despite a fond – if slightly patronizing – view of the Gaelic mind, they are enormous fun.

★ **Ian Rankin** *The Hanging Garden* and *The Falls* (both Orion/Mass Market Paperback). Superbly plotted dark stories featuring Rebus, a maverick police detective who haunts the bars of Edinburgh. Now a TV series and the subject of a guided tour in the city.

James Robertson *The Fanatic* (Fourth Estate). Stunning debut novel set in the present-day Edinburgh ghost tours; the current "ghost" becomes fascinated by the seventeenth-century character he portrays and, by delving into the history of the period, reveals secrets of the past and present.

Dorothy L. Sayers *Five Red Herrings* (New English Library/Harper). A complicated tale involving railway timetables set in Gatehouse of Fleet in Galloway, but solved, of course, by Lord Peter Wimsey.

Sir Walter Scott *The Waverley Novels* (Penguin). The books that did much to create the romanticized version of Scottish life and history. A series of critical hardback editions has been published by Edinburgh University Press: *Kenilworth*, *Tale of Old Mortality*, *Black Dwarf*, *St Ronan's Well* and *The Antiquary*. For more on Scott, see p.174.

Iain Crichton Smith *Consider the Lilies* (UK Canongate). Poetic lament about the Highland Clearances by Scotland's finest bilingual (English and Gaelic) writer.

Muriel Spark *The Prime of Miss Jean Brodie* (Penguin/HarperCollins).

Wonderful evocation of middle-class Edinburgh life and aspirations, still apparent in that city today.

Alan Spence *The Stone Garden* (UK Phoenix). Perceptive, gently humorous and well-crafted short stories based on childhood experiences in Glasgow.

Robert Louis Stevenson *Dr Jekyll and Mr Hyde* (Penguin/Bantam); *The Master of Ballantrae* (Penguin/Oxford University Press); *Weir of Hermiston* (UK Penguin). Nineteenth-century tales of intrigue and adventure. For more on Stevenson, see p.139.

Nigel Tranter *The Bruce Trilogy* (Coronet/Hodder & Stoughton). Massive tome about Robert the Bruce by a prolific and hugely popular author on Scottish themes. *The Flockmasters* (B&W) deals with the Clearances and *Kettle of Fish* (B&W) with salmon poaching in the Tweed.

★ **Alan Warner** *Morvern Callar* (Vintage/Anchor). Bleakly humorous story of a supermarket shelf-packer from Oban who finds her boyfriend has committed suicide in her kitchen and tries to put it out of her mind with the aid of sex, drugs and booze until she finds an appalling solution. It'll grip you. The sequel is *These Demented Lands* (Vintage/Anchor), and his latest, *The Sopranos* (Jonathan Cape/Harvest), follows a Catholic girls' choir to Edinburgh.

★ **Irvine Welsh** *Irvine Welsh Omnibus* (Vintage/Norton). A compendium including *Trainspotting*, *The Acid House* and *Marabou Stork Nightmares*, all of which can also be found as separate titles. Welsh trawls through the horrors of drug addiction, sexual fantasy, urban decay and hopeless youth, making you either rejoice at an authentic and unapologetic new voice for the dispossessed, or cringe. Thankfully, his unflinching attention is not without humour.

Kevin Williamson (ed.) *Children of Albion Rovers* (Rebel/Penguin). A fast-track introduction to some of the best Scottish writers of the drug-culture generation, with novellas by the likes of Irvine Welsh, Alan Warner, Gordon Legge and Laura J. Hird.

Children's fiction

Eleanor Atkinson *Greyfriars Bobby* (Penguin/Buccaneer Books). Part of Edinburgh folklore, this is the tear-jerking true story of a faithful dog who nightly visited his master's grave. Suitable for ten-year-olds and over.

George Mackay Brown *Pictures in the Cave* (UK Canongate). A collection of stories based on folk tales, told by a master poet. Suitable for nine-year-olds and over.

Kathleen Fidler *Desperate Journey* (UK Canongate). Story of a family driven from Scotland in the Sutherland Clearances across the Atlantic to Canada. *The Droving Lad* (UK Canongate) is a thriller about a boy and his first experience of herding cattle from the Highlands to the Lowlands. Suitable for nine-year-olds and over.

★ **Mairi Hedderwick** *Katie Morag and the Two Grandmothers* (Red Fox/Trafalgar Square). One of the many delightful stories of a little girl and the trouble she gets in on the west-coast island of Struay, beautifully illustrated by the author. Suitable for reading to under-fives.

Jackie Kay *The Frog Who Dreamed She Was an Opera Singer* (Bloomsbury). Collection of poems, funny and appealing, for eight-year-olds upward.

Ted Hughes *Nessie the Mannerless Monster* (Faber). A verse story about the famous monster who goes to London to see the queen. Suitable for five- to eight-year-olds.

Mollie Hunter *A Stranger Came Ashore* (HarperCollins). Set in Shetland, this a tragic and gripping historical tale. Suitable for ten-year-olds and over.

Gavin Maxwell *Ring of Bright Water* (UK Longman). Heart-warming true tale of the author's relationship with three otters. Suitable for seven-year-olds upwards.

Aileen Paterson *Maisie Goes to Glasgow* (UK Three Hill Books). There are lots of adventures of this mischievous cat, mostly set in Scotland. Suitable for five- to eight-year-olds.

Stephen Potts *Hunting Gumnor* (UK Mammoth). A haunting story set on a Scottish island, both an adventure and a fantasy, which affirms the values of island life and the creatures that live there. Suitable for ages ten and upwards.

★ **Robert Louis Stevenson** *Kidnapped* (Penguin/Modern Library). A thrilling historical adventure set in eighteenth-century Scotland. Every bit as exciting as the better-known *Treasure Island*.

Poetry

★ **George Mackay Brown** *Selected Poems 1954–1983* (John Murray). Brown's work is as haunting, beautiful and gritty as the Orkney islands which inspire it. The most recent collection is the posthumous *Travellers* (Murray), featuring work either previously unpublished or appearing only in newspapers and periodicals.

Robert Burns *Selected Poems* (Penguin). Scotland's most famous bard. Immensely popular all over the world, his best-known works are his earlier ones, including *Auld Lang Syne* and *My Love Is Like A Red, Red Rose*.

Crawford & Imlah *The New Penguin Book of Scottish Verse* (Penguin). A historical survey of Scottish verse and its many languages, from St Columba to Don Paterson.

Carol Anne Duffy *Selected Poems* (Penguin). Some of her work reflects her early childhood in Glasgow; all of it is personal and packed with striking images.

William Dunbar *The Poems of William Dunbar* (UK Mercat Press). An important literary figure in his time, his poetry reveals the concerns and attitudes to life at the court of James IV.

Douglas Dunn *Selected Poems 1964–83* (Faber). A writer of delicately wrought poetry, ranging from the intensely private to poems involved with Scottish issues. He also edited *The Faber Book of Twentieth-Century Scottish Poetry* (Faber & Faber), featuring all the big names (except for Dunn himself) and some lesser-known works.

Kathleen Jamie *The Queen of Sheba* and *The Donkey's Ears* (Penguin). Although often set in Scotland, her work has a wider significance; its tone is strong, almost angry, and its themes both personal and universal. Her latest volume, *Jizzen* (Picador), is highly acclaimed.

Jackie Kay *The Adoption Papers* and *Other Lovers* (Bloodaxe UK). Her poetry explores being black, Scottish and gay and deals with personal relationships in an accessibly intimate way.

★ **Liz Lochhead** *Bagpipe Muzak* (Penguin); *True Confessions* (Polygon). A strong straightforward style, coupled with shrewd observations, Lochhead speaks with immediacy on personal relationships.

★ **Norman MacCaig** *Selected Poems* (Chatto & Windus). Justly celebrated for its keen observation of the natural world, MacCaig's work remains intellectually challenging without being arid. His poetry, rooted in the Highlands, uses detail to explore a universal landscape. *Norman MacCaig; A Celebration* (Chapman) is an anthology written for his 85th birthday, and includes work by more than ninety writers, including Ted Hughes and Seamus Heaney.

Hugh MacDiarmid *Selected Poems* (Penguin). Immensely influential, not least for his nationalist views and his use of Scots, MacDiarmid's poetry is richly challenging. *A Drunk Man Looks at a Thistle* is acknowledged as a masterpiece of Scottish literature.

Sorley Maclean (Somhairle Macgill-Eain) *From Wood to Ridge: Collected Poems* (UK Birlinn). Written in Gaelic, his poems have been translated into bilingual editions all over the world; they deal with the sorrows of poverty, war and love.

William McGonagall *McGonagall: A Selection* (edited by Colin Walker; UK Birlinn). Verse so bad you have to read it – or perhaps not.

John McQueen and Tom Scott (eds) *The Oxford Book of Scottish Verse* (UK Oxford Paperbacks). Claims to be the most comprehensive anthology of Scottish poetry ever published.

Edwin Morgan *New Selected Poems* (UK Carcanet). A love of words and their sounds is evident in his poems, which are refreshingly varied and often experimental. He comments on the Scottish scene with shrewdness and humour.

Edwin Muir *Collected Poems* (Faber). Muir's childhood on Orkney remained with him as a dream of paradise from which he was banished to Glasgow. His poems are passionately concerned with Scotland.

Don Paterson *God's Gift to Women* and *Nil Nil* (Faber). A writer whose work examines the working class, sex and drink with a wry sense of humour and an exciting, innovative voice.

Iain Crichton Smith *Collected Poems* (Carcanet UK). Born on the Isle of Lewis, Crichton Smith wrote with feeling and sometimes bitterness, in both Gaelic and English, of the life of the rural communities, the iniquities of the Free Church, the need to revive Gaelic culture and the glory of the Scottish landscape.

Folklore and legend

Margaret Bennett *Scottish Customs from the Cradle to the Grave* (Polygon). Fascinating and sympathetic extensive oral history.

Michael Brander *Tales of the Borders* (UK Mainstream). Part social history and part guidebook, a collection of romantic nineteenth-century Border tales retold and put into historical context.

Alan J. Bruford and Donald Archie McDonald (eds) *Scottish Traditional Tales* (Polygon). A huge collection of folk stories from all over Scotland, taken from tape archives.

Neil Philip (ed) *The Penguin Book of Scottish Folk Tales* (UK Penguin). A collection of over a hundred folk tales from all over Scotland.

Nigel Tranter *Tales and Traditions of Scottish Castles* (UK Neil Wilson). The myths and legends of some of Scotland's more famous castles.

History, politics and culture

Historic Scotland (UK Stationery Office). A series of books covering many aspects of Scotland's history and prehistory, including the Picts, Vikings, Romans and Celts. All are colourful, accessible and well presented. Available at many Historic Scotland properties as well as bookshops.

Scotland's Past in Action "Building Railways"; "Feeding Scotland"; "Fishing and Whaling". Some of the titles in an attractive series of small illustrated books, produced by the National Museums of Scotland.

Adamnan (trans. John Marsden) *The Illustrated Life of Columba* (UK Llanerch). The original story of the life of St Columba, annotated and accompanied by beautiful photos of the places associated with him, in particular the Hebridean island of Iona.

Ian Adams and Meredith Somerville *Cargoes of Despair and Hope* (UK John Donald Publishing). Riveting mixture of contemporary documents and letters telling the story of Scottish emigration to North America from 1603 to 1803.

Colin Bell *Collins Scotland's Century – An Autobiography of the Nation* (HarperCollins). Richly illustrated and readable account of the social history of Scotland, based on radio interviews with people from all walks of life.

Bella Bathurst *The Lighthouse Stevensons* (HarperCollins). Fascinating account of the lives and amazing achievements of Robert Louis Stevenson's family, who built many of the island lighthouses round Scotland.

David Daiches (ed) *The New Companion to Scottish Culture* (Polygon/Subterranean). A dense, wide-ranging tome with more than 300 articles on Scottish culture in its widest sense, from eating to marriage customs to the Scottish Enlightenment.

★ **Tom Devine** *The Scottish Nation 1700–2000* (Penguin). Best post-Union history from the last Scottish Parliament to the new one.

G. Donaldson & R.S. Morpeth (ed) *A Dictionary of Scottish History* (UK John Donald). A user-friendly volume listing dates, facts and potted biographies.

Ninian Dunnett *Out on the Edge* (Canongate). A readable series of interviews with Scots, probing the national psyche.

Antonia Fraser *Mary, Queen of Scots* (Orion/Delta). An acclaimed biography of Scotland's most tragic queen, capturing the essence of both the period and the woman.

George MacDonald Fraser *The Steel Bonnets* (HarperCollins). Immensely enjoyable and erudite account of sixteenth-century cattle-rustling, feud, blackmail, murder and mayhem in the border country between England and Scotland.

Michael Lynch *Scotland: A New History* (UK Pimlico). Probably the best available overview of Scottish history, taking the story up to 1992.

James MacKay *William Wallace* (Mainstream). An authoritative biography, and the best of a rash of books capitalizing on the success of the movie *Braveheart* – the book is more of a stickler for historical fact than the film.

Fitzroy Maclean *Bonnie Prince Charlie* (Canongate). Very readable and more or less definitive biography of Scotland's most romanticized historical figure, written by the "real" James Bond.

John McLeod *No Great Mischief If You Fall* (Vintage/Trafalgar). Gloom and doom on the rape of the Highlands; an enraging, bleak but stimulating book debunking some of the myths upheld by the Highland industry.

John Prebble *Glencoe*; *Culloden*; *The Highland Clearances* (all Penguin). Emotive, subjective and accessible accounts of key events in Highland history.

John Purser *Scotland's Music* (Mainstream). Comprehensive overview of traditional and classical music in Scotland; thorough and scholarly but readable.

★ **T.C. Smout** *A History of the Scottish People 1560–1830* and *A Century of the Scottish People 1830–1950* (both Fontana). Widely acclaimed books, brimful of interest for those keen on social history. Smout combines enormous learning with a clear and entertaining style.

Martin Wallace *A Little Book of Celtic Saints* (UK Appletree Press). A small but informative volume.

Andy Wightman *Who Owns Scotland* (Canongate). A detailed and revealing breakdown of the patterns of land ownership and use in Scotland, but rather dry for general reading. *Scotland: Land and Power* (Luath) confronts the current land reform problems and suggests possible solutions.

Art, architecture and historic sites

Churches to Visit in Scotland (UK St Andres Press). Useful descriptions of location, significant features and accessibility without regard to architectural merit.

Exploring Scotland's Heritage (UK The Stationery Office). Detailed, beautifully illustrated series with the emphasis on historic buildings and archeological sites. Recently updated titles cover Orkney, Shetland, the Highlands, Aberdeen and Northeast Scotland, Fife, Perthshire and Angus, and Argyll and the Western Isles.

Lesley Astaire, Roddy Martine and Fritz von Schulenburg *Living in Scotland* (Thames & Hudson). A fascinating, if rather intense, photographic tour of the interiors of the main country homes, inhabited castles and grand town houses of Scotland.

Roger Billcliffe *The Scottish Colourists* (UK John Murray). An impressive, perhaps definitive, study of a group of artists reckoned by many to be Scotland's finest.

Jude Burkhauser *Glasgow Girls: Women in Art and Design 1880–1920* (Canongate). The lively contribution of women to the development of the Glaswegian Art Nouveau movement is recognized in this authoritative account.

Alan Crawford *Charles Rennie Mackintosh* (Thames & Hudson). Part of the World of Art series, describing the major contribution of Scotland's premier architect.

Kitty Cruft and Andrew Fraser (eds) *James Craig 1744–95* (UK EUP). Distinguished authors offer reassessments of Craig's achievement in designing Edinburgh's New Town.

Miles Glendinning (ed) *A History of Scottish Architecture from the Renaissance to the Present Day* (UK EUP). The most comprehensive work on the history of Scottish architecture.

Bill Hare *Contemporary Painting in Scotland* (UK Craftsman House). Features the work of 48 contemporary artists including John Bellany, Bruce McLean and Elizabeth Blackadder, and gives special attention to the "New Painting" that emerged in the 1980s and developed into a distinctive Scottish style. Expensive and serious.

Charles McKean, David Walker and Frank Walker *Central Glasgow* (UK Rutland Press). An architectural romp through the city centre and West End, with plenty of photographs and informed comment; part of the Rutland Press series of illustrated guides to Scottish architecture. Whilst authoritative, they are not at all stuffy and are conveniently pocket-sized. In addition, the Press has produced studies of such notable figures as James Miller, Basil Spence and Peter Womersley.

★ **Duncan MacMillan** *Scottish Art 1460–1990* (Mainstream/Trafalgar)). Lavish overview of Scottish painting with good sections on landscape, portraiture and the Glasgow Boys.

Colin McWilliam (ed) *The Buildings of Scotland* (UK Penguin). There are volumes on various regions of Scotland, including Fife, Edinburgh and Lothian, and Argyll and Bute, all of which provide comprehensive and scholarly coverage of every building of importance. Though easy to follow, they would best suit visitors intending to spend more than a couple of weeks in Scotland.

Steven Parissien *Adam Style* (Phaidon). A well-illustrated account of the birth of the Neoclassical style named for the two Scottish Adam brothers, Robert and James.

Guides and picture books

Scottish Wild Flowers; *Scottish Birds* (UK HarperCollins). Well-illustrated and informative small guides. Also in the guide series are *Clans and Tartans* and *Scottish Surnames* which are a first step on the road to genealogy.

Colin Baxter *Scotland from the Air* (UK Lomond); *Portrait of Scotland* (UK Voyageur); with Jim Crumley: *Portrait of Edinburgh* (UK Colin Baxter Photography); with Jack McLean: *The City of Glasgow* (UK Colin Baxter Photography). Best known for his ubiquitous postcards, Baxter's photographs succeed in capturing the grandeur of Scotland's moody landscapes and characterful cityscapes in many lavishly illustrated books.

Laurie Campbell & Roy Dennis *Golden Eagles* (UK Colin Baxter). Second only to the stag as a symbol of Scotland, the eagle is captured in this book in magnificent photographs.

Derek Cooper *Skye* (UK Birlinn). A gazetteer and guide and an indispensable mine of information; although written in 1970, it has been updated and revised.

★ **Hamish Haswell-Smith** *The Scottish Islands* (UK Canongate). An exhaustive and impressive gazetteer with maps and absorbing information on all the Scottish islands. Filled with attractive sketches and paintings, the book is breathtaking in its thoroughness and lovingly gathered detail.

Ranald Macinnes *The Aberdeen Guide* (UK Birlinn). Series of city walks with detailed architectural and historical background.

Magnus Magnusson and Graham White (eds) *The Nature of Scotland – Landscape, Wildlife and People* (Canongate). Glossy picture-based book on Scotland's natural heritage, from geology to farming and conservation. Good section on crofting.

Andrew Murray Scott *Discovering Dundee: The Story of a City* (UK Mercat Press). A good popular history of the city and some of its famous citizens.

N.S. Newton *Inverness* (UK John Donald). Inverness has a long history on account of its crucial position at the head of the Great Glen.

Donald Omand *The Borders Book* (UK Birlinn). An entertaining history of the much disputed land between England and Scotland, from prehistory to its present passion for rugby.

Paul Ramsay *Lochs & Glens of Scotland* (UK Collins & Brown). Informative text and stunning photographs of the Highlands that make you want to book a holiday immediately.

Cecil Sinclair *Tracing your Scottish Ancestors* (UK Mercat Press). Probably the best guide to ancestry research in the Scottish Record Office – definitely worth reading before visiting General Register House.

David Williams *The Glasgow Guide* (UK Canongate). Thirteen walks round Glasgow, with the emphasis on historical points of interest: buildings, graveyards, museums and architecture.

Michael and Elspeth Wills *Walks in Edinburgh's Old Town* (UK Mercat Press). A small guide which takes you into the nooks and crannies of Scotland's most historically intense city centre. Also *Walks in Edinburgh's New Town* (UK Mercat Press) to get you up to date.

Memoirs and travelogues

David Craig *On the Crofter's Trail* (UK Pimlico). Using anecdotes and interviews with descendants, Craig conveys the hardship and tragedy of the Highland Clearances without being mawkish.

Jim Crumley *Gulfs of Blue Air – A Highland Journey* (Mainstream). Recent travelogue mixed with nature notes and references to Scottish poets such as MacCaig and Mackay Brown.

★ **Elizabeth Grant of Rothiemurchus** *Memoirs of a Highland Lady* (Canongate). Hugely readable recollections written with wit and perception at the turn of the eighteenth century, charting social changes in Edinburgh, London and particularly Speyside.

James Hunter *Scottish Highlanders* (Mainstream). Attempts to explain the strong sense of blood ties held by people of Scottish descent all over the world; lots of history and good photographs.

★ **Samuel Johnson and James Boswell** *A Journey to the Western Isles of Scotland* and *The Journal of a Tour to the Hebrides* (Penguin/Canongate). Lively accounts of a famous journey around the islands taken by the famous lexicographer, Dr Samuel Johnson, and his biographer and friend.

Tom Morton *Spirit of Adventure: A Journey Beyond the Whisky Trails*

(Mainstream). Offbeat and funny view of Scotland's whisky industry as seen from the back of a motorcycle in appalling weather. Also *Hell's Golfer* (Mainstream), a search for the least snobbish golf courses in Scotland.

Edwin Muir *Scottish Journey* (Mainstream). A classic travelogue written in 1935 with sympathetic insight by the Orcadian writer on his return to Scotland from London.

June Skinner Sawyers *The Road North* (UK In Pinn). An interesting collection of 300 years of Scottish travel writing, divided into regions.

★ **Robert Louis Stevenson** *Edinburgh: Picturesque Notes* (Harvill Press). Charming evocation of Stevenson's birthplace – its moods, curiosities and influences on his work.

Betsy Whyte *The Yellow on the Broom* (UK Birlinn). A fascinating glimpse of childhood in a traveller family, both on the road and in council housing for part of the year to comply with school attendance.

Wildlife and outdoor pursuits

Bartholomew Walks Series (UK Bartholomew). The series covers individual areas of Scotland, including Perthshire, Loch Lomond and the Trossachs, Oban, Mull and Lochaber, and Skye and Wester Ross. Each booklet has a range of walks of varying lengths with clear maps and descriptions.

Ordnance Survey Pathfinder Series (Jarrold Publishing/Seven Hills Book Distribution). Top-quality maps, colour pictures and clear text. Titles include "Loch Lomond and the Trossachs", "Fort William and Glen Coe" and "Perthshire".

Scotland for Game, Sea and Coarse Fishing (UK Pastime Publications). General guide on what to fish, where and for how much, along with notes on records, regulations and convenient accommodation. Published in association with the Scottish Tourist Board.

Donald Bennet *The Munros* (UK Scottish Mountaineering Trust). Authoritative and attractively illustrated hillwalkers' guides to the Scottish peaks. SMT also publishes guides to districts and specific climbs, as well as *The Corbetts* by Scott Johnstone *et al.*

★ **Hamish Brown** *Hamish's Mountain Walk/Climbing the Corbetts* (Baton Wicks). The best of the travel narratives about walking in the Scottish Highlands.

Anthony Burton *The Caledonian Canal* (UK Aurum Press). A book for walkers, cyclists and boaters with maps and details of boat rental, accommodation, and the like.

Andrew Dempster *Classic Mountain Scrambles in Scotland* (UK Mainstream). Guide to hill walks in Scotland that combine straightforward walking with some rock-climbing.

Derek Douglas *The Thistle: A Chronicle of Scottish Rugby* (Mainstream). History of the game for enthusiasts, from Victorian times to the present day, with some good photos.

Richard Fitter, Alastair Fitter and Marhorie Blanney *Collins Pocket Guide to the Wild Flowers of Britain and Northern Europe* (UK HarperCollins). An excellent, easy-to-use field guide.

David Hamilton *The Scottish Golf Guide* (Canongate). An inexpensive paperback with descriptions of and useful information about 84 of Scotland's best courses from the remote to the Open Championship.

John Hancox *Collins Pocket Reference – Cycling in Scotland* (UK HarperCollins). Spiral-bound edition with over fifty road routes of all grades up and down the country, each with a useful route map. For more off-road mountain bike routes, try *Scotland: The Central Valley* by Derek Purdy (UK Haynes Publishers) in the *Ride Your Bike* series, or *101 Bike Routes in Scotland* by Harry Henniker (UK Mainstream).

Philip Lusby & Jenny Wright *Scottish Wild Plants* (UK The Stationery Office). Beautifully produced book about the rarer plants of Scotland, their discovery and conservation, produced in conjunction with the Royal Botanic Gardens of Edinburgh.

Kenny MacDonald (ed) *Scottish Football Quotations* (UK Mainstream). Shows you the humour that prevents Scottish football fans from losing heart.

Michael Madders and Julia Welstead *Where to Watch Birds in Scotland* (UK A&C Black). Region-by-region guide with maps, details on access and habitat, and notes on what to see when.

Jenny Parke *Ski & Snowboard: Scotland* (UK Luath Press). Informative book about where to find the best slopes, with loads of useful advice.

Roger Smith *The West Highland Way* (Mercat Press); *The Southern Upland Way* (UK The Stationery Office o/p). Comprehensive guides to long-distance paths, containing information on sights, history, nature and help on planning your trek, as well as specially oriented maps.

Ralph Storer *100 Best Routes on Scottish Mountains* (UK Little, Brown). A compilation of the best day-walks in Scotland, including some of the classics overlooked by the Munroing guides.

Food and drink

Annette Hope *A Caledonian Feast* (UK Mainstream). Authoritative and entertaining history of Scottish food and social life from the ninth to the twentieth centuries. Lots of recipes.

Michael Jackson *Malt Whisky Companion* (UK Dorling Kindersley). An attractively put together tome, considered by many to be the "bible" on malt whisky tasting.

Ralph Kenna *The Glasgow Pub Companion* (UK Neil Wilson). Covers about 200 pubs, both traditional and trendy.

G.W. Lockhart *The Scots and Their Fish* (UK Birlinn). Tells the history of fish and fishing in Scotland, and ends with a selection of traditional recipes.

Sue Lawrence *Scots Cooking* (Headline). This award-winning book offers traditional recipes from all over Scotland.

Claire Macdonald *The Claire Macdonald Cookbook* (UK Bantam); Seasonal Cooking (Corgi). Lady Claire Macdonald of Macdonald has become widely known in Scottish cookery circles. She promotes the use of native food and runs a successful hotel on Skye.

Charles McLean *Scotch Whisky* (Pitkin Guides). A small, thorough, fact-filled book covering malt, grain and blended whiskies, plus whisky-based liqueurs.

★ **Nick Nairn** *Wild Harvest; Wild Harvest 2; Island Harvest* (all UK BBC Books). Glossy TV tie-ins by an engaging young and talented Scottish chef, who takes up the challenge of gathering and eating from the wild. Both books feature fascinating, if difficult to re-create, recipes.

Rosemary Schrager *Rosemary, Castle Cook* (UK Everyman Chess). Famous from the TV series, the cook at posh Amhuinnsuidhe Castle on Harris yields up some of the secrets of her kitchen.

language

language

Language

Language is a thorny, complex and often highly political issue in Scotland. If you're not from Scotland yourself, you're most likely to be addressed in a variety of English, spoken in a Scottish accent. Even then, you're likely to hear phrases and words that are part of what is known as Lowland Scottish or Scots, which is now officially recognized as a distinct language in its own right. To a lesser extent, Gaelic, too, remains a living language, particularly in the *Gàidhealtachd* or Gaelic-speaking areas of the Western Isles, parts of Skye and a few scattered Hebridean islands. In Orkney and Shetland, the local dialect of Scots contains many words carried over from Norn, the Norse language spoken in the Northern Isles from the time of the Vikings until the eighteenth century (for more on this, see box on p.679).

Scots

Lowland Scottish or **Scots** is spoken by thirty percent of the Scottish population, according to the latest survey. It began life as a northern branch of Anglo-Saxon, and emerged as a distinct language in the Middle Ages. From the 1370s until the Union in 1707, it was the country's main literary and documentary language. Since the eighteenth century, however, it has been systematically repressed in preference to English.

Robbie Burns is the most obvious literary exponent of the Scots language, but there was a revival in the last century led by poets such as Hugh MacDiarmid. (For examples of the works of both writers, see "Books".) Only very recently has Scots enjoyed something of a renaissance, getting itself on the Scottish school curriculum in 1996, and achieving official recognition as a distinct language in 1998. Despite these enormous political achievements, many people (rightly or wrongly) still regard Scots as a dialect of English.

HarperCollins in the UK publishes a handy, pocket-sized Scots dictionary as a guide to the mysteries of Scottish vocabulary and idiom.

Gaelic

Scottish **Gaelic** (*Gàidhlig*, pronounced "gallic") is one of only four Celtic languages to survive into the modern age (Welsh, Breton and Irish Gaelic are the other three). Manx, the old language of the Isle of Man, died out early last century, while Cornish was finished as a community language way back in the eighteenth century. Scottish Gaelic is most closely related to Irish Gaelic and Manx – hardly surprising since Gaelic was introduced to Scotland from Ireland around the third century BC. Some folk still argue that Scottish Gaelic is merely a dialect of its parent language, Irish Gaelic, and indeed the two languages remain more or less mutually intelligible. From the fifth to the twelfth centuries, Gaelic enjoyed an expansionist phase, gradually becoming the national language, thanks partly to the backing of the Celtic church in Iona. At the end of this period, Gaelic was spoken throughout virtually all of what is now Scotland, the main exceptions being Orkney and Shetland.

From that high point onwards Gaelic began a steady decline. Even before Union with England, power, religious ideology and wealth gradually passed into non-Gaelic hands. The royal court was transferred to Edinburgh and an

Anglo-Norman legal system was put in place. The Celtic church was Romanized by the introduction of foreign clergy, and, most importantly of all, English and Flemish merchants colonized the new trading towns of the east coast. In addition, the pro-English attitudes held by the Covenanters led to strong anti-Gaelic feeling within the Church of Scotland from its inception.

The two abortive Jacobite rebellions of 1715 and 1745 furthered the language's decline, as did the Clearances that took place in the Gaelic-speaking Highlands from the 1770s to the 1820s, which forced thousands to migrate to central Scotland's new industrial belt or emigrate to North America. Although efforts were made to halt the decline in the first half of the nineteenth century, the 1872 Education Act gave no official recognition to Gaelic, and children were severely punished if they were caught speaking the language in school.

Current estimates put the number of Gaelic speakers at 86,000 (about two percent of the population), the majority of whom live in the *Gàidhealtachd*, with an extended Gaelic community of perhaps 250,000 who have some understanding of the language. Since the 1980s, the language has stabilized and even recovered, thanks to the introduction of bilingual primary and nursery schools, and a huge increase in the amount of broadcasting time given to Gaelic-language programmes. The success of rock bands such as Runrig has shown that it is possible to combine traditional Gaelic culture with popular entertainment and reach a mass audience.

Gaelic grammar and pronunciation

Gaelic is a highly complex tongue, with a fiendish, antiquated **grammar** and, with only eighteen letters, an intimidating system of spelling. **Pronunciation** is easier than it appears at first glance – one general rule to remember is that the **stress** always falls on the first syllable of a word. The general rule of syntax is that the verb starts the sentence whether it's a question or not, followed by the subject and then the object; adjectives generally follow the word they are describing.

Short and long vowels

Gaelic has both short and long vowels, the latter being denoted by an acute or grave accent.

a as in cat; before nn and ll, as in cow
à as in bar
e as in pet
é like rain
i as in sight
í like free
o as in pot
ò like enthral
ó like cow
u like scoot
ù like loo

Vowel combinations

Gaelic is littered with diphthongs, which, rather like in English, can be pronounced in several different ways depending on the individual word.

ai like cat, or pet; before dh or gh, like street
ao like the sound in the middle of colonel
ei like mate
ea like pet, or cat, and sometimes like mate; before ll or nn like cow
èa as in hear
eu like train, or fear
ia like fear
io like fear, or shorter than street
ua like wooer

Consonants

The consonants listed below are those that differ substantially from the English.

b at the beginning of a word as in big; in the middle or at the end of a word like the p in pair

bh at the beginning of a word like the v in van; elsewhere it is silent

c as in cat; after a vowel it has aspiration before it

ch always as in loch, never as in church

cn like the cr in crowd

d like the d in dog, but with the tongue pressed against the back of the upper teeth; at the beginning of a word or before e or i, like the j in jam; in the middle or at the end of a word like the t in cat; after i like the ch in church

dh before and after a, o or u is an aspirated g, rather like a gargle; before e or i like the y in yes; elsewhere silent

fh usually silent; sometimes like the h in house

g at the beginning of a word as in get; before e like the y in yes; in the middle or end of a word like the ck in sock; after i like the ch in loch

gh at the beginning of a word as in get; before or after a, o or u rather like a gargle; after i sometimes like the y in gay, but often silent

l after i and sometimes before e like the l in lot; elsewhere a peculiarly Gaelic sound produced by flattening the front of the tongue against the palate

mh like the v in van

p at the beginning of a word as in pet; elsewhere it has aspiration before it

rt pronounced as sht

s before e or i like the sh in ship; otherwise as in English

sh before a, o or u like the h in house; before e like the ch in loch

t before e or i like the ch in church; in the middle or at the end of a word it has aspiration before it; otherwise as in English

th at the beginning of a word, like the h in house; elsewhere, and in the word thu, silent

Gaelic phrases and vocabulary

The choice is limited when it comes to **teach-yourself Gaelic** courses, but the BBC *Can Seo* cassette and book is perfect for starting you off. Drier and more academic is *Teach Yourself Gaelic* (Hodder & Stoughton), which is aimed at bringing beginners to working competence. *Everyday Gaelic* by Morag MacNeill (Gairm) is the best phrasebook around.

Basic words and greetings

English - **Gaelic**
yes - **tha**
no - **chan eil**
hello - **hallo**
how are you? - **ciamar a tha thu?**
OK - **tha gu math**
thank you - **tapadh leat**
welcome - **fàilte**
come in - **thig a-staigh**
goodbye - **mar sin leat**
goodnight - **oidhche mhath**
who? - **cò?**
where is...? - **càit a bheil...?**
when? - **cuine?**
what is it? - **dé tha ann?**
morning - **madainn**
evening - **feasgar**
day - **là**
night - **oidhche**
here - **an seo**
there - **an sin**
this way - **mar seo**
that way - **mar sin**
pound/s - **not/aichean**
tomorrow - **a-màireach**
tonight - **a-nochd**
cheers - **slàinte**
yesterday - **an-dé**

today - **an-diugh**
tomorrow - **maireach**
now - **a-nise**
hotel - **taigh-òsda**
house - **taigh**
story - **sgeul**
song - **òran**
music - **ceòl**
book - **leabhar**
tired - **sgìth**
food - **lòn**
bread - **aran**
water - **uisge**
milk - **bainne**
beer - **leann**
wine - **fion**
whisky - **uisge beatha**
post office - **post oifis**
Edinburgh - **Dun Eideann**
Glasgow - **Glaschu**
America - **Ameireaga**
Ireland - **Eire**
England - **Sasainn**
London - **Lunnain**

Some useful phrases

English - **Gaelic**
It's a nice day - **Tha latha math ann**
How much is that? - **Dè tha e 'cosg?**
What's your name? - **Dè 'n t-ainm a th'ort?**
Excuse me - **Gabh mo leisgeul**
What time is it? - **Dé am uair a tha e?**
I'm thirsty - **Tha am pathadh orm**
I'd like a double room - **'Se rùm dùbailte tha mi'giarraigh**
Do you speak Gaelic? - **A bheil Gàidhlig agad?**
What is the Gaelic for ...? - **Dé a' Ghàidhlig a tha ... air?**
I don't understand - **Chan eil mi 'tuigsinn**
I don't know - **Chan eil fhios agam**
That's good - **'S math sin**
It doesn't matter - **'S coma**
I'm sorry - **Tha mi duilich**

Numbers and days

English - **Gaelic**
1 - **aon**
2 - **dà/dhà**
3 - **trì**
4 - **ceithir**
5 - **còig**
6 - **sia**
7 - **seachd**
8 - **ochd**
9 - **naoi**
10 - **deich**
11 - **aon deug**
20 - **fichead**
21 - **aon ar fhichead**
30 - **deug ar fhichead**
40 - **dà fhichead**
50 - **lethcheud**
60 - **trì fichead**
100 - **ceud**
1000 - **mìle**
Monday - **Diluain**
Tuesday - **Dimàirt**
Wednesday - **Diciadain**
Thursday - **Diardaoin**
Friday - **Dihaoine**
Saturday - **Disathurna**
Sunday - **Didòmhnaich/La na Sàbaid**

Gaelic geographical and place-name terms

The purpose of the list below is to help with place-name derivations from Gaelic and with more detailed map reading. For a list of place names derived from Norse, see box on p.679.

Gaelic - English

abhainn - river

ach or auch, from achadh - field

ail, aileach - rock

Alba - Scotland

ardan or arden, from àird - a point of land or height

aros - dwelling

ault, from allt - stream

bad - brake or clump of trees

bagh - bay

bal or bally, from baile - town, village

balloch, from bealach - mountain pass

ban - white, fair

bàrr - summit

beg, from beag - small

ben, from beinn - mountain

blair, from blàr - field or battlefield

cairn, from càrn - pile of stones

camas - bay, harbour

craig, from creag - rock

cnoc - hill

coll or colly, from coille- wood or forest

corran - a spit or point jutting into the sea

corrie, from coire - round hollow in mountainside, whirlpool

craig, from creag - rock, crag

cruach - bold hill

drum, from druim - ridge

dubh - black

dun or dum, from dùn - fort

eilean - island

ess, from eas - waterfall

fin, from fionn - white

gair or gare, from geàrr - short

garv, from garbh - rough

geodha - cove

glen, from gleann - valley

gower or gour, from gabhar - goat

inch, from innis - meadow or island

inver, from inbhir - river mouth

ken or kin, from ceann - head

knock, from cnoc - hill

kyle, from caolas - narrow strait

lag - hollow

larach - site of an old ruin

liath - grey

loch - lake

meall - round hill

mon, from monadh - hill

more, from mór - large, great

rannoch, from raineach - bracken

ross, from ros - promontory

rubha - promontory

sgeir - sea rock

sgurr - sharp point

sron - nose, prow or promontory

strath, from srath - broad valley

tarbet, from tairbeart - isthmus

tigh - house

tir or tyre, from tìr - land

torr - hill, castle

tràigh - shore

uig - shelter

uisge - water

Glossary

Auld Old.
Aye Yes.
Bairn Baby.
Baronial *see "Scottish Baronial" below*
Ben Hill or mountain.
Blackhouse Thick-walled traditional dwelling.
Bonnie Pretty.
Bothy Primitive cottage or hut; farmworker's or shepherd's mountain shelter.
Brae Slope or hill.
Brig Bridge.
Broch Circular prehistoric stone fort.
Burn Small stream or brook.
Byre Shelter for cattle; cottage.
Cairn Mound of stones.
Carse Riverside area of flat alluvium.
Ceilidh (pronounced "kay-lee") Social gathering involving dancing, drinking, singing and storytelling.
Central Belt The densely populated strip of central Scotland between the Forth and Clyde estuaries, incorporating the conurbations of Edinburgh, Glasgow and Stirling.
Clan Extended family.
Clearances Policy adopted by late eighteenth- and early nineteenth-century landowners to evict tenant crofters in order to create space for more profitable sheep-grazing. Families cleared from the Highlands were often put on emigrant ships to North America or the colonies.
Corbett A mountain between 2500ft and 3000ft high.
Corbie-stepped Architectural term; any set of steps on a gable.
Covenanters Supporter of the Presbyterian Church in the seventeenth century.
Crannog Celtic lake or bog dwelling.
Croft Small plot of farmland with house, common in the Highlands.
Crow-stepped Same as corbie-stepped.
Dolmen Grave chamber.
Dram Literally, one-sixteenth of a fluid ounce. Usually refers to any small measure of whisky.
Dun Fortified mound.
First-foot The first person to enter a household after midnight on *Hogmanay* (see below).
Firth A wide sea inlet or estuary.
Gillie Personal guide used on hunting or fishing trips.
Glen Deep, narrow mountain valley.
Harling Limestone and gravel mix used to cover buildings.
Hogmanay New Year's Eve.
Howe Valley.
Howff Meeting place; pub.
HS Historic Scotland, a government-funded heritage organization.
Ken Knowledge; understanding.
Kilt Knee-length tartan skirt worn by Highland men.
Kirk Church.
Laird Landowner; aristocrat.
Law Rounded hill.
Links Grassy coastal land; coastal golf course.
Loch Lake.
Lochan Little loch.
Mac/Mc These prefixes in Scottish surnames derive from the Gaelic, meaning "son of". In Scots "Mac" is used for both sexes. In Gaelic "Nic" is used for women: *Donnchadh Mac Aodh* is Duncan MacKay, *Iseabail Nic Aodh* is Isabel MacKay.
Machair Sandy, grassy, lime-rich coastal land, generally used for grazing.
Manse Official home of a Presbyterian minister.
Munro A mountain over 3000ft high.
Munro-bagging The sport of trying to climb as many Munros as possible.
NTS The National Trust for Scotland, a heritage organization.
Peel Fortified tower, built to withstand Border raids.
Pend Archway or vaulted passage.
Presbyterian The form of church government used in the official (Protestant) Church of

Scotland, established by John Knox during the Reformation.

Sassenach Literally "Saxon"; used by Highlanders to refer to lowlanders, though commonly used to describe the English.

Scottish Baronial Style of architecture favoured by the Scottish land-owning class featuring crow-stepped gables and round turrets.

Shinty Stick and ball game played in the Highlands, with similarities to hockey.

Smiddy Smithy.

SNH Scottish Natural Heritage, a government-funded conservation body.

SNP Scottish National Party.

Sporran Leather purse worn in front of, or at the side of, a kilt.

Tartan Check-patterned woollen cloth, particular patterns being associated with particular clans.

Thane A landowner of high rank; the chief of a clan.

Trews Tartan trousers.

Wee Small.

Wynd Narrow lane.

Yett Gate or door.

index

and small print

Index

Map entries are in **colour**

B

C

D

INDEX

E

F

G

INDEX

K

L

INDEX

M

INDEX

N

O

S

INDEX

T

INDEX

U

V

W

Y

Z

Twenty Years of Rough Guides

In the summer of 1981, Mark Ellingham, Rough Guides' founder, knocked out the first guide on a typewriter, with a group of friends. Mark had been travelling in Greece after university, and couldn't find a guidebook that really answered his needs.There were heavyweight cultural guides on the one hand – good on museums and classical sites but not on beaches and tavernas – and on the other hand student manuals that were so caught up with how to save money that they lost sight of the country's significance beyond its role as a place for a cool vacation. None of the guides began to address Greece as a country, with its natural and human environment, its politics and its contemporary life.

Having no urgent reason to return home, Mark decided to write his own guide. It was a guide to Greece that tried to combine some erudition and insight with a thoroughly practical approach to travellers' needs. Scrupulously researched listings of places to stay, eat and drink were matched by careful attention to detail on everything from Homer to Greek music, from classical sites to national parks and from nude beaches to monasteries. Back in London, Mark and his friends got their Rough Guide accepted by a farsighted commissioning editor at the publisher Routledge and it came out in 1982.

The Rough Guide to Greece was a student scheme that became a publishing phenomenon. The immediate success of the book – shortlisted for the Thomas Cook award – spawned a series that rapidly covered dozens of countries. The Rough Guides found a ready market among backpackers and budget travellers, but soon acquired a much broader readership that included older and less impecunious visitors. Readers relished the guides' wit and inquisitiveness as much as the enthusiastic, critical approach that acknowledges everyone wants value for money – but not at any price.

Rough Guides soon began supplementing the "rougher" information – the hostel and low-budget listings – with the kind of detail that independent-minded travellers on any budget might expect. These days, the guides – distributed worldwide by the Penguin group – include recommendations spanning the range from shoestring to luxury, and cover more than 200 destinations around the globe. Our growing team of authors, many of whom come to Rough Guides initially as outstandingly good letter-writers telling us about their travels, are spread all over the world, particularly in Europe, the USA and Australia. As well as the travel guides, Rough Guides publishes a series of dictionary phrasebooks covering two dozen major languages, an acclaimed series of music guides running the gamut from Classical to World Music, a series of music CDs in association with World Music Network, and a range of reference books on topics as diverse as the Internet, Pregnancy and Unexplained Phenomena. Visit **www.roughguides.com** to see what's cooking.

Rough Guide credits

Text editor: Matthew Teller
Series editor: Mark Ellingham
Editorial: Martin Dunford, Jonathan Buckley, Jo Mead, Kate Berens, Ann-Marie Shaw, Helena Smith, Judith Bamber, Orla Duane, Olivia Eccleshall, Ruth Blackmore, Geoff Howard, Claire Saunders, Gavin Thomas, Alexander Mark Rogers, Polly Thomas, Joe Staines, Richard Lim, Duncan Clark, Peter Buckley, Lucy Ratcliffe, Clifton Wilkinson, Alison Murchie, Andrew Dickson (UK); Andrew Rosenberg, Stephen Timblin, Yuki Takagaki, Richard Koss, Hunter Slaton (US)
Production: Susanne Hillen, Andy Hilliard, Link Hall, Helen Prior, Julia Bovis, Michelle Draycott, Katie Pringle, Mike Hancock, Zoë Nobes, Rachel Holmes, Andy Turner
Cartography: Melissa Baker, Maxine Repath, Ed Wright, Katie Lloyd-Jones
Picture research: Louise Boulton, Sharon Martins, Mark Thomas
Online: Kelly Cross, Anja Mutic-Blessing, Jennifer Gold, Audra Epstein, Suzanne Welles, Cree Lawson (US)
Finance: John Fisher, Gary Singh, Edward Downey, Mark Hall, Tim Bill
Marketing & Publicity: Richard Trillo, Niki Smith, David Wearn, Chloë Roberts, Demelza Dallow, Claire Southern (UK); Simon Carloss, David Wechsler, Kathleen Rushforth (US)
Administration: Tania Hummel, Julie Sanderson

Publishing information

This fifth edition published March 2002 by
Rough Guides Ltd
62–70 Shorts Gardens, London WC2H 9AH.
Penguin Putnam, Inc. 375 Hudson Street, NY 10014, USA.
Distributed by the Penguin Group
Penguin Books Ltd,
80 Strand, London WC2R ORL
Penguin Putnam, Inc.
375 Hudson Street, NY 10014, USA
Penguin Books Australia Ltd,
487 Maroondah Highway, PO Box 257, Ringwood, Victoria 3134, Australia
Penguin Books Canada Ltd,
10 Alcorn Avenue, Toronto, Ontario, Canada M4V 1E4
Penguin Books (NZ) Ltd,
182–190 Wairau Road, Auckland 10, New Zealand
Typeset in Bembo and Helvetica to an original design by Henry Iles.

Printed in Italy by LegoPrint S.p.A

888pp includes index
A catalogue record for this book is available from the British Library
ISBN 1-85828-873-8

Help us update

We've gone to a lot of effort to ensure that the fifth edition of **The Rough Guide to Scotland** is accurate and up-to-date. However, things change – places get "discovered", opening hours are notoriously fickle, restaurants and rooms raise prices or lower standards. If you feel we've got it wrong or left something out, we'd like to know, and if you can remember the address, the price, the time, the phone number, so much the better.

We'll credit all contributions, and send a copy of the next edition (or any other Rough Guide if you prefer) for the best letters. Everyone who writes to us and isn't already a subscriber will receive a copy of our full-colour twice-yearly newsletter. Please mark letters: "**Rough Guide Scotland Update**" and send to: Rough Guides, 62–70 Shorts Gardens, London WC2H 9AH, or Rough Guides, 4th Floor, 345 Hudson St, New York, NY 10014. Or send an email to: **mail@roughguides.co.uk** or **mail@roughguides.com**

Acknowledgements

The authors would like to thank the National Trust for Scotland and Historic Scotland; Caledonian MacBrayne, P&O Scottish Ferries and Orkney Ferries for help in getting round the islands; Pete Heywood, Colin Irwin and Geoff Howard for the Music piece in Contexts; Matthew Teller for his enthusiasm, his skill, his praise, his criticism and his modesty; Lucy Ratcliffe; Helena Smith; Rachel Holmes and James Morris for typesetting; Sam Kirby and Maxine Repath for cartography; Mark Thomas for photo research; and Susannah Wight for proofreading.

Rob Humphreys would also like to thank: Alasdair Enticknap for more notes on the west coast; Dick and Sue Courchée for more B&B tips; Sara & Adrian for sussing out the Small Isles; Val & Gordon for researching Skye and Outer Hebrides and for enduring the foot-and-mouth madness in Mull; Gordon (again) for border skirmishing; Val (again) for Orkney & Shetland assistance and for sorting the biblio; and Kate, Stan & Josh for coming out to Islay, Orkney & Shetland.

Donald Reid would also like to thank all those who have been generous with beds, meals, ideas, advice and good leads along the way; various tourist offices, in particular those at HOST; Andy Symington for boldly setting off to the far north and producing some redoubtable work; Barry Shelby for the Glasgow listings and loyal support; Ellie Buchanan for her contribution to the Festival material; and especially Mo for sailing the ship around with me.

Readers' letters

Many thanks to all those readers who took the time to write or email with comments, suggestions and helpful advice: Chloe Anderton-Brown, William Preston Fitzhugh, A. & J. Hewitt, Sebastian Rinken, Graeme Alexander, John Rower, Jess Day, Eric J. Sandeen, Steve Cam, T.E. Klimczyk, R.A.D. Norris, Mary Victoria, Andy Winter, Olvia Maehler, Susan Jeacle, P.L. Goldsmith, Katherine Glawe, R. Lancaster, Kelly Cross, Alex Ross, Catherine E. Herriott, Paddy & Toni Cafferky, Norman W. Leslie, R.A. Hempstock, Angus Gordon, Mrs J.M. Foggitt, Pat Corbridge, K.M. Sutherland, Karin MacKinnon, Ben Dipper, Jenny Kohn, Rick Kitson, Sandra Robertson, Philip Hatfield, Rich Rowe, John Deas, Dave Fell & Richard Garvie, John Walton, JPM, Brian Harvey & Viviane van den Boogaard, Donna Ritenour, David & Gwen Bevington, Dr A. Young, Sherry Sparrow, Robert Flemington, James S. McCormick, David Watkins & Emma Dijkstra, Mr J. Shaw, Isabel Raes, Joeri & Christophe, Barbara Phipps, Marie Bridge, Michael Patison, Stephanie Turcotte, Alan Turnball, Ann P. Howard, Geoff Muggeridge, Jodie Ivers, Nick Jones, Anna Rawlinson, Robert L. Holmes, Clare E. Livingstone, Ros Westcott, Ken Sinnock, Jenny & Ron Farmer, Steve Cann, Peter Goldsmith, Sheila Didcock, Mr A.J. Barclay, Michael Marten, Beatriz Campos, Martin Bodman, Jane Cox, Nigel Renouf and anyone else who we've inadvertently missed out.

Photo credits

Cover

Front cover (small image, top) Puffin © Mark Hannaford/Ffotograff
Front cover (small image, lower) SECC ("The Armadillo"), Glasgow © Jerry Dennis
Back cover (top) Loch Leven © Robert Harding
Back cover (lower) Rannoch Moor, Black Rock Cottage © Joe Cornish

Introduction

Loch Lomond © Donald Reid
Glen Coe, St John's church © David Crossland/Travel Ink
Otter © L. Cambell/Scotland in Focus
SECC ("The Armadillo"), Glasgow © Edmund Nägele
On the Cuillin ridge © Donald Reid
Gannets © C.K. Robeson/Scotland in Focus
Calton Hill, Edinburgh © Greg Balfour Evans
House for an Art Lover, Glasgow © Jerry Dennis
Wester Ross © Paul Harris
Whiskies © Neil Setchfield
Catacol Bay, Isle of Arran © Edmund Nägele
Finnieston Crane, Glasgow © Jerry Dennis
Lairig Ghru, Cairngorms © Scotland in Focus
Gaelic signage © Western Isles Tourist Board
Northern Lighthouse Board, Stromness © Rob Humphreys

Things not to miss

01 Glenfinnan Monument, Loch Shiel © Michael Jenner
02 Lewis chess pieces © Museum of Scotland
03 Glasgow School of Art © Jerry Dennis
04 Victoria Street, Edinburgh © Michael Jenner
05 Callanish standing stones © B. Woods/Trip
06 Glen Coe © J. Robertson/Trip
07 Edinburgh fireworks © J. Robertson/Trip
08 Isle of Staffa © A. Lambert/Trip
09 Tobermory, Mull © Edmund Nägele
10 Highland Games © Neil Egerton/Travel Ink
11 West Highland Railway © J. Byers/ Scotland in Focus
12 Kinloch Castle, Rùm © Michael Jenner
13 Dunnottar Castle © Greg Balfour Evans
14 St Magnus Cathedral © John MacPherson/Scotland in Focus
15 Hillwalking © Donald Reid
16 Iona Abbey, cloisters © Jerry Dennis
17 Caledonian forest © Laurie Campbell/Scotland in Focus
18 Aerial view of Orkney © H. Rogers/Trip
19 Isle of Eigg © J. MacPherson/Scotland in Focus
20 St Andrews, Royal & Ancient golf course © Greg Balfour Evans
21 Edinburgh Festival © F. Good/Trip
22 Melrose Abbey © D. Houghton/Trip
23 Islay © Michael Jenner
24 Burrell Collection, Glasgow © Michael Jenner
25 Loch Fyne Oyster Bar © G. Satterley/Scotland in Focus
26 Courtesy of the Shetland Folk Festival
27 Isle of Lewis © William Grey/Travel Ink
28 Cairngorms © D. Barnes/Scotland in Focus
29 View of Ailsa Craig © Edmund Nägele
30 Maes Howe, Orkney © Doug Houghton
31 Courtesy of Dundee Contemporary Arts
32 Stirling Castle © Edmund Nägele
33 Jarlshof, Shetland © Doug Houghton
34 South Harris beach © R. Weir/ Scotland in Focus
35 The Black Cuillin, Skye © Scotland in Focus
36 Bow bar, Edinburgh © Donald Reid
37 Mousa Broch, Shetland © R. Schofield/Scotland in Focus
38 Smokies © StockScotland
39 Whale-watching © Peter Cairns/ StockScotland
40 Aberlemno Pictish stone © Sea Watch Foundation

Black and white photos

Calton Hill, Edinburgh © Greg Balfour Evans
Edinburgh, Royal Mile (Canongate Tolbooth) © Greg Balfour Evans
Melrose Abbey © D. Houghton/Trip
Dumfries © Rob Humphreys
SECC ("The Armadillo"), Glasgow © Edmund Nägele
Statue of Mercury, Merchant City, Glasgow © Helena Smith
Stirling Castle © Edmund Nägele
Lake of Menteith © Helena Smith
Islay © Michael Jenner
Tobermory, Mull © Rob Humphreys
Malt whisky © William Shaw/AXIOM
Standing Stones, Lewis © B. Woods/Trip
Skye © Sasha Gusov/AXIOM
Dunnottar Castle © Greg Balfour Evans
Union Street, Aberdeen © Doug Houghton
Wester Ross © Paul Harris
Castle Urquhart, Loch Ness © H. Rogers/Trip
Ullapool and Loch Broom © Scotland in Focus
Gannets © K. Robeson/Scotland in Focus
Stones of Stenness, Orkney © Rob Humphreys
Papa Stour, Shetland © Rob Humphreys

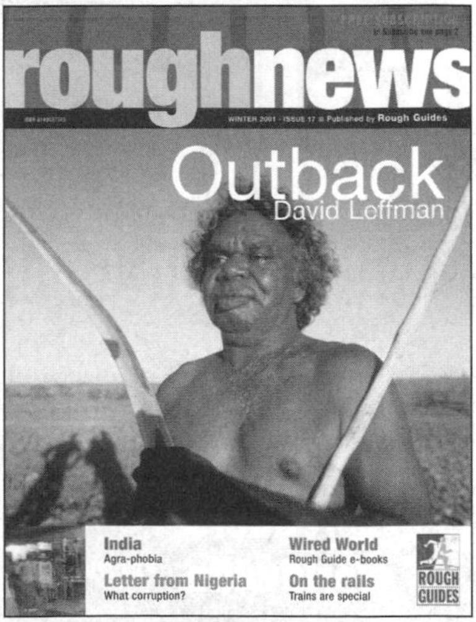